The Ernst & Young Tax Guide 2002

Critical Acclaim . . .

"This is the best tax guide of the bunch . . . the most up-to-date guide . . . ."

USA Today

"Hard to beat . . . (Ernst & Young) experts elucidate each point, giving examples, definitions and strategies that you won't learn about from the IRS."

Money

"This book contains useable tax forms, perhaps saving a trip to the library or post office, and because it delays publication until December, it has more up-to-date information on tax changes than its competitors—or even the IRS."

Chicago Sun-Times

"Best of the commercially available guides. . . . It is the only guide with the final version of federal tax forms."

New York Daily News

"Destined to become an 'old standard,' all written in plain English. . . . If you can afford just one tax book, this could be the one."

Seattle Post-Intelligencer

"The text-with-commentary approach makes the book both authoritative and easy-to-use."

People

"The simplest tax guide to understand."

CBS This Morning

"The explanations, examples, and planning advice are top-drawer."

Orlando Sentinel

"Exceptionally detailed."

The Sunday Denver Post

"An excellent book, full of clear explanations, planning hints, tax savers and sample forms."

Atlanta Journal Constitution

"Our brand-name choice for filers with lots of questions for filing and planning situations. . . ."

Fort Worth Star-Telegram

". . . a veritable fountain of information. . . ."

Milwaukee Sentinel

". . . the best of the bunch for return preparation."

Des Moines Register

2002 Tax Calendar

JANUARY

15 ❏ Final estimated tax payment for 2001 due if you did not pay your income tax (or enough of your income tax) for that year through withholding. Use Form 1040ES.

FEBRUARY

1 ❏ If you did not pay your last installment of estimated tax by January 15, file your income tax return for 2001 on this date, thereby avoiding any penalty for late payment of the last installment. Use Form 1040 or 1040A.

15 ❏ File a new Form W-4 if you can claim exemption from withholding.

MARCH

1 ❏ Farmers and fishermen must file their 2001 income tax return (Form 1040) to avoid an underpayment penalty for the last quarter of 2001 if they were required to but did not pay estimated tax on January 15.

APRIL

15 ❏ File your income tax return for 2001 (Forms 1040, 1040A, or 1040EZ) and pay any tax due.

❏ Make your 2001 IRA contribution.

❏ If you are not extending your return, make your Keogh contribution if you have self-employment income.

❏ For an automatic 4-month extension, file Form 4868 and pay any tax that you estimate will be due. Then file Form 1040 or 1040A by August 15. If you get an extension, you can't file Form 1040EZ.

❏ Pay the first installment of your 2002 estimated tax if you are not paying your 2002 income tax (or enough of it) through withholding tax.

❏ If you made any taxable gifts during 2001 (more than $10,000 per donee), file a gift tax return for that year (Form 709 or 709-A) and pay any tax due.

APRIL (CONT.)

❏ For an automatic 4-month extension, file Form 4868. (You can use one Form 4868 to file for both your income tax and gift tax extensions.)

JUNE

17 ❏ Pay the second installment of 2002 estimated tax.

30 ❏ Individuals who have signature authority or other authority over certain bank, securities, or other financial accounts in a foreign country must file Form TDF 90.22.1.

AUGUST

15 ❏ If you filed for an automatic 4-month extension to file your 2001 income tax return, file Form 1040 or Form 1040A and pay any tax, interest, and penalties due. Also make your Keogh contribution if it has not already been made. If you want an additional 2-month extension, file Form 2688.

❏ If you filed for an automatic 4-month extension to file your gift tax return for 2001, file it and pay any tax, interest, and penalties due. If you want an additional 2-month extension, file Form 2688. (You can use one Form 2688 to apply for both your income tax and gift tax second extensions.)

SEPTEMBER

16 ❏ Pay the third installment of your 2002 estimated tax.

OCTOBER

15 ❏ If you were given an automatic 4-month extension and an additional 2-month extension for your 2001 income tax return, file Form 1040 or Form 1040A and pay any tax, interest, and penalty due, and any gift tax return if due.

❏ Last day to make a Keogh contribution for calendar year 2001 if you were granted an additional 2-month extension of time to file your tax return.

DECEMBER

31 ❏ Last day to establish a Keogh (H.R. 10) plan for 2002.

The Ernst & Young
Tax Guide 2002

By the Tax Partners and
Professionals of Ernst & Young LLP

Peter W. Bernstein, Editor

John Wiley & Sons, Inc.

In the preparation of this book, every effort has been made to offer the most current, correct, and clearly expressed information possible. Nonetheless, inadvertent errors can occur, and tax rules and regulations often change.

Further, the information in the text is intended to afford general guidelines on matters of interest to taxpayers. The application and impact of tax laws can vary widely, however, from case to case, based upon the specific or unique facts involved. Accordingly, the information in this book is not intended to serve as legal, accounting, or tax advice. Readers are encouraged to consult with professional advisors for advice concerning specific matters before making any decision, and the author and publishers disclaim any responsibility for positions taken by taxpayers in their individual cases or for any misunderstanding on the part of readers.

The information in this book is based on the Internal Revenue Code as of November, 2001.

Copyright © 1989, 1990, 1991, 1992, 1993, 1994, 1995, 1996, 1997, 1998, 1999, 2000, 2001, 2002 by Ernst & Young LLP and Peter W. Bernstein Corporation
Copyright © 1984, 1985, 1986, 1987, 1988 by Arthur Young & Company and Peter W. Bernstein Corporation
Published by John Wiley & Sons, Inc.

All rights reserved.

Reproduction or translation of any part of this work beyond that permitted by Section 107 or 108 of the 1976 United States Copyright Act without the permission of the copyright owner is unlawful. Requests for permission or further information should be addressed to the Permissions Department, John Wiley & Sons, Inc., 605 Third Avenue, New York, NY 10158.

This publication is designed to provide accurate and authoritative information with regard to the subject matter covered. It is sold with the understanding that the publisher is not engaged in rendering legal, accounting, or other professional services. If legal advice or other expert assistance is required, the services of a competent professional person should be sought.

This book contains the text, charts, and figures from the Internal Revenue Service Publication 17, Your Federal Income Tax (rev. Nov. 2001) and portions of other pertinent Internal Revenue Service publications.

ISBN: 0-471-43493-0
ISSN: 1059-809X

Text design by Cindy Geist

Manufactured in the United States of America

Table of Contents

PART I

THE INCOME TAX RETURN

1

PART II

INCOME

79

80 *Chart:* Income

PART III

STANDARD DEDUCTION AND ITEMIZED DEDUCTIONS

305

Special Tables of Contents

REAL ESTATE INVESTORS' TAX GUIDE

SELF-EMPLOYED ENTREPRENEURS' TAX GUIDE

BUSINESS EXECUTIVES' TAX GUIDE

SENIOR CITIZENS' TAX GUIDE

How to Use This Guide

The Ernst & Young Tax Guide 2002 is an easy-to-use, step-by-step guide to preparing your own tax return. It has been designed with you in mind, and its format should help highlight information to save you time and money. To make sure you have the most up-to-date tax information available, we, unlike other tax guides, have waited until the beginning of December before going to press.

The book explains, in clear and simple English, important aspects of the tax laws that affect you. It covers what you need to know about your taxes—from how to file your return to how to lower the tax you'll pay next year. Throughout the book, you will find hundreds of examples illustrating how the tax law works. Sample tax forms and schedules show you how to fill out your return line by line. Here are some of the book's special features and how to use them:

- **Two Books in One.** *The Ernst & Young Tax Guide 2002* is really two books. The first book is the official Internal Revenue Service tax guide, Publication 17, *Your Federal Income Tax,* which is reproduced here. Published annually, it contains the IRS's position on many of the tax questions taxpayers face. The second book is the Ernst & Young guide. Here are comments, explanations, and tax-saving tips on what the IRS tells you—and doesn't tell you. It's no surprise that the IRS doesn't tell you everything, and what it does say often favors the U.S. government. Courts and tax professionals frequently differ with IRS opinions. The Ernst & Young text provides you with this additional material. The two books have been spliced together to give you the most well-rounded tax guide on the market. To distinguish between the two perspectives, the IRS text appears in black throughout the book, whereas Ernst & Young's comments appear in the blue boxes or in blue type.

- **TaxSavers, TaxPlanners, TaxAlerts, and TaxOrganizers.** One of the book's biggest attractions is the more than 400 *TaxSavers, TaxPlanners, TaxAlerts,* and *TaxOrganizers* that you'll find appropriately placed throughout the text. *TaxSavers* are tips that help you slash your tax bill this year and next—legally. *TaxPlanners* outline strategies that help you plan better for the upcoming year. *TaxAlerts* point out taxes and regulations that have just changed or may change in the near future, and they give you important current filing advice about issues you will want to consider as you prepare your returns. *TaxOrganizers* point out steps you can take now to make it easier to file your taxes later.

- **Tax Forms You Can Use.** *The Ernst & Young Tax Guide 2002* contains more official tax forms that you can use than any other tax guide. You'll find many of the federal tax forms that you need in Part VI, *Filling Out Your Tax Return and Tax Forms You Can Use,* along with tax tables and tax rate schedules. Simply tear the forms out and fill them in. It's perfectly acceptable to send your completed forms from this book to the IRS (don't forget to make a copy of them for your files). A listing of all the tax forms that appear in the book can be found in the Table of Contents. Also, tax forms are available electronically through the Ernst & Young Tax Corner at www.ey.com/pfc.

- **Special Tables of Contents.** We've taken great pains to ensure that this book is clearly organized for easy access. If you can't find the section you want in the regular Table of Contents, look over the *Special Tables of Contents.* All told, there are eight of these—one each for families, homeowners, investors in stocks and bonds, investors in real estate, self-employed entrepreneurs, business executives, senior citizens, and members of the armed forces. Each *Special Table of Contents* contains a listing of the major tax issues for members of that group and tells where you can find the answers in the book. In addition, we have a table of contents at the beginning of each chapter to help you find what you need.

We have drawn from the tax experience of scores of Ernst & Young LLP partners and staff from all parts of the United States to create this tax guide. Among the major accounting firms, only Ernst & Young LLP publishes a complete tax guide that is available to the general public. It provides the most complete and up-to-date tax information of any tax guide published. You also might be interested in other Ernst & Young publications: *The Ernst & Young Tax Saver's Guide 2002,* a year-round tax planner with money-saving tax strategies; *Ernst & Young's Personal Financial Planning Guide,* special tax edition, a book that walks readers through all the basics of financial planning, including special tactics tied to life's major events; *Ernst & Young's Retirement Planning Guide,* special tax edition, a book to help you secure a sound retirement; and *Ernst & Young's Financial Planning for Women,* a guide tailored to help women meet their short- and long-term financial goals.

The Ernst & Young Tax Guide Editorial Board 2002

Contributing Authors

ATLANTA
Lynn Finkelstein
Amanda K. Foster
Gregory Guthrie
Chuck Kowal
Jennifer Littrell
Susan Parsons
Scott Shows

BOSTON
Patricia Buzgo
Darlene Dahl-Legro
James Raymond

CHICAGO
Melissa Bertram
Jeffrey H. Brodsky
Helen Chan
Amy B. Corbett
Fran Decicco
Sheri L. Hatfield
Elizabeth L. Helton
Paul Manghera
Anne C. Metzger
Lorrie A. Minor
Michael J. Simmons
Sue M. Smith
Chris Yannella

DALLAS
Christopher Gold
Richard Joyner
Matthew Paladini
Leslie Shaffer

GRAND RAPIDS
Ellen W. Bolline
Chad C. Nesbit
Erin C. Nichols
Jeffrey S. Williams

MEADOWLANDS
Marcello Cosentino
Donald A. Culp
James O'Gorman

METROPARK
Jeffrey P. Bolson
Stuart E. Doctor
Margaret L. Kenney
Joanna E. Lanni
Gary P. Lubowiecki

NEW YORK
Charles R. Cangro
Peter D. Lucido
Martin Nissenbaum

PROVIDENCE
Charlene K. Butler
George R. Cobleigh
Janice C. Preston
Susan M. Simoneau

SAN DIEGO
Donald A. Blackwell

SAN JOSE
Jarrett Bostwick

WASHINGTON
Lauren D. Bazel
Diane C. Carruthers
Kara A. Getz
Walter S. Goldberg
David J. Kautter
James Kolan
Jeffrey A. Lear
Phillip D. Moseley

WOODLAND HILLS
Alev Lewis

Special thanks to James S. Turley, Chairman of Ernst & Young LLP; Richard S. Bobrow, CEO of the Americas; Dennis Purdum, Chief Operating Officer for the Americas; William J. Lipton, Vice Chairman—Tax Services; David J. Kautter, Director of National Tax; Sylvia J. Pozarnsky, National Director—Personal Financial Counseling; Martin Nissenbaum, National Director—Personal Income Tax Planning; and Jeffrey P. Bolson.

Special Acknowledgments: Robin Factor, Greg Friedman, Erika Heilman, Alexia Meyers, and Janice Weisner from John Wiley & Sons, Inc.

With more than 4,000 tax practitioners, Ernst & Young LLP has one of the largest professional tax practices in the United States. This book draws upon the experience of many of those professionals for its content.

Changes in the Tax Law You Should Know About

On June 7, 2001, President George W. Bush signed into law The Economic Growth and Tax Relief Reconciliation Act of 2001. The enactment of this $1.35 trillion ten-year tax cut represented a historic change in the tax law for individuals.

The new law provides tax relief for virtually all taxpayers in the form of rate reductions, tax-deferred (and, in some cases tax-free) wealth accumulation opportunities, and reduced estate taxes. However, many provisions of the Act are being phased-in over a number of years. Some provisions take effect in 2010 only to expire the following year.

Perhaps the Act's most unique, and controversial, feature is that all of its new provisions expire after December 31, 2010, and the rules in effect in 2001 will be reinstated—unless a future Congress takes some action to the contrary. In the meantime, there are ample tax saving opportunities for individual taxpayers, some of which are explained below.

Important Tax Changes for 2001

➤ Reduced Tax Rates

For tax years beginning in 2001, the income tax rates have been reduced. The following TaxAlert highlights these changes.

TaxAlert

10% tax rate. A portion of your income that would be subject to the 15% tax rate is subject to a reduced rate of 10%. For 2001, most individuals receive the benefits of the 10% rate through the rate reduction credit, discussed later. A person who can be claimed as a dependent on someone else's return is not eligible for the credit and will receive the benefits of the 10% rate by completing a worksheet in the form instructions.

Other tax rates. The other tax rates, 28%, 31%, 36% and 39.6% are reduced to 27.5%, 30.5%, 35.5%, and 39.1%, respectively. These reduced rates should have been reflected in amounts withheld (such as backup withholding) on certain payments made after August 6, 2001.

This table shows the phase-in of the reductions for individual tax brackets greater than 15%.

PHASE-IN OF INDIVIDUAL RATE REDUCTIONS

TAX YEAR	TAX RATES			
2000	28%	31%	36%	39.6%
2001	27.5%	30.5%	35.5%	39.1%
2002–2003	27%	30%	35%	38.6%
2004–2005	26%	29%	34%	37.6%
2006 and later	25%	28%	33%	35%

➤ Advance Payment of Income Tax

If you received an advance payment of income tax of 2001, you do not have to report this payment as income on your federal income tax return. This payment reduces your rate reduction credit, discussed next.

➤ Rate Reduction Credit

If you did not receive the maximum advance payment in 2001, you may qualify for the rate reduction credit. You can use the worksheet in your form instructions to determine whether you can claim the credit. See Chapter 37, *Other Credits Including the Earned Income Credit.*

➤ Tax Relief for Victims of Terrorist Attacks

At the time this publication was being prepared for print, Congress was considering legislation that would provide tax relief for individuals affected by terrorist attacks against the United States.

➤ Child Tax Credit

The maximum child tax credit for each child is increased to $600. The qualifications for claiming the additional child tax credit have been changed to include a qualifying individual with fewer than 3 children. See Chapter 35, *Child Tax Credit.*

TaxAlert

Child tax credits. A recent law permits you to take full advantage of nonrefundable personal tax credits—i.e., the dependent care credit, the credit for the elderly and disabled, the adoption credit, the child tax credit, the credit for interest on certain home mortgages, the Hope Scholarship and Lifetime Learning credits, and the D.C. homebuyer's credit). For 2001, the nonrefundable personal credits can be used to offset regular tax in full, not just to the extent by which your regular tax exceeds the tentative alternative minimum tax (AMT).

In addition, the provision in the law that otherwise would reduce the additional child credit for families with three or more qualifying children, will not apply for 2001. This means that families with three or more qualifying children will be allowed additional credit in 2001.

➤ Interest on Student Loans

You may be able to deduct as an adjustment to income interest paid on a qualified student loan. The maximum deduction is increased to $2,500. See Publication 970, *Tax Benefits for Higher Education.*

➤ Traditional IRA Income Limits

Generally, if you have a traditional individual retirement arrangement and are covered by an employer retirement plan, the amount of income you can have and not be affected by the deduction phaseout is increased. The amounts vary depending on filing status. See Chapter 18, *Individual Retirement Arrangements (IRAs) and Education Savings Accounts (ESAs).*

➤ Alternative Minimum Tax (AMT)

The AMT exemption amounts are increased. See Chapter 31, *How to Figure Your Tax.*

➤ Schedule D Tax Computation Simplified

The tax computation on Schedule D is now easier for most taxpayers. For information on completing Schedule D, see Chapter 17, *Reporting Gains and Losses.*

➤ Lower Capital Gain Tax Rate

A new capital gain tax rate applies to gain that is "qualified 5-year gain." Qualified 5-year gain is long-term capital gain from the sale of property that you held for more than 5 years and that would otherwise be subject to the 10% capital gain rate. See Chapter 17, *Reporting Gains and Losses.*

You can elect to treat certain assets held on January 1, 2001, as sold and then reacquired on the same date. The purpose of this election is to make any future gain on the property that would otherwise be subject to the 20% capital gain rate eligible for the 18% rate if the property is held for more than 5 years from the date reacquired.

➤ Foreign Earned Income Exclusion

The amount of foreign earned income that you can exclude increased to $78,000. See Publication 54, *Tax Guide for U.S. Citizens and Resident Aliens Abroad.*

➤ Standard Mileage Rate

The standard mileage rate for the cost of operating your car increased to 34 1/2 cents a mile for all business miles driven. See Chapter 28, *Car Expenses and Other Employee Businesses.*

➤ Minimum Required Distributions

Until final regulations are issued, proposed regulations can be relied on to determine the minimum required distribution from certain qualified plans and individual retirement arrangements (IRAs). These regulations simplify the rules for distributions during the life of the employee (or IRA owner) and for distributions after the death of that individual. In most cases, these regulations reduce the minimum required distribution. For information on IRA distributions, see Chapter 18, *Individual Retirement Arrangements (IRAs) and Education Savings Accounts (ESAs).*

➤ Standard Deduction

The standard deduction for taxpayers who do not itemize deductions on Schedule A (Form 1040) is higher in 2001 than it was in 2000. The amount depends on your filing status. See Chapter 21, *Standard Deduction.*

➤ Exemption Amount

You are allowed a $2,900 deduction for each exemption to which you are entitled. However, your exemption amount could be phased out if you have high income. See Chapter 3, *Personal Exemptions and Dependents.*

➤ Limit on Itemized Deductions

Some of your itemized deductions may be limited if your adjusted gross income is more than $132,950 ($66,475 if you are married filing separately). See Chapter 22, *Limit on Itemized Deductions.*

➤ Social Security and Medicare Taxes

The maximum wages subject to social security tax (6.2%) is increased to $80,400. All wages are subject to Medicare tax (1.45%).

➤ New Names for Certain Tax Provisions

The names used to refer to certain tax provisions have been changed.

- Medical savings accounts (MSAs) are now **Archer MSAs.** For information on Archer MSAs, see Publication 969, *Medical Savings Accounts (MSAs).*
- Education individual retirement accounts (education IRAs) are now **Coverdell education savings accounts** (Coverdell ESAs). For information on Coverdell ESAs, see Publication 970, *Tax Benefits for Higher Education.*

Important Tax Changes for 2002

This section summarizes important tax changes that take effect in 2002 and that could affect your estimated tax payments for 2002.

➤ Tax Rates Reduced

For tax years beginning in 2002, the income tax rates have been reduced. The following TaxAlert highlights these changes.

TaxAlert

10% tax rate. The 10% tax rate is reflected in the tax tables and tax schedules. You do not have to make a separate computation or figure a credit to get the benefits of this rate.
Other tax rates. The other tax rates, 27.5%, 30.5%, 35.5%, and 39.1% are reduced to 27%, 30%, 35%, and 38.6%, re-

spectively. These reduced rates should be reflected in amounts withheld (such as backup withholding) on certain payments made after 2001.

➤ Estimated Tax Safe Harbor for Higher Income Individuals

For estimated tax payments for tax years beginning in 2002, the estimated tax safe harbor for higher income individuals (other than farmers and fishermen) has been modified. If your 2001 adjusted gross income is more than $150,000 ($75,000 if you are married filing a separate return for 2002), you will have to pay the smaller of 90% of your expected tax for 2002 or **112%** of the tax shown on your 2001 return to avoid an estimated tax penalty. See Chapter 5, *Tax Withholding and Estimated Tax.*

➤ Higher Education Expenses

You may be able to deduct as an adjustment to income up to $3,000 of qualified tuition and related expenses you paid. The expenses can be for you, your spouse, or your dependent.

➤ Interest on Student Loans

Two changes apply to the deduction for student loan interest.

- The provision that limited your deduction to interest paid during the first 60 months is repealed.
- The modified AGI phaseout amounts are increased.

For more information on the deduction for student loan interest, see Publication 970.

➤ Coverdell Education Savings Accounts

The following changes apply to Coverdell education savings accounts.

- Contribution limit increases to $2,000 per beneficiary.
- The income phase out increases for joint filers.
- Qualified education expenses include elementary and secondary school expenses.
- Age limits do not apply to "special needs" beneficiaries.
- Contributions may be made until April 15 of the following year.
- Tax-free distributions can be used for special needs services.

➤ Employer-Provided Educational Assistance

The following changes apply to employer-provided educational assistance.

- Exclusion made permanent.
- Exclusion applies to graduate level courses.

➤ Qualified Tuition Programs

The qualified tuition program (formerly qualified state tuition program) includes programs established and maintained by one or more eligible educational institutions. Two other changes affect this program.

- Distributions from a state program that are used to pay qualified higher education expenses are tax free. Other distributions are subject to 10% additional tax.
- Tax-free distributions can be used for special needs services.

TaxAlert

Qualified Tuition (Section 529) Programs. Section 529 plans allow a taxpayer to either buy tuition credits or to contribute to a special higher education savings account for a designated beneficiary. These programs, which were beneficial under prior law, have become even more valuable as a result of changes made by the new law.

The most significant change made by the new law is that qualifying distributions from these programs will no longer be subject to tax. Under prior law, account earnings used for qualifying expenses were taxable to the student at the time withdrawn. Under the new law, post-2001 distributions from qualified state tuition plans will be fully excluded from gross income.

➤ Tax Benefits for Adoption

Changes apply to the adoption credit and to the exclusion for benefits under an employer-provided adoption assistance program. These changes include the following.

- The credit for children without special needs is made permanent.
- The exclusion under an adoption assistance program is made permanent.
- The credit and exclusion amounts increased to a maximum of $10,000.
- The modified AGI phaseout amounts increased.

➤ Benefits for Public Safety Officer's Survivors

For tax years beginning after 2001, a survivor annuity received by the spouse, former spouse, or child of a public safety officer killed in the line of duty will generally be excluded from the recipient's income regardless of the date of the officer's death. Survivor benefits received before 2002 are excluded only if the officer died after 1996. See Chapter 13, *Other Income.*

➤ Foreign Earned Income Exclusion

The amount of foreign earned income that you can exclude will increase to $80,000. See Publication 54.

➤ Self-Employed Health Insurance Deduction

The part of your self-employed health insurance premiums that you can deduct as an adjustment to income increases to 70%.

➤ Increased IRA Contribution and Deduction Limit

Your maximum contribution (and any allowable deduction) limit is increased. Previously, the limit was $2,000. The new limit depends on your age at the end of the year.

- If you are under age 50, the most you can contribute is the smaller of $3,000, or your taxable compensation.

- If you are age 50 or older, the most you can contribute is the smaller of $3,500, or your taxable compensation.

➤ Rollovers of IRAs into Qualified Plans

For distributions after December 31, 2001, you may be able to roll over tax free, a distribution from your IRA into a qualified plan.

➤ Rollovers of Distributions from Employer Plans

For distributions after December 31, 2001, you can roll over both the taxable and nontaxable part of a distribution from a qualified plan into a traditional IRA.

TaxPlanner

Expanded Rollover Options. Beginning in 2002:

- All IRA distributions (except for after-tax amounts) can be rolled into employer plans.
- Certain after-tax contributions to a qualified plan can be rolled over to an IRA or defined contribution plan.
- Surviving spouses will be able to roll over any distribution attributable to a decedent-employee into any eligible retirement plan in the same manner as if the spouse were the employee.

➤ Hardship Exception to the 60-day Rule

For distributions after December 31, 2001, the IRS may waive the 60-day requirement to roll over distributions from your IRA or your employer's pension plan where the failure to do so would be against equity or good conscience, including casualty, disaster, or other events beyond your reasonable control.

➤ Limit on Elective Deferrals

The maximum amount of elective deferrals under a salary reduction agreement that can be contributed to a qualified plan is increased to $11,000 ($12,000 if you are age 50 or over). However, for SIMPLE plans, the amount is increased to $7,000 ($7,500 if you are age 50 or over).

TaxPlanner

Defined Benefit Plans. For 2002, the maximum annual benefit payable at retirement in a defined benefit plan generally is the lesser of (a) 100% of average compensation or (b) $160,000. In addition, the dollar limit will no longer be adjusted based on the social security retirement age.

Instead, the dollar limit will be reduced for benefits beginning before age 62 or increased for benefits beginning after age 65.

TaxPlanner

Deduction Limit for Contributions to Profit Sharing Plans. Under prior law, the deduction for contributions to a profit sharing plan was limited to 15% of compensation. Beginning in 2002, the limit will increase to 25% of compensation.

➤ New Credit for Elective Deferrals and IRA Contributions

You may be able to take a credit of up to $1,000 for qualified retirement savings contributions.

Explanation

Tax Credit for Certain Retirement Deferrals. Beginning in 2002, joint filers with adjusted gross income (AGI) below $50,000, and single filers or those who are married filing separately with AGI below $25,000, can qualify for a tax credit of up to $1,000 for contributions or deferrals to retirement savings plans. The maximum credit is 50% of the contribution or deferral (up to $2,000). The amount of the credit is determined on a sliding scale.

TaxPlanner

Employer-Provided Retirement Advice. Beginning in 2002, qualified retirement planning services provided by an employer will constitute a fringe benefit excludable from an employee's income.

TaxPlanner

Estate, Gift, and Generation-Skipping Transfer Taxes. The estate and generation-skipping transfer (GST) tax rates are gradually reduced over the next nine years, after which these taxes are repealed for 2010 only. The top gift tax rate is also gradually reduced over the next nine years but is not repealed. For decedents dying in 2001, the exemptions amount is $675,000 for estate tax and $1,060,000 for GST tax; the tax rate is 55%, plus a 5% surtax on certain estates over $10 million. For decedents dying in 2002, the exemption amount will be $1 million for estate tax, and the $1,060,000 for the GST tax will be indexed for inflation. The tax rate will be 50% for the estate tax. The surtax will be repealed. After increasing to $1 million in 2002, the gift tax exemption will remain constant and will not be indexed for inflation.

Important 2001 Tax Reminders from the IRS

Listed below are important reminders and other items that may help you file your 2001 tax return. Many of these items are explained in more detail later in this publication.

➤ Write in Your Social Security Number

To protect your privacy, Social Security numbers (SSNs) are not printed on the peel-off label that comes in the mail with your tax instruction booklet. This means you must enter your SSN in the space provided on your tax form. If you filed a joint return for 2000 and are filing a joint return for 2001 with the same spouse, enter your names and SSNs in the same order as on your 2000 return. See Chapter 1, *Filing Information.*

➤ Taxpayer Identification Numbers

You must provide the taxpayer identification number for each person for whom you claim certain tax benefits. This applies even if the person was born in 2001. Generally, this number is the person's Social Security number (SSN). See Chapter 1, *Filing Information.*

➤ Tax from Recapture of Education Credits

You may owe this tax if you claimed an education credit in one year and in a later year you, your spouse if filing jointly, or your dependent received:

- A refund of qualified tuition and related expenses, or
- Tax-free educational assistance.

See Chapter 36, *Education Credits.*

➤ Advance Earned Income Credit

If a qualifying child lives with you and you expect to qualify for the earned income credit in 2002, you may be able to get part of the credit paid to you in advance throughout the year (by your employer) instead of waiting until you file your tax return. See Chapter 37, *Other Credits.*

➤ Individual Retirement Arrangements (IRAs) for Spouse

A married couple filing a joint return can contribute up to $2,000 each to their IRAs, even if one spouse had little or no income.

➤ Spouse Covered by Plan

Even if your spouse is covered by an employer-sponsored retirement plan, you may be able to deduct contributions to your traditional IRA if you are not covered by an employer plan.

➤ Joint Return Responsibility

Generally, both spouses are responsible for the tax and any interest or penalties on a joint tax return. In some cases, one spouse may be relieved of that responsibility for items of the other spouse that were incorrectly reported on the joint return. For details, see *Joint responsibility* in Chapter 2, *Filing Status.*

➤ Include Your Phone Number on Your Return

To promptly resolve any questions we have in processing your tax return, we would like to be able to call you. Please enter your daytime telephone number on your tax form in the space provided next to your signature.

➤ Payment of Taxes

Make your check or money order payable to "United States Treasury." You can pay your taxes by credit card, or, if you file electronically, by electronic funds withdrawal (direct debit). See Chapter 1, *Filing Information.*

➤ Faster Ways to File Your Return

The IRS offers fast, accurate ways to file your tax return information without filing a paper tax return. You can use IRS *e-file* (electronic filing). For details, see chapter 1. For details on these fast filing methods, see Chapter 1, *Filing Information.*

➤ Private Delivery Services

You may be able to use a designated private delivery service to mail your tax returns and payments. See Chapter 1, *Filing Information,* for more information.

➤ Refund on a Late Filed Return

If you were due a refund but you did not file a return, you generally must file within 3 years from the date the return was originally due to get that refund.

➤ Privacy Act and Paperwork Reduction Information

The IRS Restructuring and Reform Act of 1998, the Privacy Act of 1974, and the Paperwork Reduction Act of 1980 require that when we ask you for information we must first tell you what our legal right is to ask for the information, why we are asking for it, how it will be used, what could happen if we do not receive it, and whether your response is voluntary, required to obtain a benefit, or mandatory under the law. A complete statement on this subject can be found in the 1040 instruction booklet.

➤ Treasury Inspector General for Tax Administration

If you want to confidentially report misconduct, waste, fraud, or abuse by an IRS employee, you can call **1-800-366-4484** (1-800-877-8339 for TTY/TDD users). You can remain anonymous.

How to Avoid 25 Common Errors

1 Most importantly, check your math.

2 Double-check that your Social Security number has been correctly written on the return. If you are married, check that your spouse's Social Security number is properly listed, whether filing a joint or separate return.

3 Include your Social Security number on each page of the return so that if a page is misplaced by the IRS, it can be reattached.

4 Check that you have claimed all of your dependents, such as elderly parents who may not live with you. See Chapter 3, *Personal Exemptions and Dependents*.

5 Include on the return the Social Security numbers for all dependents including those born during 2001.

6 If you are single and have a dependent who lives with you, check to see if you qualify for the lower tax rates available to a head of household or surviving spouse.

7 You may be eligible for the earned income credit if you do NOT file as married filing separately. If you have one qualifying child and your earned income and modified adjusted gross income for 2001 are less than $28,281 ($32,121 if you have more than one qualifying child), you may qualify. If you do not have a qualifying child, but are between the ages of 25 and 65, and your earned income for 2001 and modified adjusted gross income are less than $10,710, you may qualify as well. See Chapter 37, *Other Credits Including the Earned Income Credit*.

8 If you are married, check to see if filing separate returns rather than a joint return is more beneficial.

9 Attach all copy Bs of your W-2 forms to your return in order to avoid correspondence with the IRS. If you received a Form 1099-R showing federal income tax withheld, attach copy B of that form as well.

10 You may be eligible to claim the additional standard deductions if you are blind or 65 years of age or older.

11 Be sure to sign your check and write your Social Security number, the form number, and the tax year on the face of any checks made out to the IRS. (Example: "000-00-000 - 2001 Form 1040.")

12 Be sure that your Form W-2 and all Form 1099s are correct. If they're wrong, have them corrected as soon as possible so that the IRS's records agree with the amounts you show on your return.

13 If you worked for more than one employer, be sure to claim a credit for any overpaid Social Security taxes withheld from your wages.

14 If you received a state tax refund or a refund of interest you paid on a mortgage in an earlier year, make sure you have not included too much of your refund in your income. These refunds may not be taxable if you did not get a tax benefit from deducting them. If, for example, you used the standard deduction in the year in which the taxes or interest were paid, you do not have to include the refund in income this year.

15 Deductible real property taxes should be distinguished from assessments paid for local benefits, such as repair of streets, sidewalks, sewers, curbs, gutters, and other improvements that tend to benefit specific properties. Assessments of this type generally are not deductible.

16 Make sure to sign and date your return and enter your occupation. If you are filing a joint return, be sure that your spouse also signs as required.

17 Only a portion of your Social Security benefits may be taxable. If your income does not exceed a certain amount, none of it may be taxable.

18 Check last year's tax return to see if there are any items that carry over to this year, such as charitable contributions or capital losses that exceeded the amount you were previously able to deduct.

19 If you can be claimed as a dependent on someone else's return, do not claim a personal exemption on your return. Your standard deduction may be limited as well. See Chapter 21, *Standard Deduction*.

20 Fill out Form 8606, *Nondeductible IRA Contributions*, for your contributions to an IRA account, even if you don't claim any deduction for the contribution.

21 Recheck your basis in the securities that you sold during the year, particularly shares of a mutual fund. Income and capital gains dividends that were automatically reinvested in the fund over the years increase your basis in the mutual fund and thus reduce a gain or increase a loss that you have to report. Also, any "front-end" or purchase fees are still considered part of your cost basis for tax purposes, even though they reduce your investment in a mutual fund.

22 Recheck that you have used the correct column in the Tax Rate Table or the right Tax Rate Schedule for your filing status.

23 Don't miss deadlines: December 31—set up a Keogh plan; April 15—make your IRA contribution; April 15—file your return or request an extension. Check the tax calendar periodically. See the *2002 Tax Calendar*.

24 If you regularly get large refunds, you're having too much withheld and, in effect, giving an interest-free loan to the IRS. Increasing the number of allowances you claim on W-4 form will increase your take-home pay.

25 Keep copies of all documents that you send to the IRS. Use certified mail for all important correspondence to the IRS. Don't forget to keep your records in good shape so that you can find answers to any IRS questions about your return.

50 of the Most Easily Overlooked Deductions

The following list will serve as a reminder of some deductions you can easily overlook when you prepare your return. It is not intended to be all-inclusive, nor applicable to everyone. The circumstances of your situation will determine whether you qualify. See the page reference following each item for a complete explanation.

1 Accounting fees for tax preparation services and IRS audits (p. 427)

2 Alcoholism and drug abuse treatment (p. 317)

3 Amortization of premium on taxable bonds (p. 429)

4 Appraisal fees for charitable donations or casualty losses (p. 350)

5 Appreciation on property donated to a charity (p. 358)

6 Casualty or theft losses (p. 364)

7 Cellular telephones (p. 421)

8 Cleaning and laundering services when traveling (p. 381)

9 Commissions and closing costs on sale of property (p. 197)

10 Contact lenses, eye glasses, and hearing devices (p. 317)

11 Contraceptives, if bought with a prescription (p. 317)

12 Costs associated with looking for a new job in your present occupation, including fees for résumé preparation and employment of outplacement agencies (p. 425)

13 Depreciation of home computers (p. 422)

14 Dues to labor unions (p. 426)

15 Education expenses to the extent required by law or your employer or needed to maintain or improve your skills (p. 412)

16 Employee contributions to a state disability fund (p. 326)

17 Employee's moving expenses (p. 283)

18 Federal estate tax on income with respect to a decedent (p. 429)

19 Fees for a safe-deposit box to hold investments (e.g., stock certificate) (p. 429)

20 Fees paid for childbirth preparation classes if instruction relates to obstetrical care (p. 318)

21 Fifty % of self-employment tax (p. 8)

22 Foreign taxes paid (p. 326)

23 Foster child care expenditures (p. 188)

24 Gambling losses to the extent of gambling gains (p. 430)

25 Hospital services fees (laboratory work, therapy, nursing services, and surgery) (p. 317)

26 Impairment-related work expenses for a disabled individual (p. 430)

27 Improvements to your home (p. 241)

28 Investment advisory fees (p. 428)

29 IRA trustee's administrative fees billed separately (p. 429)

30 Lead paint removal (p. 317)

31 Legal fees incurred in connection with obtaining or collecting alimony (p. 428)

32 Long-term care insurance premiums (p. 319)

33 Margin account interest expense (p. 346)

34 Medical transportation, including standard mileage deduction (p. 321) and lodging expenses incurred for medical reasons while away from home (p. 320)

35 Mortgage prepayment penalties and late fees (p. 337)

36 Out-of-pocket expenses relating to charitable activities, including the standard mileage deduction (p. 353)

37 Part of health insurance premiums if self-employed (p. 508)

38 Penalty on early withdrawal of savings (p. 102)

39 Personal liability insurance for wrongful acts as an employee (p. 421)

40 Points on a home mortgage and certain refinancings (p. 338)

41 Protective clothing required at work (p. 426)

42 Real estate taxes associated with the purchase or sale of property (p. 328)

Individual Tax Organizer

The following schedules should help you organize the data you need to prepare your 2001 federal income tax return. They are intended only to provide general guidelines and should not be regarded as all-inclusive.

TAXPAYER INFORMATION

PERSONAL DATA

Your name _____

Your spouse's name _____

Social Security number _____ Spouse's _____

Marital status at year-end: ☐ Married ☐ Single ☐ Widowed after 1998 ☐ Divorced ☐ Married but separated

DEPENDENT CHILDREN

Name (address if different from yours)	Social Security number	Date of birth	Did you provide more than half of support?	Married filing a joint return?	Full-time student for 5 months or more?	Income over $2,900

OTHER DEPENDENTS

Name (address if different from yours)	Social Security number	Relationship	Months lived in your home	Is dependent's income over $2,900	Did you provide more than half of support?

PAYMENTS AND REFUNDS OF INCOME TAXES

	FEDERAL		STATE		CITY	
	Date paid	Amount	Date paid	Amount	Date paid	Amount
2001 estimated payments, including overpayment credited from 2000 return:						
Tax refunds received in 2001[1]						

[1] Do not include interest received on refunds or paid on deficiencies. Detail these amounts in the interest sections of this organizer.

COMPENSATION

Indicate recipient: H=Husband; W=Wife.

H W	Employer name	Gross earnings	Federal income tax withheld	Social Security tax withheld	Medicare tax withheld	State tax withheld	City tax withheld

INTEREST INCOME

Indicate ownership: H=Husband; W=Wife; J=Joint.

Report all interest received by you or for your account on Forms 1099-INT or other statements of total interest received. Failure to record any such income could result in a notice from the IRS.

If the amount of interest reported on Forms 1099-INT includes interest accrued on bonds at the time of purchase, adjustments can be made.

If you invested in a tax-exempt municipal bond fund, note the fund's schedule of percentage income related to each state.

H W J		Amount
	Savings accounts, credit unions, and certificates of deposit:	
	U.S. Savings Bonds and other U.S. government securities:	
	Corporate bonds:	
	Other interest[1]:	
	Tax-exempt interest	
	Interest received on tax refunds:	

[1] *If you received interest income from seller-financed mortgages, you will need the payer's name, address, and Social Security number.*

DIVIDEND INCOME

Indicate ownership: H=Husband; W=Wife; J=Joint.

Report all dividends received by you or for your account on Forms 1099-DIV or other information statements received. Failure to record any such income could result in a notice from the IRS.

H W J	Name of corporation [identify foreign corporation with (F)]	Indicate T (taxable), C (capital gain), N (nontaxable), U (U.S obligation) X (exempt)	Dividends received	U.S. taxes withheld

SALE OR PURCHASE OF RESIDENCE

Did you sell your residence during the year or within the last two years? ☐ Yes   ☐ No
If you answered "Yes," see Chapter 16, *Selling Your Home.*

SALE OF STOCKS AND BONDS

Indicate H-Husband; W-Wife; or J-Joint.

Note: Gross proceeds from sales reported here should reconcile with Forms 1099-B received from your broker. You should explain any discrepancies to prevent an IRS inquiry stemming from their matching program.

H W J	Description (include number of shares, common or preferred, and par value of bonds)	Date Acq.	Date Sold	Gross sales price[1]	Cost or other basis plus expenses of sale[2]	Gain or (loss)[3]

[1] *List proceeds of sale or cash received in lieu of fractions on receipt of stock rights or stock dividends.*

[2] *The basis of stock should be decreased by all nontaxable dividends and increased by any reinvested dividends. See Chapter 14,* Basis of Property.

[3] *Have you acquired stock, securities, contracts, or options to sell or acquire stock*   ☐ Yes   ☐ No
or securities substantially identical to stock or securities sold at a loss within a period beginning 30 days prior to and ending 30 days after the date of sale? If "Yes," see the discussion of "Wash Sale" in Chapter 15, Sale of Property.

OTHER TRANSACTIONS

Did you exchange securities for other securities or exchange any investment property for any other property? Did any security held by you or any amounts due you become worthless during the year? Did you sell your vacation home or other property during the year? Did you realize a gain or a loss on property, in whole or in part, by destruction, theft, seizure, or condemnation (including the threat or imminence thereof)? Did you engage in any commodity transactions (including open positions on December 31) during the year? Did you engage in any transactions involving traded options?

If you answered "Yes" to any of these questions, read the applicable portions of this book.

SALE OF OTHER PROPERTY

H W J	Description	Date		Gross sales price	Cost of other basis, plus expenses of sale	Depreciation or depletion	Gain or (loss)
		Acq.	Sold				

INSTALLMENT SALES

Did you make sales during the year for which the receipt of all or part of the sales price was deferred until future years?
    If yes, discuss with your tax advisor.   ☐ Yes   ☐ No

Did you collect on any installment obligations from sales made prior to 2001?   ☐ Yes   ☐ No

For more information, see Chapter 15, *Sale of Property*.

RENT AND ROYALTY INCOME

	Property A		Property B	
Did you actively participate in the operation of the rental activity during the year? For more information on active participation, see Chapter 10, *Rental Income and Expenses*.	☐ Yes	☐ No	☐ Yes	☐ No

Location and description of property[1]
Gross rents and royalties received
Expenses

[1]*If property has been used by you or your family as a personal residence, indicate the total days held for rent but not rented, days rented, and days used by you or your family.*

PARTNERSHIPS (P), SMALL BUSINESS CORPORATIONS (S), AND ESTATES AND TRUSTS (E/T)

Retain all Forms K-1 or other information relating to entity listed below.

P S E/T	H W J	Name	Tax shelter registration number	I.D. number	Income or (loss)

PENSION AND ANNUITY INCOME

Did you receive any payments from a retirement plan?   ☐ Yes   ☐ No

If yes, write in the amount received during the year and any taxes withheld.

Did you roll over a profit-sharing or retirement plan distribution into another plan?   ☐ Yes   ☐ No

What was the starting date of your annuity?

What is the amount received in the current taxable year?

Did you receive any IRA distributions during the year?   ☐ Yes   ☐ No

Retain all Forms 1099-R or other information relating to each distribution.

Did you convert all or any part of a regular IRA into a Roth IRA during 2001?   ☐ Yes   ☐ No

If yes, amount converted.

OTHER INCOME

Description	Amount
Alimony or legal separation payments received	
Disability payments	
Other tax refunds not shown elsewhere	
Unemployment insurance compensation	
Social security benefits	
Other[1] (describe)	

[1]*The types of other income include, but are not limited to, net income from self-employment, director's fees, prizes, cancelation of debts, gambling winnings, jury fees, punitive damages (unless awarded in a wrongful death action where state law so provides), receiver's fees, and certain tuition paid by an employer (e.g., graduate courses after 6/30/96). Also, include gross income from oil and gas working interests, as well as any expenses relating to them. For more information see Chapter 13, Other Income.*

			Amount
Did you receive any income from a foreign source?	☐ Yes	☐ No	
Did you own shares in a mutual fund that retained your share of capital gains and paid the tax on it?	☐ Yes	☐ No	
Did you have any income from farm property?	☐ Yes	☐ No	
Did you have any bartering income?	☐ Yes	☐ No	

DEDUCTIONS

ADJUSTMENTS TO INCOME

Alimony or legal separation payments made in current taxable year _____

    Recipient's last name _____ and social security no. _____

Penalties for early withdrawal of savings _____

Individual Retirement Arrangements (IRAs)[1]

			Amount
Did you contribute to your own IRA?	☐ Yes	☐ No	
Type:			
☐ Regular			
☐ Roth			
☐ Education			
Did you participate in a retirement plan maintained by your employer?	☐ Yes	☐ No	
Did your spouse contribute to his/her own IRA?	☐ Yes	☐ No	
Did your spouse participate in a retirement plan maintained by his/her employer?	☐ Yes	☐ No	
Did you and your spouse contribute to a spousal IRA?	☐ Yes	☐ No	

Self-employed Keogh (HR-10) plan

	Yours	Spouse's
Amount contributed		

Have you incurred moving expenses in connection with starting work at a new permanent location? See Chapter 19, *Moving Expenses*.	☐ Yes	☐ No
Did you or your spouse receive any disability payments?	☐ Yes	☐ No

[1]*Depending on your (and your spouse's) income level and whether you (or your spouse) are an active participant in an employer-maintained retirement plan, your IRA deduction may be limited.*

MEDICAL EXPENSES

Note: You will qualify for a federal deduction only if your total unreimbursed medical expenses exceed 7.5% of your adjusted gross income.

List even if reimbursed	Amount
Medical or health insurance premiums (including amounts paid by payroll deductions)	
Medicare premiums	
Prescription drugs and insulin	
Doctors and dentists	
Hospitals	
Other medical expenses (eyeglasses, contact lenses, hearing aids, travel and lodging expenses)	
Reimbursements for medical expenses through insurance or other sources	

Note: If you are divorced or separated, have a child, and paid medical expenses for that child, include these amounts whether or not you are entitled to the dependency exemption. If you were self-employed and had a net profit for the year, were a general partner (or a limited partner receiving guaranteed payments) or if you received wages from an S corporation in which you were a more than 2% shareholder you may be able to deduct a percentage of the amount paid for health insurance on behalf of yourself, your spouse, and dependents. For more information, see Chapter 23, Medical and Dental Expenses.

TAXES

Item	Amount
Real estate taxes	
Personal property	
Vehicle licenses (allowed in some states). State of	
State or local income taxes (if not listed elsewhere)	
Other taxes (not including income taxes and other taxes listed elsewhere)	
State disability tax	

Note: Foreign income taxes paid or withheld should be listed by country.

INTEREST EXPENSES

Item	Payee	Amount
Home mortgage paid to financial institutions		
Home mortgage paid to individuals[1]		
Mortgage points on principal residence[2]		
Prepayment penalty on loans		
Brokerage accounts		
Investment interest		
Other (itemize)		

[1] *You need name(s) and social security number(s).*

[2] *Include only points, including loan origination fees, on the purchase or improvement of your principal residence. If you paid points to refinance your mortgage, see Chapter 25,* Interest Expense.

For more information, see Chapter 25, *Interest Expense.*

CHARITABLE CONTRIBUTIONS

In addition to outright gifts of cash or property, deductible contributions also include out-of-pocket expenses incurred for charity, for example, transportation (automobile mileage may be claimed at 14 cents per mile), meals and lodging away from home, and cost and upkeep of special uniforms and equipment required in the performance of donated services. You need a contemporaneous written acknowledgment from the charity to which a contribution or contributions of $250 or more was made during the year. A canceled check no longer constitutes adequate substantiation for contributions in excess of $250.

If you have sold any property to a charity for less than the property's fair market value, you will need details.

For more information, see Chapter 26, *Contributions.*

CASH CONTRIBUTIONS

Recipient	Amount[1]

If total noncash contributions have a value in excess of $500, you will need the following information:
the name and address of the donee; the date of the gift; a description of the property, how it was acquired by you, and when it was acquired by you; your tax basis; its value at the time of the donation and how the value was ascertained. Indicate (√) if any property was held by you for less than 1 year.

If you made noncash contributions of property in excess of $5,000 in value, use Form 8283, *Noncash Charitable Contributions,* with Section B, *Appraisal Summary,* completed.   □ Yes   □ No

CASUALTY LOSSES

Note: You will qualify for a deduction for a personal casualty loss only if it exceeds 10% of your adjusted gross income and only for the amount *not* covered by insurance reimbursement. See Chapter 27, *Casualty and Theft Losses,* for details.

Casualty losses include such items as losses from automobile collisions; damage from storms, fires, and floods; and damage from vandalism, theft, and other casualties.

A disaster loss is a loss that occurred in an area determined by the President of the United States to warrant federal disaster assistance. See Chapter 27, *Casualty and Theft Losses.*

Describe the casualty loss and its approximate date and location. _____

_____

_____

Indicate (√) type of property: _____ business _____ investment _____ personal

OTHER DEDUCTIONS

Note: In general, you will qualify for a federal deduction only if your total other miscellaneous deductions exceed 2% of your adjusted gross income.

Item	Amount		Item	Amount
Investment expenses: Automobile expense			Educational expense (to maintain or improve skills required by employer)	
Investment counsel fees			Meals and entertainment[1]	
Safe-deposit box			Tax advice/return fees	
Subscriptions			Union dues	
Telephone			Dues for professional organizations	
IRA fees			Business publications	
Other			Office-in-home expenses[2]	
			Other	

[1] *Only 50% of meals and entertainment expenses are deductible.*

[2] *See Chapter 30, Miscellaneous Deduction.*

EMPLOYEE BUSINESS EXPENSES

Were you reimbursed for any business expenses incurred in connection with the
performance of services for your employer?   □ Yes   □ No

If yes, answer the following questions:

A. Are you required to return reimbursement to the extent it exceeds expenses?   □ Yes   □ No

B. Are you required to submit itemized supporting documentation to your employer?   □ Yes   □ No

If you answered yes to the above questions and your reimbursement does not exceed your expenses, you are generally not required to report the reimbursement and expenses on your return. However, if your reimbursement does not equal your expenses, or if you answered no to questions A and/or B, report below the total reimbursements and expenses for the year. Certain other business expenses, even if not reimbursed, may also be deductible.

Does your employer have an accountable reimbursement plan? See Chapter 28, *Car Expenses
and Other Employee Business Expenses.*   □ Yes   □ No

Employee business expenses   Amount

_____

_____

Total amount reimbursed. (Do not include any amounts that were reported to you as
wages in box 10 of Form W-2.)   _____

Do you have substantiation (described below) for travel and entertainment expenses?   □ Yes   □ No

Information that must be available includes

- Amounts spent
- Dates of departure and return for each trip and the number of days spent on business
- Dates of entertainment
- Places of entertainment or travel
- Dates and descriptions of business gifts
- Business purposes of the travel, entertainment, or business gifts
- Business relationships with the persons entertained or to whom gifts were made

AUTOMOBILE EXPENSES

Mileage information	Automobile 1	Automobile 2
Number of months used for business during the year	_____	_____
Total mileage (include personal miles)	_____	_____
Business mileage portion of the total mileage	_____	_____
Commuting mileage portion of the total mileage	_____	_____
Original cost	_____	_____
Annual lease payments	_____	_____

Total actual expenses (business and personal for months used for business)

_____

_____

AUTOMOBILE DEPRECIATION

Year, make, model	Cost	Date acquired
Automobile _____	_____	_____

Do you have adequate or sufficient evidence to justify the deduction for the vehicles?   □ Yes   □ No

If yes, is the evidence written?   □ Yes   □ No

CHILD CARE CREDIT

If you incurred any expenses for child or dependent care so that you and your spouse could be gainfully employed or attend an educational institution as a full-time student, complete the table below.

Did your employer provide or reimburse you for the cost of child or dependent care?   ☐ Yes   ☐ No

If so, the credit must be reduced by the amount excluded from your income through your employer's dependent care assistance program.

Name of child or dependent	Name, address, and social security number or FEIN of person or organization providing care	Relationship, if any	Period of care		Amount paid
			From	To	

FOREIGN TAXES

List foreign source income and foreign income taxes paid

Country	Income		Taxes Paid	
	Type	Amount	Date paid	Amount

EMPLOYING DOMESTIC HELP

Did you employ domestic help?   ☐ Yes   ☐ No

Did you pay more than $1,300 during the year to an individual for services provided in your home?   ☐ Yes   ☐ No

If so, you may be required to pay employment taxes see Chapter 41, *What to Do If You Employ Domestic Help*.

Income and Expense Records You Should Keep in Addition to Your Income Tax Return

Some Suggestions That Could Come in Handy

INCOME	RECORDS
❏ Wages, salaries	✔ Form W-2
❏ Interest income	✔ 1099-INT, 1099-OID or Substitute 1099, such as broker statement or year-end account summary
❏ Dividend income	✔ 1099-DIV or Substitute 1099 such as broker statement or year-end account summary
❏ State tax refunds	✔ Form 1099-G, state income tax return
❏ Self-employment income	✔ Sales slips, invoices, receipts, sales tax reports, business books and records
❏ Capital gains and losses	✔ 1099-B or Substitute 1099, such as broker statement or year-end account summary showing proceeds from sales of securities or other capital assets. Records must also show your cost or other basis and the expenses of the sale. Your records must show when and how an asset was acquired (including property received as a gift or inheritance), how the asset was used, and when and how it was disposed of. To support the basis of securities, you should keep old account statements, buy/sell execution records, stock dividend and stock split information, and dividend reinvestment records (see Chapter 15, *Sale of Property*).
❏ IRA distributions	✔ 1099-R, year-end account summary
❏ Pension and annuities	✔ 1099-R, records of contributions
❏ Rents	✔ Checkbook, receipts and canceled checks, and other books and records
❏ Partnerships, S corporations	✔ Schedule K-1, record of unused passive activity losses
❏ Estates, trusts	✔ Schedule K-1, copies of last will and testament including codicils, Form 56-Notice Concerning Fiduciary Relationship, Form 1310-Statement of Person Claiming Refund due a Deceased Taxpayer, including death certificate or letters of office, Form 4810-Request for Prompt Assessment Under IRC Section 6501(d), Tax worksheets showing pre- and post-death income allocation, including copies of all 1099's received for the year of death, copies of prior three years' Form 1040, and copies of all prior-year gift tax returns.
❏ Social Security benefits	✔ Form SSA-1099
❏ Royalties	✔ 1099-MISC
❏ Unemployment compensation	✔ 1099-G
❏ Alimony	✔ Divorce settlement papers
❏ Miscellaneous income	✔ 1099-MISC and other records of amounts receicved

EXPENSE	RECORDS
❏ Domestic employee expense	✔ Canceled checks, state unemployment tax payments, see Chapter 41, *What to Do If You Employ Domestic Help*.
❏ Self-employment expense	✔ Bills, canceled checks, receipts, bank statements, all business books and records
❏ IRA contribution	✔ Year-end account summary, deposit receipt
❏ Keogh contribution	✔ Year-end account summary, deposit receipt
❏ Alimony	✔ Divorce settlement papers, canceled alimony checks
❏ Medical and dental expense	✔ Bills, canceled checks, receipts, pay stubs if employer withholds medical insurance from wages
❏ Taxes	✔ Canceled checks, mortgage statements, receipts, Form W-2
❏ Interest expense	✔ Bank statements, mortgage statements (Form 1098), canceled checks
❏ Charitable contributions	✔ Canceled checks, receipts, detailed description of noncash property contributed
❏ Miscellaneous deductions	✔ Receipts, canceled checks, or other documentary evidence (See Chapters 27 through 30.)
❏ Casualty and theft losses	✔ Description of property, photograph of damaged property, receipts, canceled checks, policy and insurance reports
❏ Exemptions	✔ Birth certificates, Social Security numbers

CREDITS	RECORDS
❏ Child and dependent care	✔ Receipts, canceled checks and name, address, and identification number of care provider
❏ Estimated taxes	✔ Canceled checks
❏ Foreign taxes	✔ Form 1099 DIV
❏ Withheld taxes	✔ Forms W-2 and 1099

PART I

The Income Tax Return

The five chapters in this part provide basic information on the tax system. They take you through the first steps of filling out a tax return—such as deciding what your filing status is, how many exemptions you can take, and which form to file. They also discuss record-keeping requirements, electronic filing, certain penalties, and the two methods used to pay tax during the year: withholding and estimated tax.

1

Filing Information

Introduction

Unlike the other certainty in life, paying taxes is the one for which you may obtain an extension. Besides explaining when you must file your tax return and what to do if you are unable to get it prepared on time, this chapter provides an introduction to the basic framework within which you file your federal income tax return. It answers a lot of the elementary questions about the procedures and calculations involved in determining your income tax.

This chapter discusses such items as who is required to file and who should file even though he or she is not required to do so. It tells you which forms to use, how

to go about preparing your tax return once you have obtained the correct forms, and where to mail your tax return once it has been completed. In addition, the chapter informs you about the penalties that may be imposed if you do not pay your taxes on time and instructs you on what to do if you discover that a previous tax return is in error. The chapter also explains what the different accounting methods are and which method may be used in preparing your return.

Remember, one of the most important features of this book is Chapter 48, 2001 Federal Tax Forms and Schedules You Can Use.

Important Changes

Who must file. Generally, the amount of income you can receive before you must file a return has been increased. See *Table 1-1, Table 1-2,* and *Table 1-3* for the specific amounts.

Third party designee. You can now allow the IRS to discuss your 2001 tax return with a friend, family member, or any other person you choose by checking the "Yes" box in the "third party designee" area of your return. See *Third Party Designee.*

Mailing your return. You may be mailing your return to a different address this year because the IRS has changed the filing location for sev-

eral areas. If you received an envelope with your tax package, please use it. Otherwise, see your form instructions for where to file.

Sign your return electronically. Create your own personal identification number (PIN) and file a completely paperless tax return with IRS *e-file.* See *Does My Return Have To Be On Paper.*

Important Reminders

Alternative filing methods. Rather than filing a return on paper, you may be able to file electronically using IRS *e-file.* For more information, see *Does My Return Have To Be On Paper,* later.

Change of address. If you change your address, you should notify the IRS. See *Change of Address,* later, under *What Happens After I File.*

Write in your social security number. You must write your social security number (SSN) in the spaces provided on your tax return. If you file a joint return, please write the SSNs in the same order as the names.

Direct Deposit of refund. Instead of getting a paper check, you may be able to have your refund deposited directly into your account at a bank or other financial institution. See *Direct Deposit* under *Refunds,* later.

Alternative payment methods. If you owe additional tax, you may be able to pay electronically. See *How To Pay,* later.

Installment agreement. If you cannot pay the full amount due with your return, you may ask to make monthly installment payments. See *Installment Agreement,* later, under *Amount You Owe.*

Service in combat zone. You are allowed extra time to take care of your tax matters if you are a member of the Armed Forces who served in a combat zone, or if you served in the combat zone in support of the Armed Forces. See *Individuals Serving in Combat Zone,* later, under *When Do I Have To File.*

Adoption taxpayer identification number. If a child has been placed in your home for purposes of legal adoption and you will not be able to get a social security number for the child in time to file your return, you may be able to get an adoption taxpayer identification number (ATIN). For more information, see *Social Security Number,* later.

Taxpayer identification number for aliens. If you or your dependent is a nonresident or resident alien who does not have and is not eligible to get a social security number, file **Form W-7** with the IRS to apply for an Individual Taxpayer Identification Number (ITIN). For more information, see *Social Security Number,* later.

1040PC format no longer accepted. The 1040PC format was a computer-generated paper tax return. The availability of electronic filing for home computer users has reduced the need for this format. The IRS no longer accepts tax returns in the 1040PC format. The IRS encourages all former 1040PC filers to use IRS *e-file.*

This chapter discusses:

• Whether you have to file a return,
• Which form to use,
• How to file electronically,
• When, how, and where to file your return,
• What happens if you pay too little or too much tax,
• What records you should keep and how long you should keep them, and
• How you can change a return you have already filed.

Do I Have To File a Return?

TaxAlert: The 2001 Tax Act

Changes in tax rate structure. The new law generally creates a new 10% rate bracket, provides a rate reduction credit for 2001, and reduces the tax rates in the brackets above 15%. The 10% rate applies to the first $6,000 of taxable income for single filers, $10,000 of taxable income for heads of household, and $12,000 of taxable income for married couples filing jointly. For 2001, all rates will effectively be reduced one-half precent per tax bracket (with the exception of the 10% and 15% brackets). Therefore, the retroactive rate cuts for 2001 are reduced to 27.5%, 30.5%, and 39.1%.

You must file a federal income tax return if you are a citizen or resident of the United States or a resident of Puerto Rico and you meet the filing requirements for any of the following categories that apply to you.

1) Individuals in general. (There are special rules for surviving spouses, executors, administrators, legal representatives, U.S. citizens living outside the United States, residents of Puerto Rico, and individuals with income from U.S. possessions.)
2) Dependents.
3) Child under age 14.
4) Self-employed persons.
5) Aliens.

The filing requirements for each category are explained in this chapter. The filing requirements apply even if you do not owe tax.

Tip. *Even if you do not have to file a return, it may be to your advantage to do so. See* Who Should File, *later.*

One return. File only **one** federal income tax return for the year regardless of how many jobs you had, how many Forms W-2 you received, or how many states you lived in during the year.

Individuals—In General

If you are a U.S. citizen or resident, whether you must file a return depends on three factors:

1) Your gross income,
2) Your filing status, and
3) Your age.

To find out whether you must file, see *Table 1-1, Table 1-2,* and *Table 1-3.* Even if no table shows that you must file, you may need to file to get money back. (See *Who Should File,* later.)

Gross income. This includes all income you receive in the form of money, goods, property, and services that is not exempt from tax. It also includes income from sources outside the United States (even if you may exclude all or part of it). Common types of income are discussed in the chapters in *Part Two* of this publication.

Community property. If you are married and your permanent home is in a community property state, half of any income described by state law as community income may be considered yours. This affects your federal taxes, including whether you must file if you do not file a joint return with your spouse. See Publication 555, *Community Property,* for more information.

Self-employed individuals. If you are self-employed, your gross income includes the amount on line 7 of Schedule C (Form 1040), *Profit or Loss From Business,* or line 1 of Schedule C-EZ (Form 1040), *Net Profit From Business.* See *Self-Employed Persons,* later, for more information about your filing requirements.

Caution. *If you do not report all of your self-employment income, you could cause your social security benefits to be lower when you retire.*

Filing status. Your filing status depends on whether you are single or married and on your family situation. Your filing status is determined on the last day of your tax year, which is December 31 for most taxpayers. See chapter 2 for an explanation of each filing status.

Age. If you are 65 or older at the end of the year, you generally can have a higher amount of gross income than other taxpayers before you must file. See *Table 1-1.* You are considered 65 on the day before your 65th birthday. For example, if your 65th birthday was on January 1, 2002, you are considered 65 for 2001.

Example
You are 65 years old and earned $8,700 of **taxable income** last year. Your husband, who is 66 years old, received a **pension** of $5,000, all of which was **taxable income.** You and your husband legally separated on December 28. If you had been living together at the end of the year, you would not have had to file an income tax return, because your combined income was less than $15,200. But, because you are living apart and your gross income was more than $8,550, you must file a return.

Table 1–1. **2001 Filing Requirements for Most Taxpayers**

To use this table, first find your marital status at the end of 2001. Then, read across the line that shows your filing status and age at the end of 2001. You must file a return if your gross income was at least the amount shown in the last column.

Gross income means all income you received in the form of money, goods, property, and services that is not exempt from tax, including any income from sources outside the United States (even if you may exclude part or all of it).

When using this table, do not include social security benefits as gross income unless you are married filing a separate return and lived with your spouse at any time in 2001. (If you must include the benefits, see chapter 12 for the amount to include.)

Also, see *Table 1–2* and *Table 1–3* for other situations when you must file a return.

Marital Status	Filing Status	Age*	Gross Income
Single (including divorced and legally separated)	Single	under 65 65 or older	$7,450 $8,550
	Head of household	under 65 65 or older	$9,550 $10,650
Married, with a child, living apart from your spouse during the last 6 months of 2001	Head of household	under 65 65 or older	$9,550 $10,650
Married, living with your spouse at the end of 2001 (or on the date your spouse died)	Married, joint return	under 65 (both spouses) 65 or older (one spouse) 65 or older (both spouses)	$13,400 $14,300 $15,200
	Married, separate return	any age	$2,900
Married, not living with your spouse at end of 2001 (or on the date your spouse died)	Married, joint or separate return	any age	$2,900
Widowed before 2001 and not remarried in 2001	Single	under 65 65 or older	$7,450 $8,550
	Head of household	under 65 65 or older	$9,550 $10,650
	Qualifying widow(er) with dependent child	under 65 65 or older	$10,500 $11,400

Surviving Spouses, Executors, Administrators, and Legal Representatives

You must file a final return for a decedent (a person who died) if both of the following are true.

- You are the surviving spouse, executor, administrator, or legal representative.
- The decedent met the filing requirements at the date of death.

For more information on rules for filing a decedent's final return, see chapter 4.

U.S. Citizens Living Outside the United States

If you are a U.S. citizen living outside the United States, you must file a return if you meet the filing requirements. For information on special tax rules that may apply to you, get Publication 54, *Tax Guide for U.S. Citizens and Resident Aliens Abroad*. It is available at most U.S. embassies and consulates. Also see *How To Get Tax Help* in the back of this publication.

Explanation
For more information about U.S. citizens living abroad, see Chapter 42, *U.S. Citizens Working Abroad.*

Residents of Puerto Rico

Generally, if you are a U.S. citizen and a resident of Puerto Rico, you must file a U.S. income tax return if you meet the filing requirements. This is in addition to any legal requirement you may have to file an income tax return for Puerto Rico.

If you are a resident of Puerto Rico for the entire year, gross income does not include income from sources within Puerto Rico, except for amounts received as an employee of the United States or a U.S. agency. If you receive income from Puerto Rican sources that is not subject to U.S. tax, you must reduce your standard deduction. As a result, the amount of income you must have before you are required to file a U.S. income tax return is lower than the applicable amount in *Table 1-1* or *Table 1-2.* See *U.S. taxation* and its discussion, *Standard deduction,* under *The Commonwealth of Puerto Rico* in Publication 570, *Tax Guide for Individuals With Income From U.S. Possessions,* for further information.

Individuals With Income From U.S. Possessions

If you had income from Guam, the Commonwealth of the Northern Mariana Islands, American Samoa, or the Virgin Islands, special rules may apply when determining whether you must file a U.S. federal income tax return. In addition, you may have to file a return with the individual island government. See Publication 570 for more information.

Table 1–2. 2001 Filing Requirements for Dependents

See chapter 3 to find out if someone can claim you as a dependent.

If your parents (or someone else) can claim you as a dependent, and any of the situations below apply to you, you must file a return. (See *Table 1–3* for other situations when you must file.)

In this table, **earned income** includes salaries, wages, tips, and professional fees. It also includes taxable scholarship and fellowship grants. (See *Scholarship and Fellowship Grants* in chapter 13.) **Unearned income** includes investment-type income such as interest, dividends, and capital gains. It also includes unemployment compensation, taxable social security benefits, pensions, annuities, and distributions of unearned income from a trust. **Gross income** is the total of your earned and unearned income.

Caution: If your gross income was $2,900 or more, you generally cannot be claimed as a dependent unless you were under age 19 **or** a full-time student under age 24. For details, see *Gross Income Test* in chapter 3.

Single dependents— Were you either age 65 or older or blind?

❑ **No.** You must file a return if any of the following apply.
- Your unearned income was more than $750.
- Your earned income was more than $4,550.
- Your gross income was more than the larger of:
  1) $750, or
  2) Your earned income (up to $4,300) plus $250.

❑ **Yes.** You must file a return if any of the following apply.
- Your earned income was more than $5,650 ($6,750 if 65 or older **and** blind).
- Your unearned income was more than $1,850 ($2,950 if 65 or older **and** blind).
- Your gross income was more than:
  1) The larger of $750, or your earned income (up to $4,300) plus $250, plus
  2) $1,100 ($2,200 if 65 or older **and** blind).

Married dependents— Were you either age 65 or older or blind?

❑ **No.** You must file a return if any of the following apply.
- Your gross income was at least $5 and your spouse files a separate return and itemizes deductions.
- Your earned income was more than $3,800.
- Your unearned income was more than $750.
- Your gross income was more than the larger of:
  1) $750, or
  2) Your earned income (up to $3,550) plus $250.

❑ **Yes.** You must file a return if any of the following apply.
- Your gross income was at least $5 and your spouse files a separate return and itemizes deductions.
- Your earned income was more than $4,700 ($5,600 if 65 or older **and** blind).
- Your unearned income was more than $1,650 ($2,550 if 65 or older **and** blind).
- Your gross income was more than:
  1) The larger of $750 or your earned income (up to $3,550) plus $250, plus
  2) $900 ($1,800 if 65 or older **and** blind).

Dependents

If you are a dependent (one who meets the dependency tests in chapter 3), see *Table 1-2* to find whether you must file a return. You also must file if your situation is described in *Table 1-3*.

Responsibility of parent. Generally, a child is responsible for filing his or her own tax return and for paying any tax on the return. But if a dependent child who must file an income tax return cannot file it for any reason, such as age, a parent, guardian, or other legally responsible person must file it for the child. If the child cannot sign the return, the parent or guardian must sign the child's name followed by the words "By (signature), parent (or guardian) for minor child."

Child's earnings. Amounts a child earns by performing services are his or her gross income. This is true even if under local law the child's parents have the right to the earnings and may actually have received

them. If the child does not pay the tax due on this income, the parent is liable for the tax.

Explanation
For more details about **dependents**, see Chapter 3, *Personal Exemptions and Dependents.*

Child Under Age 14

If a child's only income is interest and dividends (including Alaska Permanent Fund dividends) and certain other conditions are met, a parent can elect to include the child's income on the parent's return. If this election is made, the child does not have to file a return. See

Table 1–3. **Other Situations When You Must File a 2001 Return**

If any of the four conditions listed below apply, you must file a return, even if your income is less than the amount shown in *Table 1–1* or *Table 1–2.*

1. You owe any special taxes, such as:

   - Social security or Medicare tax on tips you did not report to your employer. (See chapter 7.)
   - Uncollected social security, Medicare, or railroad retirement tax on tips you reported to your employer. (See chapter 7.)
   - Uncollected social security, Medicare, or railroad retirement tax on your group-term life insurance.
   - Alternative minimum tax. (See chapter 31.)
   - Tax on a qualified retirement plan, including an individual retirement arrangement (IRA). (See chapter 18.)
   - Tax on an Archer MSA. (See Publication 969, *Medical Savings Accounts (MSAs).*)
   - Recapture of an investment credit or a low-income housing credit. (See the instructions for Form 4255, *Recapture of Investment Credit*, or Form 8611, *Recapture of Low-Income Housing Credit.*)
   - Recapture tax on the disposition of a home purchased with a federally-subsidized mortgage. (See chapter 16.)
   - Recapture of the qualified electric vehicle credit. (See chapter 37.)
   - Recapture of an education credit. (See chapter 36.)
   - Recapture of the Indian employment credit.

2. You received any advance earned income credit (EIC) payments from your employer. This amount should be shown in box 9 of your Form W–2. (See chapter 37.)

3. You had net earnings from self-employment of at least $400. (See *Self-Employed Persons* in this chapter.)

4. You had wages of $108.28 or more from a church or qualified church-controlled organization that is exempt from employer social security and Medicare taxes. (See Publication 533.)

Parent's Election To Report Child's Interest and Dividends in chapter 32.

Self-Employed Persons

You are self-employed if you:

- Carry on a trade or business as a sole proprietor,
- Are an independent contractor,
- Are a member of a partnership, or
- Are in business for yourself in any other way.

Self-employment can include work in addition to your regular full-time business activities. It also includes certain part-time work that you do at home or in addition to your regular job.

You must file a return if your gross income is at least as much as the filing requirement amount for your filing status and age (shown in *Table 1-1*). Also, you must file Form 1040 and **Schedule SE** (Form 1040), *Self-Employment Tax,* if:

1) Your net earnings from self-employment (excluding church employee income) were $400 or more, or
2) You had church employee income of $108.28 or more. (See *Table 1-3.*)

Use Schedule SE (Form 1040) to figure your self-employment tax. Self-employment tax is comparable to the social security and Medicare tax withheld from an employee's wages. For more information about this tax, get Publication 533, *Self-Employment Tax.*

Examples
A person who delivers newspapers would be subject to self-employment tax. A person working at home in a cottage industry—making quilts or pillows, for example—would be subject to self-employment tax.

In some instances, it is to your advantage to report income from self-employment, because if you do not already qualify, you will then become eligible for Social Security benefits. For more information on self-employed persons, see Chapter 38, *If You Are Self-Employed.*

TAXSAVER

Employing your spouse. In prior years, there was an advantage for a self-employed person whose earnings were slightly over the maximum tax base to employ a spouse in the business to lower his or her self-employment tax. The spouse's wages were not subject to Social Security taxes or self-employment tax. Now, however, the spouse's wages are subject to Social Security taxes. A self-employed person who has previously employed his or her spouse for this reason should consider terminating this practice.

Explanation

You are able to deduct one-half of your self-employment tax for the year in calculating your adjusted gross income. For details see Chapter 24, *Taxes You May Deduct*.

Self-employment tax has two parts: old age, survivor, and disability insurance (OASDI) and Medicare hospital insurance (HI). (The comparable Social Security tax withheld on an employee's wages consists of these same two parts.) In 2001, the cap on self-employment income subject to OASDI is $80,400. There is no limit on the amount of self-employment income subject to the HI portion of the self-employment tax.

TAXALERT

The 2002 FICA wage and self-employment income base will be $84,900.

Foreign governments or international organizations. If you are a U.S. citizen who works in the United States for an international organization, a foreign government, or a wholly owned instrumentality of a foreign government, and your employer does not deduct social security and Medicare taxes from your income, you must include your earnings from services performed in the United States when figuring your net earnings from self-employment.

Ministers. You must include income from services you performed as a minister when figuring your net earnings from self-employment, unless you have an exemption from self-employment tax. This also applies to Christian Science practitioners and members of a religious order who have not taken a vow of poverty. For more information, get Publication 517, *Social Security and Other Information for Members of the Clergy and Religious Workers*.

Aliens

Your status as an alien—resident, nonresident, or dual-status—determines whether and how you must file an income tax return.

The rules used to determine your alien status are discussed in Publication 519, *U.S. Tax Guide for Aliens*.

Resident alien. If you are a resident alien for the entire year, you must file a tax return following the same rules that apply to U.S. citizens. Use the forms discussed in this publication.

Nonresident alien. If you are a nonresident alien, the rules and tax forms that apply to you are different from those that apply to U.S. citizens and resident aliens. See Publication 519 to find out if U.S. income tax laws apply to you and which forms you should file.

Dual-status taxpayer. If you were a resident alien for part of the tax year and a nonresident alien for the rest of the year, you are a dual-status taxpayer. Different rules apply for each part of the year. For information on dual-status taxpayers, see Publication 519.

Explanation

For more information about foreign citizens living in the United States, see Chapter 43, *Foreign Citizens Living in the United States*.

Who Should File

Even if you do not have to file, you should file a federal income tax return to get money back if any of the following conditions apply.

1) You had income tax withheld from your pay.
2) You qualify for the earned income credit. See chapter 37 for more information.

3) You qualify for the additional child tax credit. See chapter 35 for more information.

Which Form Should I Use?

You must use one of three forms to file your return: Form 1040EZ, Form 1040A, or Form 1040. (But also see *Does My Return Have To Be On Paper,* later.)

Form 1040EZ

Form 1040EZ is the simplest form to use.
You can use Form 1040EZ if all of the following apply.

1) Your filing status is single or married filing jointly. If you were a nonresident alien at any time in 2001, your filing status must be married filing jointly.
2) You (and your spouse if married filing a joint return) were under age 65 on January 1, 2002, and not blind at the end of 2001.
3) You do not claim any dependents.
4) Your taxable income is less than $50,000.
5) Your income is *only* from wages, salaries, tips, unemployment compensation, Alaska Permanent Fund dividends, taxable scholarship and fellowship grants, qualified state tuition program earnings, and taxable interest of $400 or less.
6) You did not receive any advance earned income credit (EIC) payments.
7) You do not claim any adjustments to income, such as a deduction for IRA contributions or student loan interest.
8) You do not claim any credits other than the earned income credit or the rate reduction credit.

You must meet all of these requirements to use Form 1040EZ. If you do not, you must use Form 1040A or Form 1040.

TAXPLANNER

Even though it might be easier for you to file Form 1040EZ, you should carefully review your situation before doing so, especially if your income is close to the Form 1040EZ maximum level of $50,000. Check what deductions you may be able to claim if you itemize them. (You cannot claim **itemized deductions** on Form 1040EZ.) If you have deductions that can be itemized and you do not claim them, you could be significantly overpaying your tax.

Figuring tax. On Form 1040EZ, you can only use the tax table to figure your tax. You cannot use Form 1040EZ to report any other tax.

Form 1040A

If you do not qualify to use Form 1040EZ, you may be able to use Form 1040A.
You can use Form 1040A if all of the following apply.

1) Your income is *only* from wages, salaries, tips, IRA distributions, pensions and annuities, taxable social security and railroad retirement benefits, taxable scholarship and fellowship grants, interest, ordinary dividends (including Alaska Permanent Fund dividends), capital gain distributions, qualified state tuition program earnings, and unemployment compensation.
2) Your taxable income is less than $50,000.
3) Your adjustments to income are for only the following items.
   a) The deduction for contributions to an IRA.
   b) The student loan interest deduction.
4) You do not itemize your deductions.

5) Your taxes are from only the following items.
   a) Tax Table.
   b) Alternative minimum tax. (See chapter 31.)
   c) Advance earned income credit (EIC) payments, if you received any. (See chapter 37.)
   d) Recapture of an education credit.
   e) Form 8615, *Tax for Children Under Age 14 Who Have Investment Income of More Than $1,500.*
   f) Capital Gain Tax Worksheet.
6) You claim only the following credits.
   a) The credit for child and dependent care expenses. (See chapter 33.)
   b) The credit for the elderly or the disabled. (See chapter 34.)
   c) The child tax credit. (See chapter 35.)
   d) The additional child tax credit. (See chapter 35.)
   e) The education credits. (See chapter 36.)
   f) The earned income credit. (See chapter 37.)
   g) The adoption credit. (See chapter 37.)
   h) The rate reduction credit. (See chapter 37.)

You must meet all of the above requirements to use Form 1040A. If you do not, you must use Form 1040.

If you meet the above requirements, you can use Form 1040A even if you received employer-provided adoption benefits or dependent care benefits.

Caution. *If you receive a capital gain distribution that includes 28% rate gain, qualified 5-year gain, unrecaptured section 1250 gain, or section 1202 gain, you cannot use Form 1040A. You must use Form 1040.*

TaxAlert

Form 1040A lets you report most retirement income, including pension and annuity payments, taxable Social Security and railroad retirement benefits, and payments from your IRA. Furthermore, it allows you to claim the credit for the elderly or the disabled and report your estimated tax payments. If you have been filing a Form 1040 because of these items, you can qualify for the easier-to-file Form 1040A. Be aware that you still cannot claim itemized deductions on Form 1040A. If you have deductions that can be itemized, you may be better off continuing to file a Form 1040.

Form 1040

If you cannot use Form 1040EZ or Form 1040A, you must use Form 1040. You can use Form 1040 to report all types of income, deductions, and credits.

You may have received Form 1040A or Form 1040EZ in the mail because of the return you filed last year. If your situation has changed this year, it may be to your advantage to file Form 1040 instead. You may pay less tax by filing Form 1040 because you can take itemized deductions and some adjustments to income and credits you cannot take on Form 1040A or Form 1040EZ.

You must use Form 1040 if any of the following apply.

1) Your taxable income is $50,000 or more.
2) You itemize your deductions.
3) You received or paid interest on securities transferred between interest payment dates.
4) You received nontaxable distributions required to be reported as capital gains.
5) You received capital gain distributions that included 28% rate gain, qualified 5-year gain, unrecaptured section 1250 gain, or section 1202 gain.
6) You have to complete Part III of Schedule B (Form 1040) because:
   a) You received a distribution from a foreign trust, or

b) You had a bank, securities, or other financial account in a foreign country at any time during the year.
   Note. If the combined value of the foreign account(s) was $10,000 or less during all of 2001, or if the account(s) was with a U.S. military banking facility operated by a U.S. financial institution, you may be able to use Form 1040A or Form 1040EZ.
7) You had income that cannot be reported on Form 1040EZ or Form 1040A. This includes gain from the sale of property, barter income, alimony income, taxable refunds of state and local income taxes, self-employment income (including farm income), and income received as a partner in a partnership, a shareholder in an S corporation, or a beneficiary of an estate or trust.
8) You are reporting original issue discount in an amount more or less than the amount shown on Form 1099-OID.
9) You sold or exchanged capital assets or business property.
10) You claim adjustments to gross income for other than contributions to an IRA or the student loan interest deduction. If these are your only adjustments to gross income, you may be able to file Form 1040A.
11) Your Form W-2 shows uncollected employee tax (social security and Medicare tax) on tips or group-term life insurance in box 12. (See chapter 7.)
12) You received $20 or more in tips in any one month and did not report all of them to your employer. (See chapter 7.)
13) You must pay tax on self-employment income. (See Schedule SE (Form 1040), *Self-Employment Tax.*)
14) You must pay household employment taxes. (See Schedule H (Form 1040).)
15) You have to recapture an investment credit, a low-income housing credit, a qualified electric vehicle credit, or an Indian employment credit.
16) You have to recapture tax on the disposition of a home purchased with a federally-subsidized mortgage. (See chapter 16.)
17) You have to pay tax on an excess golden parachute payment.
18) You claim any credits other than the credits listed earlier under *Form 1040A.*
19) You have to file other forms with your return to report certain exclusions, taxes, or transactions. This includes the following forms.
   a) Form 2555, *Foreign Earned Income.*
   b) Form 2555-EZ, *Foreign Earned Income Exclusion.*
   c) Form 4563, *Exclusion of Income for Bona Fide Residents of American Samoa.*
   d) Form 4970, *Tax on Accumulation Distribution of Trusts.*
   e) Form 4972, *Tax on Lump-Sum Distributions.* (See chapter 11.)
   f) Form 5329, *Additional Taxes on Qualified Plans (Including IRAs) and Other Tax-Favored Accounts.*
      Note. Do not file Form 1040 only because you have to file Form 5329. File Form 5329 by itself. (See chapters 11 and 18.)
   g) Form 8271, *Investor Reporting of Tax Shelter Registration Number.*
   h) Form 8814, *Parents' Election To Report Child's Interest and Dividends.*
   i) Form 8853, *Archer MSAs and Long-Term Care Insurance Contracts.*

Does My Return Have To Be On Paper?

IRS *e-file* (electronic filing) is the preferred method of filing. It's so easy, 40 million people use it. You may be able to file a paperless return, or a return with less paper. This section explains IRS *e-file:*

- Using a tax professional,
- Using your personal computer, or
- Using a telephone (TeleFile).

Table 1–4. **Benefits of IRS *e-file***

Accuracy	• Your chance of getting an error notice from the IRS is significantly reduced.
Security	• Your privacy and security are assured.
Electronic Signatures	• Create your own Personal Identification Number (PIN) and file a completely paperless return through your tax preparation software or tax professional. There is nothing to mail!
Proof of Acceptance	• You receive an electronic acknowledgement within 48 hours confirming that the IRS has accepted your return for processing.
Fast Refunds	• You get your refund in half the time, even faster with Direct Deposit—in as few as 10 days.
FREE/Low Cost Filing	• Check out the IRS Web Site at www.irs.gov for IRS *e-file* partners offering free or low cost filing options to taxpayers who qualify.
Electronic Payment Options	• Convenient, safe and secure electronic payment options are available. *e-file* and pay in a single step. Schedule an electronic funds withdrawal from your bank account (up to and including April 15, 2002) or pay by credit card.
Federal/State Filing	• Prepare and file your federal and state tax returns together and double the benefits you get from *e-file*.

IRS *e-file*

Table 1-4 lists the benefits of IRS *e-file*. IRS *e-file* uses automation to replace most of the manual steps needed to process paper returns. As a result, the processing of *e-file* returns is faster and more accurate than the processing of paper returns. However, errors on the return or problems with its transmission can delay processing.

Example
You expect a $3,000 refund. If you can receive your refund in 3 weeks by filing electronically instead of 3 months by filing a paper form, you could save money by investing the refund sooner. Assuming you can earn 7% after tax on your money, you might save $45. However, the company that files your return electronically will usually charge you a separate fee for this service. This should be considered in your decision to file electronically.

As with a paper return, you are responsible for making sure your return contains accurate information and is filed on time.

Using *e-file* does not affect your chances of an IRS examination of your return.

State returns. In most states, you can file an electronic state return simultaneously with your federal return. For more information, check with your local IRS office, state tax agency, tax professional, or the IRS web site at **www.irs.gov.**

Refunds. You can have a refund check mailed to you, or you can have your refund deposited directly to your checking or savings account.

With *e-file,* your refund will be issued in half the time as when filing on paper. Most refunds are issued within 3 weeks. If you choose Direct Deposit, you can receive your refund in as few as 10 days.

Explanation: Direct Deposit Refunds
Direct Deposit refunds will usually be issued 2 to 3 weeks from the date the electronic return is accepted. However, the Treasury Department does not guarantee that a refund will be issued by a specific date or for the anticipated amount.

The following conditions may delay refunds and/or change refund amounts. Direct Deposit elections generally will not be honored in these cases:

1. Taxpayer owes back taxes, either individual or business.
2. Taxpayer owes delinquent child support.
3. Taxpayer has a certain delinquent debt, such as student loans.
4. The last name and Social Security number of the primary taxpayer are not the same as on last year's return. If this is the case, the return will be delayed at least 1 week for rematching.
5. The estimated tax payments reported on the return do not match the estimated tax payments recorded on the IRS master file. This generally occurs when:
   a. The spouse made separate payments and filed a joint return, or vice versa; or
   b. The return was filed before the January 15, 2002, estimated tax payment was credited to the taxpayer's account.
6. The taxpayer has a Schedule E claiming a deduction for a questionable tax shelter.
7. The taxpayer is claiming a blatantly unallowable deduction.

TaxPlanner

A refund anticipation loan (RAL) is a loan made to you based on your expected refund. The loan is a contract between you and a financial institution. Generally, the financial institution will require that you sign an authorization that permits the institution to debit your account after the refund has been credited to it. You can expect to pay a fee to the electronic filer, who with your permission submits information to the financial institution, and a fee to the financial institution. These fees are in addition to the tax preparation fee and electronic filing fee. Generally, Direct Deposit takes 2 to 3 weeks before you receive your refund. An RAL could speed up the time for you to have your money by about 2 weeks but at a relatively high "interest cost." For example, if your expected refund is $1,000 and the fee is $30, the "interest cost" to you for the 2 weeks' use of the money comes to over 75% on an annualized basis.

Offset against debts. As with a paper return, you may not get all of your refund if you owe certain past-due amounts, such as federal tax, state tax, a student loan, or child support. See *Offset Against Debts* under *Refunds,* later.

Explanation: Composition of an Electronic Return
In total, an electronic return contains the same information as a comparable return filed entirely on paper documents. An electronic return consists of:

1. Electronic portion of return—Data transmitted to the IRS electronically
2. Nonelectronic portion of return—Paper documents (filed with the IRS at a later date) that contain information that cannot be electronically transmitted, such as taxpayer signatures and documents prepared by third parties

Electronic Portion of Return
For 2001 returns, most forms and schedules, including Form 1040 and Form 1040A, can be transmitted electronically and are considered the "electronic portion" of the return.

Nonelectronic Portion of Return
Some parts of your return *cannot* be filed electronically, including the following:

- Form 8453, *U.S. Individual Income Tax Declaration for Electronic Filing,* required for all electronic returns
- Copy B Form W-2, W-2G, or 1099-R, which would normally be attached to the front of a paper return
- Other information documents that are voluntarily being included with the return by the taxpayer as supporting material

Exclusions from Electronic Filing
The following are some of the types of returns that are excluded from electronic filing:

  Decedent returns, including joint returns filed by surviving spouses
  Returns with a power of attorney currently in effect for the refund to be sent to a third party
  Returns subject to community property rules with filing status "Married Filing Separately"
  Returns with Social Security numbers within the range 900-00-0000 through 999-99-9998. These are temporary Social Security numbers

Refund inquiries. If you do not receive your refund within 4 weeks after your return was accepted by IRS, you can call TeleTax Refund Information. See *What is TeleTax* in your tax forms package for information on how to use this service.

If TeleTax has no information about your return, contact your tax professional or electronic return transmitter for the date IRS accepted your return. If your return was accepted more than 6 weeks ago, contact the IRS. Explain that you filed your return electronically and that TeleTax

has no information on it. Also, provide the first social security number shown on your return and the date the IRS accepted your return.

Balance due. If you owe tax, you must pay it by April 15, 2002, to avoid late-payment penalties and interest. You can make your payment electronically by scheduling an electronic funds withdrawal from your checking or savings account or by credit card.

See *How To Pay,* later, for information on how to pay the balance due.

VITA or TCE. The IRS Volunteer Income Tax Assistance (VITA) and Tax Counseling for the Elderly (TCE) programs may be able to help you file your return electronically. For information on these programs, call the IRS.

Personal identification number (PIN). If you *e-file* your return, you can sign your return electronically by creating your own Personal Identification Number (PIN). This PIN serves as your signature and can only be used if you file electronically using tax preparation software or through a tax professional. (It can even be used by first-time filers who were 16 or older on December 31, 2001.) To create a PIN, you must know your adjusted gross income and total tax from your 2000 tax return (prior to any adjustment). These amounts, along with your name, social security number, and date of birth, will be used to verify your identity.

If you are not eligible or choose not to use a PIN to sign your return electronically, you must complete Form 8453 or Form 8453-OL, whichever applies.

Using a Tax Professional
Many tax professionals file returns electronically for their clients. You can prepare your own return and have a professional electronically transmit it, or you can have your return prepared and transmitted by a tax professional. In either situation, you can sign your return using your PIN.

Depending on the tax professional, and the specific services requested, a fee may be charged. Look for the "Authorized IRS *e-file* Provider" sign or search for a provider near you on the IRS web site at **www.irs.gov** (click on Electronic Services).

Form 8453. Your tax professional may ask you to sign Form 8453, *U.S. Individual Income Tax Declaration for an IRS e-file Return.* Both spouses must sign if a joint return is being filed. Your tax professional will file the Form 8453 with the IRS. Your tax professional is required to give you the preparer-signed copy of your return, including a copy of the completed Form 8453. This material is for your records. Do not mail this copy to the IRS.

Using a Personal Computer
A computer with a modem and/or Internet access is all you need to file your tax return using IRS *e-file.* You can buy tax preparation software at various electronic stores or computer and office supply stores. You can download software from the Internet or prepare and file your tax return completely on-line by using a tax preparation software package on the Internet (nothing to buy or install). Best of all, you can *e-file* your tax return from the comfort of your home any time of day or night. Sign your return electronically using your PIN to complete the process. To find a list of software companies that participate in the IRS *e-file* program, visit our web site at **www.irs.gov.**

Form 8453-OL. After the IRS has accepted your return, you may have to send the IRS Form 8453-OL, *U.S. Individual Income Tax Declaration for an IRS efile On-line Return.* Form 8453-OL is available through your electronic return transmitter.

Using a Telephone (TeleFile)
If you receive a TeleFile tax package, you may be able to file your Form 1040EZ information over the phone. If you are eligible to use TeleFile, IRS will send you the TeleFile tax package automatically. You can use TeleFile only if you receive the package. You cannot order it.

To file using TeleFile, follow the instructions in the TeleFile tax package. The call takes about 10 minutes and is free. You must use a touch-tone phone.

When Do I Have To File?

April 15, 2002, is the due date for filing your 2001 income tax return if you use the calendar year. For a quick view of due dates for filing a return with or without an extension of time to file (discussed later), see *Table 1-5.*

If you use a fiscal year (a year ending on the last day of any month except December, or a 52-53 week year), your income tax return is due by the 15th day of the 4th month after the close of your fiscal year.

When the due date for doing *any* act for tax purposes—filing a return, paying taxes, etc.—falls on a Saturday, Sunday, or legal holiday, the due date is delayed until the next business day.

Filing on time. Your paper return is filed on time if it is mailed in an envelope that is properly addressed and postmarked by the due date. The envelope must have enough postage. If you send your return by registered mail, the date of the registration is the postmark date. The registration is evidence that the return was delivered. If you send a return by certified mail and have your receipt postmarked by a postal employee, the date on the receipt is the postmark date. The postmarked certified mail receipt is evidence that the return was delivered.

Private delivery services. If you use a private delivery service designated by the IRS to send your return, the postmark date generally is the date the private delivery service records in its database or marks on the mailing label. The private delivery service can tell you how to get written proof of this date.

The following are designated private delivery services.

- Airborne Express (Airborne): Overnight Air Express Service, Next Afternoon Service, and Second Day Service.
- DHL Worldwide Express (DHL): DHL "Same Day" Service and DHL USA Overnight.
- Federal Express (FedEx): FedEx Priority Overnight, FedEx Standard Overnight, and FedEx 2Day.
- United Parcel Service (UPS): UPS Next Day Air, UPS Next Day Air Saver, UPS 2nd Day Air, UPS 2nd Day Air A.M, UPS Worldwide Express Plus, and UPS Worldwide Express.

Caution. *Private delivery services cannot deliver items to P.O. boxes. You must use the U.S. Postal Service to mail any item to an IRS P.O. box address.*

Electronically filed returns. If you use IRS *e-file,* your return is considered filed on time if the authorized electronic return transmitter postmarks the transmission by the due date. An authorized electronic return transmitter is a participant in the IRS *e-file* program that transmits electronic tax return information directly to the IRS.

The electronic postmark is a record of when the authorized electronic return transmitter received the transmission of your electronically filed return on its host system. The date and time in your time zone controls whether your electronically filed return is timely.

Filing late. If you do not file your return by the due date, you may have to pay a failure-to-file penalty and interest. For more information, see *Penalties,* later. Also see *Interest* under *Amount You Owe.*

If you were due a refund but you did not file a return, you generally must file within 3 years from the date the return was originally due to get that refund.

Nonresident alien. If you are a nonresident alien and earn wages subject to U.S. income tax withholding, your 2001 U.S. income tax return (Form 1040NR or Form 1040NR-EZ) is due by:

- April 15, 2002, if you use a calendar year, or
- The 15th day of the 4th month after the end of your fiscal year if you use a fiscal year.

If you do not earn wages subject to U.S. income tax withholding, your return is due by:

- June 17, 2002, if you use a calendar year, or
- The 15th day of the 6th month after the end of your fiscal year, if you use a fiscal year.

Get Publication 519, *U.S. Tax Guide for Aliens,* for more filing information.

Filing for a decedent. If you must file a final income tax return for a taxpayer who died during the year (a decedent), the return is due by the 15th day of the 4th month after the end of the decedent's normal tax year. In most cases, for a 2001 return, this will be April 15, 2002. See *Final Return for the Decedent* in chapter 4.

Extensions of Time To File

You may be able to get an extension of time to file your return. Special rules apply if you were:

- Outside the United States, or
- Serving in a combat zone.

These rules are discussed separately.

Automatic extension. If you cannot file your 2001 return by the due date, you may be able to get an automatic 4-month extension of time to file.

Example. If your return is due on April 15, 2002, you will have until August 15, 2002, to file.

How to get the automatic extension. You can get the automatic extension by:

1) Using IRS *e-file* (electronic filing), or
2) Filing a paper form.

E-file **options.** There are three options for using *e-file* to get an extension of time to file. If you *e-file,* you will get a confirmation number when you complete the transaction. Keep the number with your records.

Complete **Form 4868,** *Application for Automatic Extension of Time To File U.S. Individual Income Tax Return,* to use as a worksheet. If you think you may owe tax when you file your return, use *Part III* of the form to estimate your balance due. Do not send Form 4868 to the IRS.

E-file by phone. You can file Form 4868 by phone any time from March 1 through April 15, 2002. You will need to provide certain infor-

Table 1–5. When To File Your 2001 Return
(For U.S. citizens and residents who file returns on a calendar year)

	For Most Taxpayers	For Certain Taxpayers Outside the U.S.
No extension requested	April 15, 2002	June 17, 2002
Automatic extension Form 4868 filed, or credit card payment made	August 15, 2002	August 15, 2002
2nd extension Form 2688 filed after getting automatic extension	October 15, 2002	October 15, 2002

mation from your tax return for 2000. If you wish to make a payment by electronic funds withdrawal, see *Electronic payment by electronic filer,* under *How To Pay,* later in this chapter.

E-file using your personal computer or a tax professional. You can use a tax software package with your personal computer or a tax professional to file Form 4868 electronically. You will need to provide certain information from your tax return for 2000. If you wish to make a payment by electronic funds withdrawal, see *Electronic payment by electronic filer,* under *How To Pay,* later in this chapter.

E-file and pay by credit card. You can get an extension by paying part or all of your estimate of tax due by using a credit card. You can do this by phone or over the Internet. You do not file Form 4868. See *Payment by credit card,* under *How To Pay,* later in this chapter.

Filing a paper Form 4868. You can get an extension of time to file by filing a paper Form 4868. Mail it to the address shown in the form instructions.

If you want to make a payment with the form, make your check or money order payable to the "United States Treasury." Write your social security number, daytime phone number, and "2001 Form 4868" on your check or money order.

TaxAlert

The IRS offers some relief to taxpayers unable to pay the amount owed with the filing of Form 4868. The IRS permits Form 4868 to be filed and an automatic 4-month extension obtained even though the tax properly estimated to be due is not paid in full when the form is filed. No late filing penalty will be assessed under these circumstances. However, it is still required that the tax liability shown on Form 4868 be properly estimated based on the information available to the taxpayer. Furthermore, unless at least 90% of the taxpayer's actual tax liability was paid prior to the original due date of the return through withholding or estimated payment, a late payment penalty of 1/2% per month will be assessed for each month from the original due date to the date of payment plus the regular rate of interest on underpayments.

When to file. You must request the automatic extension by the due date for your return. You can file your return any time before the 4-month extension period ends.

TaxSaver

An extension of time to file will not be valid if it does not show a "proper" estimate of tax liability. A proper estimate is based on all the facts and information you have at the time of filing. If your estimate is found to be improper, your extension will be invalid and you will be subject to failure-to-file penalties. See *Penalties,* later.

Some tax experts contend that you should request the maximum extension allowed for filing your return, arguing that your chances of an audit are reduced, because IRS field agents will have less time to conduct the audit. Other tax experts contend that you're better off filing on April 15, because that way you get lost in the crowd. Both theories are oversimplifications of IRS procedures.

When you file your return. Enter any payment you made related to the extension of time to file on line 64, Form 1040. If you file Form 1040EZ or Form 1040A, include that payment in your total payments on line 10 of Form 1040EZ or line 41 of Form 1040A. Also print "Form 4868" and the amount paid in the space to the left of line 10 or line 41.

Extension beyond 4 months. If you get the 4-month extension and you later find that you are not able to file within the 4-month extension period, you may be able to get 2 more months to file, for a total of 6 months.

You can apply for an extension beyond the 4-month extension either by writing a letter to the IRS or by filing **Form 2688,** *Application for Additional Extension of Time To File U.S. Individual Income Tax Return.* You should ask for the extension early so that, if it is not approved, you still will be able to file on time. Except in cases of undue hardship, a request for additional time will not be approved unless you have first used the automatic 4-month extension. Form 2688 or your letter will not be considered if you file it after the extended due date.

To get an extension beyond the automatic 4-month extension, you must give all the following information.

- The reason for requesting the extension.
- The tax year to which the extension applies.
- The length of time needed for the extension.
- Whether another extension of time to file has already been requested for this tax year.

You must sign the request for this extension, or it may be signed by your attorney, CPA, enrolled agent, or a person with a power of attorney. If you are unable to sign the request because of illness or for another good reason, a person with a close personal or business relationship to you can sign for you, stating why you could not sign the request.

E-file. Refer to your tax software package or tax preparer for ways to file Form 2688 electronically. You will need to provide certain information from your tax return for 2000. Do not mail the Form 2688 if you file electronically.

Explanation

Generally, only causes that are beyond your control will be acceptable as reasons for an additional extension. In addition to personal sickness or injury and to a death or serious illness in your immediate family, some acceptable reasons, drawn from IRS proceedings and court cases, include the following:

1. You have a substantial number of security transactions (approximately 200) during the taxable year, some quite complex, and there has not been sufficient time to gather and analyze all the required information.
2. You have invested in oil properties and received the information from the operators too late to complete your return adequately by the due date.
3. You have a complicated deduction problem with your medical expenses that is under study by your tax advisors, and it may not be resolved in time to prepare your tax return adequately.
4. You sold securities in the taxable year that you had held for some years, and you have not as yet been able to determine the tax basis of such securities. You have checked your records but may have to go back to old records of your broker to determine the correct figures.
5. A partnership on the accrual basis in which you are a member initiated a profit-sharing plan at the end of the tax year, the contribution to which depends on approval of the plan by the IRS. Such approval has not yet been received.
6. Any other situation in which there is a "reasonable cause"—for example, the destruction by fire or other casualty of your business records or a lack of funds to pay the tax when you can demonstrate that this lack occurred despite the exercise of ordinary business care and prudence.

Extension approved. If your application for this extension is approved, you will be notified by the IRS.

If the IRS later determines that the statements made on your request for this extension are false or misleading and an extension would not have been approved at the time based on the true facts, the extension is null and void. You will have to pay the failure-to-file penalty (discussed later).

Extension not approved. If your application for this extension is not approved, you must file your return by the extended due date of the automatic extension. You may be allowed to file within 10 days of the date of the notice you get from the IRS if the end of the 10-day period is later than the due date. The notice will tell you if the 10-day grace period is granted.

No further extensions. An extension of more than 6 months will not be approved if you are in the United States.

TAXPLANNER

An extension of time to file is not an extension of time to pay. If you are unable to pay the full amount of tax due with your tax return because of financial hardship, you should still file the tax return along with a "good faith" payment of as much of the tax due as you can afford to pay. You should complete Form 9465 to request the privilege of paying the remaining tax in installments. This form should be attached to the front of the return when it is filed. However, the IRS will impose a $43 fee for entering into an installment agreement. You can expect a decision back from the IRS within 30 days regarding your installment request; but **you still will be subject to interest and the failure-to-pay penalty on the unpaid tax.**

The IRS will continue to send you a bill for the unpaid tax, interest, and penalty until the total amount is paid. After the tax is completely paid, you can request in writing that the penalty be waived due to reasonable cause because of financial hardship. The IRS has total discretion in waiving penalties and may require you to prove your financial hardship.

If your tax return is already in the formal collection process (i.e., you have been contacted by an IRS official regarding a delinquent tax liability) and you are unable to pay the tax due, you may request an installment agreement with the IRS officer. If he or she agrees, the installment agreement is made using Form 433-D, and you will be required to provide financial information. You may need to seek professional tax advice if this is the case.

Individuals Outside the United States

You are allowed an automatic 2-month extension (until June 17, 2002, if you use the calendar year) to file your 2001 return and pay any federal income tax due if:

1) You are a U.S. citizen or resident, and
2) On the due date of your return:
   a) You are living outside of the United States and Puerto Rico, and your main place of business or post of duty is outside the United States and Puerto Rico, *or*
   b) You are in military or naval service on duty outside the United States and Puerto Rico.

However, if you pay the tax due after the due date (generally, April 15), interest will be charged from that date until the date the tax is paid.

See *When To File and Pay* in Publication 54 for more information.

If you served in a combat zone, see *Individuals Serving in Combat Zone,* later, for special rules that apply to you.

Married taxpayers. If you file a joint return, only one spouse has to qualify for this automatic extension. If you and your spouse file separate returns, this automatic extension applies only to the spouse who qualifies.

How to get the extension. To use this special automatic extension, you must attach a statement to your return explaining what situation qualified you for the extension. (See the situations listed under (2), earlier.)

Extensions beyond 2 months. If you cannot file your return within the automatic 2-month extension period, you may be able to get an additional 2-month extension, for a total of 4 months. Generally, you must file a paper Form 4868 by the end of the automatic extension period (usually June 17) to get this additional 2-month extension.

This additional 2-month extension of time to file is *not* an extension of time to pay. See *Payment of tax,* earlier.

Extension beyond 4 months. If you are still unable to file your return within the 4-month extension period, you may be able to get an extension for 2 more months, for a total of 6 months. See *Extension beyond 4 months,* earlier.

No further extension. An extension of more than 6 months will generally not be granted. However, if you are outside the United States and meet certain tests, you may be granted a longer extension. See *When To File and Pay* in Publication 54 for more information.

Individuals Serving in Combat Zone

The deadline for filing your tax return, paying any tax you may owe, and filing a claim for refund is automatically extended if you serve in a combat zone. This applies to members of the Armed Forces, as well as Red Cross personnel, accredited correspondents, and civilians under the direction of the Armed Forces in support of the Armed Forces.

Combat zone. For purposes of the automatic extension, the term "combat zone" includes the following areas.

1) The Persian Gulf Area, effective August 2, 1990.
2) The qualified hazardous duty area of Bosnia and Herzegovina, Croatia, and Macedonia, effective November 21, 1995.
3) The qualified hazardous duty area of the Federal Republic of Yugoslavia (Serbia/Montenegro), Albania, the Adriatic Sea, and the Ionian Sea north of the 39th parallel, effective March 24, 1999.

See Publication 3, *Armed Forces' Tax Guide,* for information about other tax benefits available to military personnel serving in a combat zone.

Extension period. The deadline for filing your return, paying any tax due, and filing a claim for refund is extended for at least 180 days after the later of:

1) The last day you are in a combat zone (or the last day the area qualifies as a combat zone), or
2) The last day of any continuous qualified hospitalization for injury from service in the combat zone.

In addition to the 180 days, your deadline is also extended by the number of days you had left to take action with the IRS when you entered the combat zone. For example, you have 3 1/2 months (January 1–April 15) to file your tax return. Any days left in this period when you entered the combat zone (or the entire 3 1/2 months if you entered it before the beginning of the year) are added to the 180 days. See *Extension of Deadline* in Publication 3 for more information.

How Do I Prepare My Return?

This section explains how to get ready to fill in your tax return and when to report your income and expenses. It also explains how to complete certain sections of the form. You may find *Table 1-6* helpful when you prepare your return.

In most cases, the IRS will mail you Form 1040, Form 1040A, or Form 1040EZ with related instructions, or a TeleFile package, based on what you filed last year. Before you fill in the form, look it over to see if you need additional forms or schedules. You may also want to read *Does My Return Have To Be On Paper,* earlier.

Table 1–6. Six Steps for Preparing Your Return

> 1—Get your records together for income and expenses.
> 2—Get the forms, schedules, and publications you need.
> 3—Fill in your return.
> 4—Check your return to make sure it is correct.
> 5—Sign and date your return.
> 6—Attach all required forms and schedules.

If you do not receive a tax return package in the mail, or if you need other forms, you can order them. See *How To Get Tax Help* in the back of this publication.

Substitute tax forms. You cannot use your own version of a tax form unless it meets the requirements explained in Publication 1167, *Substitute Printed, Computer-Prepared, and Computer-Generated Tax Forms and Schedules.*

Explanation
The tax forms provided in the back of this book meet these requirements. You may also obtain tax forms via the Internet by visiting the *Ernst & Young Tax and Financial Planning Corner* at www.ey.com/pfc.

Form W-2. If you are an employee, you should receive Form W-2 from your employer. You will need the information from this form before you prepare your return.

If you do not receive Form W-2 by January 31, 2002, contact your employer. If you still do not get the form by February 15, the IRS can help you by requesting the form from your employer. For more information, see *Form W-2* under *Credit for Withholding and Estimated Tax* in chapter 5.

Form 1099. If you received certain types of income, you may receive a Form 1099. For example, if you received taxable interest of $10 or more, the payer generally must give you a Form 1099-INT. If you have not received it by January 31, 2002, contact the payer. If you still do not get the form by February 15, call the IRS for help.

When Do I Report My Income and Expenses?

You must figure your taxable income on the basis of a tax year. A "tax year" is an annual accounting period used for keeping records and reporting income and expenses. You must account for your income and expenses in a way that clearly shows your taxable income. The way you do this is called an accounting method. This section explains which accounting periods and methods you can use.

Accounting Periods

Most individual tax returns cover a *calendar year*—the 12 months from January 1 through December 31. If you do not use a calendar year, your accounting period is a *fiscal year.* A regular fiscal year is a 12-month period that ends on the last day of any month except December. A 52–53 week fiscal year varies from 52 to 53 weeks and always ends on the same day of the week.

You must choose your accounting period when you file your first income tax return. It cannot be longer than 12 months.

TaxPlanner
To operate on a fiscal year accounting basis, you must keep your books and records based on that fiscal year. Because most individual taxpayers keep their personal financial records on a calendar year basis, it is easier to use a calendar year period.

It is virtually impossible for an individual to secure permission to change to a fiscal year accounting period without justification. Usually, the justification must be that you are involved in a cyclical business from which self-employment or partnership income flows. Furthermore, in most cases, that income has to be your sole or principal source of income.

More information. For more information on accounting periods, including how to change your accounting period, see Publication 538, *Accounting Periods and Methods.*

Accounting Methods

Your accounting method is the way you account for your income and expenses. Most taxpayers use either the cash method or an accrual method. You choose a method when you file your first income tax return. If you want to change your accounting method after that, you generally must get IRS approval.

Cash method. If you use this method, report all items of income in the year in which you actually or constructively receive them. Deduct all expenses in the year you actually pay them. This is the method most individual taxpayers use.

Explanation
Accounting methods are important because they determine when you recognize income and when you deduct expenses for tax purposes. The cash method allows you more flexibility and control over your tax liability.

Individuals who do not own and operate their own business *must* use the cash method. However, the IRS will not permit you to use the cash method if you own your own business and if inventories of unsold goods or materials are on hand at the end of the year.

TaxAlert
IRS officials have expressed the view that you may not use the cash method for any substantial business activity, even one providing only personal or professional services. The law does not support this view. Nevertheless, in conducting audits, the IRS has been aggressive in urging taxpayers to change to the accrual method of accounting.

TaxPlanner
Generally, most taxpayers who expect to be in the same tax bracket from one year to the next and who want to reduce their current tax bill as much as possible should attempt to defer income to a subsequent year and to take deductions in the current year. (If you suspect you might be in a higher tax bracket in a subsequent year, however, you would want to do just the opposite.)

You might consider lumping together your deductions in a single year. For example, in some states and cities, you may pay property, state, and local income taxes in either December or January, giving you the opportunity to pay 2 years' worth of these taxes in a single calendar year. You can also control when you make charitable contributions. To some extent, you can also control when you make interest payments on a mortgage.

Constructive receipt. You constructively receive income when it is credited to your account or set apart in any way that makes it available to you. You do not need to have physical possession of it. For example, interest credited to your bank account on December 31, 2001, is taxable income to you in 2001 if you could have withdrawn it in 2001 (even if the amount is not entered in your passbook or withdrawn until 2002).

Garnisheed wages. If your employer uses your wages to pay your debts, or if your wages are attached or garnisheed, the full amount is constructively received by you. You must include these wages in income for the year you would have received them.

Brokerage and other accounts. Profits from a brokerage account, or similar account, are fully taxable in the year you earn them. This is true even if:

1) You do not withdraw the earnings,
2) The credit balance in the account may be reduced or eliminated by losses in later years, or
3) Current profits are used to reduce or eliminate a debit balance from previous years.

Example
You sold your ABC Company stock on December 15, 2001, realizing a gain of $5,000. You did not withdraw the cash in your account until January 6, 2002. The gain is taxable income to you for 2001.

Debts paid for you. If another person cancels or pays your debts (but not as a gift or loan), you have constructively received the amount and generally must include it in your gross income for the year. See *Canceled Debts* in chapter 13 for more information.

Example
Your new employer pays the balance of the mortgage due on your home that is not covered by the selling price so you can move to Florida to work for him. The payments are not intended to be a gift or a loan to you. The amount your employer pays on the mortgage is income to you in the year that he pays it.

Payment to third party. If a third party is paid income from property you own, you have constructively received the income. It is the same as if you had actually received the income and paid it to the third party.

Payment to an agent. Income an agent receives for you is income you constructively received in the year the agent receives it. If you indicate in a contract that your income is to be paid to another person, you must include the amount in your gross income when the other person receives it.

Explanation
The IRS considers you to have received income in the year that your agent receives it, but if a person who is not your agent or creditor receives your income, then you do not have to consider that amount as income until you personally obtain it. The key question is whether you can control the receipt of the income during the year. If you can, the income is taxable to you in that year.

Example
ABC Company mailed you a $500 dividend check on December 9, 2001. The post office inadvertently delivered the check on December 31 to Mr. Wheat on the other side of town. You didn't receive the check until January 6, 2002. The $500 in dividends is taxable to you in 2002, because Mr. Wheat was not your agent. You should carefully explain this turn of events when you prepare your return because the IRS document-matching program will have a Form 1099 from ABC Company that lists the $500 as having been paid to you in 2001.

TAXPLANNER

It is possible to structure a sale of property so that the sale funds are deposited in an escrow account and then disbursed to you in the next tax year. The advantage to you in this arrangement is that you have the security of knowing that the sale proceeds exist, but, at the same time, you're able to defer taxes on the funds until they become income to you, in the following tax year. To do this, the escrow arrangement must be agreed on by both the buyer and the seller. The arrangement must follow other specific guidelines as well. You will need to seek professional advice.

Check received or available. A valid check you received or that was made available to you before the end of the tax year is constructively received by you in that year, even if you do not cash the check or deposit it in your account until the next year.

No constructive receipt. There may be facts to show that you did not constructively receive income.

Example. Alice Johnson, a teacher, agreed to her school board's condition that, in her absence, she would receive only the difference between her regular salary and the salary of a substitute teacher hired by the school board. Therefore, Alice did not constructively receive the amount by which her salary was reduced to pay the substitute teacher.

Explanation
The IRS does not consider you to have paid an expense if you use a note in lieu of cash to make the payment. In this case, you have only made a promise to pay sometime in the future. However, the IRS considers you to have made a payment if you use cash borrowed from a third party to pay an expense.

Example
If you give a note to your doctor promising to pay him for medical services already rendered, you have not yet paid the expense in the IRS's eyes. However, if you borrow money from your bank and use the cash to pay your doctor, you have paid the expense for tax purposes. Similarly, if you pay by credit card, you have made the payment for tax purposes. Paying by credit card is just like borrowing from a third party. **More information.** For more information on the determination of medical and dental expenses, see Chapter 23, *Medical and Dental Expenses,* and Publication 502, *Medical and Dental Expenses.*

Exception
Individual Retirement Arrangements. If you qualify for a tax-deductible contribution, you may take a deduction for a contribution to an Individual Retirement Arrangement (IRA) in 1 year, even though you do not make the actual cash contri-

bution to your account until the following year; that is, you may file your tax return showing a deduction for a contribution to your IRA, although you have not yet made the contribution. The deduction is valid as long as you make the contribution on or before April 15 of the following year, even if you get a filing extension. **More information.** For more information, see Chapter 18, and Publication 590, *Individual Retirement Arrangements (IRAs).*

Accrual method. If you use an accrual method, you generally report income when you earn it, rather than when you receive it. You generally deduct your expenses when you incur them, rather than when you pay them.

Income paid in advance. Prepaid income is generally included in gross income in the year you receive it. Your method of accounting does not matter as long as the income is available to you. Prepaid income includes rents or interest you receive in advance and pay for services you will perform later.

Additional information. For more information on accounting methods, including how to change your accounting method, get Publication 538.

Social Security Number

You must enter your social security number (SSN) in the space provided on your return. Be sure the SSN on your return is the same as the SSN on your social security card. If you are married, enter the SSNs for both you and your spouse, whether you file jointly or separately.

If you are filing a joint return, write the SSNs in the same order as the names. Please use this same order in submitting other forms and documents to the IRS.

Name change. If you changed your name because of marriage, divorce, etc., immediately notify your Social Security Administration (SSA) office so the name on your tax return is the same as the one the SSA has on its records. This may prevent delays in issuing your refund and safeguard your future social security benefits.

Dependent's social security number. You must provide the SSN of each dependent you claim, regardless of the dependent's age. This requirement applies to *all dependents* (not just your children) claimed on your tax return.

Exception. If your child was born and died in 2001 and you do not have an SSN for the child, you may attach a copy of the child's birth certificate instead. If you do, enter "DIED" in column 2 of line 6c.

No social security number. File **Form SS-5** with your local SSA office to get an SSN for yourself or your dependent. It usually takes about 2 weeks to get an SSN. If you or your dependent is not eligible for an SSN, see *Individual taxpayer identification number,* later.

If you are a U.S. citizen, you must show proof of age, identity, and citizenship with your Form SS-5. If you are 18 or older, you must appear in person with this proof at an SSA office.

Form SS-5 is available at any SSA office. If you have any questions about which documents you can use as proof of age, identity, or citizenship, contact your SSA office.

If your dependent does not have an SSN by the time your return is due, you may want to ask for an extension of time to file, as explained earlier under *When Do I Have To File.*

If you do not provide a required SSN or if you provide an incorrect SSN, your tax may be increased and any refund may be reduced.

Adoption taxpayer identification number (ATIN). If you are in the process of adopting a child who is a U.S. citizen or resident and cannot get an SSN for the child until the adoption is final, you can apply for an ATIN to use instead of an SSN.

File **Form W-7A** with the IRS to get an ATIN if all of the following are true.

- You have a child living with you who was placed in your home for legal adoption by an authorized placement agency.
- You cannot get the child's existing SSN even though you have made a reasonable attempt to get it from the birth parents, the placement agency, and other persons.
- You cannot get an SSN for the child from the SSA because, for example, the adoption is not final.
- You cannot get an Individual Taxpayer Identification Number (ITIN) (discussed later) for the child.
- You are eligible to claim the child as a dependent on your tax return.

After the adoption is final, you must apply for an SSN for the child. You cannot continue using the ATIN.

See Form W-7A for more information.

Nonresident alien spouse. If your spouse is a nonresident alien and you file a joint or separate return, your spouse must have either an SSN or an ITIN. If your spouse is not eligible for an SSN, see the next discussion.

Individual taxpayer identification number (ITIN). The IRS will issue you an ITIN if you are a nonresident or resident alien and you do not have and are not eligible to get an SSN. To apply for an ITIN, file **Form W-7** with the IRS. It usually takes about 30 days to get an ITIN. Enter this number on your tax return wherever your SSN is requested.

Alien dependent. If your dependent is a nonresident or resident alien who does not have and is not eligible to get a social security number (SSN), file Form W-7 with the IRS to apply for an ITIN. Enter this number on your return wherever the dependent's SSN is requested.

Caution. *An ITIN is for tax use only. It does not entitle you or your dependent to social security benefits or change the employment or immigration status of either of you under U.S. law.*

Penalty for not providing social security number. If you do not include your SSN or the SSN of your spouse or dependent as required, you may have to pay a penalty. See the discussion on *Penalties,* later, for more information.

SSN on correspondence. If you write to the IRS about your tax account, be sure to include your SSN (and the name and SSN of your spouse, if you filed a joint return) in your correspondence. Because your SSN is used to identify your account, this helps the IRS respond to your correspondence promptly.

Presidential Election Campaign Fund

This fund was set up to help pay for presidential election campaigns. You may have $3 of your tax liability go to this fund by checking the *Yes* box on Form 1040, Form 1040A, or Form 1040EZ. If you are filing a joint return, your spouse may also have $3 go to the fund. If you check *Yes,* it will not change the tax you pay or the refund you will receive.

Computations

The following information on entering numbers on your tax return may be useful in making the return easier to complete.

Rounding off dollars. You may round off cents to whole dollars on your return and schedules. If you do round to whole dollars, you must round all amounts. To round, drop amounts under 50 cents and increase amounts from 50 to 99 cents to the next dollar. For example, $1.39 becomes $1 and $2.50 becomes $3.

If you have to add two or more amounts to figure the amount to enter on a line, include cents when adding the amounts and round off only the total.

Example. You receive two W-2 forms: one showing wages of $5,000.55 and one showing wages of $18,500.73. On Form 1040, line 7, you would enter $23,501 ($5,000.55 + $18,500.73 = $23,501.28), not $23,502 ($5,001 + $18,501).

Equal amounts. If you are asked to enter the smaller or larger of two equal amounts, enter that amount.

Example. Line 1 is $500. Line 3 is $500. Line 5 asks you to enter the smaller of line 1 or 3. Enter $500 on line 5.

Negative amounts. If you need to enter a negative amount, put the amount in parentheses rather than using a minus sign. To combine positive and negative amounts, add all the positive amounts together and then subtract the negative amounts.

Attachments

Depending on the form you file and the items reported on your return, you may have to complete additional schedules and forms and attach them to your return.

Tip. *IRS e-file is paperless. There's nothing to sign, attach, or mail, not even your Forms W-2.*

Form W-2. Form W-2, *Wage and Tax Statement,* is a statement from your employer of wages and other compensation paid to you and taxes withheld from your pay. You should have a Form W-2 from each employer. Be sure to attach a copy of Form W-2 in the place indicated on the front page of your return. Attach it only to the front page of your return, not to any attachments. For more information, see *Form W-2* in chapter 5.

If you received a Form 1099-R, *Distributions From Pensions, Annuities, Retirement or Profit-Sharing Plans, IRAs, Insurance Contracts, etc.,* showing federal income tax withheld, attach a copy of that form in the place indicated on the front page of your return.

Form 1040EZ. There are no additional schedules to file with Form 1040EZ.

Form 1040A. Attach the additional schedules and forms that you had to complete behind the Form 1040A in order by number. If you are filing Schedule EIC, put it last. Do not attach items unless required to do so.

Form 1040. Attach any forms and schedules behind Form 1040 in order of the "Attachment Sequence Number" shown in the upper right corner of the form or schedule. Put forms without an attachment sequence number next. Then arrange all other statements or attachments in the same order as the forms and schedules they relate to and attach them last. Do not attach items unless required to do so.

> **TAXPLANNER**
>
> If you fail to organize your return according to the prescribed sequence numbers, the IRS, upon receipt of your return, will disassemble it and put it back together in the proper order. This procedure may result in the loss of a page of your return, causing some delay in its processing.

Third Party Designee

You can authorize the IRS to discuss your return with a friend, family member, or any other person you choose. If you check the "Yes" box in the third party designee area of your 2001 tax return and provide the information required, you are authorizing:

1) The IRS to call the designee to answer any questions that arise during the processing of your return, and
2) The designee to:
   a) Give information that is missing from your return to the IRS,
   b) Call the IRS for information about the processing of your return or the status of your refund or payments, and
   c) Respond to certain IRS notices that you have shown the designee. These notices about math errors, offsets (see *Refunds,* later), and return preparation will be sent to you, not the designee.

The authorization cannot be revoked. However, it will automatically end no later than the due date (without any extensions) for filing your 2002 tax return. This is April 15, 2003, for most people.

See your form instructions for more information.

Tip. *If you want to allow the paid preparer who signed your return to discuss it with the IRS, just enter "Preparer" in the space for the designee's name.*

Signatures

You must sign and date your return. If you file a joint return, both you and your spouse must sign the return, even if only one of you had income.

Caution. *If you file a joint return, both spouses are generally liable for the tax, and the entire tax liability may be assessed against either spouse. See chapter 2.*

If you are due a refund, it cannot be issued unless you have signed your return.

Enter your occupation in the space provided in the signature section. If you file a joint return, enter both your occupation and your spouse's occupation. Entering your daytime telephone number may help speed the processing of your return.

When someone can sign for you. You can appoint an agent to sign your return if you are:

1) Unable to sign the return because of disease or injury,
2) Absent from the United States for a continuous period of at least 60 days before the due date for filing your return, or
3) Given permission to do so by the IRS office in your area.

Power of attorney. A return signed by an agent in any of these cases must have a power of attorney (POA) attached that authorizes the agent to sign for you. You can use a POA that states that the agent is granted authority to sign the return, or you can use **Form 2848,** *Power of Attorney and Declaration of Representative.* Part I of Form 2848 must state that the agent is granted authority to sign the return.

Unable to sign. If the taxpayer is mentally incompetent and cannot sign the return, it must be signed by a court-appointed representative who can act for the taxpayer.

If the taxpayer is mentally competent but physically unable to sign the return or POA, a valid "signature" is defined under state law. It can be anything that clearly indicates the taxpayer's intent to sign. For example, the taxpayer's "X" with the signatures of two witnesses might be considered a valid signature under a state's law.

Spouse unable to sign. If your spouse is unable to sign for any reason, see *Signing a joint return* in chapter 2.

Child's return. If a child has to file a tax return but cannot sign the return, the child's parent, guardian, or another legally responsible person must sign the child's name, followed by the words "By (signature), parent (or guardian) for minor child."

Paid Preparer

Generally, anyone you pay to prepare, assist in preparing, or review your tax return must sign it and fill in the other blanks in the paid preparer's area of your return. Signature stamps and labels are not acceptable.

If the preparer is self-employed (that is, not employed by any person or business to prepare the return), he or she should check the self-employed box in the *Paid Preparer's Use Only* space on the return.

The preparer must give you a copy of your return in addition to the copy filed with the IRS.

If you prepare your own return, leave this area blank. If another person prepares your return and does not charge you, that person should not sign your return.

If you have questions about whether a preparer must sign your return, please contact any IRS office.

> **Explanation**
> *Paid preparer authorization.* In the signature area of your 2001 tax return, you are asked whether the IRS can discuss

the return with the paid preparer who signed the return. If you check the "Yes" box, you are authorizing:

1) The IRS to call the paid preparer to answer any questions that arise during the processing of your return, and
2) The paid preparer to:
   a) Give information that is missing from your return to the IRS,
   b) Call the IRS for information about the processing of your return or the status of your refund or payments, and
   c) Respond to certain IRS notices that you have shown the preparer. These notices about math errors, offsets (see *Refunds*, later), and return preparation will be sent to you, not the preparer.

The authorization cannot be revoked. However, it will automatically end no later than the due date (without any extensions) for filing your 2001 tax return. This is April 15, 2002, for most people.

See your form instructions for more information.

TaxAlert

A person who is paid to prepare all or a substantial portion of your income tax return must sign it. In addition, the IRS says that a tax consultant who is paid to review a tax return that you have already prepared and signed is also considered a tax return preparer and must sign it.

If an individual who prepares your return refuses to sign it, you are probably dealing with someone you should not rely on. While you could still file the return, you should probably consider using another tax preparer. If you have to pay the first preparer, you should report the matter to the IRS.

Refunds

When you complete your return, you will determine if you paid more income tax than you owed. If so, you can get a refund of the amount you overpaid or, if you file Form 1040 or Form 1040A, you can choose to apply all or part of the overpayment to your next year's (2002) estimated tax. You cannot have your overpayment applied to your 2002 estimated tax if you file Form 1040EZ.

Caution. *If you choose to have a 2001 overpayment applied to your 2002 estimated tax, you cannot change your mind and have any of it refunded to you after the due date of your 2001 return.*

Follow the form instructions to complete the entries to claim your refund and/or to apply your overpayment to your 2002 estimated tax.

Tip. *If your refund for 2001 is large, you may want to decrease the amount of income tax withheld from your pay in 2002. See chapter 5 for more information.*

Explanation

If you choose to apply all or part of your overpayment to your next year's estimated tax, the estimated tax installment payment is considered made on April 15. Your first installment may be reduced accordingly. For more information, see Chapter 5, *Tax Withholding and Estimated Tax* and Publication 505, *Tax Withholding and Estimated Tax.*

Direct Deposit. Instead of getting a paper check, you may be able to have your refund deposited directly into your account at a bank or other financial institution. Follow the form instructions to request Direct Deposit.

If the Direct Deposit cannot be done, the IRS will send a check instead.

Overpayment less than one dollar. If your overpayment is less than one dollar, you will not get a refund unless you ask for it in writing.

Cashing your refund check. Cash your tax refund check soon after you receive it. Checks not cashed within 12 months of the date they are issued will be canceled and the proceeds returned to the IRS.

If your check has been canceled, you can apply to the IRS to have it reissued.

Refund more or less than expected. If you receive a check for a refund you are not entitled to, or for an overpayment that should have been credited to estimated tax, do not cash the check. Call the IRS.

If you receive a check for more than the refund you claimed, do not cash the check until you receive a notice explaining the difference.

If your refund check is for less than you claimed, it should be accompanied by a notice explaining the difference. Cashing the check does not stop you from claiming an additional amount of refund.

If you did not receive a notice and you have any questions about the amount of your refund, you should wait 2 weeks. If you still have not received a notice, call the IRS.

Offset against debts. If you are due a refund but have not paid certain amounts you owe, all or part of your refund may be used to pay all or part of the past-due amount. This includes past-due federal income tax, other federal debts (such as student loans), state income tax, and child and spousal support payments. You will be notified if the refund you claimed has been offset against your debts.

Joint return and injured spouse. When a joint return is filed and only one spouse owes a past-due amount, the other spouse can be considered an *injured spouse.* An injured spouse can get a refund for his or her share of the overpayment that would otherwise be used to pay the past-due amount.

To be considered an injured spouse, you must:

1) File a joint return,
2) Have reported income (such as wages, interest, etc.),
3) Have made and reported tax payments (such as federal income tax withheld from wages or estimated tax payments), or claimed the earned income credit or other refundable credit, and
4) Have an overpayment, all or part of which may be applied against the past-due amount.

If you are an injured spouse, you can obtain your portion of the joint refund by completing **Form 8379,** *Injured Spouse Claim and Allocation.* Follow the instructions on the form.

Amount You Owe

When you complete your return, you will determine if you have paid the full amount of tax that you owe. If you owe additional tax, you should pay it with your return.

If the IRS figures your tax for you, you will receive a bill for any tax that is due. You should pay this bill within 30 days (or by the due date of your return, if later). See *Tax Figured by IRS* in chapter 31.

Caution. *If you do not pay your tax when due, you may have to pay a failure-to-pay penalty. See* Penalties, *later. For more information about your balance due, see Publication 594,* The IRS Collection Process.

Tip. *If the amount you owe for 2001 is large, you may want to increase the amount of income tax withheld from your pay or make estimated tax payments for 2002. See chapter 5 for more information.*

How To Pay

If you have an amount due on your tax return, you can pay by check, money order, or credit card. If you filed electronically, you also may be able to make your payment by electronic funds withdrawal.

Tip. *You do not have to pay if the amount you owe is less than $1.*

Payment by check or money order. If you pay by check or money order, make it out to the "United States Treasury." Please show your correct name, address, social security number, daytime telephone number, and the tax year and form number on the front of your check or money order.

For example, if you file Form 1040 for 2001 and you owe additional tax, show your name, address, social security number, daytime telephone number, and "2001 Form 1040" on the front of your check or money order. If you file an amended return (Form 1040X) for 2000 and you owe tax, show your name, address, social security number, daytime telephone number, and "2000 Form 1040X" on the front of your check or money order.

Enclose your payment with your return, but do not attach it to the form. If you filed Form 1040, please complete **Form 1040-V,** *Payment Voucher,* and enclose it with your payment and return. Form 1040-V will help us process your payment more accurately and efficiently. Follow the instructions that come with the form.

Do not mail cash with your return. If you pay cash at an IRS office, keep the receipt as part of your records.

Payment not honored. If your check or money order is not honored by your bank (or other financial institution) and the IRS does not receive the funds, you still owe the tax. In addition, you may be subject to a dishonored check penalty.

Payment by credit card. You can use your American Express®, Discover®, or MasterCard® credit card.

To pay by credit card, call a service provider and follow the recorded instructions. You can also pay by credit card over the Internet using a service provider's web site.

The service providers charge a convenience fee based on the amount you are paying. Fees may vary between the providers. You will be told what the fee is during the transaction and will have the option to continue or end the transaction. You may also obtain the convenience fee by calling the service provider's automated customer service telephone number or visiting their respective web site.

Caution. *Do not add the convenience fee to your tax payment.*

If you pay by credit card, write the confirmation number you were given at the end of the transaction and the tax payment amount in the upper left corner of page 1 of your tax return.

Service Providers

PhoneCharge Inc.

To make a payment, call	1-888-ALL-TAXX
or	1-888-255-8299
For Customer Service	1-877-851-9964
Web Address	www.1888ALLTAXX.com

Official Payments Corporation

To make a payment, call	1-800-2PAY-TAX
or	1-800-272-9829
For Customer Service	1-877-754-4413
Web Address	www.officialpayments.com

TAXPLANNER

Be careful about paying your taxes by credit card. Most of the payment options demand that you pay a "convenience fee" for using your card. Also, if you won't be paying off your balance right away, the interest your credit card charges may be much higher than the 8% interest the IRS charges for late payment.

Electronic payment by electronic filer. If you file your tax return electronically, you can make your payment electronically.

You can file and pay in a single step by authorizing an electronic funds withdrawal from your checking or savings account. This option is available through tax software packages, tax professionals, and TeleFile. If you select this payment option, you will need to have your account number, your financial institution's routing transit number, and account type (checking or savings). You can schedule the payment for any future date up to and including the return due date (April 15, 2002).

Caution. *Be sure to check with your financial institution to make sure that an electronic funds withdrawal is allowed and to get the correct routing and account numbers.*

To pay by electronic funds withdrawal from your checking or savings account when you file by TeleFile, fill in lines E, F, G, and H on the TeleFile Tax Record.

You can also file and pay in a single step by authorizing a credit card payment. This option is available through some tax software packages and tax professionals.

Estimated tax payments. Do not include any 2002 estimated tax payment in the payment for your 2001 income tax return. See chapter 5 for information on how to pay estimated tax.

Interest

Interest is charged on tax you do not pay by the due date of your return. Interest is charged even if you get an extension of time for filing.

Tip. *If the IRS figures your tax for you, interest cannot start earlier than the 31st day after the IRS sends you a bill. For information, see* Tax Figured by IRS *in chapter 31.*

Interest on penalties. Interest is charged on the failure-to-file penalty, the accuracy-related penalty, and the fraud penalty from the due date of the return (including extensions) to the date of payment. Interest on other penalties starts on the date of notice and demand, but is not charged on penalties paid within 21 calendar days from the date of the notice (or within 10 business days if the notice is for $100,000 or more).

Interest due to IRS error or delay. All or part of any interest you were charged can be forgiven if the interest is due to an unreasonable error or delay by an officer or employee of the IRS in performing a ministerial or managerial act.

A ministerial act is a procedural or mechanical act that occurs during the processing of your case. A managerial act includes personnel transfers and extended personnel training. A decision concerning the proper application of federal tax law is not a ministerial or managerial act.

The interest can be forgiven only if you are not responsible in any important way for the error or delay and the IRS has notified you in writing of the deficiency or payment. For more information, get Publication 556, *Examination of Returns, Appeal Rights, and Claims for Refund.*

Interest and certain penalties may also be suspended for a limited period if you filed your return by the due date (including extensions) and the IRS does not provide you with a notice specifically stating your liability and the basis for it before the close of the 18-month period beginning on the later of:

- The date the return is filed, or
- The due date of the return without regard to extensions.

For more information, get Publication 556.

TAXPLANNER

If you owe additional tax, it is *not* a good idea to file your return by January 31. As long as you have planned well and have paid enough in estimated taxes to avoid a penalty, you would be better off keeping any other tax you owe in your savings account, where it will earn interest for 2½ months, rather than paying your tax bill early.

Installment Agreement

If you cannot pay the full amount due with your return, you can ask to make monthly installment payments. However, you will be charged interest and may be charged a late payment penalty on the tax not paid by April 15, 2002, even if your request to pay in installments is granted. If your request is granted, you must also pay a fee. To limit the interest and penalty charges, pay as much of the tax as possible with your return. But before requesting an installment agreement, you should consider other less costly alternatives, such as a bank loan.

To ask for an installment agreement, use **Form 9465,** *Installment Agreement Request.* You should receive a response to your request within 30 days. But if you file your return after March 31, it may take longer for a reply.

Guaranteed availability of installment agreement. The IRS must agree to accept the payment of your tax liability in installments if, as of the date you offer to enter into the agreement:

1) Your total taxes (not counting interest, penalties, additions to the tax, or additional amounts) do not exceed $10,000,
2) In the last 5 years, you (and your spouse if the liability relates to a joint return) have not:
   a) Failed to file any required income tax return,
   b) Failed to pay any tax shown on any such return, or
   c) Entered into an installment agreement for the payment of any income tax,
3) You show you cannot pay your income tax in full when due,
4) The tax will be paid in full in 3 years or less, and
5) You agree to comply with the tax laws while your agreement is in effect.

Gift To Reduce the Public Debt

You can make a contribution (gift) to reduce the public debt. If you wish to do so, make a *separate* check payable to "Bureau of the Public Debt." You can send it to:

Bureau of the Public Debt
Department G
P.O. Box 2188
Parkersburg, WV 26106-2188.

Or, you can enclose the check in the envelope with your income tax return. Please do not add this gift to any tax you owe.

You can deduct this gift as a charitable contribution on next year's tax return if you itemize your deductions on Schedule A (Form 1040).

Peel-Off Address Label

After you have completed your return, peel off the label with your name and address from the inside of your tax return package and place it in the appropriate area of the Form 1040, Form 1040A, or Form 1040EZ you send to the IRS. If you have someone prepare your return, give that person your label to use on your tax return.

If you file electronically (and Form 8453 is required), use your label on Form 8453. (More information on electronic filing is found earlier in this chapter.)

The label helps the IRS to correctly identify your account. It also saves processing costs and speeds up processing so that refunds can be issued sooner.

Caution. *You must write your SSN in the spaces provided on your tax return.*

Correcting the label. Make necessary name and address changes on the label. If you have an apartment number that is not shown on the label, please write it in. If you changed your name, see the discussion under *Social Security Number,* earlier.

No label. If you did not receive a tax return package with a label, print or type your name and address in the spaces provided at the top of Form 1040 or Form 1040A. If you are married filing a separate return, do not enter your spouse's name in the space at the top. Instead, enter his or her name in the space provided on line 3.

If you file Form 1040EZ and you do not have a label, print (do not type) this information in the spaces provided.

P.O. box. If your post office does not deliver mail to your street address and you have a P.O. box, print your P.O. box number on the line for your present home address instead of your street address.

Foreign address. If your address is outside the United States or its possessions or territories, enter the information on the line for "City, town or post office, state, and ZIP code" in the following order:

1) City,
2) Province or state, and
3) Name of foreign country. (*Do not* abbreviate the name of the country.)

Follow the country's practice for entering the postal code.

TaxAlert

You are not excused from filing a return because you have not received the proper forms from the IRS. In addition to any IRS office (check the telephone book), you may usually obtain the necessary forms at your local post office, public library, or bank. Forms that you can use to file your return are provided at the back of this book. You may also obtain tax forms via the Internet by visiting the *Ernst & Young Tax and Financial Planning Corner* at www.ey.com/pfc.

Where Do I File?

After you complete your return, you must send it to the IRS. You can mail it or you may be able to file it electronically. See *Does My Return Have To Be On Paper,* earlier.

Mailing your return. If an addressed envelope came with your tax forms package, you should mail your return in that envelope.

If you do not have an addressed envelope or if you moved during the year, mail your return to the Internal Revenue Service Center for the area where you now live. A list of Service Center addresses is shown in your tax forms package.

If you are making a payment, follow any additional instructions in your tax forms package.

What Happens After I File?

After you send your return to IRS, you may have some questions. This section discusses concerns you may have about recordkeeping, your refund, and what to do if you move.

What Records Should I Keep?

You must keep records so that you can prepare a complete and accurate income tax return. The law does not require any special form of records. However, you should keep all receipts, canceled checks or other proof of payment, and any other records to support any deductions or credits you claim.

If you file a claim for refund, you must be able to prove by your records that you have overpaid your tax.

TaxPlanner

See the detailed listing of tax records to keep at the end of the *Ernst & Young Individual Tax Organizer* in the front of this book.

How long to keep records. You must keep your records for as long as they are important for the federal tax law.

Keep records that support an item of income or a deduction appearing on a return until the period of limitations for the return runs out. (A period of limitations is the period of time after which no legal action can be brought.) For assessment of tax you owe, this generally is 3 years from the date you filed the return. For filing a claim for credit or refund, this generally is 3 years from the date you filed the original return, or 2 years from the date you paid the tax, whichever is later. Returns filed before the due date are treated as filed on the due date.

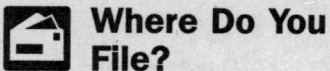 **Where Do You File?**

If an envelope addressed to "Internal Revenue Service Center" came with this booklet, please use it. If you do not have one or if you moved during the year, mail your return to the Internal Revenue Service Center shown that applies to you.

 Envelopes without enough postage will be returned to you by the post office. Your envelope may need additional postage if it contains more than five pages or is oversized (for example, it is over ¼" thick). Also, include your complete return address.

IF you live in...	THEN use this address if you:	
	Are not enclosing a check or money order...	Are enclosing a check or money order...
Florida, Georgia, North Carolina, South Carolina, West Virginia	Internal Revenue Service Center Atlanta, GA 39901-0002	Internal Revenue Service Center Atlanta, GA 39901-0102
New Jersey, New York (New York City and counties of Nassau, Rockland, Suffolk, and Westchester)	Internal Revenue Service Center Holtsville, NY 00501-0002	Internal Revenue Service Center Holtsville, NY 00501-0102
New York (all other counties), Massachusetts, Michigan, Rhode Island	Internal Revenue Service Center Andover, MA 05501-0002	Internal Revenue Service Center Andover, MA 05501-0102
Illinois, Iowa, Kansas, Minnesota, Missouri, Oklahoma, Utah, Wisconsin	Internal Revenue Service Center Kansas City, MO 64999-0002	Internal Revenue Service Center Kansas City, MO 64999-0102
Connecticut, Delaware, District of Columbia, Indiana, Maine, Maryland, New Hampshire, Pennsylvania, Vermont	Internal Revenue Service Center Philadelphia, PA 19255-0002	Internal Revenue Service Center Philadelphia, PA 19255-0102
Ohio	Internal Revenue Service Center Cincinnati, OH 45999-0002	Internal Revenue Service Center Cincinnati, OH 45999-0102
Arizona, Colorado, Idaho, Montana, New Mexico, Texas, Wyoming	Internal Revenue Service Center Austin, TX 73301-0002	Internal Revenue Service Center Austin, TX 73301-0102
Nebraska, North Dakota, South Dakota, Washington	Internal Revenue Service Center Ogden, UT 84201-0002	Internal Revenue Service Center Ogden, UT 84201-0102
Alaska, California, Hawaii, Nevada, Oregon	Internal Revenue Service Center Fresno, CA 93888-0002	Internal Revenue Service Center Fresno, CA 93888-0102
Alabama, Arkansas, Kentucky, Louisiana, Mississippi, Tennessee, Virginia	Internal Revenue Service Center Memphis, TN 37501-0002	Internal Revenue Service Center Memphis, TN 37501-0102
All APO and FPO addresses, American Samoa, nonpermanent residents of Guam or the Virgin Islands*, Puerto Rico (or if excluding income under Internal Revenue Code section 933), a foreign country: U.S. citizens and those filing Form 2555, 2555-EZ, or 4563	Internal Revenue Service Center Philadelphia, PA 19255-0215 USA	Internal Revenue Service Center Philadelphia, PA 19255-0215 USA

* Permanent residents of Guam should use: Department of Revenue and Taxation, Government of Guam, P.O. Box 23607, GMF, GU 96921; permanent residents of the Virgin Islands should use: V.I. Bureau of Internal Revenue, 9601 Estate Thomas, Charlotte Amalie, St. Thomas, VI 00802.

If you did not report income that you should have reported on your return, and it is more than 25% of the income shown on the return, the period of limitations does not run out until 6 years after you filed the return. If a return is false or fraudulent with intent to evade tax, or if no return is filed, an action can generally be brought at any time.

You may need to keep records relating to the basis of property longer than the period of limitations. Keep those records as long as they are important in figuring the basis of the original or replacement property. Generally, this means for as long as you own the property and, after you dispose of it, for the period of limitations that applies to you. See chapter 14 for information on basis.

Note. If you receive a Form W-2, keep Copy C until you begin receiving social security benefits. This will help protect those benefits, just in case there is a question about your work record or earnings in a particular year. The Social Security Administration suggests that you confirm your work record with them from time to time.

Copies of returns. You should keep copies of tax returns you have filed and the tax forms package as part of your records. They may be helpful in amending filed returns or preparing future ones.

If you need a copy of a prior year tax return, you can get it from the IRS. Use **Form 4506,** *Request for Copy or Transcript of Tax Form.* There is a charge for a copy of a return, which you must pay with Form 4506.

Transcript. You can also use Form 4506 to ask for a transcript of your return filed this year or during the 3 preceding years. It will show most lines from your original return, including accompanying forms and schedules.

Tax account information. If you need a statement of your tax account showing any later changes that you or the IRS made to the original return, you will need to ask for tax account information.

Do not use Form 4506 for tax account information. Instead, contact the IRS. You should have your name and address, social security number or employer identification number (if applicable), tax period, and form number available. You will get the following information:

- Type of return filed,
- Filing status,
- Federal income tax withheld,
- Tax shown on return,
- Adjusted gross income,
- Taxable income,
- Self-employment tax,
- Number of exemptions,
- Refund,
- Earned income credit, and
- Mortgage interest deduction or real estate tax deduction.

TAXPLANNER

We recommend that you keep all your canceled checks for 6 years. It would be wise to keep your income tax returns permanently. You should keep documents showing your basis in a piece of property for as long as you own that piece of property. If you sell a piece of property, you should keep your records showing your basis in the old property for at least 6 years after the sale.

If you do not keep the requisite records, it may be impossible for you to prove that you incurred deductible expenses or to establish your basis for gain or loss. Without such proof, the IRS can deny you a deduction. If you acquire property from an estate or by gift, it is advisable to secure a copy of the valuation of the estate or of the gift tax return so that you can determine the donor's basis in the property that you have been given. Knowing the donor's basis, you can easily determine your gain or loss when you sell the property. See Chapter 14, *Basis of Property,* for more details on determining gains and losses from the sale of property.

Example

Your parents buy a house for you as a wedding present. You sell the house 10 years later. The only record of the initial transaction is in the county real estate records. You believe there were other costs associated with the purchase, but you cannot find any records of them. If you claim the additional unsupported costs and the IRS examines your return for the year of the sale, it's likely that those costs will not be allowed. If you claim the additional costs and do not disclose on your return the lack of records to substantiate them, you could be subject to a penalty.

More information. For more information on recordkeeping, get Publication 552, *Recordkeeping for Individuals*.

Interest on Refunds

If you are due a refund, you may get interest on it. The interest rates are adjusted quarterly.

If the refund is made within 45 days after the due date of your return, no interest will be paid. If you file your return after the due date (including extensions), no interest will be paid if the refund is made within 45 days after the date you filed. If the refund is not made within this 45-day period, interest will be paid from the due date of the return or from the date you filed, whichever is later.

Accepting a refund check does not change your right to claim an additional refund and interest. File your claim within the period of time that applies. See *Amended Returns and Claims for Refund*, later. If you do not accept a refund check, no more interest will be paid on the overpayment included in the check.

Interest on erroneous refund. All or part of any interest you were charged on an erroneous refund generally will be forgiven. Any interest charged for the period before demand for repayment was made will be forgiven unless:

1) You, or a person related to you, caused the erroneous refund in any way, or
2) The refund is more than $50,000.

For example, if you claimed a refund of $100 on your return, but the IRS made an error and sent you $1,000, you would not be charged interest for the time you held the $900 difference. You must, however, repay the $900 when the IRS asks.

Past-Due Refund

If you do not get your refund within 4 weeks after filing your return, you can call TeleTax. For details on how to use this telephone service, see *What Is TeleTax?* in your tax forms package. Please wait at least 4 weeks after filing your 2001 tax return before using this service. In some cases, TeleTax may not have refund information until 6 weeks after you file.

See *IRS e-file*, earlier, for information about refund inquiries when you file an electronic return.

Change of Address

If you have moved, file your return using your new address.

If you move after you filed your return, you should give the IRS clear and concise written notification of your change of address. The notification should be sent to the Internal Revenue Service Center serving your old address or to the Customer Service Division in the local area office. You can use **Form 8822**, *Change of Address*. If you are expecting a refund, also notify the post office serving your old address. This will help in forwarding your check to your new address (unless you chose Direct Deposit of your refund).

Be sure to include your social security number (and the name and social security number of your spouse, if you filed a joint return) in any correspondence with the IRS.

What If I Made a Mistake?

Errors may delay your refund or result in notices being sent to you. If you discover an error, you can file an amended return or claim for refund.

Amended Returns and Claims for Refund

You should correct your return if, after you have filed it, you find that:

1) You did not report some income,
2) You claimed deductions or credits you should not have claimed,
3) You did not claim deductions or credits you could have claimed, or
4) You should have claimed a different filing status. (You cannot change your filing status from married filing jointly to married filing separately after the due date of the original return. However, an executor may be able to make this change for a deceased spouse.)

If you need a copy of your return, see *Copies of returns* under *What Records Should I Keep*, earlier in this chapter.

Form 1040X. Use Form 1040X, *Amended U.S. Individual Income Tax Return*, to correct the return you have already filed. An amended tax return cannot be filed electronically under the *e-file* system.

Completing Form 1040X. On Form 1040X, write your income, deductions, and credits as you originally reported them on your return, the changes you are making, and the corrected amounts. Then figure the tax on the corrected amount of taxable income and the amount you owe or your refund.

If you owe tax, pay the full amount with Form 1040X. The tax owed will not be subtracted from any amount you had credited to your estimated tax.

If you cannot pay the full amount due with your return, you can ask to make monthly installment payments. See *Installment Agreement*, earlier.

If you overpaid tax, you can have all or part of the overpayment refunded to you, or you can apply all or part of it to your estimated tax. If you choose to get a refund, it will be sent separately from any refund shown on your original return.

Filing Form 1040X. After you finish your Form 1040X, check it to be sure that it is complete. Do not forget to show the year of your original return and explain all changes you made. Be sure to attach any forms or schedules needed to explain your changes. Mail your Form 1040X to the Internal Revenue Service Center serving the area where you now live (as shown in the instructions to the form).

File a separate form for each tax year involved.

Time for filing a claim for refund. Generally, you must file your claim for a credit or refund within 3 years after the date you filed your original return or within 2 years after the date you paid the tax, whichever is later. Returns filed before the due date (without regard to extensions) are considered filed on the due date (even if the due date was a Saturday, Sunday, or legal holiday). These time periods are suspended while you are financially disabled, discussed later.

If the last day for claiming a credit or refund is a Saturday, Sunday, or legal holiday, you can file the claim on the next business day.

If you do not file a claim within this period, you may not be entitled to a credit or a refund.

Late-filed return. If you were due a refund but you did not file a return, you generally must file within 3 years from the date the return was originally due to get that refund.

Limit on amount of refund. If you file your claim within 3 years after the date you filed your return, the credit or refund cannot be more than the part of the tax paid within the 3-year period (plus any extension of time for filing your return) immediately before you filed the claim. This time period is suspended while you are financially disabled, discussed later.

Tax paid. Payments made before the due date (without regard to extensions) of the original return are considered paid on the due date.

Examples include federal income tax withheld from wages and estimated income tax.

Example 1. You made estimated tax payments of $500 and got an automatic extension of time to August 16, 1999, to file your 1998 income tax return. When you filed your return on that date, you paid an additional $200 tax. On August 15, 2002, you filed an amended return and claimed a refund of $700. Because you filed your claim within 3 years after you filed your original return, you can get a refund of up to $700, the tax paid within the 3 years plus the 4-month extension period immediately before you filed the claim.

Example 2. The situation is the same as in Example 1, except you filed your return on October 29, 1999, 2 1/2 months after the extension period ended. You paid an additional $200 on that date. On October 29, 2002, you filed an amended return and claimed a refund of $700. Although you filed your claim within 3 years from the date you filed your original return, the refund was limited to $200, the tax paid within the 3 years plus the 4-month extension period immediately before you filed the claim. The estimated tax of $500 paid before that period cannot be refunded or credited.

If you file a claim more than 3 years after you file your return, the credit or refund cannot be more than the tax you paid within the 2 years immediately before you file the claim.

Example. You filed your 1998 tax return on April 15, 1999. You paid taxes of $500. On November 1, 2000, after an examination of your 1998 return, you had to pay an additional tax of $200. On May 13, 2002, you file a claim for a refund of $300. However, because you filed your claim more than 3 years after you filed your return, your refund will be limited to the $200 you paid during the 2 years immediately before you filed your claim.

Financially disabled. The time periods are suspended for the period in which you are financially disabled. You are financially disabled if you are unable to manage your financial affairs because of a medically determinable physical or mental impairment which can be expected to result in death or which has lasted or can be expected to last for a continuous period of not less than 12 months. However, you are not treated as financially disabled during any period your spouse or any other person is authorized to act on your behalf in financial matters.

To claim that you are financially disabled, you must send in the following written statements with your claim for refund.

1) A statement from your qualified physician that includes:
   a) The name and a description of your physical or mental impairment,
   b) The physician's medical opinion that the impairment prevented you from managing your financial affairs,
   c) The physician's medical opinion that the impairment was or can be expected to result in death, or that its duration has lasted, or can be expected to last, at least 12 months,
   d) The specific time period (to the best of the physician's knowledge), and
   e) The following certification signed by the physician: "I hereby certify that, to the best of my knowledge and belief, the above representations are true, correct, and complete."
2) A statement made by the person signing the claim for credit or refund that no person, including your spouse, was authorized to act on your behalf in financial matters during the period of disability (or the exact dates that a person was authorized to act for you).

Exceptions for special types of refunds. If you file a claim for one of the items listed below, the dates and limits discussed earlier may not apply. These items, and where to get more information, are as follows.

- A bad debt. (See *Nonbusiness Bad Debts* in chapter 15.)
- A worthless security. (See *Worthless securities* in chapter 15.)
- Foreign tax paid or accrued. (See Publication 514, *Foreign Tax Credit for Individuals.*)
- Net operating loss carryback. (See Publication 536, *Net Operating Losses (NOLs) for Individuals, Estates, and Trusts.*)

- Carryback of certain business tax credits. (See Form 3800, *General Business Credit.*)
- A claim based on an agreement with the IRS extending the period for assessment of tax.
- An injured spouse claim. (See *Offset against debts,* earlier.)

Processing claims for refund. Claims are usually processed shortly after they are filed. Your claim may be accepted as filed, disallowed, or subject to examination. If a claim is examined, the procedures are the same as in the examination of a tax return.

If your claim is disallowed, you will receive an explanation of why it was disallowed.

Taking your claim to court. You can sue for a refund in court, but you must first file a timely claim with the IRS. If the IRS disallows your claim or does not act on your claim within 6 months after you file it, you can then take your claim to court. For information on the burden of proof in a court proceeding, see Publication 556, *Examination of Returns, Appeal Rights, and Claims for Refund.*

The IRS provides a fast method to move your claim to court if:

- You are filing a claim for a credit or refund based solely on contested income tax or on estate tax or gift tax issues considered in your previously examined returns, and
- You want to take your case to court instead of appealing it within the IRS.

When you file your claim with the IRS, you get the fast method by requesting in writing that your claim be immediately rejected. A notice of claim disallowance will then be promptly sent to you.

You have 2 years from the date of mailing of the notice of disallowance to file a refund suit in the United States District Court having jurisdiction or in the United States Court of Federal Claims.

Interest on refund. If you receive a refund because of your amended return, interest will be paid on it from the due date of your original return or the date you filed your original return, whichever is later, to the date you filed the amended return. However, if the refund is not made within 45 days after you file the amended return, interest will be paid up to the date the refund is paid.

Reduced refund. Your refund may be reduced by an additional tax liability that has been assessed against you.

Also, your refund may be reduced by amounts you owe for past-due child support, debts to another federal agency, or for state tax. The refund procedures discussed in this chapter will not be available to you to get back the reduction. See *Offset against debts,* earlier.

Effect on state tax liability. If your return is changed for any reason, it may affect your state income tax liability. This includes changes made as a result of an examination of your return by the IRS. Contact your state tax agency for more information.

TAXPLANNER

The IRS routinely shares information with most states that have state income taxes. If you file an amended federal tax return showing a balance due, you may avoid interest on tax due to the state and any penalties by taking the initiative and filing amended state tax returns when that is appropriate.

Penalties

The law provides penalties for failure to file returns or pay taxes as required.

Civil Penalties

If you do not file your return and pay your tax by the due date, you may have to pay a penalty. You may also have to pay a penalty if you substantially understate your tax, file a frivolous return, or fail to supply your social security number. If you provide fraudulent information on your return, you may have to pay a civil fraud penalty.

Filing late. If you do not file your return by the due date (including extensions), you may have to pay a *failure-to-file* penalty. The penalty is based on the tax not paid by the due date (without regard to extensions). The penalty is usually 5% for each month or part of a month that a return is late, but not more than 25%.

Fraud. If your failure to file is due to fraud, the penalty is 15% for each month or part of a month that your return is late, up to a maximum of 75%.

Return over 60 days late. If you file your return more than 60 days after the due date or extended due date, the minimum penalty is the smaller of $100 or 100% of the unpaid tax.

Exception. You will not have to pay the penalty if you show that you failed to file on time because of reasonable cause and not because of willful neglect.

Paying tax late. You will have to pay a *failure-to-pay* penalty of 1/2 of 1% (.50%) of your unpaid taxes for each month, or part of a month, after the due date that the tax is not paid. This penalty does not apply during the automatic 4-month extension of time to file period, if you paid at least 90% of your actual tax liability on or before the due date of your return and pay the balance when you file the return.

The monthly rate of the failure-to-pay penalty is half the usual rate (.25% instead of .50%) if an installment agreement is in effect for that month. You must have filed your return by the due date (including extensions) to qualify for this reduced penalty.

If a notice of intent to levy is issued, the rate will increase to 1% at the start of the first month beginning at least 10 days after the day that the notice is issued. If a notice and demand for immediate payment is issued, the rate will increase to 1% at the start of the first month beginning after the day that the notice and demand is issued.

This penalty cannot be more than 25% of your unpaid tax. You will not have to pay the penalty if you can show that you had a good reason for not paying your tax on time.

Combined penalties. If both the failure-to-file penalty and the failure-to-pay penalty (discussed earlier) apply in any month, the 5% (or 15%) failure-to-file penalty is reduced by the failure-to-pay penalty. However, if you file your return more than 60 days after the due date or extended due date, the minimum penalty is the smaller of $100 or 100% of the unpaid tax.

Accuracy-related penalty. You may have to pay an accuracy-related penalty if:

1) You underpay your tax because of either "negligence" or "disregard" of rules or regulations, or
2) You substantially understate your income tax.

The penalty is equal to 20% of the underpayment. The penalty will not be figured on any part of an underpayment on which the fraud penalty (discussed later) is charged.

Negligence or disregard. The term "negligence" includes a failure to make a reasonable attempt to comply with the tax law or to exercise ordinary and reasonable care in preparing a return. Negligence also includes failure to keep adequate books and records. You will not have to pay a negligence penalty if you have a reasonable basis for a position you took.

The term "disregard" includes any careless, reckless, or intentional disregard.

TAXPLANNER

The IRS has a comprehensive program to compare the amounts of income reported as paid by payers on Form 1099 series information returns with the amounts of income reported by the payees in their income tax returns. If this document-matching program discloses apparently underreported income, you will receive a notice of additional tax due that may include imposition of a 20% negligence penalty. If you receive an information return showing income paid to you that through no fault of your own you did not receive in 2001 or that for some reason is not taxable to you, you should nevertheless report as income on your return the entire amount shown by the information return and subtract from that the amount you believe to be erroneous. Following this procedure usually will avoid automatic generation of the IRS notice and the inconvenience and frustration of corresponding with the IRS to get the matter resolved.

Adequate disclosure. You can avoid the penalty for disregard of rules or regulations if you adequately disclose on your return a position that has at least a reasonable basis. See *Disclosure statement,* later.

Substantial understatement of income tax. You understate your tax if the tax shown on your return is less than the correct tax. The understatement is substantial if it is more than the larger of 10% of the correct tax or $5,000. However, the amount of the understatement is reduced to the extent the understatement is due to:

1) Substantial authority, or
2) Adequate disclosure and a reasonable basis.

Substantial authority. Whether there is or was substantial authority for the tax treatment of an item depends on the facts and circumstances. Consideration will be given to court opinions, Treasury regulations, revenue rulings, revenue procedures, and notices and announcements issued by the IRS and published in the *Internal Revenue Bulletin* that involve the same or similar circumstances as yours.

Disclosure statement. To adequately disclose the relevant facts about your tax treatment of an item, use **Form 8275,** *Disclosure Statement.* You must also have a reasonable basis for treating the item the way you did.

In cases of substantial understatement only, items that meet the requirements of Revenue Procedure 2001–11 (or later update) are considered adequately disclosed on your return without filing Form 8275.

Use **Form 8275-R,** *Regulation Disclosure Statement,* to disclose items or positions contrary to regulations.

Reasonable cause. You will not have to pay a penalty if you show a good reason (reasonable cause) for the way you treated an item. You must also show that you acted in good faith.

Explanation
The IRS's explanation of the penalty for substantial understatement and how to avoid it oversimplifies a very complex situation.

Under regulations issued by the IRS, the following items may generally be considered substantial authority:

- Internal Revenue Code and other statutory provisions
- Temporary and final IRS regulations
- Court cases
- Administrative pronouncements (including revenue rulings and revenue procedures)
- Tax treaties and regulations issued as a result of a treaty
- Congressional intent as reflected in committee reports, joint explanatory statements of managers included in conference committee reports, and statements made in Congress by one of a bill's managers prior to enactment of a bill
- General explanations of tax legislation prepared by the Joint Committee on Taxation (the Blue Book)
- Proposed IRS regulations

- Information or press releases, notices, announcements, and any other similar documents published by the IRS in the *Internal Revenue Bulletin*
- Private letter rulings, technical advice memoranda, actions on decisions, and general counsel memoranda after they have been released to the public, if they are dated after March 12, 1981

Frivolous return. You may have to pay a penalty of $500 if you file a frivolous return. A frivolous return is one that does not include enough information to figure the correct tax or that contains information clearly showing that the tax you reported is substantially incorrect.

You will have to pay the penalty if you filed this kind of return because of a frivolous position on your part or a desire to delay or interfere with the administration of federal income tax laws. This includes altering or striking out the preprinted language above the space provided for your signature.

This penalty is added to any other penalty provided by law.

Explanation
Congress enacted this penalty to attack a great variety of tax protest activities, including:

1. Irregular tax forms not in processible form
2. References to spurious constitutional arguments as a basis for not completing tax forms
3. Unallowable deductions claimed as a protest against military expenses
4. Deliberate use of incorrect Tax Tables
5. Presentation of clearly inconsistent information, such as a taxpayer who lists only two dependents while claiming 99 exemptions for withholding purposes

TaxAlert

Unlike most other penalties, the penalty for filing a frivolous return is not based on your tax liability. The penalty for filing a frivolous return will be assessed immediately and added to any other penalties.

The penalty must be paid in full upon notice and demand from IRS even if you protest the penalty.

Fraud. If there is any underpayment of tax on your return due to fraud, a penalty of 75% of the underpayment due to fraud will be added to your tax.

Joint return. The fraud penalty on a joint return does not apply to a spouse unless some part of the underpayment is due to the fraud of that spouse.

Failure to supply social security number. If you do not include your social security number (SSN) or the SSN of another person where required on a return, statement, or other document, you will be subject to a penalty of $50 for *each* failure. You will also be subject to a penalty of $50 if you do not give your SSN to another person when it is required on a return, statement, or other document.

For example, if you have a bank account that earns interest, you must give your SSN to the bank. The number must be shown on the Form 1099-INT or other statement the bank sends you. If you do not give the bank your SSN, you will be subject to the $50 penalty. (You also may be subject to "backup" withholding of income tax. See chapter 5.)

You will not have to pay the penalty if you are able to show that the failure was due to reasonable cause and not willful neglect.

Failure to furnish tax shelter registration number. A person who sells (or otherwise transfers) to you an interest in a tax shelter must give you the tax shelter registration number or be subject to a $100 penalty. If you claim any deduction, credit, or other tax benefit because of the tax shelter, you must attach **Form 8271,** *Investor Reporting of Tax Shelter Registration Number,* to your return to report this number. You will have to pay a penalty of $250 for each failure to report a tax shelter registration number on your return. The penalty can be excused if you have a reasonable cause for not reporting the number.

Criminal Penalties
You may be subject to criminal prosecution (brought to trial) for actions such as:

1) Tax evasion,
2) Willful failure to file a return, supply information, or pay any tax due,
3) Fraud and false statements, or
4) Preparing and filing a fraudulent return.

TaxAlert

In addition to any of the other penalties discussed in this section, you can be charged a penalty for paying your tax with a bad check. The penalty may not be imposed if you submit a bad check in good faith and with reasonable cause to believe that it will be paid. The penalty is 2% of the amount of the check or, if the check is less than $750, the lesser of $15 or the amount of the check.

2

Filing Status

Introduction

*One of the first things to determine in preparing your income tax return is your filing status. There are five possible choices: **single, married filing jointly, married filing separately, unmarried head of household,** and **qualifying widow or widower** with a dependent child.*

*Your choice of filing status dictates which Tax Table or Tax Rate Schedule you will use in calculating your tax liability; whether you may claim an **exemption** for a **dependent** or whether you may be claimed as a dependent; and how much income you can have before you are taxed at all.*

This chapter helps you decide which filing status you should choose so that you pay the least amount of tax.

This chapter discusses which filing status you should use. There are five filing statuses. They are:

- Single,
- Married Filing Jointly,
- Married Filing Separately,
- Head of Household, and
- Qualifying Widow(er) With Dependent Child.

Tip. *If more than one filing status applies to you, choose the one that will give you the lowest tax.*

Explanation
If your filing status changes during the year, you may not file under one status for one part of that year and under a second status for the remainder of the year. The law requires that your filing status for the entire year be determined by your status on the last day of the tax year. For example, even if you get married on December 31, you are treated as married for the entire year and you may either file as married filing jointly or married filing separately. Choose the one that will produce the lowest tax. (*Note:* If your spouse or a qualifying person died during the year, see the IRS explanation below.)

You use your filing status in determining your filing requirements (chapter 1), standard deduction (chapter 21), and correct tax (chapter 31). You also use your filing status in determining whether you are eligible to claim certain deductions and credits.

Useful Items

You may want to see:

Publication

- ☐ **501** Exemptions, Standard Deduction, and Filing Information
- ☐ **519** U.S. Tax Guide for Aliens
- ☐ **555** Community Property

Marital Status

In general, your filing status depends on whether you are considered unmarried or married. A marriage means only a legal union between a man and a woman as husband and wife.

Unmarried persons. You are considered unmarried for the whole year if, on the last day of your tax year, you are unmarried or legally separated from your spouse under a divorce or a separate maintenance decree. State law governs whether you are married or legally separated under a divorce or separate maintenance decree.

Divorced persons. If you are divorced under a final decree by the last day of the year, you are considered unmarried for the whole year.

Divorce and remarriage. If you obtain a divorce in one year for the sole purpose of filing tax returns as unmarried individuals, and at the time of divorce you intended to and did remarry each other in the next tax year, you and your spouse must file as married individuals.

Annulled marriages. If you obtain a court decree of annulment, which holds that no valid marriage ever existed, you are considered unmarried even if you filed joint returns for earlier years. You must file amended returns (Form 1040X, *Amended U.S. Individual Income Tax Return*) claiming single or head of household status for all tax years affected by the annulment that are not closed by the statute of limitations for filing a tax return. The statute of limitations generally does not expire until 3 years after your original return was filed.

Explanation

Invalid divorces. This is a very confusing subject because courts in different geographic locations disagree with each other. Furthermore, the courts and the IRS have interpreted the law differently.

Generally, you may *not* file a joint return with your second spouse unless the marital relationship with your first spouse has been severed.

While terminating a marriage is usually a matter of obtaining a divorce from a foreign or a domestic court, it is not always that straightforward. When a particular state's law does not recognize the validity of a divorce decree acquired in another jurisdiction, the IRS and the courts disagree over the status of the divorce.

The Second and Third Circuit Courts of Appeals adhere to the so-called rule of validation. Basically, this rule specifies that a divorce in any court's jurisdiction must be recognized for the purposes of tax law. Consequently, under the rule of validation, a valid joint return may be filed with a second spouse. However, the IRS, the Tax Court, and the Ninth Circuit Court of Appeals do not support the rule of validation. Instead, they maintain that a second court possessing jurisdiction may declare a prior divorce invalid. Thus, a return filed jointly by a party of the invalid divorce and a subsequent marriage partner may not be valid. Nevertheless, neither these courts nor the IRS will challenge the validity of a divorce decree until a court of competent jurisdiction has declared the divorce invalid.

Prisoners of war. You are still considered to be married if your spouse is a prisoner of war (POW) or is listed as missing in action (MIA). Even if you subsequently discover that your spouse died in action or in captivity in a prior year, you cannot alter your married filing status on prior income tax returns.

TaxSaver

When to get divorced. December is the better month to get divorced if spouses have similar incomes. In this way, you can file single returns for the entire year. January is the better month to get divorced if one spouse has considerably more income than the other and you both want to save on taxes.

The IRS contends that actions that are designed to control an individual's marital status at the close of the year for tax purposes, such as a year-end tax-motivated divorce followed by immediate remarriage, are shams and should be disregarded for tax purposes. According to the IRS, individuals retain their married status when:

1. A divorce under the laws of a foreign jurisdiction is obtained late in the year
2. At the time of the divorce the parties intend to remarry
3. The remarriage occurs in January of the next year

However, a divorce followed by cohabitation is not necessarily a sham. The IRS has recognized such arrangements and has allowed individuals to claim single filing status as long as they say that they intend to remain divorced and not remarry each other.

TaxPlanner

If you are getting a divorce, you should consider the impact of the alternative minimum tax (AMT) on special types of income and how accelerating these types of income or deferring related deductions can be taken advantage of while still filing as married filing jointly. See Chapter 31, *How to Figure Your Tax,* for additional discussion of the AMT.

Head of household or qualifying widow(er) with dependent child. If you are considered unmarried, you may be able to file as a head of household or as a qualifying widow(er) with a dependent child. See *Head of Household* and *Qualifying Widow(er) With Dependent Child* to see if you qualify.

Married persons. If you are considered married for the whole year, you and your spouse can file a joint return, or you can file separate returns.

Considered married. You are considered married for the whole year if on the last day of your tax year you and your spouse meet any one of the following tests.

1) You are married and living together as husband and wife.
2) You are living together in a *common law marriage* that is recognized in the state where you now live or in the state where the common law marriage began.
3) You are married and living apart, but not legally separated under a decree of divorce or separate maintenance.
4) You are separated under an interlocutory (not final) decree of divorce. For purposes of filing a joint return, you are not considered divorced.

Spouse died. If your spouse died during the year, you are considered married for the whole year for filing status purposes.

If you did not remarry before the end of the tax year, you can file a joint return for yourself and your deceased spouse. For the next 2 years, you may be entitled to the special benefits described later under *Qualifying Widow(er) With Dependent Child.*

If you remarried before the end of the tax year, you can file a joint return with your new spouse. Your deceased spouse's filing status is married filing separately for that year.

Married persons living apart. If you live apart from your spouse and meet certain tests, you may be *considered unmarried.* If this applies to you, you can file as head of household even though you are not divorced or legally separated. If you qualify to file as head of household instead of as married filing separately, your standard deduction will be higher. Also, your tax may be lower, and you may be able to claim the earned income credit. See *Head of Household,* later.

Single

Your filing status is *single* if, on the last day of the year, you are unmarried or legally separated from your spouse under a divorce or separate maintenance decree, and you do not qualify for another filing status. To determine your marital status on the last day of the year, see *Marital Status,* earlier.

Your filing status may be single if you were widowed before January 1, 2001, and did not remarry in 2001. However, you might be able to use another filing status that will give you a lower tax. See *Head of Household* and *Qualifying Widow(er) With Dependent Child* to see if you qualify.

How to file. You can file Form 1040EZ (if you have no dependents, are under 65 and not blind, and meet other requirements), Form 1040A, or Form 1040. If you file Form 1040A or Form 1040, show your filing status as single by checking the box on line 1. Use the *Single* column of the Tax Table or *Schedule X* of the Tax Rate Schedules to figure your tax.

Married Filing Jointly

You can choose **married filing jointly** as your filing status if you are married and both you and your spouse agree to file a joint return. On a joint return, you report your combined income and deduct your combined allowable expenses.

If you and your spouse decide to file a joint return, your tax may be lower than your combined tax for the other filing statuses. Also, your standard deduction (if you do not itemize deductions) may be higher, and you may qualify for tax benefits that do not apply to other filing statuses. You can file a joint return even if one of you had no income or deductions.

Tip. *If you and your spouse each have income, you may want to figure your tax both on a joint return and on separate returns (using the filing status of married filing separately). Choose the method that gives the two of you the lower combined tax.*

How to file. If you file as married filing jointly, you can use Form 1040 or Form 1040A. If you have no dependents, are under 65 and not blind, and meet other requirements, you can file Form 1040EZ. If you file Form 1040 or Form 1040A, show this filing status by checking the box on line 2. Use the *Married filing jointly* column of the Tax Table or *Schedule Y-1* of the Tax Rate Schedules to figure your tax.

Explanation
Marriage tax penalty. Marriage partners who earn approximately the same income may pay more tax if they file a joint return or file separate married returns than they would if they could file two single returns. This is known as "the marriage tax penalty."

Example
John and Mary were both employed during the year. Mary had a **gross income** of $30,000, and John earned $28,000. If John and Mary were wed before the end of the year, their joint tax liability after deducting personal exemptions and the standard deduction would be $6,690. However, if they postponed their marriage until next year, their combined tax liabilities for the current year, filing as single taxpayers, would be as follows:

Mary's tax:	$3,382
John's tax:	3,082
Total:	$6,464

Thus, there is a marriage tax penalty of $226. One possible solution would be to delay getting married.

TaxAlert: The 2001 Tax Act
Marriage Penalty Relief Beginning in 2005. The Economic Growth and Tax Relief Reconciliation Act of 2001 provides some long-awaited relief to those affected by the marriage tax penalty. A married couple's standard deduction is gradually increased to twice the standard deduction for an unmarried individual. This is phased in beginning in 2005 and becomes fully effective in 2009. Another bonus for married couples is the expansion of the 15% tax bracket to twice the size of the bracket for a single taxpayer. This is phased in beginning in 2005 and becomes fully effective in 2008.

Explanation
Singles' tax penalty. A single person earning the same **taxable income** as a married person whose spouse has comparatively little taxable income will pay substantially more income tax than the married person. In other words, if you marry somebody with little or no taxable income, your tax decreases. This is known as "the singles' tax penalty."

Example
Assume the same facts as in the above example, except that John had only $300 of interest income. If John and Mary were married before December 31, 2001, their joint tax liability on the gross income $30,300 would be $2,535. If they married after the end of the year, their combined tax liabilities in the current year, filing as single taxpayers, would be as follows:

Mary's tax:	$3,382
John's tax:	0
Total:	$3,382

Thus, there is a singles' tax penalty of $847. One possible solution would be to get married quickly.

TaxSaver
When to get married. If you are contemplating a winter marriage and one of you has more income than the other, choose December instead of January if you want to save on your taxes. If you have similar incomes, choose January.

Spouse died during the year. If your spouse died during the year, you are considered married for the whole year and can choose married filing jointly as your filing status. See *Spouse died,* earlier, for more information.

Divorced persons. If you are divorced under a final decree by the last day of the year, you are considered unmarried for the whole year and you cannot choose married filing jointly as your filing status.

Filing a Joint Return

Both you and your spouse must include all of your income, exemptions, and deductions on your joint return.

Accounting period. Both of you must use the same accounting period, but you can use different accounting methods. See *Accounting Periods* and *Accounting Methods* in chapter 1.

Joint responsibility. Both of you may be held responsible, jointly and individually, for the tax and any interest or penalty due on your joint return. One spouse may be held responsible for all the tax due even if all the income was earned by the other spouse.

Divorced taxpayer. You may be held jointly and individually responsible for any tax, interest, and penalties due on a joint return filed before your divorce. This responsibility may apply even if your divorce decree states that your former spouse will be responsible for any amounts due on previously filed joint returns.

Relief from joint liability. In some cases, one spouse may be relieved of joint liability for tax, interest, and penalties on a joint return for items of the other spouse that were incorrectly reported on the joint return. You can ask for relief no matter how small the liability.

There are three types of relief available.

1) Innocent spouse relief, which applies to all joint filers.
2) Separation of liability, which applies to joint filers who are divorced, widowed, legally separated, or have not lived together for the past 12 months.

3) Equitable relief, which applies to all joint filers who do not qualify for innocent spouse relief or separation of liability and to married couples filing separate returns in community property states.

You must file Form 8857, *Request for Innocent Spouse Relief,* to request any of these kinds of relief. Publication 971, *Innocent Spouse Relief,* explains these kinds of relief and who may qualify for them.

Signing a joint return. For a return to be considered a joint return, both husband and wife must generally sign the return. If your spouse died before signing the return, see *Signing the return* in chapter 4.

Spouse away from home. If your spouse is away from home, you should prepare the return, sign it, and send it to your spouse to sign so that it can be filed on time.

Injury or disease prevents signing. If your spouse cannot sign because of disease or injury and tells you to sign, you can sign your spouse's name in the proper space on the return followed by the words "By (your name), Husband (or Wife)." Be sure to also sign in the space provided for your signature. Attach a dated statement, signed by you, to the return. The statement should include the form number of the return you are filing, the tax year, the reason your spouse cannot sign, and a statement that your spouse has agreed to your signing for him or her.

Signing as guardian of spouse. If you are the guardian of your spouse who is mentally incompetent, you can sign the return for your spouse as guardian.

Spouse in combat zone. If your spouse is unable to sign the return because he or she is serving in a combat zone, such as the Persian Gulf Area or Yugoslavia, or a qualified hazardous duty area (Bosnia and Herzegovina, Croatia, and Macedonia), and you do not have a power of attorney or other statement, you can sign for your spouse. Attach a signed statement to your return that explains that your spouse is serving in a combat zone. For more information on special tax rules for persons who are serving in a combat zone, get Publication 3, *Armed Forces' Tax Guide.*

Other reasons spouse cannot sign. If your spouse cannot sign the joint return for any other reason, you can sign for your spouse only if you are given a valid power of attorney (a legal document giving you permission to act for your spouse). Attach the power of attorney (or a copy of it) to your tax return. You can use Form 2848, *Power of Attorney and Declaration of Representative.*

TaxAlert

Contrary to the IRS's assertion, the failure of one spouse to sign a return will not prevent a finding that the return was a joint return. If the facts of the case support the conclusion that the nonsigning spouse gave tacit consent to a joint filing, then a valid joint return exists.

Even when a spouse's signature is forged, a valid joint return can exist. In one case, the IRS challenged the return of a husband who, due to marital difficulties, had an unknown person forge his wife's signature. Even though his wife testified in court that she would not have signed a joint return under any circumstances, the court ruled that the joint return was valid. The court reasoned that the wife's refusal to sign was unrelated to the joint filing status claim. Furthermore, because the couple had always filed jointly in the past and the wife did nothing to indicate her disapproval of her husband's intention to continue to file jointly, the court said she had no grounds to complain after the filing was made. The court's message is: The presence or absence of an authentic signature does not constitute conclusive evidence of the intent to file jointly or singly. In addition, the refusal to sign does not necessarily mean that the intent to file a joint return was nonexistent.

Nonresident alien or dual-status alien. A joint return generally cannot be filed if either spouse is a nonresident alien at any time during the tax year. However, if one spouse was a nonresident alien or dual-status alien who was married to a U.S. citizen or resident at the end of the year, the spouses can choose to file a joint return. If you do file a joint return, you and your spouse are both treated as U.S. residents for the entire tax year. For information on this choice, see chapter 1 of Publication 519.

TaxPlanner

You may file a joint return and use the more beneficial joint tax rates if you fall into either of the following two categories:

1. As of the close of the tax year, you are a nonresident alien married to a citizen or resident of the United States.
2. You are a nonresident alien at the beginning of the tax year but a resident of the United States at the close of the tax year (i.e., a dual-status taxpayer) and you are married to a citizen or resident of the United States at the end of the tax year.

The catch is that a joint return requires that the worldwide income of both spouses for the entire year be included in taxable income.

Generally, not filing jointly means that separate returns are required. Only the worldwide income of a U.S. citizen and the worldwide income of an alien while a U.S. resident would be included in each person's taxable income. As a result, the alien spouse's income while a nonresident would be excluded. However, the more burdensome married filing separately tax rates must be used.

Married Filing Separately

You can choose **married filing separately** as your filing status if you are married. This method may benefit you if you want to be responsible only for your own tax or if this method results in less tax than a joint return. If you and your spouse do not agree to file a joint return, you may have to use this filing status.

If you live apart from your spouse and meet certain tests, you may be **considered unmarried** and may be able to file as head of household. This can apply to you even if you are not divorced or legally separated. If you qualify to file as head of household, instead of as married filing separately, your tax may be lower, you may be able to claim the earned income credit and certain other credits, and your standard deduction will be higher. The head of household filing status allows you to choose the standard deduction even if your spouse chooses to itemize deductions. See *Head of Household,* later, for more information.

Tip. *Unless you are required to file separately, you should figure your tax both ways (on a joint return and on separate returns). This way you can make sure you are using the method that results in the lowest combined tax. However, you will generally pay more combined tax on separate returns than you would on a joint return because the tax rate is higher for married persons filing separately.*

How to file. If you file a separate return, you generally report only your own income, exemptions, credits, and deductions. You can claim an exemption for your spouse if your spouse had no gross income and was not a dependent of another person. However, if your spouse had any gross income, or was the dependent of someone else, you cannot claim an exemption for him or her on your separate return.

If you file as married filing separately, you can use Form 1040A or Form 1040. Select this filing status by checking the box on line 3 of either form. You must also write your spouse's social security number and full name in the spaces provided. Use the *Married filing separately* column of the Tax Table or *Schedule Y-2* of the Tax Rate Schedules to figure your tax.

Special Rules

Special rules apply if your filing status is married filing separately.
Community property states. If you live in Arizona, California, Idaho, Louisiana, Nevada, New Mexico, Texas, Washington, or Wisconsin and file separately, your income may be considered separate income or community income for income tax purposes. See Publication 555.
Deductions, credits, and certain income. If your filing status is married filing separately:

1) You should itemize deductions if your spouse itemizes deductions, because you cannot claim the standard deduction.
2) You cannot deduct interest paid on a qualified student loan.
3) You cannot take the credit for child and dependent care expenses in most instances, and the amount that you can exclude from income under an employer's dependent care assistance program is limited to $2,500 (instead of $5,000 if you filed a joint return).
4) You cannot take the earned income credit.
5) You cannot exclude any interest income from qualified U.S. savings bonds that you used for higher education expenses.
6) You cannot take the credit for the elderly or the disabled unless you lived apart from your spouse for the entire year.
7) You cannot take the education credits (the Hope credit and the lifetime learning credit).
8) You cannot take the exclusion or credit for adoption expenses in most instances.
9) You will become subject to the limit on the child tax credit, the limit on itemized deductions, and the phaseout of the deduction for personal exemptions at income levels that are half of those for a joint return.
10) You may have to include in income more of your social security benefits (or equivalent railroad retirement benefits) than you would on a joint return. For information on social security and railroad retirement benefits, see Publication 915, *Social Security and Equivalent Railroad Retirement Benefits.*
11) You cannot roll over amounts from a traditional IRA into a Roth IRA during the year, unless you did not live with your spouse at any time during the year.
12) Your capital loss deduction limit is $1,500 (instead of $3,000 if you filed a joint return).

TaxSaver

Consider filing separate returns:

1. If you suspect that your spouse owes the IRS money. If you file a joint return, you will both be liable for any tax due.
2. If you can obtain a larger benefit from a deduction for a net operating loss against separate rather than joint income.
3. If you or your spouse has significant medical or miscellaneous expenses or casualty losses, a larger deduction may be obtained, because only medical expenses exceeding 7.5%, miscellaneous expenses exceeding 2%, and personal casualty losses exceeding 10% of adjusted gross income are deductible. Thus, the lower your adjusted gross income, the more medical or miscellaneous expenses or casualty losses will be deductible.
4. If you are getting divorced. Overall tax savings will result when a high-bracket taxpayer deducts his or her alimony payment and an ex-spouse includes that alimony payment in his or her income at a lower marginal rate.
5. If neither you nor your spouse-to-be may itemize deductions (see Chapters 21–30). The standard deduction for a single person in 2001 is $4,550. Two single individuals filing separately could claim two standard deductions totaling $9,100. That is $1,500 more than the $7,600 standard deduction for a married couple. If neither of you can itemize your deductions, postponing your marriage until the following tax year will enable you to generate an additional $1,500 of income, tax-free.
6. If both husband and wife have similar income and deductions.
7. If a spouse wishes to be responsible for only his or her tax liability.

Consider filing a joint return:

1. If only one spouse has income.
2. If, as of the close of the tax year, you are a nonresident alien married to a citizen or resident of the United States, or you are a nonresident alien at the beginning of the tax year but a resident of the United States at the close of the year and you are married to a U.S. citizen or resident of the United States at the end of the year.

Individual retirement arrangements (IRAs). You may not be able to deduct all or part of your contributions to a traditional IRA if you or your spouse were covered by an employee retirement plan at work during the year. Your deduction is reduced or eliminated if your income is more than a certain amount. This amount is lower for married individuals who file separately and lived together at any time during the year. For more information, see *How Much Can I Deduct?* in Publication 590, *Individual Retirement Arrangements (IRAs).*
Rental activity losses. If you actively participated in a passive rental real estate activity that produced a loss, you generally can deduct the loss from your nonpassive income, up to $25,000. This is called a special allowance. However, married persons filing separate returns who lived together at any time during the year cannot claim this special allowance. Married persons filing separate returns who lived apart at all times during the year are each allowed a $12,500 maximum special allowance for losses from passive real estate activities. See *Limits on Rental Losses* in chapter 10.

Joint Return After Separate Returns
You can change your filing status by filing an amended return using Form 1040X.

If you or your spouse (or both of you) file a separate return, you generally can change to a joint return any time within 3 years from the due date of the separate return or returns. This does not include any extensions. A separate return includes a return filed by you or your spouse claiming married filing separately, single, or head of household filing status.

Separate Returns After Joint Return
Once you file a joint return, you cannot choose to file separate returns for that year after the due date of the return.

Explanation
If a husband and wife fail to file for a particular year, they may still file a joint return for that period, even if the return is as much as 3 years overdue. However, once the IRS has notified each spouse individually that he or she has not filed a return that is more than 3 years overdue, they cannot file a joint return.

Exception. A personal representative for a decedent can change from a joint return elected by the surviving spouse to a separate return for the decedent. The personal representative has 1 year from the due date of the return to make the change. See chapter 4 for more information on filing a return for a decedent.

Head of Household

You may be able to file as *head of household* if you meet all of the following requirements.

1) You are unmarried or considered unmarried on the last day of the year.
2) You paid more than half the cost of keeping up a home for the year.
3) A qualifying person lived with you in the home for more than half the year (except for temporary absences, such as school). However, your dependent parent does not have to live with you. See *Special rule for parent,* later, under *Qualifying Person.* A foster child must live with you all year.

Tip. *If you qualify to file as head of household, your tax rate usually will be lower than the rates for single or married filing separately. You will also receive a higher standard deduction than if you file as single or married filing separately.*

Kidnapped children. A child may qualify you to file as head of household, even if the child has been kidnapped. For more information, see Publication 501.

How to file. If you file as head of household, you can use either Form 1040A or Form 1040. Indicate your choice of this filing status by checking the box on line 4 of either form. Use the *Head of a household* column of the Tax Table or *Schedule Z* of the Tax Rate Schedules to figure your tax.

Considered Unmarried

You are considered unmarried on the last day of the year if you are legally separated from your spouse, according to your state law, under a divorce or separate maintenance decree.

You are also considered unmarried on the last day of the tax year if you meet *all* of the following tests.

1) You file a separate return.
2) You paid more than half the cost of keeping up your home for the tax year.
3) Your spouse did not live in your home during the last 6 months of the tax year. Your spouse is considered to live in your home even if he or she is temporarily absent due to special circumstances. See *Temporary absences,* later.
4) Your home was the main home of your child, stepchild, or adopted child for more than half the year or was the main home of your foster child for the entire year. (See *Home of qualifying person,* later, for rules applying to a child's birth, death, or temporary absence during the year.)
5) You must be able for to claim an exemption for the child. However, you can still meet this test if you cannot claim the exemption only because the noncustodial parent is allowed to claim the exemption for the child. See *Exception* under *Support Test for Child of Divorced or Separated Parents* in chapter 3 for situations where the noncustodial parent is allowed to claim the exemption for the child.

The general rules for claiming an exemption for a dependent are explained in chapter 3.

Caution. *If you were considered married for part of the year and lived in a community property state (listed earlier under* Married Filing Separately*), special rules may apply in determining your income and expenses. See Publication 555 for more information.*

Nonresident alien spouse. You are considered unmarried for head of household purposes if your spouse was a nonresident alien at any time during the year and you do not choose to treat your nonresident spouse as a resident alien. However, your spouse is not a qualifying person for head of household purposes. You must have another qualifying person and meet the other tests to be eligible to file as a head of household.

Earned income credit. Even if you are considered unmarried for head of household purposes because you are married to a nonresident alien, you are still considered married for purposes of the earned income credit (unless you meet the five tests listed earlier). You are not entitled to the credit unless you file a joint return with your spouse and meet other qualifications. See Publication 596, *Earned Income Credit,* for more information.

Choice to treat spouse as resident. You are considered married if you choose to treat your spouse as a resident alien.

Keeping Up a Home

To qualify for head of household status, you must pay more than half of the cost of keeping up a home for the year. You can determine whether you paid more than half of the cost of keeping up a home by using the *Cost of Keeping Up a Home* worksheet, shown later.

Costs you include. Include in the cost of upkeep expenses such as rent, mortgage interest, real estate taxes, insurance on the home, repairs, utilities, and food eaten in the home.

Costs you do not include. Do not include in the cost of upkeep expenses such as clothing, education, medical treatment, vacations, life insurance, or transportation. Also, do not include the rental value of a home you own or the value of your services or those of a member of your household.

Cost of Keeping Up a Home

	Amount You Paid	Total Cost
Property taxes	$ _____	$ _____
Mortgage interest expense	_____	_____
Rent	_____	_____
Utility charges	_____	_____
Upkeep and repairs	_____	_____
Property insurance	_____	_____
Food consumed on the premises	_____	_____
Other household expenses	_____	_____
Totals	$ _____	$ _____
Minus total amount you paid		(_____)
Amount others paid		$ _____

If the total amount you paid is more than the amount others paid, you meet the requirement of paying more than half the cost of keeping up the home.

Qualifying Person

See *Table 2–1* to see who is a qualifying person.

Any person not described in *Table 2–1* is not a qualifying person.

Home of qualifying person. Generally, the qualifying person must live with you for more than half of the year.

Special rule for parent. You may be eligible to file as head of household even if the parent for whom you can claim an exemption does not live with you. You must pay more than half the cost of keeping up a home that was the main home for the *entire year* for your father or mother. You are keeping up a main home for your father or mother if

Table 2–1. **Who Is a Qualifying Person for Filing as Head of Household?**[1]

IF the person is your . . .	AND . . .	THEN that person is . . .
Parent, Grandparent, Brother, Sister, Stepbrother, Stepsister, Stepmother, Stepfather, Mother-in-law, Father-in-law, Half brother, Half sister, Brother-in-law, Sister-in-law, Son-in-law, or Daughter-in-law	You can claim an exemption for him or her[2]	A qualifying person.
	You cannot claim an exemption for him or her	**NOT** a qualifying person.
Uncle, Aunt, Nephew, or Niece	He or she is related to you by blood <u>and</u> you can claim an exemption for him or her[2, 3]	A qualifying person.
	He or she is not related to you by blood[3]	**NOT** a qualifying person.
	You cannot claim an exemption for him or her	
Child, Grandchild, Stepchild, or Adopted child	He or she is single	A qualifying person.[4]
	He or she is married, <u>and</u> you can claim an exemption for him or her[2]	A qualifying person
	He or she is married, <u>and</u> you cannot claim an exemption for him or her	**NOT** a qualifying person.[5]
Foster child[6]	The child lived with you all year, <u>and</u> you can claim an exemption for him or her[2]	A qualifying person.
	The child lived with you all year, <u>and</u> you cannot claim an exemption for him or her	**NOT** a qualifying person.

[1]A person cannot qualify more than one taxpayer to use the head of household filing status for the year.

[2]If you can claim an exemption for a person only because of a multiple support agreement, that person cannot be a qualifying person. See *Multiple Support Agreement*.

[3]You are related by blood to an uncle or aunt if he or she is the brother or sister of your mother or father. You are related by blood to a nephew or niece if he or she is the child or your brother or sister.

[4]This child is a qualifying person even if you cannot claim an exemption for the child.

[5]This child is a qualifying person if you could claim an exemption for the child except that the child's other parent claims the exemption under the special rules for a noncustodial parent discussed under *Support Test for Divorced or Separated Parents* in chapter 3.

[6]The term "foster child" is defined under *Exemptions for Dependents* in chapter 3.

you pay more than half the cost of keeping your parent in a rest home or home for the elderly.

TAXPLANNER

If you are providing some support for your parents—but less than half of their total support—you should investigate targeting your support payments so that you can qualify as a head of household by establishing one of your parents as a dependent. For example, when you are providing funds to your parents for their support, some type of notation should be made on your check that specifically states for whom the money is being provided. In this fashion, you can clearly demonstrate that the 50% support requirement has been satisfied for at least one of your parents.

Temporary absences. You and your qualifying person are considered to live together even if one or both of you are temporarily absent from your home due to special circumstances such as illness, education, business, vacation, or military service. It must be reasonable to assume that the absent person will return to the household after the temporary absence. You must continue to keep up the home during the absence.

Examples

One court has held that a man still qualified for head of household status even though he temporarily moved out of his home after becoming legally separated. The court believed that the man had always intended to return to his home (and, in fact, he did return). The court was also aware that he had been awarded custody of his child.

Another court has held that a man could not claim that he was the head of the household that he maintained for his son where he himself did not live because of fear of his son.

Note: If your child or stepchild is absent from the home less than 6 months under a custody agreement, the absence is considered temporary.

Death or birth. You may be eligible to file as head of household if the individual who qualifies you for this filing status is born or dies during the year. You must have provided more than half of the cost of keeping up a home that was the individual's main home for more than half the year or, if less, the period during which the individual lived.

Example. You are unmarried. Your mother, for whom you can claim an exemption, lived in an apartment by herself. She died on September 2. The cost of the upkeep of her apartment for the year until her death was $6,000. You paid $4,000 and your brother paid $2,000. Your brother made no other payments toward your mother's support. Your mother had no income. Because you paid more than half the cost of keeping up your mother's apartment from January 1 until her death, and you can claim an exemption for her, you can file as a head of household.

Explanation
Except when you are supporting and maintaining your parents, who do not have to live with you, the IRS says that you cannot qualify as head of household unless you live in the home that you are supporting and maintaining. However, some courts have said that you can maintain more than one home and still claim head of household status. The household that qualifies you as a head of household need not be your principal place of abode, but it must be the home where you and members of your household live for an adequate period of time.

Example 1
A woman who owned two homes, hundreds of miles apart, could still claim to be head of household at the home that was the principal place of residence of her adopted son, though she spent only 40% of her time there. For both homes, however, she paid more than half the cost of upkeep.

Example 2
A man could not claim to be head of household, although he paid 80–90% of the household expenses and was a member of a nearby church because he did not spend a substantial amount of time at the house. He only visited his sisters at the house, either when he was in town on business during the week or when he stopped by for Sunday dinner. The house was owned by his sisters.

Example 3
A woman who spent 85% of her time in one house and 15% in another house that was the principal residence of her daughter and grandchildren was not allowed to claim head of household status. In this case, the houses were less than 2 miles apart and the woman stayed over at her daughter's only when either she or her daughter was ill. Besides, the daughter, not her mother, rented the house, although the daughter used money given to her by her mother to pay the rent.

Example 4
The case of the two-family house. In this case, a husband, wife, and their children lived in one of the house's units and the wife's mother and unwed sister lived in the other unit. The home contained some common areas but also some partitioned areas for the private use of each family unit. A court upheld the wife's mother's claim of head of household status based on her support of her unwed daughter.

Even though the mother paid less than half of the total household expenses, she did pay more than half of the expenses attributable to her and her daughter.

Qualifying Widow(er) With Dependent Child

If your spouse died in 2001, you can use married filing jointly as your filing status for 2001 if you otherwise qualify to use that status. The year of death is the last year for which you can file jointly with your deceased spouse. See *Married Filing Jointly,* earlier.

You may be eligible to use ***qualifying widow(er) with dependent child*** as your filing status for 2 years following the year of death of your spouse. For example, if your spouse died in 2000, and you have not remarried, you may be able to use this filing status for 2001 and 2002.

This filing status entitles you to use joint return tax rates and the highest standard deduction amount (if you do not itemize deductions). This status does not entitle you to file a joint return.

How to file. If you file as qualifying widow(er) with dependent child, you can use either Form 1040A or Form 1040. Indicate your filing status by checking the box on line 5 of either form. Write the year your spouse died in the space provided on line 5. Use the *Married filing jointly* column of the Tax Table or *Schedule Y-1* of the Tax Rate Schedules to figure your tax.

Eligibility rules. You are eligible to file your 2001 return as a qualifying widow(er) with dependent child if you meet all of the following tests.

1) You were entitled to file a joint return with your spouse for the year your spouse died. It does not matter whether you actually filed a joint return.
2) You did not remarry before the end of 2001.
3) You have a child, stepchild, adopted child, or foster child for whom you can claim an exemption.
4) You paid more than half the cost of keeping up a home that is the main home for you and that child for the entire year, except for temporary absences. See *Temporary absences* and *Keeping Up a Home,* discussed earlier under *Head of Household.*

Caution. *As mentioned earlier, this filing status is only available for 2 years following the year of death of your spouse.*

Example. John Reed's wife died in 1999. John has not remarried. During 2000 and 2001, he continued to keep up a home for himself and his child (for whom he can claim an exemption). For 1999 he was entitled to file a joint return for himself and his deceased wife. For 2000 and 2001 he can file as qualifying widower with a dependent child. After 2001 he can file as head of household if he qualifies.

Death or birth. You may be eligible to file as a qualifying widow(er) with dependent child if the child who qualifies you for this filing status is born or dies during the year. You must have provided more than half of the cost of keeping up a home that was the child's main home during the entire part of the year he or she was alive.

3

Personal Exemptions and Dependents

Introduction

In 2001, you are entitled to a $2,900 **deduction** for yourself, your spouse, and each person you support who otherwise qualifies as a dependent. Each year the amount of the personal exemption is adjusted for inflation. This chapter tells you what specific qualifications you have to meet to take these deductions. It informs you about the special rules and procedures that apply to divorced and separated couples with children, widows and widowers, and residents of **community property** states. Perhaps, most importantly, this chapter suggests when it might not be a good idea to take a deduction, even though you could qualify for it.

To qualify as your **dependent**, a person must meet five tests, all of which are explained in great detail in this chapter:

1. The person must be either a relative or a full-time member of your household.
2. The person must be a citizen or resident of the United States or a resident of Canada or Mexico.
3. The person must not file a **joint return** with another person.
4. The person must receive over half of his or her **support** from you.
5. The person must have less than $2,900 in **gross income** for the year, unless he or she is your child and is either under age 19 or a full-time student under age 24.

The original intent of personal **exemptions** for dependents was to provide tax relief so that even the poorest citizen would be left with enough money after taxes

to support self and family. Obviously, a $2,900 deduction these days can save the taxpayer only a small portion of the income necessary to live, even at a subsistence level. Ironically, the higher your income level and the higher your **marginal tax rate**, the greater economic benefit you derive from these—or, for that matter, any—deductions. A $2,900 deduction is worth $435 to a married couple filing a joint return with a **taxable income** of $20,000 and a marginal tax rate of 15%. The same $2,900 deduction is worth $870 to a married couple filing a joint return with a taxable income over $109,250 and a marginal tax rate of 30%. (Once your adjusted gross income reaches a certain threshold, figuring out what the exemption is worth is more complicated. This chapter explains this in more detail.)

Also explained are the rules that phase out the value of your personal exemptions if your adjusted gross income exceeds certain amounts: $199,450 for married persons filing jointly, $166,200 for heads of household, $132,950 for single taxpayers, and $99,725 for married persons filing separate returns.

Figuring out who should claim whom as a dependent can be a difficult matter involving considerable tax planning. For example, when parents are divorced, the custodial parent may sign a declaration permitting the noncustodial parent to claim the exemption for the dependent child. Consequently, if the noncustodial parent is in a higher tax bracket, a greater tax benefit can be obtained. Either parent is entitled to claim the medical expenses paid for the child, even if that parent cannot claim the child as a dependent.

Important Changes

Exemption amount. The amount you can deduct for each exemption has increased from $2,800 in 2000 to $2,900 in 2001.

Exemption phaseout. You will lose all or part of the benefit of your exemptions if your adjusted gross income is above a certain amount. The amount at which this phaseout begins depends on your filing status. For 2001, the phaseout begins at $99,725 for married persons filing separately, $132,950 for unmarried individuals, $166,200 for heads of household, and $199,450 for married persons filing jointly. See *Phaseout of Exemptions,* later.

This chapter discusses exemptions. The following topics will be explained.

- Personal exemptions—You generally can take one for yourself and, if you are married, one for your spouse.
- Exemptions for dependents—You must meet five exemption tests for each exemption you claim. If you are entitled to claim an exemption for a dependent, that dependent cannot claim a personal exemption on his or her own tax return.
- Phaseout of exemptions—You get less of a deduction when your adjusted gross income goes above a certain amount.
- Social security number (SSN) requirement for dependents—You must list the social security number of any dependent for whom you claim an exemption.

Exemptions reduce your taxable income. Generally, you can deduct $2,900 for each exemption you claim in 2001. How you claim an exemption on your tax return depends on which form you file.

If you file Form 1040EZ, the exemption amount is combined with the standard deduction amount and entered on line 5.

If you file Form 1040A or Form 1040, follow the instructions for the form. The total number of exemptions you can claim is the total in the box on line 6d. Also complete line 24 (Form 1040A) or line 38 (Form 1040) by multiplying the total number of exemptions shown in the box on line 6d by $2,900.

Caution. *If your adjusted gross income is more than $99,725, see* Phaseout of Exemptions, *later.*

Useful Items

You may want to see:

Publication

☐ **501**   Exemptions, Standard Deduction, and Filing Information

Form (and Instructions)

☐ **2120**   Multiple Support Declaration
☐ **8332**   Release of Claim to Exemption for Child of Divorced or Separated Parents

Exemptions

There are two types of exemptions: personal exemptions and exemptions for dependents. While these are both worth the same amount, different rules apply to each type.

Personal Exemptions

You are generally allowed one exemption for yourself and, if you are married, one exemption for your spouse. These are called personal exemptions.

Your Own Exemption

You can take one exemption for yourself unless you can be claimed as a dependent by another taxpayer.

Single persons. If another taxpayer is entitled to claim you as a dependent, you cannot take an exemption for yourself. This is true even if the other taxpayer does not actually claim your exemption.

Married persons. If you file a joint return, you can take your own exemption. If you file a separate return, you can take your own exemption only if another taxpayer is not entitled to claim you as a dependent.

Your Spouse's Exemption

Your spouse is never considered your dependent. You may be able to take one exemption for your spouse only because you are married.

TAXPLANNER

An exemption for your spouse is available only if you are married to that person on the last day of your tax year. Our advice for tax-conscious lovers is: December weddings are generally better than January weddings. As for divorces, January is generally better than December.

A common-law marriage is recognized for federal tax purposes if it is recognized by the state where it was entered into. To determine if you are married in common law may require legal advice.

Other tax considerations may make a year-end wedding inadvisable. If bride and groom have equal incomes, single tax rates may be more beneficial than married tax rates. For more advice about taxes and marriage, see Chapter 2, *Filing Status.*

Joint return. On a joint return you can claim one exemption for yourself and one for your spouse.

Explanation

Filing a joint return with your spouse will prevent anyone else from claiming him or her as a dependent, even if that person was otherwise entitled to do so. However, your spouse's parents may be able to claim your spouse as a dependent if you do not file a joint return.

Example

John and Mary attended college for 6 months during 2001 and were married in November of that year. John earned $10,000 and Mary earned $2,900, during 2001. If the newlyweds file a joint income tax return, they will owe $0 in taxes. However, Mary's parents will then be unable to claim their daughter as a dependent, even though they provided more than half her support that year.

If John and Mary file as "married, filing separately," Mary will owe no tax and John will owe $330. In addition, Mary's parents, who are in the 30% tax bracket, will be entitled to claim Mary as a dependent, giving them a tax benefit of $870. Thus, if the newlyweds file separate returns, their overall tax liability combined with that of Mary's parents will be reduced by $540, (the $870 tax savings to Mary's parents less the additional $330 tax John and Mary incur by filing separate returns). If John's parents also provided half of his support in 2001 and can claim him as a dependent, the combined tax liability for everybody involved will be even lower.

Separate return. If you file a separate return, you can claim the exemption for your spouse only if your spouse had *no gross income* and was not the dependent of another taxpayer. This is true even if the other taxpayer does not actually claim your spouse's exemption. This is also true if your spouse is a nonresident alien.

Death of spouse. If your spouse died during the year, you can generally claim your spouse's exemption under the rules just explained under *Joint return* and *Separate return*.

If you remarried during the year, you cannot take an exemption for your deceased spouse.

If you are a surviving spouse without gross income and you remarry in the year your spouse died, you can be claimed as an exemption on both the final separate return of your deceased spouse and the separate return of your new spouse for that year. If you file a joint return with your new spouse, you can be claimed as an exemption only on that return.

Divorced or separated spouse. If you obtained a final decree of divorce or separate maintenance by the end of the year, you cannot take your former spouse's exemption. This rule applies even if you provided all of your former spouse's support.

> **TAXPLANNER**
>
> If you're getting divorced near the end of 2001, it may be better to postpone the divorce until January of 2002. In that way, you can claim an exemption for your spouse as well as use the married filing jointly tax rates.

Exemptions for Dependents

You are allowed one exemption for each person you can claim as a dependent. To claim the exemption for a dependent, you must meet *all five* of the dependency tests, discussed later. You can claim an exemption for your dependent even if your dependent files a return. But that dependent cannot claim his or her own personal exemption if you are entitled to do so. However, see *Joint Return Test,* later in this chapter.

Kidnapped children. You may be eligible to claim the exemption for a child, even if the child has been kidnapped. For more information, see Publication 501.

Child born alive. If your child was born alive during the year, and the dependency tests are met, you can claim the exemption. This is true even if the child lived only for a moment. State or local law must treat the child as having been born alive. There must be proof of a live birth shown by an official document, such as a birth certificate.

> **TAXPLANNER**
>
> You can take a dependency exemption for 2001 for a child born on or before December 31, 2001, but not for a baby born January 1, 2002. Plan accordingly!

> **TAXPLANNER**
>
> In addition to the personal exemption, after 1998, a tax credit may be available for each qualifying child under age 17. The per child credit for 2001 is $600 per child.

Stillborn child. You cannot claim an exemption for a stillborn child.

Death of dependent. If your dependent died during the year and otherwise met the dependency tests, you can claim the exemption for your dependent.

Example. Your dependent mother died on January 15. The five dependency tests are met. You can claim the exemption for her on your return.

Housekeepers, maids, or servants. If these people work for you, you cannot claim exemptions for them.

Child tax credit. You may be entitled to a child tax credit for each of your qualifying children for whom you can claim an exemption. For more information, see chapter 35.

Dependency tests. The following five tests must be met for you to claim an exemption for a dependent.

1) Member of Household or Relationship Test.
2) Citizen or Resident Test.
3) Joint Return Test.
4) Gross Income Test.
5) Support Test.

Member of Household or Relationship Test

To meet this test, a person must either:

1) Live with you for the entire year as a member of your household, or
2) Be related to you in one of the ways listed later under *Relatives who do not have to live with you.*

If at any time during the year the person was your spouse, that person cannot be your dependent. However, see *Personal Exemptions,* earlier.

> **Explanation**
>
> For an unrelated person to qualify as your dependent, he or she must live with you at your principal place of residence—not merely at a house that you maintain for the entire year.

Temporary absences. A person lives with you as a member of your household even if either (or both) of you are temporarily absent due to special circumstances. Temporary absences due to special circumstances include absences because of illness, education, business, vacation, or military service.

If the person is placed in a nursing home for an indefinite period of time to receive constant medical care, the absence is considered temporary.

Death or birth. A person who died during the year, but was a member of your household until death, will meet the member of household test. The same is true for a child who was born during the year and was a member of your household for the rest of the year. The test is also met if a child would have been a member except for any required hospital stay following birth.

Local law violated. A person does not meet the member of household test if at any time during your tax year the relationship between you and that person violates local law.

Relatives who do not have to live with you. A person related to you in any of the following ways does not have to live with you for the entire year as a member of your household to meet this test.

- Your child, grandchild, great grandchild, etc. (a legally adopted child is considered your child).
- Your stepchild.
- Your brother, sister, half brother, half sister, stepbrother, or stepsister.
- Your parent, grandparent, or other direct ancestor, but not foster parent.
- Your stepfather or stepmother.
- A brother or sister of your father or mother.
- A son or daughter of your brother or sister.
- Your father-in-law, mother-in-law, son-in-law, daughter-in-law, brother-in-law, or sister-in-law.

Any of these relationships that were established by marriage are not ended by death or divorce.

Explanation
A dependent must be *either* a relative described above or a full-time resident in your principal residence. Your child qualifies as a relative, even if the child is illegitimate.

While your stepchild, stepfather, and stepmother all qualify as relatives, their blood relations do not. Even so, their blood relations may qualify as your dependents if they are full-time residents in your home.

While your spouse's brother and/or sister qualify as relatives to you, their spouses do not.

Example
Amy is married to Oliver. Amy's sister Laura, along with Laura's husband, Stephen, are relatives of Amy, but only Laura is a relative of Oliver. If Amy and Oliver file a joint tax return, Laura and Stephen may both be claimed as dependents (as relatives) if they otherwise qualify. But if Amy and Oliver file married but separate returns, Stephen would not be considered a relative of Oliver and could only be claimed as a dependent by Oliver if Stephen was a full-time resident in Oliver's personal residence.

Adoption. Even if your adoption of a child is not yet final, the child is considered to be your child if he or she was placed with you for legal adoption by an authorized placement agency. Also, the child must have been a member of your household. An authorized placement agency includes any person authorized by state law to place children for legal adoption.

If the child was not placed with you by an authorized agency, the child will meet this test only if he or she was a member of your household for your entire tax year.

Example
Frank and Lisa are married. Emma, a 5-year-old orphan, is placed by an authorized adoption agency in their home in July 2001. She is a member of the household for the rest of the year. Even though Emma was not a resident of their household for 12 months during 2001, and even though she was not legally adopted by Frank and Lisa until 2002, she may be claimed as Frank and Lisa's dependent for 2001. However, if Emma had not been placed in Frank and Lisa's home by an authorized adoption agency, Frank and Lisa would not be able to claim her as a dependent.

Foster child. A foster child must live with you as a member of your household for the entire year to qualify as your dependent.
Cousin. You can claim an exemption for your cousin only if he or she lives with you as a member of your household for the entire year. A cousin is a descendant of a brother or sister of your father or mother.
Joint return. If you file a joint return, you do not need to show that a person is related to both you and your spouse. You also do not need to show that a person is related to the spouse who provides support.

For example, your spouse's uncle who receives more than half his support from you may be your dependent, even though he does not live with you. However, if you and your spouse file **separate returns,** your spouse's uncle can be your dependent only if he is a member of your household and lives with you for your entire tax year.

Citizen or Resident Test

To meet the citizen or resident test, a person must be a U.S. citizen or resident, or a resident of Canada or Mexico, for some part of the calendar year in which your tax year begins.

Explanation
Residents of Puerto Rico do not meet the citizenship test unless they are also U.S. citizens.

Children's place of residence. Children usually are citizens or residents of the country of their parents.

If you were a U.S. citizen when your child was born, the child may be a U.S. citizen although the other parent was a nonresident alien and the child was born in a foreign country. If so, and the other dependency tests are met, you can take the exemption. It does not matter if the child lives abroad with the nonresident alien parent.

Example
The IRS ruled that a U.S. citizen living in England since the age of 9, who subsequently married an Englishwoman, could not claim their son, who was born in England, as a dependent. The foreign-born child of a U.S. citizen and a nonresident alien is *not* a citizen or resident of the United States unless the American parent lived in the United States for 10 years before the child's birth. At least 5 of those 10 years must have been subsequent to age 14.

If you are a U.S. citizen who has legally adopted a child who is not a U.S. citizen or resident, and the other dependency tests are met, you can take the exemption if your home is the child's main home and the child is a member of your household for your entire tax year.
Foreign students' place of residence. Foreign students brought to this country under a qualified international education exchange program and placed in American homes for a temporary period generally are not U.S. residents and do not meet the citizen or resident test. You cannot claim exemptions for them. However, if you provided a home for a foreign student, you may be able to take a charitable contribution deduction. See *Expenses Paid for Student Living With You* in chapter 26.

Explanation
For more information about taxes for aliens, see Chapter 43, *Foreign Citizens Living in the United States.*

Joint Return Test

Even if the other dependency tests are met, you are generally not allowed an exemption for your dependent if he or she files a joint return.

Example. You supported your daughter for the entire year while her husband was in the Armed Forces. The couple files a joint return. Even though all the other tests are met, you cannot take an exemption for your daughter.
Exception. The joint return test does not apply if a joint return is filed by the dependent and his or her spouse merely as a claim for refund and no tax liability would exist for either spouse on separate returns.

Example. Your son and his wife each had less than $2,000 of wages and no unearned income. Neither is required to file a tax return. Taxes were taken out of their pay, so they file a joint return to get a refund. You are allowed to take exemptions for your son and daughter-in-law if the other dependency tests are met.

Gross Income Test

Generally, you cannot take an exemption for a dependent if that person had gross income of $2,900 or more for 2001. This test does not apply if the person is your child and is either:

Figure 3–A. **Can You Claim an Exemption for a Dependent?**

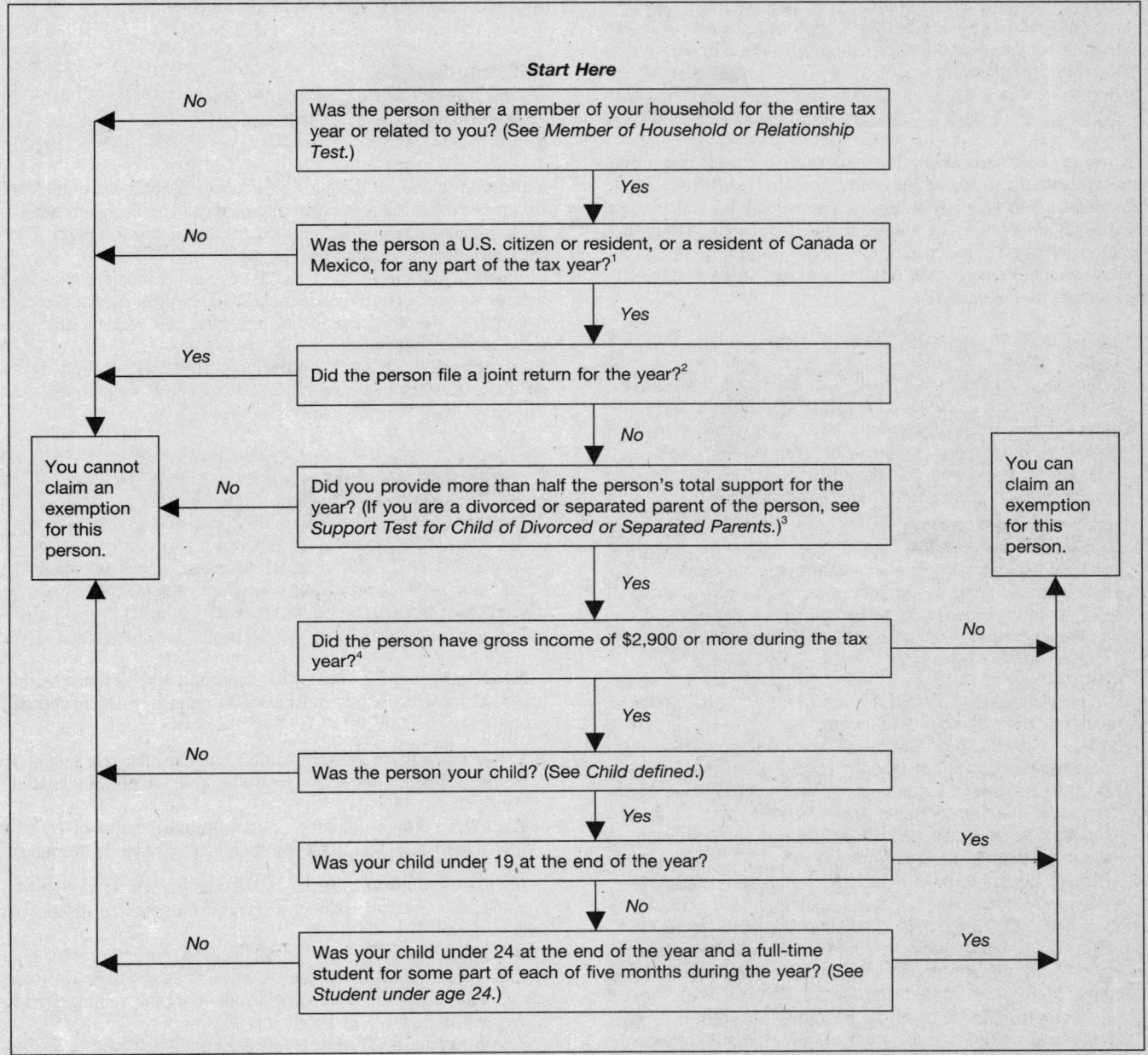

[1]If the person was your legally adopted child and lived in your home as a member of your household for the entire tax year, answer "yes" to this question.

[2]If neither the person nor the person's spouse is required to file a return, but they file a joint return only to claim a refund of tax withheld, answer "no" to this question.

[3]Answer "yes" to this question if you meet the multiple support requirements under *Multiple Support Agreement*.

[4]Gross income for this purpose does not include income received by a permanently disabled individual at a sheltered workshop. See *Disabled dependents*.

1) Under age 19 at the end of the year, or
2) A student under age 24 at the end of the year.

The exceptions for children under age 19 and students under age 24 are discussed in detail later.

If you file on a fiscal year basis, the gross income test applies to the calendar year in which your fiscal year begins.

Gross income defined. All income in the form of money, property, and services that is not exempt from tax is gross income.

In a manufacturing, merchandising, or mining business, gross income is the total net sales minus the cost of goods sold, plus any miscellaneous income from the business.

Gross receipts from rental property are gross income. Do not deduct taxes, repairs, etc., to determine the gross income from rental property.

Gross income includes a partner's share of the gross, not a share of the net, partnership income.

Example
Oscar's father retired 5 years ago and receives over half of his support from Oscar. The father is a partner in a real estate partnership, and his share of gross rental income from

the partnership is $3,000 before expenses. After expenses, his net rental income is $200. Oscar may not claim his father as a dependent because his father's share of the partnership's gross rental income exceeds the $2,900 exemption amount.

Gross income also includes all unemployment compensation and certain scholarship and fellowship grants. Scholarships received by degree candidates that are used for tuition, fees, supplies, books, and equipment required for particular courses are not included in gross income. For more information, see chapter 13.

Tax-exempt income, such as certain social security payments, is not included in gross income.

Explanation
Gross income also includes: (1) gross profit from self-employment, (2) the full gain from the sale of stock or real estate, and (3) the gain on the sale of a personal residence, even if the gain exceeds the exempted amount.

Gross income does *not* include: (1) tax-free municipal bond interest and (2) gifts received from others.

TAXSAVER
Because tax-free municipal bond interest is not included in gross income, a person who may possibly be claimed by another as a dependent may be better off holding municipal bonds rather than taxable bonds.

Example
Widower Nick, 63 years old, lives with his son and daughter-in-law. His only source of income is from the $40,000 he has to invest. If he invests in a bond yielding 8%, he would receive $3,200 of taxable income. Because that is less than his $4,550 standard deduction, Nick would not have any tax liability. However, Nick's son would not be able to claim his father as a dependent because Nick would have more than $2,900 in gross income.

If Nick invests $20,000 in the 8% bond and $20,000 in a 6% tax-free municipal bond, his annual income would be $2,800 ($1,600 + $1,200), $400 less than if he put all his money in a taxable bond. His son would now be able to claim his father as a dependent, because Nick's gross income ($1,600) would be less than $2,900. However, Nick would now have to file a tax return because his total income is more than $750, the filing requirement threshold for dependents (see Chapter 1, *Filing Information*).

The tax benefit to his son should be compared with Nick's lower yield and increased tax to see which is more beneficial.

Disabled dependents. For this gross income test, gross income does not include income received by a permanently and totally disabled individual for services performed at a sheltered workshop. The availability of medical care must be the main reason the individual is at the workshop. Also, the income must come solely from activities at the workshop that are incident to this medical care. A sheltered workshop is a school operated by certain tax-exempt organizations, or by a state, a U.S. possession, a political subdivision of a state or possession, the United States, or the District of Columbia, that provides special instruction or training designed to alleviate the disability of the individual.

Child defined. For purposes of the gross income test, your child is your son, stepson, daughter, stepdaughter, a legally adopted child, or a child who was placed with you by an authorized placement agency for your

legal adoption. A foster child who was a member of your household for your entire tax year is also considered your child.

Exception
The gross income exception for children is not available for a son-in-law or daughter-in-law.

Child under age 19. If your child is under 19 at the end of the year, the gross income test does not apply. Your child can have any amount of income and you can still claim an exemption if the other dependency tests, including the support test, are met.

Example. Marie, 18, earned $3,000. Her father provided more than half her support. Because Marie is under 19, the gross income test does not apply. If the other dependency tests were met, Marie's father can claim an exemption for her.

Student under age 24. The gross income test does not apply if your child is a student who is under age 24 at the end of the calendar year. The other dependency tests must still be met.

TAXPLANNER
You are not allowed an exemption for a child who is age 24 or older whose gross income is not less than the exemption amount ($2,900, for 2001). However, if you can't claim an exemption for your child because of this rule, the child can claim the exemption on his or her return.

Student defined. To qualify as a student, your child must be, during some part of each of 5 calendar months during the calendar year (not necessarily consecutive):

1) A full-time student at a school that has a regular teaching staff, course of study, and regularly enrolled body of students in attendance, or
2) A student taking a full-time, on-farm training course given by a school described in (1) above or a state, county, or local government.

Full-time student defined. A full-time student is a person who is enrolled for the number of hours or courses the school considers to be full-time attendance.

School defined. The term "school" includes elementary schools, junior and senior high schools, colleges, universities, and technical, trade, and mechanical schools. It does *not* include on-the-job training courses, correspondence schools, and night schools.

Example. James, 22, attends college as a full-time student. During the summer, James earned $3,000. If the other dependency tests are met, his parents can take the exemption for James.

Vocational high school students. People who work on "co-op" jobs in private industry as a part of the school's prescribed course of classroom and practical training are considered full-time students.

Night school. Your child is not a full-time student while attending school only at night. However, full-time attendance at a school can include some attendance at night as part of a full-time course of study.

Explanation
In order to qualify for the full-time student exemption, the child must be enrolled in an institution in which education is the primary purpose.

Example
A hospital providing programs for interns and residents does not qualify. However, a division of the hospital whose

primary purpose is the education of students rather than on-the-job training may qualify.

Explanation

The gross income exception for full-time students is designed to allow students to work to help pay their way through school without jeopardizing their parents' dependency deduction. However, the parents must continue to provide over half of the child's support to take the deduction.

Example

Mr. and Mrs. Johnson's 22-year-old unmarried son, Robert, graduated from college in June 2001 and got a job for the remainder of the year that paid him $10,000 in taxable income. Because Robert was a full-time student for at least 5 months during 2001, he is exempt from the gross income test. Nevertheless, Mr. and Mrs. Johnson will not be able to take a $2,900 deduction for Robert as their dependent unless they can prove that they provided half of Robert's support during the entire year. If they are entitled to take the deduction for him, Robert is not entitled to claim an exemption for himself on his return.

Assuming the exemption for Robert is more valuable on his parents' return than on Robert's own return, Robert's parents should document that they did furnish over half their son's support during the year by paying for his tuition and room and board while he was in school. Robert should have used as large a portion of his income as possible for things that do not constitute support. The more money he saved and invested in 2001, the better. Then Mr. and Mrs. Johnson would be entitled to claim Robert as a dependent and take a $2,900 deduction.

On the other hand, if Mr. and Mrs. Johnson are subject to the personal exemption phaseout, they may want to make sure that they can't claim Robert as a dependent because it does them no good. In 2001, the personal exemption phaseout begins at $199,450 for joint returns. If Mr. and Mrs. Johnson have a taxable income of $321,950, they would receive no benefit from having Robert as a dependent. They should then plan not to provide over 50% of Robert's support.

Explanation

The gross income of a married couple residing in a community property state is generally split equally between each spouse for the purposes of the dependency deduction.

Example

Henry Smith provides more than 50% of the support for his son Jim and his daughter-in-law Jan, both of whom are over 19. Jim has no income and is not a student during 2001. Jan earns $6,000. Assuming that the other four dependency tests are met, Henry Smith may claim his son Jim as a dependent in a common-law state. In a community property state, however, Henry could not claim Jim as a dependent, because each spouse is treated as having gross income of $3,000 (half of $6,000).

Support Test

Generally, you must provide more than half of a person's total support during the calendar year to meet the support test. However, there are special rules that apply in the following two situations.

1) Two or more persons provide support, but no one person provides more than half of a person's total support. See *Multiple Support Agreement,* later.
2) The person supported is the child of divorced or separated parents. See *Support Test for Child of Divorced or Separated Parents,* later.

You figure whether you have provided more than half of a person's total support by comparing the amount you contributed to that person's support with the entire amount of support that person received from all sources. This includes support the person provided from his or her own funds.

You may find *Table 3-1* helpful in figuring whether you provided more than half of a person's support.

Person's own funds not used for support. A person's own funds are not support unless they are actually spent for support.

Example. Your mother received $2,400 in social security benefits and $300 in interest. She paid $2,000 for lodging and $400 for recreation.

Even though your mother received a total of $2,700, she spent only $2,400 for her own support. If you spent more than $2,400 for her support and no other support was received, you have provided more than half of her support.

Explanation

You may be able to claim someone as a dependent even though you provide support for less than half the year. Support depends on the amount spent, not the length of time over which it is spent. As long as you provide over 50% of the total amount of a person's support for a year, you may claim that person as a dependent.

Child's wages used for own support. You cannot include in your contribution to your child's support any support that is paid for by the child with the child's own wages, even if you paid the wages.

Year support is provided. The year you provide the support is the year you pay for it, even if you do so with borrowed money that you repay in a later year.

Explanation

Only the amount actually spent on support is relevant to the support test. The funds made available for support purposes are not relevant until actually used.

Example 1

The income of a trust for the benefit of a minor was not spent for the minor's support. The parent who provided the funds for the child's support may claim the dependency deduction.

Example 2

According to a court ruling, an individual could claim a dependency deduction for his grandmother even though she received state old-age assistance payments that exceeded the amounts spent by the grandson. The grandmother did not spend all of the payments received from the state for her support. The amount of the state payments that she did spend for her support was less than what was provided to her by her grandson.

If you use a fiscal year to report your income, you must provide more than half of the dependent's support for the calendar year in which your fiscal year begins.

Table 3–1. **Worksheet for Determining Support**

Funds Belonging to the Person You Supported	
1) Total funds belonging to the person you supported, including income received (taxable and nontaxable) and amounts borrowed during the year, plus the amount in savings and other accounts at the beginning of the year	$
2) Amount used for support	$
3) Amount used for other purposes	$
4) Amount in savings and other accounts at the end of the year	$
(The total of lines 2, 3, and 4 should equal line 1)	$
Expenses for Entire Household (where the person you supported lived)	
5) Lodging (Complete item a or b)	
a) Rent paid	$
b) If not rented, show fair rental value of home. If the person you supported owned the home, include the amount in line 19.	$
6) Food	$
7) Utilities (heat, light, water, etc. not included in line 5a or 5b)	$
8) Repairs (not included in line 5a or 5b)	$
9) Other. Do not include expenses of maintaining home, such as mortgage interest, real estate taxes, and insurance.	$
10) Total household expenses (Add lines 5 through 9)	$
11) Total number of persons who lived in household	
Expenses for the Person You Supported	
12) Each person's part of household expenses (line 10 divided by line 11)	$
13) Clothing	$
14) Education	$
15) Medical, dental	$
16) Travel, recreation	$
17) Other (specify)	$
18) Total cost of support for the year (Add lines 12 through 17)	$
Did You Provide More Than Half?	
19) Amount the person provided for own support (line 2, plus line 5b if the person you supported owned the home)	$
20) Amount others provided for the person's support. Include amounts provided by state, local, and other welfare societies or agencies. Do not include any amounts included on line 1.	$
21) Amount you provided for the person's support (line 18 minus lines 19 and 20)	$
22) 50% of line 18	$

Is line 21 more than line 22?
Yes. You meet the support test for the person. If the other exemption tests are met, you may claim an exemption for the person.
No. You do not meet the support test for the person. You cannot claim an exemption for the person unless you can do so under a multiple support agreement. See *Multiple Support Agreement* in this chapter.

TAXPLANNER

You should maintain complete records of expenditures made to support anyone whom you intend to claim as a dependent. Take particular pains to maintain records of support for children of divorced parents and for children who are attending college.

The IRS has established guidelines so that members of a community property state can determine who is entitled to deduct whom as a dependent. For additional information, see IRS Publication 555.

Armed Forces dependency allotments. The part of the allotment contributed by the government and the part taken out of your military pay are both considered provided by you in figuring whether you provide more than half of the support. If your allotment is used to support persons other than those you name, you can take the exemptions for them if they otherwise qualify.

Example. You are in the Armed Forces. You authorize an allotment for your widowed mother that she uses to support herself and your sister. If the allotment provides more than half of their support, you can take an exemption for each of them, if they otherwise qualify, even though you authorize the allotment only for your mother.

Tax-exempt military quarters allowances. These allowances are treated the same way as dependency allotments in figuring support. The allotment of pay and the tax-exempt basic allowance for quarters are both considered as provided by you for support.

Tax-exempt income. In figuring a person's total support, include tax-exempt income, savings, and borrowed amounts used to support that person. Tax-exempt income includes certain social security benefits, welfare benefits, nontaxable life insurance proceeds, Armed Forces family allotments, nontaxable pensions, and tax-exempt interest.

Example 1. You provide $4,000 toward your mother's support during the year. She has earned income of $600, nontaxable social security benefit payments of $4,800, and tax-exempt interest of $200. She uses all these for her support. You cannot claim an exemption for your mother because the $4,000 you provide is not more than half of her total support of $9,600.

Example 2. Your daughter takes out a student loan of $2,500 and uses it to pay her college tuition. She is personally responsible for the loan. You provide $2,000 toward her total support. You cannot claim an exemption for your daughter because you provide less than half of her support.

Social security benefit payments. If a husband and wife each receive payments that are paid by one check made out to both of them, half of the total paid is considered to be for the support of each spouse, unless they can show otherwise.

If a child receives social security benefits and uses them toward his or her own support, the payments are considered as provided by the child.

Support provided by the state (food stamps, housing, etc.). Benefits provided by the state to a needy person generally are considered to be used for support. However, payments based on the needs of the recipient will not be considered as used entirely for that person's support if it is shown that part of the payments were not used for that purpose.

Foster care payments and expenses. Payments you receive for the support of a foster child from a child placement agency are considered support provided by the agency. Similarly, payments you receive for the support of a foster child from a state or county are considered support provided by the state or county.

If you are not in the trade or business of providing foster care to a child and your unreimbursed out-of-pocket expenses in caring for a foster child were mainly to benefit an organization qualified to receive deductible charitable contributions, the expenses are deductible as charitable contributions, but are not considered support you provided. For more information about the deduction for charitable contributions, see Publication 526. If your unreimbursed expenses are not deductible as charitable contributions, they are considered support you provided.

If you are in the trade or business of providing foster care, your unreimbursed expenses are not considered support provided by you.

Home for the aged. If you make a lump-sum advance payment to a home for the aged to take care of your relative for life and the payment is based on that person's life expectancy, the amount of support you provide each year is the lump-sum payment divided by the relative's life expectancy. The amount of support you provide also includes any other amounts that you provided during the year.

Example
Jane's mother resides in a senior citizens' home that is supported and operated by a church. It cost the church

$6,000 last year to support Jane's mother. For Jane to claim her mother as a dependent, she must prove that she has provided more than $6,000 additional support for her mother, over and above the $6,000 provided by the church.

Total Support

To figure if you provided more than half of the support of a person, you must first determine the total support provided for that person. Total support includes amounts spent to provide food, lodging, clothing, education, medical and dental care, recreation, transportation, and similar necessities.

Explanation
Money that is not included in gross income, such as certain Social Security benefits, veterans' benefits, and so on, must be considered in determining support. For example, an amount borrowed by the person, or by you, and spent for support must be included in total support.

Explanation
Here's a quick list of broad areas in which expenditures constitute support. For more details see the text below.

Lodging, including utilities and telephone
Room and board at a college or private school
Clothing, laundry, and dry cleaning
Education, including tuition, books and supplies, and music and dancing lessons
Medical expenses, including doctor, dentist, and health insurance premiums
Transportation, including purchase of a car, its maintenance, and gas
Child care, including baby-sitters, nursery school, and summer camp
Entertainment, including movies, theater, spending money, toys, and vacations
Charitable contributions on behalf of a dependent
Wedding costs
Payments to an institution for the care of an elderly parent

Generally, the IRS maintains that only expenditures necessary for essential support—basic food, housing, clothing, education, health, and transportation—qualify toward the 50% support test. The courts have been more lenient, allowing expenditures for dancing lessons, summer camp, vacations, and wedding receptions to count toward support.

Generally, the amount of an item of support is the amount of the expense incurred in providing that item. For lodging, the amount of support is the fair rental value of the lodging.

Expenses that are not directly related to any one member of a household, such as the cost of food for the household, must be divided among the members of the household.

Example. Your parents live with you, your spouse, and your two children in a house you own. The fair rental value of your parents' share of lodging is $2,000 a year, which includes furnishings and utilities. Your father receives a nontaxable pension of $4,200, which he spends equally between your mother and himself for items of support such as clothing, transportation, and recreation. Your total food expense for the household is $6,000. Your heat and utility bills amount to $1,200. Your mother has hospital and medical expenses of $600, which you pay during the year. Figure your parents' total support as follows:

	Support provided	
	Father	Mother
Fair rental value of lodging	$1,000	$1,000
Pension spent for their support	2,100	2,100
Share of food (1/6 of $6,000)	1,000	1,000
Medical expenses for mother		600
Parents' total support	$4,100	$4,700

You must apply the support test separately to each parent. You provide $2,000 ($1,000 lodging, $1,000 food) of your father's total support of $4,100—less than half. You provide $2,600 to your mother ($1,000 lodging, $1,000 food, $600 medical)—more than half of her total support of $4,700. You meet the support test for your mother, but not your father. Heat and utility costs are included in the fair rental value of the lodging, so these are not considered separately.

Lodging defined. Lodging is the fair rental value of the room, apartment, or house in which the person lives. It includes a reasonable allowance for the use of furniture and appliances and for heat and other utilities.

Fair rental value defined. This is the amount you could reasonably expect to receive from a stranger for the same kind of lodging. It is used in place of rent or taxes, interest, depreciation, paint, insurance, utilities, cost of furniture and appliances, etc. In some cases, fair rental value may be equal to the rent paid.

If you provide the total lodging, the amount of support you provide is the fair rental value of the room the person uses, or a share of the fair rental value of the entire dwelling if the person has use of your entire home. If you do not provide the total lodging, the total fair rental value must be divided depending on how much of the total lodging you provide. If you provide only a part and the person supplies the rest, the fair rental value must be divided between both of you according to the amount each provides.

Example. Your parents live rent free in a house you own. It has a fair rental value of $5,400 a year furnished, which includes a fair rental value of $3,600 for the house and $1,800 for the furniture. This does not include heat and utilities. The house is completely furnished with furniture belonging to your parents. You pay $600 for their utility bills. Utilities are not usually included in rent for houses in the area where your parents live. Therefore, you consider the total fair rental value of the lodging to be $6,000 ($3,600 fair rental value of the unfurnished house, $1,800 allowance for furnishings provided by your parents, and $600 cost of utilities) of which you are considered to provide $4,200 ($3,600 + $600).

Person living in his or her own home. The total fair rental value of a person's home that he or she owns is considered support contributed by that person.

Living with someone rent free. If you live with a person rent free in his or her home, you must reduce the amount you provide for support by the fair rental value of lodging he or she provides you.

TaxSaver

If your dependent is living in his or her own home, it may be to your mutual advantage for you to acquire a partial interest in the home and thereby become jointly liable for the mortgage and real estate taxes. By doing this, you can include 50% of the mortgage expense and real estate taxes you incur as part of your support calculation.

TaxPlanner

If your mother lives alone in her own home and you pay the mortgage and real estate taxes for her, no one is entitled

to the deduction for mortgage interest expenses, or real estate taxes. You pay them, but because you are not personally liable for them, you may not deduct them. Conversely, your mother is personally responsible for them, but she does not pay them and so she may not deduct them.

However, if you give your mother the cash and she pays the mortgage interest expenses and real estate taxes, she would be entitled to the deductions. Chances are, though, that you are in a higher tax bracket than your mother. Therefore, it would be more advantageous for you to take the deductions than for your mother to do so, because the higher the tax bracket, the more a deduction is worth.

If the house were transferred into joint ownership and you also became obligated for the mortgage, you could deduct the mortgage interest and real estate taxes you paid. In addition, you could claim your mother as a dependent. Arranging things in this manner may realize the greatest tax savings. To take full advantage of the deduction for mortgage interest, you would have to meet the special rules for qualified residence mortgages. See Chapter 25, *Interest Expense.*

Property. Property provided as support is measured by its fair market value. Fair market value is the price that property would sell for on the open market. It is the price that would be agreed upon between a willing buyer and a willing seller, with neither being required to act, and both having reasonable knowledge of the relevant facts.

Capital expenses. Capital items, such as furniture, appliances, and cars, that are bought for a person during the year can be included in total support under certain circumstances.

The following examples show when a capital item is or is not support.

Example 1. You buy a $200 power lawn mower for your 13-year-old child. The child is given the duty of keeping the lawn trimmed. Because a lawn mower is ordinarily an item you buy for personal and family reasons that benefits all members of the household, you cannot include the cost of the lawn mower in the support of your child.

Example 2. You buy a $150 television set as a birthday present for your 12-year-old child. The television set is placed in your child's bedroom. You can include the cost of the television set in the support of your child.

Example 3. You pay $5,000 for a car and register it in your name. You and your 17-year-old daughter use the car equally. Because you own the car and do not give it to your daughter but merely let her use it, you cannot include the cost of the car in your daughter's total support. However, you can include in your daughter's support your out-of-pocket expenses of operating the car for her benefit.

Example 4. Your 17-year-old son, using personal funds, buys a car for $4,500. You provide all the rest of your son's support—$4,000. Since the car is bought and owned by your son, the car's fair market value ($4,500) must be included in his support. The $4,000 support you provide is less than half of his total support of $8,500. You cannot claim an exemption for your son.

TaxSaver

In Example 4 above, the parents were not able to claim their son as a dependent because the son paid the entire $4,500 to buy the car. However, if the parents had contributed $251 toward the car's purchase, they would then have contributed more than half of their son's support and could claim the son as a dependent and get a $2,900 deduction. Assuming that the parents were in the 30% tax bracket, the deduction was worth $870 to them. The moral of the story is: Contributing to the purchase of a car or a trip in the year in which your child graduates from school may make good tax sense if the contribution assures you of 1 more year in which you can claim your child as a dependent.

Medical insurance premiums. Medical insurance premiums you pay, including premiums for supplementary Medicare coverage, are included in the support you provide.

Medical insurance benefits. Medical insurance benefits, including basic and supplementary Medicare benefits, are not part of support.

Tuition payments and allowances under the GI Bill. Amounts veterans receive under the GI Bill for tuition payments and allowances while they attend school are included in total support.

Example. During the year, your son receives $2,200 from the government under the GI Bill. He uses this amount for his education. You provide the rest of his support—$2,000. Because GI benefits are included in total support, your son is not your dependent.

Other support items. Other items may be considered as support depending on the facts in each case. For example, if you pay someone to provide child care or disabled dependent care, you can include these payments as support, even if you claim a credit for them. For information on the credit, see chapter 33.

TaxPlanner

If you contribute support to a household other than the one in which you live and that household includes more than one person who may qualify as your dependent, you may earmark portions of your support funds for specific persons. This will enable you to prove that you have provided more than 50% of the support for a certain member or members of the household. Without written corroboration, it is likely that the monies contributed will be prorated among all the members of the household, which could result in your losing a dependency exemption.

Example
You provide $5,000 of support for your parents. They live in their own apartment and spend $6,000 annually on their joint support.

Unless you have specifically designated whom your money is for, the IRS will assume that half of the money was intended for each parent. Therefore, you have not provided more than 50% of the support for either parent.

If you establish in writing that over $3,000 of your funds spent on support are for one of your parents and the balance is for the other, you will be able to claim one dependency deduction.

Do Not Include in Total Support
The following items are not included in total support.

1) Federal, state, and local income taxes paid by persons from their own income.
2) Social security and Medicare taxes paid by persons from their own income.
3) Life insurance premiums.
4) Funeral expenses.
5) Scholarships received by your child if your child is a full-time student.
6) Survivors' and Dependents' Educational Assistance payments used for support of the child who receives them.

Explanation
Savings should not be included in total support.

Example
If a child puts his or her entire after-tax earnings from a part-time job in a savings account or purchases common stock, the child is not considered to have spent any earnings toward self-support.

This is an important point to remember in the year in which a child graduates from school and gets a job for the rest of the year. Whether or not the parents may claim the child as a dependent hinges on whether or not their support payments—tuition, room and board, graduation presents, and so on—exceed the child's earnings that are not put into savings or used to pay taxes.

Multiple Support Agreement

Sometimes no one provides more than half of the support of a person. Instead, two or more persons, each of whom would be able to take the exemption but for the support test, together provide more than half of the person's support.

When this happens, you can agree that any one of you who individually provides more than 10% of the person's support, but *only one*, can claim an exemption for that person. Each of the others must sign a written statement agreeing not to claim the exemption for that year. The statements must be filed with the income tax return of the person who claims the exemption. **Form 2120,** *Multiple Support Declaration,* can be used for this purpose.

Example 1. You, your sister, and your two brothers provide the entire support of your mother for the year. You provide 45%, your sister 35%, and your two brothers each provide 10%. Either you or your sister can claim an exemption for your mother. The other must sign a Form 2120 or a similar statement agreeing not to take an exemption for her. Because neither brother provides more than 10% of the support, neither can take the exemption. Your brothers do not have to sign a Form 2120 or the written statement.

Example 2. You and your brother each provide 20% of your mother's support for the year. The remaining 60% of her support is provided equally by two persons who are not related to her. She does not live with them. Because more than half of her support is provided by persons who cannot claim an exemption for her, no one can take the exemption.

Example 3. Your father lives with you and receives 25% of his support from social security, 40% from you, 24% from his brother, and 11% from a friend. Either you or your uncle can take the exemption for your father. A Form 2120 or a similar statement from the one not taking the exemption must be attached to the return of the one who takes the exemption.

TaxPlanner

The multiple support agreement provides a tax-planning opportunity that should not be overlooked. If more than one individual provides at least 10% of the support of a dependent, and if no one individual provides over 50% support, an individual in a higher tax bracket may take the deduction, even if that individual did not provide the most support for the dependent.

Example
Four adult children jointly furnish all of the support for their elderly father. The marginal tax rate for three of the children

is 15%, but the fourth child is in the 30% bracket. Therefore, the fourth child should be designated as the one to claim the dependency deduction under the multiple support agreement, even if he or she is providing less support than the other three. The $2,900 deduction is worth $870 to the fourth child but is worth only $435 to any of the other children, because they are taxed at 15%.

Support Test for Child of Divorced or Separated Parents

The support test for a child of divorced or separated parents is based on the special rules explained here and shown in *Figure 3-B.* However, these special rules apply only if all of the following are true.

1) The parents are divorced or legally separated under a decree of divorce or separate maintenance, or separated under a written separation agreement, or lived apart at all times during the last 6 months of the calendar year.
2) One or both parents provide more than half of the child's total support for the calendar year.
3) One or both parents have custody of the child for more than half of the calendar year.

"Child" is defined earlier under *Gross Income Test.*

This discussion does not apply if the support of the child is determined under a multiple support agreement, discussed earlier.

General rule. The parent who has custody of the child for the greater part of the year (the ***custodial parent***) is generally treated as the parent who provides more than half of the child's support. It does not matter whether the custodial parent actually provided more than half of the support.

Custody. Custody is usually determined by the terms of the most recent decree of divorce or separate maintenance, or a later custody decree. If there is no decree, use the written separation agreement. If neither a decree nor agreement establishes custody, then the parent who has the physical custody of the child for the greater part of the year is considered to have custody of the child. This also applies if the validity of a decree or agreement awarding custody is uncertain because of legal proceedings pending on the last day of the calendar year.

If the parents are divorced or separated during the year and had joint custody of the child before the separation, the parent who has custody for the greater part of the rest of the year is considered to have custody of the child for the tax year.

Example 1. Under the terms of your divorce, you have custody of your child for 10 months of the year. Your former spouse has custody for the other 2 months. You and your former spouse provide the child's total support. You are considered to have provided more than half of the support of the child. However, see *Exception,* later.

Example 2. You and your former spouse provided your child's total support for 2001. For the first 8 months of the year, you had custody of your child under your 1994 divorce decree (the most recent decree at the time). On August 31, 2001, a new custody decree granted custody to your former spouse. Because you had custody for the greater part of the year, you are considered to have provided more than half of your child's support, unless the exception described next applies.

Exception. The ***noncustodial parent*** will be treated as providing more than half of the child's support if:

1) The custodial parent signs a written declaration that he or she will not claim the exemption for the child, and the noncustodial parent attaches this written declaration to his or her return,
2) A decree or agreement went into effect after 1984 and states the noncustodial parent can claim the child as a dependent without regard to any condition, such as payment of support, or

3) A decree or agreement executed before 1985 provides that the noncustodial parent is entitled to the exemption, and he or she provides at least $600 for the child's support during the year, unless the pre-1985 decree or agreement is modified after 1984 to specify that this provision will not apply.

Noncustodial parent. The noncustodial parent is the parent who has custody of the child for the shorter part of the year or who does not have custody at all.

Example. Under the terms of your 1984 divorce decree, your former spouse has custody of your child. The decree specifically states that you are entitled to the exemption. You provide at least $600 in child support during the calendar year. You are considered to have provided more than half of the child's support.

Written declaration. The custodial parent may use either **Form 8332** or a similar statement to make the written declaration to release the exemption to the noncustodial parent. The noncustodial parent must attach the form or statement to his or her tax return.

The exemption can be released for a single year, for a number of specified years (for example, alternate years), or for all future years, as specified in the declaration. If the exemption is released for more than one year, the original release must be attached to the return of the noncustodial parent for the first year of such release, and a copy must be attached for each later year.

Divorce decree or separation agreement. If your divorce decree or separation agreement went into effect after 1984 and it states you can claim the child as your dependent without regard to any condition, such as payment of support, you can attach a copy of the following pages from the decree or agreement instead of Form 8332.

1) Cover page. (Write the other parent's social security number on this page.)
2) The page that states you can claim the child as your dependent.
3) Signature page with the other parent's signature and the date of the agreement.

Caution. *If your divorce decree or separation agreement went into effect after 1984 and it states that you can claim the child as your dependent if you meet certain conditions, you must attach to your return Form 8332 or a similar statement from the custodial parent releasing the exemption.*

Child support. All child support payments actually received from the noncustodial parent are considered used for the support of the child.

Example. The noncustodial parent provides $1,200 for the child's support. This amount is considered support provided by the noncustodial parent even if the $1,200 was actually spent on things other than support.

Paid in a later year. If you fail to pay child support in the year it is due, but pay it in a later year, your payment of the overdue amount is not considered paid for the support of your child, either for the year the payment was due or for the year it is paid. It is payment of an amount you owed to the custodial parent, but it is not considered paid by you for the support of your child.

Example. You owed but failed to pay child support last year. This year, you pay all of the amount owed from last year and the full amount due for this year. Your payment of this year's child support counts as support for this year, but your payment of the amount owed from last year does not count as support either for this year or for last year.

Third-party support. Support provided by a third party for a divorced or separated parent is not included as support provided by that parent. However, see *Remarried parent,* later.

Example. You are divorced. During the entire year, you and your child live with your mother in a house she owns. The fair rental value of the lodging provided by your mother for your child is $3,000. The home provided by your mother is not included in the amount of support you provide.

Remarried parent. If you remarry, the support provided by your new spouse is treated as provided by you.

Figure 3–B. **Support Test for Children of Divorced or Separated Parents**

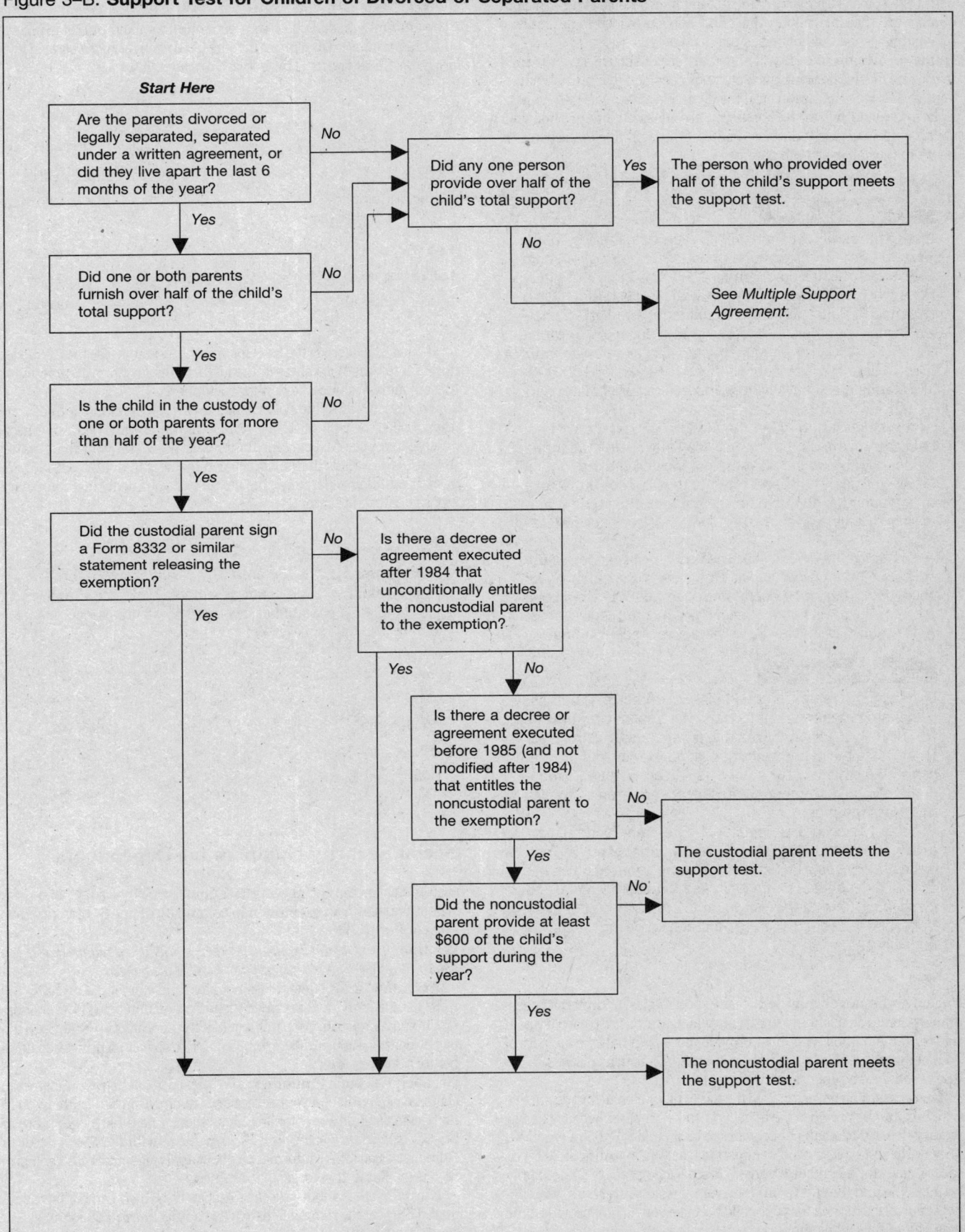

Example. You have two children from a former marriage who live with you. You have remarried and are living in a home owned by your new spouse. The fair rental value of the home provided to the children by your new spouse is treated as provided by you.

Home jointly owned. If you and your former spouse have the right to use and live in the home, each of you is considered to provide half of your child's lodging. However, if the divorce decree gives only you the right to use and live in the home, you are considered to provide your child's entire lodging. It does not matter if the legal title to the home remains in the names of both parents.

TaxPlanner

Due to the new education credits (see Chapter 36, *Education Credits,* for information about the Hope Scholarship Credit and the Lifetime Learning Credit), there are situations where the parent may not want to claim an eligible dependent. Education credits phase out for single taxpayers with modified adjusted gross income between $40,000–$50,000 and for couples filing jointly with modified adjusted gross income between $80,000–$100,000. The credits are not available to married taxpayers filing separately.

The student may claim the credits, even if the parents paid the expenses, but no one may claim the student as a dependent. The parent must not include the student on his or her tax return, and if the parent is allowed to take a dependency exemption for the student, the student may not claim a dependency exemption on his or her own tax return.

You should not claim your child as your dependent if the education tax credit will provide a greater tax benefit for your child than your tax benefit from the $2,900 exemption amount. The maximum tax benefit for a married couple, in the 30% tax bracket, to claim a child as a dependent is $870.

TaxPlanner

Generally, the parent in the higher tax bracket should be designated as the parent to claim the dependency exemption for a child, assuming that the parent meets all the tests for claiming the dependency deduction. However, if the person with the highest tax bracket is subject to the phaseout of the personal exemption, the dependency exemption may not benefit that person.

Note: The child and dependent care credit and medical expense deductions may be claimed whether or not you can claim the child as a dependent. For more information on the child and dependent care credit, see Chapter 33, *Child and Dependent Care Credit.* For more information on the medical expense deduction, see Chapter 23, *Medical and Dental Expenses.*

Parents who never married. These special rules for divorced or separated parents do not apply to parents who never married each other. If this is your situation, you must provide more than half the support of your child or enter into a multiple support agreement, as discussed earlier, to satisfy the support test.

Example. You never married the father of your child and do not live with him, but he provides the home you and your child live in. The fair rental value of the lodging he provides to your child is $3,000 a year. You provide the rest of your child's support for the year, which is $1,200. The special rules for a child of divorced or separated parents do not apply because you and the child's father never married. As a result, you cannot claim an exemption for your child because you did not provide more than half of the child's support.

Phaseout of Exemptions

The amount you can claim as a deduction for exemptions is phased out once your adjusted gross income (AGI) goes above a certain level for your filing status. These levels are as follows:

Filing Status	AGI Level Which Reduces Exemption Amount
Married filing separately	$ 99,725
Single	132,950
Head of household	166,200
Married filing jointly	199,450
Qualifying widow(er)	199,450

If your AGI exceeds the level for your filing status, use the Deduction for Exemptions Worksheet in the instructions for Form 1040 to figure the amount of your deduction for exemptions.

You must reduce the dollar amount of your exemptions by 2% for each $2,500, or part of $2,500 ($1,250 if you are married filing separately), that your AGI exceeds the amount shown for your filing status. If your AGI exceeds the amount shown by more than $122,500 ($61,250 if married filing separately), the amount of your deduction for exemptions is reduced to zero.

Explanation

The amount you can claim as a deduction for exemptions is completely phased out if your adjusted gross income exceeds the following levels:

Married filing separately	$160,975
Single	255,450
Head of household	288,700
Married filing jointly	321,950
Qualifying widow(er)	321,950

Social Security Numbers for Dependents

You must list the social security number (SSN) of *any* person for whom you claim an exemption in column (2) of line 6c of your Form 1040 or Form 1040A.

Caution. *If you do not list the dependent's SSN when required or if you list an incorrect SSN, the exemption may be disallowed.*

Note. If your dependent does not have and cannot get an SSN, you must list the individual taxpayer identification number (ITIN) or adoption taxpayer identification number (ATIN) instead of an SSN. See Taxpayer identification numbers for aliens or Taxpayer identification number for adoptees, later.

No social security number. If a person for whom you expect to claim an exemption on your return does not have an SSN, either you or that person should apply for an SSN as soon as possible by filing **Form SS-5,** *Application for a Social Security Card,* with the Social Security Administration (SSA). Information about applying for an SSN and Form SS-5 is available at your local SSA office.

It usually takes about 2 weeks to get an SSN. If you do not have a required SSN by the filing due date, you can file Form 4868 for an extension of time to file.

Deduction for Exemptions Worksheet—Line 38

1. Is the amount on Form 1040, line 34, more than the amount shown on line 4 below for your filing status?

   ☐ **No.** (STOP) Multiply $2,900 by the total number of exemptions claimed on Form 1040, line 6d, and enter the result on line 38.

   ☐ **Yes.** *Continue* ↘

2. Multiply $2,900 by the total number of exemptions claimed on Form 1040, line 6d . . . . **2.** _____

3. Enter the amount from Form 1040, line 34 . . . . **3.** _____

4. Enter the amount shown below for your filing status.

   - Single—$132,950
   - Married filing jointly or qualifying widow(er)—$199,450
   - Married filing separately—$99,725
   - Head of household—$166,200

   } . . . . **4.** _____

5. Subtract line 4 from line 3 . . . . **5.** _____

   Note. If line 5 is more than: $122,500 if single, married filing jointly, head of household, or qualifying widow(er); $61,250 if married filing separately, **stop here.** You **cannot** take a deduction for exemptions.

6. Divide line 5 by: $2,500 if single, married filing jointly, head of household, or qualifying widow(er); $1,250 if married filing separately. If the result is not a whole number, increase it to the next higher whole number (for example, increase 0.0004 to 1) . . . . **6.** _____

7. Multiply line 6 by 2% (.02) and enter the result as a decimal . . . . **7.** ____.____

8. Multiply line 2 by line 7 . . . . **8.** _____

9. **Deduction for exemptions.** Subtract line 8 from line 2. Enter the result here and on Form 1040, line 38   **9.** _____

TAX ORGANIZER

To obtain a Social Security number, fill out form SS-5 located in Chapter 48, *2001 Federal Tax Forms and Schedules You Can Use,* and file it with your local Social Security office. If you applied for a Social Security number for your child but failed to receive it by the due date for filing your return, write "Applied For" in the space provided for the number on your return.

Born and died in 2001. If your child was born and died in 2001, and you do not have an SSN for the child, you may attach a copy of the child's birth certificate instead. If you do, enter "DIED" in column (2) of line 6c of your Form 1040 or Form 1040A.

Taxpayer identification numbers for aliens. If your dependent is a resident or nonresident alien who does not have and is not eligible to get an SSN, the IRS will issue your dependent an individual taxpayer identification number (ITIN) instead of an SSN. Write the number in column (2) of line 6c of your Form 1040 or Form 1040A. To apply for an ITIN, use **Form W-7,** *Application for IRS Individual Taxpayer Identification Number.*

It usually takes about 30 days to get an ITIN.

Taxpayer identification numbers for adoptees. If you have a child who was placed with you by an authorized placement agency, you may be able to claim an exemption for the child. However, if you cannot get an SSN or an ITIN for the child, you must get an adoption taxpayer identification number (ATIN) for the child from the IRS. See **Form W-7A,** *Application for Taxpayer Identification Number for Pending U.S. Adoptions,* for details.

4

Decedents

Introduction

The death of an individual causes special income tax problems that are likely to be unfamiliar and puzzling to the survivors. Among other things, the decedent's will and state inheritance laws can create a bewildering array of questions about how income is to be allocated and which **deductions** *may be claimed and by whom. This chapter helps you sort out such questions. It is most helpful to a survivor who has to deal with a relatively uncomplicated situation and a small estate. Where the assets are large and the situation is complex, professional assistance is recommended.*

Important Changes

Rollovers by surviving spouses. For distributions after 2001, an employee's surviving spouse who receives an eligible rollover distribution may roll it over into an eligible retirement plan, including an IRA, a qualified plan, a section 403(b) annuity, or a section 457 plan. For distributions before 2002, surviving spouses could only roll the distribution over into an IRA.

Assets held on January 1, 2001. If the estate held certain assets on January 1, 2001, you can treat the assets as being sold and reacquired on the same date. Any gain on the deemed sale must be recognized and included in income. This treatment allows future gains on those assets to be taxed at a rate of 18% (instead of 20%) if the asset is held by the estate for more than 5 years from the reacquired date. For more information, see the instructions for Schedule D of Form 1041.

Estate tax return. Generally, if the decedent died during 2001, an estate tax return (Form 706) must be filed if the gross estate is more than $675,000. If death occurs in 2002, Form 706 must be filed if the gross estate is more than $1,000,000.

Estate tax repeal. The estate tax is repealed for decedents dying after 2009.

Important Reminder

Consistent treatment of estate items. Beneficiaries must generally treat estate items the same way on their individual returns as they are treated on the estate's return. For more information, see *How and When To Report* under *Distributions to Beneficiaries From an Estate* in Publication 559, *Survivors, Executors, and Administrators.*

This chapter discusses the tax responsibilities of the person who is in charge of the property (estate) of an individual who has died (decedent). It also covers the following topics.

- Filing the decedent's final return.
- Tax effects on survivors.

This chapter does **not** discuss the requirements for filing an income tax return of an estate (Form 1041). For information on Form 1041, see *Income Tax Return of an Estate—Form 1041* in Publication 559. This chapter also does not discuss the requirements for filing an estate tax return (Form 706). For information, see Form 706 and its instructions.

Explanation

Though this chapter mainly discusses the filing requirement of a final individual income tax return for a decedent, an explanation of the various potential filing requirements may be helpful. Generally, upon an individual's death, there are two types of taxes that should be addressed: estate tax and income tax.

The estate tax is reported on Form 706, *U.S. Estate Tax Return.* Form 706 is not an income tax return; rather, it is a return that is based on the value of the net assets of the decedent's "estate" at date of death. The filing deadline for Form 706 is within 9 months after the date of death unless you received an extension of time to file. In 2002, the first $1,000,000 of one's estate is generally not taxable because the IRS allows a unified credit that equals the tax calculated on $1,000,000 of assets. (*Note:* This unified credit is a once-in-a-lifetime credit and takes into account prior gifts.) Therefore, Form 706 is generally required to be filed if your gross estate (the value of the estate *without* subtracting debts and liabilities) is over $1,000,000.

TaxAlert: The 2001 Tax Act

The Economic Growth and Tax Relief Act of 2001 gradually increases the unified credit amount so that by year 2009 it will equal the tax calculated on $3,500,000 of assets. In 2010, the estate tax is scheduled to be fully repealed.

The repeal of the estate tax, however, is provided to last only for people dying in 2010. After December 31, 2010, the estate tax reverts to 2001 law.

The increase in the unified credit equivalent, the repeal of the estate tax, and the increase in the highest estate tax rate are being phased in as follows:

Year of Death	Highest Estate Tax Rate	Unified Credit Amount
2001	55% (plus possible surtax)	$675,000
2002	50%	$1,000,000
2003	49%	$1,000,000
2004	48%	$1,500,000
2005	47%	$1,500,000
2006	46%	$2,000,000
2007	45%	$2,000,000
2008	45%	$2,000,000
2009	45%	$3,500,000
2010	N/A	Full Repeal
2011	55% (plus possible surtax)	$1,000,000

TAXPLANNER

In addition to the *U.S. Estate Tax Return* (Form 706), there are two possible income tax returns that may need to be filed: Form 1040, *U.S. Individual Income Tax Return,* and Form 1041, *U.S. Income Tax Return for Estates and Trusts.* Form 1040 is generally used to report all the income that was earned and received prior to death. Any income that was earned and received after date of death is generally reported by the estate (or the trust, if the asset was held in trust) and is reported on Form 1041. This chapter focuses mainly on Form 1040 issues. Finally, if the decedent made a gift during the year of death, the personal representative may be required to file a gift tax return (Form 709) on the decedent's behalf and pay any gift tax due.

Useful Items

You may want to see:

Publication

☐ **559** Survivors, Executors, and Administrators

Form (and Instructions)

☐ **56** Notice Concerning Fiduciary Relationship
☐ **1310** Statement of Person Claiming Refund Due a Deceased Taxpayer
☐ **4810** Request for Prompt Assessment Under Internal Revenue Code Section 6501(d)

Personal Representative

A personal representative of an estate is an executor, administrator, or anyone who is in charge of the decedent's property.
Executor. Generally, an executor (or executrix) is named in a decedent's will to administer the estate (property and debts left by the decedent) and distribute properties as the decedent has directed.

Administrator. An administrator (or administratrix) is usually appointed by the court if no will exists, if no executor was named in the will, or if the named executor cannot or will not serve.
Personal representative. In general, an executor and an administrator perform the same duties and have the same responsibilities. Because a personal representative for a decedent's estate can be an executor, administrator, or anyone in charge of the decedent's property, the term *personal representative* will be used throughout this chapter.

The surviving spouse may or may not be the personal representative, depending on the terms of the decedent's will or the court appointment.

Duties

The primary duties of a personal representative are to collect all of the decedent's assets, pay the creditors, and distribute the remaining assets to the heirs or other beneficiaries.

The personal representative also must perform the following duties.

1) Notify the IRS (as discussed below) that he or she is acting as the personal representative.
2) File any income tax and estate tax return when due. (See *Final Return for the Decedent,* next.)
3) Pay any tax determined up to the date of discharge from duties.
4) Provide the payers of any interest and dividends the name(s) and identification number(s) of the new owner(s). (See *Interest and Dividend Income (Forms 1099),* later.)

For more information on the duties and responsibilities of the personal representative, see *Duties* under *Personal Representative* in Publication 559.
Notifying the IRS. File a written notice (or Form 56) with the IRS office where the returns are filed for the person (or estate) for whom you are acting. See the instructions for Form 56 for more information.

Explanation
Form 56, *Notice Concerning Fiduciary Relationship,* is used to notify the IRS of the *creation* or *termination* of a fiduciary relationship. If notification is not given to the IRS, notices of taxes due will be sent to the last known address of the decedent. This is considered sufficient notice by the IRS. Therefore, Form 56 should be filed in a timely manner so that the personal representative is not considered personally liable for the taxes due, along with possible interest and penalties.

Final Return for the Decedent

The same filing requirements that apply to individuals determine if a final income tax return must be filed for the decedent. Filing requirements are discussed in chapter 1.
Filing to get a refund. A return should be filed to obtain a refund if tax was withheld from salaries, wages, pensions, or annuities, or if estimated tax was paid, even if a return is not required to be filed. See *Claiming a refund,* later. Also, the decedent may be entitled to other credits that result in a refund. See chapters 37 and 38 for additional information on refundable credits and see chapter 35 for information on the child tax credit.
Determining income and deductions. The method of accounting regularly used by the decedent before death generally determines what income you must include and what deductions you can take on the final return. Generally, individuals use one of two methods of accounting: cash or accrual.

Cash method. If the decedent used the cash method of accounting, include only the items of income actually or constructively received before death and deduct only the expenses the decedent paid before death.

For an exception for certain medical expenses not paid before death, see *Decedents* in chapter 23.

Explanation

Actual or constructive receipt of income includes items such as uncashed payroll and **dividend** checks, if they were received or were available to the decedent before death.

Example

If the decedent's payroll check for June 1 through June 15 is available on Wednesday, June 15, but she fails to pick it up and dies on Thursday, June 16, the income is included in the decedent's final individual income tax return. However, if the decedent would not have been paid until Friday, June 17—that date appears on the check and that is the first day it could have been picked up—the income is reported as part of the estate and *not* on the final Form 1040. In the latter case, the income is called *income in respect of the decedent* and is discussed in the following section.

If the decedent was married and lived in a **community property** state—Arizona, California, Idaho, Louisiana, Nevada, New Mexico, Texas, or Washington—half of the combined income and expenses of husband and wife up to the date of death may be attributable to the decedent. Wisconsin has a marital property law that is similar to community property law.

TaxSaver

The person filing the decedent's final return may elect to include as income on that return all of the U.S. Savings Bond interest that had accumulated but had not been reported. If the decedent otherwise had low **taxable income** to report on her final return, this return could be the best one in which to recognize the interest income. To determine whether or not this is advantageous, you have to compare the tax rate of the decedent on the final individual income tax return with the tax rate of the recipient of the bonds. (For a further discussion of this point, see Chapter 8, *Interest Income*.)

Accrual method. If the decedent used an accrual method of accounting, report only those items of income that the decedent accrued, or earned, before death. Deduct those expenses the decedent was liable for before death, regardless of whether the expenses were paid.

Additional information. For more information on the cash and accrual methods, see *Accounting Methods* in chapter 1.

Who must file the return? The personal representative (defined earlier) must file the final income tax return (Form 1040) of the decedent for the year of death and any returns not filed for preceding years. A surviving spouse, under certain circumstances, may have to file the returns for the decedent. See *Joint Return,* later.

Example. Samantha Smith died on March 21, 2001, before filing her 2000 tax return. Her personal representative must file her 2000 return by April 16, 2001. Her final tax return is due April 15, 2002.

Explanation

If the decedent had not yet filed a return for the previous year, the personal representative or surviving spouse should prepare and file the return, just as the decedent would have. The only differences are: (1) the executor signs the return (see *Signing the Return,* later) and (2) the estimated tax payments that are due after the decedent died are not required to be made. If a joint return is being filed, see the discussion of estimated tax payments under *Joint Return,* later.

For the year of death, the decedent's final return covers income received and deductions paid during the period from January 1 through the date of death (assuming that the decedent was a cash-basis taxpayer).

TaxSaver

If the decedent was a member of the U.S. Armed Forces and dies while in active service in a combat zone or from wounds, disease, or other injury received in a combat zone, the decedent's income tax liability is forgiven for the tax year in which death occurred.

A decedent's income tax liability is also forgiven for any decedent who was either a military or civilian U.S. employee at death and dies from wounds or injury incurred while a U.S. employee in a terroristic or military action outside the United States.

For additional information, please seek advice from your tax advisor.

TaxSaver

A surviving spouse may be able to reduce the tax on his or her income by filing a **joint return** with the decedent. Even if a taxpayer died on January 1 with no income earned by that date, the availability of joint tax rates to the surviving spouse could be beneficial. However, if the surviving spouse marries before the end of the year, the decedent must file as married filing separately.

Filing the return. The word "DECEASED," the decedent's name, and the date of death should be written across the top of the tax return. In the name and address space, you should write the name and address of the decedent and, if a joint return, the surviving spouse. If a joint return is not being filed, the decedent's name should be written in the name space and the personal representative's name and address should be written in the remaining space.

Example. John Stone died in early 2001. He was survived by his wife Jane. The top of their final joint return on Form 1040, which includes the required information, is illustrated on the next page.

Signing the return. If a personal representative has been appointed, that person must sign the return. If it is a joint return, the surviving spouse must also sign it.

If no personal representative has been appointed, the surviving spouse (on a joint return) should sign the return and write in the signature area "Filing as surviving spouse." See *Joint return,* later.

If no personal representative has been appointed and if there is no surviving spouse, the person in charge of the decedent's property must file and sign the return as "personal representative."

TaxOrganizer

After a person dies, it may be difficult for the family or personal representative to locate the information necessary to file the final tax return (e.g., charitable contribution receipts, interest deductions, pay stubs, 1099s). However, it is important to make a diligent search and to keep these items organized. See chart on page 54 entitled "Important Tax-Related Actions to Take after a Death."

Example. Assume in the previous example that no personal representative has been appointed. The bottom of the final joint return, which shows that Jane is filing the return as the surviving spouse, is illustrated on the next page.

DECEASED   JOHN S. STONE   FEBRUARY 28, 2001

Form **1040** Department of the Treasury—Internal Revenue Service
U.S. Individual Income Tax Return 2001   IRS Use Only—Do not write or staple in this space.

For the year Jan. 1–Dec. 31, 2001, or other tax year beginning _____, 2001, ending _____, 20___

OMB No. 1545-0074

Label
(See instructions on page 19.)
Use the IRS label. Otherwise, please print or type.

CAR-RT   SORT**CR01
LP   S29   30
JOHN S & JANE M STONE
1772 OAK ST   103
SHERIDAN   WY   82801

L A B E L H E R E

I R S

Your social security number
765 : 00 : 4321

Spouse's social security number
123 : 00 : 4567

▲ **Important!** ▲
You **must** enter your SSN(s) above.

Presidential Election Campaign
(See page 19.)

Note. Checking "Yes" will not change your tax or reduce your refund.
Do you, or your spouse if filing a joint return, want $3 to go to this fund? . . . ▶

You   Spouse
☐ Yes ☐ No ☐ Yes ☐ No

Filing Status
1 ☐ Single
2 ☐ Married filing joint return (even if only one had income)

Third Party Designee
Do you want to allow another person to discuss this return with the IRS (see page 53)? ☐ **Yes.** Complete the following. ☑ **No**

Designee's name ▶ _____   Phone no. ▶ ( )   Personal identification number (PIN) ▶ ☐☐☐☐☐

Sign Here
Joint return? See page 19.
Keep a copy for your records.

Under penalties of perjury, I declare that I have examined this return and accompanying schedules and statements, and to the best of my knowledge and belief, they are true, correct, and complete. Declaration of preparer (other than taxpayer) is based on all information of which preparer has any knowledge.

Your signature	Date	Your occupation	Daytime phone number
Jane M. Stone	4/1/02	Engineer	( )
Spouse's signature. If a joint return, **both** must sign. Filing as surviving spouse	Date	Spouse's occupation	

Paid Preparer's Use Only

Preparer's signature ▶		Date	Check if self-employed ☐	Preparer's SSN or PTIN
Firm's name (or yours if self-employed), address, and ZIP code ▶			EIN	
			Phone no. ( )	

Tip. *Beginning with your tax return for 2001, you can check the "Yes" box in the "Third Party Designee" area of your return to authorize the IRS to discuss your return with a friend, family member, or any other person you choose. This allows the IRS to call the person you identified as your designee to answer any questions that may arise during the processing of your return. It also allows your designee to perform certain actions. See your income tax package for details.*

Claiming a refund. Generally, a person who is filing a return for a decedent and claiming a refund must file Form 1310 with the return. However, if the person claiming the refund is a surviving spouse filing a joint return with the decedent, or a court-appointed or certified personal representative filing an original return for the decedent, Form 1310 is not needed. The personal representative must attach to the return a copy of the court certificate showing that he or she was appointed the personal representative.

Example. Mr. Green died before filing his tax return. You were appointed the personal representative for Mr. Green's estate and you file his Form 1040 showing a refund due. You do not need Form 1310 to claim the refund if you attach a copy of the court certificate showing you were appointed the personal representative.

TaxPlanner

To make sure that refunds are not delayed, it is recommended that Form 1310 be attached to *any* return being filed for a decedent on which a refund is being claimed.

Form 1310 can also be submitted to request that a refund check issued jointly be reissued to a surviving spouse.

When and where to file. The final income tax return is due at the same time the decedent's return would have been due had death not occurred. The final return for a decedent who was a calendar year taxpayer is generally due April 15 following the year death occurred. However, when the due date falls on a Saturday, Sunday, or legal holiday, the due date is delayed until the next business day.

TaxPlanner

The personal representative or surviving spouse may request an extension of time to file the decedent's final income tax return by filing Form 4868. This will give you an additional 4 months to file the return. If additional time is required, Form 2688, *Request for Additional Time to File*, may be filed to request an additional 2-month extension. Note that an extension of time to file does not mean an extension of time to pay tax. Hence, any tax liability owed must be paid in full by the due date of the return, excluding extensions. See *When Do I Have to File?* in Chapter 1, *Filing Information*.

You may obtain Form 4868 or Form 2688 via the Internet by visiting the *Ernst & Young Tax and Financial Planning Corner* at www.ey.com/pfc.

Generally, you must file the final income tax return of the decedent with the Internal Revenue Service Center for the place where you live. A tax return for a decedent cannot be electronically filed.

Request for prompt assessment (charge) of tax. The IRS ordinarily has 3 years from the date an income tax return is filed, or its due

Important Tax-Related Actions To Take after a Death	
Action	**Comments**
Obtain at least 10 death certificates from the local county clerk, mortuary, or funeral director.	The executor or personal representative (referred to as the "executor" in this chart) must file the death certificate with the estate tax return (Form 706) for the decedent. Also, death certificates will be needed to claim life insurance proceeds, change title to bank accounts, and transfer title to other assets. Death certificates usually will not be available until a week or two after the death.
Contact life insurance companies to claim the proceeds. The executor can usually find the telephone number in the life insurance policy.	Contact the insurance company as soon as possible. Insurance companies are sometimes slow to respond, and the decedent's family may need the insurance proceeds for support.
Notify the Social Security Administration of the death. Also notify banks and investment brokers.	The telephone number for the Social Security Administration is 1-800-772-1213.
Contact an estate planning or probate attorney to determine what court filings are necessary.	Select an attorney who has at least 5 years of significant experience handling probates and administrations of estates. See the attorney as soon as possible after the death. Referrals to attorneys can be obtained from friends or relatives, or often from a local Bar Association Referral Service.
Contact an accountant regarding all tax filings that will be necessary.	The personal representative of surviving spouse must file a final income tax return for the decedent (Form 1040). No further estimated taxes for the decedent must be paid after the death of the decedent. The "probate estate" (if a probate is necessary) becomes a new taxpayer and the personal representative must file a tax return (Form 1041). The estate may select a fiscal year which may result in beneficial tax deferral. If the decedent created a "revocable living trust" during life, that trust (which becomes irrevocable at death) also becomes a new taxpayer and may also be required to file a Form 1041. However, in certain cases, the probate estate and the trust may file consolidated income tax returns.
Open an estate checking account as soon as possible—deposit all checks due to the decedent and pay all debts and expenses owed (including funeral expenses and taxes) from this account.	It is critical that accurate records are kept. Do not comingle anyone else's income or expenses with the decedent's income and expenses, including income earned and expenses paid after date of death. The executor will need accurate information to report on the decedent's final income tax return, the estate's and/or trust's income tax return, and the estate tax return.
Search through the decedent's desk, office, safe deposit box, and files to locate information which needed for the tax returns.	Specifically, look for the following: Will, codicils to the Will, trust agreements, addresses, and social security numbers of beneficiaries; checking, savings money market, and CD statements; check book registers, brokerage statements, stock certificates, bonds, retirement plan, and IRA benefit statements; life insurance and annuity policies; the last 3 years of state and federal income tax returns, all prior gift tax returns; property tax bill and deed for real estate; buy-sell or operating agreements for businesses, all outstanding bills (including last illness and funeral bills), and any undeposited checks.
Review the decedent's company retirement and benefit plans, as well as IRA's, with a tax advisor	The beneficiary of these assets must make certain decisions regarding distributions from these plans and IRA's; and the decisions made can have significant income tax consequnces.

date, whichever is later, to charge any additional tax that is due. However, as a personal representative, you may request a prompt assessment of tax after the return has been filed. This reduces the time for making the assessment to 18 months from the date the written request for prompt assessment was received. This request can be made for any income tax return of the decedent and for the income tax return of the decedent's estate. This may permit a quicker settlement of the tax liability of the estate and an earlier final distribution of the assets to the beneficiaries.

You can request prompt assessment of any of the decedent's taxes (other than federal estate taxes) for any years for which the statutory period for assessment is open. This applies even though the returns were filed before the decedent's death.

Form 4810. You can use Form 4810 to make this request. It must be filed separately from any other document. The request should be filed with the IRS office where the return was filed. If Form 4810 is not used, you must clearly indicate that you are making a request for prompt assessment under section 6501(d) of the Internal Revenue Code. You must identify the type of tax and the tax period for which the prompt assessment is requested.

Failure to report income. If you or the decedent failed to report substantial amounts of gross income (more than 25% of the gross income reported on the return) or filed a false or fraudulent return, your request for prompt assessment will not shorten the period during which the IRS may assess the additional tax. However, such a request may relieve you of personal liability for the tax if you did not have knowledge of the unpaid tax.

TAXPLANNER

A representative of a decedent's estate may be held personally liable by the IRS for later-discovered tax deficiencies if the representative has not retained enough of the estate's assets to pay those deficiencies. Therefore, many cautious representatives are slow to distribute the estate's assets to the heirs. Filing Form 4810, *A Request for Prompt Assessment*, may shorten the period in which the IRS may hold the representative responsible for not paying enough tax, thereby potentially allowing the estate's assets to be distributed more promptly. However, the request may trigger an audit of those returns.

Request for discharge from personal liability for tax. An executor can make a written request for a discharge from personal liability for a decedent's income and gift taxes. The request must be made after the returns for those taxes are filed. It must clearly indicate that the request is for discharge from personal liability under section 6905 of the Internal Revenue Code. For this purpose, an executor is an executor or administrator that is appointed, qualified, and acting within the United States.

Within 9 months after receipt of the request, the IRS will notify the executor of the amount of taxes due. If this amount is paid, the executor will be discharged from personal liability for any future deficiencies. If the IRS has not notified the executor, he or she will be discharged from personal liability at the end of the 9-month period.

Caution. *Even if the executor is discharged from personal liability, the IRS still will be able to assess tax deficiencies against the executor to the extent that he or she still has any of the decedent's property.*

Joint return. Generally, the personal representative and the surviving spouse can file a joint return for the decedent and the surviving spouse. However, the surviving spouse alone can file the joint return if no personal representative has been appointed before the due date for filing the final joint return for the year of death. This also applies to the return for the preceding year if the decedent died after the close of the preceding tax year and before the due date for filing that return. The income of the decedent that was includible on his or her return for the year up to the date of death (as explained under *Determining income and deductions,* earlier) and the income of the surviving spouse for the entire year must be included in the final joint return.

TAXPLANNER

If you are a surviving spouse and are filing a joint return with the decedent, you are not relieved of the obligation to make estimated tax payments because of the death. See Chapter 5, *Tax Withholding and Estimated Tax,* for more information on estimated tax payments.

A final joint return with the decedent cannot be filed if the surviving spouse remarried before the end of the year of the decedent's death. The filing status of the decedent in this instance is "married filing separate return."

TAXSAVER

If the decedent was married, it is important to calculate whether the tax on a joint return would be less than the total tax on two separate returns.

Ordinarily, a joint return would result in the least overall tax for married couples, but only a complete computation will tell you for sure. Remember, the joint return will include all of the income and deductions of the survivor for the entire year, but those of the decedent are included only up to the date of death. If property was owned jointly with the surviving spouse, all of the income after death is required to be reported in the joint return, because it, along with the ownership of the property, passed to the surviving spouse. However, if the property was not owned jointly and passed to an executor at death, the subsequent income on that property would be reported on the income tax return for the estate for which the executor is responsible and not on the joint return.

Personal representative may revoke joint return election. A court-appointed personal representative may revoke an election to file a joint return that was previously made by the surviving spouse alone. This is done by filing a separate return for the decedent within one year from the due date of the return (including any extensions). The joint return made by the surviving spouse will then be regarded as the separate return of that spouse by excluding the decedent's items and refiguring the tax liability.

How To Report Certain Income

This section explains how to report certain types of income on the final return. The rules on income discussed in the other chapters of this publication also apply to a decedent's final return. See chapters 6 through 17, if they apply.

Interest and Dividend Income (Forms 1099)

A Form 1099 should be received for the decedent to report interest and dividends earned before death. These amounts must be included on the decedent's final return. A separate Form 1099 should show the interest and dividends earned after the date of the decedent's death and paid to the estate or other recipient that must include those amounts on its return. You can request corrected Forms 1099 if these forms do not properly reflect the right recipient or amounts.

For example, a Form 1099-INT reporting interest payable to the decedent may include income that should be reported on the final income tax return of the decedent, as well as income that the estate or other recipient should report, either as income earned after death or as income in respect of the decedent (discussed later). For income earned after death, you should ask the payer for a Form 1099 that properly identifies the recipient (by name and identification number) and the proper amount. If that is not possible, or if the form includes an amount that represents income in respect of the decedent, report the interest, as shown next under *How to report.*

See *U.S. savings bonds acquired from decedent* in Publication 559 for information on savings bond interest that may have to be reported on the final return.

How to report. If you are preparing the decedent's final return and you have received a Form 1099-INT for the decedent that includes amounts belonging to the decedent and to another recipient (the decedent's estate or another beneficiary), report the total interest shown on Form 1099-INT on Schedule 1 (Form 1040A) or on Schedule B (Form 1040). Next, enter a subtotal of the interest shown on Forms 1099 and the interest reportable from other sources for which you did not receive Forms 1099. Then, show any interest (including any interest you receive as a nominee) belonging to another recipient separately and subtract it from the subtotal. Identify this adjustment as a "Nominee Distribution" or other appropriate designation.

Report dividend income for which you received a Form 1099-DIV, *Dividends and Distributions,* on the appropriate schedule using the same procedure.

Note. If the decedent received amounts as a nominee, you must give the actual owner a Form 1099, unless the owner is the decedent's spouse. See *General Instructions for Forms 1099, 1098, 5498, and W-2G,* for more information on filing forms 1099.

TAXPLANNER

No matter how hard you try, you will not get the payers of dividends and interest to reflect properly the amounts attributable to the decedent prior to death and the amounts that are paid to the decedent's successor in interest. It is therefore imperative that you follow the example below carefully in order to avoid bothersome inquiries from the IRS.

Example 1

Marty died on June 30, 2001. Marty owned 50 shares of ABC Corporation and 75 shares of XYZ Corporation, both of which paid a $1 per share quarterly dividend on February 1, May 1, August 1, and November 1. Upon Marty's death, all shares were transferred to his estate. XYZ Corporation has properly issued two Forms 1099-DIV. One Form 1099-DIV identifies Marty as the recipient of $150 (the dividends paid to Marty prior to death, from January 1, 2001, to June 30, 2001), and the other identifies Marty's estate as the recipient of $150 (the dividends paid to the estate, from July 1, 2001, to December 31, 2001). ABC Corporation, however, issued only one Form 1099-DIV, naming Marty as the recipient of the entire year's dividend ($200).

On Marty's final return, you must report total dividends as indicated on all Forms 1099-DIV issued in Marty's name ($150 from XYZ Corporation and $200 from ABC Corporation) on line 5, Part II of Form 1040, Schedule B. Several lines above line 6, write "Subtotal" and enter $350. Below this subtotal, write "Nominee Distribution" and enter $100 (the dividends paid by ABC Corporation to Marty's estate). Subtract the nominee distribution from the subtotal and report the net result of $250 on line 6. The same reporting procedure would apply to reporting interest. See the example below for an example of the language to put on Schedule B.

Example 2

John Johnson died on July 1, 2001. In January 2002, ABC Bank sent a Form 1099-INT to his executor reflecting interest paid during 2001 of $5,000. Because John was only alive for one-half of 2001, only one-half of the interest will be reported on his final Form 1040 for 2001. The other one-half of the interest will be reported on his estate's income tax return (Form 1041).

Schedule B of John's final Form 1040 should report the $2,500 of interest. Part I, line 1, should be completed as follows:

ABC Bank	$5,000
Less nominee distribution	($2,500)
(estate of John Johnson:	
EIN: 00-0000000)	

Part 1, line 4, would show total interest income of $2,500

The Form 1041 for the estate of John will report the other $2,500 of interest income.

TAXORGANIZER

You should keep a copy of the Forms 1099 that you receive as well as the tax worksheets showing pre- and postdeath income for a minimum of 3 years.

Accelerated Death Benefits

Accelerated death benefits are amounts received under a life insurance contract before the death of the insured individual. These benefits also include amounts received on the sale or assignment of the contract to a viatical settlement provider.

Generally, if the decedent received accelerated death benefits either on his or her own life or on the life of another person, those benefits are not included in the decedent's income. This exclusion applies only if the insured was a terminally or chronically ill individual. For more information, see *Accelerated death benefits* under *Gifts, Insurance, and Inheritances* in Publication 559.

Business Income

This section discusses some of the business income which may have to be included on the final return.

Partnership income. The death of a partner closes the partnership's tax year for that partner. Generally, it does not close the partnership's tax year for the remaining partners. The decedent's distributive share of partnership items must be figured as if the partnership's tax year ended on the date the partner died. To avoid an interim closing of the partnership books, the partners can agree to estimate the decedent's distributive share by prorating the amounts the partner would have included for the entire partnership tax year.

On the decedent's final return, include the decedent's distributive share of partnership items for the following periods.

1) The partnership's tax year that ended within or with the decedent's final tax year (the year ending on the date of death).
2) The period, if any, from the end of the partnership's tax year in (1) to the decedent's date of death.

TAXALERT

Effective for partnerships with taxable years beginning after December 31, 1997, the partnership's tax year closes with respect to a partner whose entire interest in the partnership is terminated by death. Therefore, the partnership income will have to be allocated between and reported by the decedent and the decedent's successor in interest. The final individual income tax return should include the decedent's share of partnership income and deductions for the partnership's tax year that ends within or with the decedent's last tax year (the year ending on the date of death). The final return must also include income for the period between the end of the partnership's last tax year and the date of death.

The income for the part of the partnership's tax year after the partner's death is reported by the estate or other person who has acquired the interest in the partnership.

Example

Jim, a partner in a law firm, died on December 1, 2001. The tax year for the partnership ends on June 30. Jim's partnership income for the year ending June 30, 2001, of $100,000 will be included on his 2001 individual income tax return. In addition, Jim's final income tax return for 2001 will also include his pro rata portion (154 days) of partnership income and deductions from July 1, 2001, to December 1, 2001, with the remainder to be reported to Jim's successor in interest.

TAXSAVER

Planning for partnership interests can save substantial amounts of income tax. For example, a partner should investigate the possibility of appointing his or her spouse as successor in interest to the partnership so that the income or loss for the year of death can flow onto the survivor's return and thus onto the joint return.

There is another way of ensuring the immediate transfer of the partnership interest to the spouse upon the partner's death so that the income or loss can be reported on the joint return. The spouses may own the partnership interest in joint tenancy. Be sure to check that the partnership will permit this. Also, if the executor has the assets and the legal authority to make a distribution to the spouse, all or a portion of the partnership income can be transferred to the final joint return. Prompt action may be necessary. Finally, consult with a tax advisor because there may be tax disadvantages to holding property in joint tenancy.

TaxPlanner

If a decedent had an interest in a passive activity (e.g., a partnership or S corporation), the passive activity rules still apply on the decedent's final individual tax return. For example, the death of a partner does not trigger the deduction of any suspended passive activity losses associated with that partnership. (See Chapter 13, *Other Income,* for more information on passive activity losses.) Generally, the remaining suspended losses may be transferred to the partner's successor in interest. However, these losses may have to be reduced depending on whether the interest received a step-up in basis. You should consult with your tax advisor for more information.

S corporation income. If the decedent was a shareholder in an S corporation, include on the final return the decedent's share of the S corporation's items of income, loss, deduction, and credit for the following periods.

1) The corporation's tax year that ended within or with the decedent's final tax year (the year ending on the date of death).
2) The period, if any, from the end of the corporation's tax year in (1) to the decedent's date of death.

Example

Julia Jones was a 20% partner in XYZ Partnership and a 20% shareholder in ABC Corporation, an S corporation. The tax year for both the partnership and the corporation ends on December 31. Julia died on October 1, 2001. Had she lived, Julia would have earned $100,000 of ordinary income in 2001 from the partnership and another $100,000 of ordinary income from the corporation.

Julia's final tax return for 2001 will include $75,068 (274 days) of income from ABC Corporation and $75,068 of income from XYZ Partnership. The remaining $24,932 of ABC Corporation and the $24,932 from XYZ Partnership income will be included in the tax return of the successor in interest.

Self-employment income. Include self-employment income actually or constructively received or accrued, depending on the decedent's accounting method. (See *Constructive receipt of income,* under *Income To Include,* in Publication 559 for an explanation of the concept.) For self-employment tax purposes only, the decedent's self-employment income will include the decedent's distributive share of a partnership's income or loss through the end of the month in which death occurred. For this purpose, the partnership income or loss is considered to be earned ratably over the partnership's tax year. For more information on how to compute self-employment income, see Publication 533, *Self-Employment Tax.*

Roth IRA

Any amount not previously reported must be included on the decedent's final return, if the decedent:

- Died in 2001,
- Withdrew an amount from a traditional IRA in 1998,
- Converted the amount to a Roth IRA, and
- Included the taxable conversion amount in income over the 4-year period beginning in 1998.

For more information on Roth IRAs, see Publication 590, *Individual Retirement Arrangements (IRAs).*

Coverdell Education Savings Account (ESA)

Generally, the balance in a Coverdell ESA must be distributed within 30 days after the individual for whom the account was established reaches age 30, or dies, whichever is earlier. The treatment of the Coverdell ESA at the death of an individual under age 30 depends on who acquires the interest in the account. If the decedent's estate acquires the interest, the earnings on the account must be included on the final income tax return of the decedent. The estate tax deduction, discussed later, does not apply to this amount. If a beneficiary acquires the interest, see the discussion under *Income in Respect of the Decedent,* later.

Caution. *For tax years beginning after 2001, the age 30 limit does not apply if the individual for whom the account was established or the beneficiary that acquires the account is an individual with special needs. This includes an individual who because of a physical, mental, or emotional condition (including learning disability) requires additional time to complete his or her education.*

For more information on Coverdell ESAs, see Publication 970, *Tax Benefits for Higher Education.*

Archer MSA

The treatment of an Archer MSA (medical savings account), including a Medicare+Choice MSA, at the death of the account holder depends on who acquires the interest in the account. If the decedent's estate acquires the interest, the fair market value of the assets in the account on the date of death is included in income on the decedent's final return. The estate tax deduction, discussed later, does not apply to this amount.

If a beneficiary acquires the interest, see the discussion under *Income in Respect of the Decedent,* later. For more information on Archer MSAs, see Publication 969, *Medical Savings Accounts (MSAs).*

Exemptions, Deductions, and Credits

Generally, the rules for exemptions, deductions, and credits allowed to an individual also apply to the decedent's final income tax return. Show on the final return deductible items the decedent paid (or accrued, if the decedent reported deductions on an accrual method) before death.

Exemptions

You can claim the decedent's personal exemption on the final income tax return. If the decedent was another person's dependent (for example, a parent's), you cannot claim the personal exemption on the decedent's final return.

Standard Deduction

If you do not itemize deductions on the final return, the full amount of the appropriate standard deduction is allowed regardless of the date of death. For information on the appropriate standard deduction, see chapter 21.

Itemized Deductions

If the total of the decedent's itemized deductions is more than the decedent's standard deduction, the federal income tax will generally be less if you claim itemized deductions on the final return. See chapters 23 through 30 for the types of expenses that are allowed as itemized deductions.

TaxPlanner

Funeral, burial, and probate expenses are not deductible on your income tax return. However, these may be deducted on your estate tax return.

Medical expenses. Medical expenses paid before death by the decedent are deductible, subject to limits, on the final income tax return if deductions are itemized. This includes expenses for the decedent as well as for the decedent's spouse and dependents.

Caution. *Qualified medical expenses are not deductible if paid with a tax-free distribution from an Archer MSA.*

For information on certain medical expenses that were not paid before death, see *Decedents* in chapter 23.

TaxSaver

The executor or executrix may elect to claim certain medical and dental expenses as deductions on the estate tax return or as deductions on the decedent's final income tax return. The tax should be computed both ways to see which results in more tax savings.

If an election is made to include the medical and dental expenses on the decedent's income tax return rather than on the federal estate tax return, the executor or executrix must attach a statement to the income tax return stating that he or she has not claimed the amount as an estate tax deduction and that the estate waives the right to claim the amount as a deduction.

TaxSaver

When death is expected, proper planning can save tax dollars. Deductible expenses, such as interest expense and accounting fees, that are due near the date of death may be paid before death or after death. Choose the time offering the greater tax benefit. If you arrange to pay the expenses before death, they are deductible on the decedent's final Form 1040 if deductions are itemized. If you arrange to pay them after death, they are deductible on the estate's income tax return.

Unrecovered investment in pension. If the decedent was receiving a pension or annuity and died without a surviving annuitant, you can take a deduction on the decedent's final return for the amount of the decedent's investment in the pension or annuity contract that remained unrecovered at death. The deduction is a miscellaneous itemized deduction that is not subject to the 2% limit on adjusted gross income. See chapter 30.

Deduction for Losses

A decedent's net operating loss deduction from a prior year and any capital losses (including capital loss carryovers) can be deducted only on the decedent's final income tax return. A net operating loss on the decedent's final income tax return can be carried back to prior years. You cannot deduct any unused net operating loss or capital loss on the estate's income tax return.

TaxSaver

Net operating losses (or carryover losses) from business operations and **capital losses** (or carryover losses) of the

decedent may not be carried over to the returns of executors or heirs. However, if a joint return is filed for the year of death, these losses may be used to offset the survivor's income for the entire year. In this case, it may be advantageous for the surviving spouse to incur **capital gains** and/or other income and to offset them with the capital losses and/or net operating losses that cannot be carried forward past the year of the spouse's death.

Example
Your husband died on June 30, 2001, with $10,000 in **short-term capital losses** from his personal account. Because the maximum capital loss that can be deducted in a year is $3,000, only $3,000 of those losses will be allowed on your 2001 joint return, with no carryover of the remaining $7,000. However, if you could recognize an additional $7,000 in gains before the end of the year, you could use your deceased husband's remaining $7,000 of losses to offset the gains by filing a joint return. If you waited until a later year to recognize those gains, they would be fully taxable, unless you had incurred other losses to offset them.

Credits

Any of the tax credits discussed in this publication also apply to the final return if the decedent was eligible for the credits at the time of death. These credits are discussed in chapters 33 through 37.

Tax withheld and estimated payments. There may have been income tax withheld from the decedent's pay, pensions, or annuities before death, and the decedent may have paid estimated income tax. To get credit for these tax payments, you must claim them on the decedent's final return. For more information, see *Credit for Withholding and Estimated Tax* in chapter 5.

Explanation
Exemption allowances, the standard deduction, and itemized deductions are not prorated over that part of the year during which a now deceased taxpayer was alive. However, exemptions claimed for **dependents** could be a problem if the decedent did not live long enough during the year to provide the required amount of support. In most situations, potential problems will be alleviated if the surviving spouse files a joint return with the decedent. See Chapter 3, *Personal Exemptions and Dependents,* for more information.

Tax Effect on Others

This section contains information about the effect of an individual's death on the income tax liability of the survivors (including the widow or widower and any beneficiaries) and the estate. A survivor should coordinate the filing of his or her own tax return with the personal representative handling the decedent's estate. The personal representative can coordinate filing status, exemptions, income, and deductions so that the decedent's final return and the income tax returns of the survivors and the estate are all filed correctly.

Survivors
If you are a survivor, you may qualify for certain benefits when filing your own income tax return. This section addresses some issues that may apply to you.

Gifts and inheritances. Property received as a gift, bequest, or inheritance is not included in your income. However, if property you receive in this manner later produces income, such as interest, dividends, or rent, that income is taxable to you. If the gift, bequest, or inheritance you receive is the income from property, that income is taxable to you.

If you inherited the right to receive income in respect of the decedent, see *Income in Respect of the Decedent,* later.

TaxAlert

The cost basis of any asset distributed from the decedent's estate (which he/she owned at death) via bequest or inheritance is "stepped up" to the fair market value at the date of the decedent's death or the alternate valuation date. See Chapter 14, *Basis of Property,* for more information.

Furthermore, the asset is deemed to be long-term capital gain property, so any capital appreciation on the asset will be taxed at a 10% or 20% capital gains tax rate.

Exception: If you or your spouse inherits property that you gifted to the decedent within 1 year of death, your basis in the asset is what the decedent's adjusted basis in the asset was immediately before his/her death.

TaxAlert

Fees received by an executor or administrator for duties performed for an estate are includable in the gross income of the executor or administrator but are usually not subject to self-employment tax as long as you are not in the trade or business of being an executor or administrator.

However, a bequest to the executor is not treated as income. It is merely a gift to an heir who also happens to be serving as executor. Therefore, if you are the executor and an heir, you may consider declining to take a fee, in which case you will receive a larger portion of the estate that is not subject to income tax. Contact your tax advisor to assist you in determining which course of action is more beneficial.

Joint return by surviving spouse. A surviving spouse can file a joint return for the year of death and may qualify for special tax rates for the following 2 years. For more information, see *Qualifying Widow(er) With Dependent Child* in chapter 2.

Explanation

After the 2-year period following the date of death, a surviving spouse may still be able to qualify as a **head of household** and use the Tax Table and Tax Rate Schedules for head of household. While not as beneficial as joint return rates, they are better than those for single persons. See Chapter 2, *Filing Status,* for more details.

Decedent as your dependent. If the decedent qualified as your dependent for the part of the year before death, you can claim the exemption for the dependent on your tax return, regardless of when death occurred during the year.

If the decedent was your qualifying child, you may be able to claim the child tax credit. See chapter 35.

Income in Respect of the Decedent

All gross income that the decedent would have received had death not occurred and that was not properly includible on the final return, discussed earlier, is income in respect of the decedent.

How To Report
Income in respect of a decedent must be included in the income of one of the following.

- The decedent's estate, if the estate receives it.
- The beneficiary, if the right to income is passed directly to the beneficiary and the beneficiary receives it.
- Any person to whom the estate properly distributes the right to receive it.

Tip. *If you have to include income in respect of the decedent in your gross income, you may be able to claim a deduction for the estate tax paid on that income. For more information, see* Estate Tax Deduction, *later.*

Example 1. Frank Johnson owned and operated an apple orchard. He used the cash method of accounting. He sold and delivered 1,000 bushels of apples to a canning factory for $2,000, but did not receive payment before his death. The proceeds from the sale are income in respect of the decedent. When the estate was settled, payment had not been made and the estate transferred the right to the payment to his widow. When Frank's widow collects the $2,000, she must include that amount in her return. It is not to be reported on the final return of the decedent or on the return of the estate.

Example 2. Assume the same facts as in Example 1, except that Frank used the accrual method of accounting. The amount accrued from the sale of the apples would be included on his final return. Neither the estate nor the widow will realize income in respect of the decedent when the money is later paid.

Example 3. Cathy O'Neil was entitled to a large salary payment at the date of her death. The amount was to be paid in five annual installments. The estate, after collecting two installments, distributed the right to the remaining installments to you, the beneficiary. The payments are income in respect of the decedent. None of the payments were includible in Cathy's final return. The estate must include in its income the two installments it received, and you must include in your income each of the three installments as you receive them.

Transferring your right to income. If you transfer your right to income in respect of a decedent, you must include in your income the greater of:

1) The amount you receive for the right, or
2) The fair market value of the right at the time of the transfer.

Fair market value (FMV). FMV is the price at which the property would change hands between a buyer and a seller, neither having to buy or sell, and both having reasonable knowledge of all necessary facts.

Giving your right to income as a gift. If you give your right to receive income in respect of a decedent as a gift, you must include in your income the fair market value of the right at the time you make the gift.

Example

Tom has a right to receive a payment of $10,000 that represents income in respect of his deceased father (e.g., deferred compensation). He makes a gift of his right to receive the money. He would immediately have to recognize the $10,000 as income on his tax return.

Type of income. The character or type of income that you receive in respect of a decedent is the same as it would be to the decedent if he or she were alive. If the income would be a capital gain to the decedent, it will be a capital gain to you.

Interest accrued on savings certificates. The interest accrued on savings certificates (redeemable after death without forfeiture of interest) that is for the period from the date of the last interest payment to the date of the decedent's death, but not received as of that date, is income in respect of the decedent. Interest for a period after the decedent's death that becomes payable on the certificates after death is not income in respect of the decedent, but is taxable income includible in the income of the respective recipients.

Installment obligations. If the decedent had sold property using the installment method and you have the right to collect the payments, use the same gross profit percentage the decedent would have used to figure the part of each payment that represents profit. Include in your income the same profit the decedent would have included had death not occurred. For more information on installment sales, see Publication 537, *Installment Sales.*

Explanation
Payments from an installment sale can consist in whole or in part of (1) principal payment, (2) capital gain, and (3) interest income.

If you dispose of an installment obligation acquired from a decedent (other than by transfer to the obligor), the rules explained in Publication 537 for figuring gain or loss on the disposition apply to you.

Example
Andrew sold undeveloped real estate held as an investment in 1999 for $120,000, receiving a note payable in four annual installments of $30,000 each plus interest. Andrew's basis in the land was $40,000. Andrew died before the first installment was due, and the note was transferred to Helen, Andrew's heir. Helen collected the first installment of the note, $30,000, in 2000. When Helen was in need of additional cash in early 2001, she sold the note to a bank for its fair market value of $90,000. For 2000, Helen must recognize gain on the payment she received. Using the same gross profit percentage as the decedent's ($80,000/$120,000), she would recognize a $20,000 gain, computed as follows:

$$\$30,000 \times \$80,000/\$120,000 = \$20,000$$

For 2001, Helen must recognize gain on the disposition of the installment obligation. The gain is the difference between her basis and the fair market value at the time of the disposition. Her basis in the obligation is the same as Andrew's ($40,000) less the payment of principal received by her in 2000 ($10,000). Hence, her gain is computed as follows:

$$\$90,000 - (\$40,000 - \$10,000) = \$60,000$$

Whether the gain recognized by Helen on her tax return is **ordinary income** or capital gain depends on what it would have been to Andrew had he lived to collect the payments.

Inherited IRAs. If a beneficiary receives a lump-sum distribution from a traditional IRA he or she inherited, all or some of it may be taxable. The distribution is taxable in the year received as income in respect of a decedent up to the decedent's taxable balance. This is the decedent's balance at the time of death, including unrealized appreciation and income accrued to date of death, minus any basis (nondeductible contributions). Amounts distributed that are more than the decedent's entire IRA balance (including taxable and nontaxable amounts) at the time of death are the income of the beneficiary.

If the beneficiary of a traditional IRA is the decedent's surviving spouse who properly rolls over the distribution into another traditional IRA or into a Roth IRA, the distribution is not currently taxed. For distributions after 2001, a surviving spouse can also roll over tax free the taxable part of the distribution into a qualified plan, section 403 annuity, or section 457 plan.

Example 1. At the time of his death, Greg owned a traditional IRA. All of the contributions by Greg to the IRA had been deductible contri-

butions. Greg's nephew, Mark, was the sole beneficiary of the IRA. The entire balance of the IRA, including income accruing before and after Greg's death, was distributed to Mark in a lump sum. Mark must include the total amount received in his income. The portion of the lump-sum distribution that equals the amount of the balance in the IRA at Greg's death, including the income earned before death, is income in respect of the decedent. Mark may take a deduction for any federal estate taxes that were paid on that portion.

Example 2. Assume the same facts as in Example 1, except that some of Greg's contributions to the IRA had been nondeductible contributions. To determine the amount to include in income, Mark must subtract the total nondeductible contributions made by Greg from the total amount received (including the income that was earned in the IRA both before and after Greg's death). Income in respect of the decedent is the total amount included in income less the income earned after Greg's death.

TaxAlert

In January 2001, the IRS issued new proposed regulations that simplify distribution requirements for IRAs, including distribution from inherited IRAs. Generally speaking, a beneficiary may take distributions from an inherited IRA over his or her own life expectancy. These regulations are effective for distributions for calendar years beginning on or after January 1, 2002. However, IRA owners are permitted to follow the rules for distributions in 2001.

For more information on inherited IRAs, see Publication 590.

Roth IRAs. Qualified distributions from a Roth IRA are not subject to tax. A distribution made to a beneficiary or to the Roth IRA owner's estate on or after the date of death is a qualified distribution if it is made after the 5-year tax period beginning with the first tax year in which a contribution was made to any Roth IRA of the owner.

Caution. *A distribution cannot be a qualified distribution unless it is made after 2002.*

Generally, the entire interest in the Roth IRA must be distributed by the end of the fifth calendar year after the year of the owner's death unless the interest is payable to a designated beneficiary over his or her life or life expectancy. If paid as an annuity, the distributions must begin before the end of the calendar year following the year of death. If the sole beneficiary is the decedent's spouse, the spouse can delay the distributions until the decedent would have reached age 70 1/2 or can treat the Roth IRA as his or her own Roth IRA.

Part of any distribution to a beneficiary that is not a qualified distribution may be includible in the beneficiary's income. Generally, the part includible is the earnings in the Roth IRA. Earnings attributable to the period ending with the decedent's date of death are income in respect of the decedent. Additional earnings are the income of the beneficiary.

Explanation
The new regulations mentioned above also impact Roth IRAs.

For more information on Roth IRAs, see Publication 590.

Coverdell education savings account (ESA). Generally, the balance in a Coverdell ESA must be distributed within 30 days after the individual for whom the account was established reaches age 30 or dies, whichever is earlier. The treatment of the Coverdell ESA at the death of an individual under age 30 depends on who acquires the interest in the account. If the decedent's estate acquires the interest, see the discussion under *How To Report Certain Income,* earlier.

Caution. *For tax years beginning after 2001, the age 30 limit does not apply if the individual for whom the account was established or the ben-*

eficiary that acquires the account is an individual with special needs. This includes an individual who because of a physical mental, or emotional condition (including learning disability) requires additional time to complete his or her education.

If the decedent's spouse or other family member is the designated beneficiary of the decedent's account, the Coverdell ESA becomes that person's Coverdell ESA. It is subject to the rules discussed in Publication 970.

Any other beneficiary (including a spouse or family member who is not the designated beneficiary) must include in income the earnings portion of the distribution. Any balance remaining at the close of the 30-day period is deemed to be distributed at that time. The amount included in income is reduced by any qualified higher education expenses of the decedent that are paid by the beneficiary within 1 year after the decedent's date of death. An estate tax deduction, discussed later, applies to the amount included in income by a beneficiary other than the decedent's spouse or family member.

Archer MSA. The treatment of an Archer MSA, including a Medicare+Choice MSA, at the death of the account holder depends on who acquires the interest in the account. If the decedent's estate acquires the interest, see the earlier discussion under *How To Report Certain Income.*

If the decedent's spouse is the designated beneficiary of the account, the account becomes that spouse's Archer MSA. It is subject to the rules discussed in Publication 969.

Any other beneficiary (including a spouse that is not the designated beneficiary) must include in income the fair market value of the assets in the account on the decedent's date of death. This amount must be reported for the beneficiary's tax year that includes the decedent's date of death. The amount included in income is reduced by any qualified medical expenses for the decedent that are paid by the beneficiary within 1 year after the decedent's date of death. An estate tax deduction, discussed later, applies to the amount included in income by a beneficiary other than the decedent's spouse.

Other income. For examples of other income situations concerning decedents, see *Specific Types of Income in Respect of a Decedent* in Publication 559.

Deductions in Respect of the Decedent

Items such as business expenses, income-producing expenses, interest, and taxes, for which the decedent was liable but that are not properly allowable as deductions on the decedent's final income tax return will be allowed as a deduction to one of the following when paid.

- The estate.
- The person who acquired an interest in the decedent's property (subject to such obligations) because of the decedent's death, if the estate was not liable for the obligation.

Explanation
Deductions in respect of the decedent are items that would normally be deductible by the decedent except that he or she had not paid them before death. Typical examples are real estate taxes, state income taxes, and interest expense.

TAXSAVER

Expenses in respect of a decedent are deductible on both the estate income tax return and the estate transfer tax return. The estate tax and income tax are two different taxes with two entirely unrelated sets of rules. Taking a deduction on one return does not preclude taking the same deduction on the other return. When death is anticipated, planning the best possible use of double deductions may yield significant tax savings. A professional who specializes in this area should be consulted.

Example
When Oscar died in 2001, he owed accrued interest of $100. The marginal estate tax rate for Oscar's estate is 50%, and the estate's marginal *income* tax rate is 28%. The deduction on the estate tax return is worth $50 (50% of $100), and the deduction on the estate's income tax return is worth $28. Consequently, $78 of the $100 liability is recovered through tax savings.

On the other hand, less tax savings would be realized if Oscar had paid the $100 of interest before he died. He would have been able to take the interest deduction on his personal income tax return, paying $28 less in taxes, assuming he was in the 28% bracket. When he died, he would have been net out-of-pocket $72, his estate would be $72 less, and therefore his estate tax would be reduced by $36 (50% of $72). Thus, if he had paid the expense, his total tax savings would have been $64—$28 of income tax and $36 of estate tax—instead of the $78 tax saved because he had not paid the interest before he died, thus allowing the double deduction.

Estate Tax Deduction

Income that a decedent had a right to receive is included in the decedent's gross estate and is subject to estate tax. This income in respect of a decedent is also taxed when received by the recipient (estate or beneficiary). However, an income tax deduction is allowed to the recipient for the estate tax paid on the income.

The deduction for estate tax can be claimed only for the same tax year in which the income in respect of the decedent must be included in the recipient's income. (This also is true for income in respect of a prior decedent.)

You can claim the deduction only as a miscellaneous itemized deduction on Schedule A (Form 1040). This deduction is not subject to the 2% limit on miscellaneous itemized deductions as discussed in chapter 30.

If the income in respect of the decedent is capital gain income, the gain must be reduced, but not below zero, by any estate tax deduction attributable to that gain when figuring the maximum capital gain tax, the 50% exclusion for gain on small business stock, or any net capital loss limitation.

For more information, see *Estate Tax Deduction* in Publication 559.

Explanation
The deduction for federal estate tax attributable to income in respect of a decedent is complex. The good news is that the question does not arise if there is no federal estate tax on the decedent's estate. If the amount that each individual can leave estate tax free—$675,000 in 2001 and $1,000,000 in 2002, which is equivalent to the unified credit, and the marital deduction—is large enough to eliminate any federal estate tax liability, there cannot be an income tax deduction for federal estate tax.

If the estate incurs federal estate tax, the recipient of income in respect of a decedent may be entitled to an itemized deduction on his or her income tax return.

To determine the amount that can be deducted, you must

first determine if the income and deductions in respect of the decedent result in net income. If so, you must then calculate the additional estate tax attributable to the net income in respect of the decedent.

To determine whether the items in respect of the decedent result in net income, you must deduct the total amount of deductions in respect of the decedent that appears on the estate tax return from the total amount of income in respect of the decedent that appears on that return. To calculate the additional estate tax, you must compare the actual estate tax with the estate tax that would have been paid if the net income in respect of a decedent had not been included. This amount is the deduction. The recipient's claim to the deduction is in the same proportion as his or her share in the total income in respect of the decedent.

Example

Assume that the estate tax return shows that the estate received salary income in respect of a decedent of $2,500 and had a deduction in respect of a decedent of $500 for unpaid real estate tax. The net of these two amounts is $2,000. Recomputation of the estate tax with $2,000 removed from the return shows that the estate tax caused by including these items is $740. If you, as one of two heirs of the estate, collect half of the $2,500 salary, you will be entitled to an income tax itemized deduction of half the $740, or $370.

5

Tax Withholding and Estimated Tax

Introduction

April 15 is the date by which most people file their income tax return for the previous year, but it is not the day most people actually pay their taxes. The bulk of your taxes is paid during the year, either by your employer's withholding money from your paycheck or by your making **estimated tax** *payments every quarter. The tax system operates on a pay-as-you-go policy, which generally requires that at least 90% of your tax liability be paid during the year.*

The tax law imposes severe penalties if you underwithhold or underpay your estimated taxes. Yet it is clearly not in your best interest to overwithhold or overpay estimated taxes, as the U.S. government does not pay interest on such overpayments. Therefore, it is essential that you estimate your tax liability as accurately as possible so that you neither underpay nor overpay your taxes. This chapter helps you do just that.

Salaries and wages are subject to withholding by your

employer regardless of the amount you are paid, the frequency of payment, or the form of payment. Nevertheless, you are entitled to reduce the amount of withholding by filing a completed Form W-4 with your employer. This form takes into account not only your marital status, personal **exemptions,** *and* **dependents,** *but also your estimated* **deductions** *and tax credits. Form W-4 may prove especially beneficial if you have large mortgage deductions or tax-shelter investments.*

*Estimated tax payments cover sources of income not subject to withholding—***self-employment** *income,* **interest, dividends, capital gains,** *and* **trust and estate** *income. While generally your tax withholding and estimated payments have to cover 90% of your tax liability for you to avoid paying some stiff penalties, this is not always the case. This chapter discusses all the important exceptions.*

Important Change for 2001

Estimated tax safe harbor for higher income taxpayers. For installment payments for tax years beginning in 2001, the estimated tax safe harbor for higher income individuals (other than farmers and fishermen) has been modified. If your adjusted gross income was more than $150,000 ($75,000 if you are married filing a separate return), you must have deposited

the smaller of 90% of your expected tax for 2001 or *110%* of the tax shown on your 2000 return to avoid an estimated tax penalty.

Important Changes for 2002

Tax law changes for 2002. When you figure how much income tax you want withheld from your pay and when you figure your estimated tax for 2002, consider tax law changes effective in 2002. See Publication 553, *Highlights of 2001 Tax Changes*.

TaxAlert

Refer to *Changes in the Tax Law You Should Know About* in the front of the book.

Certain withholding rates decreased. The withholding rates on the following items have been decreased.

1) **Gambling winnings.** The rate has decreased from 28% to 27%.
2) **Unemployment compensation.** The rate has decreased from 15% to 10%.
3) **Federal payments.** Withholding on certain federal payments is voluntary. The elective rates have been decreased to 7%, 10%, 15%, and 27%.
4) **Backup withholding.** The rate has decreased from 31% to 30%.
5) **Supplemental wages.** The rate has decreased from 28% to 27%.

Withholding on these items is discussed later in this chapter.

Important Reminders

Unemployment compensation. You can choose to have income tax withheld from your unemployment compensation. See *Unemployment Compensation* under *Withholding,* later, for more information.

Federal payments. You can choose to have income tax withheld from certain federal payments you get. These payments include social security and tier 1 railroad retirement benefits. For more information, see *Federal Payments* under *Withholding,* later.

Claiming withholding and estimated tax payments. When you file a federal income tax return, be sure to take credit for all federal income tax and excess social security or railroad retirement taxes withheld from your salary, wages, pensions, etc., and any backup withholding shown on Forms 1099. Also, take credit for all estimated tax payments you made for that year. For example, all estimated tax payments made for 2001 should be claimed on the tax return you file for the 2001 tax year. You should file a return and claim these credits even if you do not owe tax. See *Credit for Withholding and Estimated Tax,* later, in this chapter.

This chapter discusses how to pay your tax as you earn or receive income during the year. In general, the federal income tax is a pay-as-you-go tax. There are two ways to pay as you go.

* *Withholding.* If you are an employee, your employer probably withholds income tax from your pay. Tax may also be withheld from certain other income—including pensions, bonuses, commissions, and gambling winnings. In each case, the amount withheld is paid to the Internal Revenue Service (IRS) in your name.
* *Estimated tax.* If you do not pay your tax through withholding, or do not pay enough tax that way, you might have to pay estimated tax. People who are in business for themselves generally will have to pay their tax this way. You may have to pay estimated tax if you receive income such as dividends, interest, capital gains, rent, and royalties. Estimated tax is used to pay not only income tax, but self-employment tax and alternative minimum tax as well.

This chapter explains both of these methods. In addition, it explains:

* *Credit for withholding and estimated tax.* When you file your 2001 income tax return, take credit for all the income tax withheld from your salary, wages, pensions, etc., and for the estimated tax you paid for 2001, and
* *Underpayment penalty.* If you did not pay enough tax during the year either through withholding or by making estimated tax pay-

ments, you may have to pay a penalty. The IRS usually can figure this penalty for you. See *Underpayment Penalty* at the end of this chapter.

Useful Items

You may want to see:

Publication

- ☐ **505** Tax Withholding and Estimated Tax
- ☐ **553** Highlights of 2001 Tax Changes
- ☐ **919** How Do I Adjust My Tax Withholding?

Form (and Instructions)

- ☐ **W-4** Employee's Withholding Allowance Certificate
- ☐ **W-4P** Withholding Certificate for Pension or Annuity Payments
- ☐ **W-4S** Request for Federal Income Tax Withholding From Sick Pay
- ☐ **W-4V** Voluntary Withholding Request
- ☐ **1040-ES** Estimated Tax for Individuals
- ☐ **2210** Underpayment of Estimated Tax by Individuals, Estates, and Trusts

Withholding

This chapter discusses withholding on these types of income:

* Salaries and wages,
* Tips,
* Taxable fringe benefits,
* Sick pay,
* Pensions and annuities,
* Gambling winnings,
* Unemployment compensation, and
* Certain federal payments.

This chapter explains in detail the rules for withholding tax from each of these types of income.

This chapter also covers backup withholding on interest, dividends, and other payments.

Salaries and Wages

Income tax is withheld from the pay of most employees. Your pay includes your regular pay, bonuses, commissions, and vacation allowances. It also includes reimbursements and other expenses allowances paid under a nonaccountable plan. See *Supplemental Wages,* later, for more information about reimbursements and allowances paid under a nonaccountable plan.

Military retirees. Military retirement pay is treated in the same manner as regular pay for income tax withholding purposes, even though it is treated as a pension or annuity for other tax purposes.

Household workers. If you are a household worker, you can ask your employer to withhold income tax from your pay. Tax is withheld only if you want it withheld and your employer agrees to withhold it. If you do not have enough income tax withheld, you may have to make estimated tax payments, as discussed later under *Estimated Tax.*

Farmworkers. Income tax is generally withheld from your cash wages for work on a farm unless your employer both:

1) Pays you cash wages of less than $150 during the year, and
2) Has expenditures for agricultural labor totaling less than $2,500 during the year.

If you receive either noncash wages or cash wages not subject to withholding, you can ask your employer to withhold income tax. If your employer does not agree to withhold tax, or if not enough is withheld, you may have to make estimated tax payments, as discussed later under *Estimated Tax.*

Explanation
Generally, withholding is required on wages, regardless of the amount of wages paid, the frequency of payment, the form of payment (cash, check, stock, or other property), or the manner in which the wage is computed (hourly, weekly, yearly, or even as a percentage of employer profits).

For more information about household workers, see Chapter 41, *What to Do If You Employ Domestic Help.*

Determining Amount of Tax Withheld

The amount of income tax your employer withholds from your regular pay depends on two things.

1) The amount you earn.
2) The information you give your employer on **Form W-4.**

Form W-4 includes three types of information that your employer will use to figure your withholding.

1) Whether to withhold at the single rate or at the lower married rate.
2) How many withholding allowances you claim. (Each allowance reduces the amount withheld.)
3) Whether you want an additional amount withheld.

If your income is low enough that you will not have to pay income tax for the year, you may be exempt from withholding. This is explained under *Exemption From Withholding,* later.

Note. You must specify a filing status and a number of withholding allowances on Form W-4. You cannot specify only a dollar amount of withholding.

New job. When you start a new job, you must fill out Form W-4 and give it to your employer. Your employer should have copies of the form. If you need to change the information, you must fill out a new form.

If you work only part of the year (for example, you start working after the beginning of the year), too much tax may be withheld. You may be able to avoid overwithholding if your employer agrees to use the part-year method. See *Part-year method* in chapter 1 of Publication 505 for more information.

Changing your withholding. Events during the year may change your marital status or the exemptions, adjustments, deductions, or credits you expect to claim on your return. When this happens, you may need to give your employer a new Form W-4 to change your withholding status or number of allowances.

You ***must*** give your employer a new Form W-4 within 10 days after either of the following.

1) Your divorce, if you have been claiming married status.
2) Any event that decreases the number of withholding allowances you can claim.

Generally, you can submit a new Form W-4 whenever you wish to change the number of your withholding allowances for any other reason.

Changing your withholding for 2003. If events in 2002 will decrease the number of your withholding allowances for 2003, you ***must*** give your employer a new Form W-4 by December 1, 2002. If the event occurs in December 2002, submit a new Form W-4 within 10 days.

Explanation
You must file a new Form W-4 when it becomes reasonable for you to expect that the estimated deductions or credits you claim on your existing Form W-4 will be less than you anticipated. Conversely, you may file a new Form W-4 when it becomes reasonable to expect that your estimated deductions or credits will be more than you claim on your existing form. Examples of situations that might warrant that you file a new Form W-4 include (1) buying or selling a house, (2) refinancing or paying off a home mortgage, (3) moving to a different city, or (4) a substantial increase in medical costs.

Cumulative wage method. If you change the number of your withholding allowances during the year, too much or too little tax may have been withheld for the period before you made the change. You may be able to compensate for this if your employer agrees to use the cumulative wage withholding method for the rest of the year. You must ask in writing that your employer use this method.

To be eligible, you must have been paid for the same kind of payroll period (weekly, biweekly, etc.) since the beginning of the year.

Checking your withholding. After you have given your employer a Form W-4, you can check to see whether the amount of tax withheld from your pay is too little or too much. See *Getting the Right Amount of Tax Withheld,* later. If too much or too little tax is being withheld, you should give your employer a new Form W-4 to change your withholding.

Example
Tom is a bachelor living in an apartment. His annual income is $35,000, and he claims the standard deduction when he files his income tax return. He is currently claiming two allowances on his Form W-4. In March 2001, Tom buys a house. As a result of the increased deductions resulting from the purchase, he will itemize his deductions on his 2001 federal income tax return. He estimates that the deductions will total $11,500 and will be made up of mortgage interest, points, real estate tax, and state income tax. He revises his Form W-4 to reflect the change in his status to claim four allowances for the remainder of the year.

Note. You cannot give your employer either a payment to cover withholding for past pay periods or a payment for estimated tax.

Completing Form W-4

Form W-4 has worksheets to help you figure how many withholding allowances you can claim. The worksheets are for your own records. Do not give them to your employer.

You do not have to use the worksheets if you use a more accurate method of figuring the number of withholding allowances. See *Alternative method of figuring withholding allowances* under *Completing Form W-4 and Worksheets* in chapter 1 of Publication 505 for more information.

TAXPLANNER
The tax withheld from your salary or wage based on the revised Form W-4 that you file with your employer should be appropriate for your circumstances on an annual basis. However, the new withholding is effective only for pay periods after you file the form, and the total tax withheld for any given year may be significantly less than your actual tax liability. You should estimate your annual tax, as explained later in this chapter, and compare that estimate to the year-to-date tax withheld plus the amounts expected to be withheld based

on your revised Form W-4. If that comparison shows a substantial gap, it would be appropriate to file a new Form W-4, claiming fewer allowances or requesting a larger additional amount to be withheld in order to narrow that gap.

TaxPlanner

You are liable for severe penalties if you complete a Form W-4 with false information in an attempt to reduce your withholding below the amount you are legally allowed. The form should be filled out carefully and accurately so that the amount of your withholding is the least you are legally allowed but enough to avoid underpayment penalties.

On the other hand, contrary to the belief of many taxpayers, there is *not* a penalty for overwithholding. So much emphasis has been put on the accuracy of various worksheets that some taxpayers may have *increased* their withholding more than they actually want. If you are more comfortable claiming fewer exemptions than you are entitled to so that you can get a nice refund when you file your return, feel free to do so, but remember, it is like giving the government an interest-free loan during the year.

TaxPlanner

Your Form W-4 should be reviewed periodically as your sources and levels of income change and as your deductible expenses and credits increase or decrease.

Example 1
You have an estimated net loss from a partnership of $2,000, which you would report on Schedule E of your Form 1040. You are not required to make any payments of estimated tax. You may use your $2,000 partnership loss to figure the number of withholding allowances you may claim on your Form W-4.

Example 2
You have an estimated net loss from business of $3,000, which you would report on Schedule C. You would also otherwise be required to make payments of estimated tax on your alimony income of $3,000. You may not use your business loss to figure your withholding allowances.

Example 3
You have an estimated net loss from your farm of $5,000, which you would report on Schedule F. You would otherwise be required to make payments of estimated tax on rental income of $4,000. To figure your withholding allowances, you may include only $1,000 of your farm loss ($5,000 estimated net loss minus $4,000 income subject to estimated tax).

Example 4
You expect to have itemized deductions of $15,000, which you would report on Schedule A. You also expect to have $9,000 of self-employment income on which you would otherwise have to pay estimated tax. To figure your withholding allowances for Form W-4, you should include only $6,000 of your itemized deductions ($15,000 total itemized deductions minus the $9,000 self-employment income subject to estimated tax). This will, in effect, allow you to withhold through your salary any estimated tax due on your self-employment income. However, you will still be subject to self-employment tax on the $9,000 income.

Rules relating to when you may properly claim withholding allowances. For the purpose of figuring your withholding allowances for estimated deductions and estimated tax credits, *estimated* means the dollar amount of each item you reasonably expect to claim on your 2002 return. That dollar amount should be no more than the sum of the following:

1. The amount of each item shown or expected to be shown on your 2001 return that you also reasonably expect to show on your 2002 return
2. Additional amounts that you can determine for each item for 2002

Additional amounts that can be determined. These are amounts that are not included in (1) and that can be shown to result from identifiable events in 2001 or 2002. Amounts can be shown to result from identifiable events if the amounts relate to payments already made during 2002, to binding obligations to make payments (including payments of taxes) during 2002, and to other events or transactions that have been started and that you can prove at the time you file your Form W-4.

Amounts disallowed by the Internal Revenue Service. Generally, to figure your withholding allowances for 2002, you should not include any amount shown on your 2001 return that has been disallowed by the IRS. If you have not yet filed your 2001 return, you should not include any amount shown on your 2000 return that has been disallowed by the IRS.

Two jobs. If you have income from two jobs at the same time, complete only one set of Form W-4 worksheets. Then split your allowances between the Forms W-4 for each job. You cannot claim the same allowances with more than one employer at the same time. You can claim all your allowances with one employer and none with the other, or divide them any other way.

Example
Bill and Alice are married. Both are employed and expect to file a joint return. When they combine their expected salary and other income and then total their expected deductions and credits on a Form W-4 worksheet, they determine that they are entitled to claim 26 allowances. Bill and Alice must both file separate W-4 forms with their respective employers but may allocate the 26 allowances any way they like. Bill could claim 24 allowances and Alice could claim 2, for example, or each could claim 13 allowances.

Married individuals. If both you and your spouse are employed and expect to file a joint return, figure your withholding allowances using your combined income, adjustments, deductions, exemptions, and credits. Use only one set of worksheets. You can divide your total allowances any way, but you cannot claim an allowance that your spouse also claims.

If you and your spouse expect to file separate returns, figure your allowances separately based on your own individual income, adjustments, deductions, exemptions, and credits.

Personal allowances worksheet. Use the *Personal Allowances Worksheet* on page 1 of Form W-4 to figure your withholding allowances for exemptions and any special allowances that apply.

Example
John and Mary are married and plan to file a joint return. John's wages from his only employer are $55,000. Mary's

wages from her only employer are $1,000. Because Mary's wages are $1,000 or less, John may claim a special allowance.

Deductions and adjustments worksheet. Fill out this worksheet to adjust the number of your withholding allowances for deductions, adjustments to income, and tax credits. The *Deductions and Adjustments Worksheet* is on page 2 of Form W-4. Chapter 1 of Publication 505 explains this worksheet.

Two-earner/two-job worksheet. You may need to complete this worksheet if you have two jobs or a working spouse. You can also add to the amount, if any, on line 8 of this worksheet, any additional withholding necessary to cover any amount you expect to owe other than income tax, such as self-employment tax.

Getting the Right Amount of Tax Withheld
In most situations, the tax withheld from your pay will be close to the tax you figure on your return if you follow these two rules.

1) You accurately complete all the Form W-4 worksheets that apply to you.
2) You give your employer a new Form W-4 when changes occur.

But because the worksheets and withholding methods do not account for all possible situations, you may not be getting the right amount withheld. This is most likely to happen in the following situations.

- You are married and both you and your spouse work.
- You have more than one job at a time.
- You have nonwage income, such as interest, dividends, alimony, unemployment compensation, or self-employment income.
- You will owe additional amounts with your return, such as self-employment tax.
- Your withholding is based on obsolete Form W-4 information for a substantial part of the year.
- Your earnings are more than $150,000 if you are single or $200,000 if you are married.

To make sure you are getting the right amount of tax withheld, get Publication 919. It will help you compare the total tax to be withheld during the year with the tax you can expect to figure on your return. It also will help you determine how much additional withholding, if any, is needed each payday to avoid owing tax when you file your return. If you do not have enough tax withheld, you may have to make estimated tax payments, as explained under *Estimated Tax,* later.

TaxPlanner

In essence, overwithholding amounts to giving the government a portion of your salary as an interest-free loan. Nevertheless, underwithholding may subject you to stiff nondeductible penalties. It is therefore essential that you estimate your tax liability as accurately as possible so that you neither underwithhold nor overwithhold.

Rules Your Employer Must Follow
It may be helpful for you to know some of the withholding rules your employer must follow. These rules can affect how to fill out your Form W-4 and how to handle problems that may arise.

New Form W-4. When you start a new job, your employer should give you a Form W-4 to fill out. Your employer will use the information you give on the form to figure your withholding beginning with your first payday.

If you later fill out a new Form W-4, your employer can put it into effect as soon as possible. The deadline for putting it into effect is the start of the first payroll period ending 30 or more days after you turn it in.

No Form W-4. If you do not give your employer a completed Form W-4, your employer must withhold at the highest rate—as if you were single and claimed no allowances.

Repaying withheld tax. If you find you are having too much tax withheld because you did not claim all the withholding allowances you are entitled to, you should give your employer a new Form W-4. Your employer cannot repay any of the tax previously withheld.

However, if your employer has withheld more than the correct amount of tax for the Form W-4 you have in effect, you do not have to fill out a new Form W-4 to have your withholding lowered to the correct amount. Your employer can repay the amount that was incorrectly withheld. If you are not repaid, your Form W-2 will reflect the full amount actually withheld.

Exemption From Withholding
If you claim exemption from withholding, your employer will not withhold federal income tax from your wages. The exemption applies only to income tax, not to social security or Medicare tax.

You can claim exemption from withholding for 2002 only if *both* the following situations apply.

1) For **2001** you had a right to a refund of all federal income tax withheld because you had no tax liability.
2) For **2002** you expect a refund of all federal income tax withheld because you expect to have no tax liability.

Student. If you are a student, you are not automatically exempt. See chapter 1 to see whether you must file a return. If you work only part time or only during the summer, you may qualify for exemption from withholding.

Age 65 or older or blind. If you are 65 or older or blind, use one of the worksheets in chapter 1 of Publication 505, under *Exemption From Withholding,* to help you decide whether you can claim exemption from withholding. Do not use either of those worksheets if you will itemize deductions or claim exemptions for dependents or claim tax credits on your 2002 return. See *Itemizing deductions or claiming exemptions or tax credits* in Publication 505.

Claiming exemption from withholding. To claim exemption, you must give your employer a Form W-4. Print "EXEMPT" on line 7.

Your employer must send the IRS a copy of your Form W-4 if you claim exemption from withholding and your pay is expected to usually be more than $200 a week. If it turns out that you do not qualify for exemption, the IRS will send both you and your employer a written notice.

TaxPlanner

You should not be concerned if, by all reasonable expectations, your deductions and credits entitle you to 10 or more allowances, even though your employer must send a Form W-4 to the IRS. If you are entitled to 10 or more allowances, you should claim them. However, if you do claim 10 or more allowances, preserve your Form W-4 worksheets and supporting papers. They may be needed to satisfy the IRS that you are entitled to the allowances you are claiming.

If you claim exemption, but later your situation changes so that you will have to pay income tax after all, you must file a new Form W-4 within 10 days after the change. If you claim exemption in 2002, but you expect to owe income tax for 2003, you must file a new Form W-4 by December 1, 2002.

TaxSaver

Many students and retired persons who expect to have no federal income tax liability work part time in occupations in which they receive tips. To avoid unnecessary income tax withholding, you may file a Form W-4 with your employer, certifying that you had no federal income tax liability last year and expect to have none this year as well. Keep in mind that the exemption only applies to income tax withholding, not to Social Security or Medicare tax.

An exemption is good for only one year. You must give your employer a new Form W-4 by February 15 each year to continue your exemption.

Supplemental Wages
Supplemental wages include bonuses, commissions, overtime pay, and certain sick pay. The payer can figure withholding on supplemental wages using the same method used for your regular wages. If these payments are identified separately from your regular wages, your employer or other payer of supplemental wages can withhold income tax from these wages at a flat rate of 27%.

Expense allowances. Reimbursements or other expense allowances paid by your employer under a nonaccountable plan are treated as supplemental wages.

Reimbursements or other expense allowances paid under an accountable plan that are more than your proven expenses are treated as paid under a nonaccountable plan if you do not return the excess payments within a reasonable period of time.

For more information about accountable and nonaccountable expense allowance plans, see *Reimbursements* in chapter 28.

Penalties
You may have to pay a penalty of $500 if both of the following apply.

1) You make statements or claim withholding allowances on your Form W-4 that reduce the amount of tax withheld.
2) You have no reasonable basis for those statements or allowances at the time you prepare your Form W-4.

There is also a criminal penalty for willfully supplying false or fraudulent information on your Form W-4 or for willfully failing to supply information that would increase the amount withheld. The penalty upon conviction can be either a fine of up to $1,000 or imprisonment for up to one year, or both.

These penalties will apply if you deliberately and knowingly falsify your Form W-4 in an attempt to reduce or eliminate the proper withholding of taxes. A simple error—an honest mistake—will not result in one of these penalties. For example, a person who has tried to figure the number of withholding allowances correctly, but claims seven when the proper number is six, will not be charged a W-4 penalty.

Tips
The tips you receive while working on your job are considered part of your pay. You must include your tips on your tax return on the same line as your regular pay. However, tax is not withheld directly from tip income, as it is from your regular pay. Nevertheless, your employer will take into account the tips you report when figuring how much to withhold from your regular pay.

See chapter 7 for information on reporting your tips to your employer. For more information on the withholding rules for tip income, see Publication 531, *Reporting Tip Income.*

How employer figures amount to withhold. The tips you report to your employer are counted as part of your income for the month you report them. Your employer can figure your withholding in either of two ways.

1) By withholding at the regular rate on the sum of your pay plus your reported tips.

2) By withholding at the regular rate on your pay plus an amount equal to 27% of your reported tips.

Not enough pay to cover taxes. If your regular pay is too low for your employer to withhold all the tax (including social security tax, Medicare tax, or railroad retirement tax) due on your pay plus your tips, you can give your employer money to cover the shortage.

If you do not give your employer money to cover the shortage, your employer will first withhold as much social security tax, Medicare tax, or railroad retirement tax as possible, up to the proper amount, and then withhold income tax up to the full amount of your pay. If not enough tax is withheld, you may have to make estimated tax payments. When you file your return, you also may have to pay any social security tax, Medicare tax, or railroad retirement tax your employer could not withhold.

Allocated tips. Your employer should not withhold income tax, social security tax, Medicare tax, or railroad retirement tax on any allocated tips. Withholding is based only on your pay plus your *reported tips.* Your employer should refund to you any incorrectly withheld tax. See *Allocated Tips* in chapter 7 for more information.

Taxable Fringe Benefits

The value of certain fringe benefits you receive from your employer is considered part of your pay. Your employer generally must withhold income tax on these benefits from your regular pay for the period the benefits are paid or considered paid.

For information on fringe benefits, see *Fringe Benefits* under *Employee Compensation* in chapter 6.

Your employer can choose not to withhold income tax on the value of your personal use of a car, truck, or other highway motor vehicle provided by your employer. Your employer must notify you if this choice is made.

For more information on withholding on taxable fringe benefits, see chapter 1 of Publication 505.

Sick Pay

Sick pay is a payment to you to replace your regular wages while you are temporarily absent from work due to sickness or personal injury. To qualify as sick pay, it must be paid under a plan to which your employer is a party.

If you receive sick pay from your employer or an agent of your employer, income tax must be withheld. An agent who does not pay regular wages to you may choose to withhold income tax at a flat 27% rate.

However, if you receive sick pay from a third party who is not acting as an agent of your employer, income tax will be withheld only if you choose to have it withheld. See *Form W-4S,* later.

If you receive payments under a plan in which your employer does not participate (such as an accident or health plan where you paid all the premiums), the payments are not sick pay and usually are not taxable.

Union agreements. If you receive sick pay under a collective bargaining agreement between your union and your employer, the agreement may determine the amount of income tax withholding. See your union representative or your employer for more information.

Form W-4S. If you choose to have income tax withheld from sick pay paid by a third party, such as an insurance company, you must fill out Form W-4S, *Request for Federal Income Tax Withholding From Sick Pay.* Its instructions contain a worksheet you can use to figure the amount you want withheld. They also explain restrictions that may apply.

Give the completed form to the payer of your sick pay. The payer must withhold according to your directions on the form.

If you do not request withholding on Form W-4S, or if you do not have enough tax withheld, you may have to make estimated tax payments. If you do not pay enough estimated tax or have enough income tax withheld, you may have to pay a penalty.

Pensions and Annuities

Income tax usually will be withheld from your pension or annuity distributions, unless you choose not to have it withheld. This rule applies to distributions from:

- A traditional individual retirement arrangement (IRA),
- A life insurance company under an endowment, annuity, or life insurance contract,
- A pension, annuity, or profit-sharing plan,
- A stock bonus plan, and
- Any other plan that defers the time you receive compensation.

The amount withheld depends on whether you receive payments spread out over more than one year (periodic payments), within one year (nonperiodic payments), or as an eligible rollover distribution (ERD). You cannot choose not to have income tax withheld from an ERD.

Explanation
Nontaxable part. A part of your pension or annuity may not be taxable. See Chapter 11, *Retirement Plans, Pensions, and Annuities,* for information on figuring the nontaxable part. Income tax will not be withheld from the part of your pension or annuity that is nontaxable. Therefore, the tax withheld will be figured on, and cannot be more than, the taxable part.

TaxAlert

A distribution that is eligible for direct rollover treatment (see Chapter 11, *Retirement Plans, Pensions, and Annuities*) but is not directly rolled over is subject to mandatory 20% withholding unless the participant's eligible rollover distributions for the year are expected to be less than $200.

If a participant elects to have a portion of a distribution transferred in a direct rollover and the remainder distributed to him or her, only the portion that is distributed will be subject to the 20% withholding. A plan administrator will not be liable for tax, interest, or penalties for failure to withhold if he or she reasonably relied on information about the participant's plan received from the participant.

Note: Hardship distributions from qualified plans are not excluded from the mandatory 20% income tax withholding.

TaxPlanner

If property *other than cash* is distributed, withholding must still occur. However, if the distribution consists of cash or other property and securities of the company, withholding need not exceed the sum of the cash and fair market value of property received. Consequently, no mandatory withholding occurs where the distribution consists only of securities of the company.

TaxAlert

A written explanation of the direct rollover option and related rules (including the rules governing withholding) must generally be provided to participants not more than 90 days and not less than 30 days before the distribution date. For a series of periodic payments that are eligible for direct rollover, an initial timely notice must be given and an additional notice must be provided at least annually for as long as the payments continue.

Failure to provide such notice could cause the plan to become disqualified under the Internal Revenue Code. The IRS has issued a model notice that plan administrators are allowed to customize by deleting any portions that do not apply to the plan and adding additional information that is not inconsistent with the model notice.

Periodic Payments
Withholding from periodic payments of a pension or annuity is figured in the same way as withholding from salaries and wages. To tell the payer of your pension or annuity how much you want withheld, fill out **Form W-4P,** *Withholding Certificate for Pension or Annuity Payments,* or a similar form provided by the payer. Follow the rules discussed under *Withholding on Salaries and Wages,* earlier, to fill out your Form W-4P.

The withholding rules for pensions and annuities differ from those for salaries and wages in the following ways:

1. If you do not fill out a withholding certificate, tax will be withheld as if you were married and were claiming three withholding allowances.
2. Your certificate will not be sent to the IRS regardless of the number of allowances you claim on it.
3. You can choose not to have tax withheld, regardless of how much tax you owed last year or expect to owe this year. You do not have to qualify for exemption. See *Choosing Not to Have Income Tax Withheld,* later.
4. Tax will be withheld as if you were single and claiming no withholding allowances if:
   a) You do not give the payer your Social Security number (in the required manner), or
   b) The IRS notifies the payer, before any payment or distribution is made, that you gave it an incorrect Social Security number.

Note: Military retirement pay generally is treated in the same manner as wages and not as a pension or annuity for income tax withholding purposes. Military retirees should use Form W-4, not Form W-4P.

TaxAlert

If a series of periodic payments began prior to January 1, 1993, you determine whether post–December 31, 1992, payments are a series of substantially equal periodic payments over a specified period by taking into account all payments, including payments made before January 1, 1993. If the post–December 31, 1992, payments are not a series of substantially equal periodic payments, they will be subject to the direct rollover rules, including mandatory 20% withholding.

Nonperiodic Payments
Tax will be withheld at a 10% rate on any nonperiodic payments you receive.

Because withholding on nonperiodic payments does not depend on withholding allowances or whether you are married or single, you cannot use Form W-4P to tell the payer how much to withhold. But you can use Form W-4P to specify that an additional amount be withheld. You can also use Form W-4P to choose not to have tax withheld or to revoke a choice not to have tax withheld. See *Choosing Not to Have Income Tax Withheld,* later.

Note: The 10% rate of withholding on nonperiodic payments is less than the lowest tax rate (15%). Therefore, you may need to use Form W-4P to ask for additional withholding. If you do not have enough tax withheld, you may need to make estimated tax payments, as explained later.

Eligible Rollover Distributions

Distributions you receive that are eligible to be rolled over tax-free into qualified retirement or annuity plans are subject to a 20% withholding tax.

An *eligible rollover distribution (ERD)* is any distribution from a qualified pension or tax-sheltered annuity other than:

1. A minimum required distribution, or

2. One of a series of substantially equal periodic pension or annuity payments made over:
   a) Your life (or your life expectancy) or the joint lives of you and your beneficiary (or your life expectancies), or
   b) A specified period of 10 or more years.

The withholding rules for non-ERD distributions are discussed earlier under *Periodic Payments* and *Nonperiodic Payments.*

A distribution is subject to withholding if it is not substantially equal to the periodic payments.

For example, upon retirement you receive 30% of your accrued pension benefits in the form of a single-sum distribution with the balance payable in annuity form. The 30% distribution is an ERD subject to 20% withholding. The annuity payments are periodic payments subject to withholding only if you choose to have withholding taken out.

The payer of a distribution must withhold at a 20% rate on any part of an ERD that is not rolled over directly to another qualified plan. You cannot elect not to have withholding on these distributions.

If tax is withheld on the ERD, it will be withheld only on the taxable part. You must either:

1. Contribute to the new plan (within 60 days from the date of the distribution) an amount equal to the taxable part of the total ERD, including the amount withheld, or

2. Include in your income for the year of the distribution any amount withheld for which you did not make a matching contribution to the new plan.

The matching contribution to cover the withheld amount must be in addition to the rollover of all the taxable part that you actually received.

Therefore, if the amount you actually received is less than the taxable part of the ERD and you do not:

1. Roll over the entire amount received, and

2. Also contribute to the new plan an amount sufficient to bring the total of the rollover plus the additional amount contributed up to an amount equal to that taxable part,

you must include any difference in your income.

If the amount you actually received is more than the taxable part of the total ERD, you cannot roll over more than the taxable part. If you roll over an amount equal to the taxable part, you do not have to include any of the amount withheld in your income. If you roll over less than the taxable part, you must include in your income the difference between the amount you roll over and the taxable part.

Exception to withholding rule. The only way to avoid withholding on an ERD is to have it directly rolled over from the employer's plan to a qualified plan or IRA. This direct rollover is made only at your direction. You must first make sure that the receiving trustee agrees to accept a direct rollover. The transferor trustee must allow you to make such a rollover and provide to you, within a reasonable period of time, written instructions on how to do so. You must

also follow spousal consent and other participant and beneficiary protection rules.

TAXSAVER

If you receive an eligible rollover distribution from which the mandatory 20% withholding tax has been withheld, and you then decide you wish to roll the distribution over to an IRA within the allowed 60 days, you must come up with the 20% that was withheld from other funds within the 60-day period in order to roll the entire balance over. Otherwise the 20% that has been withheld will be treated as a taxable distribution and ineligible for rollover.

Choosing Not to Have Income Tax Withheld

You can choose not to have income tax withheld from your pension or annuity, whether the payments are periodic or nonperiodic. This rule does not apply to eligible rollover distributions. The payer will tell you how to make this choice. If you use Form W-4P, check the box on line 1 to make this choice. This choice will stay in effect until you decide you want withholding.

The payer will ignore your request not to have income tax withheld if:

1. You do not give the payer your Social Security number (in the required manner), or

2. The IRS notifies the payer, before any payment or distribution is made, that you gave it an incorrect Social Security number.

TAXPLANNER

You should choose to have no tax withheld from nonperiodic payments (total distributions within 1 year) from an employer pension or profit-sharing plan if you intend to defer taxation by putting the money directly into an Individual Retirement Arrangement (IRA).

If you choose not to have any income tax withheld from your pension or annuity, or if you do not have enough withheld, you may have to make estimated tax payments. See *Estimated Tax,* later.

If you do not pay enough tax through either estimated tax or withholding, you may have to pay a penalty. See *Underpayment Penalty,* later in this chapter.

Outside United States. If you are a U.S. citizen or resident alien and you choose not to have tax withheld from pension or annuity benefits, you must give the payer of the benefits a home address in the United States or in a U.S. possession. Otherwise, the payer must withhold tax. For example, the payer would have to withhold tax if you provide a U.S. address for a nominee, trustee, or agent to whom the benefits are to be delivered but do not provide your own home address in the United States or in a U.S. possession.

Revoking a choice not to have tax withheld. If you want to revoke your choice not to have tax withheld, the payer of your pension or annuity will tell you how. If the payer gives you Form W-4P, write "Revoked" by the checkbox on line 1 of the form.

If you get periodic payments and do not complete the rest of the form, the payer will withhold tax as if you were married and claiming three allowances. If you want tax withheld at a different rate, you must complete the rest of the form.

Notice required of payer. The payer of your pension or annuity is required to send you a notice telling you about your right to choose not to have tax withheld.

More information. For more information on taxation of annuities and distributions (including eligible rollover distributions) from qualified retirement plans, see chapter 11. For information on IRAs, see chapter 18. For more information on withholding on pensions and annuities, including a discussion of **Form W-4P,** see *Pensions and Annuities* in chapter 1 of Publication 505.

Gambling Winnings

Income tax is withheld from certain kinds of gambling winnings. For 2002, the amount withheld is 27% of the proceeds paid (the amount of your winnings minus the amount of your bet).

Gambling winnings of more than $5,000 from the following sources are subject to income tax withholding.

- Any sweepstakes, wagering pool, or lottery.
- Any other wager, if the proceeds are at least 300 times the amount of the bet.

It does not matter whether your winnings are paid in cash, in property, or as an annuity. Winnings not paid in cash are taken into account at their fair market value.

Gambling winnings from bingo, keno, and slot machines generally are not subject to income tax withholding. However, you may need to provide the payer with a social security number to avoid withholding. See *Backup withholding on gambling winnings* in Publication 505. If you receive gambling winnings not subject to withholding, you may need to make estimated tax payments. See *Estimated Tax,* later.

If you do not pay enough tax through withholding or estimated tax payments, you may be subject to a penalty. See *Underpayment Penalty,* later.

Form W-2G. If a payer withholds income tax from your gambling winnings, you should receive a Form W-2G, *Certain Gambling Winnings,* showing the amount you won and the amount withheld. Report the tax withheld on line 59 of Form 1040.

TAXPLANNER

Gambling losses are deductible, but only to the extent that you have gambling winnings to offset the losses and only if you itemize your deductions. It's very important to keep accurate records to document both your winnings and your losses.

Unemployment Compensation

You can choose to have income tax withheld from unemployment compensation. To make this choice, you will have to fill out **Form W-4V,** *Voluntary Withholding Request* (or a similar form provided by the payer) and give it to the payer. The amount withheld will be 10% of each payment.

Unemployment compensation is taxable. So, if you do not have income tax withheld, you may have to make estimated tax payments. See *Estimated Tax,* later.

If you do not pay enough tax either through withholding or estimated tax, you may have to pay a penalty. See *Underpayment Penalty,* later, for information.

Federal Payments

You can choose to have income tax withheld from certain federal payments you receive. These payments are:

1) Social security benefits,
2) Tier 1 railroad retirement benefits,
3) Commodity credit loans you choose to include in your gross income, and

4) Payments under the Agricultural Act of 1949 (7 U.S.C. 1421 et. seq.), or title II of the Disaster Assistance Act of 1988, as amended, that are treated as insurance proceeds and that you receive because:
   a) Your crops were destroyed or damaged by drought, flood, or any other natural disaster, or
   b) You were unable to plant crops because of a natural disaster described in (a).

To make this choice, you will have to fill out **Form W-4V,** *Voluntary Withholding Request,* (or a similar form provided by the payer) and give it to the payer. For 2002, you can choose to have 7%, 10%, 15%, or 27% of each payment withheld.

If you do not choose to have income tax withheld, you may have to make estimated tax payments. See *Estimated Tax,* later.

If you do not pay enough tax either through withholding or estimated tax, you may have to pay a penalty. See *Underpayment Penalty,* later, for information.

More information. For more information about the tax treatment of social security and railroad retirement benefits, see chapter 12. Get Publication 225, *Farmer's Tax Guide,* for information about the tax treatment of commodity credit loans or crop disaster payments.

Backup Withholding

Banks and other businesses that pay you certain kinds of income must file an information return (Form 1099) with the IRS. The information return shows how much you were paid during the year. It also includes your name and taxpayer identification number (TIN). TINs are explained in chapter 1.

These payments generally are not subject to withholding. However, "backup" withholding is required in certain situations. And, backup withholding can apply to most kinds of payments that are reported on Form 1099.

For 2002, the payer must withhold at a flat 30% rate in the following situations.

- You do not give the payer your TIN in the required manner.
- The IRS notifies the payer that the TIN you gave is incorrect.
- You are required, but fail, to certify that you are not subject to backup withholding.
- The IRS notifies the payer to start withholding on interest or dividends because you have underreported interest or dividends on your income tax return. The IRS will do this only after it has mailed you four notices over at least a 120-day period.

See *Backup Withholding* in chapter 1 of Publication 505 for more information.

Penalties. There are civil and criminal penalties for giving false information to avoid backup withholding. The civil penalty is $500. The criminal penalty, upon conviction, is a fine of up to $1,000, or imprisonment of up to one year, or both.

Estimated Tax

Estimated tax is the method used to pay tax on income that is not subject to withholding. This includes income from self-employment, interest, dividends, alimony, rent, gains from the sale of assets, prizes, and awards. You also may have to pay estimated tax if the amount of income tax being withheld from your salary, pension, or other income is not enough.

Estimated tax is used to pay both income tax and self-employment tax, as well as other taxes and amounts reported on your tax return. If you do not pay enough through withholding or by making estimated tax payments, you may be charged a penalty. If you do not pay enough by the due date of each payment period (see *When To Pay Estimated Tax,* later), you may be charged a penalty even if you are due a refund when you file your tax return. For information on when the penalty applies, see *Underpayment Penalty,* later.

Who Must Make Estimated Tax Payments?

If you had a tax liability for 2001, you may have to pay estimated tax for 2002.

General rule. You must make estimated tax payments for 2002 if both of the following apply.

1) You expect to owe at least $1,000 in tax for 2002 after subtracting your withholding and credits.
2) You expect your withholding and credits to be less than the smaller of:

- 90% of the tax to be shown on your 2002 tax return, or
- 100% of the tax shown on your 2001 tax return. Your 2001 tax return must cover all 12 months.

TaxAlert

For 2002, you can avoid underpayment penalties by calculating your estimated payments as 100% of your prior year's tax if your adjusted gross income (AGI) is $150,000 or less. If your AGI for 2001 is greater than $150,000, you must have 112% of your prior year's tax paid in. All taxpayers can avoid penalties for underpayment of tax if at least 90% of their *current* tax liability is paid through withholding and estimated tax payments.

Example

Tessa Lane's 2002 income tax liability is $45,000. Her adjusted gross income in 2001 was $140,000, while her 2001 tax liability was $30,000. Lane will avoid an underpayment penalty in 2002 if the total amount of tax withheld and estimated tax payments made for 2002 exceed 100% of her 2001 liability, or $30,000.

Special rules for farmers, fishermen, and higher income taxpayers. There are exceptions to the general rule for farmers, fishermen, and certain higher income taxpayers. See *Figure 5–A* and chapter 2 of Publication 505 for more information.

Aliens. Resident and nonresident aliens may also have to make estimated tax payments. Resident aliens should follow the rules in this chapter unless noted otherwise. Nonresident aliens should get **Form 1040-ES(NR)**, *U.S. Estimated Tax for Nonresident Alien Individuals.*

Avoiding estimated tax. If you receive salaries or wages, you can avoid having to make estimated tax payments by asking your employer to take more tax out of your earnings. To do this, file a new Form W-4 with your employer.

Estimated payments not required. You do not have to pay estimated tax for 2002 if you meet all three of the following conditions:

1) You had no tax liability for 2001.
2) You were a U.S. citizen or resident for the whole year.
3) Your 2001 tax year covered a 12-month period.

You had no tax liability for 2001 if your total tax was zero or you did not have to file an income tax return.

Married taxpayers. To figure whether you must make estimated tax payments, apply the rules discussed here to your separate estimated income. If you can make joint estimated tax payments, you can apply these rules on a joint basis.

You and your spouse can make joint estimated tax payments even if you are not living together.

You and your spouse cannot make joint estimated tax payments if:

1) You are legally separated under a decree of divorce or separate maintenance,
2) Either spouse is a nonresident alien, or
3) You and your spouse have different tax years.

Whether you and your spouse make joint estimated tax payments or separate payments will not affect your choice of filing a joint tax return or separate returns for 2002.

Figure 5–A. **Do You Have To Pay Estimated Tax?**

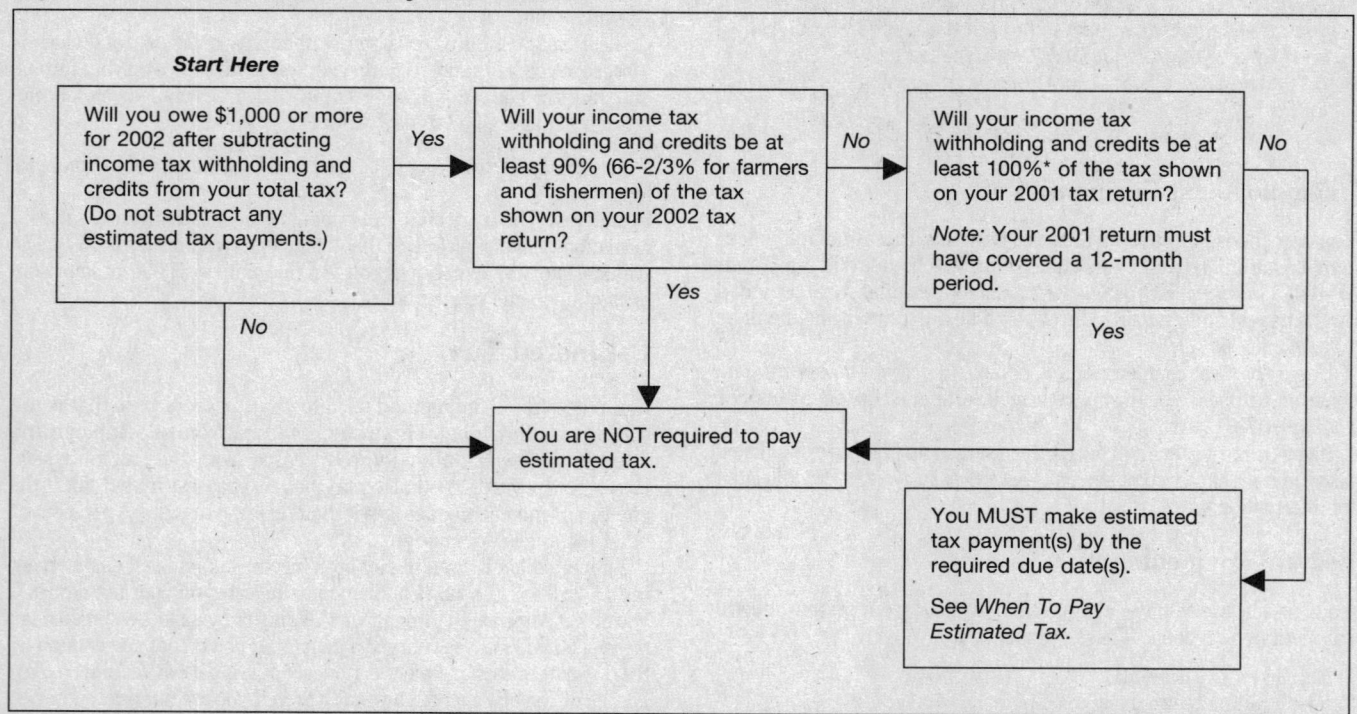

* 112% if less than two-thirds of your gross income for 2001 and 2002 is from farming or fishing and your 2001 adjusted gross income was more than $150,000 ($75,000 if your filing status for 2002 is married filing a separate return).

2001 separate returns and 2002 joint return. If you plan to file a joint return with your spouse for 2002, but you filed separate returns for 2001, your 2001 tax is the total of the tax shown on your separate returns. You filed a separate return if you filed as single, head of household, or married filing separately.

2001 joint return and 2002 separate returns. If you plan to file a separate return for 2002, but you filed a joint return for 2001, your 2001 tax is your share of the tax on the joint return. You file a separate return if you file as single, head of household, or married filing separately. To figure your share of the tax on the joint return, first figure the tax both you and your spouse would have paid had you filed separate returns for 2001 using the same filing status as for 2002. Then multiply the tax on the joint return by the following fraction:

$$\frac{\text{The tax you would have paid}}{\text{The total tax you and your spouse would}}$$
$$\text{had you filed a seperate return}$$
$$\text{have paid had you filed seperate returns}$$

Example. Joe and Heather filed a joint return for 2001 showing taxable income of $48,000 and a tax of $7,557. Of the $48,000 taxable income, $40,000 was Joe's and the rest was Heather's. For 2002, they plan to file married filing separately. Joe figures his share of the tax on the 2001 joint return as follows:

Tax on $40,000 based on a separate return	$8,172
Tax on $8,000 based on a separate return	1,204
Total	$9,376
Joe's percentage of total ($8,172 ÷ $9,376)	87%
Joe's share of tax on joint return ($7,557 × 87%)	$6,574

How To Figure Estimated Tax

To figure your estimated tax, you must figure your expected adjusted gross income, taxable income, taxes, deductions, and credits for the year.

When figuring your 2002 estimated tax, it may be helpful to use your income, deductions, and credits for 2001 as a starting point. Use your 2001 federal tax return as a guide. You can use Form 1040-ES to figure your estimated tax.

You must make adjustments both for changes in your own situation and for recent changes in the tax law. For 2002, there are several changes in the law. These changes are discussed in Publication 553, *Highlights of 2001 Tax Changes,* or visit the IRS Web Site at **www.irs.gov.**

Form 1040-ES includes a worksheet to help you figure your estimated tax. Keep the worksheet for your records.

For more complete information and examples of how to figure your estimated tax for 2002, see chapter 2 of Publication 505.

TAXPLANNER

A convenient way to figure your estimated tax is to list all your sources of income from last year. Then enter the estimated income from each source for *this* year. Add to this list all new sources of income that you expect this year. Repeat this procedure for all deductions and exemptions. If your itemized deductions are more than the standard deduction, use your itemized deductions. Then compute your estimated tax liability for 2002 based on your estimated taxable income.

After you have calculated your estimated tax liability, add any additional taxes, including self-employment taxes, that you expect to pay for the current year. Then subtract the var-

---

ious tax credits you expect to claim for the current year, and also subtract the income tax you expect to have withheld. The remaining tax liability is your estimated tax.

If your estimated tax exceeds $1,000, equal estimated tax payments generally have to be made on April 15, June 15, September 15, and January 15. Special exceptions, described later in this chapter, may reduce or eliminate this requirement.

When To Pay Estimated Tax

For estimated tax purposes, the year is divided into four payment periods. Each period has a specific payment due date. If you do not pay enough tax by the due date of each of the payment periods, you may be charged a penalty even if you are due a refund when you file your income tax return. The following chart gives the payment periods and due dates for estimated tax payments.

For the period:	Due date:
Jan. 1* through Mar. 31	April 15
April 1 through May 31	June 15
June 1 through Aug. 31	September 15
Sept. 1 through Dec. 31	January 15 next year**

*If your tax year does not begin on January 1, see *Fiscal year taxpayers,* later.
**See *January payment,* later.

Saturday, Sunday, holiday rule. If the due date for making an estimated tax payment falls on a Saturday, Sunday, or legal holiday, the payment will be on time if you make it on the next day that is not a Saturday, Sunday, or legal holiday. For example, a payment due Saturday, June 15, 2002, will be on time if you make it by Monday, June 17, 2002.

January payment. If you file your 2002 Form 1040 or Form 1040A by January 31, 2003, and pay the rest of the tax you owe, you do not need to make your estimated tax payment that would be due on January 15, 2003.

Fiscal year taxpayers. If your tax year does not start on January 1, see the Form 1040-ES instructions for your payment due dates.

When To Start

You do not have to make estimated tax payments until you have income on which you will owe the tax. If you have income subject to estimated tax during the first payment period, you must make your first payment by the due date for the first payment period. You can pay all your estimated tax at that time, or you can pay it in installments. If you choose to pay in installments, make your first payment by the due date for the first payment period. Make your remaining installment payments by the due dates for the later periods.

No income subject to estimated tax during first period. If you first have income subject to estimated tax during a later payment period, you must make your first payment by the due date for that period. You can pay your entire estimated tax by the due date for that period, or you can pay it in installments by the due date for that period and the due dates for the remaining periods. The following chart shows when to make installment payments.

If you first have income on which you must pay estimated tax:	Make a payment by:	Make later installments by:
Before Apr. 1	Apr. 15	June 15 Sep. 15 Jan. 15 next year*
After Mar. 31 and before June 1	June 15	Sep. 15 Jan. 15 next year*

| After May 31 and before Sept. 1 | Sep. 15 | Jan. 15 next year* |
| After August 31 | Jan. 15 next year* | (None) |

*See *January payment*, and *Saturday, Sunday, holiday rule* under *When to Pay Estimated Tax*, earlier.

Change in estimated tax. After making your first estimated tax payment, changes in your income, adjustments, deductions, credits, or exemptions may make it necessary for you to refigure your estimated tax. Pay the unpaid balance of your amended estimated tax by the next payment due date after the change or in installments by that date and the due dates for the remaining payment periods.

Example

In April 2002, John figured that his estimated tax for 2002 would be $12,000. Accordingly, he made his first 2002 quarterly estimated payment of $3,000 on April 15, 2002, and his second quarterly estimated payment of $3,000 on June 17, 2002. In August, John purchased a new home, and his monthly mortgage payments increased dramatically. Because John could deduct his mortgage interest payments, he reduced his third and fourth quarterly estimated payments due on September 16, 2002, and January 15, 2003, respectively.

How much to pay to avoid a penalty. To determine how much you should pay by each payment due date, see *How To Figure Each Payment*, next. If the earlier discussions of *No income subject to estimated tax during first period* or *Change in estimated tax* apply to you, you may need to read *Annualized Income Installment Method* in Publication 505, for information on how to avoid a penalty.

How To Figure Each Payment

You should pay enough estimated tax by the due date of each payment period to avoid a penalty for that period. You can figure your required payment for each period by using either the regular installment method or the annualized income installment method. These methods are described in Publication 505. If you do not pay enough each payment period, you may be charged a penalty even if you are due a refund when you file your tax return.

File Form 2210 to avoid a penalty. If your estimated tax payment for a previous period is less than one-fourth of your amended estimated tax, you may be charged a penalty for underpayment of estimated tax for that period when you file your tax return. To avoid the penalty, you must file Form 2210 with your 2002 tax return. You must also show that the total of your withholding and estimated tax payment for the period was at least as much as your annualized income installment. See chapter 4 of Publication 505 for more information.

Explanation

The discussion that follows shows in detail how to compute your annualized income installment.

Figure your installment for each payment period as follows:

1. Figure your adjusted gross income (AGI), alternative minimum taxable income (AMTI), and adjusted self-employment income (SEI) for the months in 2002 ending before the due date of the payment period. (Your AGI is your actual total taxable income minus your actual adjustments to income for the months in the period.)

2. Multiply each of the amounts in step (1) by
   a) 4, if the payment due date is April 15.
   b) 2.4, if the payment due date is June 17.
   c) 1.5, if the payment due date is September 16.
   d) 1, if the payment due date is January 15, 2003.
   These amounts are your annualized AGI, AMTI, and SEI.

3. Determine the greater of your
   a) Actual itemized deductions for the months in the period multiplied by the same figure used in step (2), or
   b) Standard deduction for the year.

4. Multiply your exemptions by the 2002 exemption amount.

5. Add the amounts from steps (3) and (4), and subtract the total from your annualized AGI determined in step (2). This amount is your annualized taxable income.

6. Figure the appropriate tax on your annualized taxable income [from step (5)], the alternative minimum tax on your annualized AMTI, and self-employment tax on SEI [from step (2)].

7. Total the amounts figured in step (6).

8. Add any additional taxes that you may owe because of events that occurred during the months in 2002 ending before the due date of the payment period. "Additional taxes" are the ones listed on lines 52–56 of the 2001 Form 1040.

9. Subtract from this total any nonrefundable credits that you may be able to claim because of events that occurred during the months in 2002 ending before the due date of the payment period. These are the credits that make up the total on line 50 of the 2001 Form 1040. If these credits are more than the total of step (7) plus additional taxes figured in step (8), use zero as the result and go on to the next step.

10. Add to the result of step (9) any of the taxes listed below that you may owe because of events that occurred during the months in 2002 ending before the due date of the payment period:
    a) Tax from recapture of an investment credit
    b) Tax on premature distributions from retirement plans (Form 5329, Part II only)
    c) Section 72 penalty taxes
    d) Excise tax on golden parachute payments

11. Add any advance earned income credit payments received during the months in 2002 ending before the due date of the payment period.

12. Subtract the following credits that apply to your situation for the months in 2002 ending before the due date of the payment period:
    a) Credit for federal tax on gasoline and special fuel
    b) Earned income credit

13. Multiply the result of step (12) by
    a) 22.5%, if the payment due date is April 15.
    b) 45%, if the payment due date is June 17.
    c) 67.5%, if the payment due date is September 16.
    d) 90%, if the payment due date is January 15, 2003.

14. Figure the total estimated tax you had to pay by the due date of each of the preceding payment periods. This is the total of the lower of the required installment or the annualized income installment for each payment period.

15. Subtract the step (14) amount from the step (13) amount.

If the annualized income installment for the payment period is less than the required installment, you only need to pay the annualized income installment.

When you pay the annualized income installment for the next payment period, you must add the difference between the required installment for that subsequent payment period (as increased) and the annualized income installment for the previous payment period to the required installment for the next payment period.

Estimated Tax Payments Not Required

You do not have to make estimated tax payments if your withholding in each payment period is at least one-fourth of your required annual payment or at least your required annualized income installment for that period. You also do not have to make estimated tax payments if you will pay enough through withholding to keep the amount you owe with your return under $1,000.

How To Pay Estimated Tax

There are five ways to pay estimated tax.

1) By crediting an overpayment on your 2001 return to your 2002 estimated tax.
2) By sending in your payment with a payment-voucher from **Form 1040-ES.**
3) By paying electronically using the Electronic Federal Tax Payment System (EFTPS).
4) By direct debit if you are filing Form 1040 or Form 1040A electronically.
5) By credit card using a pay-by-phone system.

Crediting an Overpayment

When you file your Form 1040 or Form 1040A for 2001 and you have an overpayment of tax, you can apply part or all of it to your estimated tax for 2002. On line 69 of Form 1040, or line 44 of Form 1040A, write the amount you want credited to your estimated tax rather than refunded. The amount you have credited should be taken into account when figuring your estimated tax payments.

You can use all the credited amount toward your first payment, or you can spread it out in any way you choose among any or all of your payments.

If you ask that an overpayment be credited to your estimated tax for the next year, the payment is considered to have been made on the due date of the first estimated tax installment (April 15 for calendar year taxpayers). You cannot have any of that amount refunded to you after that due date until the close of that tax year. You also cannot use that overpayment in any other way after that date.

Explanation
An overpayment that is applied to your estimated tax payment for the current year is considered to have been paid on time even if you are granted an extension and file your previous year's tax return after April 15.

Example
If you get a legal extension on your tax return from April 15 to August 15 and you actually file your return in July, you can apply any overpayment you may have made in the previous year to your estimated tax payments that were due on April 15 and June 15.

Using the Payment-Vouchers

Each payment of estimated tax must be accompanied by a payment-voucher from Form 1040-ES. If you made estimated tax payments last year, you should receive a copy of the 2002 Form 1040-ES in the mail. It will have payment-vouchers preprinted with your name, address, and social security number. Using the preprinted vouchers will speed processing, reduce the chance of error, and help save processing costs.

If you did not pay estimated tax last year, you will have to get a copy of Form 1040-ES from the IRS. After you make your first payment, a Form 1040-ES package with the preprinted vouchers will be mailed to you. Follow the instructions in the package to make sure you use the vouchers correctly.

Use the window envelopes that came with your Form 1040-ES package. If you use your own envelope, make sure you mail your payment-vouchers to the address shown in the Form 1040-ES instructions for the place where you live.

Caution. *Do not use the address shown in the Form 1040 or Form 1040A instructions.*

TaxPlanner

For a copy of Form 1040-ES, see Chapter 48, *2001 Federal Tax Forms and Schedules You Can Use.*

Explanation
The following explanation discusses in detail how to use the payment voucher:

1. Enter your Social Security number, name, and address on the voucher. If this information is preprinted on the voucher, make any corrections that are necessary. Use the preprinted voucher if you have one.

   If you are making joint estimated tax payments, your spouse's name and Social Security number should be included on the voucher. If you make joint payments and you have different last names, separate them with an "and"—for example, "John Brown and Mary Smith."
2. On the left side of the voucher, enter the amount you are paying. If you credited an overpayment on last year's return to your estimated tax for this year, subtract the amount of the overpayment that you want to apply to this payment from the amount you need to pay for the period. The result is the amount you should pay with the voucher. Enter only this amount on line 1 of the voucher. If the amount is zero, you do not have to send in a voucher.
3. Tear off the voucher at the perforation.
4. Enclose (but do not staple or otherwise attach) your check or money order with the voucher. Make your check or money order payable to the United States Treasury. Write your Social Security number and "2002 Form 1040-ES" on your check or money order.
5. Fill in the Record of Estimated Tax Payments on your Form 1040-ES package so that you will have a record of your payments.
6. Mail the voucher to the Internal Revenue Service Center for the place where you live. Use the addressed envelope that comes with your voucher or the address for your state shown in the Form 1040-ES package.

If you file a joint return and you are making joint estimated tax payments, please enter the names and social security numbers on the payment voucher in the same order as they will appear on the joint return. **Change of address.** You must notify the IRS if you are making estimated tax payments and you changed your address during the year. You must send a clear and concise written statement to the IRS Service Center where you filed your last return and provide all of the following:

- Your full name (and your spouse's full name),
- Your signature (and spouse's signature),
- Your old address (and spouse's old address if different),
- Your new address, and
- Your social security number (and spouse's social security number).

You can use Form 8822, *Change of Address,* for this purpose.

You can continue to use your old preprinted payment-vouchers until the IRS sends you new ones. However, **do not** correct the address on the old voucher.

Payment by Direct Debit or Credit Card

If you want to make estimated payments by direct debit or by credit card, see the Form 1040-ES instructions or *How To Pay Estimated Tax* in Publication 505.

Credit for Withholding and Estimated Tax

When you file your 2001 income tax return, take credit for all the income tax and excess social security or railroad retirement tax withheld from your salary, wages, pensions, etc. Also, take credit for the estimated tax you paid for 2001. These credits are subtracted from your tax. You should file a return and claim these credits, even if you do not owe tax.

If you had two or more employers and were paid wages of more than $80,400 during 2001, too much social security or railroad retirement tax may have been withheld from your wages. See *Credit for Excess Social Security Tax or Railroad Retirement Tax Withheld* in chapter 37.

Withholding

If you had income tax withheld during 2001, you should receive a statement by January 31, 2002, showing your income and the tax withheld. Depending on the source of your income, you will receive:

- Form W-2, *Wage and Tax Statement,*
- Form W-2G, *Certain Gambling Winnings,* or
- A form in the 1099 series.

Forms W-2 and W-2G. You file Form W-2 with your income tax return. File Form W-2G with your return if it shows any federal income tax withheld from your winnings.

You should get at least two copies of each form you receive. Attach one copy to the front of your federal income tax return. Keep one copy for your records. You should also receive copies to file with your state and local returns.

Example

Ted Taxpayer is employed by ABC Company, Inc. His Form W-2, box 2, reflects that he had $10,675.50 in federal tax withheld by ABC Company on wages of $46,958. His state income tax of $2,817.48 withheld for the state of Georgia is reflected in box 18 on the same amount of wages. Box 13 indicates (Code D—Code definitions can be found on the back of the W-2 form) that Ted contributed $2,546.21 to his company's 401(k) plan. That amount of income was not included in the federal or state wages, but it is included in determining how much was withheld from Ted's income for Social Security and Medicare purposes. Refer to boxes 3 and 5. The Social Security tax withheld is in box 4, and the Medicare tax withheld is in box 6. Box 14 shows any other deductions that were made from Ted's income and that he contributed $325.61 to the United Way. The pension plan box is checked in box 15 and lets Ted (and

the IRS) know that he is covered by a pension plan and therefore may be limited in his ability to make deductible IRA contributions.

Form W-2

Your employer should give you a Form W-2 for 2001 by January 31, 2002. You should receive a separate Form W-2 from each employer you worked for.

If you stop working before the end of the year, your employer can give you your Form W-2 at any time after you leave your job. However, your employer must give it to you by January 31 of the following year (or the next day that is not a Saturday, Sunday, or holiday if January 31 is a Saturday, Sunday, or holiday).

If you ask for the form, your employer must give it to you within 30 days after receiving your written request or within 30 days after your final wage payment, whichever is later.

If you have not received your Form W-2 by February 1, 2002, you should ask your employer for it. If you do not receive it by February 15, call the IRS.

Form W-2 shows your total pay and other compensation and the income tax, social security tax, and Medicare tax that was withheld during the year. Include the federal income tax withheld (as shown on Form W-2) on:

- Line 59 if you file Form 1040,
- Line 37 if you file Form 1040A, or
- Line 8 if you file Form 1040EZ.

Form W-2 is also used to report any taxable sick pay you received and any income tax withheld from your sick pay.

Form W-2G

If you had gambling winnings in 2001, the payer may have withheld 27 1/2% or 28% as income tax. If tax was withheld, the payer will give you a Form W-2G showing the amount you won and the amount of tax withheld.

Report the amounts you won on line 21 of Form 1040. Take credit for the tax withheld on line 59 of Form 1040. If you had gambling winnings, you must use Form 1040; you cannot use Form 1040A or Form 1040EZ.

The 1099 Series

Most forms in the 1099 series are not filed with your return. You should receive these forms by February 1, 2002. Keep these forms for your records. There are several different forms in this series, including:

- Form 1099-B, *Proceeds From Broker and Barter Exchange Transactions,*
- Form 1099-DIV, *Dividends and Distributions,*
- Form 1099-G, *Certain Government and Qualified State Tuition Program Payments,*
- Form 1099-INT, *Interest Income,*
- Form 1099-MISC, *Miscellaneous Income,*
- Form 1099-OID, *Original Issue Discount,*
- Form 1099-R, *Distributions From Pensions, Annuities, Retirement or Profit-Sharing Plans, IRAs, Insurance Contracts, etc.,*
- Form SSA-1099, *Social Security Benefit Statement,* and
- Form RRB-1099, *Payments by the Railroad Retirement Board.*

If you received the types of income reported on some forms in the 1099 series, you may not be able to use Form 1040A or Form 1040EZ. See the instructions to these forms for details.

Form 1099-R. Attach Form 1099-R to your return if box 4 shows federal income tax withheld. Include the amount withheld in the total on line 59 of Form 1040 or line 37 of Form 1040A. You cannot use Form 1040EZ if you received payments reported on Form 1099-R.

Backup withholding. If you were subject to backup withholding on income you received during 2001, include the amount withheld, as shown on your Form 1099, in the total on line 59 of Form 1040, or line 37 of Form 1040A.

Form Not Correct

If you receive a form with incorrect information on it, you should ask the payer for a corrected form. Call the telephone number or write to the address given for the payer on the form. The corrected Form W-2G or Form 1099 you receive will be marked "Corrected." A special form, Form W-2c, *Corrected Wage and Tax Statement,* is used to correct a Form W-2.

Form Received After Filing

If you file your return and you later receive a form for income that you did not include on your return, you should report the income and take credit for any income tax withheld by filing Form 1040X, *Amended U.S. Individual Income Tax Return.* See *Amended Returns and Claims for Refund* in chapter 1.

Separate Returns

If you are married but file a separate return, you can take credit only for the tax withheld from your own income. Do not include any amount withheld from your spouse's income. However, different rules may apply if you live in a community property state.

Community property states are listed in chapter 2. For more information on these rules, and some exceptions, see Publication 555, *Community Property.*

Fiscal Years

If you file your tax return on the basis of a fiscal year (a 12-month period ending on the last day of any month except December), you must follow special rules to determine your credit for federal income tax withholding. For a discussion of how to take credit for withholding on a fiscal year return, see *Fiscal Years* in chapter 3 of Publication 505.

> ### Explanation
> Employees on a fiscal year may suffer a delay in utilizing their credit from withheld taxes. See Chapter 43, *Foreign Citizens Living in the United States,* for an example.

Estimated Tax

Take credit for all your estimated tax payments for 2001 on line 60 of Form 1040 or line 38 of Form 1040A. Include any overpayment from 2000 that you had credited to your 2001 estimated tax. You must use Form 1040 or Form 1040A if you paid estimated tax. You cannot use Form 1040EZ.

Name changed. If you changed your name, and you made estimated tax payments using your old name, attach a brief statement to the front of your tax return indicating:

- When you made the payments,
- The amount of each payment,
- Which IRS address you sent the payments to,
- Your name when you made the payments, and
- Your social security number.

The statement should cover payments you made jointly with your spouse as well as any you made separately.

Separate Returns

If you and your spouse made separate estimated tax payments for 2001 and you file separate returns, you can take credit only for your own payments.

If you made joint estimated tax payments, you must decide how to divide the payments between your returns. One of you can claim all of the estimated tax paid and the other none, or you can divide it in any other way you agree on. If you cannot agree, you must divide the payments in proportion to each spouse's individual tax as shown on your separate returns for 2000.

Divorced Taxpayers

If you made joint estimated tax payments for 2001, and you were divorced during the year, either you or your former spouse can claim all of the joint payments, or you each can claim part of them. If you cannot agree on how to divide the payments, you must divide them in proportion to each spouse's individual tax as shown on your separate returns for 2001.

If you claim any of the joint payments on your tax return, enter your former spouse's social security number (SSN) in the space provided on the front of Form 1040 or Form 1040A. If you divorced and remarried in 2001, enter your present spouse's SSN in that space and write your former spouse's SSN, followed by "DIV," to the left of line 60, Form 1040, or line 38, Form 1040A.

Underpayment Penalty

If you did not pay enough tax either through withholding or by making estimated tax payments, you will have an underpayment of estimated tax and you may have to pay a penalty. Generally, you will *not* have to pay a penalty for 2001 if any of the following situations applies.

- The total of your withholding and estimated tax payments was at least as much as your 2000 tax (or 110% of your 2000 tax if your adjusted gross income was more than $150,000—$75,000 if your 2001 filing status is married filing separately) and you paid all required estimated tax payments on time.
- The tax balance due on your return is no more than 10% of your total 2001 tax, and you paid all required estimated tax payments on time.
- Your total 2001 tax minus your withholding is less than $1,000.
- You did not have a tax liability for 2000.
- You did not have any withholding taxes and your current year tax less any household employment taxes is less than $1,000.

Special rules apply if you are a farmer or fisherman. See *Farmers and Fishermen* in chapter 4 of Publication 505 for more information.

IRS can figure the penalty for you. If you think you owe the penalty but you do not want to figure it yourself when you file your tax return, you may not have to. Generally, the IRS will figure the penalty for you and send you a bill. However, you must complete Form 2210 and file it with your return if you are able to lower or eliminate your penalty. See chapter 4 of Publication 505.

> ### *TaxPlanner*
> The safest method of paying enough estimated tax and withholding, and thereby avoiding underpayment penalties, is to use last year's tax. The tax shown on your previous year's tax return less the tax that is expected to be withheld during the current year must be paid in estimated installments throughout the year.
>
> ### Example
> Elizabeth West's 2001 tax return indicates that her 2001 tax liability (including self-employment tax and alternative minimum tax) was $14,000. In 2002, Elizabeth estimates that her tax liability will jump to $24,000 due to several contemplated stock sales that should result in a substantial

capital gain. Elizabeth's withholding on her 2002 salary is expected to be $13,000.

Because her withholding of $13,000 during 2002 is not expected to exceed her 2001 tax of $14,000, she should increase her withholding by $1,000 during the year. Even though she will have paid less than 90% of her tax liability for 2002, she will avoid an underpayment penalty because she has paid an amount at least equal to her 2002 tax. If she made this determination early enough in the year, she could accomplish the same result by making four quarterly estimated tax payments of $250.

However, Elizabeth will have to pay an additional $10,000 ($24,000 – $14,000) when she files her 2002 tax return by April 15, 2003. Nevertheless, she will have had the use of this money from the time she sold her stock until the time she filed her 2002 tax return.

Explanation

Underpayment Penalties. You may be penalized for not paying enough tax for a particular installment period. The amount subject to the penalty is the amount by which the required installment, defined as the lesser of items 1 or 2 below, exceeds the amount paid for the quarterly period:

1. 90% of the tax shown on the return (after certain adjustments), allocated evenly to each of quarterly periods; or
2. 100% of the prior year's tax, allocated evenly to each of the quarterly periods (provided the prior year comprised 12 months and a return was filed for such year); if your 2000 adjusted gross income exceeds $150,000, you must pay 108.6% of the 2000 tax liability to avoid underpayment penalties for 2001; if your 2001 adjusted gross income exceeds $150,000, you must pay 112% of the 2001 liability to avoid underpayment penalties for 2002.

Example

Ms. Green's adjusted gross income in 2000 was $175,000, while her 2000 tax liability was $40,000. Her 2001 income tax liability is $55,000. Ms. Green will avoid an underpayment penalty in 2001 if the total amount of tax withheld and estimated tax payments exceeds 110% of her 2000 tax liability, or $44,000. To avoid a penalty in 2002, she would have to pay in $61,600 (112% of $55,000) since her adjusted gross income also exceeded $150,000 in 2001.

The underpayment penalty may also be avoided by using a special rule based on your annualized income. Under the special rule, no penalty is imposed for a quarter if the cumulative amount paid by the installment date equals or exceeds 90% of the cumulative estimated tax as computed on annualized income.

In general, the annualized method allows you to calculate your quarterly payment based on taxable income received up to the end of the latest quarter, annualized to a 12-month period. You can usually benefit from the annualized method if you do not receive your taxable income evenly throughout the year (e.g., if you are the owner of a ski shop that receives most of its revenue during the winter months).

The use of the methods for determining the underpaid amount, described above, may vary from quarter to quarter to provide the minimum underpayment amount by quarter. Remember, however, that if you pay the annualized income installment, you must add the difference between the amount you pay and the required installment to the required installment for the next period if the annualized income method is not used for the next period.

The tax computed for purposes of determining the quarterly payment required to avoid the underpayment penalty includes the self-employment tax and all other taxes (including the alternative minimum tax), minus any allowable credits.

If the amount paid for a quarterly period is greater than the amount required to avoid penalty, the excess is applied first against underpayments in prior quarters, and then against subsequent underpayments. Any penalty is assessed from the installment due date to the date paid or the original due date of the return, whichever is earlier. The rate of the penalty is the same as the rate of interest for underpayments of tax. However, the penalty is not compounded daily, whereas the interest is.

Special requirements and exceptions are provided for farmers, fishermen, and nonresident aliens.

TAXALERT

The underpayment of estimate tax penalty is not imposed where the total tax liability for the year, reduced by any withheld tax and estimated tax payments, is less than $1,000.

PART II

Income

The chapters in this part discuss many kinds of income. They explain which income is taxed and which is not. The following chart lists some of the topics covered in this part. It is divided into (1) items you generally must include in income and (2) items you generally do not include in income. See Chapters 14–17 for information on gains and losses that are reported on Schedule D (Form 1040). Casualty and theft losses are discussed in Chapter 27, *Casualty and Theft Losses.*

Chapters 18, 19, and 20 discuss three deductions that are used to figure adjusted gross income—the deduction for payments to an individual retirement arrangement (IRA), the deduction for moving expenses, and the deduction for alimony you pay. Other deductions used to figure adjusted gross income are the deductions for self-employment tax (see Chapter 24, *Taxes You May Deduct*), for the self-employed health insurance deduction (see Chapter 23, *Medical and Dental Expenses*), for payments to a Keogh retirement plan or self-employed SEP plan (see Chapter 11, *Retirement Plans, Pensions, and Annuities*), for a penalty on early withdrawal of savings (see Chapter 8, *Interest Income*), for the student loan interest deduction (see Chapter 25, *Interest Expense*), and for the medical savings account deduction (see Chapter 23, *Medical and Dental Expenses*).

INCOME

INCOME GENERALLY INCLUDES:

Alimony (Chapter 13, *Other Income*)

Bartering income (Chapter 13, *Other Income*)

Cancelled debt income (Chapter 13, *Other Income*)

Dividends (Chapter 9, *Dividends and Other Corporate Distributions*)

Gain on the sale of personal items, such as a car (Chapter 13, *Other Income*)

Gambling winnings (Chapter 13, *Other Income*)

Income from an activity not for profit (Chapter 13, *Other Income*)

Interest (Chapter 8, *Interest Income*)

Part of Social Security benefits and equivalent railroad retirement benefits (Chapter 12, *Social Security and Equivalent Railroad Retirement Benefits*)

Pensions and annuities (Chapter 11, *Retirement Plans, Pensions, and Annuities*)

Recoveries of amounts previously deducted (Chapter 13, *Other Income*)

Rental income (Chapter 10, *Rental Income and Expenses*)

Royalties (Chapter 13, *Other Income*)

Tips (Chapter 7, *Tip Income*)

Wages, salaries, and other earnings (Chapter 6, *Wages, Salaries, and Other Earnings*)

Your share of estate and trust income (Chapter 13, *Other Income*)

Your share of partnership and S Corporation income (Chapter 13, *Other Income*)

INCOME GENERALLY DOES NOT INCLUDE:

Accident and health insurance proceeds (Chapter 13, *Other Income*)

Gifts and inheritances (Chapter 13, *Other Income*)

Housing allowance for members of the clergy (Chapter 6, *Wages, Salaries, and Other Earnings*)

Interest on state and local government obligations (Chapter 8, *Interest Income*)

Life insurance proceeds (Chapter 13, *Other Income*)

Military allowances (Chapter 6, *Wages, Salaries, and Other Earnings*)

Part of scholarship and fellowship grants (Chapter 13, *Other Income*)

Part of Social Security benefits and equivalent railroad retirement benefits (Chapter 12, *Social Security and Equivalent Railroad Retirement Benefits*)

Veterans' benefits (Chapter 6, *Wages, Salaries, and Other Earnings*)

Welfare and other public assistance benefits (Chapter 13, *Other Income*)

Workers' compensation and similar payments for sickness and injury (Chapter 13, *Other Income*)

6

Wages, Salaries, and Other Earnings

Introduction

Ask most people how much they get paid, and, if they are willing to admit anything, they'll tell you what their salary is. Usually, there's more to income than that. The way the IRS sees it, "gross income means all income from whatever source derived." That means that not only is your salary subject to tax but so also are many of the fringe benefits that you might receive—everything from country club membership and employer-provided discounts to a company car. This chapter spells out in greater detail items of compensation that are taxable.

Some fringe benefits you receive from your employer are tax-free. For example, the cost of the first $50,000 of coverage in a group term life insurance plan will be tax-free if all employees in the plan are treated in the same way. And, if your employer, in a moment of detached and disinterested generosity, presents you with a Rolls-Royce as a gift, there's a chance that you will not have to pay taxes on it. This chapter prepares you—in a tax sense—for that golden moment.

Important Reminder

Foreign income. If you are a U.S. citizen or resident alien, you must report income from sources outside the United States (foreign income) on your tax return unless it is exempt by U.S. law. This is true whether you reside inside or outside the United States and whether or not you receive a Form W-2, *Wage and Tax Statement,* or Form 1099 from the foreign payer. This applies to earned income (such as wages and tips) as well as unearned income (such as interest, dividends, capital gains, pensions, rents, and royalties).

If you reside outside the United States, you may be able to exclude part or all of your foreign source earned income. For details, see Publication 54, *Tax Guide for U.S. Citizens and Resident Aliens Abroad.*

This chapter discusses wages, salaries, fringe benefits, and other compensation received for services as an employee. The topics include:

- Bonuses and awards,
- Sickness and injury benefits, and
- Special rules for certain employees.

The chapter explains what income is included in the employee's gross income and what is not included.

Explanation
One of the most important decisions you have to make in determining your correct taxable income is what payments to include. A taxable payment is not limited to cash. It may be property, stock, or other **assets.** Also, you must include in your gross income the fair market value of payments in kind.

Example 1
Your employer provides you with a car that is used for both personal and business purposes. The value of the personal use of the car is included in earnings and it is taxable to you.

Example 2
You assist a group of investors in purchasing a piece of **real estate.** In consideration of your services, the investors award you an unconditional percentage of ownership in the acquired asset. You have invested none of your personal funds. The fair market value of your ownership interest is considered as wages taxable to you in the year the transfer is completed.

Example 3
A farmer receives 50 bushels of wheat as a payment in kind. Unless specifically excluded under a government program, the farmer has income to the extent of the fair market value of the wheat.

Useful Items

You may want to see:

Publication

☐ **463**   Travel, Entertainment, Gift, and Car Expenses
☐ **503**   Child and Dependent Care Expenses
☐ **505**   Tax Withholding and Estimated Tax
☐ **525**   Taxable and Nontaxable Income

Explanation
Other useful publications and references include:
■ 15, Circular E, Employer's Tax Guide; Chapter 5. Wages and Other Compensation
■ 15-A, Employer's Supplemental Tax Guide; Chapter 6. Employee Fringe Benefits
■ 15-B, Employer's Tax Guide to Fringe Benefits; Chapter 1—Fringe Benefits Overview
■ 17, Your Federal Income Tax; Chapter 6—Wages, Salaries, and Other Earnings
These and other IRS publications are available online at www.irs.gov

Employee Compensation

This section discusses many types of employee compensation followed by a detailed explanation of fringe benefits.

Explanation
All compensation for personal services, no matter what the form of payment, must be included in gross income. Such compensation is subject to taxes in the year received, unless the taxpayer reports income on the accrual basis.

If you perform services and decide that payment for them should be made to another person, the monies remitted to the third party are taxable to you. The IRS and the courts have long held that "fruits" of a taxpayer's labor are attributable to the "tree" that grew them.

Furthermore, you may not render services and then ask your employer to hold the funds in an attempt to control artificially when the wages will be included in your taxable income.

Example
You are due compensation for work you performed. You advise the payer to hold the money because you will not require the funds immediately. The payer credits the payment due you on the company books. You do not request the money until after the close of the tax year in which the services were rendered.

The IRS may hold that you were in **constructive receipt** of the funds before year's end. The compensation may have to be included in your income for the year in which the payment could have been received, even though you were not actually paid until later.

TAXPLANNER
You will have a problem with the IRS if you ask your employer *after* you have performed the work to withhold funds in an attempt to control artificially when the wages will be included in your taxable income. If you make arrangements to defer receipt of income *prior* to commencing work, you will not have a problem.

However, if your employer forces you to take your bonus in a later year, then it is not taxable to you until the year in which you receive it.

Example
If at the beginning of the year you arrange to have your employer pay you your year-end bonus over a 5-year period, the IRS will not claim that you were in constructive receipt of the entire bonus at year's end. You may even arrange to have your employer add interest to your deferred bonus. You must, however, make these arrangements prior to performance of the work for which the bonus will be paid.

If you are an employee, you should receive Form W-2 from your employer showing the pay you received for your services. Include your pay on line 7 of Form 1040 or Form 1040A, or on line 1 of Form 1040EZ, even if you do not receive a Form W-2.

Child-care providers. If you provide child care, either in the child's home or in your home or other place of business, the pay you receive must be included in your income. If you are not an employee, you are probably self-employed and must include payments for your services on Schedule C (Form 1040), *Profit or Loss From Business,* or Schedule C-EZ (Form 1040), *Net Profit From Business.* You are generally not an employee unless you are subject to the will and control of the person who employs you as to what you are to do and how you are to do it.

Baby sitting. If you baby sit for relatives or neighborhood children, whether on a regular basis or only periodically, the rules for child-care providers apply to you.

Miscellaneous Compensation

This section discusses many types of employee compensation. The subjects are arranged in alphabetical order.

Advance commissions and other earnings. If you receive advance commissions or other amounts for services to be performed in the future and you are a cash method taxpayer, you must include these amounts in your income in the year you receive them.

If you repay unearned commissions or other amounts in the same year you receive them, reduce the amount included in your income by the repayment. If you repay them in a later tax year, you can deduct the repayment as an itemized deduction on your Schedule A (Form 1040), or you may be able to take a credit for that year. See *Repayments* in chapter 13.

Explanation
In some cases, an advance payment of a commission or salary may be considered a loan, thus permitting you to delay paying tax on that amount. If the loan is repaid, you will not have to recognize any taxable income. If the loan is forgiven,

you will recognize the amount of the loan as compensation in the year in which it was forgiven. See *Canceled Debts* in Chapter 13, *Other Income*, for a complete discussion. Commissions and salaries are considered to be income when they are paid to you or when they are applied as a reduction to your loan account.

The key question is: When may a payment be characterized as a loan? Generally, for a transaction to be considered a loan, a debtor-creditor relationship must exist at the outset. In other words, the lending party expects and will eventually receive monetary repayment. Payment in return for a future obligation to render services is *not* a loan. Thus, an advance on your wages is not a loan. Whether a payment is or is not a loan is usually a question of fact, requiring a review of each case's unique circumstances.

Example
If you receive an advance of your January 2002 salary on December 31, 2001, you will have taxable income in 2001.

TaxSaver
Generally, you should take advantage of your employer's 401(k) plan or 403(b) plan. Your contribution to the plan will not be included in your taxable wages. See Chapter 11, *Retirement Plans, Pensions, and Annuities,* for more information about these plans.

TaxPlanner
You may wish to consider a loan from your employer's qualified pension or annuity plan rather than an advance on your next year's salary. Loans are not considered taxable income to the borrower under most circumstances. See Chapter 11, *Retirement Plans, Pensions, and Annuities,* for rules regarding loans from an employer's qualified pension or annuity plan.

TaxAlert: The 2001 Tax Act
Beginning in year 2002, owners-employees such as S corporation shareholders, partners, and sole proprietors will be able to borrow from their pension plans without being subject to a penalty tax.

Allowances and reimbursements. If you receive travel, transportation, or other business expense allowances or reimbursements from your employer, get Publication 463. If you are reimbursed for moving expenses, get Publication 521, *Moving Expenses.*
Back pay awards. Include in income amounts you are awarded in a settlement or judgment for back pay. These include payments made to you for damages, unpaid life insurance premiums, and unpaid health insurance premiums. They should be reported to you by your employer on Form W-2.

Explanation
If you received an amount in settlement or judgment for back wages and liquidated damages (e.g., under Title VII as amended by the 1991 Civil Rights Act), see *Court Awards and Damages* in Chapter 13, *Other Income*. Generally, awards intended to replace lost wages are included in your taxable income. However, in certain circumstances all or a portion of the award may be excludable from your taxable income.

TaxPlanner
Prior to entering any settlement agreement, you should consult with a tax advisor to ensure that you negotiate the most tax-favorable terms.

Bonuses and awards. Bonuses or awards you receive for outstanding work are included in your income and should be shown on your Form W-2. These include prizes such as vacation trips for meeting sales goals. If the prize or award you receive is goods or services, you must include the fair market value of the goods or services in your income. However, if your employer merely promises to pay you a bonus or award at some future time, it is not taxable until you receive it or it is made available to you.

Employee achievement award. If you receive tangible personal property (other than cash, a gift certificate, or an equivalent item) as an award for length of service or safety achievement, you can generally exclude its value from your income. However, the amount you can exclude is limited to your employer's cost and cannot be more than $1,600 ($400 for awards that are not qualified plan awards) for all such awards you receive during the year. Your employer can tell you whether your award is a qualified plan award. Your employer must make the award as part of a meaningful presentation, under conditions and circumstances that do not create a significant likelihood of it being disguised pay.

However, the exclusion does not apply to the following awards.

- A length-of-service award if you received it for less than 5 years of service or if you received another length-of-service award during the year or the previous 4 years.
- A safety achievement award if you are a manager, administrator, clerical employee, or other professional employee or if more than 10% of eligible employees previously received safety achievement awards during the year.

Example. Ben Green received three employee achievement awards during the year: a nonqualified plan award of a watch valued at $250, and two qualified plan awards of a stereo valued at $1,000 and a set of golf clubs valued at $500. Assuming that the requirements for qualified plan awards are otherwise satisfied, each award by itself would be excluded from income. However, since the $1,750 total value of the awards is more than $1,600, Ben must include $150 ($1,750 − $1,600) in his income.
Government cost-of-living allowances. Cost-of-living allowances are generally included in your income. However, they are not included in your income if you are a federal civilian employee or a federal court employee who is stationed in Alaska, Hawaii, or outside the United States.

Allowances and differentials that increase your basic pay as an incentive for taking a less desirable post of duty are part of your compensation and must be included in income. For example, your compensation includes Foreign Post, Foreign Service, and Overseas Tropical differentials. For more information, get Publication 516, *U.S. Government Civilian Employees Stationed Abroad.*

Explanation
Government cost-of-living allowances paid to federal civilian employees are tax-exempt only for those employees whose compensation is set by statute.

Note received for services. If your employer gives you a secured note as payment for your services, you must include the fair market value (usually the discount value) of the note in your income for the year you receive it. When you later receive payments on the note, a proportionate part of each payment is the recovery of the fair market value that you previously included in your income. Do not include that part again in your income. Include the rest of the payment in your income in the year of payment.

If your employer gives you an unsecured note as payment for your services, payments on the note that are credited toward the principal amount of the note are compensation income when you receive them.

Retirement plan contributions. Generally, you must include in income amounts you pay into a retirement plan through payroll deductions. You recover your contributions tax free when you retire and receive benefits from the plan. See chapter 11 for more information about the tax treatment of retirement plan benefits.

Employer's contributions to qualified plan. Your employer's contributions to a qualified retirement plan for you are not included in income at the time contributed. (Your employer can tell you whether your retirement plan is qualified.) However, the cost of life insurance coverage included in the plan may have to be included. See *Group-Term Life Insurance Premiums,* later, under *Fringe Benefits.*

Elective deferrals. If you chose to set aside part of your pay for retirement under a qualified deferred compensation arrangement (for example, a section 401(k) plan), the amount you set aside (called an elective deferral) is treated as an employer contribution to a qualified plan, subject to a limit. For 2001, this limit is $10,500 for all elective deferrals. If you set aside more than $10,500, the excess must be included in your income for that year. See Publication 525 for a discussion of the tax treatment of corrective distributions of excess deferrals.

TaxAlert: The 2001 Tax Act

The current $10,500 limit on contributions to 401(k) plans is increased to $11,000 in 2002. This limit is increased by $1,000 each year until the limit reaches $15,000 in 2006. Thereafter, the limit is indexed for inflation.

Elective deferrals are not excluded from wages for social security and Medicare taxes and benefits.

If you are a federal employee, this treatment applies to your contributions to the Thrift Savings Plan.

Employer's contributions to nonqualified plan. If your employer pays into a nonqualified plan for you, you generally must include the contributions in your income as wages for the tax year in which the contributions are made. However, if your interest in the plan is subject to a substantial risk of forfeiture (meaning you have a good chance of losing it) at the time of contribution, do not include the value of your interest in your income until it is no longer subject to a substantial risk of forfeiture.

Explanation

Under a *qualified plan,* participating employees may defer taxation on an employer's contributions into their individual accounts or for their vested benefits in qualified plans until some future date of distribution. Additionally, the tax on the income the account generates may be deferred until the money is distributed to the employee.

The same deferred taxation is allowed under a *nonqualified plan* as long as the employee's interest in the plan is not transferable and is subject to substantial risk of forfeiture. However, when either of these restrictions is no longer met, the value of the account will immediately become taxable to the employee. (Whether a plan is qualified or nonqualified depends on whether or not certain statutory requirements are satisfied.)

See Chapter 11, *Retirement Plans, Pensions, and Annuities,* for suggestions about what to do when you receive distributions from qualified plans.

Severance pay. Amounts you receive as severance pay are taxable. A lump-sum payment for cancellation of your employment contract must be included in your income in the tax year you receive it.

Accrued leave payment. If you are a federal employee and receive a lump-sum payment for accrued annual leave when you retire or resign, this amount will be included as wages on your Form W-2.

If you resign from one agency and are reemployed by another agency, you may have to repay part of your lump-sum annual leave payment to the second agency. You can reduce gross wages by the amount you repaid in the same tax year in which you received it. Attach to your tax return a copy of the receipt or statement given to you by the agency you repaid to explain the difference between the wages on the return and the wages on your Forms W-2.

Outplacement services. If you choose to accept a reduced amount of severance pay so that you can receive outplacement services (such as training in resumé writing and interview techniques), you must include the unreduced amount of the severance pay in income.

However, you can deduct the value of these outplacement services (up to the difference between the severance pay included in income and the amount actually received) as a miscellaneous deduction (subject to the 2% limit) on Schedule A (Form 1040).

Sick pay. Pay you receive from your employer while you are sick or injured is part of your salary or wages. In addition, you must include in your income sick pay benefits received from any of the following payers.

1) A welfare fund.
2) A state sickness or disability fund.
3) An association of employers or employees.
4) An insurance company, if your employer paid for the plan.

However, if you paid the premiums on an accident or health insurance policy, the benefits you receive under the policy are not taxable.

Social security and Medicare taxes paid by employer. If you and your employer have an agreement that your employer pays your social security and Medicare taxes without deducting them from your gross wages, you must report the amount of tax paid for you as taxable wages on your tax return. The payment is also treated as wages for figuring your social security and Medicare taxes and your social security and Medicare benefits. However, these payments are not treated as social security and Medicare wages if you are a household worker or a farm worker.

Stock appreciation rights. Do not include a stock appreciation right granted by your employer in income until you exercise (use) the right. When you use the right, you are entitled to a cash payment equal to the fair market value of the corporation's stock on the date of use minus the fair market value on the date the right was granted. You include the cash payment in your income in the year you use the right.

Explanation

Stock appreciation rights (SARs) are rights awarded to an employee by a corporation that enable the employee to benefit over a certain period of time from the appreciation in value of the employer's stock without the employee actually owning the stock.

Example

You are given 10 SARs when your company's stock is valued at $25 per share. You may exercise your SARs at any time during a 24-month period. In the first 6 months after the SARs are awarded, the company's stock rises to $50 per share. However, you do not exercise your SARs because you expect the stock to continue to appreciate in value. Even though you have an unrealized gain of $250 [($50 less $25) × 10 SARs], you do not include it in gross income because the SARs have not been exercised.

Eighteen months after the SARs are issued, the company stock is selling for $85 per share. You exercise your SARs, and the company pays you $600 [($85 less $25) × 10 SARs]. The $600 gain must now be included in your gross income.

Stock options. If you receive a nonstatutory option to buy or sell stock or other property as payment for your services, you will usually have income either when you receive the option or when you exercise the option (use it to buy or sell the stock or other property). However, if your option is a statutory stock option, you usually will not have any income until you sell or exchange your stock. Your employer can tell you which kind of option you hold. For details, get Publication 525.

Explanation
A stock option gives you the right to buy a company's stock at a specified price within a designated time period. Generally, stock options are awarded to you by your employer as an alternative method of compensation. The option itself is not taxed when it is granted to you. The amount of income and the year when it is included in your taxable income depend on the type of option granted. There are two basic types of stock options: nonqualified stock options and incentive stock options.

Nonqualified stock options. Generally, nonqualified stock options are those *not accorded* favorable or preferred tax treatment by a specific provision of the Internal Revenue Code.

A nonqualified stock option is not taxable to you at the time the option is granted, unless the *option* is traded through a public stock exchange. Rather, you are taxed when the option is exercised on the difference between the fixed option price and the fair market value of the stock on the date you exercise your option. This amount is taxed at ordinary income rates. The basis of the stock received is generally its fair market value on the date you exercise the option. If the stock appreciates thereafter, that gain will be taxable as a capital gain when you sell it.

An advantage of the nonqualified stock option is that you do not have to invest any personal funds when the option is granted or while the option is outstanding. However, if you decide to exercise the option, you will need funds to pay the option price *and* the income tax that will be levied on your gain.

Incentive stock options. Generally, incentive stock options enable you to take advantage of a specific provision of the Internal Revenue Code.

Incentive stock options are not taxable to you at the time the option is granted, nor do you pay tax when the option is exercised. Furthermore, if you do not dispose of the stock within 2 years after the option is granted, and you hold the stock for over 12 months after you exercise the option, any gain will be taxed as a long-term capital gain. However, if you sell the stock within 1 year after the date you exercised the option, the stock loses its preferential treatment and any gain is taxed to you as ordinary income.

The spread between the option price and the fair market value of the stock upon exercise of the incentive stock option may be taxed indirectly if you are subject to alternative minimum tax. For a discussion of the alternative minimum tax, see Chapter 31, *How to Figure Your Tax*. For a further discussion of stock options, see Chapter 14, *Basis of Property*.

TaxAlert
Net capital gains, the excess of net long-term capital gain over net short-term capital loss, are taxed at a maximum marginal rate of 20% for taxpayers in the ordinary income tax brackets between 28% and 39.6%. Net capital gains are taxed at a maximum marginal rate of 10% for taxpayers in the 15% ordinary income tax bracket. For purchases of securities made after year 2000 and held more than 5 years, the maximum marginal rate will be 18% for higher income taxpayers and 8% for taxpayers in the lowest tax bracket. Taxpayers will be allowed to treat purchases prior to year 2001 as if purchased on January 1, 2001, with a special election.

TaxPlanner
You can use stock swaps to finance the exercise of stock options by giving the company stock equal in value to the price of the option.

TaxSaver
Employee stock purchase plans. Many companies have stock purchase plans that offer participating employees the opportunity to buy company stock. Employees usually contribute to the plan by authorizing payroll deductions, which are not excludable from gross income.

As an employee, you do not have to pay any tax when the plan's trustee exercises the option and purchases company stock. The stock is merely credited to your account within the plan.

At some future time, you may request to receive the stock purchased for your account. On distribution, if you immediately sell the stock, any gain will be taxed as ordinary income. The gain will generally be determined by the sale price less the amount you contributed to the plan to buy the stock. Your company should be able to provide you with all relevant information.

However, if after receiving the stock you hold it long enough to meet the long-term capital gain holding period, any gain will be treated as a long-term capital gain. Again, if you have a capital loss carryover, the fact that the sale is characterized as a capital gain could still result in a tax benefit for you.

Restricted property. Generally, if you receive property for your services, you must include its fair market value in your income in the year you receive the property. However, if you receive stock or other property that has certain restrictions that affect its value, you may not have to include the value of the property in your income in the year you receive it. For details, see *Restricted Property* in Publication 525..

Example
Your employer offers to sell you a parcel of land worth $5,000 for a bargain price of $3,500. You would have to include the $1,500 that the company, in effect, gave you as income for the year. In turn, your cost **basis** for the property would be $5,000, not the $3,500 you actually paid for it.

This example shows the importance of putting a reasonable value on the property you receive from your employer. The lower the value is, the less income you will currently report. However, your basis in the property will also be lower and you will realize a larger gain upon the subsequent sale of the property.

Dividends you receive on restricted stock are extra compensation to you. Your employer should include these payments on your Form W-2.

Explanation

A substantial risk of forfeiture occurs when your ownership of property is conditional on the performance of substantial services in the future. When you complete these services or when the property may be legally transferred by you, whichever is earlier, you must recognize as income the difference between the fair market value of the property on that date and the amount, if any, you paid for it.

TaxSaver

If you expect the value of the property to appreciate, you may choose to recognize the income generated by the property before any restrictions on your ownership are lifted. Then, if the property increases in value from the time you have recognized it as income to the time the risk of forfeiture is removed, the increase will not be taxed at that time. Instead, the tax on that appreciation will be deferred until the property is sold. You may make this choice even if you pay an amount for the property at least equal to its fair market value and therefore recognize zero taxable income currently. You must decide no later than 30 days after you receive the property if you are going to recognize the income while the property is still subject to restrictions.

If you recognize the income and then are forced to forfeit the property, you may deduct as a loss the amount you originally paid for the property. If you believe that the chances you have of forfeiting the property are high, then you should avoid recognizing the income up front.

Example 1

On December 10, 2001, your employer sold you a share of stock for $10 that had a fair market value of $110. The stock is subject to a substantial risk of forfeiture until April 1, 2003. Because the stock might have to be forfeited, you do not have to include the $100 difference between your purchase price and the fair market value of the stock in your 2001 taxable income.

Assume you did not recognize the income immediately. On April 1, 2003, the fair market value of your share of stock is $210. You must include $200 ($210 – $10) in your taxable income in 2003. Assuming you are in the 31% tax bracket, your tax is $62.

However, if you chose to recognize the income on the stock immediately, you would include $100 ($110 – $10) in your taxable income for 2001 and would incur tax of $31 if you were in the 31% tax bracket. Having made that choice, you owe no more tax until you sell the stock, at which time you will owe tax on the excess of the selling price over your $110 tax basis for the stock.

Example 2

Assume the same facts as in Example 1, except that after you recognized the income from the property in your 2001 income, you had to forfeit your claim to the property in 2002. You may deduct only the $10 you paid for the stock as a **capital loss.** You do *not* get to claim a loss on the $100 of *income* you previously reported.

Stock you chose to include in income. Dividends you receive on restricted stock you chose to include in your income in the year transferred are treated the same as any other dividends. Report them on your return as dividends. For a discussion of dividends, see chapter 9.

For information on how to treat dividends reported on both your Form W-2 and Form 1099-DIV, see *Dividends received on restricted stock* in Publication 525.

Fringe Benefits

Fringe benefits you receive in connection with the performance of your services are included in your income as compensation unless you pay fair market value for them or they are specifically excluded by law. Abstaining from the performance of services (for example, under a covenant not to compete) is treated as the performance of services for purposes of these rules.

Accounting period. You must use the same accounting period your employer uses to report your taxable noncash fringe benefits. Your employer has the option to report taxable noncash fringe benefits by using either of the following rules.

1) The ***general rule:*** benefits are reported for a full calendar year (January 1–December 31).
2) The ***special accounting period rule:*** benefits provided during the last 2 months of the calendar year (or any shorter period) are treated as paid during the following calendar year. For example, each year your employer reports the value of benefits provided during the last 2 months of the prior year and the first 10 months of the current year.

Your employer does not have to use the same accounting period for each fringe benefit, but must use the same period for all employees who receive a particular benefit.

You must use the same accounting period that you use to report the benefit to claim an employee business deduction (for use of a car, for example).

Form W-2. Your employer reports your taxable fringe benefits in box 1 (*Wages, tips, other compensation*) of Form W-2. The total value of your fringe benefits may also be noted in box 12. The value of your fringe benefits may be added to your other compensation on one Form W-2, or you may receive a separate Form W-2 showing just the value of your fringe benefits in box 1 with a notation in box 12.

Accident or Health Plan

Generally, the value of accident or health plan coverage provided to you by your employer is not included in your income. Benefits you receive from the plan are generally taxable, as explained later under *Sickness and Injury Benefits.*

Explanation

This exclusion applies to coverage provided to the taxpayer and the taxpayer's spouse and dependents.

Long-term care coverage. Contributions by your employer to provide coverage for long-term care services are generally not included in income. However, contributions made through a flexible spending or similar arrangement (such as a cafeteria plan) must be included in your income. This amount will be reported as wages in box 1 of your Form W-2.

Contributions you make to the plan are discussed in Publication 502, *Medical and Dental Expenses.*

Archer MSA contributions. Contributions by your employer to your Archer MSA (previously called a medical savings account) are not included in your income. Their total will be reported in box 12 of Form W-2 with code R. You must report this amount on Form 8853, *Archer MSAs and Long-Term Care Insurance Contracts,* and attach the form to your return.

If your employer does not make contributions to your MSA, you can make your own contributions to your MSA. These contributions are discussed in Publication 969, *Medical Savings Accounts (MSAs).* Also, see Form 8853.

Adoption Assistance

You may be able to exclude from income amounts paid or expenses incurred by your employer for qualified adoption expenses in connection with your adoption of an eligible child. See Publication 968, *Tax Benefits for Adoption,* for more information.

Adoption benefits are reported by your employer in box 12 of Form W-2 with code T. They are also included as social security and Medicare wages in boxes 3 and 5. However, they are not included as wages in box 1. To determine the taxable and nontaxable amounts, you must complete Part III of Form 8839, *Qualified Adoption Expenses.* Attach the form to your return.

De Minimis (Minimal) Benefits

If your employer provides you with a product or service and the cost of it is so small that it would be unreasonable for the employer to account for it, the value is not included in your income. Generally, the value of these benefits, such as discounts at company cafeterias, cab fares home when working overtime, and company picnics, is not included in your income.

Holiday gifts. If your employer gives you a turkey, ham, or other item of nominal value at Christmas or other holidays, you do not have to include the value of the gift in your income. However, if your employer gives you cash, a gift certificate, or a similar item that you can easily exchange for cash, you include the value of that gift as extra salary or wages regardless of the amount involved.

Educational Assistance

You can exclude from your income up to $5,250 of qualified employer-provided educational assistance. The exclusion does not apply to graduate-level courses beginning before January 1, 2002. For more information, see Publication 508, *Tax Benefits for Work-Related Education.*

> **TaxAlert: The 2001 Tax Act**
>
> Beginning in year 2002, this exclusion now applies to graduate-level courses.

Employer-Provided Vehicles

If your employer provides a car (or other highway motor vehicle) to you, your personal use of the car is usually a taxable noncash fringe benefit.

Your employer must determine the actual value of this fringe benefit to include in your income.

Tip. *Certain employer-provided transportation can be excluded from gross income. See the discussion on* Transportation, *next.*

Transportation

If your employer provides you with a qualified transportation fringe benefit, it can be excluded from your income, up to certain limits. A qualified transportation fringe benefit is:

1) Transportation in a commuter highway vehicle (such as a van) between your home and work place,
2) A transit pass, or
3) Qualified parking.

Cash reimbursement by your employer for these expenses under a bona fide reimbursement arrangement is also excludable. However, cash reimbursement for a transit pass is excludable only if a voucher or similar item that can be exchanged only for a transit pass is not readily available for direct distribution to you.

Exclusion limit. The exclusion for commuter highway vehicle transportation and transit pass fringe benefits cannot be more than a total of $65 a month, regardless of the total value of both benefits.

The exclusion for the qualified parking fringe benefit cannot be more than $175 a month, regardless of its value.

If the benefits have a value that is more than these limits, the excess must be included in your income.

> **TaxAlert**
>
> An exclusion from gross income is allowed for an employee whose employer offers the choice between cash or employer-provided parking, and the employee chooses parking. If you choose cash, the amount offered is includable in your income.

Commuter highway vehicle. This is a highway vehicle that seats at least six adults (not including the driver). At least 80% of the vehicle's mileage must reasonably be expected to be:

1) For transporting employees between their homes and work place, and
2) On trips during which employees occupy at least half of the vehicle's adult seating capacity (not including the driver).

Transit pass. This is any pass, token, farecard, voucher, or similar item entitling a person to ride mass transit (whether public or private) free or at a reduced rate or to ride in a commuter highway vehicle operated by a person in the business of transporting persons for compensation.

Qualified parking. This is parking provided to an employee at or near the employer's place of business. It also includes parking provided on or near a location from which the employee commutes to work in a commuter highway vehicle or carpool. It does not include parking at or near the employee's home.

> **Explanation**
>
> **Employer-provided vehicles.** If your employer provides a car (or other highway motor vehicle) to you, your personal use of the car is usually a taxable noncash fringe benefit.
>
> Your employer must determine the actual value of this fringe benefit to include in your income.
>
> **Note:** *Certain employer-provided transportation can be excluded from gross income.*

Group-Term Life Insurance Premiums

Generally, the cost of up to $50,000 of group-term life insurance coverage provided to you by your employer (or former employer) is not included in your income. However, you must include in income the cost of employer-provided insurance that is more than the cost of $50,000 of coverage. If you pay any part of the cost of the insurance, your entire payment reduces, dollar for dollar, the amount you would otherwise include in your income. However, you cannot reduce the amount to include in your income by:

1) Payments for coverage in a different tax year,
2) Payments for coverage through a cafeteria plan, unless the payments are after-tax contributions, or
3) Payments for coverage not taxed to you because of the exceptions discussed later in *Entire cost excluded.*

> **Explanation**
>
> The IRS has published an updated schedule for the imputed cost of life insurance coverage exceeding $50,000. The new rate schedule applies to insurance coverage provided after June 30, 1999. See Publication 535, *Business Expenses,* for more information.

The amount included in your income is reported as part of your wages in box 1 of your Form W-2. It is also shown separately in box 12 with code C.

Example

Your employer, ABC Company, pays the premiums on your $150,000 group-term life insurance policy. You are 40 years old. Every $1,000 worth of coverage costs $.10 per month. Because under the law only $50,000 worth of coverage may be excluded from your income, the cost of the additional $100,000 of life insurance, or $120 [($.10 x 12 months) x $100], has to be included in your income, even though your employer covers the cost.

If you pay any amount of the $120 directly, you may reduce, dollar for dollar, the amount of the premium that would otherwise be included in your income. Thus, if you paid $50, only $70 ($120 – $50) of the premium would be included in your income.

Group-term life insurance. This insurance is term life insurance protection (insurance for a fixed period of time) that:

1) Provides a general death benefit,
2) Is provided to a group of employees,
3) Is provided under a policy carried by the employer, and
4) Provides an amount of insurance for each employee based on a formula that prevents individual selection.

Permanent benefits. If your group-term life insurance policy includes permanent benefits, such as a paid-up or cash surrender value, you must include in your income, as wages, the cost of the permanent benefits minus the amount you pay for them. Your employer should be able to tell you the amount to include in your income.

Accidental or other death benefits. Insurance that provides accidental or other death benefits but does not provide general death benefits (travel insurance, for example) is not group-term life insurance.

Entire cost excluded. You are not taxed on the cost of group-term life insurance if any of the following circumstances apply.

1) You are permanently and totally disabled and have ended your employment.
2) Your employer is the beneficiary of the policy for the entire period the insurance is in force during the tax year.
3) A charitable organization (defined in chapter 26) is the only beneficiary of the policy for the entire period the insurance is in force during the tax year. (You are not entitled to a deduction for a charitable contribution for naming a charitable organization as the beneficiary of your policy.)

Entire cost taxed. You are taxed on the entire cost of group-term life insurance if either of the following circumstances apply.

1) The insurance is provided by your employer through a qualified employees' trust, such as a pension trust or a qualified annuity plan.
2) You are a key employee and your employer's plan discriminates in favor of key employees.

Life insurance agents. Full-time life insurance agents who are considered employees for social security and Medicare tax withholding purposes are treated as employees in applying the provisions relating to group-term life insurance under a policy carried by their employer.

More than $50,000 from one employer. If you have only one employer and you were insured at any time during the tax year for more than $50,000 under a group-term life insurance policy, your taxable income from this source is included as other compensation on the Form W-2 you receive.

More than $50,000 from two or more employers. If two or more employers provide you group-term life insurance coverage totaling more than $50,000, you must figure how much to include in your income. You must include the cost of life insurance provided to you during the tax year, regardless of when your employers paid the premiums.

Figuring the taxable cost. You figure the taxable cost for each month of coverage by multiplying the number of thousands of dollars of insurance coverage for the month (figured to the nearest tenth), less 50, by the cost from the following table. Use your age on the last day of the tax year. You must prorate the cost from the table if less than a full month of coverage is involved.

COST PER $1,000 OF PROTECTION
FOR ONE MONTH

Age	Cost
Under 25	$ .05
25 through 29	.06
30 through 34	.08
35 through 39	.09
40 through 44	.10
45 through 49	.15
50 through 54	.23
55 through 59	.43
60 through 64	.66
65 through 69	1.27
70 and older	2.06

Example. You are 51 years old and work for employers A and B. Both employers provide group-term life insurance coverage for you for the entire year. Your coverage is $35,000 with employer A and $45,000 with employer B. You pay premiums of $4.15 a month under the employer B group plan. You figure the amount to include in your income as follows:

Employer A coverage (in thousands)	$ 35
Employer B coverage (in thousands)	+ 45
Total coverage (in thousands)	$ 80
Minus: Exclusion (in thousands)	– 50
Excess amount (in thousands)	$ 30
Multiply by cost per $1,000 per month, age 51 (from table)	x .23
Cost of excess insurance for 1 month	$ 6.90
Multiply by number of full months coverage at this cost	x 12
Cost of excess insurance for tax year	$ 82.80
Minus: Premiums you paid ($4.15 x 12 months)	– 49.80
Cost to include in income as wages	$ 33.00

Special Rules for Certain Employees

This section deals with special rules for people in certain types of employment: members of the clergy, members of religious orders, people working for foreign employers, military personnel, veterans, and certain volunteers.

Clergy

If you are a member of the clergy, you must include in your income offerings and fees you receive for marriages, baptisms, funerals, masses, etc., in addition to your salary. If the offering is made to the religious institution, it is not taxable to you.

If you are a member of a religious organization and you give your outside earnings to the organization, you still must include the earnings in your income. However, you may be entitled to a charitable contribution deduction for the amount paid to the organization. See chapter 26.

Housing. Special rules apply to members of the clergy. Under these rules, you do not include in your income the rental value of a home (including utilities) or a housing allowance provided to you as part of your pay. The home or allowance must be provided as compensation for your duties as an ordained, licensed, or commissioned minister. However, you must include the rental value of the home or the housing allowance as earnings from self-employment on Schedule SE (Form 1040) if you are subject to the self-employment tax. For more information, see Publication 517, *Social Security and Other Information for Members of the Clergy and Religious Workers.*

Explanation

To qualify for the exclusions from gross income, you must be appropriately ordained, commissioned, or licensed as a minister or other member of the clergy and you must be employed by a religious organization to perform ministerial functions. You qualify as a member of the clergy if you have been appropriately ordained according to the customs of your faith. The exclusion also applies to retired ministers, but not their widows.

Exception

An ordained minister may not claim the exclusions from gross income when the crux of his or her ministry consists of preachings against communism for a nonreligious, tax-exempt organization. Such a message is not religious because anticommunism is not an adopted tenet of his or her faith.

   Sham churches. The IRS has been cracking down on individuals who declare themselves clergy of newly established churches, arrange to have all their income paid to the church, and then have the church pay their living expenses. The object of such individuals is to take advantage of a church's tax-exempt status and shield income from taxation. Individuals who set up sham churches may be subject to criminal sanctions.

Designation requirement. The church or organization that employs you must officially designate the payment as a housing allowance before the payment is made. A definite amount must be designated; the amount of the housing allowance cannot be determined at a later date.

If you are employed and paid by a local congregation, a resolution by a national church agency of your denomination does not effectively designate a housing allowance for you. The local congregation must officially designate the part of your salary that is to be a housing allowance. However, a resolution of a national church agency can designate your housing allowance if you are directly employed by the agency. If no part has been officially designated, you must include your total salary in your income.

Homeowner. If you own your home or are buying it, you can exclude your housing allowance from your income if you spend it for the down payment on the home, for mortgage payments, or for interest, taxes, utilities, repairs, etc. However, you cannot exclude more than the fair rental value of the home plus the cost of utilities, even if a larger amount is designated as a housing allowance. The fair rental value of a home includes the fair rental value of the furnishings in it.

You can deduct on Schedule A (Form 1040) the qualified mortgage interest and real estate taxes you pay on your home even if you use nontaxable housing allowance funds to make the payments. See chapters 24 and 25.

Teachers or administrators. If you are a minister employed as a teacher or administrator by a church school, college, or university, you are performing ministerial services for purposes of the housing exclu-

sion. However, if you perform services as a teacher or administrator on the faculty of a nonchurch college, you cannot exclude from your income a housing allowance or the value of a home that is provided to you.

Tip. *If you live in faculty lodging as an employee of an educational institution or an academic health center, all or part of the value of that lodging may be nontaxable under a different rule. See* Faculty lodging *in the discussion on meals and lodging in Publication 525.*

If you serve as a minister of music or minister of education or serve in an administrative or other function of your religious organization, but are not authorized to perform substantially all of the religious duties of an ordained minister in your church (even if you are commissioned as a *minister of the gospel*), the housing exclusion does not apply to you.

Theological students. The housing exclusion does not apply if you are a theological student serving a required internship as an assistant pastor, unless you are ordained, commissioned, or licensed as a minister.

Traveling evangelists. If you are an ordained minister and are providing evangelistic services, you can exclude amounts received from out-of-town churches that are designated as a housing allowance, provided you actually use them to maintain your permanent home.

Retired members of the clergy. The rental value of a home provided rent free by your church for your past services is not income if you are a retired minister. In addition, the amount of your housing allowance that you spend for utilities, maintenance, repairs, and similar expenses that are directly related to providing a home is not income to you. These amounts are also not included in net earnings from self-employment.

The general convention of a national religious denomination can designate a housing allowance for retired ministers that can be excluded from income. This applies if the local congregations authorize the general convention to establish and maintain a unified pension system for all retired clergy members of the denomination for their past services to the local churches.

A surviving spouse of a retired minister cannot exclude a housing allowance from income. If these payments were reported to you on Form 1099-R, include them on lines 16a and 16b of Form 1040, or on lines 12a and 12b of Form 1040A. Otherwise, include them on line 21 of Form 1040.

Pension. A pension or retirement pay for a member of the clergy is usually treated the same as any other pension or annuity. It must be reported on lines 16a and 16b of Form 1040 or on lines 12a and 12b of Form 1040A.

Members of Religious Orders

If you are a member of a religious order who has taken a vow of poverty, how you treat earnings that you renounce and turn over to the order depends on whether your services are performed for the order.

Services performed for the order. If you are performing the services as an agent of the order in the exercise of duties required by the order, do not include in your income the amounts turned over to the order.

If your order directs you to perform services for another agency of the supervising church or an associated institution, you are considered to be performing the services as an agent of the order. Any wages you earn as an agent of an order that you turn over to the order are not included in your gross income.

Example. You are a member of a church order and have taken a vow of poverty. You renounce any claims to your earnings and turn over to the order any salaries or wages you earn. You are a registered nurse, so your order assigns you to work in a hospital that is an associated institution of the church. However, you remain under the general direction and control of the order. You are considered to be an agent of the order and any wages you earn at the hospital that you turn over to your order are not included in your income.

Services performed outside the order. If you are directed to work outside the order, your services are not an exercise of duties required by the order unless they meet both of the following requirements.

1) They are the kind of services that are ordinarily the duties of members of the order.
2) They are part of the duties that you must exercise for, or on behalf of, the religious order as its agent.

If you are an employee of a third party, the services you perform for the third party will not be considered directed or required of you by the order. Amounts you receive for these services are included in your income, even if you have taken a vow of poverty.

Example. Mark Brown is a member of a religious order and has taken a vow of poverty. He renounces all claims to his earnings and turns over his earnings to the order.

Mark is a school teacher. He was instructed by the superiors of the order to get a job with a private tax-exempt school. Mark became an employee of the school, and, at his request, the school made the salary payments directly to the order.

Because Mark is an employee of the school, he is performing services for the school rather than as an agent of the order. The wages Mark earns working for the school are included in his income.

Foreign Employer

Special rules apply if you work for a foreign employer.

U.S. citizen. If you are a U.S. citizen who works in the United States for a foreign government, an international organization, a foreign embassy, or any foreign employer, you must include your salary in your income.

Social security and Medicare taxes. You are exempt from social security and Medicare taxes if you are employed in the United States by an international organization or a foreign government. However, you must pay self-employment tax on your earnings from services performed in the United States, even though you are not self-employed. This rule also applies if you are an employee of a qualifying wholly-owned instrumentality of a foreign government.

Non-U.S. citizen. If you are not a U.S. citizen, or if you are a U.S. citizen but also a citizen of the Philippines, and you work for an international organization in the United States, your salary from that source is exempt from tax. If you work for a foreign government in the United States, your salary from that source is exempt from tax if your work is like the work done by employees of the United States in that foreign country and the foreign government gives an equal exemption to employees of the United States in that country.

Waiver of alien status. If you are an alien who works for a foreign government or international organization and you file a waiver under section 247(b) of the Immigration and Nationality Act to keep your immigrant status, different rules may apply. See *Foreign Employer* in Publication 525.

Employment abroad. For information on income earned abroad, get Publication 54.

Military

Payments you receive as a member of a military service generally are taxed as wages except for retirement pay, which is taxed as a pension. Allowances generally are not taxed. For more information on the tax treatment of military allowances and benefits, get Publication 3, *Armed Forces' Tax Guide.*

Military retirement pay. If your retirement pay is based on age or length of service, it is taxable and must be included in your income as a pension on lines 16a and 16b of Form 1040, or on lines 12a and 12b of Form 1040A. Do not include in your income the amount of any reduction in retirement or retainer pay to provide a survivor annuity for your spouse or children under the Retired Serviceman's Family Protection Plan or the Survivor Benefit Plan.

For more information on survivor annuities, see chapter 11.

Disability. If you are retired on disability, see *Military and Government Disability Pensions* under *Sickness and Injury Benefits,* later.

Veterans' benefits. Do not include in your income any veterans' benefits paid under any law, regulation, or administrative practice administered by the Department of Veterans Affairs (VA). The following amounts paid to veterans or their families are not taxable.

1) Education, training, and subsistence allowances.
2) Disability compensation and pension payments for disabilities paid either to veterans or their families.
3) Grants for homes designed for wheelchair living.
4) Grants for motor vehicles for veterans who lost their sight or the use of their limbs.
5) Veterans' insurance proceeds and dividends paid either to veterans or their beneficiaries, including the proceeds of a veteran's endowment policy paid before death.
6) Interest on insurance dividends you leave on deposit with the VA.

Rehabilitative program payments. VA payments to hospital patients and resident veterans for their services under the VA's therapeutic or rehabilitative programs are not treated as nontaxable veterans' benefits. Report these payments as income on line 21 of Form 1040.

Volunteers

The tax treatment of amounts you receive as a volunteer worker for the Peace Corps or similar agency is covered in the following discussions.

Peace Corps. Living allowances you receive as a Peace Corps volunteer or volunteer leader for housing, utilities, household supplies, food, and clothing are exempt from tax.

Taxable allowances. The following allowances must be included in your income and reported as wages.

1) Allowances paid to your spouse and minor children while you are a volunteer leader training in the United States.
2) Living allowances designated by the Director of the Peace Corps as basic compensation. These are allowances for personal items such as domestic help, laundry and clothing maintenance, entertainment and recreation, transportation, and other miscellaneous expenses.
3) Leave allowances.
4) Readjustment allowances or termination payments. These are considered received by you when credited to your account.

Example. Gary Carpenter, a Peace Corps volunteer, gets $175 a month as a readjustment allowance during his period of service, to be paid to him in a lump sum at the end of his tour of duty. Although the allowance is not available to him until the end of his service, Gary must include it in his income on a monthly basis as it is credited to his account.

Volunteers in Service to America (VISTA). If you are a VISTA volunteer, you must include meal and lodging allowances paid to you in your income as wages.

> **Explanation**
> VISTA volunteers do not benefit from the same gross income exclusions as do members of the Peace Corps.

National Senior Services Corps programs. Do not include in your income amounts you receive for supportive services or reimbursements for out-of-pocket expenses from the following programs.

- Retired Senior Volunteer Program (RSVP).
- Foster Grandparent Program.
- Senior Companion Program.

Service Corps of Retired Executives (SCORE). If you receive amounts for supportive services or reimbursements for out-of-pocket expenses from SCORE, do not include these amounts in income.

Volunteer tax counseling. Do not include in your income any reimbursements you receive for transportation, meals, and other expenses you have in training for, or actually providing, volunteer federal income tax counseling for the elderly (TCE).

You can deduct as a charitable contribution your unreimbursed out-of-pocket expenses in taking part in the volunteer income tax assistance (VITA) program.

Sickness and Injury Benefits

This section discusses many types of sickness and injury benefits including disability benefits and military and government disability pensions..

TaxAlert: The 2001 Tax Act

Holocaust restitution payments paid to eligible individuals or their heirs on or after January 1, 2000, are exempt from taxable income. The restitution payments are also not considered in computations that included tax-exempt income (e.g., the calculation of taxable Social Security payments).

Disability Income

Generally, if you retire on disability, you must report your pension or annuity as income. There is a tax credit for people who are permanently and totally disabled. For information on this credit and the definition of permanent and total disability, see chapter 34.

Disability pensions. Generally, you must report as income any amount you receive for personal injury or sickness through an accident or health plan that is paid for by your employer. If both you and your employer pay for the plan, only the amount you receive that is due to your employer's payments is reported as income. However, certain payments may not be taxable to you. Your employer should be able to give you specific details about your pension plan and tell you the amount you paid for your disability pension. In addition to disability pensions and annuities, you may be receiving other payments for sickness and injury.

Cost paid by you. If you pay the entire cost of a health or accident insurance plan, do not include any amounts you receive from the plan for personal injury or sickness as income on your tax return. If your plan reimbursed you for medical expenses you deducted in an earlier year, you may have to include some, or all, of the reimbursement in your income. See *Reimbursement in a later year* in chapter 23.

Cafeteria plans. Generally, if you are covered by an accident or health insurance plan through a cafeteria plan, and the amount of the insurance premiums was not included in your income, you are not considered to have paid the premiums and you must include any benefits you receive in your income. If the amount of the premiums was included in your income, you are considered to have paid the premiums, and any benefits you receive are not taxable.

Explanation

If you paid disability premiums with after-tax dollars, the value of any disability benefits you receive will not be taxable. If you paid the premiums with pre-tax dollars or your employer paid the premiums, the value of benefits you receive will be taxable.

Accrued leave payment. If you retire on disability, any lump-sum payment you receive for accrued annual leave is a salary payment. The payment is not a disability payment. Include it in your income in the tax year you receive it.

Retirement and profit-sharing plans. If you receive payments from a retirement or profit-sharing plan that does not provide for disability retirement, do not treat the payments as a disability pension. The payments must be reported as a pension or annuity. For more information on pensions, see chapter 11.

How to report. If you retired on disability, you must include in income any disability pension you receive under a plan that is paid for by your employer. You must report your taxable disability payments as wages on line 7 of Form 1040 or Form 1040A, until you reach minimum retirement age. Minimum retirement age generally is the age at which you can first receive a pension or annuity if you are not disabled.

Beginning on the day after you reach minimum retirement age, payments you receive are taxable as a pension or annuity. Report the payments on lines 16a and 16b of Form 1040, or on lines 12a and 12b of Form 1040A. The rules for reporting pensions are explained in *How To Report* in chapter 11.

Military and Government Disability Pensions

Certain military and government disability pensions are not taxable.

You may be able to exclude from income amounts you receive as a pension, annuity, or similar allowance for personal injury or sickness resulting from active service in one of the following government services.

- The armed forces of any country.
- The National Oceanic and Atmospheric Administration.
- The Public Health Service.
- The Foreign Service.

Conditions for exclusion. Do not include the disability payments in your income if any of the following conditions apply.

1) You were entitled to receive a disability payment before September 25, 1975.
2) You were a member of a listed government service or its reserve component, or were under a binding written commitment to become a member, on September 24, 1975.
3) You receive the disability payments for a combat-related injury. This is a personal injury or sickness that:
   a) Results directly from armed conflict,
   b) Takes place while you are engaged in extra-hazardous service,
   c) Takes place under conditions simulating war, including training exercises such as maneuvers, or
   d) Is caused by an instrumentality of war.
4) You would be entitled to receive disability compensation from the Department of Veterans Affairs (VA) if you filed an application for it. Your exclusion under this condition is equal to the amount you would be entitled to receive from the VA.

Pension based on years of service. If you receive a disability pension based on years of service, you generally must include it in your income. But if it is a result of active service in one of the listed government services and one of the listed conditions applies, do not include in income the part of your pension that you would have received if the pension had been based on a percentage of disability. You must include the rest of your pension in your income.

Terrorist attack. Do not include in your income disability payments you receive for injuries resulting directly from a terrorist attack that occurs while you are a U.S. government employee performing official duties outside the United States. For your disability payments to be tax exempt, the Secretary of State must determine the attack was a terrorist attack.

VA disability benefits. Disability benefits you receive from the VA are not included in your income. If you are a military retiree and you receive disability benefits from other than the VA, do not include in your income the amount of disability benefits equal to the VA benefits to which you are entitled.

Retroactive VA determination. If you retire from the armed services based on years of service and are later given a retroactive service-connected disability rating by the VA, your retirement pay for the retroactive period is excluded from income up to the amount of VA disability benefits you would have been entitled to receive. You can claim a refund of any tax paid on the excludable amount (subject to the statute of limitations) by filing an amended return on Form 1040X for each previous year during the retroactive period.

If you receive a lump-sum disability severance payment and are later awarded VA disability benefits, do not include in your income the portion of the severance payment equal to the VA benefit you would have been entitled to receive in that same year. However, you must include in your income any lump-sum readjustment or other nondisability severance payment you received on release from active duty, even if you are later given a retroactive disability rating by the VA.

Long-Term Care Insurance Contracts

Long-term care insurance contracts are generally treated as accident and health insurance contracts. Amounts you receive from them (other than policyholder dividends or premium refunds) generally are excludable from income as amounts received for personal injury or sickness. To claim an exclusion for payments made on a per diem or other periodic basis under a long-term care insurance contract, you must file Form 8853 with your return.

A long-term care insurance contract is any insurance contract that only provides coverage for *qualified long-term care services.* The contract:

1) Must be guaranteed renewable,
2) Must not provide for a cash surrender value or other money that can be paid, assigned, pledged, or borrowed.
3) Must provide that refunds, other than refunds on the death of the insured or complete surrender or cancellation of the contract, and dividends under the contract may be used only to reduce future premiums or increase future benefits, and
4) Generally must not pay or reimburse expenses incurred for services or items that would be reimbursed under Medicare, except where Medicare is a secondary payer or the contract makes per diem or other periodic payments without regard to expenses.

Qualified long-term care services. Qualified long-term care services are:

1) Necessary diagnostic, preventive, therapeutic, curing, treating, mitigating, and rehabilitative services, and
2) Maintenance or personal care services required by a *chronically ill individual* as prescribed by a licensed health care practitioner.

Chronically ill individual. A chronically ill individual is one who has been certified as one of the following.

1) An individual who, for at least 90 days, is unable to perform at least two activities of daily living without substantial assistance due to loss of functional capacity. Activities of daily living are eating, toileting, transferring, bathing, dressing, and continence.
2) An individual who requires substantial supervision to be protected from threats to health and safety due to severe cognitive impairment.

The certification must have been made by a licensed health care practitioner within the previous 12 months.

Limit on exclusion. You can generally exclude from gross income up to $200 a day for 2001. The $200 is indexed for inflation. See *Limit on exclusion,* under *Long-Term Care Insurance Contracts,* under *Sickness and Injury Benefits* in Publication 525 for more information.

Workers' Compensation

Amounts you receive as workers' compensation for an occupational sickness or injury are fully exempt from tax if they are paid under a workers' compensation act or a statute in the nature of a workers' compensation act. The exemption also applies to your survivors. The exemption, however, does not apply to retirement plan benefits you receive based on your age, length of service, or prior contributions to the plan, even if you retired because of occupational sickness or injury.

Caution. *If part of your workers' compensation reduces your social security or equivalent railroad retirement benefits received, that part is considered social security (or equivalent railroad retirement) benefits and may be taxable. For more information, see Publication 915,* Social Security and Equivalent Railroad Retirement Benefits.

Return to work. If you return to work after qualifying for workers' compensation, payments you continue to receive while assigned to light duties are taxable. Report these payments as wages on line 7 of Form 1040 or Form 1040A, or on line 1 of Form 1040EZ.

Other Sickness and Injury Benefits

In addition to disability pensions and annuities, you may receive other payments for sickness or injury.

Railroad sick pay. Payments you receive as sick pay under the Railroad Unemployment Insurance Act are taxable and you must include them in your income. However, do not include them in your income if they are for an on-the-job injury.

If you received income because of a disability, see *Disability Income,* earlier.

Federal Employees' Compensation Act (FECA). Payments received under this Act for personal injury or sickness, including payments to beneficiaries in case of death, are not taxable. However, you are taxed on amounts you receive under this Act as *continuation of pay* for up to 45 days while a claim is being decided. Report this income on line 7 of Form 1040 or Form 1040A, or on line 1 of Form 1040EZ. Also, pay for sick leave while a claim is being processed is taxable and must be included in your income as wages.

You can deduct the amount you spend to buy back sick leave for an earlier year to be eligible for nontaxable FECA benefits for that period. It is a miscellaneous deduction subject to the 2% limit on Schedule A (Form 1040). If you buy back sick leave in the same year you use it, the amount reduces your taxable sick leave pay. Do not deduct it separately.

Other compensation. Many other amounts you receive as compensation for sickness or injury are not taxable. These include the following amounts.

- Compensatory damages you receive for physical injury or physical sickness, whether paid in a lump sum or in periodic payments.
- Benefits you receive under an accident or health insurance policy on which either you paid the premiums or your employer paid the premiums but you had to include them in your income.
- Disability benefits you receive for loss of income or earning capacity as a result of injuries under a no-fault car insurance policy.
- Compensation you receive for permanent loss or loss of use of a part or function of your body, or for your permanent disfigurement. This compensation must be based only on the injury and not on the period of your absence from work. These benefits are not taxable even if your employer pays for the accident and health plan that provides these benefits.

Reimbursement for medical care. A reimbursement for medical care is generally not taxable. However, this reimbursement may reduce your medical expense deduction. For more information, see chapter 23.

7

Tip Income

Introduction

Tips are one of the least-reported types of income. Recent estimates have placed the amount of annual tips going to food and beverage industry workers at $18 billion or more annually. However, these employees reported only $7 billion in income from tips on their taxes in 1998. Consequently, in April 2000, the IRS announced plans to resume a controversial audit program under which it will conduct employer-only tip examinations and assessments for FICA in cases of "flagrant violations" of tip reporting rules. This audit program focuses on cases of serious noncompliance at businesses in which tipping is customary and was effective October 1, 2000. Nevertheless, employee reporting requirements and employer withholding requirements have not changed. This chapter spells out the details.

This chapter is for employees who receive tips from customers.

All tips you receive are income and are subject to federal income tax. You must include in gross income all tips you receive directly from customers, tips from charge customers that are paid to you by your employer, and your share of any tips you receive under a tip-splitting or tip-pooling arrangement.

The value of noncash tips, such as tickets, passes, or other items of value are also income and subject to tax.

Explanation
Self-employed individuals may receive cash tips or other income from clients. This additional income is *not* considered income from tips. It is, however, considered self-employment income and must be reported to the IRS on Schedule C. See Chapter 38, *If You Are Self-Employed: How to File Schedule C*, for more information.

Reporting your tip income correctly is not difficult. You must do three things.

1) Keep a daily tip record.

2) Report tips to your employer.

3) Report all your tips on your income tax return.

This chapter will show you how to do these three things and what to do on your tax return if you have not done the first two. This chapter will also show you how to treat allocated tips.

Useful Items

You may want to see:

Publication

☐ **531** Reporting Tip Income
☐ **1244** Employee's Daily Record of Tips and Report to Employer

Form (and Instructions)

☐ **4137** Social Security and Medicare Tax on Unreported Tip Income
☐ **4070** Employee's Report of Tips to Employer

Keeping a Daily Tip Record

Why keep a daily tip record? You must keep a daily tip record so you can:

- Report your tips accurately to your employer,
- Report your tips accurately on your tax return, and
- Prove your tip income if your return is ever questioned.

How to keep a daily tip record. There are two ways to keep a daily tip record. You can either:

1) Write information about your tips in a tip diary, or
2) Keep copies of documents that show your tips, such as restaurant bills and credit card charge slips.

You should keep your daily tip record with your personal records. You must keep your records for as long as they are important for administration of the federal tax law.

If you keep a tip diary, you can use Form 4070A, *Employee's Daily Record of Tips.* To get Form 4070A, ask the Internal Revenue Service (IRS) or your employer for Publication 1244. Publication 1244 includes a year's supply of Form 4070A. Each day, write in the information asked for on the form.

TAXPLANNER

You are not required to complete Form 4070A as long as you have an alternative method of recording your tips. The IRS issues the form merely to help employees keep track of their income from tips.

Complete written records, however, are essential, particularly if you must later substantiate a claim that you did not receive all the tips your employer alleges were allocated to you.

Examples of documentary evidence are copies of restaurant bills, credit card charges, or charges under any other arrangement containing amounts added by the customer as a tip.

If you do not use Form 4070A, start your records by writing your name, your employer's name, and the name of the business if it is different from your employer's name. Then, each workday, write the date and the following information.

- Cash tips you get directly from customers or from other employees.
- Tips from credit card charge customers that your employer pays you.
- The value of any noncash tips you get, such as tickets, passes, or other items of value.
- The amount of tips you paid out to other employees through tip pools or tip splitting, or other arrangements, and the names of the employees to whom you paid the tips.

Caution. *Do not write in your tip diary the amount of any* service charge *that your employer adds to a customer's bill and then pays to you and treats as wages. This is part of your wages, not a tip.*

Explanation

An arbitrary fixed charge that your employer adds to the customer's bill is not a tip or gratuity subject to tip reporting and withholding requirements. Even if it is called a tip, the amount an employee is guaranteed from his or her employer is additional wage compensation.

Example

A club does not permit its members to tip its employees but adds 10% to each member's restaurant charges. This additional amount is set aside in a fund and is disbursed monthly to all employees. Because the employer controls the allocation of the funds, they are additional wages, not tips.

However, if a headwaiter receives one lump-sum payment to be distributed to all waiters and waitresses, then the payments are income from tips. The headwaiter would include in his income only the amount he retained, not the total he distributed.

Electronic tip record. You may use an electronic system provided by your employer to record your daily tips. You must receive and keep a paper copy of this record.

Reporting Tips to Your Employer

Why report tips to your employer? You must report tips to your employer so that:

- Your employer can withhold federal income tax and social security and Medicare taxes or railroad retirement tax,
- Your employer can report the correct amount of your earnings to the Social Security Administration or Railroad Retirement Board (which affects your benefits when you retire or if you become disabled, or your family's benefits if you die), and
- You can avoid the penalty for not reporting tips to your employer (explained later).

TAXSAVER

Your employer usually deducts the withholding due on tips from your regular wages. However, you do not have to have income tax withheld if you can claim exemption from withholding. You can claim exemption only if you had no income tax liability last year and expect none this year. See *Exemption From Withholding* in Chapter 5, *Tax Withholding and Estimated Tax,* for more information.

Example

Many students and retired persons who expect to have no federal income tax liability work part-time in occupations in which they receive tips. To avoid unnecessary income tax withholding, you may file a Form W-4 with your employer, certifying that you had no federal income tax liability last year and expect to have none this year as well.

What tips to report. Report to your employer only cash, check, or credit card tips you receive.

If your total tips for any one month from any one job are less than $20, do not report them to your employer.

Do not report the value of any noncash tips, such as tickets or passes, to your employer. You do not pay social security and Medicare taxes or railroad retirement tax on these tips.

Example

If you earn only $15 in tips in October, you do not have to report anything to your employer. However, you must still pay federal income tax on the tips when you report them on your tax return. The $15 is never subject to Social Security and Medicare taxes.

TAXPLANNER

If it is not customary to tip for a type of service, the IRS may be willing to concede that additional payments received for normal services may not be tips and may, indeed, be tax-free gifts from the customer. You would have to prove that the services performed did not extend beyond the minimum requirements of the job and that you work in an industry in which extra compensation is not traditional.

This claim would be impossible to sustain in all but the most unusual circumstances. The IRS and the courts generally presume that amounts received for performing services are taxable as compensation.

How to report. If your employer does not give you any other way to report tips, you can use Form 4070. To get a year's supply of the form, ask the IRS or your employer for Publication 1244. Fill in the information asked for on the form, sign and date the form, and give it to your employer.

If you do not use Form 4070, give your employer a statement with the following information.

- Your name, address, and social security number.
- Your employer's name, address, and business name (if it is different from the employer's name).
- The month (or the dates of any shorter period) in which you received tips.
- The total tips required to be reported for that period.

You must sign and date the statement. You should keep a copy with your personal records.

Your employer may require you to report your tips more than once a month. However, the statement cannot cover a period of more than one calendar month.

Electronic tip statement. Your employer can have you furnish your tip statements electronically.

TAXPLANNER

Prior to 1999, no provision existed for employees to furnish tip statements to employers in a form other than on paper. The regulations permit either an employer to adopt a system under which some or all of the tipped employees of the employer would furnish their tip statements electronically or the IRS could provide additional methods of demonstrating income from tips. The employer could include in its electronic system any tipped employee(s) working in any location(s).

The entry by the employee in the electronic system on a daily (or more frequent) basis, together with the daily record based on these entries provided by the employer, will satisfy the substantiation requirements.

When to report. Give your report for each month to your employer by the 10th of the next month. If the 10th falls on a Saturday, Sunday, or legal holiday, give your employer the report by the next day that is not a Saturday, Sunday, or legal holiday.

Example 1. You must report your tips received in June 2002 by July 10, 2002.

Example 2. You must report your tips received in January 2002 by February 11, 2002. February 10 is on a Sunday, and the 11th is the next day that is not a Saturday, Sunday, or legal holiday.

Explanation
The amount of tips you report to your employer is treated as income subject to withholding in the month after it has been reported.

Example
If you earn $75 in tips in October, you must report that amount to your employer by November 10. In November your employer will treat the $75 in tips in October as additional compensation subject to federal income tax withholding and Social Security tax.

TAXSAVER
If you earn $25 from tips in December 2001 but do not report it to your employer until January 2002 you may defer recognizing that $25 of income until you file your 2002 tax return.

Final report. If your employment ends during the month, you can report your tips when your employment ends.

Penalty for not reporting tips. If you do not report tips to your employer as required, you may be subject to a penalty equal to 50% of the social security and Medicare taxes or railroad retirement tax you owe on the unreported tips. (For information about these taxes, see *Reporting social security and Medicare taxes on tips not reported to your employer* under *Reporting Tips on Your Tax Return,* later.) The penalty amount is in addition to the taxes you owe.

You can avoid this penalty if you can show reasonable cause for not reporting the tips to your employer. To do so, attach a statement to your return explaining why you did not report them.

TAXALERT

During 1995, the IRS established a *voluntary* program for tip reporting by food and beverage establishments, known as the Tip Reporting Alternative Commitment (TRAC). This program is intended to increase tip reporting and compliance levels by both employees and employers. Under TRAC, an employer agrees to (1) maintain quarterly educational programs that will instruct new employees and update existing employees as to their reporting obligations; (2) comply with all federal tax requirements regarding the maintaining of records, filing of returns, and depositing of taxes; and (3) set up procedures to ensure the accurate recording of all tips. In return, the IRS agrees to base the restaurant's liability for employment taxes solely on reported tips and any unreported tips discovered during an IRS audit of an employee.

During 2000, the IRS announced that it is simplifying its voluntary income from tip compliance agreements and expanding them to all industries where tipping is customary. Under Tip Rate Determination Agreement (TRDA), the IRS and the employer work together to determine the amount of tips that employees generally receive and should report. Under TRAC, the employer agrees to educate employees and establish tip reporting procedures.

Until now, only the gaming, food and beverage, cosmetology, and barber industries were able to make TRDAs with the IRS. The IRS has now developed a TRDA and TRAC for other industries in which tipping is customary. Employers that can participate include taxicab and limousine companies, airport skycap companies, and car wash operations.

In addition to TRDA and TRAC, the IRS will now permit employers in the food and beverage industries to design their own program through Employer's Tip Reporting Alternative Commitment (EmTRAC). This is in lieu of the IRS-developed TRAC. EmTRAC will include the same employer commitments and protections as afforded under TRAC 166-47.

Employees in the food service industry should be cognizant of the increased diligence by employers and the IRS in reporting tip income. The IRS has issued draft forms of TRAC agreements that can be used as a model for various industries. Employers considering entering into TRAC agreements with the IRS should carefully determine if such an agreement is in their best interest. Consult with your tax advisors for more information.

Giving your employer money for taxes. Your regular pay may not be enough for your employer to withhold all the taxes you owe on your regular pay plus your reported tips. If this happens, you can give your employer money until the close of the calendar year to pay the rest of the taxes.

If you do not give your employer enough money, your employer will apply your regular pay and any money you give to the taxes in the following order.

1) All taxes on your regular pay.
2) Social security and Medicare taxes or railroad retirement tax on your reported tips.
3) Federal, state, and local income taxes on your reported tips.

Any taxes that remain unpaid can be collected by your employer from your next paycheck. If withholding taxes remain uncollected at the end of the year, you may be subject to a penalty for underpayment of estimated taxes. See Publication 505, *Tax Withholding and Estimated Tax,* for more information.

TAXSAVER

If your base wages are not enough to cover your necessary withholding taxes, it may be more beneficial to pay your employer money to cover the withholding deficiency *at the end of the year* instead of making payments to your employer throughout the year. Set aside sufficient cash from tips until the end of the tax year; then, give your employer enough cash to cover the remaining withholding taxes. This approach allows you access to the cash throughout the year and avoids underpayment penalties from not paying in enough taxes during the year.

If you find it easier to manage your cash flow by paying the additional taxes due on a more frequent basis, you can make estimated tax payments or pay the taxes to your employer periodically throughout the year. See Chapter 5, *Tax Withholding and Estimated Tax,* for information on estimated tax.

Caution. *You must report on your tax return any social security and Medicare taxes or railroad retirement tax that remained uncollected at the end of 2001. See* Reporting uncollected social security and Medicare taxes on tips *under* Reporting Tips on Your Tax Return, *later. These uncollected taxes will be shown in box 12 of your 2001 Form W-2 (codes A and B).*

Tip Rate Determination and Education Program

Your employer may participate in the Tip Rate Determination and Education Program. The program was developed to help employees and employers understand and meet their tip reporting responsibilities.

There are two agreements under the program—the *Tip Rate Determination Agreement (TRDA)* and the *Tip Reporting Alternative Commitment (TRAC).* In addition, employers in the food and beverage industry may be able to get approval of an employer-designed EmTRAC program. For information on the EmTRAC program, see Notice 2001–1 in Internal Revenue Bulletin No. 2001–2.

Your employer can provide you with a copy of the agreement. If you want to learn more about these agreements, contact the local tip coordinator. A list of tip coordinators is available at **www.irs.gov.**

Reporting Tips on Your Tax Return

How to report tips. Report your tips with your wages on line 1, Form 1040EZ, or line 7, Form 1040A or Form 1040.
What tips to report. You must report all tips you received in 2001, including both cash tips and noncash tips, on your tax return. Any tips you reported to your employer for 2001 are included in the wages shown in box 1 of your Form W-2. Add to the amount in box 1 only the tips you did not report to your employer.

Explanation

All voluntary payments received from customers are taxable to the employee. This includes the **fair market value** of any noncash items given to employees.

Example

Tokens given to blackjack dealers in gambling casinos are taxable as income from tips to the dealers.

Caution. *If you received $20 or more in cash and charge tips in a month and did not report all of those tips to your employer, see* Reporting social security and Medicare taxes on tips not reported to your employer, *later.*
Caution. *If you did not keep a daily tip record as required and an amount is shown in box 8 of your Form W-2, see* Allocated Tips, *later.*

If you kept a daily tip record and reported tips to your employer as required under the rules explained earlier, add the following tips to the amount in box 1 of your Form W-2.

- Cash and charge tips you received that totaled less than $20 for any month.
- The value of noncash tips, such as tickets, passes, or other items of value.

Example. John Allen began working at the Diamond Restaurant (his only employer in 2001) on June 30 and received $10,000 in wages during the year. John kept a daily tip record showing that his tips for June were $18 and his tips for the rest of the year totaled $7,000. He was not required to report his June tips to his employer, but he reported all of the rest of his tips to his employer as required.

John's Form W-2 from Diamond Restaurant shows $17,000 ($10,000 wages plus $7,000 reported tips) in box 1. He adds the $18 unreported tips to that amount and reports $17,018 as wages on his tax return.
Reporting social security and Medicare taxes on tips not reported to your employer. If you received $20 or more in cash and charge tips in a month from any one job and did not report all of those tips to your employer, you must report the social security and Medicare taxes on the unreported tips as additional tax on your return. To report these taxes, you must file a return even if you would not otherwise have to file. You must use Form 1040. (You cannot file Form 1040EZ or Form 1040A.)

TAXSAVER

Limit on Social Security and railroad retirement tax. There are limits on the amount of Social Security and railroad retirement tax that your employer withholds from your wages and reported tips. If you worked for two or more employers in 2001, you may have overpaid one or more of these taxes. You may be eligible for a credit for excess Social Security tax or railroad retirement tax, discussed in Chapter 37, *Other Credits Including the Earned Income Credit.*

TAXALERT

Since 1994, there has been no limit on the amount of wages and reported tips subject to Medicare tax. The Medicare tax rate is 1.45%. However, only the first $80,400 of wages and tips are subject to Social Security tax. The Social Security tax rate is 6.2%.

Use **Form 4137** to figure these taxes. Enter the tax on line 54, Form 1040, and attach Form 4137 to your return.

Reporting uncollected social security and Medicare taxes on tips. If your employer could not collect all the social security and Medicare taxes or railroad retirement tax you owe on tips reported for 2001, the uncollected taxes will be shown in box 12 of your Form W-2 (codes A and B). You must report these amounts as additional tax on your return. You may have uncollected taxes if your regular pay was not enough for your employer to withhold all the taxes you owe and you did not give your employer enough money to pay the rest of the taxes.

To report these uncollected taxes, you must file a return even if you would not otherwise have to file. You must use Form 1040. (You cannot file Form 1040EZ or Form 1040A.) Include the taxes in your total tax amount on line 58, and write "UT" and the total of the uncollected taxes on the dotted line next to line 58.

TaxSaver

Tips received while working at a job covered by the Railroad Retirement Tax Act or while working for most state or local governments or for some nonprofit organizations are not subject to Social Security tax and should not be included on Form 4137. See *Employers Subject to the Railroad Retirement Act* in Publication 531.

Allocated Tips

If your employer allocated tips to you, they are shown separately in box 8 of your Form W-2. They are not included in box 1 with your wages and reported tips. If box 8 is blank, this discussion does not apply to you.
What are allocated tips? These are tips that your employer assigned to you in addition to the tips you reported to your employer for the year. Your employer will have done this only if:

- You worked in a restaurant, cocktail lounge, or similar business that must allocate tips to employees, and
- The tips you reported to your employer were less than your share of 8% of food and drink sales.

Explanation

Large food or beverage establishments must report tip allocations to the IRS.

A "large food or beverage establishment" is defined as one where the employer normally employed 10 or more employees on a typical day during the preceding calendar year and where tipping is customary.

How were your allocated tips figured? The tips allocated to you are your share of an amount figured by subtracting the reported tips of all employees from 8% (or an approved lower rate) of food and drink sales (other than carryout sales and sales with a service charge of 10% or more). Your share of that amount was figured using either a method provided by an employer-employee agreement or a method provided by IRS regulations based on employees' sales or hours worked. For information about the exact allocation method used, ask your employer.

Example

The following example shows how a food and beverage establishment might determine what amount to include in the special box provided on each employee's Form W-2.

Lee's is a large food and beverage establishment that for one payroll period had gross receipts of $100,000 and reported tips of $6,200. Directly tipped employees reported $5,700, while indirectly tipped employees reported $500.

Directly tipped employees	Gross receipts for payroll period	Tips reported
Amos	$ 18,000	$1,080
Mitchell	16,000	880
Charlie	23,000	1,810
Nelson	17,000	800
Ed	12,000	450
Allan	14,000	680
	$100,000	$5,700

The allocation computations would be as follows:

1. Total tips to be allocated: $100,000 (gross receipts) × 0.08 = $8,000.
2. Tips reported by indirectly tipped employees = $500.
3. Tips to be allocated to directly tipped employees: $8,000 – $500 (indirect employees' tips) = $7,500.
4. Allocation of tips to directly tipped employees:

	Directly tipped employees' share of 8% gross		Gross receipts ratio		Employee share of 8% gross
Amos	$7,500	×	18,000/100,000	=	$1,350
Mitchell	7,500	×	16,000/100,000	=	1,200
Charlie	7,500	×	23,000/100,000	=	1,725
Nelson	7,500	×	17,000/100,000	=	1,275
Ed	7,500	×	12,000/100,000	=	900
Allan	7,500	×	14,000/100,000	=	1,050
					$7,500

5. Calculation of tip shortfall of directly tipped employees:

	Employee share of 8% gross		Tips reported		Employees' shortfall
Amos	$1,350	–	$1,080	=	$ 270
Mitchell	1,200	–	880	=	320
Charlie	1,725	–	1,810	=	—
Nelson	1,275	–	800	=	475
Ed	900	–	450	=	450
Allan	1,050	–	680	=	370
		Total shortfall		$1,885	

Because Charlie has no reporting shortfall, there is no allocation to him.
6. Total tips reported, including reported tips of indirectly tipped employees: $8,000 – $6,200 (total tips reported) = $1,800 (amount allocable among shortfall employees).
7. Allocation of tip shortfall among directly tipped employees:

	Allocable amount	×	Shortfall ratio	=	Amount of allocation
Amos	$1,800	×	270/1,885	=	$ 258
Mitchell	1,800	×	320/1,885	=	305
Nelson	1,800	×	475/1,885	=	454

Ed	1,800	×	450/1,885	=	430
Allan	1,800	×	370/1,885	=	353
			Total		$1,800

These allocated amounts must be reported by the employer on the employees' W-2s in box 8. For example, Amos would have allocated tip income of $258.

TaxPlanner

The reporting requirements for employers are only guidelines and apply only to large food or beverage establishments. Nevertheless, the courts have imposed "industry averages" on taxpayers who had no records or inadequate records.

Example

In a series of cases, the courts held that average tips for taxi drivers come to 10% of gross income. A court was willing to accept a 2% figure for tips only when the driver produced daily logs that showed the amounts of fares and tips. The court believed that the records were true and accurate.

The courts have held that the average tips for barbers and hairdressers range from 2% to 8%.

To estimate the tip income of waiters and waitresses, the IRS has used various methods, based on the total sales of the restaurant. While the courts often adjust the IRS determination, they usually accept any reasonable method the IRS uses. Recent Federal Appeals case law has held that the IRS can assess the restaurant owners for FICA taxes without attempting to first determine the unreported income of each individual employee.

Our advice is: Maintain adequate records of all amounts that you actually receive.

TaxPlanner

If the employee or employer would like to request a tip rate lower than 8%, he or she must file a petition with the district director for the IRS district in which the business is located. The petition must include specific information to justify the lower rate. An employee petition can only be filed with the consent of the majority of the directly tipped employees. The petition must state the total number of directly tipped employees and the number of employees consenting to the petition. The employer must also be notified immediately, and the employer must promptly give the district director a copy of any Form 8027, *Employers Annual Information Return of Tip Income and Allocated Tips*, filed by the employer for the prior 3 years.

Must you report your allocated tips on your return? You must report allocated tips on your tax return unless either of the following exceptions applies.

1) You kept a daily tip record, or other evidence that is as credible and as reliable as a daily tip record, as required under rules explained earlier.
2) Your tip record is incomplete, but it shows that your actual tips were more than the tips you reported to your employer plus the allocated tips.

If either exception applies, report your actual tips on your return. Do not report the allocated tips. See *What tips to report* under *Reporting Tips on Your Tax Return,* earlier.

How to report allocated tips. If you must report allocated tips on your return, add the amount in box 8 of your Form W-2 to the amount in box 1. Report the total as wages on line 7 of Form 1040. (You cannot file Form 1040EZ or Form 1040A.)

Because social security and Medicare taxes were not withheld from the allocated tips, you must report those taxes as additional tax on your return. Complete Form 4137, and include the allocated tips on line 1 of the form. See *Reporting social security and Medicare taxes on tips not reported to your employer* under *Reporting Tips on Your Tax Return,* earlier.

8

Interest Income

Introduction

Interest income is a significant portion of all income earned by Americans. The government takes pains to make sure that all such income is reported by taxpayers. That's why payers of interest, like banks, are required to report to the government the amounts of interest they pay out and to whom. If you do not supply your proper tax identification number—usually your Social Security number—to a payer of interest, tax will automatically be withheld.

Some investments permit you to delay reporting interest income. Such investments may boost the after-tax rate of return on your money, because you may pay tax on the income in a year—a retirement year, for example—when your tax rate is lower. This chapter helps you sort through some of the strategies for postponing taxes on interest income.

Important Reminder

Foreign-source income. If you are a U.S. citizen with interest income from sources outside the United States (foreign income), you must report that income on your tax return unless it is exempt by U.S. law. This is true whether you reside inside or outside the United States and whether or not you receive a Form 1099 from the foreign payer.

This chapter discusses:

- Different types of interest income,
- What interest is taxable and what interest is nontaxable,
- When to report interest income, and
- How to report interest income on your tax return.

In general, any interest that you receive or that is credited to your account and can be withdrawn is taxable income. (It does not have to be entered in your passbook.) Exceptions to this rule are discussed later in this chapter.

You may be able to deduct expenses you have in earning this income on Schedule A (Form 1040) if you itemize your deductions. See chapter 30.

Recordkeeping. You should keep a list showing sources and amounts of interest received during the year. Also, keep the forms you receive that show your interest income (Forms 1099-INT, for example) as an important part of your records.

Useful Items

You may want to see:

Publication

- ☐ **537** Installment Sales
- ☐ **550** Investment Income and Expenses
- ☐ **1212** List of Original Issue Discount Instruments

Form (and Instructions)

- ☐ **Schedule B (Form 1040)** Interest and Ordinary Dividends
- ☐ **Schedule 1 (Form 1040A)** Interest and Ordinary Dividends for Form 1040A Filers
- ☐ **3115** Application for Change in Accounting Method
- ☐ **8815** Exclusion of Interest From Series EE and I U.S. Savings Bonds Issued After 1989
- ☐ **8818** Optional Form To Record Redemption of Series EE and I U.S. Savings Bonds Issued After 1989

TAXORGANIZER

Keep the following records for at least 3 years: 1099-INT, 1099-OID, or Substitute 1099, such as broker statement or year-end account summary.

You should also keep a written record of Series EE U.S. Savings Bonds issued after 1989. This includes serial numbers, issue dates, face values, and redemption proceeds of each bond. Form 8818 may also be used.

You should also keep bills, receipts, canceled checks, and other documentation that show you paid qualified higher education expenses.

General Information

A few items of general interest are covered here.

Tax on investment income of a child under age 14. Part of a child's 2001 investment income may be taxed at the parent's tax rate. This may happen if all the following are true.

1) The child was under age 14 on January 1, 2002.
2) The child had more than $1,500 of investment income (such as taxable interest and dividends) and has to file a tax return.
3) Either parent was alive at the end of 2001.

If all these statements are true, **Form 8615,** *Tax for Children Under Age 14 Who Have Investment Income of More Than $1,500,* must be completed and attached to the child's tax return. If any of these statements is not true, Form 8615 is not required and the child's income is taxed at his or her own tax rate.

However, the parent can choose to include the child's interest and dividends on the parent's return if certain requirements are met. Use **Form 8814,** *Parents' Election To Report Child's Interest and Dividends,* for this purpose.

Explanation

You may only elect to include your child's income on your return if (1) your child's income consists solely of interest and dividends and is between $750 and $7,500, (2) your child made no estimated tax payments, (3) your child had no backup withholding, and (4) your child did not have any overpayment of tax shown on his or her 2000 return applied to the 2001 return. You may still need to file a state income tax return for your child.

For more information about the tax on investment income of children and the parents' election, see chapter 32.

Beneficiary of an estate or trust. Interest, dividends, and other investment income you receive as a beneficiary of an estate or trust is generally taxable income. You should receive a **Schedule K-1** (Form 1041), *Beneficiary's Share of Income, Deductions, Credits, etc.,* from the fiduciary. Your copy of Schedule K-1 and its instructions will tell you where to report the income on your Form 1040.

Social security number (SSN). You must give your name and SSN to any person required by federal tax law to make a return, statement, or other document that relates to you. This includes payers of interest.

SSN for joint account. If the funds in a joint account belong to one person, list that person's name first on the account and give that person's SSN to the payer. (For information on who owns the funds in a joint account, see *Joint accounts,* later.) If the joint account contains combined funds, give the SSN of the person whose name is listed first on the account.

These rules apply both to joint ownership by a married couple and to joint ownership by other individuals. For example, if you open a joint savings account with your child using funds belonging to the child, list the child's name first on the account and give the child's SSN.

Custodian account for your child. If your child is the actual owner of an account that is recorded in your name as custodian for the child, give the child's SSN to the payer. For example, you must give your child's SSN to the payer of dividends on stock owned by your child, even though the dividends are paid to you as custodian.

Penalty for failure to supply SSN. If you do not give your SSN to the payer of interest, you may have to pay a penalty. See *Failure to supply social security number* under *Penalties* in chapter 1. Backup withholding also may apply.

TAXPLANNER

If you change your name because of marriage, divorce, or any other reason, it is important to notify the Social Security Administration promptly. Otherwise, the IRS may believe it has discovered a reporting discrepancy that you will have to explain. In addition, some taxpayers who fail to notify the government of a name change do not receive credit for taxes they have paid.

Backup withholding. Your interest income is generally not subject to regular withholding. However, it may be subject to backup withholding to ensure that income tax is collected on the income. Under backup withholding, the payer of interest must withhold, as income tax, a percentage of the amount you are paid. For 2002, the percentage is 30%.

Backup withholding may also be required if the Internal Revenue Service (IRS) has determined that you underreported your interest or dividend income. For more information, see *Backup Withholding* in chapter 5.

Reporting backup withholding. If backup withholding is deducted from your interest income, the payer must give you a Form 1099-INT for the year that indicates the amount withheld. The Form 1099-INT will show any backup withholding as "Federal income tax withheld."

TAXORGANIZER

While you are not required to attach Form 1099-INT to your return, it is a good idea to do so if it indicates that you had federal tax withheld. This will provide the IRS with complete details of how your federal income tax withheld number was calculated.

Joint accounts. If two or more persons hold property (such as a savings account or bond) as joint tenants, tenants by the entirety, or tenants in common, each person's share of any interest from the property is determined by local law.

Explanation

Whether or not a person receives a share of any interest from a property depends on state law and the intentions of the parties.

Many people open a joint bank account with a friend or a relative so that the friend or relative may inherit the property more easily upon the owner's death. In such cases, no immediate transfer of property interest is intended. In these circumstances, the interest income should be reported solely by the owner who contributed the money.

Example 1
If two brothers, Tom and Bill, have a joint brokerage account in which all the funds were contributed by Tom, with no intention of conferring any immediate benefit on Bill, all of the income should be reported by Tom.

Note: To avoid an IRS deficiency notice issued through its document-matching program, Tom should make sure that his Social Security number is reported on Form 1099-INT.

Example 2
If a husband and wife own bonds as joint tenants, tenants by the entirety, or tenants in common, and they file separate tax returns, each should include his or her share of the income.

Example 3
If a parent does not transfer bonds to her child but uses joint tenancy so that ownership of the bonds will pass automatically to the child in case of her death, the income belongs to the parent. The parent's Social Security number should be used, and all income should be reported on the parent's return. The same applies to joint savings accounts, other bank accounts, and certificates of deposit.

If a parent does intend to transfer during her lifetime some or all of her bonds to a child, a proportionate amount of interest should be included in both of their tax returns. Either person's Social Security number may be used.

Note: Bonds, savings accounts, and the like that are in the name of a parent or other adult as custodian under the state's Uniform Gifts or Transfers to Minors Act should use the *child's* Social Security number.

TaxPlanner

Since only one Social Security number will be recorded by the payer of interest, the IRS's document-matching program may issue deficiency notices when interest income is split between two or more returns. This situation arises because the tax return with the Social Security number shown on the payer's records may not include the full amount of the interest paid. To reduce the chance of receiving an IRS deficiency notice, show both the full amount of the interest paid and a subtraction for "amount attributable to others," including their Social Security numbers, on Schedule B (Form 1040) in the section used for reporting distributions of income.

The person who receives the other part of the interest needn't worry. Although that person includes on his or her return an amount for which he or she does not receive a Form 1099-INT, the IRS rarely questions returns where income in excess of that computed by the government is reported.

Income from property given to a child. Property you give as a parent to your child under the Model Gifts of Securities to Minors Act, the Uniform Gifts to Minors Act, or any similar law, becomes the child's property.

Income from the property is taxable to the child, except that any part used to satisfy a legal obligation to support the child is taxable to the parent or legal guardian having that legal obligation.

Savings account with parent as trustee. Interest income from a savings account opened for a child who is a minor, but placed in the name and subject to the order of the parents as trustees, is taxable to the child if, under the law of the state in which the child resides, both of the following are true.

1) The savings account legally belongs to the child.
2) The parents are not legally permitted to use any of the funds to support the child.

Form 1099-INT. Interest income is generally reported to you on Form 1099-INT, *Interest Income,* or a similar statement, by banks, savings and loans, and other payers of interest. This form shows you the interest you received during the year. Keep this form for your records. You do not have to attach it to your tax return.

Report on your tax return the total amount of interest income that you receive for the tax year. This includes amounts reported to you on Form 1099-INT and amounts for which you did not receive a Form 1099-INT.

Explanation
The IRS contends that the figures shown on Form 1099 represent the correct amount of interest income paid to you. You have the burden of proof to demonstrate otherwise. If you have a valid reason for claiming that the correct amount is different—write on your return the amount shown on Form 1099 and then immediately show a subtraction (or addition) with an explanation for the adjustment. If you notice an error in the amount of interest stated, you should request that the payer issue a corrected Form 1099.

Example
You buy a bond on 4/1/01, which pays interest once a year on December 31. Because you bought the bond between the interest payment dates, you pay, in addition to the bond, $750 for "purchased interest" (i.e., money to reimburse the seller for the interest earned between 1/1/01 and 4/1/01). On 12/31/01, you receive a $3,000 interest payment which represents interest for the period 1/1/01 through 12/31/01. Since you did not earn the interest from 1/1 through 4/1/01, you should not have to pay income tax on this amount. Therefore, on Schedule B (Form 1040), you should report as follows:

XYZ Corporation interest	$3,000
Less amount of purchased interest	(750)

See *Bonds Sold Between Interest Dates* later in this chapter.

TaxOrganizer

You should keep copies of each Form 1099-INT you receive for a minimum of 3 years. See Chapter 1, *Filing Information,* for more information on recordkeeping.

Nominees. Generally, if someone receives interest as a nominee for you, that person will give you a Form 1099-INT showing the interest received on your behalf.

If you receive a Form 1099-INT that includes amounts belonging to another person, see the discussion on nominee distributions under *How To Report Interest Income* in chapter 1 of Publication 550, or see the Schedule 1 (Form 1040A) or Schedule B (Form 1040) instructions.

Incorrect amount. If you receive a Form 1099-INT that shows an incorrect amount (or other incorrect information), you should ask the issuer for a corrected form. The new Form 1099-INT you receive will be marked "Corrected."

Form 1099-OID. Reportable interest income may also be shown on Form 1099-OID, *Original Issue Discount.* For more information about amounts shown on this form, see *Original Issue Discount (OID),* later in this chapter.

TAX*ORGANIZER*

You should keep copies of each Form 1099-OID you receive for a minimum of 3 years. See Chapter 1, *Filing Information,* for more information on recordkeeping.

Exempt-interest dividends. Exempt-interest dividends you receive from a regulated investment company (mutual fund) are not included in your taxable income. (However, see *Information-reporting requirement,* next.) You will receive a notice from the mutual fund telling you the amount of the exempt-interest dividends that you received. Exempt-interest dividends are not shown on Form 1099-DIV or Form 1099-INT.

Information-reporting requirement. Although exempt-interest dividends are not taxable, you must show them on your tax return if you have to file. This is an information-reporting requirement and does not change the exempt-interest dividends to taxable income.

Note. Exempt-interest dividends paid from specified private activity bonds may be subject to the alternative minimum tax. See Alternative Minimum Tax in chapter 31 for more information. Chapter 1 of Publication 550 contains a discussion on private activity bonds, under State or Local Government Obligations.

TAX*SAVER*

Investment income that is exempt from federal tax may still be taxable on your state tax return. This includes interest and dividends paid or accrued to you on state, municipal, or any other type of debt obligation. However, in most states, there are also certain federally tax-exempt bonds that are also not taxable at the state level. Be sure to check your state filing requirements before you invest in federally tax-exempt obligations. Finally, be aware that interest from certain private activity bonds will result in a preference item for the Alternative Minimum Tax, even though the interest is not taxable for regular tax. See Chapter 31, *How to Figure Your Tax,* for more information on the Alternative Minimum Tax.

Interest on VA dividends. Interest on insurance dividends that you leave on deposit with the Department of Veterans Affairs (VA) is not taxable. This includes interest paid on dividends on converted United States Government Life Insurance and on National Service Life Insurance policies.

Taxable Interest

Taxable interest includes interest you receive from bank accounts, loans you make to others, and other sources. The following are some other sources of taxable interest.

Dividends that are actually interest. Certain distributions commonly called dividends are actually interest. You must report as interest so-called "dividends" on deposits or on share accounts in:

- Cooperative banks,
- Credit unions,
- Domestic building and loan associations,
- Domestic savings and loan associations,
- Federal savings and loan associations, and
- Mutual savings banks.

Money market funds. Generally, amounts you receive from money market funds should be reported as dividends, not as interest.

Money market certificates, savings certificates, and other deferred interest accounts. If you open any of these accounts, interest may be paid at fixed intervals of 1 year or less during the term of the account. You generally must include this interest in your income when you actually receive it or are entitled to receive it without paying a substantial penalty. The same is true for accounts that mature in 1 year or less and pay interest in a single payment at maturity. If interest is deferred for more than 1 year, see *Original Issue Discount (OID),* later.

Interest subject to penalty for early withdrawal. If you withdraw funds from a deferred interest account before maturity, you may have to pay a penalty. You must report the total amount of interest paid or credited to your account during the year, without subtracting the penalty. See *Penalty on early withdrawal of savings* in chapter 1 of Publication 550, for more information on how to report the interest and deduct the penalty.

Money borrowed to invest in money market certificate. The interest you pay on money borrowed from a bank or savings institution to meet the minimum deposit required for a money market certificate from the institution and the interest you earn on the certificate are two separate items. You must report the total interest you earn on the certificate in your income. If you itemize deductions, you can deduct the interest you pay as investment interest, up to the amount of your net investment income. See *Interest Expenses* in chapter 3 of Publication 550.

Example. You deposited $5,000 with a bank and borrowed $5,000 from the bank to make up the $10,000 minimum deposit required to buy a 6-month money market certificate. The certificate earned $575 at maturity in 2001, but you received only $265, which represented the $575 you earned minus $310 interest charged on your $5,000 loan. The bank gives you a Form 1099-INT for 2001 showing the $575 interest you earned. The bank also gives you a statement showing that you paid $310 interest for 2001. You must include the $575 in your income. If you itemize your deductions on Schedule A (Form 1040), you can deduct $310, subject to the net investment income limit.

TAX*PLANNER*

Note that in the example above the $310 in interest is deductible *only if* you itemize your deductions and may be further limited if you have no net investment income (see Chapter 25, *Interest Expense*). If you are not able to fully deduct the interest you pay, you may want to reconsider the investment arrangement.

Example

Assuming the same facts as in the example above, if you are in the top tax bracket, paying 39.1%, $225 of the $575 interest you earned will go to the IRS, leaving you with only $350. Since you paid $310 in interest charges (for which you receive no tax benefit if you do not itemize) to earn that $350, you have only $40 of after-tax gain on your $5,000 investment, for an after-tax rate of return of .8% on this investment.

TAX*SAVER*

You should be very interested in the after-tax rate of return on your investments. If your interest income is fully taxable, you may determine your after-tax return in the following manner. First, determine from the Tax Tables (printed in the back of this book) what you expect your highest **marginal tax rate** to be by calculating your total **taxable income** and then determining the highest rate at which it will be taxed. If the rate is, say, 31%, then the IRS gets 31% of your interest income on any investment, and you keep 69%. Thus, if you earn 10% on a bank deposit, your after-tax rate of return is really 6.9% (10% × 69%). See the chart later in this chapter in the *State or Local Government Obligations* section for a comparison of after-tax yields with the yield of municipal bonds. As the chart indicates, you should remember to include your state and local taxes when computing your marginal tax rate.

Gift for opening account. If you receive noncash gifts or services for making deposits or for opening an account in a savings institution, you may have to report the value as interest.

Explanation
Incentive items received (e.g., a toaster from a bank) may be considered income to you, not a tax-free gift. In cases such as this, you may have taxable income.

For deposits of less than $5,000, gifts or services valued at more than $10 must be reported as interest. For deposits of $5,000 or more, gifts or services valued at more than $20 must be reported as interest. The value is determined by the cost to the financial institution.

Example. You open a savings account at your local bank and deposit $800. The account earns $20 interest. You also receive a $15 calculator. If no other interest is credited to your account during the year, the Form 1099-INT you receive will show $35 interest for the year. You must report $35 interest income on your tax return.

Interest on insurance dividends. Interest on insurance dividends left on deposit with an insurance company that can be withdrawn annually is taxable to you in the year it is credited to your account. However, if you can withdraw it only on the anniversary date of the policy (or other specified date), the interest is taxable in the year that date occurs.

Explanation
Remember to distinguish between the insurance dividend and the *interest* on that dividend. An insurance dividend is the amount of your premium that is paid back to you if your insurance company achieves a lower mortality cost on policyholders than it expected. An insurance dividend is treated as an adjustment to your insurance premium and is therefore not taxable income to you unless it exceeds your premium. If you leave this dividend on deposit with the insurance company, however, any interest you receive on it should be included as interest income, just as it would be if you had left the money in the bank.

TaxPlanner
If you receive Form 1099-INT from an insurance company every year, you may have an untapped source of cash at your disposal. This form usually indicates that insurance dividends paid in prior years are accumulating in a savings account paying *passbook* rates. This money might be better invested in money market funds or other investments paying higher rates. To find out if you have money you did not know about, contact your insurance agent.

Prepaid insurance premiums. Any increase in the value of prepaid insurance premiums, advance premiums, or premium deposit funds is interest if it is applied to the payment of premiums due on insurance policies or made available for you to withdraw.

U.S. obligations. Interest on U.S. obligations, such as U.S. Treasury bills, notes, and bonds, issued by any agency or instrumentality of the United States is taxable for federal income tax purposes.

Explanation
Interest income on U.S. obligations is not subject to *state and local* income tax. Therefore, if your state has a high income tax rate, investing in U.S. obligations, rather than in instruments taxable at the state level, could mean a significant tax savings overall. Nevertheless, interest paid on **tax refunds** made by the federal government is taxable by both the state and the federal governments.

Treasury bills generally have a 13-week, 26-week, or 52-week maturity period. They are issued at a discount in the amount of $1,000 and multiples of $1,000. The difference between the discounted price you pay for the bills and the face value you receive at maturity is interest income. Generally, you report this interest income when the bill is paid at maturity.

Treasury notes have maturity periods of more than 1 year, ranging up to 10 years. Maturity periods for *Treasury bonds* are longer than 10 years. Both notes and bonds generally pay interest every 6 months. Generally, you report this interest for the year paid. For more information, see *U.S. Treasury Bills, Notes, and Bonds* in chapter 1 of Publication 550.

Explanation
The paragraph above discusses interest income only when a Treasury bill is held until maturity. When a Treasury bill is sold before maturity, the difference between the purchase price and the selling price may be part interest and part **short-term capital gain** or loss.

Example
You buy a $10,000 Treasury bill for $9,760 exactly 100 days before maturity. Thirty days later, you sell the bill for $9,850.

For tax purposes, you have earned a pro rata portion of the discount as interest income for the time you held the bill: $30/100 \times (\$10,000 - \$9,760) = \$72$. The other $18 you receive over and above the purchase price is a short-term capital gain.

TaxSaver
U.S. Treasury bills are relatively short-term investments. Their maturity dates vary from a week to a year. Since the interest income in most cases is reported at maturity—unless the bill is sold beforehand—purchasing Treasury bills with a maturity date falling in the following year offers cash basis taxpayers an opportunity to postpone interest income from one year to the next. However, if you borrow money to acquire Treasury bills, your interest expense deduction may also be deferred. See Chapter 25, *Interest Expense,* for an explanation.

For other information on Treasury notes or bonds, write to:

Bureau of the Public Debt
Attn: Customer Information
Parkersburg, WV 26106-2186

Or, on the Internet, visit: **www.publicdebt.treas.gov**

For information on series EE, series I, and series HH savings bonds, see *U.S. Savings Bonds,* later.

Interest on tax refunds. Interest you receive on tax refunds is taxable income.

Interest on condemnation award. If the condemning authority pays you interest to compensate you for a delay in paying an award, the interest is taxable.

Explanation
The interest on the award is taxable even if the condemning authority is a state or local government. The logic is as
follows: The interest arises out of the government's eminent
domain activities and not through the exercise of its borrowing power.

Installment sale payments. If a contract for the sale or exchange of
property provides for deferred payments, it also usually provides for interest payable with the deferred payments. That interest is taxable when
you receive it. If little or no interest is provided for in a deferred payment contract, part of each payment may be treated as interest. See *Unstated Interest and Original Issue Discount* in Publication 537, *Installment Sales.*

Explanation
Congress has clamped down on a device that was used
with great success. The idea was to sell a piece of real
estate at an inflated price in order to receive a larger
long-term capital gain and, in turn, agree to accept deferred payments carrying a low interest rate. The strategy
was to give up interest income taxed at ordinary rates and
replace it with a larger long-term capital gain taxed at a
lower rate.

Under legislation effective for debt instruments issued
after December 31, 1984, payments must be made on a
current basis, and certain tests are applied to determine if
the interest rate is appropriate. If it isn't, some of each
payment is recharacterized as interest. Because the rules
are very complex, you should obtain professional assistance when you are negotiating a deal and making the necessary computations.

The rules are not applicable to sales of less than
$250,000, the sale of your principal residence, or sales for
less than $1 million of a farm used by the seller as a farm.

However, in these situations, the IRS has the authority
to recharacterize a transaction if the stipulated interest rate
falls below the published federal rate. In such cases, the
IRS would reduce the amount of the capital gain and increase the interest income.

Interest on annuity contract. Accumulated interest on an annuity
contract you sell before its maturity date is taxable.

Usurious interest. Usurious interest is interest charged at an illegal
rate. This is taxable as interest unless state law automatically changes
it to a payment on the principal.

Individual retirement arrangements (IRAs). Interest on a Roth
IRA generally is not taxable. Interest on a traditional IRA is tax deferred.
You generally do not include it in your income until you make with-
drawals from the IRA. See chapter 18.

Interest income on frozen deposits. Exclude from your gross income interest on frozen deposits. A deposit is frozen if, at the end of the
year, you cannot withdraw any part of the deposit because:

1) The financial institution is bankrupt or insolvent, or
2) The state where the institution is located has placed limits on withdrawals because other financial institutions in the state are bankrupt
or insolvent.

The amount of interest you must exclude is the interest that was
credited on the frozen deposits minus the sum of:

1) The net amount you withdrew from these deposits during the year,
and

2) The amount you could have withdrawn as of the end of the year (not
reduced by any penalty for premature withdrawals of a time deposit).

If you receive a Form 1099-INT for interest income on deposits that were
frozen at the end of 2001, see *Frozen deposits* under *How To Report Interest Income* in chapter 1 of Publication 550, for information about reporting this interest income exclusion on your 2001 tax return.

The interest you exclude is treated as credited to your account in the
following year. You must include it in income when you can withdraw
it.

Example. $100 of interest was credited on your frozen deposit dur-
ing the year. You withdrew $80 but could not withdraw any more as of
the end of the year. You must include $80 in your income for the year.
You must exclude $20.

Bonds traded flat. If you buy a bond when interest has been defaulted
or when the interest has accrued but has not been paid, that interest is
not income and is not taxable as interest if paid later. When you receive
a payment of that interest, it is a return of capital that reduces the remaining cost basis. Interest that accrues after the date of purchase, however, is taxable interest income for the year it is received or accrued. See
Bonds Sold Between Interest Dates, later, for more information.

Below-market loans. A below-market loan is a loan on which no interest is charged or on which interest is charged at a rate below the applicable federal rate. See *Below-Market Loans* in chapter 1 of Publication 550 for more information.

Explanation
If you make a below-market loan, you must report as interest income any forgone interest (defined below) arising from
that loan. How you should report the income as well as the
application of the below-market loan rules and exceptions
are described in this section.

If you receive a below-market loan, you may be able to
claim a deduction for interest expense in excess of the interest that you actually paid—but only if you use the funds
to buy investment property.

Forgone interest. For any period, forgone interest is:

1. The amount of interest that would be payable for that period if interest accrued on the loan at the applicable federal rate and was payable annually on December 31,
minus
2. Any interest actually payable on the loan for the period.

The **applicable federal rate** is set by the IRS each month
and is published in the *Internal Revenue Bulletin*. You can
also contact an IRS office to get these rates.

Below-market loans. A below-market loan is a loan on
which no interest is charged or on which interest is charged
at a rate below the applicable federal rate. A below-market
loan is generally recharacterized as an arm's length transaction in which the lender is treated as having made:

1. A loan to the borrower in exchange for a note that requires the payment of interest at the applicable federal
rate, and
2. An additional payment to the borrower.

The lender's additional payment to the borrower is treated
as a gift, dividend, contribution to capital, payment of compensation, or other payment, depending on the substance
of the transaction. The borrower may have to report this payment as taxable income depending on its classification.

Loans subject to the rules. The rules for below-market
loans apply to:

Gift loans
Compensation-related loans

Corporation-shareholder loans

Tax avoidance loans

Certain loans to qualified continuing care facilities (made after October 11, 1985)

Certain other below-market loans

Exceptions

The rules for below-market loans do not apply to certain loans on days on which the total outstanding amount of loans between the borrower and lender is $10,000 or less. The rules do not apply on those days to:

1. Gift loans between individuals if the gift loan is not directly used to purchase or carry income-producing assets; or
2. Compensation-related loans or corporation-shareholder loans if the avoidance of federal tax is not a principal purpose of the loan.

A compensation-related loan is any below-market loan between an employer and an employee or between an independent contractor and a person for whom the contractor provided services.

Other loans not subject to the rules. Other loans are excluded from the below-market rules, including:

1. Loans made available by the lender to the general public on the same terms and conditions and that are consistent with the lender's customary business practice.
2. Loans subsidized by a federal, state, or municipal government that are made available under a program of general application to the public.
3. Certain employee-relocation loans.
4. Loans to or from a foreign person, unless the interest income would be effectively connected with the conduct of a U.S. trade or business and would not be exempt from U.S. tax under an income tax treaty.
5. Other loans on which the interest arrangement can be shown to have no significant effect on the federal tax liability of the lender or the borrower.
6. Certain refundable loans to a qualified continuing care facility under a continuing care contract. This exclusion may apply if the lender (resident) or the lender's spouse (resident's spouse) is age 65 or older before the close of the year. In order to qualify for the exclusion from the below-market loan rules, the continuing care facility must also provide the resident-lender (without substantial additional charge) a separate living space, meals, routine medical care, and, when necessary, long-term nursing care. For 2001, the exclusion applies only to the part of the total outstanding loan balance that is $144,100 or less. This threshold is indexed annually for inflation.

If a taxpayer structures a transaction to be a loan not subject to the below-market loan rules, and one of the principal purposes of structuring the transaction in such a way is to avoid federal tax, then the IRS may consider the loan to be a tax-avoidance scheme and, as such, subject to the rules for below-market loans.

All the facts and circumstances are used to determine if the interest arrangement of a loan has a significant effect on the federal tax liability of the lender or borrower. Some factors to be considered are:

- Whether income and deduction items generated by the loan offset each other

- The amount of such items
- The cost to the taxpayer of complying with the below-market loan provisions, if they applied
- Any reasons other than tax avoidance purposes for structuring the transaction as a below-market loan

Gift and demand loans. A gift loan is any below-market loan where the forgone interest is in the nature of a gift. A demand loan is a loan payable in full at any time upon demand by the lender. A lender who makes a gift loan or demand loan is treated as transferring an additional payment to the borrower (as a gift, dividend, etc.) in an amount equal to the forgone interest. The borrower is treated as transferring the forgone interest to the lender and may be entitled to an interest expense deduction depending on the use of the monies borrowed. The lender must report that amount as interest income. These transfers are considered to occur annually, generally on December 31.

Example

Jill's grandmother makes an interest-free loan to Jill on July 1 for $50,000. Jill has net investment income from outside sources of $5,000. The applicable federal interest rate is 5% at this time. This loan will be treated as a gift loan. On December 31, Jill will be treated as having paid her grandmother $1,250 in interest and her grandmother must report $1,250 of interest income, even though no money has changed hands.

Special rules for gift loans between individuals that do not exceed $100,000. For gift loans that do not exceed $100,000, the amount of forgone interest that is treated as transferred by the borrower to the lender is limited. This limit is the borrower's net investment income for the year, unless one of the principal purposes of the loan is the avoidance of federal tax. Also, if a borrower has net investment income of $1,000 or less for the year, the borrower's net investment income is considered to be zero and the borrower will have no interest expense deduction.

Example

Using the same facts in the above example, assume Jill has $1,100 in net investment income for the year. On December 31, Jill will be treated as having paid her grandmother $1,100 in interest (not $1,250) because of the net investment income limitation. Jill's grandmother would include the $1,100 as interest income.

Term loans. A lender who makes a below-market term loan (a loan that is not a demand loan) is treated as transferring, as a gift, dividend, etc., an additional lump-sum cash payment to the borrower on the date the loan is made. The amount of this payment is the amount of the loan minus the present value of all payments due under the loan. An amount equal to this excess is treated as original issue discount (OID). Accordingly, the OID rules of Section 1272 of the Internal Revenue Code apply. The lender must report the annual part of the OID as interest income. The borrower may be able to deduct some or all of the excess as interest expense depending on the use of the monies borrowed.

Effective dates. These rules apply to term loans made after June 6, 1984, and to demand loans outstanding after that date.

U.S. Savings Bonds

This section provides tax information on U.S. savings bonds. It explains how to report the interest income on these bonds and how to treat transfers of these bonds.

For other information on U.S. savings bonds, write to:

Bureau of the Public Debt
Attn: Savings Bond Operations Office
Parkersburg, WV 26106-1328

Or, on the Internet, visit: **www.savingsbonds.gov**

Cash method taxpayers. If you use the cash method of accounting, as most individual taxpayers do, you generally report the interest on U.S. savings bonds when you receive it. The cash method of accounting is explained in chapter 1 under *Accounting Methods.*

Accrual method taxpayers. If you use an accrual method of accounting, you must report interest on U.S. savings bonds each year as it accrues. You cannot postpone reporting interest until you receive it or the bonds mature. Accrual methods of accounting are explained in chapter 1 under *Accounting Methods.*

Series HH Bonds. These bonds are issued at face value. Interest is paid twice a year by direct deposit to your bank account. If you are a cash method taxpayer, you must report interest on these bonds as income in the year you receive it.

Series HH Bonds were first offered in 1980. Before 1980, **series H bonds** were issued. Series H bonds are treated the same as series HH bonds. If you are a cash method taxpayer, you must report the interest when you receive it.

Series H bonds have a maturity period of 30 years. Series HH bonds mature in 20 years.

Series EE and series I bonds. Interest on these bonds is payable when you redeem the bonds. The difference between the purchase price and the redemption value is taxable interest.

Series EE bonds were first offered in July 1980. They have a maturity period of 30 years. Before July 1980, **series E bonds** were issued. The original 10-year maturity period of series E bonds has been extended to 40 years for bonds issued before December 1965 and 30 years for bonds issued after November 1965. Series EE and series E bonds are issued at a discount. The face value is payable to you at maturity.

Series I bonds were first offered in 1998. These are inflation-indexed bonds issued at their face amount with a maturity period of 30 years. The face value plus accrued interest is payable to you at maturity.

If you use the cash method of reporting income, you can report the interest on series EE, series E, and series I bonds in either of the following ways.

1) **Method 1.** Postpone reporting the interest until the earlier of the year you cash or dispose of the bonds or the year they mature. (However, see *Savings bonds traded,* later.) **Note.** Series E bonds issued in 1961 and 1971 matured in 2001. If you have used method 1, you generally must report the interest on these bonds on your 2001 return.
2) **Method 2.** Choose to report the increase in redemption value as interest each year.

You must use the same method for all series EE, series E, and series I bonds you own. If you do not choose method 2 by reporting the increase in redemption value as interest each year, you must use method 1.

Tip. *If you plan to cash your bonds in the same year that you will pay for higher education expenses, you may want to use method 1 because you may be able to exclude the interest from your income. To learn how, see* Education Savings Bond Program, *later.*

Change from method 1. If you want to change your method of reporting the interest from method 1 to method 2, you can do so without permission from the IRS. In the year of change you must report all interest accrued to date and not previously reported for all your bonds.

Once you choose to report the interest each year, you must continue to do so for all series EE, series E, and series I bonds you own and for any you get later, unless you request permission to change, as explained next.

Change from method 2. To change from method 2 to method 1, you must request permission from the IRS. Permission for the change is automatically granted if you send the IRS a statement that meets all the following requirements.

1) You have typed or printed at the top, *"Change in Method of Accounting Under Section 6.01 of the Appendix of Rev. Proc. 99–49 (or later update)."*
2) It includes your name and social security number under the label in (1).
3) It identifies the savings bonds for which you are requesting this change.
4) It includes your agreement to:
   a) Report all interest on any bonds acquired during or after the year of change when the interest is realized upon disposition, redemption, or final maturity, whichever is earliest, and
   b) Report all interest on the bonds acquired before the year of change when the interest is realized upon disposition, redemption, or final maturity, whichever is earliest, with the exception of the interest reported in prior tax years.
5) It includes your signature.

You must attach this statement to your tax return for the year of change, which you must file by the due date (including extensions).

You can have an automatic extension of 6 months from the due date of your return (including extensions) to file the statement with an amended return. To get this extension, you must have filed your original return by the due date (including extensions). At the top of the statement, write *"Filed pursuant to section 301.9100–2."*

By the date you file the original statement, you must also send a copy to the address below.

Internal Revenue Service
Attention: CC:PA:T
P.O. Box 7604
Benjamin Franklin Station
Washington, DC 20044

If you use a private delivery service, send the copy to the address below.

Internal Revenue Service
Attention: CC:PA:T
1111 Constitution Avenue, NW
Room 6561
Washington, DC 20044

Instead of filing this statement, you can request permission to change from method 2 to method 1 by filing **Form 3115.** In that case, follow the form instructions for an automatic change. No user fee is required.

Explanation

Series E and Series EE bonds are unique investments from a tax viewpoint. Since you, as a cash method taxpayer, may decide not to report the increase in value of the bonds as income each year and instead may decide to report the interest income when the bonds are cashed in or when they reach final maturity (whichever is earlier), you can—to an unusual extent—control when the income is recognized. The best time to redeem the bonds is a year in which you have low taxable income and a low tax rate.

Few people choose to report income annually rather than at sale or maturity, but if you do, you would report as income the increase in the redemption value of each bond each year. All you must do is report the income on your tax return. It would be advantageous to report the income annually only if you had an income so low that your personal exemption and itemized deductions or standard deduction might otherwise be wasted. The most likely people to choose this option are children age 14 and over and retired people, both of whom may have low taxable income. (Under the Tax Reform Act of 1986, income received by children under age 14 may be taxed at their parents' rate.) Remember, once you choose to report the income each year, you must obtain permission from the IRS to change your reporting method.

Example
A 70-year-old unmarried man with only $1,500 of other income might wish to report his savings bond interest each year, since his first $8,550 of income (his standard deduction and exemption) is tax free in 2001. If he holds the bonds and reports all the income in the year they mature, his taxable income in that year might be more than $8,550, and he would therefore pay taxes he could have otherwise avoided by reporting a smaller amount of interest each year over the life of the bond.

Explanation
The interest rate on Series EE bonds varies depending upon when the bonds were purchased. The method of calculating the interest rate is different for bonds purchased prior to May 1, 1995, between May 1, 1995, and April 30, 1997, and after May 1, 1997. The Treasury site at http://www.publicdebt.treas.gov/sav/savtypes has more details.

Millions of Series E and H bonds continue to be held by the public. Most are still earning interest due to extended maturity rates. Some, however, have reached their final maturity and should be exchanged or redeemed.

Series HH bonds may be obtained in exchange for outstanding eligible Series EE bonds and Series E bonds having a combined redemption value of $500 or more. Owners who have deferred reporting interest earned on the bonds that they plan to exchange may continue to defer the interest until the year in which the Series HH bonds received in exchange are redeemed, reach final maturity, or are otherwise disposed of.

Although Series H bonds cannot be exchanged for Series HH bonds (nor can Series E bonds be exchanged for Series EE bonds), the redemption proceeds can be reinvested in new series bonds. However, any previously tax-deferred interest must be reported for federal income tax purposes in the year of redemption.

TAXPLANNER
For most bonds issued prior to May 1997, interest is credited to U.S. savings bonds at specified dates (i.e., there is no proration of interest for bonds cashed during the middle of an interest period). Thus, you should plan ahead to cash in your bonds just after (versus just before) an interest credit date.

Co-owners. If a U.S. savings bond is issued in the names of co-owners, such as you and your child or you and your spouse, interest on the bond is generally taxable to the co-owner who bought the bond.

One co-owner's funds used. If you used your funds to buy the bond, you must pay the tax on the interest. This is true even if you let the other co-owner redeem the bond and keep all the proceeds. Under these circumstances, since the other co-owner will receive a Form 1099-INT at the time of redemption, the other co-owner must provide you with another Form 1099-INT showing the amount of interest from the bond that is taxable to you. The co-owner who redeemed the bond is a "nominee." See *Nominee distributions* under *How To Report Interest Income* in chapter 1 of Publication 550 for more information about how a person who is a nominee reports interest income belonging to another person.

Both co-owners' funds used. If you and the other co-owner each contribute part of the bond's purchase price, the interest is generally taxable to each of you, in proportion to the amount each of you paid.

Community property. If you and your spouse live in a community property state and hold bonds as community property, one-half of the interest is considered received by each of you. If you file separate returns, each of you generally must report one-half of the bond interest. For more information about community property, see Publication 555, *Community Property.*

Table 8–1. These rules are also shown in *Table 8–1.*
Ownership transferred. If you bought series E, series EE, or series I bonds **entirely with your own funds** and had them reissued in your co-owner's name or beneficiary's name alone, you must include in your gross income for the year of reissue all interest that you earned on these bonds and have not previously reported. But, if the bonds were reissued in your name alone, you do not have to report the interest accrued at that time.

This same rule applies when bonds (other than bonds held as community property) are transferred between spouses incident to divorce.

Explanation
If you make a gift of Series E or Series EE bond to a child, remember that it is not possible to transfer the obligation of reporting the interest income that has already accu-

Table 8–1. **Who Pays the Tax on U.S. Savings Bond Interest**

IF ...	THEN the tax on the bond interest must be paid by ...
You buy a bond in your name and the name of another person as co-owners, using only your own funds	You.
You buy a bond in the name of another person, who is the sole owner of the bond	The person for whom you bought the bond.
You and another person buy a bond as co-owners, each contributing part of the purchase price	Both you and the other co-owner, in proportion to the amount each paid for the bond.
You and your spouse, who live in a community property state, buy a bond that is community property	You and your spouse. If you file separate returns, both you and your spouse generally pay tax on one-half of the interest.

mulated. The interest that has accumulated through the date of the gift must be reported by the donor in the year of the gift. Interest that accumulates from the date of the gift until maturity is reported by the individual receiving the gift.

Purchased jointly. If you and a co-owner each contributed funds to buy series E, series EE, or series I bonds *jointly* and later have the bonds reissued in the co-owner's name alone, you must include in your gross income for the year of reissue your share of all the interest earned on the bonds that you have not previously reported. At the time of reissue, the former co-owner does not have to include in gross income his or her share of the interest earned that was not reported before the transfer. This interest, however, as well as all interest earned after the reissue, is income to the former co-owner.

This income-reporting rule also applies when the bonds are reissued in the name of your former co-owner and a new co-owner. But the new co-owner will report only his or her share of the interest earned after the transfer.

If bonds that you and a co-owner bought *jointly* are reissued to each of you separately in the same proportion as your contribution to the purchase price, neither you nor your co-owner has to report at that time the interest earned before the bonds were reissued.

Example 1. You and your spouse each spent an equal amount to buy a $1,000 series EE savings bond. The bond was issued to you and your spouse as co-owners. You both postpone reporting interest on the bond. You later have the bond reissued as two $500 bonds, one in your name and one in your spouse's name. At that time neither you nor your spouse has to report the interest earned to the date of reissue.

Example 2. You bought a $1,000 series EE savings bond entirely with your own funds. The bond was issued to you and your spouse as co-owners. You both postpone reporting interest on the bond. You later have the bond reissued as two $500 bonds, one in your name and one in your spouse's name. You must report half the interest earned to the date of reissue.

Transfer to a trust. If you own series E, series EE, or series I bonds and transfer them to a trust, giving up all rights of ownership, you must include in your income for that year the interest earned to the date of transfer if you have not already reported it. However, if you are considered the owner of the trust and if the increase in value both before and after the transfer continues to be taxable to you, you can continue to defer reporting the interest earned each year. You must include the total interest in your income in the year you cash or dispose of the bonds or the year the bonds finally mature, whichever is earlier.

TAXSAVER

If you transfer the bonds to a revocable trust, of which you are considered the owner, you may continue to defer reporting the income. Many individuals use a revocable trust as a substitute for a will. A revocable trust is not required to pay federal income tax on income earned in the trust. Instead, all income (and deductions) is reported on your individual tax return, as if the revocable trust did not exist. In essence, you are treated as if you owned the assets outright. For more details, consult your tax advisor.

The same rules apply to previously unreported interest on series EE or series E bonds if the transfer to a trust consisted of series HH or series H bonds you acquired in a trade for the series EE or series E bonds. See *Savings bonds traded,* later.

Decedents. The manner of reporting interest income on series E, series EE, or series I bonds, after the death of the owner, depends on the accounting and income-reporting method previously used by the decedent. This is explained in chapter 1 of Publication 550.

Explanation

Income that the decedent had a right to receive at the time of death, but which is included on another's tax return (or the estate tax return), is called "income in respect of the decedent." See Chapter 4, *Decedents,* for more information.

TAXPLANNER

If the final income tax return of the decedent shows a low amount of taxable income, it would be better to include the interest income from the date of purchase of the bonds through the date of death, the choice described in (1). Otherwise, the IRS says that the interest income must be reported by the person who receives the bonds, the choice described in (2).

However, there is a third option. If the bonds are in the name of the decedent alone, their ownership passes to the estate. The estate is a separate taxable entity that files its own income tax return. If the estate has a low amount of taxable income, it might be advisable for the executor to redeem the bonds.

A point to remember is this: The unique method by which interest from U.S. savings bonds are taxed gives you an opportunity to reduce income tax by selecting the person or entity with the lowest tax rate to receive the income.

Example 1

Your uncle, a cash method taxpayer, died and left you a $1,000 Series E bond. He bought the bond for $750 and chose not to report the interest each year. At the date of death, interest of $200 had accrued on the bond and its value of $950 was included in your uncle's estate. Your uncle's executor did not choose to include the $200 accrued interest in your uncle's final income tax return.

You are a cash method taxpayer and do not choose to report the interest each year as it is earned. If you cash the bond when it reaches maturity value of $1,000, you will report $250 interest income—the difference between the maturity value of $1,000 and the original cost of $750. Also, you may deduct (as a miscellaneous deduction not subject to the 2% AGI limit) in that year any federal estate tax that was paid on the $200 of interest that was included in your uncle's estate. For more information on this subject, see Chapter 4, *Decedents.*

Example 2

If, in Example 1, the executor had chosen to include the $200 accrued interest in your uncle's final tax return, you would report only $50 as interest when you cashed the bond at maturity. This $50 is the interest earned after your uncle's death.

Example 3

Your aunt died owning Series H bonds that she got in a trade for Series E bonds. (See *Savings bonds traded.*) You were the beneficiary of these bonds. Your aunt used the cash method and did not choose to report the interest on the Series E bonds each year as it accrued. Your aunt's executor did not choose to include on her final tax return any interest earned before her death.

The income in respect of a decedent is the sum of the unreported interest on the Series E bonds and the interest, if any, payable on the Series H bonds but not received as of the date of your aunt's death. You must report any interest received during the year as income on your return. The part of the interest that was payable but not received before your aunt's death is income in respect of the decedent and may qualify for the estate tax deduction. For when to report the interest on the Series E bonds traded, see *Savings bonds traded,* below.

TaxSaver

Series EE bonds can be an interesting tax-sheltered investment in two ways. First, because most individuals are cash method taxpayers paying taxes on income as it is received, interest income from Series EE bonds is not recognized until it is received when the bonds are redeemed. But, there is a second way you can shelter your interest income from Series EE bonds for an even longer time. If, instead of redeeming the bonds when they come due, you exchange them for Series HH bonds (that pay interest semiannually), you can avoid recognition of the accumulated Series EE bonds interest until the Series HH bonds are redeemed.

Example

Salma purchases $7,500 worth of Series EE bonds, which pay interest at 4% per year. In slightly more than 7 years, the bonds will have grown in value to $10,000. Instead of redeeming them at that point, Salma exchanges them for $10,000 worth of Series HH bonds, which pay interest at the rate of 4% per year. The $2,500 of interest income earned over the years on the Series EE bonds would not be taxable at the date of exchange but would be deferred. Salma will receive $400 of taxable interest income per year on the Series HH bonds. The $2,500 of deferred interest income on the Series EE bonds would not be taxable until the Series HH bonds reach final maturity or are redeemed.

There is, however, a limitation on the purchase of Series EE bonds. An individual may purchase only up to $15,000 per year.

Savings bonds traded. If you postponed reporting the interest on your series EE or series E bonds, you did not recognize taxable income when you traded the bonds for series HH or series H bonds, unless you received cash in the trade. (You cannot trade series I bonds for series HH bonds.) Any cash you received is income up to the amount of the interest earned on the bonds traded. When your series HH or series H bonds mature, or if you dispose of them before maturity, you report as interest the difference between their redemption value and your cost. Your cost is the sum of the amount you paid for the traded series EE or series E bonds plus any amount you had to pay at the time of the trade.

Example. You own series E bonds with accrued interest of $523 and a redemption value of $2,723 and have postponed reporting the interest. You trade the bonds for $2,500 in series HH bonds and $223 in cash. You must report the $223 as taxable income in the year of the trade.

Choice to report interest in year of trade. You can choose to treat all of the previously unreported accrued interest on the series EE or series E bonds traded for series HH bonds as income in the year of the trade. If you make this choice, it is treated as a change from method 1. See *Change from method 1* under *Series EE and series I bonds,* earlier.

Form 1099-INT for U.S. savings bonds interest. When you cash a bond, the bank or other payer that redeems it must give you a Form 1099-INT if the interest part of the payment you receive is $10 or more. Box 3 of your Form 1099-INT should show the interest as the difference between the amount you received and the amount paid for the bond. However, your Form 1099-INT may show more interest than you have to include on your income tax return. For example, this may happen if any of the following are true.

1) You chose to report the increase in the redemption value of the bond each year. The interest shown on your Form 1099-INT will not be reduced by amounts previously included in income.
2) You received the bond from a decedent. The interest shown on your Form 1099-INT will not be reduced by any interest reported by the decedent before death, or on the decedent's final return, or by the estate on the estate's income tax return.
3) Ownership of the bond was transferred. The interest shown on your Form 1099-INT will not be reduced by interest that accrued before the transfer.
4) You were named as a co-owner and the other co-owner contributed funds to buy the bond. The interest shown on your Form 1099-INT will not be reduced by the amount you received as nominee for the other co-owner. (See *Co-owners,* earlier in this chapter, for more information about the reporting requirements.)
5) You received the bond in a taxable distribution from a retirement or profit-sharing plan. The interest shown on your Form 1099-INT will not be reduced by the interest portion of the amount taxable as a distribution from the plan and not taxable as interest. (This amount is generally shown on Form 1099-R, *Distributions From Pensions, Annuities, Retirement or Profit-Sharing Plans, IRAs, Insurance Contracts, etc.,* for the year of distribution.)

For more information on including the correct amount of interest on your return for (1), (2), (3), and (4) above, see *How To Report Interest Income,* later. Publication 550 includes examples showing how to report these amounts.

If you received a taxable distribution of bonds from a retirement or profit-sharing plan ((5) above), see *How To Report Interest Income* in Publication 550 for information on how to report the interest.

Tip. *Interest on U.S. savings bonds is exempt from state and local taxes. The Form 1099-INT you receive will indicate the amount that is for U.S. savings bond interest in box 3. Do not include this amount on your state or local income tax return.*

Explanation

When you redeem U.S. savings bonds, the government assumes that the difference between the issue price and the redemption amount is interest paid to you entirely at that time, even though some of the interest may already have been reported by you or someone else. The government will therefore issue a Form 1099-INT to you for the full amount.

If you should not be taxed on the full amount of interest, you should show the full amount as reported on the Form 1099-INT issued by the government on Schedule B (Form 1040) and also show a subtraction for the amount that is not taxable to you. This will help you to avoid IRS deficiency notices.

Education Savings Bond Program

You may be able to exclude from income all or part of the interest you receive on the redemption of qualified U.S. savings bonds during the year if you pay qualified higher educational expenses during the same year. This exclusion is known as the *Education Savings Bond Program.*

If you are married, you can qualify for this exclusion only if you file a joint return with your spouse.

Form 8815. Use Form 8815 to figure your exclusion. Attach the form to your Form 1040 or Form 1040A.

☐ CORRECTED (if checked)

PAYER'S name, street address, city, state, ZIP code, and telephone no.	Payer's RTN (optional)	OMB No. 1545-0112	
		2001 Form **1099-INT**	**Interest Income**

PAYER'S Federal identification number	RECIPIENT'S identification number	1 Interest income not included in box 3 $	**Copy B** **For Recipient**
RECIPIENT'S name		2 Early withdrawal penalty $	3 Interest on U.S. Savings Bonds and Treas. obligations $	This is important tax information and is being furnished to the Internal Revenue Service. If you are required to file a return, a negligence penalty or other sanction may be imposed on you if this income is taxable and the IRS determines that it has not been reported.
Street address (including apt. no.)		**4 Federal income tax withheld** $	5 Investment expenses $	
City, state, and ZIP code		6 Foreign tax paid	7 Foreign country or U.S. possession	
Account number (optional)		$		

Form **1099-INT**   (Keep for your records.)   Department of the Treasury - Internal Revenue Service

Qualified U.S. savings bonds. A qualified U.S. savings bond is a series EE bond *issued after 1989* or a series I bond. The bond must be issued either in your name (sole owner) or in your and your spouse's names (co-owners). You must be at least 24 years old before the bond's issue date.

Caution. *The date a bond is issued may be earlier than the date the bond is purchased because bonds are issued as of the first day of the month in which they are purchased.*

Beneficiary. You can designate any individual (including a child) as a beneficiary of the bond.

Verification by IRS. If you claim the exclusion, the IRS will check it by using bond redemption information from the Department of the Treasury.

Qualified expenses. Qualified higher educational expenses are tuition and fees required for you, your spouse, or your dependent (for whom you can claim an exemption) to attend an eligible educational institution.

Qualified expenses include any contribution you make to a qualified state tuition program or to a Coverdell education savings account.

Qualified expenses do not include expenses for room and board or for courses involving sports, games, or hobbies that are not part of a degree program.

Eligible educational institutions. These institutions include most public, private, and nonprofit universities, colleges and vocational schools that are accredited and are eligible to participate in student aid programs run by the Department of Education.

Reduction for certain benefits. You must reduce your qualified higher educational expenses by certain benefits the student may have received. These benefits include:

1) Qualified scholarships that are exempt from tax (see chapter 13 for information on qualified scholarships), and
2) Any other nontaxable payments (other than gifts, bequests, or inheritances) received for educational expenses, such as:
   a) Veterans' educational assistance benefits,
   b) Benefits under a qualified state tuition program, or
   c) Certain employer-provided educational assistance benefits.

Effect of other tax benefits. Do not include in your qualified expenses any expenses used to:

1) Figure an education credit on Form 8863, or
2) Figure how much of a distribution from an education IRA you can exclude from your income.

Amount excludable. If the total proceeds (interest and principal) from the qualified U.S. savings bonds you redeem during the year are not more than your qualified higher educational expenses for the year, you can exclude all of the interest. If the proceeds are more than the expenses, you can exclude only part of the interest.

To determine the excludable amount, multiply the interest part of the proceeds by a fraction. The numerator (top part) of the fraction is the qualified higher educational expenses you paid during the year. The denominator (bottom part) of the fraction is the total proceeds you received during the year.

Example. In February 2001, Mark and Joan, a married couple, cashed a qualified series EE U.S. savings bond they bought in April 1993. They received proceeds of $7,256, representing principal of $5,000 and interest of $2,256. In 2001, they paid $4,000 of their daughter's college tuition. They are not claiming an education credit for that amount, and they do not have an education IRA. They can exclude $1,244 ($2,256 × ($4,000 ÷ $7,256)) of interest in 2001. They must pay tax on the remaining $1,012 ($2,256 − $1,244) interest.

TAXPLANNER

Certain high-income taxpayers do not qualify for the tax break on Series EE bonds for educational purposes. If this is the case, you might consider buying the bonds in your child's name. When the child reaches age 14, he or she may cash them in and will be taxed at his or her rate, rather than yours, which is presumably higher.

Modified adjusted gross income limit. The interest exclusion is limited if your modified adjusted gross income (modified AGI) is:

• $55,750 to $70,750 for taxpayers filing single or head of household, and
• $83,650 to $113,650 for married taxpayers filing jointly or for a qualifying widow(er) with dependent child.

You do not qualify for the interest exclusion if your modified AGI is equal to or more than the upper limit for your filing status.

Modified AGI, for purposes of this exclusion, is adjusted gross income (line 20 of Form 1040A or line 34 of Form 1040) figured before the interest exclusion, and modified by adding back any:

1) Foreign earned income exclusion,
2) Foreign housing exclusion or deduction,

3) Exclusion of income for bona fide residents of American Samoa,

4) Exclusion for income from Puerto Rico,

5) Exclusion for adoption benefits received under an employer's adoption assistance program, and

6) Deduction for student loan interest.

Use the worksheet in the instructions for line 9, Form 8815, to figure your modified AGI. If you claim any of the exclusion or deduction items listed above (except item 6), add the amount of the exclusion or deduction (except any deduction for student loan interest) to the amount on line 5 of the worksheet, and enter the total on Form 8815, line 9, as your modified AGI.

If you have investment interest expense incurred to earn royalty income, see *Education Savings Bond Program* in chapter 1 of Publication 550.

Recordkeeping. If you claim the interest exclusion, you must keep a written record of the qualified U.S. savings bonds you redeem. Your record must include the serial number, issue date, face value, and total redemption proceeds (principal and interest) of each bond. You can use **Form 8818,** *Optional Form To Record Redemption of Series EE and I U.S. Savings Bonds Issued After 1989,* to record this information. You should also keep bills, receipts, canceled checks, or other documentation that shows you paid qualified higher educational expenses during the year.

Bonds Sold Between Interest Dates

If you sell a bond between interest payment dates, part of the sales price represents interest accrued to the date of sale. You must report that part of the sales price as interest income for the year of sale.

If you buy a bond between interest payment dates, part of the purchase price represents interest accrued before the date of purchase. When that interest is paid to you, treat it as a return of your capital investment, rather than interest income, by reducing your basis in the bond. See *Accrued interest on bonds* under *How To Report Interest Income* in chapter 1 of Publication 550 for information on reporting the payment.

Explanation
Usually, interest on a bond is paid every 6 months. When a bond is sold between interest payment dates, the seller is entitled to payment from the buyer—in addition to payment for the bond itself—for the interest earned since the issuer's last interest payment. This extra payment—often called "purchased interest" on a broker's statement—is interest income to the seller of the bond, reportable for tax purposes as of the date of the sale. The buyer of the bond should record the purchased interest separately from the price of the bond in his or her records. The purchased interest partially offsets the first interest payment made to the buyer.

If the purchased interest is paid in 2001 but the first interest payment is not received until 2002, the buyer should report the purchased interest as an adjustment to interest income in 2002, not in 2001.

Example 1
On April 1, 2001, John bought from George a $10,000 bond yielding 10%. Interest on the bond is paid on January 1 and July 1 of each year. John paid $10,250—$10,000 in principal plus $250 for interest earned from January 1 to April 1. Thus, George received $250 of interest income on April 1, 2001. John received his first interest check on July 1, 2001. Half of that $500 represented a payment of purchased interest, and the other half

represented interest income. In order to avoid any IRS notices, John should report the full $500 on Schedule B (Form 1040) and also show a subtraction for $250 of interest that he purchased.

Example 2
Assume the same facts as above, except that John bought the bond from George on October 1, 2001. John received his interest check for $500 on January 1, 2002. Half of it represented repayment of purchased interest, and the other half represented interest income. However, John may *not* deduct the $250 of purchased interest for 2001 but must wait until 2002. On the other hand, George will report his $250 of interest income on his 2001 return, since he received it on October 1, 2001.

Insurance

Life insurance proceeds paid to you as beneficiary of the insured person are usually not taxable. But if you receive the proceeds in installments, you must usually report a part of each installment payment as interest income.

For more information about insurance proceeds received in installments, see Publication 525, *Taxable and Nontaxable Income.*

Explanation
For more information on life insurance proceeds, see Chapter 13, *Other Income.*

Annuity. If you buy an annuity with life insurance proceeds, the annuity payments you receive are taxed as pension and annuity income, not as interest income. See chapter 11 for information on pension and annuity income.

Original Issue Discount (OID)

Original issue discount (OID) is a form of interest. You generally include OID in your income as it accrues over the term of the debt instrument, whether or not you receive any payments from the issuer.

A debt instrument generally has OID when the instrument is issued for a price that is less than its stated redemption price at maturity. OID is the difference between the stated redemption price at maturity and the issue price.

All instruments that pay no interest before maturity are presumed to be issued at a discount. Zero coupon bonds are one example of these instruments.

The OID accrual rules generally do not apply to short-term obligations (those with a fixed maturity date of 1 year or less from date of issue). See *Discount on Short-Term Obligations* in chapter 1 of Publication 550.

De minimis OID. You can treat the discount as zero if it is less than one-fourth of 1% (.0025) of the stated redemption price at maturity multiplied by the number of full years from the date of original issue to maturity. This small discount is known as "de minimis" OID.

Example 1. You bought a 10-year bond with a stated redemption price at maturity of $1,000, issued at $980 with OID of $20. One-fourth of 1% of $1,000 (stated redemption price) times 10 (the number of full years from the date of original issue to maturity) equals $25. Because the $20 discount is less than $25, the OID is treated as zero. (If you hold the bond at maturity, you will recognize $20 ($1,000 − $980) of capital gain.)

Example 2. The facts are the same as in *Example 1,* except that the bond was issued at $950. The OID is $50. Because the $50 discount is more than the $25 figured in *Example 1,* you must include the OID in income as it accrues over the term of the bond.

Debt instrument bought after original issue. If you buy a debt instrument with de minimis OID at a premium, the discount is not includible in income. If you buy a debt instrument with de minimis OID at a discount, the discount is reported under the market discount rules. See *Market Discount Bonds* in chapter 1 of Publication 550.

Exceptions to reporting OID. The OID rules discussed in this chapter do not apply to the following debt instruments.

1) Tax-exempt obligations. (However, see *Stripped tax-exempt obligations* under *Stripped Bonds and Coupons* in chapter 1 of Publication 550).
2) U.S. savings bonds.
3) Short-term debt instruments (those with a fixed maturity date of not more than 1 year from the date of issue).
4) Obligations issued by an individual before March 2, 1984.
5) Loans between individuals, if all the following are true.
   a) The lender is not in the business of lending money.
   b) The amount of the loan, plus the amount of any outstanding prior loans between the same individuals, is $10,000 or less.
   c) Avoiding any federal tax is not one of the principal purposes of the loan.

Explanation

The IRS interpretation is misleading with respect to tax-exempt obligations issued after September 3, 1982, and acquired after March 1, 1984. Even though interest on such obligations is tax-free, the OID rules will apply in determining the basis of the security in the event of sale, exchange, or maturity. (See the discussion later in this chapter.)

In addition, under the Technical and Miscellaneous Revenue Act of 1988, the original issue discount on a stripped tax-exempt bond may be treated as taxable interest if the stripped bond is sold at a discount rate that is higher than the original issue.

TAXPLANNER

Debt instruments issued after 1954 and before May 28, 1969 (or before July 2, 1982, if a government instrument). For these instruments, you pay no tax on the OID until the year you sell, exchange, or redeem the instrument. If a gain results, and if the instrument is a capital asset, the amount of the gain equal to the OID is taxed as ordinary interest income. The balance of the gain is capital gain. If there is a loss on the sale of the instrument, the entire loss is a capital loss and no reporting of OID is required.

Debt instruments issued after May 27, 1969 (or after July 1, 1982, if a government instrument), and before 1985. If you hold these debt instruments as capital assets, you must include a part of the discount in your gross income each year that you own the instruments. Your basis in the instrument is increased by the amount of OID that you include in your gross income.

Form 1099-OID. The issuer of the debt instrument (or your broker, if you held the instrument through a broker) should give you Form 1099-OID, *Original Issue Discount,* or a similar statement, if the total OID for the calendar year is $10 or more. Form 1099-OID will show, in box 1, the amount of OID for the part of the year that you held the bond. It also will show, in box 2, other interest that you must include in your income. A copy of Form 1099-OID will be sent to the IRS. Do not file your copy with your return. Keep it for your records.

In most cases, you must report the entire amount in boxes 1 and 2 of Form 1099—OID as interest income. But see *Refiguring OID shown on Form 1099-OID,* later in this discussion, for more information.

Nominee. If someone else is the holder of record (the registered owner) of an OID instrument that belongs to you and receives a Form 1099-OID on your behalf, that person must give you a Form 1099-OID.

Refiguring OID shown on Form 1099-OID. You must refigure the OID shown in box 1 of Form 1099-OID if either of the following apply.

1) You bought the debt instrument after its original issue and paid a premium or an acquisition premium.
2) The debt instrument is a stripped bond or a stripped coupon (including certain zero coupon instruments).

For information about figuring the correct amount of OID to include in your income, see *Figuring OID on Long-Term Debt Instruments* in Publication 1212.

Explanation

Stripped coupon bonds are coupon bonds that have been separated into component parts. The coupons represent claims for interest payments, which are paid on a periodic basis. The bond itself represents the claim for the repayment of the principal, which occurs at some future time.

Example

A 10-year, $10,000, 9% bond (interest paid semiannually) was issued on January 1, 2001, for $10,000. On April 1, 2001, when the bond had a market price of $9,900, the coupons were stripped from the bond so that they and the bond became separate assets that could be bought and sold in the marketplace. In other words, the holder could have sold the right to receive $450 semiannually for the next 9¾ years and could have independently sold the right to receive the $10,000 on January 1, 2011.

Assume that the right to receive 20 semiannual payments is worth $4,100 and the right to receive $10,000 on January 1, 2011, is worth $5,800. The tax treatment to buyer and to seller is as follows:

The seller.
1. Include the accrued interest income of $225 from January 1, 2001, through April 1, 2001, in income.
2. Increase your basis by the $225 to $10,225.
3. Allocate the basis, using **fair market value,** to the coupons [($4,100 ÷ $9,900) × $10,225 = $4,235)] and the bond [($5,800 ÷ $9,900) × $10,225 = $5,990)].
4. Compare the proceeds for what you sell—either the coupons or the bond—with the basis figured above to determine if you've had a gain or a loss.
5. The difference between the basis of what is not sold and the amount that will be received over time is considered an original issue discount (OID). That amount is treated as earned over the life of the asset. Thus, if the coupons were retained, the difference between their basis ($4,235) and the amount that will be received over time ($450 semiannually for 10 years, or $9,000) would be the original issue discount.

In this example, $4,765 in interest income must be included on your returns over the 10 years. The amount to be included in your income for each year is figured by performing a complicated computation, for which you will probably require professional assistance.

Similarly, if the bond were retained, the difference between its basis ($5,990) and the proceeds ($10,000) would be its original issue discount. Again, complicated compu-

Period	Beginning basis	interest income	OID portion	Interest portion	Ending basis
3	919,166	69,736	9,736	60,000	928,902
4	928,902	69,839	9,839	60,000	938,740
5	938,740	69,943	9,943	60,000	948,683
6	948,683	70,048	10,048	60,000	958,732
7	958,732	70,155	10,155	60,000	968,886
8	968,886	70,262	10,262	60,000	979,148
9	979,148	70,371	10,371	60,000	989,519
10	989,519	70,481	10,481	60,000	1,000,000
		$700,000	$100,000	$600,000	

The total interest income recognized for the first year will be $69,533 ($60,000 interest and $9,533 of OID). Further special computations will be required if the obligation is sold prior to maturity. Professional advice is *absolutely essential* for anyone who needs to make special OID computations.

TAXPLANNER

A zero-coupon bond is one that is purchased at a substantial discount and pays no interest during its life.

If you buy a zero-coupon bond, you do not bear the investment risk entailed in reinvesting interest payments received over the life of the bond because there are no such payments. Moreover, since the issue price and the maturity value have been derived from compound interest tables, you may figure what the precise return on your investment will be if the bond is held until it matures. This is true *only* of zero-coupon bonds.

Note: Because you do not receive the interest until a zero-coupon bond matures, the market value of the bond during the holding period can be very volatile as market interest rates change. The longer the maturity is, the more volatile is the price.

Even though the interest on a zero-coupon bond is not paid until maturity, it is included in income each year. Consequently, an individual must pay tax on income that he or she has not yet received. However, if the bonds are owned in your IRA or Keogh plan, this income is not currently taxable. [See Chapter 18, *Individual Retirement Arrangements and Education Savings Accounts.*] The advantage, however, is that you lock in an interest rate.

On the other hand, nontaxable zero-coupon bonds—such as zero-coupon municipal bonds—may be attractive to individuals in a high tax bracket for the obvious reasons that interest rates are locked in and the increase in value each year is not taxable. In this case, you increase your cost basis on the bonds each year by the amount of the original issue discount applicable to that year, even though you don't pay any federal tax on the income. You may, however, have to pay state income taxes. You will need to check your state tax rules.

Example

Assume that Jennifer purchases a 10-year $100,000, nontaxable zero-coupon bond on June 28, 2000, for $50,000. The chart below illustrates how the basis of the bond increases over the life of the bond.

---

tations are required to determine the amount included in your income each year.

The buyer. The difference between what you pay and what you will receive over time is the original issue discount. A special computation is necessary to figure how much you should include in income each year.

Form 1099-OID not received. If you had OID for the year but did not receive a Form 1099-OID, see Publication 1212, which lists total OID on certain debt instruments and has information that will help you figure OID. If your debt instrument is not listed in Publication 1212, consult the issuer for further information about the accrued OID for the year.
Refiguring periodic interest shown on Form 1099-OID. If you disposed of a debt instrument or acquired it from another holder during the year, see *Bonds Sold Between Interest Dates,* earlier, for information about the treatment of periodic interest that may be shown in box 2 of Form 1099-OID for that instrument.

Explanation

The IRS explanation about bonds issued before and after July 1, 1982, is correct. However, the Deficit Reduction Act of 1984 extended these rules to debt instruments issued by individuals after March 1, 1984. This will affect individuals who borrow and lend at a discounted rate.

The current law also makes original issue discount the general rule with regard to obligations issued after July 18, 1984, and purchased in the open market. (This law also applies to bonds issued before July 19, 1984, and purchased after April 30, 1993.) Under the prior law, the difference between the purchase price and ultimate proceeds on the sale or redemption of a debt instrument was treated as a capital gain. Now, however, if you sell property after December 31, 1984, or buy a bond in the marketplace that was issued after July 18, 1984, or a bond issued prior to July, 1984, and purchased after April 30, 1993, you must determine whether there is original issue discount and, if so, how much. Some of that amount will be included in your ordinary income each year. You will need professional help to make this calculation. For more information, see *Market discount bonds* later in this chapter.

Example

Assume that Jim purchases a publicly traded 6% $1 million bond that was issued after December 31, 1984, for $900,000. The bond has a maturity of 10 years at the time of purchase. Jim will also receive $60,000 in interest each year.

The computation of the amount of original issue discount to be included is as follows:

Post 7/1/82 debt
With coupon

Face value	$1,000,000
Purchase price	$900,000
Length of term	10
Coupon rate	6%

Period	Beginning basis	Total interest income	OID portion	Interest portion	Ending basis
1	$900,000	$69,533	$9,533	$60,000	$909,533
2	909,533	69,634	9,634	60,000	919,166

Post 7/1/82 debt
Zero-coupon

Face value	$100,000
Purchase price	$50,000
Length of term	10

Period	Beginning basis	OID	Ending basis
1	$50,000	$3,589	$53,589
2	53,589	3,846	57,435
3	57,435	4,122	61,557
4	61,557	4,418	65,975
5	65,975	4,735	70,711
6	70,711	5,075	75,786
7	75,786	5,439	81,225
8	81,225	5,830	87,055
9	87,055	6,248	93,303
10	93,303	6,697	100,000
		$50,000	

The new method for determining original issue discount illustrated above is applicable to tax-exempt bonds. The annual increase in basis is determined accordingly. However, the new original issue discount computation is *not* the method used for a tax-exempt bond issued before September 4, 1982, and acquired before March 2, 1984. Instead, a rule is used that allocates the discount proportionately over the life of the bond. The result of this is illustrated as follows.

Example
Assume the same facts as in the previous example except that the bond was purchased on July 1, 1982. The following chart illustrates how the basis of the bond increased under prior tax law.

Pre 7/1/82 debt
Zero-coupon

Face value	$100,000
Purchase price	$50,000
Length of term	10

Period	Beginning basis	OID	Ending basis
1	$50,000	$5,000	$55,000
2	55,000	5,000	60,000
3	60,000	5,000	65,000
4	65,000	5,000	70,000
5	70,000	5,000	75,000
6	75,000	5,000	80,000
7	80,000	5,000	85,000
8	85,000	5,000	90,000
9	90,000	5,000	95,000
10	95,000	5,000	100,000
		$50,000	

This is not the way interest actually accrued, and the consequence is an inflated basis for these bonds in their early years. The bizarre result: You may be able to sell these bonds and report a large capital loss even though there is no real economic loss.

Certificates of deposit (CDs). If you buy a CD with a maturity of more than 1 year, you must include in income each year a part of the total interest due and report it in the same manner as other OID.

This also applies to similar deposit arrangements with banks, building and loan associations, etc., including:

- Time deposits,
- Bonus plans,
- Savings certificates,
- Deferred income certificates,
- Bonus savings certificates, and
- Growth savings certificates.

TaxPlanner

A time deposit with a penalty for early withdrawal is one of the few investments that permits you to defer the recognition of income to a subsequent year when the investment matures rather than in the year when the interest accrues. Other examples are U.S. savings bonds and U.S. Treasury bills.

Bearer CDs. CDs issued after 1982 generally must be in registered form. Bearer CDs are CDs that are not in registered form. They are not issued in the depositor's name and are transferable from one individual to another.

Banks must provide the IRS and the person redeeming a bearer CD with a Form 1099-INT.

TaxPlanner

Market discount bonds. A market discount bond is any bond having market discount except:

1. Short-term obligations (those with fixed maturity dates of up to 1 year from the date of issue)
2. Tax-exempt obligations that you bought before May 1, 1993
3. U.S. savings bonds
4. Certain installment obligations

Market discount arises when the value of a debt obligation decreases after its issue date, generally because of an increase in interest rates. If you buy a bond on the secondary market, it may have market discount.

If you dispose of a market discount bond, you generally must recognize the gain as taxable interest income up to the amount of the bond's **accrued market discount,** if:

1. The bond was issued after July 18, 1984, or
2. You purchased the bond after April 30, 1993.

The rest of the gain is capital gain if the bond was a capital asset.

TaxAlert

Under the Revenue Reconciliation Act of 1993, the gain on the sale of a tax-exempt obligation that is acquired after April 30, 1993, for a price that is less than the face amount of the bond will be treated as *ordinary income* and not as a *capital gain* to the extent of the accrued market discount. Any remaining gain is treated as a capital gain. The gain on the sale of a tax-exempt obligation that is acquired before May 1, 1993, will be treated entirely as a capital gain.

More information. See chapter 1 of Publication 550 for more information about OID and related topics, such as market discount bonds.

State or Local Government Obligations

Generally, interest on obligations used to finance government operations is not taxable if the obligations are issued by a state, the District of Columbia, a possession of the United States, or any of their political subdivisions. This includes interest on certain obligations issued after 1982 by an Indian tribal government treated as a state.

Explanation
Assume that tax-exempt municipal bonds were previously sold to the public at par (face value) at an interest rate lower than the rate demanded by today's investors. Since the interest rate on these bonds is lower than the rate demanded by today's investors, the bonds are trading in the marketplace at a substantial discount from par. This is a market discount. If you buy these bonds now and subsequently realize a gain either when you sell them or when they reach maturity, you must report the gain as taxable interest income up to the amount of the bonds' accrued market discount and the remaining portion as capital gain if the bond was a capital asset. Similarly, if you realize a capital loss on municipal bonds, it is deductible.

The rule with regard to bonds bought at a premium is different. If you buy a bond for $11,000 that will mature for $10,000 and you hold it until maturity, you may not claim a capital loss or any kind of deduction because the tax law requires that you **amortize** the premium over the life of the bond.

TaxSaver
If you are considering selling a tax-exempt bond and purchasing another tax-exempt bond, keep in mind that for bonds purchased before May 1, 1993, you will not have to treat accrued market discount as ordinary income, but rather as a capital gain. Depending on your tax bracket, this may be a significant consideration since the top capital gains tax rate is 28%, while the top marginal rate is 39.1%. Further, while most municipal bond interest is not subject to federal tax, capital gain income and accretion of market discount are. You should be aware of this when you are deciding which bonds to buy.

Example
A $10,000, 10-year tax-exempt municipal bond, yielding 8% purchased at par, will provide $800 of tax-free interest each year, and there will be no capital gain on maturity. The total earned for the 10 years is $8,000.

Similarly, a $12,000, 10-year tax-exempt municipal bond with a 5.2% coupon ($624 interest per year) purchased on May 2, 1997, at $10,000 will yield a total of $8,240 over the life of the bond—$624 of tax-free interest each year plus $200 of taxable interest income each year if the bond is held to maturity. This represents the market discount accretion. But the taxable interest income will be subject to

tax of up to 39.1%, so the net earnings for the 10 years may be reduced to $7,458.

TaxPlanner
When you are determining whether to invest in tax-exempt securities, compare the net after-tax income from a tax-exempt investment with a similar taxable investment.

Equivalent Yield Needed from a Taxable Bond

Tax-Exempt Yield	Based on Your Combined Federal and State Marginal Tax Bracket						
	28%	31%	33%	36%	39.1%	42%	46%
4.00	5.56	5.80	5.97	6.25	6.57	6.90	7.41
4.50	6.25	6.52	6.72	7.03	7.39	7.76	8.33
5.00	6.94	7.25	7.46	7.81	8.21	8.62	9.26
5.50	7.64	7.97	8.21	8.59	9.03	9.48	10.19
6.00	8.33	8.70	8.96	9.38	9.85	10.34	11.11
6.50	9.03	9.42	9.70	10.16	10.67	11.21	12.04
7.00	9.72	10.14	10.45	10.94	11.49	12.07	12.96

Interest on arbitrage bonds issued by state or local governments after October 9, 1969, and interest on private activity bonds generally is taxable.

For more information on whether such interest is taxable or tax exempt, see *State or Local Government Obligations* in chapter 1 of Publication 550.

Information reporting requirement. If you must file a tax return, you are required to show any tax-exempt interest you received on your return. This is an information-reporting requirement only. It does not change tax-exempt interest to taxable interest.

When To Report Interest Income

When to report your interest income depends on whether you use the cash method or an accrual method to report income.

Cash method. Most individual taxpayers use the cash method. If you use this method, you generally report your interest income in the year in which you actually or constructively receive it. However, there are special rules for reporting the discount on certain debt instruments. See *U.S. Savings Bonds* and *Original Issue Discount*, earlier.

Example. On September 1, 1999, you loaned another individual $2,000 at 12%, compounded annually. You are not in the business of lending money. The note stated that principal and interest would be due on August 31, 2001. In 2001, you received $2,508.80 ($2,000 principal and $508.80 interest). If you use the cash method, you must include in income on your 2001 return the $508.80 interest you received in that year.

Constructive receipt. You constructively receive income when it is credited to your account or made available to you. You do not need to have physical possession of it. For example, you are considered to receive interest, dividends, or other earnings on any deposit or account in a bank, savings and loan, or similar financial institution, or interest on life insurance policy dividends left to accumulate, when they are credited to your account and subject to your withdrawal. This is true even if they are not yet entered in your passbook.

You constructively receive income on the deposit or account even if you must:

1) Make withdrawals in multiples of even amounts,
2) Give a notice to withdraw before making the withdrawal,
3) Withdraw all or part of the account to withdraw the earnings, or
4) Pay a penalty on early withdrawals, unless the interest you are to re-

ceive on an early withdrawal or redemption is substantially less than the interest payable at maturity.

Accrual method. If you use an accrual method, you report your interest income when you earn it, whether or not you have received it. Interest is earned over the term of the debt instrument.

Example. If, in the previous example, you use an accrual method, you must include the interest in your income as you earn it. You would report the interest as follows: 1999, $80; 2000, $249.60; and 2001, $179.20.

Coupon bonds. Interest on coupon bonds is taxable in the year the coupon becomes due and payable. It does not matter when you mail the coupon for payment.

How To Report Interest Income

Generally, you report all of your taxable interest income on line 8a, Form 1040; line 8a, Form 1040A; or line 2, Form 1040EZ.

You cannot use Form 1040EZ if your interest income is more than $400. Instead, you must use Form 1040A or Form 1040.

Form 1040A. You must complete Part I of Schedule 1 (Form 1040A) if you file Form 1040A and any of the following are true.

1) Your taxable interest income is more than $400.
2) You are claiming the interest exclusion under the Education Savings Bond Program (discussed earlier).
3) You received interest from a seller-financed mortgage, and the buyer used the property as a home.
4) You received a Form 1099-INT for tax-exempt interest.
5) You received a Form 1099-INT for U.S. savings bond interest that includes amounts you reported before 2001.
6) You received, as a nominee, interest that actually belongs to someone else.
7) You received a Form 1099-INT for interest or frozen deposits.

List each payer's name and the amount of interest income received from each payer on line 1. If you received a Form 1099-INT or Form 1099-OID from a brokerage firm, list the brokerage firm as the payer.

You cannot use Form 1040A if you must use Form 1040, as described next.

Form 1040. You must use Form 1040 instead of Form 1040A or Form 1040EZ if:

1) You forfeited interest income because of the early withdrawal of a time deposit,
2) You received or paid accrued interest on securities transferred between interest payment dates,
3) You had a financial account in a foreign country, unless the combined value of all foreign accounts was $10,000 or less during all of 2001 or the accounts were with certain U.S. military banking facilities.
4) You acquired taxable bonds after 1987 and choose to reduce interest income from the bonds by any amortizable bond premium (see *Bond Premium Amortization* in chapter 3 of Publication 550), or
5) You are reporting OID in an amount more or less than the amount shown on Form 1099-OID.

Schedule B. You must complete Part I of Schedule B (Form 1040) if you file Form 1040 and any of the following apply.

1) Your taxable interest income is more than $400.
2) You are claiming the interest exclusion under the Education Savings Bond Program (discussed earlier).

3) You had a foreign account.
4) You received interest from a seller-financed mortgage, and the buyer used the property as a home.
5) You received a Form 1099-INT for tax-exempt interest.
6) You received a Form 1099-INT for U.S. savings bond interest that includes amounts you reported before 2001.
7) You received, as a nominee, interest that actually belongs to someone else.
8) You received a Form 1099-INT for interest on frozen deposits.
9) You received a Form 1099-INT for interest on a bond that you bought between interest payment dates.
10) Statement (4) or (5) in the preceding list is true.

On line 1, Part I, list each payer's name and the amount received from each. If you received a Form 1099-INT or Form 1099-OID from a brokerage firm, list the brokerage firm as the payer.

Form 1099-INT. Your taxable interest income, except for interest from U.S. savings bonds and Treasury obligations, is shown in box 1 of Form 1099-INT. Add this amount to any other taxable interest income you received. You must report all of your taxable interest income even if you do not receive a Form 1099-INT.

If you forfeited interest income because of the early withdrawal of a time deposit, the deductible amount will be shown on Form 1099-INT in box 2. See *Penalty on early withdrawal of savings* in chapter 1 of Publication 550.

Box 3 of Form 1099-INT shows the amount of interest income you received from U.S. savings bonds. Treasury bills, Treasury notes, and Treasury bonds. Add the amount shown in box 3 to any other taxable interest income you received, unless part of the amount in box 3 was previously included in interest income. If part of the amount shown in box 3 was previously included in your interest income, see *U.S. savings bond interest previously reported,* later.

Box 4 of Form 1099-INT (federal income tax withheld) will contain an amount if you were subject to backup withholding. Report the amount from box 4 on Form 1040EZ, line 8, on Form 1040A, line 37, or on Form 1040, line 59 (federal income tax withheld).

Box 5 of Form 1099-INT shows investment expenses you may be able to deduct as an itemized deduction. See chapter 3 of Publication 550 for more information about investment expenses.

U.S. savings bond interest previously reported. If you received a Form 1099-INT for U.S. savings bond interest, the form may show interest you do not have to report. See *Form 1099-INT for U.S. savings bonds interest,* earlier, under *U.S. Savings Bonds.*

On line 1, Part I of Schedule B (Form 1040), or on line 1, Part I of Schedule 1 (Form 1040A), report all the interest shown on your Form 1099-INT. Then follow these steps.

1) Several lines above line 2, enter a subtotal of all interest listed on line 1.
2) Below the subtotal write "U.S. Savings Bond Interest Previously Reported" and enter amounts previously reported or interest accrued before you received the bond.
3) Subtract these amounts from the subtotal and enter the result on line 2.

More information. For more information about how to report interest income, see chapter 1 of Publication 550 or the instructions for the form you must file.

9

Dividends and Other Corporate Distributions

Introduction

*Most people think they know what **dividends** are. The problem is that the term is commonly used to describe a large number of items that the **IRS** does not consider to be dividends. "Dividends" paid by an insurance company to its policyholders are considered by the IRS to be a return of premiums, not dividends. "Dividends" paid by a savings and loan association to its depositors are considered to be interest, not dividends.*

*So what is a dividend? A **dividend** is a share of a corporation's profits that is distributed to shareholders. This chapter will discuss how these distributions as well as other corporate distributions are taxed. If you own stock in a company or shares in a **mutual fund** or **real estate investment trust (REIT)**, you may receive divi-*

dend distributions. The distributing company or mutual fund will send you a Form 1099-DIV at the end of the year with the total amount of dividends that you must report to the IRS on your income tax return. This chapter will explain the difference between the various tax forms you may receive and which forms you should keep in your records or attach to your income tax return.

*This chapter also discusses **dividend reinvestment plans (DRIPs)** that reinvest the dividends in the stock generating them. These plans are provided by companies for all their shareholders and should not be confused with retirement plans run by employers for the benefit of their employees.*

Important Reminder

Foreign income. If you are a U.S. citizen with dividend income from sources outside the United States (foreign income), you must report that income on your tax return unless it is exempt by U.S. law. This is true whether you reside inside or outside the United States and whether or not you receive a Form 1099 from the foreign payer.

TAXSAVER

Foreign dividends. Foreign governments often withhold tax on dividends from foreign corporations before you receive them. For example, if you are a stockholder in a Canadian company that declares a $100 dividend, you might receive only $85 because of a $15 Canadian withholding tax. Nevertheless, the $100 must be reported on

your U.S. income tax return. The $15 of foreign taxes may be claimed either as a foreign tax credit using Form 1116 or as an itemized deduction on Schedule A (Form 1040). It's generally preferable to take the tax credit. For more on this subject, see Chapter 24, *Taxes You May Deduct.*

TAXSAVER

Beginning in 1998, individuals with $300 or less of foreign taxes paid ($600 for joint filers) are able to take a foreign tax credit for that entire amount. This is an exemption from the limitation of offsetting foreign tax credits against U.S. tax liability. The exemption must be elected each year and is only available if all foreign source income is qualified passive income.

Example

You are a single individual who invests in a mutual fund that holds foreign securities. During 2001, your share of foreign taxes paid by this mutual fund is $250. When you prepare your 2001 tax return, you can claim an exemption from the foreign tax credit limitation and credit the full $250 against your U.S. tax liability.

This chapter discusses the tax treatment of:

- Ordinary dividends,
- Capital gain distributions,
- Nontaxable distributions, and
- Other distributions you may receive from a corporation or a mutual fund.

This chapter also explains how to report dividend income on your tax return.

Dividends are distributions of money, stock, or other property paid to you by a corporation. You also may receive dividends through a partnership, an estate, a trust, or an association that is taxed as a corporation. However, some amounts you receive that are called dividends are actually interest income. (See *Dividends that are actually interest* under *Taxable Interest* in chapter 8.)

Explanation

There are generally two different types of corporations: S corporations and C corporations. The treatment of distributions from S corporations to shareholders differs from that of C corporations to their shareholders.

In this chapter, the IRS is referring to C corporations only, because S corporations do not technically pay dividends. See Chapter 13, *Other Income*, for information on distributions from S corporations.

Most distributions are paid in cash (or check). However, distributions can consist of more stock, stock rights, other property, or services.

Explanation

Any distribution to a shareholder from earnings and profits is generally a dividend. However, a distribution is not a taxable dividend if it is a return of capital to the shareholder. Most distributions are in money, but they may also be in stock or other property.

An interest-free loan or below-market rate loan by a corporation to a stockholder *may* result in taxable dividend income to the stockholder.

Additionally, if you are a stockholder who uses company property for personal use, you are considered to be in **constructive receipt** of a dividend that will be taxable to you and disallowed as a tax deduction to the company. The value of a constructive dividend is the fair market value of the benefit provided to the shareholder.

Example 1

A shareholder's use of a condominium maintained by his solely owned corporation resulted in his receipt of constructive dividends because he maintained the unit as his residence. The taxpayer benefited from the corporation's payments because he did not have to pay any housing costs. The Tax Court determined the portion of the condominium expenses that was allocable to business use and

permitted the corporation to deduct that amount. The balance of the expenses was treated as constructive dividends received by the shareholder.

Example 2

A corporation sold real property to its sole shareholder at a price that was lower than the property's fair market value. The result is a constructive dividend to the shareholder and gain to the corporation.

TAXPLANNER

All personal loans from corporations should have written documentation as well as charge market interest rates. If appropriate interest is not paid on the loans, the interest amount should be treated as a constructive dividend if the corporation has sufficient earnings and profits and therefore, treated as ordinary taxable income by the individual taxpayer. By not reporting appropriately, an individual may be subject to penalties and interest on the portion of underpayment of taxes.

Useful Items

You may want to see:

Publication

☐ **514** Foreign Tax Credit for Individuals
☐ **550** Investment Income and Expenses
☐ **564** Mutual Fund Distributions

Form (and Instructions)

☐ **Schedule B (Form 1040)** — Interest and Ordinary Dividends
☐ **Schedule 1 (Form 1040A)** — Interest and Ordinary Dividends for Form 1040A Filers

TAXORGANIZER

Records you should keep. The following is a list of records that you should keep to substantiate your dividend figures in the event of an IRS or state examination. Generally, we recommend that you retain these records for 6 years. However, you should keep records related to dividend reinvestment programs for 6 years after you fully exit the program.

1099-DIV, Dividends and Distributions
Dividend Reinvestment Plan Records
Form 2439, Notice to Shareholders of Undistributed Long-Term Capital Gains
1099s with backup withholding for attachment to your tax return
Form 1096, Annual Summary and Transmittal of U.S. Information Returns
Schedule K-1 (Form 1041), Beneficiary's Share of Income, Deductions, Credits, etc.
Schedule K-1 (Form 1065), Partner's Share of Income, Credits, Deductions, etc.
Schedule K-1 (Form 1120S), Shareholder's Share of Income, Credits, Deductions, etc.

General Information

This section discusses general rules on dividend income.

Tax on investment income of a child under age 14. Part of a child's 2001 investment income may be taxed at the parent's tax rate. This may happen if all of the following are true.

1) The child was under age 14 on January 1, 2002.
2) The child had more than $1,500 of investment income (such as taxable interest and dividends) and has to file a tax return.
3) Either parent was alive at the end of 2001.

If all of these statements are true, **Form 8615,** *Tax for Children Under Age 14 Who Have Investment Income of More Than $1,500,* must be completed and attached to the child's tax return. If any of these statements is not true, Form 8615 is not required and the child's income is taxed at his or her own tax rate.

However, the parent can choose to include the child's interest and dividends on the parent's return if certain requirements are met. Use **Form 8814,** *Parents' Election To Report Child's Interest and Dividends,* for this purpose.

For more information about the tax on investment income of children and the parents' election, see chapter 32.

> **Explanation**
> A parent may elect on Form 8814 to include on his or her return the unearned income of a child under the age of 14 whose income is less than $7,500 and consists solely of interest, dividends, or Alaska Permanent Fund dividends. The election cannot be made if estimated payments were made in your child's name, if your child had an overpayment on his or her 2000 tax return which was applied to 2001, or if your child is subject to backup withholding. (See explanation of backup withholding below.) The election must be made by the due date (including extensions) of the parent's tax return. A separate election must be made for each child whose income the parents choose to report.
>
> On Form 8814, if a child (under age 14) had income over $1,500, it would be taxed as follows: The first $750 would be tax-free, the next $750 would be taxed at 15%, and the amount of income over $1,500 would be taxed at the parents' tax bracket. Note that the same overall tax result is achieved if the election is not made and the child files his or her own tax return. However, the child is required to attach Form 8615 to his or her return, which can be complicated if there is more than one child under age 14 required to file a return.

Beneficiary of an estate or trust. Dividends and other distributions you receive as a beneficiary of an estate or trust are generally taxable income. You should receive a **Schedule K-1** (Form 1041), *Beneficiary's Share of Income, Deductions, Credits, etc.,* from the fiduciary. Your copy of Schedule K-1 and its instructions will tell you where to report the income on your Form 1040.

> **Explanation**
> In addition to dividends that may be reported on Schedule K-1 (Form 1041) for beneficiaries of estates and trusts, dividends may also be reported to you on a Schedule K-1 (Form 1065) if you are a partner in a partnership or a Schedule K-1 (Form 1120S) if you are a shareholder in an S corporation. Generally, dividends reported on a Schedule K-1 should be entered on Schedule B, Part II, line 5 of Form 1040.

Social security number (SSN). You must give your name and SSN (or individual taxpayer identification number (ITIN)) to any person required by federal tax law to make a return, statement, or other document that relates to you. This includes payers of dividends. If you do not give your SSN or ITIN to the payer of dividends, you may have to pay a penalty.

For more information on SSNs and ITINs, see *Social security number (SSN)* in chapter 8.

Backup withholding. Your dividend income is generally not subject to regular withholding. However, it may be subject to backup withholding to ensure that income tax is collected on the income. Under backup withholding, the payer of dividends must withhold, as income tax, a percentage of the amount you are paid. For 2002, this percentage is 30%.

Backup withholding may also be required if the Internal Revenue Service (IRS) has determined that you underreported your interest or dividend income. For more information, see *Backup Withholding* in chapter 5.

Stock certificate in two or more names. If two or more persons hold stock as joint tenants, tenants by the entirety, or tenants in common, each person may receive a share of any dividends from the stock. Each person's share is determined by local law.

> **Explanation**
> There are many technical problems if stock is jointly registered in two or more names. You should not assume that any income earned is earned jointly. Rather, in cases where no immediate gift transfer of the property is intended, the income should be reported by the owner of the property producing the income. (See *Joint Accounts,* Chapter 8, *Interest Income,* for a complete discussion of this matter.)
>
> **TAXPLANNER**
>
> Because only one recipient's Social Security number will be recorded by the corporation paying the dividend, the IRS's document-matching program may issue deficiency notices when the income is split between two or more individuals' returns. This situation arises because the income tax return with the Social Security number shown on the company's records may not include the full amount of the dividend paid.
>
> To reduce the chance of receiving an IRS deficiency notice, show both the full amount of the dividend paid and a subtraction for "amount attributable to others" on Schedule B (Form 1040) in the section used for reporting dividends.
>
> The person who receives the other part of the dividend needn't worry. Although that person includes on his or her return an amount for which he or she does not receive a Form 1099-DIV, the IRS rarely questions returns when income in excess of that computed by the government is reported. (See the discussion regarding *Nominees* later in this chapter and *Joint Accounts* in Chapter 8, *Interest Income,* for a further discussion of this matter.)

Form 1099-DIV. Most corporations use Form 1099-DIV, *Dividends and Distributions,* to show you the distributions you received from them during the year. Keep this form with your records. You do not have to attach it to your tax return. Even if you do not receive Form 1099-DIV, you must still report all of your taxable dividend income.

> **Explanation**
> The Form 1099 that you receive must be examined carefully. If you receive a Form 1099-DIV, you have received dividends during the year on stock you own. If you receive a Form 1099-INT, you have received interest on a savings account.

TaxOrganizer

While you are not required to attach Form 1099-DIV to your return, it is a good idea to do so if it indicates that you had federal tax withheld from the dividend payment. The amount of federal income tax withheld will be shown in box 4 of Form 1099-DIV. Attaching the form will provide the IRS with a complete picture as to how the total amount of your federal income tax withheld was calculated.

Reporting tax withheld. If tax is withheld from your dividend income, the payer must give you a Form 1099-DIV that indicates the amount withheld.

Nominees. If someone receives distributions as a nominee for you, that person will give you a Form 1099-DIV, which will show distributions received on your behalf.

Explanation

A nominee is someone who, in his or her name and with his or her Social Security or federal identification number, receives income that belongs to another person. Form 1099 is used by the nominee to report the amount and type of income received on behalf of the owner.

If you receive a Form 1099 from a nominee, you should cite the source of that income on your tax return as the nominee, not the original payer of the income. If you receive a Form 1099 as a nominee for another person, see the section on nominees under *How to Report Dividend Income,* toward the end of this chapter, for a complete discussion on the filing and reporting requirements of a nominee.

Example

Brokerage Firm A collects your dividend from XYZ Corporation and reports the income to you on Form 1099. You should show the dividend as being received from Brokerage Firm A, *not* from XYZ Corporation.

Form 1099-MISC. Certain substitute payments in lieu of dividends or tax-exempt interest that are received by a broker on your behalf must be reported to you on Form 1099-MISC, *Miscellaneous Income,* or a similar statement. See *Reporting Substitute Payments* under *Short Sales* in chapter 4 of Publication 550 for more information about reporting these payments.

Incorrect amount shown on a Form 1099. If you receive a Form 1099 that shows an incorrect amount (or other incorrect information), you should ask the issuer for a corrected form. The new Form 1099 you receive will be marked "Corrected."

Dividends on stock sold. If stock is sold, exchanged, or otherwise disposed of after a dividend is declared, but before it is paid, the owner of record (usually the payee shown on the dividend check) must include the dividend in income.

TaxAlert

If stock is sold, exchanged, or otherwise disposed of after a dividend is declared, but before it is paid, the owner of record (usually the payee shown on the dividend check) must report the dividend. Even if the purchase price of the stock goes up because of the amount of the anticipated dividend, the owner of record must report such dividend.

Explanation
Dividends on stock sold. The owner of record on the date a dividend is declared receives the dividend, not the owner on the date of payment.

The following timeline illustrates when you are entitled to receive dividend payments:

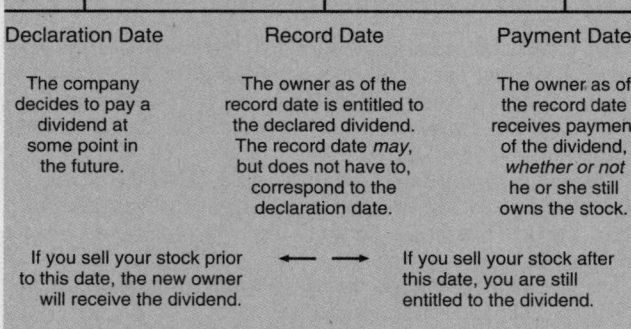

Declaration Date	Record Date	Payment Date
The company decides to pay a dividend at some point in the future.	The owner as of the record date is entitled to the declared dividend. The record date *may,* but does not have to, correspond to the declaration date.	The owner as of the record date receives payment of the dividend, *whether or not* he or she still owns the stock.
If you sell your stock prior to this date, the new owner will receive the dividend.	← →	If you sell your stock after this date, you are still entitled to the dividend.

TaxPlanner

If you buy stock on or near the date a dividend is declared, make sure you receive all amounts due. The transaction of the sale may not be recorded in time by the corporation paying the dividend, and the former stock owner may receive payment. If you do not receive a dividend due you, check with your broker as soon as possible.

If you receive a dividend to which you were not entitled in one year and pay it back in another, it is counted as income in the year received and a deduction in the year repaid. Show the deduction as a negative amount of dividend income on Schedule B (Form 1040). If the repayment is greater than $3,000, however, you may save taxes by recomputing your tax for the prior year and amending your prior year's tax return. Consult your tax advisor.

Dividends received in January. If a regulated investment company (mutual fund) or real estate investment trust (REIT) declares a dividend (including any exempt-interest dividend or capital gain distribution) in October, November, or December payable to shareholders of record on a date in one of those months but actually pays the dividend during January of the next calendar year, you are considered to have received the dividend on December 31. You report the dividend in the year it was declared.

TaxSaver

You should pay close attention to the timing of your purchase of a mutual fund. For example, if you invest in a fund near the end of the year and the fund shortly thereafter makes a year-end distribution, you will have to pay tax on the distribution even though from your point of view you are simply getting back the capital you just invested in the fund. In effect, all you've done is "bought" taxable income that the fund earned earlier in the year but had not yet paid out to shareholders. Typically, the fund's share price drops by the amount of the distribution. However, your cost basis in the mutual fund will be the predistribution price you paid for the shares.

There is one consolation: Your higher basis will reduce any capital gain on a later sale, or if you sell the fund at a loss, it will increase your capital loss. If you want to limit your tax liability and lower your basis in the shares, you should delay your purchase of fund shares until after the record date for the distribution. Usually a fund can tell you when distributions, if any, for the year are expected. Alternatively, you can consult investment publications, which indicate distribution dates for the previous year. They are usually a pretty good guide to future distribution dates.

Example
ABC Fund declares and distributes a $1 dividend on December 1. If you had purchased 1,000 shares at $10 per share on November 30, you will have to report $1,000 of income for 2001. If you bought the shares on December 2, after the record date, you will pay $9 per share and have no taxable income to report. Of course, for the shares bought on November 30, your basis would be $10 per share instead of $9.

TaxPlanner

If you are thinking of selling shares in a mutual fund, particularly near the end of the year when many funds pay dividends, you should consider redeeming your shares before any upcoming dividend payments are made by the fund. If your shares are worth more than you paid, you can maximize your capital gains on the redemption and avoid paying the higher tax rate on ordinary income that you would pay on an ordinary dividend. If your shares are worth less than you paid for them, you can minimize your capital losses by selling before the dividend. Remember, the net asset value per share of the fund (that is, the amount you would receive on the redemption of your shares) decreases by the amount of the dividend. For more about mutual funds, see Chapter 39, *Mutual Funds*.

Ordinary Dividends

Ordinary (taxable) dividends are the most common type of distribution from a corporation. They are paid out of the earnings and profits of a corporation and are ordinary income to you. This means they are not capital gains. You can assume that any dividend you receive on common or preferred stock is an ordinary dividend unless the paying corporation tells you otherwise. Ordinary dividends will be shown in box 1 of the Form 1099-DIV you receive.

Dividends used to buy more stock. The corporation in which you own stock may have a *dividend reinvestment plan.* This plan lets you choose to use your dividends to buy (through an agent) more shares of stock in the corporation instead of receiving the dividends in cash. If you are a member of this type of plan and you use your dividends to buy more stock at a price equal to its fair market value, you still must report the dividends as income.

Explanation
Many large publicly held companies allow stockholders to use their dividends to buy more shares of stock *directly* from the company. This type of program eliminates the need to use or pay commissions to an agent or broker. You should keep this cost savings in mind when considering a particular dividend reinvestment plan.

If you are a member of a dividend reinvestment plan that lets you buy more stock at a price less than its fair market value, you must report as dividend income the fair market value of the additional stock on the dividend payment date.

You also must report as dividend income any service charge subtracted from your cash dividends before the dividends are used to buy the additional stock. But you may be able to deduct the service charge. See chapter 30 for more information about deducting expenses of producing income.

In some dividend reinvestment plans, you can invest more cash to buy shares of stock at a price less than fair market value. If you choose to do this, you must report as dividend income the difference between the cash you invest and the fair market value of the stock you buy. When figuring this amount, use the fair market value of the stock on the dividend payment date.

Explanation
Dividend reinvestment plans (often called **DRIPs**)—even those in which employees may make voluntary contributions—should not be confused with retirement plans that invest in company stock. DRIPs are open to all stockholders, not just employees. Dividends are immediately reinvested to buy more shares of that company's stock. DRIPs are also subject to income taxes annually, whereas income in employee retirement plans is typically tax deferred.

DRIPs may cause confusion because some plans permit you to reinvest in shares at a discount, usually about 5%. The discount is included in the amount of dividend taxable to you.

Example
Stock of Company X is selling for $10. You are entitled to $20 in dividends on the stock you hold. Because you are in a DRIP that includes a 5% discount, your dividends will buy 2.105 shares of stock. You will report $21.05 of dividend income.

TaxAlert

A recent IRS ruling indicated that shareholders who purchase stock solely through a cash purchase plan would *not* be treated as having received a distribution of the discount amount. However, if the shareholders participate in both a DRIP *and* the cash purchase aspects of the plan, they will be treated as having received a taxable distribution of the discount amount of the stock.

TaxPlanner

Unless you're very careful, you're likely to get an IRS deficiency notice when you take advantage of a dividend reinvestment plan if you hold the shares that are producing the dividends. Problems can occur if you receive two Forms 1099. One will report the dividends paid on shares you hold. The other Form 1099 will report the discount and the dividends paid on the shares held in the plan. Be sure to reconcile the amounts and report the correct total.

Any service charge paid on a dividend reinvestment plan may be taken as an **itemized deduction** on Schedule A of Form 1040 (subject to the 2% of adjusted gross income limitation explained in Chapter 30, *Miscellaneous Deductions*). You should *not* offset your dividend income with the service charge. If you do, you may receive a notice from the IRS.

TAXPLANNER

When you sell shares acquired in a dividend reinvestment plan, you compute the gain or loss in the same way that you normally would by subtracting your cost from the proceeds of the sale. Your cost includes the amount of dividends that have been reinvested. Usually your only record of the shares' cost is the annual statement issued by the administrator of the dividend reinvestment plan. It is imperative to keep these statements as a permanent part of your records. If you don't have this information, you can contact the transfer agent who handles the company's dividend reinvestment plan. You can obtain the name from the company's investor relations office. However, some dividend reinvestment plans charge a fee for re-creating records. Alternatively, you can look up a company's dividend history in Standard & Poor's.

Example

You purchased 10 shares of ABC Mutual Fund in June 1, 1998, for $100. For the next 3 years you participated in a dividend reinvestment plan that made the following dividend distributions, which were reinvested for you: $10 on December 31, 1998, purchased 1 additional share; $15 on December 31, 1999, purchased 1 additional share; and $25 on December 31, 2000, purchased 2 additional shares. Assuming no further purchases or sales of ABC Mutual Fund, you would own 14 shares of the fund at a total cost basis of $150 in 2001.

If you sold all 14 shares in 2001 for $15 dollars per share, your gain would be $60 ($210 proceeds less $150 basis). Without proof of your dividend reinvestments, however, the IRS could argue that your basis was only the original $100 and your gain was actually $110.

Note that a portion of your $60 gain would be long-term, but the gain attributable to the 2 shares purchased on December 31, 2000, through the DRIP would be short-term, because you would not have owned these shares for more than 12 months. The short-term gain would be $5 of the total gain ($30 proceeds on 2 shares less $25 cost).

See Chapter 17, *Reporting Gains and Losses,* to determine how to calculate your gain or loss if you did not sell *all* 14 shares of ABC Mutual Fund at once.

TAXSAVER

Dividend reinvestment plans that permit you to invest at less than market price (e.g., whether by discount or reduction in commissions on purchase) may be a very good deal. In effect, you earn a higher yield because you are receiving "extra" shares.

Money market funds. Report amounts you receive from money market funds as dividend income. Money market funds are a type of mutual fund and should not be confused with bank money market accounts that pay interest.

TAXPLANNER

Dividends paid from money market funds are reported as *dividends*—not interest—even though they represent income the money market fund received on certificates of deposit and other interest-bearing investments. These dividends *must* be shown in the dividend section of Schedule B (Form 1040). If they are not, you're likely to receive a notice from the IRS requesting an explanation.

However, dividends paid or credited by a mutual savings bank, building and loan association, or savings and loan association are considered *interest*—not dividends—for income tax reporting purposes. The Form 1099 that you receive from these organizations tells you which type of income to report and generally instructs you on how to report the income.

Capital Gain Distributions

Capital gain distributions (also called capital gain dividends) are paid to you or credited to your account by **regulated investment companies** (commonly called **mutual funds**) and **real estate investment trusts (REITs).** They will be shown in box 2a of the Form 1099-DIV you receive from the mutual fund or REIT.

Report capital gain distributions as long-term capital gains regardless of how long you owned your shares in the mutual fund or REIT.

Explanation

For 2001, capital gain distributions are reported on Schedule D, line 13. For more information, see Chapter 17, *Reporting Gains and Losses.*

TAXALERT

The new law for mutual funds or real estate investment trusts states that all capital gain distributions may not be classified as strictly long-term. The 1099-DIV, Form 2439, or other supplementary form should indicate the portion of the distribution that is classified as ordinary income or long-term capital gain.

Undistributed capital gains of mutual funds and REITs. Some mutual funds and REITs keep their long-term capital gains and pay tax on them. You must treat your share of these gains as distributions, even though you did not actually receive them. However, they are not included on Form 1099-DIV. Instead, they are reported to you on **Form 2439,** *Notice to Shareholder of Undistributed Long-Term Capital Gains.*

Report undistributed capital gains as long-term capital gains in column (f) on line 11 of Schedule D (Form 1040). The tax paid on these gains by the mutual fund or REIT is shown in box 2 of Form 2439. You take credit for this tax by including it on line 65, Form 1040, and checking box a on that line. Attach Copy B of Form 2439 to your return, and keep Copy C for your records.

Basis adjustment. Increase your basis in your mutual fund or your interest in a REIT by the difference between the gain you report and the credit you claim for the tax paid.

Explanation

An investment company or mutual fund that realizes capital gains during the year has the option of whether or not to distribute the capital gains to shareholders of the mutual fund. The two different treatments are reported by shareholders as follows.

Distributed capital gains are reported to shareholders on Form 1099-DIV, box 2a. You will receive this amount in cash and must include the entire amount of the distributed capital gains in your calculation of taxable income.

Undistributed capital gains are reported to shareholders on Form 2439. You will *not* receive this amount in cash.

Rather, the mutual fund or real estate investment trust (REIT) has retained the capital gains and paid your proportionate share of the tax due. You will include the entire amount of the undistributed capital gains in your calculation of taxable income, but you will also be credited for the tax that the mutual fund paid on your behalf. In addition, you will increase your basis in the stock by the net amount not distributed to you.

Example 1
ABC Mutual Fund elects to distribute all of its 2001 capital gain. *Each shareholder will receive a pro rata share of the distribution in cash.* Each shareholder reports this distribution and pays the appropriate tax. The fund will provide each shareholder with Form 1099-DIV, which contains the amounts to be reported.

Example 2
ABC Mutual Fund elects to treat all of its 2001 capital gain as an undistributed capital gain. *The shareholders receive no cash distribution.* Each shareholder reports his or her share of capital gain and tax paid on his or her behalf by ABC Mutual Fund. These amounts are shown on the Form 2439 that each shareholder receives.

If your share of the capital gain is $1,200 and your share of the tax is $408, the $1,200 is included as capital gain income and the $408 is claimed as a credit on your individual return. Increase your basis in the stock by $792, the net amount not distributed to you ($1,200 less $408).

Explanation
You must report any undistributed gains shown on Form 2439 in addition to any capital gain distributions reported on Form 1099-DIV.

Additional information. For more information on the treatment of distributions from mutual funds, see Publication 564.

Nontaxable Distributions

You may receive a return of capital or a tax-free distribution of more shares of stock or stock rights. These distributions are not treated the same as ordinary dividends or capital gain distributions.

Return of Capital

A return of capital is a distribution that is not paid out of the earnings and profits of a corporation. It is a return of your investment in the stock of the company. You should receive a Form 1099-DIV or other statement from the corporation showing you what part of the distribution is a return of capital. On Form 1099-DIV, a nontaxable return of capital will be shown in box 3. If you do not receive such a statement, you report the distribution as an ordinary dividend.

Basis adjustment. A return of capital reduces the basis of your stock. It is not taxed until your basis in the stock is fully recovered. If you buy stock in a corporation in different lots at different times, and you cannot definitely identify the shares subject to the return of capital, reduce the basis of your earliest purchases first.

When the basis of your stock has been reduced to zero, report any additional return of capital that you receive as a capital gain. Whether you report it as a long-term or short-term capital gain depends on how long you have held the stock. See *Holding Period* in chapter 15.

Example. You bought stock in 1989 for $100. In 1992, you received a return of capital of $80. You did not include this amount in your income, but you reduced the basis of your stock to $20. You received a return of capital of $30 in 2001. The first $20 of this amount reduced your basis to zero. You report the other $10 as a long-term capital gain for 2001. You must report as a long-term capital gain any return of capital you receive on this stock in later years.

Explanation
Some mutual fund dividends may be treated as a tax-free return of capital. This occurs when the mutual fund does not have enough current or accumulated earnings and profits to cover the distribution. In this situation, the distribution is considered to be a "return of capital" (the amount you originally invested) and is nontaxable to the extent of the basis in your shares. (Your basis is generally the price at which you bought the shares plus or minus any adjustments. See Chapter 14, *Basis of Property.*) This amount will be shown in box 3 of Form 1099-DIV.

Although the distribution is tax-free, it will reduce your basis in the mutual fund shares. To the extent that the distribution is greater than your basis in your shares, you will be treated as having a gain from the sale or exchange of the shares. This gain must be reported on Schedule D (Form 1040). (See the IRS example directly preceding this explanation.)

TAX**ORGANIZER**
It is extremely important to keep accurate records of nontaxable dividends. Most people do not realize that a nontaxable dividend is usually considered a return of purchase price and then a capital gain once your cost has been recovered. Keep in mind that even nontaxable dividends can become subject to tax at some point.

Liquidating distributions. Liquidating distributions, sometimes called liquidating dividends, are distributions you receive during a partial or complete liquidation of a corporation. These distributions are, at least in part, one form of a return of capital. They may be paid in one or more installments. You will receive a Form 1099-DIV from the corporation showing you the amount of the liquidating distribution in box 8 or 9.

For more information on liquidating distributions, see chapter 1 of Publication 550.

TAX**SAVER**
If the total liquidating distributions you receive are less than the basis of your stock, you may have a capital loss. You can report a capital loss only after you have received the final distribution in liquidation that results in the redemption or cancellation of the stock. Whether you report the loss as a long-term or short-term capital loss depends on how long you held the stock. See *Holding Period* in Chapter 15, *Sale of Property.*

Example
You own stock in XYZ Corporation with a basis of $100. You received liquidating distributions of $90: $60 in 2000 and $30 in 2001. You reported the $10 loss in 2001.

Distributions of Stock and Stock Rights

Distributions by a corporation of its own stock are commonly known as stock dividends. Stock rights (also known as "stock options") are distributions by a corporation of rights to acquire the corporation's stock.

Generally, stock dividends and stock rights are not taxable to you, and you do not report them on your return.

Taxable stock dividends and stock rights. Distributions of stock dividends and stock rights are taxable to you if any of the following apply.

1) You or any other shareholder has the choice to receive cash or other property instead of stock or stock rights.
2) The distribution gives cash or other property to some shareholders and an increase in the percentage interest in the corporation's assets or earnings and profits to other shareholders.
3) The distribution is in convertible preferred stock and has the same result as in (2).
4) The distribution gives preferred stock to some common stock shareholders and common stock to other common stock shareholders.
5) The distribution is on preferred stock. (The distribution, however, is not taxable if it is an increase in the conversion ratio of convertible preferred stock made solely to take into account a stock dividend, stock split, or similar event that would otherwise result in reducing the conversion right.)

Explanation
Any transaction having the effect of increasing your proportionate interest in a corporation's assets or earnings and profits may be taxable to you, even though no stock or stock rights are actually distributed.

A number of transactions have the effect of increasing your proportionate interest in a corporation—for example, a change in the conversion ratio on certain classes of stock or a change in the redemption price of certain securities. If such a transaction occurs, you will be informed by the corporation.

The term "stock" includes rights to acquire stock, and the term "shareholder" includes a holder of rights or of convertible securities.

If you receive taxable stock dividends or stock rights, include their fair market value at the time of the distribution in your income.

Example
ABC Company gives its shareholders the option of receiving a dividend as $10 cash or as stock (thus, the distribution will be taxable to *all* shareholders). On February 15, the date of distribution, the value of 1 share of stock is $5. A shareholder who chooses stock in lieu of cash will receive 2 additional shares of stock on February 15. This shareholder will be taxed on $10, the fair market value of the stock, even though no cash was received with which to pay the tax. A shareholder who chooses cash will also be taxed on $10, but this shareholder will have the cash in hand to pay the tax.

Preferred stock redeemable at a premium. If you hold preferred stock having a redemption price higher than its issue price, the difference (the redemption premium) generally is taxable as a constructive distribution of additional stock on the preferred stock. For more information, see chapter 1 of Publication 550.

Basis. Your basis in stock or stock rights received in a taxable distribution is their fair market value when distributed. If you receive stock or stock rights that are not taxable to you, see *Stocks and Bonds* under *Basis of Investment Property* in chapter 4 of Publication 550 for information on how to figure their basis.

Fractional shares. You may not own enough stock in a corporation to receive a full share of stock if the corporation declares a stock dividend. However, with the approval of the shareholders, the corporation may set up a plan in which fractional shares are not issued, but instead are sold, and the cash proceeds are given to the shareholders. Any cash you receive for fractional shares under such a plan is treated as an amount realized on the sale of the fractional shares. You must determine your gain or loss and report it as a capital gain or loss on Schedule D (Form 1040). Your gain or loss is the difference between the cash you receive and the basis of the fractional shares sold.

Example. You own one share of common stock that you bought on January 3, 1993, for $100. The corporation declared a common stock dividend of 5% on June 30, 2001. The fair market value of the stock at the time the stock dividend was declared was $200. You were paid $10 for the fractional-share stock dividend under a plan described in the above paragraph. You figure your gain or loss as follows:

Fair market value of old stock	$200.00
Fair market value of stock dividend (cash received)	+10.00
Fair market value of old stock and stock dividend	$210.00
Basis (cost) of old stock after the stock dividend	
(($200 ÷ $210) × $100)	$ 95.24
Basis (cost) of stock dividend	
(($10 ÷ $210) × $100)	+4.76
Total	$100.00
Cash received	$ 10.00
Basis (cost) of stock dividend	−4.76
Gain	$ 5.24

Because you had held the share of stock for more than 1 year at the time the stock dividend was declared, your gain on the stock dividend is a long-term capital gain.

Explanation
It is *not* true that all amounts received with regard to fractional shares are treated as capital gains, as described in the IRS text.

A distinction is made when shareholders have the *option* of receiving cash or other property instead of fractional shares. If shareholders have this option and receive cash in lieu of fractional shares, the value received is treated as dividend income, which is taxed at ordinary rates. If the corporation issues cash in lieu of fractional shares of stock for the purpose of saving the trouble, expense, and inconvenience of issuing fractional shares, then the capital gain treatment described above applies. The transaction will be treated as though fractional shares had been received by the shareholders and were then redeemed by the corporation.

Scrip dividends. A corporation that declares a stock dividend may issue you a scrip certificate that entitles you to a fractional share. The certificate is generally nontaxable when you receive it. If you choose to have the corporation sell the certificate for you and give you the proceeds, your gain or loss is the difference between the proceeds and the portion of your basis in the corporation's stock that is allocated to the certificate.

However, if you receive a scrip certificate that you can choose to redeem for cash instead of stock, the certificate is taxable when you receive it. You must include its fair market value in income on the date you receive it.

Other Distributions

You may receive any of the following distributions during the year.
Exempt-interest dividends. Exempt-interest dividends you receive from a regulated investment company (mutual fund) are not included in

your taxable income. You will receive a notice from the mutual fund telling you the amount of the exempt-interest dividends you received. Exempt-interest dividends are not shown on Form 1099-DIV or Form 1099-INT.

Information reporting requirement. Although exempt-interest dividends are not taxable, you must show them on your tax return if you have to file a return. This is an information reporting requirement and does not change the exempt-interest dividends to taxable income.

Alternative minimum tax treatment. Exempt-interest dividends paid from specified private activity bonds may be subject to the alternative minimum tax. See *Alternative Minimum Tax* in chapter 31 for more information.

Explanation
Tax-exempt dividends are reported on line 8b of Form 1040 as tax-exempt interest. While tax-exempt dividends are exempt from federal income taxes, they may be considered an "add-back" for state and local tax purposes. This treatment depends on which state returns you are required to file. Generally, your state may require that you add back to federal adjusted gross income either all or some portion of the amount you entered on line 8b of your 1040. See your state income tax forms for guidance.

Dividends on insurance policies. Insurance policy dividends that the insurer keeps and uses to pay your premiums are not taxable. However, you must report as taxable interest income the interest that is paid or credited on dividends left with the insurance company.

If dividends on an insurance contract (other than a modified endowment contract) are distributed to you, they are a partial return of the premiums you paid. Do not include them in your gross income until they are more than the total of all net premiums you paid for the contract. (For information on the treatment of a distribution from a modified endowment contract, see *Distribution Before Annuity Starting Date From a Nonqualified Plan* under *Taxation of Nonperiodic Payments* in Publication 575, *Pension and Annuity Income.*) Report any taxable distributions on insurance policies on line 16b (Form 1040) or line 12b (Form 1040A).

Dividends on veterans' insurance. Dividends you receive on veterans' insurance policies are not taxable. In addition, interest on dividends left with the Department of Veterans Affairs is not taxable.

Patronage dividends. Generally, patronage dividends you receive in money from a cooperative organization are included in your income.

Do not include in your income patronage dividends you receive on:

1) Property bought for your personal use, or
2) Capital assets or depreciable property bought for use in your business. But you must reduce the basis (cost) of the items bought. If the dividend is more than the adjusted basis of the assets, you must report the excess as income.

These rules are the same whether the cooperative paying the dividend is a taxable or tax-exempt cooperative.

Explanation
Patronage dividends are amounts paid by a cooperative organization to one of its patrons (1) on the basis of the quantity or quality of business done with the patron, (2) pursuant to a written obligation in existence before the cooperative received the amounts paid into it by the patron, and (3) determined by reference to net earnings. In other words, patronage dividends amount to a return of some of the

amounts a patron spent with a cooperative. Patronage dividends usually occur with farm cooperatives. Any "refund" or "discount" to the patron is income.

However, if the purchase leading to receipt of the dividend was neither deductible nor considered a capital expense, the dividend really amounts to a discount or a rebate, which is not considered income.

Alaska Permanent Fund dividends. Do not report these amounts as dividends. Instead, report these amounts on line 21 of Form 1040, line 13 of Form 1040A, or line 3 of Form 1040EZ.

TAXSAVER
Dividends received on restricted stock. Restricted stock is stock that you get from your employer for services you perform and that is nontransferable and subject to a substantial risk of forfeiture. You do not have to include the value of the stock in your income when you receive it as restricted shares. However, if you get dividends on the restricted stock, you must include them in your income as wages, not dividends. At the time that the restrictions are lifted on the stock and you have full access to the stock, dividends are treated as taxable dividend income.

If you get both a 1099-DIV and a W-2, which includes the dividends on your restricted stock, it is important to report the taxable dividend amount only once on your tax return. To avoid notices generated from the IRS's document-matching program, statements must be included with your return to explain any discrepancies between the amounts reported by you and the amounts indicated on Form 1099-DIV or Form W-2.

TAXPLANNER
Election. You can choose to include in gross income the value of restricted stock as pay for services. Consult with your tax advisor if you are considering this election. If you make this choice, the dividends are treated as any other dividends.

If you elect to include in gross income the value of the restricted stock you have received, consider notifying your employer so that dividend payments on the stock are no longer included in your W-2 wages.

How To Report Dividend Income

Generally, you can use either Form 1040 or Form 1040A to report your dividend income. Report the total of your ordinary dividends on line 9 of Form 1040 or Form 1040A.

If you receive capital gain distributions, you may be able to use Form 1040A or you may have to use Form 1040. See *Capital gain distributions only* in chapter 17. If you receive nontaxable distributions required to be reported as capital gains, you must use Form 1040. You cannot use Form 1040EZ if you receive any dividend income.

Explanation
Use the following decision tree to determine which forms and schedules you may be required to file:

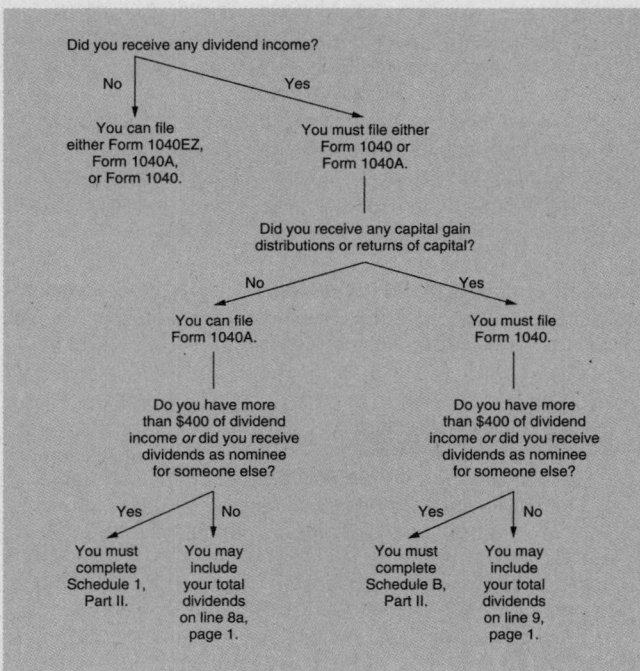

Form 1099-DIV. If you owned stock on which you received $10 or more in dividends and other distributions, you should receive a Form 1099-DIV. Even if you do not receive Form 1099-DIV, you must report all of your taxable dividend income.

See Form 1099-DIV for more information on how to report dividend income.

TaxOrganizer

You should make sure you keep a copy of all Forms 1099-DIV that you received in the mail. See sample form below.

Form 1040A. You must complete Part II of Schedule 1 (Form 1040A) and attach it to your Form 1040A, if:

1) Your ordinary dividends (box 1 of Form 1099-DIV) are more than $400, or
2) You received, as a nominee, dividends that actually belong to someone else.

List on line 5 each payer's name and the amount of ordinary dividends you received. If you received a Form 1099-DIV from a brokerage firm, list the brokerage firm as the payer.

Enter on line 6 the total of the amounts listed on line 5. Also enter this total on line 9, Form 1040A.

Explanation

Exempt-interest dividends, which are treated as interest, should not be reported on Schedule 1 of Form 1040A. The amount should be included on line 8b of page 1. See *How to Report Interest Income* in Chapter 8, *Interest Income.*

Form 1040. You must fill in Part II of Schedule B and attach it to your Form 1040, if:

1) Your ordinary dividends (box 1 of Form 1099-DIV) are more than $400, or
2) You received, as a nominee, dividends that actually belong to someone else.

Explanation

Even if your dividends are less than $400, you must report them and, to the extent that they are taxable, pay tax on them. The $400 test determines whether or not you must list each dividend payer separately on Schedule B. If your dividends total less than $400, you can include a single amount on line 9 of page 1 and avoid completing Schedule B, Part II.

☐ CORRECTED (if checked)

PAYER'S name, street address, city, state, ZIP code, and telephone no.		1 Ordinary dividends $	OMB No. 1545-0110	Dividends and Distributions
		2a Total capital gain distr. $	20**01**	
		2b 28% rate gain $	Form **1099-DIV**	
PAYER'S Federal identification number	RECIPIENT'S identification number	2c Qualified 5-year gain $	2d Unrecap. sec. 1250 gain $	**Copy B** **For Recipient**
RECIPIENT'S name		2e Section 1202 gain $	3 Nontaxable distributions $	This is important tax information and is being furnished to the Internal Revenue Service. If you are required to file a return, a negligence penalty or other sanction may be imposed on you if this income is taxable and the IRS determines that it has not been reported.
Street address (including apt. no.)		4 **Federal income tax withheld** $	5 Investment expenses $	
City, state, and ZIP code		6 Foreign tax paid $	7 Foreign country or U.S. possession	
Account number (optional)		8 Cash liquidation distr. $	9 Noncash liquidation distr. $	

Form **1099-DIV**   (Keep for your records.)   Department of the Treasury - Internal Revenue Service

If your ordinary dividends are more than $400, you must also complete Part III of Schedule B.

Explanation
Part III of Schedule B refers to a financial interest in a foreign bank, brokerage account, or trust. See the instructions for Schedule B or consult with your tax advisor for additional filing requirements, if applicable.

List on line 5, Part II of Schedule B, each payer's name and the amount of ordinary dividends you received. If your securities are held by a brokerage firm (in "street name"), list the name of the brokerage firm that is shown on Form 1099-DIV as the payer. If your stock is held by a nominee who is the owner of record, and the nominee credited or paid you dividends on the stock, show the name of the nominee and the dividends you received or for which you were credited.

TaxSaver
If you receive a Form 1099-DIV that shows your taxpayer identification number and names two or more recipients, or includes amounts belonging to another person, you must file a Form 1099-DIV with the IRS to show the proper distributions of the amounts shown. Complete the form and a Form 1096, Annual Summary and Transmittal of U.S. Information Returns, and file both forms with your Internal Revenue Service Center. Give the other person Copy B of the Form 1099-DIV that you filed as a nominee. On the forms, you should be listed as the "Payer." On Form 1099-DIV, the other owner should be listed as the "Recipient." You are not required, however, to file a Form 1099-DIV to show payments for your spouse. For more information about the reporting requirements and the penalties for failure to file (or furnish) certain information returns, see the Instructions for Forms 1099, 1098, 5498, and W-2G.

Include on line 5 dividends you received, as a nominee, that actually belong to another person (such as your child), even if you later distributed some or all of this income to others. Enter a subtotal of all your dividend income listed on line 5 several lines above line 6. Below the subtotal, write "Nominee Distribution," and show the amounts received as a nominee. Subtract these distributions from the subtotal, and enter the result on line 6.

TaxPlanner
The complexity of paperwork involved in serving as a nominee makes it clear that you should avoid doing so unless absolutely necessary. If you are a nominee and fail to file the appropriate returns, you could be penalized by the IRS.

Enter on line 6 the total of the amounts listed on line 5. Also enter this total on line 9, Form 1040.

Expenses related to dividend income. You may be able to deduct expenses related to dividend income if you itemize your deductions on Schedule A (Form 1040). See chapter 30 for general information about deducting expenses of producing income. •

Explanation
Expenses that may be deducted include custody fees, investment advisory fees, depository fees (which are usually applicable to foreign dividends), and service charges relating to dividend income. A more complete discussion of these items appears in Chapter 30, *Miscellaneous Deductions*.

Explanation
Stock sold short. If you borrow stock to make a short sale, you may have to pay the lender an amount to replace the dividends distributed while you maintain your short position. Your treatment of the payment depends on the kind of distribution for which you are reimbursing the lender of the stock. See Chapter 15, *Sale of Property*, for an explanation of a short sale.

TaxPlanner
If you borrow stock to make a short sale, and you pay the lender in lieu of the dividends distributed while you maintain your short position, you can deduct these payments provided you hold the short sale open at least 46 days (more than 1 year in the case of an extraordinary dividend as defined below), and you itemize your deductions. You deduct these expenses as investment interest on Schedule A (Form 1040).

If you close the short sale on or before the 45th day after the date of the short sale (1 year or less in the case of an extraordinary dividend), you must increase the basis of the stock used to close the short sale by that amount.

Exception
The IRS will disallow the deduction for amounts you pay in place of dividends to the extent the payments exceed the amount that you receive as ordinary income from the lender of the stock for the use of collateral with the short sale. However, this exception does not apply to payments in place of extraordinary dividends, discussed below.

Explanation
Extraordinary Dividends. If the amount of any dividend you receive on a share of preferred stock equals or exceeds 5% (10% in the case of other stock) of the amount realized on the short sale, the dividend you receive is an extraordinary dividend.

If your payment is made for a liquidating distribution or nontaxable stock distribution, or if you buy more shares equal to a stock distribution issued on the borrowed stock during your short position, you have a capital expense. You must add the payment to the cost of the stock sold short. See *Short Sales* in Publication 550 for more information about the tax treatment of short sales.

Example
Ben feels that the market value of XYZ Corporation stock is going to decline, so he sells XYZ stock to Sally. However, Ben does not hold any XYZ stock, so to effect the transaction, Ben's broker borrows XYZ stock from another customer, Robert, to deliver to Sally. Sally is now the stockholder of record.

XYZ Corporation will pay any and all dividends on this stock directly to Sally. However, Robert is entitled to the money, because he merely lent his shares to Ben. Ben, not

XYZ Corporation, will pay Robert the amount of the dividend. Ben may deduct the payment as an itemized deduction on Schedule A if he borrows the stock for more than 45 days and has not diminished his risk of loss by, for example, holding an option to buy substantially similar stock. Robert enters that amount on page 1 (Form 1040) as income from Ben.

If Ben returns the stock within 45 days, he will not be able to claim a deduction. The amount paid to Robert increases the basis of the stock sold.

More information. For more information about how to report dividend income, see chapter 1 of Publication 550 or the instructions for the form you must file.

10

Rental Income and Expenses

Rent is the income received for allowing another person to use property that you own. This income is customarily received in cash. If, in lieu of paying all or part of the rent in cash, a tenant provides you with certain services, the value of the services is rental income to you.

You may deduct any expenses directly incurred to repair or to maintain your rental property. However, certain other expenses may not be deducted in the year in which you pay for them; rather, they must be **capitalized** *and deducted over a period of years. You may also deduct any* **depreciation** *taken on your rental property. Depreciation is a noncash expense claimed in order to deduct each year a small part of what you originally paid for the property.*

There are a variety of methods by which you may depreciate property and calculate your tax deduction, and

all are explained in this chapter. In 1981, Congress adopted the **Accelerated Cost Recovery System (ACRS).** *Then, in 1986, Congress made some additional changes and adopted the* **Modified Accelerated Cost Recovery System (MACRS).** *This chapter delves into all the complexities of ACRS and MACRS and outlines strategies that will enable you to benefit from them.*

Typically, you will do better taking a current **deduction** *rather than capitalizing an expense and depreciating an item over time. But, since there are no hard and fast rules as to what must be considered a deductible expense and what must be capitalized, there are plenty of opportunities to be appropriately aggressive and save on your taxes. This chapter explains the rules and the opportunities for tax savings.*

This chapter discusses rental income and expenses. It covers the following topics.

- Rental income.
- Rental expenses.
- Personal use of dwelling unit (including vacation home).
- Depreciation.
- Limits on rental losses.
- How to report your rental income and expenses.

If you sell or otherwise dispose of your rental property, see Publication 544, *Sales and Other Dispositions of Assets.*

If you have a loss from damage to, or theft of, rental property, see Publication 547, *Casualties, Disasters, and Thefts.*

If you rent a condominium or a cooperative apartment, some special rules apply to you even though you receive the same tax treatment as other owners of rental property. See Publication 527, *Residential Rental Property,* for more information.

Useful Items

You may want to see:

Publication

- ☐ **527** Residential Rental Property
- ☐ **534** Depreciating Property Placed in Service Before 1987
- ☐ **535** Business Expenses
- ☐ **925** Passive Activity and At-Risk Rules
- ☐ **946** How To Depreciate Property

Form (and Instructions)

- ☐ **4562** Depreciation and Amortization
- ☐ **6251** Alternative Minimum Tax—Individuals
- ☐ **8582** Passive Activity Loss Limitations
- ☐ **Schedule E (Form 1040)** Supplemental Income and Loss

Rental Income

You generally must include in your gross income all amounts you receive as rent. Rental income is any payment you receive for the use or occupation of property. In addition to amounts you receive as normal rent payments, there are other amounts that may be rental income.

When to report. Report rental income on your return for the year you actually or constructively receive it, if you are a cash basis taxpayer. You are a cash basis taxpayer if you report income in the year you receive it, regardless of when it was earned. You constructively receive income when it is made available to you, for example, by being credited to your bank account.

For more information about when you constructively receive income, see *Accounting Methods* in chapter 1.

Advance rent. Advance rent is any amount you receive before the period that it covers. Include advance rent in your rental income in the year you receive it regardless of the period covered or the method of accounting you use.

Example. You sign a 10-year lease to rent your property. In the first year, you receive $5,000 for the first year's rent and $5,000 as rent for the last year of the lease. You must include $10,000 in your income in the first year.

Explanation

Some taxpayers have attempted to circumvent the rule requiring advance rent to be included in current income by structuring the payment as a "loan." The courts have generally disallowed this technique and follow this type of transaction with close scrutiny. As a general rule, if such a loan is to be repaid out of future rental proceeds, the loan will probably be considered advance rent.

However, the courts have held that an up-front payment for an option to purchase the property is not considered advance rent and, as such, does not have to be included in income where the agreement provides no provision for returning the money to the renter or applying it to the rent.

Even if there exists a promissory note, the courts will look to the parties' intent, as well as to other factors such as interest charged, whether the loan is secured, and whether the loan payment and rental dates are identified.

Security deposits. Do not include a security deposit in your income when you receive it if you plan to return it to your tenant at the end of the lease. But if you keep part or all of the security deposit during any year because your tenant does not live up to the terms of the lease, include the amount you keep in your income for that year.

If an amount called a security deposit is to be used as a final payment of rent, it is advance rent. Include it in your income when you receive it.

Explanation

Generally, the distinction between advance rent and security deposits depends on the nature of the rights and obligations that are assumed when the deposit is made. If, for example, the landlord has the option either to refund a security deposit or to apply it to a future year's rent, the courts have held that the landlord has unrestricted use of the money and that it is considered advance rent.

In cases in which the landlord is required by law to pay interest on the security deposit, the deposit generally is not considered advance rent.

TAX PLANNER

Landlords often forget whether they have treated a security deposit as a true security deposit or as advance rent. If this happens, the landlord will not be sure how to treat the refund and/or application of the security deposit at the end of the term of the lease. Be sure to note in your records exactly how you are treating the amount for tax purposes so that the tax returns for the year in which the security deposit is returned and/or applied will be easy to prepare.

TAX SAVER

When drawing up a rental agreement, it is helpful to include the following language: "that the security deposit of $xx is not to be used for the last month's rent. . . ." This helps ensure deferred recognition of the security deposit as income until such time as you determine it should not be refunded.

Payment for canceling a lease. If your tenant pays you to cancel a lease, the amount you receive is rent. Include the payment in your income in the year you receive it regardless of your method of accounting.

Explanation

Additionally, the courts have ruled that any payments you receive as consideration for modifying the terms of an existing lease must be treated as **ordinary income**. However, certain expenses incurred as a result of the cancellation or modification of a lease may be currently deductible. For example, attorney fees attributable to the *lessee's* forfeiture and termination of a lease would be currently deductible. On the other hand, if the lessor caused the termination, the expense would usually be amortized over a period of time. You should consult your tax advisor.

TAX SAVER

A payment for cancellation of a lease may be very large, depending on the time left on the lease and the agreement of the parties. As with most types of income to cash basis taxpayers, arranging for the receipt of this payment in a year in which you have a lower **marginal tax rate** may save you taxes.

Expenses paid by tenant. If your tenant pays any of your expenses, the payments are rental income. You must include them in your income.

You can deduct the expenses if they are deductible rental expenses. See *Rental Expenses,* later, for more information.

Explanation
When a tenant pays to have capital improvements constructed on the landlord's property and these improvements are *not* made in lieu of rent or other required payments, the value of these improvements is *not* income to the landlord, either when made or on termination of the lease, even though the landlord keeps the improvements at the end of the lease. However, the landlord will have no basis in the improvements and, therefore, cannot depreciate the improvements.

Example 1
Susan rents an apartment to Pam. Pam, at her own expense, constructs a wall to separate the dining area from the living room. At the end of the lease, Pam vacates the apartment, leaving the wall. Susan does not record income at any time, even though she may benefit from the capital improvement.

If Susan must incur an expense to remove the wall and restore the property, it is either deducted from income or capitalized, depending on factors discussed later in this chapter.

Example 2
Ken rents an apartment to Anthony for $550. Anthony pays for plumbing repairs of $150, which he in turn deducts out of his current month's rent. Although Ken has received only $400 from Anthony, he must report the entire rent amount of $550 as income. Ken may also be able to report the $150 for plumbing repairs as a deductible rental expense.

Other examples of landlord expenses paid by a tenant that would be considered rental income include a tenant's payment of a landlord's real estate taxes, mortgage payments, or income taxes.

TaxPlanner
It would be unusual for an expense paid by a tenant that is the responsibility of the landlord not to be deductible by the landlord as well. But such expenses do exist. Consider, for example, a building code violation fine incurred for some change made in the tenant's space by the tenant without the landlord's consent. The fine is imposed on the landlord, but the violation is the tenant's fault. The tenant pays the penalty, but the landlord still has to declare that amount as income, and, in this case, the landlord probably will not be able to deduct the amount of the fine as an expense. Most penalties are not deductible. If this is a possibility, a clause in the lease making the payment of such a penalty the responsibility of the tenant when the tenant is at fault would probably keep the payment by the tenant from being income to the landlord.

Property or services. If you receive property or services, instead of money, as rent, include the fair market value of the property or services in your rental income.

Explanation
Examples of other types of income treated as rental income include the following:

1. Amounts received from an insurance company under a policy that reimburses a property owner for rent lost because of a fire or other casualty affecting the rental property.
2. Amounts received by subletting a property to another individual. If you did receive such income, you would be able to deduct the rent you are paying to the landlord as an expense. However, you are still not the owner and therefore would not be able to depreciate the property.

If the services are provided at an agreed upon or specified price, that price is the fair market value unless there is evidence to the contrary.
Rental of property also used as a home. If you rent property that you also use as your home and you rent it fewer than 15 days during the tax year, do not include the rent you receive in your income and do not deduct rental expenses. However, you can deduct on Schedule A (Form 1040) the interest, taxes, and casualty and theft losses that are allowed for nonrental property. See *Personal Use of Dwelling Unit (Including Vacation Home),* later.
Part interest. If you own a part interest in rental property, you must report your part of the rental income from the property.

Rental Expenses

This part discusses repairs and certain other expenses of renting property that you ordinarily can deduct from your rental income. It includes information on the expenses you can deduct if you rent part of your property, or if you change your property to rental use. Depreciation, which you can also deduct from your rental income, is discussed later.

TaxSaver
You may deduct expenses on your rental property during a period in which it is *not* being rented as long as it is actively being held out for rent. This applies to a period between rentals, as well as to the period during which a property is being marketed as a rental property for the first time.

The IRS can disallow these deductions if you are unable to show you were actively seeking a profit and had a reasonable expectation of achieving one. The deduction cannot be disallowed just because your property is difficult to rent.

When to deduct. You generally deduct your rental expenses in the year you pay them.
Vacant rental property. If you hold property for rental purposes, you may be able to deduct your ordinary and necessary expenses (including depreciation) for managing, conserving, or maintaining the property while the property is vacant. However, you cannot deduct any loss of rental income for the period the property is vacant.

Example
You own a rental property that, during 2001, was vacant for about half the year. You had rental income of $12,000 during the year and ordinary and necessary expenses of $15,000, which resulted in an overall loss of $3,000. As long as you can demonstrate that you have been actively trying to rent the house (e.g., newspaper clippings advertising the property for rent), you would be able to deduct your expenses up to $12,000. The remaining $3,000 of expenses can be carried over to the next year. However, see *Losses From Real Estate Activities,* later in this chapter, for special rules and how to report rental income and expenses. See *How to Report Rental Income and Expenses,* later in this chapter.

Pre-rental expenses. You can deduct your ordinary and necessary expenses for managing, conserving, or maintaining rental property from the time you make it available for rent.

Depreciation. You can begin to depreciate rental property when it is ready and available for rent. See *Placed-in Service Date* under *Depreciation,* later.

Expenses for rental property sold. If you sell property you held for rental purposes, you can deduct the ordinary and necessary expenses for managing, conserving, or maintaining the property until it is sold.

Personal use of rental property. If you sometimes use your rental property for personal purposes, you must divide your expenses between rental and personal use. Also, your rental expense deductions may be limited. See *Personal Use of Dwelling Unit (Including Vacation Home),* later.

Part interest. If you own a part interest in rental property, you can deduct your part of the expenses that you paid.

Repairs and Improvements

You can deduct the cost of repairs to your rental property. You cannot deduct the cost of improvements. You recover the cost of improvements by taking depreciation (explained later).

Recordkeeping. Separate the costs of repairs and improvements, and keep accurate records. You will need to know the cost of improvements when you sell or depreciate your property.

Repairs. A repair keeps your property in good operating condition. It does not materially add to the value of your property or substantially prolong its life. Repainting your property inside or out, fixing gutters or floors, fixing leaks, plastering, and replacing broken windows are examples of repairs.

If you make repairs as part of an extensive remodeling or restoration of your property, the whole job is an improvement.

Improvements. An improvement adds to the value of your property, prolongs its useful life, or adapts it to new uses. Improvements include the following items.

- Putting a recreation room in an unfinished basement.
- Paneling a den.
- Adding a bathroom or bedroom.
- Putting decorative grillwork on a balcony.
- Putting up a fence.
- Putting in new plumbing or wiring.
- Putting in new cabinets.
- Putting on a new roof.
- Paving a driveway.

If you make an improvement to property, the cost of the improvement must be capitalized. The capitalized cost can generally be depreciated as if the improvement were separate property.

Explanation
The examples given by the IRS are not necessarily improvements that must be capitalized. If a so-called improvement does not prolong useful life or add to value, it is deductible currently as a repair. It is the "nature" of the repair rather than the "amount" that determines whether it is deductible or not.

Examples
Examples of capitalized expenses are as follows:

- Improvements made to property to comply with government regulations
- Expenditures to place property in a safe condition
- Facelifting to improve property's appearance
- Replacement of flashing around a building's roof
- Replacement of a gravel driveway with a cement driveway
- Replacing a floor
- Replacing or recovering a roof

Examples of deductible expenses are as follows:

- Replacing a portion of a wooden bathroom when damage has been caused by water
- Repainting or repapering a room in a rooming house when it is necessary to keep the area clean and serviceable
- Reinforcing sagging floors
- Resurfacing a parking lot
- Making piecemeal repairs to floors

TaxOrganizer

All records and receipts of your rental expenditures, and what they were specifically for, should be kept for a minimum of three years. This will allow you to substantiate items relating to your rental property if the IRS should have any questions.

It is extremely important to keep accurate records of expenditures segregated for repairs that are currently deductible and improvements that are capitalized. Generally, IRS agents give close attention to repair and maintenance deductions. Sometimes expenditures have completely been disallowed unless the taxpayer can prove each specific amount of repairs.

Other Expenses

Other expenses you can deduct from your rental income include advertising, cleaning and maintenance services, utilities, fire and liability insurance, taxes, interest, commissions for the collection of rent, ordinary and necessary travel and transportation, and other expenses, discussed next.

Explanation
While commissions paid to collect rent are deductible, commissions paid to obtain long-term rentals (greater than a 1-year period) must be capitalized and **amortized** over the life of the lease. Commissions paid to acquire the rental property must be capitalized as part of the basis of that property and recovered when the property is depreciated.

Points paid to acquire a mortgage on the rental property must be amortized over the life of the mortgage.

Other deductible expenses connected to renting include legal costs for dispossessing a tenant, property management fees, and pest control fees.

The "ordinary and necessary travel and transportation" category includes, of course, local transportation. It also covers the cost of meals and lodging on trips to inspect rental property located outside the immediate area. However, for the cost of nonlocal transportation and some other expenses to be deductible, the *primary* purpose of the trip must be to take care of the rental property. (See Chapter 28, *Car Expenses and Other Employee Business Expenses,* for a discussion of how to deduct expenses when you use your personal automobile in your trade or business.)

Example
If you take a 1-week trip to Florida and spend 1 day inspecting your rental property, *no* nonlocal transportation expenses are deductible. If, on the other hand, 6 of the 7 days are used to repair and attend to the property, *all* non-

local transportation expenses are deductible. In both cases, local transportation expenses incurred traveling to and from the property are deductible.

Rental payments for property. You can deduct the rent you pay for property that you use for rental purposes. If you buy a leasehold for rental purposes, you can deduct an equal part of the cost each year over the term of the lease.

Example 1
If you pay $1,100 rent for property and collect $1,200 in rent from a third party for the same property, you may deduct the $1,100 you pay. Your profit from the rental activity is $100.

Example 2
If you buy a 10-year lease on property from someone for $1,000, you have to pay the rent that the former owner of the lease had to pay. In turn, you report as income any rent you receive on the property. You may amortize the cost of the lease over 10 years, deducting $100 each year.

Rental of equipment. You can deduct the rent you pay for equipment that you use for rental purposes. However, in some cases, lease contracts are actually purchase contracts. If so, you cannot deduct these payments. You can recover the cost of purchased equipment through depreciation.

Explanation
A lease with an option to buy may be a purchase contract. Generally, if the sum of the rental payments on a lease with an option to buy amounts to a substantial part of what would be the purchase price, and if the option period is clearly less than the useful life of the property, the transaction is treated as a sale. Income is recognized under the installment sale rules. (See Chapter 15, *Sale of Property*, for details.)

If the lease is treated as a sale on the date the lease is entered into, rather than the date the option is exercised, there may be unwanted tax consequences for the landlord. The payments that the landlord receives will be proceeds from the sale of property, and he or she will report the gain on the installment method. The landlord may also have to report imputed interest income (see Chapter 13, *Other Income*). Consequently, the landlord might have more income and fewer deductions than expected.

TaxPlanner
The rules in this area are complex, but a careful drafting of a property agreement will reduce or eliminate the likelihood that the IRS will consider the lease a sale. Professional help should be obtained.

Insurance premiums paid in advance. If you pay an insurance premium for more than one year in advance, each year you can deduct the part of the premium payment that will apply to that year. You cannot deduct the total premium in the year you pay it.

Local benefit taxes. Generally, you cannot deduct charges for local benefits that increase the value of your property, such as charges for putting in streets, sidewalks, or water and sewer systems. These charges are nondepreciable capital expenditures. You must add them to the basis of your property. You can deduct local benefit taxes if they are for maintaining, repairing, or paying interest charges for the benefits.

TaxSaver
Whether or not you are offering property for rent, it is important to keep a file on the assessments you pay for sewers, streets, and the like. These add to your cost basis in the property and are important in determining your gain or loss if you ever sell the property. In addition, if you do rent the property out, the increase in your cost basis for any special assessment may increase your depreciation deduction, depending on the type of assessment.

Travel expenses. You can deduct the ordinary and necessary expenses of traveling away from home if the primary purpose of the trip was to collect rental income or to manage, conserve, or maintain your rental property. You must properly allocate your expenses between rental and nonrental activities. For information on travel expenses, see chapter 28.

Recordkeeping. To deduct travel expenses, you must keep records that follow the rules in chapter 28.

Local transportation expenses. You can deduct your ordinary and necessary local transportation expenses if you incur them to collect rental income or to manage, conserve, or maintain your rental property.

Generally, if you use your personal car, pickup truck, or light van for rental activities, you can deduct the expenses using one of two methods: actual expenses or the standard mileage rate. For 2001, the standard mileage rate for all business miles is 34.5 cents a mile. For more information, see chapter 28.

Recordkeeping. To deduct car expenses under either method, you must keep records that follow the rules in chapter 28. In addition, you must complete Part V of Form 4562 and attach it to your tax return.

Tax return preparation. You can deduct, as a rental expense, the part of the tax return preparation fees you paid to prepare Part I of Schedule E (Form 1040). You can also deduct, as a rental expense, any portion of the total expense you paid to resolve a tax underpayment related to your rental activities. On your 2001 Schedule E, you can deduct fees paid in 2001 to prepare Part I of your 2000 Schedule E.

TaxOrganizer
Be sure to keep a detailed diary of expenses for your rental property. Include the following:

- Date and amount paid for maintenance expenses
- Travel expenses to and from rental property (keep track of number of miles driven or actual car expenses, including the date of travel)
- Amount of tax return preparation fee paid for rental income portion of return (have your tax preparer show the amount separately on his or her invoice)

Not Rented for Profit

If you do not rent your property to make a profit, you can deduct your rental expenses only up to the amount of your rental income. Any rental expenses in excess of rental income cannot be carried forward to the next year. For more information about the rules for an activity not engaged in for profit, see chapter 1 of Publication 535.

Where to report. Report your not-for-profit rental income on line 21, Form 1040. You can include your mortgage interest (if you use the property as your main home or second home), real estate taxes, and casualty losses on the appropriate lines of Schedule A (Form 1040), *Itemized Deductions,* if you itemize your deductions.

Claim your other rental expenses, subject to the rules explained in chapter 1 of Publication 535, as miscellaneous itemized deductions on line 22 of Schedule A (Form 1040). You can deduct these expenses only if they, together with certain other miscellaneous itemized deductions, total more than 2% of your adjusted gross income.

TAXPLANNER

If you move out of your personal residence and rent it, your deductions for **real estate** tax and mortgage interest are shifted from itemized deductions on Schedule A to rental deductions on Schedule E of Form 1040. The only additional deductions you become entitled to are those for operating expenses and depreciation. Since the rental income is included in your gross income, and the amount of additional deductions you are entitled to may be small, renting out your personal residence could increase your taxable income. If you rent out your personal residence with the intention of returning to live in it in the future, a special rule governing the deduction of mortgage interest may benefit you. See *Passive Activity Limits* later in this chapter.

Property Changed to Rental Use

If you change your home or other property, (or a part of it), to rental use at any time other than at the beginning of your tax year, you must divide yearly expenses, such as depreciation, taxes, and insurance, between rental use and personal use.

You can deduct as rental expenses only the part of the expense that is for the part of the year the property was used or held for rental purposes.

You cannot deduct depreciation or insurance for the part of the year the property was held for personal use. However, you can include the home mortgage interest and real estate tax expenses for the part of the year the property was held for personal use as an itemized deduction on Schedule A (Form 1040).

Example. Your tax year is the calendar year. You moved from your home in May and started renting it on June 1. You can deduct as rental expenses seven-twelfths of your yearly expenses, such as taxes and insurance.

Starting with June, you can deduct as rental expenses the amounts you pay for items generally billed monthly, such as utilities.

Renting Part of Property

If you rent part of your property, you must divide certain expenses between the part of the property used for rental purposes and the part of the property used for personal purposes as though you actually had two separate pieces of property.

You can deduct the expenses related to the part of the property used for rental purposes, such as home mortgage interest and real estate taxes, as rental expenses on Schedule E (Form 1040). You can deduct the expenses for the part of the property used for personal purposes, subject to certain limitations, only if you itemize your deductions on Schedule A (Form 1040). You can also deduct as a rental expense a part of other expenses that normally are nondeductible personal expenses, such as expenses for electricity or painting the outside of your house. You cannot deduct any part of the cost of the first phone line even if your tenants have unlimited use of it.

You do not have to divide the expenses that belong only to the rental part of your property. For example, if you paint a room that you rent, or if you pay premiums for liability insurance in connection with renting a room in your home, your entire cost is a rental expense. If you install a second phone line strictly for your tenants' use, all of the cost of the second line is deductible as a rental expense. You can deduct depreciation, discussed later, on the part of the property used for rental purposes as well as on the furniture and equipment you use for rental purposes.

Example

Allison rents a room in her house to Gladys. Every year Allison has the house, including Gladys's room, painted for maintenance purposes. The portion of the paint and labor cost for the rented room is deducted on Schedule E. The portion that does not relate to the rented room is not deductible.

Allison pays mortgage interest and property taxes each year on this home. A percentage of this interest and tax that relates to the rental is deductible on Schedule E and the remaining amount is deductible as an itemized deduction on Schedule A.

How to divide expenses. If an expense is for both rental use and personal use, such as mortgage interest or heat for the entire house, you must divide the expense between the rental use and the personal use. You can use any reasonable method for dividing the expense. It may be reasonable to divide the cost of some items (for example, water) based on the number of people using them. However, the two most common methods for dividing an expense are one based on the number of rooms in your home and one based on the square footage of your home.

TAXPLANNER

As there are various methods of dividing expenses, you should use whichever "reasonable" method provides the best result. For more information, see *How to Divide Expenses*, later in this chapter.

Personal Use of Dwelling Unit (Including Vacation Home)

If you have *any* personal use of a dwelling unit (including vacation home) that you rent, you *must* divide your expenses between rental use and personal use. See *Figuring Days of Personal Use* and *How To Divide Expenses,* later.

If you used your dwelling unit for personal purposes long enough during 2001, it will be considered a "dwelling unit used as a home." If so, you cannot deduct rental expenses that exceed rental income for that property. See *Dwelling Unit Used as Home* and *How To Figure Rental Income and Deductions,* later. If your dwelling unit is not considered a dwelling unit used as a home, you can deduct rental expenses that exceed rental income for that property subject to certain limits. See *Limits on Rental Losses,* later.

Exception for minimal rental use. If you use the dwelling unit as a home and you rent it fewer than 15 days during the year, do not include any of the rent in your income and do not deduct any of the rental expenses. See *Dwelling Unit Used as Home,* later.

TAXSAVER

This is one of the very few instances in which the IRS considers income to be nontaxable. You should be on the lookout for opportunities to rent property for less than 15 days to take advantage of this tax loophole. Residents of Augusta, Georgia, for example, have an annual opportunity to rent their houses for a short period during the Masters golf tournament.

Explanation

In general, the tax rules governing the rental of vacation homes and other dwelling units are the same as those governing any rental property. The allowable methods of depreciation, the types of deductible expenditures, and the types of expenditures that should be capitalized are all determined in the same way for both categories of rental property. However, if you or a member of your family uses the vacation home or dwelling unit during the year, the amount of deductible expenses may be limited by special rules.

Here's an easy way to figure out whether or not you have to follow the special rules for reporting rental income outlined later:

Step 1. Determine the number of days the property was rented at **fair market value** during the year. If this number is less than 15, STOP. You may not deduct any rental expenses, and you do not report any rental income. (*Note:* You may always deduct qualified residence interest, taxes, **casualty losses,** and theft losses if you itemize deductions. To do so, simply take the deduction for the entire amount of these items on Schedule A of Form 1040.) If the number of days rented is 15 or more, you must report rental income. Proceed to Step 2.

Step 2. Determine the number of days you personally use the property. If this number does not exceed the greater of (a) 14 days or (b) 10% of the number of days for which the property was rented at fair market value, you are not subject to any special rules. After completing Step 3, you determine your rental income or loss in the same way you would for any type of rental property.

If your personal use of the property exceeds the limits above, you *are* subject to special rules limiting the amount of deductible expenses. After completing Step 3, you determine your rental income or loss using the rules discussed in this section.

Step 3. Allocate *all* expenses between the rental period and the period in which you use the property personally, using the method described in the following section. Expenses allocated to the period of personal use are not deductible, except for interest, taxes, and casualty and theft losses (see Step 1). Then determine your rental income or loss, using either the general rules for rental property or the special rules regarding the personal use of vacation homes, whichever is appropriate.

Note: See later, *Days Not Counted as Personal Use* regarding use of a home before or after renting.

Dwelling unit. A dwelling unit includes a house, apartment, condominium, mobile home, boat, vacation home, or similar property. A dwelling unit has basic living accommodations, such as sleeping space, a toilet, and cooking facilities. A dwelling unit does not include property used solely as a hotel, motel, inn, or similar establishment.

Property is used solely as a hotel, motel, inn, or similar establishment if it is regularly available for occupancy by paying customers and is not used by an owner as a home during the year.

Example. You rent a room in your home that is always available for short-term occupancy by paying customers. You do not use the room yourself, and you allow only paying customers to use the room. The room is used solely as a hotel, motel, inn, or similar establishment and is not a dwelling unit.

Explanation
A dwelling unit must provide basic living accommodations, such as sleeping space, a rest room, and cooking facilities. The Tax Court has ruled that a mini-motor home qualifies as a dwelling unit.

An outbuilding used in conjunction with the main building to provide living accommodations, such as a garage, a barn, or a greenhouse, constitutes part of the main dwelling unit. When renting one of these outbuildings, you may deduct expenses only to the extent you have income. You may not deduct a rental loss. This is so because the outbuilding is not considered separate from the main building that is being used as a personal residence or vacation home.

Rental pools and time-shares. Rental pools are agreements under which two or more vacation homes are made available for rent by their owners, who agree to share "at least substantially part of the rental income from the homes regardless [of] which of the vacation homes are actually rented." Under proposed IRS regulations, special rules apply when you are computing income, expense, and personal use days.

Also, under proposed IRS regulations, individuals owning a time-share that they rent are to treat their rental income and expense separately with respect to their unit. Consult your tax advisor.

Dwelling Unit Used as Home

The tax treatment of rental income and expenses for a dwelling unit that you also use for personal purposes depends on whether you use it as a home. (See *How To Figure Rental Income and Deductions,* later.)

You use a dwelling unit as a home during the tax year if you use it for personal purposes more than the greater of:

1) 14 days, or
2) 10% of the total days it is rented to others at a fair rental price.

See *Figuring Days of Personal Use,* later.

If a dwelling unit is used for personal purposes on a day it is rented at a fair rental price, do not count that day as a day of rental in applying (2) above. Instead, count it as a day of personal use in applying both (1) and (2) above. This rule does not apply when dividing expenses between rental and personal use.

Fair rental price. A fair rental price for your property generally is an amount that a person who is not related to you would be willing to pay. The rent you charge is not a fair rental price if it is substantially less than the rents charged for other properties that are similar to your property.

Examples
The following examples show how to determine whether you used your rental property as a home.

Example 1. You converted the basement of your home into an apartment with a bedroom, a bathroom, and a small kitchen. You rented the basement apartment at a fair rental price to college students during the regular school year. You rented to them on a 9-month lease (273 days).

During June (30 days), your brothers stayed with you and lived in the basement apartment rent free.

Your basement apartment was used as a home because you used it for personal purposes for 30 days. Rent-free use by your brother is considered personal use. Your personal use (30 days) is more than the greater of 14 days or 10% of the total days it was rented (27 days).

Example 2. You rented the guest bedroom in your home at a fair rental price during the local college's homecoming, commencement, and football weekends (a total of 27 days). Your sister-in-law stayed in the room, rent free, for the last 3 weeks (21 days) in July.

The room was used as a home because you used it for personal purposes for 21 days. That is more than the greater of 14 days or 10% of the 27 days it was rented (3 days).

Example 3. You own a cottage in a resort area. You rented it at a fair rental price for a total of 170 days during the year. For 12 of those days, the tenant was not able to use the cottage and allowed you to use it even though you did not refund any of the rent. Your family actually used the cottage for 10 of those days. Therefore, the cottage is treated as having been rented for 160 (170 – 10) days. Your family also used the cottage for 7 other days during the year.

You used the cottage as a home because you used it for personal purposes for 17 days. That is more than the greater of 14 days or 10% of the 160 days it was rented (16 days).

Use As Main Home Before or After Renting

For purposes of determining whether a dwelling unit was used as a home, do not count as days of personal use the days you used the property as your main home before or after renting it or offering it for rent in either of the following circumstances.

1) You rented or tried to rent the property for 12 or more consecutive months.
2) You rented or tried to rent the property for a period of less than 12 consecutive months and the period ended because you sold or exchanged the property.

This special rule does not apply when dividing expenses between rental and personal use.

Figuring Days of Personal Use

A day of personal use of a dwelling unit is any day that it is used by any of the following persons.

1) You or any other person who has an interest in it, unless you rent it to another owner as his or her main home under a shared equity financing agreement (defined later).
2) A member of your family or a member of the family of any other person who has a financial interest in it, unless the family member uses the dwelling unit as his or her main home and pays a fair rental price. Family includes only brothers and sisters, half-brothers and half-sisters, spouses, ancestors (parents, grandparents, etc.) and lineal descendants (children, grandchildren, etc.).
3) Anyone under an arrangement that lets you use some other dwelling unit.
4) Anyone at less than a fair rental price.

TAXSAVER

The rule relating to personal use does not apply to use by an in-law of the taxpayer who owns the property. Thus, a son-in-law could lease property at a fair market value to his mother-in-law, and it would not be treated as personal use.

Main home. If the other person or member of the family in (1) or (2) above has more than one home, his or her main home is the one lived in most of the time.

Shared equity financing agreement. This is an agreement under which two or more persons acquire undivided interests for more than 50 years in an entire dwelling unit, including the land, and one or more of the co-owners is entitled to occupy the unit as his or her main home upon payment of rent to the other co-owner or owners.

Donation of use of property. You use a dwelling unit for personal purposes if:

• You donate the use of the unit to a charitable organization,
• The organization sells the use of the unit at a fund-raising event, and
• The "purchaser" uses the unit.

TAXPLANNER

Although donating your rental property for a certain time period to a charitable organization is considered personal use, you still may be allowed to deduct certain expenses during that time on Schedule A as a charitable contribution. See Chapter 26, *Contributions,* for further details on donating your property.

Examples

The following examples show how to determine days of personal use.

Example 1. You and your neighbor are co-owners of a condominium at the beach. You rent the unit to vacationers whenever possible. The unit is not used as a main home by anyone. Your neighbor uses the unit for two weeks every year.

Because your neighbor has an interest in the unit, both of you are considered to have used the unit for personal purposes during those 2 weeks.

Example 2. You and your neighbors are co-owners of a house under a shared equity financing agreement. Your neighbors live in the house and pay you a fair rental price.

Even though your neighbors have an interest in the house, the days your neighbors live there are not counted as days of personal use by you. This is because your neighbors rent the house as their main home under a shared equity financing agreement.

Example 3. You own a rental property that you rent to your son. Your son has no interest in this dwelling unit. He uses it as his main home. He pays you a fair rental price for the property.

Your son's use of the property is not personal use by you because your son is using it as his main home, he has no interest in the property, and he is paying you a fair rental price.

Example 4. You rent your beach house to Joshua. Joshua rents his house in the mountains to you. You each pay a fair rental price.

You are using your house for personal purposes on the days that Joshua uses it because your house is used by Joshua under an arrangement that allows you to use his house.

Days Used for Repairs and Maintenance

Any day that you spend working substantially full time repairing and maintaining your property is not counted as a day of personal use. Do not count such a day as a day of personal use even if family members use the property for recreational purposes on the same day.

Explanation

If the dwelling unit is rented and you are a guest of the occupant for a brief visit, this will not constitute personal use. Of course, the longer the visit is, the more likely the IRS is to claim you were an occupant rather than a visitor. Certainly, 1 or 2 days should be no problem.

How To Divide Expenses

If you use a dwelling unit for both rental and personal purposes, divide your expenses between the rental use and the personal use based on the number of days used for each purpose. Expenses for the rental use of the unit are deductible under the rules explained in *How To Figure Rental Income and Deductions,* next.

When dividing your expenses follow these rules.

1) Any day that the unit is rented at a fair rental price is a day of rental use even if you used the unit for personal purposes that day. This rule does not apply when determining whether you used the unit as a home.
2) Any day that the unit is available for rent but not actually rented is not a day of rental use.

Example. Your beach cottage was available for rent from June 1 through August 31 (92 days). Your family uses the cottage during the last 2 weeks in May (14 days). You were unable to find a renter for the first week in August (7 days). The person who rented the cottage for July allowed you to use it over a weekend (2 days) without any reduction in or refund of rent. The cottage was not used at all before May 17 or after August 31.

You figure the part of the cottage expenses to treat as rental expenses as follows.

1) The cottage was used for rental a total of 85 days (92 – 7). The days it was available for rent but not rented (7 days) are not days of rental use. The July weekend (2 days) you used it is rental use because you received a fair rental price for the weekend.
2) You used the cottage for personal purposes for 14 days (the last 2 weeks in May).
3) The total use of the cottage was 99 days (14 days personal use + 85 days rental use).
4) Your rental expenses are 85/99 (86%) of the cottage expenses.

When determining whether you used the cottage as a home, the July weekend (2 days) you used it is personal use even though you received a fair rental price for the weekend. Therefore, you had 16 days of personal use and 83 days of rental use for this purpose. Because you used the cottage for personal purposes more than 14 days and more than 10% of the days of rental use, you used it as a home. If you have a net loss, you may not be able to deduct all of the rental expenses. See *Property Used as a Home* in the following discussion.

TAXSAVER

The Tax Court allows you to use a different allocation formula for interest and taxes than the one the IRS describes above. Under the Tax Court formula, interest and taxes are allocated in the ratio of days rented to days in the year instead of in the ratio of days rented to days used. Using the Tax Court ratio results in a smaller amount of interest and taxes being allocated to the rental property, which creates the potential for you to deduct a larger amount of your other rental expenses.

Example
You own a cabin, which you rented for June and July, lived in for 1 month, and tried to rent the rest of the year. Your rental income for the 2 months was $2,800. Your total expenses for the cabin were as follows:

Interest	$1,500
Taxes	900
Utilities	750
Maintenance	300
Depreciation	1,200

	IRS method	Tax Court method
1) Gross rental income	$2,800	$2,800
2) Minus:		
a) Part of interest for rental use		
($1,500 × 61/91)	1,005	
($1,500 × 61/365)		251
b) Part of taxes for rental use		
($900 × 61/91)	603	
($900 × 61/365)		150

	IRS	Tax Court
3) Gross rental income that is more than the interest and taxes for rental	$1,192	$2,399
4) Minus:		
a) Part of utilities for rental use (61/91)	503	503
b) Part of maintenance for rental use (61/91)	201	201
5) Gross rental income that is more than the interest, taxes, and operating expenses for rental use	$ 488	$1,695
6) Minus: Depreciation limited to the part for rental use ($1,200 × 61/91 = $804) or line 5, whichever is less	488	804
7) Net rental income	$ –0–	$ 891

Both the IRS method and the Tax Court method allocate interest expense and real estate taxes partly to Schedule E (for determining net rental income) and partly to Schedule A (for personal itemized deductions). But examine how these allocations affect Schedule A.

Total interest paid is $1,500. Since the IRS method allocates $1,005 to the rental activity, the $495 balance is allocated to Schedule A. The Tax Court method allocates only $251 to the rental activity, leaving $1,249 for a deduction on Schedule A. Similarly, the IRS method allocates $603 of the $900 in real estate taxes to the rental activity, leaving $297 for Schedule A. The Tax Court method allocates only $150 to the rental activity, leaving $750 for Schedule A.

	Schedule A		Additional itemized deduction per Tax Court method
	Tax Court method	IRS method	
Interest	$1,249	$495	$ 754
Real estate taxes	750	297	453
			$1,207

Under the Tax Court method, you end up with additional deductions of $1,207, but you also have an additional net rental income of $891. The difference is that you reduce your taxable income by $316 more than under the IRS method. This conclusion assumes that you had enough other itemized deductions to make itemizing worthwhile and that your itemized deductions are not being limited.

Under the Tax Reform Act of 1986, the concept illustrated above is even more important. Rental income is considered to be passive income and, as such, can be used to offset passive losses. For more details, see Chapter 25, *Interest Expense.*

How To Figure Rental Income and Deductions

How you figure your rental income and deductions depends on whether the dwelling unit was used as a home (see *Dwelling Unit Used as Home,* earlier) and, if used as a home, how many days the property was rented.

Property Not Used As a Home

If you do not use a dwelling unit as a home, report all the rental income and deduct all the rental expenses. See *How To Report Rental Income and Expenses,* later.

Your deductible rental expenses can be more than your gross rental income. However, see *Limits on Rental Losses,* later.

Property Used As a Home

If you use a dwelling unit as a home during the year (see *Dwelling Unit Used as Home,* earlier), how you figure your rental income and deductions depends on how many days the unit was rented.

Rented fewer than 15 days. If you use a dwelling unit as a home and you rent it fewer than 15 days during the year, do not include in income any of the rental income. Also, you cannot deduct any expenses as rental expenses.

Rented 15 days or more. If you use a dwelling unit as a home and rent it 15 days or more during the year, you include all your rental income in your income. See *How To Report Rental Income and Expenses,* later. If you had a net profit from the rental property for the year (that is, if your rental income is more than the total of your rental expenses, including depreciation), deduct all of your rental expenses. However, if you had a net loss, you may not be able to deduct all of your rental expenses.

Use *Table 10–1* to figure your deductible expenses.

Table 10–1. **Worksheet for Figuring the Limit on Rental Deductions for a Dwelling Unit Used as a Home**

Use this worksheet only if you answer "yes" to all of the following questions.
- Did you use the dwelling unit as a home this year? (See *Dwelling Unit Used as Home.*)
- Did you rent the dwelling unit 15 days or more this year?
- Is the total of your rental expenses and depreciation more than your rental income?

1. Enter rents received . . . . _____
2. a. Enter the rental portion of deductible home mortgage interest (see instructions) . . . . _____
   b. Enter the rental portion of real estate taxes . . . . _____
   c. Enter the rental portion of deductible casualty and theft losses (see instructions) . . . . . . _____
   d. Enter direct rental expenses (see instructions) . . . . _____
   e. **Fully deductible rental expenses.** Add lines 2a–2d . . . . _____
3. Subtract line 2e from line 1. If zero or less, enter zero . . . . _____
4. a. Enter the rental portion of expenses directly related to operating or maintaining the dwelling unit (such as repairs, insurance, and utilities) . . . . _____
   b. Enter the rental portion of excess mortgage interest (see instructions) . . . . . . _____
   c. Add lines 4a and 4b . . . . _____
   d. **Allowable operating expenses.** Enter the smaller of line 3 or line 4c . . . . . . _____
5. Subtract line 4d from line 3. If zero or less, enter zero . . . . _____
6. a. Enter the rental portion of excess casualty and theft losses (see instructions) . . . . . . _____
   b. Enter the rental portion of depreciation of the dwelling unit . . . . _____
   c. Add lines 6a and 6b . . . . _____
   d. **Allowable excess casualty and theft losses and depreciation.** Enter the smaller of line 5 or line 6c . . _____
7. a. **Operating expenses to be carried over to next year.** Subtract line 4d from line 4c . . . _____
   b. **Excess casualty and theft losses and depreciation to be carried over to next year.** Subtract line 6d from line 6c . . . . _____

Enter the amounts on **lines 2e, 4d, and 6d** on the appropriate lines of Schedule E (Form 1040), Part I.

Worksheet Instructions

Follow these instructions for the worksheet above. If you were unable to deduct all your expenses last year because of the rental income limit, add these unused amounts to your expenses for this year.

Line 2a. Figure the mortgage interest on the dwelling unit that you could deduct on Schedule A (Form 1040) if you had not rented the unit. **Do not** include interest on a loan that did not benefit the dwelling unit. For example, **do not** include interest on a home equity loan used to pay off credit cards or other personal loans, buy a car, or pay college tuition. Include interest on a loan used to buy, build, or improve the dwelling unit, or to refinance such a loan. Enter the rental portion of this interest on line 2a of the worksheet.

Line 2c. Figure the casualty and theft losses related to the dwelling unit that you could deduct on Schedule A (Form 1040) if you had not rented the dwelling unit. To do this, complete Section A of Form 4684, *Casualties and Thefts,* treating the losses as personal losses. On line 17 of Form 4684, enter 10% of your adjusted gross income

figured **without** your rental income and expenses from the dwelling unit. Enter the rental portion of the result from line 18 of Form 4684 on line 2c of this worksheet. **Note.** Do **not** file this Form 4684 or use it to figure your personal losses on Schedule A. Instead, figure the personal portion on a separate Form 4684.

Line 2d. Enter the total of your rental expenses that are directly related only to the rental activity. These include interest on loans used for rental activities other than to buy, build, or improve the dwelling unit. Also include rental agency fees, advertising, office supplies, and depreciation on office equipment used in your rental activity.

Line 4b. On line 2a, you entered the rental portion of the mortgage interest you could deduct on Schedule A if you had not rented the dwelling unit. Enter on line 4b of this worksheet the rental portion of the mortgage interest you could not deduct on Schedule A because it is **more than** the limit on home mortgage interest. **Do not** include interest on a loan that did not benefit the

dwelling unit (as explained in the line 2a instructions).

Line 6a. To find the rental portion of excess casualty and theft losses, use the Form 4684 you prepared for line 2c of this worksheet.

A. Enter the amount from line 10 of Form 4684 . . . . . _____

B. Enter the rental portion of **A.** _____

C. Enter the amount from line 2c of this worksheet . . . . _____

D. Subtract **C** from **B.** Enter the result here and on line 6a of this worksheet . . . . . _____

Allocating the limited deduction. If you cannot deduct all of the amount on line 4c or 6c this year, you can allocate the allowable deduction in any way you wish among the expenses included on line 4c or 6c. Enter the amount you allocate to each expense on the appropriate line of Schedule E, Part I.

Explanation
The IRS explanation is correct as far as it goes. However, four areas require clarification:

1. The starting point in determining your rental income is gross rental income, which is defined by the IRS as the gross rent received less expenses incurred to obtain tenants, such as advertising and real estate agent's fees. This definition is important because it enables you to deduct this type of expense *before* taking deductions for interest, taxes, and casualty losses, which might be enough to reduce your rental income to zero. The result may be a larger total deduction. The key point is: Start with gross rent received, deduct your expenses to obtain tenants, and then proceed through the deduction process described above.
2. The total amount of a casualty or theft loss allocated to the rental period is deductible. Ordinarily, a personal casualty or theft loss is deductible only to the extent that it is more than $100 and more than 10% of your **adjusted gross income,** but this is not the case when you are dealing with rental property. Your loss in this case would not be subject to the $100 or 10% floor limitation. (See Chapter 27, *Casualty and Theft Losses,* for further details.)
3. Your basis in the vacation home or other dwelling unit is reduced only by the amount of depreciation actually allowed as a deduction, not by the amount of depreciation allocated to the rental period. This, in effect, decreases any gain you have to recognize if you subsequently sell the property. For more details on sales of **depreciable assets,** see *Depreciation,* later in this chapter.
4. Although the deductions for operating expenses and depreciation may not reduce income below zero, the deductions for interest and real estate taxes may.

TaxSaver

When you personally use a dwelling unit for more than 14 days or more than 10% of the number of days it is rented at fair market value, it is generally to your advantage to use the Tax Court formula for computing the amount of interest and taxes allocable to the rental period. Doing so usually allows you a greater *total* deduction, since interest, taxes, and casualty losses may be deducted on Schedule A, even if they are disallowed on Schedule E.

However, when your personal use of the dwelling is less than both 15 days and 10% of the number of days it is rented at fair market value, it is to your advantage to use the IRS method of allocating interest and taxes because the net loss on the rental property will be allowed if your personal use is not substantial. (This assumes that the passive loss rules will not limit your net loss.) In this case, the IRS method does not reduce your total deduction; instead, it decreases your rental income (or increases your rental loss) and hence decreases your adjusted gross income.

Decreasing your adjusted gross income can be important, for the following reasons:

1. For 2001, if your adjusted gross income is in excess of $132,950 ($66,475 if married filing seperately), your total itemized deductions will be reduced by 3% of the excess of your adjusted gross income over $132,950 ($66,475 if married filing seperately). Therefore, a reduction in adjusted gross income will reduce the effect of this limitation.
2. If your adjusted gross income is above certain thresholds, the amount of personal exemptions you are entitled to may be decreased. Therefore, a reduction in your adjusted gross income may increase the amount you can claim for your personal exemptions.
3. The amounts of certain itemized deductions, such as medical expenses, casualty losses, and most miscellaneous itemized deductions, are determined by reference to your adjusted gross income. Decreasing your adjusted gross income potentially increases your itemized deductions for these items.
4. Many states use adjusted gross income as the starting point in computing state taxable income. Using the IRS method may reduce your state tax liability.
5. If you are subject to alternative minimum tax, this method will reduce your alternative minimum taxable income.
6. A reduction in adjusted gross income may reduce the taxable amount of Social Security payments.
7. If you are a participant in a qualified pension plan, a decrease in your adjusted gross income may allow you to deduct contributions to an IRA.

Depreciation

You recover your cost in income producing property through yearly tax deductions. You do this by *depreciating* the property; that is, by deducting some of your cost on your tax return each year.

Three basic factors determine how much depreciation you can deduct. They are: (1) your basis in the property, (2) the recovery period for the property, and (3) the depreciation method used. You cannot simply deduct your mortgage or principal payments, or the cost of furniture, fixtures and equipment, as an expense.

You can deduct depreciation only on the part of your property used for rental purposes. Depreciation reduces your basis for figuring gain or loss on a later sale or exchange.

You may have to use Form 4562 to figure and report your depreciation. See *How To Report Rental Income and Expenses,* later.

Claiming the correct amount of depreciation. You should claim the correct amount of depreciation each tax year. If, in an earlier year, you did not claim depreciation that you were entitled to deduct, you must still reduce your basis in the property by the amount of depreciation that you should have deducted. You generally cannot deduct the unclaimed depreciation in the current year or any later tax year. However, you may be able to claim the correct amount of depreciation on an amended return (Form 1040X) for the earlier year. See *Claiming the correct amount of depreciation* in Publication 527 for more information.

Example
Barbara makes improvements in the amount of $10,000 to her rental property. These improvements are capitalized and depreciated over time. In the first year the improvements are put in service, Barbara does not deduct the correct amount of depreciation. She deducts $100 and reduces her basis by that amount, when the actual depreciation amount allowable is $200. If Barbara sells the property at the beginning of the next year, her basis in the property would be $9,800 (not $9,900). This is because even though Barbara only deducted $100 as depreciation, she was *allowed* to take a depreciation deduction of $200 and her adjusted basis should reflect the correct amount of depreciation that should have been taken.

Changing your accounting method to deduct unclaimed depreciation. If you claimed less depreciation than allowable in an earlier year, you can change your accounting method to take a deduction in the current year for the unclaimed depreciation. To change your accounting method, you must have the consent of the IRS. In some instances, you can receive automatic consent. For more information, see chapter 1 of Publication 946.

Land. You can never depreciate land. The costs of clearing, grading, planting, and landscaping are usually all part of the cost of land and are not depreciable.

> ### Explanation
> When calculating your depreciation expense, be sure to separate out the cost of land from the cost of the building since land is not depreciable. Taxpayers often forget to separate these costs, and, therefore, the true adjusted basis of the building is often not reflected. These amounts are normally not allocated on your purchase agreement so you must get an estimate of the value of the land by a real estate broker or by your county. For further details, consult your tax advisor.

Depreciation Systems

There are three ways to figure depreciation. The depreciation system you use depends on the type of property and when the property was placed in service. For property used in rental activities you use:

- MACRS (Modified Accelerated Cost Recovery System) for property placed in service after 1986.
- ACRS (Accelerated Cost Recovery System) for property placed in service after 1980 but before 1987, or
- Useful lives and either straight line or an accelerated method of depreciation, such as the declining balance method, if placed in service before 1981.

Caution. *This chapter discusses MACRS only. If you need more information about depreciating property placed in service before 1987, see Publication 534,* Depreciating Property Placed in Service Before 1987.

> ### Explanation
> Depreciation may perhaps be best understood as a way of deducting the cost of an expenditure over many years. Depreciation is calculated in the same way whether you report income on the **cash** or the **accrual method.**
>
> The period of time over which you depreciate your property has long been the subject of controversy. Different taxpayers, often in the same business, have depreciated the same type of property over widely different periods. Efforts to bring more uniformity to the write-off period resulted in the introduction of the Accelerated Cost Recovery System (ACRS). ACRS was replaced with MACRS (Modified ACRS) by the Tax Reform Act of 1986. Most tangible personal property can be depreciated. Artwork is an exception. It cannot be depreciated because no useful life can be established.

If you placed property in service before 2001, continue to use the same method of figuring depreciation that you used in the past.

Section 179 election. You cannot claim the section 179 deduction for property held to produce rental income (unless renting property is your trade or business). See chapter 2 of Publication 946.

> ### Explanation
> Property that does not normally qualify for the Section 179 deduction includes:

1. Property held for the production of income
2. Real property, including buildings and their structures
3. Property acquired from certain groups or persons
4. Certain property you lease to others

The Section 179 election falls under similar guidelines to the investment tax credit qualifications. Consult your tax advisor.

No deduction greater than basis. The total of all your yearly depreciation deductions cannot be more than the cost or other basis of the property. For this purpose, your yearly depreciation deductions include any depreciation that you were allowed to claim, even if you did not claim it.

Cooperative apartments. If you rent your cooperative apartment to others, you can deduct your share of the cooperative housing corporation's depreciation. See *Cooperative apartments* in Publication 527 for information on how to figure your depreciation deduction.

> ### Explanation
> To qualify as a cooperative housing corporation, four tests must be met:
>
> 1. There is only a single class of stock outstanding.
> 2. Each stockholder must be entitled (solely because he or she owns stock) to occupy a house or an apartment owned or leased by the corporation.
> 3. There are no distributions to a stockholder that are not out of the corporation's earnings, except for partial or complete liquidation.
> 4. At least 80% of the corporation's gross income is received from the tenant-stockholders.
>
> If you are a tenant-stockholder in a co-op, you compute your depreciation deduction in the following manner:
>
> 1. Compute depreciation for all of the depreciable property owned by the corporation, using the following method:
>   a) Multiply your cost per share for the corporation stock by the total number of shares outstanding.
>   b) Add the total mortgage indebtedness on the property as of the date you purchased your stock to the amount computed in (a).
>   c) From the amount determined in (b), subtract the part of the mortgage indebtedness (existing on the date you purchased your stock) allocable to nondepreciable property, such as land. The result is the depreciable basis of the corporation's property.
>   d) Compute the depreciation, using the basis calculated in (c) and one of the allowable methods of depreciation discussed later.
> 2. From the amount of depreciation computed in (1), subtract depreciation on any rental space owned by the corporation that may not be lived in by tenant-stockholders.
> 3. Divide the number of shares of stock in the corporation you own by the total number of shares outstanding (including shares held by the corporation).
> 4. Multiply the amount calculated in (2) by the percentage determined in (3). This is your depreciation deduction, which is limited to the adjusted basis of your stock in the corporation.
>
> If you rent your co-op, you may also deduct other rental expenses, such as repairs, maintenance, commissions, and insurance fees, as well as depreciation. Whether or not you rent your co-op, you may deduct your share of the corporation's deductible interest and taxes.

MACRS

In general, tangible property placed in service during 2001 is depreciated using MACRS.

MACRS consists of two systems that determine how you depreciate your property. The main system is called the *General Depreciation System (GDS).* The second system is called the *Alternative Depreciation System (ADS).* GDS is used to figure your depreciation deduction for property used in most rental activities, unless you elect ADS.

To figure your MACRS deduction, you need to know the following information about your property:

1) Its recovery period,
2) Its placed-in-service date, and
3) Its depreciable basis.

Personal home changed to rental use. You must use MACRS to figure the depreciation on property you used as your home and changed to rental property in 2001.

Excluded property. You cannot use MACRS for certain personal property placed in service in your rental property in 2001 if it had been previously placed in service before MACRS became effective in 1987 (before August 1, 1986, if election made).

In addition, you may elect to exclude certain property from the application of MACRS. See Publication 946 for more information.

Recovery Periods Under GDS

Each item of property that can be depreciated is assigned to a property class. The recovery period of the property depends on the class the property is in. The property classes are:

- 3-year property,
- 5-year property,
- 7-year property,
- 10-year property,
- 15-year property,
- 20-year property,
- Nonresidential real property, and
- Residential rental property.

Recovery periods for property used in rental activities are shown in *Table 10–2.*

The class to which property is assigned is determined by its class life. Class lives and recovery periods for most assets are listed in *Appendix B* in Publication 946.

Additions or improvements to property. Treat depreciable additions or improvements you make to any property as separate property

Table 10–2. **MACRS Recovery Periods for Property Used in Rental Activities**

Type of Property	MACRS Recovery Period to Use	
	General Depreciation System	Alternative Depreciation System
Computers and their peripheral equipment	5 years	5 years
Office machinery, such as:		
Typewriters		
Calculators		
Copiers	5 years	6 years
Automobiles	5 years	5 years
Light trucks	5 years	5 years
Appliances, such as:		
Stoves		
Refrigerators	5 years	9 years
Carpets	5 years	9 years
Furniture used in rental property	5 years	9 years
Office furniture and equipment, such as:		
Desks		
Files	7 years	10 years
Any property that does not have a class life and that has not been designated by law as being in any other class	7 years	12 years
Fences	15 years	20 years
Roads	15 years	20 years
Shrubbery	15 years	20 years
Residential rental property (buildings or structures) and structural components such as furnaces, water pipes, venting, etc., ...	27.5 years	40 years
Additions and improvements, such as a new roof	The recovery period of the property to which the addition or improvement is made, determined as if the property were placed in service at the same time as the addition or improvement.	

items for depreciation purposes. The recovery period for an addition or improvement to property begins on the later of:

1) The date the addition or improvement is placed in service, or
2) The date the property to which the addition or improvement was made is placed in service.

The class and recovery period of the addition or improvement is the one that would apply to the underlying property if it were placed in service at the same time as the addition or improvement.

Example. You own a residential rental house that you have been renting since 1986 and are depreciating under ACRS. You put an addition onto the house and you placed it in service in 2001. You must use MACRS for the addition. Under MACRS, the addition would be depreciated as residential rental property over 27.5 years.

Placed-in-Service Date
You can begin to depreciate property when you place it in service in your trade or business or for the production of income. Property is considered placed in service in a rental activity when it is ready and available for a specific use in that activity.

Cost Basis
To deduct the proper amount of depreciation each year, you must first determine your basis in the property you intend to depreciate. The basis used for figuring depreciation is your original basis in the property increased by any additions or improvements made to the property. Your original basis is usually your cost. However, if you acquire the property in some other way, such as by inheriting it, getting it as a gift, or building it yourself, you may have to figure your original basis in another way. Other adjustments could also affect your basis. See chapter 14.

Example
You use an old truck in your business with an unrecovered cost of $6,000. You trade it in for a new truck and pay an additional $9,000 in cash. You subsequently spend $1,000 to have a heavy-duty component added. Your unadjusted basis is $16,000: the unrecovered cost of the old truck ($6,000) plus the cash paid for the new truck ($9,000) and the heavy-duty component ($1,000). Although you have one adjusted basis for your new truck, you may have to use one method of depreciation for the $6,000 unrecovered cost of the old truck and another method of depreciation for the $10,000. (See the antichurning rules covered in the section *MACRS Depreciation Under ADS* later in this chapter.)

Explanation
If you change personal use property to business or income-producing use property, the depreciable basis of the property would be the lesser of the fair market value at the date of change or the property's adjusted basis.

Example 1
Kelly purchased a house for $80,000. Before changing the property from personal to rental use, she made $6,000 of improvements. On the date of the change from personal to business use, the fair market value of the property was $90,000. The depreciable basis of the property is the lesser of the fair market value of the depreciable property at the date of the change or the property's adjusted basis. Since the adjusted basis of the house ($86,000, which consists of $80,000 cost plus $6,000 of improvements) is less than the fair market value of the house ($90,000), the depreciable basis is $86,000.

Example 2
Alternatively, if the value of the property on the date of the change from personal to business use was $84,000, the depreciable basis would be $84,000 (the lower of the adjusted basis of $86,000 or the fair market value of $84,000).

Conventions
To figure your depreciation deduction for both the year in which you place property in service and the year in which you dispose of property, you use one of the following conventions.

1) Mid-month convention.
2) Half-year convention.
3) Mid-quarter convention.

Mid-month convention. A mid-month convention is used for residential rental property in all situations. Under a mid-month convention, residential rental property placed in service, or disposed of, during any month is treated as placed in service, or disposed of, in the middle of that month.

Half-year convention. The half-year convention is used in rental activities other than residential rental property. The half-year convention treats all property placed in service, or disposed of, during a tax year as placed in service, or disposed of, in the middle of that tax year.

A half year of depreciation is allowable for the first year property is placed in service, regardless of when the property is placed in service during the tax year. For each of the remaining years of the recovery period, you will take a full year of depreciation. If you hold the property for the entire recovery period, a half year of depreciation is allowable for the year in which the recovery period ends. If you dispose of the property before the end of the recovery period, a half year of depreciation is allowable for the year of disposition.

Mid-quarter convention. A mid-quarter convention must be used in certain circumstances for property other than residential rental property. This convention applies if the total basis of such property that is placed in service in the last 3 months of a tax year is more than 40% of the total basis of all such property you place in service during the tax year.

Under a mid-quarter convention, all property placed in service, or disposed of, during any quarter of a tax year is treated as placed in service, or disposed of, in the middle of the quarter.

Exception. If the third quarter of your 2001 tax year includes September 11, 2001, you may elect to apply the half-year convention, as discussed above, to all property (other than non-residential real property and residential rental property) placed in service during your 2001 tax year. The third quarter begins on the first day of the seventh month of the tax year.

To make the election, write "Election Pursuant to Notice 2001-70" across the top of Form 4562.

Example. During the tax year, Jordan Gregory purchased the following items to use in his rental property.

- A dishwasher for $400, that he placed in service in January.
- Used furniture for $100, that he placed in service in September.
- A refrigerator for $500, that he placed in service in October.

Jordan uses the calendar year as his tax year. The total basis of all property placed in service in that year is $1,000. The $500 basis of the refrigerator placed in service during the last 3 months of his tax year exceeds $400 (40% × $1,000).

Ordinarily, Jordan must use the mid-quarter convention instead of the half-year convention for all three items. However, for 2001 he can use the half-year convention for all three items if he makes the election as discussed under *Exception* above.

Explanation
Under the modified MACRS rules, a half-year convention is used on business personal property placed in service or re-

moved from service during the year. For example, a calendar year taxpayer who has been in business all year computes his or her depreciation as if all property had been acquired on July 1.

If the taxable year is less than 12 months (usually in the case of a new business), the property will be treated as in service during half of the short tax year.

If more than 40% of your business personal property is placed in service in the last 3 months of your tax year, a special averaging convention applies. This is called a mid-quarter convention and requires property placed in service during any quarter of a tax year to be treated as placed in service at the midpoint of such quarter.

Dispositions of business personal property result in a half-year of depreciation.

Residential and nonresidential real property are treated as placed in service (or taken out of service) in the middle of the month and use a mid-month convention rather than the half-year convention described above.

Note that you may also need to compute alternative minimum tax depreciation for purposes of computing your alternative minimum taxable income. See Chapter 31, *How to Figure Your Tax*, for additional information.

MACRS Depreciation Under GDS

You can figure your MACRS depreciation deduction under GDS in one of two ways. The deduction is substantially the same both ways. (The difference, if any, is slight.) You can either:

1) Use the percentage from the optional MACRS tables, see *Table 10–3*, or
2) Actually figure the deduction using the depreciation method and convention that apply over the recovery period of the property.

Publication 946 discusses computing depreciation using the proper method and convention.

Using the Optional Tables

You can use the tables in *Table 10–3* to compute annual depreciation under MACRS. The tables show the percentages for the first 6 years. The percentages in Tables 10–3–A, 10–3–B, and 10–3–C make the change from declining balance to straight line in the year that straight line will yield a larger deduction. See *Appendix A* of Publication 946 for complete tables.

If you elect to use the straight line method for 5-, 7-, or 15-year property, or the 150% declining balance method for 5- or 7-year property, use the tables in *Appendix A* of Publication 946.

How to use the tables. The following section explains how to use the optional tables.

Figure the depreciation deduction by multiplying your ***unadjusted basis*** in the property by the percentage shown in the appropriate table. Your unadjusted basis is your depreciable basis without reduction for depreciation previously claimed.

Once you begin using an optional table to figure depreciation, you must continue to use it for the entire recovery period unless there is an adjustment to the basis of your property for a reason other than:

1) Depreciation allowed or allowable, or
2) An addition or improvement that is depreciated as a separate item of property.

If there is an adjustment for any other reason (for example, because of a deductible casualty loss), you can no longer use the table. For the year of the adjustment and for the remaining recovery period, figure depreciation using the property's adjusted basis at the end of the year and the appropriate depreciation method, as explained in *MACRS Depreciation Under GDS* in Publication 527.

Tables 10–3–A, 10–3–B, and 10–3–C. The percentages in these tables take into account the half-year and mid-quarter conventions. Use Table 10–3–A for 5-year property, Table 10–3–B for 7-year property, and Table 10–3–C for 15-year property. Use the percentage in the second column (half-year convention) unless you must use the mid-quarter convention (explained earlier). If you must use the mid-quarter convention, use the column that corresponds to the calendar year quarter in which you placed the property in service.

Example 1. You purchased a stove and refrigerator and placed them in service in February. Your basis in the stove is $300 and your basis in the refrigerator is $500. Both are 5-year property. Using the half-year convention column in Table 10–3–A, you find the depreciation percentage for year 1 is 20%. For that year, your depreciation deduction is $60 ($300 × .20) for the stove, and is $100 ($500 × .20) for the refrigerator.

For the second tax year, you find your depreciation percentage is 32%. That year's depreciation deduction will be $96 ($300 × .32) for the stove and $160 ($500 × .32) for the refrigerator.

Example 2. Assume the same facts as in Example 1, except you buy the refrigerator in October instead of February. You must use the mid-quarter convention to figure depreciation on the stove and refrigerator. The refrigerator was placed in service in the last 3 months of the tax year and its basis ($500) is more than 40% of the total basis of all property placed in service during the year ($800 × .40 = $320).

Because you placed the refrigerator in service in October, you use the fourth quarter column of Table 10–3–A and find that the depreciation percentage for year 1 is 5%. Your depreciation deduction for the refrigerator is $25 ($500 × .05).

Because you placed the stove in service in February, you use the first quarter column of Table 10–3–A and find that the depreciation percentage for year 1 is 35%. For that year, your depreciation deduction for the stove is $105 ($300 × .35).

Table 10–3–D. Use this table for residential rental property. Find the row for the month that you placed the property in service. Use the percentages listed for that month to figure your depreciation deduction. The mid-month convention is taken into account in the percentages shown in the table.

Example. You purchased a single family rental house and placed it in service in February. Your basis in the house is $80,000. Using Table 10–3–D, you find that the percentage for property placed in service in February of year 1 is 3.182%. That year's depreciation deduction is $2,546 ($80,000 × .03182).

MACRS Depreciation Under ADS

If you choose, you can use the ADS method for most property. Under ADS, you use the straight line method of depreciation.

Table 10–2 shows the recovery periods for property used in rental activities that you depreciate under ADS. See *Appendix B* in Publication 946 for other property. If your property is not listed, it is considered to have no class life. Under ADS, personal property with no class life is depreciated using a recovery period of 12 years and real property with no class life is depreciated using a recovery period of 40 years.

Use the mid-month convention for residential rental property. For all other property, use the half-year or mid-quarter convention.

Election. You choose to use ADS by entering the depreciation on line 16, Part II of Form 4562.

The election of ADS for one item in a class of property generally applies to all property in that class that is placed in service during the tax year of the election. However, the election applies on a property-by-property basis for residential rental property.

Once you choose to use ADS, you cannot change your election.

Table 10–3. Optional MACRS Tables
Table 10–3–A. MACRS 5-Year property

Year	Half-year convention	Mid-quarter convention			
		First quarter	Second quarter	Third quarter	Fourth quarter
1	20.00%	35.00%	25.00%	15.00%	5.00%
2	32.00	26.00	30.00	34.00	38.00
3	19.20	15.60	18.00	20.40	22.80
4	11.52	11.01	11.37	12.24	13.68
5	11.52	11.01	11.37	11.30	10.94
6	5.76	1.38	4.26	7.06	9.58

Table 10–3–B. MACRS 7-Year property

Year	Half-year convention	Mid-quarter convention			
		First quarter	Second quarter	Third quarter	Fourth quarter
1	14.29%	25.00%	17.85%	10.71%	3.57%
2	24.49	21.43	23.47	25.51	27.55
3	17.49	15.31	16.76	18.22	19.68
4	12.49	10.93	11.97	13.02	14.06
5	8.93	8.75	8.87	9.30	10.04
6	8.92	8.74	8.87	8.85	8.73

Table 10–3–C. MACRS 15-Year property

Year	Half-year convention	Mid-quarter convention			
		First quarter	Second quarter	Third quarter	Fourth quarter
1	5.00%	8.75%	6.25%	3.75%	1.25%
2	9.50	9.13	9.38	9.63	9.88
3	8.55	8.21	8.44	8.66	8.89
4	7.70	7.39	7.59	7.80	8.00
5	6.93	6.65	6.83	7.02	7.20
6	6.23	5.99	6.15	6.31	6.48

Table 10–3–D. Residential Rental Property (27.5-year)

	Use the row for the month of the taxable year placed in service.					
	Year 1	Year 2	Year 3	Year 4	Year 5	Year 6
Jan.	3.485%	3.636%	3.636%	3.636%	3.636%	3.636%
Feb.	3.182	3.636	3.636	3.636	3.636	3.636
March	2.879	3.636	3.636	3.636	3.636	3.636
Apr.	2.576	3.636	3.636	3.636	3.636	3.636
May	2.273	3.636	3.636	3.636	3.636	3.636
June	1.970	3.636	3.636	3.636	3.636	3.636
July	1.667	3.636	3.636	3.636	3.636	3.636
Aug.	1.364	3.636	3.636	3.636	3.636	3.636
Sept.	1.061	3.636	3.636	3.636	3.636	3.636
Oct.	0.758	3.636	3.636	3.636	3.636	3.636
Nov.	0.455	3.636	3.636	3.636	3.636	3.636
Dec.	0.152	3.636	3.636	3.636	3.636	3.636

Explanation

The antichurning rules, as they are called, are designed to prevent you from taking undue advantage of the new, faster depreciation deduction rates by engaging in transactions in which the real and beneficial ownership interest in the property does not really change. For property originally acquired after 1980 and before 1986, rather than switching to MACRS, you must continue to use the previous method of depreciation only if MACRS will yield greater depreciation deductions in the first year. For property originally acquired prior to 1980, you must continue to use the previous method of accounting in all cases.

Example 1

You own your residence, which you bought in 1975. In 2001, you move out and convert the house to rental property. Although you first put it to business use in 2001, you cannot use MACRS because the property was actually acquired prior to 1980.

Example 2

In 1984, John and Mary acquired assets that they held as community property during their married life. John died in 1987, and his property was included in his estate, which resulted in his half being revalued to current fair market value. John's half of the property can be written off under MACRS, but the IRS says that the antichurning rules prevent Mary from using MACRS on her revalued half because there was no change of ownership, the property was placed in service after 1980 and before 1986, and the MACRS yields a greater first-year deduction.

Other Rules About Depreciable Property

In addition to the rules about what methods you can use, there are other rules you should be aware of with respect to depreciable property.
Gain from disposition. If you dispose of depreciable property at a gain, you may have to report, as ordinary income, all or part of the gain. See Publication 544, *Sales and Other Dispositions of Assets.*

Explanation

When you sell an asset for more than your unrecovered cost, you face the problem of recapture, that is, reporting all or part of your gain as ordinary income as opposed to capital gain. If you sell tangible personal property at a gain, your recapture is the lower of your gain or the previous amount of depreciation.

Example

		Case 1	Case 2
1)	Cost	$1,000	$1,000
2)	Depreciation previously claimed	(600)	(600)
3)	Unrecovered cost	$ 400	$ 400
4)	Selling price	$ 900	$1,200
5)	Gain on sale (4 – 3)	$ 500	$ 800
6)	Recapture ordinary income (lower of 2 or 5)	(500)	(600)
7)	Possible capital gain (5 – 6)	$ –0–	$ 200

Note that the recapture rules generally do not apply to real property if straight-line depreciation was used. However, a new 25% tax rate may apply to depreciation recapture on real property.

TAXPLANNER

Because the maximum tax rate on ordinary income is 39.1% and the maximum tax rate on long-term capital gains is generally 20%, the depreciation recaptured may be taxed at a higher rate at the time of the sale.

TAXALERT

Under current law, leasehold improvements must be depreciated under MACRS. You generally must depreciate an addition or improvement to nonresidential real property placed in service over a 39-year period using the straight-line method beginning in the month the addition or improvement is placed in service for assets placed in service after May 12, 1993. Leasehold improvements must be depreciated over the MACRS recovery period even if it exceeds the term of the lease.

TAXORGANIZER

Make sure to keep track of all assets acquired and improvements made related to your rental properties. You should keep records of cost, depreciation method, and amount of depreciation already taken. Therefore, if any of these assets are sold, it will be easier to calculate the gain and recapture amount, if necessary.

Alternative minimum tax. If you use accelerated depreciation, you may have to file Form 6251. Accelerated depreciation includes MACRS, ACRS, and any other method that allows you to deduct more depreciation than you could deduct using a straight line method.

Limits on Rental Losses

Rental real estate activities are generally considered passive activities, and the amount of loss you can deduct is limited. Generally, you cannot deduct losses from rental real estate activities unless you have income from other passive activities. However, you may be able to deduct rental losses without regard to whether you have income from other passive activities if you "materially" or "actively" participated in your rental activity. See *Passive Activity Limits,* later.

Losses from passive activities are first subject to the at-risk rules. At-risk rules limit the amount of deductible losses from holding most real property placed in service after 1986.
Exception. If your rental losses are less than $25,000 and you actively participated in the rental activity, the passive activity limits probably do not apply to you. See *Losses From Rental Real Estate Activities,* later.
Property used as a home. If you used the rental property as a home during the year, the passive activity rules do not apply to that home. Instead, you must follow the rules explained earlier under *Personal Use of Dwelling Unit (Including Vacation Home.)*

At-Risk Rules

The at-risk rules place a limit on the amount you can deduct as losses from activities often described as tax shelters. Losses from holding real property (other than mineral property) placed in service before 1987 are not subject to the at-risk rules.

Generally, any loss from an activity subject to the at-risk rules is allowed only to the extent of the total amount you have at risk in the activity at the end of the tax year. You are considered at risk in an activity to the extent of cash and the adjusted basis of other property you contributed to the activity and certain amounts borrowed for use in the activity. See Publication 925 for more information.

Passive Activity Limits

In general, rental activities (except those meeting the exception for real estate professionals, below) are passive activities. For this purpose, a rental activity is an activity from which you receive income mainly for the use of tangible property, rather than for services.
Limits on passive activity deductions and credits. Deductions for losses from passive activities are limited. You generally cannot offset income, other than passive income, with losses from passive activities. Nor can you offset taxes on income, other than passive income, with credits resulting from passive activities. Any excess loss or credit is carried forward to the next tax year.

For a detailed discussion of these rules, see Publication 925.

Example

Assume Rob maintains a tax-sheltered investment in which he made an initial investment of $20,000. Assuming Rob had a loss of $6,000 the first year, he would be able to take the loss deduction of $6,000, but the total maximum amount of loss deductions Rob could take in future years could not exceed $14,000 ($20,000 − $6,000).

You may have to complete **Form 8582** to figure the amount of any passive activity loss for the current year for all activities and the amount of the passive activity loss allowed on your tax return.

Exception for real estate professionals. Rental activities in which you *materially participated* during the year are not passive activities if, during that year, you were a real estate professional because you met the requirements. For a detailed discussion of the requirements, see Publication 527. For a detailed discussion of material participation, see Publication 925.

Explanation

An activity is considered a rental activity for this exception if:

1. Tangible property is used by customers.
2. Income received is principally for the use of property whether or not there is a lease, service contract, or other arrangement.

An activity is not considered a rental activity for this exception if:

1. The average time the customer uses the property is 7 days or less.
2. The average time the customer uses the property is 30 days or less and personal services have been provided by the owner in connection with the rental.
3. Extraordinary personal services are provided by the owner in connection with the rental.
4. The rental of the activity is incidental to the nonrental.
5. The property is associated with a partnership, S corporation, or joint venture.

Example

Amy owns a time-share condo and rents it to a third party for a week each year. Amy paid for no additional services except for weekly cleaning of the unit through condominium dues. This property is not considered a rental activity.

Losses From Rental Real Estate Activities

If you or your spouse *actively participated* in a passive rental real estate activity, you can deduct up to $25,000 of loss from the activity from your nonpassive income. This special allowance is an exception to the general rule disallowing losses in excess of income from passive activities. Similarly, you can offset credits from the activity against the tax on up to $25,000 of nonpassive income after taking into account any losses allowed under this exception.

If you are married, filing a separate return, and lived apart from your spouse for the entire tax year, your special allowance cannot be more than $12,500. If you lived with your spouse at any time during the year and are filing a separate return, you cannot use the special allowance to reduce your nonpassive income or tax on nonpassive income.

The maximum amount of the special allowance is reduced if your modified adjusted gross income is more than $100,000 ($50,000 if married filing separately).

Active participation. You actively participated in a rental real estate activity if you (and your spouse) owned at least 10% of the rental property and you made management decisions in a significant and bona fide

sense. Management decisions include approving new tenants, deciding on rental terms, approving expenditures, and similar decisions.

TaxAlert

A recently changed regulation tightened the "partial disposition" rule, requiring a taxpayer to dispose of "substantially all" of an activity rather than a "substantial part" under an earlier proposed regulation in order to deduct associated carryover suspended losses, that is, losses from this activity that did not get deducted in prior years. You should consult your tax advisor.

More information. See Publication 925 for more information on the passive loss limits, including information on the treatment of unused disallowed passive losses and credits and the treatment of gains and losses realized on the disposition of a passive activity.

TaxSaver

If you rent out your personal residence with the intention of returning to it (say, for example, you are transferred overseas for several years), the mortgage interest on the property may not be subject to the passive loss limitation rules. This can result in significant tax savings.

Example

Rental of a dwelling unit

Rent income	$15,000
Mortgage interest	(7,000)
Real estate tax	(3,000)
Other expenses	(1,000)
Depreciation	(9,000)
Net loss subject to passive loss rules	($5,000)

This loss may be deductible on your tax return, under the active participation $25,000 limitation mentioned earlier.

Rental of a personal residence with intention of returning .

Rent income	$15,000
Real estate tax	(3,000)
Other expenses	(1,000)
Depreciation	(9,000)
Net rental (passive) income	$2,000
Mortgage interest (loss **not** subject to passive loss rules)	(7,000)
Net loss from property allowed on tax return	($5,000)

$7,000 of this loss (the portion representing qualified residence mortgage interest) may be deductible against nonpassive income. In addition, the $2,000 net passive income may offset passive losses from other passive activities.

Be aware that the depreciation deduction reduces the cost basis of your property, thereby increasing the gain upon sale of the property.

Explanation

You must meet the active participation standards both in the year in which the loss arose and in the year in which the loss is allowed. Losses that exceed $25,000 carried over from an active participation year can be used in a later year if the taxpayer continues to actively participate.

The $25,000 offset rule does not apply to the losses carried over from prior years where the taxpayer did not actively participate in the rental.

TaxAlert

A tax-saving opportunity exists depending upon how personal property and real property are grouped. Under final regulations, a taxpayer could not treat as a single activity the rental of real property and the rental of personal property (other than personal property provided in connection with real property). Further, effective for tax years beginning in January 1993, it allows a taxpayer to treat as a single activity real property provided in connection with personal property.

Example

An individual who leases $10,000 of real property (e.g., a small structure or other fixture) in connection with renting $150,000 of computer equipment could treat as one activity the rental of both the real property and the personal property.

To make an election to treat all real property as a single activity, a taxpayer must file a statement with his or her original tax return for the tax year the taxpayer is making the election.

TaxPlanner

It may not be beneficial for you to group all of your rental real estate interests together if you have interests in non-rental activities that are also passive. Consult your tax advisor for further details.

How To Report Rental Income and Expenses

If you rent buildings, rooms, or apartments, and provide only heat and light, trash collection, etc., you normally report your rental income and expenses in Part I of Schedule E (Form 1040). However, do not use that schedule to report a not-for-profit activity. See *Not Rented for Profit,* earlier.

If you provide significant services that are primarily for your tenant's convenience, such as regular cleaning, changing linen, or maid service, you report your rental income and expenses on Schedule C (Form 1040), *Profit or Loss From Business* or Schedule C-EZ, *Net Profit From Business (Sole Proprietorship)*. Significant services do not include the furnishing of heat and light, cleaning of public areas, trash collection, etc. For information, see Publication 334, *Tax Guide for Small Business (For Individuals Who Use Schedule C or C-EZ)*. You also may have to pay self-employment tax on your rental income. See Publication 533, *Self-Employment Tax.*

Form 1098. If you paid $600 or more of mortgage interest on your rental property to any one person, you should receive a Form 1098, *Mortgage Interest Statement,* or similar statement showing the interest you paid for the year. If you and at least one other person (other than your spouse if you file a joint return) were liable for, and paid interest on the mortgage, and the other person received the Form 1098, report your share of the interest on line 13 of Schedule E (Form 1040). Attach a statement to your return showing the name and address of the other person. In the left margin of Schedule E (Form 1040), next to line 13, write "See attached."

Schedule E (Form 1040)

Use Part I of Schedule E (Form 1040) to report your rental income and expenses. List your total income, expenses, and depreciation for each rental property. Be sure to answer the question on line 2.

If you have more than three rental or royalty properties, complete and attach as many Schedules E as are needed to list the properties. Complete lines 1 and 2 for each property. However, fill in the "Totals" column on only one Schedule E. The figures in the "Totals" column on that Schedule E should be the combined totals of all Schedules E.

Page 2 of Schedule E is used to report income or loss from partnerships, S corporations, estates, trusts, and real estate mortgage investment conduits. If you need to use page 2 of Schedule E, use page 2 of the same Schedule E you used to enter the combined totals in Part I.

On page 1, line 20 of Schedule E, enter the depreciation you are claiming. You must complete and attach Form 4562 for rental activities only if you are claiming:

- Depreciation on property placed in service during 2001,
- Depreciation on any property that is listed property (such as a car), regardless of when it was placed in service, or
- Any car expenses (actual or the standard mileage rate).

Otherwise, figure your depreciation on your own worksheet. You do not have to attach these computations to your return.

Example. On January 1, Justin Cole bought a townhouse and placed it in service as residential rental property. He receives $1,100 a month rental income. His rental expenses for the year are as follows:

Fire insurance (1-year policy)	$ 200
Mortgage interest	5,000
Fee paid to real estate company for collecting monthly rent	572
General repairs	175
Real estate taxes imposed and paid	800

Justin's basis for depreciation of the townhouse is $65,000. He is using MACRS with a 27.5-year recovery period. On April 1, Justin bought a new refrigerator for the rental property at a cost of $425. He uses the MACRS method with a 5-year recovery period.

Justin uses the percentage for January in *Table 10–3–D* to figure his depreciation deduction for the townhouse. He uses the percentage under "Half-year convention" in *Table 10–3–A* to figure his depreciation deduction for the refrigerator. He must report the depreciation on Form 4562.

Justin figures his net rental income or loss for the townhouse as follows:

Total rental income received		
($1,100 × 12)		$13,200
Minus Expenses:		
Fire insurance (1-year policy)	$ 200	
Mortgage interest	5,000	
Rent collection fee	572	
General repairs	175	
Real estate taxes	800	
Total expenses		6,747
Balance		$ 6,453
Minus Depreciation:		
On townhouse ($65,000 × 3.485%)	$2,265	
On refrigerator ($425 × 20%)	85	
Total depreciation		2,350
Net rental income for townhouse		$ 4,103

TaxOrganizer

Records you should keep.

1. Rental agreement
2. Records of tenant-paid improvements, real estate taxes, mortgage payments, etc.

3. A log of how many days a property is rented, used for personal purposes, or vacant
4. Proof of advertising vacant properties in newspapers, magazines, and the like
5. Lists distinguishing the nature of each repair or improvement
6. Receipts for each repair and improvement including date and amount paid
7. A log of travel expenses allocating between rental and nonrental purposes
8. A schedule showing method of division of expenses if part of property is rented
9. Schedule listing depreciable assets with respect to the rental property including amount, date purchased, life of asset, method of depreciation, and depreciation already taken
10. Carryforward of passive activity losses not utilized in prior years
11. Carryforward of rental losses in excess of $25,000 when actively participating in rental activity
12. Form 1098 or other form indicating mortgage interest paid
13. Property tax forms and receipts
14. Proof of tax preparation fees paid in relation to rental property
15. Security deposit information

11

Retirement Plans, Pensions, and Annuities

Introduction

No matter how welcome retirement may be, you're liable to encounter a host of challenging tax dilemmas that you've never before faced. For starters, the chances are good that you will have some difficulty projecting your tax liabilities. Your income will most likely be different from what it has been, and the way in which you calculate your tax will be different, too. If your **pension** *payments are not subject to mandatory withholding rules, you may have to start making* **estimated tax** *payments or you may elect to have income taxes withheld from your pension pay-*

ments. You'll have to puzzle over the complicated withdrawal requirements for an **Individual Retirement Arrangement (IRA)** *and possibly for a Keogh plan, a pension plan for the* **self-employed.** *Perhaps, most important, if you are entitled to any* **lump-sum distributions,** *you will have to make the difficult decision as to whether to roll over the funds and defer the tax or to pay the tax currently but at the low rates currently permitted by* **10-year income averaging,** *if you are eligible. This chapter helps guide you through this maze of complicated decisions.*

Important Change

Required distributions. The IRS proposed new rules that simplify the calculation of required distributions. See the discussion on required distributions under *Tax on Excess Accumulation* in Publication 575, *Pension and Annuity Income.*

Important Reminder

5-year tax option repealed. The 5-year tax option for figuring the tax on lump-sum distributions from a qualified retirement plan has been repealed. However, a plan participant can continue to choose the 10-year tax option or capital gain treatment for a lump-sum distribution that qualifies for the special treatment.

> **TAXALERT**
>
> **Repeal of the 15% tax on excess accumulations.** The 15% excise tax on excess accumulations was repealed for estates of decedents dying after December 31, 1996. Prior to January 1, 1997, a 15% estate tax was imposed on "ex-

cess accumulations" in a retirement plan, which were defined generally as the amount in a plan at the time of the participant's death that exceeds the present value of a hypothetical life annuity paying $150,000 a year ($160,000 as adjusted for inflation).

> **TAXALERT**
>
> **Involuntary distribution requirements.** A plan may not distribute your vested accrued benefit to you without your consent (and the consent of your spouse if the qualified joint and survivor annuity rules apply) unless the present value of your accrued benefit is $5,000 or less. Effective for distributions made after December 31, 2001, in determining your accrued benefit for purposes of the $5,000 limitation on involuntary distributions, employers may disregard benefits and related earnings, which are attributable to rollover contributions. In addition, upon enactment of final regulations by the Secretary of Labor, involuntary distributions that exceed $1,000 must be rolled over automatically to a designated IRA, unless you affirmatively elect to have the distribution transferred to a different IRA or a qualified plan or to receive it directly.

This chapter discusses the tax treatment of distributions you receive from:

1) An employee pension or annuity from a qualified plan,
2) A disability retirement, and
3) A purchased commercial annuity.

What is not covered in this chapter. The following topics are not discussed in this chapter:

1) **The General Rule.** This is the method generally used to determine the tax treatment of pension and annuity income from nonqualified plans. If your annuity starting date is after November 18, 1996, you generally cannot use the General Rule for a qualified plan. For more information about the General Rule, see Publication 939.
2) **Civil service retirement benefits.** If you are retired from the federal government (either regular or disability retirement), see Publication 721, *Tax Guide to U.S. Civil Service Retirement Benefits*. Publication 721 also covers the information that you need if you are the survivor or beneficiary of a federal employee or retiree who died.
3) **Individual retirement arrangements (IRAs).** Information on the tax treatment of amounts you receive from an individual retirement arrangement (IRA), as well as general information on traditional and Roth IRAs, is in chapter 18.

Useful Items

You may want to see:

Publication

☐ **575** Pension and Annuity Income
☐ **721** Tax Guide to U.S. Civil Service Retirement Benefits
☐ **939** General Rule for Pensions and Annuities

Form (and Instructions)

☐ **W-4P** Withholding Certificate for Pension or Annuity Payments
☐ **1099-R** Distributions From Pensions, Annuities, Retirement or Profit-Sharing Plans, IRAs, Insurance Contracts, etc.
☐ **4972** Tax on Lump-Sum Distributions
☐ **5329** Additional Taxes on Qualified Plans (Including IRAs) and Other Tax-Favored Accounts

Employee Pensions and Annuities

Generally, if you did not pay any part of the cost of your employee pension or annuity and your employer did not withhold part of the cost from your pay while you worked, the amounts you receive each year are fully taxable. You must report them on your income tax return.

Partly taxable payments. If you paid part of the cost of your annuity, you are not taxed on the part of the annuity you receive that represents a return of your cost. The rest of the amount you receive is taxable. Your annuity starting date (defined later) determines which method you must or may use.

If you contributed to your pension or annuity plan, you figure the tax-free and the taxable parts of your annuity payments under either the Simplified Method or the General Rule. If your annuity starting date is *after November 18, 1996,* and your payments are from a qualified plan, you *must* use the Simplified Method. Generally, you must use the General Rule only for nonqualified plans.

If your annuity starting date is *after July 1, 1986, but before November 19, 1996,* you *can* use either the General Rule or, if you qualify, the Simplified Method.

TAXALERT

If your annuity starting date is on or after November 19, 1996, you must use the Simplified Method for payments from a qualified plan unless you are age 75 and your annuity payments are guaranteed for at least 5 years.

More than one program. If you receive benefits from more than one program, such as a pension plan and a profit-sharing plan, you must figure the taxable part of each separately. Make separate computations even if the benefits from both are included in the same check. For example, benefits from one of your programs could be fully taxable, while the benefits from your other program could be taxable under the General Rule or the Simplified Method. Your former employer or the plan administrator should be able to tell you if you have more than one pension or annuity contract.

Railroad retirement benefits. Part of the railroad retirement benefits you receive is treated for tax purposes like social security benefits, and part is treated like an employee pension. For information about railroad retirement benefits treated as social security benefits, see Publication 915, *Social Security and Equivalent Railroad Retirement Benefits.* For information about railroad retirement benefits treated as an employee pension, see *Railroad Retirement* in Publication 575.

Credit for the elderly or the disabled. If you receive a pension or annuity, you may be able to take the credit for the elderly or the disabled. See chapter 34.

Explanation
Since this credit is designed to help only those taxpayers with very modest resources, you are ineligible if you receive substantial Social Security benefits or have substantial **adjusted gross income.**

Withholding and estimated tax. The payer of your pension, profit-sharing, stock bonus, annuity, or deferred compensation plan will withhold income tax on the taxable parts of amounts paid to you. You can choose not to have tax withheld except for amounts paid to you that are eligible rollover distributions. See *Eligible rollover distributions* under *Rollovers,* later. You make this choice by filing Form W-4P.

For payments other than eligible rollover distributions, you can tell the payer how to withhold by filing Form W-4P. If an eligible rollover distribution is paid directly to you, 20% will generally be withheld. There is no withholding on a direct rollover of an eligible rollover distribution. See *Direct rollover option* under *Rollovers,* later. If you choose not to have tax withheld or you do not have enough tax withheld, you may have to pay estimated tax.

For more information, see *Pensions and Annuities* under *Withholding* in chapter 5.

TAXALERT

The payer of your pension, profit-sharing, stock bonus, annuity, or deferred compensation plan is required to withhold an amount equal to 20% of any designated distribution that is an **eligible rollover distribution,** unless you elect to have that distribution paid *directly* to an **eligible retirement plan.** An eligible rollover distribution is any taxable distribution of all or a portion of an employee's balance in a qualified plan or tax-sheltered annuity arrangement. The exceptions to this are: (1) any distribution that is one of a series of substantially equal periodic payments made over the life or life expectancy of the employee (or the joint lives or life expectancies of the employee and the employee's designated beneficiary) or made over a period of 10 years or more, (2) required minimum distributions, and (3) certain corrective and deemed distributions. An **eligible retirement plan** is generally another **qualified retirement plan,** an **individual retirement account,** or an **individual retirement annuity.** Effective for distributions after December 31, 2001, an eligible retirement plan will also include a governmental Section 457 plan and a Section 403(b) tax-sheltered annuity.

If the payment made to you is not an eligible rollover distribution, the payer will withhold income tax on the taxable amounts paid to you. However, withholding from these payments is not mandatory and you can tell the payer how to withhold by filing Form W-4P, *Withholding Certificate for Pension or Annuity Payments.* If you choose not to have tax withheld, you may have to pay estimated tax.

Loans. If you borrow money from your qualified pension or annuity plan, tax-sheltered annuity program, government plan, or contract purchased under any of these plans, you may have to treat the loan as a nonperiodic distribution. This means that you may have to include in income all or part of the amount borrowed unless certain exceptions apply. Even if you do not have to treat the loan as a nonperiodic distribution, you may not be able to deduct the interest on the loan in some situations. For details, see *Loans Treated as Distributions* in Publication 575. For information on the deductibility of interest, see chapter 25.

Exception
A loan will not be considered a distribution to the extent that the loan (when added to the outstanding balance of all other loans maintained by the employer) does not exceed the lesser of (1) $50,000 or (2) the greater of either $10,000 or one-half of the participant's vested accrued benefits under the plan. The $50,000 limit is reduced by the excess of the participant's highest outstanding loan balance during the preceding 12-month period, over the outstanding balance at the date of the new loan.

In addition, the exception does not apply unless the loan by its terms must be repaid within 5 years and requires level repayments made not less frequently than quarterly over the term of the loan.

The 5-year rule (above) does not apply to loans made after December 31, 1986, in connection with the purchase of a principal residence of a participant.

TaxAlert
Interest on a loan from an employee plan is only deductible under the general loan interest rules (discussed in Chapter 25, *Interest Expense*). Even if the interest is deductible under the general rules, it will not be deductible if the loan was made to a key employee or secured by amounts attributable to an employee's salary reduction amounts. (Personal loan interest is not deductible.) Check with your plan administrator to determine whether Department of Labor regulations will affect your plan loans currently or plan loans that you intend to make.

TaxPlanner
Plan loans are a good way to provide for children's college expenses, a housing down payment, or any other family need. The interest paid helps your account grow at an at-

tractive rate if the plan credits interest paid on the loan to your account.

Elective deferrals. Some retirement plans allow you to elect to have part of your compensation contributed by your employer to a retirement fund, rather than have it paid to you. You do not pay tax on this money until you receive it in a distribution from the plan. Generally, you may not defer more than a total of $10,500 for all qualified plans by which you are covered.

Elective deferrals generally include elective employer contributions to cash or deferred arrangements [known as *Section 401(k) plans*] and elective contributions to Section 501(c)(18)(D) plans, salary reduction simplified employee pension (SARSEP) plans, SIMPLE plans, and tax-sheltered annuities.

Certain deferrals that are not included in your gross income are included in compensation. Therefore, the amounts deferred in certain employee benefit plans will increase the tax-deferred amount that can be contributed by the employer at the election of the employee.

TaxPlanner
There are several special rules used to determine the limit on employee elective deferrals. If the deferrals are otherwise permitted under these special rules, there is an annual limit on elective deferrals—$10,500 for 2001. This is an aggregate limit for each individual that takes into consideration all deferrals by that individual during the year to Section 401(k) plans, Section 403(b) tax-sheltered annuities, SIMPLE plans, and SARSEPs. The limit applies even if the employee makes deferrals to plans sponsored by different employers or to different types of plans [such as a 401(k) plan and a SIMPLE IRA].

In 2002, the dollar limit on annual elective deferrals will be increased to $11,000. In 2003 and thereafter, the limits will be increased in $1,000 annual increments until the limits reach $15,000 in 2006. The dollar limit will be indexed in $500 increments thereafter.

Example
Assume Steve works for Employer A from January 2001 to April 2001 and defers $3,000 to Employer A's Section 401(k) plan during this time. If Steve leaves in May 2001 to work for Employer B for the remainder of the year, the most Steve could defer to Employer B's Section 401(k) plan for the remainder of 2001 is $7,500.

Alternatively, assume Steve works for Employer A from January 2001 to August 2001 and defers $5,000 to Employer A's Section 401(k) plan. In September, Steve leaves to work for Employer B, which sponsors a SIMPLE IRA for its employees. Steve will only be allowed to defer $5,500 to the SIMPLE IRA for 2001—$10,500 aggregate limit less $5,000 already deferred to Employer A's Section 401(k) plan—even though SIMPLE IRAs generally allow employee deferrals of up to $6,500.

TaxAlert
Effective for taxable years beginning after December 31, 2001, the otherwise applicable dollar limits on elective deferrals for a Section 401(k) plan, a Section 403(b) tax-sheltered annuity, a SEP, or a SIMPLE plan or deferrals under an eligible Section 457 plan are increased for individuals who have attained at least age 50 by the end of the year. The additional amount of elective contributions that may be

made by an eligible individual participating in such a plan is the lesser of (1) the applicable dollar amount (as described below) or (2) the participant's compensation for the year reduced by any other elective deferrals of the participant for the year. The applicable dollar amount for catch-up contributions under a Section 401(k) plan, a Section 403(b) tax-sheltered annuity, a SEP or an eligible Section 457 plan is $1,000 for taxable years beginning in 2002, $2,000 for 2003, $3,000 for 2004, $4,000 for 2005, and $5,000 for 2006 and thereafter. The applicable dollar amount for catch-up contributions under a SIMPLE plan is $500 for taxable years beginning in 2002, $1,000 for 2003, $1,500 for 2004, $2,000 for 2005, and $2,500 for 2006 and thereafter.

TAXALERT

If you realize that you made excess elective deferrals (the limit for 2001 is $10,500) in any given calendar year, be certain to notify your plan administrator(s) as soon as possible. The excess deferral amount will be taxable to you in the year of the deferral. In addition, if this excess deferral is not distributed to you by the following April 15, the excess deferral amount will again be taxed to you when it is ultimately distributed to you upon your retirement or separation from the employer. If the excess deferral is distributed to you by the following April 15, however, it will not be taxed a second time when distributed (although the income attributable to the excess deferral will be taxed to you). Excess deferrals in 2001 must be distributed by April 15, 2002.

Matching contributions for the self-employed do not count toward your elective deferral limit. Although employer matching contributions do not generally count against the 2001 $10,500 limit on employee elective deferrals, a special rule previously required self-employed persons to count matching contributions against this limit. For tax years beginning after 1997 (after 1996 for SIMPLE plans), employer matching contributions will not count toward a self-employed person's elective deferral limit.

Elective deferrals can be made to SARSEPs established before 1997. After December 31, 1996, elective deferrals can be made to SIMPLE plans.

TAXPLANNER

The benefits of Section 401(k) plans are substantial. The elective deferrals are not subject to federal, most state, and local income taxes until they are withdrawn. Earnings on the elective deferrals are also not subject to income tax until they are withdrawn. An employer matching contribution program, which is deductible to the employer within certain limits, can encourage employees to make elective contributions. Finally, on withdrawal, a lump-sum distribution can escape immediate income tax or excise tax if it is deposited into a rollover account. For more information, see *Rollovers* later in this chapter.

TAXPLANNER

Section 403(b) plans (tax-sheltered annuity, or TSA plans), which are available to employees of certain tax-exempt organizations, educational organizations, and state and local governments, offer many of the same benefits that 401(k) plans offer. The elective deferrals are not subject to federal income tax, most state income taxes, and most local income taxes until they are withdrawn. Earnings on elective deferrals are also not subject to income tax until they are withdrawn. Rollovers are permitted for qualifying distributions to help avoid immediate income tax or excise taxes, if applicable. Effective for distributions made after December 31, 2001, eligible rollover distributions from a TSA plan can be rolled over into a qualified retirement plan, another TSA plan, or an IRA.

Prior to 1997, tax-exempt organizations (except for certain grandfathered organizations) were not permitted to adopt 401(k) plans but were able to offer TSA plans. State and local governments (other than rural cooperative plans and certain Indian tribal governments) also cannot provide 401(k) plans to their employees, although they may also offer a TSA plan.

TAXSAVER

Individuals earning limited amounts of self-employment income may be able to shelter all or a substantial portion of the income by utilizing a SIMPLE IRA. (*Note:* Unless you are self-employed, SIMPLE IRAs may only be established by your employer.) Although an individual may only defer $6,500 to a SIMPLE IRA, these deferrals are not limited to a certain percentage of an individual's compensation as is the case with other plans. For example, an individual with $10,000 in self-employment income (e.g., director's fees) could defer $6,500 (or 65%) of the income into a SIMPLE IRA. In addition to the $6,500 employee deferral, either a 3% matching contribution or a 2% employer contribution would be required to satisfy the SIMPLE IRA rules. On the other hand, the same individual could only contribute 15% of the income (after reduction for self-employment taxes and the 15% contribution itself) into a SEP, or approximately $1,205. See the discussion in Chapter 18, *Individual Retirement Arrangements (IRAs) and Education Savings Accounts (ESAs),* for more details on the requirements for SIMPLE IRAs. The following illustrates the advantages of using a SIMPLE IRA to defer limited amounts of income.

Example

Amy earned $10,000 in director's fees, has elected to defer 100% of such income to the SIMPLE IRA, and will utilize the matching contribution. A 15% SEP is shown for comparison. *Note:* This example assumes that Amy has made no other elective deferrals for the year [such as to a 401(k) plan], so the full $10,500 limit on elective deferrals is available.

	SIMPLE IRA	15% SEP
Self-employment income	$10,000	$10,000
Less ½ self-employment tax (7.65%)	(765)	(765)
Net self-employment income	$ 9,235	$ 9,235
Times deferral percentage	100%	13.043% (effective)
Elective deferral	(cap) $ 6,500	$ 1,205
Match of 3%	$ 277	$ 0
Total	$ 6,777	$ 1,205

For information about tax-sheltered annuities, see Publication 571, *Tax-Sheltered Annuity Programs for Employees of Public Schools and Certain Tax-Exempt Organizations.*

TAXALERT: THE 2001 TAX ACT

Effective for taxable years beginning after December 31, 2001 and before January 1, 2007, a temporary nonrefundable tax credit will be provided to eligible individuals in an amount equal to a percentage (see the table below) of their qualified retirement savings contribution not to exceed $2,000. Only individuals with a joint return with adjusted gross income of $50,000 or less, a head-of-household return of $37,500 or less, or a single return of $25,000 or less are eligible for the credit. The credit is available with respect to elective deferrals to a Section 401(k) plan, a Section 403(b) tax-sheltered annuity, or a governmental Section 457 plan, a SIMPLE, or a SEP, and with respect to contributions to a traditional or Roth IRA, and voluntary after-tax employee contributions to a qualified retirement plan.

Adjusted Gross Income

Joint Return		Head of Household		All Other Cases		Applicable
Over	Not over	Over	Not over	Over	Not over	Percentage
	$30,000		$22,500		$15,000	50%
$30,000	32,500	$22,500	24,375	$15,000	16,250	20%
32,500	50,000	24,375	37,500	16,250	25,000	10%
50,000		37,500		25,000		0%

Qualified plans for self-employed individuals. Qualified plans set up by self-employed individuals are sometimes called Keogh or H.R. 10 plans. Qualified plans can be set up by sole proprietors, partnerships (but not a partner), and corporations. They can cover self-employed persons, such as the sole proprietor or partners, as well as regular (common-law) employees.

Distributions from a qualified plan are usually fully taxable because most recipients have no cost basis. If you have an investment (cost) in the plan, however, your pension or annuity payments from a qualified plan are taxed under the Simplified Method. For more information about qualified plans, see Publication 560, *Retirement Plans for Small Business*.

Deferred compensation plans of state and local governments and tax-exempt organizations. If you participate in one of these non-qualified plans (known as *section 457 plans*), you will not be taxed currently on your pay that is deferred under the plan. You or your beneficiary will be taxed on this deferred pay only when it is distributed or otherwise made available to either of you.

For information on the limits on deferrals under section 457 plans and how to treat excess deferrals, see *Retirement Plan Contributions* under *Employee Compensation* in Publication 525.

Distributions of deferred pay are not eligible for the 10-year tax option and rollover treatment (discussed later). Distributions are, however, subject to the tax for failure to make minimum distributions. See *Required distributions not made,* under *Tax on Excess Accumulation,* later.

For general information on these deferred compensation plans, see *Section 457 Deferred Compensation Plans* in Publication 575.

Cost (Investment in the Contract)

Before you can figure how much, if any, of your pension or annuity benefits is taxable, you must determine your cost (your investment in the contract). Your total cost in the plan includes everything that you paid. It also includes amounts your employer paid that were taxable at the time paid. Cost does not include any amounts you deducted or excluded from income.

From this total cost paid or considered paid by you, subtract any re-funds of premiums, rebates, dividends, unpaid loans, or other tax-free amounts you received by the later of the annuity starting date or the date on which you received your first payment.

TAXSAVER

You may or may not have any cost (investment) in your plan for unrepaid loans. If you received a loan from a plan but did not repay the loan according to the repayment schedule (a default), the amount of the loan that was in default was probably reported to you as taxable income in the year you failed to make the required payments. The amount of the unrepaid loan that has already been taxed to you reduces the amount that can be distributed to you and should not be included in your cost. However, if you repay part or all of the loan to the plan after the loan has been taxed to you because of a default, your repayments will increase your cost in the plan. Your plan administrator should properly track your loan repayments and determine your cost in the plan.

Your *annuity starting date* is the later of the first day of the first period for which you received a payment, or the date the plan's obligation became fixed.

Your employer or the organization that pays you the benefits (plan administrator) should show your cost in Box 5 of your Form 1099-R.

Foreign employment contributions. If you worked in a foreign country and your employer contributed to your retirement plan, a part of those payments may be considered part of your cost. This applies to contributions that were made:

1) Before 1963,
2) After 1962 for work if you performed the services under a plan that existed on March 12, 1962, or
3) After 1996 if you performed the services of a foreign missionary.

Explanation

Your cost includes contributions by your employer if you were required to include the amounts in your gross income. If you were employed abroad before 1963, your cost also includes amounts contributed by your employer before 1963 that would have been excludable from your gross income if paid directly to you.

Simplified Method

Under the Simplified Method, you figure the tax-free part of each monthly annuity payment by dividing your cost by the total number of expected monthly payments. For an annuity that is payable for the lives of the annuitants, this number is based on the annuitants' ages on the annuity starting date and is determined from a table. For any other annuity, this number is the number of monthly annuity payments under the contract.

Who must use the Simplified Method. You must use the Simplified Method if your annuity starting date is after November 18, 1996, *and* you receive pension or annuity payments from a qualified plan or annuity, *unless* you were at least 75 years old and entitled to annuity payments from a qualified plan that are guaranteed for 5 years or more.

Who must use the General Rule. You must use the General Rule if you receive pension or annuity payments from:

1) A nonqualified plan (such as a private annuity, a purchased commercial annuity, or a nonqualified employee plan), or
2) A qualified plan if you are age 75 or older on your annuity starting date and your annuity payments are guaranteed for at least 5 years.

You can use the General Rule for a qualified plan if your annuity starting date is before November 19, 1996 (but after July 1, 1986), and you do not qualify to use, or choose not to use, the Simplified Method.

You generally cannot use the General Rule for a qualified plan if your annuity starting date is after November 18, 1996. Complete information on the General Rule, including the tables you need, is contained in Publication 939.

Tip. If you are age 75 or older, *and your annuity starting date is after November 18, 1996, you must use the General Rule if the payments are guaranteed for at least 5 years. You must use the Simplified Method if the payments are guaranteed for less than 5 years.*

Note. If you are not sure whether your retirement plan is a qualified plan (that meets certain Internal Revenue Code requirements), ask your employer or plan administrator.

Guaranteed payments. Your annuity contract provides guaranteed payments if a minimum number of payments or a minimum amount (for example, the amount of your investment) is payable even if you and any survivor annuitant do not live to receive the minimum. If the minimum amount is less than the total amount of the payments you are to receive, barring death, during the first 5 years after payments begin (figured by ignoring any payment increases), you are entitled to less than 5 years of guaranteed payments.

If you are the survivor of a deceased retiree, you can use the Simplified Method if the retiree used it.

Exclusion limit. Your annuity starting date determines the total amount that you can exclude from your taxable income over the years.

If your annuity starting date is after 1986, your exclusion is limited to your cost. If it was before January 1, 1987, you can continue to take your monthly exclusion for as long as you receive your annuity.

If your annuity starting date is after 1986, any unrecovered cost at your (or the last annuitant's) death is allowed as a miscellaneous itemized deduction on the final return of the decedent. This deduction is not subject to the 2%-of-adjusted-gross-income limit.

How to use it. Complete the Simplified Method Worksheet to figure your taxable annuity for 2001. If the annuity is payable only over your life, use your age at the birthday preceding your annuity starting date. For annuity starting dates beginning in 1998, if your annuity is payable over your life and the lives of other individuals, use your combined ages at the birthdays preceding the annuity starting date.

Caution. *If your annuity starting date begins in 1998 and your annuity is payable over the lives of more than one annuitant, the total number of monthly annuity payments expected to be received is based on the combined ages of the annuitants at the annuity starting date. However, if your annuity starting date began before January 1, 1998, the total number of monthly annuity payments expected to be received is based on the primary annuitant's age at the annuity starting date.*

Tip. *Be sure to keep a copy of the completed worksheet; it will help you figure your taxable annuity in later years.*

Example. Bill Kirkland, age 65, began receiving retirement benefits on January 1, 2001, under a joint and survivor annuity. Bill's annuity starting date is January 1, 2001. The benefits are to be paid for the joint lives of Bill and his wife, Kathy, age 65. Bill had contributed $31,000 to a qualified plan and had received no distributions before the annuity starting date. Bill is to receive a retirement benefit of $1,200 a month, and Kathy is to receive a monthly survivor benefit of $600 upon Bill's death.

Bill must use the Simplified Method to figure his taxable annuity because his payments are from a qualified plan and he is under age 75. Because his annuity is payable over the lives of more than one annuitant, he uses his and Kathy's combined ages and Table 2 at the bottom of the worksheet in completing line 3 of the worksheet. His completed worksheet is shown in Table 11-1.

Bill's tax-free monthly amount is $100 ($31,000 ÷ 310 as shown on line 4 of the worksheet). Upon Bill's death, if Bill has not recovered the full $31,000 investment, Kathy will also exclude $100 from her $600 monthly payment. The full amount of any annuity payments received after 310 payments are paid must be included in gross income.

If Bill and Kathy die before 310 payments are made, a miscellaneous

itemized deduction will be allowed for the unrecovered cost on the final income tax return of the last to die. This deduction is not subject to the 2%-of-adjusted-gross-income limit.

Tip. *Had Bill's retirement annuity payments been from a nonqualified plan, he would have used the General Rule. He uses the Simplified Method Worksheet because his annuity payments are from a qualified plan.*

Survivors

If you receive a survivor annuity because of the death of a retiree who had reported the annuity under the *Three-Year Rule,* include the total received in income. (The retiree's cost has already been recovered tax free.)

If the retiree was reporting the annuity payments under the *General Rule,* apply the same exclusion percentage the retiree used to your initial payment called for in the contract. The resulting tax-free amount will then remain fixed. Any increases in the survivor annuity are fully taxable.

If the retiree was reporting the annuity payments under the *Simplified Method,* the part of each payment that is tax free is the same as the tax-free amount figured by the retiree at the annuity starting date. See *Simplified Method,* earlier.

In any case, if the annuity starting date is after 1986, the total exclusion over the years cannot be more than the cost.

If you are the survivor of an employee, or former employee, who died before becoming entitled to any annuity payments, you must figure the taxable and tax-free parts of your annuity payments.

Estate tax. If your annuity was a joint and survivor annuity that was included in the decedent's estate, an estate tax may have been paid on it. You can deduct, as a miscellaneous itemized deduction, the part of the total estate tax that was based on the annuity. This deduction is not subject to the 2%-of-adjusted-gross-income limit. The deceased annuitant must have died after the annuity starting date. (For details, see section 1.691(d)-1 of the regulations.) This amount cannot be deducted in one year. It must be deducted in equal amounts over your remaining life expectancy.

Explanation

The deduction for an annuity that is included in the decedent's estate has become very rare. Since the exemptions for estate tax have been greatly increased and the marital deduction is now unlimited (and current law now repeals the estate tax effective in 2010), it is unusual for any estate tax to be paid on a joint and survivor annuity. However, some people do qualify.

Example

Alexander dies while receiving an annuity worth $10,000. Alexander's beneficiary will receive $1,000 per year for the next 15 years. The estate tax figured with the annuity included is $4,500 more than when figured without the annuity.

The recipient may claim an itemized deduction (not subject to the 2%-of-adjusted-gross-income limitation) each year of $300 ($1,000/$15,000 × $4,500). In this computation, the $15,000 represents the total dollars that will be received over the 15-year period.

How To Report

If you file Form 1040, report your total annuity on line 16a and the taxable part on line 16b. If your pension or annuity is fully taxable, enter it on line 16b; do not make an entry on line 16a.

If you file Form 1040A, report your total annuity on line 12a and the taxable part on line 12b. If your pension or annuity is fully taxable, enter it on line 12b; do not make an entry on line 12a.

Table 11–1 **Simplified Method Worksheet**
(Keep for Your Records)

1. Enter the total pension or annuity payments received this year. Also, enter this amount on Form 1040, line 16a, or Form 1040A, line 12a	**1.** _____ 14,400
2. Enter your cost in the plan at the annuity starting date plus any death benefit exclusion	**2.** _____ 31,000
3. Enter the appropriate number from Table 1 below. **But** if your annuity starting date was **after** 1997 **and** the payments are for your life and that of your beneficiary, enter the appropriate number from **Table 2** below	**3.** _____ 310
4. Divide line 2 by the number on line 3	**4.** _____ 100
5. Multiply line 4 by the number of months for which this year's payments were made. If your annuity starting date was *before* 1987, skip lines 6 and 7 and enter this amount on line 8. Otherwise, go to line 6	**5.** _____ 1,200
6. Enter the amount, if any, recovered tax free in years after 1986	**6.** _____ –0–
7. Subtract line 6 from line 2	**7.** _____ 31,000
8. Enter the *smaller* of line 5 or line 7	**8.** _____ 1,200
9. **Taxable amount.** Subtract line 8 from line 1. Enter the result, but not less than zero. Also, add this amount to the total on Form 1040, line 16b, or Form 1040A, line 12b. If your Form 1099–R shows a larger amount, use the amount on this line instead of the amount from Form 1099–R	**9.** _____ 13,200

TABLE 1 FOR LINE 3 ABOVE

	AND your annuity starting date was—	
IF the age at annuity starting date was...	**before** November 19, 1996, enter on line 3...	**after** November 18, 1996, enter on line 3...
55 or under	300	360
56–60	260	310
61–65	240	260
66–70	170	210
71 or older	120	160

TABLE 2 FOR LINE 3 ABOVE

IF the combined ages at annuity starting date were...	THEN enter on line 3...
110 or under	410
111–120	360
121–130	310
131–140	260
141 or older	210

More than one annuity. If you receive more than one annuity and at least one of them is not fully taxable, enter the total amount received from *all* annuities on line 16a, Form 1040, or line 12a, Form 1040A, and enter the taxable part on line 16b, Form 1040, or line 12b, Form 1040A. If all the annuities you receive are fully taxable, enter the total of all of them on line 16b, Form 1040, or line 12b, Form 1040A.

Joint return. If you file a joint return and you and your spouse each receive one or more pensions or annuities, report the total of the pensions and annuities on line 16a, Form 1040, or line 12a, Form 1040A, and report the taxable part on line 16b, Form 1040, or line 12b, Form 1040A.

Explanation
If you receive a lump-sum distribution and, to avoid the current tax, decide to roll it over into another retirement vehicle, such as an IRA, you still are required to show the total amount received on line 16a (or line 12a, Form 1040A). However, on line 16b (or line 12b, Form 1040A) you would show the taxable amount as zero. Also, enter "Rollover" next to line 16b (or line 12b, Form 1040A).

Lump-Sum Distributions

If you receive a lump-sum distribution from a qualified employee plan or qualified employee annuity and the plan participant was born before 1936, you may be able to elect optional methods of figuring the tax on the distribution. The part from active participation in the plan before 1974 may qualify as capital gain subject to a 20% tax rate. The part from participation after 1973 (and any part from participation before 1974 that you do not report as capital gain) is ordinary income. You may be able to use the 10-year tax option, discussed later, to figure tax on the ordinary income part.

Caution. *The 5-year tax option for figuring the tax on lump-sum distributions has been repealed.*

Use Form 4972 to figure the separate tax on a lump-sum distribution using the optional methods. The tax figured on Form 4972 is added to the regular tax figured on your other income. This may result in a smaller tax than you would pay by including the taxable amount of the distribution as ordinary income in figuring your regular tax.

Lump-sum distribution defined. A lump-sum distribution is the distribution or payment in 1 tax year of a plan participant's entire balance from all of the employer's qualified plans of one kind (for example, pension, profit-sharing, or stock bonus plans). A distribution from a non-qualified plan (such as a privately purchased commercial annuity or a section 457 deferred compensation plan of a state or local government or tax-exempt organization) cannot qualify as a lump-sum distribution.

The participant's entire balance from a plan does not include certain forfeited amounts. It also does not include any deductible voluntary employee contributions allowed by the plan after 1981 and before 1987. For more information about distributions that do not qualify as lump-sum distributions, see *Distributions that do not qualify* under *Lump-Sum Distributions* in Publication 575.

TAXPLANNER

If you change jobs and plan to participate in your new employer's plan, you may want to consider a "plan-to-plan" transfer to the new plan if your new employer cooperates. If an amount is transferred from one qualified plan to another, no amount will be required to be withheld on the amount transferred from your old employer's plan. While there is nothing in the law that requires your new employer to accept transferred amounts, some employers may do this as an accommodation to new employees.

Plan-to-plan transfers have certain advantages over rollovers, discussed below. One advantage is that your periods of service for both employers would be counted by the plan for purposes of the 10-year averaging computation.

TAXALERT

A qualified plan must allow participants the option of a direct rollover to other qualified plans or an IRA. Like plan-to-plan transfers, however, there is nothing in the law that requires your new employer to accept these amounts. If the new employer's plan will not accept these amounts, they could be transferred directly from your old employer's plan to an IRA.

How to treat the distribution. If you receive a lump-sum distribution, you may have the following options for how you treat the taxable part.

1) Report the part of the distribution from participation before 1974 as a capital gain (if you qualify) and the part from participation after 1973 as ordinary income.
2) Report the part of the distribution from participation before 1974 as a capital gain (if you qualify) and use the 10-year tax option to figure the tax on the part from participation after 1973 (if you qualify).
3) Use the 10-year tax option to figure the tax on the total taxable amount (if you qualify).
4) Roll over all or part of the distribution. See *Rollovers,* later. No tax is currently due on the part rolled over. Report any part not rolled over as ordinary income.
5) Report the entire taxable part of the distribution as ordinary income on your tax return.

The first three options are explained in the following discussions.

Electing optional lump-sum treatment. You can choose to use the 10-year tax option or capital gain treatment only once after 1986 for any plan participant. If you make this choice, you cannot use either of these optional treatments for any future distributions for the participant.

Taxable and tax-free parts of the distribution. The taxable part of a lump-sum distribution is the employer's contributions and income earned on your account. You may recover your *cost* in the lump sum and any *net unrealized appreciation (NUA)* in employer securities tax free.

Cost. In general, your cost is the total of:

1) The plan participant's nondeductible contributions to the plan,
2) The plan participant's taxable costs of any life insurance contract distributed,
3) Any employer contributions that were taxable to the plan participant, and
4) Repayments of any loans that were taxable to the plan participant.

You must reduce this cost by amounts previously distributed tax free.

NUA. The NUA in employer securities (box 6 of Form 1099-R) received as part of a lump-sum distribution is generally tax free until you sell or exchange the securities. (For more information, see *Distributions of employer securities* under *Taxation of Nonperiodic Payments,* in Publication 575.)

Explanation

Employer securities distributed as part of a lump-sum distribution may have increased in value after they were purchased by the trust that is making the distribution. This increase is called "net unrealized appreciation." It is not taxed at the time of the lump-sum distribution.

If you later sell these securities, any gain is taxed as a **long-term capital gain** (i.e., as if held for 12 months)—up to the amount of your NUA. Any gain above this amount is a long-term capital gain only if the employee holds the stock for more than 12 months prior to selling it.

You may also elect not to use this treatment on your tax return and instead treat the capital gain (NUA) as part of your lump-sum distribution. This may be desirable if you have tax losses that can offset the amount of NUA.

You may not claim a loss if you receive stock that is worth less than your total contributions to the plan. You may claim a loss when you sell the stock if it is sold for less than the amount of your own after-tax employee contributions allocated to the shares of stock sold.

Example

Assume that Widget Company's pension trust used the company's contribution for Sarah Jones to purchase 100 shares of Widget Company common stock at $10 per share on January 15, 1988. These securities were given to Sarah Jones as part of a lump-sum distribution on January 1, 2001, when their value had risen to $15 per share. Sarah is taxed on the $10 per share that was contributed by Widget, but she is not taxed on the NUA of $5 per share on January 1, 2001.

If Sarah sold the 100 shares of Widget Company stock on January 12, 2001, for $25 per share, the $500 gain [($15 − $10) × 100 shares] attributed to NUA would be taxed as long-term capital gain. The gain of $1,000 [($25 − $5 − $10) × 100 shares] would be taxed as a short-term capital gain, since Sarah held the securities for less than 12 months from the distribution date.

If Sarah had made her own after-tax contributions of $1,700 to the pension trust and received Widget Company stock valued at only $1,000 at the time of the lump-sum distribution, she could not have claimed a loss at that time. However, if she later sold the stock, she would compare her proceeds with $1,700 to determine if she had a gain or a loss on the sale.

TaxPlanner

There is no mandatory 20% withholding requirement for employer securities distributed in an eligible rollover distribution. See *Rollovers*, later in this chapter. Therefore, it may be beneficial under some circumstances for you to receive an eligible rollover distribution consisting of employer securities or employer securities and cash, rather than all cash.

Capital Gain Treatment

Capital gain treatment applies only to the taxable part of a lump-sum distribution resulting from participation in the plan before 1974. The amount treated as capital gain is taxed at a 20% rate. You can elect this treatment only once for any plan participant, and only if the plan participant was born before 1936.

Complete Part II of Form 4972 to choose the 20% capital gain election. For more information, see *Capital Gain Treatment* under *Lump-Sum Distributions* in Publication 575.

10-Year Tax Option

The 10-year tax option is a special formula used to figure a separate tax on the ordinary income part of a lump-sum distribution. You pay the tax only once, for the year in which you receive the distribution, not over the next 10 years. You can elect this treatment only once for any plan participant, and only if the plan participant was born before 1936.

The ordinary income part of the distribution is the amount shown in box 2a of the Form 1099-R given to you by the payer, minus the amount, if any, shown in box 3. You also can treat the capital gain part of the distribution (box 3 of Form 1099-R) as ordinary income for the 10-year tax option if you do **not** choose capital gain treatment for that part.

Complete Part III of Form 4972 to choose the 10-year tax option. You must use the special tax rates shown in the instructions for Part III to figure the tax. Publication 575 illustrates how to complete Form 4972 to figure the separate tax.

Rollovers

If you withdraw cash or other assets from a qualified retirement plan in an eligible rollover distribution, you can defer tax on the distribution by rolling it over to another qualified retirement plan or a traditional IRA.

For this purpose, a qualified retirement plan generally is:

1) A qualified employee plan, or
2) A qualified employee annuity.

Caution. *This discussion applies only to traditional IRAs.*

In general, the most you can roll over is the part that would be taxable if you did not roll it over. You cannot roll over your contributions, other than your deductible employee contributions. You do not pay tax on the amount that you roll over. This amount, however, is generally taxable later when it is paid to you or your survivor.

You must generally complete the rollover by the 60th day following the day on which you receive the distribution from your employer's plan. (This 60-day period is extended for the period during which the distribution is in a frozen deposit in a financial institution.) For all rollovers to an IRA, you must irrevocably elect rollover treatment by written notice to the trustee or issuer of the IRA.

Tip. *The 60-day period may be extended for distributions made after 2001 in certain cases of casualty, disaster, or other events beyond your reasonable control.*

Eligible rollover distributions. Generally, you can roll over any part of the taxable portion of most nonperiodic distributions from a qualified retirement plan, unless it is a required minimum distribution.

Hardship distributions. Hardship distributions from 401(k) plans and similar employer-sponsored retirement plans are no longer treated as eligible rollover distributions.

TaxPlanner

Since hardship distributions are no longer considered eligible rollover distributions, they will not be subject to the mandatory 20% withholding rules that normally apply to eligible rollover distributions. If you are receiving a hardship distribution, you can reduce the amount withheld from the distribution and retain more cash to satisfy the need giving rise to the hardship by filing a Form W-4P with your plan administrator. See the earlier discussion in this chapter on *Withholding and Estimated Tax*.

TaxPlanner

For distributions after December 31, 1999, if you receive a hardship distribution and another event occurs such as the employee's separation from service or attainment of age 59½ so that the distribution is permitted without regard to hardship, then the amount distributed after that event is eligible for rollover treatment. This rule applies regardless of whether the qualified plan or TSA plan characterizes the distribution as a hardship distribution.

For distributions after December 31, 1999, if a portion of a distribution that includes a hardship distribution is not includible in gross income (e.g., after-tax contributions), then the portion of the distribution that is not includible in gross income is first allocated to the hardship distribution. This rule increases the amount of your eligible rollover distribution.

Direct rollover option. You can choose to have the administrator of your old plan transfer the distribution directly from your old plan to the new plan (if permitted) or traditional IRA. If you decide on a rollover, it is generally to your advantage to choose this direct rollover option. Under this option, the plan administrator would not withhold tax from your distribution.

TaxAlert

Upon the issuance of final regulations, plan sponsors will be required to roll over distributions of less than $5,000 but more than $1,000 to an IRA selected by the plan sponsor, unless you affirmatively elect to have the distribution transferred to a different IRA or a qualified plan or to receive it directly.

Withholding tax. If you choose to have the distribution paid to you, it is taxable in the year distributed unless you roll it over to a new plan or IRA within 60 days. The plan administrator must withhold income tax of 20% from the taxable distribution paid to you. (See *Pensions and Annuities* under *Withholding* in chapter 5.)

Caution. *If you decide to roll over an amount equal to the distribution before withholding, your contribution to the new plan or IRA must include other money (for example, from savings or amounts borrowed) to replace the amount withheld.*

The administrator must give you a written explanation of your distribution options within a reasonable period of time before making an eligible rollover distribution.

Explanation

Remember, if you do not wish to include the property received as part of a distribution in the rollover, you cannot roll over cash in place of the property received (such as stock) unless the actual property is sold. The proceeds from the bona fide sale may then be included in the rollover. If the plan in which you participate makes eligible rollover distributions, the plan administrator (usually the employer) is required by law to give you a written explanation of how the rollover rules work.

Generally, an **eligible rollover distribution** means any distribution of all or any portion of an employee's balance in a qualified plan. Eligible rollover distributions do not include the following.

- Required minimum distributions (e.g., distributions required to be made to more than 5% owners who have attained age 70½)
- Distributions that are part of a series of substantially equal payments that are received at least annually over the life or life expectancy of the employee (or the joint lives or life expectancies of the employee and the employee's designated beneficiary) or made over a period of at least 10 years
- Distributions not includable in gross income (e.g., distributions that represent a return of an employee's after-tax contributions)
- Certain corrective distributions made because of the plan's violation of the Internal Revenue Code's limitations
- Loans treated as distributions because they violate the Internal Revenue Code's plan loan rules
- Loans in default that are treated as distributions
- Certain dividends paid on employer securities
- Hardship distributions of elective deferrals (and all other hardship distributions after December 31, 2001)

Eligible rollover distributions can be rolled over in one of two ways. First, you can transfer funds in a **direct rollover** where the plan trustee transfers some or all of your eligible rollover distribution directly to the trustee of an eligible retirement plan.

TaxPlanner

A **direct rollover** may be accomplished by wire transfer, by mailing a check to the trustee of the recipient plan, or even by providing you with a check and instructing you to deliver it to an eligible retirement plan. However, the check must be made payable only to the trustee or custodian of the eligible retirement plan, not to you.

Explanation

You cannot be precluded from dividing an eligible rollover distribution by electing to make a direct rollover of a portion of the distribution and to receive a distribution of the remaining portion. However, your employer may preclude you from electing to have a portion of an eligible rollover

distribution paid on a direct rollover if that portion is less than $500.

TaxPlanner

Employers may, but need not, exclude eligible rollover distributions that are less than $200 from the direct rollover option. Employers are not required to withhold from distributions of less than $200. However, amounts of $200 or less may still be eligible for rollover by you within 60 days after receipt (see discussion below).

An employer is not required to allow employees to have a direct rollover paid to more than one recipient plan. Therefore, if you wish to diversify an IRA investment, for example, you can subsequently roll over a distribution to another IRA or utilize an IRA trustee-to-trustee transfer. If an amount is subsequently transferred to a second IRA, it cannot be rolled over again for 1 year. However, there is no limit on direct IRA trustee-to-trustee transfers.

Tip. The withholding requirement can be avoided on a distribution received currently simply by having amounts transferred directly to an IRA and then immediately withdrawing them from the IRA.

TaxAlert

Plan administrators are required to give plan participants a written notice explaining the direct rollover option and related tax rules. You may consider the decision whether to have your benefits paid in a direct rollover or paid directly to you for at least 30 days after you receive this notice, unless you waive this right.

Explanation

There is a second way amounts can be rolled over. If your funds are not transferred into a direct rollover (e.g., where the plan trustee has made the check payable to you), you may nonetheless roll over some or all of your eligible rollover distribution to an eligible retirement plan. You must complete the rollover by the 60th day following the day on which you receive the distribution. In this case, 20% of the distribution will be withheld as income tax by the plan administrator making the distribution, and in order to roll over the full distribution, you will have to use other funds to make up the 20% withheld. If you do not make up the amount withheld, you will be taxed on the amount withheld and may also owe a 10% early distribution tax on such amount. See *Tax on Early Distributions* later in this chapter.

Deductible voluntary employee contributions. If you receive an eligible rollover distribution from your employer's qualified plan of a part of the balance of your accumulated deductible voluntary employee contributions, you can roll over tax free any part of this distribution. The rollover can be either to a traditional IRA or to certain other qualified plans.

TaxSaver

One of the most difficult decisions you have to make when you near retirement is what to do with your qualified pension or profit-sharing plan. There are usually four choices:

1. **Lump-sum distribution.** If you were born before 1936, you may be eligible to pay tax based on 10-year income averaging (discussed above) and retain the rest of the distribution to invest as you see fit.

2. **Annuity.** The qualified plan pays you and/or your surviving spouse an annuity, the value of which is determined by how much of an annuity the lump-sum distribution would have bought from an insurance carrier based on your life expectancy. When you and your spouse die, nothing further is paid. If your plan requires that a joint and survivor annuity be offered to married participants, then, in order to elect out of the annuity alternative, your spouse must consent to another form of distribution, such as a lump-sum distribution.

3. **Rollover to an IRA.** There is no income tax required to be withheld on any portion of an eligible rollover distribution that is rolled over directly to an eligible retirement plan. The principal continues to earn income without tax until it is withdrawn. Withdrawals are taxed at ordinary income rates and are required to begin not later than April 1 of the calendar year following the calendar year in which the employee attains age 70½. Withdrawals are to be made over the life of such employee or over the lives of such employee and a designated beneficiary (or over a period not extending beyond the life expectancy of such employee or the joint life expectancy of such employee and a designated beneficiary).

4. **Retention in the plan.** If you have more than $5,000 vested in the plan, the plan must permit you to leave your account balance in the qualified plan until you reach age 62 or a stipulated normal retirement age, if later. This may be advantageous if you don't need the money right away, depending on the investment return of the plan. If you have less than $5,000 vested in the plan, the plan may require that you receive your account balance in a lump sum whether or not you consent.

Example

You have $100,000 in the company's qualified plan, and you will reach the retirement age of 65 shortly. You may have the following options, depending on the plan's distribution provisions:

1. You and your spouse may receive a joint and survivor annuity of $12,000 every year through the year of death of the last to die. Each payment will be subject to tax at ordinary rates, which may be as high as 39.1%, depending on which tax bracket you're in. The total that you and/or your spouse will receive will depend on your life spans and your actual marginal tax rates in each year that you live. This is the joint and 100% survivor annuity option. Most plans permit more than one annuity option. As an alternative, if your plan permits, you could elect to receive more during your lifetime and have your spouse receive less upon your death, so long as your spouse receives no less than 50% of the amount you receive.

2. You may roll over the entire amount into an IRA. You will have to begin receiving payments, which will be taxed at ordinary income rates, no later than April 1 of the year following the year you reach age 70½.

3. The plan invests solely in a guaranteed insurance contract that has a fixed rate of 8.5% for 2001. This rate may be so attractive that you may elect to defer the receipt of your account balance until a later year, if you qualify.

4. No current tax is paid or withheld if the entire amount is rolled over to a qualified plan of a new employer. (Remember that while a qualified plan is required to offer the direct rollover option, there is no requirement that another qualified plan accept such rollovers.) You will pay tax when withdrawals occur.

5. If you will be self-employed during the year in which you retire, you can roll over your qualified pension plan into a Keogh plan. The virtue of rolling over your pension into a Keogh plan instead of an IRA is that you can be taxed using the 10-year averaging method (discussed above) if you withdraw the money from the account in a lump-sum distribution. You cannot use the 10-year averaging method if you roll over your qualified pension plan into an IRA. Many people find it easy to arrange to be self-employed in the year in which they retire. If the plan-to-plan transfer is done properly, you can preserve your pretransfer service from the old plan for purposes of the 5-year minimum participation requirement.

In this example, the choice between options 1, 2, and 3 is tricky and requires analysis under various assumptions of interest rates, life expectancy, medical expenses, current needs, and tax rates. Professional help is necessary and well worth the cost.

Methods 4 and 5 may also save you time and keep your investments consolidated in one account while preserving your option to be taxed using the 10-year averaging method. Consult your tax advisor if you think you qualify for these two alternatives.

Rollover by surviving spouse. You may be able to roll over tax free all or part of a distribution from a qualified retirement plan you receive as the surviving spouse of a deceased employee. The rollover rules apply to you as if you were the employee except that you generally can roll over the distribution only into a traditional IRA.

Tip. *You can roll over a distribution made after 2001 into a qualified retirement plan or a traditional IRA.*

A beneficiary other than the employee's surviving spouse cannot roll over a distribution.

Alternate payee under qualified domestic relations order. You may be able to roll over all or any part of a distribution from a qualified retirement plan that you receive under a qualified domestic relations order (QDRO). If you receive the distribution as an employee's spouse or former spouse (not as a nonspousal beneficiary), the rollover rules apply to you as if you were the employee. You can roll over the distribution from the plan into a traditional IRA or to another eligible retirement plan. See Publication 575 for more information on benefits received under a QDRO.

Explanation

If you have not designated a beneficiary for any salary that, because of death, you will not collect, the money will generally be paid into your estate. In that case, it would be reported as income on the estate's income tax return. Any distribution attributable to an employee that is paid to the employee's surviving spouse is treated in the same manner as if the spouse were the employee. The same rule applies if any distribution attributable to an employee is paid to a spouse or a former spouse as an "alternate payee" under a QDRO. A distribution made to the surviving spouse of an employee (or an alternate payee under a QDRO) is an eligible rollover distribution if it meets the requirements explained above. For further details, consult your tax advisor.

TAXPLANNER

Be certain to inform your plan administrator if you wish to change the beneficiary of your qualified retirement plan. Generally, the designated beneficiary on file with your plan administrator will be treated as the beneficiary of your plan even if you have subsequently changed the beneficiary under other agreements, such as a divorce settlement. It is a good idea to review your beneficiary designations each time you have a change in family status (e.g., marriage or divorce).

Retirement bonds. If you redeem a retirement bond, you can defer the tax on the amount received by rolling it over to an IRA or qualified employer plan as discussed in Publication 590.

For more information on the rules for rolling over distributions, see Publication 575.

Special Additional Taxes

To discourage the use of pension funds for purposes other than normal retirement, the law imposes additional taxes on early distributions of those funds and on failures to withdraw the funds timely. Ordinarily, you will not be subject to these taxes if you roll over all early distributions you receive, as explained earlier, and begin drawing out the funds at a normal retirement age, in reasonable amounts over your life expectancy. These special additional taxes are the taxes on:

- Early distributions, and
- Excess accumulation (not receiving minimum distributions).

These taxes are discussed in the following sections.

If you must pay either of these taxes, report them on **Form 5329.** However, you do not have to file Form 5329 if you owe only the tax on early distributions and your Form 1099-R shows a "1" in box 7. Instead, enter 10% of the taxable part of the distribution on line 55 of Form 1040 and write "No" on the dotted line next to line 55.

Even if you do not owe any of these taxes, you may have to complete Form 5329 and attach it to your Form 1040. This applies if you received an early distribution and your Form 1099-R does not show distribution code "2," "3," or "4" in box 7 (or the code shown is incorrect).

Tax on Early Distributions

Most distributions (both periodic and nonperiodic) from qualified retirement plans and nonqualified annuity contracts made to you before you reach age 59 1/2 are subject to an additional tax of 10%. This tax applies to the part of the distribution that you must include in gross income.

For this purpose, a *qualified retirement plan* is:

1) A qualified employee plan,
2) A qualified employee annuity plan, or
3) A tax-sheltered annuity plan.

Caution. *A state or local government section 457 deferred compensation plan is also treated as a qualified retirement plan to the extent that any distribution made after 2001 is attributable to amounts the plan received in a direct transfer or rollover from one of the plans listed above.*

5% rate on certain early distributions from deferred annuity contracts. If an early withdrawal from a deferred annuity is otherwise subject to the 10% additional tax, a 5% rate may apply instead. A 5% rate applies to distributions under a written election providing a specific schedule for the distribution of your interest in the contract if, as of March 1, 1986, you had begun receiving payments under the election. On line 4 of Form 5329, multiply by 5% instead of 10%. Attach an explanation to your return.

Exceptions to tax. Certain early distributions are excepted from the early distribution tax. If the payer knows that an exception applies to your early distribution, distribution code "2," "3," or "4" should be shown in box 7 of your Form 1099-R and you do not have to report the distribution on Form 5329. If an exception applies but distribution code "1" (early distribution, no known exception) is shown in box 7, you must file Form 5329. Enter the taxable amount of the distribution shown in box 2a of your Form 1099-R on line 1 of Form 5329. On line 2, enter the amount that can be excluded and the exception number shown in the Form 5329 instructions.

Tip. *If distribution code "1" is incorrectly shown on your Form 1099-R for a distribution received when you were age 59 1/2 or older, include that distribution on Form 5329. Enter exception number "11" on line 2.*

The early distribution tax does not apply to any distribution that meets one of the following exceptions.

General exceptions. The tax does not apply to distributions that are:

- Made as part of a series of substantially equal periodic payments (made at least annually) for your life (or life expectancy) or the joint lives (or joint life expectancies) of you and your designated beneficiary (if from a qualified retirement plan, the payments must begin after your separation from service),
- Made because you are totally and permanently disabled, or
- Made on or after the death of the plan participant or contract holder.

TAXPLANNER

You should carefully consider whether equal periodic distributions commencing before you attain age 59½ will be sufficient to satisfy your income needs. Although these distributions are not subject to the 10% early distribution tax, they *will* be subject to this tax if the amount of the distributions is modified either before you attain age 59½ or before the end of the calendar 5-year period beginning with the date of the first distribution (even if this period ends after you attain age 59½). In the year the distributions are modified, you will have to pay the 10% penalty tax on all of the distributions you have received to date, plus interest.

Additional exceptions for qualified retirement plans. The tax does not apply to distributions that are:

- From a qualified retirement plan after your separation from service in or after the year you reached age 55,
- From a qualified retirement plan to an alternate payee under a qualified domestic relations order,
- From a qualified retirement plan to the extent you have deductible medical expenses (medical expenses that exceed 7.5% of your adjusted gross income), whether or not you itemize your deductions for the year,
- From an employer plan under a written election that provides a specific schedule for distribution of your entire interest if, as of March 1, 1986, you had separated from service and had begun receiving payments under the election.
- From an employee stock ownership plan for dividends on employer securities held by the plan, or
- From a qualified retirement plan due to an IRS levy of the plan.

Additional exceptions for nonqualified annuity contracts. The tax does not apply to distributions that are:

- From a deferred annuity contract to the extent allocable to investment in the contract before August 14, 1982,

- From a deferred annuity contract under a qualified personal injury settlement,
- From a deferred annuity contract purchased by your employer upon termination of a qualified employee plan or qualified employee annuity plan and held by your employer until your separation from service, or
- From an immediate annuity contract (a single premium contract providing substantially equal annuity payments that start within one year from the date of purchase and are paid at least annually).

TaxSaver

Note that the 10% excise tax also does not apply in the year of distribution if you roll over a qualifying distribution (including a direct rollover of an eligible rollover distribution). This is because the tax is applied only to taxable distributions. This helps to make rollovers an even more attractive alternative.

TaxOrganizer

On Form 1099-R, distributions should be coded by the payer without regard to whether a rollover is made or anticipated. Thus, for purposes of 1099-R reporting, a rollover that is planned or has already occurred should not be considered an exception to the early distribution penalty.

Example

If Ben Jones withdraws the total balance in his qualified plan, informs the IRA trustees that the funds will be rolled over, is under age 59½, and meets no other exception under the early distribution rules, the Form 1099-R should contain a code 1, "early distribution, no known exception." If Mr. Jones then rolls over his distribution, he should properly report the rollover on his federal income tax return to avoid the early (premature) distribution penalty.

Tax on Excess Accumulation

To make sure that most of your retirement benefits are paid to you during your lifetime, rather than to your beneficiaries after your death, the payments that you receive from qualified retirement plans must begin no later than on your *required beginning date* (defined next).

Unless the rule for 5% owners applies, *you must begin* to receive distributions from your qualified retirement plan by April 1 of the year that follows the *later* of:

1) The calendar year in which you reach age 70 1/2, or
2) The calendar year in which you retire.

However, your plan may require you to begin to receive distributions by April 1 of the year that follows the year in which you reach age 70 1/2, even if you have not retired.

For this purpose, a *qualified retirement plan* includes a:

1) Qualified employee plan,
2) Qualified employee annuity plan,
3) Section 457 deferred compensation plan, or
4) Tax-sheltered annuity plans (for benefits accruing after 1986).

Age 70 1/2. You reach age 70 1/2 on the date that is 6 calendar months after the date of your 70th birthday.

For example, if you are retired and your 70th birthday was on July 1, 2000, you were age 70 1/2 on January 1, 2001. Your required beginning date is April 1, 2002. If your 70th birthday was on June 30, 2000, you were age 70 1/2 on December 30, 2000, and your required beginning date is April 1, 2001, unless you had not yet retired.

5% owners. If you are a 5% owner of the company maintaining your qualified retirement plan, you must begin to receive distributions by April 1 of the calendar year that follows the year in which you reach age 70 1/2, regardless of when you retire.

Required distributions. By the required beginning date, as explained above, you must either:

1) Receive your entire interest in the plan (for a tax-sheltered annuity, your entire benefit accruing after 1986), or
2) Begin receiving periodic distributions in annual amounts calculated to distribute your entire interest (for a tax-sheltered annuity, your entire benefit accruing after 1986) over your life or life expectancy or over the joint lives or joint life expectancies of you and a designated beneficiary (or over a shorter period).

TaxAlert

The life expectancy tables are set to be modified in the near future to reflect current longer life expectancies. When implemented, this will generally result in lower minimum required distributions.

Additional information. For more information on this rule and how to figure the required amount to be distributed, see *Tax on Excess Accumulation* in Publication 575.

Required distributions not made. If you do not receive required minimum distributions, you are subject to an additional excise tax. The tax equals 50% of the difference between the amount that must be distributed and the amount that was distributed during the tax year. You can get this excise tax waived if you establish that the shortfall in distributions was due to reasonable error and that you are taking reasonable steps to remedy the shortfall.

Explanation

Effective for years beginning after December 31, 1996, all plans [except traditional IRAs; see *When Must I Withdraw IRA Assets? (Required Distributions)* in Chapter 18, *Individual Retirement Arrangements (IRAs)*] must begin to make minimum distributions to you (unless you are a more than 5% owner) no later than April 1 of the calendar year following the later of:

1. The calendar year in which you reach age 70½, or
2. The calendar year in which you retire.

Although plans must begin making minimum distributions by the later of the calendar year after you retire or the year after you turn 70½, they are not required to wait until you actually retire. They may begin making minimum distributions in the year after you reach retirement age under the plan. Your plan administrator can provide details on the provisions of your plan.

The requirement that distributions to a more than 5% owner begin by April 1 of the calendar year after the year in which he or she reaches 70½ continues to be effective.

Plans can, but are not required to, permit individuals who were receiving minimum distributions on December 31, 1996, but who have not yet retired, to stop receiving distributions until they retire. You should ask your employer or plan administrator if this is permitted under your plan.

TaxPlanner

If you work beyond age 70½, it may be advantageous to delay the minimum distributions (if your plan allows) and allow the amounts in the retirement plan to grow on a tax-deferred basis. The advantage of delaying distributions is reduced for defined benefit plan participants due to a special rule that requires the amount of the minimum distributions to be increased when the participant ultimately retires and begins receiving distributions. Consult your plan administrator or tax advisor for more information on the decision to delay minimum distributions.

TAXPLANNER

Because the penalty for failure to receive required minimum distributions is severe, you must take steps to ensure that you receive these amounts on a timely basis. Many financial institutions do not inform their IRA holders when it is time to begin receiving distributions. Recently proposed regulations would require IRA trustees to report to the Internal Revenue Service and the IRA owner the amount required to be distributed from the IRA for each calendar year. These requirements are still being worked out.

TAXPLANNER

If you have made after-tax contributions to your employer's retirement plan [e.g., contributions other than pre-tax salary deferrals to a 401(k) plan or 403(b) tax-sheltered annuity], you may be able to satisfy the minimum distribution rules without being taxed for the first year (or possibly the first 2 years) the minimum distributions are required. This may be accomplished by: (1) electing to receive a lump-sum distribution from your retirement plan or IRA by April 1 of the year the minimum distributions are required to begin, (2) retaining the portion of the distribution that represents the tax-free return of your after-tax employee contributions, and (3) electing to roll over the remaining amount of the lump-sum distribution to another qualified retirement plan or IRA.

Example

Assume Dawn reaches age 70½ in 2000 and elects to retire in 2000. Also assume that Dawn has made a total of $40,000 in after-tax employee contributions to her employer's retirement plan over the years and has a balance of $100,000 in the plan as of the end of 2000. Dawn must receive the minimum required distribution for 2000 by April 1, 2001. In addition, she must receive the minimum required distribution for 2001 by December 31, 2001. Assume the minimum required distribution amounts are $15,000 and $20,000 for 2000 and 2001, respectively.

Since taxpayers may only roll over amounts that are otherwise taxable to them, Dawn is not allowed to roll over the $40,000 attributable to her after-tax employee contributions—only the $60,000 may be rolled over to an IRA. Accordingly, Dawn elects to receive a lump-sum distribution of her entire $100,000 account balance by April 1, 2001; retains the $40,000 attributable to her after-tax employee contributions; and rolls over $60,000 to an IRA within 60 days of the distribution. She will not be taxed on the $40,000 she did not roll over since this is a nontaxable return of her after-tax employee contributions. More importantly, the IRS has ruled that such nontaxable amounts may be used to satisfy the minimum distribution requirements. In this example, the $40,000 distributed to Dawn by April 1, 2001, exceeded both the $15,000 that was required to be distributed by April 1, 2001, and the $20,000 that was required to be distributed to her by December 31, 2001.

State insurer delinquency proceedings. You might not receive the minimum distribution because of state insurer delinquency proceedings for an insurance company. If your payments are reduced below the minimum due to these proceedings, you should contact your plan administrator. Under certain conditions, you will not have to pay the excise tax.

Form 5329. You must file a Form 5329 if you owe a tax because you did not receive a minimum required distribution from your qualified retirement plan.

Disability Pensions

If you retired on disability, you must include in income any disability pension you receive under a plan that is paid for by your employer. You must report your taxable disability payments as wages on line 7 of Form 1040 or Form 1040A until you reach minimum retirement age. Minimum retirement age generally is the age at which you can first receive a pension or annuity if you are not disabled.

You may be entitled to a tax credit if you were permanently and totally disabled when you retired. For information on this credit, see chapter 34.

Beginning on the day after you reach minimum retirement age, payments you receive are taxable as a pension or annuity. Report the payments on lines 16a and 16b of Form 1040, or on lines 12a and 12b of Form 1040A.

For more information on how to report disability pensions, including military and certain government disability pensions, see chapter 6.

Purchased Annuities

If you privately purchased an annuity contract from a commercial organization, such as an insurance company, you generally must use the General Rule to figure the tax-free part of each annuity payment. For more information about the General Rule, get Publication 939. Also, see *Variable Annuities* in Publication 575 for the special provisions that apply to these annuity contracts.

Sale of annuity. Gain on the exchange of an annuity contract is ordinary income to the extent that the gain is due to interest accumulated on the contract and the exchange is for a life insurance or endowment contract. You do not recognize gain or loss on an exchange of an annuity contract solely for another annuity contract if the insured or annuitant remains the same. See *Transfers of Annuity Contracts* in Publication 575 for more information about exchanges of annuity contracts.

Explanation

Publication 575 contains a brief discussion of the main features of variable commercial annuities and the rules that apply to these contracts to figure the tax-free part of each annuity payment.

Purchased annuities are subject to the General Rule if your annuity starting date is before November 19, 1996. If you sell an annuity before its maturity date, the insurance company determines the amount of interest income and provides you with that information.

TAXSAVER

Annuities are popular investments because the amount you contribute grows over time through the accumulation of interest. The interest income is not currently taxable to you and is reported as income only in later years, when payments are made from the annuity. The taxable payments are most likely to be made after you've retired. Therefore, an annuity may be a good way in which to earn income and defer taxes. Nowadays, it is more important than ever to investigate the financial strength and credit rating of the insurance company issuing the annuity.

Social Security and Equivalent Railroad Retirement Benefits

Introduction

Social Security income and equivalent railroad retirement benefits used to be tax free. That's no longer the case. Now, you may have to pay income tax on amounts you receive. However, figuring out whether the benefits you receive are taxable is not easy. You will be required to puzzle through complicated rules, obtain information, and make numerous computations. This chapter will simplify your task. Among other things, it includes worksheets to help you make the necessary calculations.

This chapter explains the federal income tax rules for social security benefits and equivalent tier 1 railroad retirement benefits. It explains:

- How to figure whether your benefits are taxable,
- How to use the social security benefits worksheet (with examples),
- How to report your taxable benefits, and
- How to treat repayments that are more than the benefits you received during the year.

Social security benefits include monthly survivor and disability benefits. They do not include supplemental security income (SSI) payments, which are not taxable.

Equivalent tier 1 railroad retirement benefits are the part of tier 1 benefits that a railroad employee or beneficiary would have been entitled to receive under the social security system. They are commonly called the social security equivalent benefit (SSEB) portion of tier 1 benefits.

If you received these benefits during 2001, you should have received a Form SSA-1099 or Form RRB-1099 (Form SSA-1042S or Form RRB-1042S if you are a nonresident alien). These forms show the amounts received and repaid, and taxes withheld for the year. You may receive more than one of these forms for the same year. You should add the amounts shown on all forms you receive for the year to determine the "total" amounts received and repaid, and taxes withheld for that year. See the *Appendix* at the end of Publication 915 for more information.

TaxAlert

Revocation of exemption from Social Security coverage.
If you are a minister, a member of a religious order not under a vow of poverty, or Christian Science practitioner who previously elected exemption from Social Security coverage and self-employement tax, you now have a limited period of time to revoke that exemption. You can revoke the exemption during the 15½-month period from January 1, 2001, to April 15, 2002. This period is extended beyond April 15, 2002, if you get an extension to file your 2001 return. The revocation will be effective for either 2000 or 2001 and all later years. You will be covered under the Social Security system, and your earnings will be subject to self-employment tax during those years. Once you revoke the exemption, you can never again elect exemption from Social Security coverage.
You must file Form 2031 to revoke the exemption.

Note. When the term "benefits" is used in this chapter, it applies to both social security benefits and equivalent tier 1 railroad retirement benefits.
Caution. Legislation in 2000 removed the "earnings test" for social security recipients who work and are ages 65 through 70. This change has no effect on the federal income tax rules for social security benefits.

What is not covered in this chapter. This chapter does not cover the tax rules for the following railroad retirement benefits:

- Non-social security equivalent benefit (NSSEB) portion of tier 1 benefits,
- Tier 2 benefits,
- Vested dual benefits, and
- Supplemental annuity benefits.

For information on these benefits, see Publication 575, *Pension and Annuity Income.*

This chapter also does not cover the tax rules for foreign social security or railroad retirement benefits. These benefits are taxable as annuities, unless they are exempt from U.S. tax under a treaty. For more information, see Publication 915.

Useful Items

You may want to see:

Publication

- ☐ **575** Pension and Annuity Income
- ☐ **590** Individual Retirement Arrangements (IRAs)
- ☐ **915** Social Security and Equivalent Railroad Retirement Benefits

Forms (and Instructions)

- ☐ **1040-ES** Estimated Tax for Individuals
- ☐ **W-4V** Voluntary Withholding Request

TAXPLANNER

For additional Social Security and retirement information, you may want to consult the following Web sites: www.ssa.gov, www.rrb.gov, and www.seniors.gov.

Are Any of Your Benefits Taxable?

To find out whether any of your benefits are taxable, compare the *base amount* for your filing status with the total of:

1) One-half of your benefits, plus
2) All your other income, including tax-exempt interest.

When making this comparison, do not reduce your other income by any *exclusions* for:

- Interest from qualified U.S. savings bonds,
- Employer-provided adoption benefits,
- Foreign earned income or foreign housing, or
- Income earned in American Samoa or Puerto Rico by bona fide residents.

TAXPLANNER

If you want to plan ahead, you can request an estimate of your Social Security benefits by filing Form SSA-7004-PC, *Your Social Security Statement.* Copies of the form can be obtained from your local Social Security office, by calling (800) 772-1213, or by visiting www.ssa.gov on the World Wide Web.

Explanation
Taxation of benefits. In figuring if any of your benefits are taxable, use the amount shown in box 5 of the Form SSA-1099 or Form RRB-1099 you received. If you received more than one form, add together the amount in box 5 of each form.

SSI payments. If you received any SSI payments during the year, do not include these payments in your Social Security benefits received. SSI payments are made under Title XVI of the Social Security Act. They are not taxable for federal income tax purposes.

Form SSA-1099. If you received or repaid Social Security benefits during 2001, you will receive Form SSA-1099, *Social Security Benefit Statement.* An IRS Notice 703 will be enclosed with your Form SSA-1099. This notice includes a worksheet you can use to determine if any of your benefits may be taxable. Keep this notice for your own records. Do *not* mail it to either the Internal Revenue Service or the SSA.

Every person who received Social Security benefits will receive a Form SSA-1099, even if the benefit is combined with another person's in a single check. If you receive benefits on more than one Social Security record, you may get more than one Form SSA-1099.

Form RRB-1099. If you received or repaid the Social Security equivalent portion of tier 1 railroad retirement benefits or special guaranty benefits during 2001, you will receive Form RRB-1099, *Payments by the Railroad Retirement Board.*

Each beneficiary will receive his or her own Form RRB-1099. If you receive benefits on more than one railroad retirement record, you may get more than one Form RRB-1099.

Figuring total income. To figure the total of one-half of your benefits plus your other income, use the worksheet later in this discussion. If the total is more than your base amount, part of your benefits may be taxable.

Explanation
The filing requirements for individuals are based on income, age, and filing status (e.g., married filing jointly, single). See Chapter 1, *Filing Information.*

If you are married and file a joint return for 2001, you and your spouse must combine your incomes and your benefits to figure whether any of your combined benefits are taxable. Even if your spouse did not receive any benefits, you must add your spouse's income to yours to figure whether any of your benefits are taxable.

Tip. *If the only income you received during 2001 was your social security or the SSEB portion of tier 1 railroad retirement benefits, your benefits generally are not taxable and you probably do not have to file a return. If you have income in addition to your benefits, you may have to file a return even if none of your benefits are taxable.*

Base amount. Your base amount is:

- $25,000 if you are single, head of household, or qualifying widow(er),
- $25,000 if you are married filing separately and *lived apart* **from your spouse for** *all* **of 2001,**
- $32,000 if you are married filing jointly, or
- $-0- if you are married filing separately and **lived with** your spouse at any time during 2001.

Explanation

Social Security and railroad retirement benefits are partially taxable if your *total income* (defined below) is more than $32,000 for married taxpayers filing jointly and $25,000 for single filers. If you are married filing separately *and* you lived with your spouse at any time during the year, your base amount is $0, which means that your Social Security retirement benefits are partially taxable regardless of your income level. Your *total income* is the sum of your adjusted gross income, tax-exempt income, excluded foreign source income, excluded interest from U.S. savings bonds (interest excluded in connection with the payment of qualified education expenses), and one-half of your Social Security retirement benefits.

Tax-exempt income is *not taxable* for federal purposes, even if you receive Social Security benefits. However, it is one of the items taken into consideration in determining whether or not your income exceeds the threshold amount so that your Social Security benefits are taxable.

TAXSAVER

If you expect your total income (defined above) to exceed the base amount ($32,000 if you are filing a joint return, $25,000 if you are filing single), you may wish to consider the following strategies.

- *Defer the recognition of income* by investing in U.S. savings bonds. Generally, the increase in value of the bonds issued at a discount (Series E and EE) is not taxable until you surrender the bonds. Additionally, if you hold the bonds until death, your heirs will recognize the income (assuming you did not elect to include in income the annual increase in the value of the bond).
- *Stagger the recognition of income* so that you have alternating years of higher income. Depending on your income level, you could structure income so that your Social Security benefits are taxed every other year. For example, when considering sources of cash flow, surrender U.S. savings bonds, make withdrawals from IRAs, and sell appreciated property in alternate years. You could also schedule the maturity dates of U.S. Treasury notes and bills to ensure that your income is under the base amount in certain years.
- If you have earned income, *consider contributing to your company's 401(k) plan or a deductible Individual Retirement Arrangement (IRA) account* (see Chapter 18, *Individual Retirement Arrangements (IRAs)*, to determine if you qualify) to decrease your adjusted gross income and also reduce the taxable portion of your Social Security benefits.

TAXALERT

Tax-exempt income is added to your adjusted gross income for purposes of calculating how much, if any, of your Social Security benefits will be subject to tax. Keep this in mind when evaluating the after-tax rate of return of tax-exempt investments vs. taxable investments.

Worksheet. You can use the following worksheet to figure the amount of income to compare with your base amount. This is a quick way to check whether some of your benefits may be taxable.

A. Write in the amount from *box 5* of all your Forms SSA-1099 and RRB-1099. Include the full amount of any lump-sum benefit payments received in 2001, for 2001 and earlier years. (If you received more than one form, combine the amounts from box 5 and write in the total.) .... A. _____

Note: If the amount on line A is zero or less, stop here; none of your benefits are taxable this year.

B. Enter one-half of the amount on line A................................. B. _____

C. Add your taxable pensions, wages, interest, dividends, and other taxable income and write in the total .... C. _____

D. Write in any tax-exempt interest income (such as interest on municipal bonds) plus any exclusions from income (listed earlier) .... D. _____

E. Add lines B, C, and D and write in the total .... E. _____

*Note. Compare the amount on line E to your **base amount** for your filing status. If the amount on line E equals or is less than the **base amount** for your filing status, none of your benefits are taxable this year. If the amount on line E is more than your **base amount**, some of your benefits may be taxable. You then need to complete Worksheet 1 in Publication 915 (or in your tax form instruction booklet).*

Example. You and your spouse (both over 65) are filing a joint return for 2001, and you both received social security benefits during the year. In January 2002, you received a Form SSA-1099 showing net benefits of $6,600 in box 5. Your spouse received a Form SSA-1099 showing net benefits of $2,400 in box 5. You also received a taxable pension of $17,000 and interest income of $500. You did not have any tax-exempt interest income. Your benefits are not taxable for 2001 because your income, as figured in the following worksheet, is not more than your base amount ($32,000) for married filing jointly.

Even though none of your benefits are taxable, you must file a return for 2001 because your taxable gross income ($17,500) exceeds the minimum filing requirement amount for your filing status.

A. Write in the amount from *box 5* of all your Forms SSA-1099 and RRB-1099. Include the full amount of any lump-sum benefit payments received in 2001, for 2001 and earlier years. (If you received more than one form, combine the amounts from box 5 and write in the total.) .... A. $9,000

Note: If the amount on line A is zero or less, stop here; none of your benefits are taxable this year.

B. Enter one-half of the amount on line A. .... B.   4,500

C. Add your taxable pensions, wages, interest, dividends, and other taxable income and write in the total .... C.   17,500

D. Write in any tax-exempt interest income (such as interest on municipal bonds) plus any exclusions from income (listed earlier) .... D.   -0-

E. Add lines B, C, and D and write in the total .... E. $22,000

*Note: Compare the amount on line E to your **base amount** for your filing status. If the amount on line E equals or is less than the **base amount** for your filing status, none of your benefits are taxable this year. If the amount on line E is more than your **base amount**, some of your benefits may be taxable. You then need to complete Worksheet 1 in Publication 915 (or in your tax form instruction booklet).*

Who is taxed. The person who has the legal right to receive the benefits must determine whether the benefits are taxable. For example, if you and your child receive benefits, but the check for your child is made out in your name, you must use only your part of the benefits to see whether any benefits are taxable to you. One-half of the part that belongs to your child must be added to your child's other income to see whether any of those benefits are taxable to your child.

TAXORGANIZER

You should maintain a copy of Form(s) SSA-1099, RRB-1099, and Form 1042F for 3 years following the due date (including extensions) of your income tax return.

Repayment of benefits. Any repayment of benefits you made during 2001 must be subtracted from the gross benefits you received in 2001. It does not matter whether the repayment was for a benefit you received in 2001 or in an earlier year. If you repaid more than the gross benefits you received in 2001, see *Repayments More Than Gross Benefits,* later.

Your gross benefits are shown in box 3 of Form SSA-1099 or RRB-1099. Your repayments are shown in box 4. The amount in box 5 shows your net benefits for 2001 (box 3 minus box 4). Use the amount in box 5 to figure whether any of your benefits are taxable.

Tax withholding and estimated tax. You can choose to have federal income tax withheld from your social security benefits and/or the SSEB portion of your tier 1 railroad retirement benefits. If you choose to do this, you must complete a Form W-4V. For 2002, you can choose withholding at 7%, 10%, 15%, or 27% of your total benefit payment.

If you do not choose to have income tax withheld, you may have to request additional withholding from other income or pay estimated tax during the year. For details, get Publication 505, *Tax Withholding and Estimated Tax,* or the instructions for Form 1040-ES.

How To Report Your Benefits

If part of your benefits are taxable, you must use Form 1040 or Form 1040A. You cannot use Form 1040EZ.

Reporting on Form 1040. Report your net benefits (the amount in box 5 of your Form SSA-1099 or Form RRB-1099) on line 20a and the taxable part on line 20b. If you are married filing separately and you lived apart from your spouse for all of 2001, also enter "D" to the left of line 20a.

Reporting on Form 1040A. Report your net benefits (the amount in box 5 of your Form SSA-1099 or Form RRB-1099) on line 14a and the taxable part on line 14b. If you are married filing separately and you lived apart from your spouse for all of 2001, also enter "D" to the right of the word "benefits" on line 14a.

Benefits not taxable. If none of your benefits are taxable, do not report any of them on your tax return. But if you are married filing separately and you lived apart from your spouse for all of 2001, make the following entries. On Form 1040, enter "D" to the left of line 20a and "-0-" on line 20b. On Form 1040A, enter "D" to the right of the word "benefits" on line 14a and "-0-" on line 14b.

TAXORGANIZER

Summary of How to Report Your Benefits

	Form 1040	Form 1040A	Form 1040EZ
Net benefits	Line 20a	Line 14a	Cannot use Form
Taxable benefits	Line 20b	Line 14b	Cannot use Form

How Much Is Taxable?

If part of your benefits are taxable, how much is taxable depends on the total amount of your benefits and other income. Generally, the higher that total amount, the greater the taxable part of your benefits.

Maximum taxable part. Generally, up to 50% of your benefits will be taxable. However, up to 85% of your benefits can be taxable if either of the following situations applies to you.

1) The total of one-half of your benefits and all your other income is more than $34,000 ($44,000 if you are married filing jointly).
2) You are married filing separately and *lived with your spouse* at any time during 2001.

Explanation
After determining whether or not your Social Security retirement benefits are taxable, you must then determine

what percentage (either 50% or 85%) of the total benefit is taxable. If you are filing a joint return and your *total income* (adjusted gross income + tax-exempt income + excluded foreign source income + excluded interest income from U.S. savings bonds + one-half of your Social Security retirement benefits) is less than $44,000 but greater than $34,000, a maximum of 50% of your Social Security retirement benefits is subject to federal tax. If, however, your *total income* exceeds $44,000, up to 85% of your Social Security retirement benefits will be included in income and taxed accordingly.

TAXSAVER

Many states allow a deduction for the amount of Social Security retirement benefits taxed at the federal level. Consult your tax advisor or state income tax authority for details.

Which worksheet to use. A worksheet to figure your taxable benefits is in the instructions for your Form 1040 or Form 1040A. You can use either that worksheet or *Worksheet 1* in Publication 915, unless any of the following situations applies to you.

1) You contributed to a traditional individual retirement arrangement (IRA) and your IRA deduction is limited because you or your spouse is covered by a retirement plan at work. In this situation you *must* use the special worksheets in Appendix B of Publication 590 to figure both your IRA deduction and your taxable benefits.
2) Situation (1) does not apply and you take an exclusion for interest from qualified U.S. savings bonds (Form 8815), for adoption benefits (Form 8839), for foreign earned income or housing (Form 2555 or Form 2555-EZ), or for income earned in American Samoa (Form 4563) or Puerto Rico by bona fide residents. In this situation, you *must* use *Worksheet 1* in Publication 915 to figure your taxable benefits.
3) You received a lump-sum payment for an earlier year. In this situation, also complete *Worksheet 2 or 3* and *Worksheet 4* in Publication 915. See *Lump-sum election.*

Lump-sum election. You must include the taxable part of a lump-sum (retroactive) payment of benefits received in 2001 in your 2001 income, even if the payment includes benefits for an earlier year.

Tip. *This type of lump-sum benefit payment should not be confused with the lump-sum death benefit that both the SSA and RRB pay to many of their beneficiaries. No part of the lump-sum death benefit is subject to tax.*

Generally, you use your 2001 income to figure the taxable part of the total benefits received in 2001. However, you may be able to figure the taxable part of a lump-sum payment for an earlier year separately, using your income for the earlier year. You can elect this method if it lowers your taxable benefits.

Making the election. If you received a lump-sum benefit payment in 2001 that includes benefits for one or more earlier years, follow the instructions in Publication 915 under *Lump-Sum Election* to see whether making the election will lower your taxable benefits. That discussion also explains how to make the election.

Caution. *Since the earlier year's taxable benefits are included in your 2001 income, no adjustment is made to the earlier year's return. Do not file an amended return for the earlier year.*

TAXPLANNER

Estimated tax. Generally, tax is not withheld on Social Security benefits. This means that you may have to pay estimated tax during the year if these benefits are taxable and you do not have enough taxes withheld from other income. However, you may request to have federal income tax withheld from your benefits at 7%, 10%, 15%, 27% or 30%, but no other percentage or amount is allowed. This request is made by completing Form W-4V, *Voluntary Withholding Request,* and giving it to the agency making the payments. See Chapter 5, *Tax Withholding and Estimated Tax,* for more information on estimated tax.

Examples

The following are a few examples you can use as a guide to figure the taxable part of your benefits.

Example 1. George White is single and files Form 1040 for 2001. He received the following income in 2001:

Fully taxable pension	$18,600
Wages from part-time job	9,400
Taxable interest income	990
Total	$28,990

George also received social security benefits during 2001. The Form SSA-1099 he received in January 2002 shows $5,980 in box 5. To figure his taxable benefits, George completes the worksheet shown here.

Worksheet 1. Figuring Your Taxable Benefits

1. Enter the total amount from *box 5* of *ALL* your Forms SSA-1099 and RRB-1099 .... **5,980**

Note. *If line 1 is zero or less, stop here; none of your benefits are taxable. Otherwise, go on to line 2.*

2. Enter one-half of line 1 .... **2,990**

3. Enter the total of the amounts from:

   Form 1040: Lines 7, 8a, 8b, 9–14, 15b, 16b, 17–19, and 21.

   Form 1040A: lines 7, 8a, 8b, 9, 10, 11b, 12b, and 13 .... **28,990**

4. *Form 1040A filers:* Enter the total of any exclusions for qualified U.S. savings bond interest (Form 8815, line 14) or for adoption benefits (Form 8839, line 26).

   Form 1040 filers: Enter the total of any exclusions/adjustments for:

   • Qualified U.S. savings bond interest (Form 8815, line 14),

   • Adoption benefits (Form 8839, line 26),

   • Foreign earned income or housing (Form 2555, lines 43 and 48, or Form 2555-EZ, line 18), and

   • Certain income of bona fide residents of American Samoa (Form 4563, line 15) or Puerto Rico .... **-0-**

5. Add lines 2, 3, and 4 .... **31,980**

6. *Form 1040A filers:* Enter the amount from Form 1040A, line 16

   Form 1040 filers: Enter the amount from Form 1040, line 32, minus any amount on Form 1040, line 24 .... **-0-**

7. Subtract line 6 from line 5 .... **31,980**

8. Enter $25,000 ($32,000 if married filing jointly; $0 if married filing separately and you lived with your spouse at any time during 2001) **25,000**

9. Subtract line 8 from line 7. If zero or less, enter -0- **6,980**

Note. *If line 9 is zero or less, stop here; none of your benefits are taxable. (Do not enter any amounts on Form 1040, line 20a or 20b or on Form 1040A, line 14a or 14b. But if you are married filing separately and you lived apart from your spouse for all of 2001, enter "D" to the left of line 20a, Form 1040, or to the right of the word "benefits" on line 14a, Form 1040A. Also enter -0- on Form 1040, line 20b or on Form 1040A, line 14b.) Otherwise, go on to line 10.*

10. Enter $9,000 ($12,000 if married filing jointly; $0 if married filing separately and you lived with your spouse at any time in 2001) **9,000**

11. Subtract line 10 from line 9. If zero or less, enter -0- .... **-0-**

12. Enter the *smaller* of line 9 or line 10 .... **6,980**

13. Enter one-half of line 12 .... **3,490**

14. Enter the *smaller* of line 2 or line 13 .... **2,990**

15. Multiply line 11 by 85% (.85). If line 11 is zero, enter -0- .... **-0-**

16. Add lines 14 and 15 .... **2,990**

17. Multiply line 1 by 85% (.85) **5,083**

18. **Taxable benefits.** Enter the *smaller* of line 16 or line 17 .... **2,990**

   • Enter the amount from line 1 above on Form 1040, line 20a or on Form 1040A, line 14a.

   • Enter the amount from line 18 above on Form 1040, line 20b or on Form 1040A, line 14b.

The amount on line 18 of George's worksheet shows that $2,990 of his social security benefits is taxable. On line 20a of his Form 1040, George enters his net benefits of $5,980. On line 20b, he enters his taxable part of $2,990.

Example 2. Ray and Alice Hopkins file a joint return on Form 1040A for 2001. Ray is retired and received a fully taxable pension of $15,500. He also received social security benefits, and his Form SSA-1099 for 2001 shows net benefits of $5,600 in box 5. Alice worked during the year and had wages of $14,000. She made a deductible payment to her IRA account of $1,000. Ray and Alice have two savings accounts with a total of $250 in interest income. They complete Worksheet 1 and find that none of Ray's social security benefits are taxable. They leave lines 14a and 14b of their Form 1040A blank.

Worksheet 1. Figuring Your Taxable Benefits

1. Enter the total amount from *box 5* of *ALL* your Forms SSA-1099 and RRB-1099 .... **5,600**

Note. *If line 1 is zero or less, stop here; none of your benefits are taxable. Otherwise, go to line 2.*

2. Enter one-half of line 1 .... **2,800**

3. Enter the total of the amounts from:

   Form 1040: Lines 7, 8a, 8b, 9–14, 15b, 16b, 17–19, and 21.

   Form 1040A: lines 7, 8a, 8b, 9, 10, 11b, 12b and 13 .... **29,750**

4. *Form 1040A filers:* Enter the total of any exclusion for qualified U.S. savings bond interest (Form 8815, line 14) or for adoption benefits (Form 8839, line 26).

   Form 1040 filers: Enter the total of any exclusions/adjustments for:

   • Qualified U.S. savings bond interest (Form 8815, line 14),

   • Adoption benefits (Form 8839, line 26),

   • Foreign earned income or housing (Form 2555, lines 43 and 48, or Form 2555-EZ, line 18), and

   • Certain income of bona fide residents of American Samoa (Form 4563, line 15) or Puerto Rico .... **-0-**

5. Add lines 2, 3, and 4 .... **32,550**

6. *Form 1040A filers:* Enter the amount from Form 1040A, line 16

   Form 1040 filers: Enter the amount from Form 1040, line 32, minus any amount on Form 1040, line 24 .... **1,000**

7. Subtract line 6 from line 5 .... **31,550**

8. Enter $25,000 ($32,000 if married filing jointly; $0 if married filing separately and you lived with your spouse at any time during 2001) **32,000**

9. Subtract line 8 from line 7. If zero or less, enter -0- .... **-0-**

Note. *If line 9 is zero or less, stop here; none of your benefits are taxable. (Do not enter any amounts on Form 1040, line 20a or 20b or on Form 1040A, line 14a or*

14b. But if you are married filing separately and you lived apart from your spouse for all of 2001, enter "D" to the left of line 20a, Form 1040, or to the right of the word "benefits" on line 14a, Form 1040A. Also enter -0- on Form 1040, line 20b or on Form 1040A, line 14b.) Otherwise, go on to line 10.

10. Enter $9,000 ($12,000 if married filing jointly; $0 if married filing separately and you lived with your spouse at any time in 2001) ...... _____

11. Subtract line 10 from line 9. If zero or less, enter -0- .... _____

12. Enter the *smaller* of line 9 or line 10 .... _____

13. Enter one-half of line 12... _____

14. Enter the *smaller* of line 2 or line 13 .... _____

15. Multiply line 11 by 85% (.85). If line 11 is zero, enter -0- .... _____

16. Add lines 14 and 15 .... _____

17. Multiply line 1 by 85% (.85) .... _____

18. **Taxable benefits.** Enter the *smaller* of line 16 or line 17 .... _____

- Enter the amount from line 1 above on Form 1040, line 20a or on Form 1040A, line 14a.

- Enter the amount from line 18 above on Form 1040, line 20b or on Form 1040A, line 14b

Example 3. Joe and Betty Johnson file a joint return on Form 1040 for 2001. Joe is a retired railroad worker and in 2001 received the social security equivalent benefit (SSEB) portion of tier 1 railroad retirement benefits. Joe's Form RRB-1099 shows $10,000 in box 5. Betty is a retired government worker and receives a fully taxable pension of $38,000. They had $2,300 in interest income plus interest of $200 on a qualified U.S. savings bond. The savings bond interest qualified for the exclusion. Thus, they have a total income of $40,300 ($38,000 + $2,300). They figure their taxable benefits by completing Worksheet 1.

Worksheet 1. Figuring Your Taxable Benefits

1. Enter the total amount from *box 5* of **ALL** your Forms SSA-1099 and RRB-1099 10,000

Note. *If line 1 is zero or less, stop here; none of your benefits are taxable. Otherwise, go to line 2.*

2. Enter one-half of line 1.. 5,000

3. Enter the total of the amounts from:

   Form 1040: Lines 7, 8a, 8b, 9–14, 15b, 16b, 17–19, and 21.

   Form 1040A: lines 7, 8a, 8b, 9, 10, 11b, 12b, and 13 40,300

4. *Form 1040A filers:* Enter the total of any exclusions for qualified U.S. savings bond interest (Form 8815, line 14) or for adoption benefits (Form 8839, line 26).

   Form 1040 filers: Enter the total of any exclusions/adjustments for:

   - Qualified U.S. savings bond interest (Form 8815, line 14),

   - Adoption benefits (Form 8839, line 26),

   - Foreign earned income or housing (Form 2555, lines 43 and 48, or Form 2555-EZ, line 18), and

   - Certain income of bona fide residents of American Samoa (Form 4563, line 15) or Puerto Rico...................................... 200

5. Add lines 2, 3, and 4 45,500

6. *Form 1040A filers:* Enter the amount from Form 1040A, line 16
   Form 1040A filers: Enter the amount from Form 1040, line 32, minus any amount on Form 1040, line 24 .... -0-

7. Subtract line 6 from line 5 45,500

8. Enter $25,000 ($32,000 if married filing jointly; $0 if married filing separately and you lived with your spouse at any time during 2001) 32,000

9. Subtract line 8 from line 7. If zero or less, enter -0- 13,500

Note. *If line 9 is zero or less, stop here; none of your benefits are taxable. (Do not enter any amounts on Form 1040, line 20a or 20b or on Form 1040A, line 14a or 14b. But if you are married filing separately and you lived apart from your spouse for all of 2001, enter "D" to the left of line 20a, Form 1040, or to the right of the word "benefits" on line 14a, Form 1040A. Also enter -0- on Form 1040, line 20b or on Form 1040A, line 14b.) Otherwise, go on to line 10.*

10. Enter $9,000 ($12,000 if married filing jointly; $0 if married filing separately and you lived with your spouse at any time in 2001) 12,000

11. Subtract line 10 from line 9. If zero or less, enter -0- 1,500

12. Enter the *smaller* of line 9 or line 10 12,000

13. Enter one-half of line 12... 6,000

14. Enter the *smaller* of line 2 or line 13 5,000

15. Multiply line 11 by 85% (.85). If line 11 is zero, enter -0- 1,275

16. Add lines 14 and 15 6,275

17. Multiply line 1 by 85% (.85) 8,500

18. **Taxable benefits.** Enter the *smaller* of line 16 or line 17 6,275

- Enter the amount from line 1 above on Form 1040, line 20a or on Form 1040A, line 14a.

- Enter the amount from line 18 above on Form 1040, line 20b or on Form 1040A, line 14b

More than 50% of Joe's net benefits are taxable because the income on line 7 of the worksheet ($45,500) is more than $44,000. Joe and Betty enter $10,000 on line 20a, Form 1040, and $6,275 on line 20b, Form 1040.

Deductions Related to Your Benefits

You may be entitled to deduct certain amounts related to the benefits you receive.

Disability payments. You may have received disability payments from your employer or an insurance company that you included as income on your tax return in an earlier year. If you received a lump-sum payment from SSA or RRB, and you had to repay the employer or insurance company for the disability payments, you can take an itemized deduction for the part of the payments you included in gross income in the earlier year. If the amount you repay is more than $3,000, you may be able to claim a tax credit instead. Claim the deduction or credit in the same way explained under *Repayments More Than Gross Benefits*, later.

Legal expenses. You can usually deduct legal expenses that you pay or incur to produce or collect taxable income or in connection with the determination, collection, or refund of any tax.

Legal expenses for collecting the ***taxable*** part of your benefits are deductible as a miscellaneous itemized deduction on line 22, Schedule A (Form 1040).

TAXALERT

If your adjusted gross income exceeds $132,950 ($66,475 for married persons filing separately) in 2001, certain itemized deductions claimed on your return may be phased out. See Chapter 30, *Miscellaneous Deductions*, for details.

Repayments More Than Gross Benefits

In some situations, your Form SSA-1099 or Form RRB-1099 will show that the total benefits you repaid (box 4) are more than the gross benefits (box 3) you received. If this occurred, your net benefits in box 5 will be a negative figure (a figure in parentheses) and none of your benefits will be taxable. If you receive more than one form, a negative figure in box 5 of one form is used to offset a positive figure in box 5 of another form for that same year.

If you have any questions about this negative figure, contact your local SSA office or your local U.S. RRB field office.

Joint return. If you and your spouse file a joint return, and your Form SSA-1099 or RRB-1099 has a negative figure in box 5, but your spouse's does not, subtract the amount in box 5 of your form from the amount in box 5 of your spouse's form. You do this to get your net benefits when figuring if your combined benefits are taxable.

Example. John and Mary file a joint return for 2001. John received Form SSA-1099 showing $3,000 in box 5. Mary also received Form SSA-1099 and the amount in box 5 was ($500). John and Mary will use $2,500 ($3,000 minus $500) as the amount of their net benefits when figuring if any of their combined benefits are taxable.

Explanation
Social Security benefits are determined on a cash basis, just like most other income of individuals. Accordingly, repayments of prior-year amounts reduce current-year benefits.

TaxSaver

The SSA can reduce your monthly benefits if you have earned income in excess of the threshold amounts (explained below) and are under age 65. The retirement earnings test has been eliminated for individuals attaining normal retirement age—currently age 65. However, a test remains in effect for individuals ages 62 through 64. A modified test applies for the year an individual reaches age 65. For the year in which an individual reaches 65, each $3 of income earned in 2001 over $25,000 (up from $17,000 in 2000) will reduce your Social Security benefits by $1. The $25,000 threshold applies only for months prior to attaining age 65. There is no limit on earnings beginning the month an individual attains age 65. For individuals between the ages of 62 and 64, each $2 of income earned in 2001 over $10,680 (up from $10,080 in 2000) will reduce your Social Security benefits by $1. Other exceptions apply during the initial year you receive Social Security retirement benefits. Consult the SSA for further explanation.

Threshold Amounts for Earned Income in Retirement

	2001	2002
Age 65*	$25,000	$30,000
Age 62–64	$10,680	Subject to automatic adjustment

*Threshold applies only for months prior to attaining normal retirement age—currently age 65.

TaxAlert

If you were born after 1937, your "normal retirement age" will occur later than age 65. Normal retirement age is the age at which full (100%) Social Security retirement benefits are available. Currently, age 65 is considered normal retirement age. However, beginning with individuals who attain age 62 in the year 2000 (born in 1938), the normal retirement age increases over the next 22 years, leveling off at age 67 for individuals who were born in 1960 or later. In other words, the normal retirement age for individuals born between 1955 and 1969 will be age 66, plus 2 months for every year after 1954. Refer to the chart below entitled "Scheduled Increases in Social Security Normal Retirement Age."

Scheduled Increases in Social Security Normal Retirement Age

Birth Year	Year Worker Attains Age 62	Normal Retirement Age
1938	2000	65 + 2 months
1939	2001	65 + 4 months
1940	2002	65 + 6 months
1941	2003	65 + 8 months
1942	2004	65 + 10 months
1943	2005	66
1944	2006	66
1945	2007	66
1946	2008	66
1947	2009	66
1948	2010	66
1949	2011	66
1950	2012	66
1951	2013	66
1952	2014	66
1953	2015	66
1954	2016	66
1955	2017	66 + 2 months
1956	2018	66 + 4 months
1957	2019	66 + 6 months
1958	2020	66 + 8 months
1959	2021	66 + 10 months
1960	2022	67
1961 and subsequent years	2023 and later	67

Repayment of benefits received in an earlier year. If the total amount shown in box 5 of all of your Forms SSA-1099 and RRB-1099 is a negative figure, you can take an itemized deduction for the part of this negative figure that represents benefits you included in gross income in an earlier year.

If this deduction is $3,000 or less, it is subject to the 2%-of-adjusted-gross-income limit that applies to certain miscellaneous itemized deductions. Claim it on line 22, Schedule A (Form 1040).

TaxAlert

If your adjusted gross income exceeds $132,950 ($64,475 for married persons filing separately) in 2001, certain itemized deductions claimed on your return may be phased out. See Chapter 30, *Miscellaneous Deductions,* for details.

If this deduction is more than $3,000, you should figure your tax two ways:

1) Figure your tax for 2001 with the itemized deduction included on line 27 of Schedule A.
2) Figure your tax for 2001 in the following steps.
   a) Figure the tax without the itemized deduction included on line 27 of Schedule A.

b) For each year after 1983 for which part of the negative figure represents a repayment of benefits, refigure your taxable benefits as if your total benefits for the year were reduced by that part of the negative figure. Then refigure the tax for that year.

c) Subtract the total of the refigured tax amounts in (b) from the total of your actual tax amounts.

d) Subtract the result in (c) from the result in (a).

Compare the tax figured in methods (1) and (2). Your tax for 2001 is the smaller of the two amounts. If method (1) results in less tax, take the itemized deduction on line 27, Schedule A (Form 1040). If method (2) results in less tax, claim a credit for the applicable amount on line 65 of Form 1040 and write "I.R.C. 1341" in the margin to the left of line 65. If both methods produce the same tax, deduct the repayment on line 27, Schedule A (Form 1040).

Explanation

This confusing computation allows you to reduce your current tax by the greater of two amounts: 1) the amount of tax you would save by taking the deduction this year or 2) what you paid in tax the prior year because of including the amount in income.

13

Other Income

Introduction

Your salary, interest you earn, dividends received, a gain from the sale of securities—all of these, of course, are taxable income.

Unfortunately, so are a lot of other things: a debt forgiven by a friend, jury pay, a free trip you receive from a travel agency for organizing a group of tourists, and royalties you earn on a book. All of these are taxable income to you, too.

The general rule is that anything that enriches you should be included in your gross income, unless it is specifically excluded by the tax law.

Indeed, some things are excluded from taxation. Gen-

erally, you don't have to pay income tax on life insurance proceeds that you receive because of the death of the insured. Most gifts and inheritances are tax-free income. The value of the vegetables you grow in your garden and eat yourself is not taxable. This chapter tells you what kind of income is taxable, what kind of income is not taxable, and how you can tell the difference.

This chapter includes a discussion on passive activity losses. Passive investments include all rental activities, all limited partnerships, and those other businesses in which the taxpayer is not involved in the operations on a regular, continuous, and substantial basis.

This chapter discusses many kinds of income and explains whether they are taxable or nontaxable.

- Income that is taxable must be reported on your tax return and is subject to tax.
- Income that is nontaxable may have to be shown on your tax return but is not subject to tax.

This chapter begins with discussions of the following income items.

- Bartering.
- Canceled debts.
- Life insurance proceeds.
- Partnership income.
- S Corporation income.
- Recoveries (including state income tax refunds).
- Rents from personal property.
- Repayments.
- Royalties.
- Unemployment benefits.
- Welfare and other public assistance benefits.

These discussions are followed by brief discussions of many income items arranged in alphabetical order.

You must include on your return all income you receive in the form of money, property, and services unless the tax law states that you do not include them. Some items, however, are only partly excluded from income.

Useful Items

You may want to see:

Publication

- ☐ **520** Scholarships and Fellowships
- ☐ **525** Taxable and Nontaxable Income
- ☐ **544** Sales and Other Dispositions of Assets
- ☐ **550** Investment Income and Expenses

Bartering

Bartering is an exchange of property or services. You must include in your income, at the time received, the fair market value of property or services you receive in bartering. If you exchange services with another person and you both have agreed ahead of time as to the value of the services, that value will be accepted as fair market value unless the value can be shown to be otherwise.

Generally, you report this income on Schedule C, *Profit or Loss From Business,* or Schedule C-EZ, *Net Profit From Business* (Form 1040). But if the barter involves an exchange of something other than services, such as in *Example 3* below, you may have to use another form or schedule instead.

Explanation
The Internal Revenue Service (IRS) explanation is correct in stating that if you exchange your property and/or services for the property and/or services of another, you have taxable income. However, when you exchange property for property, you generally recognize income only to the extent that the fair market value of the property you receive exceeds your **adjusted basis** in the property you give up (note that an exception to this general rule is for like-kind exchanges). The proper way of determining gain on exchanges of property and your **basis** in the property you receive are discussed in Chapter 14, *Basis of Property*, and Chapter 15, *Sale of Property*.

Example 1. You are a self-employed attorney who performs legal services for a client, a small corporation. The corporation gives you shares of its stock as payment for your services. You must include the fair market value of the shares in your income on Schedule C or Schedule C-EZ (Form 1040) in the year you receive them.

Example 2. You are self-employed and a member of a barter club. The club uses "credit units" as a means of exchange. It adds credit units to your account for goods or services you provide to members, which you can use to purchase goods and services offered by other members of the barter club. The club subtracts credit units from your account when you receive goods or services from other members. You must include in your income the value of the credit units that are added to your account, even though you may not actually receive goods or services from other members until a later tax year.

Example 3. You own a small apartment building. In return for 6 months rent-free use of an apartment, an artist gives you a work of art she created. You must report as rental income on Schedule E, *Supplemental Income and Loss* (Form 1040), the fair market value of the artwork, and the artist must report as income on Schedule C or Schedule C-EZ (Form 1040) the fair rental value of the apartment.

Form 1099-B from barter exchange. If you exchanged property or services through a barter exchange, you should receive Form 1099-B, *Proceeds From Broker and Barter Exchange Transactions,* or a similar statement from the barter exchange by January 31, 2002. It should show the value of cash, property, services, credits, or scrip you received from exchanges during 2001. The IRS will also receive a copy of Form 1099-B.

Canceled Debts

Generally, if a debt you owe is canceled or forgiven, other than as a gift or bequest, you must include the canceled amount in your income. You have no income from the canceled debt if it is intended as a gift to you. A debt includes any indebtedness for which you are liable or which attaches to property you hold.

If the debt is a nonbusiness debt, report the canceled amount on line 21 of Form 1040. If it is a business debt, report the amount on Schedule C or C-EZ (Form 1040) (or on Schedule F, *Profit or Loss From Farming* (Form 1040), if you are a farmer).

TaxPlanner
Family members often make interest-free or below-market interest loans to one another. The IRS may recharacterize these loans as arm's length transactions and impute interest income to the lender and interest expense to the borrower, which are then reported on their respective tax returns. See Chapter 8, *Interest Income,* for further discussion of below-market loans. You should consult your tax advisor about how to report any below-market loan transactions.

Form 1099-C. If a federal government agency, financial institution, or credit union cancels or forgives a debt you owe of $600 or more, you will receive a Form 1099-C, *Cancellation of Debt.* The amount of the canceled debt is shown in box 2.

Interest included in canceled debt. If any interest is forgiven and included in the amount of canceled debt in box 2, the amount of interest will also be shown in box 3. Whether or not you must include the interest portion of the canceled debt in your income depends on whether the interest would be deductible if you paid it. See *Deductible debt,* under *Exceptions,* later.

If the interest would not be deductible (such as interest on a personal loan), include in your income the amount from box 2 of Form 1099-C. If the interest would be deductible (such as on a business loan), include in your income the net amount of the canceled debt (the amount shown in box 2 less the interest amount shown in box 3).

Discounted mortgage loan. If your financial institution offers a discount for the early payment of your mortgage loan, the amount of the discount is canceled debt. You must include the canceled amount in your income.

TaxSaver
Proceed cautiously if the financial institution that holds your mortgage offers you a substantial discount on your loan balance in exchange for a prepayment on it. While this might at first appear very attractive, remember that you will have to pay ordinary income tax on the amount of the discount offered, which may considerably reduce any advantage to you. Your money might be put to better use in investments with a high after-tax yield or in paying off expensive consumer credit.

Stockholder debt. If you are a stockholder in a corporation and the corporation cancels or forgives your debt to it, the canceled debt is dividend income to you.

If you are a stockholder in a corporation and you cancel a debt owed to you by the corporation, you generally do not realize income. This is because the canceled debt is considered as a contribution to the capital of the corporation equal to the amount of debt principal that you canceled.

Exceptions
There are several exceptions to the inclusion of canceled debt in income. These are explained next.

Nonrecourse debt. If you are not personally liable for the debt (nonrecourse debt), different rules apply. You may have a gain or loss if nonrecourse debt is canceled or forgiven in conjunction with the foreclosure or repossession of property to which the debt attaches. See Publication 544 for more information.

Student loans. Certain student loans contain a provision that all or part of the debt incurred to attend the qualified educational institution will be canceled if you work for a certain period of time in certain professions for any of a broad class of employers.

You do not have income if your student loan is canceled after you agreed to this provision and then performed the services required. To qualify, the loan must have been made by:

1) The federal government, a state or local government, or an instrumentality, agency, or subdivision thereof,
2) A tax-exempt public benefit corporation that has assumed control of a state, county, or municipal hospital, and whose employees are considered public employees under state law, or
3) An educational institution:
   a) Under an agreement with an entity described in (1) or (2) that provided the funds to the institution to make the loan, or
   b) As part of a program of the institution designed to encourage students to serve in occupations or areas with unmet needs and under which the services provided are for or under the direction of a governmental unit or a tax-exempt section 501(c)(3) organization.

A loan to refinance a qualified student loan will also qualify if it was made by an educational institution or a tax-exempt 501(c)(3) organization under its program designed as described in (3)(b) above.

Section 501(c)(3) organizations are defined in Publication 525.

Deductible debt. You do not have income from the cancellation of a debt if your payment of the debt would be deductible. This exception applies only if you use the cash method of accounting. For more information, see chapter 5 of Publication 334, *Tax Guide for Small Business*.

Price reduced after purchase. Generally, if the seller reduces the amount of debt you owe for property you purchased, you do not have income from the reduction. The reduction of the debt is treated as a purchase price adjustment and reduces your basis in the property.

Excluded debt. Do not include a canceled debt in your gross income in the following situations.

1) The debt is canceled in a bankruptcy case under title 11 of the U.S. Code. See Publication 908, *Bankruptcy Tax Guide*.
2) The debt is canceled when you are insolvent. However, you cannot exclude any amount of canceled debt that is more than the amount by which you are insolvent. See Publication 908.
3) The debt is qualified farm debt and is canceled by a qualified person. See chapter 4 of Publication 225, *Farmer's Tax Guide*.
4) The debt is qualified real property business debt. See chapter 5 of Publication 334.

TaxAlert

The 1993 Tax Act changed the rules about how certain real property business debts can be treated. Under prior law, if you were solvent (i.e., not in bankruptcy) and you wished to discharge certain business real property debts, the amount of the debt discharged would be counted as gross income to you. Under the current tax law, if you are a solvent taxpayer, you can elect to exclude from your income some or all of the discharge of qualified real property business indebtedness. The amount that can be excluded from income cannot exceed the basis of the depreciable real property. In addition, the amount excluded from your income is considered a reduction in the basis of the property. If you subsequently dispose of the property, the amount of the reduction in the basis of the property is treated as depreciation for purposes of computing how much ordinary income must be recaptured in order to calculate your tax.

There are certain limitations on the amount of debt that you can discharge and exclude from your income. The amount you may exclude from your income may not exceed the principal amount of the debt (immediately before the discharge) of the real property that is security for the debt. For this purpose, the fair market value of the property is reduced by the outstanding principal amount of any other qualified real property business indebtedness secured by the property. You should consult with your tax advisor.

Example

Assume on July 1, 2001, Christine owns a building worth $150,000, used in her trade or business, that is subject to a first mortgage debt of $110,000 and a second mortgage debt of $90,000. Christine agrees with her second mortgagee to reduce the second mortgage debt to $30,000, resulting in a discharge of indebtedness income in the amount of $60,000. Assuming that Christine has sufficient basis in business real property to absorb the reduction, Christine can elect to exclude $50,000 of that discharge from her gross income. Why $50,000? The $50,000 amount is the excess of her combined mortgage debts ($200,000) over the fair market value of the estate ($150,000) immediately before the discharge of the indebtedness. However, $10,000, the amount of the debt relief over the excluded amount in this example, would be considered income to Christine in 2001 and therefore subject to tax. The logic here is that because of the discharge of the indebtedness, Christine gained $10,000 in equity in the property at its current fair market value.

Life Insurance Proceeds

Life insurance proceeds paid to you because of the death of the insured person are not taxable unless the policy was turned over to you for a price. This is true even if the proceeds were paid under an accident or health insurance policy or an endowment contract.

Proceeds not received in installments. If death benefits are paid to you in a lump sum or other than at regular intervals, include in your income only the benefits that are more than the amount payable to you at the time of the insured person's death. If the benefit payable at death is not specified, you include in your income the benefit payments that are more than the present value of the payments at the time of death.

Proceeds received in installments. If you receive life insurance proceeds in installments, you can exclude part of each installment from your income.

To determine the excluded part, divide the amount held by the insurance company (generally the total lump sum payable at the death of the insured person) by the number of installments to be paid. Include anything over this excluded part in your income as interest.

Example

Suppose you receive a $100,000 life insurance death benefit that you elect to receive over 10 annual installments. Any amount that you receive in excess of $10,000 each year will be considered taxable income to you.

Surviving spouse. If your spouse died before October 23, 1986, and insurance proceeds paid to you because of the death of your spouse are received in installments, you can exclude up to $1,000 a year of the interest included in the installments. If you remarry, you can continue to take the exclusion.

More information. For more information, see *Life Insurance Proceeds* in Publication 525.

TAX SAVER

Interest option on insurance. If an insurance company pays you only interest on proceeds from life insurance left on deposit with them, the interest you are paid is taxable.

Example

Assume you are a beneficiary of a life insurance death benefit. If the payment structure of the benefit is such that you are only receiving the interest, then your entire payment would be considered taxable. The individual (or successor beneficiary) who will be receiving the principal of the benefit would receive it income tax free. Special exclusion ratio rules apply to individuals receiving annuity death benefits in the form of principal and interest.

If your spouse died before October 23, 1986, and you chose to receive only the interest from your insurance proceeds, the $1,000 interest exclusion for a surviving spouse does not apply. If you later decide to receive the proceeds from the policy in installments, you can take the interest exclusion from the time you begin to receive the installments.

Surrender of policy for cash. If you surrender a life insurance policy for cash, you must include in income any proceeds that are more than the cost of the life insurance policy. In general, your cost (or investment in the contract) is the total of premiums that you paid for the life insurance policy, less any refunded premiums, rebates, dividends, or unrepaid loans that were not included in your income.

Example

Assuming you terminated a life insurance policy with a cash value of $50,000 and of that amount you only paid $40,000 in net premiums, $10,000 would be considered taxable income to you at that time.

However, if you exchange one life insurance policy for another policy, it is possible that you may not have a taxable transaction. See your tax advisor.

You should receive a Form 1099-R showing the total proceeds and the taxable part. Report these amounts on lines 16a and 16b of Form 1040, or lines 12a and 12b of Form 1040A.

Endowment proceeds. Endowment proceeds paid in a lump sum to you at maturity are taxable only if the proceeds are more than the cost of the policy. To determine your cost, add the aggregate amount of premiums (or other consideration) paid for the contract and subtract any amount that you previously received under the contract and excluded from your income. Include the part of the lump sum payment that is more than your cost in your income.

TAX SAVER

There are a number of ways in which insurance proceeds may be paid. The choice may have been made by the deceased, or the choice may belong to the recipient of the proceeds. In either case, proper planning may save tax dollars and increase wealth.

Generally, the insured should not decide how the insurance benefits are to be paid, unless he or she is worried that the beneficiary, be it a child or a spouse, might squander the money. Absent that, determining the method of payment should be left to the beneficiary, who, after the death of the insured, is in the best position to consider potential investments, as well as tax benefits.

Explanation

Endowment contracts, much like whole life insurance contracts, require you, as the owner, to pay annual premiums in return for a certain sum of cash that is paid when you reach a specified age or upon death. Unless you choose to receive the endowment proceeds in installments, the excess of the proceeds over the cost of the policy is taxable in the year of maturity, *even if the proceeds are not received until a later year.* The excess of the proceeds is taxed as ordinary income, not as capital gain. The cost of the endowment contract is the total amount of the premiums you paid for it, not its cash value at the time of maturity or when you surrender it.

However, if you agree to take the proceeds as an annuity within 60 days after the lump-sum payment becomes available and before you receive any cash, you are not considered to have received the lump sum for tax purposes. The lump sum is taxed as an annuity; that is, you are taxed on the amounts as you receive them each year.

The Technical and Miscellaneous Revenue Act of 1988 included a provision designed to discourage the use of a life insurance contract as a tax shelter. For certain contracts entered into or materially changed after June 21, 1988, you may be required to treat distributions first as income and then as recovery of investment. Distributions are defined for this purpose to include a loan. In certain circumstances, an additional 10% tax will be imposed on the amount that is includable in gross income. Consult your tax advisor to determine if you are subject to this provision.

Deceased public safety officers. If you are a survivor of a public safety officer who died in the line of duty, you may be able to exclude from income certain amounts you receive.

Bureau of Justice Assistance payments. If you are a surviving dependent of a public safety officer (law enforcement officer or firefighter) who died in the line of duty, do not include in your income the death benefit paid to you by the Bureau of Justice Assistance.

Governmental plan annuity. If you receive a survivor annuity as the child or spouse (or former spouse) of a public safety officer who was killed in the line of duty after 1996, you generally do not have to include it in income. This exclusion applies to the amount of the annuity that is based on the officer's service as a public safety officer.

Caution. *Beginning in 2002, this exclusion applies regardless of when the officer was killed.*

For this purpose, the term **public safety officer** includes police and law enforcement officers, firefighters and rescue squad and ambulance crews. See Publication 525 for more information.

Accelerated Death Benefits

Certain amounts paid as accelerated death benefits under a life insurance contract or viatical settlement before the individual's death are excluded from income if the insured is terminally or chronically ill.

Viatical settlement. This is the sale or assignment of any part of the death benefit under a life insurance contract to a viatical settlement provider. A viatical settlement provider is a person who regularly engages in the business of buying or taking assignment of life insurance contracts on the lives of insured individuals who are terminally or chronically ill and who meets the requirements of section 101(g)(2)(B) of the Internal Revenue Code.

Exclusion for terminal illness. Accelerated death benefits are fully excludable if the insured is a terminally ill individual. This is a person who has been certified by a physician as having an illness or physical condition that can reasonably be expected to result in death within 24 months from the date of the certification.

Exclusion for chronic illness. If the insured is a chronically ill individual who is not terminally ill, accelerated death benefits paid on the basis of costs incurred for qualified long-term care services are fully excludable. Accelerated death benefits paid on a per diem or other periodic basis are excludable up to a limit. This limit applies to the total of the accelerated death benefits and any periodic payments received from long-term care insurance contracts. For information on the limit and the definitions of *chronically ill individual* and *long-term care insurance contracts*, see *Long-Term Care Insurance Contracts* under *Sickness and Injury Benefits* in chapter 6.

Exception. The exclusion does not apply to any amount paid to a person (other than the insured) who has an insurable interest in the life of the insured because the insured:

- Is a director, officer, or employee of the other person, or
- Has a financial interest in the person's business.

Form 8853. To claim an exclusion for accelerated death benefits made on a per diem or other periodic basis, you must file Form 8853, *Archer MSAs and Long-term Care Insurance Contracts,* with your return. You do not have to file Form 8853 to exclude accelerated death benefits paid on the basis of actual expenses incurred.

Partnership Income

A partnership generally is not a taxable entity. The income, gains, losses, deductions, and credits of a partnership are *passed through* to the partners based on each partner's distributive share of these items.

Schedule K-1 (Form 1065). Although a partnership generally pays no tax, it must file an information return on Form 1065, *U.S. Return of Partnership Income,* and send Schedule K-1 (Form 1065) to each partner. In addition, the partnership will send each partner a copy of the *Partner's Instructions for Schedule K-1 (Form 1065)* to help each partner report his or her share of the partnership's income, deductions, credits, and tax preference items.

Recordkeeping. Keep Schedule K-1 (Form 1065) for your records. Do not attach it to your Form 1040.

Explanation

General. A partnership includes a group, pool, joint venture, or other unincorporated organization that carries on a business or financial operation. Most entities that qualify for partnership treatment can elect out of partnership treatment under the "check-the-box" regulations. See your tax advisor for more information.

Limited liability companies. A number of states permit the formation of limited liability companies (LLCs). In an LLC, members and designated managers are not personally liable for any debts of the company. In addition, if certain corporate characteristics are not present, the entity can be treated as a partnership and as a result enjoy the same federal income tax benefits that apply to partnerships. If the entity is appropriately established, LLCs combine the benefits of corporate limited liability with the advantages of partnership taxation. In addition to LLCs, one may consider the formation of a limited liability partnership (LLP). Consult your tax advisor or attorney to find out if these are options for your business in the state you live in.

Reporting income. Because a partnership is not a taxable entity, all tax items are passed through to the partners. A partnership is required to give you a Schedule K-1, Partner's Share of Income, Credits, Deductions, etc. A Schedule K-1 will list your distributive share of income, gains, losses, deductions, and credits that is required to be included in your individual tax return. If, for example, the Schedule K-1 indicates interest income of $100, you will need to include $100 as interest income on your Schedule B, Form 1040. (See Chapter 8, *Interest Income*.)

Basis. Because the partnership's income and losses flow directly through to you, such income or losses will affect your tax basis in the partnership. It is important that you maintain and update this tax-basis calculation every year for two reasons: First, your distributive share of the partnership losses is limited to the adjusted basis of your interest in the partnership at the end of the partnership year in which the losses took place. Second, in the year you sell your partnership interest, you will need to know your tax basis in order to calculate your gain or loss. To determine the adjusted basis of your interest in the partnership, begin with your initial investment and your initial share of your partnership liabilities and make the following adjustments.

Additions to basis

1. Your distributive share of the partnership's taxable income
2. Your share of any tax-exempt income earned by the partnership
3. Your share of the excess of partnership deductions for depletion over the basis of partnership property subject to depletion
4. Any additional capital you contribute
5. Your share of any increase in partnership liabilities

Subtractions from basis

1. Any cash distributions you receive
2. The basis that you take in any property distributed to you by the partnership
3. Your share of oil and gas depletion claimed by the partnership
4. Your distributive share of partnership losses
5. Your share of nondeductible, noncapital expenditures made by the partnership
6. Your share of any decrease in partnership liabilities

The partnership agreement usually covers the distribution of profits, losses, and other items. However, if there is no agreement for sharing a specific item of gain or loss, generally, each partner's distributive share is figured according to the partner's interest in the partnership.

In addition, *special "at-risk" rules apply* to a partnership engaged in any activity.

You may deduct your share of a partnership loss from any activity only up to the total amount that you are at risk in the activity at the end of the partnership's tax year.

The amount you are at risk in an activity is the cash and the adjusted basis of other property you contributed to the activity. Also, you are at risk for any amounts borrowed for use in the activity for which you either are personally liable or have pledged property, except property used in the activity, as security.

Generally, you are not at risk for:

1. Any nonrecourse loans used to finance the activity, to acquire property used in the activity, or to acquire your interest in the activity, unless they are secured by property not used in the activity;

2. Amounts for which you are protected against loss by guarantees, stop-loss agreements, or other similar arrangements; or

3. Amounts borrowed from interested or related parties if your partnership is engaged in certain activities.

For more information on the at-risk rules, see Publication 925, *Passive Activities and At-Risk Rules.*

In addition to the factors discussed above, your amount at risk is affected by the operating results of the activity itself. Income from the activity increases the amount you are at risk. Losses from the activity decrease the amount you are at risk. The at-risk amount is determined at the end of each tax year. Any loss in excess of that amount is disallowed for that year. It may, however, be carried over to future years, and to the extent that you subsequently have amounts at risk, it may be deducted in those years.

Under prior law, a partnership engaged in real estate activity was not subject to the at-risk rules. The Tax Reform Act of 1986 extended the at-risk rules to include real estate activities placed in service after December 31, 1986, but makes exceptions for third-party nonrecourse debt from commercial lenders and certain other parties.

In addition to the at-risk rules, the income from real estate partnerships is also subject to the passive activity rules. See the discussion, *Passive Activity Limitations and At-Risk Limitations,* at the end of this chapter. Also, consult your tax advisor for further information.

When to report partnership income. Generally, partnership income is treated as paid to you on the last day of the partnership year. (See Chapter 4, *Decedents,* for exceptions relating to partnership interests held by a decedent.) Generally, you must include your distributive share of partnership items on your return for your tax year in which the last day of the partnership year falls. If you receive income from a partnership other than in your capacity as a partner, however, you must report the income in the year in which it was received. For instance, if you sell property to your partnership at a gain, the gain is generally included in income when you receive the sale proceeds, regardless of when your partnership's tax year ends.

Estimated tax payments. A partner must take into account his or her share of the partnership's income or deductions to date at *each* estimated tax payment date. Often, this information is not readily available. If you are a member of a partnership, you may protect yourself from underpayment penalties by basing your payments on one of the exceptions described in Chapter 5, *Tax Withholding and Estimated Tax.*

However, if a partner moves from one state to another, and if the states involved follow federal rules, the partnership income or loss should be reported in the state income tax return for the state in which the partner resides when the partnership's year ends.

Sale of partnership interest. If you have a gain or a loss from the sale or exchange of a partnership interest, it is treated as a gain or a loss from the sale of a capital asset. The gain or loss is the difference between the amount you receive and the adjusted basis of your interest in the partnership. If you are relieved of any debts of the partnership, you must include these debts in the amount you receive.

However, you may have ordinary income as well as capital gain or loss on the sale of your partnership interest if the sale involves uncollected accounts receivable or inventory items that have increased in value. Consult your tax advisor for further help.

For more information on partnerships, get Publication 541, *Partnerships.*

S Corporation Income

In general, an S corporation does not pay tax on its income. Instead, the income, losses, deductions, and credits of the corporation are *passed through* to the shareholders.

Schedule K-1 (Form 1120S). An S corporation must file a return on Form 1120S, *U.S. Income Tax Return for an S Corporation,* and send Schedule K-1 (Form 1120S) to each shareholder. In addition, the S corporation will send each shareholder a copy of the *Shareholder's Instructions for Schedule K-1 (Form 1120S)* to help each shareholder report his or her share of the S corporation's income, losses, credits, and deductions.

Recordkeeping. Keep Schedule K-1 (Form 1120S) for your records. Do not attach it to your Form 1040.

Explanation

Shareholder's return. Generally, S corporation distributions are a nontaxable return of your basis in the corporation's stock. However, in certain cases, part of the distributions may be taxable as a dividend or as a long-term or short-term capital gain, or as both. The corporation's distributions may be in the form of cash or property.

All current-year income or loss and other tax items are taxed to you at the corporation's year-end. Generally, these items passed through to you as a shareholder will increase or decrease the basis of your S corporation stock as appropriate. Dividends are paid only from prior-year earnings (generally retained earnings from years prior to 1983 or prior to becoming an S corporation). Generally, property (including cash) distributions, except dividend distributions, are considered a return of capital to the extent of your basis in the stock of the corporation. Distributions in excess of basis are treated as a gain from the sale or exchange of property.

You should receive from the S corporation in which you are a shareholder a copy of the Shareholder's Instructions for Schedule K-1 (Form 1120S), together with a copy of Schedule K-1 (Form 1120S), showing your share of the income, credits, and deductions of the S corporation for the tax year. Your distributive share of the items of income, gain, loss, deduction, or credit of the S corporation must be shown separately on your Form 1040. The character of these items generally is the same as if you had realized or incurred them personally.

Individuals form an S corporation to get the legal benefits of a corporation, such as limited liability, while retaining the tax benefits of an individual. Usually, an S corporation does not pay federal income tax. One exception is a tax on certain gains that is paid by the S corporation, but normally, the individual owners of the corporation pay tax or accrue tax benefits on their personal returns based on the corporation's profits and losses.

Income from an S corporation is included in an individual's return as if the S corporation did not exist. Dividends that the S corporation receives are included as dividends on your return on Schedule B (Form 1040). Capital gains are included as capital gains on Schedule D (Form 1040). Types of income from an S corporation that are not treated specially on an individual's return are combined and included on Schedule E (Form 1040). If you have losses from a subchapter S corporation when you are not an active participant in the corporation's business activities, your losses will be subject to the passive activity limitations. See the section on Passive Activity Losses at the end of this chapter.

Estimated tax payments. A shareholder must take into account his or her share of the S corporation's income or deductions to date at *each* estimated tax payment date. Often, this information is not readily available. If you are a member of an S corporation, you may protect yourself from underpayment penalties by basing your payments on one of the exceptions described in Chapter 5, *Tax Withholding and Estimated Tax.*

Generally, an S corporation must have its tax year-end on December 31. However, under certain circumstances, an S corporation may operate on a **fiscal year;** that is, its tax year may end on a date other than December 31. Your return should include all S corporation income for its operating year that ends within your tax year.

Example

If your S corporation's year ends on October 31, your return for 2001 will include the income items for the corporation's entire year that ended October 31, 2001, even though that means including 2 months of 2000.

Deducting losses. You may deduct any losses of the S corporation for the year up to the amount of your basis.

Basis in an S corporation. Your basis in an S corporation at the end of a year is your investment (stock and loans), with the following adjustments.

Additions to basis

1. Your distributive share of the S corporation's separately and nonseparately stated taxable income
2. Your share of tax-exempt income earned by the S corporation
3. Any additional capital that you contribute
4. Deductions for depletion in excess of the basis of the property
5. A loan to the corporation directly from the shareholder; however, a guarantee of a third-party loan by a shareholder does not qualify as an addition to basis

Subtractions from basis

1. Generally, any cash distributed and the fair market value of property distributed (other than taxable dividends), but not below zero
2. Your distributive share of the S corporation's separately and nonseparately stated items of loss and deduction
3. Your share of nondeductible, noncapital expenditures made by the S corporation
4. Your share of the deductions for depletion for any oil and gas property held by the S corporation to the extent that the deduction does not exceed the proportionate share of the property's adjusted basis allocated to you

Example 1

Your basis in an S corporation is $20,000. The corporation makes a distribution to you of $30,000 in cash or property. You would have to recognize income of $10,000.

Example 2.

Your basis in an S corporation is $20,000. If it reports losses of $30,000, you may deduct only $20,000 for the year. The other $10,000 worth of losses is carried over until you have more basis.

All you need to prepare your individual tax return is the Form K-1 provided by the S corporation. It tells you what the numbers are and where to put them on your Form 1040.

TaxPlanner

An S corporation is just one of several alternatives to consider as a vehicle to conduct economic activities, but it does offer some of the best features of a regular corporation, a partnership, and a sole proprietorship.

1. As in a regular corporation, the stockholders of an S corporation are normally immune from liabilities in excess of their investment.
2. Like a regular corporation, the S corporation structure is convenient for transferring equity to children as part of your estate planning and the gradual transition of management and control to your heirs or successors. As shareholders, the children then report their proportionate share of S corporation income and losses on their respective tax returns.
3. Like a partnership or sole proprietorship, the S corporation permits the investors to deduct operating losses. Just as important, profits are not taxed twice, as they are in a regular corporation. A regular corporation itself pays taxes, and so do the individuals who receive a share of those profits when dividends are paid. An S corporation is, except in certain circumstances, exempt from taxes—at least at the federal level.

For more information on S corporations and their shareholders, see the instructions for Form 1120S.

Recoveries

A recovery is a return of an amount you deducted or took a credit for in an earlier year. The most common recoveries are refunds, reimbursements, and rebates of deductions itemized on Schedule A (Form 1040). You may also have recoveries of non-itemized deductions (such as payments on previously deducted bad debts) and recoveries of items for which you previously claimed a tax credit.

Tax benefit rule. You must include a recovery in your income in the year you receive it up to the amount by which the deduction or credit you took for the recovered amount reduced your tax in the earlier year. For this purpose, any increase to an amount carried over to the current year that resulted from the deduction or credit is considered to have reduced your tax in the earlier year. For more information, get Publication 525.

Federal income tax refund. Refunds of federal income taxes are not included in your income because they are never allowed as a deduction from income.

TaxAlert

Advance Refund Checks

The 2001 Tax Act established a new 10% income tax bracket for the first portion of taxable income currently taxed at 15%. This new tax bracket was not incorporated into the 2001 wage withholding tables, so the Department of Treasury issued refund checks to taxpayers starting in summer 2001. The 2001 advance refund amount is a maximum of $300 for single taxpayers and married taxpayers filing sep-

State and Local Income Tax Refund Worksheet

1. Enter the income tax refund from **Form(s) 1099-G** (or similar statement). But **do not** enter more than the amount on your 2000 Schedule A (Form 1040), line 5 . . . . **1.** _____

2. Enter your total allowable itemized deductions from your 2000 Schedule A (Form 1040), line 28 . . . . **2.** _____

   Note. If the filing status on your 2000 Form 1040 was married filing separately and your spouse itemized deductions in 2000, skip lines 3, 4, and 5, and enter the amount from line 2 on line 6.

3. Enter the amount shown below for the filing status claimed on your **2000** Form 1040.
   - Single—$4,400
   - Married filing jointly or qualifying widow(er)—$7,350
   - Married filing separately—$3,675
   - Head of household—$6,450

   . . . **3.** _____

4. Did you fill in line 35a on your 2000 Form 1040?
   - ☐ **No.** Enter -0-.
   - ☐ **Yes.** Multiply the number on line 35a of your 2000 Form 1040 by: $850 if your 2000 filing status was married filing jointly or separately or qualifying widow(er); $1,100 if your 2000 filing status was single or head of household.

   4. _____

5. Add lines 3 and 4 . . . . **5.** _____
6. Is the amount on line 5 less than the amount on line 2?
   - ☐ **No.** (STOP) None of your refund is taxable.
   - ☐ **Yes.** Subtract line 5 from line 2 . . . . **6.** _____
7. **Taxable part of your refund.** Enter the **smaller** of line 1 or line 6 here and on Form 1040, line 10 . . . . **7.** _____

arate returns, $500 for heads of households, and $600 for married taxpayers filing jointly. The advance refund check is a reduction of tax and *should not* be included as taxable income on your 2001 federal income tax return.

State income tax refund. If you received a state or local income tax refund (or credit or offset) in 2001, you must include it in income if you deducted the tax in an earlier year. You should receive Form 1099-G, *Certain Government and Qualified State Tuition Program Payments,* from the payer by January 31, 2002. The IRS will also receive a copy of the Form 1099-G.

Explanation
The above worksheet can be used to determine the taxable amount of your state and local income tax refund.

Mortgage interest refund. If you received a refund or credit in 2001 of mortgage interest paid in an earlier year, the amount should be shown in box 3 of your Form 1098, *Mortgage Interest Statement.* Do not subtract the refund amount from the interest you paid in 2001. You may have to include it in your income under the rules explained in the following discussions.

Interest on recovery. Interest on any of the amounts you recover must be reported as interest income in the year received. For example, report any interest you received on state or local income tax refunds on line 8a of Form 1040.

Explanation
Although the amount of a state tax refund may not be included in gross income, any interest you receive on federal or state refunds is taxable.

Recovery and expense in same year. If the refund or other recovery and the expense occur in the same year, the recovery reduces the deduction or credit and is not reported as income.

Recovery for 2 or more years. If you receive a refund or other recovery that is for amounts you paid in 2 or more separate years, you must allocate, on a pro rata basis, the recovered amount between the years in which you paid it. This allocation is necessary to determine the amount of recovery from any earlier years and to determine the amount, if any, of your allowable deduction for this item for the current year. For information on how to compute the allocation, see *Recoveries* in Publication 525.

Itemized Deduction Recoveries
If you recover any amount that you deducted in an earlier year on Schedule A (Form 1040), you must generally include the full amount of the recovery in your income in the year you receive it.

Where to report. Enter your state or local income tax refund on line 10 of Form 1040, and the total of all other recoveries as other income on line 21 of Form 1040. You cannot use Form 1040A or Form 1040EZ.

Standard deduction limit. You are generally allowed to claim the standard deduction if you do not itemize your deductions. Only your itemized deductions that are more than your standard deduction are subject to the recovery rule (unless you are required to itemize your deductions). If your total deductions on the earlier year return were not more than your income for that year, include in your income this year the smaller of:

1) Your recoveries, or
2) The amount by which your itemized deductions exceeded the standard deduction.

Example. For 2000, you filed a joint return. Your taxable income was $20,000 and you were not entitled to any tax credits. The standard deduction that you could have claimed was $7,350, and you had itemized deductions of $9,000. In 2001, you received the following recoveries for amounts deducted on your 2000 return:

Medical expenses	$200
State and local income tax refund	400
Refund of mortgage interest	325
Total recoveries	**$925**

None of the recoveries were more than the deductions taken for 2000.

Because your total recoveries are less than the amount by which your itemized deductions exceeded the standard deduction ($9,000 − 7,350 = $1,650), you must include your total recoveries in your income for 2001. Report the state and local income tax refund of $400 on line 10 of Form 1040 and the balance of your recoveries, $525, on line 21 of Form 1040.

TaxPlanner

The IRS correctly points out that the recovery of certain amounts you deducted is not income if you did not itemize your deductions in the year in which you paid these expenses. However, if the payer of the refund submits a Form 1099 or Form 1099-G to the IRS, we suggest that you attach a statement to your return including the item in income and then subtracting it out explaining why the item does not represent taxable income. This may prevent an inquiry from the IRS.

If you were subject to the alternative minimum tax in 2000, you may not have obtained any benefit for all or part of your state income tax deduction. This is because state income taxes are not deductible for purposes of computing the alternative minimum tax. (The alternative minimum tax is explained in Chapter 31, *How to Figure Your Tax*.) You will want to compute carefully the amount of the refund you received in 2001 that did not give you any tax benefit in 2000. Attach a statement in your return explaining why the item does not represent taxable income.

This will require a "with-and-without" computation. If your prior-year tax was not lower *with* the deduction, you did not receive a benefit, and, therefore, the refund is *not* taxable income when received.

If, in 2000, you itemized your deductions and had your itemized deductions scaled back due to a high adjusted gross income (AGI), generally your refund will be included in your income for 2001.

The amount of a refund that would be included in income in the year of receipt is the difference between (1) the prior year's reduced itemized deductions and (2) the reduced itemized deductions (or standard deduction, if greater) that you would have taken had you paid and deducted the proper amount in the first place and received a later refund or recovery.

Example

Tracy had $528,950 of AGI in 2000, paid $40,000 in state income taxes during 2000, and had no other itemized deductions. Tracy had $12,000 of itemized deductions disallowed (3% × $400,000). She received a $5,000 state tax refund in 2001. If Tracy had only paid in the correct $35,000 of state taxes in 2000, she would still have had $12,000 in itemized deductions disallowed. She received a tax benefit to the extent of the $5,000 difference between her $28,000 deduction ($40,000 less $12,000) for 2000 and the $23,000 2000 deduction she would have claimed had she paid in the correct tax in 2000 ($35,000 less $12,000). Thus, the entire $5,000 state tax refund ($28,000 less $23,000) is includable in Tracy's 2001 income.

Standard deduction for earlier years. To determine if amounts recovered in 2001 must be included in your income, you must know the standard deduction for your filing status for the year the deduction was claimed. Standard deduction amounts for 2000, 1999, and 1998 are in Publication 525.

Explanation
The following table can be used as a reference to determine the amount of standard deduction allowed in previous years.

	2000	1999	1998
Single	4,400	4,300	4,250
Married filing jointly/qualifying widower	7,350	7,200	7,100
Married filing separately	3,675	3,600	3,550
Head of household	6,450	6,350	6,250

Example. You filed a joint return for 2000 with taxable income of $25,000. Your itemized deductions were $8,700. The standard deduction that you could have claimed was $7,350. In 2001 you recovered $2,400 of your 2000 itemized deductions. None of the recoveries were more than the actual deductions for 2000. Include $1,350 of the recoveries in your 2001 income. This is the smaller of your recoveries ($2,400) or the amount by which your itemized deductions were more than the standard deduction ($8,700 − 7,350 = $1,350).

Recovery limited to deduction. You do not include in your income any amount of your recovery that is more than the amount you deducted in the earlier year. The amount you include in your income is limited to the smaller of:

1) The amount deducted on Schedule A (Form 1040), or
2) The amount recovered.

Example. During 2000 you paid $1,700 for medical expenses. From this amount you subtracted $1,500, which was 7.5% of your adjusted gross income. Your actual medical expense deduction was $200. In 2001, you received a $500 reimbursement from your medical insurance for your 2000 expenses. The only amount of the $500 reimbursement that must be included in your income for 2001 is $200—the amount actually deducted.

Explanation
Sometimes you get some money back in a year after you paid and deducted it (e.g., a refund of state income tax or real estate tax). To the extent that you got a tax benefit in the earlier year, and *only* to that extent, you must include the refund in income.

Example
In 2001, Stan and Lori received a refund of $1,000 for real estate taxes they paid in 2000. In 2000, they had $8,000 of itemized deductions, all of which was from their real estate taxes. The 2000 standard deduction was $7,350. Because they only have to report the amount of the refund to the extent they received a tax benefit, in 2001, they would include $650 ($8,000 − $7,350) of the refund in income.

Other recoveries. See *Recoveries* in Publication 525 if:

1) You have recoveries of items other than itemized deductions, or
2) You received a recovery for an item for which you claimed a tax credit (other than investment credit or foreign tax credit) in a prior year.

Rents from Personal Property

If you rent out personal property, such as equipment or vehicles, how you report your income and expenses is generally determined by:

1) Whether or not the rental activity is a business, and
2) Whether or not the rental activity is conducted for profit.

Generally, if your primary purpose is income or profit and you are involved in the rental activity with continuity and regularity, your rental activity is a business. See Publication 535 for details on deducting expenses for both business and not-for-profit activities.

Reporting business income and expenses. If you are in the business of renting personal property, report your income and expenses on Schedule C or C-EZ (Form 1040). The form instructions have information on how to complete them.

Reporting nonbusiness income. If you are not in the business of renting personal property, report your rental income on line 21 of Form 1040. List the type and amount of the income on the dotted line to the left of the amount you report on line 21.

Reporting nonbusiness expenses. If you rent personal property for profit, include your rental expenses in the total amount you enter on line 32 of Form 1040. Also enter the amount and "PPR" on the dotted line to the left of line 32.

If you do not rent personal property for a profit, your deductions are limited and you cannot report a loss to offset other income. See *Activity not for profit,* under *Other Income,* later.

Repayments

If you had to repay an amount that you included in your income in an earlier year, you may be able to deduct the amount repaid from your income for the year in which you repaid it. Or, if the amount you repaid is more than $3,000, you may be able to take a credit against your tax for the year in which you repaid it. Generally, you can claim a deduction or credit only if the repayment qualifies as an expense or loss incurred in your trade or business or in a for-profit transaction.

Type of deduction. The type of deduction you are allowed in the year of repayment depends on the type of income you included in the earlier year. You generally deduct the repayment on the same form or schedule on which you previously reported it as income. For example, if you reported it as self-employment income, deduct it as a business expense on Schedule C or C-EZ (Form 1040) or Schedule F (Form 1040). If you reported it as a capital gain, deduct it as a capital loss on Schedule D (Form 1040). If you reported it as wages, unemployment compensation, or other nonbusiness income, deduct it as a miscellaneous itemized deduction on Schedule A (Form 1040).

Repayment—$3,000 or less. If the amount you repaid was $3,000 or less, deduct it from your income in the year you repaid it. If you must deduct it as a miscellaneous itemized deduction, enter it on line 22 of Schedule A (Form 1040).

Repayment—over $3,000. If the amount you repaid was more than $3,000, you can deduct the repayment, as described earlier. However, you can instead choose to take a tax credit for the year of repayment if you included the income under a *claim of right.* This means that at the time you included the income, it appeared that you had an unrestricted right to it. If you qualify for this choice, figure your tax under both methods and compare the results. Use the method (deduction or credit) that results in less tax.

Method 1. Figure your tax for 2001 claiming a deduction for the repaid amount. If you must deduct it as a miscellaneous itemized deduction, enter it on line 27 of Schedule A (Form 1040).

Method 2. Figure your tax for 2001 claiming a credit for the repaid amount. Follow these steps.

1) Figure your tax for 2001 *without* deducting the repaid amount.
2) Refigure your tax from the earlier year without including in income the amount you repaid in 2001.

3) Subtract the tax in (2) from the tax shown on your return for the earlier year. This is the credit.
4) Subtract the answer in (3) from the tax for 2001 figured without the deduction (Step 1).

If method 1 results in less tax, deduct the amount repaid. If method 2 results in less tax, claim a credit for the amount repaid on line 65 of Form 1040, and write "I.R.C. 1341" next to line 65.

An example of this computation can be found in Publication 525.

Example

For tax year 2000, you were married with no dependents. You filed a joint return with your spouse and reported taxable income of $90,000 (after all deductions and exemptions). Your return showed a tax liability of $19,500, which you paid. In 2001, you had to return $5,000 that you had received and had included in your 2000 gross income. Your marital and filing statuses were the same in 2001 as in 2000, and your taxable income for 2001 is $115,000 (after all deductions and exemptions).

To determine how to treat the repayment on your 2001 return, the following calculations must be performed.

Method 1

	2001 taxable income	$115,000
	Less: Deduction for repayment	(5,000)
	Revised 2001 taxable income	$110,000
	Tax using method 1	**$24,947**

Method 2

	2001 taxable income	$115,000
	Recomputed 2001 tax liability	$ 26,496
(a)	2000 taxable income as previously reported	$ 90,000
	Less: Deduction for repayment	(5,000)
	2000 taxable income w/out repayment	$ 85,000
	Recomputed 2000 tax liability	$ 18,100
(b)	2000 tax as reported	$ 19,500
	Recomputed 2000 tax liability (w/out repayment)	(18,100)
	Difference	$ 1,400
(c)	Recomputed 2001 tax liability	$ 26,496
	Difference from (b)	(1,400)
	Tax using method 2	**$ 25,096**

To determine which method should be used to account for your repayment in 2001, you must now compare the two methods and choose the one that generates the lower tax liability. In the above example, method 1 generates the lesser tax liability; therefore, you would deduct the $5,000 repayment on your 2001 tax return.

Note that these two methods will only result in different tax liabilities if you fall into different marginal tax brackets in each year (e.g., in 2000, you are in the 28% marginal tax bracket and in 2001, you are in the 31% tax bracket).

Repaid social security benefits. If you repaid social security benefits, see *Repayment of benefits* in chapter 12.

Royalties

Royalties from copyrights, patents, and oil, gas, and mineral properties are taxable as ordinary income.

You generally report royalties in Part 1 of Schedule E (Form 1040). However, if you hold an operating oil, gas, or mineral interest or are in business as a self-employed writer, inventor, artist, etc., report your income and expenses on Schedule C or Schedule C-EZ (Form 1040).

Copyrights and patents. Royalties from copyrights on literary, musical, or artistic works, and similar property, or from patents on inventions, are amounts paid to you for the right to use your work over a specified period of time. Royalties are generally based on the number of units sold, such as the number of books, tickets to a performance, or machines sold.

Oil, gas, and minerals. Royalty income from oil, gas, and mineral properties is the amount you receive when natural resources are extracted from your property. The royalties are based on units, such as barrels, tons, etc., and are paid to you by a person or company who leases the property from you.

Explanation

Income from a working interest in an oil or gas property is reported on Schedule C and is generally subject to self-employment tax, even though you may not actively participate in the operations that produce the income. Such income, however, is not eligible for Individual Retirement Arrangement (IRA) or Keogh plan contributions, because it is not earned by personal services you performed.

Depletion. If you are the owner of an economic interest in mineral deposits or oil and gas wells, you can recover your investment through the depletion allowance. For information on this subject, see chapter 10 of Publication 535, *Business Expenses.*

Explanation

Two methods are used to compute the depletion allowance: cost depletion and percentage depletion.

Each year, you must compute the depletion allowance using both methods and use the method that results in a greater deduction. No matter which method is used, you must reduce your basis in the property by the amount of allowance that is claimed each year. Once your basis has been reduced to zero, then the percentage method will be used until the property is sold or is no longer producing.

Cost depletion. A report will be issued each year showing the number of units produced during the year and the revised number of units that are left to be extracted. You can add the number of units produced to the number of units left to be extracted at the end of the year to obtain your total number of units for the beginning of the year. Many reports contain units shown as both barrels and MCFs (1,000 cubic feet of gas). The MCF units will need to be converted to barrels in order to compute the cost depletion allowance. The conversion rate is 6 MCFs = 1 barrel. After determining the number of units left to be extracted at the beginning of the year, then divide that number into your adjusted basis in the property at the beginning of the year. This gives you your cost per unit.

Your current depletion deduction is computed by multiplying the cost per unit by the number of units extracted and sold during that year. Your basis will be reduced by the amount of depletion deducted each year. Once your basis has been reduced to zero, you may no longer claim cost depletion.

Percentage depletion. To compute the percentage depletion allowance, you take a percentage of the gross income from the property. Different percentage rates are specified for different types of property. (Timber is excluded from this method.) Percentage depletion is limited to 50% (100% in the case of oil and gas properties, except properties qualifying for marginal production depletion that have no net income limitation) of the income from the property, computed before the deduction for depletion. Additionally, percentage depletion is limited to 65% of the taxpayer's total taxable income, computed without any deduction for percentage depletion, net operating loss carryback, or capital loss carryback. Any part of the percentage depletion allowance disallowed because of the 65% limitation may be carried over into future years. Unlike cost depletion, you may claim percentage depletion even though your basis in the property has been reduced to zero. If cost depletion results in a greater deduction than percentage depletion on a property-by-property comparison, then cost depletion must be taken on that property.

Example

A small independent producer of crude oil invests $1 million to lease a well. Her geologists estimate that the well will yield 1 million barrels of oil. During 2001, she pumped 7,500 barrels of oil and sold 6,000 of them at $30 per barrel. The oil cost $15 per barrel to produce.

The permissible rate for percentage depletion for an independent producer of crude oil is 15%, unless the property qualifies as marginal production property. Marginal production depletion rates are set by the IRS and are based on the prior year's average oil price. For 2001, the marginal production depletion rate was 15%. The independent oil producer computes her depletion allowance as follows:

Cost Depletion Method

Cost depletion:	
Depletable cost per unit ($1,000,000 ÷ 1,000,000 = $1)	
Cost depletion (6,000 × $1)	$6,000

Percentage Depletion Method

Sales (6,000 × $30)		$180,000
Less: Production costs (6,000 × $15)		90,000
Income		$ 90,000
Gross income from property	$180,000	
Percentage depletion ($180,000 × 15%)	$ 27,000	(A)
Limitation (100% of the $90,000 income computed above from the property, except for properties qualifying for marginal prodution depletion that do not have net income limits for years beginning after December 31, 1997, and before January 1, 2002)	$ 90,000	(B)
Percentage depletion, lesser of A or B	$ 27,000	

Because percentage depletion is more advantageous than cost depletion, the independent oil producer must use percentage depletion on her oil well. However, there is a further limitation—percentage depletion may not exceed 65% of taxable income computed without depletion. Please consult your tax advisor.

Adjusted Cost Basis at 12/31/2001	
Original cost basis	$1,000,000
Less: Depletion deduction	(27,000)
Adjusted basis (use for cost)	$ 973,000

Coal and iron ore. Under certain circumstances, you can treat amounts you receive from the disposal of coal and iron ore as payments from the sale of a capital asset, rather than as royalty income. For information about gain or loss from the sale of coal and iron ore, get Publication 544.

Sale of property interest. If you sell your complete interest in oil, gas, or mineral rights, the amount you receive is considered payment for the sale of section 1231 property, not royalty income. Under certain circumstances, the sale is subject to capital gain or loss treatment on Schedule D (Form 1040). For more information on selling section 1231 property, see chapter 3 of Publication 544. If you retain a royalty, an overriding royalty, or a net profit interest in a mineral property for the life of the property, you have made a lease or a sublease, and any cash you receive for the assignment of other interests in the property is ordinary income subject to a depletion allowance.

Explanation

The sale of most items producing royalty income is treated as a capital transaction. However, this is not true for copyrights and other property created by your personal efforts. The purpose of this exception is to prevent people such as authors from receiving capital gain treatment for their literary efforts. For more information, see Chapter 15, *Sale of Property.*

Part of future production sold. If you own mineral property but sell part of the future production, you generally treat the money you receive from the buyer at the time of the sale as a loan from the buyer. Do not include it in your income or take depletion based on it.

When production begins, you include all the proceeds in your income, deduct all the production expenses, and deduct depletion from that amount to arrive at your taxable income from the property.

Explanation

If you are paid royalties or bonuses for the production of oil before production actually begins, you may qualify for a depletion allowance in the year in which the advance royalty or bonus is included in your income. You should consult your tax advisor for further clarification of this point.

Unemployment Benefits

The tax treatment of unemployment benefits you receive depends on the type of program paying the benefits.

Unemployment compensation. You must include in your income all unemployment compensation you receive. You should receive a Form 1099-G, *Certain Government and Qualified State Tuition Program Payments,* showing the amount paid to you. Generally, you enter unemployment compensation on line 19 of Form 1040, line 13 of Form 1040A, or line 3 of Form 1040EZ.

Types of unemployment compensation. Unemployment compensation generally includes any amount received under an unemployment compensation law of the United States or of a state. It includes the following benefits.

- Benefits paid by a state or the District of Columbia from the Federal Unemployment Trust Fund.
- State unemployment insurance benefits.
- Railroad unemployment compensation benefits.
- Disability payments from a government program paid as a *substitute* for unemployment compensation. (Amounts received as workers' compensation for injuries or illness are *not* unemployment compensation. See chapter 6 for more information.)
- Trade readjustment allowances under the Trade Act of 1974.
- Benefits under the Airline Deregulation Act of 1978.
- Unemployment assistance under the Disaster Relief Act Amendments of 1974.

Government program. If you contribute to a governmental unemployment compensation program and your contributions are not deductible, amounts you receive under the program are not included as unemployment compensation until you recover your contributions.

Repayment of unemployment compensation. If you repaid in 2001 unemployment compensation you received in 2001, subtract the amount you repaid from the total amount you received and enter the difference on line 19 of Form 1040, line 13 of Form 1040A, or line 3 of Form 1040EZ. On the dotted line next to your entry write "Repaid" and the amount you repaid. If you repaid unemployment compensation in 2001 that you included in income in an earlier year, you can deduct the amount repaid on Schedule A (Form 1040) if you itemize deductions. For more information, see *Repayments,* earlier.

Tax withholding. You can choose to have federal income tax withheld from your unemployment compensation. To make this choice, complete Form W-4V, *Voluntary Withholding Request,* and give it to the paying office. Tax will be withheld at 15% of your payment.

Caution. *If you do not choose to have tax withheld from your unemployment compensation, you may be liable for estimated tax. For more information on estimated tax, see chapter 5.*

Supplemental unemployment benefits. Benefits received from an employer-financed fund (to which the employees did not contribute) are not unemployment compensation. They are taxable as wages and are subject to withholding for income tax and social security and Medicare taxes. Report these payments on line 7 of Form 1040 or Form 1040A or on line 1 of Form 1040EZ.

Repayment of benefits. You may have to repay some of your supplemental unemployment benefits to qualify for trade readjustment allowances under the Trade Act of 1974. If you repay supplemental unemployment benefits in the same year you receive them, reduce the total benefits by the amount you repay. If you repay the benefits in a later year, you must include the full amount of the benefits received in your income for the year you received them.

Deduct the repayment in the later year as an adjustment to gross income on Form 1040. (You cannot use Form 1040A or Form 1040EZ.) Include the repayment on line 32 of Form 1040, and write "Sub-Pay TRA" and the amount on the dotted line next to line 32. If the amount you repay in a later year is more than $3,000, you may be able to take a credit against your tax for the later year instead of deducting the amount repaid. For more information on this, see *Repayments,* earlier.

Private unemployment fund. Unemployment benefit payments from a private fund to which you voluntarily contribute are taxable only if the amounts you receive are more than your total payments into the fund. Report the taxable amount on line 21 of Form 1040.

Payments by a union. Benefits paid to you as an unemployed member of a union from regular union dues are included in your gross income on line 21 of Form 1040.

Guaranteed annual wage. Payments you receive from your employer during periods of unemployment, under a union agreement that guarantees you full pay during the year, are taxable as wages. Include them on line 7 of Form 1040 or Form 1040A or on line 1 of Form 1040EZ.

State employees. Payments similar to a state's unemployment compensation may be made by the state to its employees who are not covered by the state's unemployment compensation law. Although the payments are fully taxable, do not report them as unemployment compensation. Report these payments on line 21 of Form 1040.

Welfare and Other Public Assistance Benefits

Do not include in your income benefit payments from a public welfare fund, such as payments due to blindness. Payments from a state fund for the victims of crime should not be included in the victims' incomes if they are in the nature of welfare payments. Do not deduct medical expenses that are reimbursed by such a fund. You must include in your income any welfare payments obtained fraudulently.

Alaska residents. Payments the state of Alaska makes to its citizens who meet certain age and residency tests that are not based on need are not welfare benefits. Include them in income on line 21 of Form 1040.

Persons with disabilities. If you have a disability, you must include in income compensation you receive for services you perform unless the compensation is otherwise excluded. However, you do not include in income the value of goods, services, and cash that you receive, not in return for your services, but for your training and rehabilitation because you have a disability. Excludable amounts include payments for transportation and attendant care, such as interpreter services for the deaf, reader services for the blind, and services to help mentally retarded persons do their work.

Disaster relief grants. Grants made under the Disaster Relief Act of 1974 to help victims of natural disasters are not included in income. Do not deduct casualty losses or medical expenses that are specifically reimbursed by these disaster relief grants. Unemployment assistance payments under the Act are taxable unemployment compensation. See *Unemployment compensation,* earlier.

Mortgage assistance payments. Payments made under section 235 of the National Housing Act for mortgage assistance are not included in the homeowner's income. Interest paid for the homeowner under the mortgage assistance program cannot be deducted.

Nutrition Program for the Elderly. Food benefits you receive under the Nutrition Program for the Elderly are not taxable. If you prepare and serve free meals for the program, include in your income as wages the cash pay you receive, even if you are also eligible for food benefits.

Payments to reduce cost of winter energy. Payments made by a state to qualified people to reduce their cost of winter energy use are not taxable.

Explanation

Other Sickness and Injury Benefits

In addition to welfare or insurance benefits, you may receive other payments for sickness or injury. Table 13–1 gives a general overview of some of these payments.

Workers' compensation. Amounts you receive as workers' compensation for an occupational sickness or injury are fully exempt from tax if they are paid under a workers' compensation act or a statute in the nature of a workers' compensation act. The exemption also applies to your survivor(s). The exemption from tax, however, does not apply to retirement benefits you receive based on your age, length of service, or prior contributions to the plan, even if you retired because of occupational sickness or injury.

Note. If part of your workers' compensation reduces your Social Security or equivalent railroad retirement benefits received, that part is considered Social Security (or equivalent railroad retirement) benefits and may be taxable. For more information, see Publication 915, *Social Security and Equivalent Railroad Retirement Benefits.*

Return to work. If you return to work after qualifying for workers' compensation, payments you continue to receive while assigned to light duties are taxable. Report these payments as wages on line 7 of Form 1040 or Form 1040A or on line 1 of Form 1040EZ.

Federal Employees' Compensation Act (FECA). Payments received under this Act for personal injury or sickness, including payments to beneficiaries in case of death, are not taxable. However, you are taxed on amounts you receive under this Act as "continuation of pay" for up to 45 days while a claim is being decided. Report this income on line 7 of Form 1040 or Form 1040A or on line 1 of Form 1040EZ. Also, pay for sick leave while a claim is being processed is taxable and must be included in your income as wages.

The IRS has ruled that the subsidized portion of health benefits provided by an employer to an employee's domestic partner, who does not qualify as a spouse or a dependent, will be taxable as wages to the employee.

You can deduct the amount you spend to "buy back" sick leave for an earlier year to be eligible for nontaxable FECA benefits for that period. It is a miscellaneous deduction subject to the 2% limit on Schedule A (Form 1040). If you buy back sick leave in the same year you use it, the amount reduces your taxable sick leave pay. Do not deduct it separately.

Other compensation. Many other amounts you receive as compensation for injury or illness are not taxable. These include:

- **Compensatory damages** you receive for physical injury or physical illness, whether paid in a lump sum or in periodic payments,
- **Benefits you receive under an accident or health insurance policy** on which either you paid the premiums or your employer paid the premiums but you had to include them in your gross income,
- **Disability benefits** you receive for loss of income or earning capacity as a result of injuries under a "no-fault" car insurance policy, and
- **Compensation you receive for permanent loss or loss of use** of a part or function of your body, or for your permanent disfigurement. This compensation must be based only on the injury and not on the period of your absence from work. These benefits are exempt from tax even if your employer pays for the accident and health plan that provides these benefits.

Only damages received on account of personal injury or sickness are nontaxable according to the Small Business Job Protection Act of 1996. Punitive damages will be taxable—other than those received in a wrongful death action where state law stipulates that they are nontaxable. This law is effective for amounts received after August 20, 1996, unless there was a binding settlement in effect on September 13, 1995.

Reimbursement for medical care. A reimbursement for medical care is generally not taxable. However, this reimbursement may reduce your medical expense deduction. For more information, see Chapter 23, *Medical and Dental Expenses.* See Table 13–1.

Other Income

The following brief discussions are arranged in alphabetical order. Income items that are discussed in greater detail in another publication include a reference to that publication.

Table 13–1. **Are Your Sickness and Injury Benefits Taxable?**

*This table is intended as a general overview. Additional rules may apply depending on your situation. For more information about your benefits, see **Other Sickness and Injury Benefits.***

Type of Benefit	General Rule
Workers' compensation	<u>Not taxable</u> if paid under a workers' compensation act or a statute in the nature of a workers' compensation act <u>and</u> paid due to a work-related sickness or injury. However, payments received after returning to work are <u>taxable</u>.
Federal Employees' Compensation Act (FECA)	<u>Not taxable</u> if paid because of personal injury or sickness. However, payments received as "continuation of pay" for up to 45 days while a claim is being decided and pay received for sick leave while a claim is being processed are <u>taxable</u>.
Compensatory damages	<u>Not taxable</u> if received for injury or sickness.
Accident or health insurance benefits	<u>Not taxable</u> if you paid the insurance premiums.
Disability benefits	<u>Not taxable</u> if received for loss of income or earning capacity due to an injury covered by a "no-fault" automobile policy.
Compensation for permanent loss or loss of use of a part or function of your body, or for permanent disfigurement	<u>Not taxable</u> if paid due to the injury. The payments must be figured without regard to any period of absence from work.
Reimbursements for medical care	<u>Not taxable</u>—but the reimbursement may reduce your medical expense deduction.

Activity not for profit. You must include on your return income from an activity from which you do not expect to make a profit. An example of this type of activity is a hobby or a farm you operate mostly for recreation and pleasure. Enter this income on line 21 of Form 1040. Deductions for expenses related to the activity are limited. They cannot total more than the income you report and can be taken only if you itemize deductions on Schedule A (Form 1040). See *Not-for-Profit Activities* in chapter 1 of Publication 535 for information on whether an activity is considered carried on for a profit.

Explanation

An activity will be presumed to have been for profit if it results in a profit in at least 3 out of 5 consecutive tax years whether the activity is held individually, in trust, as a partnership, or as an S corporation. However, for the breeding, training, showing, or racing of horses, the activity must result in a profit in at least 2 out of 7 consecutive tax years. If the activity meets this test, it is presumed to be carried on for profit and the limits will not apply.

If you have engaged in an activity for less than 3 years, you can postpone the determination that the activity is not for profit by filing Form 5213, *Election to Postpone Determination*. Get Publication 535, *Business Expenses*, for more information.

It is possible that the IRS may treat you as engaged in a profit-making activity, even if you do not have a profit for 3 or more years during a period of 5 consecutive tax years. The IRS determines the activity's status—for profit or as a hobby—by considering the facts and circumstances surrounding the case. Some factors that will be considered include the following:

1. The manner in which you carry on the activity. For example, do you conduct your actions in a businesslike manner (records, activity details, separate bank accounts, etc.)?
2. The expertise possessed by you and your advisors
3. The time and effort you expend in carrying on the activity
4. Any expectation you have that assets used in the activity may appreciate in value
5. Prior success in similar or dissimilar activities
6. Your history of income or loss with respect to the activity
7. The amount of occasional profits, if any, that you earn through the activity
8. Your financial status. For example, the fact that you do not have substantial income from other sources may indicate that you are engaging in the activity for profit
9. Elements of personal pleasure or recreation

These factors are not exclusive, and no one factor or number of factors is determinative.

TaxPlanner

If an activity does show a profit for any 3 of 5 consecutive years (2 of 7 years for horse farms), there is a presumption by law that you are engaged in the activity for profit. The IRS has the burden of proving that the activity is only a hobby. However, if you do not meet the 3-year test and the IRS determines that the activity is a hobby, then you have the burden of proving your profit motive.

You would normally not file Form 5213, *Election to Postpone Determination with Respect to the Presumption That an Activity Is Engaged in for Profit,* until the IRS has examined records from one of the early years in which you engaged in the activity and has concluded that it is a hobby. Then, to prevent the IRS from assessing a tax on the years under examination, you should file Form 5213.

However, by filing the form, you agree to extend the period for which the IRS may collect additional taxes by disallowing the losses until 2 years after the examination period is over.

Also, by filing, you virtually guarantee that the IRS will carefully examine all years during the period under examination. Because the IRS previously concluded that the activity is a hobby, it is almost certain to reach the same conclusion again.

Advance payment of the rate reduction credit. If you received a check from the IRS during 2001 for the advance payment of the rate reduction credit, do not report it on your tax return. It is not taxable. For more information about the rate reduction credit, see chapter 38.

Alaska Permanent Fund dividend income. If you received a payment from Alaska's mineral income fund (Alaska Permanent Fund dividend), report it as income on line 21 of Form 1040, line 13 of Form 1040A, or line 3 of Form 1040EZ. The state of Alaska sends each recipient a document that shows the amount of the payment with the check. The amount is also reported to IRS.

Alimony. Include in your income on line 11 of Form 1040 any alimony payments you receive. Amounts you receive for child support are not income to you. Alimony and child support payments are discussed in chapter 20.

TaxPlanner

While alimony payments you receive are taxable, property settlements arising out of divorce are not. You should bear this in mind when considering the tax consequences of a divorce. See Chapter 20, *Alimony,* for more details.

TaxSaver

Receipt of alimony payments is considered compensation for purposes of making an IRA contribution. See Chapter 18, *Individual Retirement Arrangements and Education Savings Accounts,* for more details.

Campaign contributions. These contributions are not income to a candidate unless they are diverted to his or her personal use. To be exempt from tax, the contributions must be spent for campaign purposes or kept in a fund for use in future campaigns. However, interest earned on bank deposits, dividends received on contributed securities, and net gains realized on sales of contributed securities are taxable and must be reported on Form 1120-POL, *U.S. Income Tax Return for Certain Political Organizations.* Excess campaign funds transferred to an office account must be included in the officeholder's income on line 21 of Form 1040 in the year transferred.

Cash rebates. A cash rebate you receive from a dealer or manufacturer of an item you buy is not income.

Example. You buy a new car for $9,000 cash and receive a $400 rebate check from the manufacturer. The $400 is not income to you. Your cost is $8,600. This is your basis on which you figure gain or loss if you sell the car, and depreciation if you use it for business.

Explanation

The IRS realistically views rebates as another way of offering a price reduction to induce you to buy a product. Similarly, the dividends that a life insurance company pays you are a reduction of your premium rather than an addition to your gross income.

Casualty insurance and other reimbursements. You generally should not report these reimbursements on your return. Get Publication 547, *Casualties, Disasters, and Thefts,* for more information.

Child support payments. You should not report these payments on your return. Get Publication 504, *Divorced or Separated Individuals,* for more information.

Court awards and damages. To determine if settlement amounts you receive by compromise or judgment must be included in your income, you must consider the item that the settlement replaces. Include the following as ordinary income.

1) Interest on any award.
2) Compensation for lost wages or lost profits in most cases.
3) Punitive damages. It does not matter if they relate to a physical injury or physical sickness.
4) Amounts received in settlement of pension rights (if you did not contribute to the plan).
5) Damages for:
   a) Patent or copyright infringement,
   b) Breach of contract, or
   c) Interference with business operations.
6) Back pay and damages for emotional distress received to satisfy a claim under Title VII of the Civil Rights Act of 1964.

Do not include in your income compensatory damages for personal physical injury or physical sickness (whether received in a lump sum or installments).

Explanation

Compensation from a discrimination lawsuit and compensation damages awarded from an Employee Retirement and Income Security Act lawsuit are generally included in your income.

Emotional distress. Damages you receive for emotional distress due to a physical injury or sickness are treated as received for the physical injury or sickness. Do not include them in your income. If the emotional distress is due to a personal injury that is unrelated to a physical injury or sickness (for example, employment discrimination or injury to reputation), you must include the damages in your income, except for any damages you receive for medical care due to that emotional distress. Emotional distress includes physical symptoms that result from emotional distress, such as headaches, insomnia, and stomach disorders.

Explanation

Only damages received on account of personal injury or sickness are nontaxable according to the Small Business Job Protection Act of 1996. Punitive damages will be taxable, unless they are received in a wrongful death action in which state law stipulates that they are nontaxable. This law is effective for amounts received after August 20, 1996, unless there was a binding settlement in effect on September 13, 1995.

TAXSAVER

The legal expense that you incur in the process of getting a damage award may be claimed as an itemized deduction (subject to the 2%-of-AGI floor) only if the award is included in your gross income. If the award is only partially included in your gross income, you may deduct only a proportional amount in legal fees. Thus, if the entire award is excluded from your gross income, none of your legal fees are deductible.

TAXSAVER

A technique now being used in large personal injury cases is the so-called structured settlement, in which the defendant's insurance company offers an **annuity** to the injured party instead of a **lump-sum distribution.** The IRS has ruled that the entire amount of the annuity payments may be excluded from the recipient's gross income, even though the recipient is, in effect, receiving interest.

Credit card insurance. Generally, if you receive benefits under a credit card disability or unemployment insurance plan, the benefits are taxable to you. These plans make the minimum monthly payment on your credit card account if you cannot make the payment due to injury, illness, disability, or unemployment. Report on line 21 of Form 1040 the amount of benefits you received during the year that is more than the amount of the premiums you paid during the year.

Energy conservation subsidies. You can exclude from gross income any subsidy provided, either directly or indirectly, by public utilities for the purchase or installation of an energy conservation measure for a dwelling unit.

Energy conservation measure. This includes installations or modifications that are primarily designed to reduce consumption of electricity or natural gas, or improve the management of energy demand.

Dwelling unit. This includes a house, apartment, condominium, mobile home, boat, or similar property. If a building or structure contains both dwelling and other units, any subsidy must be properly allocated.

Estate and trust income. An estate or trust, unlike a partnership, may have to pay federal income tax. If you are a beneficiary of an estate or trust, you may be taxed on your share of its income distributed or required to be distributed to you. However, there is never a double tax. Estates and trusts file their returns on Form 1041, *U.S. Income Tax Return for Estates and Trusts,* and your share of the income is reported to you on Schedule K-1 of Form 1041.

Explanation

Generally speaking, there are three types of trusts: (1) a trust that is required to distribute all the income it earns during the year (simple trust), (2) a trust that has the choice of whether to distribute all, part, or none of the income (complex trust), and (3) a trust where the person creating the trust is treated as the owner of the trust's assets (grantor

trust). The taxability of these trusts varies. A beneficiary of a simple trust must report all the income (though generally not capital gains), whether actually distributed or not, on his or her income tax return (Form 1040). A beneficiary of a complex trust will only report the income of the trust to the extent of distributions actually made by the trust to the beneficiary. A beneficiary of a grantor trust must report all income, gains, and deductions on the beneficiary's return, as they are not taxed on a trust return.

Current income required to be distributed. If you are the beneficiary of a trust that must distribute all of its current income, you must report your share of the distributable net income, whether or not you have actually received it.

Example

A beneficiary of a trust that is required to distribute all of its current income receives a Schedule K-1 reporting $100 of interest income. However, the beneficiary has not received any distributions from the trust. The beneficiary must report the $100 of interest income on Schedule B of Form 1040 even though the beneficiary has not received any distributions.

Current income not required to be distributed. If you are the beneficiary of an estate or trust and the fiduciary has the choice of whether to distribute all or part of the current income, you must report:

1) All income that is required to be distributed to, whether or not it is actually distributed, plus
2) All other amounts actually paid or credited to you,

up to the amount of your share of distributable net income.

Explanation

When an estate earns income before the assets have all been distributed, it is taxed like a complex trust. Many people find this area of estate taxation very confusing, and for good reason. Gifts and inheritances are not gross income to the recipient. However, money or property that you inherit may earn some interest, dividends, or rent while the estate is being settled. It is that income that must be reported either by you or by the estate. Ordinarily, the executor of the estate files an income tax return for the estate, reporting the income, but he or she may shift the tax burden of that income to the beneficiaries if the property has already been distributed to them. See Chapter 4, *Decedents,* for more detail.

TAXALERT

In some instances, adjustments for the alternative minimum tax could flow through a trust to the beneficiary. See Chapter 31, *How to Figure Your Tax,* for more details.

How to report. Treat each item of income the same way that the estate or trust would treat it. For example, if a trust's dividend income is distributed to you, you report the distribution as dividend income on your return. The same rule applies to distributions of tax-exempt interest and capital gains.

The fiduciary of the estate or trust must tell you the type of items making up your share of the estate or trust income and any credits you are allowed on your individual income tax return.

Losses. Losses of estates and trust generally are not deductible by the beneficiaries.

Exception

There are significant exceptions to the rule that losses of estates and trusts are not deductible by the beneficiaries. When an estate or a trust terminates, the beneficiaries are frequently allowed a deduction for certain expenses that the estate or trust had but was unable to use as a deduction. These items are (1) net operating loss carryovers, (2) certain excess deductions in the year of termination, and (3) capital loss carryovers.

When an estate is terminated, it is not unusual for the attorney's and executor's fees to be paid in the year in which the estate is closed. If such expenses and the net operating loss carryover exceed the estate's income for that year, the excess is deductible by the beneficiaries. This deduction may be claimed only by itemizing deductions on Schedule A (Form 1040). These deductions are subject to the 2% rule on miscellaneous itemized deductions. This means that they are only deductible to the extent that total miscellaneous itemized deductions exceed 2% of AGI.

A capital loss carryover from an estate or a trust may be used in the beneficiaries' current or subsequent returns to reduce capital gains and/or to generate a deduction subject to the limitation that only $3,000 of capital losses in excess of capital gains may be deducted each year.

When to report estate and trust income. You must include your share of the estate or trust income on your return for your tax year in which the last day of the estate or trust tax year falls.

The trustee of the trust or estate will provide you with a Form K-1 that tells you each item of income and deductions, and where they are to be reported on your personal tax return.

TaxSaver

It may be a good idea if you are the beneficiary of a trust to inform the trustee of your tax situation so that all possible tax-saving alternatives can be explored. Amounts that are *not* required to be distributed currently, according to the terms of the trust, may sometimes be distributed at the discretion of the trustee. There may be substantial tax advantages to the timing, amounts, and methods of such distributions. You and the trustee should consult with a professional who specializes in this area.

TaxPlanner

If you are receiving trust income, you should consider if it is necessary for you to make estimated tax payments or increase your withholding taxes as a result of this additional income. See Chapter 5, *Tax Withholding and Estimated Tax.*

Grantor trust. Income earned by a grantor trust is taxable to the grantor, not the beneficiary, if the grantor keeps certain control over the trust. (The grantor is the one who transferred property to the trust.) This rule applies if the property (or income from the property) put into the trust will or may revert (be returned) to the grantor or the grantor's spouse.

Generally, a trust is a grantor trust if the grantor has a reversionary interest valued (at the date of transfer) at more than 5% of the value of the transferred property.

TaxAlert

Even though the grantor is taxed on the trust income, the trustee of a grantor trust may need to file Form 1041 if the trust income reaches a level that requires a return. The items of income, deduction, and credit are treated as owned by the grantor, or another person, and are reported on a separate statement that is attached to Form 1041.

The IRS issued final regulations during 1996 that provide guidance for optional methods of reporting trust income by a grantor trust. For example, alternative methods of reporting include the issuance of a Form 1099 directly from the payer of income to the grantor for inclusion on the grantor's individual tax return; the issuance of a Form 1099 by the trust to the grantor; or the filing of a Form 1041 by the trustee of the grantor trust.

The rules can get complicated, especially if there is more than one grantor. You should consult with your tax advisor for more information.

Fees for services. Include all fees for your services in your income. Examples of these fees are amounts you receive for services you perform as:

1) A corporate director,
2) An executor or administrator of an estate,
3) A notary public, or
4) An election precinct official.

Nonemployee compensation. If you are *not an employee* and the fees for your services from the same payer total $600 or more for the year, you may receive a Form 1099-MISC. You may need to report your fees as self-employment income. See *Self-Employed Persons,* in chapter 1, for a discussion of when you are considered self-employed.

Corporate director. Corporate director fees are self-employment income. Report these payments on Schedule C (Form 1040) or Schedule C-EZ (Form 1040).

Executor or administrator of an estate. If you are not in the trade or business of being an executor (for instance, you are the executor of a friend's or relative's estate), report these fees on line 21 of Form 1040. If you provide the services as a trade or business, report them as self-employment income on Schedule C (Form 1040) or Schedule C-EZ (Form 1040).

Notary public. Report payments for these services on Schedule C (Form 1040) or Schedule C-EZ (Form 1040). These payments are *not* subject to self-employment tax. (See the separate instructions for Schedule C (Form 1040) for details.)

Election precinct official. You should receive a Form W-2 showing payments for services performed as an election official or election worker. Report these payments on line 7 of Form 1040 or Form 1040A, or on line 1 of Form 1040EZ.

Explanation

Self-employment income. Chapter 38, *If You Are Self-Employed,* includes a more comprehensive discussion of self-employment income.

Corporate director fees and executor fees (if you are in the trade or business of being an executor) are considered self-employment income. For both employees and self-employed individuals, the 2001 wage base is $80,400 for Old Age, Survivor, and Disability Insurance (OASDI) and is unlimited for Medicare. The OASDI rate is 12.4% and the Medicare rate is 2.9%. These rates are applied to 92.35% of your self-employment income. Thus, if a person earns self-employment income of $100,000, he or she will pay self-employment tax of $12,648 [i.e., ($80,400 × 15.3%) plus [($100,000 × 92.35%) − $80,400] × 2.9%]; see Schedule SE. However, if your net earnings from self-employment are less than $400, no self-employment tax is payable.

Fees are self-employment income only if you present yourself as being in the trade or business that produces the fees. Therefore, unless you *regularly* appear as a witness, act as an executor or trustee, or judge elections, the fees earned will not be self-employment income subject to self-employment tax.

Clergy fees. Fees received by clergy for performing funerals, marriages, baptisms, or other services must be included in gross income.

TaxSaver

A member of the clergy, however, can request to be exempt from the self-employment tax on such income by filing Form 4361, *Application for Exemption from Self-Employment Tax for Use by Ministers, Members of Religious Orders, and Christian Science Practitioners.*

TaxPlanner

Any business that pays you more than $600 in fees should provide you with a Form 1099. A copy of this form should also be filed with the IRS by the business. Individual payers are not required to file this form. However, you are not excused from your responsibility to report the income just because you do not receive a Form 1099.

Professional fees. Fees received by a doctor, lawyer, and so on should be shown on Schedule C, Profit or Loss from Business, *not* in the Miscellaneous Income section on line 21 of Form 1040. Otherwise, the IRS's document-matching program may generate unwarranted notices, suggesting that you have underpaid your tax.

Explanation

Sole proprietorship (self-employment) income. Unlike a partnership or a regular corporation, a sole proprietorship is not a separate entity. In a sole proprietorship, you and your business are one and the same. You report gross profit or loss for the year from the sole proprietorship on Form 1040, Schedule C (or Schedule C-EZ if you meet certain requirements), and it becomes part of your AGI. In addition to owing income tax on such income, you, as the sole proprietor, will usually be liable for self-employment tax, and you may also be required to make payments of estimated taxes. In order to avoid a penalty for underpayment of estimated taxes, you must make estimated tax payments for 2002 if you expect to owe at least $1,000 in tax for 2002 after subtracting your withholding and credits, and you expect your withholding and credits to be less than the smaller of:

1) 90% of the tax to be shown on your 2002 tax return, or
2) 100% of the tax shown on your 2001 tax return (or 112% if your 2001 AGI exceeds $150,000). See Chapter 5, *Tax Withholding and Estimated Tax.*

A net loss from the business can generally be deducted in computing your AGI.

Your profit (or loss) is computed as income less your allowable deductions. Income includes cash, property, and services received by the business from all sources, unless specifically excluded under the tax code. Allowable deductions include all necessary and ordinary expenses incurred in connection with the business. For sole proprietorships in the business of selling goods or inventory, the primary expense will be the cost of goods sold. The cost of goods sold represents the cost of materials, labor, and overhead included in the inventory sold during the year. Other expenses that you deduct on Schedule C include salaries and wages, interest on loans used in the business, rent, depreciation, bad debts, travel and entertainment, insurance, real estate taxes, and so on.

If you operate your own business or have other self-employment income, such as babysitting or selling crafts, see these other publications for more information.

- Publication 334, *Tax Guide for Small Business*
- Publication 535, *Business Expenses*
- Publication 533, *Self-Employment Tax*

TaxSaver

Note: If you receive fees that are self-employment income, you may contribute to a **Keogh plan, Simplified Employee Plan IRA, or SIMPLE IRA.** See Chapter 18, *Individual Retirement Arrangements and Education Savings Accounts,* for details.

Foster-care providers. Payments you receive from a state, political subdivision, or tax-exempt child-placement agency for providing care to qualified foster individuals in your home generally are not included in your income. However, you must include in your income payments received for the care of more than 5 individuals age 19 or older and certain difficulty-of-care payments.

A qualified foster individual is a person who:

1) Is living in a foster family home, and
2) Was placed there by:
   a) An agency of a state or one of its political subdivisions, or
   b) If the individual is under age 19, a tax-exempt child placement agency licensed by a state or one of its political subdivisions.

TaxPlanner

If a foster child lives with you in your home for the entire year, you are entitled to claim the child as a dependent if you provide more than half of his or her support. This is often the case when you care for the children of relatives. By claiming the child as a dependent, you may receive an additional exemption of $2,900 for 2001. Thus, it may be worthwhile for you to calculate whether you are in fact providing more than half the child's support. (See Chapter 33, *Child and Dependent Care Credit,* for details.)

Difficulty-of-care payments. These are additional payments that are designated by the payer as compensation for providing the additional care that is required for physically, mentally, or emotionally handicapped qualified foster individuals. A state must determine that the additional compensation is needed, and the care for which the payments are made must be provided in your home.

You must include in your income difficulty-of-care payments received for more than:

1) 10 qualified foster individuals under age 19, or
2) 5 qualified foster individuals age 19 or older.

Maintaining space in home. If you are paid to maintain space in your home for emergency foster care, you must include the payment in your income.

Reporting taxable payments. If you receive payments that you must include in your income, you are in business as a foster-care provider and you are self-employed. Report the payments on Schedule C or Schedule C-EZ (Form 1040). Get Publication 587, *Business Use of Your Home (Including Use by Day-Care Providers),* to help you determine the amount you can deduct for the use of your home.

Free tour. If you received a free tour from a travel agency for organizing a group of tourists, you must include its value in your income. Report the fair market value of the tour on line 21 of Form 1040 if you are not in the trade or business of organizing tours. You cannot deduct your expenses in serving as the voluntary leader of the group at the group's request. If you organize tours as a trade or business, report the tour's value on Schedule C (Form 1040) or Schedule C-EZ (Form 1040).

Gambling winnings. You must include your gambling winnings in income on line 21 of Form 1040. If you itemize your deductions on Schedule A (Form 1040), you can deduct gambling losses you had during the year, but only up to the amount of your winnings. See chapter 30 for information on recordkeeping.

Lotteries and raffles. Winnings from lotteries and raffles are gambling winnings. In addition to cash winnings, you must include in your income the fair market value of bonds, cars, houses, and other non-cash prizes.

Tip. *If you win a state lottery prize payable in installments, see Publication 525 for more information.*

TaxPlanner

If you win a large lottery, proper financial planning can help you minimize the tax bite. You should consult with a financial planner or your tax advisor.

Form W-2G. You may have received a Form W-2G, *Certain Gambling Winnings,* showing the amount of your gambling winnings and any tax taken out of them. Include the amount from box 1 on line 21 of Form 1040. Be sure to include any amount from box 2 on line 59 of Form 1040.

Explanation

While a winner of the Canadian government lottery does not have to pay Canadian tax on the winnings, a U.S. citizen or resident who wins does have to pay U.S. tax on the amount. Citizens and residents of the United States have to report all income, including foreign income. See Chapter 42, *U.S. Citizens Working Abroad,* and Chapter 43, *Foreign Citizens Living in the United States,* for more information about worldwide income.

TaxPlanner

Because you may not win money gambling until late in the year and gambling losses are deductible only up to the amount of your winnings, you should plan ahead by keeping losing racetrack, lottery, and other gambling tickets. In that way, if you do win, you will be able to itemize your gambling losses. It's also a good idea to keep a diary of gambling losses incurred during the entire year. Note that losses from one kind of gambling are deductible against gains from another kind. These losses are claimed as miscellaneous itemized deductions but are not subject to the 2%-of-AGI floor and are reported on Schedule A, line 27.

Gifts and inheritances. Generally, property you receive as a gift, bequest, or inheritance is not included in your income. However, if property you receive this way later produces income such as interest, divi-

dends, or rents, that income is taxable to you. If property is given to a trust and the income from it is paid, credited, or distributed to you, that income is also taxable to you. If the gift, bequest, or inheritance is the income from the property, that income is taxable to you.

Explanation

Items given to you as an incentive to enter into a business transaction are not tax-free gifts. For example, incentive items such as small appliances or dinnerware given to you by a bank as an incentive to open an account are treated as taxable interest income to you and must be reported at their fair market value.

Inherited pension or IRA. If you inherited a pension or an individual retirement arrangement (IRA), you may have to include part of the inherited amount in your income. See chapter 11 if you inherited a pension. See chapter 18 if you inherited an IRA.

Hobby losses. Losses from a hobby are not deductible from other income. A hobby is an activity from which you do not expect to make a profit. See *Activity not for profit,* earlier.

Caution. *If you collect stamps, coins, or other items as a hobby for recreation and pleasure, and you sell any of the items, your gain is taxable as a capital gain. (See chapter 17.) However, if you sell items from your collection at a loss, you cannot deduct the loss.*

Explanation

While a *net* loss from the sale of stamps, coins, or other items that you collect for a hobby may not be deducted, a loss from the sale of these items may be offset against a gain from the sale of similar items occurring in the same year.

Example

You sell several stamps at a gain of $1,000. You may offset up to $1,000 in losses from the sale of other stamps against this gain. The result is that there is no taxable gain. All of the sales should be listed separately on Schedule D.

TaxSaver

If you are planning to sell an item in your collection that has appreciated in value and your collection also contains an item that has decreased in value, you may want to sell both in the same year to incur the least amount of tax. In short, clean out the junk to establish losses in a year when you have gains.

Holocaust victims restitution. Under new law enacted in 2001, the federal tax treatment of payments received by Holocaust victims (or their heirs) as restitution for Nazi persecution has been clarified. Restitution payments received after December 31, 1999 (and interest earned on the payments, including interest earned on amounts held in certain escrow accounts or funds) are not taxable. You also do not include them in any computations in which you would ordinarily add excludable income to your adjusted gross income, such as the computation to determine the taxable part of social security benefits. If the payments are made in property, your basis in the property is its fair market value when you receive it.

Excludable restitution payments are payments or distributions made by any country or any other entity because of persecution of an individual on the basis of race, religion, physical or mental disability, or sexual orientation by Nazi Germany, any other Axis regime, or any other Nazi-controlled or Nazi-allied country, whether the payments are made under a law or as a result of a legal action. They include compensation or reparation for property losses resulting from Nazi persecution, including proceeds under insurance policies issued before and during World War II by European insurance companies.

Amending your 2000 return. If your treatment of restitution payments received in 2000 was different from the treatment described above and caused you to pay more tax, you should file an amended return for 2000 on Form 1040X, *Amended U.S. Individual Income Tax Return.* To claim a refund of tax, you should generally file the amended return by April 15, 2004. See the form instructions for more information.

Illegal income. Illegal income, such as stolen or embezzled funds, must be included in your income on line 21 of Form 1040, or on Schedule C or Schedule C-EZ (Form 1040) if from your self-employment activity.

Explanation

It is not necessary for the activity that produces income to be legal for the income to be taxable. Income from illegal activities, such as embezzlement, drug dealing, bookmaking, and bootlegging, is taxable. Al Capone, the notorious Chicago bootlegger during Prohibition, was convicted of income tax evasion because he did not report his illegal income.

Embezzlement income is taxable in the year in which the funds are stolen. If the embezzler pays back the stolen funds in a later year, he or she can claim a deduction in the year of repayment.

Indian fishing rights. If you are a member of a qualified Indian tribe that has fishing rights secured by treaty, executive order, or an Act of Congress as of March 17, 1988, do not include in your income amounts you receive from activities related to those fishing rights. The income is not subject to income tax, self-employment tax, or employment taxes.

TaxAlert

Investment clubs. An investment club is a group of friends, neighbors, business associates, or others who pool limited or stated amounts of funds to invest in stock or other securities. The club may or may not have a written agreement, charter, or bylaws. Usually, the group operates informally with members pledging a regular amount to be paid into the club monthly. Some clubs have a committee that gathers information on securities, selects the most promising, and recommends that the club invest in them. Other clubs rotate the investigatory responsibilities among all their members. Most require all members to vote for or against all investments, sales, exchanges, or other transactions.

How the income from an investment club is reported on your tax return depends on how the club operates. Most clubs operate as partnerships and are treated as such for federal tax purposes. Others operate as corporations, trusts, or associations taxed as corporations.

Members of an investment club should include their share of each type of the club's income on their returns. For example, dividends are reported on Schedule B, Part II, line 5, and capital gains are reported on Schedule D.

The expenses incurred by the club to produce or to collect income, to manage investment property, or to determine any tax due are also reported separately. You may deduct your share of these items on Schedule A as a miscellaneous deduction if you itemize your deductions.

Note: These expenses—along with some others—must exceed 2% of your AGI to be deductible as miscellaneous itemized deductions.

TaxAlert

Depending on how your investment club is organized, it may be required to file a separate partnership, corporation, or trust tax return. More details are explained in IRS Publication 550, some of which follow.

Tax returns and identifying numbers. Investment clubs must file either **Form 1065**, *U.S. Partnership Return of Income;* **Form 1041**, *U.S. Income Tax Return for Estates and Trusts;* or **Form 1120**, *U.S. Corporation Income Tax Return.* Certain small corporations may be able to file **Form 1120-A**, *U.S. Corporation Short-Form Income Tax Return.* See the instructions for Forms 1120 and 1120-A.

Form SS-4. Each club must have an employer identification number (EIN) to use when filing its return. The club's EIN also may have to be given to the payer of dividends. If your club does not have an EIN, use Form SS-4, Application for Employer Identification Number. Mail the completed Form SS-4 to the IRS Center where you file the club's tax return. Form SS-4 can be found in Chapter 48, *2001 Federal Tax Forms and Schedules You Can Use.*

Stock in name of club. When stock is recorded in the name of the investment club, the club must give its own EIN to the payer of dividends.

If the club is a partnership or a trust, the dividends distributed to the partners or beneficiaries must be shown on Form 1065 or Form 1041, respectively. The partners' or the beneficiaries' identifying numbers also must be shown on the return.

If the club is an association taxed as a corporation, any distribution it makes that qualifies as a dividend must be reported on Forms 1096 and 1099-DIV if total distributions to the shareholder are $10 or more for the year.

Stock in name of member. When stock is recorded in the name of one club member, this member must give his or her Social Security number to the payer of dividends. (When stock is held in the names of two or more club members, the Social Security number of only one member must be given to the payer.) This member is considered as the record owner for the actual owner of the stock, the investment club. This member is a "nominee" and must file Form 1099-DIV, showing the club to be the owner of the dividend, his or her Social Security number, and the EIN of the club.

Example

In order to avoid any matching notices from the IRS, the nominee should report the dividend income on his or her tax return on line 5, Part II, of Form 1040, Schedule B and then subtract out the nominee distribution.

ABC company	$100
Less: Nominee distribution	($100)

No Social Security coverage for investment club earnings. If an investment club partnership's activities are limited to investing in savings certificates, stock, or securities and collecting interest or dividends for its members' accounts, the members' share of income is not earnings from self-employment. You cannot voluntarily pay the self-employment tax in order to increase your Social Security coverage and ultimate benefits.

For more information about investment clubs, see Publication 550.

Interest on frozen deposits. In general, you exclude from your income the amount of interest earned on a frozen deposit. See *Interest income on frozen deposits* in chapter 8.

Interest on qualified savings bonds. You may be able to exclude from income the interest from qualified U.S. savings bonds you redeem if you pay qualified higher educational expenses in the same year. For more information on this exclusion, see *Education Savings Bond Program* under *U.S. Savings Bonds* in chapter 8.

Job interview expenses. If a prospective employer asks you to appear for an interview and either pays you an allowance or reimburses you for your transportation and other travel expenses, the amount you receive is generally not taxable. You include in income only the amount you receive that is more than your actual expenses.

Jury duty. Jury duty pay you receive must be included in your income on line 21 of Form 1040. If you must give the pay to your employer because your employer continues to pay your salary while you serve on the jury, you can deduct the amount turned over to your employer as an adjustment to your income. Include the amount you repay your employer on line 32 of Form 1040. Write "Jury Pay" and the amount on the dotted line next to line 32.

Explanation
Jury fees. This item is often overlooked. Just because a fee is paid by a government body does not mean that it is not subject to tax. However, the Tax Court has ruled that the mileage allowance received by a juror to cover the cost of transportation between the court and his or her home is not included in income. In addition, if you are required to give your jury pay to your employer, you can claim a deduction for the amount paid over. You can claim this deduction whether or not you itemize your deductions. You would report the income on line 21 of Form 1040 and, if you give your jury pay to your employer, report it as an adjustment on line 32 and write "Jury Pay" next to the amount.

Kickbacks. You must include kickbacks, side commissions, push money, or similar payments you receive in your income on line 21 of Form 1040, or on Schedule C or Schedule C-EZ (Form 1040), if from your self-employment activity.

Example. You sell cars and help arrange car insurance for buyers. Insurance brokers pay back part of their commissions to you for referring customers to them. You must include the kickbacks in your income.

TAXSAVER
Note received for services. If your employer gives you a note as payment for your services, you must include the fair market value (usually the discount value) of the note in your income as wages for the year you receive it. When you later receive payments on the note, part of each payment is a recovery of the fair market value that you previously included in your income. Do not include that part in your income again. Include the rest of the payment in your income in the year of payment.

The fair market value of a note is extremely difficult to determine, unless the note may be sold to a third party, and even then its worth may be difficult to determine.

If the issuer of the note is insolvent, the fair market value of the note may be zero. In this case, any money you subsequently get from the issuer is taxed as ordinary income in the year in which you receive it. Similarly, if the value of the note is less than its face value, any amount that you subsequently receive from the issuer that is greater than the recognized value of the note is taxed as ordinary income in the year in which it is received.

A note's fair market value may be less than its face amount if, based on the facts and circumstances at the time the note is issued, it is uncertain that you will be able to collect the face amount. A note may also be considered to be worth less than its face amount if the interest rate that it pays is below the market rate or the collateral pledged against the note is limited.

If you think the note you receive may be worth more or less than its face value, consult your tax advisor about how to report the transaction.

Medical savings accounts (MSAs). You do not generally include in income amounts you withdraw from your Archer MSA or Medicare+Choice MSA if you use the money to pay for qualified medical expenses. Generally, qualified medical expenses are those you can deduct on Schedule A (Form 1040), *Itemized Deductions*. For more information about qualified medical expenses, see chapter 23. For more information about Archer MSAs or Medicare+Choice MSAs, see Publication 969, *Medical Savings Accounts (MSAs)*.

Caution. *You cannot buy health insurance with distributions from your MSA unless you are receiving unemployment benefits, buying continuation coverage required by federal law, or buying long-term care insurance.*

TAXSAVER
Contributions to an MSA can also be deductible. See Chapter 23, *Medical and Dental Expenses,* for details.

Taxable distributions and penalty. If you use the money from your MSA for any purpose besides qualified medical expenses, it will be taxable income that you must report on your tax return. In addition to the tax, you will be charged a 15% penalty for an early distribution. The penalty will not be charged if you are disabled, age 65, or die during the year.

Prizes and awards. If you win a prize in a lucky number drawing, television or radio quiz program, beauty contest, or other event, you must include it in your income. For example, if you win a $50 prize in a photography contest, you must report this income on line 21 of Form 1040. If you refuse to accept a prize, do not include its value in your income.

Explanation
An individual wins a prize in a charitable fundraising raffle and refuses to accept the prize, returning the prize to the charity. The individual need not include the value of the prize as income on his or her return. Likewise, the individual is not entitled to a charitable deduction.

Prizes and awards in goods or services must be included in your income at their fair market value.

Explanation
Fair market value is the price at which property would be exchanged between a willing buyer and a willing seller when neither party is compelled to buy or to sell. When merchandise is received as a prize, fair market value is the suggested retail price, unless some other measure of fair market value can be readily ascertained. Other ways to measure

fair market value that have been approved by the courts include the following:

1. **Resale value.** The Tax Court has ruled that, in some cases, the fair market value of an item is what you could realize by selling it.
2. **Value to the recipient.** If you receive a prize that is not something you would ordinarily purchase, the Tax Court has said that you may discount the value of the prize.

Example 1

An individual received a new car as an award from her employer. The Tax Court ruled that the amount to be considered as income was not what the employer had paid for the car but how much the recipient would have realized by selling the car immediately after it was received.

Example 2

Taxpayers received two first-class cruise tickets from a game show. The tickets were nontransferable and had to be used within 1 year. The Tax Court found that the tickets were not something that the taxpayers would normally have acquired but were a luxury that would otherwise have been beyond their means. Accordingly, the Tax Court permitted an amount less than the retail price of the tickets in the taxpayers' gross income.

There is no standardized technique to determine the amount to be included in gross income in cases similar to these. Our advice is this: If you believe that you can justify a value less than normal retail price, it may be worthwhile to include the lower amount in taxable income.

Employee awards or bonuses. Cash awards or bonuses given to you by your employer for good work or suggestions generally must be included in your income as wages. However, certain noncash employee achievement awards can be excluded from income. See *Bonuses and awards* in chapter 6.

Pulitzer, Nobel, and similar prizes. If you were awarded a prize in recognition of past accomplishments in religious, charitable, scientific, artistic, educational, literary, or civic fields, you generally must include the value of the prize in your income. However, you do not include this prize in your income if you meet *all* of the following requirements.

1) You were selected without any action on your part to enter the contest or proceeding.
2) You are not required to perform substantial future services as a condition to receiving the prize or award.
3) The prize or award is transferred by the payer directly to a governmental unit or tax-exempt charitable organization as designated by you.

See Publication 525 for more information about the conditions that apply to the transfer.

Railroad retirement annuities. The following types of payments are treated as pension or annuity income and are taxable under the rules explained in chapter 12.

1) Tier 1 railroad retirement benefits that are more than the *social security equivalent benefit.*
2) Tier 2 benefits.
3) Vested dual benefits.

Sale of home. You may be able to exclude from income all or part of any gain from the sale or exchange of a personal residence. See chapter 16.

Sale of personal items. If you sold an item you owned for personal use, such as a car, refrigerator, furniture, stereo, jewelry, or silverware,

your gain is taxable as a capital gain. Report it on Schedule D (Form 1040). You cannot deduct a loss.

However, if you sold an item you held for investment, such as gold or silver bullion, coins, or gems, any gain is taxable as a capital gain and any loss is deductible as a capital loss.

Scholarships and fellowships. A candidate for a degree can exclude amounts received as a qualified scholarship or fellowship. A qualified scholarship or fellowship is any amount you receive that is for:

1) Tuition and fees to enroll at or attend an educational organization, or
2) Fees, books, supplies, and equipment required for courses at the educational institution.

Amounts used for room and board *do not* qualify. Get Publication 520 for more information on qualified scholarships and fellowship grants.

Payments for services. Payments you receive for services required as a condition of receiving a scholarship or fellowship grant must be included in your income, even if the services are required of all candidates for the degree. This includes amounts received for teaching and research. Include these payments on line 7 of Form 1040 or Form 1040A, or on line 1 of Form 1040EZ.

For information about the rules that apply to a tax-free qualified tuition reduction provided to employees and their families by an educational institution, see Publication 520.

VA payments. Allowances paid by the Department of Veterans Affairs are not included in your income. These allowances are not considered scholarship or fellowship grants.

Scholarship prizes. Scholarship prizes won in a contest are not scholarships or fellowships if you do not have to use the prizes for educational purposes. You must include these amounts in your income on line 21 of Form 1040, whether or not you use the amounts for educational purposes.

Explanation

Employer-Provided Educational Assistance

Certain educational expenses paid by your employer are excludable if they have been provided under an educational assistance program as defined in the IRS code. The program must be specifically defined in a written plan by the employer. The plan cannot discriminate in favor of highly compensated employees, nor can more than 5% of the amounts paid by an employer be provided to individuals who make up more than 5% of the ownership of the employer.

Up to $5,250 of employer-provided tuition reimbursement, whether or not the courses are job-related, may be excluded from your income each calendar year.

Educational expenses that do not qualify under an Employer Provided Assistance Program as defined in the IRS code may still be excludable from income as a working condition fringe benefit. In general, expenses qualify for exclusion if they 1) maintain or improve skills required in your employment or business or 2) meet the express requirements of your employer, or applicable law, imposed as a condition of employment. However, educational expenditures that are made to meet minimum educational requirements or that qualify you for a new trade or business, such as a law degree, are not deductible. Therefore, only expenses for education related to your present work are deductible. These deductions are subject to limitations and would be reported on Schedule A.

Education expenditures include such items as tuition, books, supplies, lab fees, and certain travel and transportation costs. Employees enrolled in undergraduate courses that are fully reimbursed by their employer are not eligible for either the Hope Scholarship Credit or the Lifetime Learning Credit for that year. However, if your employer does not reimburse you for all of your expenses, such as books and supplies, you may be eligible to receive an education credit based on these expenses. See Chapter 36, *Education Credits,* for more information on these credits.

TaxAlert

For classes beginning before December 31, 2001, only undergraduate courses qualify for the exclusion. However, a new provision applies to courses beginning after December 31, 2001 that extends the exclusion to graduate courses.

State tuition programs. If you receive distributions from a qualified state tuition program, only the amount that is more than the amount contributed to the program is taxable.

Qualified state tuition programs are defined in Publication 970. For more information on a specific program, contact the state or agency that established and maintains it.

Explanation

A qualified state tuition program (QSTP) is a program established and maintained by a state under which a person may: (1) prepay tuition benefits on behalf of a beneficiary so that the beneficiary is entitled to a waiver or payment of qualified higher education expenses, or (2) contribute to an account that is established for paying qualified higher education expenses of the beneficiary.

TaxAlert

Under the 2001 Tax Act, distributions made after December 31, 2001 from qualified state tuition programs are excludable from gross income as long as the distributions are used to pay for qualified higher education expenses.

TaxSaver

If the amounts saved through the QSTP are used to pay for college, the student or the student's parents may still be able to claim the Hope Scholarship Credit or the Lifetime Learning Credit. See Chapter 36, *Education Credits.*

Transporting school children. Do not include in your income a school board mileage allowance for taking children to and from school if you are not in the business of taking children to school. You cannot deduct expenses for providing this transportation.

Union benefits and dues. Amounts deducted from your pay for union dues, assessments, contributions, or other payments to a union cannot be excluded from your income.

You may be able to deduct some of these payments as a miscellaneous deduction subject to the 2% limit if they are related to your job and if you itemize your deductions on Schedule A (Form 1040). For more information, see *Union Dues and Expenses* in chapter 30.

Strike and lockout benefits. Benefits paid to you by a union as strike or lockout benefits, including both cash and the fair market value of other property, are usually included in your income as compensation. You can exclude these benefits from your income only when the facts clearly show that the union intended them as gifts to you.

Utility rebates. If you are a customer of an electric utility company and you participate in the utility's energy conservation program, you may receive on your monthly electric bill either:

1) A reduction in the purchase price of electricity furnished to you (rate reduction), or
2) A nonrefundable credit against the purchase price of the electricity.

The amount of the rate reduction or nonrefundable credit is not included in your income.

Passive Activity Limitations and At-Risk Limitations

Explanation

Under current law, individuals, estates, trusts, closely held corporations, and personal service corporations are generally prohibited from deducting net losses generated by passive activities. In addition, tax credits from passive activities are generally limited to the tax liability attributable to such activities. Disallowed passive activity losses are suspended and carried forward indefinitely to offset passive activity income generated in future years. Similar carryforward treatment applies to suspended credits.

Note that these rules relate to passive income/losses and do not apply to portfolio income/losses. Portfolio income/losses include interest, dividends, annuities, and royalties, as well as gain or loss from the disposition of income-producing or investment property that is not derived in the ordinary course of a trade or business.

Defining passive activities. A passive activity involves the conduct of any trade or business in which you do not materially participate. You are treated as a material participant only if you are involved in the operations of the activity on a regular, continuous, and substantial basis. If you are not a material participant in an activity but your spouse is, you are treated as being a material participant and the activity is not considered passive.

Seven tests. The IRS has seven tests you can meet to be considered a material participant. If you satisfy one of these tests, you will be considered a material participant in any activity. These tests are:

1. You participate more than 500 hours per taxable year.
2. Your participation during the taxable year constitutes substantially all of the participation of all individuals involved.
3. You participate for more than 100 hours during the taxable year and no one else participates more than you participated.
4. The activity is a significant participation activity (SPA) for the taxable year, and your participation in all SPAs during the taxable year exceeds 500 hours. An SPA is an activity in which an individual participates for more than 100 hours but does not otherwise meet a material participation test.
5. You materially participated in any 5 of the 10 preceding taxable years.
6. The activity is a personal service activity, and you materially participated for any 3 preceding taxable years. A personal service activity involves performance of personal services in the fields of health, law, engineering, architecture, accounting, actuarial sciences, performing arts, consulting, or any other business in which capital is not a material income-producing factor.
7. Based on all the facts and circumstances, your participation is regular, continuous, and substantial during the taxable year.

Defining an activity. The proper grouping of business operations into one or more activities is important in determining the allocation of suspended losses, measuring material participation, separating rental and nonrental activities, and determining when a disposition of an activity has occurred. IRS regulations define an activity as any "appropriate economic unit for measuring gain or loss." What constitutes an "appropriate economic unit" is determined by looking at all facts and circumstances. The regulations list five factors that are to be given the greatest weight. They are:

1. Similarities and differences in types of business
2. The extent of common control
3. The extent of common ownership
4. Geographical location
5. Interdependence between the activities

Generally, taxpayers must be consistent from year to year in determining the business operations that consti-tute an activity. Consult your tax advisor for more information.

"At-Risk" Limitation Provisions
The deduction for business losses is generally limited to the amount by which you are considered to be "at risk" in the activity. You are considered at risk for the amount of cash you have invested in the venture and the basis of property invested plus certain amounts borrowed for use in the activity.

Borrowed amounts that are considered at risk are (1) loans for which you are personally liable for repayment or (2) loans secured by property, other than that used in the activity. Generally, liabilities that are secured by property within the activity for which you are not otherwise personally liable are not considered to be at risk. An exception: If nonrecourse financing—financing for which you are not personally liable—is secured against real property used in the activity, you may be considered at risk for the amount of financing.

The law provides a broad list of activities (including the holding of real estate acquired after 1986) that are subject to the at-risk provisions. If the "at-risk" provisions apply to you, you should consult with your tax advisor.

Passive Activity Losses
The passive activity rules limit deductions and credits from passive trade or business activities. Deductions attributable to passive activities, to the extent they exceed income from passive activities, generally may not be deducted against other income, such as wages, portfolio income, or business income that is not derived from a passive activity. Deductions that are suspended under these rules are carried forward indefinitely and are treated as deductions from passive activities in succeeding years. Suspended losses are allowed in full when a taxpayer disposes of his or her entire interest in a passive activity to an unrelated person. For dispositions made after January 1, 1995, you must dispose of "substantially all" of a passive activity in order to deduct that same portion. You may also be able to deduct suspended losses in a passive activity if your interest is disposed of in other ways, including abandonment and death of the taxpayer. "See Disposition of Passive Activity," discussed later. Special rules may apply; you should consult your tax advisor.

Rental Real Estate
As discussed above, generally, a trade or business activity is passive unless the taxpayer *materially participates* in that activity. Rental real estate activities, however, are passive regardless of the level of the taxpayer's participation. A special rule permits the deduction of up to $25,000 of losses from certain rental real estate activities (even though they are considered passive) if the taxpayer actively participates in them. This special rule is available in full to taxpayers with AGI of $100,000 or less and phases out for taxpayers with AGI between $100,000 and $150,000. For further information about rental real estate passive rules, see Chapter 10, *Rental Income and Expenses*.

Real Estate Professionals
Passive activity limitations for certain real estate professionals are more liberal than they used to be. Taxpayers who satisfy certain eligibility thresholds and materially participate in rental real estate activities may treat any losses as losses from a nonpassive activity and may use these losses against all sources of taxable income.

Eligibility. Only individuals and closely held C corporations can qualify for this special rule. An individual taxpayer will qualify for any tax year if more than one-half of the personal services (with more than 750 hours) performed in trades or businesses by the taxpayer during such a tax year are performed in real property trades or businesses in which the taxpayer materially participates. A real property trade or business includes any real property development, redevelopment, construction, reconstruction, acquisition, conversion, rental, operation, management, leasing, or brokerage trade or business. Personal services performed as an employee are not considered in determining material participation unless the employee has more than a 5% ownership in the business during any part of the tax year. However, independent contractor realtor services would qualify for this purpose. For closely held C corporations, the eligibility requirements are met if more than 50% of the corporation's gross receipts for the tax year are derived from real property trades or businesses in which the corporation materially participates.

Example 1
During 2001, a self-employed real estate developer earned $100,000 in development fees from projects the developer spent 1,200 hours developing. In addition, the developer incurred rental real estate losses of $200,000 from properties that the developer spent over 800 hours managing during 2001. The developer performs no other personal services during the year and has no other items of income or deduction. Because the developer (1) materially participated in the rental real estate activity, (2) performed more than 750 hours in real property trades or businesses, and (3) performed more than 50% of the developer's total personal service hours in real estate trades or businesses in which the developer materially participated, the developer will have a net operating loss of $100,000 to carry back (and the excess to carry forward) to offset any source of income.

This rule for real estate professionals' passive loss relief is a two-step process. First, you must demonstrate eligibility for the relief provision by achieving the required levels of personal services in real estate trades or businesses. Thereafter, you would get relief from the passive loss limitations only for your rental real estate activities for which you satisfy the material participation standards.

For spouses filing joint returns, each spouse's personal services are taken into account separately. However, in determining material participation, the participation of the other spouse is taken into account as required under current law.

Example 2

A husband and wife filing a joint return meet the eligibility requirements if, during the tax year, *one spouse* performs more than 750 hours representing at least half of his or her personal services in a real estate trade or business in which either spouse materially participates.

Aggregation of Activities

Whether a taxpayer *materially participates* in his or her rental real estate activities is determined generally as if each interest of the taxpayer in rental real estate is a separate activity. However, the taxpayer may elect to treat all interest in rental real estate as one activity.

The election permitting a taxpayer to aggregate his or her rental real estate activities for testing for material participation is not intended to alter the rules with respect to material participation through limited partnership interest. Generally, no interest as a limited partner is treated as an interest with respect to which a taxpayer materially participates. However, Treasury regulations provide that a limited partner is considered to materially participate in the activities conducted through the partnership in certain situations where (1) the limited partner is also a general partner at all times during the partnership's tax year, (2) the limited partner materially participates in the activity during any 5 of the preceding 10 years, or (3) the activity is a personal service activity in which the limited partner materially participated for any 3 preceding years.

Losses attributable to limited partnership interests are considered passive, except where regulations provide otherwise. In general, working interests in any oil or gas property held directly or through an entity that does not limit the taxpayer's liability are *not* considered passive, whether or not the taxpayer is a material participant.

The IRS has issued regulations with regard to the aggregation of activities in order to satisfy the material participation tests for real estate professionals. These rules are very complex and hold potential tax traps for the unwary. We recommend that you consult with your tax advisor if you believe that electing to aggregate activities may be beneficial to you.

Example 1

Three brothers own a hardware store as partners. Two of them consider it their full-time job, because it is their only source of income. The third brother lives 200 miles away and is consulted only on major issues. The two brothers who work at the store meet the material participation test. The third brother has a passive investment.

Example 2

Bonnie owns a one-sixteenth interest in four different racehorses. She does not own the stables where the horses are trained and fed. She is not involved in the daily care of the horses. She pays her fair share of the costs and offers advice regarding when and where the horses are to be run. Bonnie has significant salary income from a full-time job and from managing her portfolio. Bonnie is probably not a material participant.

Example 3

Andrea is a limited partner in a partnership. She is not a material participant.

Example 4

Chris owns rental property. He has a passive investment.

Exception

An exception to the general rule that does not allow grouping rental activities with business activity is that, in certain instances, passive rental losses can offset income from business activities. For this exception to apply, you must own the same proportionate ownership interest in each activity.

Example

Jack and Jill are married and file a joint return. Jack owns and operates a grocery store that generates net income for the current year. Jill owns the building, of which 25% is rented to Jack's grocery store activity (grocery store rental). The building rental activities generate a net loss in the current year.

Because they file a joint return, Jack and Jill are treated as one taxpayer. Therefore, the sole owner of the grocery store activity is also the sole owner of the rental activity. Consequently, each owner of the business activity has the same proportionate ownership interest in the rental activity. Accordingly, both activities may be grouped together; thus, the net income from Jack's grocery store can be offset by the amount of net loss from Jill's building rental activities. See your tax advisor for more information if you think this exception applies to your situation.

TAXPLANNER

You should try to realign your personal finances so that you maximize your interest expense deductions. If you borrowed money to purchase a passive investment, any interest on the loan will be considered part of your passive investment loss. If you are in a real estate limited partnership, you may be able to have all the partners contribute additional capital so that the passive loss is reduced or limited. Your capital contribution could come from your other investments or from a mortgage on a personal residence. If you have untapped appreciation in your personal residence, you can borrow against it and deduct the interest cost subject to certain limitations. Make sure, however, that any mortgage does not exceed the limits applicable to your situation, because such disallowed interest would be considered nondeductible personal interest.

Disposition of Passive Activity

Previously disallowed losses (but not credits) are recognized in full when the taxpayer disposes of his or her entire interest in the passive activity in a fully taxable transaction. However, suspended losses are not deductible when the taxpayer sells the interest to a related party. Rather, the losses remain with the individual (and may offset passive income) until the related purchaser disposes of the interest in a taxable transaction to an unrelated person. Various other types of dispositions trigger suspended losses, including abandonment, death of the taxpayer, gifts, and installment sales of entire interests, although special rules apply.

A sale in a taxable year beginning before January 1, 1987, reported on the installment method and included in income after December 31, 1986, would be considered income from a passive activity.

Example

Bob disposes of rental property in 1986 under the installment sale method and properly reports $2,000 of taxable gain in his 1986 through 2001 tax returns. Bob may treat the 1987 through 2001 gains as income from a passive activity and may offset other passive losses in these years.

Basis of Property

Introduction

The gain or loss you realize on the disposition of property—whether through a sale or exchange—is measured by the difference between the selling price and your **basis.** *In many cases, the basis of an* **asset** *is no more than your cost. However, if you acquire property in exchange for services, by inheritance, or in exchange for other property, different factors besides cost are likely to have a crucial bearing on determining your tax basis.*

This chapter tells you how to calculate the basis of property. Particular attention is given to some of the more complicated situations that may arise. You'll learn, for instance, how to calculate your basis in a particular piece of property by referring to other assets you already hold. To help you determine which expenditures increase your basis in a piece of property and which do not, comprehensive lists of allowable—but often overlooked—expenditures are provided.

This chapter discusses how to figure your basis in property. It is divided into the following sections.

- Cost basis.
- Adjusted basis.
- Basis other than cost.

Basis is the amount of your investment in property for tax purposes. Use the basis of property to figure gain or loss on the sale, exchange, or other disposition of property. Also use it to figure deductions for depreciation, amortization, depletion, and casualty losses. You must keep accurate records of all items that affect the basis of property so you can make these computations.

Explanation

This chapter does not reflect the provisions of the law that deal with bankruptcy. If any of your debts were canceled by a creditor or were discharged because you became bankrupt, the basis of your assets might be affected. For information about the effect these provisions may have on basis, see the *Debt Cancelation* section in Publication 908, *Bankruptcy Tax Guide.*

Publication 908 discusses the technical rules related to bankruptcy, but here are several key points to remember:

1. The tax treatment of a forgiven debt depends on how the debt arose. For example, a personal loan from a relative, when it was unrelated to a business or an investment, is not taxed if it is forgiven. Instead, it is considered a gift. If the amount is over $10,000, the person forgiving the loan might have to file a gift tax return and pay gift tax.
2. On the other hand, a business loan forgiven for business reasons is taxed. In this case, you may pay the tax on a forgiven loan or opt for a reduction in the basis of your assets by an amount equal to the debt forgiven. The result is that you are not able to deduct as much in depreciating the asset. Thus, if it is sold before it is fully depreciated, you have either a larger gain or a smaller loss on the asset than you would if you paid the tax directly. After 1986, a *solvent* taxpayer may make this election only if the loan is "purchase money debt," in which case the forgiveness is treated as a purchase price adjustment of the related asset.

3. If you declare personal bankruptcy, you are not taxed on any debt you owe that is forgiven or canceled. You also are not taxed on any debt you owe that is forgiven or canceled if a business you own goes into bankruptcy. However, you may be required to reduce the **net operating loss carryforwards** and **tax credit carryforwards** that otherwise would be available in subsequent years to offset income and reduce your income tax liability. One strategy to avoid losing these tax benefits is to reduce the basis of depreciable property or real property held as inventory, by an amount equal to the debt forgiven.

If you use property for both business and personal purposes, you must allocate the basis based on the use. Only the basis allocated to the business use of the property can be depreciated.

Your original basis in property is adjusted (increased or decreased) by certain events. If you make improvements to the property, increase your basis. If you take deductions for depreciation or casualty losses, reduce your basis.

Useful Items

You may want to see:

Publication

- [ ] **15-B** Employer's Tax Guide to Fringe Benefits
- [ ] **523** Selling Your Home
- [ ] **525** Taxable and Nontaxable Income
- [ ] **535** Business Expenses
- [ ] **537** Installment Sales
- [ ] **544** Sales and Other Dispositions of Assets
- [ ] **550** Investment Income and Expenses
- [ ] **551** Basis of Assets
- [ ] **564** Mutual Fund Distributions
- [ ] **946** How To Depreciate Property

Cost Basis

The basis of property you buy is usually its cost. The cost is the amount you pay in cash, debt obligations, other property, or services. Your cost also includes amounts you pay for the following items.

- Sales tax.
- Freight.
- Installation and testing.
- Excise taxes.
- Legal and accounting fees (when they must be capitalized).
- Revenue stamps.
- Recording fees.
- Real estate taxes (if assumed for the seller).

In addition, the basis of real estate and business assets may include other items.

TaxAlert

If you perform services for an entity and in exchange receive stock or a partnership interest, the fair market value (FMV) of what you receive is treated as compensation. Your basis in the stock or partnership interest is equal to the amount of compensation reported by you, increased by the amount, if any, paid for the stock or partnership interest. For more information, see Chapter 6, *Wages, Salaries, and Other Earnings.*

TaxSaver

If you receive an equity interest in a business in exchange for services rendered, you should consider reducing the stated value of the equity interest. You may do this if the shares are not marketable and/or if they represent only a minority holding.

Loans with low or no interest. If you buy property on any time-payment plan that charges little or no interest, the basis of your property is your stated purchase price minus any amount considered to be unstated interest. You generally have unstated interest if your interest rate is less than the applicable federal rate.

For more information, see *Unstated Interest and Original Issue Discount* in Publication 537.

Explanation

If you buy personal property or educational services by contract and carrying charges are separately stated but interest cannot be ascertained, the Internal Revenue Service (IRS) assumes that interest is being charged at the rate of 6% per annum on the average unpaid balance of the contract during the tax year. Your tax basis is determined by subtracting the interest from the total contract cost of the property. You may deduct the interest in the year in which it is, in effect, being paid. But see Chapter 25, *Interest Expense,* for possible limitations on your deductions.

Real Property

Real property, also called real estate, is land and generally anything built on, growing on, or attached to land.

If you buy real property, certain fees and other expenses you pay are part of your cost basis in the property.

If you buy buildings and the land on which they stand for a lump sum, allocate the basis among the land and the buildings so you can figure the allowable depreciation on the buildings. Land is not depreciable. Allocate the cost according to the fair market values of the land and buildings at the time of purchase.

Fair market value (FMV) is the price at which the property would change hands between a willing buyer and a willing seller, neither having to buy or sell, who both have reasonable knowledge of all the necessary facts. Sales of similar property on or about the same date may be helpful in figuring the FMV of the property.

Assumption of mortgage. If you buy property and assume (or buy subject to) an existing mortgage on the property, your basis includes the amount you pay for the property plus the amount to be paid on the mortgage.

Settlement costs. You can include in the basis of property you buy the settlement fees and closing costs you pay for buying the property. (A fee for buying property is a cost that must be paid even if you buy the property for cash.) You cannot include fees and costs for getting a loan on the property.

The following are some of the settlement fees or closing costs you can include in the basis of your property.

- Abstract fees (abstract of title fees).
- Charges for installing utility services.

Table 14–1. **Examples of Adjustments to Basis**

Increases to Basis	Decreases to Basis

• Capital improvements:
  – Putting an addition on your home
  – Replacing an entire roof
  – Paving your driveway
  – Installing central air conditioning
  – Rewiring your home
	• Exclusion from income of subsidies for energy conservation measures

• Assessments for local improvements:
  – Water connections
  – Sidewalks
  – Roads
	• Casualty or theft loss deductions and insurance reimbursements
	
	• Credit for qualified electric vehicles
	
	• Section 179 deduction
	
	• Depreciation

• Costs of restoring damaged property after a casualty loss	• Deduction for clean-fuel vehicles and clean-fuel refueling property
• Legal fees for defending and perfecting a title	• Nontaxable corporate distributions
• Zoning costs	

- Legal fees (including title search and preparation of the sales contract and deed).
- Recording fees.
- Surveys.
- Transfer taxes.
- Owner's title insurance.
- Any amounts the seller owes that you agree to pay, such as back taxes or interest, recording or mortgage fees, charges for improvements or repairs, and sales commissions.

Explanation
If the real property is used in your trade or business or as a rental, you cannot elect to deduct transfer taxes in lieu of adding them to your basis.

Settlement costs *do not include* amounts placed in escrow for the future payment of items such as taxes and insurance.

The following are some of the settlement fees and closing costs you *cannot* include in the basis of property.

1) Casualty insurance premiums.
2) Rent for occupancy of the property before closing.
3) Charges for utilities or other services related to occupancy of the property before closing.
4) Fees for refinancing a mortgage.
5) Charges connected with getting a loan. The following are examples of these charges.
  a) Points (discount points, loan origination fees).
  b) Mortgage insurance premiums.
  c) Loan assumption fees.
  d) Cost of a credit report.
  e) Fees for an appraisal required by a lender.

Real estate taxes. If you pay real estate taxes the seller owed on real property you bought, and the seller did not reimburse you, treat those taxes as part of your basis. You cannot deduct them as taxes.

If you reimburse the seller for taxes the seller paid for you, you can usually deduct that amount as an expense in the year of purchase. Do not include that amount in the basis of your property. If you did not reimburse the seller, you must reduce your basis by the amount of those taxes.

Points. If you pay points to get a loan (including a mortgage, second mortgage, line of credit, or a home equity loan), do not add the points to the basis of the related property. Generally, you deduct the points over the term of the loan. For more information on how to deduct points, see *Points* in chapter 5 of Publication 535.

Explanation
The following costs increase your tax basis:

1. Interest on debt incurred to finance the construction or production of real property, long-lived personal property with a useful life of 20 years or more, and other tangible property requiring more than 2 years (1 year in the case of property costing more than $1 million) to produce or construct or reach a productive stage. Additionally, interest incurred to finance property produced under a long-term contract increases your tax basis to the extent that income is not reported under the percentage-of-completion method.

These rules do *not* apply to interest incurred during the construction of real property to be used as your principal residence or second home. (For a definition of principal residence, see Chapter 16, *Selling Your Home*. But see Chapter 25, *Interest Expense*, for other rules affecting how much interest you may be able to deduct on a residence.)

2. The costs of defending or perfecting a title, architect's fees, and financing and finder's fees. Points, usually up-front payments on a mortgage charged to purchasers or borrowers, may be deducted as interest. See Chapter 25, *Interest Expense*, for more information and the timing of the deduction.

3. Certain start-up costs for a business. These include legal fees for the drafting of documents, accounting fees, and other similar expenses directly associated with the organization of a business. The costs of organizing a partnership, such as the expenses incurred in raising capital, putting together a prospectus, and paying commissions on the sale of investment units, also increase your basis, as does the cost of investigating the creation or acquisition of an active trade or business. See Chapter 38, *If You Are Self-Employed*, for further information.

Some taxpayers who are starting a new business try to deduct the expenses incurred before the business actually begins. The IRS, however, may not accept these as current **deductions,** and it may either require that you deduct the expenses over a number of years or decide that the expenses should increase your basis in the business. The IRS allows you to amortize certain business start-up and organizational costs over 60 months if an election statement providing certain information is included in a tax return that you file on a timely basis. If you currently neither deduct nor amortize an expense, the tax benefit is obtained when the entity is sold or ceases operation. Therefore, it is important to include the election with your tax return for the year in which the costs are first incurred.

Unlike costs of organizing a partnership or starting up its business, costs of selling partnership interests (syndication costs) may not be amortized or deducted. (For further discussion, see *Adjusted Basis*, following.)

TaxSaver

Increasing your tax basis by as much as possible subsequently reduces the amount of gain or increases the amount of loss realized when you dispose of the property.

TaxAlert

Individuals do not derive any tax benefit from **realizing a loss** related to the disposition of personal property. Personal property includes any property that is not considered an investment (such as a refrigerator), as well as any property that is not used in a trade or business.

TaxSaver

If you pay interest, taxes, and other carrying charges on unimproved and unproductive real estate but cannot deduct these expenses because you do not itemize your deductions, consider treating them as **capital expenditures,** which increase your basis and reduce your gain on sale. This election is made on an annual basis and must be renewed each year that you want to continue capitalizing these costs.

Example

Jane rents an apartment and has few **itemized deductions.** She borrows money to purchase an unimproved lot in Florida. She incurs $1,000 in interest expense on the borrowed funds and pays $100 in real estate taxes in each of the 5 years she holds the property. If Jane elects to capitalize the interest and taxes, she increases her basis by $5,500 over the 5 years.

TaxOrganizer

You should keep a copy of the closing statement you receive when you are either buying or selling real property.

Points on home mortgage. Special rules may apply to points you and the seller pay when you get a mortgage to buy your main home. If certain requirements are met, you can deduct the points in full for the year in which they are paid. Reduce the basis of your home by any seller-paid points. For more information, see *Points* in chapter 25.

Adjusted Basis

Before figuring gain or loss on a sale, exchange, or other disposition of property or figuring allowable depreciation, depletion, or amortization, you must usually make certain adjustments (increases and decreases) to the basis of the property. The result of these adjustments to the basis is the adjusted basis (see Table 14–1).

Explanation

Note that you may need to make a separate calculation of basis when figuring your **alternative minimum tax (AMT)**. You must take into consideration the impact that AMT adjustments, such as depreciation, have on basis in property. For a discussion of the AMT, see Chapter 31, *How to Figure Your Tax.*

Increases to Basis

Increase the basis of any property by all items properly added to a capital account. These include the cost of any improvements having a useful life of more than 1 year. Other items added to the basis of property include the cost of extending utility service lines to the property and legal fees, such as the cost of defending and perfecting title.

Improvements. Add the cost of improvements to your basis in the property if they increase the value of the property, lengthen its life, or adapt it to a different use. For example, improvements include putting a recreation room in your unfinished basement, adding another bathroom or bedroom, putting up a fence, putting in new plumbing or wiring, installing a new roof, or paving your driveway.

TaxSaver

When you sell your home, your gain or loss is measured by the difference between the price you receive on the sale and your basis. Any improvements you have made will have increased your basis and will now decrease your tax liability. It is important that you keep adequate records of all improvements.

Among the improvements and other costs that increase your basis are the following:

1. Replacing the roof
2. Installing permanent storm windows
3. Installing new plumbing
4. Installing a new heating or air conditioning system
5. Installing a new furnace
6. Restoring a run-down house

7. Landscaping: adding new trees, shrubs, or lawn
8. Building a swimming pool, tennis court, or sauna
9. Constructing or improving a driveway
10. Constructing walks
11. Constructing patios and decks
12. Constructing walls
13. Payment of real estate commissions
14. Payment of legal fees stemming from improvements, zoning, and so on
15. Payment of closing costs
16. Cost of appliances

Many of the items listed above, such as real estate commissions and closing costs, appear on the closing statement you receive when you purchase the property.

It is important to distinguish between expenditures that constitute additions to basis and those that constitute repairs. If the asset is used in a trade or a business, repairs are deductible but do not increase its basis. If the asset is personal, the costs of repairs are not deductible and do not increase the asset's basis. (For a more complete discussion of this matter, see Chapter 10, *Rental Income and Expenses*.)

As noted by the IRS, your basis in property is reduced by money you receive as a return of capital. See Chapter 9, *Dividends and Other Corporate Distributions*, for further details.

Example

You buy land and a building for $25,000 for use as a parking lot. You pay $3,000 to have the building torn down, and you sell some of the materials you salvage from it for $5,000. You figure your adjusted basis in the property by taking your $25,000 initial cost, adding the $3,000 you spent for tearing down the building, and subtracting the $5,000 you received for the materials you salvaged. Your adjusted basis for the lot is $23,000. The money you received from the sale of the salvaged materials is not income, and the cost of tearing down the building is not deductible.

TaxOrganizer

You should keep a copy of all invoices you receive for improvements that increase your basis in real property.

Assessments for local improvements. Add assessments for improvements such as streets and sidewalks to the basis of the property if they increase the value of the property assessed. Do not deduct them as taxes. However, you can deduct as taxes assessments for maintenance, repairs, or interest charges on the improvements.

Example. Your city changes the street in front of your store into an enclosed pedestrian mall and assesses you and other affected property owners for the cost of the conversion. Add the assessment to your property's basis. In this example, the assessment is a depreciable asset.

Explanation

For further discussion of assessments and how to treat them, see Chapter 24, *Taxes You May Deduct.*

Decreases to Basis

The following items reduce the basis of your property.

- The section 179 deduction.
- The deduction for clean-fuel vehicles and clean-fuel vehicle refueling property.

- Nontaxable corporate distributions (see chapter 9).
- Deductions previously allowed (or allowable) for amortization, depreciation, and depletion.
- Exclusion of subsidies for energy conservation measures (see *Energy conservation subsidies* in chapter 13).
- Credit for qualified electric vehicles.
- Postponed gain from the sale of your home.
- Casualty and theft losses and insurance reimbursements.
- Certain canceled debt excluded from income.
- Rebates received from a manufacturer or seller.
- Easements.
- Gas-guzzler tax.
- Adoption tax benefits.

Casualties and thefts. If you have a casualty or theft loss, decrease the basis of your property by any insurance proceeds or other reimbursement and by any deductible loss not covered by insurance.

You must increase your basis in the property by the amount you spend on repairs that substantially prolong the life of the property, increase its value, or adapt it to a different use. To make this determination, compare the repaired property to the property before the casualty.

For more information on casualty and theft losses, see chapter 27.

Easements. The amount you receive for granting an easement is generally considered to be from the sale of an interest in real property. It reduces the basis of the affected part of the property. If the amount received is more than the basis of the part of the property affected by the easement, reduce your basis in that part to zero and treat the excess as a recognized gain.

If the gain is on a capital asset, see chapter 17 for information about how to report it. If the gain is on property used in a trade or business, see Publication 544 for information about how to report it.

Depreciation and section 179 deduction. Decrease the basis of your qualifying business property by any section 179 deduction you take and the depreciation you deducted, or could have deducted, on your tax returns under the method of depreciation you selected.

For more information about depreciation and the section 179 deduction, see Publication 946.

Explanation

For additional information on the Section 179 deduction, see Chapter 38, *If You Are Self-Employed: How to File Schedule C.* Also see *How to Begin Depreciating Your Property* in Publication 946.

Explanation

If you discover that you deducted less depreciation than you could have claimed on your prior returns, you should consider filing amended returns to claim a refund if the statute of limitations (generally, 3 years from the date you filed the original return) has not expired.

The IRS has introduced a procedure that may permit you to change your method of accounting to allow you to claim the allowable amount. Consult your tax advisor.

Credit for qualified electric vehicles. If you claim the credit for a qualified electric vehicle, you must reduce your basis in that vehicle by the lesser of the following amounts.

- $4,000.
- 10% of the vehicle's cost.

This basis reduction rule applies even if the credit allowed is less than the reduction. For more information on this credit, see chapter 12 in Publication 535.

Deduction for clean-fuel vehicle and refueling property. If you take the deduction for clean-fuel vehicles or clean-fuel vehicle refueling property, decrease the basis of the property by the amount taken. For more information about these deductions, see chapter 12 in Publication 535.

Exclusion of subsidies for energy conservation measures. You can exclude from gross income any subsidy you received from a public utility company for the purchase or installation of an energy conservation measure for a dwelling unit. Reduce the basis of the property for which you received the subsidy by the excluded amount. For more information about this subsidy, see chapter 13.

Postponed gain from sale of home. If you postponed gain from the sale of your main home before May 7, 1997, you must reduce the basis of your new home by the amount of the postponed gain. For more information on the rules for the sale of a home, see Publication 523.

Example

You owned a duplex used as rental property that cost you $40,000, of which $35,000 was allocated to the building and $5,000 to the land. You added an improvement to the duplex that cost $10,000. In February last year the duplex was damaged by fire. Up to that time you had been allowed depreciation of $23,000. You sold some salvaged material for $1,300 and collected $19,700 from your insurance company. You deducted a casualty loss of $1,000 on your income tax return for last year. You spent $19,000 of the insurance proceeds for restoration of the duplex, which was completed this year. You must use the duplex's adjusted basis after the restoration to determine depreciation for the rest of the property's recovery period. Figure the adjusted basis of the duplex as follows:

Original cost of duplex		$35,000
Addition to duplex		10,000
Total cost of duplex		$45,000
Minus: Depreciation		23,000
Adjusted basis before casualty		$22,000
Minus: Insurance proceeds	$19,700	
Deducted casualty loss	1,000	
Salvage proceeds	1,300	22,000
Adjusted basis after casualty		$ –0–
Add: Cost of restoring duplex		19,000
Adjusted basis after restoration		$19,000

Your basis in the land is its original cost of $5,000.

Basis Other Than Cost

There are many times when you cannot use cost as basis. In these cases, the fair market value or the adjusted basis of the property can be used. Fair market value (FMV) and adjusted basis were discussed earlier.

Property Received for Services

If you receive property for your services, include its FMV in income. The amount you include in income becomes your basis. If the services were performed for a price agreed on beforehand, it will be accepted as the FMV of the property if there is no evidence to the contrary.

Explanation
If you receive property by inheritance or as a gift, special rules apply. The basis of the property you inherit is usually its FMV at the time of the donor's death. (For more details, see *Inherited Property*, discussed later in this chapter.) The basis of property you get as a gift is generally the same as the donor's basis. If, however, the FMV of the property is less than the donor's basis at the time you receive the gift, your basis for the purpose of figuring whether you have a gain or a loss when you sell the property is the gift's FMV at the time you receive it. (See *Property Received as a Gift*, discussed later in this chapter.)

Restricted property. If you receive property for your services and the property is subject to certain restrictions, your basis in the property is its FMV when it becomes substantially vested. However, this rule does not apply if you make an election to include in income the FMV of the property at the time it is transferred to you, less any amount you paid for it. Property becomes substantially vested when your rights in the property or the rights of any person to whom you transfer the property are not subject to a substantial risk of forfeiture. For more information, see *Restricted Property* in Publication 525.

Explanation
For a full discussion of this subject, see *Property Received for Services* in Chapter 6, *Wages, Salaries, and Other Earnings*.

Bargain purchases. A bargain purchase is a purchase of an item for less than its FMV. If, as compensation for services, you buy goods or other property at less than FMV, include the difference between the purchase price and the property's FMV in your income. Your basis in the property is its FMV (your purchase price plus the amount you include in income).

If the difference between your purchase price and the FMV is a qualified employee discount, do not include the difference in income. However, your basis in the property is still its FMV. See *Employee Discounts* in Publication 15-B.

Examples
Airline, railroad, or subway employees need not include as income free travel provided by their employer if the employer does not incur any substantial additional cost in providing such travel.

Employee clothing discounts, discount brokerage fees, and lodging and meal discounts can also qualify as nontaxable compensation. Employees are eligible for such tax-free benefits only if the merchandise or services are also offered to customers in the ordinary course of the employer's business. The amount of the tax-free discount is subject to specific dollar limitations.

Business use of a company car, parking at or near your business premises, business periodicals, and any other property or service provided by your employer can be excluded from your taxable income if you would be allowed to take a business deduction had you paid for the benefit yourself.

Other nontaxable fringe benefits from employers include medical savings account (MSA) contributions, free medical services, reimbursement of medical expenses, gifts of $25 or less, payments of premiums for up to $50,000 of group term life insurance coverage, tuition given to children of university employees, dinner money for employees working overtime, and meals furnished to employees on the employer's business premises for the convenience of the employer.

Taxable Exchanges

A taxable exchange is one in which the gain is taxable or the loss is deductible. A taxable gain or deductible loss also is known as a recognized gain or loss. If you receive property in exchange for other property in a taxable exchange, the basis of the property you receive is usually its FMV at the time of the exchange.

Involuntary Conversions

If you receive property as a result of an involuntary conversion, such as a casualty, theft, or condemnation, you can figure the basis of the replacement property using the basis of the converted property.

Similar or related property. If you receive property similar or related in service or use to the converted property, the replacement property's basis is the same as the converted property's basis on the date of the conversion, with the following adjustments.

1) Decrease the basis by the following.
   a) Any loss you recognize on the conversion.
   b) Any money you receive that you do not spend on similar property.
2) Increase the basis by the following.
   a) Any gain you recognize on the conversion.
   b) Any cost of acquiring the replacement property.

Money or property not similar or related. If you receive money or property not similar or related in service or use to the converted property, and you buy replacement property similar or related in service or use to the converted property, the basis of the replacement property is its cost decreased by the gain not recognized on the conversion.

TAXSAVER

You can elect to exclude the gain if within 2 years following the year in which the involuntary gain was realized you buy new property that is similar or related in service or use to the old property. If this election is made, a gain will be recognized to the extent that the gain realized exceeds the difference between the cost of the replacement property and the adjusted basis of the old property. The basis of the new property is the cost of the new property decreased by the amount of gain that is not recognized.

The 1993 Tax Act extended the replacement period for your principal residence or any of its contents if it is converted involuntarily as a result of a disaster. The new replacement period was extended to 4 years after the close of the first year in which conversion was realized. This provision is effective for property in presidentially declared disaster areas on or after September 1, 1991.

Example. The state condemned your property. The adjusted basis of the property was $26,000 and the state paid you $31,000 for it. You realized a gain of $5,000 ($31,000 − $26,000). You bought replacement property similar in use to the converted property for $29,000. You recognize a gain of $2,000 ($31,000 − $29,000), the unspent part of the payment from the state. Your unrecognized gain is $3,000, the difference between the $5,000 realized gain and the $2,000 recognized gain. The basis of the replacement property is figured as follows:

Cost of replacement property	$29,000
Minus: Gain not recognized	3,000
Basis of replacement property	$26,000

Allocating the basis. If you buy more than one piece of replacement property, allocate your basis among the properties based on their respective costs.

TAXPLANNER

When you buy more than one asset for a single amount, such as land with buildings or the operating assets of a business, your costs must be reasonably allocated among the different assets. While the IRS may always question whether or not you have allocated these costs fairly, the IRS is unlikely to do so if the allocation has been contractually agreed to by the parties involved, particularly if you and the seller have adverse interests. Therefore, it may often be to your advantage to have the allocation spelled out in the purchase agreement.

If you are acquiring a trade, business, or investment asset, a favorable allocation of costs may have tax advantages. For example, raw land may not be depreciated, but buildings may. A favorable allocation between land and buildings enables you to claim more depreciation. The 1993 Tax Act provided that the costs of specified intangible assets (such as goodwill, covenant-not-to-compete, franchise, etc.) will be amortized over a 15-year period. Thus, while you can now amortize costs allocated to certain intangible assets, allocating more cost to operating assets instead may create an income tax advantage because of the more rapid depreciation methods available for equipment. However, while the allocation of purchase price to tangible assets (e.g., equipment) will generally produce a favorable income tax result, this allocation can cause state and local sales and use taxes and business property taxes to be imposed on the tangible assets acquired.

The 1993 Tax Act also provided that if you dispose of a specified intangible asset that was acquired in a transaction, but you retain other specified intangible assets acquired in the same transaction, you may not claim a loss as a result of the disposition. Instead, the bases of the retained specified intangible assets are increased by the amount of the unrecognized loss.

For information about asset allocations, see Chapter 38, *If You Are Self-Employed: How to File Schedule C.*

A provision of the Tax Reform Act of 1986 that is still in effect mandates that the residual method must be used to allocate the purchase price of acquired assets. Under the residual method, the amount allocated to the value of goodwill and going concern value is the excess of the purchase price over the FMV of the tangible assets and the other identifiable intangible assets.

For certain types of acquisitions of assets used in a trade or a business, the buyer and seller must file Form 8594 with the IRS, showing how the purchase price was allocated among various classes of assets. For more information, consult your tax advisor.

Nontaxable Exchanges

A nontaxable exchange is an exchange in which you are not taxed on any gain and you cannot deduct any loss. If you receive property in a nontaxable exchange, its basis is generally the same as the basis of the property you transferred. See *Nontaxable Trades* in chapter 15.

Like-Kind Exchanges

The exchange of property for the same kind of property is the most common type of nontaxable exchange. To qualify as a like-kind exchange, the property traded and the property received must be both of the following.

1) Qualifying property.
2) Like-kind property.

The basis of the property you receive is generally the same as the basis of the property you gave up. If you trade property in a like-kind exchange and also pay money, the basis of the property received is the basis of the property you gave up increased by the money you paid.

Qualifying property. In a like-kind exchange, you must hold for investment or for productive use in your trade or business both the property you give up and the property you receive.

Like-kind property. There must be an exchange of like property. The exchange of real estate for real estate or personal property for similar personal property is an exchange of like property.

Example. You trade in an old truck used in your business with an adjusted basis of $1,700 for a new one costing $6,800. The dealer allows you $2,000 on the old truck, and you pay $4,800. This is a like-kind exchange. The basis of the new truck is $6,500 (the adjusted basis of the old one, $1,700, plus the amount you paid, $4,800).

If you sell your old truck to a third party for $2,000 instead of trading it in and then buy a new one from the dealer, you have a taxable gain of $300 on the sale ($2,000 sale price minus $1,700 basis). The basis of the new truck is the price you pay the dealer.

> **Explanation**
> In general, all gains and losses realized on sales and other dispositions of property are taxable, but an exception is made when business or investment property is traded or exchanged for "like-kind" property. In this case, the newly acquired property is viewed as a continuation of the investment in the original property, so the tax basis does not change. The reason to make tax-free exchanges is not to avoid taxes but to defer them while realizing some other investment aims. (For more details on nontaxable exchanges, see Chapter 15, *Sale of Property.*)

Partially nontaxable exchange. A partially nontaxable exchange is an exchange in which you receive unlike property or money in addition to like property. The basis of the property you receive is the basis of the property you gave up, with the following adjustments.

1) Decrease the basis by the following amounts.
   a) Any money you receive.
   b) Any loss you recognize on the exchange.
2) Increase the basis by the following amounts.
   a) Any additional costs you incur.
   b) Any gain you recognize on the exchange.

Allocation of basis. Allocate the basis first to the unlike property, other than money, up to its FMV on the date of the exchange. The rest is the basis of the like property.

More information. See *Like-Kind Exchanges* in chapter 1 of Publication 544 for more information.

Property Transferred From a Spouse

The basis of property transferred to you or transferred in trust for your benefit by your spouse is the same as your spouse's adjusted basis. The same rule applies to a transfer by your former spouse that is incident to divorce. However, adjust your basis for any gain recognized by your spouse or former spouse on property transferred in trust. This rule applies only to a transfer of property in trust in which the liabilities assumed, plus the liabilities to which the property is subject, are more than the adjusted basis of the property transferred.

If the property transferred to you is a series E, series EE, or series I U.S. savings bond, the transferor must include in income the interest accrued to the date of transfer. Your basis in the bond immediately after the transfer is equal to the transferor's basis increased by the interest income includible in the transferor's income. For more information on these bonds, see chapter 8.

The transferor must give you, at the time of the transfer, the records needed to determine the adjusted basis and holding period of the property as of the date of the transfer.

For more information about the transfer of property from a spouse, see chapter 15.

Property Received as a Gift

To figure the basis of property you receive as a gift, you must know its adjusted basis to the donor just before it was given to you, its FMV at the time it was given to you, and any gift tax paid on it.

> **Explanation**
> If a gift tax return was filed, you should examine it for information on the donor's tax basis.

FMV less than donor's adjusted basis. If the FMV of the property at the time of the gift is less than the donor's adjusted basis, your basis depends on whether you have a gain or a loss when you dispose of the property. Your basis for figuring gain is the same as the donor's adjusted basis plus or minus any required adjustments to basis while you held the property. Your basis for figuring loss is its FMV when you received the gift plus or minus any required adjustments to basis while you held the property. See *Adjusted Basis,* earlier.

Example. You received an acre of land as a gift. At the time of the gift, the land had an FMV of $8,000. The donor's adjusted basis was $10,000. After you received the property, no events occurred to increase or decrease your basis. If you later sell the property for $12,000, you will have a $2,000 gain because you must use the donor's adjusted basis at the time of the gift ($10,000) as your basis to figure gain. If you sell the property for $7,000, you will have a $1,000 loss because you must use the FMV at the time of the gift ($8,000) as your basis to figure loss.

If the sales price is between $8,000 and $10,000, you have neither gain nor loss.

> **Example**
> Owen owns a building in which his adjusted basis is $40,000. The fair market value of the building, however, is only $30,000. Owen gives the building to Jim. Jim's basis is $40,000—Owen's adjusted basis—for determining depreciation and for computing a gain on the sale of the building. Jim's basis is $30,000—the FMV at the time of the gift—for computing a loss on the sale of the building.
> *Note:* If the FMV of the building increases to $35,000, Jim may sell the property without recognizing a gain or a loss. His proceeds of $35,000 would be greater than the basis used for computing a loss on the sale and less than the basis used for computing a gain on the sale.
>
> **TaxPlanner**
> If the FMV of property that you intend to give as a gift is less than your adjusted basis in the property, you might want to sell the property and then make a gift of the proceeds. In this way, you recognize a loss on the sale of the property. This could provide you with a tax savings. The recipient of the gift will receive the same amount of value, but in cash rather than property. Had the recipient received property, he

or she would not be able to deduct the loss you had on the property when the recipient sold it because the recipient's basis in the property for computing a loss is the property's FMV at the time the gift is made.

Business property. If you hold the gift as business property, your basis for figuring any depreciation, depletion, or amortization deduction is the same as the donor's adjusted basis plus or minus any required adjustments to basis while you hold the property.

FMV equal to or greater than donor's adjusted basis. If the FMV of the property is equal to or greater than the donor's adjusted basis, your basis is the donor's adjusted basis at the time you received the gift. Increase your basis by all or part of any gift tax paid, depending on the date of the gift, explained later.

Also, for figuring gain or loss from a sale or other disposition or for figuring depreciation, depletion, or amortization deductions on business property, you must increase or decrease your basis (the donor's adjusted basis) by any required adjustments to basis while you held the property. See *Adjusted Basis,* earlier.

Gift received before 1977. If you received a gift before 1977, increase your basis in the gift (the donor's adjusted basis) by any gift tax paid on it. However, do not increase your basis above the FMV of the gift at the time it was given to you.

Gift received after 1976. If you received a gift after 1976, increase your basis in the gift (the donor's adjusted basis) by the part of the gift tax paid on it that is due to the net increase in value of the gift. Figure the increase by multiplying the gift tax paid by a fraction. The numerator of the fraction is the net increase in value of the gift and the denominator is the amount of the gift.

The net increase in value of the gift is the FMV of the gift minus the donor's adjusted basis. The amount of the gift is its value for gift tax purposes after reduction by any annual exclusion and marital or charitable deduction that applies to the gift. For information on the gift tax, see Publication 950, *Introduction to Estate and Gift Taxes.*

Example. In 2001, you received a gift of property from your mother that had an FMV of $50,000. Her adjusted basis was $20,000. The amount of the gift for gift tax purposes was $40,000 ($50,000 minus the $10,000 annual exclusion). She paid a gift tax of $9,000 on the property. Your basis is $26,750, figured as follows:

Fair market value	$50,000
Minus: Adjusted basis	- 20,000
Net increase in value	$30,000
Gift tax paid	$ 9,000
Multiplied by ($30,000 ÷ $40,000)	x .75
Gift tax due to net increase in value	$ 6,750
Adjusted basis of property to your mother	+20,000
Your basis in the property	$26,750

Inherited Property

Your basis in property you inherit from a decedent is generally one of the following.

1) The FMV of the property at the date of the individual's death.
2) The FMV on the alternate valuation date if the personal representative for the estate chooses to use alternate valuation.
3) The value under the special-use valuation method for real property used in farming or another closely held business, if chosen for estate tax purposes.
4) The decedent's adjusted basis in land to the extent of the value ex-

cluded from the decedent's taxable estate as a qualified conservation easement.

If a federal estate tax return does not have to be filed, your basis in the inherited property is its appraised value at the date of death for state inheritance or transmission taxes.

TAXALERT: THE 2001 TAX ACT

Please note that under the new tax law (see *Changes in the Tax Law You Should Know About* located at the beginning of this guide), the step-up in basis rules are to be replaced with a carryover basis system. As of the date of this publication, the carryover basis rules had yet to be determined by Congress.

Explanation

The alternate valuation date is the earlier of the date 6 months after death and the date on which the estate's assets are distributed, sold, exchanged, or disposed of. Alternate valuation may be elected only if it is necessary to file an estate tax return. Furthermore, use of the alternate valuation date must result in a decrease in the estate tax. The election must be made for all property included in the estate.

TAXSAVER

Choosing an alternate valuation date may be helpful in reducing estate tax if the market value of the assets in the estate is declining. However, if this is the case, the tax basis of those assets must also be reduced; this means increased income taxes in the future if the market value of the assets rises and they are then sold. Thus, the decision to elect the alternate valuation date to reduce estate tax should be balanced against a possible increase in future income taxes.

For more information, see the instructions to Form 706, *U.S. Estate Tax Return.*

Explanation

If a decedent used property that he or she owned for farming, trade, or business purposes at the date of death, the executor of the decedent's estate may, under most conditions, choose the special-use valuation method for that property. This means that the property is included in the decedent's estate at the value based on its *current use* and not at the value based on what its most lucrative use might be. For example, if the land is being used for farming, its value is figured on its worth as farmland and not on what it might be worth if used for industrial purposes.

The following conditions must be met before you use the special-use valuation method:

1. The decedent must have been a resident or a citizen of the United States.
2. The property must pass to a qualified heir, meaning an ancestor of either the decedent or his or her spouse or one of their lineal descendants.
3. The property must be located in the United States and must be used in a trade or a business.
4. The property must have been used by the decedent in a trade or a business for 5 of the past 8 years. The 8-year period is measured from the earliest of the decedent's death, disablement, or retirement.

5. The value of the real and personal property used in the farm or closely held business must form at least one-half of the decedent's gross estate. (Gross estate is the total amount of the decedent's assets.)
6. At least one-quarter of the value of the gross estate must be qualified real property. (Livestock and farm machinery are not considered qualified real property. Real estate is.)

The maximum amount that the special-use method can decrease the value of the estate is $750,000, increased each year for cost-of-living adjustments.

TAX*SAVER*

In community property states, the basis of the surviving spouse's one-half share of the community property will also receive a step-up in basis, normally to its FMV, at the date of the decedent spouse's death.

TAX*ORGANIZER*

If you receive property by inheritance, you should request a copy of the estate tax return from the executor of the estate to determine your basis in the inherited property.

Property Changed to Business or Rental Use

When you hold property for personal use and change it to business use or use it to produce rent, you must figure its basis for depreciation. An example of changing property held for personal use to business use would be renting out your former personal residence.
Basis for depreciation. The basis for depreciation is the lesser of the following amounts.

1) The FMV of the property on the date of the change.
2) Your adjusted basis on the date of the change.

Example. Several years ago, you paid $160,000 to have your house built on a lot that cost $25,000. Before changing the property to rental use last year, you paid $20,000 for permanent improvements to the house and claimed a $2,000 casualty loss deduction for damage to the house. Because land is not depreciable, you can only include the cost of the house when figuring the basis for depreciation.

Your adjusted basis in the house when you changed its use was $178,000 ($160,000 + $20,000 − $2,000). On the same date, your property had an FMV of $180,000, of which $15,000 was for the land and $165,000 was for the house. The basis for figuring depreciation on the house is its FMV on the date of the change ($165,000) because it is less than your adjusted basis ($178,000).
Sale of property. If you later sell or dispose of the property, the basis you use will depend on whether you are figuring gain or loss.
Gain. The basis for figuring a gain is your adjusted basis when you sell the property.
Example. Assume the same facts as in the previous example except that you sell the property at a gain after being allowed depreciation deductions of $37,500. The basis for figuring gain is $165,000 ($178,000 + $25,000 (land) − $37,500).
Loss. Figure the basis for a loss starting with the smaller of your adjusted basis or the FMV of the property at the time of the change to business or rental use. Then adjust this amount for the period after the change in the property's use, as discussed earlier under *Adjusted Basis,* to arrive at a basis for loss.
Example. Assume the same facts as in the previous example, except that you sell the property at a loss after being allowed depreciation deductions of $37,500. In this case, you would start with the FMV on the date of the change to rental use ($180,000), because it is less than the ad-

justed basis of $203,000 ($178,000 + $25,000) on that date. Reduce that amount ($180,000) by the depreciation deductions to arrive at a basis for loss of $142,500 ($180,000 − $37,500).

Stocks and Bonds

The basis of stocks or bonds you buy generally is the purchase price plus any costs of purchase, such as commissions and recording or transfer fees. If you get stocks or bonds other than by purchase, your basis is usually determined by the FMV or the previous owner's adjusted basis, as discussed earlier.

You must adjust the basis of stocks for certain events that occur after purchase. For example, if you receive additional stock from nontaxable stock dividends or stock splits, divide the adjusted basis of the old stock by the number of shares of old and new stock. This rule applies only when the additional stock received is identical to the stock held. Also reduce your basis when you receive nontaxable distributions. They are a return of capital.

Example. In 1999 you bought 100 shares of XYZ stock for $1,000 or $10 a share. In 2000 you bought 100 shares of XYZ stock for $1,600 or $16 a share. In 2001 XYZ declared a 2-for-1 stock split. You now have 200 shares of stock with a basis of $5 a share and 200 shares with a basis of $8 a share.
Other basis. There are other ways to figure the basis of stocks or bonds depending on how you acquired them. For detailed information, see *Stocks and Bonds* under *Basis of Investment Property* in chapter 4 of Publication 550.
Identifying stocks or bonds sold. If you can adequately identify the shares of stock or the bonds you sold, their basis is the cost or other basis of the particular shares of stocks or bonds. If you buy and sell securities at various times in varying quantities and you cannot adequately identify the shares you sell, the basis of the securities you sell is the basis of the securities you acquired first. For more information about identifying securities you sell, see *Stocks and Bonds* under *Basis of Investment Property* in chapter 4 of Publication 550.

TAX*PLANNER*

If your portfolio consists of various lots of the same stock acquired at different times and at different costs, some care must be exercised when a sale of a portion of these shares is contemplated. For example, assume that you own five different lots of ABC Motors stock acquired at different times and ranging in cost basis between $40 and $80 per share. If the stock is currently selling for $60 per share and you sell a lot with a basis of $40 per share, you recognize a gain; on the other hand, if you sell a lot having a basis of $80 per share, you sustain a loss. The situation may be far more complicated if the company has paid **stock dividends** or has split its stock one or more times.

It may be advisable to take any shares that you receive as the result of a stock dividend or a stock split and combine them with the shares that gave rise to the dividend or split. Have your broker convert all such related stock certificates into one certificate. Thus, each block of stock having a distinguishable cost basis is separately maintained. Although you are certainly not required to do this, it simplifies your record-keeping task and makes it much easier for you to compute your gain or loss when you sell the shares.

TAX*ORGANIZER*

You should keep a copy of your broker confirmation statement as a record for your cost basis in the shares of stock you have purchased during the year.

Explanation

For tax purposes, the selling instructions given to your broker or fund representative must be in writing. Even if stock certificates from a different lot are actually delivered to the transfer agent, you may consider the stock sold as you specified, provided that you identified the shares to be sold and received written confirmation of your orders.

TAXPLANNER

Incentive stock options. If the shares you are selling were acquired by exercising an Incentive Stock Option (ISO) with previously owned employer shares, special rules will apply in determining the basis of the ISO shares.

The sale or transfer of stock acquired through the exercise of an ISO within 2 years of the option's grant date and within 1 year of the option's exercise date is known as a "disqualifying disposition." If the sale constitutes a disqualifying disposition of the ISO shares, the lowest basis shares are considered to be sold first, regardless of your effort to identify and sell specific shares. For more information, see Chapter 6, *Wages, Salaries, and Other Earnings*, and Publication 525, *Taxable and Nontaxable Income*.

Charitable contributions. If you own several blocks of appreciated shares, it is generally to your advantage to give away those shares with the lowest tax basis. When you make a contribution of the stock, you should be especially careful to designate which shares are being contributed. Let your stockbroker or transfer agent and the charity know the date you purchased the shares that you are now donating. It's important to take these steps at the time you are making the gift. For more information, see Chapter 26, *Contributions*.

TAXALERT

The 1993 Tax Act provides that unrealized gains from contributions of appreciated property will no longer be subject to the AMT. (The 1993 Tax Act repealed the provision that treated the untaxed appreciation deducted as a charitable contribution as a tax preference item for the purpose of calculating the AMT.) For more information, see Chapter 26, *Contributions*.

Mutual fund shares. If you sell mutual funds you acquired at various times and prices, you can choose to use an average basis. For more information, see *Average Basis* in Publication 564.

Explanation

For further discussion, see Chapter 17, *Reporting Gains and Losses*. Also, mutual funds are discussed in Chapter 39, *Mutual Funds*.

Bond premium. If you buy a taxable bond at a premium and choose to amortize the premium, reduce the basis of the bond by the amortized premium you deduct each year. See *Bond Premium Amortization* in chapter 3 of Publication 550 for more information. Although you cannot deduct the premium on a tax-exempt bond, you must amortize the premium each year and reduce your basis in the bond by the amortized amount.

Example

On January 15, 2000, Elizabeth purchases for $120,000 a tax-exempt obligation maturing on January 15, 2007, with a stated principal amount of $100,000, payable at maturity. The obligation provides for unconditional payments of interest of $9,000, payable on January 15 of each year. The interest payments on the obligation are qualified stated interest. The amount of bond premium is $20,000 ($120,000 − $100,000).

Based on the remaining payment schedule of the bond and Elizabeth's basis in the bond, Elizabeth's yield is 5.48%, compounded annually. The bond premium that must be amortized on January 15, 2001, is $2,420.55 ($9,000 − $6,579.45). The bond premium amortized is the excess of the qualified stated interest allocable to the period ($9,000) over the product of the adjusted acquisition price at the beginning of the period ($120,000) and Elizabeth's yield (5.48%, compounded annually). However, Elizabeth may not claim the amortization as a deduction on her tax return.

Original issue discount (OID) on debt instruments. You must increase your basis in an OID debt instrument by the OID you include in income for that instrument. See *Original Issue Discount* in chapter 8.

Tax-exempt bonds. OID on tax-exempt bonds is generally not taxable. However, there are special rules for figuring the basis of these bonds issued after September 3, 1982, and acquired after March 1, 1984. See chapter 4 of Publication 550.

Explanation

For further discussion of original issue discount, including some recent changes in the law, see Chapter 8, *Interest Income*.

TAXSAVER

Automatic investment service and dividend reinvestment plans. If you take part in an automatic investment service, your cost basis per share of stock, including fractional shares, bought by the bank or other agent is your proportionate share of the agent's cost of all shares purchased at the same time plus the same share of the brokerage commission paid by the agent. If you take part in a **dividend** reinvestment plan and you receive stock from the corporation at a discount, your cost is the full FMV of the stock on the dividend payment date. You must include the amount of the discount in your income as an additional dividend.

Special rules apply in determining the basis of stock you acquired through a **stock dividend** or a **stock right. Stock dividends** are distributions by a corporation of its own stock. Usually, stock dividends are not taxable to the shareholder. However, for exceptions to this rule, see Chapter 9, *Dividends and Other Corporate Distributions*. If stock dividends are not taxable, you must allocate your basis for the stock between the old and the new stock in proportion to the FMV of each on the date of the distribution of the new stock.

New and old stock identical. If the new stock you received as a dividend is the same as the old stock on which the dividend is declared, both new and old shares probably have equal FMVs and you can divide the adjusted basis of the old stock by the number of shares of old and new stock. The result is your basis for each share of stock.

Example

You owned one share of common stock that you bought for $45. The corporation distributed two new shares of common stock for each share you held. You then had three shares of common stock, each with a basis of $15 ($45 ÷ 3). If you owned two shares before the distribution, one bought for $30 and the other for $45, you would have six shares after the distribution: three with a basis of $10 each and three with a basis of $15 each.

Explanation

New and old stock not identical. If the new stock you received as a nontaxable dividend is not the same as the old stock on which the dividend was declared, the FMVs of the old stock and the new stock will probably be different, so you should allocate the adjusted basis of your old stock between the old stock and the new stock in proportion to the FMVs of each on the date of the distribution of the new stock.

Example 1

This example shows how to account for stock splits and stock dividends.

| | Block 1 | | |
	Shares	Total Cost	Cost per Share
Jan. 15, 1997	100	$3,000	$ 30
2 for 1 stock split	100	–0–	
Dec. 31, 1997	200	$3,000	$ 15
Nov. 30, 1997			
10% stock dividend	20		
Dec. 31, 1997	220	$3,000	$13.636

| | Block 2 | | |
	Shares	Total Cost	Cost per Share
Nov. 30, 1997	100	$2,000	$ 20
10% stock dividend	10		
Dec. 31, 1997	110	$2,000	$18.182

The original cost of each block of stock must be divided by the number of shares on hand at any given date to arrive at basis per share.

Example 2

This example shows how to account for nontaxable stock dividends with an FMV that is different from the value of the original stock held.

	Shares	Total Cost	Cost per Share	Total FMV	FMV per Share
Feb. 7, 1997 Purchased common stock	1,000	$14,000	$14	$14,000	$14
Aug. 30, 1997 10% stock dividend of preferred stock. FMV of original stock is $22 per share.	100			$ 1,000	$10

1,000 shares × $14 = $14,000	Cost of originating stock

1,000 shares × $22 = $22,000	Market value of original stock
100 shares × $10 = $ 1,000	Market value of preferred stock
$22,000/$23,000 × $14,000 = $13,391	Cost of original stock apportioned to such stock
$1,000/$23,000 × $14,000 = $609	Cost of original stock apportioned to the preferred stock

Explanation

If your stock dividend is taxable on receipt, the original basis of your new stock is its FMV on the date of distribution. Your holding period is determined from the date of distribution.

Stock rights are rarely taxable when you receive them. For more information, see Chapter 9, *Dividends and Other Corporate Distributions.*

If you receive stock rights that are taxable, the basis of the rights is their FMV at the time of distribution.

If you receive stock rights that are not taxable and you allow them to expire, they have no basis.

If you exercise or sell the nontaxable stock rights and if, at the time of distribution, the rights had an FMV of 15% or more of the FMV of the old stock, you must divide the adjusted basis of the stock between the stock and the stock rights. Use a ratio of the FMV of each to the FMV of both at the time of distribution of the rights. If the FMV of the stock rights is less than 15%, their basis is zero unless you choose to allocate a part of the basis of the old stock to the rights. You make this allocation on your return for the tax year in which the rights are received.

Basis of new stock. If you exercise the stock rights, the basis of the new stock is its cost plus the basis of the stock rights exercised. The holding period of the new stock begins on the date on which you exercised the stock rights.

Example

You own 100 shares of Tan Company stock, which cost you $22 per share. The Tan Company gave you 10 stock rights that would allow you to buy 10 additional shares of stock at $26 per share. At the time the rights were distributed, the stock had a market value of $30, without the rights, and each right had a market value of $3. The market value of the stock rights is less than 15% of the market value of the stock, but you choose to divide the basis of your stock between the stock and the rights. You figure the basis of the rights and the basis of the old stock as follows:

100 shares × $22 = $2,200, basis of old stock

100 shares × $30 = $3,000, market value of old stock

10 rights × $3 = $30, market value of rights

30/3,030 × $2,200 = $21.78, basis of rights

3,000/3,030 × $2,200 = $2,178.22, new basis of old stock

If you sell the stock rights, the basis for figuring gain or loss is $2.178 per right. If you exercise the stock rights, the basis of the new stock you receive is $28.178 per share, the subscription price paid ($26), plus the basis of the stock rights exercised ($2.178 each). The remaining basis of the 100 shares of old stock for figuring gain or loss on a later sale is $2,178.22, or $21.7822 per share.

Explanation

Other basis rules. There are many other special rules you must follow in determining your basis in certain types of property. Here are some examples.

If you receive stock of one corporation in exchange for stock of another corporation in certain types of corporate reorganizations, your basis in the stock received will be equal to the basis of the stock you exchanged.

Certain types of tax credits may reduce basis in whole or in part. For example, if you claim rehabilitation credits on a building, the basis of the property is reduced by the amount of the credit.

If you lease real property on which the lessee makes improvements and the value of such improvements is excluded from income, your basis in the improvements is zero.

If you sell property to charity in a bargain sale, your basis for determining the gain from the sale is reduced by the ratio of the total basis of the property to its FMV.

For more information, you should consult your tax advisor.

15

Sale of Property

Introduction

Any time you sell or exchange a piece of property at a gain—whether it be your house, a stock you own, or something you use in your trade or business—you usually have to pay taxes on the transaction. That, of course, doesn't mean that sales and exchanges should be avoided, but the manner in which you choose to dispose of an **asset** *may determine how much you will have to pay in taxes. This chapter describes the various options available to you and the tax consequences of each.*

Because the amounts involved in sales and exchanges of property are often quite large relative to other items that make up your income, this chapter merits careful attention. It not only spells out how you deter-mine the way in which various transactions are taxed but also offers suggestions about how to minimize or defer the tax burdens that you may incur.

In addition, this chapter discusses **bad debts.** *When a borrower cannot repay a loan, it is known as a bad debt. Some loans are made in connection with a trade or a business, some are made for purely personal reasons, and still others are made to make a profit. All sorts of rules have to be followed, and not every bad debt qualifies for a deduction. This chapter spells out what kind of documentation you need to prove that the money you lost was a bona fide debt and that there is no chance of repayment—the two conditions that must be met for you to take a deduction.*

Important Reminder

Foreign income. If you are a U.S. citizen with investment property from sources outside the United States, you must report all gains and losses from the sale of that property on your tax return unless it is exempt by U.S. law. This is true whether you reside inside or outside the United States and whether or not you receive a Form 1099 from the foreign payer.

This chapter discusses the tax consequences of selling or trading investment property. It explains:

- What is a sale or trade,
- When you have a nontaxable trade,
- What to do with a related party transaction,
- Whether the property you sell is a capital asset or a noncapital asset,
- Whether you have a capital or ordinary gain or loss from the sale of property,
- How to determine your holding period, and

- When you can make a tax-free rollover of a gain from selling certain securities.

Sales not discussed in this publication. Certain sales or trades of property are discussed in other publications.

Installment sales are covered in Publication 537, *Installment Sales.*

Transfers of property at death are covered in Publication 559, *Survivors, Executors, and Administrators.*

Transactions involving business property are covered in Publication 544, *Sales and Other Dispositions of Assets.*

Dispositions of an interest in a passive activity are covered in Publication 925, *Passive Activity and At-Risk Rules.*

Sales of a main home are covered in chapter 16.

Publication 550, *Investment Income and Expenses (Including Capital Gains and Losses),* provides more detailed discussion about sales and trades of investment property. Publication 550 includes information about the rules covering nonbusiness bad debts, straddles, section 1256 contracts, puts and calls, commodity futures, short sales, and wash sales. It also discusses investment-related expenses.

TaxSaver

Noncorporate taxpayers who held qualified small business stock (QSBS) for more than 5 years could exclude from gross income 50% of any gain realized from the sale or exchange of the stock. This exclusion is limited to the greater of:

1. 10 times the taxpayer's basis in the stock; or
2. $10 million in gain from all of the taxpayer's transactions in stock of that corporation (held for more than 5 years).

The rules for determining whether stock is qualified small business stock can be summarized as follows:

- The stock must be newly issued stock and issued after August 10, 1993.
- The stock cannot be acquired in exchange for other stock.
- The issuing corporation must be a C corporation but may not be a cooperative, Domestic International Sales Corporation (DISC), former DISC, real estate investment trust (REIT), regulated investment company (RIC), Real Estate Mortgage Investment Conduit (REMIC), a corporation having a possessions tax credit election in effect nor owning a subsidiary that has a possessions tax credit election in effect.
- At least 80% of the corporation's assets must be used in the active conduct of a qualifed trade or business or in the start-up of a future qualified trade or business.
- A qualified trade or business is any business other than one involving the performance of services in the fields of health, law, engineering, architecture, accounting, actuarial science, performing arts, consulting, athletics, financial services, brokerage services, or any other trade or business where the principal asset of the business is the reputation or skill of one or more employees. A qualified trade or business also cannot involve the businesses of banking, insurance, financing, leasing, investing or similar businesses, farming or certain businesses involving natural resource extraction or production, and businesses operating a hotel, motel, restaurant, or similar business.
- The corporation may not have greater than $50 million in gross assets (i.e., the sum of cash plus the aggregate fair market value of other corporate property) at the time the qualified small business stock is issued. If the corporation meets this test at the time of issuance of the stock, a subsequent event that violates this rule will not disqualify stock that previously qualified.

Note: Under certain circumstances, the gain on the sale of publicly traded securities will not be taxed if the proceeds from the sale are used to acquire common stock in a specialized small business investment company (SSBIC) within a 60-day period. See Publication 550, Investment Income and Expenses, for a detailed description of these additional requirements.

Useful Items

You may want to see:

Publication

Form (and Instructions)

Sales and Trades

If you sold property such as stocks, bonds, or certain commodities through a broker during the year, you should receive, for each sale, a *Form 1099-B, Proceeds From Broker and Barter Exchange Transactions,* or an equivalent statement from the broker. You should receive the statement by January 31 of the next year. It will show the gross proceeds from the sale. The IRS will also get a copy of Form 1099-B from the broker.

Use Form 1099-B (or an equivalent statement received from your broker) to complete Schedule D of Form 1040.

What is a Sale or Trade?

This section explains what is a sale or trade. It also explains certain transactions and events that are treated as sales or trades.

A sale is generally a transfer of property for money or a mortgage, note, or other promise to pay money. A trade is a transfer of property for other property or services and may be taxed in the same way as a sale.

Sale and purchase. Ordinarily, a transaction is not a trade when you voluntarily sell property for cash and immediately buy similar property to replace it. The sale and purchase are two separate transactions. But see *Like-kind exchanges* under *Nontaxable Trades,* later.

Example
You sell your car to your brother and buy a new one from a dealer. You have entered into two separate transactions.

Redemption of stock. A redemption of stock is treated as a sale or trade and is subject to the capital gain or loss provisions unless the redemption is a dividend or other distribution on stock.

Dividend versus sale or trade. Whether a redemption is treated as a sale, trade, dividend, or other distribution depends on the circumstances in each case. Both direct and indirect ownership of stock will be considered. The redemption is treated as a sale or trade of stock if:

1) The redemption is not essentially equivalent to a dividend (see chapter 9),
2) There is a substantially disproportionate redemption of stock,
3) There is a complete redemption of all the stock of the corporation owned by the shareholder, or
4) The redemption is a distribution in partial liquidation of a corporation.

Redemption or retirement of bonds. A redemption or retirement of bonds or notes at their maturity is generally treated as a sale or trade.

Surrender of stock. A surrender of stock by a dominant shareholder who retains control of the corporation is treated as a contribution to capital rather than as an immediate loss deductible from taxable income. The surrendering shareholder must reallocate his or her basis in the surrendered shares to the shares he or she retains.

Worthless securities. Stocks, stock rights, and bonds (other than those held for sale by a securities dealer) that became worthless during the tax year are treated as though they were sold on the last day of the tax year. This affects whether your capital loss is long-term or short-term. See *Holding Period,* later.

If you are a cash basis taxpayer and make payments on a negotiable promissory note that you issued for stock that became worthless, you can deduct these payments as losses in the years you actually make the payments. Do not deduct them in the year the stock became worthless.

Explanation
A security is considered worthless when it has no recognizable value. You should be able to establish that the worthless security had value in the year preceding the year in which you take the deduction and that an identifiable event reduced the value to zero, causing the loss in the year in which you deduct it. A drop in the value of a stock, even though substantial, does not constitute worthlessness. The courts have held that if stock is sold for a very nominal sum (e.g., less than 1 cent per share), that is proof of worthlessness.

TaxPlanner
The deduction for a worthless security must be taken in the year the security becomes worthless, even if it is sold for a nominal sum in the following year. If you do not learn that a security has become worthless until a later year, you should file an amended return for the year in which it became worthless. Because it may be difficult to determine exactly when a stock becomes worthless, the capital loss deduction should be claimed in the earliest year a claim may be reasonably made.

If you hold securities that seem to be on the verge of worthlessness, it may be easier to sell them now and take your capital loss without waiting for proof of worthlessness.

When securities are bought on credit, the timing of the deduction for worthlessness depends on the type of debt you have incurred. If the stock is purchased by giving the seller a note and the stock becomes worthless before the note is paid off, you may deduct the loss only as you make the payments on the note. However, if you borrow the funds from a third party, you may deduct the loss in the year in which the stock becomes worthless. In either case, an accrual basis taxpayer takes the deduction in the year the security becomes worthless.

TaxOrganizer
You should keep any documents indicating the date on which the security becomes worthless. Examples of sufficient documentation are bankruptcy documents and financial statements.

How to report loss. Report worthless securities on line 1 or line 8 of Schedule D (Form 1040), whichever applies. In columns (c) and (d), write "Worthless." Enter the amount of your loss in parentheses in column (f).

Filing a claim for refund. If you do not claim a loss for a worthless security on your original return for the year it becomes worthless, you can file a claim for a credit or refund due to the loss. You must use Form 1040X, *Amended U.S. Individual Income Tax Return,* to amend your return for the year the security became worthless. You must file it within 7 years from the date your original return for that year had to be filed, or 2 years from the date you paid the tax, whichever is later. For more information about filing a claim, see *Amended Returns and Claims for Refund* in chapter 1.

Exceptions
While an exchange is generally taxable, the following "exchanges" are not:

- The extension of the maturity date of promissory notes
- The exercise of an option to convert a bond into stock of the issuing corporation, if the conversion privilege is provided for in the bond
- The conversion of security interests to stock in the same corporation subsequent to certain reorganizations (one example: the exchange of common stock for preferred stock)

TaxPlanner
You may save taxes by carefully planning major sales and exchanges. It may be better to wait until after the end of the year before finalizing a sale so that a gain may be deferred until the next year. Alternatively, you may want to finalize the sale before the end of the year to take advantage of any losses in the current year. Professional advice should be obtained before, not after, a major transaction.

Explanation
Estates. The transfer of property of a decedent to the executor or administrator of the estate, or to the heirs or beneficiaries, generally is not a sale or exchange. No taxable gain or deductible loss results from the transfer.

Easements. Granting or selling an easement usually is not a taxable sale of property. Instead, the amount received for the easement is subtracted from the **basis** of the property. If only a part of an entire tract of property is permanently affected by the easement, only the basis of that part is reduced by the amount received. Any amount received that is more than the basis of the property to be reduced is a taxable gain. The transaction is reported as if it were a sale of the property.

If you transfer a perpetual easement for consideration, the transaction will be treated as a sale of property.

Life estate, etc. The entire amount you realize from disposing of a life interest in property, an interest in property for a set number of years, or an income interest in a trust is a taxable gain if you first got the interest as a gift, inheritance, or transfer in trust. Your basis in the property is considered to be zero. This rule does not apply if all interests in the property are disposed of at the same time.

Example 1
Your father dies, leaving his farm to you for life, with a remainder interest to your younger brother. You decide to sell your life interest in the farm. The entire amount you receive is a taxable gain, and your basis in the farm is disregarded.

Example 2
The facts are the same as in Example 1, except that your younger brother joins you in selling the farm. Because the entire interest in the property is conveyed, your taxable gain is the amount by which your share of the proceeds exceeds your adjusted basis in the farm.

Note: In Example 2, each brother's gain is computed by allocating the tax basis between them. The basis for the entire property—the **fair market value** at the date of the decedent's death—is adjusted for **depreciation** and improvements. Then, using actuarial tables, you compute the value of the life interest and of the **remainder interest** at the date of sale.

The younger brother could sell his remainder interest in the property independently of his brother, using his separate basis in computing his gain or loss on the sale. However, the older brother may not get the benefit of his basis in the property if he sells his life interest separately. The moral of the story is: Sometimes you save on taxes if you get along with your brother.

Sale versus lease. Just because a document says that it is a lease does not necessarily make it a lease for tax purposes. The rules are very complicated and not completely clear. Professional help is advisable. See Publication 544, *Sales and Other Dispositions of Assets.*

Installment sales. Some sales are made under a plan that provides for part or all of the sales price to be paid in a later year. These are called installment sales. If you finance the buyer's purchase of your property instead of the buyer getting a loan or mortgage from a bank, you probably have an installment sale.

You report your gain on an installment sale only as you actually receive payment. You are taxed only on the part of each payment that represents your profit on the sale. In this way, the installment method of reporting income relieves you of paying tax on income that you have not yet collected.

The first step in using the installment method is to find what portion of each installment payment represents a gain. This is determined by calculating the gross profit percentage, which is your gross profit divided by the contract price. Apply this percentage to all payments you receive in a year.

Gross profit is the selling price less the adjusted basis of the property sold. The selling price includes any cash you receive, the fair market value of any property received from the buyer, plus the amount of any existing mortgage on the property that the buyer took subject to or assumed.

Contract price is the selling price less any mortgage encumbrance on the property. However, if the amount of the mortgage is more than the adjusted basis of the property, then the selling price is reduced only by the adjusted basis, so the gross profit percentage is 100%.

Example 3

In 1980, Able bought commercial **real estate** for $100,000. He put $20,000 down and took out a mortgage for $80,000. By 1997, Able had reduced the mortgage to $40,000 and had an adjusted basis in the real estate of $85,000 (original cost, less depreciation, plus improvements). Able sold the real estate to Baker for $190,000. To pay Able, Baker assumed the rest of the mortgage and made three installment payments of $50,000 each.

Able figures his gross profit as follows:

Selling price	$190,000
Less adjusted tax basis	85,000
Gross profit	$105,000

Able figures his contract price as follows:

Selling price	$190,000
Less mortgage assumed	40,000
Contract price	$150,000

Able's gross profit percentage is 70% (gross profit divided by contract price). Able must report 70% of all contract-price collections as a taxable gain in the year they are received.

TaxSaver

Using the installment sale method may spread out your gain over several years and may result in a lower total tax on your gain.

By taking only a portion of the gain into income each year, you may avoid reaching a higher tax bracket. Even if you are already in the highest bracket, use of the installment sale method may still be beneficial, because taxes may be deferred to later years.

A disadvantage of the installment sale method is that if you are the seller, you do not obtain the sale proceeds immediately and therefore cannot reinvest them elsewhere.

TaxSaver

Installment sale treatment is not obligatory. You may elect not to follow the installment sale rules, in which case your total gain is recognized in the year of the sale.

While it is generally advantageous to defer recognition of a gain or part of a gain by using the installment sale method, under certain circumstances, accelerating recognition may result in overall tax savings. For example, if you expect your income in future years to be much higher than it is now or if you currently have a **capital loss** that may be offset by a gain, you may want to recognize your gain immediately.

The Tax Reform Act of 1986 limited the ability to defer tax by restricting use of the installment sale method to certain kinds of property. For example, the installment sale method may no longer be used for sales of publicly traded stocks or securities. However, you may sell other types of property, such as real property used in your business or for rental, under an installment sale and still defer the tax on the gain.

If you decide not to use the installment sale reporting method, indicate this decision on either Schedule D (Form 1040) or Form 4797 by the date your tax return for the year of the sale is due. (Schedule D is used to report sales of capital assets. Form 4797 is used to report sales of trade or business property and other noncapital assets.) Once you decide not to use the installment sale method, you may change your decision only with the consent of the IRS.

If you choose not to use the installment method and you are a **cash basis** taxpayer, remember that you may discount (reduce the stated value of) any installment payments that you are to receive at a later date. Therefore, the total gain on the sale you report should be discounted because you do not receive the total payment at the time of the sale.

TaxAlert

Sales at a loss do not qualify for installment sale reporting. Also, under changes made by the Revenue Act of 1987, sales by dealers or by persons who regularly sell personal property on the installment basis no longer qualify for the installment method.

Explanation

The gain you have from an installment sale will be treated as **capital gain** if the property you sold was a capital asset (discussed later). However, if you took depreciation **deductions** on the assets, including the section 179 deduction, part of your gain may be treated as **ordinary income.**

Example

On January 31, 1998, Susan sells property for $4,000 on which she has a $1,000 gain. Half of the gain is taxable at ordinary rates.

If Susan receives the initial $2,000 payment in 1998, she is receiving one-half the proceeds and must report one-half of the gain, or $500. Because the ordinary income portion must be reported first, the entire $500 is treated as an **ordinary gain.** When Susan receives the second $2,000 payment, she reports the second half of the gain, $500, as a capital gain.

Explanation

Any depreciation claimed on personal property must be recaptured as ordinary income in the year of sale, even if there are no payments received in the year of sale. The depreciation recapture for real property is generally limited to the amount by which the depreciation claimed exceeds the amount available under the straight-line method of depreciation. The adjusted basis of the property being sold is increased by the amount of recaptured income that you include in your gross income in the year of sale so that the gain recognized in future years is decreased.

Example

Assume that Sam sold tangible personal property to Betty in 1995 for $100,000 to be paid in installments over 5 years, beginning in 1997. Interest is payable at market rates. The property was originally purchased for $30,000. Because of depreciation, it has an adjusted basis of $20,000. There is a gain of $80,000 ($100,000 − $20,000), of which $10,000 is recaptured income to be reported on Sam's 1995 return.

The $10,000 that is included in Sam's income in the year of sale is added to the $20,000 adjusted basis to figure how much income Sam must report using the installment method. Therefore, Sam's gross profit is $70,000 ($100,000 − $30,000). Sam's gross profit percentage is 70%.

On each of the $20,000 payments that Sam receives from 1997 through 2001, $14,000 would be included in his income ($20,000 × 70%).

Explanation

The installment sale rules contain a number of very important limitations.

Sales to a spouse or an 80% controlled entity. If you sell depreciable property to your spouse or to a partnership or corporation of which you own 80% or more, you must report all of the gain in the year of the sale, despite any installment payment schedules set up under the sale agreement. The same rule may also apply to the sale of property to a trust of which you (or your spouse) is a beneficiary.

Sales to other relatives. If you sell property, other than marketable securities, to a related person on an installment basis and that person resells (or makes a gift of) the property within 2 years, you have to recognize any additional gain in the year of the resale.

If you sell marketable securities to a related person and that person resells the property, you have to recognize any additional gain, unless the sale takes place after you have received all the installment payments due to you. There is no 2-year cutoff date as with other kinds of property, noted above. See the special rules regarding publicly traded property, below.

A related person includes your spouse, children, grandchildren, and parents. A related person is also any partnership in which you are a partner, any estates and trusts of which you are a beneficiary, any grantor trusts of which you are treated as an owner, and any corporation in which you own at least half of the total value of the stock.

The normal 3-year statute of limitations for tax assessments by the IRS is extended for resales of installment property by a related person. In these cases, the statute of limitations will not expire until 2 years after you report to the IRS that a resale took place.

Nontaxable trades. Special rules apply to the exchange of like-kind property, which is tax free. However, nonlike-kind property included in the exchange is taxable. The installment method may be used for the nonlike-kind property. For a further discussion of this subject, see *Nontaxable Trades.*

Like-kind exchanges. For like-kind exchanges involving related parties, both parties must hold the property for more than 2 years for the original exchange to qualify as tax free. This rule is applicable to both parties to the transaction, even though only one party avails himself or herself of like-kind treatment. Also, real property located in the United States and real property located outside the United States no longer qualify as property of a like kind. These changes are generally effective for transfers after July 10, 1989.

Disposing of installment obligations. If you sell property on an installment basis and then later dispose of the installment note, you may have to report a gain or a loss. Generally, the amount of your gain or loss is equal to the difference between your basis in the installment note and the amount you receive when you dispose of the note.

Example

Toni sells real estate on an installment basis for a $200,000 note receivable and has a $120,000 gross profit from the sale. After she collects $100,000 (and reports a profit of $60,000, half her gross profit), she sells the remaining $100,000 note receivable to a bank for $95,000. Toni reports a $55,000 profit in the year of the sale of the note (the remaining $60,000 of gross profit less the $5,000 loss on the sale of the note).

Explanation

A disposition for this purpose is not limited to a sale of the installment note. For example, if you make a sale of property after December 31, 1988, for more than $150,000, and you assign the installment obligation as collateral security for a loan, the IRS will treat this as a disposition. This is because you would have deferred the gain on the sale while obtaining the use of the money through a loan.

Publicly traded property. The installment method cannot be used for sales of publicly traded property, including stock or securities that are traded on an established securities market.

Repossessing property sold under the installment method. If you sell property on an installment plan, you may have to repossess it if, for example, the buyer defaults on his or her obligation. When repossession takes place, you may have to report a gain or a loss. You follow different rules for determining your gain or loss, depending on whether the property being repossessed is personal property or real property.

Personal property. If you repossess personal property sold under an installment plan, you must compare the fair market value of the property recovered with your basis in the installment notes plus any expenses you had in connection with repossession. Under the installment method, your basis is the face value of the note still outstanding less the amount of unreported profit on the original sale. (If you did not use the installment reporting method, your basis is the value of the property at the time of the original sale less payments of principal received to date.)

Your gain or loss is of the same character (short term or long term) as the gain or loss realized on the original sale if you used the installment method. If you did not, any gain resulting from repossession is treated as ordinary income. Any loss is an **ordinary loss** if the property is business property. If it is nonbusiness property, any loss resulting from repossession is treated as a short-term capital loss.

Real property. If you have to repossess your former residence because the buyer defaults and you excluded the gain (see Chapter 16, *Selling Your Home,* for details), no gain or loss is recognized if you resell the house within 1 year of repossession. If the property is not resold within 1 year, you may have to recognize the gain. The amount of tax you may have to pay on the gain will depend on whether the house you repossessed was originally sold before or after May 6, 1997. For houses sold before May 7, 1997, $125,000 of the gain could have been excluded or the gain could have been deferred by acquiring a replacement home. For houses sold after May 6, 1997, up to $250,000 or $500,000 of the gain may be excluded (see Chapter 16, *Selling Your Home,* for more information). You may never deduct a loss on repossession because you may not deduct losses on property used primarily for personal purposes.

Computing your gain or loss on repossessed real property. Generally, your gain or loss on property that you have repossessed equals (1) the total amount of payments you have received under the installment sale minus (2) the amount of taxable gain you have already reported on the installment sale.

The gain you report on the repossessed property is limited, however, to the gross profit you expected on the installment sale less repossession costs and the amount of taxable gain you have already reported on the installment sale. Your basis in the repossessed property is your adjusted basis at the time of the originial sale less deferred gain on repossession.

Example

Linda Smith sold a building that was not her personal residence to Ann Carter in 1990 for $100,000, payable in 10 annual installments. Linda's basis in the building was $70,000, and no mortgage was outstanding. The expected gross profit in the sale was $30,000, and the gross profit percentage was 30%.

In 1996, Ann failed to pay the sixth installment. By then, Linda had recognized $15,000 of gain from the $50,000 in payments received. She repossessed the building, incurring legal fees of $1,000 in the process. Linda's gain is computed as follows:

Gain

Payments received	$50,000
Less: Taxable gain already reported on sale	15,000
Gain subject to limitation	$35,000

Limitation on gain

Gross profit expected on installment sale	$30,000
Less: Repossession costs	1,000
Less: Taxable gain already reported on sale	15,000
Limitation	$14,000

Linda must report a $14,000 gain on repossession. Her basis in the reacquired building is $49,000, figured by taking $70,000 (her original adjusted basis) and subtracting $21,000 ($35,000 − $14,000), the amount of gain on repossession unrecognized because of the limitation on gain.

TAXPLANNER

Computing interest on installment sales. Special rules may apply regarding the amount of interest to be recognized on installment sales of more than $3,000.

If the amount of interest is not specifically stated in the sales agreement or if the stated interest is at an unrealistically low rate, you must calculate unstated or imputed interest. In general, you have unstated interest if (1) the sum of all payments due more than 6 months after the date of sale exceeds (2) the present value of such payments and the present value of any interest payment provided for in the contract. Present value is determined by using a so-called testing rate compounded semiannually. If there is unstated interest, you are required to *impute* interest using the testing rate. The testing rate is calculated by using the applicable federal rate (AFR). The AFR is based on average market yields of U.S. obligations. The AFR may be the short-, medium-, or long-term rate that U.S. obligations are yielding, depending on the length of the contract.

The testing rate is equal to *110% of the AFR* at the time the sale is made. If unstated interest results using the testing rate, then interest must be computed using the testing rate, compounded semiannually.

Example

On June 1, 1999, Nicholas and Alexandra sell their limousine for $45,000, to be paid in three annual installments of $15,000 each on June 1, 1999, 2000, and 2001. No interest is stated in the sales contract. Their basis in the car is $35,000.

Because $30,000, the sum of the payments due more than 6 months after the sale, exceeds $26,314, the present value of such payments discounted at 9% semiannually, there is unstated interest.

The imputed interest over the 2 years is $3,686 (9% compounded semiannually). This amount must be subtracted from the selling price when the gain on the sale is computed:

Stated selling price	$45,000
Less: Unstated interest	3,686
Adjusted selling price	$41,314
Less: Basis	35,000
Gain on sale	$ 6,314
Gross profit percentage: ($6,314 ÷ $41,314)	15.3%

Imputed interest is important to consider for two reasons: (1) It alters the amount of gain on a sale, and (2) it is deductible as an interest expense by the buyer, subject to limitations (see Chapter 25, *Interest Expense*), and must be reported as interest income by the seller.

Note: If all of the installment payments are due within 1 year after the date of sale, it is not necessary to figure your imputed interest. Additionally, payments received within the first 6 months of a sale have no imputed interest. The AFR will be determined by the IRS every month.

buyer even if the amount of the note is more than the fair market value of the property.

Example. You sell stock that you had pledged as security for a bank loan of $8,000. Your basis in the stock is $6,000. The buyer pays off your bank loan and pays you $20,000 in cash. The amount realized is $28,000 ($20,000 plus $8,000). Your gain is $22,000 ($28,000 minus $6,000).

TAX*ORGANIZER*

You should keep a copy of your sales agreements, loan agreements, and closing statements associated with any installment sale.

How To Figure Gain or Loss

You figure gain or loss on a sale or trade of property by comparing the amount you realize with the adjusted basis of the property.

Gain. If the amount you realize from a sale or trade is more than the adjusted basis of the property you transfer, the difference is a gain.

Loss. If the adjusted basis of the property you transfer is more than the amount you realize, the difference is a loss.

Adjusted basis. The adjusted basis of property is your original cost or other original basis properly adjusted (increased or decreased) for certain items. See chapter 14 for more information about determining the adjusted basis of property.

Amount realized. The amount you realize from a sale or trade of property is everything you receive for the property. This includes the money you receive plus the fair market value of any property or services you receive.

If you finance the buyer's purchase of your property and the debt instrument does not provide for adequate stated interest, the unstated interest will reduce the amount realized. For more information, see Publication 537.

Fair market value. Fair market value is the price at which the property would change hands between a buyer and a seller, neither being forced to buy or sell and both having reasonable knowledge of all the relevant facts.

The fair market value of notes or other debt instruments you receive as a part of the sale price is usually the best amount you can get from selling them to, or discounting them with, a bank or other buyer of debt instruments.

TAX*PLANNER*

An appraisal by a qualified person is usually accepted by both the courts and the IRS as the fair market value. The appraiser should be familiar with valuation methods accepted in the particular field (real estate, art objects, equipment and machinery, etc.). For real estate, a local appraiser is better qualified than an out-of-towner. In other fields, prior experience in the field is more important. It may be prudent to obtain an appraisal at the date of the transaction, just in case it is needed later.

TAX*ORGANIZER*

You should keep a copy of your appraisal report of any property sold in order to verify its value.

Example. You trade A Company stock with an adjusted basis of $7,000 for B Company stock with a fair market value of $10,000, which is your amount realized. Your gain is $3,000 ($10,000 minus $7,000). If you also receive a note for $6,000 that has a discount value of $4,000, your gain is $7,000 ($10,000 plus $4,000 minus $7,000).

Debt paid off. A debt against the property, or against you, that is paid off as a part of the transaction, or that is assumed by the buyer, must be included in the amount realized. This is true even if neither you nor the buyer is personally liable for the debt. For example, if you sell or trade property that is subject to a nonrecourse loan, the amount you realize generally includes the full amount of the note assumed by the

Example

You sell property and the buyer pays you $20,000 cash and assumes an existing mortgage on the property of $8,000. You bought the property for $6,000 and added improvements costing $10,000. Your selling expenses were $1,400. Your gain on the sale is figured as follows:

Amount realized

Cash	$20,000	
Mortgage assumed by buyer	8,000	$28,000

Minus: Adjusted basis

Cost	$ 6,000	
Improvements	10,000	
Total	$16,000	
Plus: Selling expenses	1,400	$17,400

| **Gain** | | **$10,600** |

Payment of cash. If you trade property and cash for other property, the amount you realize is the fair market value of the property you receive. Determine your gain or loss by subtracting the cash you pay plus the adjusted basis of the property you traded in from the amount you realize. If the result is a positive number, it is a gain. If the result is a negative number, it is a loss.

Explanation

If you receive a mortgage or a trust note, payments include some interest income in addition to principal.

Example

Assume that a $10,000 installment note with a discounted value of $8,000 is given by an individual to a cash basis taxpayer in payment for a capital asset with a basis of $7,000. The taxpayer recognizes $1,000 ($8,000 − $7,000) as a capital gain. As each installment is paid, eight-tenths ($8,000 ÷ $10,000) of the payment is a return of principal and two-tenths is interest income.

Explanation

If you are an **accrual basis** taxpayer—and most people are not—use the full face value of the note in computing your gain or loss on the sale. Consequently, payments on the note are returns of principal.

If you are a cash basis taxpayer, and if the installment note is given by a corporation and the discounted value of the note is used to compute your gain on the sale of a capital asset, the income to be recognized is a capital gain. If the note is given by an individual, the income is taxable as ordinary income.

Example

A cash basis taxpayer sells a capital asset to a corporation in exchange for a $10,000 note with an interest rate of 9%. Because current interest rates are more than 9% or because of the corporation's low credit status, the note has a discounted value of $8,000, 80% of its face value. The tax-payer uses the $8,000 value to compute gain or loss on the sale. When the corporation later pays the note, the $2,000 difference, which must be reported as income, is treated as a capital gain. If an individual had issued the note, the $2,000 gain to the taxpayer realized on payment of the note would be taxed as ordinary income.

Explanation
Property used partly for business. If you sell or exchange property that you used for both business and personal purposes, the gain or loss on the sale or exchange must be figured as though you had sold two separate pieces of property. You must divide the selling price, selling expenses, and the basis between the business and personal parts. Depreciation is deducted from the basis of the business part. Gain or loss realized on the business part of the property may be treated as capital gain or loss, or as ordinary gain or loss (see Publication 544, *Sales and Other Dispositions of Assets*). Any gain realized on the personal part of the property is a capital gain. A loss on the personal part is not deductible.

No gain or loss. You may have to use a basis for figuring gain that is different from the basis used for figuring loss. In this case, you may have neither a gain nor a loss. See *Basis Other Than Cost* in chapter 14.

TaxSaver

If you plan to give away a capital asset that has depreciated in value, consider selling it and giving away the proceeds instead, particularly if the would-be recipient of the property would likely sell it in the immediate future. By selling, you realize a capital loss and the consequent tax savings. At the same time, the would-be recipient of the property, who might have been unable to claim a capital loss because he or she would have had a different basis in the property, receives assets of the same value, only in cash instead of property.

Nontaxable Trades

This section discusses trades that generally do not result in a taxable gain or deductible loss. For more information on nontaxable trades, see chapter 1 of Publication 544.

Like-kind exchanges. If you trade business or investment property for other business or investment property of a like kind, you do not pay tax on any gain or deduct any loss until you sell or dispose of the property you receive. To be nontaxable, a trade must meet all six of the following conditions.

1) The property must be business or investment property. You must hold both the property you trade and the property you receive for productive use in your trade or business or for investment. Neither property may be property used for personal purposes, such as your home or family car.
2) The property must not be held primarily for sale. The property you trade and the property you receive must not be property you sell to customers, such as merchandise.
3) The property must not be stocks, bonds, notes, choses in action, certificates of trust or beneficial interest, or other securities or evidences of indebtedness or interest, including partnership interests. However, you can have a nontaxable trade of corporate stocks under a different rule, as discussed later.

4) There must be a trade of like property. The trade of real estate for real estate, or personal property for similar personal property is a trade of like property. The trade of an apartment house for a store building, or a panel truck for a pickup truck, is a trade of like property. The trade of a piece of machinery for a store building is not a trade of like property. Real property located in the United States and real property located outside the United States are not like property. Also, personal property used predominantly within the United States and personal property used predominantly outside the United States are not like property.
5) The property to be received must be identified within 45 days after the date you transfer the property given up in the trade.
6) The property to be received must be received by the earlier of:
   a) The 180th day after the date on which you transfer the property given up in the trade, or
   b) The due date, including extensions, for your tax return for the year in which the transfer of the property given up occurs.

Explanation
The term *like kind* refers to a property's nature or character, not its grade or quality. With real estate, for example, the location of the property and whether or not it has been improved are factors that affect only grade or quality, not its nature. Property held for productive use in a trade or a business may be exchanged for property held for investment.

Examples
Like-kind exchanges include the following:

- Improved for unimproved real estate when exchanged by a person who does not deal in real estate
- A used car for a new one to be used for the same purpose

The following are *not* considered like-kind exchanges:

- Personal property (such as a boat) for real property
- Gold numismatic coins for gold bullion (the IRS ruled that an investment in gold coins was an investment in the coins themselves, while the investment in bullion was an investment in the world gold market)
- Gold bullion for silver bullion
- Male livestock for female livestock
- U.S. real property for real property located outside the United States

TaxAlert

For exchanges after April 10, 1991, depreciable, tangible personal property may be exchanged for either like-kind or like-class property and may qualify for **like-kind exchange treatment.** Like-class properties are depreciable, tangible personal properties within the same "general asset classes" as defined in the Standard Industrial Classification Manual (see Publication 544, *Sales and Other Dispositions of Assets*).

For exchanges of multiple properties after April 10, 1991, you are not required to make a property-by-property comparison if you

1. Separate the properties into two or more exchange groups, or
2. Transfer or receive more than one property within a single exchange group.

If you trade property with a related party in a like-kind exchange, a special rule may apply. See *Related Party Transactions,* later in this chapter. Also, see chapter 1 of Publication 544 for more information on exchanges of business property and special rules for exchanges using qualified intermediaries or involving multiple properties.

Partially nontaxable exchange. If you receive cash or unlike property in addition to like property, and the above six conditions are met, you have a partially nontaxable trade. You are taxed on any gain you realize, but only up to the amount of the cash and the fair market value of the unlike property you receive. You cannot deduct a loss.

Example

You exchange real estate held for investment that has an adjusted basis of $8,000 for other real estate that you want to hold for investment. The real estate you receive has a fair market value of $10,000, and you also receive $1,000 in cash. Although the total gain realized on the transaction is $3,000, only $1,000 (cash received) is included in your income.

TaxSaver

Assume that you are to receive property that is worth less than the property you are to give up and you expect to make improvements on the new property. Rather than receive money or unlike property from the other owner to make up the difference in value, you might ask her to make the improvements on her property before the transfer. In that way, you reduce the amount of unlike property included in the exchange and therefore reduce the amount of tax you have to pay on the transfer. What is the incentive for the other owner? Making the improvement might induce you to make the deal.

TaxSaver

If the amount of liabilities you assume in an exchange is less than the amount of liabilities you give up, the difference is treated as cash received. Consequently, if you assume a mortgage that is less than the mortgage you had been carrying on the exchanged property, you recognize gain as if you had received cash for the difference.

If you receive cash but assume more debt than you were relieved of, you cannot offset the cash received with the debt assumed. In this case, you should have the buyer pay down some of the debt you are assuming rather than paying you the cash directly. You may be able to borrow the difference against the property at a later date.

Like property and unlike property transferred. If you give up unlike property in addition to the like property, you must recognize gain or loss on the unlike property you give up. The gain or loss is the difference between the adjusted basis of the unlike property and its fair market value.

Like property and money transferred. If conditions (1)–(6) are met, you have a nontaxable trade even if you pay money in addition to the like property.

Basis of property received. To figure the basis of the property received, see *Nontaxable Exchanges* in chapter 14.

How to report. You must report the trade of like property on **Form 8824.** If you figure a recognized gain or loss on Form 8824, report it on Schedule D of Form 1040 or on **Form 4797,** *Sales of Business Property,* whichever applies.

For information on using Form 4797, see chapter 4 of Publication 544.

TaxSaver

A like-kind exchange is a useful planning tool in deferring tax on appreciated property if you intend to reinvest in a similar property within a relatively short period. No gain or loss is recognized in a deferred like-kind exchange if you meet the following requirements:

1. You must follow specific procedures to identify replacement property within 45 days after relinquishing the old property.
2. You must receive the replacement property within 180 days after relinquishing the old property.
3. You must structure the exchange to comply with one or more of the guidelines described in the final regulations. The reason for this step is that if the exchange does not fall within one of the guidelines, then the exchange could be subject to scrutiny by the IRS.

Taxpayers should design their transactions to comply with one of the following IRS guidelines:

1. You cannot have an immediate ability or unrestricted right to receive money or other property pursuant to the security or guarantee arrangement. However, the replacement property may be secured or guaranteed before you actually receive like-kind replacement property by one or more of the following:
   a. Mortgage, deed of trust, or other security interest in property
   b. Standby letter of credit meeting certain specifications and a guarantee of a third party
2. You may not have an immediate ability or unrestricted right to receive, pledge, borrow, or otherwise obtain the benefits of the cash or cash equivalent held in an escrow account or qualified trust. However, the replacement property may be secured by cash or a cash equivalent if the cash or cash equivalent is held in a qualified escrow account or in a qualified trust.
3. You may not have an immediate ability or unrestricted right to receive, pledge, borrow, or otherwise obtain the benefits of money or other property held by a qualified intermediary. However, you may use a qualified intermediary in a deferred exchange if the qualified intermediary is unrelated to you (see the IRS final regulations for details). A qualified intermediary may be an escrow or title company.

More than one IRS guideline can be used in the same deferred exchange, but the terms and conditions of each must be separately satisfied. You should consult your tax advisor if you are contemplating a like-kind exchange.

Corporate stocks. The following trades of corporate stocks generally do not result in a taxable gain or a deductible loss.

Corporate reorganizations. In some instances, a company will give you common stock for preferred stock, preferred stock for common stock, or stock in one corporation for stock in another corporation. If this is part of a merger, recapitalization, transfer to a controlled corporation, bankruptcy, corporate division, corporate acquisition, or other corporate reorganization, you do not recognize gain or loss.

Stock for stock of the same corporation. You can exchange common stock for common stock or preferred stock for preferred stock in the same corporation without having a recognized gain or loss. This is true for a trade between two stockholders as well as a trade between a stockholder and the corporation.

Convertible stocks and bonds. You generally will not have a recognized gain or loss if you convert bonds into stock or preferred stock into common stock of the same corporation according to a conversion privilege in the terms of the bond or the preferred stock certificate.

Property for stock of a controlled corporation. If you transfer property to a corporation solely in exchange for stock in that corporation, and immediately after the trade you are in control of the corporation, you ordinarily will not recognize a gain or loss. This rule applies both to individuals and to groups who transfer property to a corporation. It does not apply if the corporation is an investment company.

For this purpose, to be in control of a corporation, you or your group of transferors must own, immediately after the exchange, at least 80% of the total combined voting power of all classes of stock entitled to vote and at least 80% of the outstanding shares of each class of nonvoting stock of the corporation.

If this provision applies to you, you must attach to your return a complete statement of all facts pertinent to the exchange.

Additional information. For more information on trades of stock, see *Nontaxable Trades* in chapter 4 of Publication 550.

Explanation
The statement must include the following information:

- A description of the property transferred, with its cost or other basis
- The kind of stock received, including the number of shares and fair market value
- The principal amount and fair market value of any securities received
- The amount of money received, if any
- A description of any liabilities assumed by the corporation in the transaction, including the corporate business reason for the assumption

Generally, when you transfer property to a corporation that you alone will control in exchange for its stock, no gain or loss is recognized. "Control" means that you or your group of investors owns at least 80% of the outstanding voting stock and at least 80% of the shares of all other classes of outstanding stock. However, if you receive property other than stock, then you may have to recognize a gain equal to that additional property's value. Moreover, if the property you transfer to the corporation has been depreciated, all or a portion of your gain may be ordinary income rather than a capital gain.

Example
You transfer machinery that has an adjusted basis of $10,000 and a fair market value of $25,000 to a corporation that you and your associates will control in exchange for stock worth $20,000 and $5,000 in cash. You realize a $15,000 gain on the transfer of the machinery.

The transfer would have been tax free if all you had received in return was stock. However, you have to report a gain of $5,000 for the cash received. Furthermore, if you previously claimed $5,000 or more in depreciation on the machinery, all of the $5,000 you received is treated as ordinary income under the depreciation recapture rules. For a complete discussion of depreciation, see Chapter 10, *Rental Income and Expenses.*

Explanation
There has been much litigation over the issue of momentary control—a situation that arises when investors hold the required 80% of stock only briefly and then dispose of a portion of it. Generally, momentary control is not sufficient to ensure preferential tax treatment if there was an agreement or prearranged plan for subsequent disposition of the stock acquired in the exchange.

Condemnations and involuntary exchanges. Condemnation is the process by which private property is legally taken by governments or certain entities, such as public utilities, in exchange for money or property.

If the condemnation award you receive is more than your adjusted basis in the condemned property, you have a gain. This gain may be postponed if you receive similar property instead of cash or if replacement property is purchased with the cash you receive. If you purchase replacement property, it must be put to a use similar to that of the original property. It also must be purchased within 2 years from the close of the first year in which any part of the gain on condemnation is realized. For business real property, the purchase must be made within 3 years.

If the condemnation award you receive is less than your basis in the property, you have a loss. This loss is not deductible if the property was your residence. Your loss, however, may be deducted if the property was used in a trade or a business or for the production of income.

Insurance policies and annuities. You will not have a recognized gain or loss if you trade:

1) A life insurance contract for another life insurance contract or for an endowment or annuity contract,
2) An endowment contract for an annuity contract or for another endowment contract that provides for regular payments beginning at a date not later than the beginning date under the old contract, or
3) An annuity contract for another annuity contract.

The insured or annuitant must be the same under both contracts. Exchanges of contracts not included in this list, such as an annuity contract for an endowment contract, or an annuity or endowment contract for a life insurance contract, are taxable.

Demutualization of life insurance companies. If you received stock or cash in exchange for your equity interest as a policyholder or an annuitant, you generally will not have a recognized gain or loss. See *Demutualization of Life Insurance Companies* in Publication 550.

U.S. Treasury notes or bonds. You can trade certain issues of U.S. Treasury obligations for other issues designated by the Secretary of the Treasury, with no gain or loss recognized.

Transfers Between Spouses

Generally, no gain or loss is recognized on a transfer of property from an individual to (or in trust for the benefit of) a spouse, or if incident to a divorce, a former spouse. This nonrecognition rule does not apply if the recipient spouse or former spouse is a nonresident alien. The rule also does not apply to a transfer in trust to the extent the adjusted basis of the property is less than the amount of the liabilities assumed plus any liabilities on the property.

Any transfer of property to a spouse or former spouse on which gain or loss is not recognized is treated by the recipient as a gift and is not considered a sale or exchange. The recipient's basis in the property will be the same as the adjusted basis of the giver immediately before the transfer. This carryover basis rule applies whether the adjusted basis of the transferred property is less than, equal to, or greater than either its fair market value at the time of transfer or any consideration paid by the recipient. This rule applies for purposes of determining loss as well as gain. Any gain recognized on a transfer in trust increases the basis.

A transfer of property is incident to a divorce if the transfer occurs within 1 year after the date on which the marriage ends, or if the transfer is related to the ending of the marriage.

Explanation

For transfers of property incident to divorce to a former spouse who is a nonresident alien, gain or loss may be recognized to the spouse who transferred the property based on the fair market value of the property transferred.

The law also provides that a transfer of stock between spouses or incident to divorce will not cause income to be recognized to the spouse who transferred the property if the stock was acquired by exercising an incentive stock option. The same results occur even if the spouse who transferred the property did not hold the stock for the required holding period. For more information on the tax treatment of incentive stock options, see *Stock Options* in Chapter 6, *Wages, Salaries, and Other Earnings.*

Related Party Transactions

Special rules apply to the sale or trade of property between related parties.

TaxPlanner

Special rules are imposed on taxpayers who try to avoid taxation on property gains by passing the property on to a trust. A special tax is imposed on a trust when the trust sells appreciated property within 2 years of having received it. The property may have been acquired by gift, through a bargain purchase, or as a transfer from another trust. The trust's gain is taxed at the highest rate that the donor of the property would have had to pay had he or she reported the gain on the sale in the same year in which the trust did.

Exception

This special tax is not imposed on a sale or an exchange that occurs within 2 years of the transfer of property if the sale or exchange takes place after the death of the donor of the property.

The purpose of the special tax is to prevent the grantor from taking advantage of a lower tax bracket in a trust. The law assumes, except in the case of death, that if the property is sold within 2 years, this was the plan all along.

Gain on sale or trade of depreciable property. Your gain from the sale or trade of property to a related party may be ordinary income, rather than capital gain, if the property can be depreciated by the party receiving it. See chapter 2 of Publication 544 for more information.

Like-kind exchanges. Generally, if you trade business or investment property for other business or investment property of a like kind, no gain or loss is recognized. See *Like-kind exchanges* earlier under *Nontaxable Trades.*

This rule also applies to trades of property between related parties, defined next under *Losses on sales or trades of property.* However, if either you or the related party disposes of the like property within 2 years after the trade, you both must report any gain or loss not recognized on the original trade on your return filed for the year in which the later disposition occurs.

Losses on sales or trades of property. You cannot deduct a loss on the sale or trade of property, other than a distribution in complete liquidation of a corporation, if the transaction is directly or indirectly between you and the following **related parties.**

1) Members of your family. This includes only your brothers and sisters, half-brothers and half-sisters, spouse, ancestors (parents, grandparents, etc.), and lineal descendants (children, grandchildren, etc.).
2) A partnership in which you directly or indirectly own more than 50% of the capital interest or the profits interest.
3) A corporation in which you directly or indirectly own more than 50% in value of the outstanding stock. (See *Constructive ownership of stock,* later.)
4) A tax-exempt charitable or educational organization that is directly or indirectly controlled, in any manner or by any method, by you or by a member of your family, whether or not this control is legally enforceable.

In addition, a loss on the sale or trade of property is not deductible if the transaction is directly or indirectly between the following related parties.

1) A grantor and fiduciary, or the fiduciary and beneficiary, of any trust.
2) Fiduciaries of two different trusts, or the fiduciary and beneficiary of two different trusts, if the same person is the grantor of both trusts.
3) A trust fiduciary and a corporation of which more than 50% in value of the outstanding stock is directly or indirectly owned by or for the trust, or by or for the grantor of the trust.
4) A corporation and a partnership if the same persons own more than 50% in value of the outstanding stock of the corporation and more than 50% of the capital interest, or the profits interest, in the partnership.
5) Two S corporations if the same persons own more than 50% in value of the outstanding stock of each corporation.
6) Two corporations, one of which is an S corporation, if the same persons own more than 50% in value of the outstanding stock of each corporation.
7) An executor and a beneficiary of an estate (except in the case of a sale or trade to satisfy a pecuniary bequest).
8) Two corporations that are members of the same controlled group. (Under certain conditions, however, these losses are not disallowed but must be deferred.)
9) Two partnerships if the same persons own, directly or indirectly, more than 50% of the capital interests or the profit interests in both partnerships.

Multiple property sales or trades. If you sell or trade to a related party a number of blocks of stock or pieces of property in a lump sum, you must figure the gain or loss separately for each block of stock or piece of property. The gain on each item may be taxable. However, you cannot deduct the loss on any item. Also, you cannot reduce gains from the sales of any of these items by losses on the sales of any of the other items.

Indirect transactions. You cannot deduct your loss on the sale of stock through your broker if, under a prearranged plan, a related party buys the same stock you had owned. This does not apply to a trade between related parties through an exchange that is purely coincidental and is not prearranged.

Constructive ownership of stock. In determining whether a person directly or indirectly owns any of the outstanding stock of a corporation, the following rules apply.

Rule 1. Stock directly or indirectly owned by or for a corporation, partnership, estate, or trust is considered owned proportionately by or for its shareholders, partners, or beneficiaries.

Rule 2. An individual is considered to own the stock that is directly or indirectly owned by or for his or her family. Family includes only brothers and sisters, half-brothers and half-sisters, spouse, ancestors, and lineal descendants.

Rule 3. An individual owning, other than by applying rule 2, any stock in a corporation is considered to own the stock that is directly or indirectly owned by or for his or her partner.

Rule 4. When applying rule 1, 2, or 3, stock constructively owned by a person under rule 1 is treated as actually owned by that person. But stock constructively owned by an individual under rule 2 or rule 3 is not treated as owned by that individual for again applying either rule 2 or rule 3 to make another person the constructive owner of the stock.

Property received from a related party. If you sell or trade at a gain property that you acquired from a related party, you recognize the gain only to the extent it is more than the loss previously disallowed to the related party. This rule applies only if you are the original transferee and you acquired the property by purchase or exchange. This rule does not apply if the related party's loss was disallowed because of the wash sale rules described in chapter 4 of Publication 550 under *Wash Sales.*

Example 1. Your brother sells you stock for $7,600. His cost basis is $10,000. Your brother cannot deduct the loss of $2,400. Later, you sell the same stock to an unrelated party for $10,500, realizing a gain of $2,900. Your reportable gain is $500—the $2,900 gain minus the $2,400 loss not allowed to your brother.

Example 2. If, in *Example 1,* you sold the stock for $6,900 instead of $10,500, your recognized loss is only $700 (your $7,600 basis minus $6,900). You cannot deduct the loss that was not allowed to your brother.

Explanation

Transactions between a trust and the relative of a trust beneficiary may be indirect related-party transactions. Similarly, the sale of stock by one spouse followed by the purchase by the other spouse of an equal number of the same corporation's shares is an indirect sale between related parties, even though both spouses deal through brokers on the New York Stock Exchange. However, if there is a significant time lapse between the two transactions—a month or more—the transactions are not considered linked.

Capital Gains and Losses

This section discusses the tax treatment of gains and losses from different types of investment transactions.

Character of gain or loss. You need to classify your gains and losses as either ordinary or capital gains or losses. You then need to classify your capital gains and losses as either short-term or long-term. If you have long-term gains and losses, you must identify your 28% rate gains and losses. If you have a net capital gain, you must also identify your qualified 5-year gain and any unrecaptured section 1250 gain.

The correct classification and identification helps you figure the limit on capital losses and the correct tax on capital gains. Reporting capital gains and losses is explained in chapter 17.

Capital or Ordinary Gain or Loss

If you have a taxable gain or a deductible loss from a transaction, it may be either a capital gain or loss or an ordinary gain or loss, depending on the circumstances. Generally, a sale or trade of a capital asset (defined next) results in a capital gain or loss. A sale or trade of a noncapital asset generally results in ordinary gain or loss. Depending on the circumstances, a gain or loss on a sale or trade of property used in a trade or business may be treated as either capital or ordinary, as explained in Publication 544. In some situations, part of your gain or loss may be a capital gain or loss, and part may be an ordinary gain or loss.

Capital Assets and Noncapital Assets

For the most part, everything you own and use for personal purposes, pleasure, or investment is a *capital asset.* Some examples are:

- Stocks or bonds held in your personal account,
- A house owned and used by you and your family,
- Household furnishings,
- A car used for pleasure or commuting,
- Coin or stamp collections,
- Gems and jewelry, and
- Gold, silver, or any other metal.

Any property you own is a capital asset, except the following *noncapital assets.*

1) *Property held mainly for sale to customers* or property that will physically become a part of the merchandise that is for sale to customers.
2) *Depreciable property* used in your trade or business, even if fully depreciated.
3) *Real property* used in your trade or business.
4) *A copyright, a literary, musical, or artistic composition, a letter or memorandum,* or similar property:
   a) Created by your personal efforts,
   b) Prepared or produced for you as a letter, memorandum, or similar property, or
   c) Acquired under circumstances (for example, by gift) entitling you to the basis of the person who created the property or for whom it was prepared or produced.
5) *Accounts or notes receivable* acquired in the ordinary course of a trade or business for services rendered or from the sale of property described in (1).
6) *U.S. Government publications* that you received from the government free or for less than the normal sales price, or that you acquired under circumstances entitling you to the basis of someone who received the publications free or for less than the normal sales price.
7) *Certain commodities derivative financial instruments* held by commodities derivatives dealers.
8) *Hedging transactions,* but only if the transaction is clearly identified as a hedging transaction before the close of the day on which it was acquired, originated, or entered into.
9) *Supplies* of a type you regularly use or consume in the ordinary course of your trade or business.

Example

You bought a car for personal use and later sold it for less than you paid for it. The loss is not deductible. However, if you had sold it for more than you paid for it, the gain would be taxable. A loss would be deductible only if, or to the extent that, the car was used for business. If it was sold at a loss, the loss would be deductible. If the car had been stolen, you would have had a theft loss.

Note: In determining the amount of the loss, what you paid for the car would have to be reduced by any depreciation allowed as a deduction. This would reduce the amount of the loss you could claim.

Explanation

While losses on personal property generally are not deductible, losses associated with a trade or a business may be. However, property originally held for personal use may be converted to business use under certain circumstances (and vice versa). There are very few court cases in this area, and those that exist do not provide much guidance about how long property must be rented before it is considered converted to business use. Each case depends on the specific facts and circumstances. In general, if a residence has been rented for a period of years, there is strong evidence that it has been converted to rental property.

Examples

In one case, a residence was rented out for several months under a bona fide lease. The property could not be reoccupied by the owner during the term of the lease. The owner's motive for leasing the house was to make money. The court held that the property had been converted to rental use.

In another case, a building was remodeled to make it fit for business purposes. This was considered to be strong evidence that the property was being converted to rental use.

Note: There are no clear-cut guidelines for what constitutes conversion to business use. However, simply listing the property with a rental agent is not sufficient. The guidelines in Chapter 16, *Selling Your Home*, may be helpful.

Investment Property

Investment property is a capital asset. Any gain or loss from its sale or trade is generally a capital gain or loss.

TAXPLANNER

If you collect gold, silver, stamps, antiques, and the like, you should be aware that losses from the sale or trade of such property generally are not deductible. In order to claim a loss, you must be able to show that your primary purpose in collecting the property was to make a profit. Furthermore, you must show that you were not collecting the items purely as a hobby or for personal enjoyment. Obviously, there may be a very fine line between a hobby and a profit-making activity.

Example

The Tax Court did *not* allow a taxpayer to deduct a loss on the sale of antiques he used to furnish his home. The taxpayer argued that he was speculating on large increases in the value of the antiques. The Tax Court emphasized his personal use of the antiques and noted that most of the taxpayer's sales of antiques were merely a means of financing the acquisition of more antiques.

Gold, silver, stamps, coins, gems, etc. These are capital assets except when they are held for sale by a dealer. Any gain or loss you have from their sale or trade generally is a capital gain or loss.

Stocks, stock rights, and bonds. All of these (including stock received as a dividend) are capital assets except when held for sale by a securities dealer. However, if you own small business stock, see *Losses on Section 1244 (Small Business) Stock* and *Losses on Small Business Investment Company Stock* in chapter 4 of Publication 550.

Personal use property. Property held for personal use only, rather than for investment, is a capital asset, and you must report a gain from its sale as a capital gain. However, you cannot deduct a loss from selling personal use property.

Discounted Debt Instruments

Treat your gain or loss on the sale, redemption, or retirement of a bond or other debt instrument originally issued at a discount or bought at a discount as capital gain or loss, except as explained in the following discussions.

Short-term government obligations. Treat gains on short-term federal, state, or local government obligations (other than tax-exempt obligations) as ordinary income up to your ratable share of the acquisition discount. This treatment applies to obligations that have a fixed maturity date not more than 1 year from the date of issue. *Acquisition discount* is the stated redemption price at maturity minus your basis in the obligation.

However, do not treat these gains as income to the extent you previously included the discount in income. See *Discount on Short-Term Obligations* in chapter 1 of Publication 550.

Short-term nongovernment obligations. Treat gains on short-term nongovernment obligations as ordinary income up to your ratable share of original issue discount (OID). This treatment applies to obligations that have a fixed maturity date of not more than 1 year from the date of issue.

However, to the extent you previously included the discount in income, you do not have to include it in income again. See *Discount on Short-Term Obligations* in chapter 1 of Publication 550.

Tax-exempt state and local government bonds. If these bonds were originally issued at a discount before September 4, 1982, or you acquired them before March 2, 1984, treat your part of the OID as tax-exempt interest. To figure your gain or loss on the sale or trade of these bonds, reduce the amount realized by your part of the OID.

If the bonds were issued after September 3, 1982, and acquired after March 1, 1984, increase the adjusted basis by your part of the OID to figure gain or loss. For more information on the basis of these bonds, see *Discounted Debt Instruments* in chapter 4 of Publication 550.

Example

On March 1, 1984, Kathy bought a $10,000 tax-exempt state government bond for $9,000 that was originally issued at $8,500 on September 3, 1982. Kathy must treat her part of the original issue discount (OID) as tax-exempt interest. The accumulated OID from the date of issue to the date Kathy purchased the bond was $600. On August 15, 1996, Kathy sold the bond for $9,800. Kathy must report a $100 capital gain on the sale. The market discount in the bond is the original issue price ($8,500) plus the accumulated OID from the date of issue that represented interest to any earlier holders ($600) and minus the price Kathy paid for the bond ($9,000). As a result, the market discount is $100 ($9,100 − $9,000). The remaining difference of $700 ($9,800 − $9,100) is treated as tax-exempt interest.

Any gain from market discount is usually taxable on disposition or redemption of tax-exempt bonds. If you bought the bonds before May 1, 1993, the gain from market discount is capital gain. If you bought the bonds after April 30, 1993, the gain is ordinary income.

You figure the market discount by subtracting the price you paid for the bond from the sum of the original issue price of the bond and the amount of accumulated OID from the date of issue that represented interest to any earlier holders. For more information, see *Market Discount Bonds* in chapter 1 of Publication 550.

A loss on the sale or other disposition of a tax-exempt state or local government bond is deductible as a capital loss.

Explanation

You must accrue OID on tax-exempt state and local government bonds issued after September 3, 1982, and acquired after March 1, 1984. Your adjusted basis at the time of disposition is figured by adding accrued OID to your basis. You must accrue OID on tax-exempt obligations under the same method used for OID on corporate obligations issued after July 1, 1982.

> **Example**
> On March 2, 1984, Julie bought a $10,000 tax-exempt state government bond for $9,100 that was originally issued at $8,500 on September 4, 1982. On August 15, 1996, Julie sold the bond for $9,800. Julie previously accrued $500 of OID tax-exempt interest over the period she held the bond. Julie must report a $200 capital gain on the sale of the bond [$9,800 − ($9,100 + $500)].

Redeemed before maturity. If a state or local bond that was issued *before June 9, 1980,* is redeemed before it matures, the OID is not taxable to you.

If a state or local bond issued *after June 8, 1980,* is redeemed before it matures, the part of the OID that is earned while you hold the bond is not taxable to you. However, you must report the unearned part of the OID as a capital gain.

Example. On July 1, 1990, the date of issue, you bought a 20-year, 6% municipal bond for $800. The face amount of the bond was $1,000. The $200 discount was OID. At the time the bond was issued, the issuer had no intention of redeeming it before it matured. The bond was callable at its face amount beginning 10 years after the issue date.

The issuer redeemed the bond at the end of 11 years (July 1, 2001) for its face amount of $1,000 plus accrued annual interest of $60. The OID earned during the time you held the bond, $73, is not taxable. The $60 accrued annual interest also is not taxable. However, you must report the unearned part of the OID ($127) as a capital gain.

Long-term debt instruments issued after 1954 and before May 28, 1969 (or before July 2, 1982, if a government instrument). If you sell, trade, or redeem for a gain one of these debt instruments, the part of your gain that is not more than your ratable share of the OID at the time of the sale or redemption is ordinary income. The rest of the gain is capital gain. If, however, there was an intention to call the debt instrument before maturity, all of your gain that is not more than the entire OID is treated as ordinary income at the time of the sale. This treatment of taxable gain also applies to corporate instruments issued after May 27, 1969, under a written commitment that was binding on May 27, 1969, and at all times thereafter.

Long-term debt instruments issued after May 27, 1969 (or after July 1, 1982, if a government instrument). If you hold one of these debt instruments, you must include a part of the OID in your gross income each year that you own the instrument. Your basis in that debt instrument is increased by the amount of OID that you have included in your gross income. See *Original Issue Discount (OID)* in chapter 8 for information about the OID that you must report on your tax return.

If you sell or trade the debt instrument before maturity, your gain is a capital gain. However, if at the time the instrument was originally issued there was an intention to call it before its maturity, your gain generally is ordinary income to the extent of the entire OID reduced by any amounts of OID previously includible in your income. In this case, the rest of the gain is a capital gain.

Market discount bonds. If the debt instrument has market discount and you chose to include the discount in income as it accrued, increase your basis in the debt instrument by the accrued discount to figure capital gain or loss on its disposition. If you did not choose to include the discount in income as it accrued, you must report gain as ordinary interest income up to the instrument's accrued market discount. The rest of the gain is capital gain. See *Market Discount Bonds* in chapter 1 of Publication 550.

A different rule applies to market discount bonds issued before July 19, 1984, and purchased by you before May 1, 1993. See chapter 4 of Publication 550.

Retirement of debt instrument. Any amount that you receive on the retirement of a debt instrument is treated in the same way as if you had sold or traded that instrument.

Notes of individuals. If you hold an obligation of an individual that was issued with OID after March 1, 1984, you generally must include the OID in your income currently, and your gain or loss on its sale or retirement is generally capital gain or loss. An exception to this treatment applies if the obligation is a loan between individuals and all of the following requirements are met.

1) The lender is not in the business of lending money.
2) The amount of the loan, plus the amount of any outstanding prior loans, is $10,000 or less.
3) Avoiding federal tax is not one of the principal purposes of the loan.

If the exception applies, or the obligation was issued before March 2, 1984, you do not include the OID in your income currently. When you sell or redeem the obligation, the part of your gain that is not more than your accrued share of the OID at that time is ordinary income. The rest of the gain, if any, is capital gain. Any loss on the sale or redemption is capital loss.

> **Explanation**
> There are other kinds of sales or trades that many individuals enter into. Some of these transactions—short sales, put options, wash sales—are discussed below. The tax rules are very complicated. Professional advice should be obtained if you plan to invest in any of these transactions.
>
> **Short sales.** A short sale occurs when the seller borrows the property delivered to the buyer and, at a later date, either buys substantially identical property and delivers it to the lender or makes delivery out of such property held by the seller at the time of the sale. The holding period on a short sale is usually determined by the length of time the seller actually holds the property that is eventually delivered to the lender to close the short sale.
>
> **Example**
> Even though you do not own any stock in the Ace Corporation, you contract to sell 100 shares of it, which you borrow from your broker. After 13 months, when the price of the stock has fallen, you buy 100 shares of Ace Corporation stock and immediately deliver them to your broker to close out the short sale. Your gain is treated as a short-term capital gain because your holding period for the delivered property is less than 1 day.
>
> **Explanation**
> **Long and short positions.** If you have held substantially identical property to the property sold short for 1 year or less on the date of the short sale, the following two rules apply:
>
> 1. Any gain on closing a short sale is a short-term gain.
> 2. The holding period of the substantially identical property begins on the date of the closing of the short sale or on the date of the sale, gift, or other disposition of this property, whichever comes first.
>
> These two rules also apply if you acquire substantially identical property after the originating short sale and before the closing of the short sale.
>
> **Example**
> On February 6, 1996, you bought 100 shares of Able Corporation stock for $1,000. On July 6, 1996, you sold short 100 shares of similar Able stock for $1,600. On November 6, 1996, you purchased 100 more shares of Able stock for

$1,800 and used them to close the short sale. On this short sale, you realized a $200 short-term capital loss.

On February 7, 1997, you sold for $1,800 the stock originally bought on February 6, 1996. Although you have actually held this stock for more than 1 year, by using rule 2, the holding period is treated as having begun on November 6, 1996, the date of the closing of the short sale. The $800 gain realized on the sale is therefore a short-term capital gain.

TAXALERT

Short sales take away the tax benefits of long-term holding periods with respect to any substantially identical stock held in a long position, unless you have already met the long-term holding requirement at the time you make the short sale.

Treatment of losses. If, on the date of a short sale of a capital asset, you have held substantially identical property for more than 1 year, any loss you have on the short sale is treated as a long-term capital loss, even though the property used to close the sale was held for 1 year or less.

TAXORGANIZER

You should keep a copy of your broker confirmation statement for the purchase of any securities or options. Also, keep a copy of the Form 1099-B provided by your broker for any sales of securities or options.

TAXPLANNER

Short sales against the box. Selling short against the box means that you are selling borrowed securities while owning substantially identical securities that you later deliver to close the short sale.

Under prior law, a gain or loss on a transaction designed to reduce or eliminate risk of loss, such as a short sale against the box, or an "equity swap," was not recognized until the transaction was effectively "closed."

Under the Taxpayer Relief Act of 1997, you will generally be required to recognize gain (but not loss) upon entering into a constructive sale after June 8, 1997, of any appreciated position in stock, a partnership interest, or certain debt instruments that has the effect of eliminating your risk of loss and upside gain potential. You will be treated as making a constructive sale of an appreciated position when you do one of the following: (1) enter into a short sale of the same or substantially identical property; (2) enter into an offsetting contract with respect to the same or substantially identical property (an equity swap, for example); or (3) enter into a futures or forward contract to deliver the same or substantially identical property. In addition, future Treasury regulations are expected to expand these rules to other transactions that have substantially the same effects as the ones described in the IRS Code.

Exceptions

The 1997 law changes provide certain exceptions to these new rules. One of the most important is that it continues to allow short sales against the box, so long as the following requirements are met:

1. The transaction is closed within 30 days of the close of the taxable year; and
2. You hold the appreciated financial position throughout the 60-day period beginning on the date such transaction is closed, and you do not enter into certain positions that would diminish the risk of loss during that time.

TAXPLANNER

Purchasing put options. Acquiring a put option means that you are buying an option contract to sell 100 shares of stock at a set price during a specific time period. Investors who own appreciated securities that they are not yet ready to sell because of tax reasons often buy put options as a way of protecting their securities against possible price declines.

If the stock price subsequently increases, you obtain the benefit of the price increase less the cost of the put, which expires as worthless. If the stock price declines, however, you may either sell your shares at the put option price or sell the put option separately.

Example

Jim Smith purchased 100 shares of XYZ stock in July 1997 at $25 per share. The selling price in November 1997 was $55. Jim could have sold his shares in November and realized a $30 per-share gain, but it would have been taxed in 1997. Since Jim believed that the stock still had some upward potential and also wanted to postpone recognizing the gain, he bought a put option with an expiration date in March 1998, giving him the right to sell his stock at $55 per share. He locked in his gain and limited his loss to the cost of the put option.

Tax treatment of put options

1. If you sell the put—in lieu of exercising it—the gain or loss is a short-term or long-term capital gain or loss, depending on how long the put has been held.
2. If you neither sell nor exercise the put, the expiration is treated as a sale or an exchange of the put on the expiration date. Whether the loss you incur is a short-term or long-term capital loss depends on how long the put has been held.
3. If you exercise the put, its cost increases your basis in the underlying securities and thus is included in computing your gain or loss at the time of the securities' sale. Whether the gain or loss is short-term or long-term usually depends on the holding period of the underlying stock at the time the put option was acquired.

TAXPLANNER

Stock index options. Unlike a put option, which is based on shares in a specific company, a stock index option represents a group of stocks. For example, an index option is available that is keyed to Standard & Poor's 500 stock averages. Investors use stock index options to reduce portfolio exposure to general market or industry fluctuations and to improve their return on investment. Stock index options may also be used to protect current paper gains (gains you have on paper but have not yet realized) and to save taxes when a taxpayer owns appreciated stock that has not been held long enough to qualify for long-term capital gain treatment.

If you expect the stock market to go down, you might purchase stock index put options. If the market does go down, the put options gain in value, perhaps offsetting the loss in any appreciated stock you might hold.

TaxPlanner

Writing covered call options. If you have stock that has appreciated in value but want (1) to defer the gain until the following year and (2) to provide yourself with protection from market declines, consider writing a covered call option with an expiration date next year. A covered call is the selling of an option to purchase shares that you own at a specified price within a set time frame. If the purchaser of the call doesn't exercise it until next year (or lets it lapse), both the amount you receive from selling the call and the proceeds from disposition of the stock are not reported until the following year.

One disadvantage is that you give up the opportunity to benefit from a price increase in the stock you own above the option exercise price.

Example

Bill purchased 100 shares of XYZ stock for $20 per share on December 21, 1996. On December 22, 1997, the stock was selling for $50 per share, but Bill wanted to defer the gain until 1998 and protect himself against a market decline. Bill wrote a covered call option, agreeing to sell his 100 shares for $50 per share at any time within the next 3 months. He received $3 per share for selling this call option. Bill has acquired protection against a market decline because he now has $3 per share in the bank. If the person who bought the option does not exercise it, Bill reports the $3 per share as a short-term capital gain in 1998. If the option is exercised, the $3 per share is added to the $50 per-share exercise price.

If the stock had continued to appreciate, Bill could have bought other shares of the stock in the open market to deliver against the call, or he could have chosen to purchase, or buy back, the option. A short-term loss would have been realized when the option position was closed in either of these two ways.

Explanation

Wash sales. Losses from wash sales or exchanges of stocks or securities are not deductible. However, the gain from these sales is taxable. Commodity futures contracts are not stock or securities and are not covered by the wash sale rule. Any position of a straddle acquired after June 23, 1981, however, is covered by the wash sale rule. This includes futures contracts. See Publication 550, *Investment Income and Expenses.*

A wash sale occurs when you sell stock or securities, and, within 30 days before or after the sale, you buy, acquire in a taxable exchange, or acquire a contract or option to buy substantially identical stock. The substantially identical stock may be acquired by subscription for newly issued stock as well as by buying old stock. However, the unallowable loss is added to the basis of the newly acquired stock or security.

Example

You buy 100 shares of X stock for $1,000. At a later date, you sell these shares for $750. Then, within 30 days of the sale, you acquire 100 shares of the same stock for $800. Your loss of $250 on the sale is not deductible. However, the unallowed loss ($250) is added to the cost of the new stock ($800) to get the basis of the new stock ($1,050).

Explanation

For purposes of the wash sale rule, a short sale is considered complete on the date the short sale is entered into if on that date

1. You own (or, on or before that date, you enter into a contract or option to acquire) stock or securities identical to those sold short, and
2. You later deliver such stock or securities to close the short sale

Otherwise, a short sale is not considered complete until the property is delivered to close the sale.

Example

On June 3, you buy 100 shares of stock for $1,000. You sell short 100 shares of the stock for $750 on October 7. On October 8, you buy 100 shares of the same stock for $750. You close the short sale on November 18 by delivering the shares bought on June 3. The $250 loss ($1,000 – $750) is not deductible because the date of entering into the short sale (October 7) is deemed to be the date of sale for wash sale purposes and substantially identical stock was purchased within 30 days from the date of the sale. Therefore, the wash sale rule applies, and the loss is not deductible.

Explanation

Options. Gain or loss from the sale or exchange of a purchased option to buy or sell property that is a capital asset in your hands, or would be if you acquired it, is a capital gain or loss.

If you do not exercise an option to buy or sell, and you have a loss, the option is treated as having been sold or exchanged on the date that it expired.

The capital asset treatment does not apply

1. To a gain from the sale or exchange of an option, if the gain from the sale of the property underlying the option would be ordinary income, or
2. To a dealer in options, if the option is part of inventory, or
3. To a loss from failure to exercise a fixed-price option acquired on the same day the property identified in the option was acquired; such loss is not deductible.

If you grant an option on stocks, securities, commodities, or commodity futures and it is not exercised, the amount you receive (if you are not in the business of granting options) is treated as a short-term capital gain reportable on Schedule D (Form 1040), regardless of the classification of the property in your hands. If the option is exercised, you add the option payment to other amounts you receive to figure the amount you realize on the sale of the property. The classification of your gain or loss is then determined by the type of property you sold.

Your holding period for property acquired under an option to purchase begins on the day after the property was acquired, not the day after the option was acquired.

Commodity futures. A commodity future is a contract for the sale or purchase of some fixed amount of a commodity at a future date for a fixed price. The contracts are treated as either (1) hedges to ensure against unfavorable price changes in a commodity bought or sold in the course of business or (2) capital investments.

Gains and losses on hedging contracts for a commodity purchased in the ordinary course of a trade or a business to ensure the price of, and an adequate supply of, the commodity for use in the business are treated as ordinary business gains and losses.

Straddles. A straddle is a position that offsets an interest an investor has in personal property other than stock. It may take the form of a futures contract, an option, or cash. The purpose of a straddle is to reduce an individual's risk of property loss.

Example

Karen bought an option to have 5,000 bushels of wheat delivered to her in June 1997. At the same time, she bought an option to deliver 5,000 bushels of wheat in July 1997. Karen has a straddle.

Explanation

The treatment of straddles are designed to prevent the deferral of income and the conversion of ordinary income to capital gains.

Example 1

ABC stock is selling at $30. Peter purchases two options on ABC. He purchases a call to buy 100 shares of the stock for $25 per share and a put to sell 100 shares of the stock for $35 per share. As long as the stock does not stay at $30, one of the options will produce a gain and the other one will produce a loss.

Assume that by the end of the year the price of ABC is $34. The value of the call should have increased by $400, and the value of the put should have declined by $400. Under prior law, Peter could have repurchased the call and recognized the loss on his tax return, while the gain on the put could have been deferred to the following year.

Under current law, Peter cannot recognize the loss on the call until he recognizes the offsetting gain on the put.

Example 2

James purchases 100 shares of BCD stock on August 2, 1997, at $40 per share. On November 1, the BCD sells at $46 per share. James sells a call due in February, 1998, for $100. In December, the stock is selling for $50, and James repurchases the call for $400. James has a $300 short-term loss, which under prior law was deductible. Also, when he sells BCD in the following year, he could have a long-term gain. The loss cannot be deducted until the year in which the call is closed. The holding period of BCD stock is also changed. If James sells BCD in February 1998 for $50 per share, he would have a short-term gain of $700 to report (the $1,000 gain on the stock minus the $300 loss on the call).

Note: There are many special terms, rules, and exceptions to learn if you want to try your luck on these investment strategies. You should study the markets and the tax law very carefully.

TaxAlert

The 1993 Tax Act provides that specific types of capital gains can be treated as ordinary income for certain additional financial transactions. Certain gains from the sale of any conversion transaction entered into after April 30, 1993, can now be treated as ordinary income.

A conversion transaction occurs when substantially all of the expected return from an investment is attributable to the time value of the net investment. In addition, if the transaction falls within one of the following classifications, it will be considered a conversion transaction:

1. Acquiring property, and on a contemporaneous basis, contracting to sell the same property for a determined price
2. Certain straddles
3. Any transaction that is marketed as or sold as producing capital gains
4. Other transactions that the U.S. Treasury Department will describe in future regulations

A special rule exempts options dealers and commodities traders from the above provisions, but anti-abuse rules prevent limited partners or entrepreneurs from unduly profiting by this exception.

The amount of gain that can be considered ordinary income will not exceed the amount of interest that would have accrued on your net investment in the property at a rate equal to 120% of the applicable federal rate for the period of time you held the investment. This amount is then reduced by the amount of ordinary income that was recognized from the conversion transaction and any interest expense in connection with purchasing the property.

Example

Suzanne acquires stock for $10,000 on January 1, 1996, and on that same day agrees to sell it to Rick for $11,500 on January 1, 1998. Assume that the applicable federal rate is 5%. On January 1, 1998, Suzanne delivers the stock to Rick in exchange for $11,500. If the transaction was not a conversion transaction, Suzanne would have recognized a $1,500 capital gain ($11,500 − $10,000).

However, the 1993 Tax Act considers this arrangement a conversion transaction. Thus, $1,236 of her gain would be recharacterized as ordinary income (120% of 5% compounded for two years, applied to an investment of $10,000).

Computation of ordinary gain	
Investment	$10,000
Applicable rate (120% × 5%)	6%
	600
Investment	10,000
Amount after first year	10,600
Applicable rate (120% × 5%)	6%
	636
Amount after first year	10,600
	11,236
Investment	(10,000)
Ordinary income	$1,236

The difference between the ordinary income and the appreciation, $264 ($1,500 − $1,236), is classified as a long-term capital gain.

Additional requirements are imposed on conversion transactions with respect to built-in losses, options dealers, commodities traders, and limited partners and limited entrepreneurs in an entity that deals in options or trades in commodities.

Because the application of these rules is complex, you should consult your tax advisor when considering a potential conversion transaction.

Sale of business. The sale of a business is not usually the sale of one asset. If you sell your business or your interest in a business and need more information, see Publication 544, *Sales and Other Dispositions of Assets*.

Canceling a sale of real property. If you sell real property to an individual and the sales contract gives the buyer the right to return the property to you for the amount paid, you may not have to recognize gain or loss on the sale. You will not recognize gain or loss if the property is returned to you within the same tax year as the sale. However, if the property is returned to you in a future tax year, you must recognize gain or loss in the year of the sale. In the year in which the property is returned to you, your new basis in the property will be equal to the amount of cash, notes, or other property you give back to the buyer.

Lease canceled or sold. If a tenant receives payments for the cancellation of a lease on property used as the tenant's home, a gain is taxed as a capital gain, but any loss is not deductible. If the lease was used in the tenant's trade or business, gain or loss may be capital or ordinary, as explained in Publication 544, *Sales and Other Dispositions of Assets*.

Payments received by a landlord. If a landlord receives payments for cancellation of a lease, they are ordinary income and not capital gains.

Subleases. When you transfer leased property under an arrangement in which the new occupant takes over your monthly lease payments and also pays you an amount each month for relinquishing use of the property, a sublease has been entered into and payments you receive are ordinary income.

Repossession of real property. If real property that is a capital asset in your hands is repossessed by the seller under the terms of the sales contract or by foreclosure of a mortgage, you may have a capital gain or loss. The gain or loss is the difference between your adjusted basis in the property (purchase price with adjustments) and the full amount of your obligation cancelled, plus any money received, in exchange for the property. Losses on repossessions of property held for personal use, however, are not deductible. See Publication 537, *Installment Sales.* Also see the discussion of installment sales in this chapter.

Subdivision of land. If you own a tract of land, and, in order to sell or exchange it, you subdivide it into individual lots or parcels, you may receive capital gains treatment on at least a part of the proceeds if you meet the following four conditions:

1. You are not a dealer in real estate.
2. You have not made any major improvement on the tract while you held it that substantially enhances the value of the lot or parcel sold, and no such improvement will be made as part of the contract of sale with the buyer. A substantial improvement is generally one that increases the value of the property by more than 10%. Some improvements that are considered substantial are structural work on commercial and residential buildings, laying down hard-surface roads, and installing utility services.
3. You have held the land for at least 5 years, unless you got it by inheritance or devise.
4. You did not previously hold the tract or any lot or parcel on such tract mainly for sale to customers in the ordinary course of your trade or business (unless the tract previously would have qualified for this treatment), and, during the same tax year in which the sale occurred, you were not holding any other land for sale to customers in the ordinary course of trade or business.

For tax years beginning after December 31, 1996, this treatment will also apply to S corporations.

Gain on sale of lots. If your land meets these tests, the gain realized on the sale or exchange will be treated in the following manner.

If you sell less than six lots or parcels from the same tract, the entire gain is a capital gain. In figuring the number of lots or parcels sold, two or more adjoining lots sold to a single buyer in a single sale are counted as only one parcel.

When you sell or exchange the sixth lot or parcel from the same tract, the amount by which 5% of the selling price is more than the expenses of the sale is treated as ordinary income, and the rest of any gain will be a capital gain. Five percent of the selling price of all lots sold or exchanged from the tract in the tax year in which the sixth lot is sold or exchanged, and in later years, is treated as ordinary income.

If you sell the first six lots of a single tract in 1 year, to the extent of gain, the lesser of 5% of the selling price of each lot sold or the gain is treated as ordinary income. On the other hand, if you sold the first three lots in a single tract in 1 year and the next three lots in the following year, the 5% rule would apply only to the gains realized in the second year.

The selling expenses of the sale must first be deducted from the part of the gain treated as ordinary income, and any remaining expenses must be deducted from the part treated as a capital gain. You may not deduct the selling expenses from other income as ordinary business expenses.

Example 1

You sold five lots from a single tract last year. This year, you sell the sixth lot for $20,000. Your basis for this lot is $10,000, and your selling expenses are $1,500. Your gain is $8,500, all of which is capital gain, figured as follows:

Selling price		$20,000
Minus:		
Basis	$10,000	
Expense of sale	1,500	11,500
Gain from sale of lot		$ 8,500
5% of selling price	$ 1,000	
Minus: Expense of sale	1,500	
Gain reported as ordinary income		–0–
Gain reported as capital gain		$ 8,500

Because the selling expenses are more than 5% of the selling price, none of the gain is treated as ordinary income.

Example 2

Assume in Example 1 that the selling expenses are $800. The amount of gain is $9,200, of which $200 is ordinary income and $9,000 is capital gain, figured as follows:

Selling price		$20,000
Minus:		
Basis	$10,000	
Expense of sale	800	10,800
Gain from sale of lot		$ 9,200
5% of selling price	$ 1,000	
Minus: Expense of sale	800	
Gain reported as ordinary income		200
Gain reported as capital gain		$ 9,000

Explanation

Loss on sale of lots. The 5% rule does not apply to losses. If you sell a lot at a loss, it will be treated as a capital loss if you held it for investment.

For more information on subdivision of land, see Publication 544, *Sales and Other Dispositions of Assets.*

Inventions. An invention is usually a capital asset in the hands of the inventor, whether or not a patent has been applied for or has been obtained. The inventor is the individual whose efforts created the property and who qualifies as the original and first inventor or joint inventor.

If you are an inventor and transfer all substantial rights to patent property, you may get special tax treatment, as described below, if the transfer is not to your employer or to a related person.

If, for a consideration paid to the inventor, you acquire all the substantial rights to patent property before the invention is reduced to practice (tested and operated successfully under operating conditions), you may, when you dispose of your interest, get special tax treatment, if you are not the employer of the inventor or related to the inventor (as described later). However, if you buy patent property after it is reduced to practice, it may be treated as either a capital or a noncapital asset, depending on the circumstances.

Special tax treatment. If you are the inventor or an individual who acquired all the substantial rights to the patent property before the invention was reduced to practice, and you transfer all the substantial rights or an undivided interest in all such rights, the transfer will be treated as a sale or an exchange of a long-term capital asset. This rule applies even if you have not held the patent property for more than 1 year and whether or not the payments received are made periodically during the transferee's use of the patent or are contingent on the productivity, use, or disposition of the property transferred.

Courts have enforced the substantial rights requirement very strictly. Generally, a patent seller must be able to show that any rights he or she retains are insubstantial in order to treat the sale of rights in the patent property as a long-term capital gain.

The U.S. Courts of Appeals for the Sixth, Seventh, and Ninth Circuits have overturned lower court rulings that allowed patent owners transferring exclusive rights to impose geographical limitations within the United States on the person purchasing the patent. However, the official IRS position is that a transfer of all substantial rights may be limited to one or more countries.

Payment for the patent may be received by the seller in a lump sum, as an installment sale, as a fixed percentage of all future profits from the patent, or as a fee per item produced. All these methods qualify for capital gains treatment, even if the total amount of payment is uncertain.

Transfers between related parties. The special tax treatment does not apply if the transfer is either directly or indirectly between you and certain related parties.

Copyrights. Literary, musical, or artistic compositions, or similar property, are not treated as capital assets if your personal efforts created them or if you got the property in such a way that all or part of your basis in the property is determined by reference to a person whose personal efforts created the property (e.g., if you got the property as a gift). The sale of such property, whether or not it is copyrighted, results in ordinary income.

However, if you get such property, or a copyright to it, in any other way, the amounts you got for granting the exclusive use or right to exploit the work throughout the life of the copyright are treated as being received from the sale of property. It does not matter if the payment is a fixed amount or a percentage of receipts from the sale, performance, exhibition, or publication of the copyright work, or an amount based on the number of copies sold, performances given, or exhibitions made. It also does not matter if the payment is made over the same period as that covering the grantee's use of the copyrighted work.

Deposit in Insolvent or Bankrupt Financial Institution

If you lose money you have on deposit in a qualified financial institution that becomes insolvent or bankrupt, you may be able to deduct your loss in one of three ways.

1) Ordinary loss,
2) Casualty loss, or
3) Nonbusiness bad debt (short-term capital loss).

Ordinary loss or casualty loss. If you can reasonably estimate your loss, you can choose to treat the estimated loss as either an ordinary loss or a casualty loss in the current year. Either way, you claim the loss as an itemized deduction.

If you claim an ordinary loss, report it as a miscellaneous itemized deduction on line 22 of Schedule A (Form 1040). The maximum amount you can claim is $20,000 ($10,000 if you are married filing separately) reduced by any expected state insurance proceeds. Your loss is subject to the 2%-of-adjusted-gross-income limit. You cannot choose to claim an ordinary loss if any of the deposit is federally insured.

If you claim a casualty loss, attach **Form 4684,** *Casualties and Thefts,* to your return. Each loss must be reduced by $100. Your total casualty losses for the year are reduced by 10% of your adjusted gross income.

You cannot choose either of these methods if:

1) You own at least 1% of the financial institution,
2) You are an officer of the institution, or
3) You are related to such an owner or officer. You are related if you and the owner or officer are "related parties," as defined earlier under *Related Party Transactions,* or if you are the aunt, uncle, nephew, or niece of the owner or officer.

If the actual loss that is finally determined is more than the amount you deducted as an estimated loss, you can claim the excess loss as a bad debt. If the actual loss is less than the amount deducted as an estimated loss, you must include in income (in the final determination year) the excess loss claimed. See *Recoveries* in Publication 525, *Taxable and Nontaxable Income.*

TAXPLANNER

Whether you elect to claim a casualty or an ordinary loss in the year in which the requirements for the election are met will depend on a number of factors. First, you must compare the available **casualty loss deduction** (after reducing your loss by $100 plus 10% of your adjusted gross income) to your **ordinary loss deduction** (after adding the loss to other miscellaneous itemized deductions and reducing the total by 2% of adjusted gross income). The ordinary loss election is available on deposits of up to $20,000 ($10,000 if you are married and file a separate return), which are not federally insured. The $20,000 limitation applies to each financial institution, not each deposit or each tax year. This is important if you hold deposits in more than one institution.

The election to claim an ordinary loss, once made, cannot be revoked unless you obtain the consent of the IRS.

You should also consider whether it is better to forgo either election and claim the entire amount as a **capital loss** from a nonbusiness bad debt (see *Nonbusiness Bad Debts*, following). This might be advisable if you have sufficient capital gain income with which to offset the capital loss. Consult with your financial advisor when considering these elections.

Example

Judy Porter estimates that she has incurred a total loss of her $30,000 bank account with an insolvent financial institution. Her account is not federally insured. Judy's adjusted gross income (AGI) is $70,000, and she has no miscellaneous itemized deductions. Judy wants to review the tax consequences of electing to claim the estimated loss as either a casualty loss or an ordinary loss, which is treated as a miscellaneous itemized deduction.

The net deduction available under each method is as follows:

	Casualty loss	Ordinary loss
Estimated loss	$30,000	$20,000*
$100 casualty loss limitation	(100)	n/a
10% AGI limitation	(7,000)	n/a
2% AGI limitation	n/a	(1,400)
Net deduction available	$22,900	$18,600

* Limited to $20,000 per institution.

In addition, if the loss actually sustained by Judy exceeds the amount deducted as an estimated loss, she can claim the excess loss as a bad debt in the year in which that loss is finally determined. Thus, if Judy elects to treat the estimated loss as an ordinary loss and she determines in a subsequent year that her entire balance of $30,000 was lost, she could claim an additional $10,000 deduction for bad debts. This would increase her cumulative deductions under this alternative to a total amount of $28,600.

TAX*ORGANIZER*

You should obtain information and documentation to substantiate when a debt or deposit becomes worthless. The following items are examples of documentation supporting the worthlessness of debts and deposits: bankruptcy filings, news reports, and financial statements.

Nonbusiness bad debt. If you choose to treat the loss as a bad debt, see *How to report bad debts*, later.

Sale of Annuity

The part of any gain on the sale of an annuity contract before its maturity date that is based on interest accumulated on the contract is ordinary income.

Nonbusiness Bad Debts

If someone owes you money that you cannot collect, you have a bad debt. You may be able to deduct the amount owed to you when you figure your tax for the year the debt becomes worthless. A debt must be genuine for you to deduct a loss. A debt is genuine if it arises from a debtor-creditor relationship based on a valid and enforceable obligation to repay a fixed or determinable sum of money.

Explanation

Determining when a debt becomes worthless. It's not always easy to tell when a debt has become worthless, but the following factors are some indications to look for: (1) bankruptcy of the debtor, (2) termination of the debtor's business, (3) debtor's disappearance or departure from the country, (4) debtor's death, (5) receivership of the debtor, (6) a monetary judgment against the debtor that cannot be collected, and (7) drop in value of property securing the debt.

A sharp decline in the debtor's business may support a finding of worthlessness. In one case, a court allowed a taxpayer to take a bad debt deduction when the small, closely held company that had borrowed the money had to cancel some of its business contracts, had severe cash flow problems, and was unable to obtain bank loans to carry on. However, in other cases, the courts have stressed that a debt is not worthless if the borrower remains a viable going concern engaged in business, even if it is suffering a business decline and losing a lot of money.

If a foreclosure sale of pledged or mortgaged property yields less than the principal amount of the defaulted debt, worthlessness may exist. If the creditor shows that the remaining unpaid debt is uncollectible, he or she may take a bad debt deduction in the year of the foreclosure sale.

If a seller of real property reacquires the property to satisfy a debt that is secured by the property, no debt is considered to become worthless.

If an amount is owed by two or more debtors jointly, inability to collect from one of the debtors does not justify a deduction for a proportionate amount of the debt.

TAX*PLANNER*

It is important to know when a debt becomes worthless because you may not take a loss in a subsequent year. Because, in many cases, it may be difficult to determine when a debt loses its value, you should claim a deduction at the earliest time you reasonably believe the debt to be worthless. If you discover you have overlooked a bad debt deduction that you should have taken, amend your return for that year. The statute of limitations for bad debts generally runs 7 years from the due date of the tax return filed for the year in which the debt became worthless.

TAX*PLANNER*

A debt becomes worthless when a prudent person would abandon the effort to collect the debt. This may mean that you expended a lot of effort trying to collect or that you didn't try at all. You have the burden of proving that the debt is worthless.

In most circumstances, it is wise to obtain the opinion of an attorney about whether or not collection efforts are warranted. His or her opinion should be based on objective facts establishing the loss.

Whenever possible, you should also obtain copies of the debtor's financial statements. If they show a positive net worth, then, in order to establish a debt as worthless, you have to demonstrate that the **assets** are not worth what the statements claim or that another creditor has a claim on those assets that takes precedence over yours.

You should document any steps you have taken to recover the amount owed to you. Also, you should get a copy of the debtor's financial statements to substantiate the inability to pay back the loan.

Bad debts that you did not get in the course of operating your trade or business are nonbusiness bad debts. To be deductible, nonbusiness bad debts must be totally worthless. You cannot deduct a partly worthless nonbusiness debt.

Basis in bad debt required. To deduct a bad debt, you must have a basis in it—that is, you must have already included the amount in your income or loaned out your cash. For example, you cannot claim a bad debt deduction for court-ordered child support not paid to you by your former spouse. If you are a cash method taxpayer (as most individuals are), you generally cannot take a bad debt deduction for unpaid salaries, wages, rents, fees, interest, dividends, and similar items.

Explanation

The distinction between business and nonbusiness bad debts is generally clear. Business bad debts usually occur because of credit transactions with customers, employees, and others closely related to a trade or a business. The dominant motive in these transactions is to support the business activity. Nonbusiness bad debts frequently arise from casual loans, such as those made to friends or acquaintances. But there is often confusion between business and nonbusiness bad debts in the following areas:

1. **You make loans frequently, but making loans is not a full-time business.** The IRS's position is that business bad debt treatment is limited to those situations in which the taxpayer derives his or her main source of income from credit transactions. Whether or not you are in a trade or business is a question of fact. The greater the regularity of the activity, however, the more likely that a trade or business exists.

Example

You occasionally lend money to individuals starting new businesses. That is an investment activity, not a trade or a business.

2. **You make a loan to a corporation in which you are an employee and a stockholder.** You are allowed a business bad debt deduction if the loan was made primarily to protect your salary. If the loan was made primarily to protect your investment, it is considered a nonbusiness loan. The larger your investment is in a company and the smaller your salary is from it, the greater the chance that a court will determine that a loan you make to the company is for nonbusiness purposes.

TAXPLANNER

If you make advances to a corporation you own, the IRS may attempt to recharacterize the advances as equity capital rather than bona fide loans. This might postpone a deduction for a bad debt until the year in which your stock is wholly worthless. Therefore, it is important that you properly document advances you make to the corporation as bona fide loans. Generally, written, interest-bearing instruments with fixed repayment terms will qualify as bona fide debt.

TAXPLANNER

If you want a loan to a family member to be considered a bona fide debt, you should document the transaction so that it is clear that both parties expect and intend repayment of the loan.

A child may borrow money from his or her parents for a business venture. To indicate that the borrowed money is not intended as a gift, the parents should draft a note saying who owes whom money. (The parties might check with a lawyer about the exact form the note should take.) If the note calls for partial payments of the debt, each payment should be made on time. This provides evidence that a legitimate creditor-debtor relationship exists. To further support their status as creditors, parents may consider investigating the business in which the child is investing the borrowed money. An arm's length lender typically makes such an investigation.

It's also a good idea for the note from the parents to provide that the money be repaid with interest. Charging interest provides another bit of evidence that the loan between parents and child is a valid arm's length transaction. Failure to charge adequate interest can also have important gift and income tax consequences. For details, see Chapter 8, *Interest Income.*

Example 1

Gail lends her son $20,000, which the son then invests in a new business venture. Gail draws up a note that provides for a specific repayment schedule and a stated rate of interest. Collateral is also established on the note to provide Gail with some security. Later, before any payments on the note have been made, the son's business venture fails. Despite repeated efforts to collect the debt, Gail is able to recover only a small amount based on the collateral established at the time of the loan.

Gail may take a bad debt deduction of $20,000, less the amount of collateral she recovered. Gail's son may deduct his loss as a business loss.

Example 2

Assume the same facts as in Example 1 except that Gail does not document the loan. No note is drawn up, and no specific provisions are made about when her son will repay the loan. If the son's business venture fails, he may deduct his loss. The mother, however, may not take a bad debt deduction.

Explanation

Loans in your business. If you are in a business or a profession, you may have bad debts that come from loans you make to your clients. If you are not in the business of lending money and the loans have no close relationship to your business or profession, these bad debts are nonbusiness bad debts.

Mechanics' and suppliers' liens. Workers and material suppliers sometimes file liens against property because of debts owed by a builder or a contractor. If you pay off such a lien to avoid foreclosure and loss of your property, you are entitled to repayment from the builder or contractor. If the debt is uncollectible, you may take a deduction for a bad debt.

Insolvency of contractor. You can take a bad debt deduction for the amount you deposit with a contractor if the contractor becomes insolvent and you are unable to recover (collect) your deposit. If the deposit is for work that is not related to your trade or business, it is a nonbusiness bad debt deduction.

Secondary liability on home mortgage. If you sell your home and the purchaser assumes your mortgage, you may remain secondarily liable for repayment of the mortgage loan. If the purchaser defaults on the loan, you may have to make up the difference if the house is then sold for less than the amount outstanding on the mortgage. You can take a bad debt deduction for the amount you pay to satisfy the mortgage if you cannot collect it from the purchaser.

Corporate securities that become worthless are generally deductible as capital losses. This includes shares of stock, stock rights, bonds, debentures, notes, or certificates, as explained in Chapter 17, *Reporting Gains and Losses.*

TAXPLANNER

Frequently, it is difficult to establish the year in which a corporate security becomes worthless. One guide is a publication called *Capital Changes Reporter,* published by Commerce Clearing House. The section called Worthless Securities provides a current list of companies whose securities have lost their value.

It is even more difficult to determine when a closely held business becomes worthless. It is not necessary for the company to declare bankruptcy. If you are aware that a company is insolvent, you may be able to take a loss. If the business continues to operate and has more than nominal assets, however, it may be only temporarily insolvent. If that is the case, you may not be able to take a loss.

Explanation

Recovery of a bad debt. Any amount recovered for a bad debt deducted in a previous year generally must be included in your income in the year in which the amount was recovered. However, you may exclude the amount recovered up to the amount of the deduction that did not reduce your income subject to tax in the year deducted. Recovery of amounts deducted in previous years is discussed in Chapter 13, *Other Income.*

Example

In 1993 Bill had a $25,000 **long-term capital gain,** a $25,000 bad debt loss, and other deductions totaling $2,480. Bill had no **taxable income** for 1993.

In 1998, Bill recovered the entire $25,000 debt. To figure how much he should include in his 1998 income, see the calculations below.

	1993 with bad debt	1993 without bad debt
Income:		
Net long-term capital gain	$25,000	$25,000
Bad debt loss	(25,000)	
Adjusted gross income	–0–	$25,000
Less:		
Standard deductions	–0–	$3,000
Personal exemption	–0–	$1,950
Taxable income	–0–	$20,050

The calculations show that Bill's 1993 taxable income was reduced by $20,050 by including the bad debt. Therefore, $20,050 is included in Bill's taxable income for 1998, the year in which he collected the $25,000 debt.

Explanation

Business bad debts. There are two crucial differences in the treatment of business bad debts and nonbusiness bad debts:

1. Business bad debts are treated as **ordinary losses,** which may be deducted directly from gross income. Nonbusiness bad debts are short-term capital losses and should be shown on Schedule D along with your short-term and long-term gains and losses from other sources. The maximum capital loss that you may use to offset your other income each year is $3,000. See Chapter 17, *Reporting Gains and Losses,* for further information.
2. A business bad debt may be just *partially* worthless and still give rise to a tax deduction. A nonbusiness bad debt has to be totally worthless.

Example

Janet Jones, an accrual basis taxpayer, performs some plumbing work for XYZ Corporation and sends them an invoice for $20,000 in 1996. In 1997, Janet learns that XYZ Corporation will not be able to pay the entire amount of the bill. She may claim a bad debt deduction for the amount of the invoice that is worthless.

Explanation

Some businesses use the **reserve method** of computing bad debt expense in keeping their books. Under this method, an estimate of accounts for services expected to be uncollectible is computed, based on prior years' experience, and the amount is placed in reserve as bad debt expense.

The reserve method is no longer allowed for tax purposes, except for certain financial institutions. Therefore, a business bad debt will be allowed only if it is **specifically charged off** the taxpayer's books during the year. Therefore, if you own a business with a large number of accounts receivable, to maximize your allowable tax deduction, you should carefully review old accounts at year-end to make sure all worthless accounts are written off.

A special rule applies to taxpayers using the accrual method of accounting for amounts to be received for the performance of services: You are not required to include in income any portion of accrued income for services performed that, on the basis of experience, will not be collected. This rule does not apply if interest is required to be paid on a receivable amount or if there is any penalty for failure to pay such amount on time.

The IRS guidelines that spell out how a taxpayer estimates uncollectible amounts for services are somewhat complex. You should consult your tax advisor if these special rules apply to your situation.

Guarantees. If you guarantee payment of another person's debt and then have to pay it off, you may be able to take a bad debt deduction for your loss. It does not matter in what capacity you make the guarantee, whether as guarantor, endorser, or indemnitor.

To qualify for a bad debt deduction, the guarantee must either be entered into with a profit motive or be related to your trade or business or employment.

A worthless debt qualifies as a *nonbusiness bad debt* if you can show that your reason for making the guarantee was to protect your investment or to make a profit. If you make the guarantee as a favor to friends and are not given anything in return, it is considered a gift and you may not take a deduction.

You are justified in taking the deduction if you can show that you *expected* to receive something in return at a future time. The expectation must be reasonable.

Example 1

A taxpayer who ran a successful car rental operation loaned money to her brother-in-law to assist him in starting his own car rental business. The taxpayer received a promissory note due 1 year after the date of the loan, with a stated rate of interest. The brother-in-law's business venture was a flop, and the taxpayer eventually took a bad debt deduction. The court allowed the deduction, pointing out that at the time the loan was made, the brother-in-law was solvent and there was a reasonable expectation that the rental business would serve as a source of repayment.

Example 2

A taxpayer loaned his brother-in-law about $2,000 over a 2-year period to help him support the taxpayer's sister and her children. During the entire period, the brother-in-law was low on cash and his business was failing. There was no record of the loan or any understanding about how it would be repaid. The court ruled that the taxpayer could not take a bad debt deduction because there was no reasonable expectation that the loan would be repaid. Instead, the court said that the $2,000 "loan" should be considered a gift.

How to report bad debts. Deduct nonbusiness bad debts as short-term capital losses on Schedule D (Form 1040).

In Part I, line 1 of Schedule D, enter the name of the debtor and "statement attached" in column (a). Enter the amount of the bad debt in parentheses in column (f). Use a separate line for each bad debt.

For each bad debt, attach a statement to your return that contains:

1) A description of the debt, including the amount, and the date it became due,
2) The name of the debtor, and any business or family relationship between you and the debtor,
3) The efforts you made to collect the debt, and
4) Why you decided the debt was worthless. For example, you could show that the borrower has declared bankruptcy, or that legal action to collect would probably not result in payment of any part of the debt.

Filing a claim for refund. If you do not deduct a bad debt on your original return for the year it becomes worthless, you can file a claim for a credit or refund due to the bad debt. To do this, use Form 1040X, *Amended U.S. Individual Income Tax Return,* to amend your return for the year the debt became worthless. You must file it within 7 years from the date your original return for that year had to be filed, or 2 years from the date you paid the tax, whichever is later. For more information about filing a claim, see *Amended Returns and Claims for Refund* in chapter 1.

Additional information. For more information, see *Nonbusiness Bad Debts* in Publication 550. For information on business bad debts, see chapter 11 of Publication 535, *Business Expenses.*

Losses on Small Business Stock

You can deduct as an ordinary loss, rather than as a capital loss, your loss on the sale, trade, or worthlessness of section 1244 stock. Report the loss on **Form 4797,** line 10. Any gain on this stock is capital gain and is reported on Schedule D (Form 1040) if the stock is a capital asset in your hands. See *Losses on Section 1244 (Small Business) Stock* in chapter 4 of Publication 550.

Losses on Small Business Investment Company Stock

See *Losses on Small Business Investment Company Stock* in chapter 4 of Publication 550.

Explanation

While individuals who own certain stock in a small business investment company may be allowed to deduct as an ordinary loss a loss on the sale, exchange, or worthlessness of their stock, the amount that may be claimed is subject to an annual limit of $50,000 ($100,000 on **joint returns**) per taxpayer.

Ordinary loss treatment is generally available only to the original owner. If you obtain stock in a small business corporation or investment company through purchase, gift, inheritance, or the like, you may not claim ordinary losses. Similarly, if small business stock is owned through a partnership, to claim a loss, you must have been a partner when the stock was issued. If you were not a partner at such time and the partnership later distributed the stock to the partners, you may not take an ordinary loss deduction.

To qualify for ordinary loss treatment, you must own Section 1244 stock. This is the stock of a small business corporation or investment company with total capital of under $1 million that meets a *passive income test.* To meet this test, the aggregate of any gross receipts generated over the last 5 years by royalties, rents, dividends, interest, annuities, and sales of stock or securities must be less than 50% of total gross receipts taken in by the corporation in the 5-year period. In addition, the corporation's stock must have been issued for money or property other than securities. Stock that is convertible into other securities of the corporation is not treated as Section 1244 stock.

TAXPLANNER

The loss limitation of $50,000 per taxpayer is an annual limitation. Therefore, if you are considering a sale of Section 1244 stock that is expected to produce a loss of over $50,000, you should consider structuring the transaction so that stock sales will take place in more than 1 year.

Example

Craig, a bachelor, has owned 10,000 shares of qualified small business stock for several years. The stock has a basis of $150,000. He plans to dispose of the stock but expects to realize only $50,000 on the sale. If he sells all 10,000 shares in 1997, he will recognize a $100,000 loss in 1 year. Only $50,000 will be deductible as an ordinary loss. The other $50,000 will be treated as a long-term capital loss. The long-term capital loss can be offset against other capital gains, but the excess can be deducted at the rate of only $3,000 per year.

If Craig sells 5,000 shares in 1997 and 5,000 shares in 1998 and receives the same price, he will still have a total loss of $100,000. Yet, because $50,000 of the loss will be recognized in 1997 and the other $50,000 in 1998, Craig may treat both losses as ordinary losses, which makes the total $100,000 loss fully deductible.

Craig should use Form 4797 to report the Section 1244 loss as a sale of a noncapital asset.

Holding Period

If you sold or traded investment property, you must determine your holding period for the property. Your holding period determines whether any capital gain or loss was a short-term or long-term capital gain or loss.

Long term or short term. If you hold investment property *more than 1 year,* any capital gain or loss is a *long-term* capital gain or loss. If you hold the property *1 year or less,* any capital gain or loss is a *short-term* capital gain or loss.

To determine how long you held the investment property, begin counting on the date after the day you acquired the property. The day you disposed of the property is part of your holding period.

Example. If you bought investment property on February 5, 2000 and sold it on February 5, 2001, your holding period is not more than 1 year and you will have a short-term capital gain or loss. If you sold it on February 6, 2001, your holding period is more than 1 year and you will have a long-term capital gain or loss.

Securities traded on established market. For securities traded on an established securities market, your holding period begins the day after the trade date you bought the securities, and ends on the trade date you sold them.

Caution. *Do not confuse the trade date with the settlement date, which is the date by which the stock must be delivered and payment must be made.*

Example. You are a cash method, calendar year taxpayer. You sold stock at a gain on December 28, 2001. According to the rules of the stock exchange, the sale was closed by delivery of the stock three trading days after the sale, on January 3, 2002. You received payment of the sales price on that same day. Report your gain on your 2001 return, even though you received the payment in 2002. The gain is long term or short term depending on whether you held the stock more than 1 year. Your holding period ended on December 28. If you had sold the stock at a loss, you would also report it on your 2001 return.

TaxSaver

If you sell stock at the end of the year, your December statement from your broker may not reflect the sale. The broker may not record the transaction until the closing date, which could be the following year. To avoid the penalties associated with underreporting, be sure to examine your January statement as well. You should also receive Form 1099-B from your broker. This form should list all your sales for the year based on the trade date.

TaxAlert: The 2001 Tax Act

Qualified five-year gain property election. Beginning in 2001, if you are in the fifteen percent (15%) tax bracket, and you own an asset that you acquired in 1996 or earlier and have held the asset for more that 5 years and 1 day, you will pay an eight percent (8%) capital gains rate rather than a ten percent (10%) capital gains rate if the asset was sold in 2001.

In addition, beginning in 2001, if you are in a tax bracket *higher* than 15% and are subject to the twenty percent (20%) capital gains rate, you may be eligible to have an eighteen percent (18%) capital gains rate applied to "qualified 5-year gain property" provided certain requirements are met. In order to qualify for the 18% rate, the gain must be long-term capital gain from property held for more than 5 years, and such property must have been acquired (purchased) on or after January 1, 2001. Thus, assuming that you hold the property for at least 5 years and 1 day, in 2006 when you sell the property, you will receive the benefit of the 18% capital gains rate.

Alternatively, if you have assets that you purchased prior to January 1, 2001, different rules apply. In this instance, you may make an *irrevocable election* to treat the asset as if it was sold for its fair market value (it's closing price) on January 2, 2001 (i.e., a "deemed sale"), and then treat the asset as "qualified 5-year gain property" upon a future sale more than 5 years and 1 day from the date of the deemed sale. Thus, if the election is made you will: (1) pay taxes on the gain at the time of the deemed sale [i.e., you will pay taxes on the difference between your basis and the fair market value (FMV) of the property on the date of the deemed sale]; (2) own an asset with a new basis equal to the FMV of the property on the date of the deemed sale; and (3) start a new holding period for purposes of having the 18% capital gains rate apply in year 2006 (provided the asset is held for at least 5 years and 1 day prior to being sold in 2006).

Examples of assets that qualify as qualified 5-year gain property are the following:

- Capital assets (e.g., publicly traded securities)

Assets that do not qualify as qualified 5-year gain property are:

- Unrecaptured Section 1250 gain
- Collectibles
- Qualified small business stock
- Personal residences

Should you make the election? In making this election, you should consider whether the payment of the taxes today (those due on the gain from the deemed sale) are significantly less than the total savings from the benefit of the lower tax rate (18%) 5 years from now. The concept to focus on here is the "time value of money," and in this instance, if the election is made, not only are you out of pocket the amount of taxes paid, but you have also lost the opportunity to invest the proceeds used to pay the taxes over the next 5 years.

TaxSaver

Making the election (discussed directly above) might make sense if you have capital loss carryforwards and wished to use these losses in the current year. In this instance, you might choose to make the election and incur the capital gains, and then use these gains to offset your losses rather than deduct these losses on a carryforward basis of $3,000/year. If your situation appears to be one in which making this election might be beneficial, please consult your tax advisor.

TaxSaver

If you own highly appreciated stock that you acquired during or before 1996, a gift of this stock to your children and then having your children sell the stock may provide some benefits. So long as your children are in the 15% tax bracket and are not subject to the "kiddie tax" (a tax imposed on children under the age of 14), the children will owe long-term capital gains taxes on the proceeds of 8%. This is so because the child is permitted to "tack" on the parent's holding period for the stock, and is treated as if he or she acquired the stock on the date the parent did. Provided the sale takes place more than 5 years and 1 day after the date on which the stock was originally acquired, the 8% long-term capital gains rate is applied.

TAXSAVER

The election should not be made for property with built-in losses. If such an election is made, the losses are not deductible in the current or in future years. Thus, if you believe the value of the asset will increase over the next 5 years, an alternative solution might be for you to sell the property and recognize the loss, and then reacquire the property 31 days from that date. If this is the case, consult your tax advisor to ensure that all of the requirements for such a transaction are met and that you don't run afoul of the "wash-sale" rules.

How to Make the Election. Taxpayers must make this election on their 2001 income tax return filed in year 2002.

Nontaxable trades. If you acquire investment property in a trade for other investment property and your basis for the new property is determined, in whole or in part, by your basis in the old property, your holding period for the new property begins on the day following the date you acquired the old property.

Property received as a gift. If you receive a gift of property and your basis is determined by the donor's adjusted basis, your holding period is considered to have started on the same day the donor's holding period started.

If your basis is determined by the fair market value of the property, your holding period starts on the day after the date of the gift.

Inherited property. If you inherit investment property, your capital gain or loss on any later disposition of that property is treated as a long-term capital gain or loss. This is true regardless of how long you actually held the property.

Real property bought. To figure how long you have held real property bought under an unconditional contract, begin counting on the day after you received title to it or on the day after you took possession of it and assumed the burdens and privileges of ownership, whichever happened first. However, taking delivery or possession of real property under an option agreement is not enough to start the holding period. The holding period cannot start until there is an actual contract of sale. The holding period of the seller cannot end before that time.

Loss on mutual fund or REIT stock held 6 months or less. If you hold stock in a mutual fund or real estate investment trust (REIT) for 6 months or less and then sell it at a loss, special rules may apply. See chapter 4 of Publication 550.

Automatic investment service. In determining your holding period for shares bought by the bank or other agent, full shares are considered bought first and any fractional shares are considered bought last. Your holding period starts on the day after the bank's purchase date. If a share was bought over more than one purchase date, your holding period for that share is a split holding period. A part of the share is considered to have been bought on each date that stock was bought by the bank with the proceeds of available funds.

Stock dividends. The holding period for stock you received as a taxable stock dividend begins on the date of distribution.

The holding period for new stock you received as a nontaxable stock dividend begins on the same day as the holding period of the old stock. This rule also applies to stock acquired in a "spin-off," which is a distribution of stock or securities in a controlled corporation.

Nontaxable stock rights. Your holding period for nontaxable stock rights begins on the same day as the holding period of the underlying stock. The holding period for stock acquired through the exercise of stock rights begins on the date the right was exercised.

Rollover of Gain From Publicly Traded Securities

You may qualify for a tax-free rollover of certain gains from the sale of publicly traded securities. This means that if you buy certain replacement property and make the choice described in this section, you postpone part or all of your gain.

You postpone the gain by adjusting the basis of the replacement property as described in *Basis of replacement property,* later. This postpones your gain until the year you dispose of the replacement property.

You qualify to make this choice if you meet all the following tests.

1) You sell publicly traded securities at a gain. Publicly traded securities are securities traded on an established securities market.
2) Your gain from the sale is a capital gain.
3) During the 60-day period beginning on the date of the sale, you buy replacement property. This replacement property must be either common stock or a partnership interest in a specialized small business investment company (SSBIC). This is any partnership or corporation licensed by the Small Business Administration under section 301(d) of the Small Business Investment Act of 1958, as in effect on May 13, 1993.

Amount of gain recognized. If you make the choice described in this section, you must recognize gain only up to the following amount:

1) The amount realized on the sale, minus
2) The cost of any common stock or partnership interest in an SSBIC that you bought during the 60-day period beginning on the date of sale (and did not previously take into account on an earlier sale of publicly traded securities).

If this amount is less than the amount of your gain, you can postpone the rest of your gain, subject to the limit described next. If this amount is equal to or more than the amount of your gain, you must recognize the full amount of your gain.

Limit on gain postponed. The amount of gain you can postpone each year is limited to the smaller of:

1) $50,000 ($25,000 if you are married and file a separate return), or
2) $500,000 ($250,000 if you are married and file a separate return), minus the amount of gain you postponed for all earlier years.

Basis of replacement property. You must subtract the amount of postponed gain from the basis of your replacement property.

How to report and postpone gain. See chapter 4 of Publication 550 for details on how to report and postpone the gain.

16

Selling Your Home

Introduction

Your home is probably the most valuable asset you own and may increase in value. Consequently, you may have a significant gain—and lots of taxes to pay—when you sell it. With careful planning, you may avoid these taxes altogether. Alternatively, some homes will be sold at a loss. Unfortunately, a loss on the sale of your home is generally not deductible. This chapter tells you what you should and shouldn't do when you're considering selling your home.

Your home is probably your best tax shelter. The tax system continues to give many breaks to homeowners. You may deduct the cost of real estate taxes and, subject to certain limitations, the cost of interest paid on your mortgage. (See Chapter 25, Interest Expense, for an explanation of the limitations on deducting home mortgage interest.) You can completely exclude up to $250,000 of gain ($500,000 if you're married filing jointly) on the sale of your home. Some states continue to allow various types of residential energy conservation and solar energy tax credits against your state income tax liability. Refer to your state's tax return instruction guide to determine if such credits are available.

Any gain you are required to recognize on the sale of a home will be treated as long-term capital gain if the home was held for more than 1 year. Currently, the maximum tax rate applicable to net capital gains is 20%, which is significantly lower than the top tax rate applicable to ordinary income, and may be as low as 10%. See Capital Gain Tax Computation in Chapter 17, Reporting Gains and Losses.

Important Reminders

Change of address. If you change your mailing address, be sure to notify the IRS using Form 8822, *Change of Address*. Mail it to the Internal Revenue Service Center for your old address. (Addresses for the Service Centers are on the back of the form.)

Home sold with undeducted points. If you have not deducted all the points you paid to secure a mortgage on your old home, you may be able to deduct the remaining points in the year of the sale. See *Mortgage ending early* under *Points* in chapter 25.

This chapter explains the tax rules that apply when you sell your main home. Generally, your main home is the one in which you live most of the time.

Gain. If you have a gain from the sale of your main home, you may be able to exclude up to $250,000 of the gain from your income ($500,000 on a joint return in most cases). Any gain not excluded is taxable.

Loss. You cannot deduct a loss from the sale of your main home.

Worksheets. Publication 523, *Selling Your Home,* includes worksheets to help you figure the adjusted basis of the home you sold, the gain (or loss) on the sale, and the amount of the gain that you can exclude.

Reporting the sale. Do not report the sale of your main home on your tax return unless you have a gain and at least part of it is taxable. Report any taxable gain on Schedule D (Form 1040). You may also have to include Form 4797, *Sales of Business Property.* See *Reporting the Gain* in chapter 2 of Publication 523.

Who may need to read chapter 3 in Publication 523. Chapter 3 of Publication 523 explains the rules that applied to sales before May 7, 1997. You may still need to know those rules, but only if you sold your main home at a gain before May 7, 1997, and all three of the following statements are true.

1) You postponed the gain on the sale.
2) The 2-year period you had to replace that home (your replacement period) was suspended while you either:
   a) Served in the Armed Forces, or
   b) Lived and worked outside the United States.

3) You have not already reported to the IRS your purchase of a new home within your replacement period, or a taxable gain resulting from the end of your replacement period.

If all three statements are true or you have questions, see chapter 3 of Publication 523.

Useful Items

You may want to see:

Publication

☐ **523**   Selling Your Home
☐ **530**   Tax Information for First-Time Homeowners

Form (and Instructions)

☐ **Schedule D (Form 1040)**   Capital Gains and Losses
☐ **8822**   Change of Address
☐ **8828**   Recapture of Federal Mortgage Subsidy

Main Home

Usually, the home you live in most of the time is your main home and can be a:

- House,
- Houseboat,
- Mobile home,
- Cooperative apartment, or
- Condominium.

To exclude gain under the rules of this chapter, you generally must have owned and lived in the property as your main home for at least 2 years during the 5-year period ending on the date of sale.

Land. If you sell the land on which your main home is located, but not the house itself, you cannot exclude any gain you have from the sale of the land.

Example. On March 2, 2001, you sell the land on which your main home is located. You buy another piece of land and move your house to it. This sale is not considered a sale of your main home, and you cannot exclude tax on any gain on the sale of the land.

More than one home. If you have more than one home, you can exclude gain only from the sale of your main home. You must include in income the gain from the sale of any other home. If you have two homes and live in both of them, your main home is ordinarily the one you live in most of the time.

Example 1. You own and live in a house in the city. You also own a beach house, which you use during summer months. The house in the city is your main home.

Example 2. You own a house, but you live in another house that you rent. The rented house is your main home.

Explanation

If you own more than one property, it is important to determine which is your principal, or main, residence. The IRS will not issue a ruling on whether or not a home qualifies as a principal residence. The gain on the sale of your principal residence may be excluded, but the gain on the sale of your nonprincipal residence or rental property is taxed in the year of the sale.

To determine which is your principal residence, the IRS considers the following: where you vote, the address you use on your tax returns, the address you claim to be your residence in other financial dealings, where your children go to school, where you work, where your car is registered, and where you belong to social and religious groups.

That the property is currently rented or has been rented in the past does not mean that you may not consider it to be your principal residence. For example, a property that is rented out for a brief period while you are away or while you are trying to sell it should not affect the property's status as your principal residence. In order to exclude the gain, the home's status as your principal residence at the time of sale is no longer relevant as long as it was your principal residence for 2 of the 5 years prior to the date of sale.

Property used partly as your main home. If you use only part of the property as your main home, the rules discussed in this chapter apply only to the gain or loss on the sale of that part of the property. For details, see *Property used partly as your home and partly for business or rental during the year of sale* under *Business Use or Rental of Home,* later.

How To Figure Gain or Loss

To figure the gain or loss on the sale of your main home, you must know the *selling price,* the *amount realized,* and the *adjusted basis.*

Selling price. The selling price is the total amount you receive for your home. It includes money, all notes, mortgages, or other debts assumed by the buyer as part of the sale, and the fair market value of any other property or any services you receive.

Payment by employer. You may have to sell your home because of a job transfer. If your employer pays you for a loss on the sale or for your selling expenses, do *not* include the payment as part of the selling price. Your employer will include it in box 1 of your Form W-2 and you will include it in your gross income as wages on line 7 of Form 1040.

TAXSAVER

Selling your home to your employer. If during 2001 you sold your home directly to your employer at **fair market value,** no portion of the proceeds is treated as additional compensation. Any gain is excluded under the regular rules for home sales. However, if your home was sold to your employer at an amount above fair market value, part of the proceeds would be treated as compensation or ordinary income.

Option to buy. If you grant an option to buy your home and the option is exercised, add the amount you receive for the option to the selling price of your home. If the option is not exercised, you must report the amount as ordinary income in the year the option expires. Report this amount on line 21 of Form 1040.

Form 1099-S. If you received Form 1099-S, *Proceeds From Real Estate Transactions,* box 2 (gross proceeds) should show the total amount you received for your home.

However, box 2 will not include the fair market value of any property other than cash or notes, or any services, you received or will receive. Instead, box 4 will be checked.

If you can exclude the entire gain, the person responsible for closing the sale generally will not have to report it on Form 1099-S. You will use sale documents and other records to figure the total amount you received for your home.

Amount realized. The amount realized is the selling price minus selling expenses.

    Selling expenses. Selling expenses include:

- Commissions,
- Advertising fees,
- Legal fees, and
- Loan charges paid by the seller, such as loan placement fees or "points."

Explanation
Other selling expenses. The following items are also considered selling expenses: (1) broker's fees, (2) fees for drafting a contract of sale, (3) fees for drafting the deed, (4) escrow fees, (5) geological surveys, (6) maps, (7) title insurance, (8) recording fees, (9) abstracts of title, (10) title certificate, (11) title opinion, and (12) title registration.

Adjusted basis. While you owned your home, you may have made adjustments (increases or decreases) to the basis. This adjusted basis is used to figure gain or loss on the sale of your home. For information on how to figure your home's adjusted basis, see *Basis* later.

Amount of gain or loss. To figure the amount of gain or loss, compare the amount realized to the adjusted basis.

    Gain on sale. If the amount realized is more than the adjusted basis, the difference is a gain and, except for any part you can exclude, generally is taxable.

    Loss on sale. If the amount realized is less than the adjusted basis, the difference is a loss. A loss on the sale of your main home cannot be deducted.

TaxSaver

Loss on sale of a house held for investment. While you cannot deduct a loss on the sale of your home, if you own a house as an investment (and do not use it for personal purposes), you may be able to deduct any loss realized.

Example
Tom bought a house in 1986. From 1986 to 1991, Tom lived in the house with his mother. In 1991, Tom died and bequeathed the house to his mother. Tom's mother continued to live in the house until 2001, at which time she sold it at a loss. She cannot deduct the loss because it is a loss from the sale of a personal residence. Assume instead that Tom bequeathed the house to his friend Carmine, and Carmine held the house as an investment (and did not use it for personal purposes) from 1991 to 2001. If Carmine sold the house at a loss in 2001, he would have a deductible loss because it is generated from the sale of property held for investment and not from the sale of a personal residence. See Chapter 17, *Reporting Gains and Losses*, for limitations on deductibility of capital losses and for the treatment of losses from the sale of property used in a trade or business.

Explanation
If you convert your residence to rental property, your basis for purposes of calculating depreciation and a loss on sale is limited to the lesser of your adjusted basis or the value of the residence on the date of conversion. Your basis, however, for calculating a gain is your adjusted basis less allowable depreciation.

Example
Assume you have a residence with a basis of $150,000, which you convert to business use when its fair market value is $125,000. You would use $125,000 as your basis for calculating depreciation. If you subsequently sold the residence for $130,000 after having deducted $4,000 for depreciation, you would not recognize a gain or loss because a loss results on the gain calculation and a gain results on the loss calculation.

	Gain Calculation	Loss Calculation
Selling price	$130,000	$130,000
Less:		
Adjusted basis	146,000	121,000
Gain/(loss)	($16,000)	$9,000

Jointly owned home. If you and your spouse sell your jointly owned home and file a joint return, you figure your gain or loss as one taxpayer.

    Separate returns. If you file separate returns, each of you must figure your own gain or loss according to your ownership interest in the home. Your ownership interest is determined by state law.

    Joint owners not married. If you and a joint owner other than your spouse sell your jointly owned home, each of you must figure your own gain or loss according to your ownership interest in the home. Each of you applies the rules discussed in this chapter on an individual basis.

Trading homes. If you trade your old home for another home, treat the trade as a sale and a purchase.

    Example. You owned and lived in a home that had an adjusted basis of $41,000. A real estate dealer accepted your old home as a trade-in and allowed you $50,000 toward a new home priced at $80,000. This is treated as a sale of your old home for $50,000 with a gain of $9,000 ($50,000 – $41,000).

    If the dealer had allowed you $27,000 and assumed your unpaid mortgage of $23,000 on your old home, your sales price would still be $50,000 (the $27,000 trade-in allowed plus the $23,000 mortgage assumed).

Foreclosure or repossession. If your home was foreclosed on or repossessed, you have a sale.

    You figure the gain or loss from the sale in generally the same way as gain or loss from any sale. But the amount of your gain or loss depends, in part, on whether you were personally liable for repaying the debt secured by the home. Get Publication 523 for more information.

    Form 1099-A and Form 1099-C. Generally, you will receive Form 1099-A, *Acquisition or Abandonment of Secured Property,* from your lender. This form will have the information you need to determine the amount of your gain or loss and any ordinary income from cancellation of debt. If your debt is canceled, you may receive Form 1099-C, *Cancellation of Debt.*

Abandonment. If you abandon your home, you may have ordinary income. If the abandoned home secures a debt for which you are personally liable and the debt is canceled, you have ordinary income equal to the amount of the canceled debt. Get Publication 523 for more information.

Transfer to spouse. If you transfer your home to your spouse, or to your former spouse incident to your divorce, you generally have no gain or loss. This is true even if you receive cash or other consideration for the home. Therefore, the rules in this chapter do not apply.

    More information. If you need more information, see *Transfer to spouse* in Publication 523 and *Property Settlements* in Publication 504, *Divorced or Separated Individuals.*

Basis

You need to know your basis in your home to determine any gain or loss when you sell it. Your basis in your home is determined by how you got the home. Your basis is its cost if you bought it or built it. If you got it in some other way (inheritance, gift, etc.), its basis is either its fair market value when you got it or the adjusted basis of the person you got it from.

While you owned your home, you may have made adjustments (increases or decreases) to your home's basis. The result of these adjustments is your home's **adjusted basis,** which is used to figure gain or loss on the sale of your home.

You can find more information on basis and adjusted basis in chapter 14 of this publication and in Publication 523.

Settlement fees or closing costs. When you bought your home, you may have paid settlement fees or closing costs in addition to the contract price of the property. You can include in your basis the settlement fees and closing costs you paid for buying the home. You cannot include in your basis the fees and costs for getting a mortgage loan. A fee for buying the home is any fee you would have had to pay even if you paid cash for the home.

Chapter 14 lists some of the settlement fees and closing costs that you can include in the basis of property, including your home. It also lists some settlement costs that cannot be included in basis.

In addition to the items listed in chapter 14, you *cannot* include in basis:

1) Any fee or cost that you deducted as a moving expense (allowed for certain fees and costs before 1994), and
2) VA funding fees.

Adjusted Basis

Adjusted basis is your basis *increased* or *decreased* by certain amounts.

Increases to basis. These include any:

1) Additions and other improvements that have a useful life of more than 1 year.
2) Special assessments for local improvements, and
3) Amounts you spent after a casualty to restore damaged property.

Decreases to basis. These include any:

1) Gain you postponed from the sale of a previous home before May 7, 1997,
2) Deductible casualty losses,
3) Insurance payments you received or expect to receive for casualty losses,
4) Payments you received for granting an easement or right-of-way,
5) Depreciation allowed or allowable if you used your home for business or rental purposes,
6) Residential energy credit (generally allowed from 1977 through 1987) claimed for the cost of energy improvements that you added to the basis of your home,
7) Adoption credit you claimed for improvements added to the basis of your home,
8) Nontaxable payments from an adoption assistance program of your employer that you used for improvements you added to the basis of your home,
9) First-time homebuyer credit (allowed to certain first-time buyers of a home in the District of Columbia), and
10) Energy conservation subsidy excluded from your gross income because you received it (directly or indirectly) from a public utility after 1992 to buy or install any energy conservation measure. An energy conservation measure is an installation or modification that is primarily designed either to reduce consumption of electricity or natural gas or to improve the management of energy demand for a home.

Improvements. These add to the value of your home, prolong its useful life, or adapt it to new uses. You add the cost of additions and other improvements to the basis of your property.

Examples. Putting a recreation room or another bathroom in your unfinished basement, putting up a new fence, putting in new plumbing or wiring, putting on a new roof, or paving your unpaved driveway are improvements. An addition to your house, such as a new deck, a sunroom, or a garage, is also an improvement.

TaxSaver

Shrubs and trees. The Tax Court has held that shrubbery and trees may qualify as improvements to be added to the basis of the taxpayer's property.

Repairs. These maintain your home in good condition but do not add to its value or prolong its life. You do not add their cost to the basis of your property.

Examples. Repainting your house inside or outside, fixing your gutters or floors, repairing leaks or plastering, and replacing broken window panes are examples of repairs.

Recordkeeping. You should keep records to prove your home's adjusted basis. Ordinarily, you must keep records for 3 years after the due date for filing your return for the tax year in which you sold your home. But if you sold a home before May 7, 1997, and postponed tax on any gain, the basis of that home affects the basis of the new home you bought. Keep records proving the basis of both homes as long as they are needed for tax purposes.

The records you should keep include:

- Proof of the home's purchase price and purchase expenses,
- Receipts and other records for all improvements, additions, and other items that affect the home's adjusted basis,
- Any worksheets you used to figure the adjusted basis of the home you sold, the gain or loss on the sale, the exclusion, and the taxable gain,
- Any Form 2119 that you filed to postpone gain from the sale of a previous home before May 7, 1997, and
- Any worksheets you used to prepare Form 2119, such as the *Adjusted Basis of Home Sold Worksheet* or the *Capital Improvements Worksheet* from the Form 2119 instructions.

TaxOrganizer

Documenting the basis in your home. The following documentation should be maintained to support the basis in your home upon sale:

- Receipts for all the above listed increases to basis
- Closing statement from purchase of home to support all transfer taxes, attorney's fees, and other fees (survey, inspection, appraisal)
- Annual statements from cooperative housing corporations (co-ops) regarding maintenance payments used to reduce the indebtedness owed by the corporation

TaxPlanner

Other documents you can use. If you lose your original receipts, other documents may be used to substantiate the cost of improvements to your home. Cancelled checks, contracts, before and after photographs, and building permits may be acceptable to the IRS. If all documentation is lost, you should figure your basis by getting estimates of the cost of similar improvements made at the same time you made yours.

For more information on basis and adjusted basis, see Chapter 14, *Basis of Property.*

Excluding the Gain

You may qualify to exclude from your income all or part of any gain from the sale of your main home. This means that, if you qualify, you will not have to pay tax on the gain up to the limit described under *Maximum Amount of Exclusion,* next. To qualify, you must meet the ownership and use tests described later.

You can choose not to take the exclusion. In that case, you must include in income your entire gain.

TaxPlanner

Reasons behind the exclusion. This exclusion encourages taxpayers to base future housing decisions on personal and nontax financial considerations following the sale of a residence. For example, if you are planning a postretirement move to a lower-cost area, you can trade down to a less expensive residence rather than feeling pressured to reinvest the sales proceeds in a new home of equal or greater value simply to reduce taxes. You will then be able to invest the equity you had tied up in your home in higher-growth or income-producing assets.

The exclusion also eases record-keeping requirements for most taxpayers by eliminating the need to document minor home improvements. In addition, there is no limit on the number of times you can use the exclusion as long as you meet the requirements each time.

Maximum Amount of Exclusion

You can exclude the entire gain on the sale of your main home up to:

1) $250,000, or
2) $500,000 if all of the following are true.
   a) You are married and file a joint return for the year.
   b) Either you or your spouse meets the ownership test.
   c) Both you and your spouse meet the use test.
   d) During the 2-year period ending on the date of the sale, neither you nor your spouse excluded gain from the sale of another home.

TaxAlert

Trading up. This provision of the tax law is not an advantage for taxpayers who have traded up homes over a long period and now must sell a high-priced home and realize a significant profit.

Example

The Fishes are married filing jointly. The Fishes bought a home in 1966 for $20,000, sold it later for $50,000, and purchased a replacement home for $60,000. The Fishes repeatedly sell and buy homes over the years, each time purchasing a more expensive replacement home. The Fishes have owned a home for the last 5 years that now is worth $800,000, with accumulated and unrecognized gain of

$600,000. If the Fishes were to sell that home for $800,000, capital gains tax would be imposed on $100,000 (the $600,000 of accumulated profit minus the $500,000 exclusion).

Reduced Maximum Exclusion

You can claim an exclusion, but the maximum amount of gain you can exclude will be reduced, if either of the following is true.

1) You did not meet the ownership and use tests, but you sold the home due to:
   a) A change in place of employment,
   b) Health, or
   c) Unforeseen circumstances, to the extent provided in regulations (as discussed later).
2) Your exclusion would have been disallowed because of the rule described in *More Than One Home Sold During 2-Year Period,* later, except that you sold the home due to:
   a) A change in place of employment,
   b) Health, or
   c) Unforeseen circumstances, to the extent provided in regulations (as discussed next).

Example

Steve and Tina purchase a home in 2000. In 2001, Steve's employer transfers him to another city. They owned the home as their principal residence for 12 months. They can exclude up to $250,000 of gain ($500,000 times the ratio of 12 months/24 months).

Use *Worksheet 3* in Publication 523 to figure your reduced maximum exclusion.

Unforeseen circumstances. The IRS has not issued regulations defining unforeseen circumstances. You cannot claim an exclusion based on unforeseen circumstances until the IRS issues final regulations or other appropriate guidance.

More Than One Home Sold During 2-Year Period

You cannot exclude gain on the sale of your home if, during the 2-year period ending on the date of the sale, you sold another home at a gain and excluded all or part of that gain. If you cannot exclude the gain, you must include it in your income.

However, you can still claim an exclusion if you sold the home due to:

1) A change in place of employment,
2) Health, or
3) Unforeseen circumstances, to the extent provided in regulations (as discussed earlier).

The maximum amount you can exclude is reduced. See *Reduced Maximum Exclusion,* earlier.

Ownership and Use Tests

To claim the exclusion, you must meet the ownership and use tests. This means that during the *5-year period* ending on the date of the sale, you must have:

1) *Owned* the home for at least *2 years* (the ownership test), *and*
2) *Lived in* the home as your main home for at least *2 years* (the use test).

Exception. If you owned and lived in the property as your main home for less than 2 years, you can still claim an exclusion in some cases. The maximum amount you can claim will be reduced. See *Reduced Maximum Exclusion,* earlier.

Period of ownership and use. The required 2 years of ownership and use during the 5-year period ending on the date of the sale do not have to be continuous.

You meet the tests if you can show that you owned and lived in the property as your main home for either 24 full months or 730 days (365 × 2) during the 5-year period ending on the date of sale.

> ### Explanation
> The home you sold must have been owned and lived in as a principal residence by you for 2 of the 5 years prior to its sale. They key terms to remember are "owned" and "lived in" for 2 years.

Temporary absence. Short temporary absences for vacations or other seasonal absences, even if you rent the property during the absences, are counted as periods of use. See *Ownership and use tests met at different times,* later.

Example. Professor Paul Beard, who is single, bought and moved into a house on August 28, 1998. He lived in it as his main home continuously until January 5, 2000, when he went abroad for a 1-year sabbatical leave. During part of the period of leave, the house was unoccupied, and during the rest of the period, he rented it. On January 5, 2001, he sold the house at a gain.

Because his leave was not a short temporary absence, he cannot include the period of leave to meet the 2-year use test. He cannot exclude any part of his gain, unless he sold the house due to a change in place of employment or health, as explained under *Reduced Maximum Exclusion,* earlier. Even if he did sell the house due to a change in place of employment or health, he cannot exclude the part of the gain equal to the depreciation he claimed while renting the house. See *Depreciation for business use after May 6, 1997,* later.

> ### Example
> Maurice and Mavis purchase a home in 2001. The following year, Maurice is transferred overseas for 5 years, during which time the house is rented. When Maurice and Mavis return, Maurice's employer sends Maurice to another city in the United States, instead of back to the home purchased in 2001. Maurice and Mavis sell the original house without ever reoccupying it. They are generally not eligible for any exclusion as they did not live in the house at any time during the last 5 years prior to sale.
>
> ### TaxSaver
> **Status of your home.** Unlike under prior law, the status of the home when you sell it is now irrelevant. Even if you haven't lived in it for 3 years at the time of sale, the exclusion is still available if you meet the 2-year rule.

Ownership and use tests met at different times. You can meet the ownership and use tests during different 2-year periods. However, you must meet both tests during the 5-year period ending on the date of the sale.

Example. In 1992, Helen Jones lived in a rented apartment. The apartment building was later changed to a condominium, and she bought her apartment on December 1, 1998. In 1999, Helen became ill and on April 14 of that year she moved to her daughter's home. On July 10, 2001, while still living in her daughter's home, she sold her apartment.

Helen can exclude gain on the sale of her apartment because she met the ownership and use tests. Her 5-year period is from July 11, 1996, to July 10, 2001, the date she sold the apartment. She owned her apartment from December 1, 1998, to July 10, 2001 (over 2 years). She lived in the apartment from July 11, 1996 (the beginning of the 5-year period), to April 14, 1999 (over 2 years).

Cooperative apartment. If you sold stock in a cooperative housing corporation, the ownership and use tests are met if, during the 5-year period ending on the date of sale, you:

1) Owned the stock for at least 2 years, and
2) Lived in the house or apartment that the stock entitles you to occupy as your main home for at least 2 years.

Exception for individuals with a disability. There is an exception to the use test if during the 5-year period before the sale of your home:

1) You become physically or mentally unable to care for yourself, and
2) You owned and lived in your home as your main home for a total of at least 1 year.

Under this exception, you are considered to live in your home during any time that you own the home during any time that you own the home and live in a facility (including a nursing home) that is licensed by a state or political subdivision to care for persons in your condition.

If you meet this exception to the use test, you still have to meet the 2-out-of-5-year ownership test to claim the exclusion.

Gain postponed on sale of previous home. For the ownership and use tests, you may be able to add the time you owned and lived in a previous home to the time you lived in the home on which you wish to exclude gain. You can do this if you postponed all or part of the gain on the sale of the previous home because of buying the home on which you wish to exclude gain.

Previous home destroyed or condemned. For the ownership and use tests, you add the time you owned and lived in a previous home that was destroyed or condemned to the time you owned and lived in the home on which you wish to exclude gain. This rule applies if any part of the basis of the home you sold depended on the basis of the destroyed or condemned home. Otherwise, you must have owned and lived in the *same* home for 2 of the 5 years before the sale to qualify for the exclusion.

Married Persons

If you and your spouse file a joint return for the year of sale, you can exclude gain if either spouse meets the ownership and use tests. (But see *Maximum Amount of Exclusion,* earlier.)

> ### Example
> In October 2000, Karen, who is single, sells the home she has been living in as a principal residence for the past 4 years and has a gain of $75,000 on the sale. The entire $75,000 qualifies for the exclusion. On December 1, 2000, Karen marries Ray. On February 2, 2001, Ray sells the home he has owned and been living in as a principal residence for over 2 years and has a gain of $350,000 on the sale. Ray can only exclude $250,000 of the gain even if he and Karen file a joint tax return. The $500,000 exclusion does not apply for two reasons. First, Karen sold her home within the 2-year period ending on the date Ray sold his home. Second, Karen did not use Ray's home as her principal residence for at least 2 of the 5 years before the sale.

Example 1—one spouse sells a home. Emily sells her home in June 2001. She marries Jamie later in the year. She meets the ownership and use tests, but Jamie does not. She can exclude up to $250,000 of gain on a separate or joint return for 2001.

Example 2—each spouse sells a home. The facts are the same as in *Example 1* except that Jamie also sells a home. He meets the ownership and use tests on his home. Emily and Jamie can each exclude up to $250,000 of gain.

Death of spouse before sale. If your spouse died before the date of sale, you are considered to have owned and lived in the property as your main home during any period of time when your spouse owned and lived in it as a main home.

Home transferred from spouse. If your home was transferred to you by your spouse (or former spouse if the transfer was incident to divorce), you are considered to have owned it during any period of time when your spouse owned it.

Use of home after divorce. You are considered to have used property as your main home during any period when:

1) You owned it, and
2) Your spouse or former spouse is allowed to live in it under a divorce or separation instrument.

> **Explanation**
> This new provision removes the old requirement that the home be your residence at the time of sale. It should have the effect of reducing much litigation.

Business Use or Rental of Home

You may be able to exclude your gain from the sale of a home that you have used for business or to produce rental income. But you must meet the ownership and use tests.

Example 1. On May 30, 1995, Amy bought a house. She moved in on that date and lived in it until May 31, 1997, when she moved out of the house and put it up for rent. The house was rented from June 1, 1997, to March 31, 1999. Amy moved back into the house on April 1, 1999, and lived there until she sold it on January 31, 2001. During the 5-year period ending on the date of the sale (February 1, 1996–January 31, 2001), Amy owned and lived in the house for more than 2 years as shown in the table below.

Five Year Period	Used as Home	Used as Rental
2/1/96–5/31/97	16 months	
6/1/97–3/31/99		22 months
4/1/99–1/31/01	22 months	
	38 months	22 months

Amy can exclude gain up to $250,000. But she cannot exclude the part of the gain equal to the depreciation she claimed for renting the house, as explained after *Example 2.*

Example 2. William owned and used a house as his main home from 1995 through 1998. On January 1, 1999, he moved to another state. He rented his house from that date until April 30, 2001, when he sold it. During the 5-year period ending on the date of sale (May 1, 1996–April 30, 2001), William owned and lived in the house for 32 months (more than 2 years). He can exclude gain up to $250,000. However, he cannot exclude the part of the gain equal to the depreciation he claimed for renting the house, as explained next.

Depreciation for business use after May 6, 1997. If you were entitled to take depreciation deductions because you used your home for business purposes or as rental property, you cannot exclude the part of your gain equal to any depreciation allowed or allowable as a deduction for periods after May 6, 1997. If you can show by adequate records or other evidence that the depreciation deduction allowed was less than the amount allowable, the amount you cannot exclude is the smaller figure.

Example. Ray sold his main home in 2001 at a $30,000 gain. He meets the ownership and use tests to exclude the gain from his income. However, he used part of the home for business in 2000 and claimed $500 depreciation. He can exclude $29,500 ($30,000 – $500) of his gain. He has a taxable gain of $500.

Property used partly as your home and partly for business or rental during the year of sale. In the year of sale you may have used part of your property as your home and part of it for business or to produce income. Examples are:

- A working farm on which your house was located,
- An apartment building in which you lived in one unit and rented out the others,
- A store building with an upstairs apartment in which you lived, or
- A home with a room used for business (home office) or to produce income.

If you sell the entire property you should consider the transaction as the sale of two properties. The sale of the part of your property used for business or rental is reported on Form 4797. For more information, see *Property used partly as your home and partly for business or rental during the year of sale* under *Business Use or Rental of Home* in chapter 2 of Publication 523.

> **Example**
> You own a four-unit apartment house. You live in one unit and rent three units. You sell the apartment house for cash. Your records show the following:
>
> **Apartment house**
>
> | | |
> |---|---|
> | Cost | $ 80,000 |
> | Capital improvements | 20,000 |
> | | $100,000 |
> | Minus: Depreciation (on three rented units only) | 40,000 |
> | Adjusted basis | $ 60,000 |
> | Selling price | $120,000 |
> | Selling expense | 8,000 |
>
> Because one-fourth of the apartment building is your home, you figure the gain on which tax which is excluded as follows:
>
> | | Personal (1/4) | Rental (3/4) |
> |---|---|---|
> | 1) Selling price | $30,000 | $90,000 |
> | 2) Selling expense | 2,000 | 6,000 |
> | 3) Amount realized (adjusted sales price) | $28,000 | $84,000 |
> | 4) Basis (including improvements) | $25,000 | $75,000 |
> | 5) Depreciation | –0– | 40,000 |
> | 6) Adjusted basis | $25,000 | $35,000 |
> | 7) Gain [(3) minus (6)] | $ 3,000 | $49,000 |
> | 8) Gain not excluded | | $49,000 |
> | 9) Gain excluded | $ 3,000 | |
>
> The gain of $49,000 on the three-fourths of the building that was rental property is subject to tax in the year of sale. This gain is reported on Form 4797, Gains and Losses from Sales or Exchanges of Assets Used in a Trade or Business

and Involuntary Conversions. The gain on the one-fourth that was your home is excluded.

TAXSAVER

Improvements to rental property. If improvements have been made solely to rental units, their cost should be specifically allocated to the rental part of the property. This allocation will decrease the gain on the business portion of the property, which is taxable in the year of sale.

Keep detailed records of improvements. Be careful to specify whether the improvements were made exclusively to either the business or the personal portion of the residence, or whether they improved the residence as a whole.

Example
Jane Smith purchases a two-family house. The two units in the house are identical. Jane rents one out and uses the other as her personal residence. The house costs $80,000—$20,000 for the land and $60,000 ($30,000 per unit) for the building. Jane remodels the kitchen in the rental unit. The job costs $10,000, which is added to the basis of the rental unit, increasing it to $40,000. Once the unit is rented, depreciation may be claimed on this $40,000 basis.

When the property is sold, the selling price must be apportioned between the business and personal portions of the residence. If, at the time of sale, the adjusted basis of the rental unit, including the amount allocated to land, is $28,000, and if $60,000 of the selling price is allocated to the rental unit, there is currently a taxable gain of $32,000. Without the $10,000 kitchen expense, the adjusted basis would be only $18,000, increasing the currently taxable gain to $42,000.

Explanation
The apportionment of the selling price between the business and personal portions of a house should be based on the relative fair market value of each portion. Substantial improvements made to each portion of the property should be considered in determining the amount of the selling price that is allocated to each part.

Consequently, the allocation of the sales price, as well as the allocation of the cost of the improvements, may affect the amount of gain to be deferred or taxed on the sale of property used partly as your principal home. Evidence to support a particular allocation of the sales price can include a real estate broker's appraisal or the negotiated terms of the sales contract.

Special Situations

The situations that follow may affect your exclusion.

Expatriates. You cannot claim the exclusion if the expatriation tax applies to you. The expatriation tax applies to U.S. citizens who have renounced their citizenship (and long-term residents who have ended their residency) if one of their principal purposes was to avoid U.S. taxes. See chapter 4 of Publication 519, *U.S. Tax Guide for Aliens,* for more information about expatriation tax.

Home destroyed or condemned. If your home was destroyed or condemned, any gain (for example, because of insurance proceeds you received) qualifies for the exclusion.

Any part of the gain that cannot be excluded (because it is more than the limit) may be postponed under the rules explained in:

- Publication 547, *Casualties, Disasters, and Thefts,* in the case of a home that was destroyed, or

- Chapter 1 of Publication 544, *Sales and Other Dispositions of Assets,* in the case of a home that was condemned.

Sale of remainder interest. Subject to the other rules in this chapter, you can choose to exclude gain from the sale of a remainder interest in your home. If you make this choice, you cannot choose to exclude gain from your sale of any other interest in the home that you sell separately.

Exception for sales to related persons. You cannot exclude gain from the sale of a remainder interest in your home to a related person. Related persons include your brothers and sisters, half-brothers, and half-sisters, spouse, ancestors (parents, grandparents, etc.), and lineal descendants (children, grandchildren, etc.). Related persons also include certain corporations, partnerships, trusts, and exempt organizations.

Reporting the Gain

Do *not* report the 2001 sale of your main home on your tax return unless:

- You have a gain and you do not qualify to exclude all of it, or
- You have a gain and you choose not to exclude it.

If you have any taxable gain on the sale of your main home that cannot be excluded, report the entire gain realized on Schedule D (Form 1040). Report it on line 1 or line 8 of Schedule D, depending on how long you owned the home. If you qualify for an exclusion, show it on the line directly below the line on which you report the gain. Write "Section 121 exclusion" in column (a) of that line and show the amount of the exclusion in column (f) as a loss (in parentheses).

If you used the home for business or to produce rental income during the year of sale, you must use Form 4797 to report the sale of the business or rental part (or the sale of the entire property if used entirely for business or rental in that year). See *Business Use or Rental of Home* in chapter 2 of Publication 523.

Installment sale. Some sales are made under arrangements that provide for part or all of the selling price to be paid in a later year. These sales are called "installment sales." If you finance the buyer's purchase of your home yourself, instead of having the buyer get a loan or mortgage from a bank, you probably have an installment sale. You may be able to report the part of the gain you cannot exclude on the installment basis.

Use Form 6252, *Installment Sale Income,* to report the sale. Enter your exclusion on line 15 of Form 6252.

Seller-financed mortgage. If you sell your home and hold a note, mortgage, or other financial agreement, the payments you receive generally consist of both interest and principal. You must report the interest you receive as part of each payment separately as interest income. If the buyer of your home uses the property as a main or second home, you must also report the name, address, and social security number (SSN) of the buyer on line 1 of either Schedule B (Form 1040) or Schedule 1 (Form 1040A). The buyer must give you his or her SSN and you must give the buyer your SSN. Failure to meet these requirements may result in a $50 penalty for each failure. If you or the buyer does not have and is not eligible to get an SSN, see *Social Security Number* in chapter 1.

More information. For more information on installment sales, see Publication 537, *Installment Sales.*

Recapture of Federal Subsidy

If you financed your home under a federally subsidized program (loans from tax-exempt qualified mortgage bonds or loans with mortgage credit certificates), you may have to recapture all or part of the benefit you received from that program when you sell or otherwise dispose of your home. You recapture the benefit by increasing your federal income tax for the year of the sale. You may have to pay this recapture tax even if you can exclude your gain from income; that exclusion does not affect the recapture tax.

Loans subject to recapture rules. The recapture applies to loans that:

1) Came from the proceeds of qualified mortgage bonds, or
2) Were based on mortgage credit certificates.

The recapture also applies to assumptions of these loans.

When the recapture applies. The recapture of the federal mortgage subsidy applies only if you meet *both* of the following conditions.

1) You sell or otherwise dispose of your home:
   a) At a gain, and
   b) During the first 9 years after the date you closed your mortgage loan.
2) Your income for the year of disposition is more than that year's adjusted qualifying income for your family size for that year (related to the income requirements a person must meet to qualify for the federally subsidized program).

When recapture does not apply. The recapture does *not* apply if any of the following situations apply to you:

- Your mortgage loan was a qualified home improvement loan of not more than $15,000,

- The home is disposed of as a result of your death,
- You dispose of the home more than 9 years after the date you closed your mortgage loan,
- You transfer the home to your spouse, or to your former spouse incident to a divorce, where no gain is included in your income,
- You dispose of the home at a loss,
- Your home is destroyed by a casualty, and you repair it or replace it on its original site within 2 years after the end of the tax year when the destruction happened, or
- You refinance your mortgage loan (unless you later meet all of the conditions listed previously under *When the recapture applies*).

Notice of amounts. At or near the time of settlement of your mortgage loan, you should receive a notice that provides the federally subsidized amount and other information you will need to figure your recapture tax.

How to figure and report the recapture. The recapture tax is figured on Form 8828, *Recapture of Federal Mortgage Subsidy*. If you sell your home and your mortgage is subject to recapture rules, you must file Form 8828 even if you do not owe a recapture tax. Attach Form 8828 to your Form 1040. For more information, see Form 8828 and its instructions.

17

Reporting Gains and Losses

Introduction

One of the best ways to save tax dollars is to generate long-term capital gains: profits you make from the sale of assets such as stocks, bonds, and real éstate. To qualify for long-term capital gains treatment, all you have to do is hold a capital asset for more than 1 year and the gain is subject to a lower tax rate. If you held the capital asset for more than 5 years, you may be eligible for an even lower rate.

The tax benefit of generating long-term capital gains is substantial. Under the tax law, the top tax rate applicable to long-term capital gains is 20%. Accordingly,

you can achieve substantial tax savings by generating net capital gains in lieu of ordinary income. Your net capital gain equals net long-term capital gains less net short-term capital losses. The lower rates apply to property held for more than 12 months. A 28% rate applies to collectibles held over 12 months.

These rate differences will have a profound effect on tax planning and investing. This chapter will provide you with examples of how the rules work. It also provides advice on year-end planning.

Important Change

8% capital gain rate. Beginning in 2001, the 10% capital gain rate is lowered to 8% for qualified 5-year gain. For more information, see *Capital Gain Tax Rates,* later.

This chapter discusses how to report capital gains and losses from sales, exchanges, and other dispositions of investment property on Schedule D of Form 1040. The discussion includes:

- How to report short-term gains and losses,
- How to report long-term gains and losses,
- How to figure capital loss carryovers,
- How to figure your tax using the lower tax rates on a net capital gain, and
- An illustrated example of how to complete Schedule D.

If you sell or otherwise dispose of property used in a trade or business or for the production of income, see Publication 544, *Sales and Other Dispositions of Assets,* before completing Schedule D.

Useful Items

You may want to see:

Publication

- ☐ **537** Installment Sales
- ☐ **544** Sales and Other Dispositions of Assets
- ☐ **550** Investment Income and Expenses

Form (and Instructions)

- ☐ **Schedule D (Form 1040)** Capital Gains and Losses
- ☐ **4797** Sales of Business Property
- ☐ **6252** Installment Sale Income
- ☐ **8582** Passive Activity Loss Limitations

Schedule D

Report capital gains and losses on Schedule D (Form 1040). Enter your sales and trades of stocks, bonds, etc., and real estate (if not required to be reported on another form) on line 1 of Part I or line 8 of Part II, as appropriate. Include all these transactions even if you did not receive a Form 1099-B, *Proceeds From Broker and Barter Exchange Transactions,* or Form 1099-S, *Proceeds From Real Estate Transactions* (or substitute statement). You can use Schedule D-1 as a continuation schedule to report more transactions.

Explanation
Characterizing your gain or loss. When you sell or dispose of property, you must determine whether your gain or loss is capital or ordinary. Only capital gains and capital losses are reported on Schedule D, while ordinary gains and losses are reported elsewhere. This distinction is significant because (1) you can use capital losses to offset gains only to the extent of capital gains plus $3,000, and (2) net capital gains may be subject to a lower tax rate than ordinary in-

come. Any unused capital losses can be carried over to the next year.

Example

Assume that Alan has $12,000 of capital losses and $4,000 of capital gains in 2001. Alan can deduct only $7,000 of his capital losses in 2001, which is equal to his $4,000 of capital gains plus $3,000. The remaining $5,000 of losses ($12,000 gross losses minus $7,000 of losses used) may be carried over and used in later years, subject to the $3,000 limitation. If Alan's losses were ordinary, he could have used all of them in 2001, unless subject to other limitations by special provisions of the Internal Revenue Code.

Explanation

Determining your capital gains rate. For 2001, the capital gains rate depends on the type of property sold, the holding period prior to sale, your overall income level, and when the property is sold. Short-term capital gains are subject to your ordinary income rates. Long-term capital gains are subject to either an 8%, 10%, or 20% rate, depending on the above factors. Net capital gains are the excess of (1) net long-term capital gains over (2) net short-term capital losses.

Example 1

Erik bought 3,000 shares of ABC Company on April 1, 2000, when the price of the stock was $20/share. On June 1, 2001, he sold all of his ABC holdings for $25/share, realizing a profit of $15,000. Erik files a joint return with his wife with a combined taxable income that places him in the 35.5% tax bracket. Because he held the ABC stock for more than 12 months, Erik is eligible for the favorable capital gain tax rates. As a 35.5% taxpayer, his long-term capital gain on ABC stock would be taxed at 20%.

Example 2

Cheryl bought stock on January 2, 1990, for $3,000 and sold it on June 30, 2001 for $4,000. Cheryl is in the 15% bracket in 2001. Since she held the stock for more than 5 years, her gain of $1,000 is taxed at 8%.

TAXPLANNER

Long-term capital gains vs. ordinary income. The difference between the top marginal rate of 39.1% and the top rate on net capital gains of 20% is significant—a 19.1% difference. Even as ordinary tax rates fall each year over the next several years, there's still a significant difference between capital gain and ordinary rates. Accordingly, taxpayers should try to generate long-term capital gains, as opposed to ordinary income, whenever possible. It should be noted, however, that the tax law recharacterizes gains from certain conversion transactions into ordinary income. See later in this chapter for an explanation of conversion transactions.

Example

Nancy is in the top 39.1% marginal tax bracket for 2001 and 2002 and has the following unrealized capital gains and losses:

Stock A: Unrealized short-term capital gain	$ 10,000
Stock B: Unrealized long-term capital loss (20%)	($13,000)
Stock C: Unrealized long-term capital gain (20%)	$ 15,000

Assume that Nancy sells all three stocks in 2001. Nancy will compute her net capital gain for the year as follows:

Net long-term capital gain	$ 2,000
Net short-term capital gain	$10,000
Total gains	$12,000

Nancy has a net capital gain of $12,000. Nancy will pay $400 of tax on her net long-term capital gain ($2,000 × 20%) and $3,910 on her short-term capital gains, which are taxed at her regular 39.1% rate ($10,000 × 39.1%). Thus, Nancy will pay a total tax of $4,310 ($400 + $3,910) on her capital gains.

Assume instead that Nancy sells stocks A and B in 2001 but waits until 2002 to sell stock C.

Nancy will have a net long-term capital loss of ($3,000) for 2001 ($10,000 gain on stock A, less $13,000 loss on stock B). Nancy will be allowed to offset the $3,000 capital loss against her ordinary income, giving her a $1,173 tax saving for 2001.

Nancy will also have a $15,000 net long-term capital gain in 2002 from the sale of stock C. This will represent a net capital gain subject to the maximum 20% rate on net capital gains. Nancy will pay $3,000 of tax in 2002 on her net capital gain ($15,000 × 20%).

By using tax planning, Nancy's total liability on her capital gains would be $1,827 ($3,000 for 2001, less $1,173 of tax savings in 2001). As compared to the $4,310 of tax liability without tax planning, Nancy has saved $2,483. Furthermore, Nancy also delayed the payment of the tax by waiting until 2002 to trigger some of her gains.

The tax savings to Nancy may be small relative to the investment ramifications of holding stock C for a longer period. Nancy must therefore balance the potential tax savings against her overall investment strategy.

Explanation

A capital gain or loss results from (1) the sale or exchange of a capital asset or (2) net Section 1231 gains being treated as a capital gain.

Almost everything you own and use for personal purposes or investment purposes is a capital asset. For example, stocks, bonds, jewelry, and household furnishings generally are all capital assets. Most properties held in a business (e.g., inventory, accounts receivable, machinery) are not capital assets. See Chapter 15, *Sale of Property*, for a further elaboration on what constitutes a capital asset.

A net Section 1231 gain is also treated as a capital gain, while a net Section 1231 loss is treated as an ordinary loss. A Section 1231 gain or loss is any gain or loss from the sale or exchange of real property or depreciable personal property used in your trade or business and held by you for more than 1 year. Any depreciation recapture must be separately computed on the sale of depreciable property and reported as ordinary income. Thus, the portion of the gain that is considered depreciation recapture is ordinary income, rather than a Section 1231 gain. The computation of depreciation recapture is discussed in more detail at the end of this chapter.

Section 1231 gains also include recognized gains on the involuntary conversion of (1) property used in a trade or a business and held for more than 1 year, and (2) any capital asset held for more than 1 year and held in connection with a trade or a business or a transaction entered into for profit. Net involuntary conversion losses on these properties are not Section 1231 losses but are deductible as ordinary losses. An involuntary conversion is the loss of property resulting from destruction (complete or partial), theft, seizure, requisition, or condemnation. An involuntary conversion also includes the sale or exchange of property under the threat or imminence of seizure, requisition, or condemnation.

For more information, see Publication 544, *Sales and Other Dispositions of Assets*.

Tax treatment of gains and losses. Once the disposition is properly classified, you can determine whether your gains and losses will be considered ordinary, capital, or nondeductible.

Capital losses resulting from the sale of business or investment property are reported on Schedule D. These may be used to offset any other capital gains, including capital gains from business and investment property, which are also reported on Schedule D.

Losses on the sale of personal-use property (e.g., a family car) cannot be used to offset capital gains. These losses are not reported on your income tax return. Capital gains on the sale of personal-use property are taxable, however, and are reported on Schedule D.

You must aggregate all of your Section 1231 gains and losses during the year to determine the tax treatment of these items. Net Section 1231 gains are treated as capital, while net Section 1231 losses are treated as ordinary. Under a special look-back rule, if you have a net Section 1231 gain in 2001, the gain will be treated as ordinary income to the extent of any Section 1231 losses in the preceding 5 years (which were not previously used to recharacterize gains). Remember, any gain resulting in depreciation recapture is ordinary income and as a result is not considered in these computations. Fill out Form 4797 to report these items. Ordinary gains and losses are generally included in gross income. The capital gain portion is reported on Schedule D.

Capital gains and losses reported on Schedule D are further classified under long-term and short-term. Net Section 1231 gains are long-term. For other classifications, see the discussion in Chapter 15, *Sale of Property*.

TaxAlert

Recharacterizing capital gains. The Internal Revenue Code contains a provision that recharacterizes capital gains from certain conversion transactions as ordinary income. The purpose of this provision is to prohibit taxpayers from taking advantage of the favorable tax rate on capital gains by entering into transactions that are, in effect, loans but that, because of their form, generate capital gains. In a conversion transaction, the taxpayer is in the economic position of a lender, and substantially all of the taxpayer's return is attributable to the amount of time the investment is held. In order to be a conversion transaction, a transaction must satisfy at least one of the following four criteria: (1) The transaction consists of the acquisition of property by the taxpayer and a substantially contemporaneous agreement to sell the same or substantially identical property in the future; (2) the transaction is a straddle (see Chapter 15, *Sale of Property*); (3) the transaction is one that is marketed or sold to the taxpayer on the basis that it would have the economic characteristics of a loan but the interest-like return would be taxed as capital gain; or (4) the transaction is described in regulations promulgated by the Secretary of the Treasury.

Installment sales. You cannot use the installment method to report a gain from the sale of stock or securities traded on an established securities market. You must report the entire gain in the year of sale (the year in which the trade date occurs).

TaxAlert

Date of installment payments. For purposes of the dates that determine the rate at which capital gains are taxed, the date you receive an installment payment is relevant, not the actual date of sale.

Passive activity gains and losses. If you have gains or losses from a passive activity, you may also have to report them on **Form 8582**. In some cases, the loss may be limited under the passive activity rules. Refer to Form 8582 and its separate instructions for more information about reporting capital gains and losses from a passive activity.

Explanation

For 2001, the gain or loss realized upon the sale or disposition of an interest in a passive activity must be combined with other items of income, expense, gain, or loss from investments in passive activities in order to determine the amount of passive activity losses that will be deductible on Form 1040. See Chapter 13, *Other Income*, for more information.

TaxPlanner

Passive capital gains. If you generate a passive capital gain, you will be allowed to deduct passive losses to the extent of the passive gain as explained above. In addition, that passive capital gain can still be offset by capital losses on Schedule D.

Form 1099-B transactions. If you sold property, such as stocks, bonds, or certain commodities, through a broker, you should receive Form 1099-B or equivalent statement from the broker. Use the Form 1099-B or the equivalent statement to complete Schedule D.

Report the gross proceeds shown in box 2 of Form 1099-B as the *gross sales price* in column (d) of either line 1 or line 8 of Schedule D, whichever applies. However, if the broker advises you, in box 2 of Form 1099-B, that gross proceeds (gross sales price) less commissions and option premiums were reported to the IRS, enter that *net sales price* in column (d) of either line 1 or line 8 of Schedule D, whichever applies. If the net amount is entered in column (d), do not include the commissions and option premiums in column (e).

Form 1099-S transactions. If you sold or traded reportable real estate, you generally should receive from the real estate reporting person a Form 1099-S showing the gross proceeds.

"Reportable real estate" is defined as any present or future ownership interest in any of the following:

1) Improved or unimproved land, including air space,
2) Inherently permanent structures, including any residential, commercial, or industrial building,
3) A condominium unit and its accessory fixtures and common elements, including land, and
4) Stock in a cooperative housing corporation (as defined in section 216 of the Internal Revenue Code).

A "real estate reporting person" could include the buyer's attorney, your attorney, the title or escrow company, a mortgage lender, your broker, the buyer's broker, or the person acquiring the biggest interest in the property.

Your Form 1099-S will show the gross proceeds from the sale or exchange in box 2. Follow the instructions for Schedule D to report these transactions and include them on line 1 or 8 as appropriate.

Reconciling Forms 1099 with Schedule D. Add the following amounts reported to you for 2001 on Forms 1099-B and 1099-S (or on substitute statements):

1) Proceeds from transactions involving stocks, bonds, and other securities, and
2) Gross proceeds from real estate transactions (other than the sale of your main home if you had no taxable gain) not reported on another form or schedule.

If this total is more than the total of lines 3 and 10 of Schedule D, attach a statement to your return explaining the difference.

Explanation
Amounts reported to you on Form 1099-B are also reported to the IRS. The IRS matches the amounts reported on Forms 1099-B to your return to make sure you reported all of your security sales. The amounts reported on Forms 1099-B should equal the sum of the amounts on lines 3 and 10 in column (d). If not, you will probably receive a letter from the IRS asking you to explain the difference. If the amounts are different, you should attach a schedule to your return explaining why.

TaxOrganizer
Documents you need for Schedule D. Taxpayers who sell stocks, bonds, or other property through a broker should maintain the following documentation in order to facilitate the completion of Schedule D:

- Confirmations received from the broker documenting all sales transactions executed. These can be used to ensure the accuracy of any Forms 1099-B received.
- Confirmations received from the broker documenting all purchase transactions executed. These will be needed to calculate any gains or losses realized upon the sale of the property. The confirmations will also be needed to determine if any gains or losses are long-term or short-term.

TaxPlanner
Real property tax. The person reporting a real estate transaction is also responsible for including on Form 1099-S the portion of any real property tax that is property allocable to the purchaser. Thus, property tax allocable from the date of sale to year-end is reported on Form 1099-S. Note that if the purchaser agrees to pay the taxes the seller owed on the new home (up to the date of sale), these taxes are not treated as taxes paid by the purchaser but instead are treated as part of the purchaser's cost. Accordingly, these amounts are not included on Form 1099-S as real property tax allocable to the purchaser. Instead, these amounts are included on Form 1099-S as part of the seller's proceeds.

Sale of property bought at various times. If you sell a block of stock or other property that you bought at various times, report the short-term gain or loss from the sale on one line in Part I of Schedule D and the long-term gain or loss on one line in Part II. Write "Various" in column (b) for the "Date acquired." See the *Comprehensive Example* later in this chapter.

Sale expenses. Add to your cost or other basis any expense of sale such as brokers' fees, commissions, state and local transfer taxes, and option premiums. Enter this adjusted amount in column (e) of either Part I or Part II of Schedule D, whichever applies, unless you reported the net sales price amount in column (d).

For more information about adjustments to basis, see chapter 14.

Caution. *Property held for personal use only, rather than for investment, is a capital asset and you must report a gain from its sale as a capital gain. However, you cannot deduct a loss from selling personal use property.*

Explanation
Most property you own and use for personal purposes or for pleasure, such as your house, furniture, and car, falls under the heading of capital asset. A gain on the sale of this kind of property is treated as a capital gain, but no loss is recognized for income tax purposes unless the property was used for business or investment purposes. If you realize a loss on property used for both business and personal purposes, the portion of the loss that is allocated to the business portion of the property may be deductible.

Short-term gains and losses. Capital gain or loss on the sale or trade of investment property held 1 year or less is a short-term capital gain or loss. You report it in Part I of Schedule D. If the amount you report in column (f) is a loss, show it in parentheses.

You combine your share of short-term capital gains or losses from partnerships, S corporations, and fiduciaries, and any short-term capital loss carryover, with your other short-term capital gains and losses to figure your net short-term capital gain or loss on line 7 of Schedule D.

Long-term gains and losses. A capital gain or loss on the sale or trade of property held more than 1 year is a long-term capital gain or loss. You report it in Part II of Schedule D. If the amount in column (f) is a loss, show it in parentheses.

Explanation
The shortest length of time that qualifies for long-term status is 1 year plus 1 day. Your holding period begins on the day after you buy the property and includes the day you sell it.

Example
Donald pays $1,000 for Corporation X stock on July 1, 2000. His holding period begins on July 2, 2000. Donald sells the stock on July 1, 2001, for $1,500. His holding period runs from July 2, 2000 (the day after he purchased the stock), through July 1, 2001 (the day he sold the stock). Donald has a short-term capital gain of $500 because he has held the stock for exactly 1 year.

Assume instead that Donald sells the stock on July 2, 2001. His holding period runs from July 2, 2000, through July 2, 2001. His holding period is now in excess of 1 year (1 year and 1 day), so Donald's gain will be long term.

You also report the following in Part II of Schedule D:

1) Undistributed long-term capital gains from a regulated investment company (mutual fund) or real estate investment trust (REIT),
2) Your share of long-term capital gains or losses from partnerships, S corporations, and fiduciaries,
3) All capital gain distributions from mutual funds and REITs not reported directly on line 10 of Form 1040A or line 13 of Form 1040, and
4) Long-term capital loss carryovers.

Explanation
Dividends from mutual funds, which are technically known as **regulated investment companies,** are frequently composed of a combination of long-term capital gains and ordinary income. The nature of the gain is determined by how long the mutual fund has held the underlying property that generates the income, not how long you have held the mutual fund shares. Consequently, you may have a long-term capital gain, although you have held the mutual fund shares for less than the required long-term holding period.

Determination of cost basis and holding period. Mutual fund shares may be acquired on various dates, in various quantities, and at various prices. Some individuals may purchase shares through participation in dividend reinvestment or payroll deduction plans. Shares may also be sold on a periodic basis. As a result, individuals often encounter difficulty in determining their cost basis and hence gain or loss on the sale of their mutual fund shares. Under present law, four methods may be used by mutual fund shareholders to determine the cost basis of shares sold. They are

1. The specific identification method
2. The FIFO (first in, first out) method
3. The single-category method using the average approach
4. The double-category method using the average approach

The specific identification method. In order to *specifically identify* the shares sold, the following requirements must be met:

1. Specific instructions to the broker or agent must be given by the customer, indicating the particular shares to be sold. These instructions must be given at the time of sale or transfer.
2. Written *confirmation* of this request must be received from the broker or agent within a reasonable time after the sale.

The individual shareholder bears the burden of proof that he or she owned and chose to sell the specific shares at the time of sale.

TAXPLANNER

Managing gains and losses. This specific identification method provides an investor with the greatest opportunity to manage his or her reported gain or loss. For example, if a shareholder has other capital losses during the year and wishes to generate capital gains, he or she can specifically identify those shares acquired at the *lowest prices* as the shares being sold. One problem with this method, particularly with mutual funds, is the inability of transfer agents to confirm, in writing, specific shares sold to the shareholder.

Explanation
The FIFO method. Under the FIFO (first in, first out) method, the basis of shares acquired first represents the cost of the shares sold. In other words, the *oldest shares* held by the taxpayer are considered to be the first sold. The FIFO method is also a *default* method. If specific identification procedures are not or cannot be followed and the average basis approach (discussed below) is not elected, then the FIFO method will apply.

TAXALERT

Trap for the unwary. In a rising market, the FIFO method produces the *greatest gain* (and least loss) and hence, generally, the most tax.

Explanation
The single- and double-category methods using the average approach. The average basis method must be *elected* by the individual shareholder by attaching a statement to his or her income tax return, for each year the choice applies. The election must indicate whether the single-category method or the double-category method (discussed below) is being used. Once the election is made, it must continue to be used for *all* accounts in the *same* mutual fund. The average method permits the taxpayer to calculate his or her gain or loss based on the average price paid for the shares.

With the single-category method, all shares are included in a single category; that is, the basis of each share is the total adjusted basis of all shares at the time of disposition divided by the total shares. In determining the holding period (long- or short-term), the shares disposed of are considered to be those shares acquired *first* (using a FIFO-type method, discussed earlier).

With the double-category method, all shares in an account are separated into two categories:

1. Short-term—shares held for 1 year or less
2. Long-term—shares held *more* than 1 year

The average cost for each category is calculated; that is, the basis of each share in a category is the total adjusted basis of all shares in that category divided by the total shares in that category. The shareholder can specify from which category shares are sold. The custodian or agent must confirm this to the shareholder in writing. If no selection is made, the shares in the long-term category are deemed to be sold first. After a share has been held for more than 1 year, it must be transferred from the short-term to the long-term category.

Explanation
Mutual fund dividends. If an individual who purchases shares in a mutual fund receives a capital gain dividend and then sells the shares at a loss within 6 months after purchase, the loss is treated as a *long-term* capital loss to the extent of the capital gain dividend received. Just as important, you may have to pay taxes on a capital gain dividend when you have not had a profit on your investment.

Example
You pay $10,000 for ABC Mutual Fund on June 30. On July 1, ABC Mutual Fund pays you a long-term capital gain dividend of $1,000. The same day, the value of your ABC shares drops to $9,000. You haven't made any money on your investment, but you still have to pay a tax on the capital gain dividend.

TAXSAVER

When to generate losses. If at the end of the year you find that you have only short-term capital gains, you might consider generating capital losses by selling assets that have declined in value. Short-term gains are taxed as ordinary income, but you can avoid paying tax on them by offsetting them against both short-term and long-term losses.

Explanation
Sales or load charges. When a person invests in a mutual fund, he or she may be subject to a sales or load charge, which is similar to a commission. When shares are sold or redeemed, the sales or load charge is generally taken into account as part of the purchaser's basis for purposes of computing gain or loss on the sale.

If an investor exchanges shares in a mutual fund for shares in the same "family" or complex of funds, an additional sales or load charge may be waived or reduced if the investor acquires a reinvestment right (i.e., the right to acquire stock of one or more mutual funds without the payment of all or part of the standard load charge) on the original purchase. If such an exchange occurs within 90 days of the original purchase of mutual fund shares, the original sales or load charge will not be included as basis in determining the gain or loss on the exchange. This rule only applies to the extent that the additional sales or load charge is waived or reduced on the exchange. To the extent that the sales or load charge is not treated as basis in computing gain or loss, such a charge will be taken into account on shares subsequently sold.

Example

On January 1, 2001, Kurt Norton purchased 100 shares of mutual fund X for $110, which included a $10 sales or load charge. On January 20, 2001, Kurt exchanged these shares for 50 shares of mutual fund X1, worth $115. Mutual fund X1 is in the same family as mutual fund X. The sales or load charge of $10 on Kurt's purchase of mutual fund X1 was waived. Kurt's gain or loss on the exchange is computed as follows:

Sales price of mutual fund X	$115
Cost basis of mutual fund X	100
Gain (loss)	$ 15

The sales or load charge of $10 on the purchase of mutual fund X did not affect the taxable gain or loss on the exchange but will become part of the basis of mutual fund X1.

For more about mutual funds see Chapter 39, *Mutual Funds.*

The result after combining these items with your other long-term capital gains and losses is your net long-term capital gain or loss (line 16 of Schedule D).

28% rate gain or loss. Enter in column (g) the amount, if any, from column (f) that is a 28% rate gain or loss. Enter any loss in parentheses.

A 28% rate gain or loss is:

• Any collectibles gain or loss, or
• The part of your gain on qualified small business stock that is equal to the section 1202 exclusion.

For more information, see *Capital Gain Tax Rates,* later.

Capital gain distributions only. You do not have to file Schedule D if **all** of the following are true.

1) The only amounts you would have to report on Schedule D are capital gain distributions from box 2a of Form 1099-DIV (or substitute statement).
2) You do not have an amount in box 2b, 2c, 2d, or 2e of any Form 1099-DIV (or substitute statement).
3) You do not file Form 4952 or, if you do, the amount on line 4e of that form is not more than zero.

If all the above statements are true, report your capital gain distributions directly on line 13 of Form 1040 and check the box on that line. Also, use the *Capital Gain Tax Worksheet* in the Form 1040 instructions to figure your tax.

You can report your capital gain distributions on line 10 of Form 1040A, instead of on Form 1040, if both of the following are true.

1) None of the Forms 1099-DIV (or substitute statements) you received have an amount in box 2b, 2c, 2d, or 2e.
2) You do not have to file Form 1040 for any other capital gains or any capital losses.

Total net gain or loss. To figure your total net gain or loss, combine your net short-term capital gain or loss (line 7) with your net long-term capital gain or loss (line 16). Enter the result on line 17, Part III of Schedule D. If your losses are more than your gains, see *Capital Losses,* next. If both lines 16 and 17 are gains and line 39 of Form 1040 is more than zero, see *Capital Gain Tax Rates,* later.

Capital Losses

If your capital losses are more than your capital gains, you can claim a capital loss deduction. Report the deduction on line 13 of Form 1040, enclosed in parentheses.

Example 1

You have capital gains and losses for the year as follows:

	Short-term	Long-term
Gains	$ 700	$ 400
Losses	800	2,000

Your net deductible capital loss is $1,700, which you figure as follows:

Short-term capital losses	$ 800	
Minus: Short-term capital gains	700	
Net short-term capital loss		$ 100
Long-term capital losses	$2,000	
Minus: Long-term capital gains	400	
Net long-term capital loss		$1,600
Net deductible capital loss		$1,700

Your deduction is limited to the lesser of $3,000 ($1,500 if married filing separately) or your capital loss of $1,700. The amount of your capital loss carryover is limited to this $1,700 or your taxable income (adjusted as described later under *Figuring Your Carryover*), whichever is smaller.

Example 2

You have a net long-term capital loss of $1,600 and a net short-term capital gain of $450. Your deductible capital loss is $1,150 ($1,600 – $450).

Limit on deduction. Your allowable capital loss deduction, figured on Schedule D, is the lesser of:

1) $3,000 ($1,500 if you are married and file a separate return), or
2) Your total net loss as shown on line 17 of Schedule D.

You can use your total net loss to reduce your income dollar for dollar, up to the $3,000 limit.

Capital loss carryover. If you have a total net loss on line 17 of Schedule D that is more than the yearly limit on capital loss deductions, you can carry over the unused part to the next year and treat it as if you had incurred it in that next year. If part of the loss is still unused, you can carry it over to later years until it is completely used up.

When you figure the amount of any capital loss carryover to the next year, you must take the current year's allowable deduction into account, whether or not you claimed it.

When you carry over a loss, it remains long term or short term. A long-term capital loss you carry over to the next tax year will reduce that year's long-term capital gains before it reduces that year's short-term capital gains.

Figuring your carryover. The amount of your capital loss carryover is the amount of your total net loss that is more than the lesser of:

1) Your allowable capital loss deduction for the year, or
2) Your taxable income increased by your allowable capital loss deduction for the year and your deduction for personal exemptions.

If your deductions are more than your gross income for the tax year, use your negative taxable income in computing the amount in item (2).

Complete the *Capital Loss Carryover Worksheet* in the Schedule D (Form 1040) instructions to determine the part of your capital loss for 2001 that you can carry over to 2002.

Example. Bob and Gloria sold securities in 2001. The sales resulted in a capital loss of $7,000. They had no other capital transactions. Their taxable income was $26,000. On their joint 2001 return, they can deduct $3,000. The unused part of the loss, $4,000 ($7,000 − $3,000), can be carried over to 2002.

If their capital loss had been $2,000, their capital loss deduction would have been $2,000. They would have no carryover.

Use short-term losses first. When you figure your capital loss carryover, use your short-term capital losses first, even if you incurred them after a long-term capital loss. If you have not reached the limit on the capital loss deduction after using short-term losses, use the long-term losses until you reach the limit.

Explanation

A net loss may be carried forward until it is exhausted or until the taxpayer dies. This carryforward may be used to reduce your tax when you have a capital gain sometime in the future. Even if you do not have future gains, the carryforward loss may be used to offset taxable income up to $3,000 per year.

Decedent's capital loss. A capital loss sustained by a decedent during his or her last tax year (or carried over to that year from an earlier year) can be deducted only on the final income tax return filed for the decedent. The capital loss limits discussed earlier still apply in this situation. The decedent's estate cannot deduct any of the loss or carry it over to following years.

TaxPlanner

If the decedent filed a joint return in the year of death, the surviving spouse may offset gains recognized after the decedent's death but before the end of the tax year against the decedent's capital loss carryforward. Therefore, if the surviving spouse has assets that have appreciated in value, he or she should consider selling them in the year of the decedent's death. For a further discussion of this point, see Chapter 4, *Decedents.*

Joint and separate returns. If you and your spouse once filed separate returns and are now filing a joint return, combine your separate capital loss carryovers. However, if you and your spouse once filed a joint return and are now filing separate returns, any capital loss carryover from the joint return can be deducted only on the return of the person who actually had the loss.

Capital Gain Tax Rates

The tax rates that apply to a net capital gain are generally lower than the tax rates that apply to other income. These lower rates are called the maximum capital gain rates.

The term "net capital gain" means the amount by which your net long-term capital gain for the year is more than your net short-term capital loss.

TaxPlanner

Long-term investment strategies. Investment strategies that emphasize capital appreciation over current income can significantly enhance your after-tax portfolio returns. For example, "buy-and-hold" investors should keep growth-oriented investments outside of tax-deferred accounts to benefit from the capital gains tax relief. Long-term gains in a tax-deferred account are taxed at ordinary income rates—currently as high as 39.1%—when withdrawn. Outside a tax-deferred account, those same long-term gains would be taxed at the more favorable capital gains rate. In addition, new investments in tax-deferred variable annuities will require much longer holding periods to outperform "comparable" investments held in a taxable account. Although mutual funds have not—with some notable exceptions—historically paid considerable attention to the impact of taxes on shareholder returns, more fund families are developing "tax-managed" funds that seek to minimize taxable distributions to shareholders.

To take advantage of the 8%, 10%, and 20% rates, you should specifically identify shares of securities and/or mutual funds held more than 12 months prior to executing the sale. For tax purposes, the selling instructions given to the broker or fund representative must be in writing. Confirmation of the instructions should be kept in your personal files.

High-income taxpayers who have the option of deferring current compensation may be better off paying tax currently and reinvesting the after-tax proceeds in assets expected to appreciate over the long-term. This may apply, for example, in the case of a corporate executive with significant nonqualified stock option holdings where the current option spread—and, thus, the associated current tax liability—is small but the outlook for the company's stock price is favorable.

TaxPlanner

Effective in 2001, the maximum capital gains for assets that are held more than 5 years are 8% and 18% (corresponding to the 10% and 20% rates for property held between 12 months and 5 years). However, the 18% rate only applies to assets which are purchased after December 31, 2000 and held for at least five years. For assets purchased before January 1, 2001, you will be able to elect to treat these assets as if you sold them on January 1 or 2 of 2001 in order to start your holding period over. This election is discussed in more detail in Chapter 15, *Sale of Property.*

The maximum capital gain rate can be 8%, 10%, 20%, 25%, or 28%. See *Table 17-1* for details.

The maximum capital gain rate does not apply if it is higher than your regular tax rate.

Example. You have a net capital gain from selling collectibles, so the capital gain rate would be 28%. Because you are single and your taxable income is $25,000, your regular tax rate is 15%. All your taxable income will be taxed at the 15% rate. The 28% rate does not apply.

Investment interest deducted. If you claim a deduction for investment interest, you may have to reduce the amount of your net capital gain that is eligible for the capital gain tax rates. Reduce it by the amount of the net capital gain you choose to include in investment income when figuring the limit on your investment interest deduction. This is done on lines 21-23 of Schedule D. For more information about the limit on investment interest, see chapter 3 of Publication 550.

Table 17–1. **What Is Your Maximum Capital Gain Rate?**

IF your net capital gain is from ...	THEN your maximum capital gain rate is ...
Collectibles gain	28%
Gain on qualified small business stock equal to the section 1202 exclusion	28%
Unrecaptured section 1250 gain	25%
Other gain,[1] and the regular tax rate that would apply is 27.5% or higher	20%
Other gain,[1] and the regular tax rate that would apply is lower than 15%	8% or 10%[2]

[1] "Other gain" means any gain that is not collectibles gain, gain on qualified small business stock, or unrecaptured section 1250 gain.

[2] The rate is 8% only for qualified 5-year gain.

TAXPLANNER

Net capital gains. Net capital gains are not included in "investment income" for purposes of determining a taxpayer's deduction for investment interest expense. However, you can elect to include capital gains as investment income. This election can be made for all or just a portion of your capital gains. In addition, you can make one election for regular tax purposes and another for alternative minimum tax purposes. If you make such an election, you must reduce the amount of capital gains that are otherwise eligible for the maximum 20% tax rate by the amount included as investment income.

8% rate. Beginning in 2001, the 10% capital gain rate is lowered to 8% for "qualified 5-year gain."

Qualified 5-year gain. This is long-term capital gain from the sale of property that you held for more than 5 years and that would otherwise be subject to the 10% capital gain rate.

Collectibles gain or loss. This is gain or loss from the sale or trade of a work of art, rug, antique, metal (such as gold, silver, and platinum bullion), gem, stamp, coin, or alcoholic beverage held more than 1 year.

Gain on qualified small business stock. If you realized a gain from qualified small business stock that you held more than 5 years, you generally can exclude one-half of your gain from income. The taxable part of your gain equal to your section 1202 exclusion is a 28% rate gain. See *Gains on Qualified Small Business Stock* in chapter 4 of Publication 550.

Unrecaptured section 1250 gain. Generally, this is any part of your capital gain from selling section 1250 property (real property) that is due to depreciation (but not more than your net section 1231 gain), reduced by any net loss in the 28% group. Use the worksheet in the Schedule D instructions to figure your unrecaptured section 1250 gain. For more information about section 1250 property and section 1231 gain, see chapter 3 of Publication 544.

Explanation
Computing depreciation recapture. If you sell property at a gain, you must generally compute the portion of your gain that is depreciation recapture. Depreciation recapture is treated as ordinary income. The portion of the gain that is not depreciation recapture is treated as a Section 1231 gain. Complete Form 4797 to determine the amount of your gain that is depreciation recapture.

Sale of depreciable personal property. The depreciation recapture rules for depreciable personal property are relatively simple, compared to the rules for real property. De-

preciation recapture is the *lesser* of (1) the gain recognized or (2) depreciation taken on the property since 1961. Note that, under these rules, if depreciable personal property is sold at less than its original cost, the full gain will inevitably be depreciation recapture.

Example
In 1999, Alan bought personal property that he used in his trade for $5,000. Alan sold the property for $2,500 in 2001. He had already taken $3,662 in depreciation. Alan computes his gain or loss as follows:

Sales price		$2,500
Purchase price	$5,000	
Less: Depreciation taken	3,662	
Adjusted basis		1,338
Gain on sale		$1,162

Alan's gain on the sale is $1,162, which is less than the $3,662 of depreciation he had taken on the property. Therefore, his depreciation recapture is $1,162. Because this represents the full gain on the sale, no portion of the gain is treated as a Section 1231 gain and all of it will be treated as ordinary income.

Assume instead that the property had appreciated and that Alan sold the property for $6,000:

Sales price	$6,000
Adjusted basis (computed above)	1,338
Gain on sale	$4,662

Because the depreciation Alan took on the property ($3,662) is less than the gain on the sale ($4,662), Alan reports the $3,662 depreciation taken as depreciation recapture. The remaining $1,000 of his gain ($4,662 – $3,662) is treated as a Section 1231 gain.

Explanation
Sale of depreciable real estate. The depreciation recapture rules relating to the sale of real estate are quite complex. These rules depend on (1) when you placed the property in service, (2) what method of depreciation was used, and (3) whether the property was residential rental property or held for business use. It should be noted that no depreciation recapture should occur for real property acquired after 1986

because straight-line depreciation is the only method available for such property.

Real property acquired before 1976. If you acquired the real estate before 1976 and used the straight-line method of depreciation, there is no depreciation recapture on sale. If you used an accelerated method, you must go through a number of computations to determine depreciation recapture.

Step 1. Compute the excess depreciation for post-1975 years, which is the difference between the depreciation deductions you took using an accelerated method and the amount you would have taken had you used the straight-line method for the years you depreciated the property after 1975.

Step 2. Compare this amount to your overall gain on the sale. If your overall gain is less than this amount, then the overall gain is the amount of your depreciation recapture and you can stop here. If the overall gain is greater than the post-1975 excess depreciation, go on to Step 3.

Step 3. Subtract the excess depreciation computed in Step 1 from the total overall gain to compute the remaining gain. Then compute the excess depreciation for the years 1970 through 1975, using the same method as in Step 1. Take the smaller of the remaining gain or the excess depreciation for 1970 through 1975, as computed above.

If the property is *not* residential rental property, then the depreciation recapture is the sum of the excess depreciation computed in Step 1, plus the amount computed in Step 3. If the property is residential rental property, you must then compute the "applicable percentage," which depends on how many full months you owned the property. If you held the property less than 100 months, the applicable percentage is 100%. If you held the property for more than 100 full months, the applicable percentage is 100% minus the number of full months you held the property in excess of 100 months.

Multiply this percentage by the amount calculated in Step 3. Add this result to the amount calculated in Step 1 to get the total amount of gain treated as depreciation recapture.

Property acquired after 1975 and before 1981. Generally, all of the excess accelerated depreciation over straight-line depreciation up to the amount of gain has to be recaptured on sale. Certain kinds of property—government-assisted housing, low-income housing, certain rehabilitation expenses, and Title V loan property—are exempt from this rule. In these special cases, 100% of accelerated depreciation has to be recaptured for the first 100 months the property is held. After that, the recapture percentage declines 1% each month so that after 16 2/3 years there is no further recapture.

Nonresidential real property acquired after 1980 and before 1987. If the accelerated rates under the Accelerated Cost Recovery System (ACRS) are used on commercial real property, the entire amount of depreciation is subject to recapture on sale of the property. This means, in essence, that any gain up to the amount of depreciation previously claimed is treated as ordinary income. However, if straight-line ACRS is used, then none of the depreciation has to be recaptured at the time of sale.

Residential real property acquired after 1980 and before 1987. Any gain on the sale of *residential rental property* is ordinary income if the deductions taken under the accelerated ACRS method of depreciation exceed the depreciation allowed under the 15-year straight-line method of depreciation. However, any gain you incur in excess of the amount you have to recapture is treated as a capital gain. For property acquired after March 15, 1984, the ACRS period is 18 years, and, for property acquired after May 8, 1985, the ACRS period is 19 years.

Using Schedule D. You apply these rules by using Part IV of Schedule D (Form 1040) to figure your tax. Use Part IV if both of the following are true.

1) You have a net capital gain. You have a net capital gain if both lines 16 and 17 of Schedule D are gains. (Line 16 is your net long-term capital gain or loss. Line 17 is your net long-term capital gain or loss combined with any net short-term capital gain or loss.)

2) Your taxable income on Form 1040, line 39, is more than zero.

If you have any collectibles gain, gain on qualified small business stock, or unrecaptured section 1250 gain, you may have to use the *Schedule D Tax Worksheet* in the Schedule D instructions to figure your tax. See the directions below line 19 of Schedule D.

See the *Comprehensive Example,* later, for an example of how to figure your tax on Schedule D using the capital gain rates.

Using Capital Gain Tax Worksheet. If you have capital gain distributions but do not have to file Schedule D (Form 1040), figure your tax using the *Capital Gain Tax Worksheet* in the instructions for Form 1040A or Form 1040. For more information, see *Capital gain distributions only,* earlier.

New 18% rate beginning in 2006. Beginning in 2006, the 20% maximum capital gain rate will be lowered to 18% for qualified 5-year gain from property with a holding period that begins after 2000. See chapter 4 of Publication 550 for more information.

Comprehensive Example

Emily Jones is single and, in addition to wages from her job, she has income from stocks and other securities. For the 2001 tax year, she had the following capital gains and losses, which she reports on Schedule D. All the Forms 1099 she received showed net sales prices. Her filled-in Schedule D is shown in this chapter.

Capital gains and losses—Schedule D. Emily sold stock in two different companies that she held for less than a year. In June, she sold 100 shares of Trucking Co. stock that she had bought in February. She had an adjusted basis of $650 in the stock and sold it for $900, for a gain of $250. In July, she sold 25 shares of Computer Co. stock that she bought in June. She had an adjusted basis in the stock of $2,500 and she sold it for $2,000, for a loss of $500. She reports these short-term transactions on line 1 in Part I of Schedule D.

Emily had three other stock sales that she reports as long-term transactions on line 8 in Part II of Schedule D. In February, she sold 60 shares of Car Co. for $2,100. She had inherited the Car Co. stock from her father. Its fair market value at the time of his death was $2,500, which became her basis. Her loss on the sale is $400. Because she had inherited the stock, her loss is a long-term loss, regardless of how long she and her father actually held the stock. She enters the loss in column (f) of line 8.

In June, she sold 500 shares of Furniture Co. stock for $14,000. She had bought 100 of those shares in 1990, for $1,000. She had bought 100 more shares in 1992 for $2,200, and an additional 300 shares in 1995 for $1,500. Her total basis in the stock is $4,700. She has a $9,300 ($14,000 – $4,700) gain on this sale, which she enters in column (f) of line 8. Because she held all 500 shares for more than 5 years, the entire gain is qualified 5-year gain.

In December, she sold 20 shares of Toy Co. for $4,100. This was qualified small business stock that she had bought in September 1996. Her basis is $1,100, so she has a $3,000 gain which she enters in column (f) of line 8. Because she held the stock more than 5 years, she has a $1,500 section 1202 exclusion. She enters that amount in column (g) as a 28% rate gain and claims the exclusion on the line below by entering $1,500 as a loss in column (f).

She received a Form 1099-B (not shown) from her broker for each of these transactions.

Capital loss carryover from 2000. Emily has a capital loss carryover to 2001 of $800, of which $300 is short-term capital loss, and $500 is long-term capital loss. She enters these amounts on lines 6 and 14 of Schedule D.

She kept the completed *Capital Loss Carryover Worksheet* in her 2000 Schedule D instructions (not shown), so she could properly report her loss carryover for the 2001 tax year without refiguring it.

Tax computation. Because Emily has gains on both lines 16 and 17 of Schedule D and has taxable income, she goes to Part IV of Schedule D to figure her tax. But because line 15 of Schedule D is more than zero (due to her section 1202 gain from selling qualified small business stock), she must use the *Schedule D Tax Worksheet* to figure her tax instead. She must also complete the *Qualified 5-Year Gain Worksheet* (not shown) in her Schedule D instructions.

After entering the gain from line 17 on line 13 of her Form 1040, she completes the rest of Form 1040 through line 39. She enters the amount from that line, $30,000, on line 1 of the Schedule D Tax Worksheet. After filing out the worksheet and the rest of that worksheet, she figures her tax is $4,235. This is less than the $4,876 tax she would have figured without the capital gain tax rates.

Reconciliation of Forms 1099-B. Emily makes sure that the total of the amounts reported in column (d) of lines 3 and 10 of Schedule D is not less than the total of the amounts shown on the Forms 1099-B she received from her broker. For 2001, the total of each is $23,100.

**SCHEDULE D
(Form 1040)**

Department of the Treasury
Internal Revenue Service

Capital Gains and Losses

▶ Attach to Form 1040.   ▶ See Instructions for Schedule D (Form 1040).

▶ Use Schedule D-1 to list additional transactions for lines 1 and 8.

OMB No. 1545-0074

2001

Attachment
Sequence No. **12**

Name(s) shown on Form 1040

Emily Jones

Your social security number

111 : 00 : 1111

Part I — Short-Term Capital Gains and Losses—Assets Held One Year or Less

(a) Description of property (Example: 100 sh. XYZ Co.)	(b) Date acquired (Mo., day, yr.)	(c) Date sold (Mo., day, yr.)	(d) Sales price (see page D-5 of the instructions)	(e) Cost or other basis (see page D-5 of the instructions)	(f) Gain or (loss) Subtract (e) from (d)	
1 100 sh Trucking Co.	2-12-01	6-12-01	900	650	250	
25 sh Computer Co.	6-29-01	7-30-01	2,000	2,500	(500)	

2 Enter your short-term totals, if any, from Schedule D-1, line 2	**2**		
3 **Total short-term sales price amounts.** Add lines 1 and 2 in column (d)	**3**	2,900	
4 Short-term gain from Form 6252 and short-term gain or (loss) from Forms 4684, 6781, and 8824	**4**		
5 Net short-term gain or (loss) from partnerships, S corporations, estates, and trusts from Schedule(s) K-1	**5**		
6 Short-term capital loss carryover. Enter the amount, if any, from line 8 of your 2000 Capital Loss Carryover Worksheet	**6**	(300)	
7 **Net short-term capital gain or (loss).** Combine lines 1 through 6 in column (f).	**7**	(550)	

Part II — Long-Term Capital Gains and Losses—Assets Held More Than One Year

(a) Description of property (Example: 100 sh. XYZ Co.)	(b) Date acquired (Mo., day, yr.)	(c) Date sold (Mo., day, yr.)	(d) Sales price (see page D-5 of the instructions)	(e) Cost or other basis (see page D-5 of the instructions)	(f) Gain or (loss) Subtract (e) from (d)	(g) 28% rate gain or (loss) * (see instr. below)
8 60 sh Car Co.	INHERITED	2-3-01	2,100	2,500	(400)	
500 sh Furniture Co.	VARIOUS	6-27-01	14,000	4,700	9,300	
20 sh Toy Co.	9-20-96	12-15-01	4,100	1,100	3,000	1,500
Section 1202 exclusion					(1,500)	

9 Enter your long-term totals, if any, from Schedule D-1, line 9	**9**			
10 **Total long-term sales price amounts.** Add lines 8 and 9 in column (d)	**10**	20,200		
11 Gain from Form 4797, Part I; long-term gain from Forms 2439 and 6252; and long-term gain or (loss) from Forms 4684, 6781, and 8824	**11**			
12 Net long-term gain or (loss) from partnerships, S corporations, estates, and trusts from Schedule(s) K-1.	**12**			
13 Capital gain distributions. See page D-1 of the instructions	**13**			
14 Long-term capital loss carryover. Enter in both columns (f) and (g) the amount, if any, from line 13 of your 2000 Capital Loss Carryover Worksheet	**14**	(500)	(500)
15 Combine lines 8 through 14 in column (g)	**15**		1,000
16 **Net long-term capital gain or (loss).** Combine lines 8 through 14 in column (f)	**16**	9,900	
	Next: Go to Part III on the back.			

***28% rate gain or loss** includes all "collectibles gains and losses" (as defined on page D-6 of the instructions) and up to 50% of the eligible gain on qualified small business stock (see page D-4 of the instructions).

For Paperwork Reduction Act Notice, see Form 1040 instructions.   Cat. No. 11338H   Schedule D (Form 1040) 2001

Part III   **Taxable Gain or Deductible Loss**

17   Combine lines 7 and 16 and enter the result. If a loss, go to line 18. If a gain, enter the gain on Form 1040, line 13, and complete Form 1040 through line 39 . . . . **17** | 9,350

      Next: • If both lines 16 and 17 are gains **and** Form 1040, line 39, is more than zero, complete Part IV below.

            • Otherwise, skip the rest of Schedule D and complete Form 1040.

18   If line 17 is a loss, enter here and on Form 1040, line 13, the **smaller** of **(a)** that loss or **(b)** ($3,000) (or, if married filing separately, ($1,500)). Then complete Form 1040 through line 37   **18** ( )

      Next: • If the loss on line 17 is more than the loss on line 18 **or** if Form 1040, line 37, is less than zero, skip **Part IV** below and complete the **Capital Loss Carryover Worksheet** on page D-6 of the instructions before completing the rest of Form 1040.

            • Otherwise, skip **Part IV** below and complete the rest of Form 1040.

Part IV   **Tax Computation Using Maximum Capital Gains Rates**

19   Enter your unrecaptured section 1250 gain, if any, from line 17 of the worksheet on page D-7 of the instructions . . . . .   **19** | -0-

      If line 15 or line 19 is more than zero, complete the worksheet on page D-9 of the instructions to figure the amount to enter on lines 22, 29, and 40 below, and skip all other lines below. Otherwise, go to line 20.

20   Enter your taxable income from Form 1040, line 39 . . . . .   **20**

21   Enter the **smaller** of line 16 or line 17 of Schedule D **21**

22   If you are deducting investment interest expense on Form 4952, enter the amount from Form 4952, line 4e. Otherwise, enter -0-   **22** | -0-

23   Subtract line 22 from line 21. If zero or less, enter -0- **23**

24   Subtract line 23 from line 20. If zero or less, enter -0- **24**

25   Figure the tax on the amount on line 24. Use the Tax Table or Tax Rate Schedules, whichever applies   **25**

26   Enter the **smaller** of:
    • The amount on line 20 **or**
    • $45,200 if married filing jointly or qualifying widow(er);
      $27,050 if single;
      $36,250 if head of household; or
      $22,600 if married filing separately   } . . .   **26**

      If line 26 is greater than line 24, go to line 27. Otherwise, skip lines 27 through 33 and go to line 34.

27   Enter the amount from line 24 . . . .   **27**

28   Subtract line 27 from line 26. If zero or less, enter -0- and go to line 34   **28**

29   Enter your qualified 5-year gain, if any, from line 7 of the worksheet on page D-8 . . .   **29** | 9,300

30   Enter the **smaller** of line 28 or line 29 . . . .   **30**

31   Multiply line 30 by 8% (.08) **31**

32   Subtract line 30 from line 28 . . . .   **32**

33   Multiply line 32 by 10% (.10) **33**

      If the amounts on lines 23 and 28 are the same, skip lines 34 through 37 and go to line 38.

34   Enter the **smaller** of line 20 or line 23 . . . .   **34**

35   Enter the amount from line 28 (if line 28 is blank, enter -0-) . . .   **35**

36   Subtract line 35 from line 34 . . . .   **36**

37   Multiply line 36 by 20% (.20) **37**

38   Add lines 25, 31, 33, and 37 . . . .   **38**

39   Figure the tax on the amount on line 20. Use the Tax Table or Tax Rate Schedules, whichever applies   **39**

40   **Tax on all taxable income (including capital gains). Enter the smaller of line 38 or line 39 here and on Form 1040, line 40** . . . .   **40** | 4,235

Schedule D Tax Worksheet—Line 40

Keep for Your Records

Complete this worksheet only if line 15 or line 19 of Schedule D is more than zero. Otherwise, complete Part IV of Schedule D to figure your tax. **Exception: Do not** use Schedule D, Part IV, or this worksheet to figure your tax if line 16 or line 17 of Schedule D or Form 1040, line 39, is zero or less; instead, see the instructions for Form 1040, line 40.

1. Enter your taxable income from Form 1040, line 39 . . . . **1.** 30,000

2. Enter the **smaller** of line 16 or line 17 of Schedule D . . . **2.** 9,350

3. If you are claiming investment interest expense on Form 4952, enter the amount from line 4e. Otherwise, enter -0-. **Also enter this amount on Schedule D, line 22** . . . **3.** -0-

4. Subtract line 3 from line 2. If zero or less, enter -0- **4.** 9,350

5. Combine lines 7 and 15 of Schedule D. If zero or less, enter -0- **5.** 450

6. Enter the **smaller** of line 5 above or Schedule D, line 15, but not less than zero **6.** 450

7. Enter the amount from Schedule D, line 19 . . . . . . **7.** -0-

8. Add lines 6 and 7 . . . . **8.** 450

9. Subtract line 8 from line 4. If zero or less, enter -0- **9.** 8,900

10. Subtract line 9 from line 1. If zero or less, enter -0- **10.** 21,100

11. Enter the **smaller** of:

   • The amount on line 1 **or**
   • \$45,200 if married filing jointly or qualifying widow(er);
   \$27,050 if single;
   \$36,250 if head of household; or
   \$22,600 if married filing separately **11.** 27,050

12. Enter the **smaller** of line 10 or line 11 . . . . **12.** 21,100

13. Subtract line 4 from line 1. If zero or less, enter -0- . . . **13.** 20,650

14. Enter the **larger** of line 12 or line 13 . . . . ▶ **14.** 21,100

15. Figure the tax on the amount on line 14. Use the Tax Table or Tax Rate Schedules, whichever applies ▶ **15.** 3,169

   If lines 11 and 12 are the same, skip lines 16 through 21 and go to line 22. Otherwise, go to line 16.

16. Subtract line 12 from line 11 . . . . ▶ **16.** 5,950

17. Enter your qualified 5-year gain, if any, from the worksheet on page D-8. **Also enter this amount on Schedule D, line 29** . **17.** 9,300

18. Enter the **smaller** of line 16 above or line 17 above **18.** 5,950

19. Multiply line 18 by 8% (.08) **19.** 476

20. Subtract line 18 from line 16 . . . . **20.** -0-

21. Multiply line 20 by 10% (.10) . . . . **21.** -0-

   If lines 1 and 11 are the same, skip lines 22 through 34 and go to line 35. Otherwise, go to line 22.

22. Enter the **smaller** of line 1 or line 9 . . . . **22.** 8,900

23. Enter the amount from line 16. If blank, enter -0- **23.** 5,950

24. Subtract line 23 from line 22 . . . . ▶ **24.** 2,950

25. Multiply line 24 by 20% (.20) **25.** 590

   If line 7 is zero, skip lines 26 through 31 and go to line 32. Otherwise, go to line 26.

26. Enter the **smaller** of line 4 or line 7 . . . . **26.**

27. Add lines 4 and 14 . . . . **27.**

28. Enter the amount from line 1 above . **28.**

29. Subtract line 28 from line 27. If zero or less, enter -0- . . **29.**

30. Subtract line 29 from line 26. If zero or less, enter -0- . . . . . . ▶ **30.**

31. Multiply line 30 by 25% (.25) . . . . **31.**

   If line 6 is zero, skip lines 32 through 34 and go to line 35. Otherwise, go to line 32.

32. Add lines 14, 16, 24, and 30 . . . . **32.** 30,000

33. Subtract line 32 from line 1 . . . . **33.** -0-

34. Multiply line 33 by 28% (.28) . . . . **34.** -0-

35. Add lines 15, 19, 21, 25, 31, and 34 . . . . **35.** 4,235

36. Figure the tax on the amount on line 1. Use the Tax Table or Tax Rate Schedules, whichever applies . **36.** 4,876

37. **Tax on all taxable income (including capital gains).** Enter the **smaller** of line 35 or line 36. Also enter this amount on Schedule D, line 40, and Form 1040, line 40 . . . . **37.** 4,235

Individual Retirement Arrangements (IRAs) and Education Savings Accounts (ESAs)

Introduction

There are three different IRA options, each with different eligibility requirements and characteristics. In addition, there are education savings accounts (formerly known as education IRAs).

- *Deductible IRAs save you taxes this year and every year you make a contribution. If you are eligible, your annual contribution of up to $2,000 is deductible. In addition, you defer paying taxes on the income earned by the funds in your IRA until withdrawal.*

- *Nondeductible IRAs are known as such because your annual contribution is not deductible. If you are eligible, you can contribute up to $2,000. You can defer paying taxes on the income earned in your IRA until withdrawal.*

- *If you are eligible, you can make an annual contribution of up to $2,000 to a Roth IRA. The contribution is not deductible, but any income earned by the funds in your IRA are tax-exempt upon withdrawal if they meet certain requirements.*

- *Coverdell education savings accounts (formerly education IRAs) are used exclusively to pay qualified higher education expenses. If you are eligible, you can make a nondeductible contribution of up to $500 per year for each beneficiary. Withdrawals from an education savings account are tax-exempt if they met certain requirements.*

Eligibility requirements for all three kinds of IRAs and education savings accounts are described in this chapter. The 2001 Tax Act expanded contribution limits to traditional, Roth, and education savings accounts. Highlights of the 2001 Tax Act are as follows:

- *Increases both traditional and Roth IRA contribution limits up to $3,000 in 2002 through 2004; $4,000 in 2005 through 2007; and $5,000 in 2008.*

- *Implements IRA "catch-up" contributions—an increase for individuals age 50 and above of $500 in 2002 through 2005 and $1,000 in 2006 through 2008.*

The following chart summarizes the new contribution limits:

	Over 50	Other
2002	$3,500	$3,000
2003	$3,500	$3,000
2004	$3,500	$3,000
2005	$4,500	$4,000
2006	$5,000	$4,000
2007	$5,000	$4,000
2008	$6,000	$5,000

- *Increases the contribution limit to an education savings account from $500 to $2,000 beginning in 2002.*

This chapter also discusses retirement plans for the self-employed—simplified employee pensions (SEPs), (pages 274–275).

Important Changes for 2001

Coverdell education savings accounts (formerly education IRAs). Education IRAs have been renamed Coverdell education savings accounts. Coverdell education savings accounts are covered at the end of this chapter. They are also covered in Publication 970, *Tax Benefits for Higher Education.*

Modified AGI limit for traditional IRAs. For 2001, if you are covered by a retirement plan at work, your deduction for contributions to a traditional IRA will be reduced (phased out) if your modified adjusted gross income (AGI) is between:

- $53,000 and $63,000 for a married couple filing a joint return or a qualifying widow(er),
- $33,000 and $43,000 for a single individual or head of household, or
- $-0- and $10,000 for a married individual filing a separate return.

For all filing statuses other than married filing a separate return, the upper and lower limits of the phaseout range increased by $1,000. For more information, see *How Much Can I Deduct?* under *Traditional IRAs.*

Simplified rules for minimum required distributions. New rules which became effective in 2001 simplify how minimum required distributions are figured. For most people, the new simplified rules result in lower minimum required distributions. For more information, see *When Must I Withdraw IRA Assets? (Required Distributions)* in chapter 1 of Publication 590, *Individual Retirement Arrangements (IRAs).*

Important Changes for 2002

Increased traditional IRA contribution and deduction limit. The most that can be contributed to your traditional IRA for 2002 is the smaller of the following amounts:

- Your compensation that you must include in income for the year, or
- *$3,000* (up from $2,000).

If you are 50 years of age or older in 2002, the most that can be contributed to your traditional IRA for 2002 is the smaller of the following amounts:

- Your compensation that you must include in income for the year, or
- *$3,500* (up from $2,000).

For more information, see *How Much Can Be Contributed?* under *Traditional IRAs.*

Besides being able to contribute a larger amount in 2002, you may be able to deduct a larger amount. See *How Much Can I Deduct?* under *Traditional IRAs.*

Modified AGI limit for traditional IRA contributions increased. For 2002, if you are covered by a retirement plan at work, your deduction for contributions to a traditional IRA will be reduced (phased out) if your modified adjusted gross income (AGI) is between:

- $54,000 and $64,000 for a married couple or a qualifying widow(er) filing a joint return,
- $34,000 and $44,000 for a single individual or head of household, or
- $-0- and $10,000 for a married individual filing a separate return.

For all filing statuses other than married filing a separate return, the upper and lower limits of the phaseout range increased by $1,000. See *How Much Can I Deduct?* under *Traditional IRAs.*

Credit for IRA contributions. For tax years beginning after December 31, 2001, if you are an eligible individual, you may be able to claim a credit for a percentage of your qualified retirement savings contributions, such as contributions to your traditional or Roth IRA. To be eligible, you must be at least 18 years old as of the end of the year, and you cannot be a student or an individual for whom someone else claims a personal exemption. Also, your adjusted gross income (AGI) must be below a certain amount.

For more information, see Publication 553, *Highlights of 2001 Tax Changes.*

Rollovers from traditional IRAs into qualified plans. For distributions after December 31, 2001, you can roll over, tax free, a distribution from your IRA into a qualified plan. The part of the distribution that you can roll over is the part that would otherwise be taxable (includible in your income). Qualified plans may, but are not required to, accept such rollovers. Rules applicable to other rollovers, such as the 60-day time limit, apply. For more information, see *Rollovers* under *Traditional IRAs.*

Rollovers of distributions from employer plans. For distributions after December 31, 2001, you can rollover both the taxable and nontaxable part of a distribution from a qualified plan into a traditional IRA. If you have both deductible and nondeductible contributions in your IRA, you will have to keep track of your basis so you will be able to determine the taxable amount once distributions from the IRA begin.

For more information, see Publication 553, *Highlights of 2001 Tax Changes.*

Rollovers of deferred compensation plans of state and local governments (section 457 plans) into traditional IRAs. Before 2002, you could not roll over, tax free, an eligible rollover distribution from a governmental deferred compensation plan into a traditional IRA.

Beginning with distributions after December 31, 2001, if you participate in an eligible deferred compensation plan of a state or local government, you may be able to roll over part of your account tax free into an eligible retirement plan such as a traditional IRA. The most that you can roll over is the amount that would be taxed if the rollover were not an eligible rollover distribution. You cannot roll over any part of the distribution that would not be taxable. The rollover may be either direct or indirect.

For more information, see Publication 553, *Highlights of 2001 Tax Changes.*

Rollovers of traditional IRAs into deferred compensation plans of state and local governments (section 457 plans). Before 2002, you could not roll over tax free a distribution from a traditional IRA into a governmental deferred compensation plan.

Beginning with distributions after December 31, 2001, if you participate in an eligible deferred compensation plan of a state or local government, you may be able to roll over a distribution from your traditional IRA into a deferred compensation plan of a state or local government. Qualified plans may, but are not required to, accept such rollovers.

For more information, see Publication 553, *Highlights of 2001 Tax Changes.*

Rollovers of traditional IRAs into tax-sheltered annuities (section 403(b) plans). Before 2002, you could not roll over tax free a distribution from a traditional IRA into a tax-sheltered annuity.

Beginning with distributions after December 31, 2001, you may be able to roll over distributions tax free from a traditional IRA into a tax-sheltered annuity. You cannot roll over any amount that would not have been taxable.

Although a tax-sheltered annuity is allowed to accept such a rollover, it is not required to do so.

For more information, see Publication 553, *Highlights of 2001 Tax Changes.*

Participants born before 1936. If you were born before 1936, you may be able to use capital gain and averaging treatment on certain lump-sum distributions from qualified plans, but you will lose the opportunity to use capital gain or averaging treatment on distributions from a qualified plan if you roll over IRA contributions to that plan. You can retain such treatment if the rollover is from a conduit IRA. For more information on conduit IRAs, see *IRA as a holding account (conduit IRA) for rollovers to other eligible plans* in chapter 1 of Publication 590.

No rollovers of hardship distributions into IRAs. For distributions made after December 31, 2001, no hardship distribution can be rolled over into an IRA. For more information about what can be rolled over, see *Rollover From Employer's Plan Into an IRA* under *Traditional IRAs.*

Hardship exception to the 60-day rollover rule. Generally, a rollover is tax free only if you make the rollover contribution by the 60th day after the day you receive the distribution. Beginning with distributions after December 31, 2001, the IRS may waive the 60-day requirement where it would be against equity or good conscience not to do so.

For more information, see *Time Limit for Making a Rollover Contribution* under *Traditional IRAs.*

Increased Roth IRA contribution limit. If contributions on your behalf are made only to Roth IRAs, your contribution limit for 2002 generally is the lesser of:

- *$3,000* (up from $2,000), or
- Your taxable compensation.

If you are 50 years of age or older in 2002 and contributions on your behalf are made only to Roth IRAs, your contribution limit for 2002 generally is the lesser of:

- *$3,500* (up from $2,000), or
- Your taxable compensation.

However, if your modified AGI is above a certain amount, your contribution limit may be reduced. For more information, see *How Much Can Be Contributed?* under *Roth IRAs.*

Contributions to both traditional and Roth IRAs for same year. If contributions are made on your behalf to both a Roth IRA and a traditional IRA, your contribution limit for 2002 is the lesser of:

- *$3,000* (*$3,500* if you are 50 years of age or older in 2002) (up from $2,000) minus all contributions (other than employer contributions under a SEP or SIMPLE IRA plan) for the year to all IRAs other than Roth IRAs, or
- Your taxable compensation minus all contributions (other than employer contributions under a SEP or SIMPLE IRA plan) for the year to all IRAs other than Roth IRAs.

However, if your modified AGI is above a certain amount, your contribution limit may be reduced. For more information, see *How Much Can Be Contributed?* under *Roth IRAs.*

Important Reminders

IRA interest. Although interest earned from your IRA is generally not taxed in the year earned, it is ***not tax-exempt*** interest. ***Do not*** report this interest on your tax return as tax-exempt interest.

Form 8606. If you make nondeductible contributions to a traditional IRA and you do not file Form 8606, *Nondeductible IRAs and Coverdell ESAs,* with your tax return, you may have to pay a $50 penalty.

Spousal IRAs. In the case of a married couple filing a joint return, up to $2,000 for 2001 ($3,000 for 2002 or $3,500 for 2002 if 50 or older) can be contributed to IRAs (other than SIMPLE IRAs) on behalf of each spouse, even if one spouse has little or no compensation. See *Spousal IRA limit* under *How Much Can Be Contributed?* and under *Can I contribute to a Roth IRA for my spouse?* under *Roth IRAs,* later.

Caution. *Employer contributions under a SEP plan are not counted when figuring the limits just discussed. SEP plans are discussed in chapter 3 of Publication 590.*

Spouse covered by employer plan. If you are not covered by an employer retirement plan and you file a joint return, you may be able to deduct all of your contributions to a traditional IRA, even if your spouse is covered by a plan. See *How Much Can I Deduct?* under *Traditional IRAs.*

Distributions for higher education expenses. You can take distributions from your traditional IRA or Roth IRA for qualified higher education expenses without having to pay the 10% additional tax on early distributions. For more information, see Publication 590.

Distributions for first home. You can take distributions of up to $10,000 from your traditional or Roth IRA to buy, build, or rebuild a first home without having to pay the 10% additional tax on early distributions. For more information, see Publication 590.

Roth IRA. You cannot claim a deduction for any contributions to a Roth IRA. But, if you satisfy the requirements, all earnings are tax free and neither your nondeductible contributions nor any earnings on them are taxable when you withdraw them. See *Roth IRAs,* later.

TaxSaver

Retirement savings through IRAs. Wealth can be built up much faster in an IRA or other tax-deferred retirement plan than in your own investment program. Since you do not have to pay income tax as your earnings accumulate within the plan, your investments compound in value more quickly. A person in the 31% tax bracket, for example, could end up with 1.8 times more money after tax on a $2,000 deductible IRA contribution held for 20 years than if he or she did not make the contribution. If the person's **marginal tax rate** drops to 15% in retirement, he or she could have 2.2 times more money after tax.

Example

Note: This example uses federal tax rates in effect as of January 1, 2001, in order to simplify the calculations. Generally, lower federal tax rates are being phased in beginning July 1, 2001.)

If in 1986 you invested $2,000 in an IRA that earns 10% per year, it will be worth $9,283 in 2006 after all taxes are paid if you are in the 31% bracket. If in 2005 you retire and drop into the 15% tax bracket, your original $2,000 investment will be worth $11,437 after all taxes are paid.

However, if you do not have an IRA, your $2,000 is subject to tax immediately. If you are in the 31% bracket, you are left with only $1,380. Investing that $1,380 in 1986 in a non-IRA investment earning 10%, you will have only $5,241 in 2006 after taxes are paid if you remain in the 31% bracket.

TaxAlert

Note that your tax bracket may be as high as 39.1% in 2001 (lower federal tax rates are being phased in resulting in a maximum rate of 35% by 2006). Therefore, the savings resulting from an IRA may be even greater than indicated in the example.

An individual retirement arrangement (IRA) is a personal savings plan that offers you tax advantages to set aside money for your retirement.

This chapter discusses:

1) The rules for a *traditional IRA* (those that are not Roth or SIMPLE IRAs), and
2) The *Roth IRA,* which features nondeductible contributions and tax-free distributions.

> **Explanation.**
> For a discussion of Simplified Employee Pensions (SEPs) and Saving Investment Match Plan for Employees (SIMPLEs), see page 275 later in this chapter.

For more information on these plans and employees' SEP-IRAs and SIMPLE IRAs that are part of these plans, see Publication 590.

Useful Items

You may want to see:

Publication

☐ **590**   Individual Retirement Arrangements (IRAs)

Form (and Instructions)

☐ **5329**   Additional Taxes on Qualified Plans (including IRAs) and Other Tax-Favored Accounts
☐ **8606**   Nondeductible IRAs and Coverdell ESAs

> **TAXPLANNER**
>
> Self-employed persons and independent contractors often overlook the benefits available to them from establishing an IRA. The only requirement for contributing to an IRA is that you have not reached age 70½ (*note:* this does not apply to Roth IRAs) and have earned income, which includes income from your business, provided that your personal efforts create a major portion of the business income. Therefore, a self-employed person could establish both a Keogh plan and an IRA. For more information on retirement plans for the self-employed, see Chapter 11, *Retirement Plans, Pensions, and Annuities.*

> **TAXSAVER**
>
> You are a sole proprietor, and you hire your spouse or child to perform bona fide services, such as bookkeeping, as an employee. Assuming that the family member works in a genuine employment relationship, the salary paid is compensation for personal services and should be included in the family member's gross income. The family member's salary is a deductible expense to you. This gross income would entitle that family member to make a contribution to an IRA of up to $2,000.
>
> Your spouse's wages constitute wages subject to Social Security tax, so this strategy may work to your disadvantage.
>
> Be prepared to defend the genuine employment relationship of your spouse against an IRS attack.

Traditional IRAs

In this chapter the original IRA (sometimes called an ordinary or regular IRA) is referred to as a "traditional IRA." Two advantages of a traditional IRA are:

1) You may be able to deduct some or all of your contributions to it, depending on your circumstances, and,
2) Generally, amounts in your IRA, including earnings and gains, are not taxed until they are distributed.

What Is a Traditional IRA?

A traditional IRA is any IRA that is not a Roth IRA or a SIMPLE IRA.

Who Can Set Up a Traditional IRA?

You can set up and make contributions to a traditional IRA if:

1) You (or, if you file a joint return, your spouse) received taxable compensation during the year, and
2) You were not age 70 1/2 by the end of the year.

What is compensation? Compensation includes wages, salaries, tips, professional fees, bonuses, and other amounts you receive for providing personal services. The IRS treats as compensation any amount properly shown in box 1 *(Wages, tips, other compensation)* of Form W-2, *Wage and Tax Statement,* provided that amount is reduced by any amount properly shown in box 11 *(Nonqualified plans).* Scholarship and fellowship payments are compensation for this purpose only if shown in box 1 of Form W-2. Compensation also includes commissions and taxable alimony and separate maintenance payments.

Self-employment income. If you are self-employed (a sole proprietor or a partner), compensation is the net earnings from your trade or business (provided your personal services are a material income-producing factor) reduced by the total of:

1) The deduction for contributions made on your behalf to retirement plans, and
2) The deduction allowed for one-half of your self-employment taxes.

Compensation includes earnings from self-employment even if they are not subject to self-employment tax because of your religious beliefs. See Publication 533, *Self-Employment Tax,* for more information.

What is not compensation? Compensation does *not* include any of the following items.

- Earnings and profits from property, such as rental income, interest income, and dividend income.
- Pension or annuity income.
- Deferred compensation received (compensation payments postponed from a past year).
- Income from a partnership for which you do not provide services that are a material income-producing factor.
- Any amounts you exclude from income, such as foreign earned income and housing costs.

> **Explanation**
> For purposes of figuring out your contribution to your IRA, compensation includes sales commissions, the net income from your business, and partnership income that is subject to self-employment tax. Business and partnership income must be reduced by any contributions to a Keogh or SEP plan you make. Compensation does not include nontaxable amounts, deferred compensation, severance pay, or pension distributions. If you have multiple sources of self-employment income and/or partnership income subject to self-employment

tax, all gains and losses from these sources must be aggregated for purposes of computing compensation from self-employment. If the result is a gain, it is added to your wages, possibly permitting you to make a larger deductible contribution to your IRA. If the result of your self-employment activities is a loss, however, you need not account for it in determining your IRA contribution. Income earned outside the United States is compensation to the extent that it is taxable in the United States. Your foreign earned income must be adjusted for any foreign income exclusion. For more information, see Chapter 42, *U.S. Citizens Working Abroad: Tax Treatment of Foreign Earned Income.*

When and How Can a Traditional IRA Be Set Up?

You can set up a traditional IRA at any time. However, the time for making contributions for any year is limited. See *When Can Contributions Be Made,* later.

You can set up different kinds of IRAs with a variety of organizations. You can set up an IRA at a bank or other financial institution or with a mutual fund or life insurance company. You can also set up an IRA through your stockbroker. Any IRA must meet Internal Revenue Code requirements.

Kinds of traditional IRAs. Your traditional IRA can be an individual retirement account or annuity. It can be part of either a simplified employee pension (SEP) or an employer or employee association trust account.

Explanation
The basic difference between the two types of IRA accounts—Individual Retirement Arrangements and Individual Retirement Annuities—lies in the type of investment and the method of funding it. The Individual Retirement Arrangement is generally a type of trust with varied investments, such as stocks, bonds, savings accounts, certificates of deposit, credit union accounts, common trust funds, and **real estate**, among other things. An Individual Retirement Annuity is an investment in an insurance contract.

TAXPLANNER
Self-directed IRAs. If you want to actively manage your IRA investments, you may consider setting up a self-directed IRA. To do so, without having to obtain preapproval from the IRS, you may use Form 5305, a model trust form, and Form 5305-A, a model custodial account agreement. However, keep in mind that even if you use these model forms, you still will have to find a financial institution to administer your account.

TAXALERT
In deciding whether or not to create a self-directed IRA, keep in mind that an investment in the following collectibles is disallowed:

- Artworks
- Coins (unless state issued, U.S. minted gold, and silver coins of 1 ounce or less)
- Stamps
- Gems
- Antiques
- Rugs
- Alcoholic beverages
- Metals

How Much Can Be Contributed?

There are limits and other rules that affect the amount that can be contributed and the amount you can deduct. These limits and other rules are explained below.

Community property laws. Except as discussed later under *Spousal IRA limit,* each spouse figures his or her limit separately, using his or her own compensation. This is the rule even in states with community property laws.

Brokers' commissions. Brokers' commissions paid in connection with your traditional IRA are subject to the contribution limit.

Trustees' fees. Trustees' administrative fees are not subject to the contribution limit.

Caution. *Contributions to your traditional IRAs reduce the limit for contributions to Roth IRAs. (See Roth IRAs, later.)*

General limit. The most that can be contributed to your traditional IRA is *the smaller of* the following amounts:

1) Your compensation (defined earlier) that you must include in income for the year, or
2) $2,000 for 2001 ($3,000 for 2002 or $3,500 for 2002 if you are 50 or older).

This is the most that can be contributed regardless of whether the contributions are to one or more traditional IRAs or whether all or part of the contributions are nondeductible. (See *Nondeductible Contributions,* later.)

Example 1. Betty, who is single, earned $24,000 in 2001. Her IRA contributions for 2001 are limited to $2,000.

Example 2. John, a college student working part time, earned $1,500 in 2001. His IRA contributions for 2001 are limited to $1,500, the amount of his compensation.

Spousal IRA limit. If you file a joint return and your taxable compensation is less than that of your spouse, the most that can be contributed for the year to your IRA is the smaller of the following amounts:

1) $2,000 for 2001 ($3,000 for 2002 or $3,500 for 2002 if you are 50 or older), or
2) The total compensation includible in the gross income of both you and your spouse for the year, reduced by the following two amounts.
   a) Your spouse's contribution for the year to a traditional IRA.
   b) Any contribution for the year to a Roth IRA on behalf of your spouse.

This means that the total combined contributions that can be made for the year to your IRA and your spouse's IRA can be as much as $4,000 for 2001 ($6,000 for 2002, or $6,500 for 2002 if only one of you is 50 or older, or $7,000 for 2002 if both of you are 50 or older).

Example 1
A wife holds a job, and her husband does not. The two spouses file a joint return. They may contribute up to $4,000 to their respective IRAs. The contribution can be split between the husband's and wife's accounts in any way they wish, as long as no more than $2,000 is allocated to either account.

Example 2
The working wife died during the year after earning over $4,000. The nonworking husband is allowed to put $2,000 in his spousal IRA for the year, as long as he files a joint return with his deceased wife. A payment cannot be made to the decedent's IRA for the year of death.

Community property laws should be disregarded when you are determining if you are eligible to make payments to an IRA for your nonworking spouse. Thus, your nonworking spouse is not considered to have earned half your income.

When Can Contributions Be Made?

As soon as you set up your traditional IRA, contributions can be made to it through your chosen sponsor (trustee or other administrator). Contributions to a traditional IRA must be in the form of money (cash, check, or money order). Property cannot be contributed.

Contributions must be made by due date. Contributions can be made to your traditional IRA for a year at any time during the year or by the due date for filing your return for that year, *not* including extensions. For most people, this means that contributions for 2001 must be made by April 15, 2002.

Age 70 1/2 rule. Contributions cannot be made to your traditional IRA for the year in which you reach age 70 1/2 or for any later year.

Designating year for which contribution is made. If an amount is contributed to your traditional IRA between January 1 and April 15, you should tell the sponsor to which year (the current year or the previous year) the contribution is for. If you do not tell the sponsor which year it is for, the sponsor can assume, and report to the IRS, that the contribution is for the current year (the year the sponsor received it).

Filing before a contribution is made. You can file your return claiming a traditional IRA contribution before the contribution is actually made. However, the contribution must be made by the due date of your return, *not* including extensions.

> ### TaxPlanner
>
> You can make your 2001 IRA contribution as late as April 15, 2002. However, funding your IRA as early as possible maximizes your ending balance. For example, assume you have 20 years until retirement, make the maximum $4,000 contribution for you and your spouse, and the account earns 8%. If you make your contributions at year-end, your ending IRA balance will be $183,048. If you make your contributions at the beginning of the year, your ending account balance will be $197,692, an increase of $14,644.

> ### TaxPlanner
>
> If you do not have the cash available to make your 2001 IRA contribution by April 15, 2002, the deadline for 2001 contributions, you could "borrow" money by distributing part or all of an existing IRA account to yourself and use the money to make your 2001 IRA contribution to a different account. You would have to complete the rollover within 60 days of the withdrawal, meaning that you would have to come up with the funds to complete the rollover or possibly be subject to the 10% penalty for early withdrawal. *Note:* You may only roll over an IRA fund to a new IRA once in a 1-year period.
>
> Alternatively, if you want the $2,000-per-year IRA deduction but are not particularly concerned about accumulating income tax-free in your IRA, you can take advantage of the 60-day rollover period so that you have some extra spending money for 2 months.
>
> For more information about rollovers, see the discussion later in this chapter.

Contributions not required. You do not have to contribute to your traditional IRA for every tax year, even if you can.

How Much Can I Deduct?

Generally, you can deduct the lesser of:

- The contributions to your traditional IRA for the year, or
- The general limit (or the spousal IRA limit, if it applies).

However, if you or your spouse was covered by an employer retirement plan, you may not be able to deduct this amount. See *Limit if Covered by Employer Plan,* later.

Trustees' fees. Trustees' administrative fees that are billed separately and paid in connection with your traditional IRA are not deductible as IRA contributions. However, they may be deductible as a miscellaneous itemized deduction on Schedule A (Form 1040). See chapter 30.

Brokers' commissions. Brokers' commissions are part of your IRA contribution and, as such, are deductible subject to the limits.

Full deduction. If neither you nor your spouse was covered for any part of the year by an employer retirement plan, you can take a deduction for total contributions to one or more traditional IRAs of up to the lesser of:

1) $2,000 for 2001 ($3,000 for 2002 or $3,500 for 2002 if you are 50 or older), or
2) 100% of your compensation.

This limit is reduced by any contributions made to a 501(c)(18) plan on your behalf.

Spousal IRA. In the case of a married couple with unequal compensation who file a joint return, the deduction for contributions to the traditional IRA of the spouse with less compensation is limited to the lesser of:

1) $2,000 for 2001 ($3,000 for 2002 or $3,500 for 2002 if 50 or older), or
2) The total compensation includible in the gross income of both spouses for the year reduced by the following two amounts.
   a) The IRA deduction for the year of the spouse with the greater compensation.
   b) Any contributions for the year to a Roth IRA on behalf of the spouse with more compensation.

This limit is reduced by any contributions to a 501(c)(18) plan on behalf of the spouse with less compensation.

Note. If you were divorced or legally separated (and did not remarry) before the end of the year, you cannot deduct any contributions to your spouse's IRA. After a divorce or legal separation, you can deduct only contributions to your own IRA and your deductions are subject to the rules for single individuals.

Covered by an employer retirement plan. If you or your spouse was covered by an employer retirement plan at any time during the year for which contributions were made, your deduction may be further limited. This is discussed later under *Limit If Covered by Employer Plan.* Limits on the amount you can deduct do not affect the amount that can be contributed. See *Nondeductible Contributions,* later.

Are You Covered by an Employer Plan?

The Form W-2 you receive from your employer has a box used to indicate whether you were covered for the year. The "Retirement plan" box should be checked if you were covered.

Reservists and volunteer firefighters should also see *Situations in Which You Are Not Covered,* later.

If you are not certain whether you were covered by your employer's retirement plan, you should ask your employer.

> ### TaxPlanner
>
> We recommend that you check your Form W-2 to ensure that the coverage status is accurate. The rules used to determine if you are covered by an employer's plan will depend on the type of plan maintained by your employer. If you are not sure what type of plan your employer maintains, you should ask your employer. The information may also be found in the Summary Plan Description, which can be obtained from your employer. Generally, you will be considered covered if:

1. Your employer maintains a defined benefit pension plan and you meet the plan's eligibility requirements.
2. Your employer maintains a defined contribution money purchase plan, you meet the plan's eligibility requirements, and your employer is required to make a contribution to your account.
3. Your employer maintains a profit-sharing plan and makes a contribution, a forfeiture is allocated to your account, or you make any contribution with respect to a plan year ending with or within your tax year.

Example
Assume that you first became eligible to participate in your employer's profit-sharing plan on July 1, 2001. Your employer makes a contribution for the plan year ending on June 30, 2002. You will not be considered an active participant until 2002, since that is the first tax year during which an allocation was made to your account.

4. Your employer maintains a 401(k), a SEP, or a 403(b) plan, and, if for the year ending with or within your tax year, you elect to defer any compensation.

Federal judges. For purposes of the IRA deduction, federal judges are covered by an employer retirement plan.

For Which Year(s) Are You Covered?
Special rules apply to determine the tax years for which you are covered by an employer plan. These rules differ depending on whether the plan is a defined contribution plan or a defined benefit plan.
Tax year. Your tax year is the annual accounting period you use to keep records and report income and expenses on your income tax return. For most people, the tax year is the calendar year.
Defined contribution plan. Generally, you are covered by a defined contribution plan for a tax year if amounts are contributed or allocated to your account for the plan year that ends with or within that tax year.

A defined contribution plan is a plan that provides for a separate account for each person covered by the plan. Types of defined contribution plans include profit-sharing plans, stock bonus plans, and money purchase pension plans.
Defined benefit plan. If you are eligible to participate in your employer's defined benefit plan for the plan year that ends within your tax year, you are covered by the plan. This rule applies even if you:

- Declined to participate in the plan,
- Did not make a required contribution, or
- Did not perform the minimum service required to accrue a benefit for the year.

A defined benefit plan is any plan that is not a defined contribution plan. Types of defined benefit plans include pension plans and annuity plans.
No vested interest. If you accrue a benefit for a plan year, you are covered by that plan even if you have no vested interest in (legal right to) the account or the accrual.

Situations in Which You Are Not Covered
Unless you are covered under another employer plan, you are not covered by an employer plan if you are in one of the situations described below.
Social security or railroad retirement. Coverage under social security or railroad retirement is not coverage under an employer retirement plan.
Benefits from a previous employer's plan. If you receive retirement benefits from a previous employer's plan, you are not covered by that plan.

Reservists. If the only reason you participate in a plan is because you are a member of a reserve unit of the armed forces, you may not be covered by the plan. You are not covered by the plan if *both* of the following conditions are met.

1) The plan you participate in is established for its employees by:
   a) The United States,
   b) A state or political subdivision of a state, or
   c) An instrumentality of either (a) or (b) above.
2) You did not serve more than 90 days on active duty during the year (not counting duty for training).

Volunteer firefighters. If the only reason you participate in a plan is because you are a volunteer firefighter, you may not be covered by the plan. You are not covered by the plan if *both* of the following conditions are met.

1) The plan you participate in is established for its employees by:
   a) The United States,
   b) A state or political subdivision of a state, or
   c) An instrumentality of either (a) or (b) above.
2) Your accrued retirement benefits at the beginning of the year will not provide more than $1,800 per year at retirement.

Limit if Covered by Employer Plan
If either you or your spouse was covered by an employer retirement plan, you may be entitled to only a partial (reduced) deduction or no deduction at all, depending on your income and your filing status.

Your deduction begins to decrease (phase out) when your income rises above a certain amount and is eliminated altogether when it reaches a higher amount. These amounts vary depending on your filing status.

To determine if your deduction is subject to phaseout, you must determine your modified adjusted gross income (AGI) and your filing status. Then use *Table 18-1* or *18-2* to determine if the phaseout applies.
Social security recipients. Instead of using *Table 18-1* or *18-2*, use the worksheets in *Appendix B* of Publication 590 if, for the year, *all* of the following apply.

- You received social security benefits.
- You received taxable compensation.
- Contributions were made to your traditional IRA.
- You or your spouse was covered by an employer retirement plan.

Use those worksheets to figure your IRA deduction, your nondeductible contribution, and the taxable portion, if any, of your social security benefits.
Deduction phaseout. If you were covered by an employer retirement plan, your IRA deduction may be reduced or eliminated depending on your filing status and modified AGI as shown in *Table 18-1*.
Tip. *For 2002, if you are covered by a retirement plan at work, your IRA deduction will not be reduced (phased out) unless your modified AGI is between:*

- *$34,000 and $44,000 for a single individual (or head of household),*
- *$54,000 and $64,000 for a married couple (or a qualifying widow(er)) filing a joint return, or*
- *$-0- (no increase) and $10,000 for a married individual filing a separate return.*

For all filing statuses other than married filing a separate return, the upper and lower limits of the phaseout range will increase by $1,000.

If your spouse is covered. If you are not covered by an employer retirement plan, but your spouse is, and you did not receive any social security benefits, your IRA deduction is reduced or eliminated entirely depending on your filing status and modified AGI as shown in *Table 18-2*.
Filing status. Your filing status depends primarily on your marital status. For this purpose, you need to know if your filing status is single or head of household, married filing jointly or qualifying widow(er), or married filing separately. If you need more information on filing status, see chapter 2.

Table 18–1. Effect of Modified AGI[1] on Deduction if Covered by Retirement Plan at Work

If you are covered by a retirement plan at work, use this table to determine if your modified AGI affects the amount of your deduction.

IF your filing status is ...	AND your modified adjusted gross income (modified AGI) is ...	THEN you can take ...
Single or **Head of Household**	Less than $33,000	A full deduction
	At least $33,000 but less than $43,000	A partial deduction
	$43,000 or more	No deduction
Married Filing Jointly or **Qualifying Widow(er)**	Less than $53,000	A full deduction
	At least $53,000 but less than $63,000	A partial deduction
	$63,000 or more	No deduction
Married Filing Separately[2]	Less than $10,000	A partial deduction
	$10,000 or more	No deduction

[1] Modified AGI (adjusted gross income). See *Modified adjusted gross income.*
[2] If you did not live with your spouse at any time during the year, your filing status is considered Single for this purpose (therefore, your IRA deduction is determined under the "Single" column).

Table 18–2. Effect of Modified AGI[1] on Deduction if NOT Covered by Retirement Plan at Work

If you are not covered by a retirement plan at work, use this table to determine if your modified AGI affects the amount of your deduction.

IF your filing status is ...	AND your modified adjusted gross income (modified AGI) is ...	THEN you can take ...
Single, Head of Household, or **Qualifying Widow(er)**	Any amount	A full deduction
Married Filing Jointly or **Separately** with a spouse who *is not* covered by a plan at work	Any amount	A full deduction
Married Filing Jointly with a spouse who *is* covered by a plan at work	Less than $150,000	A full deduction
	At least $150,000 but less than $160,000	A partial deduction
	$160,000 or more	No deduction
Married Filing Separately with a spouse who *is* covered by a plan at work[2]	Less than $10,000	A partial deduction
	$10,000 or more	No deduction

[1] Modified AGI (adjusted gross income). See *Modified adjusted gross income.*
[2] You are entitled to the full deduction if you did not live with your spouse at any time during the year.

Lived apart from spouse. If you did not live with your spouse at any time during the year and you file a separate return, your filing status, for this purpose, is single.

Example

Joe and Mary are both employed. During 2001, Mary's compensation was $43,000, and she was not covered by her employer's retirement plan. Joe's compensation was $20,000, and he was covered by his employer's plan. If Joe and Mary file a joint return, Mary can claim a deduction for an IRA contribution since she is not covered by her employer's retirement plan. However, Joe cannot claim an IRA contribution deduction. If Joe and Mary didn't live together at all during the year and file separate returns, Joe can deduct an IRA contribution of $2,000 (subject to the adjusted gross income limitation), while Mary can deduct $2,000, since she is not covered by her employer's plan.

If they lived together for part of the year and file separate returns, neither can make a deductible IRA contribution.

Modified adjusted gross income (AGI). How you figure your modified AGI depends on whether you are filing Form 1040 or Form 1040A. If you made contributions to your IRA for 2001 and received a distribution from your IRA in 2001, see Publication 590.

Caution. *Do not assume that your modified AGI is the same as your compensation. Your modified AGI may include income in addition to your compensation (discussed earlier), such as interest, dividends, and income from IRA distributions.*

Form 1040. If you file Form 1040, refigure the amount on page 1 "adjusted gross income" line without taking into account any of the following amounts.

- IRA deduction.
- Student loan interest deduction.
- Foreign earned income exclusion.
- Foreign housing exclusion or deduction.
- Exclusion of qualified savings bond interest shown on Form 8815, *Exclusion of Interest From Series EE and I U.S. Savings Bonds Issued After 1989 (For Filers With Qualified Higher Education Expenses).*
- Exclusion of employer-paid adoption expenses shown on Form 8839, *Qualified Adoption Expenses.*

This is your modified AGI.

Form 1040A. If you file Form 1040A, refigure the amount on page 1 "adjusted gross income" line without taking into account any of the following amounts.

- IRA deduction.
- Student loan interest deduction.
- Exclusion of qualified savings bond interest shown on Form 8815.
- Exclusion of employer-paid adoption expenses shown on Form 8839.

This is your modified AGI.

Both contributions for 2001 and distributions in 2001. If **all three** of the following occurred, any IRA distributions you received in 2001 may be partly tax free and partly taxable.

1) You received distributions in 2001 from one or more traditional IRAs.
2) You made contributions to a traditional IRA for 2001.
3) Some of those contributions may be nondeductible contributions depending on whether your IRA deduction for 2001 is reduced.

If all three of the above occurred, you must figure the taxable part of the traditional IRA distribution before you can figure your modified AGI. To do this, you can use *Worksheet 1-1, Figuring the Taxable Part of Your IRA Distribution* in Publication 590.

If at least one of the above did *not* occur, figure your modified AGI using *Worksheet 18-1* in this chapter.

How to figure your reduced IRA deduction. You can figure your reduced IRA deduction *for either* Form 1040 or Form 1040A by using the worksheets in chapter 1 of Publication 590. Also, the instructions for Form 1040 and Form 1040A include similar worksheets that you may be able to use instead.

Reporting Deductible Contributions

If you file Form 1040, enter your IRA deduction on line 23 of that form. If you file Form 1040A, enter your IRA deduction on line 16. You cannot deduct IRA contributions on Form 1040EZ.

Nondeductible Contributions

Although your deduction for IRA contributions may be reduced or eliminated, contributions can be made to your IRA up to the general limit ($2,000 for 2001 ($3,000 for 2002 or $3,500 for 2002 if 50 or older) or 100% of compensation, whichever is less) or the spousal IRA limit (if it applies). The difference between your total permitted contributions and your IRA deduction, if any, is your nondeductible contribution.

Example. Martin Jones is single. In 2001, he was covered by a retirement plan at work. His salary was $52,312. His modified AGI was $55,000. Martin made a $2,000 IRA contribution for 2001. Because he was covered by a retirement plan and his modified AGI was over $43,000, he cannot deduct his $2,000 IRA contribution. However, he can choose to designate this contribution as a nondeductible contribution, as explained next.

> **Explanation**
> The chief advantage of nondeductible IRA contributions is that since the income compounds on a tax-deferred basis, the ending balance will be substantially larger under an IRA. In deciding whether to make nondeductible contributions, you should compare the IRA's rate of return against other investments, such as tax-exempt municipal bonds and annuity contracts, and after-tax rates of return on taxable investments. You must also consider the tax effect when you begin taking distributions. The taxation of IRA distributions is discussed below.

Form 8606. To designate contributions as nondeductible, you must file Form 8606.

You do not have to designate a contribution as nondeductible until you file your tax return. When you file, you can even designate otherwise deductible contributions as nondeductible.

You must file Form 8606 to report nondeductible contributions even if you do not have to file a tax return for the year.

Failure to report nondeductible contributions. If you do not report nondeductible contributions, all of the contributions to your traditional IRA will be treated as deductible. All distributions from your IRA will be taxed unless you can show, with satisfactory evidence, that nondeductible contributions were made.

Penalty for overstatement. If you overstate the amount of nondeductible contributions on your Form 8606 for any tax year, you must pay a penalty of $100 for each overstatement, unless it was due to reasonable cause.

Penalty for failure to file Form 8606. You will have to pay a $50 penalty if you do not file a required Form 8606, unless you can prove that the failure was due to reasonable cause.

> **Explanation**
> The law subjecting taxpayers to a $50 fine for failure to file Form 8606 was enacted retroactive to 1987. If you should have filed Form 8606 for a prior tax year but failed to do so, you should consider amending your return. See Chapter 1, *Filing Information*, for additional details regarding amending your return.

Worksheet 18–1. Figuring Your Modified AGI

Use this worksheet to figure your modified adjusted gross income for traditional IRA purposes.

1.	Enter your adjusted gross income (AGI) shown on line 19, Form 1040A, or line 33, Form 1040 figured without taking into account line 16, Form 1040A, or line 23, Form 1040 . . . . **1.**	
2.	Enter any *Student loan interest deduction* from line 17, Form 1040A, or line 24, Form 1040 . . . . **2.**	
3.	Enter any *Foreign earned income exclusion* from line 18, Form 2555–EZ, or line 40, Form 2555 . . . . **3.**	
4.	Enter any *Foreign housing exclusion* from line 34, Form 2555, or *Foreign housing deduction* from line 48, Form 2555 . . . . **4.**	
5.	Enter any *Excluded qualified savings bond interest* shown on line 3, Schedule 1, Form 1040A, or line 3, Schedule B, Form 1040 (from line 14, Form 8815) . . . . **5.**	
6.	Enter any *Exclusion of employer-paid adoption expenses* shown on line 26, Form 8839 . . . . **6.**	
7.	Add lines 1 through 6. This is your **Modified AGI** for traditional IRA purposes . . . . **7.**	

Tax on earnings on nondeductible contributions. As long as contributions are within the contribution limits, none of the earnings or gains on those contributions (deductible or nondeductible) will be taxed until they are distributed. See *When Can I Withdraw or Use IRA Assets,* later.

Cost basis. You will have a cost basis in your IRA if there are nondeductible contributions. Your cost basis is the sum of the nondeductible contributions to your IRA minus any withdrawals or distributions of nondeductible contributions.

Inherited IRAs

If you inherit a traditional IRA, that IRA becomes subject to special rules.

If you inherit a traditional IRA from your deceased spouse, you can choose to treat it as your own by making contributions (including rollover contributions) to it.

If you inherit a traditional IRA from anyone other than your deceased spouse, you cannot treat the inherited IRA as your own. This means that contributions (including rollover contributions) cannot be made to the IRA and you cannot roll over any amounts out of the inherited IRA.

If you inherit a traditional IRA from your deceased spouse, you can generally roll it over into another traditional IRA established for you or you can choose to treat the inherited IRA as your own.

For more information, see the discussion of inherited IRAs under *Rollover From One IRA Into Another,* later.

Can I Move Retirement Plan Assets?

Traditional IRA rules permit you to transfer, tax free, assets (money or property) from other retirement plans (including traditional IRAs) to a traditional IRA. The rules permit the following kinds of transfers.

- Transfers from one trustee to another.
- Rollovers.
- Transfers incident to a divorce.

Transfers to Roth IRAs. Under certain conditions, you can move assets from a traditional IRA to a Roth IRA. See *Can I Move Amounts Into a Roth IRA?* under *Roth IRAs,* later.

Trustee-to-Trustee Transfer

A transfer of funds in your traditional IRA from one trustee directly to another, either at your request or at the trustee's request, is ***not a rollover.*** Because there is no distribution to you, the transfer is tax free. Because it is not a rollover, it is not affected by the 1-year waiting period required between rollovers, discussed later under *Rollover From One IRA Into Another.* For information about direct transfers to IRAs from retirement plans other than IRAs, see Publication 590.

Rollovers

Generally, a rollover is a tax-free distribution to you of cash or other assets from one retirement plan that you contribute (roll over) to another retirement plan. The contribution to the second retirement plan is called a "rollover contribution."

> **Explanation**
> When you receive a property distribution (e.g., shares of stock) from your IRA or a qualified employer plan, you may roll over the property received into an IRA. You are also permitted to sell the property and roll over the sale of the proceeds into an IRA. You may *not* retain the property distribution and roll over the property's cash equivalent.

Note. The amount you roll over tax free is generally taxable when the new plan distributes that amount to you or your beneficiary.

Kinds of rollovers to an IRA. There are two kinds of rollover contributions to a traditional IRA.

1) You put amounts you receive from one traditional IRA into the same or another traditional IRA.
2) You put amounts you receive from an employer's qualified retirement plan for its employees into a traditional IRA.

Distributions after December 31, 2001, can be rolled over into a traditional IRA from:

1) A deferred compensation plan of a state or local government (section 457 plan), or
2) A tax-sheltered annuity (section 403(b)).

For more information, see Publication 553, *Highlights of 2001 Tax Changes.*

Treatment of rollovers. You cannot deduct a rollover contribution, but you must report the rollover distribution on your tax return as discussed later under *Reporting rollovers from IRAs* and under *Reporting rollovers from employer plans.*

Kinds of rollovers from an IRA. For distributions after December 31, 2001, you can roll over, tax free, a distribution from your IRA into a qualified plan, including a deferred compensation plan of a state or local government (section 457 plan) and a tax-sheltered annuity (section 403(b) plan). The part of the distribution that you can roll over is the part that would otherwise be taxable (includible in your income). Qualified plans may, but are not required to, accept such rollovers. Rules applicable to other rollovers, such as the 60-day time limit, apply.

Time limit for making a rollover contribution. You, generally, must make the rollover contribution by the 60th day after the day you receive the distribution from your traditional IRA or your employer's plan.

For distributions made after December 31, 2001, the IRS may waive the 60-day requirement where the failure to do so would be against equity or good conscience, such as a casualty, disaster, or other event beyond your reasonable control.

Extension of rollover period. If an amount distributed to you from a traditional IRA or a qualified employer retirement plan is a frozen deposit at any time during the 60-day period allowed for a rollover, special rules extend the rollover period. For more information, get Publication 590.

Rollover From One IRA Into Another

You can withdraw, tax free, all or part of the assets from one traditional IRA if you reinvest them within 60 days in the same or another traditional IRA. Because this is a rollover, you cannot deduct the amount that you reinvest in an IRA.

Waiting period between rollovers. If you make a tax-free rollover of any part of a distribution from a traditional IRA, you cannot, within a 1-year period, make a tax-free rollover of any later distribution from that same IRA. You also cannot make a tax-free rollover of any amount distributed, within the same 1-year period, from the IRA into which you made the tax-free rollover.

The 1-year period begins on the date you receive the IRA distribution, not on the date you roll it over into an IRA.

Example. If you have two traditional IRAs, IRA-1 and IRA-2, and you make a tax-free rollover of a distribution from IRA-1 into a new traditional IRA (IRA-3), you can also make a tax-free rollover of a distribution from IRA-2 into IRA-3 (or into any other traditional IRA) within 1 year of the distribution from IRA-1. These can both be tax-free rollovers because you have not received more than one distribution from either IRA within 1 year. However, you cannot, within the 1-year period, make a tax-free rollover of any distribution from IRA-3 into another traditional IRA.

Exception. There is an exception to the rule that amounts rolled over tax free into an IRA cannot be rolled over tax free again within the

1-year period beginning on the date of the original distribution. The exception applies to a distribution which meets **all three** of the following requirements.

1) It is made from a failed financial institution by the Federal Deposit Insurance Corporation (FDIC) as receiver for the institution.
2) It was **not** initiated by either the custodial institution or the depositor.
3) It was made because:
   a) The custodial institution is insolvent, and
   b) The receiver is unable to find a buyer for the institution.

Partial rollovers. If you withdraw assets from a traditional IRA, you can roll over part of the withdrawal tax free and keep the rest of it. The amount you keep will generally be taxable (except for the part that is a return of nondeductible contributions) and may be subject to the 10% additional tax on early distributions, discussed later under *Early Distributions.*

Required distributions. Amounts that must be distributed during a particular year under the required distribution rules (discussed later) *are not eligible for rollover* treatment.

Inherited IRAs. If you inherit a traditional IRA from your spouse, you generally can roll it over into a traditional IRA established for you, or you can choose to make the inherited IRA your own.

For distributions after December 31, 2001, your rollover options increase. You may still roll over your spouse's IRA into your traditional IRA, but to the extent a distribution is taxable, you can roll it over into your qualified plan, your qualified employee annuity (section 403(a) annuity), your tax-sheltered annuity (section 403(b) annuity), or your deferred compensation plan of your state or local government (section 457 plan).

Not inherited from spouse. If you inherit a traditional IRA from someone other than your spouse, you cannot roll it over or allow it to receive a rollover contribution. You must withdraw the IRA assets within a certain period. For more information, see Publication 590.

Reporting rollovers from IRAs. Report any rollover from one traditional IRA to the same or another traditional IRA on lines 15a and 15b, Form 1040 or lines 11a and 11b, Form 1040A.

Enter the total amount of the distribution on line 15a, Form 1040 or line 11a, Form 1040A. If the total amount on line 15a, Form 1040 or line 11a, Form 1040A was rolled over, enter zero on line 15b, Form 1040 or line 11b, Form 1040A. Otherwise, enter the taxable portion of the part that was not rolled over on line 15b, Form 1040 or line 11b, Form 1040A.

Rollover From Employer's Plan Into an IRA

If you receive an *eligible rollover distribution* from your (or your deceased spouse's) employer's qualified pension, profit-sharing or stock bonus plan, annuity plan, or tax-sheltered annuity plan (403(b) plan), you can roll over all or part of it into a traditional IRA.

For distributions made after December 31, 2001, if you receive an eligible rollover distribution from your (or your deceased spouse's) governmental deferred compensation plan (section 457 plan), you can roll over all or part of it into a traditional IRA.

TaxAlert

Income tax withholding may apply to distributions made from qualified employer plans. Withholding at a rate of 20% is required on a distribution unless it is transferred directly from your employer to an IRA trustee or another employer plan.

The withholding rules do *not* apply to distributions from IRAs [or Simplified Employee Pensions (SEPs), discussed later]. However, if you wish to roll over a qualified plan distribution to an IRA, be sure to transfer the amount directly from your employer to an IRA trustee or another employer plan. Otherwise, 20% of the distribution will be withheld

---

while *100%* of the distribution must be rolled over within 60 days. If you don't have the money to cover the 20% shortage, income taxes (and possibly a 10% penalty) will be due on the amount not rolled over.

For further information, see Chapter 11, *Retirement Plans, Pensions, and Annuities.*

Eligible rollover distribution. Generally, an eligible rollover distribution is the taxable part of any distribution of all or part of the balance to your credit in a qualified retirement plan *except:*

1) A minimum required distribution,
2) Hardship distributions from 401(k) plans and certain 403(b) plans, or
3) Any of a series of substantially equal periodic distributions paid at least once a year over:
   a) Your lifetime or life expectancy,
   b) The lifetimes or life expectancies of you and your beneficiary, or
   c) A period of 10 years or more.

The taxable parts of most other distributions are eligible rollover distributions. See Publication 575, *Pension and Annuity Income,* for additional exceptions.

For distributions made after December 31, 2001, no hardship distribution is an eligible rollover distribution.

Maximum rollover. The most that you can roll over is the taxable part of any eligible rollover distribution (defined earlier). All of the distribution you receive generally will be taxable unless you have made nondeductible employee contributions to the plan.

Explanation

You may withdraw the balance in your IRA and reinvest it in another IRA with no tax consequences if the money is reinvested within 60 days after the funds are distributed. This type of rollover may be done only once in a 1-year period. This rule applies to each separate IRA you own.

Example

You have two or more IRAs. You can roll over a single distribution from each or all of them to a new IRA or to another existing IRA within a 1-year period.

TaxPlanner

If you transfer funds directly between trustees of your IRA and you never actually control or use the account assets, you may transfer your account as often as you like.

All or part of a **lump-sum distribution** from a qualified employer benefit plan may be transferred to an IRA. You may effect a partial rollover—and be taxed at **ordinary income** rates—only on the portion of the money not reinvested within 60 days. This portion is not eligible for any special tax treatment, which it might have been had the entire amount in your employer benefit plan been reported as current income. As mentioned earlier, withholding at a rate of 20% is required on a qualified employer plan distribution unless it is transferred directly from your employer to the trustee of an IRA.

TaxAlert

A partial distribution from a qualified plan is eligible for rollover treatment as long as it is *not*:

1. A required minimum distribution (e.g., for individuals who have attained age 70½); or

2. A distribution that is part of a series of substantially equal payments that are received at least annually over life, life expectancy, or a period of at least 10 years.

For more details, see Chapter 11, *Retirement Plans, Pensions, and Annuities.*

TaxPlanner

Not all distributions from qualified employer benefit plans may be rolled over into an IRA. IRAs are specifically prohibited from investing in life insurance contracts. Therefore, if your employer plan distributes to you both cash and a life insurance policy, the value of the life insurance policy (except for your contributions) is currently taxable to you. If this is the case, you should consider rolling over the life insurance contract into another qualified pension, profit-sharing, or stock bonus plan that allows investments in life insurance contracts.

TaxPlanner

According to the IRS, it is your responsibility to make sure that the rollover is completed within 60 days. The IRS issued a ruling that a taxpayer flunked the 60-day test when her broker failed to perform her specific and timely instructions. The taxpayer did not discover the problem until after the 60-day period had expired. Nevertheless, the IRS ruled that there is no leeway under the existing law.

The IRS has consistently maintained this position, but the Tax Court has ruled that a rollover will not fail the 60-day requirement as a result of a bookkeeping error made by an IRA trustee, as long as the taxpayer established and transferred assets to an IRA within the 60-day period.

A court has held that a tax-free rollover can be made only if the employer's plan and trust are tax-exempt when the distribution is made. In this case, the IRS retroactively revoked the tax-exempt status of the trust. This made the distribution ineligible for a rollover.

Reversing a long-standing position, the IRS now argues that once you have made a rollover, you cannot change your mind and report the distribution as taxable income.

You may roll over a lump-sum distribution from a former spouse's IRA or employee plan that was transferred to you by a divorce decree or written agreement incident to the divorce.

Reporting rollovers from employer plans. To report a rollover from an employer retirement plan to a traditional IRA, use lines 16a and 16b, Form 1040, or lines 12a and 12b, Form 1040A. Do not use lines 15a or 15b, Form 1040, or lines 11a or 11b, Form 1040A.

More Information on Rollovers

For more information on rollovers, get Publication 590.

Transfers Incident to Divorce

If an interest in a traditional IRA is transferred from your spouse or former spouse to you by a divorce or separate maintenance decree or a written document related to such a decree, the interest in the IRA, starting from the date of the transfer, is treated as your IRA. **The transfer is tax free.** For detailed information, see Publication 590.

When Can I Withdraw or Use IRA Assets?

There are rules limiting use of your IRA assets and distributions from it. Violation of the rules generally results in additional taxes in the year of violation. See *What Acts Result in Penalties.*

Explanation

Since 1987, IRA distributions have been taxed in a manner similar to annuities. If you do not make nondeductible contributions, all distributions from an IRA account are taxed as ordinary income. You may not use special 10-year averaging on a lump-sum distribution from your IRA, even if the account is a rollover from a qualified plan. If you made nondeductible contributions, a portion of the distribution may be excludable from income. The excludable amount is computed as follows:

$$\frac{\text{Undistributed Nondeductible Contributions}}{\text{Total IRA Account Balance}} \times \frac{\text{Distribution}}{\text{Amount}}$$

Example

Assume that Mary has made a $2,000 nondeductible contribution and that the total account balance is $20,000. In 2001, she takes a $5,000 distribution. Her tax-free amount is:

$$\$2,000 / \$20,000 \times \$5,000 = \$500$$

TaxOrganizer

Undistributed nondeductible contributions are obtained from the last Form 8606 you filed. Therefore, make sure you always keep the most recent copy in your files.

TaxPlanner

Money that you withdraw from your IRA is treated as a distribution to you and may trigger the 10% penalty that is imposed on premature distributions. However, it is possible to "borrow" temporarily from your IRA by terminating the arrangement and rolling over the funds to a new IRA within 60 days. That money and any income you earn on it are not considered premature distributions. However, you may not contribute any money that you do earn to your new IRA account. Instead, you have to keep that money—and pay tax on it.

Age 59 1/2 rule. Generally, if you are under age 59 1/2, you must pay a 10% additional tax on the distribution of any assets (money or other property) from your traditional IRA. Distributions before you are age 59 1/2 are called early distributions.

The 10% additional tax applies to the part of the distribution that you have to include in gross income. It is in addition to any regular income tax on that amount.

Exceptions. There are several exceptions to the age 59 1/2 rule. Even if you receive a distribution before you are age 59 1/2, you may not have to pay the 10% additional tax if you are in one of the following situations.

- You have **unreimbursed medical expenses** that are more than 7.5% of your adjusted gross income.
- The distributions are not more than the cost of your **medical insurance.**
- You are **disabled.**
- You are the **beneficiary** of a deceased IRA owner.
- You are receiving distributions in the form of an **annuity.**

- The distributions are not more than your qualified *higher education expenses.*
- You use the distributions to buy, build, or rebuild a *first home.*
- The distribution is due to an *IRS levy* of the qualified plan.

Most of these exceptions are explained in Publication 590.

Note. Distributions that are timely and properly rolled over, as discussed earlier, are not subject to either regular income tax or the 10% additional tax. Certain withdrawals of excess contributions after the due date of your return are also tax free and therefore not subject to the 10% additional tax. (See *Excess contributions withdrawn after due date of return,* later.) This also applies to transfers incident to divorce, as discussed earlier.

Contributions returned before the due date. If you made IRA contributions for 2001, you can withdraw them tax free by the due date of your return. If you have an extension of time to file your return, you can withdraw them tax free by the extended due date. You can do this if, for each contribution you withdraw, *both* of the following conditions apply.

- You did not take a deduction for the contribution.
- You also withdraw any interest or other income earned on the contribution. You can take into account any loss on the contribution while it was in the IRA when calculating the amount that must be withdrawn. If there was a loss, the net income earned on the contribution may be a negative amount.

Note. If the trustee of your IRA is unable to calculate the amount you must withdraw, get IRS *Notice 2000-39.* The notice explains the IRS-approved method of calculating the amount you must withdraw. This notice can be found in many libraries and IRS offices.

You must include in income any earnings on the contributions you withdraw. Include the earnings in income for the year in which you made the contributions, not in the year in which you withdraw them.

Caution. *Generally, except for any part of a withdrawal that is a return of nondeductible contributions (basis), any withdrawal of your contributions after the due date (or extended due date) of your return will be treated as a taxable distribution. Another exception is the return of an excess contribution as discussed under* What Acts Result in Penalties, *later.*

Early distributions tax. The 10% additional tax on distributions made before you reach age 59 1/2 does not apply to these tax-free withdrawals of your contributions. However, the distribution of interest or other income must be reported on Form 5329 and, unless the distribution qualifies as an exception to the age 59 1/2 rule, it will be subject to this tax.

When Must I Withdraw IRA Assets? (Required Distributions)

You cannot keep funds in your traditional IRA indefinitely. Eventually they *must* be distributed. If there are no distributions, or if the distributions are not large enough, you may have to pay a 50% excise tax on the amount not distributed as required. See *Excess Accumulations (Insufficient Distributions),* later. The requirements for distributing IRA funds differ depending on whether you are the IRA owner or the beneficiary of a decedent's IRA.

Required distributions not eligible for rollover. Amounts that must be distributed (required distributions) during a particular year are not eligible for rollover treatment.

IRA owners. If you are the owner of a traditional IRA, by April 1 of the year following the year in which you reach age 70 1/2, you must either:

1) Receive the entire balance in your IRA, or
2) Start receiving periodic distributions from your IRA.

April 1 of the year following the year in which you reach age 70 1/2 is referred to as the *required beginning date.*

Periodic distributions. If you do not receive the entire balance in your traditional IRA by the required beginning date, you must start to receive periodic distributions over one of the following periods:

1) Your life,
2) The lives of you and your *designated beneficiary,*
3) A period that does not extend beyond your life expectancy, or
4) A period that does not extend beyond the joint life and last survivor expectancy of you and your designated beneficiary.

Distributions after the required beginning date. The minimum required distribution for any year after your 70 1/2 year must be made by December 31 of that later year.

TAXALERT

In 2001, the IRS issued new proposed regulations simplifying the minimum distribution rules. The regulations are effective for distributions for calendar years beginning on or after January 1, 2002. However, IRA owners may follow these regulations beginning in 2001.

Explanation

The purpose of an IRA is to provide retirement income. Therefore, when you reach age 70½, you are expected to begin withdrawing the proceeds in your IRA rather than continue to let the funds accumulate and use the IRA as a tool to build your estate. If you don't withdraw the minimum amounts yearly, a 50% nondeductible tax is levied on the amount of the minimum payment left in your IRA.

You must start receiving minimum payments from your IRA by April 1 of the year after the year in which you reach age 70½.

It is only your first distribution (the distribution for the year you reach age 70½) that may be delayed until April 1 of the following year. The second distribution must be made by December 31 of the same year. You must determine what effect the doubling of distributions will have on your tax liability.

Generally, the minimum distribution is based on the joint life expectancy of both you and a survivor who is assumed to be no more than 10 years younger (see IRS Publication 590 for the appropriate life expectancy table). Alternatively, if your spouse is more than 10 years younger than you, the minimum distribution is based on you and your spouse's joint expectancy (see IRS Publication 590 for the appropriate life expectancy table). Using this alternate method will result in a lower minimum distribution than the general method due to using a longer life expectancy.

It's worth noting that your IRA fund may continue to grow, even if you make the required distributions. For example, if the table used indicates a life expectancy of 20 years, you must withdraw only one-twentieth (5%) of your IRA funds in that year. If the funds in your IRA are earning income at the rate of 10%, your account will continue to grow.

TAXALERT

Once distributions are required, a minimum distribution *must* be made each year based on the age of the IRA owner and the appropriate life expectancy table.

Example 1

Jack Jones, who became 70½ years old on May 1, 2001, has an IRA with a December 31, 2000, balance of $80,000. By looking at tables published by the IRS, he finds that his life expectancy for purposes of his IRA is 25.3 years. This is the life expectancy for a person who is 71, which he will be during 2001. To figure his minimum distribution, he divides the amount in his IRA by 25.3. He must receive a distribution of $3,162 prior to April 1, 2002, to avoid a penalty.

Example 2

In Example 1 above, assume Jack Jones is married and his wife turns 60 in 2001. Jack can use 26.0 years for his life expectancy since his wife is more than 10 years younger than him. The distribution required by April 1, 2002, is $3,077.

TAXPLANNER

You are always permitted to take more out of your IRA than the minimum amount you calculated.

TAXPLANNER

If a participant in an IRA dies, the tax rules that apply to IRA distributions depend on whether the beneficiary is a spouse and whether the participant had reached 70½—the age at which minimum distributions are required from an IRA before death.

If your spouse is a beneficiary. If you die before age 70½ *and* distributions have not yet begun, your spouse could simply retitle your IRA account in his or her name and continue deferring tax, treating your IRA as his or her own (e.g., name new heirs). Otherwise, your spouse would have to begin distributions based on his or her life expectancy by the later of:

- December 31 of the calendar year in which you would have reached age 70½, or
- December 31 of the calendar year that follows the calendar year of your death.

If you live past age 70½ and distributions have begun, your surviving spouse can treat the IRA as his or her own IRA. Otherwise, your spouse would continue receiving minimum distributions over his or her own life expectancy (he or she can always take larger distributions if needed).

If your spouse is not the beneficiary. The options available to a non–spouse beneficiary receiving IRA assets are more limited. Your beneficiary would have to receive distributions from the account:

- By December 31 of the fifth year following the year of the owner's death, or
- In installments intended to last the beneficiary's lifetime (these installments must begin no later than December 31 of the calendar year that follows the calendar year of your death)

However, a non–spouse recipient cannot completely defer income taxes the way that a spouse beneficiary can by simply rolling the money over.

TAXPLANNER

The minimum distribution rules do not apply to Roth IRAs (see Roth IRAs for more details).

TAXPLANNER

Keogh plans. The same withdrawal techniques described in TaxPlanners 1 through 3 may be used with a Keogh plan, a retirement arrangement that self-employed people may set up.

Note: If you have a Keogh plan, you may not receive a distribution before age 59½ unless you become totally disabled; see exceptions below.

TAXPLANNER

Employee stock bonus plans and company profit-sharing plans. The main attraction of having your employer put some of your compensation into a stock bonus plan or a company profit-sharing plan is that you are not currently taxed on the contributions to or the earnings in the plan. In addition, these plans have certain advantages that IRAs do not:

1. Withdrawals may be made at any age because of retirement, separation from service, or hardship.
2. Borrowing is permitted if the loan is repaid within 5 years.
3. A lump-sum distribution may qualify for 10-year averaging.

Beneficiaries. If you are the beneficiary of a decedent's traditional IRA, the requirements for distributions from that IRA depend on whether distributions that satisfy the minimum distributions requirement have begun.

More information. For more information, including how to figure your minimum required distribution each year and how to figure your required distribution if you are a beneficiary of a decedent's IRA, see Publication 590.

Are Distributions Taxable?

In general, distributions from a traditional IRA are taxable in the year you receive them.

Exceptions. Exceptions to this general rule are rollovers and tax-free withdrawals of contributions, discussed earlier, and the return of nondeductible contributions, discussed later under *Distributions Fully or Partly Taxable.*

Caution. *Although a conversion of a traditional IRA is considered a rollover for Roth IRA purposes, it is not an exception to the general rule for distributions from a traditional IRA. Conversion distributions are includable in your gross income subject to these rules and the special rules for conversions explained in chapter 2 of Publication 590.*

Ordinary income. Distributions from traditional IRAs that you include in income are taxed as ordinary income.

No special treatment. In figuring your tax, you cannot use the 10-year tax option or capital gain treatment that applies to lump-sum distributions from qualified employer plans.

Distributions Fully or Partly Taxable

Distributions from your traditional IRA may be fully or partly taxable, depending on whether your IRA includes any nondeductible contributions.

Fully taxable. If only deductible contributions were made to your traditional IRA (or IRAs, if you have more than one), you have **no basis** in your IRA. Because you have no basis in your IRA, any distributions are fully taxable when received. See *Reporting taxable distributions on your return,* later.

Partly taxable. If you made nondeductible contributions to any of your traditional IRAs, you have a **cost basis** (investment in the contract) equal to the amount of those contributions. These nondeductible contributions are not taxed when they are distributed to you. They are a return of your investment in your IRA.

Explanation

A distribution from an IRA is fully taxable, unless it represents a timely withdrawal of an excess contribution, it is rolled over into another IRA within the required 60-day period, or it represents a return of nondeductible contributions.

If you reach age 59½ and are entitled to withdraw the funds in your IRA without penalty but you decide not to, you are not taxed until an actual distribution is made. However, in the following situations, all or part of your IRA is currently taxed:

1. The occurrence of a prohibited transaction causes the entire amount in your individual retirement *account* to be treated as distributed and therefore taxable to you. For instance, if you loan yourself the money in your IRA, the entire amount is then currently taxable to you. However, if you engage in a prohibited transaction with your individual retirement *annuity*, only the amount of the prohibited transaction is subject to a 5% excise tax (see *Prohibited Transactions*, following).
2. The pledging of an IRA *account* causes the portion pledged to be treated as distributed. For example, if you have an IRA with a value of $7,500 that you pledge as security for a $5,000 bank loan, you are taxed on the $5,000.
3. The pledging of an IRA *annuity* causes the entire account to be treated as distributed.

If you are under age 59½ and distribute part of your IRA in any of the ways described above, a 10% tax penalty is applied to the distributed portion.

Exceptions

The nondeductible 10% penalty tax on premature distributions does not apply if you are disabled and the early distribution is made because of your disability. Beginning in 1987, you will not be subject to the 10% penalty if the IRA is distributed as a life annuity (see *Early Distributions*, later).

Only the part of the distribution that represents nondeductible contributions (your cost basis) is tax free. If nondeductible contributions have been made, distributions consist partly of nondeductible contributions (basis) and partly of deductible contributions, earnings, and gains (if there are any). Until all of your basis has been distributed, each distribution is partly nontaxable and partly taxable.

Form 8606. You must complete Form 8606 and attach it to your return if you receive a distribution from a traditional IRA and have ever made nondeductible contributions to any of your traditional IRAs. Using the form, you will figure the nontaxable distributions for 2001 and your total IRA basis for 2001 and earlier years.

Note. If you are required to file Form 8606, but you are not required to file an income tax return, you still *must* file Form 8606. Send it to the IRS at the time and place you would otherwise file an income tax return.

Distributions reported on Form 1099-R. If you receive a distribution from your traditional IRA, you will receive Form 1099-R, *Distributions From Pensions, Annuities, Retirement or Profit-Sharing Plans, IRAs, Insurance Contracts, Etc.*, or a similar statement. IRA distributions are shown in boxes 1 and 2 of Form 1099-R. A number or letter code in box 7 tells you what type of distribution you received from your IRA.

TAXORGANIZER

Keep Form 1099-R with your records to substantiate IRA distributions and federal income tax withholding.

Withholding. Federal income tax is withheld from distributions from traditional IRAs unless you choose not to have tax withheld. See chapter 5.

Explanation

You may elect at any time not to have taxes withheld on the distribution. Before electing not to withhold, however, you must review your withholdings from other sources and estimated payments. See Chapter 5, *Tax Withholding and Estimated Tax*, for underpayment penalties.

IRA distributions delivered outside the United States. In general, if you are a U.S. citizen or resident alien and your home address is outside the United States or its possessions, you cannot choose exemption from withholding on distributions from your traditional IRA.

Reporting taxable distributions on your return. Report fully taxable distributions, including early distributions, on line 15b, Form 1040 (no entry is required on line 15a), or line 11b, Form 1040A. If only part of the distribution is taxable, enter the total amount on line 15a, Form 1040, or line 11a, Form 1040A, and the taxable part on line 15b, Form 1040, or line 11b, Form 1040A. You cannot report distributions on Form 1040EZ.

What Acts Result in Penalties?

The tax advantages of using traditional IRAs for retirement savings can be offset by additional taxes and penalties if you do not follow the rules. For example, there are additions to the regular tax for using your IRA funds in prohibited transactions. There are also additional taxes for the following activities.

- Investing in collectibles.
- Making excess contributions.
- Taking early distributions.
- Allowing excess amounts to accumulate (failing to take required distributions).

There are penalties for overstating the amount of nondeductible contributions and for failure to file a Form 8606, if required.

Prohibited Transactions

Generally, a prohibited transaction is any improper use of your traditional IRA by you, your beneficiary, or any disqualified person.

Disqualified persons include your fiduciary and members of your family (spouse, ancestor, lineal descendent, and any spouse of a lineal descendent).

The following are examples of prohibited transactions with a traditional IRA.

- Borrowing money from it.
- Selling property to it.
- Receiving unreasonable compensation for managing it.
- Using it as security for a loan.
- Buying property for personal use (present or future) with IRA funds.

Effect on an IRA account. Generally, if you or your beneficiary engages in a prohibited transaction in connection with your traditional IRA account at any time during the year, the account stops being an IRA as of the first day of that year.

Effect on you or your beneficiary. If you or your beneficiary engage in a prohibited transaction with your traditional IRA account at any time during the year, you (or your beneficiary) must include the fair market value of all of the IRA assets in your gross income for that year. The fair market value is the price at which the IRA assets would change hands between a willing buyer and a willing seller, when neither has any need to buy or sell, and both have reasonable knowledge of the relevant facts.

You must use the fair market value of the assets as of the first day of the year you engaged in the prohibited transaction. You may have to pay the 10% additional tax on early distributions, discussed later.

Taxes on prohibited transactions. If someone other than the owner or beneficiary of a traditional IRA engages in a prohibited transaction, that person may be liable for certain taxes. In general, there is a 15% tax on the amount of the prohibited transaction and a 100% additional tax if the transaction is not corrected.

More information. For more information on prohibited transactions, get Publication 590.

Investment in Collectibles

If your traditional IRA invests in collectibles, the amount invested is considered distributed to you in the year invested. You may have to pay the 10% additional tax on early distributions, discussed later.

Collectibles. These include:

- Art works,
- Rugs,
- Antiques,
- Metals,
- Gems,
- Stamps,
- Coins,
- Alcoholic beverages, and
- Certain other tangible personal property.

Exception. Your IRA can invest in one, one-half, one-quarter, or one-tenth ounce U.S. gold coins, or one ounce silver coins minted by the Treasury Department. It can also invest in certain platinum coins and certain gold, silver, palladium, and platinum bullion.

Explanation

The rules relating to prohibited transactions are designed to prevent the manipulation of IRA funds by the person who has set the funds aside for his or her retirement.

A qualified plan run by your employer that engages in a prohibited transaction is subject to a 5% tax on that transaction. Your IRA, which may have been part of your employer's plan, does not lose its tax-exempt status.

Although an investment in tangible property, such as artworks, precious metals or gems, antiques, or alcoholic beverages, is not technically a prohibited transaction, the cost of the item is treated as a distribution from your IRA. The amount is included in your income and may be subject to the 10% premature distribution penalty tax.

This rule is designed to prevent you from directing your IRA to invest in property that the trustee could conceivably allow you to keep in your home for your personal enjoyment.

In order to help sell U.S.-issued gold and silver coins, Congress removed the penalty for such coins acquired after October 1, 1986.

Excess Contributions

Generally, an excess contribution is the amount contributed to your traditional IRA(s) for the year that is more than the smaller of:

- Your taxable compensation for the year, or
- $2,000 for 2001 ($3,000 for 2002 or $3,500 for 2002 if 50 or older).

Example

You contribute $4,000 to IRAs you have set up for you and your nonworking spouse. You put $2,050 into your account and $1,950 into your spouse's account. There is a $50 excess contribution to your account. Only $3,950 ($2,000 + $1,950) can be contributed and deducted on your joint income tax return. In order to obtain the full $4,000 contribution, you can withdraw the $50 excess contribution from your account and put it into your spouse's account. This must be done no later than April 15, 2002.

Tax on excess contributions. In general, if the excess contribution for a year and any earnings on it are not withdrawn by the date your return for the year is due (including extensions), you are subject to a 6% tax. You must pay the 6% tax each year on excess amounts that remain in your traditional IRA at the end of your tax year. The tax cannot be more than 6% of the value of your IRA as of the end of your tax year.

Excess contributions withdrawn by due date of return. You will not have to pay the 6% tax if you withdraw an excess contribution made during a tax year *and* you also withdraw interest or other income earned on the excess contribution. You must complete your withdrawal by the date your tax return for that year is due, including extensions.

How to treat withdrawn contributions. Do not include in your gross income an excess contribution that you withdraw from your traditional IRA before your tax return is due if *both* the following conditions are met.

1) No deduction was allowed for the excess contribution.
2) You withdraw the interest or other income earned on the excess contribution.

You can take into account any loss on the contribution while it was in the IRA when calculating the amount that must be withdrawn. If there was a loss, the net income earned on the contribution may be a negative amount.

How to treat withdrawn interest or other income. You must include in your gross income the interest or other income that was earned on the excess contribution. Report it on your return for the year in which the excess contribution was made. Your withdrawal of interest or other income may be subject to an additional 10% tax on early distributions, discussed later.

Explanation

Excess payments you withdraw before the due date of the return are not subject to the 6% excise tax, provided that the full amount of income attributable to the excess contribution is also distributed. The income portion of the distribution is then included in your income in the year in which the excess contribution was made. The withdrawn income may be subject to the 10% tax on premature distributions (see *Early Distributions*, following).

Excess contributions withdrawn after due date of return. In general, you must include all distributions (withdrawals) from your traditional IRA in your gross income. However, if the following conditions are met, you can withdraw excess contributions from your IRA and not include the amount withdrawn in your gross income.

1) Total contributions (other than rollover contributions) for 2001 to your IRA were not more than $2,000.
2) You did not take a deduction for the excess contribution being withdrawn.

The withdrawal can take place at any time, even after the due date, including extensions, for filing your tax return for the year.

Explanation

Excess payments may also be adjusted by deducting the correct amount in the current year and applying the excess to the following year's contribution.

Example

If you mistakenly contributed $2,000 to your IRA in 2000, when you were entitled to only a $1,500 contribution, you may reduce your 2001 contribution by the excess $500. If you are entitled to a $1,500 contribution in 2001, you should then contribute no more than $1,000 that year. To make this application work, you must deduct only $1,500 for 2000—not the actual $2,000 you contributed. Although you are still subject to the 6% tax on the $500 excess contribution in 2000, if you reduce the following year's contribution to $1,000, there is no excess contribution remaining in your IRA and no tax would be imposed for 2001.

You would receive a $1,500 deduction for 2001 consisting of the $1,000 you actually contributed in 2001 plus the excess contribution from 2000.

Excess contribution deducted in an earlier year. If you deducted an excess contribution in an earlier year for which the total contributions were $2,000 or less, you can still remove the excess from your traditional IRA and not include it in your gross income. To do this, file Form 1040X, *Amended U.S. Individual Income Tax Return,* for that year and do not deduct the excess contribution on the amended return. Generally, you can file an amended return within 3 years after you filed your return, or 2 years from the time the tax was paid, whichever is later.

Excess due to incorrect rollover information. If an excess contribution in your traditional IRA is the result of a rollover and the excess occurred because the information the plan was required to give you was incorrect, you can withdraw the excess contribution. The limits mentioned above are increased by the amount of the excess that is due to the incorrect information. You will have to amend your return for the year in which the excess occurred to correct the reporting of the rollover amounts in that year. Do not include in your gross income the part of the excess contribution caused by the incorrect information.

Early Distributions

You must include early distributions of taxable amounts from your traditional IRA in your gross income. Early distributions are also subject to an *additional 10% tax.* See the discussion of Form 5329 under *Reporting Additional Taxes,* later, to figure and report the tax.
Early distributions defined. Early distributions are amounts distributed from your traditional IRA account or annuity before you are age 59 1/2.

TaxPlanner

Since you may largely determine when you pay tax on money in your IRA by controlling when you distribute the funds, the arrangement provides unusual opportunities for tax planning.

Your best bet is to make your withdrawal during a year in which you have low **taxable income** so that you may recognize your IRA distribution at a lower tax cost than you might otherwise be able to. For example, you might withdraw the funds in your IRA in a year in which you are unemployed or have a loss on your business activities. Or you might distribute them in a year in which you have extraordinarily large deductible expenses, such as medical costs or **casualty losses.**

Another good time to take your IRA funds is when most of your income derives from a lump-sum distribution that qualifies for **10-year averaging.** Such income is reported on a separate schedule and does not raise your marginal tax rate on other income.

Thus, if your taxable income is low enough, it might be worthwhile to take a premature distribution before you are age 59½ and pay the 10% penalty.

TaxPlanner

If you are fortunate enough to have sufficient income without taking any distributions from your IRA, you may wish to postpone withdrawing money from your IRA as long as possible. Distributions do not have to begin until April 1 of the calendar year *following* the year in which you reach age 70½. See *Required Distributions,* earlier.

Exceptions. In certain situations, you may not have to pay the 10% additional tax even if amounts are distributed from your IRA before you are age 59 1/2. These situations are listed below.

- You have *unreimbursed medical expenses* that are more than 7.5% of your adjusted gross income.
- The distributions are not more than the cost of your *medical insurance.*
- You are *disabled.*
- You are the *beneficiary* of a deceased IRA owner.
- You are receiving distributions in the form of an *annuity.*
- The distributions are not more than your qualified *higher education expenses.*
- You use the distributions to buy, build, or rebuild a *first home.*
- The distribution is due to an *IRS levy* of the qualified plan.

Most of these exceptions are explained in Publication 590.

Note. Distributions that are timely and properly rolled over, as discussed earlier, are not subject to either regular income tax or the 10% additional tax (as explained earlier under *Excess Contributions*). This also applies to transfers incident to divorce, as discussed under *Can I Move Retirement Plan Assets,* earlier.

TaxPlanner

The life annuity exception may be beneficial if you retire before age 55, your employer's plan does not provide for a life annuity, you don't want to pay the penalty and taxes on the distribution, but you need supplemental income. You will not be subject to the penalty if the plan distribution is rolled over into an IRA and then distributed as part of a series of substantially equal periodic payments (made no less frequently than annually) over your life expectancy or the joint life expectancies of you and a beneficiary.

Note that, using the life annuity exception, you would not be making a single withdrawal. Rather, you would effectively be receiving an annuity in which the payments will be substantially equal. Modifying the payments before you reach age 59½, or, in any event, within 5 years of the date of the first payment, will result in the imposition of the 10% penalty tax that would have applied absent the exception, plus interest.

The IRS has identified three methods available for determining whether distributions from an IRA are considered to be "substantially equal periodic payments."

1. **The "straight life expectancy" method:** To use this method, you divide the balance in the individual retirement account at the end of each year by the beneficiary's life expectancy, as determined from tables published by the IRS. Under this method, distributions may vary from year to year due to:
   (a) account balance changes resulting from earnings and distributions during the year, and
   (b) changes in the beneficiary's life expectancy as the beneficiary gets older.

2. **The amortization method:** This method involves determining an annuity payment based on the balance in the individual retirement account, the beneficiary's life expectancy, and an assumed interest rate. Under this method, you would essentially be able to choose among various distribution amounts: IRS rules allow you to select from several interest rate assumptions and between two published life expectancy tables. However, once the annuity amount has been determined, it will not change from year to year.

3. **The annuity factor method:** This method involves determining an annuity payment by dividing the balance in the individual retirement account by an annuity factor derived from a reasonable mortality table using a reasonable rate of interest. As under the amortization method, once determined, the annuity amount will not change.

Note that the substantially equal periodic payment exception (described above) is applied on an IRA-by-IRA basis. Therefore, an IRA owner who wants the flexibility in the future to increase the annual withdrawal amounts can divide an existing IRA into several IRAs before distributions begin. Substantially equal periodic distributions can be taken prior to 59½ from only one of the IRAs. In the future, if additional payments are needed, distributions can be taken from one or more of the other IRAs.

The straight life expectancy method (method 1, above) is the easiest to use but will result in the smallest annual distribution. The amortization and annuity factor methods result in larger distributions and are more difficult to compute, respectively, than the straight life expectancy method.

Since the rules regarding substantially equal periodic payments are complex and substantial penalties apply for failure to comply, you should consult your tax advisor when planning to take early distributions from your IRA(s).

Additional 10% tax. The additional tax on early distributions is 10% of the amount of the early distribution that you must include in your gross income. This tax is in addition to any regular income tax resulting from including the distribution in income.

Nondeductible contributions. The tax on early distributions does not apply to the part of a distribution that represents a return of your nondeductible contributions (basis).

More information. For more information on early distributions, see Publication 590.

Excess Accumulations (Insufficient Distributions)

You cannot keep amounts in your traditional IRA indefinitely. Generally, you must begin receiving distributions by April 1 of the year following the year in which you reach age 70 1/2 (your 70 1/2 year). The minimum required distribution for any year after your 70 1/2 year must be made by December 31 of that later year.

Tax on excess. If distributions are less than the minimum required distribution for the year, you may have to pay a 50% excise tax for that year on the amount not distributed as required.

Request to excuse the tax. If the excess accumulation is due to reasonable error, and you have taken, or are taking, steps to remedy the insufficient distribution, you can request that the tax be excused.

If you believe you qualify for this relief, do the following.

1) File Form 5329 with your Form 1040.
2) Pay any tax you owe on excess accumulations.
3) Attach a letter of explanation.

If the IRS approves your request, it will refund the excess accumulations tax you paid.

Exemption from tax. If you are unable to make required distributions because you have a traditional IRA invested in a contract issued by an insurance company that is in state insurer delinquency proceedings, the 50% excise tax does not apply if the conditions and requirements of Revenue Procedure 92-10 are satisfied.

TaxAlert

If you cannot receive required distributions from your IRA because your insurance company is in state insurer delinquency proceedings, consult a tax advisor to see if you can avoid the 50% excise tax.

More information. For more information on excess accumulations, see Publication 590.

Reporting Additional Taxes

Generally, you must use Form 5329 to report the tax on excess contributions, early (premature) distributions, and excess accumulations.

Filing Form 1040. If you file Form 1040, complete Form 5329 and attach it to your Form 1040. Enter the total amount of IRA tax due on line 55, Form 1040.

Note. If you have to file an individual income tax return and Form 5329, you must use Form 1040.

Not filing Form 1040. If you do not have to file a Form 1040 but do have to pay one of the IRA taxes mentioned earlier, file the completed Form 5329 with the IRS at the time and place you would have filed your Form 1040. Be sure to include your address on page 1 and your signature and date on page 2. Enclose, but do not attach, a check or money order payable to the United States Treasury for the tax you owe, as shown on Form 5329. Write your social security number and "2001 Form 5329" on your check or money order.

Form 5329 not required. You do not have to use Form 5329 if *any* of the following conditions exist.

- Distribution code 1 (early distribution) is shown in box 7 of Form 1099-R. If you do not owe any other additional tax on a distribution, multiply the taxable part of the early distribution by 10% and enter the result on line 55 of Form 1040. Write "No" next to line 55 to indicate that you do not have to file Form 5329. However, if you owe this tax and also owe any other additional tax on a distribution, do not enter this 10% additional tax directly on your Form 1040. You must file Form 5329 to report your additional taxes.

- You qualify for an exception to the additional tax on early distributions. You do not have to report the exception if distribution code 2, 3, or 4 is shown in box 7 of Form 1099-R. However, if one of those codes is not shown, or the code shown is incorrect, you must file Form 5329 to report the exception.

- You properly rolled over all distributions you received during the year.

Worksheet 18–2. **Modified Adjusted Gross Income for Roth IRA Purposes**
Use this worksheet to figure your modified adjusted gross income for Roth IRA purposes.

1. Enter your adjusted gross income (Form 1040, line 33 or Form 1040A, line 19)	1. _____
2. Enter any income resulting from the conversion of an IRA (other than a Roth IRA) to a Roth IRA	2. _____
3. Subtract line 2 from line 1	3. _____
4. Enter any traditional IRA deduction (Form 1040, line 23 or Form 1040A, line 16)	4. _____
5. Enter any student loan interest deduction (Form 1040, line 24 or Form 1040A, line 17)	5. _____
6. Enter any foreign earned income exclusion (Form 2555, line 40 or Form 2555–EZ, line 18)	6. _____
7. Enter any foreign housing exclusion or deduction (Form 2555, line 34 or 48)	7. _____
8. Enter any exclusion of bond interest (Form 8815, line 14)	8. _____
9. Enter any exclusion of employer-paid adoption expenses (Form 8839, line 26)	9. _____
10. Add the amounts on line 3 through 9. This is your **modified adjusted gross income** for Roth IRA purposes	10. _____

Roth IRAs

Regardless of your age, you may be able to establish and make nondeductible contributions to a retirement plan called a Roth IRA. **Tip.** *You can make contributions for 2001 by the due date (not including extensions) for filing your 2001 tax return. This means that most people can make contributions for 2001 by April 15, 2002.*
Contributions not reported. You do not have to report Roth IRA contributions on your return.

What Is a Roth IRA?

A Roth IRA is an individual retirement plan that, except as explained in this chapter, is subject to the rules that apply to a traditional IRA (defined below). It can be either an account or an annuity. Individual retirement accounts and annuities are described in Publication 590.

To be a Roth IRA, the account or annuity must be designated as a Roth IRA when it is set up. Neither a SEP-IRA nor a SIMPLE IRA can be designated as a Roth IRA.

Unlike a traditional IRA, you cannot deduct contributions to a Roth IRA. But, if you satisfy the requirements, qualified distributions (discussed later) are tax free. Contributions can be made to your Roth IRA after you reach age 70 1/2 and you can leave amounts in your Roth IRA as long as you live.
Traditional IRA. A traditional IRA is any IRA that is not a Roth IRA or SIMPLE IRA.

Can I Contribute to a Roth IRA?

Generally, you can contribute to a Roth IRA if you have taxable **compensation** (defined later) and your **modified AGI** (defined later) is less than:

- $160,000 for married filing jointly,
- $10,000 for married filing separately and you lived with your spouse at any time during the year, and
- $110,000 for single, head of household, qualifying widow(er) or married filing separately and you did not live with your spouse at any time during the year.

Is there an age limit for contributions? Contributions can be made to your Roth IRA regardless of your age.

Can I contribute to a Roth IRA for my spouse? You can contribute to a Roth IRA for your spouse provided the contributions satisfy the spousal IRA limit (discussed in *How Much Can Be Contributed?* under *Traditional IRAs*) and your modified AGI is less than:

- $160,000 for married filing jointly,
- $10,000 for married filing separately and you lived with your spouse at any time during the year, and
- $110,000 for married filing separately and you did not live with your spouse at any time during the year.

Compensation. Compensation includes wages, salaries, tips, professional fees, bonuses, and other amounts received for providing personal services. It also includes commissions, self-employment income, and taxable alimony and separate maintenance payments.
Modified AGI. Your modified AGI for Roth IRA purposes is your adjusted gross income (AGI) as shown on your return modified as follows.

1) *Subtract* any income resulting from the conversion of an IRA (other than a Roth IRA) to a Roth IRA (conversion income).
2) *Add* the following deductions and exclusions:
   a) Traditional IRA deduction,
   b) Student loan interest deduction,
   c) Foreign earned income exclusion,
   d) Foreign housing exclusion or deduction,
   e) Exclusion of qualified savings bond interest shown on Form 8815, and
   f) Exclusion of employer-paid adoption expenses shown on Form 8839.

You can use *Worksheet 18-2* to figure your modified AGI.

How Much Can Be Contributed?
The contribution limit for Roth IRAs depends on whether contributions are made only to Roth IRAs or to both traditional IRAs and Roth IRAs.
Roth IRAs only. If contributions are made only to Roth IRAs, your contribution limit generally is the lesser of:

- $2,000 for 2001 ($3,000 for 2002 or $3,500 for 2002 if you are 50 or older), or
- Your taxable compensation.

However, if your modified AGI is above a certain amount, your contribution limit may be reduced, as explained later under *Contribution limit reduced.*

Roth IRAs and traditional IRAs. If contributions are made to both Roth IRAs and traditional IRAs established for your benefit, your contribution limit for Roth IRAs generally is the same as your limit would be if contributions were made only to Roth IRAs, but then reduced by all contributions (other than employer contributions under a SEP or SIMPLE IRA plan) for the year to all IRAs other than Roth IRAs.

This means that your contribution limit is the lesser of:

- $2,000 for 2001 ($3,000 for 2002 or $3,500 for 2002 if you are 50 or older) minus all contributions (other than employer contributions under a SEP or SIMPLE IRA plan) for the year to all IRAs other than Roth IRAs, or
- Your taxable compensation minus all contributions (other than employer contributions under a SEP or SIMPLE IRA plan) for the year to all IRAs other than Roth IRAs.

However, if your modified AGI is above a certain amount, your contribution limit may be reduced, as explained later under *Contribution limit reduced.*

Simplified employee pensions (SEPs) are discussed in chapter 3 of Publication 590. Savings incentive match plans for employees (SIMPLE) are discussed in chapter 4 of Publication 590.

Contribution limit reduced. If your modified AGI is above a certain amount, your contribution limit is gradually reduced. Use *Table 18-3* to determine if this reduction applies to you.

Figuring the reduction. If the amount you can contribute to your Roth IRA is reduced, see Publication 590 for how to figure the reduction.

When Can I Make Contributions?

You can make contributions to a Roth IRA for a year at any time during the year or by the due date of your return for that year (not including extensions).

> **Explanation: Roth IRAs**
> Roth IRAs are retirement-savings vehicles. By permitting tax-free withdrawals, contributions made early in a taxpayer's working life receive the greatest tax benefit.

> **Example 1**
> John is 25 years old on January 1, 2001. On January 1 of each year, he contributes $2,000 to a Roth IRA. The account earns 8% per year. John retires on January 1, 2041, at age 65 (immediately after he makes his last Roth IRA contribution). He will have accumulated $561,000 toward retirement—all available tax free.

> **Example 2**
> Jim is also 25 years old on January 1, 2001. Rather than make his $2,000 Roth contribution on January 1 of each year, he waits until April 15 of the next year to make his contribution. His account also earns 8% per year. In order to retire with the same amount as John, he must wait until April 15, 2042, to retire. Alternatively, if he retires on January 1, 2041, he will only have accumulated $505,000 toward retirement—$56,000 less than John.

> **Example 3**
> Mary is 16 years old and earns wages of $2,000 in 2001. Her father gifts her $2,000, which she uses to open a Roth IRA on December 31, 2001. If the account earns 8% per year, it will be worth approximately $94,000 (tax free) if she retires at age 66.

What If I Contribute Too Much?

A 6% excise tax applies to any *excess contribution* to a Roth IRA. **Excess contributions.** These are the contributions to your Roth IRAs for a year that equal the *total* of:

1) Amounts contributed for the tax year to your Roth IRAs (other than amounts properly and timely rolled over from a Roth IRA or properly converted from a traditional IRA, as described later) that are more than your contribution limit for the year, plus
2) Any excess contributions for the preceding year, reduced by the total of:
   a) Any distributions out of your Roth IRAs for the year, plus
   b) Your contribution limit for the year minus your contributions to all your IRAs for the year.

Table 18-3. **Effect of Modified AGI on Roth IRA Contribution**

This table shows whether your contribution to a Roth IRA is affected by the amount of your modified adjusted gross income (modified AGI).

IF you have taxable compensation and your filing status is ...	AND your modified AGI is ...	THEN ...
Married Filing Jointly	Less than $150,000	You can contribute up to $2,000 for 2001 ($3,000 for 2002 or $3,500 for 2002 if age 50 or older).
	At least $150,000 but less than $160,000	The amount you can contributed is reduced as explained under *Contribution limit reduced.*
	$160,000 or more	You cannot contribute to a Roth IRA.
Married Filing Separately and you lived with your spouse at any time during the year	Zero (-0-)	You can contribute up to $2,000 for 2001 ($3,000 for 2002 or $3,500 for 2002 if 50 or older).
	More than zero (-0-) but less than $10,000	The amount you can contribute is reduced as explained under *Contribution limit reduced.*
	$10,000 or more	You cannot contribute to a Roth IRA.
Single, Head of Household, Qualifying Widow(er), or **Married Filing Separately** and you did not live with your spouse at any time during the year	Less than $95,000	You can contribute up to $2,000 for 2001 ($3,000 for 2002 or $3,500 for 2002 if age 50 or older).
	At least $95,000 but less than $110,000	The amount you can contribute is reduced as explained under *Contribution limit reduced.*
	$110,000 or more	You cannot contribute to a Roth IRA.

Withdrawal of excess contributions. For purposes of determining excess contributions, any contribution that is withdrawn on or before the due date (including extensions) for filing your tax return for the year is treated as an amount not contributed. This treatment applies only if any earnings on the contributions are also withdrawn and are reported as income earned and receivable in the year the contribution was made.

Applying excess contributions. If contributions to your Roth IRA for a year were more than the limit, you can apply the excess contribution in one year to a later year if the contributions for that later year are less than the maximum allowed for that year.

Can I Move Amounts Into a Roth IRA?

You may be able to convert amounts from either a traditional, SEP, or SIMPLE IRA into a Roth IRA. You may be able to recharacterize contributions made to one IRA as having been made directly to a different IRA. You can roll amounts over from one Roth IRA to another Roth IRA.

Conversions

You can convert a traditional IRA or a SIMPLE IRA to a Roth IRA. The conversion is treated as a rollover, regardless of the conversion method used. Most of the rules for rollovers, described under *Rollover From One IRA Into Another* under *Traditional IRAs,* earlier, apply to these rollovers. However, the 1-year waiting period does not apply.

Conversion methods. You can convert amounts from a traditional IRA to a Roth IRA in *any* of the following three ways.

1) *Rollover.* You can receive a distribution from a traditional IRA and roll it over (contribute it) to a Roth IRA within 60 days after the distribution.
2) *Trustee-to-trustee transfer.* You can direct the trustee of the traditional IRA to transfer an amount from the traditional IRA to the trustee of the Roth IRA.
3) *Same trustee transfer.* If the trustee of the traditional IRA also maintains the Roth IRA, you can direct the trustee to transfer an amount from the traditional IRA to the Roth IRA.

Same trustee. Conversions made with the same trustee can be made by redesignating the traditional IRA as a Roth IRA, rather than opening a new account or issuing a new contract.

Converting from any traditional IRA. You can convert amounts from a traditional IRA into a Roth IRA if, for the tax year you make the withdrawal from the traditional IRA, *both* of the following requirements are met.

1) Your modified AGI (explained earlier) is not more than $100,000.
2) You are not a married individual filing a separate return. (See *Lived apart from spouse* under *Filing status,* earlier.)

Required distributions. Amounts that must be distributed from your traditional IRA for a particular year (including the calendar year in which you reach age 70 1/2) under the required distribution rules (discussed under *Traditional IRAs,* earlier) cannot be converted.

Inherited IRAs. If you inherited a traditional IRA from someone other than your spouse, you cannot convert it to a Roth IRA.

Income. You must include in your gross income distributions from a traditional IRA that you would have to include in income if you had not converted them into a Roth IRA. You do not include in gross income any part of a distribution from a traditional IRA that is a return of your basis, as discussed earlier under *Traditional IRAs.*

If you must include any amount in your gross income, you may have to make estimated tax payments. See chapter 5.

How to treat 1998 conversions. If you converted amounts from a traditional IRA in 1998 to a Roth IRA, any amount you had to include in income as a result of the distribution is generally included ratably over a 4-year period, beginning with 1998. This means you included one-quarter of the amount in income in 1998, 1999, 2000, and must include the final one-quarter in 2001.

TAXPLANNER

You can choose to change a Roth Conversion IRA back into a regular IRA and once again convert the regular IRA back into a Roth IRA. Generally, you can only do this once in a calendar year. Such a change can be beneficial in a situation where you converted a regular IRA into a Roth IRA at a time when stock market values were high and then they subsequently dropped significantly. You can avoid paying tax on the "vanished" profits by recharacterizing the Roth IRA as a regular IRA and then converting back to a Roth IRA when stock values are lower.

Death of Roth IRA owner during 4-year period. If a Roth IRA owner who is including amounts ratably over the 4-year period died in 2001, any amounts not included must generally be included in the owner's (decedent's) gross income for 2001.

Note. You may have elected to include the entire amount in income in 1998. If you did, this discussion does not apply to you.

TAXPLANNER

Even if you're past the age when minimum required distributions (MRDs) from traditional IRAs have begun, you can still convert the IRA to a Roth IRA, thereby eliminating the requirement to make additional lifetime distributions from the account. *Note: You cannot roll over the current-year MRD to a Roth IRA as part of a conversion.*

TAXPLANNER

Partial conversions are permissible. You can also convert one or more separate IRAs. However, in determining the tax consequences of a partial conversion—whether from a single IRA or separate accounts—normal IRA distribution rules apply. Thus, the tax consequences depend on the value of *all* IRAs, as well as your total nondeductible contributions to all IRAs.

Example

Suppose you have two IRAs, each with a current value of $50,000. One was funded entirely with deductible contributions, while the other was funded entirely with nondeductible contributions totaling $20,000. If you converted either IRA in full, you would recognize $40,000 of income. *Note that this result occurs regardless of the IRA converted.*

Value of IRA converted	$50,000
Total nondeductible contributions	$20,000 (a)
Percentage of the total value of all IRAs converted	%50 (b)
Nondeductible contributions deemed rolled over (a) × (b)	($10,000)
Gross income inclusion	($40,000)

TAXALERT

At this time, many states have adopted the new federal tax rules governing Roth IRAs, although some have not.

Without new state legislation, a Roth IRA could be subject to state tax in a variety of ways. To avoid traps, consult your tax advisor for details before establishing a Roth IRA.

TAXPLANNER

Whether to convert or not can be a perplexing issue. It depends on many factors, such as your income tax bracket at the time of conversion versus your tax bracket in the future (e.g., during retirement), investment rates of return, your age and life expectancy, whether you have sufficient funds *outside of your IRA* with which to pay the taxes attributable to the conversion, and to what extent you'll need the funds in your IRA during retirement (vs. accumulating wealth primarily for your heirs). Like many complex financial decisions, it pays to run the numbers. Consult with your financial advisor about whether a Roth IRA conversion makes sense for you.

Converting from a SIMPLE IRA. Generally, you can convert an amount in your SIMPLE IRA to a Roth IRA under the same rules explained earlier under *Converting from any traditional IRA.*

However, you cannot convert any amount distributed from the SIMPLE IRA during the 2-year period beginning on the date you first participated in any SIMPLE IRA plan maintained by your employer.

More information. For more detailed information on conversions, see Publication 590.

Rollover From a Roth IRA

You can withdraw, tax free, all or part of the assets from one Roth IRA if you contribute them within 60 days to another Roth IRA. Most of the rules for rollovers explained under *Rollover From One IRA Into Another* under *Traditional IRAs,* earlier, apply to these rollovers.

Failed Conversions

If, when you converted amounts from a traditional IRA or SIMPLE IRA (including a transfer by redesignation) into a Roth IRA, you expected to have modified AGI of less than $100,000 and a filing status other than married filing separately, but events changed these facts, you have made a failed conversion.

Adverse consequences. If the converted amount (contribution) is not recharacterized (explained later), the contribution will be treated as a regular contribution to the Roth IRA and subject to the following tax consequences.

1) A 6% excise tax per year will apply to any excess contribution not withdrawn from the Roth IRA.
2) The distributions from the traditional IRA must be included in your gross income.
3) The 10% additional tax on early distributions may apply to any distribution.

How to avoid. You must move the amount converted (including all earnings from the date of conversion) into a traditional IRA by the due date (including extensions) for your tax return for the year during which you made the conversion to the Roth IRA. You do not have to include this distribution (withdrawal) in income. See *Recharacterizations,* next, for more information.

Recharacterizations

You may be able to treat a contribution made to one type of IRA as having been made to a different type of IRA. This is called recharacterizing the contribution. More detailed information is in Publication 590.

No deduction allowed. No deduction is allowed for the contribution to the first IRA and any net income transferred with the recharacterized contribution is treated as earned in the second IRA.

How to recharacterize a contribution. To recharacterize a contribution, you generally must have the contribution transferred from the first IRA (the one to which it was made) to the second IRA in a trustee-to-trustee transfer. If the transfer is made by the due date (including extensions) for your tax return for the year during which the contribution was made, you can elect to treat the contribution as having been originally made to the second IRA instead of to the first IRA. It will be treated as having been made to the second IRA on the same date that it was actually made to the first IRA.

Required notifications. To recharacterize a contribution, you must notify both the trustee of the first IRA (the one to which the contribution was actually made) and the trustee of the second IRA that you have elected to treat, for federal tax purposes, the contribution as having been made to the second IRA rather than the first. You must make the notifications by the date of the transfer. Only one notification is required if both IRAs are maintained by the same trustee. The notification(s) must include all of the following information.

- The type and amount of the contribution to the first IRA that is to be recharacterized.
- The date on which the contribution was made to the first IRA and the year for which it was made.
- A direction to the trustee of the first IRA to transfer in a trustee-to-trustee transfer the amount of the contribution and any net income allocable to the contribution to the trustee of the second IRA. If there was a loss while the contribution was in the first IRA, the net income that must be transferred may be a negative amount.
- The name of the trustee of the first IRA and the name of the trustee of the second IRA.
- Any additional information needed to make the transfer.

Note. If the trustee of your first IRA is unable to calculate the amount of net income you must transfer, get IRS Notice 2000-39. The notice explains the IRS-approved method of calculating the amount you must transfer.

Reporting a recharacterization. If you elect to recharacterize a contribution to one IRA as a contribution to another IRA, you must report the recharacterization on your tax return as directed by Form 8606 and its instructions. You must treat the contribution as having been made to the second IRA.

Are Distributions From My Roth IRA Taxable?

You do not include in your gross income *qualified distributions* or distributions that are a return of your regular contributions from your Roth IRA(s). You also do not include distributions from your Roth IRA that you roll over tax free into another Roth IRA. You may have to include part of other distributions in your income. See *Ordering rules for distributions,* later.

What are qualified distributions? A qualified distribution is any payment or distribution from your Roth IRA that meets the following requirements.

1) It is made after the 5-taxable-year period beginning with the first taxable year for which a contribution was made to a Roth IRA set up for your benefit, and
2) The payment or distribution is:
   a) Made on or after the date you reach age 59 1/2,
   b) Made because you are disabled,
   c) Made to a beneficiary or to your estate after your death, or
   d) To pay certain qualified first-time homebuyer amounts discussed in Publication 590.

Additional tax on distributions of conversion contributions within 5-year period. If, within the 5-year period starting with the year in which you made a conversion contribution of an amount from a traditional IRA to a Roth IRA, you take a distribution from a Roth IRA of an amount attributable to the portion of the conversion contribution that you had to include in income, you generally must pay the 10% additional tax on early distributions. (See *Ordering Rules for Distributions,* later, to determine the amount, if any, of the distribution that is attributable to the conversion contribution.) The 5-year period is separately determined for each conversion contribution.

Additional tax on other early distributions. The taxable part of other distributions from your Roth IRA(s) that are not qualified distributions is subject to the additional tax on early distributions. See Publication 590 for more information.

Ordering rules for distributions. If you receive a distribution from your Roth IRA that is *not* a qualified distribution, part of it may be taxable. There is a set order in which contributions (including conversion contributions) and earnings are considered to be distributed from your Roth IRA. Regular contributions are distributed first. See Publication 590 for more information.

Explanation

The Roth IRA includes a special ordering rule that allows early withdrawals (before age 59½), also known as non-qualified distributions. This rule provides that amounts withdrawn are first considered to come from contributions. After all original contributions have been withdrawn, remaining amounts are considered to have arisen from earnings within the IRA. Distribution of these amounts are taxable and could be subject to an early withdrawal penalty. Early withdrawals from a Roth IRA, therefore, are tax free and penalty free as long as the taxpayer is withdrawing contributions, not accumulated earnings.

Am I required to take distributions when I reach age 70 1/2? You are not required to take distributions from your Roth IRA at any age. The minimum distribution rules that apply to traditional IRAs do not apply to Roth IRAs while the owner is alive. However, after the death of a Roth IRA owner, certain of the minimum distribution rules that apply to traditional IRAs also apply to Roth IRAs.

TAXPLANNER

There are no minimum required distributions (MRDs) for a Roth IRA *during the life of the account owner*. This means that your account can stay intact for as long as you live, allowing investment earnings to grow on a tax-free basis. In addition, if you're married, your spouse—if named the beneficiary of the account—can "step into your shoes" (e.g., by establishing a Roth IRA rollover account) and continue to defer distributions during the remainder of his or her lifetime.

Following your death (or the death of your surviving spouse if he or she were named the account beneficiary and rolled over the account after your death), the normal post-mortem MRD rules would apply (see *Required Distributions* earlier). Since there is technically no required beginning date for making MRDs from a Roth IRA during your life, the schedule of required distributions after your death would be determined by your designated beneficiary who can receive distributions over his or her remaining life expectancy, so long as the first MRD is made by December 31 in the year following the year of your death. The ability to delay distributions until after your death, and then have the account gradually distributed tax free to heirs over their lifetimes, creates a useful way to transfer wealth from one generation to another.

More information. For more detailed information on Roth IRAs, see Publication 590.

Explanation: Simplified Employee Pensions (SEPs)

A simplified employee pension is a written plan that allows an employer to make contributions toward an employee's retirement without becoming involved in more complex retirement plans. If you are self-employed, you can contribute to your own SEP.

The SEP rules permit an employer to contribute and deduct each year to each participating employee's SEP up to 15% of the employee's compensation or $25,500, whichever is less. (The $25,500 is based on compensation being limited to $170,000. This amount is adjusted annually for inflation, but the amount contributed can never exceed $30,000 in any one year.) If you are self-employed, special rules apply when figuring the maximum deduction for these contributions. In determining the percentage limit on contributions, compensation is net earnings from self-employment, taking into account the contributions to the SEP.

TAXSAVER

Even if your employer makes contributions to an SEP for your account, you can make contributions to your own IRA. The IRA deduction rules, previously discussed, apply to any amounts you contribute to your IRA.

TAXSAVER

A self-employed person can claim a deduction to an SEP as long as the contribution is made by the due date of the return, including extensions. Even if you failed to set up a plan by December 31, you can still establish an SEP after the end of the year and make a timely payment.

TAXALERT

SEPs permitting salary reduction contributions cannot be established after 1996, although SEPs that allowed elective deferrals before 1997 can continue to do so.

Explanation: Saving Incentive Match Plans for Employees (SIMPLE)

For tax years after 1996, your employer can establish a new type of retirement plan called the savings incentive match plan for employees. In general, employers with 100 or fewer employees earning at least $5,000 and who do not maintain another employer-sponsored retirement plan are eligible to set up SIMPLE plans, which were created by the Small Business Job Protection Act of 1996. SIMPLE plans, which are not subject to some of the complicated rules that apply to other types of retirement plans, can be adopted as an IRA or as a part of a 401(k) plan. All employees who earn more than $5,000 a year must be eligible to participate, and self-employed individuals may also participate in SIMPLE plans. In general, contributions to a SIMPLE plan are not taxable until withdrawn.

The employer generally must either match elective employee contributions (limited to $6,000 annually) dollar for dollar up to 3% of compensation or make a "nonelective" contribution of 2% of compensation on behalf of each eligible employee. No other contributions may be made to a

SIMPLE account. Contributions to a SIMPLE account generally are deductible by the employer; however, matching contributions are deductible only if made by the due date (including extensions) of the employer's tax return.

TaxAlert: The 2001 Tax Act

Beginning in 2002, the limit on maximum annual elective deferrals to a SIMPLE plan will increase as follows:

Year	Amount
2002	$7,000
2003	$8,000
2004	$9,000
2005	$10,000

Employers are given a 2-year grace period to maintain a SIMPLE plan once they are no longer eligible to participate.

TaxSaver

If you earn limited amounts of self-employment income, a SIMPLE IRA may allow you to shelter the maximum amount from taxes. Although employee elective contributions to SIMPLE IRAs are capped at $6,000 per year for 2001, contributions are not subject to a percentage-of-compensation limitation as they are in a Keogh plan. Thus, if you received $10,000 in self-employment income, you could deduct a contribution of $6,000 (or 60%) to a SIMPLE IRA, plus any matching contributions.

Coverdell Education Savings Accounts

Education IRAs have been renamed Coverdell Education Savings Accounts, hereafter referred to as Educational Savings Accounts.

You may be able to contribute up to $500 each year to an education savings account for a child under age 18. Contributions to an education savings account are not deductible.

Any individual (including the child) can contribute to a child's education savings account if the individual's *modified adjusted gross income* (defined later) is less than $110,000 ($160,000 on a joint return). The $500 maximum contribution for each contributor is gradually reduced if the individual's modified adjusted gross income is between $95,000 and $110,000 (between $150,000 and $160,000 on a joint return). See *Who Can Contribute to an Education Savings Account?*, later.

Explanation

There is no limit on the number of education savings accounts that can be established designating the same child as the beneficiary. However, *total* contributions for the child during any tax year cannot be more than $500.

Amounts deposited in the accounts grow tax free until distributed (withdrawn).

If, for a year, distributions from an account are not more than a child's *qualified higher education expenses* (defined later) at an *eligible educational institution* (defined later), the distributions are not taxable. See *Are Distributions Taxable*, later, for more information.

What Is an Education Savings Account?

An education savings account is a trust or custodial account created only for the purpose of paying the *qualified higher education expenses* (defined later) of the designated beneficiary of the account. To be treated as an education savings account, the account must be designated as such when it is created. It must be created or organized in the United States.

Account requirements. The document creating and governing the account must be in writing and must satisfy certain requirements. See Publication 590.

Designated beneficiary. The designated beneficiary is the individual on whose behalf the trust or custodial account has been established.

Qualified higher education expenses. These are expenses required for the enrollment or attendance of the designated beneficiary at an *eligible educational institution.* The following are qualified higher education expenses.

1) Tuition.
2) Fees.
3) Books.
4) Supplies.
5) Equipment.
6) Amounts contributed to a qualified state tuition program. State tuition programs are discussed in Publication 970, *Tax Benefits for Higher Education.*
7) Room and board if the designated beneficiary is at least a half-time student at an eligible educational institution. A student is enrolled at least half-time if he or she is enrolled for at least half the full-time academic workload for the course of study the student is pursuing as determined under the standards of the institution where the student is enrolled. Room and board is limited to:
    a) The school's posted room and board charge for students living on-campus, or
    b) $2,500 each year for students living off-campus and not at home.

Eligible educational institution. This is any college, university, vocational school, or other postsecondary educational institution eligible to participate in the student aid programs administered by the Department of Education. It includes virtually any accredited public, nonprofit, or proprietary (privately owned profit-making) postsecondary institution.

Who Can Contribute to an Education Savings Account?

Any individual (including the designated beneficiary) can contribute to a child's education savings account if the individual's modified adjusted gross income (discussed later) for the tax year is less than $110,000 ($160,000 for married taxpayers filing jointly).

TaxAlert: The 2001 Tax Act

In 2002, the contribution phase-out range for joint filers increases to $190,000–$220,000 (double the single filer phase-out range of $95,000–$110,000).

Contributions can be made to one or several education savings account for the same child provided that the total contributions are not more than the *contribution limit* (defined later) for a tax year.

Qualified state tuition program. No contributions can be made to an education savings account on behalf of a beneficiary if any amount is contributed during the tax year to a qualified state tuition program on behalf of the same beneficiary. For more information on state tuition programs see Publication 970.

Contribution Limits

There are two yearly limits, one on the total amount that can be contributed for each designated beneficiary (child) and one on the amount that any individual can contribute for any one child for a year.

Limit for each child. The total of all contributions to all education savings accounts set up for the benefit of any one designated beneficiary (child) cannot be more than $500 for a tax year. This includes contributions (other than rollovers) to all the child's education savings accounts from all sources. Rollovers are discussed at *Can Education Savings Account Assets Be Moved?,* later.

Limit for each contributor. You can contribute up to $500 for each child for any tax year. This is the most you can contribute for the benefit of any one child for any year, regardless of the number of education savings accounts set up for the child. This limit may be reduced as explained next.

TAXALERT

In 2001, the annual $500 contribution limit is measured on a calendar year basis (unlike regular IRAs where the contributor has until April 15 of the next year to make a contribution). Therefore, education savings account contributors with AGI near the phaseout limits must carefully calculate the amount they can contribute by the end of the calendar year. Beginning in 2002, the taxpayer has until April 15 of the following year to make a contribution.

TAXPLANNER

If your AGI is above the limits previously discussed, you cannot make a contribution to an education savings account on behalf of any individual. However, you can gift the $500 to the individual and then the individual can make the contribution to his or her education savings account.

Distributions. Distributions from an education savings account are excludable from gross income to the extent that the distribution does not exceed qualified higher education expenses (e.g., postsecondary tuition, fees, books, supplies, equipment, and certain room and board expenses) incurred by the beneficiary during the year the distribution is made. The beneficiary can be enrolled at an eligible educational institution on a full-time, half-time, or less than half-time basis.

Reduced limit for certain contributors. If your *modified adjusted gross income* (defined next) is between $95,000 and $110,000 (between $150,000 and $160,000 if filing a joint return), your $500 limit for each child is gradually reduced. If your modified adjusted income is $110,000 or more ($160,000 or more if filing a joint return), you cannot contribute to anyone's education savings account. See Publication 590 for more information.

Modified adjusted gross income. Your modified adjusted gross income for the purpose of determining the contribution limit is the adjusted gross income shown on your return, increased by the following exclusions from your income.

1) Foreign earned income of U.S. citizens or residents living abroad.
2) Housing costs of U.S. citizens or residents living abroad.
3) Income from sources within:
   a) Puerto Rico,
   b) Guam,
   c) American Samoa, or
   d) The Northern Mariana Islands.

Additional tax on excess contributions. A 6% excise tax applies each year to excess contributions that are in an education savings account at the end of the year. Excess contributions are the *total* of the following three amounts.

1) Contributions to any child's education savings account for the year that are more than $500 or, if less, the total of each contributor's limit for the year, as discussed earlier.
2) All contributions to a child's education savings account for the year if any amount is also contributed during the year to a qualified state tuition program on behalf of the same child. However, amounts distributed from the education savings account to be contributed to the qualified state tuition program are not excess contributions.
3) Excess contributions for the preceding year, reduced by the total of the following two amounts:
   a) Distributions (other than those rolled over as discussed later) made during the year, and
   b) The contribution limit for the current year minus the amount contributed for the current year.

When Contributions Can Be Made

You can make contributions to an education savings account for a year at any time during the year. The last day you could have made a contribution for 2001 was December 31, 2001.

Other Contribution Rules

You can contribute only cash to an education savings account. You also cannot contribute to an education savings account after the beneficiary reaches age 18.

Can Education Savings Account Assets Be Moved?

You can roll over assets from one education savings account to another. You can also change the designated beneficiary or transfer the beneficiary's interest to a spouse or former spouse.

Rollovers

Any amount distributed from an education savings account and rolled over to another education savings account for the benefit of the same designated beneficiary or a member of the designated beneficiary's family is not taxable. This rule applies only if the beneficiary of the new education savings account is under age 30 on the date of the rollover contribution to the new education savings account.

An amount is rolled over if it is paid to another education savings account within 60 days after the date of the distribution.

Members of the beneficiary's family. The beneficiary's spouse and the following individuals (and their spouses) are members of the designated beneficiary's family.

1) The beneficiary's child, grandchild, or stepchild.
2) A brother, sister, stepbrother, or stepsister of the beneficiary.
3) A son or daughter of the beneficiary's brother or sister.
4) The father, mother, grandfather, grandmother, stepfather, or stepmother of the beneficiary.
5) A brother or sister of the beneficiary's father or mother.
6) The beneficiary's son-in-law, daughter-in-law, father-in-law, mother-in-law, brother-in-law, or sister-in-law.

Caution. *Only one rollover per education savings account is allowed during the 12-month period ending on the date of the payment or distribution.*

Changing the Designated Beneficiary

The designated beneficiary can be changed to certain members of the beneficiary's family (listed earlier). There are no tax consequences if, at the time of the change, the new beneficiary is under age 30.

Transfer Because of Divorce

The transfer of a designated beneficiary's interest in an education savings account to his or her spouse or former spouse under a divorce or separation instrument is not a taxable transfer. After the transfer, the interest will be treated as an education savings account in which the spouse or former spouse is the designated beneficiary.

Are Distributions Taxable?

Distributions that are not more than the designated beneficiary's qualified higher education expenses during the year are generally tax free. The portion of any distribution that is more than the education expenses may be taxable.

What Determines the Tax Treatment of Distributions?

The tax treatment of distributions (withdrawals) from an education savings account depends, in part, on the qualified higher education expenses that a designated beneficiary has in a tax year.

Distribution not more than expenses. Generally, a distribution is tax-free if it is not more than the designated beneficiary's qualified higher education expenses in a tax year.

Caution. *You cannot take a tax deduction or credit for educational expenses you use as the basis for a tax-free distribution from an education savings account.*

Waiver of tax-free treatment. If you are the designated beneficiary, you can waive the tax-free treatment of the education savings account distribution and elect to pay any tax that would otherwise be owed on the distribution. You or your parents may then be eligible to claim a Hope credit or lifetime learning credit for qualified higher education expenses paid with the distribution in that tax year.

Distributions more than expenses. Generally, if the total distributions for a tax year are more than the qualified higher education expenses, a portion of the amount distributed is taxable and the beneficiary must include it in income. For more information, see Publication 590.

Additional tax. Generally, if you receive a taxable distribution, you must pay a **10%** additional tax on the amount you must include in income.

Exceptions. There are exceptions to the 10% additional tax for special situations such as the death or disability of the designated beneficiary. For more information, see Publication 590.

When Must Education Savings Account Assets Be Distributed?

Generally, any assets remaining in an education savings account **must** be distributed when either one of the following two events occurs.

1) The designated beneficiary reaches age 30. In this case, the remaining assets must be distributed within 30 days after he or she reaches age 30.
2) The designated beneficiary dies before reaching age 30. In this case, the remaining assets must generally be distributed within 30 days after the date of death.

Exception for transfer to surviving spouse or family member. If an education savings account is transferred or rolled over to a surviving spouse or other family member (defined earlier) under age 30 when distribution is required under these rules, there are no income tax consequences as a result of the transfer.

More information. For a more detailed discussion of these rules, see Publication 590.

19

Moving Expenses

Introduction

The good news about moving expenses is that you usually may deduct them if you move because you change jobs. The not-so-good news is that, because no two moves are alike, there are several tests you must meet in order to claim the deductions and disagreements with the IRS over moving expenses are frequent.

Moving expenses are deducted from your gross income in arriving at your adjusted gross income (AGI). This can be advantageous, since you do not have to itemize your expenses to receive the benefit of the deduction.

Some tax breaks associated with moving have been

eliminated. In general, meals bought in connection with a move, expenses related to searching for a residence or living in temporary quarters, and expenses incurred in selling, purchasing, or leasing a residence in connection with a move are not deductible expenses.

If you are interested in deducting as much of your move as possible, the first rule you should follow is to keep adequate records of all of your moving-related expenditures. Receipts, plus a log of your activities, generally suffice. The other ins and outs of moving expenses are detailed in this chapter.

Important Change

Standard mileage rate. The standard mileage rate for moving expenses has been increased to 12 cents a mile. See *Travel by car* under *Deductible Moving Expenses.*

Important Reminder

Change of address. If you change your mailing address, be sure to notify the IRS using **Form 8822,** *Change of Address.* Mail it to the Internal Revenue Service Center for your old address. Addresses for the Service Centers are on the back of the form.

This chapter explains the deduction of certain expenses of moving to a new home because you changed job locations or started a new job. This includes the following topics.

- Who can deduct moving expenses.
- What moving expenses are deductible.
- What moving expenses are not deductible.
- How to report moving expenses.

You may qualify for the moving expense deduction whether you are self-employed or an employee. However, you must meet the requirements explained under *Who Can Deduct Moving Expenses.*

Moves to locations outside the United States. This chapter does not discuss moves outside the United States. If you are a United States citizen or resident alien who moved outside the United States or its pos-

sessions because of your job or business, see Publication 521, *Moving Expenses,* for special rules that apply to your move.

TaxORGANIZER

Records You Should Keep
- Receipts for:
  Professional mover's fees
  Rental of moving truck and/or equipment
  Storage and insurance of household goods and personal effects
  Cost of lodging while traveling from former home to new home
  Parking fees and tolls during move
- Mileage for use of car or actual expenses (gas and oil) while traveling from former home to new home

Useful Items

You may want to see:

Publication

☐ **521**   Moving Expenses

Form (and Instructions)

☐ **3903**   Moving Expenses
☐ **8822**   Change of Address

Who Can Deduct Moving Expenses

You can deduct your allowable moving expenses if your move is closely related to the start of work. You also must meet the distance test and the time test. These two tests are discussed later. After you have read the distance and time test rules, you may want to use *Figure 19–A* to help you decide if your move qualifies.

Related to the Start of Work

Your move must be closely related, both in time and in place, to the start of work at your new job location.

Closely related in time. You can generally consider moving expenses incurred within 1 year from the date you first reported to work at the new location as closely related in time to the start of work. It is not necessary that you arrange to work before moving to a new location, as long as you actually do go to work.

If you do not move within 1 year of the date you begin work, you ordinarily cannot deduct the expenses unless you can show that circumstances existed that prevented the move within that time.

Example. Your family moved more than a year after you started work at a new location. You delayed the move for 18 months to allow your child to complete high school. You can deduct your allowable moving expenses.

> **Explanation**
> You must make the actual move within a year of starting a new job, unless circumstances prevent you from doing so. Although not moving your family so that your child may complete high school in the same school is an acceptable reason, not moving because you haven't sold your home is not. Good intentions are not enough.

Figure 19–A. **Qualifying Moves Within the United States (Non-Military)**[1]

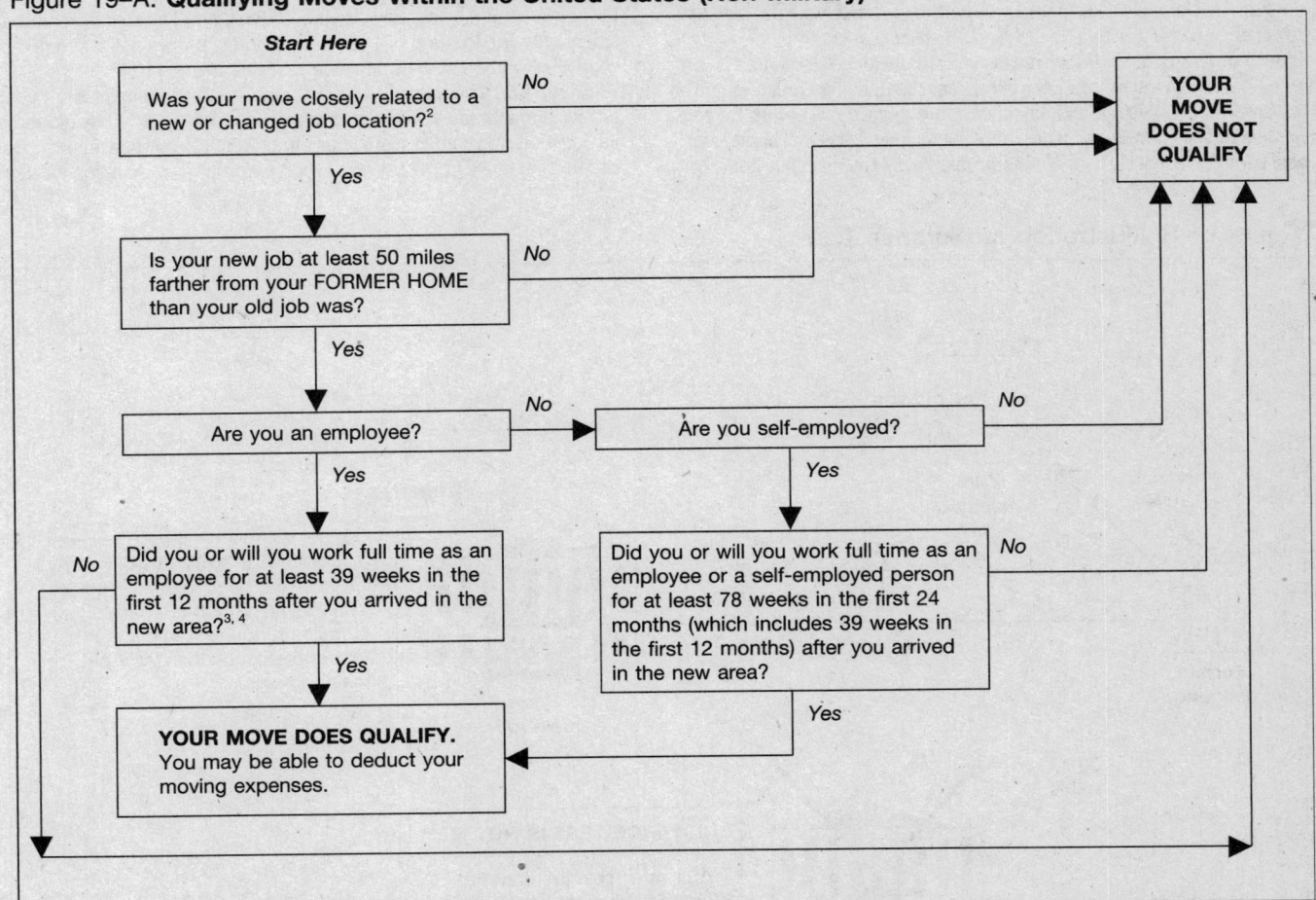

[1]Military persons should see *Members of the Armed Forces* for special rules that apply to them.

[2]Your move must be closely related to the start of work at your new job location. See *Related to Start of Work.*

[3]If you deduct expenses and do not meet this test later, you must either file an amended tax return or report your moving expense deduction as other income. See *Time test not yet met.*

[4]If you become self-employed during the first 12 months, answer YES if your combined time as a full-time employee and self-employed person equals or will equal at least 78 weeks in the first 24 months (including 39 weeks in the first twelve months) after you arrived in the new area.

Closely related in place. You can generally consider your move closely related in place to the start of work if the distance from your new home to the new job location is not more than the distance from your former home to the new job location. A move that does not meet this requirement may qualify if you can show that:

1) You are required to live at that home as a condition of your employment, or
2) You will spend less time or money commuting from your new home to your new job location.

Explanation

Assume that your new home is 60 miles from your new job but that your former home was only 55 miles from your new job. If you want to deduct your moving expenses, you must give the IRS an acceptable reason why you now drive farther than you would have if you hadn't moved. An acceptable reason might be that from your new home you are able to use a freeway or a commuter train or bus that saves you time and/or money, whereas before you had to drive across town on local streets all the way to work.

Retirees or survivors. You may be able to deduct the expenses of moving to the United States or its possessions even if the move is not related to the start of work at a new job location. You must have worked outside the United States or be a survivor of someone who did. See *Retirees or Survivors Who Move to the United States,* later.

Home defined. Your *home* means your main home (residence). It can be a house, apartment, condominium, houseboat, house trailer, or similar dwelling. It does not include other homes owned or kept up by you or members of your family. It also does not include a seasonal home, such as a summer beach cottage. Your *former home* means your home before you left for your new job location. Your *new home* means your home within the area of your new job location.

TaxSaver

First-time job seekers, such as high school and college graduates, and people reentering the labor force after a substantial period of unemployment may deduct moving expenses.

You must move from a former principal home to a new principal home, which means that you must have a principal home from which to move. According to one court, a college graduate could not deduct his expenses to move to his new job location because his student residence was not his principal home.

Distance Test

Your move will meet the distance test if your new main job location is *at least 50 miles* farther from your former home than your old main job location was from your former home. For example, if your old main job location was 3 miles from your former home, your new main job location must be at least 53 miles from that former home.

The distance between a job location and your home is the shortest of the more commonly traveled routes between them. The distance test considers only the location of your former home. It does not take into account the location of your new home. See *Figure 19–B.*

Example. You moved to a new home less than 50 miles from your former home because you changed main job locations. Your old main job location was 3 miles from your former home. Your new main job location is 60 miles from that home. Because your new main job location

Figure 19–B. **Illustration of Distance Test**

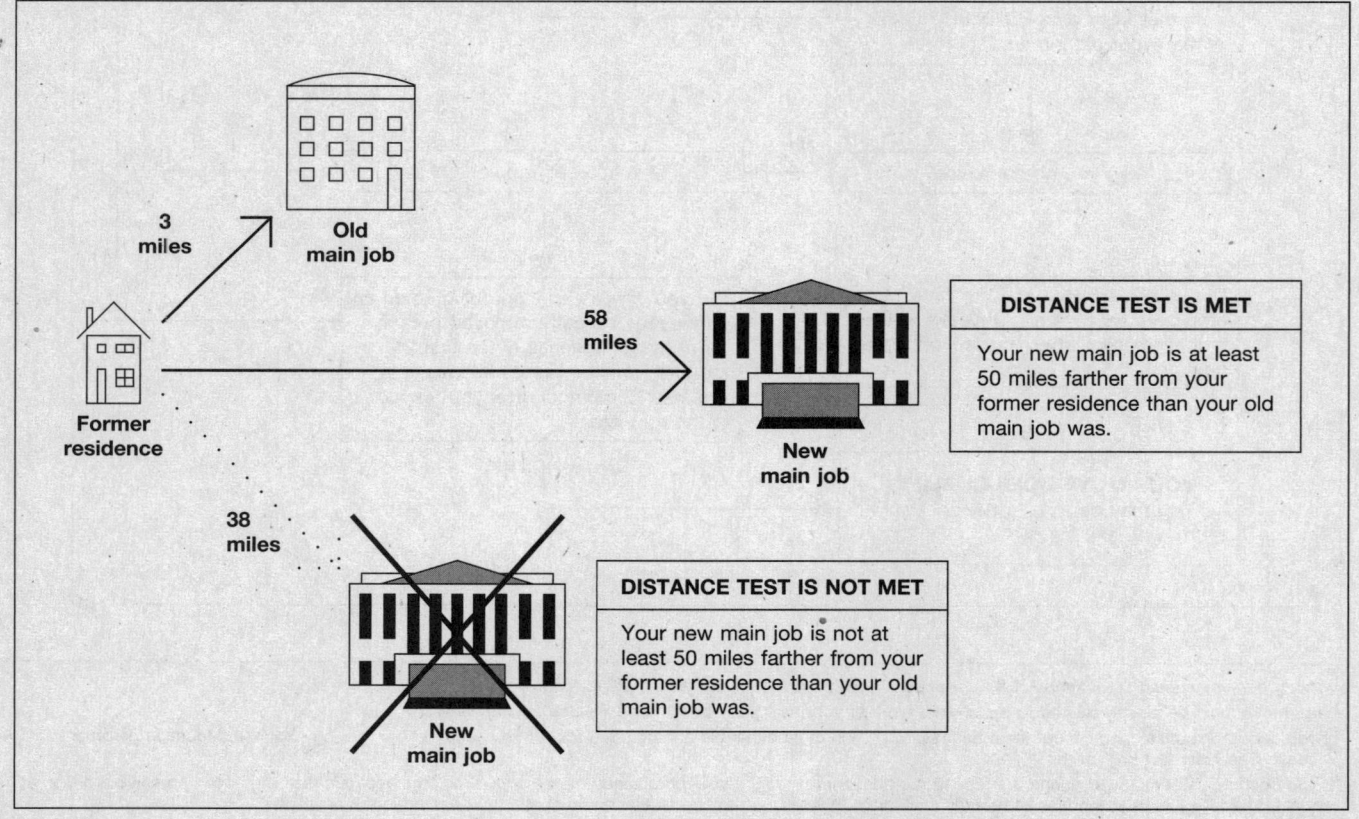

is 57 miles farther from your former home than the distance from your former home to your old main job location, you meet the distance test.

Explanation

The key is that your new job location must be at least 50 miles farther from your former home than your old job location. The IRS doesn't care how far away you live from your new office in absolute terms. To be able to deduct moving expenses, your new job has to be 50 miles farther from your former home than your old job used to be.

Example

Even though you may now live 55 miles from your office, the fact that your office is only 45 miles more from your old home than it used to be means that you will not be able to deduct your moving expenses.

You can tell whether you meet the distance test simply by subtracting the total miles from your *old* home to the old job from the total miles from the old home to the new job. The difference must be 50 miles or greater.

First job or return to full-time work. If you go to work full time for the first time, your place of work must be at least 50 miles from your former home to meet the distance test.

If you go back to full-time work after a substantial period of part-time work or unemployment, your place of work must also be at least 50 miles from your former home.

Explanation

Two months of unemployment is not long enough to qualify as a substantial period of unemployment. If you had only a brief break in employment, you must meet the same distance requirement that you would if you had been working continuously.

Exception for Armed Forces. If you are in the Armed Forces and you moved because of a permanent change of station, you do not have to meet the distance test. See *Members of the Armed Forces,* later.

Main job location. Your main job location is usually the place where you spend most of your working time. If there is no one place where you spend most of your working time, your main job location is the place where your work is centered, such as where you report for work or are otherwise required to "base" your work.

Union members. If you work for several employers on a short-term basis and you get work under a union hall system (such as a construction or building trades worker), your main job location is the union hall.

More than one job. If you have more than one job at any time, your main job location depends on the facts in each case. The more important factors to be considered are:

- The total time you spend at each place,
- The amount of work you do at each place, and
- How much money you earn at each place.

Example 1

A consultant working on an assignment in Detroit—a city that was not his main job location—was allowed by the Tax Court to deduct moving expenses when, at the request of his employer, he moved from Canton, Ohio, to Dallas, Texas, even though he continued the consulting assignment in Detroit. The Tax Court's rationale was that Detroit was only a temporary place of work and that the moving ex-

penses arose from a shift from one principal place of work— Canton—to another—Dallas.

Example 2

A government employee moved to Washington, D.C., from Honolulu but took a temporary leave of absence from her job to go to Texas to continue her studies. The Tax Court ruled that she could not deduct her moving expenses to Washington, D.C., since her location during the time of her leave was not in the "general location" of her new workplace.

A person on leave is still considered to be a full-time employee and must meet the distance requirements as though he or she were actually working at his or her new business location. In this example, the employee would have had to remain in Washington, D.C., for the required 39 weeks in the year (see below) following her move from Honolulu for her moving expenses to have been deductible.

Time Test

To deduct your moving expenses, you also must meet one of the following two time tests.

1) The time test for employees.
2) The time test for self-employed persons.

See *Table 19–1* for a summary of these tests.

Time test for employees. If you are an employee, you must work full time for at least *39 weeks during the first 12 months* after you arrive in the general area of your new job location. Full-time employment depends on what is usual for your type of work in your area.

For purposes of this test, the following four rules apply.

1) You count only your full-time work as an employee, not any work you do as a self-employed person.
2) You do not have to work for the same employer for all 39 weeks.
3) You do not have to work 39 weeks in a row.
4) You must work full time within the same general commuting area for all 39 weeks.

Explanation

The courts have held that the mere enrollment in an employment registry does not by itself constitute full-time employment.

Example

A registered nurse moved to California, where she enrolled with a nursing registry that facilitated the employment of nurses. Even though it may be the customary method to obtain a job in a hospital in California, the mere enrollment in the registry does not establish the taxpayer as a full-time employee.

Temporary absence from work. You are considered to have worked full time during any week you are temporarily absent from work because of illness, strikes, lockouts, layoffs, natural disasters, or similar causes. You are also considered to have worked full time during any week you are absent from work for leave or vacation provided for in your work contract or agreement.

Seasonal work. If your work is seasonal, you are considered to be working full time during the off-season only if your work contract or agreement covers an off-season period and that period is less than 6

Table 19–1. Satisfying the Time Test for Employees and Self-Employed Persons

IF you are...	THEN you satisfy the time test by meeting...
An employee	The 39-week test for employees.
Self-employed and an employee but unable to satisfy the 39-week test for employees	The 78-week test for self-employed persons.
Both self-employed and an employee at the same time	The 78-week test for a self-employed person or the 39-week test for an employee based on your principal place of work.
Self-employed	The 78-week test for self-employed persons.

months. For example, a school teacher on a 12-month contract who teaches on a full-time basis for more than 6 months is considered to have worked full time for the entire 12 months.

Explanation

According to the IRS, a seasonal employee under contract for less than 39 weeks of work does not meet the 39-week test unless the contract is extended and the employee actually works the required additional time or is prevented from doing so involuntarily, for example, because of illness, natural disaster, or a similar cause.

Time test for self-employed persons. If you are self-employed, you must work full time for at least *39 weeks during the first 12 months AND* for a total of at least *78 weeks during the first 24 months* after you arrive in your new job location. For purposes of this test, the following three rules apply.

1) You count any full-time work you do either as an employee or as a self-employed person.
2) You do not have to work for the same employer or be self-employed in the same trade or business for the 78 weeks.
3) You must work within the same general commuting area for all 78 weeks.

If you were both an employee and self-employed, see *Table 19–1* for the requirements.

Self-employment. You are self-employed if you work as the sole owner of an unincorporated business or as a partner in a partnership carrying on a business. You are not considered self-employed if you are semiretired, are a part-time student, or work only a few hours each week.

Full-time work. You can count only those weeks during which you work full time as a week of work. Whether you work full time during any week depends on what is usual for your type of work in your area.

For more information, see *Time test for self-employed persons* in Publication 521.

Joint return. If you are married and file a joint return and both you and your spouse work full time, either of you can satisfy the full-time work test. However, you cannot combine the weeks your spouse worked with the weeks you worked to satisfy that test.

TaxSaver

If you file separate returns, each person must meet the time test individually and deduct only his or her own expenses.

The time test may be met by either spouse if a joint return is filed. However, weeks worked by both husband and wife cannot be added together to meet the time test.

If you and your spouse are living together, and if both of you have been working full-time but one of you loses your job, you obtain the maximum tax benefits by filing a joint return. This is the case even if you reside in a **community property** state. Moving expenses paid by both husband and wife may be aggregated and are deductible in full.

Time test not yet met. You can deduct your moving expenses on your 2001 tax return even if you have not yet met the time test by the date your 2001 return is due. You can do this if you expect to meet the 39-week test in 2002, or the 78-week test in 2002 or 2003. If you deduct moving expenses but do not meet the time test in 2002 or 2003, you must either:

1) Report your moving expense deduction as other income on your Form 1040 for the year you cannot meet the test, or
2) Amend your 2001 return.

Use Form 1040X, *Amended U.S. Individual Income Tax Return,* to amend your return.

If you do not deduct your moving expenses on your 2001 return and you later meet the time test, you can file an amended return for 2001 to take the deduction.

Exceptions to the Time Test

You do not have to meet the time test if one of the following applies.

1) You are in the Armed Forces and you moved because of a permanent change of station. See *Members of the Armed Forces,* later.
2) You moved to the United States because you retired. See *Retirees or Survivors Who Move to the United States,* later.
3) You are the survivor of a person whose main job location at the time of death was outside the United States. See *Retirees or Survivors Who Move to the United States,* later.
4) Your job at the new location ends because of death or disability.
5) You are transferred for your employer's benefit or laid off for a reason other than willful misconduct. For this exception, you must have

obtained full-time employment and you must have expected to meet the test at the time you started the job.

Explanation
The courts have held and the IRS agrees that if, after moving for job-related purposes, you are fired or laid off, involuntarily lose your job (for other than willful misconduct), or are required to move again by your employer before the 39 weeks are up, you are still able to deduct your moving expenses. Death and disability also exempt a taxpayer from the 39-week requirement. However, if you voluntarily take a leave of absence—even if employment benefits continue—you may not count the leave period toward the 39 weeks.

Example
A taxpayer who terminated his employment voluntarily after working in his new location only 37 weeks (even though he did so in order to start a different job elsewhere) was not allowed the deduction for his original moving costs.

TaxSaver
Since you have 2 years to fulfill the time requirement, you should assume that you will meet it and deduct moving expenses in the year in which you incur them. Even if you expect to incur more moving expenses later, do not wait to deduct those that you already have incurred. Any later expenses that qualify may be deducted in a subsequent year.

If you fail to meet the time test later, you may either file an amended return and repay any tax due along with interest or report as income the amount you previously deducted. In some cases, the 2-year period may be extended.

Example
A woman was allowed to deduct moving expenses incurred 30 months after her transfer because she waited until her child finished school before moving her family. The IRS rule is: You have to demonstrate that there is a good reason for the delay.

Members of the Armed Forces
If you are a member of the Armed Forces on active duty and you move because of a permanent change of station, you do not have to meet the *distance and time tests,* discussed earlier. You can deduct your unreimbursed allowable moving expenses.

A permanent change of station includes:

1) A move from your home to your first post of active duty,
2) A move from one permanent post of duty to another, and
3) A move from your last post of duty to your home or to a nearer point in the United States. The move must occur within 1 year of ending your active duty or within the period allowed under the Joint Travel Regulations.

Spouse and dependents. If a member of the Armed Forces dies, is imprisoned, or deserts, a permanent change of station for the spouse or dependent includes a move to:

- The place of enlistment,
- The member's, spouse's, or dependent's home of record, or
- A nearer point in the United States.

If the military moves you and your spouse and dependents to or from separate locations, the moves are treated as a single move to your new main job location.

More information. For more information on moving expenses for members of the Armed Forces, and instructions for completing Form 3903, see *Members of the Armed Forces* in Publication 521.

Explanation
If a service member's family can't move to his or her new permanent location, the cost of moving the family to a new location is still deductible.

A service member's family may deduct expenses for a move to the foreign country to which the service member is transferred, even if the family obtains only 90-day tourist visas. The IRS recognizes the family as being part of the service member's household, residing with him or her before and after the move.

In general, a dislocation allowance received by armed services personnel is excludable from wages.

Retirees or Survivors Who Move to the United States
If you are a retiree who was working abroad or a survivor of a decedent who was working abroad and you move to the United States or one of its possessions, you do not have to meet the *time test,* discussed earlier. However, you must meet the requirements discussed below under *Retirees who were working abroad* or *Survivors of decedents who were working abroad.*

United States defined. For this section of the chapter, the term "United States" includes the possessions of the United States.

Retirees who were working abroad. You can deduct moving expenses for a move to a new home in the United States when you permanently retire. However, both your former main job location and your former home must have been outside the United States.

Permanently retired. You are considered permanently retired when you cease gainful full-time employment or self-employment. If, at the time you retire, you intend your retirement to be permanent, you will be considered retired though you later return to work. Your intention to retire permanently may be determined by:

1) Your age and health,
2) The customary retirement age for people who do similar work,
3) Whether you are receiving retirement payments from a pension or retirement fund, and
4) The length of time before you return to full-time work.

Explanation
A retiree may deduct the cost of moving back to a residence in the United States without having to be employed on returning. Although there is no timetable for the move specified in the law, it must be "in connection with the bona fide retirement of an individual." Moving expenses incurred after a lengthy delay following retirement may not be deductible.

Survivors of decedents who were working abroad. If you are the spouse or the dependent of a person whose main job location at the time of death was outside the United States, you can deduct moving expenses if the following five requirements are met.

1) The move is to a home in the United States.
2) The move begins within 6 months after the decedent's death. (When a move begins is described later.)
3) The move is from the decedent's former home.
4) The decedent's former home was outside the United States.
5) The decedent's former home was also your home.

When a move begins. A move begins when one of the following events occurs.

1) You contract for your household goods and personal effects to be moved to your home in the United States, but only if the move is completed within a reasonable time.
2) Your household goods and personal effects are packed and on the way to your home in the United States.
3) You leave your former home to travel to your new home in the United States.

Deductible Moving Expenses

If you meet the requirements discussed earlier under *Who Can Deduct Moving Expenses,* you can deduct the reasonable expenses of:

1) Moving your household goods and personal effects (including in-transit or foreign-move storage expenses), and
2) Traveling (including lodging but not meals) to your new home.

Caution. *You cannot deduct any expenses for meals.*

Reasonable expenses. You can deduct only those expenses that are reasonable for the circumstances of your move. For example, the cost of traveling from your former home to your new one should be by the shortest, most direct route available by conventional transportation. If, during your trip to your new home, you stop over, or make side trips for sightseeing, the additional expenses for your stopover or side trips are not deductible as moving expenses.

TAXPLANNER

Qualified moving expenses not paid or reimbursed by your employer will be allowed as a deduction in calculating your adjusted gross income. Moving expenses paid for by your employer directly or through reimbursement will be excludable from your gross income and wages for income and employment tax purposes, unless you actually deducted the expenses in a prior taxable year.

Travel by car. If you use your car to take yourself, members of your household, or your personal effects to your new home, you can figure your expenses by deducting either:

1) Your **actual expenses,** such as gas and oil for your car, if you keep an accurate record of each expense, or
2) The **standard mileage rate** of 12 cents a mile.

Whether you use actual expenses or the standard mileage rate to figure your expenses, you can deduct parking fees and tolls you paid in moving. You cannot deduct any part of general repairs, general maintenance, insurance, or depreciation for your car.

Explanation

The mileage rate used for moving expenses—12 cents per mile—is less than the rate used for business expenses—34.5 cents per mile.

The IRS has resisted any attempt to include depreciation of an automobile as a moving expense, maintaining that depreciation does not apply to a personal automobile.

Member of household. You can deduct moving expenses you pay for yourself and members of your household. A member of your household is anyone who has both your former and new home as his or her home. It does not include a tenant or employee, unless you can claim that person as a dependent.

Explanation

The costs of moving dependent children who do not reside with the parents before the move are not deductible, even if the parents and children move to the new location simultaneously. The reason is that the children were not members of the former household.

Location of move. There are different rules for moving within or to the United States than for moving outside the United States. This chapter only discusses moves within or to the United States. The rules for moves outside the United States can be found in Publication 521.

Household Goods and Personal Effects

You can deduct the cost of packing, crating, and transporting your household goods and personal effects and those of the members of your household from your former home to your new home. If you use your own car to move your things, see *Travel by car,* earlier. You can include the cost of storing and insuring household goods and personal effects within **any period of 30 consecutive days** after the day your things are moved from your former home and before they are delivered to your new home.

Explanation

A yacht is not considered a part of household goods or personal effects. The rationale given by the courts is that Congress intended moving expenses to cover only items that you must move from your old home to a new location. For you to claim a deductible moving expense for an item, it must be "intimately associated" with your home. A yacht is not.

However, the courts have upheld the deductibility of costs associated with moving a sailboat that the taxpayer owned for 4 years and frequently used. The taxpayer proved that he was "intimately associated" with the boat. This "intimate association" enabled the boat to be characterized as a "personal effect," thereby making all expenses associated with moving it deductible.

TAXSAVER

The cost of moving your mobile home qualifies as a moving expense, as does the cost of disconnecting or connecting appliances that you are required to move.

One court held that the cost of installing a telephone in a newly purchased home did not qualify as a deductible expense. However, now that many taxpayers own their own telephones, it would seem that the cost of disconnecting and connecting them would be a deductible expense incurred while moving household goods from one location to another.

You can deduct any costs of connecting or disconnecting utilities required because you are moving your household goods, appliances, or personal effects.

You can deduct the cost of shipping your car and household pets to your new home. You can deduct the cost of moving your household goods and personal effects from a place other than your former home. Your deduction is limited to the amount it would have cost to move them from your former home.

Caution. *You cannot deduct the cost of moving furniture you buy on the way to your new home.*

Explanation

Moving furniture that was in storage at the time of the move is deductible as long as the actual cost of moving it does not exceed what the cost of moving it would have been had the furniture been located at your former home.

Example

You are a resident of North Carolina and have been in college pursuing a degree for the last 4 years. Because of the small size of your apartment, you stored some of your furniture with your parents in Georgia.

You get a job in Washington, D.C. It costs you $1,100 to move the furniture from Georgia to Washington, D.C. If the furniture in Georgia had been shipped from North Carolina, your former home, it would have cost only $600. You may deduct only $600 of the $1,100 charge.

Note: If you lived in a dormitory or other rented quarters in North Carolina but you went home to Georgia for the summers, were considered an out-of-state or nonresident student in North Carolina, and otherwise maintained most of the major elements of residency (voting, automobile registration, charge accounts, etc.) in Georgia, you could argue that Georgia was your former home. In that case, all moving expenses would be deductible.

Travel Expenses

You can deduct the cost of transportation and lodging for yourself and members of your household while traveling from your former home to your new home. This includes expenses for the day you arrive.

You can include any lodging expenses you had in the area of your former home within one day after you could no longer live in your former home because your furniture had been moved.

You can deduct expenses for only one trip to your new home for yourself and members of your household. However, all of you do not have to travel together or at the same time. If you use your own car, see *Travel by car*, earlier.

Explanation

The courts allowed the cost of an escort as a moving expense when a taxpayer's mobile home broke down en route—the breakdown was attributable solely to the move. The charge for moving a mobile home by a professional mover is deductible. However, the replacement cost of tires for the mobile home does not qualify as a deductible moving expense. The reason is that new tires are essentially capital improvements.

TaxAlert

Travel expenses from your former home to your new home are only deductible as moving expenses when incurred after obtaining employment in the area to which you are moving.

Nondeductible Expenses

You cannot deduct the following items as moving expenses.

- Any part of the purchase price of your new home.

Explanation

No deduction is allowed for the costs of selling your former home (or settling an unexpired lease) and purchasing your new home (or the acquisition of a new lease).

- Car tags.
- Driver's license.
- Expenses of buying or selling a home.
- Expenses of getting or breaking a lease.
- Home improvements to help sell your home.
- Loss on the sale of your home.

Explanation

Under no circumstances is a loss on the sale of your personal residence deductible as a moving expense, or as any other kind of expense, even if the move forced you to sell at a loss. However, if any portion of your home was used for income-producing purposes, then the portion of the loss allocable to such use may be deductible. For more information see Chapter 16, *Selling Your Home.*

Although you may not deduct property taxes and interest as moving expenses, you may claim them as itemized deductions.

- Losses from disposing of memberships in clubs.
- Meal expenses.
- Mortgage penalties.
- Pre-move househunting expenses.
- Real estate taxes.
- Refitting of carpets and draperies.
- Security deposits (including any given up due to the move).
- Storage charges except those incurred in transit and for foreign moves.
- Temporary living expenses.

Explanation

Many moving costs represent real economic losses to you but are not deductible as moving expenses when you are computing your **taxable income.** These nondeductible moving costs are simply considered personal expenses, whether or not you are reimbursed for them. If you itemize your deductions, you might be able to deduct some costs that are not deductible as moving expenses.

Mortgage penalties that are loan prepayment penalties are usually deductible as interest. Real estate taxes are deductible. In many states, automobile tags are deductible as personal property taxes. A portion of your driver's license may be deductible as automobile transportation expenses.

You may not deduct the cost of buying new drapes.

Househunting trips and temporary housing expenses are not deductible. Also, the cost of meals incurred in connection with a move are not deductible. In addition, expenses associated with the purchase, sale, or lease of a residence are not deductible.

Example 1

The IRS has ruled that the costs associated with the transfer of a U.S. government employee were not deductible, since the employee initiated the transfer, even when the transfer was in the interest of the government. The transfer must be a requirement of the employer and not merely for the benefit of the employee.

Example 2

A taxpayer replaced carpeting and drapes at her newly leased apartment because of her husband's allergies. The costs were for the comfort of the taxpayer rather than moving expenses. A deduction was not allowed.

No double deduction. You cannot take a moving expense deduction and a business expense deduction for the same expenses. You must decide if your expenses are deductible as moving expenses or as business expenses. For example, expenses you have for travel, meals, and lodging while temporarily working at a place away from your regular place of work may be deductible as business expenses if you are considered away from home on business. Generally, your work at a single location is considered temporary if it is realistically expected to last (and does in fact last) for 1 year or less. See *Temporary Assignment or Job* in chapter 28 for information on deducting your expenses.

TaxSaver

If you are denied a deduction for moving expenses on the grounds that the move is only temporary (generally a year or less), you may still deduct your expenses for travel, meals, and lodging while away from home as business expenses.

Example

A professor who went on a 10-month sabbatical for post-doctoral research training could not deduct the expense of moving his household and personal goods. He could, however, deduct his traveling expenses, as well as the cost of his meals and lodging, while away.

How To Report

The following discussions explain how to report your moving expenses and any reimbursements or allowances you received for your move.

Form 3903. Use Form 3903 to report your moving expenses.

Where to deduct. Deduct your moving expenses on line 26 of Form 1040. The amount of moving expenses you can deduct is shown on line 5 of Form 3903.

Caution. *You cannot deduct moving expenses on Form 1040EZ or Form 1040A.*

Reimbursements. If you received a reimbursement for your allowable moving expenses, how you report this amount and your expenses depends on whether the reimbursement was paid to you under an accountable plan or a nonaccountable plan.

For more information on reimbursements, see Publication 521.

TaxSaver

If your employer purchases your former residence, the real estate commission that is avoided is not income to you, although the gain on the sale of the residence is taxed as a **capital gain**, subject to the residence replacement rules, discussed in Chapter 16, *Selling Your Home.*

Any reimbursement by your employer for a loss on the sale of your home must be included in your income. You may not deduct the loss on your home, though you may deduct the amount attributable to the real estate commission, if any, as a selling expense.

If your employer purchases your former home from you at **fair market value** and there is a subsequent decline in its worth, the loss is sustained by your employer. The home's drop in value does not affect you.

If your employer purchases your former home from you at *more* than fair market value, the excess is ordinary taxable income to you and not capital gain. You could not exclude that excess from your income, even if you purchased a new home for more than you got in total for the old one.

Note: The excess is not treated as gain on the sale of a residence that otherwise could be reinvested in a new residence. See Chapter 16, *Selling Your Home.*

Explanation

Some employers use third-party relocation service companies to buy your home from you. If the third party pays any direct home-selling costs that are normally imposed on the seller by local law and/or custom, then you will be treated as having received taxable income.

Example

An employer agreed to pay home-selling costs but required that the employee repay them if he terminated employment within a stipulated period of time. The IRS held that an enforceable debt was created and that the employee had taxable income to report when the debt was cancelled (or not paid). The employer must report the income on Form W-2.

When To Deduct Expenses

If you were not reimbursed, deduct your allowable moving expenses either in the year you incurred them or in the year you paid them.

Example. In December 2000, your employer transferred you to another city in the United States, where you still work. You are single and were not reimbursed for your moving expenses. In 2000, you paid for moving your furniture. You deducted these expenses in 2000. In January 2001, you paid for travel to the new city. You can deduct these additional expenses in 2001.

Explanation

Your employer may give you a flat amount of money to cover all your moving expenses, some of which may not be deductible. The IRS says that the employer must apply the reimbursement first to the deductible moving expenses that are not subject to withholding and then deduct withholding and social security tax from the remainder.

TaxAlert

Be sure to take into account reimbursement for nondeductible expenses when you are figuring your **estimated tax** payments.

Reimbursed expenses. If you are reimbursed for your expenses, you may be able to deduct your allowable expenses either in the year you incurred them or in the year you paid them. If you use the cash method of accounting, you can choose to deduct the expenses in the year you are reimbursed even though you paid the expenses in a different year.

If you are reimbursed for your expenses in a year after you paid the expenses, you may want to delay taking the deduction until the year you receive the reimbursement. If you do not choose to delay your deduction until the year you are reimbursed, you must include the reimbursement in your income.

Choosing when to deduct. If you use the cash method of accounting, which is used by most individuals, you can choose to deduct moving expenses in the year your employer reimburses you if:

1) You paid the expenses in a year before the year of reimbursement, or
2) You paid the expenses in the year immediately after the year of reimbursement but by the due date, including extensions, for filing your return for the reimbursement year.

TaxSaver

You generally deduct your moving expenses in the year in which you pay them. However, if you receive a reimbursement in one year and don't pay the expenses until the next year, you still may deduct the expenses in the earlier year, as long as you pay them before the due date, including extensions, for filing your return for the year of reimbursement. You should deduct your expenses in the year in which you will save the most taxes.

You should report your moving expense deduction on Form 3903.

How to make the choice. You can choose to deduct moving expenses in the year you received reimbursement by taking the deduction on your return, or amended return, for that year.

Caution. *You cannot deduct any moving expenses for which you received a reimbursement that was not included in your income. (Reimbursements are discussed in Publication 521.)*

20

Alimony

Introduction

*Designing a divorce decree, a separation agreement, or a support decree is rarely an easy task. Marital settlements are so diverse and so complex that no two situations are the same. One common element, however, is likely to be the payment of **alimony**—an amount subject to one of these settlement agreements that is not considered **child support** or a property settlement and that meets certain specific tests. If certain circumstances are met, alimony is a deduction from gross income for the spouse who pays it and included in the income of the spouse who receives it.*

Alimony may take many different forms. The payment by one spouse of the other spouse's share of mortgage and other costs for jointly owned property may be considered alimony. The payment of life insurance premiums on policies irrevocably assigned to a spouse may *also be considered alimony. Alimony may even include the payment of medical and dental expenses. This chapter discusses what should and should not be considered an alimony payment.*

The Deficit Reduction Act of 1984 completely restructured the alimony rules. The old rules still apply to alimony payments made under pre-1985 divorce and separation agreements—unless those agreements have been specifically modified. For related information refer to dependency exemption (see Chapter 3, Personal Exemptions and Dependents), the child care credit (see Chapter 33, Child and Dependent Care Credit), head of household status (see Chapter 2, Filing Status), and the earned income credit (see Chapter 37, Other Credits Including the Earned Income Credit).

This chapter discusses the rules that apply if you pay or receive alimony. It covers the following topics:

- What payments are alimony,
- What payments are not alimony, such as child support,
- How to deduct alimony you paid,
- How to report alimony income you received, and
- Whether you must recapture the tax benefits of alimony. Recapture means adding back in your income all or part of a deduction you took in a prior year.

Alimony is a payment to or for a spouse or former spouse under a divorce or separation instrument. It does not include voluntary payments that are not made under a divorce or separation instrument.

Alimony is deductible by the payer and must be included in the spouse's or former spouse's income. Although this chapter is generally written for the payer of the alimony, the recipient can use the information to determine whether an amount received is alimony.

To be alimony, a payment must meet certain requirements. Different requirements apply to payments under instruments executed after 1984 and to payments under instruments executed before 1985. This chapter discusses the rules for payments under instruments executed after 1984. For the rules for payments under pre-1985 instruments, see Publication 504, *Divorced or Separated Individuals.*

> **Explanation**
> An outline of alimony rules that apply to divorce and separation instruments executed before 1985 and not modified after 1984 is shown on page 300.

Use *Table 20-1* in this chapter as a guide to determine whether certain payments are considered alimony.

Definitions. The following definitions apply throughout this chapter.

Spouse or former spouse. Unless otherwise stated in the following discussions about alimony, the term "spouse" includes former spouse.

Divorce or separation instrument. The term "divorce or separation instrument" means:

1) A decree of divorce or separate maintenance or a written instrument incident to that decree,
2) A written separation agreement, or
3) A decree or any type of court order requiring a spouse to make payments for the support or maintenance of the other spouse. This includes a temporary decree, an interlocutory (not final) decree, and a decree of alimony *pendente lite* (while awaiting action on the final decree or agreement).

Table 20–1. **Alimony Requirements (Instruments executed after 1984)**

Payments ARE alimony if all of the following are true:	**Payment are NOT alimony if any of the following are true:**
Payments are required by a divorce or separation instrument.	Payment is designated as child support.
Payer and recipient spouse do not file a joint return.	Payment is a noncash property settlement.
Payment is in cash (including checks or money orders).	Payments are spouse's part of community income.
Payment is not designated in the instrument as not alimony.	Payments are to keep up the payer's property.
Spouses legally separated under a decree of divorce or separate maintenance are not members of the same household.	Payments are not required by a divorce or separation instrument.
Payments are not required after death of the recipient spouse.	
Payment is not designated as child support.	
These payments are deductible by the payer and includible in income by the recipient.	*These payments are neither deductible by the payer nor includible in income by the recipient.*

Useful Items

You may want to see:

Publication

☐ **504**   Divorced or Separated Individuals

General Rules

The following rules apply to alimony regardless of when the divorce or separation instrument was executed.

Payments not alimony. Not all payments under a divorce or separation instrument are alimony. Alimony does not include any of the following.

1) Child support.
2) Noncash property settlements.
3) Payments that are your spouse's part of community income. (See *Community Property* in Publication 504.)
4) Payments to keep up the payer's property.
5) Use of property.

Explanation

Other Payments Not Deductible as Alimony
Do not deduct as alimony the following:

1. Any payment not required by the decree or agreement
2. Any payment that does not arise out of the marital relationship but that is required by the decree or agreement, such as repayment of a loan to your spouse

3. Any payment you make before the decree or agreement
4. Any payment you agreed to make before the decree or agreement and paid later
5. Any payment you make after your former spouse's remarriage
6. Any payment you make after your divorced spouse's death, even though required by the decree or agreement
7. Any payment you make that is part of a property settlement

Payments to a third party. Cash payments (including checks and money orders) to a third party on behalf of your spouse under the terms of your divorce or separation instrument may be alimony if they otherwise qualify. These include payments for your spouse's medical expenses, housing costs (rent, utilities, etc.), taxes, tuition, etc. The payments are treated as received by your spouse and then paid to the third party.

Life insurance premiums. Alimony includes premiums you must pay under your divorce or separation instrument for insurance on your life to the extent your spouse owns the policy.

Explanation

The ownership of a life insurance policy must be assigned to your former spouse before you may deduct the premiums you pay as alimony. In addition, your former spouse must be the irrevocable beneficiary of the policy. Your children may be irrevocable contingent beneficiaries.

If your children are the beneficiaries of a life insurance policy and your former spouse is a contingent beneficiary, you still control the policy. The premiums you pay on it are not considered alimony.

For the premiums to be considered alimony, your former spouse's benefit from the life insurance policy must be measurable in dollars. If your former spouse would benefit from the policy only under certain contingencies, the economic advantage cannot be measured and your premiums would not be considered alimony.

Payments for jointly-owned home. If your divorce or separation instrument states that you must pay expenses for a home owned by you and your spouse or former spouse, some of your payments may be alimony.

Mortgage payments. If you must pay all the mortgage payments (principal and interest) on a jointly-owned home, and they otherwise qualify, you can deduct one-half of the total payments as alimony. If you itemize deductions and the home is a qualified home, you can claim the other half of the interest in figuring your deductible interest. Your spouse must report one-half of the payments as alimony received. If your spouse itemizes deductions and the home is a qualified home, he or she can claim one-half of the interest on the mortgage in figuring deductible interest.

Taxes and insurance. If you must pay all the real estate taxes or insurance on a home held as *tenants in common,* you can deduct one-half of these payments as alimony. Your spouse must report one-half of these payments as alimony received. If you and your spouse itemize deductions, you can each claim one-half of the real estate taxes and none of the home insurance.

If your home is held as *tenants by the entirety* or *joint tenants,* none of your payments for taxes or insurance are alimony. But if you itemize deductions, you can claim all of the real estate taxes and none of the home insurance.

Other payments to a third party. If you made other third-party payments, see Publication 504 to see whether any part of the payments qualifies as alimony.

Instruments Executed After 1984

The following rules for alimony apply to payments under divorce or separation instruments executed after 1984.

Exception for instruments executed before 1985. There are two situations where the rules for instruments executed after 1984 apply to instruments executed before 1985.

1) A divorce or separation instrument executed before 1985 and then modified after 1984 to specify that the after-1984 rules will apply.
2) A temporary divorce or separation instrument executed before 1985 and incorporated into, or adopted by, a final decree executed after 1984 that:
   a) Changes the amount or period of payment, or
   b) Adds or deletes any contingency or condition.

For the rules for alimony payments under pre-1985 instruments not meeting these exceptions, see *Instruments Executed Before 1985* in Publication 504.

Example 1. In November 1984, you and your former spouse executed a written separation agreement. In February 1985, a decree of divorce was substituted for the written separation agreement. The decree of divorce did not change the terms for the alimony you pay your former spouse. The decree of divorce is treated as executed before 1985. Alimony payments under this decree are not subject to the rules for payments under instruments executed after 1984.

Example 2. Assume the same facts as in *Example 1* except that the decree of divorce changed the amount of the alimony. In this example, the decree of divorce is not treated as executed before 1985. The alimony payments are subject to the rules for payments under instruments executed after 1984.

Explanation

For divorce decrees and separation agreements executed or revised after 1984, payments may not be deductible, even if there is a legal obligation to make them. Payments would be deductible only if all the other requirements were fulfilled.

TAXPLANNER

Don't overlook the opportunity to use the new rules on an old divorce.

Example

Bob and Mary were divorced in 1975, with Mary agreeing to pay Bob $2,000 per month in qualifying alimony payments. Mary was a stockbroker earning top dollars in 1975. Bob had never had a full-time job. In 1997, Mary's fortunes are not so rosy, whereas Bob is a top Los Angeles real estate broker.

Bob and Mary could agree that, in 1997, Mary will pay less money to Bob but that it won't be considered alimony. If Mary's marginal tax bracket has dropped to 15% and Bob's tax bracket is 31%, Mary could pay Bob as little as 69% of what her normal payment is ($1,380), and both would win. Mary would be out-of-pocket less than the $1,700 after tax she would have were she to deduct the usual $2,000 payment at her 15% bracket; Bob would receive the same amount after taxes ($1,380) as if he had received the $2,000 as taxable alimony at his 31% bracket.

Alimony requirements. A payment to or for a spouse under a divorce or separation instrument is alimony if the spouses do not file a joint return with each other and *all* the following requirements are met.

1) The payment is in cash.
2) The instrument does not designate the payment as not alimony.
3) The spouses are not members of the same household at the time the payments are made. This requirement applies only if the spouses are legally separated under a decree of divorce or separate maintenance.
4) There is no liability to make any payment (in cash or property) after the death of the recipient spouse.
5) The payment is not treated as child support.

Each of these requirements is discussed next.

Payment must be in cash. Only cash payments, including checks and money orders, qualify as alimony. The following do not qualify as alimony.

- Transfers of services or property (including a debt instrument of a third party or an annuity contract).
- Execution of a debt instrument by the payer.
- The use of property.

TAXPLANNER

According to the IRS, an annuity contract given to a spouse is a transfer of property and not a cash payment. Therefore, the spouse giving the annuity contract would not be entitled to a deduction for alimony. The spouse receiving the annuity contract has the same investment cost as the spouse giving it. The only taxable income to the receiving spouse would be the amounts received in excess of cost.

If you are the alimony payer and you want to ensure a tax

deduction, you can use distributions from an annuity contract that you own to make future alimony payments rather than transfer the annuity contract to your spouse.

Payments to a third party. Cash payments to a third party under the terms of your divorce or separation instrument can qualify as a cash payment to your spouse. See *Payments to a third party* under *General Rules,* earlier.

Also, cash payments made to a third party at the written request of your spouse qualify as alimony if ***all*** the following requirements are met.

1) The payments are in lieu of payments of alimony directly to your spouse.
2) The written request states that both spouses intend the payments to be treated as alimony.
3) You receive the written request from your spouse before you file your return for the year you made the payments.

Explanation

Medical and dental expenses. If you paid your spouse's medical and dental expenses under a decree or agreement, you may deduct them as alimony. However, a payment of unusually large medical expenses in a given year might trigger excess front-loading rules. The result could be that you lose the deduction for payments under the recapture rules (see a discussion of recapture rules later), even though they are required as part of the divorce or separation agreement.

Your spouse must report these payments as alimony received and may include them as medical expenses if he or she is itemizing deductions.

Note: The spouse who pays the medical bills saves tax by claiming the amounts as alimony rather than as medical expenses. Alimony is fully deductible from adjusted gross income, whether or not the payer itemizes deductions. For medical expenses, only those exceeding 7.5% of adjusted gross income are deductible.

TAXSAVER

If you pay medical insurance premiums on behalf of a former spouse, you may be entitled to an additional deduction.

Example

A husband who had not been directly ordered by the courts to carry medical insurance for his former wife but who was ordered to pay her reasonable medical expenses was allowed to deduct premiums paid as alimony. (He could not deduct the premiums as a medical expense.) His former wife had to include the amount that her former husband paid for the insurance premiums as income. Both parties treated as alimony the premiums and any actual medical expenses paid that were not reimbursed by insurance payments.

Note: The husband may have created a larger deduction for alimony by taking out an insurance policy on his former wife, since he may deduct the cost of the premiums (his out-of-pocket cost) whether or not his former wife incurs any actual medical expenses. Conversely, the former wife may pay a tax on an amount from which she derives no direct benefit.

Payments designated as not alimony. You and your spouse can designate that otherwise qualifying payments are not alimony. You do this by including a provision in your divorce or separation instrument that states the payments are not deductible as alimony by you and are excludable from your spouse's income. For this purpose, any instrument (written statement) signed by both of you that makes this designation and that refers to a previous written separation agreement is treated as a written separation agreement. If you are subject to temporary support orders, the designation must be made in the original or a later temporary support order.

Your spouse can exclude the payments from income only if he or she attaches a copy of the instrument designating them as not alimony to his or her return. The copy must be attached each year the designation applies.

Spouses cannot be members of the same household. Payments to your spouse while you are members of the same household are not alimony if you are legally separated under a decree of divorce or separate maintenance. A home you formerly shared is considered one household, even if you physically separate yourselves in the home.

You are not treated as members of the same household if one of you is preparing to leave the household and does leave no later than 1 month after the date of the payment.

Exception. If you are not legally separated under a decree of divorce or separate maintenance, a payment under a written separation agreement, support decree, or other court order may qualify as alimony even if you are members of the same household when the payment is made.

Explanation

Separated and living apart. The courts have traditionally held that spouses living under the same roof are not separated. However, some courts have looked to the facts and circumstances surrounding each case to determine whether or not spouses living in the same house who seldom see each other and who incur duplicate living expenses are, in fact, separated. The Appeals Courts have been reluctant to deal with the highly personalized questions that must be asked to determine whether or not the parties are truly living apart.

Liability for payments after death of recipient spouse. If you must continue to make payments for any period after your spouse's death, none of the payments made before or after the death are alimony.

The divorce or separation instrument does not have to expressly state that the payments cease upon the death of your spouse if, for example, the liability for continued payments would end under state law.

Example. You must pay your former spouse $10,000 in cash each year for 10 years. Your divorce decree states that the payments will end upon your former spouse's death. You must also pay your former spouse or your former spouse's estate $20,000 in cash each year for 10 years. The death of your spouse would not terminate these payments under state law.

The $10,000 annual payments are alimony. But because the $20,000 annual payments will not end upon your former spouse's death, they are not alimony.

Substitute payments. If you must make any payments in cash or property after your spouse's death as a substitute for continuing otherwise qualifying payments, the otherwise qualifying payments are not alimony. To the extent that your payments begin, accelerate, or increase because of the death of your spouse, otherwise qualifying payments you made may be treated as payments that were not alimony. Whether or not such payments will be treated as not alimony depends on all the facts and circumstances.

Example 1. Under your divorce decree, you must pay your former spouse $30,000 annually. The payments will stop at the end of 6 years or upon your former spouse's death, if earlier.

Your former spouse has custody of your minor children. The decree provides that if any child is still a minor at your spouse's death, you must pay $10,000 annually to a trust until the youngest child reaches the age of majority. The trust income and corpus (principal) are to be used for your children's benefit.

These facts indicate that the payments to be made after your former spouse's death are a substitute for $10,000 of the $30,000 annual payments. $10,000 of each of the $30,000 annual payments is not alimony.

Example 2. Under your divorce decree, you must pay your former spouse $30,000 annually. The payments will stop at the end of 15 years or upon your former spouse's death, if earlier. The decree provides that if your former spouse dies before the end of the 15-year period, you must pay the estate the difference between $450,000 ($30,000 × 15) and the total amount paid up to that time. For example, if your spouse dies at the end of the tenth year, you must pay the estate $150,000 ($450,000 − $300,000).

These facts indicate that the lump-sum payment to be made after your former spouse's death is a substitute for the full amount of the $30,000 annual payments. None of the annual payments are alimony. The result would be the same if the payment required at death were to be discounted by an appropriate interest factor to account for the prepayment.

Child support. A payment that is specifically designated as child support or treated as specifically designated as child support under your divorce or separation instrument is not alimony. The designated amount or part may vary from time to time. Child support payments are neither deductible by the payer nor taxable to the payee.

Specifically designated as child support. A payment will be treated as specifically designated as child support to the extent that the payment is reduced either:

1) On the happening of a contingency relating to your child, or
2) At a time that can be clearly associated with the contingency.

A payment may be treated as specifically designated as child support even if other separate payments are specifically designated as child support.

TAXPLANNER

Since child support payments are considered fixed, any reductions in child support that are not part of the original decree or a subsequent court-approved modified divorce decree are considered reductions in alimony, not child support. Therefore, be sure to have the court approve any child support reductions so that you can continue to deduct the full alimony payments.

Example

After a taxpayer remarried, his son from his previous marriage began to live with him. The taxpayer and his former wife agreed that, as a result, his child support payments should be eliminated. Even though both former spouses agreed that the payment reductions applied to child support, the courts held that they applied to alimony because the taxpayer and his former spouse did not obtain a modification of their divorce decree in court.

Contingency relating to your child. A contingency relates to your child if it depends on any event relating to that child. It does not matter whether the event is certain or likely to occur. Events relating to your child include the child's:

- Becoming employed,
- Dying,
- Leaving the household,
- Leaving school,
- Marrying, or
- Reaching a specified age or income level.

Clearly associated with a contingency. Payments are presumed to be reduced at a time clearly associated with the happening of a contingency relating to your child only in the following situations.

1) The payments are to be reduced not more than 6 months before or after the date the child will reach 18, 21, or local age of majority.
2) The payments are to be reduced on two or more occasions that occur not more than 1 year before or after a different one of your children reaches a certain age from 18 to 24. This certain age must be the same for each child, but need not be a whole number of years.

In all other situations, reductions in payments are not treated as clearly associated with the happening of a contingency relating to your child.

Either you or the IRS can overcome the presumption in the two situations above. This is done by showing that the time at which the payments are to be reduced was determined independently of any contingencies relating to your children. For example, if you can show that the period of alimony payments is customary in the local jurisdiction, such as a period equal to one-half of the duration of the marriage, you can treat the amount as alimony.

Explanation

Child Support in Agreements Executed Before 1985

Child support amounts may not be inferred for payments made under agreements executed before 1985 and not revised. You may not assume that portions of the alimony payments are used by a former spouse for support of a child. The U.S. Supreme Court has held that payments are not treated as child support payments unless they are expressly designated as such in the governing document.

Example

If the agreement that was executed before 1985 and has not been revised says "alimony and child support of $1,000 per month until the child reaches age 18 and then $750 per month," the entire payment can be treated as alimony.

Explanation

Child Support in Agreements Executed After 1984

Child support amounts *may* be inferred for payments made under agreements executed or revised after 1984, even if such payments are not specifically earmarked. However, such payments will be reduced upon certain contingencies related to the child. Such contingencies would include the child attaining a certain age or income level, dying, marrying, leaving school, leaving the spouse's household, or getting a job.

Payments that are reduced at a time that can clearly be associated with a contingency will be treated as child support. For example, if a payment was to stop at a certain calendar date that just happened to be the child's nineteenth birthday, that payment would be considered child support.

The parent who has custody of the child is entitled to take the dependency exemption for the child, as long as the parents themselves could have claimed the exemption had they filed a joint return. This will not apply if:

1. There is a multiple support agreement in effect specifying who gets the exemption.
2. The custodial parent relinquishes the exemption in writing (using language in IRS Form 8332).
3. There is an executed, pre-1985 divorce or separation agreement in effect that provides that the noncustodial

parent who also furnishes at least $600 of child support can claim the exemption.

Note: The custodial parent is still entitled to claim the dependent care credit, even if he or she relinquishes the dependency exemption to the noncustodial parent.

A parent can deduct medical expenses that he or she paid directly for a child's benefit, even though the dependency exemption for the child is claimed by the other parent. This is the case as long as a multiple-support agreement is not in effect.

TAXPLANNER

In 2001, *single* taxpayers with adjusted gross income over $132,950 and taxpayers filing as head of household with adjusted gross income exceeding $166,200 will not receive the full benefit of the deduction for personal exemptions. Taxpayers with adjusted gross income above these thresholds will have the amount of each personal and dependent exemption simultaneously reduced at a rate of 2% for each $2,500 (or fraction thereof) by which adjusted gross income exceeds the applicable threshold. In other words, each personal and dependent exemption is fully phased out for single taxpayers with adjusted gross income of $255,450, and for heads of households with adjusted gross income of $288,700. As a result, the former spouse with less adjusted gross income may receive a greater tax benefit from claiming the children as dependents than would the spouse with higher income.

How To Deduct Alimony Paid

You can deduct alimony you paid, whether or not you itemize deductions on your return. You must file Form 1040. You cannot use Form 1040A or Form 1040EZ.

Enter the amount of alimony you paid on line 31a of Form 1040. In the space provided on line 31b, enter your spouse's social security number.

If you paid alimony to more than one person, enter the social security number of one of the recipients. Show the social security number and amount paid to each other recipient on an attached statement. Enter your total payments on line 31a.

Caution. *If you do not provide your spouse's social security number, you may have to pay a $50 penalty and your deduction may be disallowed.*

Explanation

Even if the validity of a divorce decree is questioned, your spouse must include periodic payments that you make under such a divorce decree in income. You may deduct the payments as alimony. A divorce decree is valid for tax purposes until a court having proper jurisdiction declares it invalid.

The IRS generally recognizes a state court as having proper jurisdiction if that court has personal jurisdiction over the parties involved or if that court has jurisdiction over the subject matter of the action.

Example 1

In the process of separating, a husband and wife entered into a support agreement under a state court. The husband later obtained a Mexican divorce that said nothing about the support agreement. The state considered the divorce to be valid. Even though the Mexican divorce decree made no mention of the support payments, the payments were considered alimony because the original state support agreement had never been invalidated.

Example 2

A husband who obtained a Mexican divorce was later sued by his former wife for support payments and for a legal separation under state law. The state court granted the former wife the support payments. The Mexican divorce was not recognized by the state, but the payments were considered to be alimony.

How To Report Alimony Received

Report alimony you received on line 11 of Form 1040. You cannot use Form 1040A or Form 1040EZ.

Caution. *You must give the person who paid the alimony your social security number. If you do not, you may have to pay a $50 penalty.*

Recapture Rule

If your alimony payments decrease or terminate during the first 3 calendar years, you may be subject to the recapture rule. If you are subject to this rule, you have to include in income in the third year part of the alimony payments you previously deducted. Your spouse can deduct in the third year part of the alimony payments he or she previously included in income.

The 3-year period starts with the first calendar year you make a payment qualifying as alimony under a decree of divorce or separate maintenance or a written separation agreement. Do not include any time in which payments were being made under temporary support orders. The second and third years are the next 2 calendar years, whether or not payments are made during those years.

The reasons for a reduction or termination of alimony payments that can require a recapture include:

- A change in your divorce or separation instrument,
- A failure to make timely payments,
- A reduction in your ability to provide support, or
- A reduction in your spouse's support needs.

When to apply the recapture rule. You are subject to the recapture rule in the third year if the alimony you pay in the third year decreases by more than $15,000 from the second year or the alimony you pay in the second and third years decreases significantly from the alimony you pay in the first year.

When you figure a decrease in alimony, do not include the following amounts.

1) Payments made under a temporary support order.
2) Payments required over a period of at least 3 calendar years of a fixed part of your income from a business or property, or from compensation for employment or self-employment.
3) Payments that decrease because of the death of either spouse or the remarriage of the spouse receiving the payments.

Figuring the recapture. For a blank worksheet for you to use to figure recaptured alimony, see *Table 3* in Publication 504.

Including the recapture in income. If you must include a recapture amount in income, show it on Form 1040, line 11 ("Alimony received"). Cross out "received" and print "recapture." On the dotted line next to the amount, enter your spouse's last name and social security number.

Deducting the recapture. If you can deduct a recapture amount, show it on Form 1040, line 31a ("Alimony paid"). Cross out "paid" and print "recapture." In the space provided, enter your spouse's social security number.

TaxSaver

If the payments are spread out equally over the 3 years, they are all deductible. Also, payments in year 3 are more beneficial than those made in year 2. In the example presented in IRS Publication 504, $5,000 of alimony paid in year 3 rather than year 2 drops the recapture amount from $22,500 to $15,000.

Other Alimony Issues/Rules

Explanation

Transfer of property. If property is transferred in settlement of marital rights, the spouse making the transfer does not recognize either gain or loss on the transfer, whether the property has appreciated or declined in value. The transfer is treated like a gift, and the spouse receiving the property takes the basis of the transferring spouse. This is true even if the spouse receiving the property pays cash and the transaction is cast in the form of a sale.

The following are exceptions to the nonrecognition rules:

1. Transfer of an installment note to a trust will cause the deferred gain to be recognized.
2. Transfer of property subject to liabilities in excess of basis will cause the excess to be recognized.

TaxPlanner

The transfer between spouses of a note receivable that arose from an installment sale will not be considered a disposition for purposes of accelerating the reporting of previously deferred income. Instead, the recipient of the installment note will have the same tax posture as the spouse who made the transfer.

Explanation

Transfer of business property. The law is silent on the status of unrealized income from normal business accounts receivable that may be transferred. There is no recapture of investment tax credit or depreciation on the transfer of business property. The spouse making the transfer must provide permanent records of cost basis, accumulated depreciation, holding period, and investment-credit recapture potential to the other spouse. There is no penalty for failure to do so, however.

TaxPlanner

A spouse who is to receive property with a tax basis substantially less than its current value should carefully evaluate the tax consequences of disposing of it. The recipient may be subject to tax from recapture of investment tax credit and depreciation and should obtain the advice of competent counsel on such matters.

Example

As part of the divorce property settlement, Kyle gives Mary a computer that he used for 4 years in his sole proprietorship business. Kyle paid $5,000 for the computer, claimed investment credit on it, and claimed depreciation of $3,950. Since the computer ceased to be business property when it was given to Mary, she must recapture part of the investment credit claimed by Kyle. Further, Mary must pay ordinary income tax on her profit if she sells the computer for more than $1,050. See Chapter 17, *Reporting Gains and Losses,* and Chapter 37, *Other Credits.*

Explanation

Trust property. If income-producing property is placed in trust to pay alimony, the alimony payments are not included or deducted from income. This rule applies whether the alimony payments are made out of the trust income or principal. Trust distributions must be reported as income by your spouse. If your obligation to pay alimony is stated in a divorce decree, other court order, or written separation agreement, your spouse reports the distributions as alimony on line 11 of Form 1040. If your obligation is not so stated, your spouse reports the income distributions as income received from a trust, on Schedule E (Form 1040).

You may also set up a trust to pay both alimony and child support. If your former spouse remarries and you are no longer required to pay alimony, the trust may continue disbursing monies for child support.

TaxPlanner

If a trust that is set up to disburse alimony payments holds municipal bonds, the distributions to the former spouse are nontaxable to the extent that they are attributable to the trust's municipal bond income. Also, if the distributions from the trust exceed the trust's income, the excess distribution of trust principal is not taxable.

Explanation

Insurance, endowment, or annuity. If an insurance or endowment policy or an annuity contract is purchased to discharge alimony or support called for in a divorce decree, the payer does not include in, or deduct from, income payments made under the contract. The recipient must include the payments in income.

Annulments. Generally, state laws blur the distinction between a divorce and an annulment. The rules on alimony often apply to an annulment decree as well as to a divorce decree. You should examine the law of the state in which you reside to determine if this is the case.

Example

In New York, a marriage was annulled due to the wife's insanity. The husband was required to provide for her care and maintenance. Since under the general rules of law the annulment would be considered a divorce, the husband's payments were treated as alimony.

TaxPlanner

Expenses of a home. If part of an alimony award is used to pay such expenses as real estate taxes, insurance, mortgage interest, and utilities for a home owned by a divorced couple, the facts in each case determine the amount deductible by one spouse and includable by the other spouse. Two facts to consider are the type of ownership and the kinds of expenses that must be paid. However, in each case, the payments must cover a period of more than 10 years or otherwise qualify as periodic payments if made pursuant to a pre-1985 agreement.

Ownership

You should check your state law, ownership documents, and your divorce decree to determine what type of ownership you have.

1. **Joint tenants or tenants by the entirety.** You and your former spouse own a home jointly as **tenants by the en-**

tirety or **joint tenants** with a right of survivorship. You are both jointly and individually responsible for the entire mortgage balance. If your divorce decree states that your former spouse is to pay the mortgage (principal and interest) on the property from money that he or she receives from you as support, then your former spouse must include one-half of each principal and interest payment as income from alimony and you may deduct one-half of each principal and interest payment as alimony.

Your former spouse may deduct one-half of the interest if your former spouse itemizes deductions on Schedule A (Form 1040). If you itemize your deductions, it is not clear how your share of the interest should be handled. It may be deductible under the home mortgage rules if your children live there and you are not already deducting interest on two personal residences. Or it might be considered investment interest, since as far as you are concerned, the property is now just an investment. Lastly, it could be personal interest and therefore not deductible.

2. **Tenants in common.** If you and your former spouse own a home as **tenants in common,** your former spouse owns half of the property. Therefore, you may deduct as alimony amounts you pay on your former spouse's half of the property for principal, interest, insurance, and taxes. Your former spouse must include these amounts in income.

If your former spouse itemizes deductions on Schedule A (Form 1040), he or she may deduct as taxes and interest the part you paid for real estate taxes and interest on your former spouse's half of the property. He or she may not deduct amounts for insurance. Insurance is a nondeductible personal expense.

Amounts you paid on your half of the property are not deductible as alimony, nor are they includable in income by your former spouse. If you itemize your deductions on Schedule A (Form 1040), you may deduct the part you pay for real estate taxes and interest on your half of the property. You may not deduct insurance payments on your half of the property.

3. **Your former spouse owns the home.** If the home is owned by your former spouse, under a decree or agreement you pay the real estate taxes, mortgage payments, and insurance premiums on it, you may deduct these payments as alimony. Your former spouse must include these payments in income.

If your former spouse itemizes deductions on Schedule A (Form 1040), he or she may deduct the part of each payment that is for taxes and interest on the mortgage.

4. **You own the home.** If the home you own is lived in rent-free by your former spouse, you may not deduct your mortgage payments or the fair rental value of the home as alimony. However, if you itemize your deductions, you may deduct on Schedule A (Form 1040) any real estate taxes and interest you pay on the property.

Rent. If, under a divorce or separate maintenance decree or written separation agreement, you must pay rent to a third-party lessor to provide housing for your spouse or former spouse, you may deduct the rent payments as alimony. Your former spouse must include these payments in income.

Utilities. If your former spouse is the one who has the right to use the home, regardless of the type of ownership, you may deduct as alimony the amount you pay for utilities under a decree or agreement. Your former spouse must include these amounts in income.

There are many consequences of property ownership that must be considered in a divorce settlement. Any payments made by you for the mortgage, property taxes, insurance, and so on are considered alimony *only* if the house belongs to your former spouse. If you transfer your interest in the property to your children, payments to cover their portion of the mortgage payments would be treated as child support, not alimony.

Example

John and Mary owned a home that cost them $150,000. In their divorce, the court decree holds that Mary can remain in the home until their son, who is 10 years old, reaches 18. Mary must pay rent to John for using his half of the house. In 1998, the house is sold and John and Mary together receive $250,000.

Upon sale of the home, Mary is subject to tax on the gain on the home sale. Assuming she meets the requirements, she can exclude up to $250,000 of her portion of the total gain. See Chapter 16, *Selling Your Home.*

John was a landlord during the rental years and probably claimed related expenses and depreciation on his tax return. If the rent charged was reasonable, John could deduct any losses, subject to the restrictions on passive activities.

Upon sale, John is subject to tax on his entire portion of the gain.

TAXPLANNER

Other aspects of obtaining a divorce. IRS Publication 504, *Divorced or Separated Individuals,* examines more closely some of the tax aspects of obtaining a divorce, including the tax treatment of costs incurred in working out a settlement.

Court costs and legal fees related to the divorce are not deductible. However, the portion of these fees attributable to obtaining alimony is deductible as an itemized deduction, since it is an expense associated with the production of income. Any additional costs incurred to obtain alimony are also deductible, as are costs for tax advice.

Be sure to have itemized invoices for professional services. Deductible items should be specifically listed on any bill. You may claim only the deductible portion of your own legal expenses. You may not deduct the legal expenses of your spouse. Those expenses also may not be considered alimony payments.

Some part of your legal fees may give you a tax benefit, even though the fees are not spent for obtaining alimony or tax advice. For example, if part of your legal fees may be allocated to obtaining property, the tax basis of the property should be increased by the amount of such fees. If the property is business property, you will have larger **depreciation** deductions and a smaller gain if the property is sold.

There are several additional aspects that you should consider in a year in which you become divorced:

1. **Revising Form W-4.** Form W-4 should be changed if you are no longer able to claim as many withholding allowances due to your change in marital status. This may occur because you no longer file a joint return with your former spouse. It also may occur if you are not entitled to a dependency exemption for one or more of your chil-

dren. When you revise your Form W-4, your employer adjusts your tax withholding to reflect the changes in your marital status or number of dependents.

2. **Estimated taxes on alimony.** If you are receiving alimony, you may be required to make estimated tax payments, since alimony is not covered by withholding. (See Chapter 5, *Tax Withholding and Estimated Tax.*)

3. **Allocating joint estimated tax payments between you and your former spouse.** If you and your former spouse are divorced during the year and have been making joint estimated tax payments, the payments you have already made may be applied to either person's separate return or may be divided between you, as the two of you see fit. If no allocation can be agreed on, the estimated payments should be applied between the separate returns in proportion to the taxes due on each.

Example

Your return shows a tax liability of $5,100. Your former spouse's return shows a tax liability of $2,300. You would be entitled to apply 69% [$5,100 ÷ ($5,100 + $2,300)] of your total joint estimated payments against your tax liability.

4. **Retirement plans.** An employee's interest in a qualified retirement plan can be allocated between a current and a former spouse by a qualified domestic relations order. Benefits so allocated are taxed to the current and former spouses when the payments are actually received.

   If the benefits are received by anyone other than the employee or the current or former spouses, the benefits are taxed to the employee, not the recipient.

5. **Federal income taxes withheld.** Taxes withheld from your income are treated the same way as the income that generates them. If salary is split equally between you and your spouse because of community property rules, then the tax withholding is also divided evenly between the two of you.

6. **Alimony and your IRA.** All taxable alimony or separate maintenance payments received by an individual under a decree of divorce or separate maintenance are treated as eligible compensation for making IRA contributions. See Chapter 18, *Individual Retirement Arrangements (IRAs) and Education Savings Accounts (ESAs),* for details.

Instruments Executed Before 1985

Here is an outline of the old alimony rules that apply to divorce or separation instruments executed *before* 1985 and *not* changed after 1984.

Payments you make under a court decree of divorce or separation are included in the income of your spouse or former spouse and may be deducted as alimony by you if they are:

1. Required under a decree of divorce or separation, or a written instrument incident to that decree
2. Based on a marital or family relationship
3. Paid after the date the decree became effective
4. Periodic instead of a lump sum

Payments made before the divorce decree or separate maintenance agreement issued by the court do not qualify as alimony. The divorce need not be final for the payments to be considered alimony, but the payments must be ordered by the court and, if made under pre-1985 agreements, must satisfy a legal obligation arising from the marriage.

Payments you make under a written separation agreement executed after August 16, 1954, or materially altered or modified after that date, are included in the income of your spouse and may be deducted as alimony by you if they are:

1. Based on a marital or family relationship
2. Paid after the agreement is put into effect and while you and your spouse are separated and living apart
3. Paid during a tax year for which you do not file a **joint return** with the spouse who gets these payments
4. Periodic instead of a lump sum

To be binding, a written agreement must state the amount of the support payments, the length of time over which the payments are to be made, and the items of support covered by the payments. The agreement does not have to mention specifically that the couple is separated.

The written separation agreement must be accepted by both parties. One spouse may not merely designate payments as alimony. The courts have held that a letter from a husband to a wife defining various payments as support do not meet the requirements of a written agreement, even if the payments are accepted by the wife. The agreement takes effect when it has been signed by both parties, no matter what the date is on the agreement.

Example

A wife signed a separation agreement and sent it to her husband. The husband signed it before a notary public but did not return it to the wife for several months. The husband, who had been out of the country, began sending the wife support payments before she received the signed agreement. The court held that the agreement became effective when signed by the husband. All payments were viewed as alimony.

Explanation

Payments you make under a decree for support or any type of court order, including a temporary decree, entered into after March 1, 1954, or changed by a court after that date, are included in the income of your spouse and may be deducted as alimony by you if they are:

1. Required under the decree or court order
2. Paid while you and your spouse are separated and living apart
3. Paid during a tax year for which you do not file a joint return with the spouse who gets these payments
4. Periodic instead of a lump sum

Payments you make under a decree for support or any type of court order qualify as alimony, even though the decree is not pursuant to a divorce or **legal separation** agreement. These payments must be specified as being for a spouse, not a child.

Spouses separated under an interlocutory decree retain the relationship of husband and wife, even though payments made pursuant to this type of decree qualify as alimony. However, if payments are being made under an interlocutory decree issued prior to March 1, 1954, and that decree has not yet been revised, the payments are not considered alimony.

Temporary alimony. If you do not file a joint return, you may deduct periodic payments you make under a decree of alimony *pendente lite* (while awaiting action on the final decree or agreement) entered after March 1, 1954. Your spouse must include the payments in income.

Remarriage of former spouse. You may not deduct payments you make under a divorce decree to your former spouse after the spouse remarries, if you have no legal obligation to continue to make the payments. Legal obligation to continue to make the payments would be determined under the law of the state in which your divorce was granted. However, your former spouse must still report the payments as miscellaneous income (not alimony), unless it can be shown that they were gifts, were payments on a loan, or were otherwise excludable from income.

Example 1

In 1984, you were divorced from your spouse. The divorce decree calls for you to pay your former spouse $400 a month as alimony. In April 1997, your former spouse remarried, but you were not aware of this, and you continued to make the payments.

Under the state law in which you got your divorce, your legal obligation to make the payments ends if your former spouse remarries. Even though you were unaware that your former spouse remarried, you cannot deduct the payments you made after April 1997. However, your former spouse must include the payments in gross income.

Example 2

Assume the same facts as in Example 1, except that you were aware of your former spouse's remarriage and you continued to make the payments but considered them a gift. In this situation, your former spouse does not have to include the payments made after April 1997 in gross income, and you may not deduct them.

Explanation

Periodic payments in a community property state to a separated spouse are deductible as alimony only if they are more than that spouse's part of the **community income.**

Example

You live in a community property state. You are separated, and your spouse has no income. Under a written support agreement, you pay your spouse periodic payments of $12,000 of your $20,000 total yearly community income. Under your state law, earnings of a spouse living separate and apart from the other spouse continue as community property. On your separate returns, each of you must report $10,000 gross income (half of the total community income). In addition, your spouse must report $2,000 as alimony received on line 11 of Form 1040. You may deduct $2,000 as alimony paid on line 31a of Form 1040.

Note: If you did *not* make any payments to your spouse or notify him or her of the amount of the community income, the IRS can require that you report the entire $20,000 as your income.

Explanation

A couple's property continues to be considered community property by the IRS until a final divorce is granted. This is true, even though some states—Louisiana, for example—might retroactively recognize the date of separation as the time when property is no longer shared. Consequently, until a final divorce is granted, a spouse should treat as alimony only those payments that are more than his or her share of the community income. Furthermore, alimony paid to a former spouse is generally considered as having been paid from community income when you and your current spouse file separate returns.

Example

A California resident was divorced and remarried. His new wife was a **nonresident alien,** and they filed separate tax returns. The courts held that he could deduct only half of the alimony payments made to his former wife because he failed to prove that the alimony payments were made from separate income property that he did not share with his new wife. Therefore, his new wife was, in effect, paying half of his alimony payments to his former wife. Her payments were not deductible as alimony.

Explanation

Periodic payments are payments of a fixed amount (e.g., $400 a month) for an indefinite period or payments of an indefinite amount (e.g., 10% of a salary that changes from year to year) for either a fixed or an indefinite period. They need not be made at regular intervals.

Even if a state court describes payments made under a divorce decree as payments for property rights, they may be periodic payments if they are made to fulfill a legal support obligation.

Installment payments that you make to take care of your alimony obligation (the amount you must pay under the decree) generally are not considered periodic payments if the total obligation is stated in the decree or agreement. They may not be deductible at all, or they may be only partly deductible, depending mainly on the period over which you must make the payments.

In general, courts have held that if an amount specified in the divorce decree can be determined by arithmetical means, it is considered a principal sum. Payments to reach a principal sum are installment payments, not periodic payments, and generally are not deductible as alimony if they are paid over a period of 10 years or less. The following are property settlement payments, not periodic payments:

- Repayment of a debt between husband and wife in equal annual installments
- Repayment on an annual basis of the wife's interest in community property retained by the husband

Example

A woman purchased a residence in her name. Her former husband had the right to use the residence for his lifetime. The woman was not allowed to deduct the fair rental value of the property as alimony, and the man did not have to include the value in his income as periodic payments. The IRS ruled that, according to state law, the woman was making a one-time transfer of property to her former husband. Such a transfer does not qualify as alimony.

Explanation

If the period stated is 10 years or less, the payments generally are not considered periodic, and, therefore, you may not deduct them. However, if the payments are subject to certain specific contingencies, they are deductible periodic payments, even though under the decree they are for a specified period of 10 years or less. Alimony payments are considered subject to contingencies if they are to end or change in amount on

1. The death of either spouse
2. The remarriage of the spouse receiving them
3. A change in the economic status (amount of money or property owned) of either spouse

The contingency may be set forth in the terms of the decree or agreement, or it may be imposed by local law. The payments must be in the nature of alimony or an allowance for support.

Example

Under the terms of a settlement agreement approved by the divorce decree, you agreed to pay your former spouse $19,000. Of this amount, you paid $14,000 as soon as the decree was entered. You pay the remaining $5,000 for 25 months at $200 a month. The payments will stop if your former spouse dies or remarries. You may not deduct the $14,000 that is a lump-sum payment, and your former spouse does not include it in income. Because the monthly payments of $200 will stop if your former spouse dies or remarries, they are periodic payments. You may deduct them, and your former spouse must include them in income.

Explanation

If the period stated is more than 10 years and the payments are not subject to contingencies, you may deduct a certain amount of each installment payment paid during the year as a periodic payment and your spouse must include it in income. The amount is limited to 10% of the total amount to be paid over the entire time called for by the decree. This 10% limit applies to installment payments made on a timely basis and to amounts due in a future tax year but paid in advance. The limit does not apply to amounts due in a prior tax year, but paid in a later tax year. If the payments are made for more than 10 years and are subject to contingencies, you may deduct them in full as periodic payments.

Example

Your decree states that you must pay your former spouse $150,000 in installments of $20,000 a year for 5 years and $5,000 a year for the following 10 years. The payments are not subject to any contingencies. You may deduct only 10% of the $150,000, or $15,000, during each of the first 5 years. During the last 10 years, you may deduct the entire $5,000 you pay each year.

Explanation

The 10% rule is relevant only when the amounts of alimony payments required by the divorce decree are not paid evenly over the specified payment period. The intention of the 10% rule is to prevent property settlements from being disguised as alimony. Alimony is deductible; a property settlement is not. The 10% rule does not apply if the payments would cease on the occurrence of certain contingencies.

TAXPLANNER

Although you may deduct only 10% of the total amount of fixed payments in any one year, you may be able to claim a greater deduction than you would normally if you alter the timing of the payments.

Example 1

A husband is obligated to pay $160,000 over a 15-year period by paying $20,000 a year for the first 5 years and $6,000 a year for the last 10 years. Because he may deduct only 10% of the total fixed amount in any one year, only $16,000 (10% of $160,000) of the $20,000 paid in each of the first 5 years is deductible. The $4,000-per-year difference ($20,000 paid less $16,000 deductible) is not deductible by the husband or taxable to his former spouse.

In the fifth year, however, the husband makes a payment of only $16,000, instead of the required $20,000. That entire amount is deductible, since it is not more than 10% of the total amount due. If in the sixth year of payments he makes a $10,000 payment (the $6,000 he owes for that year plus the $4,000 from the year before), he may again deduct the entire amount. The $10,000 payment is less than the 10% limitation. Also, back alimony is not subject to the 10% rule. Thus, by shifting the timing of his payments, the husband may take a greater deduction.

Note: The 10% rule does apply to the advance payment of alimony. If in the above example the husband wants to make the $6,000-a-year payments for years 6, 7, and 8 in the sixth year, he may deduct only $16,000 (10% of the total amount due) of the $18,000 paid.

Example 2

Mr. Oldster got behind in his alimony payments. He made a lump-sum settlement of the amounts he owed, as well as future alimony. The amount paid was less than the total amount due and was also less than the amount of delinquent alimony. Since there was no designation of the amounts, he was allowed to deduct the total payment as back alimony.

TAXPLANNER

There are certain circumstances in which what appears to be a lump-sum payment may, in fact, be deductible as alimony.

According to an IRS ruling, a lump-sum payment to a former spouse for the remaining portion of alimony payments to which he or she is entitled qualifies as alimony.

Example

A couple divorced, and the divorce decree stipulated that the wife pay $81,000 in alimony, $3,600 per year for 22½ years. After 10 years, the husband could elect to receive the present value of the remaining payments. Since the payments spanned more than 10 years, they were considered periodic. However, because of the 10% limitation rule, the husband had to include only $8,100, 10% of the total payments received over the 22½ years, in his income for the year in which he received the lump-sum payment [(10% × $3,600) × 22.5].

Note: This opinion was given by the IRS before 1985.

TAXPLANNER

For installment payments to qualify as periodic payments, the last payment must be made more than 10 years after the decree became effective. There have been numerous errors made in implementing the effective dates of agreements and the ending of the 10-year period.

Example

According to a divorce decree, a husband must make payments at the beginning of each month for 120 months, beginning with the month after the decree becomes final. If the decree became final on December 15, 1984, the first payment was due January 1, 1985. The one hundred twentieth and final payment is due December 1, 1994—14 days short of 10 years. Since the payment period falls short of the 10-year-plus requirement, the payments are not deductible as alimony.

Exception

The 10-year rule will not apply to an agreement executed before 1985 if it has been modified after 1984 and expressly provides that the new rules will apply. If a pre-1985 agreement has been modified and there is a change in the term of payment, the new alimony rules enacted in 1984 will apply when expressly indicated.

PART III

Standard Deduction and Itemized Deductions

After you have figured your adjusted gross income, you are ready to subtract the deductions used to figure taxable income. You can subtract either the standard deduction or itemized deductions. Itemized deductions are deductions for certain expenses that are listed on Schedule A (Form 1040). The 10 chapters in this part discuss the standard deduction, each itemized deduction, and the limit on some of your itemized deductions if your adjusted gross income exceeds certain amounts. See Chapter 21, *Standard Deduction* for the factors to consider when deciding whether to subtract the standard deduction or itemized deductions.

TAKE THE STANDARD DEDUCTION IF:

- Your standard deduction is more than the total itemized deductions you can claim (Chapters 21, *Standard Deduction,* and 22, *Limit on Itemized Deductions*).

YOU CANNOT TAKE THE STANDARD DEDUCTION IF:

- You are filing a tax return with a short tax year,

- You were a nonresident or a dual-status alien during the year (Chapter 21, *Standard Deduction*), or

- You are married filing separately, and your spouse itemizes deductions.

ITEMIZE YOUR DEDUCTIONS IF:

- You cannot take the standard deduction (Chapter 21, *Standard Deduction*).

or

- You had large uninsured medical and dental expenses (Chapter 23, *Medical and Dental Expenses*),

- You paid taxes and interest on your home (Chapters 24, *Taxes You May Deduct* and 25, *Interest Expense*),

- You made large charitable contributions (Chapter 26, *Contributions*),

- You had large uninsured casualty or theft losses (Chapter 27, *Casualty and Theft Losses*),

- You had employee business expenses (Chapter 28, *Car Expenses and Other Employee Business Expenses*),

- You had employee educational expenses (Chapter 29, *Tax Benefits for Work-Related Education*), or

- You had various miscellaneous expenses (Chapter 30, *Miscellaneous Deductions*),

and

- Your total itemized deductions are more than the standard deduction you can claim (Chapter 21, *Standard Deduction*).

21

Standard Deduction

Introduction

Taxpayers who do not itemize their deductions are eligible for the standard deduction. However, you should determine whether itemizing deductions or taking the applicable standard deduction produces greater tax savings. In determining the amount of your standard deduction, you must consider many factors, including filing status, age, blindness, unearned income, and whether

or not someone is claiming you as an exemption. Higher deductions are allowed if you or your spouse is over age 65 or is totally or partially blind. On the other hand, if another taxpayer can claim you as a dependent, your standard deduction may be limited. This chapter, which includes several useful worksheets, will help you to figure out what your standard deduction is.

Important Changes

Increase in standard deduction. The standard deduction for taxpayers who do not itemize deductions on Schedule A of Form 1040 is higher in 2001 than it was in 2000. The amount depends on your filing status. *2001 Standard Deduction Tables* are shown at the end of this chapter.

Itemized deductions. The amount you can deduct for itemized deductions is limited if your adjusted gross income is more than $132,950 ($66,475 if you are married filing separately). See chapter 22 for more information.

This chapter discusses:

- How to figure the amount of your standard deduction,
- The standard deduction for dependents, and
- Who should itemize deductions.

Most taxpayers have a choice of either taking a standard deduction or itemizing their deductions. The standard deduction is a dollar amount that reduces the amount of income on which you are taxed.

The standard deduction is a benefit that eliminates the need for many taxpayers to itemize actual deductions, such as medical expenses, charitable contributions, or taxes. The standard deduction is higher for taxpayers who are 65 or older or blind. If you have a choice, you should use the method that gives you the lower tax.

You benefit from the standard deduction if your standard deduction is more than the total of your allowable itemized deductions.

Figuring the Amount

Before figuring the amount of your standard deduction, you must determine if you are eligible to take it.

Persons not eligible for the standard deduction. Your standard deduction is *zero* and you should itemize any deductions you have if:

1) You are married and filing a separate return, and your spouse itemizes deductions,
2) You are filing a tax return for a short tax year because of a change in your annual accounting period, or
3) You are a nonresident or dual-status alien during the year. You are considered a dual-status alien if you were both a nonresident and resident alien during the year.

Note. If you are a nonresident alien who is married to a U.S. citizen or resident at the end of the year, you can choose to be treated as a U.S. resident. (See Publication 519, *U.S. Tax Guide for Aliens.*) If you make this choice, you can take the standard deduction.

Explanation
Married persons who file separate returns must be consistent in claiming the standard deduction or itemizing deductions. If one spouse itemizes deductions, the other spouse must also itemize deductions and cannot claim the standard deduction.

A tax return filed for a decedent through the date of death is not considered a short tax year so that the decedent is entitled to the full standard deduction.

Example
John Thomas dies on June 15, 2001. John's final tax return will cover the period from January 1 through June 15.

The full amount of the standard deduction may be claimed on John's final return.

Caution. *If an exemption for you can be claimed on another person's return (such as your parents' return), your standard deduction may be limited. See* Standard Deduction for Dependents, *later.*

TaxAlert

The key word is *can*.
You cannot forgo an otherwise allowable dependent deduction in order to increase that dependent's standard deduction.

Standard Deduction Amount

Generally, the standard deduction amounts are adjusted each year for inflation. The standard deduction amounts for most taxpayers for 2001 are shown in *Table 21-1*.

Decedent's final return. The amount of the standard deduction for a decedent's final return is the same as it would have been had the decedent continued to live. However, if the decedent was not 65 or older at the time of death, the higher standard deduction for age cannot be claimed.

Higher Standard Deduction for Age (65 or Older)

If you do not itemize deductions, you are entitled to a higher standard deduction if you are age 65 or older at the end of the year. You are considered 65 on the day before your 65th birthday. Therefore, you can take a higher standard deduction for 2001 if your 65th birthday was on or before January 1, 2002.

Use *Table 21-2* to figure the standard deduction amount.

Higher Standard Deduction for Blindness

If you are blind on the last day of the year and you do not itemize deductions, you are entitled to a higher standard deduction as shown in *Table 21-2*. You qualify for this benefit if you are totally or partly blind.

Partly blind. If you are partly blind, you must get a certified statement from an eye doctor or registered optometrist that:

1) You cannot see better than 20/200 in the better eye with glasses or contact lenses, or
2) Your field of vision is not more than 20 degrees.

If your eye condition will never improve beyond these limits, the statement should include this fact. You must keep the statement in your records.

If your vision can be corrected beyond these limits only by contact lenses that you can wear only briefly because of pain, infection, or ulcers, you can take the higher standard deduction for blindness if you otherwise qualify.

Spouse 65 or Older or Blind

You can take the higher standard deduction if your spouse is age 65 or older or blind and:

1) You file a joint return, or
2) You file a separate return and can claim an exemption for your spouse because your spouse had no gross income and an exemption for your spouse could not be claimed by another taxpayer.

Caution. *You cannot claim the higher standard deduction for an individual other than yourself and your spouse.*

TaxSaver

Itemizing vs. standard deduction. In calculating your taxable income, you should use the larger of your itemized deductions or your standard deduction. By doing some planning, it may be possible to use the standard deduction in some years and to itemize deductions in others.

Example

In December 2001, Bill and Barbara Chapman add up their itemized deductions for 2001 and find that the total is only $3,250. At that time, they receive an annual real estate tax bill for $2,950, which can be paid anytime before January 31, 2002. A religious organization that the Chapmans are affiliated with is also requesting a $1,400 contribution for its building fund. If the Chapmans make both expenditures in 2001, they will receive no tax benefit from these tax-deductible expenditures because their itemized deductions would total $7,600, the same as their standard deduction. If they make the expenditures in 2002, they might generate more than the standard deduction for that year. Postponing would be a better strategy.

Examples

The following examples illustrate how to determine your standard deduction using *Tables 21-1* and *21-2*.

Example 1. Larry, 46, and Donna, 33, are filing a joint return for 2001. Neither is blind. They decide not to itemize their deductions. They use *Table 21-1*. Their standard deduction is $7,600.

Example 2. Assume the same facts as in Example 1, except that Larry is blind at the end of 2001. Larry and Donna use *Table 21-2*. Their standard deduction is $8,500.

Example 3. Bill and Terry are filing a joint return for 2001. Both are over age 65. Neither is blind. If they do not itemize deductions, they use *Table 21-2*. Their standard deduction is $9,400.

Standard Deduction for Dependents

The standard deduction for an individual for whom an exemption can be claimed on another person's tax return is generally limited to the greater of:

1) $750, or
2) The individual's earned income for the year plus $250 (but not more than the regular standard deduction amount, generally $4,550).

Explanation

Although the reduction in the standard deduction available to your dependent children is well publicized, the reduction for dependent parents is not so well known.

Example

Assume that your 61-year-old widowed mother has $6,750 of interest income. If she is not your dependent, she has no tax liability. Her $4,550 standard deduction plus her $2,900 personal exemption eliminate her taxable income. As your dependent, her standard deduction drops to $750 and she loses her personal exemption entirely. Her taxable income would be $6,000 and her tax would be $600. You might pay less tax because of the additional $2,900 dependent exemption (assuming your exemptions are not phased out because your income is too high), but no one will benefit from the remaining unused standard deduction of $3,800 ($4,550 − $750).

However, if the individual is 65 or older or blind, the standard deduction may be higher.

If an exemption for you can be claimed on someone else's return, use *Table 21-3* to determine your standard deduction.

2001 Standard Deduction Tables

Caution: If you are married filing a separate return and your spouse itemizes deductions, or if you are a dual-status alien, you cannot take the standard deduction even if you were 65 or older or blind.

Table 21–1. Standard Deduction Chart for Most People*

IF your Filing Status is ...	Your Standard Deduction is:
Single	$4,550
Married filing joint return or Qualifying widow(er) with dependent child	7,600
Married filing separate return	3,800
Head of household	6,650

*DO NOT use this chart if you were 65 or older or blind, OR if someone else can claim an exemption for you (or your spouse if married filing jointly). Use Table 21–2 or 21–3 instead.

Table 21–2. Standard Deduction Chart for People Age 65 or Older or Blind*

Check the correct number of boxes below. Then go to the chart.
You   65 or older ☐   Blind ☐
Your spouse, if claiming spouse's exemption   65 or older ☐   Blind ☐

Total number of boxes you checked ☐

IF your Filing Status is ...	AND the Number in the Box Above is ...	THEN your Standard Deduction is:
Single	1	$5,650
	2	6,750
Married filing joint return or Qualifying widow(er) with dependent child	1	8,500
	2	9,400
	3	10,300
	4	11,200
Married filing separate return	1	4,700
	2	5,600
	3	6,500
	4	7,400
Head of household	1	7,750
	2	8,850

*If someone else can claim an exemption for you (or your spouse if married filing jointly), use Table 21–3 instead.

Table 21–3. Standard Deduction Worksheet for Dependents*

If you were 65 or older or blind, check the correct number of boxes below. Then go to the worksheet.
You   65 or older ☐   Blind ☐
Your spouse, if claiming spouse's exemption   65 or older ☐   Blind ☐

Total number of boxes you checked ☐

1. Enter your **earned income** (defined below). If none, enter -0-.	1. _____
2. Additional amount	2. $250
3. Add lines 1 and 2.	3. _____
4. Minimum amount	4. $750
5. Enter the **larger** of line 3 or line 4.	5. _____
6. Enter the amount shown below for your filing status. • Single, enter $4,550 • Married filing separate return, enter $3,800 • Married filing jointly or Qualifying widow(er) with dependent child, enter $7,600 • Head of household, enter $6,650	6. _____
7. **Standard deduction.** a. Enter the **smaller** of line 5 or line 6. If under 65 and not blind, stop here. This is your standard deduction. Otherwise, go on to line 7b.	7a. _____
b. If 65 or older or blind, multiply $1,100 ($900 if married or qualifying widow(er) with dependent child) by the number in the box above.	7b. _____
c. Add lines 7a and 7b. This is your standard deduction for 2001.	7c. _____

Earned income includes wages, salaries, tips, professional fees, and other compensation received for personal services you performed. It also includes any amount received as a scholarship that you must include in your income.

*Use this worksheet ONLY if someone else can claim an exemption for you (or your spouse if married filing jointly).

Earned income defined. Earned income is salaries, wages, tips, professional fees, and other amounts received as pay for work you actually perform.

For purposes of the standard deduction, earned income also includes any part of a *scholarship or fellowship grant* that you must include in your gross income. See *Scholarship and Fellowship Grants* in chapter 13 for more information on what qualifies as a scholarship or fellowship grant.

Example 1. Michael is single. His parents claim an exemption for him on their 2001 tax return. He has interest income of $780 and wages of $150. He has no itemized deductions. Michael uses *Table 21-3* to find his standard deduction. He enters $150 (his earned income) on line 1, $400 ($150 plus $250) on line 3, $750 (the larger of $400 and $750) on line 5, and $4,550 on line 6. The amount of his standard deduction, on line 7a, is $750 (the smaller of $750 and $4,550).

Example 2. Joe, a 22-year-old full-time college student, is claimed on his parents' 2001 tax return. Joe is married and files a separate return. His wife does not itemize deductions on her separate return.

Joe has $1,500 in interest income and wages of $3,600. He has no itemized deductions. Joe finds his standard deduction by using *Table 21-3*. He enters his earned income, $3,600, on line 1. He adds lines 1 and 2 and enters $3,850 on line 3. On line 5 he enters $3,850, the larger of lines 3 and 4. Since Joe is married filing a separate return, he enters $3,800 on line 6. On line 7a he enters $3,800 as his standard deduction because it is smaller than $3,850, the amount on line 5.

Explanation
The $3,800 limitation applies only to a married dependent who files a separate return.

Example 3. Amy, who is single, is claimed on her parents' 2001 tax return. She is 18 years old and blind. She has interest income of $1,300 and wages of $2,900. She has no itemized deductions. Amy uses *Table 21-3* to find her standard deduction. She enters her wages of $2,900 on line 1. She adds lines 1 and 2 and enters $3,150 on line 3. On line 5 she enters $3,150, the larger of lines 3 and 4. Since she is single, Amy enters $4,550 on line 6. She enters $3,150 on line 7a. This is the smaller of the amounts on lines 5 and 6. Because she checked one box in the top part of the worksheet, she enters $1,100 on line 7b. She then adds the amounts on lines 7a and 7b and enters her standard deduction of $4,250 on line 7c.

Who Should Itemize

You should itemize deductions if your total deductions are more than the standard deduction amount. Also, you should itemize if you do not qualify for the standard deduction, as discussed earlier under *Persons not eligible for the standard deduction.*

You should first figure your itemized deductions and compare that amount to your standard deduction to make sure you are using the method that gives you the greater benefit.

Caution. *You may be subject to a limit on some of your itemized deductions if your adjusted gross income (AGI) is more than $132,950 ($66,475 if you are married filing separately). See chapter 22 and the instructions for Schedule A (Form 1040), line 28, for more information on figuring the correct amount of your itemized deductions.*

TaxAlert

If you're over the limit. Allowable itemized deductions (other than medical expenses, casualty and theft losses, and investment interest) are reduced by an amount equal to 3% of a taxpayer's adjusted gross income in excess of $132,950 ($66,475 for married persons filing a separate return). However, these allowable itemized deductions are not reduced by more than 80%. You should consider this limitation, if applicable, in determining the benefits from itemizing deductions. See Chapter 22, *Limit on Itemized Deductions*, for more details.

When to itemize. You may benefit from itemizing your deductions on Schedule A (Form 1040) if you:

1) Do not qualify for the standard deduction, or the amount you can claim is limited,
2) Had large uninsured medical and dental expenses during the year,
3) Paid interest and taxes on your home,
4) Had large unreimbursed employee business expenses or other miscellaneous deductions,
5) Had large uninsured casualty or theft losses,
6) Made large contributions to qualified charities, or
7) Have total itemized deductions that are more than the standard deduction to which you otherwise are entitled.

These deductions are explained in chapters 23–30.

If you decide to itemize your deductions, complete Schedule A and attach it to your Form 1040. Enter the amount from Schedule A, line 28, on Form 1040, line 36.

Itemizing for state tax or other purposes. If you choose to itemize even though your itemized deductions are less than the amount of your standard deduction, write "IE" (itemized elected) next to line 36 (Form 1040).

Changing your mind. If you do not itemize your deductions and later find that you should have itemized—or if you itemize your deductions and later find you should not have—you can change your return by filing Form 1040X, *Amended U.S. Individual Income Tax Return.* See *Amended Returns and Claims for Refund* in chapter 1 for more information on amended returns.

Married persons who filed separate returns. You can change methods of taking deductions only if you and your spouse both make the same changes. Both of you must file a consent to assessment for any additional tax either one may owe as a result of the change.

You and your spouse can use the method that gives you the lower total tax, even though one of you may pay more tax than you would have paid by using the other method. You both must use the same method of claiming deductions. If one itemizes deductions, the other should itemize because he or she will not qualify for the standard deduction. (See *Persons not eligible for the standard deduction,* earlier.)

22

Limit on Itemized Deductions

Introduction

The tax law limits the amount of certain itemized deductions that individuals can use to reduce their taxable income. For example, the threshold for deducting medical expenses is 7.5% of adjusted gross income; miscellaneous deductions are limited to those in excess of 2% of adjusted gross income; and home mortgage interest expense is subject to various limitations.

Congress has placed an additional "overall" limitation on the deductibility of a certain group of itemized deductions. In 2001, this limitation applies only if your adjusted gross income is greater than $132,950 ($66,475 if married filing separately). Itemized deductions that are subject to this limitation include taxes, home mort-

gage interest, charitable contributions, and miscellaneous itemized deductions. The total of this group of deductions must be reduced by 3% of the amount of your adjusted gross income in excess of $132,950 ($66,475 if married filing separately). This limitation is applied after you have used any other limitations that exist in the law, such as the adjusted gross income limitation for charitable contributions and the mortgage interest expense limitations.

Medical expenses, casualty and theft losses, investment interest expense, and gambling losses are not subject to this rule. The threshold amount is indexed annually for inflation.

This chapter discusses the overall limit on itemized deductions. The topics include:

* Who is subject to the limit,
* Which itemized deductions are limited, and
* How to figure the limit.

Useful Items

You may want to see:

Form (and Instructions)

☐ **Schedule A (Form 1040)** Itemized Deductions

Are You Subject to the Limit?

You are subject to the limit on certain itemized deductions if your adjusted gross income (AGI) is more than $132,950 ($66,475 if you are married filing separately). Your AGI is the amount on line 34 of your Form 1040.

This limit does not apply to estates or trusts.

Which Itemized Deductions Are Limited?

The following Schedule A (Form 1040) deductions are subject to the overall limit on itemized deductions.

* Taxes—line 9.
* Interest—lines 10, 11, and 12.
* Gifts to charity—line 18.
* Job expenses and most other miscellaneous deductions—line 26.
* Other miscellaneous deductions—line 27, excluding gambling and casualty or theft losses.

Which Itemized Deductions Are Not Limited?

The following Schedule A (Form 1040) deductions are not subject to the overall limit on itemized deductions. However, they are still subject to other applicable limits.

* Medical and dental expenses—line 4.
* Investment interest expense—line 13.
* Casualty and theft losses from personal use property—line 19.
* Casualty and theft losses from income-producing property—line 27.
* Gambling losses—line 27.

Explanation
Whether a particular deduction will be limited or not depends on the character of the deduction.

Example 1
Martin and Dodi Stone file a joint income tax return. They have an adjusted gross income of $332,950. The Stones' only itemized deductions are $20,000 of home mortgage

interest and $8,000 of real estate taxes. Because both of these itemized deductions are subject to the limitation, their total deductions of $28,000 must be reduced by 3% of $200,000 (the amount by which AGI exceeds $132,950), or $6,000. They may reduce their taxable income by total itemized deductions of $22,000 ($28,000 − $6,000).

Example 2

Assume the same facts as above, except that the Stones live in a downtown apartment, and their only itemized deduction is $28,000 of otherwise allowable investment interest expense. Because investment interest expense is not subject to the 3% limitation, the entire $28,000 will be deductible.

How Do You Figure the Limit?

If your itemized deductions are subject to the limit, the total of all your itemized deductions is reduced by the smaller of:

1) 3% of the amount by which your AGI exceeds $132,950 ($66,475 if married filing separately), or
2) 80% of your itemized deductions that are affected by the limit. See *Which Itemized Deductions Are Limited,* earlier.

Before you figure the overall limit on itemized deductions, you must first complete lines 1 through 27 of Schedule A (Form 1040), including any appropriate forms (such as Form 2106, Form 4684, etc.).

The overall limit on itemized deductions is figured after you have applied any other limit on the allowance of any itemized deduction. These other limits include charitable contribution limits (chapter 26), the limit on certain meals and entertainment (chapter 28), and the 2%-of-adjusted-gross-income limit on certain miscellaneous deductions (chapter 30).

Itemized Deductions Worksheet. After you have completed Schedule A (Form 1040) through line 27, you can use the *Itemized Deductions Worksheet* in the Form 1040 instructions for Schedule A to figure your limit. Enter the result on line 28 of Schedule A. Keep the worksheet for your records.

Tip. *You should compare the amount of your standard deduction to the amount of your itemized deductions after applying the limit. Use the greater amount when completing line 36 of your Form 1040. See chapter 21 for information on how to figure your standard deduction.*

Example

For tax year 2001, Bill and Terry Willow are filing a joint return on Form 1040. Their adjusted gross income is $255,250. Their Schedule A itemized deductions are as follows:

Taxes—line 9	$17,900
Interest—lines 10, 11, and 12	45,000
Investment interest expense—line 13	41,000
Gifts to charity—line 18	21,000
Job expenses—line 26	17,240
Total	**$142,140**

The Willows' investment interest expense deduction ($41,000 from line 13 of Schedule A) is not subject to the overall limit on itemized deductions.

The Willows use the *Itemized Deductions Worksheet* in the Form 1040 instructions for Schedule A to figure their overall limit. Their completed worksheet is shown in *Table 22-1.*

Of their $142,140 total itemized deductions, the Willows can deduct only $138,471 ($142,140 − $3,669). They enter $138,471 on Schedule A, line 28.

Table 22-1. Itemized Deductions Worksheet (Keep for Your Records)

1. Add the amounts on Schedule A, lines 4, 9, 14, 18, 19, 26, and 27. **1.** 142,140
2. Add the amounts on Schedule A, lines 4, 13, and 19, plus any gambling and casualty or theft losses included on line 27. **2.** 41,000

> **CAUTION** Be sure your total gambling and casualty or theft losses are clearly identified on the dotted lines next to line 27.

3. Is the amount on line 2 less than the amount on line 1?

   ☐ **No.** **STOP** Your deduction is not limited. Enter the amount from line 1 above on Schedule A, line 28.

   ☑ **Yes.** Subtract line 2 from line 1 **3.** 101,140
4. Multiply line 3 above by 80% (.80) **4.** 80,912
5. Enter the amount from Form 1040, line 34 **5.** 255,250
6. Enter: $132,950 if single, married filing jointly, head of household, or qualifying widow(er); $66,475 if married filing separately. **6.** 132,950
7. Is the amount on line 6 less than the amount on line 5?

   ☐ **No.** **STOP** Your deduction is not limited. Enter the amount from line 1 above on Schedule A, line 28.

   ☑ **Yes.** Subtract line 6 from line 5 **7.** 122,300
8. Multiply line 7 above by 3% (.03) **8.** 3,669
9. Enter the **smaller** of line 4 or line 8 **9.** 3,669
10. **Total itemized deductions.** Subtract line 9 from line 1. Enter the result here and on Schedule A, line 28 **10.** 138,471

TaxSaver

Using the 3% limitation. In certain situations, it is possible for the 3% limitation to reduce allowable itemized deductions below the standard deduction amount. You should consider this possibility when you are choosing whether to itemize your deductions or to use the standard deduction.

Example

Arthur and Karen White have adjusted gross income of $232,950. They have no mortgage on their home; however, they pay annual real estate taxes of $5,500. Each year they contribute $2,500 to their favorite charity. The Whites would compute their taxable income as follows:

Adjusted gross income		$232,950
Itemized deductions		
Real estate taxes	$5,500	
Charitable contibutions	2,500	
Total	$8,000	
Less 3% of AGI in excess of $132,950	3,000	
Allowable itemized deductions	$5,000	
Standard deduction if married, filing a joint return	$7,600	
Greater of standard deduction or allowable itemized deductions		(7,600)
Personal Exemptions		(4,176)
Taxable Income		$221,174

Note: The personal exemptions have been reduced according to the phaseout rules discussed in Chapter 3, *Personal Exemptions and Dependents.*

TaxPlanner

Bunching. If your itemized deductions are subject to this 3% limitation, you may want to consider a technique called "bunching." Bunching is effective if you are able to accumulate deductions so that they are high in one year and low in the next.

Example

Assume the same facts as in the previous example. This time, however, the Whites are able to *postpone* payment of their 2001 real estate taxes until January 2002, and they can also pay $1,500 of their $2,500 charitable contributions in early 2002. Then next year, in December 2002, they will *accelerate* these payments to make sure that they fall in 2002 and not 2003. The Whites will end up with the following expenses for 2001 and 2002:

	2001	2002
2001 Real estate taxes	—	$5,500
2001 Charitable contributions	$1,000	1,500
2002 Real estate taxes	—	$5,500
2002 Charitable contributions	—	2,500
Total	$1,000	$15,000

By bunching the expenses, the Whites may use the $7,600 standard deduction in 2001 and itemized deductions of $12,000 ($15,000 less the 3% limit of $3,000) in 2002. Total deductions equal $19,600 for the 2 years ($7,600 + $12,000). In 2002, they will have reduced their taxable income by an additional $4,400 ($12,000 – $7,600). Without bunching, the Whites would have been limited to the standard deduction in each year. (These calculations assume that the standard deduction and the itemized deduction limit will not change in 2002.)

23

Medical and Dental Expenses

Introduction

Deductible medical expenses include payments for the diagnosis, cure, mitigation, treatment, and prevention of disease. Payments with respect to any part or function of the body are allowed, as are payments for the prevention or alleviation of mental illness. You may include even your cab or bus fare to the doctor's office. But you may not include expenditures that are merely beneficial to your general health or purely cosmetic medical procedures—like vacation costs or hair transplants, for example.

*Unfortunately, while almost any medical expense qualifies for the deduction, it's difficult to take an actual **deduction on** your tax return, and it's getting more difficult.*

*Your medical expenses must total more than 7.5% of your **adjusted gross income** before you can take any deduction. In other words, someone with an adjusted gross income of $30,000 in 2001 has to have more than $2,250 of medical expenses before he or she may deduct any of them.*

Note: Your 2001 itemized deductions may be subject to certain overall limitations if your adjusted gross income exceeds $132,950 ($66,475 if married filing separately). However, deductions for medical expenses are not subject to the overall limitation. See Chapter 22, Limit on Itemized Deductions for more information on this subject.

Important Change

Standard mileage rate. The standard mileage rate allowed for out-of-pocket expenses for your car when you use your car for medical reasons is now 12 cents a mile. See *Transportation* under *What Expenses Are Deductible*.

This chapter will help you determine:

- The definition of medical care,
- What expenses you can include this year,
- How much of the expenses you can deduct,
- Whose medical expenses you can include,
- What medical expenses are deductible,
- How you treat reimbursements, and
- How to report the deduction on your tax return.

Useful Items

You may want to see:

Publication

☐ **502** Medical and Dental Expenses

Form (and Instructions)

☐ **Schedule A (Form 1040)** Itemized Deductions

What Is the Definition of Medical Care?

Medical care means amounts paid for the diagnosis, cure, mitigation, treatment, or prevention of disease, and for treatments affecting any part or function of the body. The medical care expenses must be primarily to alleviate or prevent a physical or mental defect or illness.

Medical care expenses include the premiums you pay for insurance that covers the expenses of medical care, and the amounts you pay for transportation to get medical care. Medical care expenses also include limited amounts paid for any qualified long-term care insurance contract.

TaxAlert

Marijuana and other controlled substances. The IRS has ruled that the cost of marijuana or any other federally controlled substance, even if recommended by a physician in a state whose laws permit such purchase and use, is not deductible. The U.S. Supreme Court has, in effect, upheld this ruling.

What Expenses Can You Include This Year?

You can include only the medical and dental expenses you paid this year, regardless of when the services were provided. If you pay medical expenses by check, the day you mail or deliver the check generally is the date of payment. If you use a "pay-by-phone" or "on-line" account to pay your medical expenses, the date reported on the statement of the financial institution showing when payment was made is the date of payment. You can include medical expenses you charge to your credit card in the year the charge is made. It does not matter when you actually pay the amount charged.

TaxPlanner

Timing your medical expenses. Medical expenses don't usually lend themselves to tax planning. However, because a medical deduction is available *only* in the year of payment, you may be able to maximize your deduction if you can control the timing of your payment.

To determine the most beneficial year of payment, you need to assess your situation prior to the end of the year. If it is clear that your current-year medical expenses will not exceed the nondeductible floor—7.5% of your adjusted gross income—try to defer payment of any medical bills until after year-end. You may be able to salvage a deduction next year.

If you can schedule major or minor surgery in nonemergency cases, you should compare this year's medical deductions with what they are liable to be next year to choose the more beneficial time. It is the date of payment—not the date of surgery—that determines the year in which you may deduct the expense. Remember, putting the charge on a credit card counts as payment at that time.

If you suspect that your adjusted gross income is going to drop substantially next year, defer the payment of medical bills. However, if you think your adjusted gross income is going to skyrocket next year, pay those bills now and try to salvage a deduction.

Exception
Prepaid medical expenses generally are not deductible until the year of treatment.

When do you include a decedent's medical expenses? Medical expenses for a decedent that are paid from his or her estate are treated as paid at the time the medical services were provided if they are paid within the 1-year period beginning with the day after the date of death. See *Decedent* under *Whose Medical Expenses Can You Include,* later, for an exception.

Medical expenses paid before death by the decedent are included in figuring any deduction for medical and dental expenses on the decedent's final income tax return. This includes expenses for the decedent's spouse and dependents as well as for the decedent.

How Much of the Expenses Can You Deduct?

You can deduct only the amount of your medical and dental expenses that is **more than 7.5%** of your adjusted gross income (line 34, Form 1040).

In this chapter, the term "7.5% limit" is used to refer to 7.5% of your adjusted gross income. The phrase "subject to the 7.5% limit" is also used. This phrase means that you must subtract 7.5% (.075) of your adjusted gross income from your medical expenses to figure your medical expense deduction.

Example. Your adjusted gross income is $20,000, 7.5% of which is $1,500. You paid medical expenses of $800. You cannot deduct any of your medical expenses because they are not more than 7.5% of your adjusted gross income.

Separate returns. If you and your spouse live in a noncommunity property state and file separate returns, each of you can include only the medical expenses each actually paid. Any medical expenses paid out of a joint checking account in which you and your spouse have the same interest are considered to have been paid equally by each of you, unless you can show otherwise.

Community property states. If you and your spouse live in a community property state and file separate returns, any medical expenses paid out of community funds are divided equally. Each of you should include half the expenses. If medical expenses are paid out of the separate funds of one spouse, only the spouse who paid the medical expenses can include them. If you live in a community property state, are married, and file a separate return, see Publication 555, *Community Property.*

TaxPlanner

If your spouse's medical expenses exceed yours. You should consider filing separate returns whenever the medical expenses of either spouse substantially exceed those of the other spouse. Compute and compare your tax liability if you and your spouse were to file jointly with the potential tax liability if you were to file separately before deciding which filing status to choose.

Whose Medical Expenses Can You Include?

You can include medical expenses you pay for yourself and for the individuals discussed in this section.

Spouse. You can include medical expenses you paid for your spouse. To claim these expenses, you must have been married either at the time your spouse received the medical services or at the time you paid the medical expenses.

Example 1. Mary received medical treatment before she married Bill. Bill paid for the treatment after they married. Bill can include these expenses in figuring his medical expense deduction even if Bill and Mary file separate returns.

If Mary had paid the expenses before she and Bill married, Bill could not include Mary's expenses in his separate return. Mary would include the amounts she paid during the year in her separate return. If they filed a joint return, the medical expenses both paid during the year would be used to figure their medical expense deduction.

Example 2. This year, John paid medical expenses for his wife Louise, who died last year. John married Belle this year and they file a joint return. Because John was married to Louise when she incurred the medical expenses, he can include those expenses in figuring his medical deduction for this year.

Dependent. You can include medical expenses you paid for your dependent. To claim these expenses, the person must have been your dependent either at the time the medical services were provided or at the time you paid the expenses. A person generally qualifies as your dependent for purposes of the medical expense deduction if:

1) That person lived with you for the entire year as a member of your household or is related to you,
2) That person was a U.S. citizen or resident, or a resident of Canada or Mexico, for some part of the calendar year in which your tax year began, and
3) You provided over half of that person's total support for the calendar year.

You can include the medical expenses of any person who is your dependent even if you cannot claim an exemption for him or her on your return.

Example. In 2000 your son was your dependent. In 2001 he no longer qualified as your dependent. However, you paid $800 in 2001 for medical expenses your son incurred in 2000 when he was your dependent. You can include the $800 in figuring your medical expense deduction for 2001. You cannot include this amount on your 2000 tax return.

TAXPLANNER

If you pay medical expenses for others. If you pay medical expenses on behalf of an individual who does not qualify as your dependent and your payment is made directly to the provider of the medical service, the payment is not deductible for income tax purposes. However, your payment will not be considered a gift to the individual either. An unlimited gift tax exclusion is available for qualifying medical expenses paid on any individual's behalf directly to the provider of the medical service. This exclusion is also available for transfers that would otherwise be subject to the generation-skipping transfer tax. The generation-skipping transfer tax, imposed at a flat 55% rate in 2001 in addition to any gift or estate tax incurred, is applied to transfers that are made to persons two or more generations below the donor. The flat rate goes down (and up) over the next years as follows:

2002	50%
2003	49%
2004	48%
2005	47%
2006	46%
2007-2009	45%
2010	0%
2011+	55%

You should consult your tax advisor if you are interested in pursuing this type of tax planning.

Example
A grandparent pays medical expenses directly to the hospital on a grandchild's behalf. The payments will reduce the grandparent's taxable estate and will not be subject to gift tax or generation-skipping transfer tax. This could result in significant tax savings.

Adopted child. You can include medical expenses that you paid for a child before adoption, if the child qualified as your dependent when the medical services were provided or when the expenses were paid. If you pay back an adoption agency or other persons for medical expenses they paid under an agreement with you, you are treated as having paid those expenses provided you clearly substantiate that the payment is directly attributable to the medical care of the child. But if you pay back medical expenses incurred and paid before adoption negotiations began, you cannot include them as medical expenses.

Tip. *You may be able to take a credit or exclusion for other expenses related to adoption. See Publication 968,* Tax Benefits for Adoption, *for more information.*

Child of divorced or separated parents. If either parent can claim a child as a dependent under the rules for divorced or separated parents, each parent can include the medical expenses he or she pays for the child even if an exemption for the child is claimed by the other parent.

Support claimed under a multiple support agreement. A multiple support agreement is used when two or more people provide more than half of a person's support, but no one alone provides more than half. If you are considered to have provided more than half of a person's support under such an agreement, you can include medical expenses you pay for that person, even if you cannot claim the person as a dependent.

Any medical expenses paid by others who joined you in the agreement cannot be included as medical expenses by anyone. However, you can include the entire unreimbursed amount you paid for medical expenses.

Example. You and your three brothers each provide one-fourth of your mother's total support. Under a multiple support agreement, you claim your mother as a dependent. You paid all of her medical expenses. Your brothers repaid you for three-fourths of these expenses. In figuring your medical expense deduction, you can include only one-fourth of your mother's medical expenses. Your brothers cannot include any part of the expenses. However, if you and your brothers share the nonmedical support items and you separately pay all of your mother's medical expenses, you can include the amount you paid for her medical expenses in your medical expenses.

Decedent

The survivor or personal representative of a decedent can choose to treat certain expenses paid by the decedent's estate for the decedent's medical care as paid by the decedent at the time the medical services were provided. The expenses must be paid within the 1-year period beginning with the day after the date of death. If you are the survivor or personal representative making this choice, you must attach a statement to the decedent's Form 1040 (or the decedent's amended return, Form 1040X) saying that the expenses have not been and will not be claimed on the estate tax return.

Caution. *Qualified medical expenses paid before death by the decedent are not deductible if paid with a tax-free distribution from any Medicare+Choice MSA or Archer MSA.*

Amended returns and claims for refund are discussed in chapter 1.

What if you pay medical expenses of a deceased spouse or dependent? If you paid medical expenses for your deceased spouse or dependent, include them as medical expenses on your Form 1040 in the year paid, whether they are paid before or after the decedent's death. The expenses can be included if the person was your spouse or dependent either at the time the medical services were provided or at the time you paid the expenses.

TAXPLANNER

Decedent's medical expenses. The alternatives presented above offer several options in planning for a decedent's medical expenses. If payment is deferred until after death but paid by the decedent's estate within the 1-year period that begins the day after the date of death, the expenses may be deducted on the decedent's estate tax return or the decedent's final income tax return, whichever is more beneficial. On the other hand, the expenses can be paid and deducted by the surviving spouse, if this is more advantageous. Consult your tax advisor when you are determining which option provides the greatest tax benefit to you.

What Medical Expenses Are Deductible?

Use *Table 23–1* in this chapter as a guide to determine which medical and dental expenses you can include on Schedule A (Form 1040). See Publication 502 for information about other expenses you can include.

TaxOrganizer

If the IRS challenges your deduction. In case the IRS challenges your deduction of medical expenses, you should keep the following information in order to support your claim for medical expenses incurred:

- Receipts and cancelled checks evidencing payment of medical expenses
- A permanent record of the name and address of the provider of medical care, the amount of the expenses, and the date paid
- Documentation that the expense was to obtain medical treatment, that medicine was prescribed, and that the expense was incurred on a doctor's recommendation

After reviewing the checklist, you may still be wondering whether a particular expense is deductible or not. The most comprehensive listing of items that you may and may not include when figuring your medical expenses appears in Publication 502, *Medical and Dental Expenses.*

Examples
Here are more examples of deductible items:

- A wig, if it is essential to your mental health and not just for enhancing your personal appearance
- Cosmetic surgery that is medically necessary (meaning-

Table 23–1. **Medical and Dental Expenses Checklist**

You can include:		You cannot include:	
• Birth control pills prescribed by your doctor • Capital expenses for equipment or improvements to your home needed for medical care (see Publication 502) • Cost of fertility enhancement procedures • Cost and care of guide dogs or other animals aiding the blind, deaf, and disabled • Cost of lead-based paint removal (see Publication 502) • Cost of vasectomy • Expenses of an organ donor • Hospital services fees (lab work, therapy, nursing services, surgery, etc.) • Laser eye surgery—to promote the correct function of the eye • Legal abortion • Legal operation to prevent having children • Long-term care contracts, qualified (see Publication 502) • Meals and lodging provided by a hospital during medical treatment • Medical and hospital insurance premiums • Medical services fees (from doctors, dentists, surgeons, specialists, and other medical practitioners)	• Oxygen equipment and oxygen • Part of life-care fee paid to retirement home designated for medical care • Prescription medicines (prescribed by a doctor) and insulin • Psychiatric care at a specially equipped medical center (includes meals and lodging) • Social Security tax, Medicare tax, FUTA, and state employment tax for worker providing medical care (see *Wages for nursing services,* later) • Special items (artificial limbs, false teeth, eye-glasses, contact lenses, hearing aids, crutches, wheelchair, etc.) • Special school or home for mentally or physically disabled persons (see Publication 502) • Stop-smoking programs • Transportation for needed medical care • Treatment at a drug or alcohol center (includes meals and lodging provided by the center) • Wages for nursing services (see Publication 502)	• Archer MSAs (see Publication 969) • Bottled water • Cost of nutritional supplements, vitamins, herbal supplements, "natural medicines", etc., unless you can only obtain them legally with a physician's prescription • Diaper service • Expenses for your general health (even if following your doctor's advice) such as— —Health club dues —Household help (even if recommended by a doctor) —Social activities, such as dancing or swimming lessons —Trip for general health improvement	• Funeral, burial, or cremation expenses • Ilegal operation or treatment • Life insurance or income protection policies, or policies providing payment for loss of life, limb, sight, etc. • Maternity clothes • Medical insurance included in a car insurance policy covering all persons injured in or by your car • Medicine you buy without a prescription • Nursing care for a healthy baby • Surgery for purely cosmetic reasons • Toothpaste, toiletries, cosmetics, etc.

fully promotes the proper function of the body or prevents or treats illness or disease) and not just for enhancing personal appearance

- Special diet food that is necessary and prescribed by a doctor to the extent that the cost exceeds the amount spent for normal nutritional needs
- Orthopedic shoes in excess of the cost of normal shoes
- Fees paid to someone to accompany and guide a blind person
- Costs attributable to a dog or other animal that assists individuals with physical disabilities
- Fees paid for a note taker for a deaf person
- Legal fees to obtain guardianship over a mental patient who has refused to accept therapy voluntarily
- Fees paid for childbirth preparation classes if instruction relates to obstetrical care
- Costs of a weight loss program for treatment of a specific disease, such as hypertension or obesity
- Costs of a wheelchair lift and its installation in a van
- Reasonable costs for home modifications or improvements to accommodate a handicapped person's condition when incurred for the purpose of medical care or directly related to medical care
- Legal fees necessary to authorize medical treatment for mental illness
- Expenses incurred for radial keratotomy (i.e., eye surgery to correct nearsightedness)

TAXSAVER

Physical and dental exams. The cost of periodic physical and dental exams can be included as a deductible medical expense. Usually, these expenses are too small to be deductible because only expenses over 7.5% of your adjusted gross income can be deducted. However, in years where other medical expenses have been incurred, the inclusion of these expenses in calculating your medical expense deduction can lead to tax savings.

Explanation

Drugs that may be obtained without a prescription (aspirin, skin ointments, etc.) are not deductible, even though they may be recommended or prescribed by a physician.

TAXPLANNER

Medical fees and school tuition. Some schools include a fee for medical care in the amount charged for tuition. Because you may deduct only the amount allocated to medical care if it is separately stated, an itemized bill should be requested.

Explanation

Whether or not an expense is deductible is determined by the nature of the services rendered, not by the qualifications and/or experience of the person rendering them. For example, the services do not necessarily need to be performed by a nurse, as long as the services rendered are generally considered nursing services. These include services connected with caring for the patient's condition, such as giving medication or changing bandages, as well as bathing and grooming the patient.

Examples

The courts allowed deductions for payments to a daughter for the care of her arthritic mother to the extent that they were for medical care.

In another instance, the courts allowed a deduction for the compensation paid to a "personal attendant" who was not a registered or a practical nurse. The deduction was permitted because the invalid was recovering from surgery and was in need of constant attendance.

TAXPLANNER

Two choices, one deduction. An expense may qualify for the child care credit (see Chapter 33, *Child and Dependent Care Credit*), or it may be considered a medical expense. However, the same expense may not be used for both benefits. You should analyze each benefit based on your marginal tax rate and your medical expense deduction limitation (7.5% of adjusted gross income) to determine how best to classify the expense.

Explanation

Payment for psychoanalysis that is required as part of your training to be a psychoanalyst may be a deductible educational expense necessary for professional training. The law specifically permits an itemized deduction for the cost of psychoanalytic training undertaken by psychiatrists as education expenses, because the training maintains or improves skills required in their trade or business and does not qualify them for a new trade or business. (See Chapter 29, *Employees' Educational Expenses*.) The courts have also allowed deductions for expenses incurred by a clinical psychologist in studying to become a psychoanalyst and expenses incurred by a psychiatrist for psychoanalytic training as a condition to accepting the directorship of a child study center.

However, when a psychiatric residency was undertaken to qualify a taxpayer for a new profession, the expenses were not deductible.

TAXSAVER

Capital expenses. You may include in medical expenses all or part of the amounts you pay for special equipment installed in your home, or for improvements, if the main reason for the purchase is for medical care. The amount of your medical expense deduction, however, will depend on the extent to which the equipment or improvement has increased the value of the property. To the extent a capital improvement adds value to your home, it increases the cost basis of your home. Any amount paid above the added value is currently deductible as a medical expense. A U.S. District Court recently held that this deduction is available in the year the home becomes habitable. So if a home is built over a period of years, the amount paid over the added value is all deductible in the year you can move into it, making it easier to get above the 7.5% adjusted gross income (AGI) threshhold.

Example

You have a heart ailment. On your doctor's advice, you install an elevator in your home so that you will not need to climb stairs. The elevator costs $2,000. According to competent appraisals, the elevator increases the value of your home by $1,400. The $600 difference is a medical expense. However, you may include the total cost of $2,000 in medical expenses if the elevator does not increase the value of your home.

TAXSAVER

Appraisals. The cost of an appraisal obtained to determine the increase in value of your home is also deductible, but not as a medical expense. The appraisal cost is an expense associated with the determination of your tax liability and can be included as a miscellaneous itemized deduction. See Chapter 30, *Miscellaneous Deductions*.

Explanation
Operating and upkeep expenses. If a capital expense qualifies as a medical expense, amounts paid for operation or upkeep also qualify as a medical expense, as long as the medical reason for the capital expense still exists. These expenses are medical expenses even if none or only part of the original expense was deductible.

Example
Assume the same facts as in the above example, except that the elevator increased the value of your home by $2,000. In this case, you are not entitled to a medical deduction for the cost of the elevator. However, the costs of electricity to operate the elevator and repairs to maintain it are deductible, as long as the medical reason for the elevator exists.

Exception
An exception to the general rule exists for expenditures incurred to accommodate the condition of a physically handicapped person that generally do not increase the value of a personal residence. These expenses are deductible in full as a medical expense. Examples of expenses made for the primary purpose of accommodating a personal residence to the handicapped condition of a taxpayer, the taxpayer's spouse, or dependents who reside there include:

- Construction of entrance or exit ramps to the residence
- Widening doorways at entrances or exits to the residence
- Widening or otherwise modifying hallways and interior doorways
- Installing railings, support bars, or other modifications to bathrooms
- Lowering or making other modifications to kitchen cabinets and equipment
- Altering the location or otherwise modifying electrical outlets and fixtures
- Installing porch lifts and other forms of lifts (an elevator, however, may also add to the fair market value of the residence, and any deduction would have to be decreased to that extent)
- Modifying fire alarms, smoke detectors, and other warning systems
- Modifying stairs
- Adding handrails or grab bars, whether or not in bathrooms
- Modifying hardware on doors
- Modifying areas in front entrance and exit doorways
- Grading of ground to provide access to the residence

According to the IRS, other similar expenditures may also be incurred in accommodating a personal residence to the handicapped condition of a taxpayer or a dependent. However, only reasonable costs for accommodating a handicapped person's condition will be considered incurred for the purpose of medical care. Additional costs attributable to personal desires are not deductible.

Example
You are physically handicapped and confined to a wheelchair. You incur expenses to widen doorways and lower kitchen cabinets in your residence to permit access by you. These expenses are deductible, subject to the 7.5% threshold discussed above.

TaxPlanner
Medically related capital improvements. If you have to make a medically related capital improvement, you should request a written recommendation from your doctor. In addition, obtain a reliable written appraisal from a real estate appraiser or a valuation expert. Be prepared to prove to what extent the value of your property was or was not increased.

TaxPlanner
Swimming pools. It is often difficult to obtain a medical deduction for the installation of a swimming pool. The IRS has held that swimming pools generally fall within the category of recreational or luxury items and will look at various facts when it is determining the deduction for the cost of a swimming pool, including:

- Whether the primary purpose of the pool is for medical care
- Whether the expenditure is related to medical care
- Whether the pool does more than serve the convenience and/or comfort of the taxpayer

You should contact your tax advisor if you intend to install a swimming pool for medical reasons.

Insurance Premiums

You can include in medical expenses insurance premiums you pay for policies that cover medical care. Policies can provide payment for:

- Hospitalization, surgical fees, X-rays, etc.,
- Prescription drugs,
- Replacement of lost or damaged contact lenses,
- Membership in an association that gives cooperative or so-called "free-choice" medical service, or group hospitalization and clinical care, or
- Qualified long-term care insurance contracts (subject to additional limitations). See *Qualified Long-term Care Insurance Contracts* in Publication 502.

TaxAlert
You can now treat premiums paid for qualified long-term care insurance as a deductible medical expense subject to dollar limits based on your age.

Age:	Annual deductible limit:
40 or less	$230
Over 40 to less than 50	430
Over 50 to less than 60	860
Over 60 to less than 70	2,290
Over 70	2,860

Explanation
Amounts you pay to receive medical care from a health maintenance organization (HMO) are treated as medical insurance premiums.

TaxSaver

Cafeteria plans. Employees who pay all or part of their medical insurance premiums via employer plans should ask their employer to investigate a flexible spending arrangement, which is sometimes referred to as a cafeteria plan.

Example

You are in the 27.5% tax bracket, and you pay $2,000 to cover your medical insurance premiums. Because medical expenses are deductible only if they exceed 7.5% of your adjusted gross income, chances are that you are not able to deduct your payments for medical insurance.

If your company offers medical insurance as part of a cafeteria plan, you may opt to have your wages reduced by $2,000 under a salary reduction plan to cover the cost of the insurance. The cut in wages reduces your income tax, producing a federal tax savings in this case of $550. Additional tax savings may also be enjoyed because of lower state income taxes and reduced FICA taxes. Otherwise, you must earn $2,759 (before taxes) to be left with the $2,000 (after taxes) needed to pay your medical insurance premiums.

You **cannot** deduct insurance premiums paid with pretax dollars. You cannot include the premiums because they are not included in box 1 of your Form W-2.

If you have a policy that provides more than one kind of payment, you can include the premiums for the medical care part of the policy if the charge for the medical part is reasonable. The cost of the medical part must be separately stated in the insurance contract or given to you in a separate statement.

Employer-sponsored health insurance plan. Do not include in your medical and dental expenses on Schedule A (Form 1040) any insurance premiums paid by an employer-sponsored health insurance plan unless the premiums are included in box 1 of your Form W-2. Also, do not include on Schedule A (Form 1040) any other medical and dental expenses paid by the plan unless the amount paid is included in box 1 of your Form W-2.

Flexible spending arrangement. Contributions made by your employer to provide coverage for qualified long-term care services under a flexible spending or similar arrangement must be included in your income. This amount will be reported as wages in box 1 of your Form W-2.

Medicare A. If you are covered under social security (or if you are a government employee who paid Medicare tax), you are enrolled in Medicare A. The payroll tax paid for Medicare A is not a medical expense. If you are not covered under social security (or were not a government employee who paid Medicare tax), you can voluntarily enroll in Medicare A. In this situation the premiums paid for Medicare A can be included as a medical expense on your tax return.

Medicare B. Medicare B is a supplemental medical insurance. Premiums you pay for Medicare B are a medical expense. If you applied for it at age 65 or after you became disabled, you can deduct the monthly premiums you paid. If you were over age 65 or disabled when you first enrolled, check the information you received from the Social Security Administration to find out your premium.

Prepaid insurance premiums. Premiums you pay before you are age 65 for insurance for medical care for yourself, your spouse, or your dependents after you reach age 65 are medical care expenses in the year paid if they are:

1) Payable in equal yearly installments, or more often, and
2) Payable for at least 10 years, or until you reach age 65 (but not for less than 5 years).

Unused sick leave used to pay premiums. You must include in gross income cash payments you receive at the time of retirement for unused sick leave. You must also include in gross income the value of unused sick leave that, at your option, your employer applies to the cost of your continuing participation in your employer's health plan after you retire. You can include this cost of continuing participation in the health plan as a medical expense.

If you participate in a health plan where your employer automatically applies the value of unused sick leave to the cost of your continuing participation in the health plan (and you do not have the option to receive cash), do not include the value of the unused sick leave in gross income. You cannot include this cost of continuing participation in that health plan as a medical expense.

Health Insurance Costs for Self-Employed Persons

If you were self-employed and had a net profit for the year, you may be able to deduct, as an adjustment to income, up to 60% of the amount paid for health insurance on behalf of yourself, your spouse, and dependents. If you itemize your deductions, include the remaining premiums with all other medical care expenses on Schedule A (Form 1040), subject to the 7.5% limit. See chapter 7 of Publication 535, *Business Expenses,* for more information.

TaxAlert

If you are self-employed and have a net profit for the year, you can deduct an increasing percentage of the amount you pay for health insurance on behalf of yourself, your spouse, and dependents. This percentage for years after 2001 is as follows:

Tax year beginning in:	Applicable percentage:
2002	70
2003 and thereafter	100

This deduction cannot be greater than the taxpayer's net earnings from his or her trade or business. The same deduction is available to S corporation shareholders.

Meals and Lodging

You can include in medical expenses the cost of meals and lodging at a hospital or similar institution if your main reason for being there is to receive medical care. See *Nursing home,* later.

You may be able to include in medical expenses the cost of lodging not provided in a hospital or similar institution. You can include the cost of such lodging while away from home if you meet all of the following requirements.

1) The lodging is primarily for and essential to medical care.
2) The medical care is provided by a doctor in a licensed hospital or in a medical care facility related to, or the equivalent of, a licensed hospital.
3) The lodging is not lavish or extravagant under the circumstances.
4) There is no significant element of personal pleasure, recreation, or vacation in the travel away from home.

The amount you include in medical expenses for lodging cannot be more than $50 for each night for each person. Lodging is included for a person for whom transportation expenses are a medical expense because that person is traveling with the person receiving the medical care. For example, if a parent is traveling with a sick child, up to $100 per night can be included as a medical expense for lodging. Meals are not included.

Nursing home. You can include in medical expenses the cost of medical care in a nursing home or home for the aged for yourself, your spouse, or your dependents. This includes the cost of meals and lodging in the home if the main reason for being there is to get medical care.

Do not include the cost of meals and lodging if the reason for being in the home is personal. You can, however, include in medical expenses the part of the cost that is for medical or nursing care.

Example 1
A businessman who became ill while out of town was allowed to deduct the costs of his meals and hotel room when, due to a shortage of hospital rooms, he was required to move into a hotel. He had not recovered sufficiently to return home. The courts found that the test of deductibility was *not* the nature of the institution (i.e., whether it was a hospital or a similar institution) but the condition of the individual and the nature of the services.

Example 2
The parents of a mentally ill son rented an apartment to be close to the son's clinic. They were not allowed to deduct its costs because no care was received in the apartment, and the apartment had not been altered in any way to facilitate their son's treatment. Therefore, the court held that the parents had not incurred any expenses for their son's care in the apartment.

Transportation

You can include in medical expenses amounts paid for transportation primarily for, and essential to, medical care.
You can include:

- Bus, taxi, train, or plane fares, or ambulance service,
- Transportation expenses of a parent who must go with a child who needs medical care,
- Transportation expenses of a nurse or other person who can give injections, medications, or other treatment required by a patient who is traveling to get medical care and is unable to travel alone, and
- Transportation expenses for regular visits to see a mentally ill dependent, if these visits are recommended as a part of treatment.

You cannot include:

- Transportation expenses to and from work even if your condition requires an unusual means of transportation, or
- Transportation expenses if, for nonmedical reasons only, you choose to travel to another city, such as a resort area, for an operation or other medical care prescribed by your doctor.

TaxAlert
The IRS has ruled that transportation costs and registration fees for attending a medical conference on a chronic disease suffered by a dependent are deductible medical expenses. The cost of meals and lodging cannot be deducted.

Explanation
Although the IRS has repeatedly denied *any* deduction for commuting expenses to get to one's place of work—even for disabled individuals—under certain circumstances, a deduction may be permitted for transportation required for medical reasons.

Example
If, at your doctor's advice, you take a job for the purposes of occupational therapy, you may deduct your commuting expenses. Because the employment is prescribed therapy, the expense of going to and from work is incurred in the course of obtaining occupational therapy and thus is deductible as medical transportation.

Explanation
The courts have, however, allowed a deduction for the costs of meals as well as lodging and transportation between a taxpayer's home and the out-of-state clinic where treatment was obtained when the trip was made for medical reasons. The meals were considered to be part of the transportation costs. In addition, because the taxpayer's husband had to accompany his spouse on the trip, his food costs en route were also deductible.

The expenses of a move to a different climate may be deductible if the principal purpose of the move is to alleviate an illness.

TaxAlert
The Tax Court has recently ruled that a couple could not deduct depreciation as a medical expense for a modified van in which they transported their disabled son, who had spina bifida. The Court said that depreciation is not a medical expense. They did allow the cost of necessary modifications to the van.

Car expenses. You can include out-of-pocket expenses for your car, such as gas and oil, when you use your car for medical reasons. You cannot include depreciation, insurance, general repair, or maintenance expenses.

If you do not want to use your actual expenses, you can use a standard rate of *12 cents a mile* for use of your car for medical reasons.

You can also include the cost of parking fees and tolls. You can add these fees and tolls to your medical expenses whether you use actual expenses or use the standard mileage rate.

Example. Bill Jones drove 2,800 miles for medical reasons during the year. He spent $200 for gas, $5 for oil, and $50 for tolls and parking. He wants to figure the amount he can include in medical expenses both ways to see which gives him the greater deduction.

He figures the actual expenses first. He adds the $200 for gas, the $5 for oil, and the $50 for tolls and parking for a total of $255.

He then figures the standard mileage amount. He multiplies the 2,800 miles by 12 cents a mile for a total of $336. He then adds the $50 tolls and parking for a total of $386.

Bill includes the $386 of car expenses with his other medical expenses for the year because the $386 is more than the $255 he figured using actual expenses.

Disabled Dependent Care Expenses

Some disabled dependent care expenses may qualify as medical expenses or as work-related expenses for purposes of taking a credit for dependent care. (See chapter 33.) You can choose to apply them either way as long as you do not use the same expenses to claim both a credit and a medical expense deduction.

Explanation
Special care for the handicapped. The costs of sending a mentally or physically handicapped person to a special school or home, including certain advance payments for life-

time care, may be included in medical expenses. See Publication 502, *Medical and Dental Expenses*, for more information about medical care expenses for a handicapped person. Enter the amount you paid for special care on line 1, Schedule A (Form 1040).

The distinguishing characteristic of a special school is the content of its curriculum, which must be designed to enable the student to compensate for or overcome a handicap in order to prepare him or her for future normal education and living. The curriculum of a special school may include some ordinary education, but this must be incidental to the primary purpose of the school.

If a handicapped person attends a school that is not a special school, only those costs that are specifically attributable to medical care are deductible expenses. A school that offers small classes and individual attention does not qualify as a special school.

Example
In addition to the regular tuition for a private school, the parents of a handicapped child paid a special fee for a language development program designed to help students with learning disabilities. Although no deduction was allowed for the regular tuition, the cost of the special course was deductible as a medical expense.

Impairment-Related Work Expenses (Business or Medical)

If you are disabled and have expenses which are necessary for you to be able to work (impairment-related work expenses), you can take a business deduction for these expenses, rather than a medical deduction. You are disabled if you have:

- A physical or mental disability (for example, blindness or deafness) that functionally limits your being employed, or
- A physical or mental impairment (for example, a sight or hearing impairment) that substantially limits one or more of your major life activities, such as performing manual tasks, walking, speaking, breathing, learning, or working.

You can deduct impairment-related expenses as business expenses if they are:

- Necessary for you to do your work satisfactorily,
- For goods or services not required or used, other than incidentally, in your personal activities, and
- Not specifically covered under other income tax laws.

Example. You are blind. You must use a reader to do your work. You use the reader both during your regular working hours at your place of work and outside your regular working hours away from your place of work. The reader's services are only for your work. You can deduct your expenses for the reader as business expenses.

Example 1
You are confined to a wheelchair. Sometimes you must go out of town on business. Your friend or spouse goes with you to help with such things as carrying your luggage or getting up steps. You do not pay your helper a salary, but you do pay for your helper's travel, meals, and lodging while on such trips. You have learned how to take care of yourself and to do your job in your hometown without a helper. Be-

cause the expenses for the transportation, meals, and lodging of your helper are directly related to doing your job, you may deduct them as miscellaneous deductions on Form 1040.

Example 2
Assume the same facts as in the example above, except you are dependent on your friend's help at home as well as while traveling on business. The expenses of the friend are medical expenses, not business expenses.

If, in the above example, your spouse goes with you on the out-of-town business trips, you may deduct as medical expenses only the out-of-pocket costs for your spouse's transportation. Expenses for your spouse's meals and lodging are not deductible.

How Do You Treat Reimbursements?

You can deduct as medical expenses only those amounts paid during the taxable year for which you received no insurance or other reimbursement.

Insurance Reimbursement

You must reduce your total medical expenses for the year by all reimbursements for medical expenses that you receive from insurance or other sources during the year. This includes payments from Medicare.

Generally, you do not reduce medical expenses by payments you receive for:

- Permanent loss or use of a member or function of the body (loss of limb, sight, hearing, etc.) or disfigurement that is based on the nature of the injury without regard to the amount of time lost from work,
- Loss of earnings, or
- Damages for personal injury or sickness.

You do not have a medical deduction if you are reimbursed for all of your medical expenses for the year.

Excess reimbursement. If you are reimbursed more than your medical expenses, you may have to include the excess in income. You may want to use *Figure 23–A* to help you decide if any of your reimbursement will be taxable income.

Premiums paid by you. If you pay the entire premium for your medical insurance or all of the costs of a plan similar to medical insurance, you generally do not include an excess reimbursement in your gross income.

Premiums paid by you and your employer. If both you and your employer contribute to your medical insurance plan and your employer's contributions are not included in your gross income, you must include in your gross income the part of an excess reimbursement that is from your employer's contribution.

You can figure the percentage of the excess reimbursement you must include in gross income using the following formula.

$$\frac{\text{Amount paid by employer}}{\text{Total annual cost of policy}} = \frac{\text{Percent of excess}}{\text{reimbursement that is taxable}}$$

Explanation
Insurance reimbursements. Reimbursements from insurance or other sources received during the year in which the medical expense is paid reduce the medical deduction to the extent of the reimbursement.

Figure 23–A. **Is Your Excess Medical Reimbursement Taxable?**

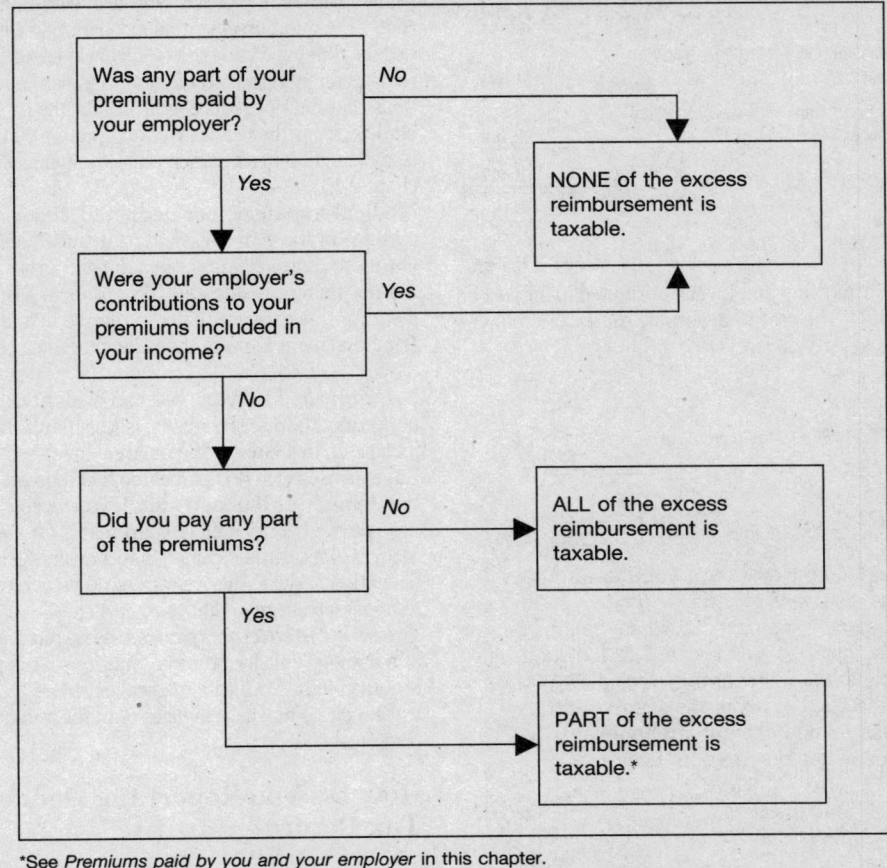

*See *Premiums paid by you and your employer* in this chapter.

If total reimbursements exceed total medical expenses for the year, the excess reimbursement may have to be included in income. The determining factor of whether or not the excess reimbursement has to be included in income depends on who paid the premium for the insurance policy.

If you pay the entire premium for medical insurance, none of the excess reimbursement is includible in income. On the other hand, if you share the cost of the premium with, for example, your employer, the part of the excess reimbursement attributable to the employer's contribution to the premium must be included in income.

Example 1

John's annual medical insurance premium is $3,000. John's employer pays $900 of the premium, and John pays $2,100 of the premium. In 2001, John incurs $5,000 of medical expenses, and his insurance company reimburses him $5,500, an excess reimbursement of $500. The amount of the excess reimbursement that must be included in John's income is $150 ($900/$3,000 × $500).

Example 2

Assume the same facts as in the example above, except John pays for the entire medical insurance premium himself. The $500 excess insurance reimbursement would *not* be included in income.

Example. You are covered by your employer's medical insurance policy. The annual premium is $2,000. Your employer pays $600 of that amount and the balance of $1,400 is taken out of your wages. The part of any excess reimbursement you receive under the policy that is from your employer's contributions is figured as follows:

$$\frac{\$600}{\$2,000} = 30\%$$

You must include in your gross income 30% (.30) of any excess reimbursement you received for medical expenses under the policy.

Premiums paid by your employer. If your employer or your former employer pays the total cost of your medical insurance plan and your employer's contributions are not included in your income, you must report all of your excess reimbursement as other income.

More than one policy. If you are covered under more than one policy, the costs of which are paid by both you and your employer, you must first divide the medical expense among the policies to figure the excess reimbursement from each policy. Then divide the policy costs to figure the part of any excess reimbursement that is from your employer's contribution.

Example. You are covered by your employer's health insurance policy. The annual premium is $1,200. Your employer pays $300, and the balance of $900 is deducted from your wages. You also paid the entire premium ($250) for a personal health insurance policy.

During the year, you paid medical expenses of $3,600. In the same year, you were reimbursed $2,400 under your employer's policy and $1,600 under your personal policy.

You figure the part of any excess reimbursement you receive that is from your employer's contribution as follows:

Step 1.

Reimbursement from employer's policy $2,400

Reimbursement from your policy 1,600

Total reimbursement **$4,000**

Amount of medical expenses from your policy [($1,600 ÷ $4,000)
× $3,600 total medical expenses] $1,440

Amount of medical expenses from your employer's policy [($2,400
÷ $4,000) × $3,600 total medical expenses] 2,160

Total medical expenses **$3,600**

**Excess reimbursement from your
employer's policy** ($2,400 − $2,160) .... $ 240

Step 2. Because both you and your employer contributed to the cost of this policy, you must divide the cost to determine the excess reimbursement from your employer's contribution.

Employer's contribution in relation to the
annual cost of the policy ($300 ÷ $1,200) 25%

**Amount to report as other income on line 21,
Form 1040** (25% × $240) **$60**

Example

John pays $1,800 and his employer pays $600 toward the $2,400 annual premium for health insurance policy no. 1. Additionally, John pays the entire premium, $500, for health insurance policy no. 2. During 2001, John paid $7,200 of medical expenses and in the same year was reimbursed $5,000 under the first policy and $3,000 under the second policy.

The portion of excess reimbursement attributable to the employer's contribution is computed as follows:

Reimbursement from policy no. 1 .... $5,000
Reimbursement from policy no. 2 3,000

  Total reimbursement $8,000

Amount of reimbursed medical expenses from policy no. 1
($5,000/$8,000 × $7,200 total medical expenses) $4,500

Amount of reimbursed medical expenses from policy no. 2
($3,000/$8,000 × $7,200 total medical expenses) 2,700

  Total medical expenses $7,200

Excess reimbursement from policy no. 1
($5,000 − $4,500) .... $ 500

The employer's contribution to the annual cost of policy no. 1 is 25% ($600/$2,400). Consequently, John must include $125 in income for 2001 ($500 × 25%).

None of the excess reimbursement from policy no. 2, $300 ($3,000 − $2,700), must be included in income, because John paid the entire premium of the policy.

Reimbursement in a later year. If you are reimbursed in a later year for medical expenses you deducted in an earlier year, you must report the reimbursement as income up to the amount you previously deducted as medical expenses. However, do not report as income the reimbursement you received up to the amount of your medical deductions that did not reduce your tax for the earlier year. For more information about the recovery of an amount that you claimed as an itemized deduction in an earlier year, see Itemized Deduction Recoveries in chapter 13.

Medical expenses not deducted. If you did not deduct a medical expense in the year you paid it because your medical expenses were not more than 7.5% of your adjusted gross income, or because you did not itemize deductions, do not include in income the reimbursement for this expense that you receive in a later year. However, if the reimbursement is more than the expense, see *Excess reimbursement,* earlier.

Example. Last year, you had medical expenses of $500. You cannot deduct the $500 because it is less than 7.5% of your adjusted gross income. If, in a later year, you are reimbursed for any of the $500 medical expenses, you do not include that amount in your gross income.

Settlement of damage suit. If you receive an amount in settlement of a personal injury suit, the part that is for medical expenses deducted in an earlier year is included in income in the later year if your medical deduction in the earlier year reduced your income tax in that year. See *Reimbursement in a later year,* earlier.

Future medical expenses. If you receive an amount in settlement of a damage suit for personal injuries that is properly allocable or determined to be for future medical expenses, you must reduce any medical expenses for these injuries until the amount you received has been completely used.

How Do You Report the Deduction on Your Tax Return?

Once you have determined which medical care expenses you can include when figuring your deduction, you must report the deduction on your tax return.

What Tax Form Do You Use?

You figure your medical expense deduction on lines 1–4 of **Schedule A,** Form 1040. You cannot claim medical expenses on Form 1040A or Form 1040EZ. If you need more information on itemized deductions or you are not sure if you can itemize, see chapters 21 and 22.

Enter the amount you paid for medical and dental care on line 1, Schedule A (Form 1040). This should be your expenses that were not reimbursed by insurance or any other sources.

You can deduct only the amount of your medical and dental expenses that is more than 7.5% of your adjusted gross income shown on line 34, Form 1040. For an example, see the partial Schedule A at the end of this chapter.

SCHEDULES A&B
(Form 1040)

Department of the Treasury
Internal Revenue Service

Schedule A—Itemized Deductions

(Schedule B is on back)

▶ **Attach to Form 1040.** ▶ **See Instructions for Schedules A and B (Form 1040).**

OMB No. 1545-0074

2001

Attachment
Sequence No. **07**

Name(s) shown on Form 1040

Bill and Helen Jones

Your social security number

000 00 0000

Medical and Dental Expenses				
	1	**Caution.** Do not include expenses reimbursed or paid by others.		
		Medical and dental expenses (see page A-2) . . .	1	3,434
	2	Enter amount from Form 1040, line 34 | 2 | 33,000 |		
	3	Multiply line 2 above by 7.5% (.075).	3	2,475
	4	Subtract line 3 from line 1. If line 3 is more than line 1, enter -0-	4	959

24

Taxes You May Deduct

Introduction

You have been allowed to deduct taxes you pay—other than your federal income tax—ever since the nation's income tax was first enacted. The underlying theory is that taxes are an involuntary expenditure and therefore should be deducted from an individual's **gross income.** *But there is a practical consideration as well: The payment of state and local taxes makes it more difficult for an individual to meet the federal tax bill.*

The taxes you may deduct include two of the most significant. They are state and local taxes you pay on property you own and on your income. Taxes you pay to a foreign government may also be deducted. These and other taxes that you may deduct from your federal income tax are described in this chapter.

Note: *Your 2001 itemized deductions may be subject to certain limitations if your adjusted gross income exceeds $132,950 ($66,475 if married filing separately). See Chapter 22,* Limit on Itemized Deductions, *for more information on the deduction limitations.*

Important Reminder

Limit on itemized deductions. If your adjusted gross income is more than $132,950 ($66,475 if you are married filing separately), the overall amount of your itemized deductions may be limited. See chapter 22 for more information about this limit.

This chapter discusses which taxes you can deduct if you itemize deductions on Schedule A (Form 1040). It also explains which taxes you can deduct on other schedules or forms and which taxes you cannot deduct.

This chapter covers:

- Income taxes (state, local, or foreign),
- Real estate taxes (state, local, or foreign),
- Personal property taxes (state or local), and
- Taxes and fees you cannot deduct.

At the end of the chapter is a section that explains which form you use to deduct the different types of taxes.

Table. Use *Table 24-1* as a guide to determine which taxes you can deduct.

Business taxes. You can deduct certain taxes only if they are ordinary and necessary expenses of your trade or business or of producing income. For information on these taxes, see Publication 535, *Business Expenses.*

State or local taxes. These are taxes imposed by the 50 states, U.S. possessions, or any of their political subdivisions (such as a county or city), or by the District of Columbia.

Indian tribal government. An Indian tribal government that is recognized by the Secretary of the Treasury as performing substantial government functions will be treated as a state for this purpose. Income taxes, real estate taxes, and personal property taxes imposed by that Indian tribal government (or by any of its subdivisions that are treated as political subdivisions of a state) are deductible.

Foreign taxes. These are taxes imposed by a foreign country or any of its political subdivisions.

Useful Items

You may want to see:

Publication

☐ **514** Foreign Tax Credit for Individuals
☐ **530** Tax Information for First-Time Homeowners

Form (and Instructions)

☐ **Schedule A (Form 1040)** Itemized Deductions
☐ **Schedule E (Form 1040)** Supplemental Income and Loss
☐ **Form 1116** Foreign Tax Credit

Tests To Deduct Any Tax

The following two tests must be met for any tax to be deductible by you.

Table 24–1. **Which Taxes Can You Deduct?**

	You Can Deduct	You Cannot Deduct
Income Taxes	State and local income taxes. Foreign income taxes. Employee contributions to state funds listed under *Contributions to state benefit funds.*	Federal income taxes. Employee contributions to private or voluntary disability plans.
Real Estate Taxes	State and local real estate taxes. Foreign real estate taxes. Tenant's share of real estate taxes paid by cooperative housing corporation.	Taxes for local benefits (with exceptions). Trash and garbage pickup fees (with exceptions). Rent increase due to higher real estate taxes. Homeowners association charges.
Personal Property Taxes	State and local personal property taxes.	
Other Taxes	Taxes that are expenses of your trade or business or of producing income. One-half of self-employment tax paid. Taxes on property producing rent or royalty income. Occupational taxes.	Many taxes, such as state and local sales taxes and federal excise taxes. See *Taxes and Fees You Cannot Deduct.*
Fees and Charges	Fees and charges that are expenses of your trade or business or of producing income.	Fees and charges, such as fees for driver's licenses or charges for water bills. See *Taxes and Fees You Cannot Deduct.*

1) The tax must be imposed on you.
2) The tax must be paid during your tax year.

The tax must be imposed on you. Generally, you can deduct only taxes that are imposed on you.

Generally, you can deduct property taxes only if you are the property owner. If your spouse owns property and pays real estate taxes on it, the taxes are deductible on your spouse's separate return or on your joint return.

The tax must be paid during your tax year. If you are a cash basis taxpayer, you can deduct only those taxes actually paid during your tax year. If you pay your taxes by check, the day you mail or deliver the check is generally the date of payment. If you use a pay-by-phone account, the date reported on the statement of the financial institution showing when payment was made is the date of payment. If you contest a tax liability and are a cash basis taxpayer, you can deduct the tax only in the year it is actually paid.

If you use an accrual method of accounting, see Publication 538, *Accounting Periods and Methods,* for more information.

Income Taxes

This section discusses the deductibility of state and local income taxes (including employee contributions to state benefit funds) and foreign income taxes.

State and Local Income Taxes

You can deduct state and local income taxes.
Exception. You cannot deduct state and local income taxes you pay on income that is exempt from federal income tax, unless the exempt income is interest income. For example, you cannot deduct the part of a state's income tax that is on a cost-of-living allowance that is exempt from federal income tax.

What To Deduct
Your deduction may be for withheld taxes, estimated tax payments, or other tax payments as follows.
Withheld taxes. Deduct state and local income taxes withheld from your salary in the year they are withheld. For 2001, these taxes will be

shown in boxes 17 and 19 of your Form W-2. You may also have state or local income tax withheld on Form W-2G (box 14), Form 1099-MISC (box 16), or Form 1099-R (boxes 10 and 13).
Estimated tax payments. Deduct estimated tax payments you made during the year under a pay-as-you-go plan of a state or local government. However, you must have a reasonable basis for making the estimated tax payments. Any estimated state or local tax payments you make that are not reasonably determined in good faith at the time of payment are not deductible. For example, you made an estimated state income tax payment. However, the estimate of your state tax liability shows that you will get a refund of the full amount of your estimated payment. You had no reasonable basis to believe you had any additional liability for state income taxes and you cannot deduct the estimated tax payment.
Refund applied to taxes. Deduct any part of a refund of prior-year state or local income taxes that you chose to have credited to your 2001 estimated state or local income taxes.

Do not reduce your deduction by either of the following items.

- Any state or local income tax refund (or credit) you expect to receive for 2001.
- Any refund of (or credit for) prior year state and local income taxes you actually received in 2001.

See *Refund (or credit) of state or local income taxes,* later.

Explanation
Generally, all state, county, city, and municipal income taxes are deductible in the year in which you pay them—including the state and local taxes applicable to interest income that is not taxable at the federal level.

Example
You have the following income:

Salary	$18,000
Municipal bond income (exempt from federal tax but taxable by your state)	2,000
Total income	$20,000

If your state income tax is $1,000, then 10%, or $100, is attributable to the federally exempt income. Nevertheless, you may deduct the entire $1,000 on your federal return.

TaxPlanner

Municipal bonds. Municipal bonds issued by your state frequently are not subject to your state's income tax, whereas obligations for other states usually are subject to the state tax.

Be sure to use your effective state rate after the federal tax benefit when you are deciding between investing in a state tax-exempt municipal bond or an obligation that is subject to your state's tax.

TaxPlanner

Deducting expenses. If you deduct an expense when you pay it rather than when the expense is incurred, as most people do, you may deduct the following:

1. State income tax withheld from salary in 2001
2. State **estimated tax** payments made in 2001 for 2001
3. Fourth-quarter state estimated tax payment for 2000 made in January 2001
4. State income tax paid with your 2000 state income tax return filed in 2001
5. State income tax paid in 2001 with a request for a filing extension for your 2000 state income tax return
6. Additional state income tax paid in 2001 as a result of an **audit** or an amended return

In most states, the fourth-quarter estimated tax payment is due in January of the following year. A January 2002, payment for the last quarter of 2001 is deductible on your 2002 return. If, however, the payment is made by December 31, 2001, it is deductible on your 2001 return. If you can accelerate your payment by a few weeks, you can accelerate your **deduction** for state income taxes by a full year.

TaxAlert

Taxpayers have been denied deductions when state estimated tax payments made on December 31 were substantially in excess of their actual tax liability. To be assured of a deduction, you must be able to prove that the tax payment was based on a reasonable estimate of your actual tax bill. Also, be sure not to prepay your state taxes if you're in an alternative minimum tax position.

TaxOrganizer

You should keep cancelled checks for payments of state estimated income tax (or any deductible tax) in order to support your claim for deductible taxes.

Separate federal returns. If you and your spouse file separate state, local, and federal income tax returns, you each can deduct on your federal return only the amount of your own state and local income tax.

Joint state and local returns. If you and your spouse file joint state and local returns and separate federal returns, each of you can deduct on your separate federal return part of the state and local income taxes. You can deduct only the amount of the total taxes that is proportionate to your gross income compared to the combined gross income of you and your spouse. However, you cannot deduct more than the amount you actually paid during the year. You can avoid this calculation if you and your spouse are jointly and individually liable for the full amount of the state and local income taxes. If so, you and your spouse

can deduct on your separate federal returns the amount you each actually paid.

Joint federal return. If you file a joint federal return, you can deduct the total of the state and local income taxes both of you paid.

TaxPlanner

If you file joint state returns and separate federal returns. If you plan on filing a joint state return with your spouse and separate federal returns, and if you are both jointly and individually liable for the full amount of the state tax, the state tax should be paid, to the extent possible, by the person in the higher separate federal income tax bracket. (For advice on filing jointly or separately, see Chapter 2, *Filing Status.*)

Contributions to state benefit funds. As an employee, you can deduct mandatory contributions to state benefit funds that provide protection against loss of wages. Mandatory payments made to the following state benefit funds are deductible as state income taxes on line 5 of Schedule A (Form 1040).

- California.
- New Jersey.
- New York Nonoccupational Disability Benefit Fund.
- Rhode Island Temporary Disability Benefit Fund.
- Washington State Supplemental Workmen's Compensation Fund.

Caution. *Employee contributions to private or voluntary disability plans are not deductible.*

Refund (or credit) of state or local income taxes. If you receive a refund of (or credit for) state or local income taxes in a year after the year in which you paid them, you may have to include the refund in income on line 10 of Form 1040 in the year you receive it. This includes refunds resulting from taxes that were overwithheld, applied from a prior year return, not figured correctly, or figured again because of an amended return. If you did not itemize your deductions in the previous year, do not include the refund in income. If you deducted the taxes in the previous year, include all or part of the refund on line 10, Form 1040, in the year you receive the refund. For a discussion of how much to include, see *Recoveries* in chapter 13.

Explanation

If you received a refund of taxes that you paid in an earlier year, such as 1999 or 2000, do not use that refund to reduce your deduction for taxes that you paid during 2001.

However, if you receive a refund of taxes in the same year in which you paid the taxes, you would use the refund to reduce your deduction for taxes.

Example

You paid $4,000 of estimated state income taxes for 2000 in four equal payments. You made your fourth payment in January 2001. You were not subject to state income tax withholding in 2000. In 2001, you received a $400 tax refund based on your 2000 state income tax return. One hundred dollars (25% of $400) of the refund is attributable to your 2001 payment. Your deduction for state and local income taxes paid in 2001 includes $900 ($1,000 − $100) plus any other payments you made during 2001 and any amount withheld during 2001. The amount of your state tax refund to be reported as income in 2001 would be $300 ($400 − $100).

TAX SAVER

Reducing the amount of the reported refund will reduce your adjusted gross income. If your adjusted gross income is lower, you may benefit from greater itemized deductions.

TAX PLANNER

If you subtract part of the refund from your other tax payments, the income reported by you will not match the amount reported to the IRS by the state on Form 1099-G. You may then receive a notice proposing an additional assessment of tax. You may avoid the notice by attaching an explanation to your return.

Explanation

An overpayment of state income tax that is to be credited against the estimated state tax for the following year is treated as though it were refunded to you. The overpayment may then be deducted as an estimated tax payment.

Example

Your 2000 state return showed an overpayment of $500, which you indicated was to be credited against your 2001 state estimated tax declaration. In addition, you made three quarterly state estimated tax payments of $500 each during 2001. On your 2001 Form 1040, you report a tax refund of $500 on line 10 and a deduction on Schedule A of $2,000.

TAX ORGANIZER

When you receive your Form 1099-G from your state or local government, keep it as documentation of your refund.

Foreign Income Taxes

Generally, you can take either a deduction or a credit for income taxes imposed on you by a foreign country or a U.S. possession. However, you cannot take a deduction or credit for foreign income taxes paid on income that is exempt from U.S. tax under the foreign earned income exclusion or the foreign housing exclusion. For information on these exclusions, get Publication 54, *Tax Guide for U.S. Citizens and Resident Aliens Abroad*. For information on the foreign tax credit, get Publication 514.

Explanation

If you have income from foreign sources, you may be required to pay foreign taxes on that income, or foreign taxes may be withheld on that income before you receive it.

Most foreign income stems from an investment in a foreign company. For example, if you invest in the stock of a Canadian oil company or an Australian mining company, foreign income taxes are withheld from the **dividends** you receive. To avoid having that income taxed twice—once by the foreign country and again by the United States—the tax law allows you either a deduction or a credit for the foreign income tax. See Chapter 37, *Other Credits Including the Earned Income Credit*, for more about foreign income taxes.

TAX PLANNER

Credit for foreign taxes. It is usually better to take a credit for foreign taxes than to deduct them as itemized deductions. Credits reduce your U.S. tax on a dollar-for-dollar

basis, whereas a deduction just reduces the amount of income subject to tax. However, if your foreign tax credit is limited and must be carried over to future years, you may want to consider taking a deduction now instead of waiting for a credit. See Chapter 42, *U.S. Citizens Working Abroad: Tax Treatment of Foreign Earned Income*, for more information on foreign tax credit limitations. The following example shows how a credit is usually more advantageous.

Example

You and your spouse had **adjusted gross income** of $70,000 in 2001, $20,000 of which was from foreign sources. You file a joint return and have no **dependents**. You had to pay $2,000 in foreign income taxes on dividend income received from sources within a foreign country. If your itemized deductions are otherwise $8,200, your added deduction for the foreign income tax reduces your U.S. tax by $550. If, however, you choose to claim a credit for the $2,000 foreign tax, your U.S. tax is reduced by the full $2,000. Therefore, you have an additional tax benefit of $1,450 by taking the credit.

TAX PLANNER

If you invest in stock of a foreign company. If you have invested in stock of a foreign company and the stock is being held by your stockbroker, ask him or her for the information that permits you to determine your foreign tax credit. In most instances, monthly statements received from brokers show only the *net* amount of foreign dividends received, *after* the foreign income tax has been deducted.

Credit for foreign taxes is available without limitation, if all your foreign income is from passive sources (interest, dividends, royalties, etc.) and the taxes are $300 or less ($600 or less if you are married filing jointly). See Chapter 37, *Other Credits Including the Earned Income Credit*, for more information about the foreign tax credit.

Example

Your brokerage statement shows foreign dividend income of $850. Upon inquiry, you determine that foreign income taxes of $150 have been withheld. Therefore, you should report $1,000 ($850 + $150) of dividend income. You then may be entitled to take a foreign tax credit of $150 or an itemized deduction of $150.

TAX ORGANIZER

For your files, you should keep your broker's statement showing any amount of foreign taxes paid.

Real Estate Taxes

Deductible real estate taxes are any state, local, or foreign taxes on real property levied for the general public welfare. The taxes must be based on the assessed value of the real property and must be charged uniformly against all property under the jurisdiction of the taxing authority.

Deductible real estate taxes generally do not include taxes charged for local benefits and improvements that increase the value of the property. They also do not include itemized charges for services (such as trash collection) to specific property or people, even if the charge is paid to the taxing authority. For more information about taxes and charges that are not deductible, see *Real Estate-Related Items You Cannot Deduct*, later.

Tenant-shareholders in a cooperative housing corporation. Generally, you can deduct your share of the real estate taxes the corporation paid or incurred on the property. The corporation should provide you with a statement showing you your share of the taxes. For more information, see *Special Rules for Cooperatives* in Publication 530.

Explanation
Generally, you may deduct only those real estate taxes assessed against property that you own.

Examples
No deduction was allowed for real estate taxes when

- A taxpayer paid, under court order, real estate taxes on his aunt's house, in which he resided.
- A guarantor paid real estate taxes on foreclosed property.
- The executor of an estate paid real estate taxes on a residence belonging to the estate, which she was occupying.
- A tenant-shareholder in a cooperative housing corporation paid his proportionate share of real estate taxes levied on recreational facilities owned and maintained by another corporation.
- A husband paid real estate taxes on property previously transferred to his wife. He had guaranteed payment if his wife defaulted but was not otherwise obligated. He will not be able to claim a deduction unless his wife actually defaults.

The Tax Court has held that sons could not deduct real estate taxes they paid on a house owned by their father and uncle because they did not have a beneficial interest in the property under California law.

You may, however, deduct real estate taxes when you have a beneficial interest in property, if the payment is made to protect that interest.

Examples
Deductions have been allowed in the following instances:

- By a donor of real estate who retained the right to use the property for 5 years
- By a lessee in Hawaii who leased property for 15 years or more and was the "deemed owner" for Hawaiian real estate purposes
- By a lessee who was permitted under local law to have his name entered on the tax assessment roll
- By a U.S. citizen who had a condominium in a foreign country, where he was not permitted to have legal title

TAX ORGANIZER

Real estate documents you need. You should keep a copy of your real estate tax bill in order to support your claim for the real estate tax deduction. Also, if you purchased a new house during the year, you should keep the closing statement. Typically, the closing statement will show the amount of taxes you paid to the seller at the time of the purchase.

Buyers and sellers of real estate. If you bought or sold real estate during the year, the real estate taxes must be divided between the buyer and the seller.

The buyer and the seller must divide the real estate taxes according to the number of days in the *real property tax year* (the period to which the tax imposed relates) that each owned the property. The seller is treated as paying the taxes up to, but not including, the date of sale. The buyer is treated as paying the taxes beginning with the date of sale. This applies regardless of the lien dates under local law. Generally, this information is included on the settlement statement provided at the closing.

If you (the seller) cannot deduct taxes until they are paid because you use the cash method of accounting, and the buyer of your property is personally liable for the tax, *you are considered to have paid your part of the tax at the time of the sale.* This lets you deduct the part of the tax to the date of sale even though you did not actually pay it. However, you must also include the amount of that tax in the selling price of the property. The buyer must include the same amount in his or her cost of the property.

You figure your deduction for taxes on each property bought or sold during the real property tax year as follows.

1. Enter the total real estate taxes for the real property tax year _____

2. Enter the number of days in the real property tax year that you owned the property .... _____

3. Divide line 2 by 365 .... _____

4. Multiply line 1 by line 3. This is your deduction. Enter it on line 6 of Schedule A (Form 1040) ....

Note. Repeat steps 1 through 4 for each property you bought or sold during the real property tax year.

Delinquent taxes. Do not divide delinquent taxes between the buyer and seller if the taxes are for any real property tax year before the one in which the property is sold. Even if the buyer agrees to pay the delinquent taxes, the buyer cannot deduct them. The buyer must add them to the cost of the property. The seller can deduct these taxes paid by the buyer. However, the seller must include them in the selling price.

Examples. The following examples illustrate how real estate taxes are divided between buyer and seller.

Example 1. Dennis and Beth White's real property tax year for both their old home and their new home is the calendar year, with payment due August 1. The tax on their old home, sold on May 7, was $620. The tax on their new home, bought on May 3, was $732. Dennis and Beth are considered to have paid a proportionate share of the real estate taxes on the old home even though they did not actually pay them to the taxing authority. On the other hand, they can claim only a proportionate share of the taxes they paid on their new property even though they paid the entire amount.

Dennis and Beth owned their old home during the real property tax year for 126 days (January 1 to May 6, the day before the sale). They figure their deduction for taxes on their old home as follows.

TAXES ON OLD HOME

1. Enter the total real estate taxes for the real property tax year.............. $620

2. Enter the number of days in the real property tax year that you owned the property 126

3. Divide line 2 by 365 .... .345

4. Multiply line 1 by line 3. This is your deduction. Enter it on line 6 of Schedule A (Form 1040) $214

Since the buyers of their old home paid all of the taxes, Dennis and Beth also include the $214 in the selling price of the old home. (The buyers add the $214 to their cost of the home.)

Dennis and Beth owned their new home during the real property tax year for 243 days (May 3 to December 31, including their date of purchase). They figure their deduction for taxes on their new home as follows.

TAXES ON NEW HOME

1. Enter the total real estate taxes for the real property tax year.............. $732

2. Enter the number of days in the real property tax year that you owned the property 243

3. Divide line 2 by 365 .... .666

4. Multiply line 1 by line 3. This is your deduction. Enter it on line 6 of Schedule A (Form 1040) $488

Since Dennis and Beth paid all of the taxes on the new home, they add $244 ($732 paid less $488 deduction) to their cost of the new home. (The sellers add this $244 to their selling price and deduct the $244 as a real estate tax.)

Dennis and Beth's real estate tax deduction for their old and new homes is the sum of $214 and $488, or $702. They will enter this amount on line 6 of Schedule A (Form 1040).

Example 2. George and Helen Brown bought a new home on May 3, 2001. Their real property tax year for the new home is the calendar year. Real estate taxes for 2000 were assessed in their state on January 1, 2001. The taxes became due on May 31, 2001, and October 31, 2001.

The Browns agreed to pay all taxes due after the date of purchase. Real estate taxes for 2000 were $680. They paid $340 on May 31, 2001, and $340 on October 31, 2001. These taxes were for the 2000 real property tax year. The Browns cannot deduct them since they did not own the property until 2001. Instead, they must add $680 to the cost of their new home.

In January 2002, the Browns receive their 2001 property tax statement for $752, which they will pay in 2002. The Browns owned their new home during the 2001 real property tax year for 243 days (May 3 to December 31). They will figure their 2002 deduction for taxes as follows.

1. Enter the total real estate taxes for the real property tax year.............. $752

2. Enter the number of days in the real property tax year that you owned the property 243

3. Divide line 2 by 365 .... .666

4. Multiply line 1 by line 3. This is your deduction. Claim it on line 6 of Schedule A (Form 1040) $501

The remaining $251 ($752 paid less $501 deduction) of taxes paid in 2002, along with the $680 paid in 2001, is added to the cost of their new home.

Because the taxes up to the date of sale are considered paid by the seller on the date of sale, the seller is entitled to a 2001 tax deduction of $931. This is the sum of the $680 for 2000 and the $251 for the 122 days the seller owned the home in 2001. The seller must also include the $931 in the selling price when he or she figures the gain or loss on the sale. The seller should contact the Browns in January 2002 to find out how much real estate tax is due for 2001.

Form 1099-S. For certain sales or exchanges of real estate, the person responsible for closing the sale (generally the settlement agent) prepares Form 1099-S, *Proceeds From Real Estate Transactions,* to report certain information to the IRS and to the seller of the property. Box 2 of the form is for the gross proceeds of the sale and should include the portion of the seller's real estate tax liability that the buyer will pay after the date of sale. The buyer includes these taxes in the cost basis of the property, and the seller both deducts this amount as a tax paid and includes it in the sales price of the property.

For a real estate transaction that involves a home, any real estate tax the seller paid in advance but that is the liability of the buyer appears in box 5 of Form 1099-S. The buyer deducts this amount as a real estate tax, and the seller reduces his or her real estate tax deduction (or includes it in income) by the same amount. See *Refund (or rebate),* later.

Explanation

Frequently, when property is sold, the amount of the real estate taxes for the "real property tax year" is not yet known, so an allocation is made on the closing statement at the time of sale based on the tax bill for the preceding year.

If the actual real estate tax bill for the real property tax year is greater than the amount used in the original allocation, the seller is entitled to a deduction greater than that shown on the real estate closing statement. The difference between the deductible amount and the amount allocated on the closing statement is considered additional proceeds of the sale.

The buyer is entitled to deduct his or her allocable share of the actual bill. The excess of the amount that he or she pays over (1) the deductible amount and (2) the amount paid or received at the closing is added to the cost of the property.

TAXPLANNER

When to deduct real estate taxes. If the real estate taxes are actually paid after the year of the sale, the seller may deduct his or her share of the taxes either in the year of the sale or in the year in which the tax is paid, whichever produces the greatest tax advantage.

The situation is slightly different for the buyer. If the buyer is liable for payment of the tax, he or she may deduct his or her allocated share of the tax only in the year in which the payment is made. If the seller is liable for payment of the tax, the buyer may deduct his or her allocated share either in the year of the sale or in the year of payment.

Taxes placed in escrow. If your monthly mortgage payment includes an amount placed in escrow (put in the care of a third party) for real estate taxes, you may not be able to deduct the total amount placed in escrow. You can deduct only the real estate tax that the third party actually paid to the taxing authority. If the third party does not notify you of the amount of real estate tax that was paid for you, contact the third party or the taxing authority to find the proper amount to show on your return.

TAXPLANNER

When to accelerate a tax payment. Most lenders arrange for payment of taxes out of escrow accounts on the tax due date. When the due date is shortly after the end of the calendar year, it may be advantageous to accelerate the payment in order to get the deduction for payment a year earlier.

Example

Real estate taxes of $1,200 for the year 2001 become due and payable on February 1, 2002. The taxpayer made monthly escrow payments of $100 each during 2001. If the taxes were paid from the escrow account on the February 1, 2002, due date, the $1,200 is a 2002 deduction. However, if the taxes were paid by December 31, 2001, the $1,200 is a 2001 deduction.

TAXORGANIZER

Escrow statements. Be sure to keep your yearly escrow statement, which should indicate the amount of real estate taxes paid from the escrow account.

Tenants by the entirety. If you and your spouse held property as tenants by the entirety and you file separate returns, each of you can deduct only the taxes each of you paid on the property.

Divorced individuals. If you divorce or separation agreement states that you must pay the real estate taxes for a home owned by you and your spouse, part of your payments may be deductible as alimony and part as real estate taxes. See Publication 504, *Divorced or Separated Individuals,* for information.

Minister's and military personnel housing allowances. If you are a minister or a member of the uniformed services and receive a housing allowance that you can exclude from income, you still can deduct all of the real estate taxes you pay on your home.

Refund (or rebate). If you receive a refund or rebate in 2001 of real estate taxes you paid in 2001, you must reduce your deduction by the amount refunded to you. If you receive a refund or rebate in 2001 of real estate taxes you deducted in an earlier year, you generally must include the refund or rebate in income in the year you receive it. However, you only need to include the amount of the deduction that reduced your tax in the earlier year. For more information, see *Recoveries* in chapter 13. **Tip.** *If you did not itemize deductions in the year you paid the tax, do not report the refund as income.*

Real Estate-Related Items You Cannot Deduct

Payments for the following items generally are not deductible as real estate taxes.

- Taxes for local benefits.
- Itemized charges for services (such as trash and garbage pickup fees).
- Transfer taxes (or stamp taxes).
- Rent increases due to higher real estate taxes.
- Homeowners' association charges.

Taxes for local benefits. Deductible real estate taxes generally do not include taxes charged for local benefits and improvements that increase the value of your property. These include assessments for streets, sidewalks, water mains, sewer lines, public parking facilities, and similar improvements. You should increase the basis of your property by the amount of the assessment.

Local benefit taxes are deductible only if they are for maintenance, repair, or interest charges related to those benefits. If only a part of the taxes is for maintenance, repair, or interest, you must be able to show the amount of that part to claim the deduction. If you cannot determine what part of the tax is for maintenance, repair, or interest, none of it is deductible.

Taxes for local benefits may be included in your real estate tax bill. If your taxing authority (or mortgage lender) does not furnish you a copy of your real estate tax bill, ask for it. You should use the rules above to determine if the local benefit tax is deductible.

Explanation
Real property taxes are deductible if they are levied for the welfare of the general public and are levied at a proportionate rate against all property within the taxing jurisdiction.

Real property taxes should be distinguished from assessments paid for local benefits, such as repair of streets, sidewalks, sewers, curbs, gutters, and other improvements that tend to benefit specific properties. Assessments of this type generally are not deductible.

A property owner often has the option of paying a special assessment in one payment or spreading the assessment over a period of years. In either case, the assessment itself is not deductible. However, payment of certain special assessments may increase the tax basis of your home. (See Chapter 14, *Basis of Property,* for a full discussion of this matter.) If an assessment on business or investment property is paid in installments, any interest charged is deductible. If the property is personal rather than business property, the interest would not be deductible. See Chapter 25, *Interest Expense.*

The IRS and the courts have held that the following *are* deductible as real property taxes:

- Assessments for the repair and resurfacing of streets, but not the lengthening or widening of them
- Wheeling, West Virginia, police and fire department charges imposed on owners of buildings and **tangible personal property**

The IRS and some courts have held that the following *are not* deductible as real property taxes:

- Delinquency penalties on California real property taxes
- California utility users' tax
- New York State renters' tax
- Prince George's County, Maryland, renters' tax
- Duluth sprinkling tax
- Vermont land gains tax
- Title registration fees
- Municipal water tax
- Monthly sewer user fees
- Building permit fees
- Sewer assessments
- Mortgage recording tax

If you pay real estate taxes this year but you are not itemizing your deductions, see Chapter 14, *Basis of Property.*

Different rules apply to real estate taxes paid during the period in which you are making improvements intended for business use. These rules are discussed in Chapter 25, *Interest Expense.*

Itemized charges for services. An itemized charge for services to specific property or people is not a tax, even if the charge is paid to the taxing authority. For example, you cannot deduct the charge as a real estate tax if it is:

- A unit fee for the delivery of a service (such as a $5 fee charged for every 1,000 gallons of water you use),
- A periodic charge for a residential service (such as a $20 per month or $240 annual fee charged to each homeowner for trash collection), or
- A flat fee charged for a single service provided by your government (such as a $30 charge for mowing your lawn because it was allowed to grow higher than permitted under your local ordinance).

Caution. *You must look at your real estate tax bill to determine if any nondeductible itemized charges, such as those just listed, are included in the bill. If your taxing authority (or mortgage lender) does not furnish you a copy of your real estate tax bill, ask for it.*

Exception. Service charges used to maintain or improve services (such as trash collection or police and fire protection) are deductible as real estate taxes if:

1) The fees or charges are imposed at a like rate against all property in the taxing jurisdiction,
2) The funds collected are not earmarked; instead, they are commingled with general revenue funds, and
3) Funds used to maintain or improve services are not limited to or determined by the amount of these fees or charges collected.

Explanation
If the cost of providing certain services, such as garbage collection or sanitary measures, is paid for out of the general real estate tax fund, the entire amount of your real estate tax bill is deductible. If, however, the amount charged for such services is separately stated or paid into a specific fund, that amount is not deductible.

Transfer taxes (or stamp taxes). Transfer taxes and similar taxes and charges on the sale of a personal home are not deductible. If they are paid by the seller, they are expenses of the sale and reduce the amount realized on the sale. If paid by the buyer, they are included in the cost basis of the property.

Rent increase due to higher real estate taxes. If your landlord increases your rent in the form of a tax surcharge because of increased real estate taxes, you cannot deduct the increase as taxes.

Homeowners' association charges. These charges are not deductible because they are imposed by the homeowners' association, rather than the state or local government.

Personal Property Taxes

Personal property tax is deductible if it is a state or local tax that is:

1) Charged on personal property,
2) Based *only* on the value of the personal property, and
3) Charged on a yearly basis, even if it is collected more than once a year, or less than once a year.

A tax that meets the above requirements can be considered charged on personal property even if it is for the exercise of a privilege. For example, a yearly tax based on value qualifies as a personal property tax even if it is called a registration fee and is for the privilege of registering motor vehicles or using them on the highways.

Example. Your state charges a yearly motor vehicle registration tax of 1% of value plus 50 cents per hundredweight. You paid $32 based on the value ($1,500) and weight (3,400 lbs.) of your car. You can deduct $15 (1% × $1,500) as a personal property tax, since it is based on the value. The remaining $17 ($.50 × 34), based on the weight, is not deductible.

> **Explanation**
> Most state automobile license fees are not based on the value of the automobile and, therefore, are not deductible as personal property taxes. Deductions have been allowed for all or part of the automobile license fees or taxes in Arizona, California, Colorado, Connecticut, Georgia, Indiana, Iowa, Maine, Massachusetts, Minnesota, Mississippi, Montana, Nebraska, Nevada, New Hampshire, Oklahoma, Washington, and Wyoming.
>
> In addition, a portion of the Oklahoma annual license registration fees for automobiles, house trailers, mobile homes, travel trailers, and boats is deductible. A portion of the Colorado specific ownership tax on motor vehicles, trailers, and mobile homes is also deductible.

Taxes and Fees You Cannot Deduct

Many federal, state, and local government taxes are not deductible because they do not fall within the categories discussed earlier. Other taxes and fees, such as federal income taxes, are not deductible because the tax law specifically prohibits a deduction for them.

Taxes and fees that are generally not deductible include the following items.

- *Estate, inheritance, legacy, or succession taxes.* These taxes are generally not deductible. However, you can deduct the estate tax attributable to income in respect of a decedent if you, as a beneficiary, must include that income in your gross income. In that case, deduct the estate tax as a miscellaneous deduction that is not subject to the 2%-of-adjusted-gross-income limit. For more information, see *Estate Tax Deduction* in Publication 559, *Survivors, Executors, and Administrators.*
- *Federal income taxes.* This includes taxes withheld from your pay.
- *Fines.* You cannot deduct penalties for violation of any law, including forfeiture of related collateral deposits.
- *Gift taxes.*
- *License fees.* You cannot deduct license fees for personal purposes (such as marriage, driver's, and dog license fees).

- *Social security.* This includes social security, Medicare, or railroad retirement taxes withheld from your pay.
- *Social security and other employment taxes for household workers.* You generally cannot deduct the social security or other employment taxes you pay on the wages of a household worker. However, you may be able to include them in medical or child care expenses. For more information, see chapters 23 and 33.

> **Explanation**
> Other taxes that are *not* deductible include the following:
>
> 1. Federal and state excise taxes on telephone service
> 2. Federal gasoline taxes
> 3. Federal excise taxes on tobacco products and alcoholic beverages
> 4. Federal excise taxes on automobiles with low gas mileage (the "gas guzzler" tax) or luxury automobiles
> 5. Foreign taxes on income earned by U.S. citizens and U.S. **resident aliens** who qualify for the foreign **earned income** exclusion
> 6. Passport fees
> 7. Occupancy taxes
> 8. Penalties assessed as taxes

Many taxes and fees other than those listed above are also nondeductible, unless they are ordinary and necessary expenses of a business or income producing activity. For other nondeductible items, see *Real Estate-Related Items You Cannot Deduct,* earlier.

> **TAXALERT**
>
> **Excise taxes on cars.** An excise tax is imposed on automobiles, except those used exclusively in the purchaser's trade or business of transporting persons or property (e.g., taxicabs). The excise tax on automobiles purchased in 2001 is 4% of the excess of the purchase price over $38,000. Because the luxury tax on automobiles is an excise tax, it is not deductible on your personal income tax return unless the purchase is connected with your business or an income-producing activity. The luxury excise tax rate is 3% in 2002 and the tax is scheduled to expire after 2002.

Where To Deduct

You deduct taxes on the following schedules.

State and local income taxes. These taxes are deducted on line 5 of Schedule A (Form 1040), even if your only source of income is from business, rents, or royalties.

Foreign income taxes. Generally, income taxes you pay to a foreign country or U.S. possession can be claimed as an itemized deduction on line 8 of Schedule A (Form 1040), or as a credit against your U.S. income tax on line 43 of Form 1040. To claim the credit, you may have to complete and attach Form 1116. For more information, see chapter 38 or the instructions for Form 1040 or get Publication 514.

Real estate taxes and personal property taxes. These taxes are deducted on lines 6 and 7 of Schedule A (Form 1040), unless they are paid on property used in your business in which case they are deducted on Schedule C (Form 1040). Taxes on property that produces rent or royalty income are deducted on Schedule E (Form 1040).

Self-employment tax. Deduct one-half of your self-employment tax on line 27, Form 1040.

Other taxes. All other deductible taxes are deducted on line 8 of Schedule A (Form 1040).

25

Interest Expense

Introduction

Interest expense is the amount of money you pay for the use of borrowed money. Depending on the use of the borrowed funds, certain types of interest expense may be deducted from your income.

To calculate your deduction, you must first segregate your borrowings into five categories: (1) amounts used for investments generating portfolio income (interest, dividends, etc.), (2) amounts used for investment in passive activities (see Chapter 13, Other Income), (3) amounts used to purchase or improve a personal residence, (4) amounts used in an active trade or business, and (5) amounts used for personal reasons. However, remember that no portion of your personal interest expense is deductible.

The interest paid on the other four categories of borrowings are subject to different rules regarding deductibility. This chapter will explain those rules and how to account for the use of your borrowings.

Your 2001 itemized deductions may be subject to certain limitations if your adjusted gross income exceeds $132,950 ($66,475 for married persons filing separately). This general limitation does not apply to investment interest expense, but it does apply to home mortgage interest expense. See Chapter 22, Limit on Itemized Deductions, for more information on this subject.

Important Reminders

Personal interest. Personal interest is not deductible. Examples of personal interest include interest on a loan to purchase an automobile for personal use and credit card and installment interest incurred for personal expenses. But you may be able to deduct interest you pay on a qualified student loan. For details, see Publication 970, *Tax Benefits for Higher Education.*

Limit on itemized deductions. Certain itemized deductions (including home mortgage interest) are limited if your adjusted gross income is more than $132,950 ($66,475 if you are married filing a separate return). For more information, see chapter 22.

This chapter discusses interest. Interest is the amount you pay for the use of borrowed money.

Explanation
Loan payments generally are divided between principal and interest. In the absence of any specific division, partial payments are presumed to apply first to interest and then to principal. However, if a single payment is made in full settlement of an outstanding debt, the payment is first applied to the remaining principal balance and then to interest.

The types of interest you can deduct as itemized deductions on Schedule A (Form 1040) are:

- Home mortgage interest, including certain points, and
- Investment interest.

This chapter explains these deductions. It also explains where to deduct other types of interest and lists some types of interest you cannot deduct.

Use *Table 25–1* to find out where to get more information on various types of interest, including investment interest.

Useful Items

You may want to see:

Publication

☐ **936** Home Mortgage Interest Deduction

Home Mortgage Interest

Generally, home mortgage interest is any interest you pay on a loan secured by your home (main home or a second home). The loan may be a mortgage to buy your home, a second mortgage, a line of credit, or a home equity loan.

You can deduct home mortgage interest only if you meet all the following conditions.

- You must file Form 1040 and itemize deductions on Schedule A (Form 1040).
- You must be legally liable for the loan. You cannot deduct payments you make for someone else if you are not legally liable to make them. Both you and the lender must intend that the loan be repaid. In addition, there must be a true debtor-creditor relationship between you and the lender.

Explanation

Interest paid to a related person is deductible, as long as it is paid for a bona fide debt. For example, parents may deduct interest paid on amounts borrowed from their minor children if the interest is otherwise deductible. If the borrower is not legally liable for the debt, or if there is no intent for the loan to be repaid, it is not a bona fide debt and interest payments are not deductible.

To deduct interest that you pay, the interest must be your liability. When two or more persons are jointly liable for the payment of interest, the person actually making the interest payment is entitled to the entire deduction.

It is not necessary to have a fixed percentage interest rate applied to the money that you have borrowed for the interest to be deducted. What is necessary is that the amount of interest paid can be definitely determined. It is usually based on a written agreement between the lender and the borrower.

Low-interest and interest-free loans, which were once popular between family members, now have severe limitations applied to them. See Chapter 8, *Interest Income*.

- The mortgage must be a secured debt on a qualified home. (Generally, your mortgage is a secured debt if you put your home up as collateral to protect the interests of the lender. The term "qualified home" means your main home or second home. For details, see Publication 936.)

Explanation

To be fully deductible as home mortgage interest, the interest must be on a debt that is secured by property that is a qualified residence. A qualified residence is property that is owned by you and used as a principal or second residence. A residence may, among other things, be a house, a cooperative apartment, a condominium, a house trailer, or a houseboat. To be considered a qualified residence, a houseboat must include basic living accommodations, including sleeping space, a toilet, and cooking facilities.

TAXPLANNER

You may treat a home currently under construction as a qualified home for a period of up to 24 months if it becomes a qualifying residence as of the time that it is ready for occupancy.

Amount Deductible

In most cases, you will be able to deduct all of your home mortgage interest. Whether you can deduct all of it depends on the date you took out the mortgage, the amount of the mortgage, and your use of its proceeds.

Fully deductible interest. If all of your mortgages fit into one or more of the following three categories at all times during the year, you can deduct all of the interest on those mortgages. (If any one mortgage fits into more than one category, add the debt that fits in each category to your other debt in the same category.)

The three categories are:

1) Mortgages you took out on or before October 13, 1987 (called *grandfathered debt*).

Explanation

All mortgage indebtedness existing on October 13, 1987 (grandfathered debt), is treated as acquisition indebtedness, regardless of the amount. The interest on this indebtedness is fully deductible.

Individuals who refinanced and increased their mortgage indebtedness before October 14, 1987, may have greater interest deductions than those individuals who waited until later because new or refinanced indebtedness is limited in amount, as explained in this chapter.

Example

When you are refinancing pre-October 14, 1987, mortgage debt, the amount that exceeds the existing debt does not qualify as grandfathered debt. The excess may be treated as home acquisition or home equity indebtedness, but the total qualifying indebtedness cannot exceed the fair market value of the residence. Grandfathered debt refinanced after October 13, 1987, generally retains its status as grandfathered debt only for the remaining term of the original debt.

Example

An original mortgage note incurred prior to October 14, 1987, to purchase a qualified residence had been reduced to $100,000 in 2001, when the value of the residence was $175,000. If this mortgage is refinanced, $100,000 of the new mortgage note is treated as grandfathered debt. Up to $75,000 may be treated as home acquisition or home equity indebtedness. If the indebtedness exceeds the value of the residence ($175,000), the excess must be allocated in accordance with the use of the excess amount.

2) Mortgages you took out after October 13, 1987, to buy, build, or improve your home (called *home acquisition debt*), but only if throughout 2001 these mortgages plus any grandfathered debt totaled $1 million or less ($500,000 or less if married filing separately).

Explanation

This limitation applies only to loans incurred to purchase, construct, or improve a home.

TaxPlanner

Is your loan large enough? When you are purchasing or constructing a home, consider your future financial needs carefully. The original loan can never be refinanced to increase the amount available for this limitation.

If you believe that you will need money for personal uses in the near future, you may want to increase the original mortgage at the time of acquisition or improvement to meet those future needs. Otherwise, if you later obtain a home equity loan, the interest on only $100,000 of the loan ($50,000 if married filing separately) is deductible as mortgage interest.

3) Mortgages you took out after October 13, 1987, other than to buy, build, or improve your home (called **home equity debt**), but only if throughout 2001 these mortgages totaled $100,000 or less ($50,000 or less if married filing separately) **and** totaled no more than the fair market value of your home reduced by (1) and (2).

TaxSaver

The benefits of home equity loans. Many taxpayers are pursuing home equity loans as a means of paying off their credit card balances, automobile loans, and other types of consumer expenditures. There are two major benefits of home equity borrowing:

1. Interest on up to $100,000 of home equity loans ($50,000 if married filing separately) is tax-deductible, whereas personal interest is not.
2. Home equity loans are less expensive than other types of credit. For example, the rate for home equity loans may be 9% or less. In comparison, the interest rates for credit cards and unsecured personal loans can exceed 18%.

Although home equity loans present several benefits, you should remember that if you are unable to pay off the loan, your house is in jeopardy—not the items that you purchased with the borrowed funds.

The dollar limits for the second and third categories apply to the combined mortgages on your main home and second home.

Explanation
According to the IRS, the fair market value of your home cannot be less than the adjusted purchase price on the last day of the taxable year.

Example
John Joyce purchases a home in August 2001 for $150,000. He makes improvements costing $10,000 to the home during 2001, but these improvements add only $5,000 to the value of the home.

Although the value of the home at the end of 2001 is only $155,000, John is allowed to use $160,000, the cost of the home plus improvements, as the fair market value.

TaxSaver

If your mortgage is above the limit. If part of your mortgage is in excess of the qualified mortgage limitation and you

have investments that produce taxable income, you could sell some of your investments and use the proceeds to reduce your mortgage principal in order to meet the qualified mortgage limitation. You could then reborrow the funds and trace them to the purchase of new investments. Interest expense on the newly invested loan proceeds remains fully deductible, subject to the investment income limitations discussed later in this chapter. Remember to consider transaction costs of switching investments and the "wash sale" rule discussed in Chapter 15, *Sale of Property*. For additional information, consult your tax advisor.

See *Part II* of Publication 936 for more detailed definitions of grandfathered, home acquisition, and home equity debt.

You can use *Figure 25–A* to check whether your home mortgage interest is fully deductible.

Explanation
A second home may also be a qualified residence. A second home may be one that you do not occupy, a home that you occupy part of the year, or a home that you rent out. If the home is rented out, it is subject to the use requirements relating to vacation homes. It qualifies as your home only if you used it more than the greater of:

1. 14 days, or
2. 10% of the number of days during the year that it was rented at a fair rental or held out for sale.

If a dwelling is not rented at any time during the year, it may be treated as a qualified residence, even if it is not used by you. For this purpose, the IRS states that "rented" includes holding the residence out for rental or for resale.

Example
Mary owns a vacation home in Northern Michigan. Because of business pressures, she is unable to use the home in 2000 or 2001 and lists the home for sale on November 1, 2001.

The house qualifies as a residence in 2000. It is not considered her residence in 2001, because Mary did not use the house for more than the greater of 14 days or 10% of the number of days it was held out for sale (10% x 61 days = 6 days).

TaxPlanner

If, in the above example, members of Mary's family use the home for 15 days in 2001, she will be considered to have used it for the same period of time and the home will be considered her residence. Members of Mary's family include her brothers or sisters, husband, children and grandchildren, and parents or grandparents.

TaxPlanner

If you own more than two homes, you may not deduct interest on the mortgages secured by more than two of these homes during any one year as home mortgage interest.

You must include your main residence as one of the homes. You may choose any one of your other homes as a qualified residence and may change this choice for each tax year.

However, you cannot choose to treat one home as a

Figure 25–A. **Is My Home Mortgage Interest Fully Deductible?**

(Instructions: Include balances of ALL mortgages secured by your main home and second home. Answer YES only if the answer is true at ALL times during the year.)

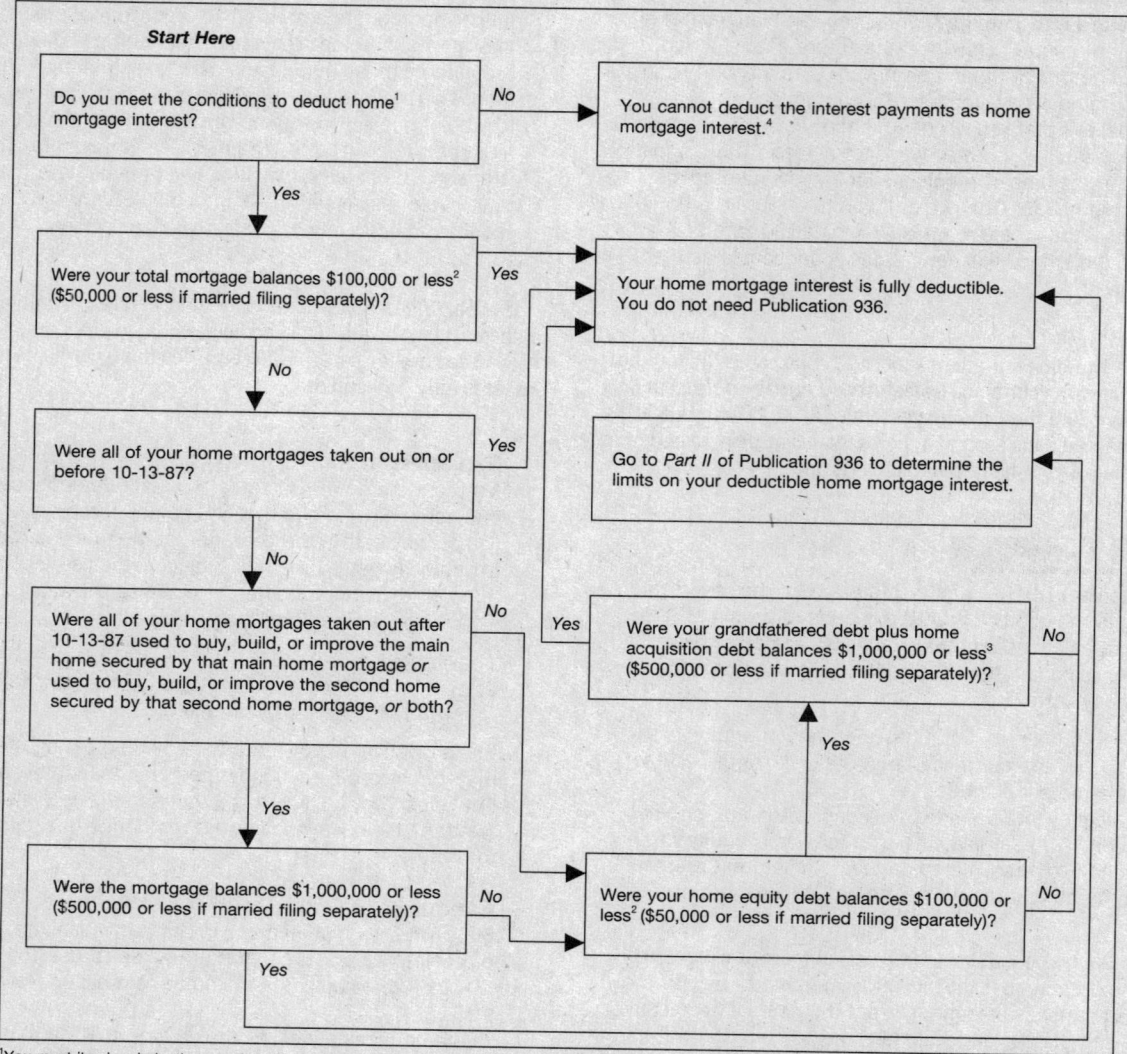

[1]You must itemize deductions on Schedule A (Form 1040) and be legally liable for the loan. The loan must be a secured debt on a qualified home. See *Home Mortgage Interest*.

[2]If all mortgages on your main or second home exceed the home's fair market value, a lower limit may apply. See *Home equity debt limit* under *Home Equity Debt* in *Part II* of Publication 936.

[3]Amounts over the $1,000,000 limit ($500,000 if married filing separately) qualify as home equity debt if they are not more than the total home equity debt limit. See Publication 936 for more information about grandfathered debt, home acquisition debt, and home equity debt.

[4]See *Table 25–1* for where to deduct other types of interest payments.

second residence for part of a year and another home as a second residence for the remainder of the year if both of these homes were owned by you during the entire year and neither home was your main residence during that year.

Limits on deduction. You cannot fully deduct interest on a mortgage that does not fit into any of the three categories listed above. If this applies to you, see *Part II* of Publication 936 to figure the amount of interest you can deduct.

Special Situations

This section describes certain items that can be included as home mortgage interest and others that cannot. It also describes certain special situations that may affect your deduction.

Late payment charge on mortgage payment. You can deduct as home mortgage interest a late payment charge if it was not for a specific service performed in connection with your mortgage loan.

Explanation

The Tax Court in one case broadly interpreted the phrase "specific services" and ruled that a taxpayer was not allowed to deduct late charges on a home mortgage loan as mortgage interest. The Court determined in that case that the late charges related to the specific service of collecting the late payment. Furthermore, the formula used in calculating the late charge did not resemble standard interest computations, because the late charge was the same whether the payment was 1 day or 1 year late.

Mortgage prepayment penalty. If you pay off your home mortgage early, you may have to pay a penalty. You can deduct that penalty as home mortgage interest provided the penalty is not for a specific service performed or cost incurred in connection with your mortgage loan.

Sale of home. If you sell your home, you can deduct your home mortgage interest (subject to any limits that apply) paid up to, but not including, the date of sale.

Example. John and Peggy Harris sold their home on May 7. Through April 30, they made home mortgage interest payments of $1,220. The settlement sheet for the sale of the home showed $50 interest for the 6-day period in May up to, but not including, the date of sale. Their mortgage interest deduction is $1,270 ($1,220 + $50).

Prepaid interest. If you pay interest in advance for a period that goes beyond the end of the tax year, you must spread this interest over the tax years to which it applies. You can deduct in each year only the interest that qualifies as home mortgage interest for that year. However, see *Points,* later.

Example 1

When Dan borrowed $10,000 on a mortgage on November 1, 2001, he prepaid 16 months of interest ($1,600). The $1,600 of prepaid interest is considered to be paid, and therefore deductible, equally over the 16-month period ($100 per month). Dan should deduct $200 in 2001, $1,200 in 2002, and $200 in 2003.

Example 2

On March 27, Eric signed a mortgage note for $1,200 and agreed to repay it in 12 equal installments, beginning on April 28. Interest of $96 was subtracted from the face value of the note, and Eric received $1,104. If Eric uses the cash method of accounting, as most people do, interest is considered to be paid in 12 installments of $8 each ($96 ÷ 12). Eric may deduct $72 ($8 × 9 months) for the first year and $24 ($8 × 3 months) in the following year.

No deduction is permitted for the interest if payment for an installment period is not made. Therefore, if Eric were to miss two installment payments in the first year, he could deduct only $56 ($8 × 7 months).

Mortgage interest credit. You may be able to claim a mortgage interest credit if you were issued a mortgage credit certificate (MCC) by a state or local government. Figure the credit on **Form 8396,** *Mortgage Interest Credit.* If you take this credit, you must reduce your mortgage interest deduction by the amount of the credit.

For more information on the credit, see chapter 37.

Ministers' and military housing allowance. If you are a minister or a member of the uniformed services and receive a housing allowance that is not taxable, you can still deduct your home mortgage interest.

Mortgage assistance payments. If you qualify for mortgage assistance payments under section 235 of the National Housing Act, part or all of the interest on your mortgage may be paid for you. You cannot deduct the interest that is paid for you.

No other effect on taxes. Do not include these mortgage assistance payments in your income. Also, do not use these payments to reduce other deductions, such as real estate taxes.

Divorced or separated individuals. If a divorce or separation agreement requires you or your spouse or former spouse to pay home mortgage interest on a home owned by both of you, the payment of interest may be alimony. See the discussion of *Payments for jointly-owned home* in chapter 20.

Redeemable ground rent. If you make annual or periodic rental payments on a redeemable ground rent, you can deduct them as mortgage interest.

Payments made to end the lease and to buy the lessor's entire interest in the land are not ground rents. You cannot deduct them. For more information, see Publication 936.

Nonredeemable ground rent. Payments on a nonredeemable ground rent are not mortgage interest. You can deduct them as rent if they are a business expense or if they are for rental property.

Rental payments. If you live in a house before final settlement on the purchase, any payments you make for that period are rent and not interest. This is true even if the settlement papers call them interest. You cannot deduct these payments as home mortgage interest.

Mortgage proceeds invested in tax-exempt securities. You cannot deduct the home mortgage interest on grandfathered debt or home equity debt if you used the proceeds of the mortgage to buy securities or certificates that produce tax-free income. Grandfathered debt and home equity debt are defined earlier under *Amount Deductible.*

Refunds of interest. If you receive a refund of interest in the same tax year you paid it, you must reduce your interest expense by the amount refunded to you. If you receive a refund of interest you deducted in an earlier year, you generally must include the refund in income in the year you receive it. However, you need to include it only up to the amount of the deduction that reduced your tax in the earlier year. This is true whether the interest overcharge was refunded to you or was used to reduce the outstanding principal on your mortgage.

If you received a refund of interest you overpaid in an earlier year, you generally will receive a Form 1098, *Mortgage Interest Statement,* showing the refund in box 3. For information about Form 1098, see *Mortgage Interest Statement,* later.

For more information on how to treat refunds of interest deducted in earlier years, see *Recoveries* in chapter 13.

Example

During 2001, you paid $2,000 in interest on your adjustable rate mortgage. On December 31, 2001, a $200 interest refund for 2001 was credited to your account. Your net deduction for interest on your loans is $1,800 ($2,000 paid minus $200 refunded).

Refunds of interest paid must be included in income if they represent a return of interest deducted in a prior year. If you receive a refund in 2001 for interest paid in 2000 and *did not itemize* your deductions in 2000, the refund is *not included* in your 2001 income. If you receive the refund in 2001 and you *did itemize* your deductions in 2000, the refund is generally *included* in your 2001 income to the extent the deduction reduced your tax in 2000.

Points

The term "points" is used to describe certain charges paid, or treated as paid, by a borrower to obtain a home mortgage. Points may also be called loan origination fees, maximum loan charges, loan discount, or discount points.

A borrower is treated as paying any points that a home seller pays for the borrower's mortgage. See *Points paid by the seller,* later.

Explanation

Usually, for federally regulated mortgage loans, points will be designated on the Uniform Settlement Statement (also known as Form HUD-1) as "loan origination fee," "loan discount," "discount points," or simply "points."

General rule. You generally cannot deduct the full amount of points in the year paid. Because they are prepaid interest, you generally must deduct them over the life (term) of the mortgage.

Explanation
Deducting points. Generally, taxpayers are prohibited from deducting prepaid interest in the year of payment. Rather, they must capitalize the prepaid interest and deduct it ratably over the term of the loan.

However, as discussed below, an exception exists for taxpayers who buy, build, or improve their principal residences and pay "points" in order to obtain a lower interest rate on their loans. The term "points" is a fee paid by the borrower that is like prepaid interest. To be deductible, the charge must represent interest paid for the use of money and must be *paid before* the time for which it represents a charge for the use of the money. Furthermore, the home must be the taxpayer's principal residence. You should note that the IRS has ruled that you can elect *not* to currently deduct points and to amortize them over the life of a loan. Such an election may be advantageous if the deduction does not benefit you in the year of purchase (e.g., you're not itemizing your deductions).

Exception. You can fully deduct points in the year paid if you meet all the following tests. (You can use *Figure 25–B* as a quick guide to see whether your points are fully deductible in the year paid.)

1) Your loan is secured by your main home. (Your main home is the one you live in most of the time.)
2) Paying points is an established business practice in the area where the loan was made.
3) The points paid were not more than the points generally charged in that area.
4) You use the cash method of accounting. This means you report income in the year you receive it and deduct expenses in the year you pay them. (If you want more information about this method, see *Accounting Methods* in chapter 1.)
5) The points were not paid in place of amounts that ordinarily are stated separately on the settlement statement, such as appraisal fees, inspection fees, title fees, attorney fees, and property taxes.
6) The funds you provided at or before closing, plus any points the seller paid, were at least as much as the points charged. The funds you provided do not have to have been applied to the points. They can include a down payment, an escrow deposit, earnest money, and other funds you paid at or before closing for any purpose. You cannot have borrowed these funds from your lender or mortgage broker.
7) You use your loan to buy or build your main home.
8) The points were computed as a percentage of the principal amount of the mortgage.
9) The amount is clearly shown on the settlement statement (such as the Uniform Settlement Statement, Form HUD-1) as points charged for the mortgage. The points may be shown as paid from either your funds or the seller's.

Note. If you meet all of these tests, you can choose to either fully deduct the points in the year paid, or deduct them over the life of the loan.
Home improvement loan. You can also fully deduct in the year paid points paid on a loan to improve your main home, if tests (1) through (6) are met.
Caution. Second home. *The Exception does not apply to points you pay on loans secured by your second home. You can deduct these points only over the life of the loan.*
Exception does not apply. If you do not qualify under the exception, or choose not to deduct the full amount of points in the year paid, see *Points* in chapter 5 of Publication 535, *Business Expenses,* for the rules on when and how much you can deduct. However, if the points relate to refinancing a home mortgage, see *Refinancing,* later.

Amounts charged for services. Amounts charged by the lender for specific services connected to the loan are not interest. Examples of these charges are:

1) Appraisal fees,
2) Notary fees,
3) Preparation costs for the mortgage note or deed of trust,
4) Mortgage insurance premiums, and
5) VA funding fees.

You cannot deduct these amounts as points either in the year paid or over the life of the mortgage. For information about the tax treatment of these amounts and other settlement fees and closing costs, get Publication 530, *Tax Information for First-Time Homeowners.*

TAXPLANNER
Pointers about points. To get a deduction for points, make sure that the loan document clearly establishes that the points were not paid for any specific services that the lender performed or agreed to perform in connection with the borrower's account under the loan contract. Charges should be separately itemized on the financing and settlement statements.

Points paid by the seller. The term "points" includes loan placement fees that the seller pays to the lender to arrange financing for the buyer.
Treatment by seller. The seller **cannot** deduct these fees as interest. But they are a selling expense that reduces the amount realized by the seller. See chapter 16 for information on the sale of your home.
Treatment by buyer. The buyer reduces the basis of the home by the amount of the seller-paid points and treats the points as if he or she had paid them. If all the tests under the *Exception,* earlier, are met, the buyer can deduct the points in the year paid. If any of those tests is not met, the buyer deducts the points over the life of the loan.
For information about basis, see chapter 14.

Explanation
Points paid by the seller, including those charged to the seller, in connection with the buyer's home mortgage loan are considered points paid by the buyer. Therefore, points paid by the seller may be fully deductible by the buyer in the year paid (see discussion of *Points* above.)

Funds provided are less than points. If you meet all the tests in the *Exception,* earlier, except that the funds you provided were less than the points charged to you (test 6), you can deduct the points in the year paid, up to the amount of funds you provided. In addition, you can deduct any points paid by the seller.
Example 1. When you took out a $100,000 mortgage loan to buy your home in December, you were charged one point ($1,000). You meet all the tests for deducting points in the year paid, except the only funds you provided were a $750 down payment. Of the $1,000 charged for points, you can deduct $750 in the year paid. You spread the remaining $250 over the life of the mortgage.
Example 2. The facts are the same as in *Example 1,* except that the person who sold you your home also paid one point ($1,000) to help you get your mortgage. In the year paid, you can deduct $1,750 ($750 of the amount you were charged plus the $1,000 paid by the seller). You spread the remaining $250 over the life of the mortgage. You must reduce the basis of your home by the $1,000 paid by the seller.
Excess points. If you meet all the tests in the *Exception,* earlier, except that the points paid were more than are generally paid in your area (test 3), you deduct in the year paid only the points that are generally

Figure 25–B. **Are My Points Fully Deductible This Year?**

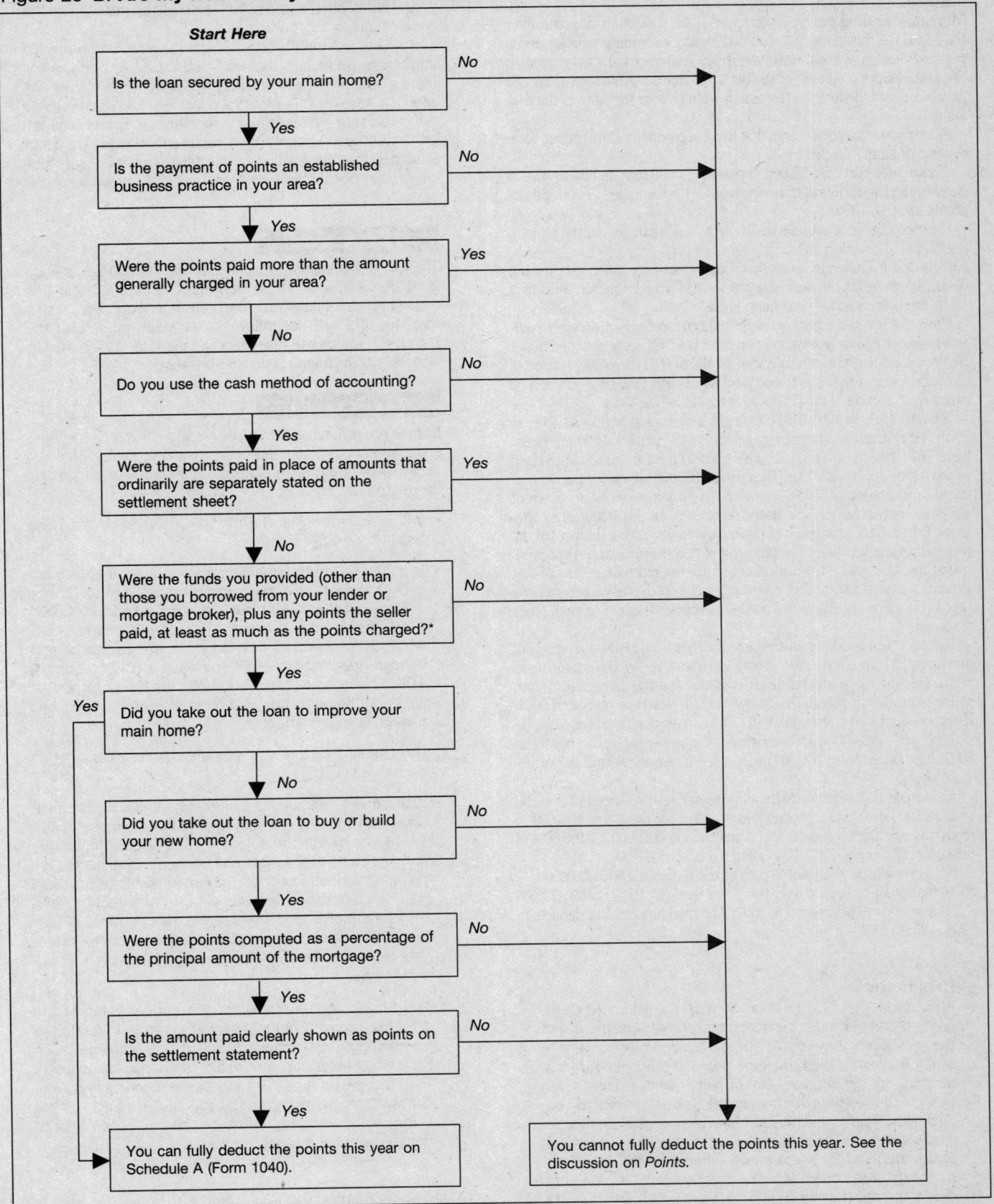

*The funds you provided do not have to have been applied to the points. They can include a down payment, an escrow deposit, earnest money, and other funds you paid at or before closing for any purpose.

charged. You must spread any additional points over the life of the mortgage.

Mortgage ending early. If you spread your deduction for points over the life of the mortgage, you can deduct any remaining balance in the year the mortgage ends. However, if you refinance the mortgage with the same lender, you cannot deduct any remaining balance of spread points. Instead, deduct the remaining balance over the term of the new loan.

A mortgage may end early due to a prepayment, refinancing, foreclosure, or similar event.

Example. Dan paid $3,000 in points in 1993 that he had to spread out over the 15-year life of the mortgage. He had deducted $1,600 of these points through 2000.

· Dan prepaid his mortgage in full in 2001. He can deduct the remaining $1,400 of points in 2001.

Refinancing. Generally, points you pay to refinance a mortgage are not deductible in full in the year you pay them. This is true even if the new mortgage is secured by your main home.

However, if you use part of the refinanced mortgage proceeds to *improve your main home* and you meet the first six tests listed under *Exception*, earlier, you can fully deduct the part of the points related to the improvement in the year you paid them with your own funds. You can deduct the rest of the points over the life of the loan.

Example 1. In 1991, Bill Fields got a mortgage to buy a home. In 2001, Bill refinanced that mortgage with a 15-year $100,000 mortgage loan. The mortgage is secured by his home. To get the new loan, he had to pay three points ($3,000). Two points ($2,000) were for prepaid interest, and one point ($1,000) was charged for services, in place of amounts that ordinarily are stated separately on the settlement statement. Bill paid the points out of his private funds, rather than out of the proceeds of the new loan. The payment of points is an established practice in the area, and the points charged are not more than the amount generally charged there. Bill's first payment on the new loan was due July 1. He made six payments on the loan in 2001 and is a cash basis taxpayer.

Bill used the funds from the new mortgage to repay his existing mortgage. Although the new mortgage loan was for Bill's continued ownership of his main home, it was not for the purchase or improvement of that home. He cannot deduct all of the points in 2001. He can deduct two points ($2,000) ratably over the life of the loan. He deducts $67 [($2,000 ÷ 180 months) × 6 payments] of the points in 2001. The other point ($1,000) was a fee for services and is not deductible.

Example 2. The facts are the same as in *Example 1*, except that Bill used $25,000 of the loan proceeds to improve his home and $75,000 to repay his existing mortgage. Bill deducts 25% ($25,000 ÷ $100,000) of the points ($2,000) in 2001. His deduction is $500 ($2,000 × 25%).

Bill also deducts the ratable part of the remaining $1,500 ($2,000 − $500) that must be spread over the life of the loan. This is $50 [($1,500 ÷ 180 months) × 6 payments] in 2001. The total amount Bill deducts in 2001 is $550 ($500 + $50).

Explanation

According to the IRS, points paid when you refinance an existing mortgage must be deducted ratably over the life of the new loan. They are not fully deductible in the year in which they were paid because they were not paid in connection with the improvement or purchase of a home, even though the original loan met the requirements for deductibility. Points paid on a refinanced mortgage are fully deductible in the year paid to the extent additional loan proceeds are used for home improvement and the points are paid with funds you provide. If only a portion of the loan proceeds is used for home improvement, then only a corresponding portion of the points is fully deductible in the year

paid. The balance of the points is deducted ratably over the life of the loan.

However, an Eighth Circuit Court decision allowed a full immediate deduction for points paid by taxpayers in obtaining a permanent mortgage on their home, the proceeds of which were used to pay off a short-term, 3-year mortgage with a balloon payment and a recently obtained home improvement loan secured by a second mortgage. The court indicated that the permanent mortgage obtained was sufficiently "in connection with" the original purchase of the home.

TaxAlert

The IRS has disagreed with this court decision and still argues that points paid for a loan to refinance a mortgage on a taxpayer's principal residence are not deductible. Therefore, the IRS will not follow the decision outside of the Eighth Circuit (Arkansas, Iowa, Minnesota, Missouri, Nebraska, North Dakota, and South Dakota).

TaxPlanner

Before you refinance. Before you refinance your home mortgage, you should consider both tax and financial factors.

For the interest to remain fully deductible, the following tax-related factors should be considered:

- Whether the term of the mortgage should be extended beyond the original term.

- In general, the total of all mortgage balances should not exceed the lesser of the fair market value of the house or $1.1 million ($1 million acquisition debt and $100,000 home equity debt) or, if married filing separately, $550,000. However, see previous discussion of refinanced grandfather debt if you have a pre-October 14, 1987, mortgage. Other limitations may also apply. See limits on the deduction of mortgage interest, discussed previously in this chapter.

The financial factors you may also want to consider include the following:

- If there are refinancing costs, you should determine how many months it would take to recoup these costs. To do so, divide the total amount of estimated refinancing costs (deductible and nondeductible) by the anticipated reduction in your monthly mortgage payment (i.e., the difference between your existing monthly payment of principal and interest and the new monthly payment). If you will recover your refinancing costs before you sell your home, then refinancing may be a smart thing to do.

- You should evaluate whether the current value of the after-tax savings from a lower interest rate exceeds the up-front cost of refinancing. Specifically, consider such factors as taxes, present value, and opportunity costs (lost income on funds used to pay refinancing charges). Software programs can assist you in evaluating whether it may be beneficial to refinance. You may also want to consult your tax advisor.

Limits on deduction. You cannot fully deduct points on a mortgage unless the mortgage fits into one of the categories listed earlier under *Fully deductible interest*. See Publication 936 for details.

Mortgage Interest Statement

If you paid $600 or more of mortgage interest (including certain points) during the year on any one mortgage, you generally will receive a **Form 1098,** *Mortgage Interest Statement,* or a similar statement from the mortgage holder. You will receive the statement if you pay interest to a person (including a financial institution or a cooperative housing corporation) in the course of that person's trade or business. A governmental unit is a person for purposes of furnishing the statement.

You should receive the statement for each year by January 31 of the following year. A copy of this form will also be sent to the IRS.

TAXORGANIZER

When you receive Form 1098, keep it with your other important tax documents.

Explanation

An individual who "takes back" a mortgage indebtedness when selling a residence is not required to prepare a Form 1098 or otherwise notify the debtor of the amount of interest paid. He or she must include the interest income on his or her tax return as seller-financed mortgage interest income and report the payer's name and amount received.

The statement will show the total interest you paid during the year. If you purchased a main home during the year, it will also show the deductible points paid during the year, including seller-paid points. However, it should not show any interest that was paid for you by a government agency.

As a general rule, Form 1098 will include only points that you can fully deduct in the year paid. However, certain points not included on Form 1098 also may be deductible, either in the year paid or over the life of the loan. See *Points,* earlier, to determine whether you can deduct points not shown on Form 1098.

Prepaid interest on Form 1098. If you prepaid interest in 2001 that accrued in full by January 15, 2002, this prepaid interest may be included in box 1 of Form 1098. However, you cannot deduct the prepaid amount for January 2002 in 2001. (See *Prepaid interest,* earlier.) You will have to figure the interest that accrued for 2002 and subtract it from the amount in box 1. You will include the interest for January 2002 with the other interest you pay for 2002. See *How To Report,* later.

Refunded interest. If you received a refund of mortgage interest you overpaid in an earlier year, you generally will receive a Form 1098 showing the refund in box 3. See *Refunds of interest,* earlier.

Investment Interest

This section discusses the interest expenses you may be able to deduct as an investor.

If you borrow money to buy property you hold for investment, the interest you pay is investment interest. You can deduct investment interest subject to the limit discussed later. However, you cannot deduct interest you incurred to produce tax-exempt income. Nor can you deduct interest expenses on straddles.

Investment interest does not include any qualified home mortgage interest or any interest taken into account in computing income or loss from a passive activity.

Investment Property

Property held for investment includes property that produces interest, dividends, annuities, or royalties not derived in the ordinary course of a trade or business. It also includes property that produces gain or loss (not derived in the ordinary course of a trade or business) from the sale or trade of property producing these types of income or held for investment (other than an interest in a passive activity). Investment property also includes an interest in a trade or business activity in which you did not materially participate (other than a passive activity).

Partners, shareholders, and beneficiaries. To determine your investment interest, combine your share of investment interest from a partnership, S corporation, estate, or trust with your other investment interest.

Allocation of Interest Expense

If you borrow money for business or personal purposes as well as for investment, you must allocate the debt among those purposes. Only the interest expense on the part of the debt used for investment purposes is treated as investment interest. The allocation is not affected by the use of property that secures the debt.

Limit on Deduction

Generally, your deduction for investment interest expense is limited to the amount of your *net investment income.*

You can carry over the amount of investment interest that you could not deduct because of this limit to the next tax year. The interest carried over is treated as investment interest paid or accrued in that next year.

You can carry over disallowed investment interest to the next tax year even if it is more than your taxable income in the year the interest was paid or accrued.

Net Investment Income
Determine the amount of your net investment income by subtracting your investment expenses (other than interest expense) from your investment income.

Investment income. This generally includes your gross income from property held for investment (such as interest, dividends, annuities, and royalties). Investment income does not include Alaska Permanent Fund dividends.

Choosing to include net capital gain. Investment income generally does not include net capital gain from disposing of investment property (including capital gain distributions from mutual funds). However, you can choose to include all or part of your net capital gain in investment income.

You make this choice by completing line 4e of Form 4952 according to its instructions.

If you choose to include any amount of your net capital gain in investment income, you must reduce your net capital gain that is eligible for the lower capital gains tax rates by the same amount.

Tip. *Before making this choice, consider the overall effect on your tax liability. Compare your tax if you make this choice with your tax if you do not.*

Investment income of child reported on parent's return. Investment income includes the part of your child's interest and dividend income that you choose to report on your return. If the child does not have Alaska Permanent Fund dividends or capital gain distributions, this is the amount on line 6 of Form 8814, *Parents' Election To Report Child's Interest and Dividends.*

Child's Alaska Permanent Fund dividends. If part of the amount you report is your child's Alaska Permanent Fund dividends, that part does not count as investment income. To figure the amount of your child's income that you can consider your investment income, start with the amount on line 6 of Form 8814. Multiply that amount by a percentage that is equal to the Alaska Permanent Fund dividends divided by the total amount of interest and dividend income on lines 1a and 2 of Form 8814. Subtract the result from the amount on line 6 of Form 8814.

Child's capital gain distributions. If part of the amount you report is your child's capital gain distributions, that part (which is reported on line 13 of Schedule D or line 13 of Form 1040) generally does not count as investment income. However, you can choose to include all or part of it in investment income. See chapter 3 of Publication 550 to figure the amount to include.

Your investment income also includes the amount on line 6 of Form 8814 (or, if applicable, the amount figured under *Child's Alaska Permanent Fund dividends*, earlier.

Investment expenses. Investment expenses include all income-producing expenses (other than interest expense) relating to investment property that are allowable deductions after applying the 2% limit that applies to miscellaneous itemized deductions. Use the smaller of:

1) The investment expenses included on line 22 of Schedule A (Form 1040), or
2) The amount on line 26 of Schedule A.

Losses from passive activities. Income or expenses that you used in computing income or loss from a passive activity are not included in determining your investment income or investment expenses (including investment interest expense). See Publication 925, *Passive Activity and At-Risk Rules*, for information about passive activities.

Form 4952

Use Form 4952, *Investment Interest Expense Deduction*, to figure your deduction for investment interest.

Exception to use of Form 4952. You do not have to complete Form 4952 or attach it to your return if you meet all of the following tests.

• Your investment interest expense is not more than your investment income from interest and ordinary dividends.
• You have no other deductible investment expenses.
• You have no disallowed investment interest expense from 2000.

If you meet all of these tests, you can deduct all of your investment interest.

More Information

For more information on investment interest, see *Investment Expenses* in chapter 3 of Publication 550.

Items You Cannot Deduct

Some interest payments are not deductible. Certain expenses similar to interest also are not deductible. Nondeductible expenses include the following items.

• Personal interest (discussed later).
• Service charges (however, see *Other Expenses* in chapter 30).
• Annual fees for credit cards.
• Loan fees.
• Credit investigation fees.
• FHA mortgage insurance premiums and VA funding fees.
• Interest to purchase or carry tax-exempt securities.

Explanation
While the general rule is that interest paid on a debt incurred to purchase or carry tax-exempt obligations is not deductible, this does not mean that if you hold tax-exempt obligations, all interest expense deductions are disallowed. The courts have consistently held that there must be a sufficiently direct relationship between the incurring of the debt and the carrying of the tax-exempt obligation before the interest is disallowed. However, if you have significant interest expense and municipal bond income, you may lose your interest deductions.

The IRS has ruled that a direct relationship between debt and the purchase of tax-exempt obligations exists when the debt proceeds are used for, and are directly traceable to,

the purchase of tax-exempts. A direct relationship between debt and the carrying of tax-exempt obligations exists when tax-exempts are used as collateral for a loan.

If only part of a debt you have is related to the holding of tax-exempt obligations, only that part of the interest paid is not allowed.

Example
Barry and Tricia borrow $10,000 from a bank and invest $2,500 of the proceeds in tax-exempt obligations. In this case, 25% ($2,500 ÷ $10,000) of the interest they pay on the loan is not deductible as investment interest.

TAXPLANNER
Don't worry about whether or not you use debt to acquire or carry tax-exempt obligations if your investment in tax-exempts is "insubstantial." The IRS defines "insubstantial" as being less than 2% of the average **adjusted basis** of your portfolio investments and business assets.

Penalties. You cannot deduct fines and penalties for violations of law, regardless of their nature.

TAXPLANNER
If you used borrowed funds to pay interest. To get an interest deduction when you use borrowed funds to pay interest, you need to be careful in structuring the transaction. Generally, the IRS says that meeting an interest obligation by giving a new note or increasing the amount due on an old note does *not* constitute payment. A deduction would be allowed only when the renewed note is paid. If, however, you borrow the money to pay the interest from a *different creditor*, the interest deduction would be allowed.

Nevertheless, the Tax Court allowed an interest deduction when the purpose of the second loan was not limited to the payment of interest on the first loan and the taxpayer showed that he could have paid the interest with other funds. You can't be too cautious in this area. Borrow from a second lender whenever possible.

TAXPLANNER
Margin interest. Stockbrokers charge you interest on a margin account—an account in which you place the money you have borrowed from your broker to purchase stocks or bonds. For the interest to be deductible, there must be a subsequent payment to your broker in cash. Alternatively, you may specifically allocate proceeds from dividends, interest, or stock sales to cover the interest. Merely charging the account does not constitute payment.

Personal Interest

Personal interest is not deductible. Personal interest is any interest that is not home mortgage interest, investment interest, business interest, or other deductible interest. It includes the following items.

• Interest on car loans (unless you use the car for business).
• Interest on federal, state, or local income tax.
• Finance charges on credit cards, retail installment contracts, and revolving charge accounts incurred for personal expenses.
• Late payment charges by a public utility.

TAXPLANNER

When you are faced with the necessity of purchasing both a house and a large-ticket consumer item (e.g., a car), you should consider the tax nature of the debt, particularly the value of the deductible interest on acquisition debt compared to loans that are repaid with nondeductible interest. Your future plans to purchase consumer items should play an important role in your mortgage and other financing decisions. In addition, if you plan ahead, you can avoid the additional costs of refinancing your mortgage or taking out a home equity loan in order to make your consumer purchases.

Example 1

Suppose you plan to finance the purchase of a car next year. If you take out a longer-term mortgage with lower payments than you might otherwise have done, you can apply the difference to your car payments. This will enable you to reduce the term of your car loan, which most likely will be financed at a higher rate than your mortgage and paid for with nondeductible interest.

Example 2

You are considering purchasing a new house and a new car within a relatively short time period. You may want to decrease your down payment on the house so that there will be extra cash available for a down payment on the car. By paying a larger down payment on the car, your nondeductible interest will be less. Conversely, by decreasing your down payment on the house, you gain a tax benefit in the form of higher mortgage interest deductions.

Tip. *You may be able to deduct interest you pay on a qualified* **student loan.** *For details, see Publication 970.*

Explanation

Student loan interest deduction. You can claim a deduction for interest paid on qualified education loans that include indebtedness incurred for your benefit or the benefit of your spouse, or any dependent at the time the indebtedness is incurred. Qualified loans also include refinancings or consolidations of the original loans. You can claim this deduction whether or not you itemize your deductions.

The deduction is allowed only for interest paid on a qualified education loan during the first 60 months in which interest payments are required on each loan outstanding (the original loan or loans and subsequent refinancing of those loans are treated as one loan for purposes of counting the first 60 months). Months during which the qualified education loan is deferred or in forbearance do not count against the 60-month period. No deduction is allowed for individuals claimed as dependents on another taxpayer's return for the tax year.

The maximum deduction is $2,500 in 2001.

The deduction is phased out for individual single taxpayers with modified adjusted gross income (AGI) of $40,000–$55,000 and for couples filing jointly with modified AGI of $60,000–$75,000.

The deduction is effective for the first 60 months of interest payments due and paid after December 31, 1997, on any qualified education loan. Old loans entered into before the date of enactment qualify, but only for the first 60 months of payments under those loans.

TAXALERT

Effective for the 2002 tax year the student loan interest deduction will no longer be limited to the first 60 months of interest payments. In addition, the income phase out ranges for the deduction will be raised. The new phase out range for single taxpayers will be increased to $50,000 – 65,000 (from $40,000 – $55,000) and to $100,000 – $130,000 (from $60,000 – $75,000) for taxpayers filing joint returns.

TAXSAVER

What loans can't include. Education loans include loans covering both tuition and room and board. However, loans cannot include educational expenses that are paid through amounts from an employer educational assistance program or from amounts withdrawn from a Coverdell education savings account. It is unclear how students or the IRS will be able to separate these expenses from the total loans received and payments made on those loans.

The U.S. Treasury is authorized to require lenders to report to borrowers the amount that constitutes deductible student loan interest. The government is also to devise a method for borrowers to certify to lenders that loan proceeds are being used to pay for qualified educational expenses.

As with the education tax credits, this deduction is another factor to consider in determining whether or not a working student should be claimed as a dependent. Parents with income above the income thresholds cannot claim this deduction.

For further information about claiming the student loan interest deduction and a worksheet, see Chapter 47, *Filling Out Form 1040,* line 24, Student Loan Interest Deduction.

Explanation

Interest you pay on loans acquired to purchase life insurance is also personal interest and generally is not deductible under current law.

TAXPLANNER

If you have loans outstanding for personal purposes, consider paying off these loans and substituting a different form of indebtedness.

Example

You have a $5,000 indebtedness on your credit card account. The funds were used for various personal purposes, and the interest is not deductible. You also have a $5,000 certificate of deposit (CD) that matures in 2001. Use the $5,000 from the maturity of the CD to pay off the credit card indebtedness. If you wish, you may borrow new funds for investment in a new CD. The interest on the new borrowings will be investment interest. The rules for deducting investment interest expense are more lenient than those for personal interest. Be sure to calculate the amount you would earn after taxes on such a borrowing/investment.

Allocation of Interest

If you use the proceeds of a loan for more than one purpose (for example, personal and business), you must allocate the interest on the loan to each use. However, you do not have to allocate home mortgage interest if it is fully deductible, regardless of how the funds are used.

You allocate interest (other than fully deductible home mortgage interest) on a loan in the same way as the loan itself is allocated. You do this by tracing disbursements of the debt proceeds to specific uses. For details on how to do this, see chapter 5 of Publication 535.

Explanation

There are five types of interest expense, each of which has different limitations on deductibility:

1. Personal interest is not deductible (except for a limited amount of student loan interest described earlier in this chapter). Personal interest generally includes interest on credit card debts and on automobile loans. If you have to incur debt, try to make the debt related to either trade or business interest, investment interest, passive activity interest, or qualified residence interest.
2. Trade or business interest is fully deductible. Generally, it is interest on debt that relates to your trade or business. However, trade or business interest is *not* deductible if it is in connection with the trade or business of performing services as an employee.
3. Investment interest deductions may be limited because the deduction cannot exceed your net investment income for the taxable year. Any excess investment interest that is not deductible in the taxable year may be deducted in following years.
4. Passive activity interest is interest that is used to offset passive activity income. Generally, a passive activity is any interest in a real estate or other activity in which you do not materially participate. For tax purposes, you are considered a material participant if you are involved in the operations of the activity on a regular, continuous, and substantial basis. For additional discussion, see Chapter 13, *Other Income.*
5. Interest on a debt secured by a qualified residence is deductible within the limitations discussed in this chapter.

TaxSaver

When interest on debt used for investment exceeds investment income, the remaining investment interest may be deducted if it is qualified residence interest.

Example

In 2001, you purchase stock for $200,000, using a 9.0% home equity loan. Your investment income is $5,000.

Interest on your home equity loan	$18,000
Interest on portion of loan up to $100,000	9,000
Balance investment interest expense	$9,000
Deductible investment interest equal to investment income	5,000
Investment interest expense carryover to 2002	$4,000

TaxSaver

Regardless of the rules pertaining to passive income limitations, interest on debt used for a passive activity may be deducted if it is qualified residence interest.

Example 1

Phil borrowed money to purchase a one-fourth interest in a partnership that manages an apartment building. In 2001, Phil paid $16,000 interest on the loan. His share of income and expenses was $60,000 and $40,000, respectively. Phil's passive income is $4,000 ($60,000 − $40,000 − $16,000). If his share of the partnership's expenses had been $50,000 instead of $40,000, Phil's $16,000 in in-

terest expense would have resulted in a passive loss of $6,000 ($60,000 − $50,000 − $16,000). This loss can be carried over to future years in which there is additional passive income.

Example 2

Karen Moore has the following income and expenses in 2001:

Wages	$79,000
Dividends	10,000
Short-term capital gain from sale of stock	2,000
Long-term capital gain taxed at 20%	1,000
Interest	8,000
Adjusted gross income (AGI)	$100,000
Investment interest expense	$21,000
Investment fees	2,500
Unreimbursed employee expenses	1,000

Karen's total miscellaneous itemized deductions are $3,500 ($2,500 + $1,000). After considering the 2% floor limitation, her allowable miscellaneous itemized deductions are $1,500 [$3,500 − (2% × $100,000 AGI)]. Therefore, Karen's net investment income is $18,500 [($10,000 + $2,000 + $8,000) − $1,500]. Because the long-term capital gain is taxed at 20%, it is not considered investment income. Karen could elect to treat the gain as ordinary income and would then be allowed to treat the $1,000 as investment income. Note that, in computing the allowable deductions, the noninvestment expenses were disallowed *before* the investment expenses.

Explanation

The proceeds of loans, other than qualified mortgage loans, which were used for mixed purposes, must be allocated to each applicable category.

Example

Joan borrows $100,000 on September 1, 2001, at an interest rate of 12% and deposits the funds in one checking account. Joan uses the money to purchase investment securities ($30,000 on September 1), a personal automobile ($30,000 on October 1), and equipment for her business ($40,000 on November 1). Joan pays interest of $1,000 at the end of each month.

Under the allocation rules, the interest on the loan is considered investment interest unless the proceeds are traceable to other purposes. The allocation is made as follows:

	Investment interest		Personal interest		Business interest	
September	100%	$1,000	—		—	
October	70%	700	30%	$300	—	
November	30%	300	30%	300	40%	$400
December	30%	300	30%	300	40%	400
Total		$2,300		$900		$800

When repayments of the debt are made, the repayment amounts are allocated first to nondeductible personal expenditures, then to investment and passive activity expenditures, and then to business expenditures.

TaxOrganizer

The accounting for interest expense on loans used for mixed purposes is extremely complex.

To simplify your tax records, establish separate loan and bank accounts for each category of expenditure.

TaxSaver

Interest on a qualified mortgage loan is not required to be allocated and is fully deductible when paid.

Although borrowing against your residence may ensure deductibility of the interest expense, the residence serves as collateral on the loan and may be foreclosed in the event of default.

How To Report

You must file Form 1040 to deduct any home mortgage interest expense on your tax return. Where you deduct your interest expense generally depends on how you use the loan proceeds. See *Table 25–1* for a summary of where to deduct your interest expense.

Home mortgage interest and points. Deduct the home mortgage interest and points reported to you on Form 1098 on line 10 of Schedule A (Form 1040). If you paid more deductible interest to the financial institution than the amount shown on Form 1098, show the larger deductible amount on line 10. Attach a statement explaining the difference and print "See attached" next to line 10.

Deduct home mortgage interest that was *not* reported to you on Form 1098 on line 11 of Schedule A (Form 1040). If you paid home mortgage interest to the person from whom you bought your home, show that person's name, address, and taxpayer identification number (TIN) on the dotted lines next to line 11. The seller must give you this number and you must give the seller your TIN. A Form W-9 can be used for this purpose. Failure to meet any of these requirements may result in a $50 penalty for each failure. The TIN can be either a social security number, an individual taxpayer identification number (issued by the Internal Revenue Service), or an employer identification number. See *Social Security Number* in chapter 1 for more information about TINs.

TaxAlert

Seller-financed mortgages. If you pay interest on a seller-financed mortgage, you are required to include the following information on line 11 of Schedule A (Form 1040):

- The seller's Social Security number or identification number
- The seller's name and address

You must also provide the seller with your Social Security or identification number. Obviously, the best time to exchange this information is at the closing. However, this rule also applies to prior agreements. If you do not have the seller's identification number, or have not provided the seller with your Social Security number, you should meet the requirements as soon as possible to reduce the potential for penalties.

If you can take a deduction for points that were *not* reported to you on Form 1098, deduct those points on line 12 of Schedule A (Form 1040). **More than one borrower.** If you and at least one other person (other than your spouse if you file a joint return) were liable for and paid interest on a mortgage that was for your home, and the other person received a Form 1098 showing the interest that was paid during the year, attach a statement to your return explaining this. Show how much of the interest each of you paid, and give the name and address of the person who received the form. Deduct your share of the interest on line 11 of Schedule A (Form 1040), and print "See attached" next to the line.

If you are the payer of record on a mortgage on which there are other borrowers entitled to a deduction for the interest shown on the Form 1098 you received, deduct only your share of the interest on line 10 of Schedule A (Form 1040). You should let each of the other borrowers know what his or her share is.

Mortgage proceeds used for business or investment. If your home mortgage interest deduction is limited but all or part of the mortgage proceeds were used for business, investment, or other deductible

Table 25–1. Where To Deduct Your Interest

Type of Interest	Where to deduct	Where to find information
Student loan interest	Form 1040, line 24 or Form 1040A, line 17	Publication 970
Deductible home mortgage interest and points reported on Form 1098	Schedule A (Form 1040), line 10	Publication 936
Deductible home mortgage interest *not* reported on Form 1098	Schedule A (Form 1040), line 11	Publication 936
Points *not* reported on Form 1098	Schedule A (Form 1040), line 12	Publication 936
Investment interest (other than interest incurred to produce rents or royalties)	Schedule A (Form 1040), line 13	Publication 550
Business interest (non-farm)	Schedule C or C-EZ (Form 1040)	Publication 535
Farm business interest	Schedule F (Form 1040)	Publications 225 and 535
Interest incurred to produce rents or royalties	Schedule E (Form 1040)	Publications 527 and 535
Personal interest	Not Deductible	

activities, see *Table 25–1*. It shows where to deduct the part of your excess interest that is for those activities.

Investment interest. Deduct investment interest, subject to certain limits discussed in Publication 550, on line 13 of Schedule A (Form 1040).

Explanation

A deduction is allowed for interest paid on indebtedness incurred to purchase or hold investment property. Investment property includes any property producing interest, dividends, annuities, royalties, or certain gains.

The amount of investment interest that may be deducted is limited to the amount of investment income less allowable expenses, other than interest, that are directly connected with the production of investment income. The allowable expenses include those expenses that are deducted on your tax return, after the 2% of adjusted gross income limitation on miscellaneous deductions. (For more information, see Chapter 30, *Miscellaneous Deductions*.)

If the investment interest paid exceeds investment income, the excess may be carried forward to offset investment income in future years.

No deduction is allowed for interest paid on indebtedness incurred to hold obligations that are exempt from federal taxation.

Example 1

In 2001, Lorraine borrows $83,000 to purchase White Company securities. During the same year, she earns $30,000 of net investment income and incurs $10,000 of interest expense on her loan. Lorraine can deduct the $10,000 interest expense as investment interest on Schedule A (Form 1040).

Example 2

George and Lisa Johnson, who file a joint return, have the following income and deductions in 2001:

Salary	$30,000
Interest and dividend income	20,000
Short-term capital gain	5,000
Adjusted gross income	$55,000
Investment advisory fees	$2,000
Investment interest expense	$31,000

Their deduction for investment interest is figured as follows:

Investment income	$25,000
Direct expense ($2,000 – 2% of $55,000)	900
Net investment income	$24,100
Investment interest deduction	$24,100

The $6,900 ($31,000 – $24,100) of investment interest expense that is not allowed as a deduction may be carried forward to 2002.

TaxAlert

Net long-term capital gains from the disposition of investment property are no longer defined as investment income for purposes of computing the limitation on investment interest deductions. You may, however, elect to include net long-term capital gain amounts in investment income for this purpose if you also reduce by the same amount the net long-term capital gain that is eligible for the special maximum capital gains rates. Short-term capital gains may still be included in the computation of investment income. For an additional discussion of reporting gains and losses, see Chapter 17, *Reporting Gains and Losses*.

Explanation

The 2% limitation on miscellaneous deductions applies first to deductions other than investment expenses.

Example

In the above example, if George and Lisa Johnson also had tax preparation fees of $500, the $1,100 (2% limitation) would reduce this amount first. The remainder, $600, would then reduce the investment expense, leaving $1,400 to be subtracted from investment income.

Explanation

Deduct interest on margin accounts on Schedule A (Form 1040) for the year in which you paid it. Interest on these accounts is considered paid when the broker is paid or when the interest becomes available to the broker through your account.

Deduct interest on money borrowed to buy a money market certificate on Schedule A (Form 1040). You must include the total interest you earn on the certificate in your income.

Example

You deposited $5,000 with a bank and borrowed another $5,000 from the same bank to make up the $10,000 minimum deposit required to buy a 6-month money market certificate. The certificate earned $250 at maturity in 2001, but you received only $100, which represents the $250 you earned minus $150 interest charged on your $5,000 loan. The bank gives you a Form 1099-INT, Statement of Recipients of Interest Income, showing the $250 interest you earned. The bank also gives you a statement showing that you paid $150 interest for 2001. You must include the $250 in your income. You may deduct $150 on Schedule A (Form 1040) if you itemize your deductions.

TaxPlanner

The amount that you forfeit to a bank or a savings institution as a penalty for premature withdrawal of funds from an account is deductible from your **gross income** in figuring your **adjusted gross income.** You need not itemize to get this deduction.

Amortization of bond premium. There are various ways to treat the premium you pay to buy taxable bonds. See *Bond Premium Amortization* in Publication 550.

TaxSaver

Premiums on taxable bonds. There are various ways to treat the premium you pay to buy taxable bonds. You may deduct amortizable bond premiums directly from interest income. This could be beneficial whether or not you itemize your deductions.

Explanation

Tax-exempt bonds. You must amortize the premium and reduce the basis of tax-exempt bonds. However, you may not deduct the amortized premium. See Publication 535, *Business Expenses*.

Market discounts. You may be able to deduct only some of the interest expense incurred to acquire or carry marketable bonds with market discounts. For debt obligations issued after July 18, 1984, the interest expense deduction will be limited to the sum of:

1. Interest income from marketable bonds
2. The interest expense in excess of interest income in (1) and accrued market discount

The disallowed interest expense is deferred until the bond is sold or matures and is deducted then. The interest limitation does not apply to tax-exempt obligations purchased before May 1, 1993, U.S. savings bonds, obligations with a maturity of 1 year or less, and certain installment obligations.

Example

Sam acquires a $100,000, 9% interest-bearing bond for $90,000 on January 2, 2001. The bond was originally issued at face value in 1996. It matures in 2011, 10 years after Sam purchased it. Sam borrowed money to acquire the bond. In 2001, Sam paid $10,200 in interest on the debt. The allowable interest deduction for the year is figured as follows:

(a)	Interest expense	$10,200
(b)	Interest income ($100,000 × 9%)	(9,000)
(c)	Net interest expense	$ 1,200
(d)	Accrued market discount ($10,000 ÷ 10 yrs.)	(1,000)
(e)	Net interest expense in excess of accrued market discount	$ 200

Total allowable interest expense is $9,200 [(b) + (e)]. The remaining $1,000 will be allowed as a deduction in the year in which the bond matures or is sold.

Sam may elect to include the accrued market discount in income for the tax years to which it's attributable, thus allowing all interest expense to be deductible. If Sam makes this election, it will apply to all market discount bonds he acquires.

See the discussion in this chapter regarding limitations on the deduction of investment interest.

Income-producing rental or royalty interest. Deduct interest on a loan for income-producing rental or royalty property that is not used in your business in Part I of Schedule E (Form 1040).

Example. You rent out part of your home and borrow money to make repairs. You can deduct only the interest payment for the rented part in Part I of Schedule E (Form 1040). Deduct the rest of the interest payment on Schedule A (Form 1040) if it is deductible home mortgage interest.

26

Contributions

Introduction

Americans give billions of dollars to charity each year. One explanation for that generosity may be that the federal government encourages charitable giving. It has long been the policy of the government to allow individuals tax **deductions** *for charitable contributions they make. In effect, Uncle Sam is contributing part of every dollar you give to charity.*

Even so, there are lots of rules governing charitable contributions, and it's important that you know them. This chapter tells you how to maximize your allowable charitable deductions and minimize your taxes. You'll learn why, for example, you might want to consider giving shares of stock instead of cash to your favorite charity. Just as important, the chapter tells you how to document your contributions.

Your 2001 itemized deductions may be subject to certain limitations if your adjusted gross income exceeds $132,950 ($66,475 if married filing separately).

For more information on this subject see Chapter 22, Limit on Itemized Deductions.

Important Reminders

Disaster relief. You can deduct contributions earmarked for flood relief, hurricane relief, or other disaster relief to a qualified organization (defined later under *Organizations That Qualify To Receive Deductible Contributions*). However, you cannot deduct contributions earmarked for relief of a particular individual or family.

Written acknowledgment required. You can claim a deduction for a contribution of $250 or more only if you have a written acknowledgment of your contribution from the qualified organization or if you have certain payroll deduction records. For more information, see *Records To Keep,* later in this chapter.

Payment partly for goods or services. A qualified organization must give you a written statement if you make a payment that is **more** than $75 and is partly a contribution and partly for goods or services. The statement must tell you that you can deduct only the amount of your payment that is more than the value of the goods or services you received. It must also give you a good faith estimate of the value of those goods or services. See *Contributions From Which You Benefit,* later in this chapter, for more information.

This chapter explains how to claim a deduction for your charitable contributions. It discusses:

- Organizations that are qualified to receive deductible charitable contributions,
- The types of contributions you can deduct,
- How much you can deduct,
- What records to keep, and
- How to report your charitable contributions.

A **charitable contribution** is a donation or gift to, or for the use of, a qualified organization. It is voluntary and is made without getting, or expecting to get, anything of equal value.

Form 1040 required. To deduct a charitable contribution, you must file Form 1040 and itemize deductions on Schedule A. The amount of your deduction may be limited if certain rules and limits explained in this chapter apply to you.

Useful Items

You may want to see:

Publication

☐ **78** Cumulative List of Organizations
☐ **526** Charitable Contributions
☐ **561** Determining the Value of Donated Property

Form (and Instructions)

☐ **Schedule A (Form 1040)** Itemized Deductions
☐ **8283** Noncash Charitable Contributions

Organizations That Qualify To Receive Deductible Contributions

You can deduct your contributions only if you make them to a *qualified organization.* To become a qualified organization, most organizations other than churches and governments, as described below, must apply to the IRS.

Tip. *You can ask any organization whether it is a qualified organization, and most will be able to tell you. Or you can check IRS Publication 78, which lists most qualified organizations. You may find Publication 78 in your local library's reference section, or on the internet at* **www.irs.gov.** *You can also call the Tax Exempt/Government Entities Customer Service at 1-877-829-5500 to find out if an organization is qualified.*

Types of Qualified Organizations

Generally, only the five following types of organizations can be qualified organizations.

1) *A community chest, corporation, trust, fund, or foundation* organized or created in or under the laws of the United States, any state, the District of Columbia, or any possession of the United States (including Puerto Rico). It must be organized and operated only for one or more of the following purposes.
   a) Religious.
   b) Charitable.
   c) Educational.
   d) Scientific.
   e) Literary.
   f) The prevention of cruelty to children or animals.

   Certain organizations that foster national or international amateur sports competition also qualify.

Examples
Contributions to the following U.S. and political subdivisions have been allowed:

• Contributions to the National Park Foundation
• Money donated to a state by an individual to defray expenses of hosting a governor's conference
• Contributions to a state for a parade incidental to a presidential inauguration

The IRS has ruled that the following are *not deductible* as contributions:

• Payments made to a state hospital for the purpose of reimbursing the state for the care of a person confined in the hospital do not constitute contributions made to a state for exclusively public purposes.
• The amount spent by a tenant for additions or improvements to government-owned housing is not deductible as a charitable contribution. Such amounts represent a nondeductible personal, living, or family expense.

2) *War veterans' organizations,* including posts, auxiliaries, trusts, or foundations, organized in the United States or any of its possessions.
3) *Domestic fraternal societies,* orders, and associations operating under the lodge system.

   Note. Your contribution to this type of organization is deductible only if it is to be used solely for charitable, religious, scientific, literary, or educational purposes, or for the prevention of cruelty to children or animals.

4) *Certain nonprofit cemetery* companies or corporations.

   Note. Your contribution to this type of organization is not deductible if it can be used for the care of a specific lot or mausoleum crypt.

5) *The United States* or any state, the District of Columbia, a U.S. possession (including Puerto Rico), a political subdivision of a state or U.S. possession, or an Indian tribal government or any of its subdivisions that perform substantial government functions.

   Note. To be deductible, your contribution to this type of organization must be made solely for public purposes.

Examples. Qualified organizations include:

• Churches, a convention or association of churches, temples, synagogues, mosques, and other religious organizations.
• Most nonprofit charitable organizations such as the Red Cross and the United Way.
• Most nonprofit educational organizations, including the Girl and Boy Scouts of America, colleges, museums, and day-care centers if substantially all the child care provided is to enable individuals (the parents) to be gainfully employed and the services are available to the general public. However, if your contribution is a substitute for tuition or other enrollment fee, it is not deductible as a charitable contribution, as explained later under *Contributions You Cannot Deduct.*
• Nonprofit hospitals and medical research organizations.
• Utility company emergency energy programs, if the utility company is an agent for a charitable organization that assists individuals with emergency energy needs.
• Nonprofit volunteer fire companies.
• Public parks and recreation facilities.
• Civil defense organizations.

Certain foreign charitable organizations. Under income tax treaties with Canada, Israel, and Mexico, you may be able to deduct contributions to certain Canadian, Israeli, or Mexican charitable organizations. The organization must meet tests that are essentially the same as the tests that qualify U.S. organizations to receive deductible contributions. For additional information on the deduction of contributions to Canadian charities, see Publication 597, *Information on the United States–Canada Income Tax Treaty.* If you need more information on how to figure your contribution to Mexican and Israeli charities, see Publication 526.

Explanation
Any organization can tell you if it is a qualified organization. Generally, charitable contributions must be made to organizations to be deductible. However, the courts have upheld contributions made to certain individuals on the grounds that the contribution was made to him or her as an

agent for the organization. Consider the following cases in which deductions were allowed:

- An individual established a scholarship fund consisting of a personal checking account. Recipients were picked by school principals on the basis of need and scholastic merit. Each check was signed by the donor and made payable jointly to the scholar and the school. The donor was not involved in the selection process.
- A host family acting as a caretaker for an individual under a Department of Public Welfare/Medical Assistance Program is entitled to deduct as a charitable contribution any unreimbursed out-of-pocket expenses incurred in supporting a participant.
- A taxpayer directed his bank to send a check to a specifically named missionary. He instructed the bank to inform the missionary that the check was for Presbyterian mission work. The Tax Court held that this was really a contribution to the church through the missionary as an agent for the church.

Exception

The Supreme Court ruled that funds transferred by parents directly to their sons while they served as unpaid missionaries were not charitable contributions "for the use of" the church, even though the funds were requested by the church.

Contributions You Can Deduct

Generally, you can deduct your contributions of money or property that you make to, or for the use of, a qualified organization. A gift or contribution is "for the use of" a qualified organization when it is held in a legally enforceable trust for the qualified organization or in a similar legal arrangement.

If you give property to a qualified organization, you generally can deduct the fair market value of the property at the time of the contribution. See *Contributions of Property,* later in this chapter.

Your deduction for charitable contributions is generally limited to 50% of your adjusted gross income, but in some cases 20% and 30% limits may apply. See *Limits on Deductions,* later.

Table 26-1 lists some examples of contributions you can deduct and some that you cannot deduct.

Explanation

Fair market value generally is the price that property would sell for on the open market. It takes into account many fac-

Table 26–1. Examples of Charitable Contributions—A Quick Check

Use the following lists for a quick check of contributions you can or cannot deduct. See the rest of this chapter for more information and additional rules and limits that may apply.

Deductible As Charitable Contributions	Not Deductible As Charitable Contributions
Money or property you give to:	Money or property you give to:
• Churches, synagogues, temples, mosques, and other religious organizations	• Civic leagues, social and sports clubs, labor unions, and chambers of commerce
• Federal, state, and local governments, if your contribution is solely for public purposes (for example, a gift to reduce the public debt)	• Foreign organizations (except certain Canadian, Israeli, and Mexican charities)
• Nonprofit schools and hospitals	• Groups that are run for personal profit
• Public parks and recreation facilities	• Individuals
• Salvation Army, Red Cross, CARE, Goodwill Industries, United Way, Boy Scouts, Girl Scouts, Boys and Girls Clubs of America, etc.	• Groups whose purpose is to lobby for law changes
• War veterans groups	• Homeowners' associations
	• Individuals
	• Political groups or candidates for public office
Costs you pay for a student living with you, sponsored by a qualified organization	Cost of raffle, bingo, or lottery tickets
Out-of-pocket expenses when you serve a qualified organization as a volunteer	Dues, fees, or bills paid to country clubs, lodges, fraternal orders, or similar groups
	Tuition
	Value of your time or services
	Value of blood given to a blood bank

tors that affect the value of property on the date of the contribution.

Example

If you give used clothing to the Salvation Army, the fair market value is the price that typical buyers actually pay for clothing of this age, condition, style, and use. Usually, such items are worth far less than what you paid for them.

TaxPlanner

Determining fair market value. A valuable tool for determining fair market value is IRS Publication 561, *Determining the Value of Donated Property*. The publication helps donors and appraisers determine the value of property given to qualified organizations and includes the kind of information you must have to support the charitable deduction you claim on your return.

A sale or purchase of similar property reasonably close to the date of your contribution is usually the best indication of fair market value. Replacement cost and opinions of experts are also valid methods for determining value.

IRS Publication 561 discusses pitfalls to be avoided in determining the value of donated property. Some pitfalls and how to avoid them are the following:

1. The best evidence of fair market value depends on actual transactions, not on some artificial estimate.
2. Do not consider unexpected events occurring after your donation of property in making the valuation. Generally, you should only consider facts known at the time of the gift.
3. Past events are not necessarily reliable in predicting future earnings and fair market value. For example, a taxpayer contributes all rights in a patent to a charitable organization. The patent has a history of high earnings, but the current trend reflects declining earnings. In this case, more emphasis should be placed on the earnings trend rather than on the earnings history.

The cost of an appraisal is not deductible as a charitable contribution, but it may be claimed as a miscellaneous itemized deduction.

You are required to obtain a qualified appraisal for certain noncash donations. A qualified appraisal must be made by an independent party. The charity or any person or entity related to the charity cannot render the appraisal. Appraisals are required for the donation of property with a claimed value in excess of $5,000. If you make gifts of two or more items of similar property during the year, the claimed value of all of those items will be added together in determining whether the $5,000 limit is exceeded. Appraisals are not required for the contribution of publicly traded stock and are required only for the contribution of nonpublicly traded securities if their claimed value exceeds $10,000.

The appraisal may not be made by the organization receiving the gift, the party from whom the taxpayer acquired the property, the taxpayer, or certain persons related to any of these persons.

The appraisal fee cannot be based on a percentage of the appraised value of the gift.

Form 8283, containing an acknowledgment of receipt of the property by the receiving organization and a certification by the appraiser, must be filed with the tax return on which the deduction is taken.

TaxSaver

In a recent case, the Tax Court disallowed a deduction for the contribution of stock in a prominent tax-preparation corporation because the taxpayers failed to get and attach an appraisal to their return.

TaxAlert

Accurate assessments. It is very important to get an accurate assessment of donated property because you may be liable for a special penalty if you overstate its value. You may be liable for the penalty if the value claimed on your return is more than 200% of the correct amount.

The penalty is 20% of the tax underpayment attributable to the overvaluation and may increase to 40% if the value claimed is 400% or more of the correct amount.

Contributions From Which You Benefit

If you receive a benefit as a result of making a contribution to a qualified organization, you can deduct only the amount of your contribution that is *more than the value of the benefit* you receive.

If you pay more than fair market value to a qualified organization for merchandise, goods, or services, the amount you pay that is more than the value of the item can be a charitable contribution. For the excess amount to qualify, you must pay it with the intent to make a charitable contribution.

Example 1. You pay $65 for a ticket to a dinner-dance at a church. All of the proceeds of the function go to the church. The ticket to the dinner-dance has a fair market value of $25. When you buy your ticket, you know that its value is less than your payment. To figure the amount of your charitable contribution, you subtract the value of the benefit you receive ($25) from your total payment ($65). You can deduct $40 as a contribution to the church.

Example 2. At a fund-raising auction conducted by a charity, you pay $600 for a week's stay at a beach house. The amount you pay is no more than the fair rental value. You have not made a deductible charitable contribution.

Examples

Even though it appears that the taxpayer received a benefit, the following charitable contributions were allowed by the courts and the IRS:

- A tornado destroyed several homes in a town. The local chapter of the American Red Cross provided food and temporary shelter to an individual whose home was destroyed. Motivated by gratitude, the individual made a contribution to the local chapter of the American Red Cross.
- A taxpayer owned a home in an area served by a volunteer fire department. No state or local taxes were used to support the fire department. The taxpayer made a contribution to its annual fund drive.
- A taxpayer's daughter was a member of a local unit of the Girl Scouts of America. The taxpayer made a contribution to that group.
- A taxpayer had a **dependent** parent who was a resident of a home for the elderly that was a member organization of a combined charity fund. The taxpayer made an unrestricted contribution to the combined charity fund, which distributed the contributions to the member organizations according to a formula.

- A taxpayer made a contribution for repairs to a chapel on his land used by the Catholic Church.
- A taxpayer donated fire-damaged buildings to a fire department for use in fire drills. The clearing of the land by the fire drills increased the value of the land. The court approved the deduction, saying that the benefit to the taxpayer was only incidental to the contribution.
- A real estate developer donated a piece of land to the local school board for a school site. The court held that the developer was not required by law to donate the land and did not receive any particular benefit.

Exceptions

A deduction for a charitable contribution was *not* permitted in the following instances:

- A person contributed a computer to a university, and the donor reserved the right to use the computer for 12 weeks per year.
- A person released frontage to a county for widening a road in order to obtain the required approval by the county planning commission of the development plan for certain lots prior to their sale. (However, the cost of the frontage is part of the total cost **basis** of the remaining property for determining the gain or loss on the sale of the property.)
- The amount paid by a taxpayer to purchase building bonds issued by a church was not a gift made to the church. However, if the taxpayer had subsequently given the bonds to the church, he would have been entitled to a charitable deduction for their fair market value at the time of the gift.
- A person made contributions to a nonprofit organization formed by parents of pupils attending a private school. The organization provided school bus transportation for members' children. The contributions served a private rather than a public interest.
- A taxpayer paid a fee to a nonprofit corporation for the privilege of taking up residence in a home operated by the corporation. This fee, along with a required entrance fee, entitled the taxpayer to lifetime care in the home. The fee represented a personal expense.

Athletic events. If you make a payment to, or for the benefit of, a college or university and, as a result, you receive the right to buy tickets to an athletic event in the athletic stadium of the college or university, you can deduct 80% of the payment as a charitable contribution.

If any part of your payment is for tickets (rather than the right to buy tickets), that part is not deductible. In that case, subtract the price of the tickets from your payment. 80% of the remaining amount is a charitable contribution.

Example 1. You pay $300 a year for membership in an athletic scholarship program maintained by a university (a qualified organization). The only benefit of membership is that you have the right to buy one season ticket for a seat in a designated area of the stadium at the university's home football games. You can deduct $240 (80% of $300) as a charitable contribution.

Example 2. The facts are the same as in Example 1 except that your $300 payment included the purchase of one season ticket for the stated ticket price of $120. You must subtract the usual price of a ticket ($120) from your $300 payment. The result is $180. Your deductible charitable contribution is $144 (80% of $180).

Charity benefit events. If you pay a qualified organization more than fair market value for the right to attend a charity ball, banquet, show, sporting event, or other benefit event, you can deduct only the amount that is more than the value of the privileges or other benefits you receive.

If there is an established charge for the event, that charge is the value of your benefit. If there is no established charge, your contribution is that part of your payment that is more than the reasonable value of the right to attend the event. Whether you use the tickets or other privileges has no effect on the amount you can deduct. However, if you return the ticket to the qualified organization for resale, you can deduct the entire amount you paid for the ticket.

Caution. *Even if the ticket or other evidence of payment indicates that the payment is a "contribution," this does not mean you can deduct the entire amount. If the ticket shows the price of admission and the amount of the contribution, you can deduct the contribution amount.*

Example. You pay $40 to see a special showing of a movie for the benefit of a qualified organization. Printed on the ticket is "Contribution—$40." If the regular price for the movie is $8, your contribution is $32 ($40 payment − $8 regular price).

Explanation

The IRS requires that charities determine the fair market value of benefits offered in exchange for contributions in advance of the solicitation and state in the solicitation, as well as in the receipt, tickets, or other documents, what portion of the contribution is deductible. The charity may advise donors that the full amount of a contribution is deductible if any of the following applies:

- The fair market value of all the benefits received in conjunction with the contribution is not more than the lesser of 2% of the payment or $76.
- The contribution is at least $38, and the only benefits received in connection with the payment are token items, such as bookmarks, calendars, key chains, mugs, posters, and T-shirts, bearing the organization's name or logo (i.e., low-cost articles with a cost not in excess of $7.60).
- The charity distributes unordered items to patrons. The distributed item must be accompanied by a request for a contribution and by a statement that the item can be retained whether or not a contribution is made. The aggregate cost per patron of these items cannot exceed $7.60.

Example 1

In 2001, a nonprofit broadcast organization sends its patrons a listener's guide for 1 year in return for a contribution of $40. The cost of the production and distribution of the listener's guide is $6 per year per patron, and its fair market value is $8. The listener's guide is not available to nonmembers by paid subscription or through newsstand sales. Because the cost of the listener's guide is $6 and it is received in return for a contribution of $40, the broadcast organization may advise its patrons that the full amount of the payment is a deductible contribution. However, if the cost of the publication exceeds $7.60, the charitable organization would be required to inform its patrons of the amount by which they should reduce their charitable deductions.

Example 2

Assume the same facts as in Example 1, except that the nonprofit broadcast organization also gives its patrons a coffee mug with the organization's logo. The cost of the mug to the organization is $3. Its fair market value is $5. The aggregate cost of the guide and the mug ($9) exceeds the 2001 limit of $7.60. The organization should inform its patrons that $27 of their contribution is deductible and $13 (the fair market value of the guide and the mug) is not.

Note: The result would be the same even if these benefits were received separately in return for two separate contributions of $20 each.

Membership fees or dues. You may be able to deduct membership fees or dues you pay to a qualified organization. However, you can deduct only the amount that is more than the value of the benefits you receive. You cannot deduct dues, fees, or assessments paid to country clubs and other social organizations. They are not qualified organizations.

Certain membership benefits can be disregarded. Both you and the organization can disregard certain membership benefits you get in return for an annual payment of ***$75 or less*** to the qualified organization. You can pay more than $75 to the organization if the organization does not require a larger payment for you to get the benefits. The following benefits are covered under this rule.

1) Any rights or privileges, other than those discussed under *Athletic events,* earlier, that you can use frequently while you are a member, such as:
   a) Free or discounted admission to the organization's facilities or events,
   b) Free or discounted parking,
   c) Preferred access to goods or services, and
   d) Discounts on the purchase of goods and services.
2) Admission, while you are a member, to events that are open only to members of the organization, if the organization reasonably projects that the cost per person (excluding any allocated overhead) is not more than $7.60. This amount may be adjusted annually for inflation.

Token items. You can deduct your entire payment to a qualified organization as a charitable contribution if both of the following are true.

1) You get a small item or other benefit of token value.
2) The qualified organization correctly determines that the value of the item or benefit you received is not substantial and informs you that you can deduct your payment in full.

Written statement. A qualified organization must give you a written statement if you make a payment to it that is ***more than $75*** and is partly a contribution and partly for goods or services. The statement must tell you that you can deduct only the amount of your payment that is more than the value of the goods or services you received. It must also give you a good faith estimate of the value of those goods or services.

The organization can give you the statement either when it solicits or when it receives the payment from you.

Exception. An organization will not have to give you this statement if one of the following is true.

1) The organization is:
   a) The type of organization described in (5) under *Types of Qualified Organizations,* earlier, or
   b) Formed only for religious purposes, and the only benefit you receive is an intangible religious benefit (such as admission to a religious ceremony) that generally is not sold in commercial transactions outside the donative context.
2) You receive only items whose value is not substantial, as described under *Token items,* earlier.
3) You receive only membership benefits that can be disregarded, as described earlier.

Expenses Paid for Student Living With You

You may be able to deduct some expenses of having a student live with you. You can deduct ***qualifying expenses*** for a foreign or American student who:

1) Lives in your home under a written agreement between you and a ***qualified organization*** as part of a program of the organization to provide educational opportunities for the student,

2) Is not your dependent or relative, and
3) Is a full-time student in the twelfth or any lower grade at a school in the United States.

You can deduct up to $50 a month for each full calendar month the student lives with you.

Tip. *Any month when conditions (1) through (3) above are met for 15 days or more counts as a full month.*

For additional information, see *Expenses Paid for Student Living With You* in Publication 526.

Mutual exchange program. You cannot deduct the costs of a foreign student living in your home under a mutual exchange program through which your child will live with a family in a foreign country.

Explanation
The deduction is limited to amounts that you actually spend for the well-being of the student during the taxable year while the student is a member of the household and a full-time student. Amounts you pay for the student's books, tuition, food, clothing, transportation, medical and dental care, and entertainment qualify for the deduction. Depreciation on your home, the fair market value of lodging at your home, or similar items are not considered an amount spent by you and are not deductible.

If you are compensated or reimbursed for the costs of having a student live with you, you may not take a deduction for any part of these costs.

Out-of-Pocket Expenses in Giving Services

You may be able to deduct some amounts you pay in giving services to a qualified organization. The amounts must be:

- Unreimbursed,
- Directly connected with the services,
- Expenses you had only because of the services you gave, and
- Not personal, living, or family expenses.

Explanation
Unreimbursed out-of-pocket expenses incurred in rendering services to qualified charities are considered contributions made "to" the charitable entities rather than "for the use of" the charitable entities, and, as such, the deduction may be subject to the 50% limit rather than the 30% limit. See *Limits on Deductions,* later, to determine if further limitations apply.

Table 26-2 contains questions and answers that apply to some individuals who volunteer their services.

Conventions. If you are a ***chosen representative*** attending a convention of a qualified organization, you can deduct actual unreimbursed expenses for travel and transportation, including a reasonable amount for meals and lodging, while away from home overnight in connection with the convention. However, see *Travel,* later.

You cannot deduct personal expenses for sightseeing, fishing parties, theater tickets, or nightclubs. You also cannot deduct travel, meals and lodging, and other expenses for your spouse or children.

You cannot deduct your expenses in attending a church convention if you go only as a member of your church rather than as a chosen representative. You can deduct unreimbursed expenses that are directly connected with giving services for your church during the convention.

Uniforms. You can deduct the cost and upkeep of uniforms that are not suitable for everyday use and that you must wear while performing donated services for a charitable organization.

Table 26–2. **Volunteers' Questions and Answers**

If you do volunteer work for a qualified organization, the following questions and answers may apply to you. All of the rules explained in this chapter also apply. See, in particular, **Out-of-Pocket Expenses in Giving Services.**	
Question	**Answer**
I do volunteer work 6 hours a week in the office of a qualified organization. The receptionist is paid $6 an hour to do the same work I do. Can I deduct $36 a week for my time?	No, you cannot deduct the value of your time or services.
The office is 30 miles from my home. Can I deduct any of my car expenses for these trips?	Yes, you can deduct the costs of gas and oil that are directly related to getting to the qualified organization where you are a volunteer. If you don't want to figure your actual costs, you can deduct 14 cents for each mile.
I volunteer as a Red Cross nurse's aide at a hospital. Can I deduct the cost of uniforms that I must wear?	Yes, you can deduct the cost of buying and cleaning your uniforms if the hospital is a qualified organization, the uniforms are not suitable for everyday use, and you must wear them when volunteering.
I pay a babysitter to watch my children while I do volunteer work for a qualified organization. Can I deduct these costs?	No, you cannot deduct payments for child care expenses as a charitable contribution, even if they are necessary so you can do volunteer work for a qualified organization. (If you have child care expenses so you can work for pay, see chapter 33.)

Foster parents. You may be able to deduct as a charitable contribution some of the costs of being a foster parent (foster care provider) if you have no profit motive in providing the foster care and are not, in fact, making a profit. A qualified organization must designate the individuals you take into your home for foster care.

You can deduct expenses that meet both of the following requirements.

1) They are unreimbursed out-of-pocket expenses to feed, clothe, and care for the foster child.
2) They must be mainly to benefit the qualified organization.

Explanation
You may deduct reasonable, unreimbursed out-of-pocket expenses you spend for underprivileged children to attend athletic events, movies, or dinners. It must be part of an event sponsored on behalf of a qualifying organization. Expenses for yourself are not deductible.

Unreimbursed expenses that you cannot deduct as charitable contributions may be considered support provided by you in determining whether you can claim the foster child as a dependent. For details see chapter 3.

Example. You cared for a foster child because you wanted to adopt her, not to benefit the agency that placed her in your home. Your unreimbursed expenses are not deductible as charitable contributions.

Car expenses. You can deduct unreimbursed out-of-pocket expenses, such as the cost of gas and oil, that are directly related to the use of your car in giving services to a charitable organization. You cannot deduct any part of general repair and maintenance expenses, depreciation, registration fees, or the costs of tires or insurance.

If you do not want to deduct your actual expenses, you can use a standard mileage rate of **14 cents a mile** to figure your contribution.

You can deduct parking fees and tolls, whether you use your actual expenses or the standard mileage rate.

You must keep reliable written records of your car expenses. For more information, see *Car expenses* under *Records To Keep,* later.

Travel. Generally, you can claim a charitable contribution deduction for travel expenses necessarily incurred while you are away from home performing services for a charitable organization only if there is **no significant element of personal pleasure,** recreation, or vacation in the travel. This applies whether you pay the expenses directly or in-

directly. You are paying the expenses indirectly if you make a payment to the charitable organization and the organization pays for your travel expenses.

The deduction for travel expenses will not be denied simply because you enjoy providing services to the charitable organization. Even if you enjoy the trip, you can take a charitable contribution deduction for your travel expenses if you are on duty in a genuine and substantial sense throughout the trip. However, if you have only nominal duties, or if for significant parts of the trip you do not have any duties, you cannot deduct your travel expenses.

Example 1. You are a troop leader for a tax-exempt youth group and take the group on a camping trip. You are responsible for overseeing the setup of the camp and for providing the adult supervision for the other activities during the entire trip. You participate in the activities of the group and really enjoy your time with them. You oversee the breaking of camp and you transport the group home. You can deduct your travel expenses.

Example 2. You sail from one island to another and spend 8 hours a day counting whales and other forms of marine life. The project is sponsored by a charitable organization. In most circumstances, you cannot deduct your expenses.

Example 3. You work for several hours each morning on an archaeological dig sponsored by a charitable organization. The rest of the day is free for recreation and sightseeing. You cannot take a charitable contribution deduction even though you work very hard during those few hours.

Example 4. You spend the entire day attending a charitable organization's regional meeting as a chosen representative. In the evening you go to the theater. You can claim your travel expenses as charitable contributions, but you cannot claim the cost of your evening at the theater.

Daily allowance (per diem). If you provide services for a charitable organization and receive a daily allowance to cover reasonable travel expenses, including meals and lodging while away from home overnight, you must include in income the amount of the allowance that is more than your deductible travel expenses. You can deduct your necessary travel expenses that are more than the allowance.

Deductible travel expenses. These include:

- Air, rail, and bus transportation,
- Out-of-pocket expenses for your car,
- Taxi fares or other costs of transportation between the airport or station and your hotel,
- Lodging costs, and
- The cost of meals.

Because these travel expenses are not business related, they are not subject to the same limits as business-related expenses. For information on business travel expenses, see *Travel Expenses* in chapter 28.

Contributions You Cannot Deduct

There are some contributions that you cannot deduct, such as those made to individuals and those made to nonqualified organizations. (See *Contributions to Individuals* and *Contributions to Nonqualified Organizations,* next). There are others that you can deduct only part of, as discussed later under *Contributions From Which You Benefit.*

Contributions To Individuals

You cannot deduct contributions to specific individuals, including the following.

- Contributions to fraternal societies made for the purpose of paying medical or burial expenses of *deceased members.*
- Contributions to *individuals who are needy or worthy.* This includes contributions to a qualified organization if you indicate that your contribution is for a specific person. *But* you can deduct a contribution that you give to a qualified organization that in turn helps needy or worthy individuals if you do not indicate that your contribution is for a specific person.
- Payments to *a member of the clergy* that can be spent as he or she wishes, such as for personal expenses.
- Expenses you paid *for another person* who provided services to a qualified organization.

  Example. Your son does missionary work. You pay his expenses. You cannot claim a deduction for your son's unreimbursed expenses related to his contribution of services.

- Payments to a hospital that are for services for *a specific patient's care* or for services for a specific patient. You cannot deduct these payments even if the hospital is operated by a city, a state, or other qualified organization.

TaxPlanner

Direct contributions to needy individuals. Direct contributions to needy or worthy individuals are not deductible. But, if you can show that the economic benefit derived by the specific individual is less than the contribution to the organization in whose care the individual is placed, the excess may be deductible.

Example
An individual made a contribution to a school for crippled children that her son attended. The donor required that a portion of her contribution be used to purchase a wheelchair for the exclusive use of her son. She was allowed a deduction for a charitable contribution for the amount by which the contribution exceeded the cost of the wheelchair. (The cost of the wheelchair may qualify as a medical expense.)

Contributions To Nonqualified Organizations

You cannot deduct contributions to organizations that are not qualified to receive tax-deductible contributions, including the following.

1) *Certain state bar associations* if:
   a) The state bar is not a political subdivision of a state,
   b) The bar has private, as well as public, purposes, such as promoting the professional interests of members, and

   c) Your contribution is unrestricted and can be used for private purposes.
2) *Chambers of commerce* and other business leagues or organizations.
3) *Civic leagues and associations.*
4) *Communist organizations.*
5) *Country clubs* and other social clubs.
6) *Foreign organizations* other than:
   a) A U.S. organization that transfers funds to a charitable foreign organization if the U.S. organization controls the use of the funds or if the foreign organization is only an administrative arm of the U.S. organization, or

Example
A contribution to the U.S. Red Cross is deductible, even though some portion of the contribution may be used outside the United States. If you make a contribution to a U.S. organization *directing* that it be sent to a foreign charitable organization to be used abroad, a deduction may not be allowed because the real recipient is not a domestic organization.

   b) Certain Canadian, Israeli, or Mexican charitable organizations. See *Certain foreign charitable organizations* under *Organizations That Qualify To Receive Deductible Contributions,* earlier.

Explanation
The Canadian, Mexican, and Israeli tax treaties provide that contributions to charitable organizations (other than charitable contributions to a college or a university at which you or a member of your family is or was enrolled) are subject to the U.S. percentage limits on charitable contributions, applied to your income from sources in each of these countries.

The organizations must meet the qualifications that U.S. charitable organizations must meet. The organization can tell you if it qualifies for deductible charitable contributions.

7) *Homeowners' associations.*
8) *Labor unions.* But you may be able to deduct union dues as a miscellaneous itemized deduction, subject to the 2%-of-adjusted-gross-income limit, on Schedule A (Form 1040). See chapter 30.
9) *Political organizations and candidates.*

Contributions From Which You Benefit

If you receive or expect to receive a financial or economic benefit as a result of making a contribution to a qualified organization, you cannot deduct the part of the contribution that represents the value of the benefit you receive. These contributions include the following.

- Contributions for *lobbying.* This includes amounts that you earmark for use in, or in connection with, influencing specific legislation.
- Contributions to a *retirement home* that are clearly for room, board, maintenance, or admittance. Also, if the amount of your contribution depends on the type or size of apartment you will occupy, it is not a charitable contribution.
- Costs of *raffles, bingo, lottery, etc.* You cannot deduct as a charitable contribution amounts you pay to buy raffle or lottery tickets or to play bingo or other games of chance. For more information on how to report gambling winnings and losses, see *Gambling Losses Up To the Amount of Gambling Winnings* in chapter 30.
- Dues to *fraternal orders* and similar groups. However, see *Membership fees or dues,* earlier, under *Contributions You Can Deduct.*

- *Tuition,* or amounts you pay instead of tuition, even if you pay them for children to attend parochial schools or qualifying nonprofit daycare centers. You also cannot deduct any fixed amount you may be required to pay in addition to the tuition fee to enroll in a private school, even if it is designated as a "donation."

Explanation

Tuition-type payments disguised as a charitable contribution are not deductible. Certain rules have been established by the IRS to determine whether an item is a tuition payment or a charitable contribution.

No deduction for a charitable contribution is allowed if *at least one* of the following conditions exists:

1. A contract under which a taxpayer agrees to make a "contribution," and that contract contains provisions ensuring the admission of the taxpayer's child
2. A plan allowing taxpayers either to pay tuition or to make "contributions" in exchange for schooling
3. The designation of a contribution for the direct benefit of a particular child
4. The otherwise unexplained denial of admission or readmission to a school of children of taxpayers who are financially able but who do not contribute

Other factors that are considered in deciding if a contribution is deductible include the following:

1. The absence of a significant tuition charge
2. Substantial or unusual pressure to contribute applied to parents of students
3. Contribution appeals made as part of the admissions or enrollment process
4. The absence of significant potential sources of revenue for operating the school other than contributions by parents of students
5. The contribution amounts are the same for all families or are paid pursuant to published guidelines for donations

Value of Time or Services

You cannot deduct the value of your time or services, including:

- *Blood donations* to the Red Cross or to blood banks, and
- *The value of income lost* while you work as an unpaid volunteer for a qualified organization.

TaxPlanner

Services to a charitable organization. If you contribute *your* services to a charitable organization, you are not permitted to take a charitable deduction for the value of your time or services. However, you are entitled to take a charitable deduction if you acquire the right to services to be performed by another and then gratuitously transfer that right to the charity.

Example

You purchase a series of six golf lessons from a local golf professional. Because you are unable to use the lessons, you donate them to your church for use in their raffle. The cost of the six lessons is deductible as a charitable contribution.

Personal Expenses

You cannot deduct personal, living, or family expenses, such as:

- **The cost of meals** you eat while you perform services for a qualified organization, unless it is necessary for you to be away from home overnight while performing the services, or
- *Adoption expenses,* including fees paid to an adoption agency and the costs of keeping a child in your home before adoption is final. However, you may be able to claim a tax credit for these expenses, and/or exclude from your gross income adoption expenses paid or reimbursed by your employer. See *Adoption Credit* in chapter 37 and Publication 968, *Tax Benefits for Adoption.*

You also may be able to claim an exemption for the child. See *Adoption* in chapter 3.

Appraisal Fees

Fees that you pay to find the fair market value of donated property are not deductible as contributions. You can claim them, subject to the 2%-of-adjusted-gross-income limit, as miscellaneous deductions on Schedule A (Form 1040). See chapter 30.

Contributions of Property

If you contribute property to a qualified organization, the amount of your charitable contribution is generally the fair market value of the property at the time of the contribution. However, if the property has increased in value, you may have to make some adjustments to the amount of your deduction. See *Giving Property That Has Increased in Value,* later.

Explanation

If you permit a charitable organization to use your property without charge (or at a minimal rate), no charitable deduction is allowed.

TaxSaver

The IRS, however, will allow charitable deductions for the cost of operation, maintenance, and repair of property directly related to the charitable organization's use of the property.

If you donate the use of your yacht to the church for use in their raffle, no income tax deduction is allowed for the rental value or other value of the donated use. Direct operating costs, such as fuel, used in connection with the donated use are allowable as a charitable contribution.

For information about the records you must keep and the information you must furnish with your return if you donate property, see *Records To Keep* and *How To Report,* later.

Partial interest in property. Generally, you cannot deduct a charitable contribution (not made by a transfer in trust) of less than your entire interest in property. A contribution of the right to use property is a contribution of less than your entire interest in that property and is not deductible. For exceptions and more information, see *Partial Interest in Property Not in Trust* in Publication 561.

Explanation

This rule does not apply to a contribution of a partial interest in property if that interest is your entire interest in the property, such as an income interest.

Nevertheless, there are some situations in which you may claim a deduction for a charitable contribution that is less than your entire interest in the property.

1. **Undivided part of your entire interest.** A contribution of an undivided part of your entire interest in property must consist of a part of each and every substantial interest or right you own in the property and must extend over the entire term of your interest in the property.

Example 1

If you own 100 acres of land and give 50 acres to a qualified organization, you may deduct the charitable contribution.

A court allowed a taxpayer a deduction when a 10% undivided interest in 44 works of art was donated to an art museum. The art museum did not take physical possession of the works of art at any time within a period that extended for more than a year after the donation. It was held that the art museum clearly had the right to possession for 10% of the days in the year and the fact that the museum did not exercise that right was not relevant.

2. **Remainder interest in a personal home or farm.** You may take a charitable deduction for a gift to a qualified organization of a **remainder interest** in a personal home or a farm if the gift is irrevocable.

Example 2

If you transfer a remainder interest in your home to your church but keep the right to live there for life, you may take a deduction for the value of the remainder interest transferred.

3. **Valuation of a partial interest in property.** The amount of the deduction for a charitable contribution of a partial interest in property is the fair market value of the partial interest at the time of the contribution. If the contribution is a remainder interest in real property, **depreciation** (figured on the **straight-line** method) and **depletion** of the property must be taken into account in determining its value. This future value must be further discounted at a rate set by the government. The rate is published each month, and you may use the rate for the month in which the contribution is made or, if you elect, the rate in either of the preceding 2 months. You should use the rate that produces the largest charitable deduction.

No deduction is allowed for the value of an interest in property transferred in trust unless the donor's entire interest is contributed to a qualified organization or unless the interest is an income interest or a remainder interest.

TaxPlanner

A deduction for a charitable contribution of an income interest in property made by a transfer in trust is allowed if the income interest is either a guaranteed **annuity** interest or a **unitrust** interest. A unitrust interest is the irrevocable right to receive payment of a fixed percentage of the net fair market value of the trust **assets** determined on a yearly basis, while an annuity interest is a right to receive a fixed percentage of the initial fair market value of the new assets.

A deduction for a charitable contribution of a remainder interest in trust is allowed if the trust is (1) a **pooled income fund,** (2) a charitable remainder annuity trust, or (3) a charitable remainder unitrust.

The use of these trusts may be very beneficial both to the individual and to the individual's favorite charity. Individuals with substantial wealth should consult their tax and legal advisors about using these mechanisms.

TaxAlert

Charitable remainder trusts. A special rule applies to charitable remainder trusts that require that the present value of the amount passing to a charity and the amount of the charitable deduction be no less than 10% of the fair market value of property contributed to the trust. Also, the annual annuity percentage of the charitable remainder trust cannot exceed 50%. Please consult your tax advisor regarding these special rules.

Future interests in tangible personal property. You can deduct the value of a charitable contribution of a future interest in tangible personal property only after all intervening interests in and rights to the actual possession or enjoyment of the property have either expired or been turned over to someone other than yourself, a related person, or a related organization.

Future interest. This is any interest that is to begin at some future time, regardless of whether it is designated as a future interest under state law.

Explanation

The amount of the deduction is the value of the future interest when you and the related person no longer have an interest in the tangible personal property. When these interests end, the deduction is allowed to you, even if there are other outstanding interests that must end before the future interest is realized by the qualified organization.

Example

In 2001, you transferred a painting to your daughter to use and enjoy for life. When your daughter dies, the painting will go to the local art museum. If your daughter irrevocably transfers her life interest to an unrelated person in a later year, you may take a charitable deduction in that year, but not sooner. The amount of your deduction is the value of the future interest in the painting at the time of the transfer to the unrelated person.

Determining Fair Market Value

This section discusses general guidelines for determining the fair market value of various types of donated property. Fair market value is the price at which property would change hands between a willing buyer and a willing seller, neither having to buy or sell, and both having reasonable knowledge of all the relevant facts. Publication 561 contains a more complete discussion.

Used clothing and household goods. Generally, the fair market value of used clothing and household goods is far less than its original cost.

For used clothing, you should claim as the value the price that buyers of used items actually pay in used clothing stores, such as consignment or thrift shops.

Example. Dawn Greene donated a coat to a thrift store operated by her church. She paid $300 for the coat 3 years ago. Similar coats in the thrift store sell for $25. The fair market value of the coat is therefore $25. Dawn's donation is limited to $25.

See *Household Goods* in Publication 561 for information on the valuation of household goods, such as furniture, appliances, and linens.

Cars, boats, and aircraft. If you contribute a car, boat, or aircraft to a charitable organization, you must determine its fair market value.

Certain commercial firms and trade organizations publish guides, commonly called "blue books," containing complete dealer sale prices or dealer average prices for recent model years. The guides may be published monthly or seasonally, and for different regions of the country. These guides also provide estimates for adjusting for unusual equipment, unusual mileage, and physical condition. The prices are not "official" and these publications are not considered an appraisal of any specific donated property. But they do provide clues for making an appraisal and suggest relative prices for comparison with current sales and offerings in your area.

Example. You donate your car to a local high school for use by their students studying automobile repair. Your credit union told you that the "blue book" value of the car is $1,600. However, your car needs extensive repairs and, after some checking, you find that you could sell it for $750. You can deduct $750, the *true* fair market value of the car, as a charitable contribution.

Large quantities. If you contribute a large number of the same item, fair market value is the price at which comparable numbers of the item are being sold.

Giving Property That Has Decreased in Value

If you contribute property with a fair market value that is less than your basis in it, your deduction is limited to fair market value. You cannot claim a deduction for the difference between the property's basis and its fair market value.

TaxPlanner

If investment property that you are planning to donate has declined in value, you may wish to consider selling it and giving the proceeds to the charitable organization. By following this strategy, you get the deduction (subject to limitations) for the capital loss, as well as the deduction for the charitable cash gift.

Giving Property That Has Increased in Value

If you contribute property with a fair market value that is more than your basis in it, you may have to reduce the fair market value by the amount of appreciation (increase in value) when you figure your deduction.

Your "basis" in property is generally what you paid for it. See chapter 14 if you need more information about basis.

Different rules apply to figuring your deduction, depending on whether the property is:

1) Ordinary income property, or
2) Capital gain property.

Ordinary income property. Property is ordinary income property if its sale at fair market value on the date it was contributed would have resulted in ordinary income or in short-term capital gain. Examples of ordinary income property are inventory, works of art created by the donor, manuscripts prepared by the donor, and capital assets held 1 year or less.

The amount you can deduct for a contribution of ordinary income property is its fair market value less the amount that would be ordinary income or short-term capital gain if you sold the property for its fair market value. Generally, this rule limits the deduction to your basis in the property.

Example. You donate stock that you held for 5 months to your church. The fair market value of the stock on the day you donate it is $1,000, but you paid only $800 (your basis). Because the $200 of appreciation would be short-term capital gain if you sold the stock, your deduction is limited to $800 (fair market value less the appreciation).

Explanation
Ordinary income property. If, on the date it was contributed, the sale of the property would have resulted in ordinary income or a short-term capital gain to the donor, it is ordinary income property. Examples of ordinary income property include inventory, letters, and memoranda given by the person who prepared them (or the person for whom they were prepared) and any property that was acquired and held for 1 year or less.

Example
You contribute inventory to your church with a fair market value of $20,000 and a cost of $8,000. Because the inventory is property that had previously been held for sale in the ordinary course of business, you would have recognized ordinary income of $12,000 had the property been sold. Therefore, your contribution of $20,000 is reduced by $12,000. Your deduction is limited to $8,000.

Capital gain property. Property is capital gain property if its sale at fair market value on the date of the contribution would have resulted in long-term capital gain. It includes capital assets held more than 1 year, as well as certain real property and depreciable property used in your trade or business and, generally, held more than 1 year.

Amount of deduction—general rule. When figuring your deduction for a gift of capital gain property, you usually can use the *fair market value* of the gift.

Exceptions. In certain situations, you must reduce the fair market value by any amount that would have been long-term capital gain if you had sold the property for its fair market value. Generally, this means reducing the fair market value to the property's cost or other basis.

Example
An individual purchased stock in 1982 for $1,000. He contributed it to his church in 2001, at which time it was worth $20,000. His charitable contribution deduction is $20,000, the fair market value at the date of the contribution.

Explanation
You usually may deduct a gift of capital gain property at its fair market value. However, your deduction is limited to your adjusted basis in the property in the following instances:

1. If the capital gain property is contributed to certain private foundations. (A private foundation receives only small or no contributions from the general public.)

TaxAlert

Contributions to private foundations. Contributions of qualified appreciated stock to private foundations are deductible at full market value subject to the 20% limitation, discussed later. If, on the date of contribution, market quotes are readily available and the sale of the stock would result in a long-term capital gain, it is qualified appreciated stock. An example would be shares of IBM that qualify for long-term capital gain treatment.

2. If you choose the 50% limit instead of the special 30% limit, discussed later. (See *Limit on Deductions*, later.)
3. If the property contributed is **tangible personal property** that is put to an unrelated use by the charity, that is, a use that is unrelated to the purpose or function of the charitable organization for which it was granted its tax-exempt status.

Example

If a painting you contribute to an educational institution is placed in the organization's library for display and study by art students, the use is *not* an unrelated use. But, if the painting is sold and the proceeds are used by the organization for educational purposes, the use is unrelated and your deduction is limited to the painting's cost.

TAXPLANNER

Before you donate a gift of tangible personal property, attempt to determine whether the use will be related to the charitable organization's exempt function. In such circumstances, ask the charitable organization to prepare a statement of intended use and retain it in your tax return file.

TAXSAVER

If you donate appreciated securities that you have held for more than a year, not only can you take a deduction based on the fair market value of the securities, but you will also avoid paying tax on the appreciation. Consequently, the cost of your contribution is reduced by the tax deduction you claim and the tax you avoided by not selling the property. In most cases, the charity does not incur any tax when it sells the property. Be careful, though, if the securities are the subject of a tender offer or other purchase agreement. The Tax Court has ruled that a gift of securities subject to such an agreement will result in income to the donor for the gain.

Example

You own stock worth $1,000. When you bought the stock more than a year ago, it cost you $100. If you sell the stock and donate the $1,000 to your favorite charity, you incur capital gains tax—possibly as much as $180, depending on what tax bracket you're in. If you contribute the stock directly to the charity, the $900 gain is not subject to tax if the property was held for more than a year.

TAXSAVER

To get the maximum tax benefit from a contribution of appreciated property, be sure that the property qualifies for long-term capital gain treatment if it is sold.

Example

You purchased stock for $1,000 on January 12, 2000. The stock was donated to your church on January 8, 2001, at which time it was worth $3,000. Because the $2,000 of appreciation would have been a short-term capital gain if you had sold the stock, your deduction is limited to $1,000. If, however, you had waited to make your donation to the church until January 13, 2001, and the stock was still worth $3,000, you would have been able to deduct $3,000.

TAXALERT

You can recognize a charitable contribution for the full fair market value of appreciated property for both regular and alternative minimum tax purposes.

Bargain sales. A bargain sale of property to a qualified organization (a sale or exchange for less than the property's fair market value) is partly a charitable contribution and partly a sale or exchange. A bargain sale may result in a taxable gain.

Explanation

The calculation of the gain on a bargain sale requires that you properly allocate your tax basis in the property sold. For example, consider the following facts:

Asset:	FMV	$1,000	
	Adjusted basis	$ 500	
Sold to ABC Charity for		$ 500	
Gain to taxpayer		$ 250	(Calculated as follows:)

$$\frac{\text{Sale price}}{\text{FMV}} \times \text{Adjusted basis}$$

$$\frac{\$500}{\$1,000} \times \$500 = \$250 \text{ allocated adjusted basis}$$

Gain = amount received − allocated adjusted basis

Gain = $500 − $250

Gain = $250

Charitable deduction is $500

More information. For more information on donated appreciated property, see *Giving Property That Has Increased in Value* in Publication 526.

When To Deduct

You can deduct your contributions only in the year you actually make them in cash or other property (or in a later carryover year, as explained later under *Carryovers*). This applies whether you use the cash or an accrual method of accounting.

Time of making contribution. Usually, you make a contribution at the time of its unconditional delivery.

Checks. A check that you mail to a charity is considered delivered on the date you mail it.

Credit card. Contributions charged on your bank credit card are deductible in the year you make the charge.

Pay-by-phone account. If you use a pay-by-phone account, the date you make a contribution is the date the financial institution pays the amount. This date should be shown on the statement the financial institution sends to you.

Stock certificate. A gift to a charity of a properly endorsed stock certificate is completed on the date of mailing or other delivery to the charity or to the charity's agent. However, if you give a stock certificate to your agent or to the issuing corporation for transfer to the name of the charity, your gift is not completed until the date the stock is transferred on the books of the corporation.

Promissory note. If you issue and deliver a promissory note to a charitable organization as a contribution, it is not a contribution until you make the note payments.

Option. If you grant an option to buy real property at a bargain price to a charitable organization, you cannot take a deduction until the organization exercises the option.

Borrowed funds. If you make a contribution with borrowed funds, you can deduct the contribution in the year you make it, regardless of when you repay the loan.

Limits on Deductions

If your total contributions for the year are 20% or less of your adjusted gross income, you do not need to read this section. The limits discussed here do not apply to you.

The amount of your deduction may be limited to either ***20%, 30%, or 50%*** of your adjusted gross income, depending on the type of property you give and the type of organization you give it to. These limits are described below.

If your contributions are more than any of the limits that apply, see *Carryovers* under *How To Figure Your Deduction When Limits Apply* in Publication 526.

50% Limit

This limit applies to the total of all charitable contributions you make during the year. This means that your deduction for charitable contributions cannot be more than 50% of your adjusted gross income for the year.

The 50% limit is the only limit that applies to gifts to organizations listed below under *50% limit organizations.* But there is one **exception.** The 30% limit also applies to such gifts if they are gifts of capital gain property for which you figure your deduction using fair market value without reduction for appreciation. (See *30% Limit,* later.)

50% limit organizations. You can ask any organization whether it is a 50% limit organization and most will be able to tell you. Or you may check IRS Publication 78 or call the Tax Exempt/Government Entities Customer Service at the number listed earlier under *Organizations that Qualify To Receive Deductible Contributions.* The following is a partial list of the types of organizations that are 50% limit organizations.

1) Churches, and conventions or associations of churches.
2) Educational organizations with a regular faculty and curriculum that normally have a regularly enrolled student body attending classes on site.
3) Hospitals and certain medical research organizations associated with these hospitals.
4) Publicly supported charities.
5) Private operating foundations.
6) Private nonoperating foundations that make qualifying distributions of 100% of contributions within 2 1/2 months following the year they receive the contribution.
7) Certain private foundations whose contributions are pooled in a common fund, the income and principal of which are paid to public charities.

30% Limit

This limit applies to the following contributions.

- Gifts of capital gain property to 50% limit organizations. (For other gifts of capital gain property, see *20% Limit,* later.) However, the 30% limit does not apply when you choose to reduce the fair market value of the property by the amount that would have been long-term capital gain if you had sold the property. Instead, only the 50% limit applies. For more information, see the rules for electing the 50% limit for capital gain property under *How To Figure Your Deduction When Limits Apply* in Publication 526.
- Gifts (other than gifts of capital gain property as explained under *20% Limit,* later) **for the use of** any organization.
- Gifts (other than capital gain property as explained under *20% Limit,* later) to all qualified organizations other than 50% limit organizations. This includes gifts to veterans' organizations, fraternal societies, nonprofit cemeteries, and certain private nonoperating foundations.

20% Limit

This limit applies to all gifts of capital gain property to or for the use of qualified organizations (other than gifts of capital gain property to 50% limit organizations).

Explanation
An organization can tell you whether contributions to it qualify for the 50%, 30%, or 20% limit.
    Contributions to any charitable organization are limited to 50% of your adjusted gross income. This includes a gift of an income interest in trust to a charitable organization.

How to figure your deduction. To figure your deduction, first you consider gifts to charitable organizations that qualify for the 50% limit. Second, you consider gifts to which the 20% and 30% limits apply. Third, you consider gifts of capital gain property to which the special 30% limit for capital gain property applies.

Example 1
Your adjusted gross income is $50,000 for 2001. On September 1, 2001, you gave your church $2,000 cash plus land, with a fair market value of $30,000 and a basis to you of $10,000. You had held the land for investment for more than 1 year. You also gave $5,000 cash to a private foundation to which the 30% limit applies. Because your allowable contributions—$32,000 ($2,000 + $30,000)—to an organization to which the 50% limit applies are more than $25,000 (50% of $50,000), your deductions subject to the 30% limit are not allowable. The $2,000 cash donated to the church is considered first. The deduction for the gift of land does not have to be reduced by the appreciation in value and is limited to $15,000 (30% × $50,000). The unused part ($15,000) may be carried over for 5 years. Therefore, in 2001, your deduction is limited to $17,000 ($2,000 + $15,000). The $5,000 contribution to the private foundation may also be carried over for 5 years.

Example 2
Your 2001 adjusted gross income was $50,000. During the year, you gave $5,000 cash to a private foundation, to which the 30% limit applies. You made no other charitable contributions. The entire $5,000 is deductible, because 30% of $50,000 is greater than $5,000.

TaxPlanner
Contributions of inventory property that was acquired during the taxable year in which the gift was made are not subject to the percentage limitation rules. The cost of these items is claimed as part of the cost of goods sold.

TaxPlanner
To ease the restrictions on charitable contribution limitations, you may consider making a series of smaller gifts over several years rather than one or two large gifts per year.

Carryovers

You can carry over your contributions that you are not able to deduct in the current year because they exceed your adjusted-gross-income limits. You can deduct the excess in each of the next 5 years until it is used up, but not beyond that time. For more information, see *Carryovers* in Publication 526.

Explanation
For contributions made to private nonoperating foundations that are in excess of 30% of your adjusted gross income, or 20% for capital gain property, you may continue to deduct the excess in each of the next 5 years until it is used up.
    You may not carry over gifts to certain veterans' organizations, fraternal societies, and nonprofit cemetery companies to which the 20% limit applies.
    For other contributions in excess of the percentage limitations, you may deduct the amount carried over in the fol-

lowing year to the extent that it is not more than the applicable percentage of your adjusted gross income for that year less the amount donated to qualified organizations during that year. In other words, current-year contributions are considered *before* prior-year carryovers. The excess can be carried over for 5 years.

The carryover amounts retain their respective limitation percentages in the carryover year.

Excess contributions can be carried over only to subsequent returns of the person who made the gift. However, if the person who made the gift dies, the carryover is lost.

Example 1
You had adjusted gross income of $20,000 in 2000. During the year, you contributed $11,000 cash to your church. You deducted $10,000 in 2000 (50% of $20,000) and carried over $1,000. In 2001, you had adjusted gross income of $20,000 and contributed $9,000 during the year. You can deduct the entire amount that you carried over from 2000. However, if you had contributed $9,500 during 2001, you could deduct only $500 of the $1,000 you carried over, carrying over the balance of $500 to 2002.

Example 2
Your adjusted gross income for 2001 and 2002 is $50,000 and $20,000, respectively. During 2001, you contributed long-term capital gain property valued at $25,000 to your church. In 2001, you deducted $15,000 (30% of $50,000) and carried over $10,000. In 2002, however, your carryover deduction is limited to 30% of $20,000, or $6,000; the remaining $4,000 will have to be carried over to 2003.

Explanation
If a gift of long-term capital gain property subject to the 30% limitation is made and, for some unforeseen reasons, cannot be utilized entirely in the current year or in carryover years, you may elect to reduce its value by 100% of the gain and deduct the lower net value of the gift under the 50% limitation.

Example
Julia Walsh makes a contribution of long-term capital gain property that cost her $40,000 and now has a fair market value of $50,000. Julia dies during the taxable year. Her adjusted gross income on her final return is $80,000.

Without the election mentioned above, Julia's deduction would be limited to $24,000 (30% × $80,000). However, if the value of the property is reduced by $10,000, the deduction is increased to $40,000.

Records To Keep

You must keep records to prove the amount of the cash and noncash contributions you make during the year. The kind of records you must keep depends on the amount of your contributions and whether they are cash or noncash contributions.

TaxOrganizer

If the IRS raises questions. In case the IRS questions your charitable contribution deductions, you should keep the following information to support your claim for charitable contribution deductions:

- Canceled checks evidencing payments of charitable contributions

- Receipts (letter or other written communication) from the charitable organization showing the name of the organization, the date of the contribution, and the amount of the contribution
- Other reliable written records that include the information described above (records may be considered reliable if they were made at or near the time of the contribution, were regularly kept by you, or if, in the case of small donations, you have emblems, buttons, or other tokens that are regularly given to persons making small cash contributions)
- Copies of appraisals (if you are claiming a deduction in excess of $5,000) or other determinations of the market value of the contribution

Note. An organization generally must give you a written statement if it receives a payment from you that is more than $75 and is partly a contribution and partly for goods or services. (See *Contributions From Which You Benefit* under *Contributions You Can Deduct,* earlier.) Keep the statement for your records. It may satisfy all or part of the recordkeeping requirements explained in the following discussions.

Cash Contributions

Cash contributions include those paid by cash, check, credit card, or payroll deduction. They also include your out-of-pocket expenses when donating your services.

For a contribution made in cash, the records you must keep depend on whether the contribution is:

1) Less than $250, or
2) $250 or more.

Amount of contribution. In figuring whether your contribution is $250 or more, do not combine separate contributions. For example, if you gave your church $25 each week, your weekly payments do not have to be combined. Each payment is a separate contribution.

If contributions are made by payroll deduction, the deduction from each paycheck is treated as a separate contribution.

If you made a payment that is partly for goods and services, as described earlier under *Contributions From Which You Benefit,* your contribution is the amount of the payment that is more than the value of the goods and services.

Contributions of Less Than $250
For each cash contribution that is less than $250, you must keep one of the following items.

1) A canceled check, *or* a legible and readable account statement that shows:
   a) If payment was by check—the check number, amount, date posted, and to whom paid.
   b) If payment was by electronic funds transfer—the amount, date posted, and to whom paid.
   c) If payment was charged to a credit card—the amount, transaction date, and to whom paid.
2) A receipt (or a letter or other written communication) from the charitable organization showing the name of the organization, the date of the contribution, and the amount of the contribution.
3) Other reliable written records that include the information described in (2). Records may be considered reliable if they were made at or near the time of the contribution, and were regularly kept by you, or if, in the case of small donations, you have emblems, buttons, or other tokens that are regularly given to persons making small cash contributions.

Car expenses. If you claim expenses directly related to use of your car in giving services to a qualified organization, you must keep reliable written records of your expenses. Whether your records are considered reliable depends on all the facts and circumstances. Generally, they may be considered reliable if you made them regularly and at or near the time you had the expenses.

Your records must show the name of the organization you were serving and the date each time you used your car for a charitable purpose. If you use the standard mileage rate of 14 cents a mile, your records must show the miles you drove your car for the charitable purpose. If you deduct your actual expenses, your records must show the costs of operating the car that are directly related to a charitable purpose.

See *Car expenses,* earlier, under *Out-of-Pocket Expenses in Giving Services,* for the expenses you can deduct.

Contributions of $250 or More

You can claim a deduction for a contribution of $250 or more only if you have an acknowledgment of your contribution from the qualified organization or certain payroll deduction records.

If you made more than one contribution of $250 or more, you must have either a separate acknowledgment for each or one acknowledgment that shows your total contributions.

TAXALERT

Written acknowledgments. You are required to obtain a contemporaneous written acknowledgment from any charitable organization to which a contribution of $250 or more is made in order to deduct that contribution. *Contemporaneous* for this purpose means that you must obtain the written acknowledgment on or before the earlier of (1) the date on which your 2001 return is actually filed or (2) the due date for the return, including extensions.

A canceled check does not constitute adequate substantiation for a cash contribution of the amount. The written acknowledgment will have to state the amount of cash and a description (but not the value) of any property other than cash contributed. It must also state whether the charitable organization provided any goods or services in consideration for the contribution, and, if so, a description and good faith estimate of the value of goods or services provided. If the goods or services provided as consideration for the contribution consist solely of intangible religious benefits, a statement to that effect will have to be included in the written acknowledgment.

Note that the primary responsibility lies with you, not the charitable organization, to request and maintain the required substantiation in your records.

For any contribution over $75 for which the charity provides goods or services, such as a dinner, the charity must provide a statement to the donor that reports the estimated value of the goods or services received by the donor in exchange for the contribution. A payment to a charity is deductible only to the extent that it exceeds the value of any goods or services received in return.

TAXPLANNER

Separate payments. In general, separate payments are not combined for purposes of the substantiation requirement. Therefore, you could deduct separate contributions of less than $250 from each paycheck or make monthly payments to a charity without running afoul of the requirement. However, you could not, for example, simply write multiple checks on the same day in order to avoid substantiation. Similarly, separate payments made at different times with respect to different fundraising events are not totaled in order to determine whether the charity must inform the donor of the value of any benefit received in return for a donation in excess of $75.

Acknowledgment. The acknowledgment must meet these tests.

1) It must be written.
2) It must include:
   a) The amount of cash you contributed,
   b) Whether the qualified organization gave you any goods or services as a result of your contribution (other than certain token items and membership benefits), and
   c) A description and good faith estimate of the value of any goods or services described in (b). If the only benefit you received was an intangible religious benefit (such as admission to a religious ceremony) that generally is not sold in a commercial transaction outside the donative context, the acknowledgment must say so and does not need to describe or estimate the value of the benefit.
3) You must get it on or before the earlier of:
   a) The date you file your return for the year you make the contribution, or
   b) The due date, including extensions, for filing the return.

Payroll deductions. If you make a contribution by payroll deduction, you do not need an acknowledgment from the qualified organization. But if your employer deducted $250 or more from a single paycheck, you must keep:

1) A pay stub, Form W-2, or other document furnished by your employer that proves the amount withheld, and
2) A pledge card or other document from the qualified organization that states the organization does not provide goods or services in return for any contribution made to it by payroll deduction.

Out-of-pocket expenses. If you render services to a qualified organization and have unreimbursed out-of-pocket expenses related to those services, you can satisfy the written acknowledgment requirement just discussed if:

1) You have adequate records to prove the amount of the expenses, and
2) By the required date, you get an acknowledgment from the qualified organization that contains:
   a) A description of the services you provided,
   b) A statement of whether or not the organization provided you any goods or services to reimburse you for the expenses you incurred,
   c) A description and a good faith estimate of the value of any goods or services (other than intangible religious benefits) provided to reimburse you, and
   d) A statement of any intangible religious benefits provided to you.

Noncash Contributions

For a contribution not made in cash, the records you must keep depend on whether your deduction for the contribution is:

1) Less than $250,
2) At least $250 but not more than $500,
3) Over $500 but not more than $5,000, or
4) Over $5,000.

Amount of contribution. In figuring whether your contribution is $250 or more, do not combine separate contributions. If you received goods or services in return, as described earlier in *Contributions From Which You Benefit,* reduce your contribution by the value of those goods or services. If you figure your deduction by reducing the fair market value of the donated property by its appreciation, as described earlier in *Giving Property That Has Increased in Value,* your contribution is the reduced amount.

Deductions of Less Than $250

If you make any noncash contribution, you must get and keep a receipt from the charitable organization showing:

1) The name of the charitable organization,
2) The date and location of the charitable contribution, and
3) A reasonably detailed description of the property.

Tip. *A letter or other written communication from the charitable organization acknowledging receipt of the contribution and containing the information in (1), (2), and (3) will serve as a receipt.*

You are not required to have a receipt where it is impractical to get one (for example, if you leave property at a charity's unattended drop site).

Additional records. You must also keep reliable written records for each item of donated property. Your written records must include the following information.

1) The name and address of the organization to which you contributed.
2) The date and location of the contribution.
3) A description of the property in detail reasonable under the circumstances. For a security, keep the name of the issuer, the type of security, and whether it is regularly traded on a stock exchange or in an over-the-counter market.
4) The fair market value of the property at the time of the contribution, and how you figured the fair market value. If it was determined by appraisal, keep a signed copy of the appraisal.
5) The cost or other basis of the property if you must reduce its fair market value by appreciation. Your records should also include the amount of the reduction and how you figured it. If you choose the 50% limit instead of the special 30% limit on certain capital gain property, you must keep a record showing the years for which you made the choice, contributions for the current year to which the choice applies, and carryovers from preceding years to which the choice applies. See *How To Figure Your Deduction When Limits Apply* in Publication 526 for information on how to make the capital gain property election.
6) The amount you claim as a deduction for the tax year as a result of the contribution, if you contribute less than your entire interest in the property during the tax year. Your records must include the amount you claimed as a deduction in any earlier years for contributions of other interests in this property. They must also include the name and address of each organization to which you contributed the other interests, the place where any such tangible property is located or kept, and the name of any person in possession of the property, other than the organization to which you contributed.
7) The terms of any conditions attached to the gift of property.

Deductions of At Least $250 But Not More Than $500

If you claim a deduction of at least $250 but not more than $500 for a noncash charitable contribution, you must get and keep an acknowledgment of your contribution from the qualified organization. If you made more than one contribution of $250 or more, you must have either a separate acknowledgment for each or one acknowledgment that shows your total contribution.

The acknowledgment must contain the information in items (1) through (3) listed under *Deductions of Less Than $250,* earlier, and your written records must include the information listed in that discussion under *Additional records.*

The acknowledgment must also meet these tests.

1) It must be written.
2) It must include:
   a) A description (but not necessarily the value) of any property you contributed,
   b) Whether the qualified organization gave you any goods or services as a result of your contribution (other than certain token items and membership benefits), and

c) A description and good faith estimate of the value of any goods or services described in (b). If the only benefit you received was an intangible religious benefit (such as admission to a religious ceremony) that generally is not sold in a commercial transaction outside the donative context, the acknowledgment must say so and does not need to describe or estimate the value of the benefit.
3) You must get the acknowledgment on or before the earlier of:
   a) The date you file your return for the year you make the contribution, or
   b) The due date, including extensions, for filing the return.

Deductions Over $500

You are required to give additional information if you claim a deduction over $500 for noncash charitable contributions. See *Records To Keep* in Publication 526 for more information.

Explanation

A receipt is not required if you deposit property at a charity's unattended drop site unless you claim that the property is worth more than $250. However, you must maintain a written record of the contribution, listing the items contributed and the date and location of the contribution.

You are required to file Form 8283, *Noncash Charitable Contributions,* if you claim a deduction of over $500 for noncash contributions. Additionally, there are special rules for noncash contributions in excess of $5,000, discussed previously in this chapter.

For contributions having a fair market value of more than $500 but less than $5,000, the donor must provide the following information:

- The name and address of the donee organization
- The description of the donated property
- The date of the contribution
- The date it was acquired by the donor
- How it was acquired by the donor
- The donor's cost or adjusted basis (except for publicly traded securities or property held for more than 12 months)
- The fair market value of the contribution
- The method used to determine the fair market value (e.g., appraisal, thrift shop value, catalog, market quote, or comparable sales)

Form 8283 must be filed with the tax return on which the deduction is taken.

Qualified Conservation Contribution

If the gift was a "qualified conservation contribution," your records must also include the fair market value of the underlying property before and after the gift and the conservation purpose furthered by the gift. See *Qualified conservation contribution* in Publication 561 for more information.

How To Report

Enter your cash contributions (including out-of-pocket expenses) on line 15, Schedule A (Form 1040).

Enter your noncash contributions on line 16 of Schedule A (Form 1040).

If your total deduction for all noncash contributions for the year is over $500, you must also file **Form 8283.** See *How To Report* in Publication 526 for more information.

27

Casualty and Theft Losses

Introduction

Almost anytime something you own is stolen, damaged, or destroyed in an accident or by an act of nature and you are not compensated by insurance, you are eligible for a tax **deduction.** *The loss need not be connected in any way to your trade or business, and it may include such personal items as jewelry, furs, and antiques. That's small comfort if everything you own has been demolished in a terrible earthquake or a devastating hurricane, but it's something.*

In order to claim a **casualty loss deduction,** *you must prove first that the casualty occurred. The most difficult task is substantiating the value of the property you have lost. That gorgeous necklace that your grandmother gave you may be worth a substantial amount, but, unless you can prove it, you're going to have a difficult time claiming a tax deduction if it is stolen. Recordkeeping and documentation are extremely important.*

No matter how good your records are, you must first pass two general limitations on the amount of your casualty and theft loss. First, you may not deduct the first $100 of any loss. Second and more significant, you are able to deduct casualty and theft losses only when the total amount you lost in any year (reduced by $100 per casualty) exceeds 10% of your **adjusted gross income.** *(The rules for deducting business losses are different. They are also discussed in this chapter.)*

This chapter spells out which casualty losses are deductible. You'll also learn about the details that should be considered in deciding when to take your deduction. Most importantly, this chapter discusses the records and other evidence you need to support any claim that you make.

Generally, for 2001, your itemized deductions are limited if your adjusted gross income exceeds $132,950 ($66,475 for married persons filing separately). However, this additional limitation does not apply to casualty or theft losses.

Important Change

Postponed tax deadlines in disaster areas. The IRS may postpone for up to 120 days certain tax deadlines of taxpayers who are affected by a presidentially declared disaster. The tax deadlines the IRS may postpone include those for filing income and employment tax returns, paying income and employment taxes, and making contributions to a traditional IRA or Roth IRA. For more information, see *Postponed tax deadlines,* later, under *Disaster Area Loss.*

This chapter explains the tax treatment of personal (not business related) casualty losses, theft losses, and losses on deposits.

Explanation
This chapter, however, does include a discussion on what to do if a loss is partly business and partly personal. For ex-

ample, if your basement flooded and damage occurred to both personal property and business property from your home office located in the basement, the loss would be partly business and partly personal. See page 374 for more information.

The chapter also explains the following topics.

- How to figure the amount of your loss.
- How to treat insurance and other reimbursements you receive.
- The deduction limits.
- When and how to report a casualty or theft.

Forms to file. When you have a casualty or theft, you have to file Form 4684. You will also have to file one or more of the following forms.

- Schedule A (Form 1040), *Itemized Deductions*
- Schedule D (Form 1040), *Capital Gains and Losses*

Explanation
For details on which form to use, see *How to Report Gains and Losses,* later.

Condemnations. For information on condemnations of property, see *Involuntary Conversions* in chapter 1 of Publication 544.

Workbook for casualties and thefts. Publication 584 is available to help you make a list of your stolen or damaged personal-use property and figure your loss. It includes schedules to help you figure the loss on your home, its contents, and your motor vehicles.

Other sources of information. For information on a casualty or theft loss of business or income-producing property, see Publication 547.

For information on a condemnation of your home, see *Involuntary Conversions* in chapter 1 of Publication 544.

TaxOrganizer

Records you should keep. If you have a casualty or theft loss, you should retain the following items:

- Documentation of date, time, and place of occurrence of the casualty or theft
- Police reports
- Insurance reports including evidence of amount of reimbursed, if any
- Original receipts (if applicable)
- Repair bills
- Form 1099 (if applicable)

Useful Items

You may want to see:

Publication

☐ **544** Sales and Other Dispositions of Assets
☐ **547** Casualties, Disasters, and Thefts
☐ **584** Casualty, Disaster, and Theft Loss Workbook (Personal-Use Property)

Form (and Instructions)

☐ **Schedule A (Form 1040)** Itemized Deductions
☐ **Schedule D (Form 1040)** Capital Gains and Losses
☐ **4684** Casualties and Thefts

Casualty

A casualty is the damage, destruction, or loss of property resulting from an identifiable event that is sudden, unexpected, or unusual.

- A *sudden* event is one that is swift, not gradual or progressive.
- An *unexpected* event is one that is ordinarily unanticipated and unintended.
- An *unusual* event is one that is not a day-to-day occurrence and that is not typical of the activity in which you were engaged.

Deductible losses. Deductible casualty losses can result from a number of different causes, including the following.

- Car accidents (but see *Nondeductible losses,* next, for exceptions).

Explanation
Damage resulting from faulty but not intentionally reckless driving is a casualty loss. Damage incurred while an automobile was operated by an unauthorized person is also a casualty loss.

The following are examples of casualty losses involving automobiles:

- The loss of an automobile that fell through the ice while the taxpayer was ice fishing
- Damage to an automobile starter caused by a child who pressed the starter button while the automobile's engine was operating

- Earthquakes.
- Fires (but see *Nondeductible losses,* next, for exceptions).
- Floods.
- Government-ordered demolition or relocation of a home that is unsafe to use because of a disaster as discussed under *Disaster Area Losses* in Publication 547.
- Hurricanes.
- Mine cave-ins.
- Shipwrecks.
- Sonic booms.
- Storms.
- Tornadoes.
- Vandalism.
- Volcanic eruptions.

Explanation
Losses caused by a person's own negligence are deductible, as are losses that occur even though they could have been foreseen or prevented. The courts have also *allowed* casualty loss deductions in the following cases:

Animals and insects

- Damage caused by a mass attack of southern pine beetles capable of destroying a tree in 5 to 10 days
- Death of a horse by swallowing the lining of a hat

Drought

- Cracking of foundation walls due to soil shrinkage
- Death of trees and plants within 3 to 4 months as a result of extraordinary drought

Earthquakes and landslides

- Collapse of a garage wall due to subsoil hydraulic action
- Damage caused by a mine cave-in (a deduction was allowed even though the landslide was reasonably foreseeable)

Household

- Bursting of hot water boiler caused by air obstruction in water pipes
- Damage to furniture dropped 16 floors by movers
- Damage caused by a flood due to faulty construction (however, the cost of repairing the defect was not deductible)

Lightning

- Any damage by lightning

Personal belongings

- Damage to a diamond ring inadvertently dropped in a kitchen garbage disposal
- Damage to a ring caused by a husband slamming a car door on his wife's finger

Septic tank

- Damage by a tractor plowing the ground

Storms

- Damage to a beach due to abnormal rains
- Damage to a home by ice and snow
- Damage to a beach house that was caused by a hurricane but was not discovered until 2 years later, when the floorboards and porch buckled (the loss was deductible in the year in which the damage was discovered)
- Property damage due to unusually high water levels caused by storms

Trees, shrubs, and landscaping

- Damage caused by accidental application of chemical weed killer to a lawn
- Damage to trees caused by blizzards and snowstorms
- Loss of trees, shrubs, and grass due to fire

Vandalism

- Damage to household appliances caused by vandals who broke into a house under construction
- Damage and destruction of art objects by vandals

Nondeductible losses. A casualty loss is not deductible if the damage or destruction is caused by the following.

- Accidentally breaking articles such as glassware or china under normal conditions.
- A family pet.
- A fire if you willfully set it or pay someone else to set it.
- A car accident if your willful negligence or willful act caused it. The same is true if the willful act or willful negligence of someone acting for you caused the accident.
- Progressive deterioration (explained next).

Progressive deterioration. Loss of property due to progressive deterioration is not deductible as a casualty loss. This is because the damage results from a steadily operating cause or a normal process, rather than from a sudden event. The following are examples of damage due to progressive deterioration.

- The steady weakening of a building due to normal wind and weather conditions.
- The deterioration and damage to a water heater that bursts. *But* the rust and water damage to rugs and drapes caused by the bursting of a water heater *does qualify* as a casualty.

Explanation
The following also do *not* qualify as casualty losses: damage from faulty construction that caused walls and floors to settle, dry rot to a wooden sloop, and the decline in value of a piece of land affected by gradual deterioration. However, the breaking up of a driveway caused by weather conditions over a 4-month period has been allowed.

- Most losses of property caused by droughts. To be deductible, a drought-related loss generally must be incurred in a trade or business or in a transaction entered into for profit.

Explanation
A water well that ran dry because of a drought may not be deducted as a casualty loss. The courts have also *disallowed* deductions for casualty losses in the following cases:

Animals and insects

- Damage to shrubs eaten by a horse
- Damage to an antique vase by a cat
- Damage to a fur coat by moths
- Loss of a valuable dog that strayed off

Automobiles

- Damage to a fuel pump and muffler caused by high stones in a road (the taxpayer was unable to prove that it was more than wear and tear)
- Damage caused by a tire blowout due to overloading
- Damage caused by exposure to salt water
- Payments to the owner of a house into which a woman accidentally drove her car
- The forced sale of an automobile due to divorce
- Damage caused by potholes in the road

Earthquakes and landslides

- Any additional loss in value due to buyer resistance (a deduction is allowed only for physical damage)

Household items

- Sale of household items by a storage company (the sale was not an unexpected occurrence)

Personal belongings

- The loss of a ring from the owner's finger
- The accidental disposal of tissues in which two rings were wrapped
- The accidental dropping of eyeglasses or a watch
- The loss of baggage and contents in transit

Shipwreck

- The snapping of a propellor on a yacht that was not the result of a shipwreck or other casualty

Trees, shrubs, and landscaping

- Damage to trees from Dutch elm disease (the disease is progressive and not sudden or unexpected)
- The gradual suffocation of a root system over a 16-month period
- Damage to palm trees caused by lethal yellowing

- Termite or moth damage.
- The damage or destruction of trees, shrubs, or other plants by a fungus, disease, insects, worms, or similar pests. *But,* a sudden destruction due to an unexpected or unusual infestation of beetles or other insects may result in a casualty loss.

Explanation
The following are also *not* considered casualty losses: damage to trees and plants caused by moths, damage caused by rat infestation, the death of a horse from colic, and the loss of livestock due to disease.

Theft

A theft is the taking and removing of money or property with the intent to deprive the owner of it. The taking of property must be illegal under the laws of the state where it occurred and it must have been done with criminal intent.

Explanation
A theft loss is deducted in the year of discovery, not the year of the theft, unless they both occur in the same year. If, in the year of discovery, an insurance claim exists and there is a reasonable expectation of recovering the cost of the asset from the insurance company, no deduction is permitted.

Theft includes the taking of money or property by the following means.

- Blackmail.
- Burglary.
- Embezzlement.
- Extortion.
- Kidnapping for ransom.
- Larceny.
- Robbery.
- Threats.

Examples
A taxpayer from New York was allowed a deduction for a theft loss for money given to fortune-tellers. Under New York law, fortune-telling is a crime. The taxpayer's testimony and receipts were sufficient proof of the amounts paid to the fortune-tellers.

A moving company placed an individual's belongings in storage until a price dispute could be resolved. A court ruled that because there was a reasonable likelihood that the individual would recover his property, no theft loss was allowed.

Mislaid or lost property. The simple disappearance of money or property is not a theft. However, an accidental loss or disappearance of property can qualify as a casualty if it results from an identifiable event that is sudden, unexpected, or unusual.

Example. A car door is accidentally slammed on your hand, breaking the setting of your diamond ring. The diamond falls from the ring and is never found. The loss of the diamond is a casualty.

Explanation
Another type of loss you may experience is seizure, requisition, or condemnation. For example, the government might seize your home in order to build a new highway. For further discussion, see Chapter 14, *Basis of Property*, and Chapter 15, *Sale of Property*.

Loss on Deposits

A loss on deposits can occur when a bank, credit union, or other financial institution becomes insolvent or bankrupt. If you incurred this type of loss, you can choose one of the following ways to deduct the loss.

- As a casualty loss.
- As an ordinary loss.
- As a nonbusiness bad debt.

Explanation
For more information see *Special Treatment for Losses on Deposits in Insolvent or Bankrupt Financial Institutions* in the instructions for Form 4684.

Casualty loss or ordinary loss. You can choose to deduct a loss on deposits as a casualty loss or as an ordinary loss for any year in which you can reasonably estimate how much of your deposits you have lost in an insolvent or bankrupt financial institution. The choice is generally made on the return you file for that year and applies to all your losses on deposits for the year in that particular financial institution. If you treat the loss as a casualty or ordinary loss, you cannot treat the same amount of the loss as a nonbusiness bad debt when it actually becomes worthless. Once you make this choice, you cannot change it without approval of the Internal Revenue Service.

Explanation
A casualty or ordinary loss is deductible in the year incurred. It is subject to $100 per event and 10% of your adjusted gross income limitations (see *Deduction Limits* later).

Example
In 2001, Molly had an adjusted gross income of $25,000 and a loss of $7,100.

Casualty loss (minus $100 floor)	$7,000
Less: 10% of AGI (10% x $25,000)	2,500
Itemized deduction	$4,500

For 2001, Molly would have a $4,500 itemized deduction with no further tax deduction in the following tax year.

Nonbusiness bad debt. If you do not choose to deduct the loss as a casualty loss or as an ordinary loss, you must wait until the actual loss is determined before you can deduct the loss as a nonbusiness bad debt.

Explanation
A nonbusiness bad debt arises from loans between individuals and not those connected with your business. If you elect to treat the loss as a nonbusiness bad debt, the loss is treated as a short-term capital loss. Capital losses, net of capital gains, are subject to the $3,000 capital loss limitation in any 1 year, with any excess over the annual limit being deductible in following tax years. See Chapter 17, *Reporting Gains and Losses*, for a further explanation of the limitations regarding the deductibility of capital losses.

Example
If Molly chose to treat her loss as a nonbusiness bad debt, she would have a $3,000 loss in 2001, a $3,000 loss in 2002, and $1,100 loss in 2003, assuming no other capital gains or losses in these years. Her total allowable deduction is $7,100.

How to report. The kind of deduction you choose for your loss on deposits determines how you report your loss. If you choose:

- Casualty loss—report it on Form 4684 first and then on Schedule A (Form 1040).
- Ordinary loss—report it on Schedule A (Form 1040).
- Nonbusiness bad debt—report it on Schedule D (Form 1040).

More information. For more information, see *Special Treatment for Losses on Deposits in Insolvent or Bankrupt Financial Institutions* in the instructions for Form 4684.

Explanation
Deducted loss recovered. If you recover an amount you deducted as loss in an earlier year, you may have to include the amount recovered in your income for the year of recovery. If any part of the original deduction did not reduce your tax in the earlier year, you do not have to include that part of the recovery in your income. For more information, see *Taxable and Nontaxable Income* in Publication 525.

Proof of Loss

To deduct a casualty or theft loss, you must be able to prove that you had a casualty or theft. You must be able to support the amount you claim for the loss as discussed next.

Casualty loss proof. For a casualty loss, your records should show all the following.

1) The type of casualty (car accident, fire, storm, etc.) and when it occurred.
2) That the loss was a direct result of the casualty.
3) That you were the owner of the property or, if you leased the property from someone else, that you were contractually liable to the owner for the damage.

Theft loss proof. For a theft loss, your records should show all the following.

1) When you discovered that your property was missing.
2) That your property was stolen.
3) That you were the owner of the property.

TaxPlanner
It is important that you have records that will prove your deduction. If you do not have the actual records to support your deduction, you can use other satisfactory evidence that is sufficient to establish your deduction.

TaxOrganizer
Proving a theft took place. For a loss from theft to be deductible, you must be able to prove that a theft has taken place. Therefore, if you think a theft may have occurred, you should file a report with the police and attach a copy of the police report to your return. The report should tell of any evidence of breaking and entering and of any witness to the removal of the property. It is not necessary that the police investigate the alleged incident.

TaxOrganizer
Supporting evidence. If you are going to claim a deduction for a casualty or theft loss, it is important that you gather as much supporting evidence as possible. Newspaper clippings about a storm, police reports, and insurance reports may all be helpful in proving the nature of the casualty or theft and when it occurred. You have the burden of proof to establish that a casualty occurred and that your loss was a direct result of the casualty.

Explanation
If there is no positive proof that a theft occurred, all details and evidence should be presented. If evidence points to a theft, the Tax Court has allowed a deduction. However, if the evidence points to a mysterious (unexplained) disappearance, deductions will be disallowed.

Determining the decrease in market value of household items and personal belongings is often difficult. A certain percentage of the original cost of an item has often been used both by the IRS and by the courts to determine the fair market value of a particular item. Therefore, if you can produce evidence of the original cost of the items that were lost or damaged, you may help your case.

TaxOrganizer
If the property is leased. Losses are deductible only by the owner of the property, unless the property is leased and the lessee is obligated to repair casualty damage to the property.

Examples
If you purchase an automobile for your son or daughter and put the title to the automobile in the child's name, any casualty or theft loss is deductible by the child—not by you.

If you damage another person's property, you may not deduct any payments you make to restore or replace that property.

Members of social clubs may not deduct an assessment to repair hurricane damage to club property.

Amount of Loss

Figure the amount of your loss using the following steps.

1) Determine your adjusted basis in the property before the casualty or theft.
2) Determine the decrease in fair market value of the property as a result of the casualty or theft.
3) From the smaller of the amounts you determined in (1) and (2), subtract any insurance or other reimbursement you received or expect to receive.

Explanation
Calculate your loss, taking into consideration any reimbursements you may receive. Your loss is limited to the lesser of your cost or the reduction in fair market value.

Proof of the amount of a casualty loss is as important as proving the existence of the casualty. There are numerous court cases in which the taxpayers have shown the existence of a casualty but failed to establish a loss amount and were therefore denied a casualty loss deduction.

Example 1
A ruby ring valued at $5,000 is stolen from your house. The ring was purchased by your great-grandfather and was handed down through three generations by means of nontaxable gifts. The amount of the loss is limited to the cost of the ring to your great-grandfather.

Example 2

A homeowner was not entitled to a casualty loss deduction resulting from hurricane damage to trees located on his property. A real estate agent's appraisal was not accepted as competent to show any decline in the fair market value of the property. Thus, the decrease in the fair market value of the property as a result of the casualty was zero.

TaxOrganizer

Establishing the amount of your loss may be difficult, but the time you spend documenting the loss may be of great value in reducing your tax. You should make a list of all stolen, lost, damaged, or destroyed items as soon after the theft, disaster, or casualty as possible. IRS Publication 584, *Disaster and Casualty Loss Workbook*, may be useful. It has schedules to help you calculate a loss on your home and its contents and on your automobile, van, truck, or motorcycle.

It is equally important to retain records that help you establish the adjusted basis of valuable property. In other words, you should keep as supporting documentation receipts and documents establishing the original purchase price, costs of improvements, portions sold, or losses.

In a 1999 court opinion, a taxpayer was denied a casualty loss deduction because she failed to establish either her basis in or the fair market value of the property.

For personal-use property and property used in performing services as an employee, apply the deduction limits, discussed later, to determine the amount of your deductible loss.

Explanation

Gain from reimbursement. If your reimbursement is more than your adjusted basis in the property, you have a gain. This is true even if the decrease if the fair market value (FMV) of the property is more than your adjusted basis. If you have a gain, you may have to pay tax on it or you may be able to postpone reporting the gain. See *Insurance and Other Reimbursements,* later.

Leased property. If you are liable for casualty damage to property you lease, your loss is the amount you must pay to repair the property minus any insurance or the reimbursement you receive or expect to receive.

Explanation

Business or income-producing property. If you have business or income-producing property, such as rental property, and it is stolen or completely destroyed, the decrease in FMV is not considered. Your loss is figured as follows: Your adjusted basis in the property minus any salvage value minus any insurance or other reimbursement you receive or expect to receive.

Adjusted Basis

Adjusted basis is your basis (usually cost) increased or decreased by various events, such as improvements and casualty losses. For more information, see chapter 14.

TaxPlanner

Separate computations. Generally, if a single casualty or theft involves more than one item of property, you must figure the loss on each item separately; then combine the losses to determine the total loss from that casualty of theft.

Exception for personal-use real property. In figuring a casualty loss on personal-use real property, the entire property (including any improvements, such as buildings, trees, and shrubs) is treated as one item. Figure the loss using the smaller of the following:

- The decrease in FMV of the entire property
- The adjusted basis of the entire property

Decrease in Fair Market Value

Fair market value (FMV) is the price for which you could sell your property to a willing buyer when neither of you have to sell or buy and both of you know all the relevant facts.

The decrease in FMV is the difference between the property's fair market value immediately before and immediately after the casualty or theft.

FMV of stolen property. The FMV of property immediately after a theft is considered to be zero, since you no longer have the property.

Example

Several years ago, you purchased silver dollars at face value for $150. This is your adjusted basis in the property. Your silver dollars were stolen this year. The FMV of the coins was $1,000 when stolen, and insurance did not cover them. Your theft loss is $150.

Recovered stolen property. Recovered stolen property is your property that was stolen and later returned to you. If you recover property after you had already taken a theft loss deduction, you must refigure your loss using the smaller of the property's adjusted basis (explained earlier) or the decrease in FMV from the time it was stolen until the time it was recovered. Use this amount to refigure your total loss for the year in which the loss was deducted.

If your refigured loss is less than the loss you deducted, you generally have to report the difference as income in the recovery year. But report the difference only up to the amount of the loss that reduced your tax. For more information on the amount to report, see *Recoveries* in chapter 13.

Example

Your personal automobile is stolen. You paid $7,000 for it, and, on the day it was stolen, it had a fair market value of $5,500. Several days later, your automobile is found damaged and abandoned. The fair market value is reduced to $3,000 because of the damage. Your loss is $2,500. The decrease in market value ($5,500 – $3,000) is less than your cost of $7,000. Therefore, your deduction is limited to $2,500.

Figuring Decrease in FMV—Items To Consider

To figure the decrease in FMV because of a casualty or theft, you generally need a competent appraisal. But other measures can also be used to establish certain decreases.

Appraisal. An appraisal to determine the difference between the FMV of the property immediately before a casualty or theft and immediately afterward should be made by a competent appraiser. The appraiser must recognize the effects of any general market decline that may occur along with the casualty. This information is needed to limit any deduction to the actual loss resulting from damage to the property.

Several factors are important in evaluating the accuracy of an appraisal, including the following.

- The appraiser's familiarity with your property before and after the casualty or theft.
- The appraiser's knowledge of sales of comparable property in the area.
- The appraiser's knowledge of conditions in the area of the casualty.
- The appraiser's method of appraisal.

TaxPlanner

You may be able to use an appraisal that you used to get a federal loan (or a federal loan guarantee) as the result of a presidentially declared disaster to establish the amount of your disaster loss. For more information on disasters, see *Disaster Area Loss,* under *When to Report Gain or Loss,* later.

TaxSaver

Damaged trees. If a casualty occurs that damages or destroys trees or shrubs on your residential property and you do not plan to repair or replace them, make sure that the appraiser's valuation documenting the decrease in the value of the property considers the estimated cleanup costs.

Explanation

An appraisal obtained for the purpose of getting a loan of federal funds or a loan guarantee from the federal government as a result of a presidentially declared disaster could also be used to establish the amount of a disaster loss. Consult your tax advisor to be certain you comply with IRS guidelines.

Appraisal fee. The appraisal fee is not a part of the casualty or theft loss. It is an expense in determining your tax liability. You can deduct it as a miscellaneous deduction subject to the 2%-of-adjusted-gross-income limit on Schedule A (Form 1040). For information about miscellaneous deductions, see chapter 30.

TaxSaver

If you have property appraised because you have a casualty loss and the loss turns out not to be deductible because it does not exceed 10% of your adjusted gross income (see *10% Rule,* later), the cost of the appraisal is still deductible as a miscellaneous deduction subject to the 2%-of-adjusted-gross-income limit on Schedule A.

Cost of cleaning up or making repairs. The cost of repairing damaged property is not part of a casualty loss. Neither is the cost of cleaning up after a casualty. But you can use the cost of cleaning up or making repairs as a measure of the decrease in FMV if you meet all the following conditions.

- The repairs are actually made.
- The repairs are necessary to bring the property back to its condition before the casualty.

- The amount spent for repairs is not excessive.
- The repairs take care of the damage only.
- The value of the property after the repairs is not, due to the repairs, more than the value of the property before the casualty.

Explanation

Courts have held that cleanup expenses are deductible in the following circumstances:

- Replanting of damaged trees necessary to restore the property to its approximate value before the casualty
- Removing destroyed or damaged trees and shrubs, less any salvage value received
- The cost of replacing a windstorm-damaged carport

Note: Losses must be reduced by the $100 deductible limit and any money paid by an insurance company.

TaxSaver

If the fair market value of your property is decreased. If the repairs do not bring the property back to its condition before the casualty, it may be that the decrease in fair market value is greater than the cost of the repairs. The greater loss is deductible.

Example

As a result of a boating accident, the fair market value of your boat drops from $6,000 to $2,500. You originally paid $5,000 for the boat. You spend $2,000 on repairs, which actually increase the market value of the boat to $4,800. Nevertheless, you are entitled to a deduction of $3,500, which is the decrease in market value as a result of the casualty ($6,000 − $2,500).

Landscaping. The cost of restoring landscaping to its original condition after a casualty may indicate the decrease in FMV. You may be able to measure your loss by what you spend on the following.

- Removing destroyed or damaged trees and shrubs minus any salvage you receive.
- Pruning and other measures taken to preserve damaged trees and shrubs.
- Replanting necessary to restore the property to its approximate value before the casualty.

Explanation

The IRS takes the position that ornamental trees and shrubbery are an integral part of the **real property** and have no separate value. Therefore, the loss from damage to landscaping is measured by the decline in the fair market value of the entire property, not of an individual tree.

This treatment generally works to your advantage. If you originally planted the trees, your basis in them is probably substantially less than the decline in their fair market value. However, because the trees are regarded as an integral part of the property, your basis for figuring your loss is not just your basis for the trees but your basis for the entire property.

Example

You purchased a lot 10 years ago for $12,000 and spent $2,000 for shrubs and saplings. The entire property is now worth $20,000. A fire destroys all of the now mature shrubs and trees and reduces the market value of the property to $11,000. You are entitled to a deduction of

$9,000. Even though you paid only $2,000 for the trees, you paid $14,000 for the entire property. Because the decline in value of $9,000 is less than your basis of $14,000, you may deduct the entire decrease in fair market value.

TAXSAVER

Storm damage. After a storm, damaged or fallen mature trees are often replaced with saplings. You should argue that the replacements—the saplings—are worth less than the fallen trees and a loss greater than the cost of the saplings should be allowed. It pays to be aggressive when claiming casualty losses for trees. Even though the IRS does not compute the amount of a loss by assigning values to individual trees or shrubs, that should not stop you from doing so to bolster your claim.

Car value. Books issued by various automobile organizations that list your car may be useful in figuring the value of your car. You can modify the book's retail value by such factors as mileage and the condition of your car to figure its value. The prices are not "official," but they may be useful in determining value and suggesting relative prices for comparison with current sales and offerings in your area. If your car is not listed in the books, determine its value from other sources. A dealer's offer for your car as a trade-in on a new car is not usually a measure of its true value.

Figuring Decrease in FMV—Items Not To Consider
The following items are generally not considered when establishing the decrease in the FMV of your property.
Replacement cost. The cost of replacing stolen or destroyed property is not part of a casualty or theft loss.

Example

You bought a new chair 4 years ago for $300. In April, a fire destroyed the chair. You estimate that it would cost $500 to replace it. If you had sold the chair before the fire, you estimate that you could have received only $100 for it because it was 4 years old. The chair was not insured. Your loss is $100, the FMV of the chair before the fire. It is not $500, the replacement cost.

Cost of protection. The cost of protecting your property against a casualty or theft is not part of a casualty or theft loss. For example, you cannot deduct the amount you spend on insurance or to board up your house against a storm.

Explanation
If the property is business property, these expenses are deductible as business expenses.

If you make permanent improvements to your property to protect it against a casualty or theft, add the cost of these improvements to your basis in the property. An example would be the cost of a dike to prevent flooding.

Explanation
Burglar alarms. The costs of protecting your property against potential casualty are not deductible. This includes such items as burglar alarms and smoke detectors.

Related expenses. Any incidental expenses you have due to a casualty or theft, such as expenses for the treatment of personal injuries, for temporary housing, or for a rental car, are not part of your casualty or theft loss.

TAXSAVER

However, incidental expenses may be deductible as business expenses if the damaged or stolen property is business property.

Explanation
Money spent for temporary lodging at a hotel or an apartment while your residence is being repaired or rebuilt, the cost of water purchased due to well contamination, the cost of putting up a fence around a fire-damaged residence, and the towing of an automobile to a garage for repairs are all personal expenses that may not be deducted.

Sentimental value. Do not consider sentimental value when determining your loss. If a family portrait, heirloom, or keepsake is damaged, destroyed, or stolen, you must base your loss only on its fair market value.
Decline in market value of property. A decrease in the value of your property because it is in or near an area that suffered a casualty, or that might again suffer a casualty, is not to be taken into consideration. You have a loss only for actual casualty damage to your property. However, if your home is in a federally declared disaster area, see *Disaster Area Losses* in Publication 547.

Explanation
Taxpayers have been unable to take deductions for such things as a decline in market value of a house because it is near a newly opened highway or because of the stigma of a previous fire. There must be actual physical damage to the property that is the immediate and direct result of a casualty. However, a court case has held that an owner could deduct as a casualty loss the decrease in fair market value due to permanent buyer resistance resulting from changes made to the neighborhood following a flood.

Photographs. Photographs taken after a casualty will be helpful in establishing the condition and value of the property after it was damaged. Photographs showing the condition of the property after it was repaired, restored, or replaced may also be helpful.

The cost of photographs obtained for this purpose is not a part of the loss. You can claim this cost as a miscellaneous itemized deduction subject to the 2%-of-adjusted-gross-income limit on Schedule A (Form 1040). For information about miscellaneous deductions, see chapter 30.

TAXORGANIZER

Photographs or videotapes of your home and its contents may be useful in other ways as well. First, they may provide evidence of value before the casualty. Recent photos or tapes may, for example, be used to prove that the property was in good condition prior to the casualty. Second, they may assist you in determining what items are missing or were destroyed in a fire or theft. People often do not have an accurate inventory of household items. Photos or tapes serve as useful reminders.

The photographs or videotapes should be updated annually and kept outside your house, preferably in a safe-deposit box. They may be even more important in dealing with your insurance claim than they are in helping you with the IRS.

Insurance and Other Reimbursements

If you receive an insurance payment or other type of reimbursement, you must subtract the reimbursement when you figure your loss. You do not have a casualty or theft loss to the extent you are reimbursed.

If you expect to be reimbursed for part or all of your loss, you must subtract the expected reimbursement when you figure your loss. You must reduce your loss even if you do not receive payment until a later tax year. See *Reimbursement Received After Deducting Loss,* later.

Failure to file a claim for reimbursement. If your property is covered by insurance, you should file a timely insurance claim for reimbursement of your loss. Otherwise, you cannot deduct this loss as a casualty or theft loss. However, this rule does not apply to the portion of the loss not covered by insurance (for example, a deductible).

Example. You have a car insurance policy with a $500 deductible. Because your insurance did not cover the first $500 of an auto collision, the $500 would be deductible (subject to the deduction limits discussed later). This is true even if you do not file an insurance claim, since your insurance policy would never have reimbursed you for the deductible.

Gain from reimbursement. If your reimbursement is more than your adjusted basis in the property, you have a gain. This is true even if the decrease in the FMV of the property is more than your adjusted basis. If you have a gain, you may have to pay tax on it, or you may be able to postpone reporting the gain. See Publication 547 for more information on how to treat a gain from a reimbursement for a casualty or theft.

Explanation
You do not have to report a gain that results from a reimbursement that exceeds your basis in the lost, damaged, or destroyed property if you use the entire reimbursement to purchase property that is either similar or related in use to the original property. Instead, the recognition of the gain is postponed until the replacement property is sold. Your basis in the replacement property is its cost minus any postponed gain. With a home, the gain may not be taxable under the new rules for exclusion of gain on home sales (see the rules discussed in Chapter 16, *Selling Your Home*).

You are allowed a certain amount of time to select and purchase the replacement property. This time period begins on the day of the casualty or theft and ends 2 years after the close of the tax year in which the reimbursement is received. Thus, if your house was robbed on August 1, 1999, and your insurance company reimbursed you for your loss on May 1, 2000, you would have until December 31, 2002, to repair or replace the damaged goods. If the cost of the replacement property is less than the reimbursement received, the unspent part of the reimbursement must be recognized as a gain.

Types of Reimbursements
The most common type of reimbursement is an insurance payment for your stolen or damaged property. Other types of reimbursements are discussed next. Also see the *Instructions for Form 4684.*

Employer's emergency disaster fund. If you receive money from your employer's emergency disaster fund and you must use that money to rehabilitate or replace property on which you are claiming a casualty loss deduction, you must take that money into consideration in computing the casualty loss deduction. Take into consideration only the amount you used to replace your destroyed or damaged property.

Example. Your home was extensively damaged by a tornado. Your loss after reimbursement from your insurance company was $10,000. Your employer set up a disaster relief fund for its employees. Employees receiving money from the fund had to use it to rehabilitate or replace their damaged or destroyed property. You received $4,000 from the fund and spent the entire amount on repairs to your home. In figuring your casualty loss, you must reduce your unreimbursed loss ($10,000) by the $4,000 you received from your employer's fund. Your casualty loss before applying the deduction limits discussed later is $6,000.

Explanation
If you have use and occupancy insurance for your business and are reimbursed for loss of business income, it does not reduce your casualty or theft loss. However, the reimbursement is considered income and is taxed in the same way as your other business income.

Cash gifts. If you receive excludable cash gifts as a disaster victim and there are no limits on how you can use the money, you do not reduce your casualty loss by these excludable cash gifts. This applies even if you use the money to pay for repairs to property damaged in the disaster.

Example. Your home was damaged by a hurricane. Relatives and neighbors made cash gifts to you which were excludable from your income. You used part of the cash gifts to pay for repairs to your home. There were no limits or restrictions on how you could use the cash gifts. Because it was an excludable gift, the money you received and used to pay for repairs to your home does not reduce your casualty loss on the damaged home.

Insurance payments for living expenses. You do not reduce your casualty loss by insurance payments you receive to cover living expenses in either of the following situations.

- You lose the use of your main home because of a casualty.
- Government authorities do not allow you access to your main home because of a casualty or threat of one.

Inclusion in income. If these insurance payments are more than the temporary increase in your living expenses, you must include the excess in your income. Report this amount on line 21 of Form 1040.

A temporary increase in your living expenses is the difference between the actual living expenses you and your family incurred during the period you could not use your home and your normal living expenses for that period. Actual living expenses are the reasonable and necessary expenses incurred because of the loss of your main home. Generally, these expenses include the amounts you pay for the following.

- Rent for suitable housing.
- Transportation.
- Food.
- Utilities.
- Miscellaneous services.

Normal living expenses consist of these same expenses that you would have incurred but did not because of the casualty.

Example. As a result of a fire, you vacated your apartment for a month and moved to a motel. You normally pay $525 a month rent. None was charged for the month the apartment was vacated. Your motel rent for this month was $1,200. You normally pay $200 a month for food. Your food expenses for the month you lived in the motel were $400. You received $1,100 from your insurance company to cover your living expenses. You determine the payment you must include in income as follows.

1) Insurance payment for living expenses............................ $1,100

2) Actual expenses during the month
   you are unable to use your home because
   of the fire $1,600

3) Normal living expenses 725

4) Temporary increase in living expenses:
   Subtract line 3 from line 2 875

5) Amount of payment includible in income:
   Subtract line 4 from line 1. .... $225

Tax year of inclusion. You include the taxable part of the insurance payment in income for the year you regain the use of your main home or, if later, for the year you receive the taxable part of the insurance payment.

Example. Your main home was destroyed by a tornado in August 1999. You regained use of your home in November 2000. The insurance payments you received in 1999 and 2000 were $1,500 more than the temporary increase in your living expenses during those years. You include this amount in income on your 2000 Form 1040. If, in 2001, you receive further payments to cover the living expenses you had in 1999 and 2000, you must include those payments in income on your 2001 Form 1040.

Disaster relief. Food, medical supplies, and other forms of assistance you receive do not reduce your casualty loss unless they are replacements for lost or destroyed property. These items are not taxable income to you.

Explanation

Disaster unemployment assistance payments are unemployment benefits that are taxable.

Reimbursement Received After Deducting Loss

If you figured your casualty or theft loss using your expected reimbursement, you may have to adjust your tax return for the tax year in which you receive your actual reimbursement. This section explains the adjustment you may have to make.

Actual reimbursement less than expected. If you later receive less reimbursement than you expected, include that difference with your other losses (if any) on your return for the year in which you can reasonably expect no more reimbursement.

Example. Your personal car had an FMV of $2,000 when it was destroyed in a collision with another car last year. The accident was due to the negligence of the other driver. At the end of the year, there was a reasonable prospect that the owner of the other car would reimburse you in full. You subtracted the expected reimbursement when you figured your loss. You did not have a deductible loss last year.

This January, the court awarded you a judgment of $2,000. However, in July it became apparent that you will be unable to collect any amount from the other driver. You can deduct the loss this year subject to the limits discussed later.

TAXPLANNER

Even though there is no formal IRS ruling, many IRS auditors tend to disallow any deduction for the unreimbursed amount if you are fully insured and settle your claim with the insurance carrier for less than the amount of the loss by signing a proof of loss statement. The proof of loss statement sets the value of the loss between you and the insurance company. Generally, the IRS auditor will only allow a deduction of the unreimbursed loss if he or she is convinced that you have attempted all reasonable remedies against the insurer.

Actual reimbursement more than expected. If you later receive more reimbursement than you expected after you claimed a deduction for the loss, you may have to include the extra reimbursement in your income for the year you receive it. However, if any part of the original deduction did not reduce your tax for the earlier year, do not include that part of the reimbursement in your income. You do not refigure your tax for the year you claimed the deduction. For more information, see *Recoveries* in chapter 13.

Example

Last year, a hurricane destroyed your motorboat. Your loss was $3,000, and you estimated that your insurance would cover $2,500 of it. Because you did not itemize deductions on your return last year, you could not deduct the loss. When the insurance company reimburses you for the loss, you do not report any of the reimbursement as income. This is true even if it is for the full $3,000 because you did not deduct the loss on your return. The loss did not reduce your tax.

Caution. *If the total of all the reimbursements you receive is more than your adjusted basis in the destroyed or stolen property, you will have a* **gain** *on the casualty or theft. If you have already taken a deduction for a loss and you receive the reimbursement in a later year, you may have to include the gain in your income for the later year. Include the gain as ordinary income up to the amount of your deduction that reduced your tax for the earlier year. See Publication 547 for more information on how to treat a gain from the reimbursement of a casualty or theft.*

Actual reimbursement same as expected. If you receive exactly the reimbursement you expected, you do not have any amount to include in your income or any loss to deduct.

Example. Last December, you had a collision while driving your personal car. Repairs to the car cost $950. You had $100 deductible collision insurance. Your insurance company agreed to reimburse you for the rest of the damage. Because you expected a reimbursement from the insurance company, you did not have a casualty loss deduction last year.

Due to the $100 rule (discussed later under *Deduction Limits*), you cannot deduct the $100 deductible you paid. When you receive the $850 from the insurance company this year, do not report it as income.

Example

A taxpayer suffered a casualty loss from vandalism and filed a claim with her insurance company in the year of the loss. The insurance company denied any liability for the damage. Consequently, the taxpayer filed suit against the insurance company. A court held that the taxpayer could not deduct the loss in the year in which it was incurred, because a reasonable possibility of recovery still existed. No deduction was allowed while the suit against the insurance company was still pending.

Single Casualty on Multiple Properties

Personal property. If a single casualty or theft involves more than one item of personal property, you must figure the loss on each item separately. Then combine the losses to determine your total loss from that casualty or theft. Personal property is any property that is not real property.

Example. A fire in your home destroyed an upholstered chair, an oriental rug, and an antique table. You did not have fire insurance to cover your loss. (This was the only casualty or theft you had during the

Table 27–1. **How To Apply the Deduction Limits**

	$100 Rule	10% Rule
General Application	You must reduce each casualty or theft loss by $100 when figuring your deduction. Apply this rule after you have figured the amount of your loss.	You must reduce your total casualty or theft loss by 10% of your adjusted gross income. Apply this rule after you reduce each loss by $100 (the $100 rule).
Single Event	Apply this rule only once, even if many pieces of property are affected.	Apply this rule only once, even if many pieces of property are affected.
More Than One Event	Apply to the loss from each event.	Apply to the total of all your losses from all events.
More Than One Person— With Loss From the Same Event (other than a married couple filing jointly)	Apply separately to each person.	Apply separately to each person.
Married Couple— With Loss From the Same Event — Filing Jointly	Apply as if you were one person.	Apply as if you were one person.
Filing Separately	Apply separately to each spouse.	Apply separately to each spouse.
More Than One Owner (other than a married couple filing jointly)	Apply separately to each owner of jointly owned property.	Apply separately to each owner of jointly owned property.

year.) You paid $750 for the chair and you established that it had an FMV of $500 just before the fire. The rug cost $3,000 and had an FMV of $2,500 just before the fire. You bought the table at an auction for $100 before discovering it was an antique. It had been appraised at $900 before the fire. You figure your loss on each of these items as follows:

	Chair	Rug	Table
1) Basis (cost)	$ 750	$3,000	$ 100
2) FMV before fire	$ 500	$2,500	$ 900
3) FMV after fire	–0–	–0–	–0–
4) Decrease in FMV	$ 500	$2,500	$ 900
5) Loss (smaller of (1) or (4))	$ 500	$2,500	$ 100
6) Total loss			$3,100

Real property. In figuring a casualty loss on personal-use real property, treat the entire property (including any improvements, such as buildings, trees, and shrubs) as one item. Figure the loss using the smaller of the adjusted basis or the decrease in FMV of the entire property.

Example. You bought your home a few years ago. You paid $160,000 ($20,000 for the land and $140,000 for the house). You also spent $2,000 for landscaping. This year a fire destroyed your home. The fire also damaged the shrubbery and trees in your yard. The fire was your only casualty or theft loss this year. Competent appraisers valued the property as a whole at $200,000 before the fire, but only $30,000 after the fire. (The loss to your household furnishings is not shown in this example. It would be figured separately, as explained earlier under *Personal property*.) Shortly after the fire, the insurance company paid you $155,000 for the loss. You figure your casualty loss as follows:

1) Adjusted basis of the entire property (land, building, and landscaping)	$162,000
2) FMV of entire property before fire	$200,000
3) FMV of entire property after fire	30,000
4) Decrease in FMV of entire property	$170,000
5) Loss (smaller of (1) or (4))	$162,000

6) Subtract insurance	155,000
7) Amount of loss	$ 7,000

Deduction Limits

After you have figured your casualty or theft loss, you must figure how much of the loss you can deduct. If the loss was to property for your personal use or for your family's, there are *two limits* on the amount you can deduct for your casualty or theft loss.

1) You must reduce each casualty or theft loss by $100 ($100 rule).
2) You must further reduce the total of all your losses by 10% of your adjusted gross income (10% rule).

You make these reductions on Form 4684.

These rules are explained next and *Table 27–1* summarizes how to apply the $100 rule and the 10% rule in various situations. For more detailed explanations and examples, see Publication 547.

Property used partly for business and partly for personal purposes. When property is used partly for personal purposes and partly for business or income-producing purposes, the casualty or theft loss deduction must be figured separately for the personal-use part and for the business or income-producing part. You must figure each loss separately because the $100 rule and the 10% rule apply only to the loss on the personal-use part of the property.

Explanation
Business or income-producing property. A loss on business property, property that earns you rent or royalty income, or other income-producing property is not subject to either the $100 rule or the 10% rule. For business or income-producing property, you must figure your loss separately for each item that is stolen, damaged, or destroyed. If casualty damage occurs both to a building and to trees on the same piece of property, the loss is measured separately for each.

Total loss of business or income-producing property. If you have business or income-producing property that is completely lost because of a casualty or theft, your deductible loss is your basis in the property minus any salvage value and minus any insurance or other reimbursement you receive or expect to receive. It does not matter what the decrease in fair market value is.

Example

You owned machinery that you used in your business. The machinery had an adjusted basis of $25,000 when it was completely destroyed by fire. Its fair market value just before the fire was $20,000. Because this was business property, and because it was completely destroyed, your deductible loss is your adjusted basis in the machinery, $25,000, decreased by salvage value and by any insurance or other reimbursement. Fair market value is not considered when you are figuring your loss, even though it is less than your basis in the machinery.

Explanation

Partial loss of business or income-producing property. If business or income-producing property is damaged but not completely destroyed in a casualty, the loss is the decrease in value because of the casualty or your adjusted basis in the property, whichever is less. From this amount (the lesser of your adjusted basis or the decrease in value), you must subtract any insurance or other reimbursement you receive or expect to receive.

TaxSaver

If your car is stolen. If your automobile is stolen or destroyed, you may be able to deduct more than the value listed in one of the various books issued by automobile organizations. If you use the automobile for business, you must make a separate calculation of the business and personal portions of the loss. This may produce a larger loss.

Example

Blair Hunt's automobile, which cost $8,000, is stolen. The "blue book"—one of the books published by automobile organizations—values his automobile at $5,000. Blair used the automobile for business 40% of the time and has taken $800 depreciation.

	Business portion	Personal portion
Value before theft	$2,000	$3,000
Value after theft	–0–	–0–
Decrease in value	$2,000	$3,000
Adjusted basis:		
Original cost	$3,200	$4,800
Depreciation	(800)	–0–
Adjusted basis	$2,400	$4,800

Blair's casualty loss before the $100 limitation is $5,400, computed as follows:

Business portion—adjusted basis	$2,400
Personal portion—the lower of the decrease in value or the adjusted basis	3,000
Total	$5,400

TaxSaver

By reporting the business loss on Schedule C (if self-employed), you can reduce your self-employment income and, hence, your self-employment tax.

$100 Rule

After you have figured your casualty or theft loss, you must reduce that loss by $100. This reduction applies to each total casualty or theft loss. It does not matter how many pieces of property are involved in an event. Only a single $100 reduction applies.

Explanation

The $100 rule and the 10% rule do not apply if the loss is on business property, property that earns you rent or royalty income, or other income-producing property.

Example. A hailstorm damages your home and your car. Determine the amount of loss, as discussed earlier, for each of these items. Since the losses are due to a single event, you combine the losses and reduce the combined amount by $100.

Single event. Generally, events closely related in origin cause a single casualty. It is a single casualty when the damage is from two or more closely related causes, such as wind and flood damage caused by the same storm.

10% Rule

You must reduce the total of all your casualty or theft losses by 10% of your adjusted gross income. Apply this rule after you reduce each loss by $100. If you have both gains and losses from casualties or thefts, see *Gains and losses,* later in this discussion.

Example 1. In June, you discovered that your house had been burglarized. Your loss after insurance reimbursement was $2,000. Your adjusted gross income is $29,500. You first apply the $100 rule and then the 10% rule. Figure your theft loss deduction as follows.

1) Loss after insurance	$2,000
2) Subtract $100	100
3) Loss after $100 rule	$1,900
4) Subtract 10% of $29,500 AGI	2,950
5) **Theft loss deduction**	–0–

You do not have a theft loss deduction because your loss ($1,900) is less than 10% of your adjusted gross income ($2,950).

Explanation

More than one loss. If you have more than one casualty or theft loss during your tax year, reduce each loss by any reimbursement and by $100. Then you must reduce the total of *all* your losses by 10% of your adjusted gross income.

Example 2. In March, you had a car accident that totally destroyed your car. You did not have collision insurance on your car, so you did not receive any insurance reimbursement. Your loss on the car was $1,200. In November, a fire damaged your basement and totally destroyed the furniture, washer, dryer, and other items stored there. Your loss on the basement items after reimbursement was $1,700. Your adjusted gross income is $25,000. You figure your casualty loss deduction as follows.

	Car	Basement
1) Loss	$1,200	$1,700
2) Subtract $100 per incident	100	100
3) Loss after $100 rule	$1,100	$1,600

Table 27–2. **When To Deduct a Loss**

IF you have a loss...	THEN deduct it in the year...
From a casualty,	The loss occurred.
In a presidentially declared disaster area,	The disaster occurred or the year immediately before the disaster.
From a theft,	The theft was discovered.
On a deposit treated as a:	
• Casualty,	• A reasonable estimate can be made.
• Bad debt,	• Deposits are totally worthless.
• Ordinary loss,	• A reasonable estimate can be made.

4) Total loss	$2,700
5) Subtract 10% of $25,000 AGI	2,500
6) Casualty loss deduction	**$ 200**

Gains and losses. If you had both gains and losses from casualties or thefts to personal-use property, you must compare your total gains to your total losses. Do this after you have reduced each loss by $100.

Losses more than gains. If your losses are more than your recognized gains, subtract your gains from your losses and reduce the result by 10% of your adjusted gross income. The rest is your deductible loss.

Example

Your theft loss after reducing it by reimbursements and by $100 is $2,700. Your casualty gain is $700. Because your loss is more than your gain, you must reduce your $2,000 net loss ($2,700 – $700) by 10% of your adjusted gross income.

Gains more than losses. If your recognized gains are more than your losses, subtract your losses from your gains. The difference is treated as capital gain and must be reported on Schedule D (Form 1040). The 10% rule does not apply to your losses.

Example 1

Your theft loss after reducing it by reimbursements and by $100 is $600. Your casualty gain is $1,600. Because your gain is more than your loss, you must report the $1,000 net gain ($1,600 – $600) on Schedule D.

Example 2

During 2001, a storm completely destroyed your summer cottage, resulting in a casualty gain of $5,000 after you were reimbursed by your insurance company. Later in the year, your home was broken into on two separate occasions. Jewelry, silverware, and other items of personal property were stolen each time. The loss (after the $100 rule) on the first theft was $900 and on the second theft was $4,000. Your 2000 adjusted gross income is $25,000.

1) Loss on first theft	$ 900
2) Plus: loss on second theft	4,000
3) Total losses	$4,900
4) Gain on cottage	5,000
5) Net gain for 1999	$100

The $100 gain will be reported on Form 4684. See *Insurance and Other Reimbursements*, regarding recognition of gains discussed earlier.

When To Report Gain or Loss

If you receive an insurance or other reimbursement that is more than your adjusted basis in the destroyed or stolen property, you have a gain from the casualty or theft. You must include this gain in your income in the year you receive the reimbursement, unless you choose to postpone the gain as explained in Publication 547.

If you have a loss, see *Table 27–2.*

Loss on deposits. If your loss is a loss on deposits in an insolvent or bankrupt financial institution, see *Loss on Deposits,* earlier.

Casualty loss. Generally, you can deduct a casualty loss only in the tax year in which the casualty occurred. This is true even if you do not repair or replace the damaged property until a later year.

Theft loss. You can generally deduct a theft loss only in the year you discover your property was stolen. You must be able to show that there was a theft, but you do not have to know when the theft occurred. However, you should show when you discovered that your property was missing.

Disaster Area Loss

If you have a casualty loss in a Presidentially declared disaster area, you can choose to deduct the loss on your tax return for either of the following years.

1) The year the casualty occurred.
2) The year immediately preceding the year the casualty occurred.

TaxSaver

If you were affected by one of the 2001 disasters, you may get speedier action on your return by writing on the front of the return that a disaster loss is being claimed.

TaxPlanner

If you are not in need of an immediate tax refund, you may want to wait to file until near the April 15th deadline. By waiting, you may be able to determine which tax year provides greater tax savings from the deduction and to choose that year to claim the loss. For more information, consult your tax advisor.

Explanation

A loss in a federally declared disaster area may be deducted on the tax return for the year in which the disaster occurs or in the immediately preceding tax year if certain requirements are met. First, the loss must have been from a disaster in an area that the President says needs federal assistance. Second, the tax return for the preceding year must be amended by the date it is due, or, if that date has already passed, by the date the tax return for the year of the disaster is due. In both instances, extensions are allowed. Generally, you would have until April 15, 2002, to amend a 2000 return to report a 2001 disaster loss. An amended return is filed on Form 1040X. A listing of federal disaster areas may be obtained from your newspaper, from local officials, or from the Federal Emergency Management Agency's website (www.fema.gov/disasters).

TaxPlanner

To determine whether you should claim the disaster loss on your current year's return or on your return for the preceding year, you should calculate the tax effects of claiming the loss in both years. Once you make a choice, it becomes irrevocable 90 days after you file your amended return or on the date on which the return for the year of the loss is due, whichever comes later.

Postponed tax deadlines. The IRS may postpone for up to 120 days certain tax deadlines of taxpayers who are affected by a Presidentially declared disaster. The tax deadlines the IRS may postpone include those for filing income and employment tax returns, paying income and employment taxes, and making contributions to a traditional IRA or Roth IRA.

If any tax deadline is postponed, the IRS will publicize the postponement in your area by publishing a news release, revenue ruling, revenue procedure, notice, announcement, or other guidance in the Internal Revenue Bulletin (IRB).

Who is eligible. If the IRS postpones a tax deadline, the following taxpayers are eligible for the postponement.

- Any individual whose main home is located in a covered disaster area (defined later).
- Any business entity or sole proprietor whose principal place of business is located in a covered disaster area.
- Any relief worker affiliated with a recognized government or philanthropic organization who is assisting in a covered disaster area.
- Any individual, business entity, or sole proprietor whose records are needed to meet a postponed deadline, provided those records are maintained in a covered disaster area. The main home or principal place of business does *not* have to be located in the covered disaster area.
- Any estate or trust that has tax records necessary to meet a postponed tax deadline, provided those records are maintained in a covered disaster area.
- The spouse on a joint return with a taxpayer who is eligible for postponements.
- Any other person determined by the IRS to be affected by a Presidentially declared disaster.

Covered disaster area. This is an area of a Presidentially declared disaster area in which the IRS has decided to postpone tax deadlines for up to 120 days.

Abatement of interest. In addition to postponing the tax deadlines, the IRS may grant an extension to file income tax returns and pay income tax. In this case, the IRS will abate the interest for the length of the extension period and for the length of any postponement.

More information. For more information, see *Disaster Area Losses* in Publication 547.

How To Report Gains and Losses

Use Form 4684 to report a gain or a deductible loss from a casualty or theft. If you have more than one casualty or theft, use a separate Form 4684 to determine your gain or loss for each event. Combine the gains and losses on one Form 4684. Follow the form instructions as to which lines to fill out.

If you have a:	Report it on:
Gain	Schedule D (Form 1040)
Loss	Schedule A (Form 1040)

Adjustments to basis. If you have a casualty or theft loss, you must decrease your basis in the property by any deductible loss and any insurance or other reimbursement. Amounts you spend to restore your property after a casualty increase your adjusted basis. See *Adjusted Basis* in chapter 14 for more information.

Net operating loss (NOL). If your casualty or theft loss deduction is more than your income, you may have an NOL. You can use an NOL to lower your tax in an earlier year, allowing you to get a refund for tax you have already paid. Or, you can use it to lower your tax in a later year. You do not have to be in business to have an NOL from a casualty or theft loss. For more information, see Publication 536, *Net Operating Losses (NOLs) for Individuals, Estates, and Trusts.*

TaxPlanner

If your loss exceeds your income. If your casualty loss exceeds your income, you should fill out Form 1045, *Application for Tentative Refund*, to see whether you have a net operating loss. When filling out this form, treat your casualty losses as business deductions rather than nonbusiness deductions. If your casualty loss results in a net operating loss, then your net operating loss can be carried back to offset your taxable income, and you may get a refund of prior-year taxes.

For example, a 2001 net operating loss caused by a casualty loss should be carried back first to 1998, any remaining loss should be carried back to 1999, and then to 2000. If any loss still remains, it can be carried forward for the next 20 years. Alternatively, you may elect on your 2001 tax return not to carry back your net operating loss but carry it forward only. See the discussion in Chapter 38, *If You Are Self-Employed: How to File Schedule C*, and you may also want to consult your tax advisor. You should compare the refund available from a carryback to the expected tax benefits in the future in order to determine whether you should make the election.

TaxAlert

Effective for losses occurring in 1998 or later, Congress changed the carryback period for most net operating losses from 3 years to 2 years and the carryforward period from 15 years to 20 years. However, the carryback period for net operating losses caused by casualty and theft losses remains at 3 years.

Car Expenses and Other Employee Business Expenses

Introduction

If you are traveling on business and your employer does not reimburse your expenses, you may deduct many of them on your income tax return. If you use your automobile partly for business purposes, you may be able to deduct some of your operating expenses. If you entertain a business associate at a restaurant or nightclub, you may probably deduct that expense, too. Within strict limits, business gifts are also deductible.

You must be able to prove the business purpose, as well as the amount of the expense, to claim a deduction for employee expenses. All expenses should be substantiated with receipts and records indicating the time, place, and business nature of the expense. This chapter explains business-related expenses for travel, transportation, entertainment, and gifts that you may deduct on your income tax return. It also discusses the reporting and record-keeping requirements for these expenses.

Important Change

Standard mileage rate. The standard mileage rate for the cost of operating your car in 2001 is 34 1/2 cents a mile for all business miles.

Car expenses and use of the standard mileage rate are explained under *Transportation Expenses,* later.

TaxAlert

Employer-provided parking. Before 1998, you had to include in income the fair market value of parking you received from your employer if you received it in place of compensation. For 2001, you can exclude up to $180 per month of employer-provided parking, even if you choose it instead of cash or your employer reduces your compensation to provide the parking. The $180 is indexed for inflation.

Important Reminders

Standard meal allowance. The standard meal allowance (also referred to as the limit on meals and incidental expenses (M&IE rate)) for most small localities in the United States is $30. However, the standard meal allowance is higher for most major cities and many other localities in the continental United States. See Publication 1542, *Per Diem Rates.* These rates (allowances/limits) are also listed in Appendix A of Chapter 41, Part 301 of the Code of Federal Regulations. If you have a computer, you can find them on the Internet at **www.policyworks. gov/perdiem.** Click on "Domestic per diem rates." Use of the standard meal allowance is explained under *What Travel Expenses Are Deductible,* later.

Meal expenses when subject to "hours of service" limits. Generally, you can deduct only 50% of your business-related meal expenses while traveling away from your tax home for business purposes. You can deduct a higher percentage if the meals take place during or incident to any period subject to the Department of Transportation's "hours of service" limits. (These limits apply to certain workers who are under certain federal regulations.) The percentage is 60% for 2001. See *Exceptions to the 50% limit* under *50% Limit,* later.

Limits that apply to employee deductions. If you are an employee, deduct your work-related expenses discussed in this chapter as a miscellaneous itemized deduction on Schedule A (Form 1040). Generally, the amount of miscellaneous itemized deductions you can deduct is limited to the amount that is more than 2% of your adjusted gross income. It may be further limited if your adjusted gross income is more than $132,950 ($66,475 if you are married filing separately). For more information, see chapter 22 and the instructions for Schedule A (Form 1040).

You may be able to deduct the ordinary and necessary business-related expenses you have for:

- Travel,
- Entertainment,
- Gifts, or
- Transportation.

An *ordinary expense* is one that is common and accepted in your field of trade, business, or profession. A *necessary expense* is one that is helpful and appropriate for your business. An expense does not have to be indispensable to be considered necessary.

This chapter explains:

- What expenses are deductible,
- What records you need to prove your expenses,
- How to treat any expense reimbursements you may receive, and
- How to report your expenses on your return.

Explanation

All employee-related expenses and certain transportation expenses are classified as miscellaneous itemized deductions. Included in this category are expenses incurred by employees that are fully or partially reimbursed or not reimbursed at all by their employer. Also included are any expenses for traveling away from home or for transportation.

The total of all miscellaneous itemized expenses (including those mentioned previously, as well as those discussed in Chapter 30, *Miscellaneous Deductions*) must be reduced by 2% of adjusted gross income. Only the amount over 2% can be claimed as an itemized deduction and generate a tax benefit.

In 2001, your total itemized deductions will be reduced by the lesser of (1) 3% of the excess of your adjusted gross income over $132,950 ($66,475 if married filing separately) or (2) 80% of the aggregate of certain itemized deductions. As a result, depending on your adjusted gross income and other itemized deductions in the current year versus those amounts anticipated in the subsequent year, it may be possible to time the payment of employee-related expenses to maximize your deduction.

If you incur expenses as an employee, seek any reimbursement you are entitled to from your employer. The courts have held that transportation expenses, such as taxi fares and automobile-operating expenses, may not be deducted directly by an employee unless the amount of the expenses exceeds the reimbursement. You cannot deduct such expenses on your own tax return because you simply don't bother to request reimbursement from your employer, even if such reimbursement is not requested based on a belief that it would not be reimbursed.

Example 1

A salesman incurred business expenses but did not submit them to his company for reimbursement because they were incurred due to mistakes he made and, therefore, were his responsibility. The courts held that these expenses were not deductible by the salesman because they were expenses of another taxpayer. Generally, the payment of an obligation of another is not considered an ordinary and necessary expense.

Example 2

An employee was told that all unessential travel would have to be curtailed. Therefore, he knew he might incur business mileage for which he would not be reimbursed. As a result, he sought and obtained reimbursement for only a portion of the total business use of his automobile. The Tax Court held that because this employee did not have any of his travel expenses rejected by his employer, he had no reasonable basis to conclude that his unreimbursed business miles would not be reimbursed. Consequently, no tax deduction was allowed for any business mileage.

Exception

When it is company policy to reimburse employees for mileage but employees are verbally instructed by company field representatives not to seek reimbursement, you may rightfully deduct unreimbursed automobile expenses.

TAXPLANNER

You should seek reimbursement for all business mileage incurred on your private automobile. To the extent that reimbursement is denied by your employer, a deduction is available.

Who does not need to use this publication. If you are an employee, you will not need to read this chapter if *all* of the following are true.

1) You fully accounted to your employer for your work-related expenses.
2) You received full reimbursement for your expenses.
3) Your employer required you to return any excess reimbursement and you did so.
4) Box 12 of your Form W-2, *Wage and Tax Statement,* shows no amount with a code **L.**

If you meet these four conditions, there is no need to show the expenses or the reimbursements on your return. See *Reimbursements,* later, if you would like more information on reimbursements and accounting to your employer.

Tip. *If you meet these conditions and your employer included reimbursements on your Form W-2 in error, ask your employer for a corrected Form W-2.*

Explanation

For more information regarding the business use of your home, see Chapter 30, *Miscellaneous Deductions*.

Useful Items

You may want to see:

Publication

☐ **463** Travel, Entertainment, Gift, and Car Expenses
☐ **535** Business Expenses
☐ **1542** Per Diem Rates

Form (and Instructions)

☐ **Schedule A (Form 1040)** Itemized Deductions
☐ **Schedule C (Form 1040)** Profit or Loss From Business
☐ **Schedule C-EZ (Form 1040)** Net Profit From Business
☐ **Schedule F (Form 1040)** Profit or Loss From Farming
☐ **Form 2106** Employee Business Expenses
☐ **Form 2106-EZ** Unreimbursed Employee Business Expenses

Travel Expenses

If you temporarily travel away from your tax home, you can use this section to determine if you have deductible travel expenses. This section defines "travel expenses," "tax home," "temporary assignment," and the "standard meal allowance." It also discusses the rules for travel inside and outside the United States and deductible convention expenses.

Travel expenses defined. For tax purposes, travel expenses are the ordinary and necessary expenses (defined earlier) of traveling away from home for your business, profession, or job.

You will find examples of deductible travel expenses in *Table 28-1*.

Example 1
The courts held that a stockholder of a corporation could not deduct the expense of operating his personal automobile while performing services for the corporation. The stockholder was not an employee or officer of the corporation. He was not reimbursed for his expenses. The courts held that the stockholder's interest in the corporation was too remote for the expense to be an ordinary business expense.

Example 2
A government employee was allowed to deduct unreimbursed expenses incurred in the use of his private airplane for business purposes. He was also allowed to depreciate the business portion of the airplane's use.

TAXPLANNER

For you to deduct a business expense, a board resolution or a policy statement from the company that employs you should indicate that you may have to incur certain expenses for which you will not be reimbursed in order for you to fulfill your job.

TAXPLANNER

You are able to deduct only 50% of most business meal and entertainment costs. Other allowable unreimbursed entertainment expenses will be grouped with certain other of your miscellaneous itemized deductions. You will be allowed a tax deduction to the extent that all these deductions exceed 2% of your adjusted gross income.

Traveling away from home. You are traveling away from home if:

1) Your duties require you to be away from the general area of your tax home (defined later) substantially longer than an ordinary day's work, and
2) You need to sleep or rest to meet the demands of your work while away from home.

This rest requirement is not satisfied by merely napping in your car. You do not have to be away from your tax home for a whole day or from dusk to dawn as long as your relief from duty is long enough to get necessary sleep or rest.

Example 1. You are a railroad conductor. You leave your home terminal on a regularly scheduled round-trip run between two cities and return home 16 hours later. During the run, you have 6 hours off at your turnaround point where you eat two meals and rent a hotel room to get necessary sleep before starting the return trip. You are considered to be away from home.

Example 2. You are a truck driver. You leave your terminal and return to it later the same day. You get an hour off at your turnaround point to eat. Because you are not off to get necessary sleep and the brief time off is not an adequate rest period, you are not traveling away from home. You cannot deduct travel expenses.

Members of the Armed Forces. If you are a member of the U.S. Armed Forces on a permanent duty assignment overseas, you are not traveling away from home. You cannot deduct your expenses for meals and lodging. You cannot deduct these expenses even if you have to maintain a home in the United States for your family members who are not allowed to accompany you overseas. If you are transferred from one permanent duty station to another, you may have deductible moving expenses, which are explained in chapter 19.

A naval officer assigned to permanent duty aboard a ship that has regular eating and living facilities has a tax home aboard ship for travel expense purposes.

Tax Home

To determine whether you are traveling away from home, you must first determine the location of your tax home.

Generally, your tax home is your regular place of business or post of duty, regardless of where you maintain your family home. It includes the *entire city or general area* in which your business or work is located.

If you have more than one regular place of business, your tax home is your main place of business. See *Main place of business or work,* later.

If you do not have a regular or a main place of business because of the nature of your work, then your tax home may be the place where you regularly live. See *No main place of business or work,* later.

If you do not have a regular place of business or post of duty and there is no place where you regularly live, you are considered a *transient (an itinerant)* and your tax home is wherever you work. As a transient, you cannot claim a travel expense deduction because you are never considered to be traveling away from home.

Main place of business or work. If you have more than one place of work, consider the following when determining which one is your main place of business or work.

1) The total time you ordinarily spend in each place.
2) The level of your business activity in each place.
3) Whether your income from each place is significant or insignificant.

Example. You live in Cincinnati where you have a seasonal job for 8 months each year and earn $25,000. You work the other 4 months in Miami, also at a seasonal job, and earn $9,000. Cincinnati is your main place of work because you spend most of your time there and earn most of your income there.

No main place of business or work. You may have a tax home even if you do not have a regular or main place of work. Your tax home may be the home where you regularly live.

Table 28–1. **Travel Expenses You Can Deduct**
This chart summarizes expenses you can deduct when you travel away from home for business purposes.

IF you have expenses for:	THEN you can deduct the costs of:
Transportation	Travel by airplane, train, bus, or car between your home and your business destination. If you were provided with a ticket or you are riding free as a result of a frequent traveler or similar program, your cost is zero. If you travel by ship, see *Luxury Water Travel* and *Cruise ships* (under *Conventions*) in Publication 463 for additional rules and limits.
Taxi, commuter bus, and airport limousine	Fares for these and other types of transportation that take you between: • The airport or station and your hotel, and • The hotel and the work location of your customers or clients, your business meeting place, or your temporary work location.
Baggage and shipping	Sending baggage and sample or display material between your regular and temporary work locations.
Car	Operating and maintaining your car when traveling away from home on business. You can deduct actual expenses or the standard mileage rate as well as business-related tolls and parking. If you rent a car while away from home on business, you can deduct only the business-use portion of the expenses.
Lodging and meals	Your lodging and meals if your business trip is overnight or long enough that you need to stop for sleep or rest to properly perform your duties. Meals include amounts spent for food, beverages, taxes, and related tips. See *Meals* for additional rules and limits.
Cleaning	Dry cleaning and laundry.
Telephone	Business calls while on your business trip. This includes business communication by fax machine or other communication devices.
Tips	Tips you pay for any expenses in this chart.
Other	Other similar ordinary and necessary expenses related to your business travel. These expenses might include transportation to or from a business meal, public stenographer's fees, computer rental fees, and operating and maintaining a house trailer.

Factors used to determine tax home. If you do not have a regular or main place of business or work, use the following three factors to determine where your tax home is.

1) You perform part of your business in the area of your main home and use that home for lodging while doing business in the area.
2) You have living expenses at your main home that you duplicate because your business requires you to be away from that home.
3) You have not abandoned the area in which both your historical place of lodging and your claimed main home are located; you have a member or members of your family living at your main home; or you often use that home for lodging.

If you satisfy all three factors, your tax home is the home where you regularly live. If you satisfy only two factors, you may have a tax home depending on all the facts and circumstances. If you satisfy only one factor, you are a *transient,* your tax home is wherever you work and you cannot deduct travel expenses.

Example 1
A retired federal district judge was allowed a travel expense deduction for travel from his personal residence, considered his tax home, to the courthouse for recalled active duty.

Example 2
After a taxpayer's employment in Cape Canaveral, Florida, was terminated, the taxpayer obtained temporary contract jobs in Virginia, Florida, North Carolina, Vermont, and Alabama. The Tax Court rejected the IRS assertion that the taxpayer had no tax home and allowed deductions for travel, meals, and lodging because he maintained a "tax home" in Cape Canaveral. The court noted that such deductions were allowed because the taxpayer returned to his Cape Canaveral home during periods of unemployment, and the taxpayer had a valid business purpose for maintaining his permanent address.

Example. You are single and live in Boston in an apartment you rent. You have worked for your employer in Boston for a number of years. Your employer enrolls you in a 12-month executive training program. You do not expect to return to work in Boston after you complete your training.

During your training, you do not do any work in Boston. Instead, you receive classroom and on-the-job training throughout the United States. You keep your apartment in Boston and return to it frequently. You use your apartment to conduct your personal business. You also keep up your community contacts in Boston. When you complete your training, you are transferred to Los Angeles.

You do not satisfy factor (1) because you did not work in Boston. You satisfy factor (2) because you had duplicate living expenses. You also satisfy factor (3) because you did not abandon your apartment in Boston as your main home, you kept your community contacts, and you frequently returned to live in your apartment. You have a tax home in Boston.

Explanation
According to the IRS, a home is a "regular place of abode in a real and substantial sense." The criteria are as follows:

1. You work in the same vicinity as your claimed abode and use it while doing business.
2. Your living expenses incurred at your claimed abode are duplicated when you're away on business.
3. You (a) have not abandoned the vicinity in which your place of lodging and claimed abode are both located; (b) have a family member or members (marital or lineal) currently residing at your claimed abode; or (c) use the claimed abode frequently.

If you maintain no fixed home, the burden of proof is on you to show the business portion of your daily expenses.

Example 1
A traveling salesman could not establish Reno, Nevada, as his tax home, even though he maintained a post office box and a bank account there, had dealings with a local stockbroker, bought an automobile there, stored his personal belongings there, and filed an income tax return from the city. He did not maintain a permanent place in Reno but stayed in hotels while he was there. Since no tax home was established, he could deduct only the business portion of his daily expenses. However, no expenses were allowed, since he did not maintain the necessary records.

Example 2
A traveling saleswoman maintained a room in her sister's home at a nominal rent. She worked for an employer in the same city, who paid her a per diem when she was away from that city. She had established a home for travel expense purposes.

Example 3
A college professor held a tenured position at a university located in Texas. While studying for her Ph.D. in Hawaii, she maintained a credit union account, a houseboat on which she paid property taxes, a post office box, and a library card in Texas and also stored almost all of her possessions there. She returned to the university after receiving her degree. The court ruled that her stay was not for an indefinite period, and she was able to deduct her lodging expenses in Hawaii.

Travel to family home. If you (and your family) do not live at your tax home, you cannot deduct the cost of traveling between your tax home and your family home. You also cannot deduct the cost of meals and lodging while at your tax home. See *Example 1* that follows.

If you are working temporarily in the same city where you and your family live, you may be considered as traveling away from home. See *Example 2,* below.

Example 1. You are a truck driver and you and your family live in Tucson. You are employed by a trucking firm that has its terminal in Phoenix. At the end of your long runs, you return to your home terminal in Phoenix and spend one night there before returning home. You cannot deduct any expenses you have for meals and lodging in Phoenix or the cost of traveling from Phoenix to Tucson. This is because Phoenix is your tax home.

Example 2. Your family home is in Pittsburgh, where you work 12 weeks a year. The rest of the year you work for the same employer in Baltimore. In Baltimore, you eat in restaurants and sleep in a rooming house. Your salary is the same whether you are in Pittsburgh or Baltimore.

Because you spend most of your working time and earn most of your salary in Baltimore, that city is your tax home. You cannot deduct any expenses you have for meals and lodging there. However, when you return to work in Pittsburgh, you are away from your tax home even though you stay at your family home. You can deduct the cost of your round trip between Baltimore and Pittsburgh. You can also deduct your part of your family's living expenses for meals and lodging while you are living and working in Pittsburgh.

Example 1
A famous baseball player was not allowed to deduct expenses for meals and lodging in Los Angeles, California, even though he maintained a home in another state. The court found his tax home to be Los Angeles, since it was his principal place of business.

Example 2
A member of the Marine Corps was stationed in Japan. His family remained in California, since they were not allowed to accompany him to his principal place of duty. The marine was not allowed to deduct travel expenses. His tax home was Japan, his principal place of duty. See *Members of the Armed Forces,* later.

Explanation
Where you earn the most money is the principal test for deciding where your tax home is.

Example
The IRS required a taxpayer to claim as his tax home a city away from the home in which his family resided. He earned 75% of his income in the city away from his family and 25% of his income in the city where his family lived. Since his tax home was different from his personal residence, he could deduct travel expenses incurred while living with his family.

Explanation
The distance between your residence and your place of employment is not a factor in determining whether expenses away from home are being incurred.

Example
The courts ruled that a taxpayer's personal decision to live a great distance from the location of his permanent employment did not render his meal and lodging expenses deductible. His place of business was his tax home.

Temporary Assignment or Job

You may regularly work at your tax home and another location. It may not be practical to return home from this other location at the end of each work day.

Temporary assignment vs. indefinite assignment. If your assignment or job away from your main place of work is *temporary,* your tax home does not change. You are considered to be away from home for the whole period you are away from your main place of work. You can deduct your travel expenses, if they otherwise qualify for deduction. Generally, a temporary assignment in a single location is one that is realistically expected to last (and does in fact last) for one year or less.

However, if your assignment or job is *indefinite,* the location of the assignment or job becomes your new tax home and you cannot deduct your travel expenses while there. An assignment or job in a single location is considered indefinite if it is realistically expected to last for more than one year, whether or not it actually lasts for more than one year.

If your assignment is indefinite, you must include in your income any amounts you receive from your employer for living expenses, even if they are called travel allowances and you account to your employer for them. You may be able to deduct the cost of relocating to your new tax home as a moving expense. See chapter 19 for more information.

Example 1

A construction worker who had been regularly employed near his home took a job in a city 250 miles away when construction got very slow in his hometown. He lived in his own trailer at the new job location. The job was expected to last 16 months, after which he planned to return home to his family. He frequently visited his hometown and continued to search for work there. *Previously,* the IRS had ruled that the worker was temporarily away from his home and *could* deduct his meals and lodging. However, under the most recent ruling, the worker's meals and lodging expenses would *not* be deductible because the assignment was expected to last longer than a year.

Example 2

A worker sold his residence in his home city, ceased to search for work there, and bought a new home at a new job location. The IRS ruled that the worker's stay was indefinite. He could not deduct the cost of his meals and lodging.

Example 3

Bill Horton, a professional hockey player, was allowed to deduct the cost of meals and lodging while playing hockey in San Diego, California. The Tax Court ruled that his tax home was in Michigan, where he maintained his house. A limited contract and the seasonal nature of the hockey profession caused the court to classify the San Diego job as temporary.

Example 4

A professional gambler spent equal amounts of time each year in Tampa and Gainesville, Florida; engaged in an equal amount of activity in both places; derived equal amounts of income in both places; and rented an apartment in each location. The court ruled that the activities were not temporary because they were "seasonal and recurring" activities. Therefore, the costs of both apartments were not deductible.

Exception for federal crime investigations or prosecutions. If you are a federal employee participating in a federal crime investigation or prosecution, you are not subject to the one-year rule. This means you may be able to deduct travel expenses even if you are away from your tax home for more than one year.

For you to qualify, the Attorney General must certify that you are traveling:

1) For the federal government,
2) In a temporary duty status, and
3) To investigate or prosecute, or provide support services for the investigation or prosecution of, a federal crime.

You can deduct your otherwise allowable travel expenses throughout the period of certification.

Determining temporary or indefinite. You must determine whether your assignment is temporary or indefinite when you start work. If you expect an assignment or job to last for one year or less, it is temporary unless there are facts and circumstances that indicate otherwise. An assignment or job that is initially temporary may become indefinite due to changed circumstances. A series of assignments to the same location, all for short periods but that together cover a long period, may be considered an indefinite assignment.

Explanation

If employment away from home in a single location is realistically expected to last for more than 1 year, or if there is no realistic expectation that the employment will last for 1 year or less, the employment is indefinite regardless of whether it actually exceeds 1 year.

Employment is temporary if work away from home in a single location is realistically expected to last (and does in fact last) for 1 year or less, in the absence of any facts and circumstances indicating otherwise.

TaxAlert

Employment away from home in a single location lasting more than 1 year is not treated as temporary. However, if employment away from home was initially expected to be for 1 year or less, and then expectations changed for it to be for more than 1 year, the employment will be considered temporary up to the point that the time length expectations changed.

Example 1

A taxpayer accepts work in a city 250 miles from the city in which she is regularly employed. She expects the work to be completed in 18 months but in fact completes the work in 10 months. The taxpayer's travel expenses are not deductible because the taxpayer's employment is indefinite. Even though the work actually lasted less than 1 year, the employment is still indefinite because the taxpayer realistically expected the work to last longer than 1 year.

Example 2

The facts are the same except that the taxpayer expects the work to be completed in 9 months. After 8 months, however, the taxpayer is asked to remain for 7 more months (for an actual stay of 15 months). The taxpayer's travel expenses are deductible only during the first 8 months of employment because only during those months did the taxpayer realistically expect the employment to be temporary.

Going home on days off. If you go back to your tax home from a temporary assignment on your days off, you are not considered away from home while you are in your hometown. You cannot deduct the cost of your meals and lodging there. However, you can deduct your travel expenses, including meals and lodging, while traveling between your temporary place of work and your tax home. You can claim these expenses up to the amount it would have cost you to stay at your temporary place of work.

If you keep your hotel room during your visit home, you can deduct the cost of your hotel room. In addition, you can deduct your expenses of returning home up to the amount you would have spent for meals had you stayed at your temporary place of work.

Probationary work period. If you take a job that requires you to move, with the understanding that you will keep the job if your work is satisfactory during a probationary period, the job is indefinite. You cannot deduct any of your expenses for meals and lodging during the probationary period.

What Travel Expenses Are Deductible?

Once you have determined that you are traveling away from your tax home, you can determine what travel expenses are deductible.

You can deduct ordinary and necessary expenses you have when you travel away from home on business. The type of expense you can deduct depends on the facts and your circumstances.

Table 28-1 summarizes travel expenses you may be able to deduct. You may have other deductible travel expenses that are not covered there, depending on the facts and your circumstances.

Explanation

Ordinarily, you can deduct expenses that you incurred to produce or collect income, or to manage, conserve, or maintain property held for producing income only on Schedule A (Form 1040). Therefore, you must itemize your deductions to claim these expenses. See Chapter 30, *Miscellaneous Deductions*.

To be deductible, an expense must be closely associated with an activity that is expected to produce income or must be incurred maintaining property that is held to produce income. Such expenses are deductible only if you itemize.

Travel and other costs of attending investment seminars are specifically disallowed.

Example 1

Transportation expenses to attend a stockholders' meeting are not deductible, unless you can demonstrate that you played a fairly substantial role in the meeting. Otherwise, it is not clear that the expenses were incurred to produce income.

Example 2

The courts held that an individual who spent his lunch hour at brokerage houses could not deduct his travel expenses because he could not establish the relationship between his visits and his investment activities.

When you travel away from home on business, you should keep records of all the expenses you have and any advances you receive from your employer. You can use a log, diary, notebook, or any other written record to keep track of your expenses. The types of expenses you need to record, along with supporting documentation, are described in *Table 28-2.*

Separating costs. If you have one expense that includes the costs of meals, entertainment, and other services (such as lodging or transportation), you must allocate that expense between the cost of meals and entertainment and the cost of other services. You must have a reasonable basis for making this allocation. For example, you must allocate your expenses if a hotel includes one or more meals in its room charge.

Travel expenses for another individual. If a spouse, dependent, or other individual goes with you (or your employee) on a business trip or to a business convention, you generally cannot deduct his or her travel expenses.

Employee. You can deduct the travel expenses of someone who goes with you if that person:

1) Is your employee,
2) Has a bona fide business purpose for the travel, and
3) Would otherwise be allowed to deduct the travel expenses.

Business associate. If a business associate travels with you and meets the conditions in (2) and (3) above, you can deduct the travel expenses you have for that person. A business associate is someone with whom you could reasonably expect to actively conduct business. A business associate can be a current or prospective (likely to become) customer, client, supplier, employee, agent, partner, or professional advisor.

Bona fide business purpose. A bona fide business purpose exists if you can prove a real business purpose for the individual's presence. Incidental services, such as typing notes or assisting in entertaining customers, are not enough to make the expenses deductible.

Example. Jerry drives to Chicago on business and takes his wife, Linda, with him. Linda is not Jerry's employee. Linda occasionally types notes, performs similar services, and accompanies Jerry to luncheons and dinners. The performance of these services does not establish that her presence on the trip is necessary to the conduct of Jerry's business. Her expenses are not deductible.

Jerry pays $115 a day for a double room. A single room costs $90 a day. He can deduct the total cost of driving his car to and from Chicago, but only $90 a day for his hotel room. If he uses public transportation, he can deduct only his fare.

TaxAlert

The tax law denies a deduction for travel expenses paid or incurred for a spouse, dependent, or other individual accompanying you on business travel, unless certain requirements are met. For the expenses to be deductible, your traveling companion must: (1) be a bona fide employee of the person paying or reimbursing the expenses; (2) be traveling for a bona fide business purpose; and (3) have expenses that are otherwise deductible. The denial of the deduction does not apply to expenses that would otherwise qualify as deductible moving expenses.

Meals

You can deduct the cost of meals in either of the following two situations.

1) It is necessary for you to stop for substantial sleep or rest to properly perform your duties while traveling away from home on business.
2) The meal is business-related entertainment.

Business-related entertainment is discussed under *Entertainment Expenses,* later. The following discussion deals only with meals that are not business-related entertainment.

Lavish or extravagant. You cannot deduct expenses for meals that are lavish or extravagant. An expense is not considered lavish or extravagant if it is reasonable based on the facts and circumstances. Expenses will not be disallowed merely because they are more than a fixed dollar amount or take place at deluxe restaurants, hotels, nightclubs, or resorts.

50% limit on meals. You can figure your meal expenses using either of the following two methods.

1) Actual cost.
2) The standard meal allowance.

Both of these methods are explained below. But, regardless of the method you use, you generally can deduct only 50% of the unreimbursed cost of your meals.

TaxAlert

Meal expenses when subject to hours of service limits. Generally, you can deduct only 50% of your business-related meal expenses while traveling away from your tax home for busi-

Table 28-2. **How To Prove Certain Business Expenses**

IF you have expenses for:	THEN you must keep records that show details of the following elements.			
	Amount	**Time**	**Place or Description**	**Business Purpose and Business Relationship**
Travel	Cost of each separate expense for travel, lodging, and meals. Incidental expenses may be totaled in reasonable categories such as taxis, daily meals for traveler, etc.	Dates you left and returned for each trip and number of days spent on business.	Destination or area of your travel (name of city, town, or other designation).	Purpose: Business purpose for the expense or the business benefit gained or expected to be gained. Relationship: N/A
Entertainment	Cost of each separate expense. Incidental expenses such as taxis, telephones, etc., may be totaled on a daily basis.	Date of entertainment. (Also see *Business Purpose.*)	Name and address or location of place of entertainment. Type of entertainment if not otherwise apparent. (Also see *Business Purpose.*)	Purpose: Business purpose for the expense or the business benefit gained or expected to be gained. For entertainment, the nature of the business discussion or activity. If the entertainment was directly before or after a business discussion: the date, place, nature, and duration of the business discussion, and the identities of the persons who took part in both the business discussion and the entertainment activity. Relationship: Occupations or other information (such as names, titles, or other designations) about the recipients that shows their business relationship to you. For entertainment, you must also prove that you or your employee was present if the entertainment was a business meal.
Gifts	Cost of the gift.	Date of the gift.	Description of the gift.	
Transportation	Cost of each separate expense. For car expenses, the cost of the car and any improvements, the date you started using it for business, the mileage for each business use, and the total miles for the year.	Date of the expense. For car expenses, the date of the use of the car.	Your business destination.	Purpose: Business purpose for the expense. Relationship: N/A

ness purposes. If you consume the meals during or incident to any period subject to the Department of Transportation's hours of service limits, you can deduct a higher percentage. The percentage is 60% for 2001, and it gradually increases to 80% by the year 2008.

Individuals subject to the Department of Transportation's hours of service limits include the following persons:

1. Certain air transportation workers (such as pilots, crew, dispatchers, mechanics, and control tower operators) who are under Federal Aviation Administration regulations
2. Interstate truck operators and bus drivers who are under Department of Transportation regulations
3. Certain railroad employees (such as engineers, conductors, train crews, dispatchers, and control operations personnel) who are under Federal Railroad Administration regulations
4. Certain merchant mariners who are under Coast Guard regulations

For more information on business meal expenses, see Publication 463.

If you are reimbursed for the cost of your meals, how you apply the 50% limit depends on whether your employer's reimbursement plan was accountable or nonaccountable. If you are not reimbursed, the 50% limit applies whether the unreimbursed meal expense is for business travel or business entertainment. The 50% limit is explained later under *Entertainment Expenses.* Accountable and nonaccountable plans are discussed later under *Reimbursements.*

Actual cost. You can use the actual cost of your meals to figure the amount of your expense before reimbursement and application of the 50% deduction limit. If you use this method, you must keep records of your actual cost.

Standard meal allowance. Generally, you can use the "standard meal allowance" method as an alternative to the actual cost method. It allows you to use a set amount for your daily **meals and incidental expenses (M&IE),** instead of keeping records of your actual costs. The set amount varies depending on where and when you travel. In this chapter, "standard meal allowance" refers to the federal rate for M&IE, discussed later under *Amount of standard meal allowance.* If you use the standard meal allowance, you still must keep records to prove the time, place, and business purpose of your travel. See *Recordkeeping,* later.

Incidental expenses. These include, but are not limited to, your costs for the following items.

1) Laundry, cleaning and pressing of clothing.
2) Fees and tips for persons who provide services, such as porters and baggage carriers.

Incidental expenses do not include taxicab fares, lodging taxes, or the costs of telegrams or telephone calls.

Explanation
Incidental expenses include items such as laundry expenses and fees and tips for waiters and baggage handlers; however, they do not include taxicab fares or the costs of telegrams or telephone calls.

Caution. *Federal employees should refer to the federal travel regulations at* **www.policyworks.gov/ftr** *for changes affecting their claims for reimbursement of these expenses.*

50% limit may apply. If you use this method for meal expenses and you are not reimbursed or you are reimbursed under a nonaccountable plan, you can generally deduct only 50% of the standard meal allowance. If you are reimbursed under an accountable plan and you are deducting amounts that are more than your reimbursements, you can deduct only 50% of the excess amount. The 50% limit is explained later under *Entertainment Expenses.* Accountable and nonaccountable plans are discussed later under *Reimbursements.*

Caution. *There is no optional standard lodging amount similar to the standard meal allowance. Your allowable lodging expense deduction is your actual cost.*

Who can use the standard meal allowance? You can use the standard meal allowance whether you are an employee or self-employed, and whether or not you are reimbursed for your traveling expenses.

Who cannot use the standard meal allowance. You cannot use the standard meal allowance if you are related to your employer as defined next.

Related to employer. You are related to your employer if:

1) Your employer is your brother or sister, half brother or half sister, spouse, ancestor, or lineal descendant,
2) Your employer is a corporation in which you own, directly or indirectly, more than 10% in value of the outstanding stock, or
3) Certain relationships (such as grantor, fiduciary, or beneficiary) exist between you, a trust, and your employer.

You may be considered to indirectly own stock, for purposes of (2), if you have an interest in a corporation, partnership, estate, or trust that owns the stock or if a member of your family or your partner owns the stock.

Use of the standard meal allowance for other travel. You can use the standard meal allowance to figure your meal expenses when you travel in connection with investment and other income-producing property. You can also use it to figure your meal expenses when you travel for qualifying educational purposes. You *cannot* use the standard meal allowance to figure the cost of your meals when you travel for medical or charitable purposes.

Amount of standard meal allowance. The standard meal allowance is the federal M&IE rate. For travel in 2001, the rate is *$30 a day* for most small localities in the United States. Most major cities and many other localities in the United States are designated as high-cost areas, qualifying for higher standard meal allowances. Locations qualifying for rates of $34, $38, $42, or $46 a day are listed in Publication 1542.

If you travel to more than one location in one day, use the rate in effect for the area where you stop for sleep or rest. If you work in the transportation industry, however, see *Special rate for transportation workers,* later.

TaxPlanner
Whether or not you receive meal money from your employer, you may claim the standard meal allowance and therefore minimize your record-keeping problems. If you are self-employed, you may also claim the standard meal allowance.

Standard meal allowance for areas outside the continental United States. The standard meal allowance rates do not apply to travel in Alaska, Hawaii, or any other locations outside the continental United States. The federal per diem rates for these locations are published monthly in the *Maximum Travel Per Diem Allowances for Foreign Areas.*

Your employer may have these rates available, or you can purchase the publication from the:

Superintendent of Documents
U.S. Government Printing Office
P.O. Box 371954
Pittsburgh, PA 15250-7954

You can also order it by calling the Government Printing Office at 1-202-512-1800 (not a toll-free number).

Per diem rates are also available on the Internet. If you have a computer and a modem, you can access foreign per diem rates at:

www.state.gov

You can access domestic per diem rates at:

www.policyworks.gov/perdiem

Special rate for transportation workers. You can use a special standard meal allowance if you work in the transportation industry. You are in the transportation industry if your work:

1) Directly involves moving people or goods by airplane, barge, bus, ship, train, or truck, and
2) Regularly requires you to travel away from home and, during any single trip, usually involves travel to areas eligible for different standard meal allowance rates.

If this applies to you, you can claim a *$38 a day* standard meal allowance ($42 for travel outside the continental United States).

Using the special rate for transportation workers eliminates the need for you to determine the standard meal allowance for every area where you stop for sleep or rest. If you choose to use the special rate for any trip, you must use the special rate (and not use the regular standard meal allowance rates) for all trips you take that year.

Travel for days you depart and return. For both the day you depart for and the day you return from a business trip, you must prorate the standard meal allowance (figure a reduced amount for each day). You can do so by one of two methods.

1) *Method 1:* You can claim 3/4 of the standard meal allowance, or
2) *Method 2:* You can prorate using any method that you consistently apply and that is in accordance with reasonable business practice.

Example. Jen is employed in New Orleans as a convention planner. In March, her employer sent her on a 3-day trip to Washington, DC, to attend a planning seminar. She left her home in New Orleans at 10 A.M. on Wednesday and arrived in Washington, DC, at 5:30 P.M. After spending two nights there, she flew back to New Orleans on Friday and arrived back home at 8:00 P.M. Jen's employer gave her a flat amount to cover her expenses and included it with her wages.

Under Method 1, Jen can claim 2 1/2 days of the standard meal allowance for Washington, DC: 3/4 of the daily rate for Wednesday and Friday (the days she departed and returned), and the full daily rate for Thursday.

Under Method 2, Jen could also use any method that she applies consistently and that is in accordance with reasonable business practice. For example, she could claim 3 days of the standard meal allowance even though a federal employee would have to use method 1 and be limited to only 2 1/2 days.

Travel in the United States

The following discussion applies to travel in the United States. For this purpose, the United States includes the 50 states and the District of Columbia. The treatment of your travel expenses depends on how much of your trip was business related and on how much of your trip occurred within the United States. See *Part of Trip Outside the United States,* later.

Trip Primarily for Business
You can deduct all your travel expenses if your trip was entirely business related. If your trip was primarily for business and, while at your business destination, you extended your stay for a vacation, made a personal side trip, or had other personal activities, you can deduct your business-related travel expenses. These expenses include the travel costs of getting to and from your business destination and any business-related expenses at your business destination.

Example. You work in Atlanta and take a business trip to New Orleans. On your way home, you stop in Mobile to visit your parents. You spend $630 for the 9 days you are away from home for travel, meals, lodging, and other travel expenses. If you had not stopped in Mobile, you would have been gone only 6 days, and your total cost would have been $580. You can deduct $580 for your trip, including the round-trip transportation to and from New Orleans. The deduction for your meals is subject to the 50% limit on meals mentioned earlier.

Trip Primarily for Personal Reasons
If your trip was primarily for personal reasons, such as a vacation, the entire cost of the trip is a nondeductible personal expense. However, you can deduct any expenses you have while at your destination that are directly related to your business.

A trip to a resort or on a cruise ship may be a vacation even if the promoter advertises that it is primarily for business. The scheduling of incidental business activities during a trip, such as viewing videotapes or attending lectures dealing with general subjects, will not change what is really a vacation into a business trip.

Explanation
The courts have not allowed expenses to be deducted for trips whose primary purpose is pleasure but whose secondary purpose is the investigation of business rental properties. If the primary purpose of the trip is to search for rental properties, all travel expenses can be deducted.

TaxOrganizer

Careful records should be maintained when family members are along on business trips. If a spouse or other family member on a trip serves a business purpose, care should be taken to document that fact. Otherwise, the incremental travel expenses attributed to the additional person may not be deducted. Receipts and a diary of your activities will be of assistance in documenting the purpose of your trip.

Part of Trip Outside the United States
If part of your trip is outside the United States, use the rules described later under *Travel Outside the United States* for that part of the trip. For the part of your trip that is inside the United States, use the rules for travel in the United States. Travel outside the United States does not include travel from one point in the United States to another point in the United States. The following discussion can help you determine whether your trip was entirely within the United States.

Public transportation. If you travel by public transportation, any place in the United States where that vehicle makes a scheduled stop is a point in the United States. Once the vehicle leaves the last scheduled stop in the United States on its way to a point outside the United States, you apply the rules under *Travel Outside the United States.*

Example. You fly from New York to Puerto Rico with a scheduled stop in Miami. You return to New York nonstop. The flight from New York to Miami is in the United States, so only the flight from Miami to Puerto Rico is outside the United States. Because there are no scheduled stops between Puerto Rico and New York, all of the return trip is outside the United States.

Private car. Travel by private car in the United States is travel between points in the United States, even when you are on your way to a destination outside the United States.

Example. You travel by car from Denver to Mexico City and return. Your travel from Denver to the border and from the border back to Denver is travel in the United States, and the rules in this section apply. The rules under *Travel Outside the United States* apply to your trip from the border to Mexico City and back to the border.

Travel Outside the United States

If any part of your business travel is outside the United States, some of your deductions for the cost of getting to and from your destination may be limited. For this purpose, the United States includes the 50 states and the District of Columbia.

How much of your travel expenses you can deduct depends in part upon how much of your trip outside the United States was business related.

See chapter 1 of Publication 463 for information on luxury water travel.

Travel Entirely for Business or Considered Entirely for Business
You can deduct all your travel expenses of getting to and from your business destination if your trip is entirely for business or considered entirely for business.

Travel entirely for business. If you travel outside the United States and you spend the entire time on business activities, you can deduct all of your travel expenses.

Travel considered entirely for business. Even if you did not spend your entire time on business activities, your trip is considered entirely for business if you meet at least one of the following four exceptions.

Exception 1—No substantial control. Your trip is considered entirely for business if you did not have substantial control over arranging the trip. The fact that you control the timing of your trip does not, by itself, mean that you have substantial control over arranging your trip.

You do not have substantial control over your trip if you:

1) Are an employee who was reimbursed or paid a travel expense allowance,
2) Are not related to your employer, and
3) Are not a managing executive.

"Related to your employer" was defined earlier in this chapter under *Who cannot use the standard meal allowance?*

A "managing executive" is an employee who has the authority and responsibility, without being subject to the veto of another, to decide on the need for the business travel.

A self-employed person generally has substantial control over arranging business trips.

Exception 2—Outside United States no more than a week. Your trip is considered entirely for business if you were outside the United States for a week or less, combining business and nonbusiness activities. One week means seven consecutive days. In counting the days, do not count the day you leave the United States, but do count the day you return to the United States.

Exception 3—Less than 25% of time on personal activities. Your trip is considered entirely for business if:

1) You were outside the United States for more than a week, and
2) You spent less than 25% of the total time you were outside the United States on nonbusiness activities.

For this purpose, count both the day your trip began and the day it ended.

Exception 4—Vacation not a major consideration. Your trip is considered entirely for business if you can establish that a personal vacation was not a major consideration, even if you have substantial control over arranging the trip.

Travel Primarily for Business

If you travel outside the United States primarily for business but spend some of your time on nonbusiness activities, you generally cannot deduct all of your travel expenses. You can only deduct the business portion of your cost of getting to and from your destination. You must make an allocation between your business and nonbusiness activities to determine your deductible amount. These travel allocation rules are discussed in chapter 1 of Publication 463.

Tip. *You do not have to allocate your travel expense deduction if you meet one of the four exceptions listed earlier under* Travel considered entirely for business. *In those cases, you can deduct the total cost of getting to and from your destination.*

Explanation
A business day is established if, during any part of the day, you are required to be present at a business-related event. Weekends falling between business days may be considered business days, but if they fall at the end of your business meetings and you remain for personal reasons, they are not business days. Transportation days are business days when you travel to your destination on a direct route.

TAXPLANNER
If, in order to take advantage of lower plane fares, your employer reimburses your travel expenses for staying overnight on Saturday at the end of a business trip, the meals and lodging costs for Saturday can be deducted by your employer and excluded from your income to the extent the costs do not exceed the cost savings. The IRS privately ruled that these travel expenses relating to the Saturday night away are deductible even though the day is spent sight-seeing.

Travel Primarily for Personal Reasons

If you travel outside the United States primarily for vacation or for *investment* purposes, the entire cost of the trip is a nondeductible *personal expense.* If you spend some time attending brief professional seminars or a continuing education program, you can deduct your registration fees and other expenses you have that are directly related to your business.

Conventions

You can deduct your travel expenses when you attend a convention if you can show that your attendance benefits your trade or business. You cannot deduct the travel expenses for your family.

If the convention is for *investment,* political, social, or other nonbusiness purposes, you cannot deduct the expenses.

Caution. *Your appointment or election as a delegate does not, in itself, determine whether you can deduct travel expenses. You can deduct your travel expenses only if your attendance is connected to your own trade or business.*

Convention agenda. The convention agenda or program generally shows the purpose of the convention. You can show your attendance at the convention benefits your trade or business by comparing the agenda with the official duties and responsibilities of your position. The agenda does not have to deal specifically with your official duties and responsibilities; it will be enough if the agenda is so related to your position that it shows your attendance was for business purposes.

Explanation
To determine whether a trip is primarily for business, the courts have used the following guidelines:

1. The amount of time spent on personal activity compared with the amount of time spent on business activity
2. The location of the convention (the setting of a convention at a resort does not mean that the expense is disallowed, but a more businesslike setting increases the strength of your case)
3. The attitude of your sponsor toward the purpose of the meeting

The courts must also be satisfied that the primary purpose of the convention is business related.

Conventions held outside the North American area. See chapter 1 of Publication 463 for information on conventions held outside the North American area.

Explanation
The amount of expenses you incur when you travel on an ocean liner or cruise ship may not be fully deductible. Generally, the amount of the deduction is limited to twice the per diem rate of an employee of the executive branch of the U.S. government multiplied by the number of days you travel on the ship. For travel on or after January 1, 1995, the executive per diem rate is $204. For travel prior to 1995, lower per diem rates applied. However, if you attend a convention while aboard the cruise ship, you may still deduct up to $2,000 per individual per calendar year if the following requirements are met:

1. The meeting must be directly related to the active conduct of a business.
2. The cruise ship must be registered in the United States and may travel only to ports in the United States or its possessions.
3. You attach to your return a written statement signed by you that includes:
   a) The total days of the trip, excluding the days of transporation to and from the cruise ship port
   b) The number of hours each day that you devoted to scheduled business activities
   c) A program of the scheduled business activities of the meeting
4. You attach to your return a written statement signed by an officer of the organization or group sponsoring the meeting that includes:
   a) A schedule of the business activities of each day of the meeting
   b) The number of hours you attended the scheduled business activities

Example
You have a business meeting in Puerto Rico and choose to travel by ship. You spend 6 days on the cruise ship from

the time you depart until the time you return. The total cost of the 6-day cruise package is $3,000. You may deduct only $2,000 of the $3,000 costs.

Entertainment Expenses

You may be able to deduct business-related entertainment expenses you have for entertaining a client, customer, or employee.

You can deduct entertainment expenses only if they are both ordinary and necessary (defined earlier) and meet one of the following two tests.

1) Directly-related test.
2) Associated test.

Both of these tests are explained in Publication 463.

Caution. *The amount you can deduct for entertainment expenses may be limited. Generally, you can deduct only 50% of your unreimbursed entertainment expenses. This limit is discussed later under* 50% Limit.

Club dues and membership fees. You cannot deduct dues (including initiation fees) for membership in any club organized for:

1) Business,
2) Pleasure,
3) Recreation, or
4) Other social purpose.

This rule applies to any membership organization if one of its principal purposes is either:

1) To conduct entertainment activities for members or their guests, or
2) To provide members or their guests with access to entertainment facilities.

The purposes and activities of a club, not its name, will determine whether or not you can deduct the dues. You cannot deduct dues paid to:

1) Country clubs,
2) Golf and athletic clubs,
3) Airline clubs,
4) Hotel clubs, and
5) Clubs operated to provide meals under circumstances generally considered to be conducive to business discussions.

Entertainment. Entertainment includes any activity generally considered to provide entertainment, amusement, or recreation. Examples include entertaining guests at nightclubs; at social, athletic, and sporting clubs; at theaters; at sporting events; on yachts; or on hunting, fishing, vacation, and similar trips. You cannot deduct expenses for entertainment that are lavish or extravagant. If you buy a ticket to an entertainment event for a client, you generally cannot deduct more than the face value of the ticket, even if you paid a higher price.

Gift or entertainment. Any item that might be considered either a gift or entertainment generally will be considered entertainment. However, if you give a customer packaged food or beverages that you intend the customer to use at a later date, treat it as a gift.

If you give a customer tickets to a theater performance or sporting event and you do not go with the customer to the performance or event, you have a choice. You can treat the cost of the tickets as either a gift expense or an entertainment expense, whichever is to your advantage.

You can change your treatment of the tickets at a later date by filing an amended return. Generally, an amended return must be filed within 3 years from the date the original return was filed or within 2 years from the time the tax was paid, whichever is later.

If you go with the customer to the event, you must treat the cost of the tickets as an entertainment expense. You cannot choose, in this case, to treat the cost of the tickets as a gift expense.

Separating costs. If you have one expense that includes the costs of entertainment, and other services (such as lodging or transportation),

you must allocate that expense between the cost of entertainment and the cost of other services. You must have a reasonable basis for making this allocation. For example, you must allocate your expenses if a hotel includes entertainment in its lounge on the same bill with your room charge.

A meal as a form of entertainment. Entertainment includes the cost of a meal you provide to a customer or client, whether the meal is a part of other entertainment or by itself. A meal expense includes the cost of food, beverages, taxes, and tips for the meal. To deduct an entertainment-related meal, you or your employee must be present when the food or beverages are provided.

Caution. *You cannot claim the cost of your meal both as an entertainment expense and as a travel expense.*

Taking turns paying for meals or entertainment. If a group of business acquaintances take turns picking up each others' meal or entertainment checks without regard to whether any business purposes are served, no member of the group can deduct any part of the expense.

Trade association meetings. You can deduct expenses for entertainment that are directly related to, and necessary for, attending business meetings or conventions of certain exempt organizations *if* the expenses of your attendance are related to your active trade or business. These organizations include business leagues, chambers of commerce, real estate boards, trade associations, and professional associations.

> **Explanation**
> The courts have held that costs of entertaining fellow employees are not deductible, even though the entertaining may have contributed to high morale and increased productivity.

Additional information. For more information on entertainment expenses, including discussions of the directly-related and associated tests, see chapter 2 of Publication 463.

50% Limit

In general, you can deduct only 50% of your business-related meal and entertainment expenses. (If you are subject to the Department of Transportation's "hours of service" limits, you can deduct a higher percentage. See *Individuals subject to "hours of service" limits,* later.)

The 50% limit applies to employees or their employers, and to self-employed persons (including independent contractors) or their clients, depending on whether the expenses are reimbursed.

Figure 28-A summarizes the general rules explained in this section.

The 50% limit applies to business meals or entertainment expenses you have while:

1) Traveling away from home (whether eating alone or with others) on business,
2) Entertaining customers at your place of business, a restaurant, or other location, or
3) Attending a business convention or reception, business meeting, or business luncheon at a club.

> **TAXALERT**
> The tax law denies a deduction for amounts paid or incurred for membership in any club organized for business, pleasure, recreation, or other social purpose.

Included expenses. Expenses subject to the 50% limit include:

- Taxes and tips relating to a business meal or entertainment activity,
- Cover charges for admission to a nightclub,
- Rent paid for a room in which you hold a dinner or cocktail party, and
- Amounts paid for parking at a sports arena.

However, the cost of transportation to and from a business meal or a business-related entertainment activity is not subject to the 50% limit.

Application of 50% limit. The 50% limit on meal and entertainment expenses applies if the expense is otherwise deductible and is not covered by one of the exceptions discussed later in this section.

The 50% limit also applies to certain meal and entertainment expenses that are not business-related. It applies to meal and entertainment expenses incurred for the production of income, including rental or royalty income. It also applies to the cost of meals included in deductible educational expenses.

When to apply the 50% limit. You apply the 50% limit after determining the amount that would otherwise qualify for a deduction. You first determine the amount of meal and entertainment expenses that would be deductible under the other rules discussed in this chapter.

Example 1. You spend $100 for a business-related meal. If $40 of that amount is not allowable because it is lavish and extravagant, the remaining $60 is subject to the 50% limit. Your deduction cannot be more than $30 (.50 × $60).

Example 2. You purchase two tickets to a concert and give them to a client. You purchased the tickets through a ticket agent. You paid $150 for the two tickets, which had a face value of $60 each ($120 total). Your deduction cannot be more than $60 (.50 × $120).

Explanation

Although entertaining a client or a business associate often makes sound business sense, entertainment deductions have sometimes been abused. For this reason, Congress has imposed limitations on the deductibility of entertainment expenses. Only 50% of otherwise allowable entertainment expenses are deductible. The 50% disallowance generally applies to all taxpayers, regardless of the nature of the business. Even before the 50% disallowance, entertainment expenses are subject to stringent record-keeping requirements and must pass one of two tests:

1. **Directly related test.** The expenditure is directly related to the active conduct of your business.
2. **Associated with test.** The expenditure is associated with the active conduct of your business, and the entertainment directly precedes or follows a substantial, bona fide business discussion.

Business meals—those that have a business purpose as opposed to a social and personal one—are not subject to these entertainment rules if they occur in surroundings conducive to business discussion, the taxpayer or an employee

Figure 28–A. Does the 50% Limit Apply to Your Expenses?
There are exceptions to these rules. See *Exceptions to the 50% Limit.*

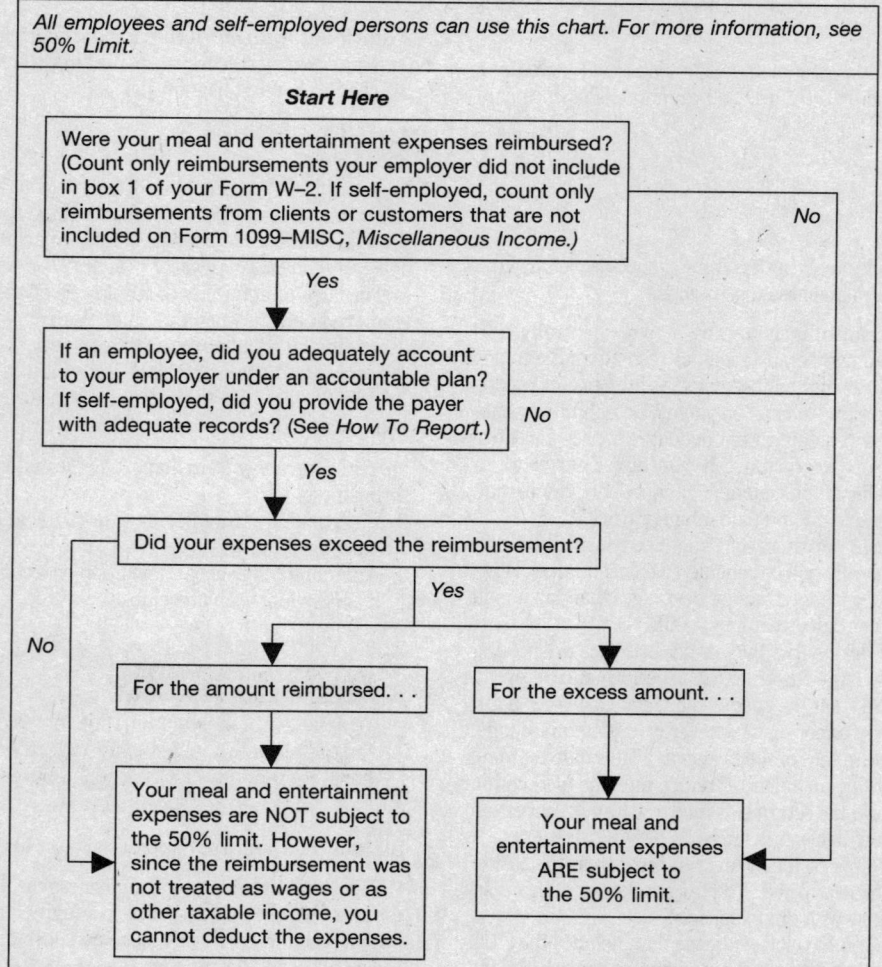

of the taxpayer is present when the food or beverages are served, and the expenses are properly substantiated.

Deductions for entertainment or business meals may not be taken if such expenses are considered lavish or extravagant.

Example
State police officers who are required to eat meals while on duty in public places were permitted to deduct expenses for these meals. The court found that the officers were significantly restricted by their employment regarding the time and place they were permitted to eat and that the meals were often subject to business-related interruptions.

Explanation
Entertainment directly related to business. The directly related test is satisfied if all of the following are true:

- You expect to derive income or some other specific business benefit (other than mere goodwill) at some indefinite future time. However, it is not necessary to demonstrate that you actually receive the benefit.
- You actively engage in a business meeting, discussion, or other bona fide business transaction with the person being entertained.
- Your principal purpose of the combined business-entertainment activity is the *active conduct* of your business. It is not necessary to devote more time to business than to the entertainment to meet this requirement.

Certain entertainment activities generally do not meet the directly related test unless proven otherwise. If you are not present for the entertainment, if the group entertained includes persons other than business associates (such as spouses), or if there are substantial distractions (as may occur in nightclubs, theaters, sporting events, and vacation resorts), your activity may fail the directly related test.

The IRS gives taxpayers some relief from these strict rules when the activity is clearly in a business setting. For example, expenditures made to further your business by providing a hospitality room at a convention are treated as entertainment expenses directly related to business. Additionally, situations in which no meaningful personal or social relationship exists between you and the persons entertained are often considered to have occurred in a business setting. For example, entertaining business and civic leaders at the opening of a new hotel or theatrical production—for the purpose of obtaining business publicity rather than creating or maintaining goodwill—is a deductible entertainment expense directly related to business.

Example
An attorney paid for the costs of an annual fishing trip with three business associates who were sources of referrals to his law practice. He also used his cabin 75% of the time for entertaining business clients. The attorney could not prove that substantial and bona fide business discussions occurred during the fishing trip or on any of the occasions when business clients used the cabin. He showed that, at most, he had just a generalized expectation of deriving income or other business benefits at some indefinite future time from those entertained. As a result, he was denied deductions for these expenses because they did not meet the directly related test.

Explanation
Entertainment associated with business. If an entertainment expenditure does not meet the directly related requirements, it may still be deductible if it passes the associated with test. An entertainment activity passes the associated with test only if it satisfies two conditions:

- The activity has a clear business purpose.
- The entertainment directly precedes or follows a substantial, bona fide business discussion.

The desire to obtain new business and the intent to maintain an existing business relationship—goodwill—are objectives that have a clear business purpose. A substantial, bona fide business discussion occurs when you actively engage in a business transaction to obtain some business benefit and the business meeting, negotiation, or discussion is substantial in relation to the entertainment. However, it is not necessary to spend more time on business than on entertainment.

Example
Bonnie McDonald, an independent consultant, spends 4 hours delivering a new management program to a group of executives in her client's New Orleans office. After the meeting, Bonnie takes the group to the French Quarter for dinner and a show. Dixieland jazz is played throughout dinner.

The entertainment passes the associated with test and is therefore deductible (subject to the 50% limitation) because Bonnie is maintaining a business relationship and the entertainment follows a substantial business meeting. The expense would not pass the directly related test because (1) goodwill generally does not qualify and (2) substantial distractions exist.

Explanation
Entertainment directly precedes or follows a substantial business discussion if it occurs on the same day. If the entertainment and business discussion do not occur on the same day, the facts and circumstances of each case determine whether or not the entertainment and the business discussion occur close enough in time so that the expenses can be deducted.

Example
A group of business associates come to Denver and hold substantial discussions with a taxpayer. Entertainment for the business guests on the evening prior to or after the day of the business discussions is generally regarded as directly preceding or following the business discussion. Therefore, 50% of the entertainment expenses are deductible.

Explanation
Deducting goodwill entertainment. Generally, entertaining for goodwill alone is not deductible. However, you may deduct goodwill expenditures when

- The goodwill occurs during a quiet business lunch or dinner.
- The goodwill precedes or follows a substantial business discussion (i.e., passes the associated with test).

Example 1
Liz Brown, a partner of a management consulting firm, plans a dinner party in a New York City hotel. She invites a number of current and prospective clients. Business is only casually discussed; her main goal is to cultivate goodwill. The

expense for the dinner party is not deductible. The goodwill is a clear business purpose, but the dinner is not preceded or followed by a substantial business discussion.

Example 2

After considering the tax cost of the nondeductible goodwill expenses, Liz Brown holds a second dinner party, but she adds a formal presentation, which is substantial in relation to the time spent cultivating goodwill. The costs of the refreshments and dinner qualify as goodwill entertainment, since the entertainment is associated with business and the goodwill (the business purpose) is preceded by a substantial business discussion (the presentation). As a result, 50% of the qualifying expenses are deductible.

Explanation

Out-of-pocket entertaining costs at clubs and lodges. Congress has made it clear that out-of-pocket entertainment costs—that otherwise qualify as directly related or associated with business expenses—may still be partially deducted, even if they are incurred at an entertainment facility. Again, 50% of such costs may not be deducted.

An entertainment facility is usually **real property,** such as a fishing camp, a ski lodge, an apartment, or a hotel suite, that may also include personal property, such as a yacht, an airplane, or an automobile. You may own or rent the facility or just be a member of a club or organization, such as a country club or a sporting group, that provides use of a facility.

Example

Mike Franklin, a sports equipment manufacturer, takes a customer to a hunting lodge on an overnight trip. Immediately after the trip, the customer discusses products and market projections. The discussion ends with the customer placing his semiannual order.

In this instance, 50% of the costs of the meals, hunting rights, drinks in the nightclub, and transportation to and from the lodge are deductible. These costs qualify as entertainment associated with business and followed by a substantial business discussion (i.e., the expenses pass the associated with test). Because 50% of the entertainment costs would have been deductible if not incurred at an entertainment facility, they are also deductible even though the hunting lodge is an entertainment facility. These costs are not directly associated with the operation and maintenance of the place. However, the cost of the lodging is associated with the operation and maintenance of the facility. Therefore, the lodging expense, though partially deductible if incurred at a nonentertainment facility (e.g., a hotel instead of the hunting lodge), is not deductible.

Explanation

Deductions for the costs of tickets to cultural, theatrical, or sporting events are severely limited. In addition to meeting the directly related or associated with tests, the allowable portion of the ticket cost is limited to the face value of the ticket. The allowable portion of the ticket cost must be further reduced because only 50% of the allowable expense may be deducted.

Example

You pay a scalper $150 for three tickets to a sporting event. The face value of each ticket is $20. Your deduction is limited to $30 ($20 face value × three tickets × 50%). A similar rule also applies to the cost of luxury sky boxes at sports arenas. Costs for the business use of a suite, an apartment, an automobile, or an airplane are generally deductible. Personal use of an entertainment facility may be considered compensation, and the individual may be subject to tax.

Exceptions to the 50% Limit

Generally, business-related meal and entertainment expenses are subject to the 50% limit. *Figure 28-A* can help you determine if the 50% limit applies to you.

Your meal or entertainment expense is *not* subject to the 50% limit if the expense meets either of the following exceptions.

Employee's reimbursed expenses. If you are an employee, you are not subject to the 50% limit on the amount of expenses for which your employer reimburses you under an accountable plan. Accountable plans are discussed later under *Reimbursements.*

Exceptions

Entertainment test exceptions. Expenses incurred in the following situations generally are not subject to the directly related and associated with tests:

- Business meals in surroundings normally considered conducive to a business discussion
- Recreational and social activities primarily benefiting employees (e.g., company picnics, office Christmas parties, and golf outings)
- Business meetings of employees, stockholders, agents, or directors
- Attendance at a business meeting of a tax-exempt business league (e.g., a chamber of commerce, a board of trade, or a professional organization)
- Employee entertainment or recreation that is treated as compensation on the employee's income tax return and as wages for withholding purposes
- Nonemployee entertainment or recreation that is treated as income on the nonemployee's tax return and reported to him or her on an informational return (Form 1099)

Exceptions to the 50% limit. Expenses incurred in the following situations are not subject to the 50% disallowance provision:

- Reimbursed meal or entertainment expenses
- Employer-paid recreational expenses for employees (e.g., a holiday party)
- Entertainment taxable to the recipient
- Entertainment expenses made available to the general public
- Entertainment expenses related to charitable fundraising sports events

Individuals subject to "hours of service" limits. You can deduct a higher percentage of your meal expenses if the meals take place during or incident to any period subject to the Department of Transportation's "hours of service" limits. The percentage is 60% for 2001, and it gradually increases to 80% by the year 2008.

Individuals subject to the Department of Transportation's "hours of service" limits include the following persons.

1) Certain air transportation workers (such as pilots, crew, dispatchers, mechanics, and control tower operators) who are under Federal Aviation Administration regulations.

2) Interstate truck operators and bus drivers who are under Department of Transportation regulations.

3) Certain railroad employees (such as engineers, conductors, train crews, dispatchers, and control operations personnel) who are under Federal Railroad Administration regulations.

4) Certain merchant mariners who are under Coast Guard regulations.

Gift Expenses

If you give gifts in the course of your trade or business, you can deduct all or part of the cost. This section explains the limits and rules for deducting the costs of gifts.

$25 limit. You can deduct no more than $25 for business gifts you give directly or indirectly to any one person during your tax year. A gift to a company that is intended for the eventual personal use or benefit of a particular person or a limited class of people will be considered an indirect gift to that particular person or to the individuals within that class of people who receive the gift.

If you give a gift to a member of a customer's family, the gift is generally considered to be an indirect gift to the customer. This rule does not apply if you have a bona fide, independent business connection with that family member and the gift is not intended for the customer's eventual use.

If you and your spouse both give gifts, both of you are treated as one taxpayer. It does not matter whether you have separate businesses, are separately employed, or whether each of you has an independent connection with the recipient. If a partnership gives gifts, the partnership and the partners are treated as one taxpayer.

Incidental costs. Incidental costs, such as engraving on jewelry, or packaging, insuring, and mailing, are generally not included in determining the cost of a gift for purposes of the $25 limit.

A cost is incidental only if it does not add substantial value to the gift. For example, the cost of gift wrapping is an incidental cost. However, the purchase of an ornamental basket for packaging fruit is not an incidental cost if the value of the basket is substantial compared to the value of the fruit.

Exceptions. The following items are not considered gifts for purposes of the $25 limit.

1) An item that costs $4 or less and:
   a) Has your name clearly and permanently imprinted on the gift, and
   b) Is one of a number of identical items you widely distribute.

   Examples include pens, desk sets, and plastic bags and cases.

2) Signs, display racks, or other promotional material to be used on the business premises of the recipient.

Explanation
Business gifts are subject to close scrutiny. The IRS views this area as one of potential abuse. Business gifts are subject to strict substantiation requirements. The date of the gift and the name of the recipient must be noted in your records to uphold the deduction.

The business gift limitations do not apply to the following types of donations:

- Fellowship grants or scholarships
- Achievement prizes and awards
- Death benefits to an employer's survivors

Examples
The cost of beer offered by a service station owner to entice customers into his service station was allowed as a business gift deduction. The courts held that the expenses were directly related to the active conduct of his business and were incurred to sell additional goods and services.

Wine samples distributed in connection with a public offering of stock were allowed as a business gift subject to the $25 per recipient limitation.

Gift or entertainment. Any item that might be considered either a gift or entertainment generally will be considered entertainment. However, if you give a customer packaged food or beverages that you intend the customer to use at a later date, treat it as a gift.

If you give a customer tickets to a theater performance or sporting event and you do not go with the customer to the performance or event, you have a choice. You can treat the cost of the tickets as either a gift expense or an entertainment expense, whichever is to your advantage.

You can change your treatment of the tickets at a later date by filing an amended return. Generally, an amended return must be filed within 3 years from the date the original return was filed or within 2 years from the time the tax was paid, whichever is later.

If you go with the customer to the event, you must treat the cost of the tickets as an entertainment expense. You cannot choose, in this case, to treat the cost of the tickets as a gift expense.

TaxPlanner
It is usually to your advantage to define a particular item as an entertainment expense rather than as a gift. Although entertainment expenses are subject to the 50% limitation, there is no fixed dollar limitation on the deduction, though the expenses must be considered ordinary and necessary.

Transportation Expenses

This section discusses expenses you can deduct for business transportation when you are not traveling away from home as defined earlier. These expenses include the cost of transportation by air, rail, bus, taxi, etc., and the cost of driving and maintaining your car.

Transportation expenses include the ordinary and necessary costs of all of the following.

- Getting from one workplace to another in the course of your business or profession when you are traveling within your tax home. (Tax home is defined earlier under *Travel Expenses.*)
- Visiting clients or customers.
- Going to a business meeting away from your regular workplace.
- Getting from your home to a temporary workplace when you have one or more regular places of work. These temporary workplaces can be either within the area of your tax home or outside that area.

Transportation expenses do ***not*** include expenses you have while traveling away from home overnight. Those expenses are travel expenses, which are discussed earlier. However, if you use your car while traveling away from home overnight, use the rules in this section to figure your car expense deduction. See *Car Expenses,* later.

Illustration of transportation expenses. *Figure 28-B* illustrates the rules for when you can deduct transportation expenses when you have a regular or main job away from your home. You may want to refer to it when deciding whether you can deduct your transportation expenses.

Explanation
If you are on temporary active duty and maintain an active business elsewhere, you may deduct expenses for meals and lodging.

Temporary work location. If you have one or more regular places of business away from your home and you commute to a temporary work location in the same trade or business, you can deduct the expenses of the daily round-trip transportation between your home and the temporary location.

Explanation

If your employment at a work location is realistically expected to (and does in fact) last for 1 year or less, the employment is temporary unless there are facts and circumstances that would indicate otherwise. If your employment at a work location is realistically expected to last for more than 1 year, or if there is no realistic expectation that the employment will last for 1 year or less, the employment is not temporary, regardless of whether it actually lasts for more than 1 year. If employment at a work location initially is realistically expected to last for 1 year or *less*, but at some later date the employment is realistically expected to last *more* than 1 year, that employment will be treated as temporary (unless there are facts and circumstances that would indicate otherwise) until the date you determine it will last more than 1 year. It will not be treated as temporary after the date you determine it will last more than 1 year.

Note: The above definition of "temporary work location" is the result of a recent change. Under the former definition, "temporary" meant an irregular or short-term basis (generally a matter of days or weeks).

TaxPlanner

You can file an amended return on Form 1040X, *Amended U.S. Individual Income Tax Return*, for any year that is affected by this change. However, you generally must file the amendment within 3 years from the time you filed the return or within 2 years from the time you paid the tax, whichever is later.

If your employment at a work location is realistically expected to last (and does in fact last) for one year or less, the employment is temporary unless there are facts and circumstances that would indicate otherwise.

If your employment at a work location is realistically expected to last for more than 1 year or if there is no realistic expectation that the employment will last for 1 year or less, the employment is not temporary, regardless of whether it actually lasts for more than 1 year.

If employment at a work location initially is realistically expected to last for 1 year or less, but at some later date the employment is realistically expected to last more than 1 year, that employment will be treated as temporary (unless there are facts and circumstances that would indicate otherwise) until your expectation changes. It will not be treated as temporary after the date you determine it will last more than 1 year.

If the temporary work location is beyond the general area of your regular place of work and you stay overnight, you are traveling away from home. You may have deductible travel expenses as discussed earlier in this chapter.

No regular place of work. If you have no regular place of work but ordinarily work in the metropolitan area where you live, you can deduct daily transportation costs between home and a temporary work site *outside* that metropolitan area.

Generally, a metropolitan area includes the area within the city limits and the suburbs that are considered part of that metropolitan area.

You cannot deduct daily transportation costs between your home and temporary work sites *within* your metropolitan area. These are nondeductible commuting costs.

TaxPlanner

The IRS has ruled that a taxpayer may deduct the expenses of daily transportation between his or her residence and any temporary work site as long as he or she has a regular work site.

Based on this ruling by the IRS, the Tax Court allowed a logger to deduct his expenses of traveling between his residence and various cutting sites because the court held the logger's residence was his *regular* place of business.

However, in response to this decision by the Tax Court, the IRS issued a new ruling that stated that daily transportation expenses incurred in going between a taxpayer's residence and a work location are nondeductible commuting expenses unless one of the following three exceptions applies:

1. A taxpayer may deduct daily transportation expenses incurred in going between the taxpayer's residence and a temporary work location *outside* the metropolitan area where the taxpayer lives and normally works. However, unless paragraph (2) or (3) below applies, daily transportation expenses incurred in going between the taxpayer's residence and a temporary work location *within* that metropolitan area are nondeductible commuting expenses.
2. If a taxpayer has one or more *regular* work locations away from the taxpayer's residence, the taxpayer may deduct daily transportation expenses incurred in going between the taxpayer's residence and a temporary work location in the same trade or business, regardless of the distance.
3. If a taxpayer's residence is the taxpayer's *principal* place of business (as opposed to a regular place of business), the taxpayer may deduct daily transportation expenses incurred in going between the residence and another work location in the same trade or business, regardless of whether the other work location is regular or temporary and regardless of the distance.

Explanation

It is important to note the difference between a principal place of business and a regular place of business. A principal place of business is determined by a facts-and-circumstances test. Among the facts and circumstances to be taken into account in determining an individual's principal place of business are the following:

1. The portion of total income from business activities that is attributable to activities at each location
2. The portion of time spent in business activities in each location
3. The facilities available to the taxpayer at each location

The regular place of business standard is less stringent than the principal place of business standard. A regular place of business is defined as any location at which the taxpayer works or performs services on a regular basis.

Two places of work. If you work at two places in one day, whether or not for the same employer, you can deduct the expense of getting from one workplace to the other. However, if for some personal reason you do not go directly from one location to the other, you cannot deduct more than the amount it would have cost you to go directly from the first location to the second.

Transportation expenses you have in going between home and a part-time job on a day off from your main job are commuting expenses. You cannot deduct them.

Figure 28–B. **When Are Transportation Expenses Deductible?**
Most employees and self-employed persons can use this chart.
(Do not use this chart if your home is your principal place of business.
See *Office in the home*.)

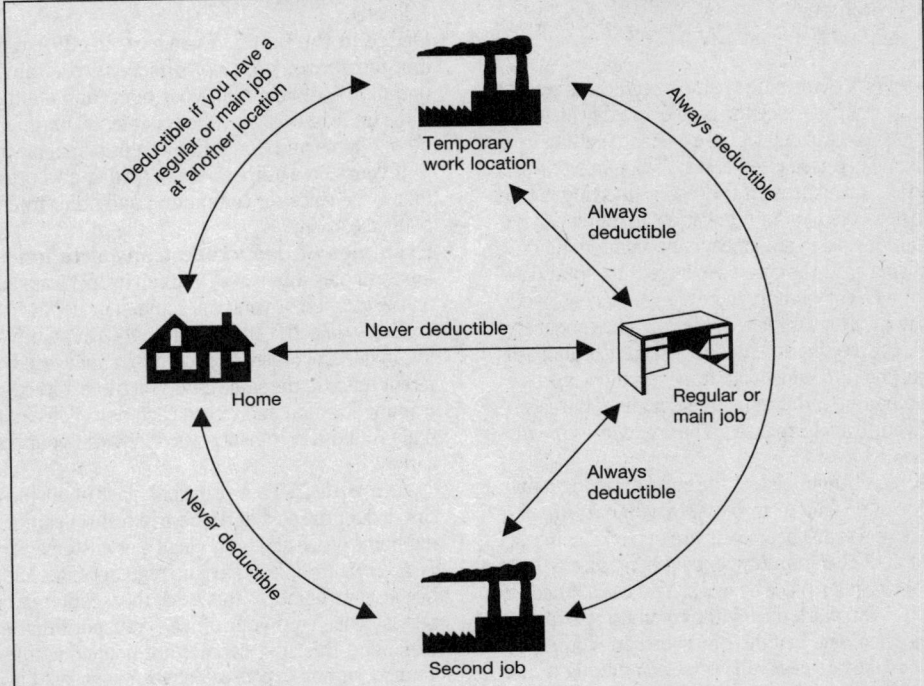

Home: The place where you reside. Transportation expenses between your home and your main or regular place of work are personal commuting expenses.

Regular or main job: Your principal place of business. If you have more than one job, you must determine which one is your regular or main job. Consider the time you spend at each, the activity you have at each, and the income you earn at each.

Temporary work location: A place where your work assignment is realistically expected to last (and does in fact last) one year or less. Unless you have a regular place of business, you can only deduct your transportation expenses to a temporary work location <u>outside</u> your metropolitan area.

Second job: If you regularly work at two or more places in one day, whether or not for the same employer, you can deduct your transportation expenses of getting from one workplace to another. You cannot deduct your transportation costs between your home and a second job on a day off from your main job.

Example 1
A doctor who practiced at a private clinic could not deduct the automobile expenses incurred on his regular and emergency trips between his home and the hospital. Under the hospital rules, the doctor was required to visit the hospital daily, as well as to spend a day on call each month. The court ruled that since the hospital was an integral and regular place of business for the doctor, his travel was a nondeductible commuting expense.

Example 2
A doctor could not deduct the cost of traveling between his office at home and the clinic where he practiced. Although he kept his medical and business records in his office in the home, he didn't see patients there. The court ruled that it was neither a principal business office nor a focal point for his medical practice and disallowed the deduction.

Example 3
A doctor who maintained two separate offices was denied a deduction for the costs of commuting between his residence and the places where he conducted his medical practices. He was, however, permitted to deduct commuting costs between his offices and to the hospital where he made his rounds.

Example 4
A college professor who maintained a home office was not allowed to deduct transportation expenses from his home to the college. The court determined that the focal point of his activities was the college at which he taught.

Exception

A police officer was allowed to claim a deduction for automobile expenses traveling to and from work because he was under orders to consider himself at work from the moment he left home until he returned.

Armed Forces reservists. A meeting of an Armed Forces reserve unit is a second place of business if the meeting is held on a day on which you work at your regular job. You can deduct the expense of getting from one workplace to the other as just discussed under *Two places of work.*

You usually cannot deduct the expense if the reserve meeting is held on a day on which you do not work at your regular job. In this case, your transportation generally is considered a nondeductible commuting cost. However, you can deduct your transportation expenses if the location of the meeting is temporary and you have one or more regular places of work.

If you ordinarily work in a particular metropolitan area but not at any specific location and the reserve meeting is held at a temporary location outside that metropolitan area, you can deduct your transportation expenses.

If you travel away from home overnight to attend a guard or reserve meeting, you can deduct your travel expenses. These expenses are discussed earlier under *Travel Expenses.*

Commuting expenses. You cannot deduct the costs of taking a bus, trolley, subway, or taxi, or of driving a car between *your home* and your main or regular place of work. These costs are personal commuting expenses. You cannot deduct commuting expenses no matter how far your home is from your regular place of work. You cannot deduct commuting expenses even if you work during the commuting trip.

Example. You had a telephone installed in your car. You sometimes use that telephone to make business calls while commuting to and from work. Sometimes business associates ride with you to and from work, and you have a business discussion in the car. These activities do not change the trip from personal to business. You cannot deduct your commuting expenses.

Parking fees. Fees you pay to park your car at your place of business are nondeductible commuting expenses. You can, however, deduct business-related parking fees when visiting a customer or client.

Advertising display on car. Putting display material that advertises your business on your car does not change the use of your car from personal use to business use. If you use this car for commuting or other personal uses, you still cannot deduct your expenses for those uses.

Car pools. You cannot deduct the cost of using your car in a nonprofit car pool. Do not include payments you receive from the passengers in your income. These payments are considered reimbursements of your expenses. However, if you operate a car pool for a profit, you must include payments from passengers in your income. You can then deduct your car expenses (using the rules in this chapter).

Hauling tools or instruments. Hauling tools or instruments in your car while commuting to and from work does not make your car expenses deductible. However, you can deduct any additional costs you have for hauling tools or instruments (such as for renting a trailer you tow with your car).

Example

A teacher could not deduct the expenses for an automobile she used to carry books and teaching materials to her classes, even though she could not store them at the school. She also used her automobile on days on which she came to school just to attend meetings. It took an hour to drive to school. Getting there by alternative means of transportation took 1½ hours and was very inconvenient. The court concluded that she would have driven even if she didn't have to transport books and that her expenses were merely commuting costs and not deductible.

Union members' trips from a union hall. If you get your work assignments at a union hall and then go to your place of work, the costs of getting from the union hall to your place of work are nondeductible commuting expenses. Although you need the union to get your work assignments, you are employed where you work, not where the union hall is located.

Office in the home. If you have an office in your home that qualifies as a *principal place of business,* you can deduct your daily transportation costs between your home and another work location in the same trade or business. (See chapter 30 for information on determining if your home office qualifies as a principal place of business.)

If your home office does not qualify as a principal place of business, follow the rules for commuting and other transportation expenses explained earlier.

Examples of deductible transportation expenses. The following examples show when you can deduct transportation expenses based on the location of your work and your home.

Example 1. You regularly work in an office in the city where you live. Your employer sends you to a one-week training session at a different office in the same city. You travel directly from your home to the training location and return each day. You can deduct the cost of your daily round-trip transportation between your home and the training location.

Example 2. Your principal place of business is in your home. You can deduct the cost of round-trip transportation between your qualifying home office and your client's or customer's place of business.

Example 3. You have no regular office, and you do not have an office in your home. In this case, the location of your first business contact is considered your office. Transportation expenses between your home and this first contact are nondeductible commuting expenses. Transportation expenses between your last business contact and your home are also nondeductible commuting expenses. Although you cannot deduct the costs of these first and last trips, you can deduct the costs of going from one client or customer to another.

Car Expenses

If you use your car for business purposes, you may be able to deduct car expenses. You generally can use one of two methods to figure your deductible expenses: actual expenses or the standard mileage rate.

If you use actual expenses to figure your deduction for a car you lease, there are rules that affect the amount of your lease payments that you can deduct. See *Leasing a car* under *Actual Car Expenses,* later.

In this chapter, "car" includes a van, pickup, or panel truck.

Explanation

Fixed and variable rate. Under certain circumstances, employees' business expenses for car expenses will be deemed substantiated when their employer reimburses such expenses with a mileage allowance different from the 34.5-cents-per-mile standard mileage rate.

TAXPLANNER

A court held that it was sufficient for a salesman to maintain records of personal miles driven only. The difference between his total mileage and his personal mileage represented his business mileage.

The courts have allowed a taxpayer a deduction for depreciation of a car used in business, even though his travel records were not very accurate or complete. Depreciation of a business asset is not subject to the strict record-keeping requirements that other types of travel expenses are. A deduction for depreciation is allowed if you can simply show that the car was used for business.

Tip. *You may be entitled to a tax credit for an electric vehicle (see chapter 37) or a deduction from gross income for a part of the cost of a clean-fuel vehicle that you place in service during the year. The vehicle must meet certain requirements, and you do not have to use it in your business to qualify for the credit or the deduction. For more information, see chapter 12 of Publication 535.*

Rural mail carriers. If you are a rural mail carrier, you may be able to treat the amount of qualified reimbursement you received as the amount of your allowable expense. Because the qualified reimbursement is treated as paid under an accountable plan, your employer should not include the amount of reimbursement in your income. And, since the reimbursement equals the expense, you have no deduction to report on your tax return.

A "qualified reimbursement" is the amount of reimbursement you receive that meets both of the following conditions.

1) It is given as an equipment maintenance allowance (EMA) to employees of the U.S. Postal Service.
2) It is at the rate contained in the 1991 collective bargaining agreement. Any later agreement cannot increase the qualified reimbursement amount by more than the rate of inflation.

See your employer for information on your reimbursement.

Caution. *If you are a rural mail carrier and received a qualified reimbursement, you cannot use the standard mileage rate.*

Standard Mileage Rate

You may be able to use the standard mileage rate to figure the deductible costs of operating your car for business purposes. For 2001, the standard mileage rate is *34 1/2 cents* a mile for all business miles.

TaxAlert

New standard mileage rate. For tax year 2001 the optional federal standard mileage rates for business, charitable, and medical use of an automobile are:

	2001
Business	34.5¢
Charitable	14¢
Medical	12¢

Caution. *If you use the standard mileage rate for a year, you* **cannot** *deduct your actual car expenses for that year.*

You generally can use the standard mileage rate regardless of whether you are reimbursed and whether any reimbursement is more or less than the amount figured using the standard mileage rate. See *Reimbursements* under *How To Report,* later.

Choosing the standard mileage rate. If you want to use the standard mileage rate for a car you own, you must choose to use it in the first year the car is available for use in your business. Then in later years, you can choose to use either the standard mileage rate or actual expenses.

If you want to use the standard mileage rate for a car you lease, you must use it for the entire lease period. For leases that began on or before December 31, 1997, the standard mileage rate must be used for the entire portion of the lease period (including renewals) that is after that date.

If you choose to use the standard mileage rate, you are considered to have chosen not to use the depreciation methods under the Modified Accelerated Cost Recovery System (MACRS). This is because the standard mileage rate includes an allowance for depreciation that is not expressed in terms of years. If you change to the actual expenses method in a later year, but before your car is fully depreciated, you have to estimate the remaining useful life of the car and use straight line depreciation. For more information about depreciation included in the standard mileage rate, see the exception in *Methods of depreciation* under *Depreciation Deduction* in chapter 4 of Publication 463.

Explanation
If you select the actual cost method (operating expenses and ACRS or MACRS), the standard mileage rate may never be used for that automobile. However, if you use the standard mileage rate for the first year, you may switch to the actual cost method, but you then must use a straight-line depreciation rate for the remaining estimated life of the automobile. Generally, actual expenses exceed the monies you may claim by using the standard mileage rate. As long as you keep adequate records, you will probably be better off claiming actual expenses.

Standard mileage rate not allowed. You cannot use the standard mileage rate if you:

1) Use the car for hire (such as a taxi),
2) Use two or more cars at the same time (as in fleet operations),
3) Claimed a depreciation deduction for the car using ACRS or MACRS depreciation in an earlier year,
4) Claimed a section 179 deduction on the car,
5) Claimed actual car expenses after 1997 for a car you leased, or
6) Are a rural mail carrier who received a qualified reimbursement. (See *Rural mail carriers,* earlier.)

Example
A newspaper deliveryman contracted to distribute newspapers on two delivery routes. Although the deliveryman's wife never contracted with the newspaper, she operated one route. He and his wife each used a separate car to deliver the newspapers. The courts held that the deliveryman and his wife were precluded from using standard mileage rates rather than actual automobile expenses because the two delivery routes constituted one single business operation.

Two or more cars. If you own two or more cars that are used for business at the same time, you cannot use the standard mileage rate for the business use of any car. However, you may be able to deduct your actual expenses for operating each of the cars in your business. See *Actual Car Expenses* in chapter 4 of Publication 463 for information on how to figure your deduction.

You are *not* using two or more cars for business at the same time if you alternate using (use at different times) the cars for business.

Example 1. Marcia, a salesperson, owns a car and a van that she alternates using for calling on her customers. She can use the standard mileage rate for the business mileage of the car and the van.

Example 2. Maureen owns a car and a van that are both used in her housecleaning business. Her employees use the van and she uses the car to travel to the various customers. Maureen cannot use the standard mileage rate for the car or the van. This is because both vehicles are used in Maureen's business at the same time. She must use actual expenses for both vehicles.

Parking fees and tolls. In addition to using the standard mileage rate, you can deduct any business-related parking fees and tolls. (Parking fees that you pay to park your car at your place of work are nondeductible commuting expenses.)

TaxAlert

Employer-provided parking. Before 1998, you had to include in income the fair market value of parking you received from your employer if you received it in place of compensation. For 2001, you can exclude up to $180 per month of employer-provided parking, even if you choose it instead of cash or your employer reduces your compensation to provide the parking. The $180 is indexed for inflation.

Actual Car Expenses

If you do not use the standard mileage rate, you may be able to deduct your actual car expenses.

Tip. *If you qualify to use both methods, you may want to figure your deduction both ways to see which gives you a larger deduction.*

Actual car expenses include the costs of:

Depreciation	Lease payments	Registration fees
Garage rent	Licenses	Repairs
Gas	Oil	Tires
Insurance	Parking fees	Tolls

Business and personal use. If you use your car for both business and personal purposes, you must divide your expenses between business and personal use. You can divide your expense based on the miles driven for each purpose.

Example. You are a contractor and drive your car 20,000 miles during the year: 12,000 miles for business use and 8,000 miles for personal use. You can claim only 60% (12,000 ÷ 20,000) of the cost of operating your car as a business expense.

Explanation

To claim a deduction for car expenses properly, you must establish that you are entitled to the deduction because the car was used at least partially for business. The deduction will be allowed only to the extent of business use. If you can establish that you are entitled to the deduction but are unable to establish the precise amount of the deduction, the court will apply its own best judgment to make an approximation of the business portion of the expenses.

Example 1

A doctor who is constantly on emergency call may not deduct all of his automobile expenses and depreciation. He must calculate how much of the automobile's use is business and how much is personal. The business portion is deductible.

Example 2

A construction worker who kept a log book of miles driven but failed to distinguish between business and personal mileage was not allowed to take any deduction.

Example 3

A salesman was able to prove that he used his automobile exclusively for business except for his round trip to and from work of 16 miles. However, he was unable to establish how many miles were dedicated to business use. The court concluded that his business use was 75% and his personal use was 25%.

Interest on car loans. If you are an employee, you cannot deduct any interest paid on a car loan. This interest is treated as personal interest and is not deductible. However, if you are self-employed and use your car in that business, see chapter 5 of Publication 535.

Tip. *If you use a home equity loan to purchase your car, you may be able to deduct the interest. See chapter 25 for more information.*

TaxPlanner

If an employee who owns a home finances the purchase of an automobile through a loan secured by the home, the interest would be fully deductible as home mortgage interest if the employee is within the $100,000 home equity indebtedness rules.

Taxes paid on your car. If you are an employee, you can deduct personal property taxes paid on your car if you itemize deductions. Enter the amount paid on line 7 of Schedule A (Form 1040). (See chapter 24 for more information on taxes.) If you are not an employee, see your form instructions for information on how to deduct personal property taxes paid on your car.

You cannot deduct luxury or sales taxes, even if you use your car 100% for business. Luxury and sales taxes are part of your car's basis and are recovered through depreciation, discussed later.

Explanation

Sales taxes on business automobiles were deductible prior to 1987. These amounts must now be added to the basis of the automobile and must be depreciated.

Fines and collateral. You cannot deduct fines and collateral you pay for traffic violations.

Depreciation and section 179 deductions. Generally, the cost of a car, plus sales tax, luxury tax, and improvements, is a capital expense. Because the benefits last longer than one year, you generally cannot deduct a capital expense. However, you can recover this cost by claiming a section 179 deduction (the deduction allowed by section 179 of the Internal Revenue Code) and/or a depreciation deduction. By using depreciation, you recover the cost over more than one year by deducting part of it each year. The section 179 deduction and the depreciation deduction are discussed in more detail in chapter 4 of Publication 463.

Explanation

For more information on the Section 179 deduction, see Chapter 38, *If You Are Self-Employed: How to File Schedule C.*

For more information on depreciation, see Chapter 10, *Rental Income and Expenses.*

Generally, there are limits on both of these deductions. Special rules apply if you use your car 50% or less in your work or business.

Explanation

Severe limitations on deductions apply after June 18, 1984, on luxury automobiles and automobiles used for both business and personal purposes. These limitations are adjusted for inflation for automobiles placed in service after 1988. The inflation adjustment is based on the automobile component of the Consumer Price Index, and any increase is rounded to the nearest $100. For automobiles placed in service in 2000, the maximum depreciation allowance is:

$3,060	for the first taxable year in its recovery period
$4,900	for the second taxable year in its recovery period
$2,950	for the third taxable year in its recovery period
$1,775	for each later taxable year in its recovery period, limited to the remaining undepreciated cost

These limitations are proportionately reduced for business usage less than 100%.

Explanation

If qualified business use of a vehicle purchased after 1986 is over 50%, then you can claim 200% declining balance depreciation over a 5-year period. Declining balance depreciation is described in Chapter 10, *Rental Income and Expenses*. Qualified business use means direct use in your trade or business, including your job. It does not include looking after your investments. However, if you use your automobile more than 50% in your trade or business, you can then use accelerated 5-year depreciation for the part used for looking after your investments.

If qualified business use is 50% or less, depreciation must be calculated on a straight-line basis over 5 years, with a proration of the maximum deduction. Although a 5-year life rate is used, only a half-year's depreciation is deductible in the first year. The other half-year is not deductible until the sixth year. Again, depreciation in excess of the allowed amounts is carried over to future years to depreciate fully the business portion of the asset.

Example

You buy an automobile in 2001 and use it 60% for business, 10% for looking after your investments, and 30% for personal use. You can deduct 70% of your depreciation, calculated using accelerated depreciation. If you use your automobile only 45% for business and 25% for looking after your investments, you can still deduct 70%, but it must be computed on a straight-line basis.

Leasing a car. If you lease a car that you use in your business, you can use the standard mileage rate or actual expenses to figure your deductible car expense.

Deductible payments. If you choose to use actual expenses, you can deduct the part of each lease payment that is for the use of the car in your business. You cannot deduct any part of a lease payment that is for personal use of the car, such as commuting.

You must spread any advance payments over the entire lease period. You cannot deduct any payments you make to buy a car, even if the payments are called lease payments.

If you lease a car for 30 days or more, you may have to reduce your lease payment deduction by an "inclusion amount." For information on reporting lease inclusion amounts, see *Leasing a Car* in chapter 4 of Publication 463.

TaxPlanner

If you buy an automobile and finance it, you cannot deduct any of the interest charges. If you finance the car by taking out a home equity loan, the interest will be deductible as home mortgage interest. See Chapter 8, *Interest Income*. However, if you are **self-employed** and use your car in your trade or business, you may deduct 100% of the business portion of the interest charges. If you simply use your car as an **employee**, you may pay less tax by leasing a car rather than buying it because you can deduct your lease payments subject to the business use rules discussed elsewhere in this chapter.

Leasing an automobile. Deducting employee business expenses for the cost of a leased automobile is similar to doing so for an automobile you own. You may deduct the portion of the total lease payments that is attributable to business use, using the ratio of business miles to total miles to make the calculation. This deduction represents

the depreciation and financing costs. Normal operating costs and maintenance (if not included in the lease) and business parking may also be deducted.

The luxury automobile rules are intended to impose the same unfavorable treatment for leased automobiles as for purchased automobiles. If you lease an automobile for business use, you can deduct the lease payments and operating expenses for that business use. If you lease an automobile and the value exceeds certain levels, you are deemed to have received additional income.

Note: You must recapture a portion of your lease payment deductions and report them as income if your business use of the automobile falls below 50%.

See Publications 534, *Depreciation*, and 917, *Business Use of a Car*, for further details and the tables for computing the lease adjustments.

Sale, Trade-in, or Other Disposition

If you sell, trade in, or otherwise dispose of your car, you may have a taxable gain or a deductible loss. This is true whether you used the standard mileage rate or actual car expenses to deduct the business use of your car. Chapter 15 has information on sales of property. For details on how to report the disposition, see Publication 544.

Explanation

Unreimbursed automobile expenses are deductible only as miscellaneous itemized deductions. Employees formerly classified as "outside sales representatives" are also subject to this provision.

As a result, these expenses will be deductible only to the extent that, when aggregated with your other miscellaneous itemized deductions, they exceed 2% of your adjusted gross income.

TaxSaver

In some cases, you may be able to deduct a greater mileage rate than the IRS customarily permits. For example, the courts have allowed truck drivers who were reimbursed at a greater rate than the standard rate to deduct the greater rate. The truck drivers had kept detailed weekly records of their trucks' operating costs.

TaxSaver

If you own an expensive business automobile, the standard mileage rate is probably inadequate to cover your operating costs. You should keep detailed records of your total expenses so that you may claim a larger deduction than you would be able to by using the standard mileage rate.

Recordkeeping

If you deduct travel, entertainment, gift, or transportation expenses, you must be able to prove (substantiate) certain elements of the expense. This section discusses the records you need to keep to prove these expenses.

If you keep timely and accurate records, you will have support to show the IRS if your tax return is ever examined. You will also have proof of expenses that your employer may require if you are reimbursed under an accountable plan. These plans are discussed later under *Reimbursements*.

TAXPLANNER

Good recordkeeping is a good business practice and a must for tax purposes. A clear and consistent set of records is the first step in justifying your expense deduction. Reasonable estimates of expenses are no longer acceptable, even if the estimate is moderate in relation to the income generated.

Form 4562, which is used to show your automobile depreciation, specifically asks whether you have evidence to support your business use percentage.

You must maintain adequate records or sufficient evidence, either written or oral, that will corroborate your own statement. Sufficient evidence includes account books, trip sheets, expense reports, appointment calendars, statements of witnesses, and certain accountings to an employer. Contemporaneous logs are no longer required, but a report made at the event would be more credible than records prepared at a later date.

If you are required to turn in the original copies of your receipts and logbooks to your employer, you should make copies for yourself. If the confidentiality of names is a consideration, special arrangements might have to be made with your employer to make necessary information available if and when it is needed.

When records are lost in circumstances beyond your control, such as destruction by fire, flood, earthquake, or other casualty, the IRS is more lenient in accepting reconstructed records and secondary evidence than it is when records are not available because of carelessness or mysterious disappearance.

Example

Travel expense records were lost during a change of residence resulting from marital problems. The court ruled that marital difficulties did not constitute a casualty warranting the use of reconstructed records.

How To Prove Expenses

Table 28-2 is a summary of records you need to prove each expense discussed in this chapter. You must be able to prove the elements listed across the top portion of the chart. You prove them by having the information and receipts (where needed) for the expenses listed in the first column.

Caution. *You cannot deduct amounts that you approximate or estimate.*

You should keep adequate records to prove your expenses or have sufficient evidence that will support your own statement. You must generally prepare a written record for it to be considered adequate. This is because written evidence is more reliable than oral evidence alone. However, if you prepare a record in a computer memory device with the aid of a logging program, it is considered an adequate record.

What Are Adequate Records?

You should keep the proof you need in an account book, diary, statement of expense, or similar record. You should also keep documentary evidence that, together with your records, will support each element of an expense.

Documentary evidence. You generally must have documentary evidence, such as receipts, canceled checks, or bills, to support your expenses.

Exception. Documentary evidence is not needed if any of the following conditions apply.

1) You have meals or lodging expenses while traveling away from home for which you account to your employer under an accountable plan and you use a per diem allowance method that includes meals and/or lodging. (Accountable plans and per diem allowances are discussed later under *Reimbursements.*)
2) Your expense, other than lodging, is less than $75.
3) You have a transportation expense for which a receipt is not readily available.

TAXALERT

The IRS has significantly eased its recordkeeping rules for employers and employees by raising the requirement for many business receipts from $25 to $75 starting October 1, 1995.

The tax law disallows an otherwise allowable deduction for any expense for traveling, entertainment, gifts, or listed property, unless the expense is substantiated by adequate records. Taxpayers are required to maintain documentary evidence (such as receipts) for (1) any lodging expenditure and (2) any other expenditure of $25 or more. However, the $25 receipt threshold, which was established in 1962, has been amended. Effective for expenditures incurred on or after October 1, 1995, the receipt threshold has been increased from $25 to $75.

Adequate evidence. Documentary evidence ordinarily will be considered adequate if it shows the amount, date, place, and essential character of the expense.

For example, a hotel receipt is enough to support expenses for business travel if it has all of the following information.

1) The name and location of the hotel.
2) The dates you stayed there.
3) Separate amounts for charges such as lodging, meals, and telephone calls.

A restaurant receipt is enough to prove an expense for a business meal if it has all of the following information.

1) The name and location of the restaurant.
2) The number of people served.
3) The date and amount of the expense.

If a charge is made for items other than food and beverages, the receipt must show that this is the case.

Canceled check. A canceled check, together with a bill from the payee, ordinarily establishes the cost. However, a canceled check by itself does not prove a business expense without other evidence to show that it was for a business purpose.

TAXPLANNER

You must maintain detailed records and report the required information on your tax return if you wish to claim a deduction for expenses that exceed reimbursements. You must keep these records, even though you do not have to give the completely detailed information to your employer because reimbursements by your employer meet the IRS per diem standards.

Duplicate information. You do not have to record information in your account book or other record that duplicates information shown on a receipt as long as your records and receipts complement each other in an orderly manner.

You do not have to record amounts your employer pays directly for any ticket or other travel item. However, if you charge these items to your employer, through a credit card or otherwise, you must keep a record of the amounts you spend.

Timely-kept records. You should record the elements of an expense or of a business use at or near the time of the expense or use and support it with sufficient documentary evidence. A timely-kept record has more value than a statement prepared later when generally there is a lack of accurate recall.

You do not need to write down the elements of every expense on the day of the expense. If you maintain a log on a weekly basis which accounts for use during the week, the log is considered a timely-kept record.

If you give your employer, client, or customer an expense account statement, it can also be considered a timely-kept record. This is true if you copy it from your account book, diary, statement of expense, or similar record.

Proving business purpose. You must generally provide a written statement of the business purpose of an expense. However, the degree of proof varies according to the circumstances in each case. If the business purpose of an expense is clear from the surrounding circumstances, then you do not need to give a written explanation.

Confidential information. You do not need to put confidential information relating to an element of a deductible expense (such as the place, business purpose, or business relationship) in your account book, diary, or other record. However, you do have to record the information elsewhere at or near the time of the expense and have it available to fully prove that element of the expense.

What If I Have Incomplete Records?

If you do not have complete records to prove an element of an expense, then you must prove the element with:

1) Your own written or oral statement, containing specific information about the element, and
2) Other supporting evidence that is sufficient to establish the element.

Destroyed records. If you cannot produce a receipt because of reasons beyond your control, you can prove a deduction by reconstructing your records or expenses. Reasons beyond your control include fire, flood, and other casualty.

Separating and Combining Expenses

This section explains when expenses must be kept separate and when expenses can be combined.

Separating expenses. Each separate payment is generally considered a separate expense. For example, if you entertain a customer or client at dinner and then go to the theater, the dinner expense and the cost of the theater tickets are two separate expenses. You must record them separately in your records.

Combining items. You can make one daily entry in your record for reasonable categories of expenses. Examples are taxi fares, telephone calls, or other incidental travel costs. Meals should be in a separate category. You can include tips for meal-related services with the costs of the meals.

Expenses of a similar nature occurring during the course of a single event are considered a single expense. For example, if during entertainment at a cocktail lounge, you pay separately for each serving of refreshments, the total expense for the refreshments is treated as a single expense.

Allocating total cost. If you can prove the total cost of travel or entertainment but you cannot prove how much it cost for each person who participated in the event, you may have to allocate the total cost among you and your guests on a pro rata basis. An allocation would be needed, for example, if you did not have a business relationship with all of your guests.

If your return is examined. If your return is examined, you may have to provide additional information to the IRS. This information could be needed to clarify or to establish the accuracy or reliability of information contained in your records, statements, testimony, or documentary evidence before a deduction is allowed.

How Long To Keep Records and Receipts

You must keep records as long as they may be needed for the administration of any provision of the Internal Revenue Code. Generally, this means you must keep your records that support your deduction (or an item of income) for 3 years from the date you file the income tax return on which the deduction is claimed. A return filed early is considered filed on the due date. For a more complete explanation, get Publication 583, *Starting a Business and Keeping Records.*

> **Explanation**
> If you use your automobile less than 50% for business and claim actual expenses, you must keep those records for at least 6 years (the straight-line, useful life depreciation period).

Reimbursed for expenses. Employees who give their records and documentation to their employers and are reimbursed for their expenses generally do not have to keep copies of this information. However, you may have to prove your expenses if any of the following conditions apply.

1) You claim deductions for expenses that are more than reimbursements.
2) Your expenses are reimbursed under a nonaccountable plan.
3) Your employer does not use adequate accounting procedures to verify expense accounts.
4) You are related to your employer, as defined earlier under *Who cannot use the standard meal allowance.*

See the next section, *How To Report,* for a discussion of reimbursements, adequate accounting, and nonaccountable plans.

> **Explanation**
> If you have expenses greater than your reimbursement and want to deduct them, you are required to put a statement in your tax return showing the total of all expenses you incurred and all reimbursements you received for that year. This information may be given in broad categories, such as transportation, meals and lodging while **away from home overnight,** entertainment expenses, and other business expenses. The statement must show the total of any charges paid or borne directly by your employer through credit cards or any other means. See *Records* for more details.
>
> **Self-employed** persons and independent contractors must be able to show that the expenses were directly related to, or associated with, their business.
>
> **Example**
> An accountant was not allowed to deduct expenses incurred at a country club because she failed to indicate the business purpose of the activities that generated the expenses and she did not maintain a detailed record of the persons entertained on each occasion. Lacking any documentation to the contrary, a court concluded that there was a likelihood that the expenses were at least partially personal.

Additional information. Chapter 5 of Publication 463 has more information on recordkeeping, including examples.

How To Report

This section explains where and how to report the expenses discussed in this chapter. It discusses reimbursements and how to treat them under accountable and nonaccountable plans. It also explains rules for fee-basis officials, certain performing artists, and certain disabled employees. This section ends with an illustration of how to report travel, entertainment, gift, and car expenses on Form 2106-EZ.

Explanation
Employees receiving the standard meal allowance under a nonaccountable plan (discussed below) may claim 50% of the standard meal allowance as a miscellaneous itemized deduction, subject to the 2% limitation. Reimbursements under accountable plans are not included in the employee's taxable compensation. Therefore, such employees receive no deduction, and the 50% limitation applies to the employer's deduction.

Self-employed. You must report your income and expenses on Schedule C or C-EZ (Form 1040) if you are a sole proprietor, or on Schedule F (Form 1040) if you are a farmer. You do not use Form 2106 or 2106-EZ. See your form instructions for information on how to complete your tax return. You can also find information in Publication 535 if you are a sole proprietor, or in Publication 225, *Farmer's Tax Guide,* if you are a farmer.

Both self-employed and an employee. If you are both self-employed and an employee, you must keep separate records for each business activity. Report your business expenses for self-employment on Schedule C, C-EZ, or F (Form 1040), as discussed earlier. Report your business expenses for your work as an employee on Form 2106 or 2106-EZ, as discussed next.

Employee. If you are an employee, you generally must complete Form 2106 to deduct your travel, transportation, and entertainment expenses. However, you can use the shorter Form 2106-EZ instead of Form 2106 if you meet both of the following conditions.

1) You are an employee deducting expenses attributable to your job.
2) You were not reimbursed by your employer for your expenses (amounts included in box 1 of your Form W-2 are not considered reimbursements).
3) If you are claiming car expenses, you use the standard mileage rate.

For more information on how to report your expenses on Forms 2106 and 2106-EZ, see *Completing Forms 2106 and 2106-EZ,* later.

Gifts. If you did not receive any reimbursements (or the reimbursements were all included in box 1 of your Form W-2), the only business expense you are claiming is for gifts, and the rules for certain individuals (such as performing artists), discussed later under *Special Rules,* do not apply to you, do not complete Form 2106 or 2106-EZ. Instead, claim the amount of your deductible gifts directly on line 20 of Schedule A (Form 1040).

Statutory employees. If you received a Form W-2 and the "Statutory employee" box in box 13 was checked, you report your income and expenses related to that income on Schedule C or C-EZ (Form 1040). Do not complete Form 2106 or 2106-EZ.

Statutory employees include full-time life insurance salespersons, certain agent or commission drivers, traveling salespersons, and certain homeworkers.

Example 1
John Smith, a salesman working on behalf of a principal, solicits orders from wholesalers and restaurants for merchandise intended for resale. John reports his income and expenses on Schedule C as a statutory employee.

Example 2
An agent-driver engaged in distributing meat, vegetables, bakery goods, beverages (other than milk), or dry cleaning services is classified as a statutory employee.

Caution. *If you are entitled to a reimbursement from your employer but you do not claim it, you cannot claim a deduction for the expenses to which that* **unclaimed reimbursement** *applies.*

Explanation
While you may not claim a deduction for an expense that your employer would reimburse, you may be entitled to a deduction for a work-related expense that you feel was necessary to do your job but that your employer does not reimburse.

Example
You are a technician who works in a laboratory in which your employer requires you to wear a certain type of uniform while on the job. The uniform is unsuitable for street wear. Your employer refuses to reimburse you for the cost of the uniform. You are entitled to deduct the expense on your own income tax return.

Reimbursement for personal expenses. If your employer reimburses you for nondeductible personal expenses, such as for vacation trips, your employer must report the reimbursement as wage income in box 1 of your Form W-2. You cannot deduct personal expenses.

Reimbursements

This section explains what to do when you receive an advance or are reimbursed for any of the employee business expenses discussed in this chapter.

If you received an advance, allowance, or reimbursement for your expenses, how you report this amount and your expenses depends on whether the reimbursement was paid to you under an accountable plan or a nonaccountable plan.

This section explains the two types of plans, how per diem and car allowances simplify proving the amount of your expenses, and the tax treatment of your reimbursements and expenses.

TaxSaver
If the various requirements discussed below are met, reimbursements are excluded from the employee's gross income for income tax as well as employment tax purposes. Amounts considered paid under a nonaccountable plan are subject to income tax as well as to employment taxes. A tax deduction is allowable as a miscellaneous itemized deduction, subject to applicable limitations, for employee business expenses reimbursed under a nonaccountable plan.

No reimbursement. You are not reimbursed or given an allowance for your expenses if you are paid a salary or commission with the understanding that you will pay your own expenses. In this situation, you have no reimbursement or allowance arrangement, and you do not have to read this section on reimbursements. Instead, see *Completing Forms 2106 and 2106-EZ,* later, for information on completing your tax return.

TaxSaver
You may claim a deduction for business expenses even if you don't receive specific reimbursements from your employer. You should have your employer supply you with a written document explaining that your compensation plan is

based on the expectation that you will incur various travel, transportation, automobile, entertainment, and business gift expenses.

Travel, transportation, automobile expenses, entertainment, business gifts, and other expenses should be reported as miscellaneous deductions on Schedule A of Form 1040.

If you are repeatedly spending money for business expenses, it is probably advantageous for you to make an arrangement with your employer to adjust your salary and/or commission downward and to give you an expense allowance. This could help you justify your deductions if you are subject to an IRS examination.

Reimbursement, allowance, or advance. A reimbursement or other expense allowance arrangement is a system or plan that an employer uses to pay, substantiate, and recover the expenses, advances, reimbursements, and amounts charged to the employer for employee business expenses. Arrangements include per diem and car allowances.

A per diem allowance is a fixed amount of daily reimbursement your employer gives you for your lodging, meal, and incidental expenses when you are away from home on business. (The term "incidental expenses" is defined earlier under *Meals.*) A car allowance is an amount your employer gives you for the business use of your car.

Your employer should tell you what method of reimbursement is used and what records you must provide.

Accountable Plans

To be an accountable plan, your employer's reimbursement or allowance arrangement must include all three of the following rules.

1) Your expenses must have a business connection—that is, you must have paid or incurred deductible expenses while performing services as an employee of your employer.
2) You must adequately account to your employer for these expenses within a reasonable period of time.
3) You must return any excess reimbursement or allowance within a reasonable period of time.

See *Adequate Accounting* and *Returning Excess Reimbursements,* later.

Explanation
For a reimbursement or other expense allowance arrangement to be an accountable plan, it must satisfy the substantiation requirement. Generally, for each expense item and for each business use, the employee must report the amount, time, place, and business purpose.

Example 1
An employer proposed to reimburse its district manager's business expenses in lieu of paying additional salary. This would result in a portion of the district manager's salary being recharacterized as paid under a reimbursement or other expense allowance arrangement, and, thus, it would fail the reimbursement requirement. Therefore, the reimbursements would be subject to employment taxes since they would not be paid under an arrangement that is an accountable plan.

Example 2
Where a taxpayer did not substantiate expenses or return excess allowance amounts, such amounts were paid under a nonaccountable plan and, thus, were includible in gross income.

Exception 1
The substantiation requirement for expense amounts related to business meals and lodging can be satisfied by using a per diem allowance. Per diem reimbursements of such expenses are not included in taxable income to the extent of the government rate.

Exception 2
The substantiation requirement for expenses relating to the business use of an employee's private automobile can be satisfied by using the standard mileage rate (34.5-cents-per-business-mile) or the fixed-and-variable-rate allowance. Under the fixed-and-variable-rate allowance method, an employer reimburses an employee's business mileage expenses using a flat rate or a stated schedule of fixed and variable rate payments that incorporates specific rules to approximate the employee's actual automobile expenses.

An *excess reimbursement or allowance* is any amount you are paid that is more than the business-related expenses that you adequately accounted for to your employer.

The definition of *reasonable period of time* depends on the facts and circumstances of your situation. However, regardless of the facts and circumstances of your situation, actions that take place within the times specified in the following list will be treated as taking place within a reasonable period of time.

1) You receive an advance within 30 days of the time you have an expense.
2) You adequately account for your expenses within 60 days after they were paid or incurred.
3) You return any excess reimbursement within 120 days after the expense was paid or incurred.
4) You are given a periodic statement (at least quarterly) that asks you to either return or adequately account for outstanding advances *and* you comply within 120 days of the statement.

TAXALERT
It is imperative that the substantiation be done and that excess amounts be returned within a reasonable period of time. If the reasonable time requirement is not met, the unsubstantiated or excess amounts are treated as reimbursements under a nonaccountable plan.

Employee meets accountable plan rules. If you meet the three rules for accountable plans, your employer should not include any reimbursements in your income in box 1 of your Form W-2. If your expenses equal your reimbursement, you do not complete Form 2106. You have no deduction since your expenses and reimbursement are equal. **Tip.** *If your employer included reimbursements in box 1 of your Form W-2 and you meet all three rules for accountable plans, ask your employer for a corrected Form W-2.*

Accountable plan rules not met. Even though you are reimbursed under an accountable plan, some of your expenses may not meet all three rules. Those expenses that fail to meet all three rules for accountable plans are treated as having been reimbursed under a nonaccountable plan (discussed later).

TAXPLANNER
A plan providing per diem allowances or mileage allowances that are reasonably calculated not to exceed the employee's

expenses will satisfy the requirement for the return of excess reimbursement, even though the employee is not required to return the excess allowance. However, the employee must return the portion of the allowance attributable to unsubstantiated days or miles of travel.

Example

An employee receives a monthly mileage allowance of $124, based on anticipated business miles of 400 per month, reimbursed at the rate of 35 cents per mile. The 35-cent-per-mile rate is reasonably calculated not to exceed the employee's expenses. The employee travels and substantiates only 300 business miles. The requirement to return the excess is satisfied if the employee is required to return the $35 (100 miles × 35 cents) advance allowance that is attributable to the 100 unsubstantiated business miles. The employee is not required to return the $1.50 (300 miles × .5 cent) reimbursement amount in excess of the 34.5-cent standard mileage rate for substantiated business miles.

Reimbursement of nondeductible expenses. You may be reimbursed under your employer's accountable plan for expenses related to that employer's business, some of which are deductible as employee business expenses and some of which are not deductible. The reimbursements you receive for the nondeductible expenses do not meet rule (1) for accountable plans, and they are treated as paid under a nonaccountable plan.

Example. Your employer's plan reimburses you for travel expenses while away from home on business and also for meals when you work late at the office, even though you are not away from home. The part of the arrangement that reimburses you for the nondeductible meals when you work late at the office is treated as paid under a nonaccountable plan.

Tip. *The employer makes the decision whether to reimburse employees under an accountable plan or a nonaccountable plan. If you are an employee who receives payments under a nonaccountable plan, you cannot convert these amounts to payments under an accountable plan by voluntarily accounting to your employer for the expenses and voluntarily returning excess reimbursements to the employer.*

Adequate Accounting

One of the three rules for an accountable plan is that you must adequately account to your employer for your expenses. You adequately account by giving your employer a statement of expense, an account book, a diary, or a similar record in which you entered each expense at or near the time you had it, along with documentary evidence (such as receipts) of your travel, mileage, and other employee business expenses. (See Table 28-2, earlier, for details you need to enter in your record and documents you need to prove certain expenses.)

You must account for *all* amounts you received from your employer during the year as advances, reimbursements, or allowances. This includes amounts you charged to your employer by credit card or other method. You must give your employer the same type of records and supporting information that you would have to give to the IRS if the IRS questioned a deduction on your return. You must pay back the amount of any reimbursement or other expense allowance for which you do not adequately account or that is more than the amount for which you accounted.

Per Diem and Car Allowances

If your employer reimburses you for your expenses using a per diem or car allowance, you can generally use the allowance as proof for the amount of your expenses. A per diem or car allowance satisfies the adequate accounting requirements for the amount of your expenses only if all four of the following conditions apply.

1) Your employer reasonably limits payments of your expenses to those that are ordinary and necessary in the conduct of the trade or business.
2) The allowance is similar in form to and not more than the federal rate (discussed later).
3) You prove the time (dates), place, and business purpose of your expenses to your employer (as explained in *Table 28-2*) within a reasonable period of time.
4) You are not related to your employer (as defined earlier under *Who cannot use the standard meal allowance*). If you are related to your employer, you must be able to prove your expenses to the IRS even if you have already adequately accounted to your employer and returned any excess reimbursement.

If the IRS finds that an employer's travel allowance practices are not based on reasonably accurate estimates of travel costs (including recognition of cost differences in different areas for per diem amounts), you will not be considered to have accounted to your employer. In this case, you must be able to prove your expenses to the IRS.

The federal rate. The federal rate can be figured using any one of the following methods.

1) For per diem amounts:
   a) The regular federal per diem rate.
   b) The standard meal allowance.
   c) The high-low rate.
2) For car expenses:
   a) The standard mileage rate.
   b) A fixed and variable rate (FAVR).

Regular federal per diem rate. The regular federal per diem rate is the highest amount that the federal government will pay to its employees for lodging, meal, and incidental expenses (or meal and incidental expenses only) while they are traveling away from home in a particular area. The rates are different for different locations. Your employer should have these rates available. (Employers can get Publication 1542, which gives the rates in the continental United States for the current year.)

The standard meal allowance. The standard meal allowance (discussed earlier) is the federal rate for meals and incidental expenses (M&IE). The rate for most small localities in the United States is $30. Most major cities and many other localities qualify for higher rates. The rates for all localities within the continental United States are listed in Publication 1542.

You receive an allowance only for meals and incidental expenses when your employer does one of the following.

1) Provides you with lodging (furnishes it in kind).
2) Reimburses you, based on your receipts, for the actual cost of your lodging.
3) Pays the hotel, motel, etc., directly for your lodging.
4) Does not have a reasonable belief that you had (or will have) lodging expenses, such as when you stay with friends or relatives or sleep in the cab of your truck.
5) Computes the allowance on a basis similar to that used in computing your compensation, such as number of hours worked or miles traveled.

High-low rate. This is a simplified method of computing the federal per diem rate for travel within the continental United States. It eliminates the need to keep a current list of the per diem rate for each city.

Under the high-low method, the per diem amount for travel during January through September of 2001 is $201 (including $42 for M&IE) for certain high-cost locations. All other areas have a per diem amount of $124 (including $34 for M&IE). (Employers can get Publication 1542 (Revised March 2001), which gives the areas eligible for the $201 per diem amount under the high-low method for all or part of this period.)

Caution. *Effective October 1, 2001, the per diem rates under this method increased. The increased rate for certain high-cost locations is $204 (including $42 for M&IE). The increased rate for all other locations is $124 (including $34 for M&IE). However, an employer can continue to use the* *lower rates described in the preceding paragraph for the remainder of 2001 if those rates and locations are used consistently during October, November, and December for all employees. Employers who did not use the high-low method during the first 9 months of 2001 cannot begin to use it before 2002. See Revenue Procedure 2001-47 for more information.*

Prorating the standard meal allowance on partial days of travel. The standard meal allowance is for a full 24-hour day of travel. If you travel for part of a day, such as on the days you depart and return, you must prorate the full-day M&IE rate. This rule also applies if your employer uses the regular federal per diem rate or the high-low rate.

You can use either of the following methods to figure the federal M&IE for that day.

1) *Method 1:*
   a) For the day you depart, add 3/4 of the standard meal allowance amount for that day.
   b) For the day you return, add 3/4 of the standard meal allowance amount for the preceding day.
2) *Method 2:* Prorate the standard meal allowance using any method that you consistently apply and that is in accordance with reasonable business practice.

The standard mileage rate. This is a set rate per mile that you can use to compute your deductible car expenses. For 2001, the standard mileage rate is ***34 1/2 cents a mile*** for all business miles. This rate is adjusted periodically.

Fixed and variable rate (FAVR). This is an allowance your employer may use to reimburse your car expenses. Under this method, your employer pays an allowance that includes a combination of payments covering fixed and variable costs, such as a cents-per-mile rate to cover your variable operating costs (such as gas, oil, etc.) plus a flat amount to cover your fixed costs (such as depreciation (or lease payments), insurance, etc.). If your employer chooses to use this method, your employer will request the necessary records from you.

Reporting your expenses with a per diem or car allowance. If your reimbursement is in the form of an allowance received under an accountable plan, the following two facts affect your reporting.

1) The federal rate.
2) Whether the allowance or your actual expenses were more than the federal rate.

The following discussions explain where to report your expenses depending upon how the amount of your allowance compares to the federal rate.

Allowance LESS than or EQUAL to the federal rate. If your allowance is less than or equal to the federal rate, the allowance will not be included in box 1 of your Form W-2. You do not need to report the related expenses or the allowance on your return if your expenses are equal to or less than the allowance.

However, if your actual expenses are more than your allowance, you can complete Form 2106 and deduct the excess amount on Schedule A (Form 1040). If you are using actual expenses, you must be able to prove to the IRS the total amount of your expenses and reimbursements for the entire year. If you are using the standard meal allowance or the standard mileage rate, you do not have to prove that amount.

Example. Nicole drives 10,000 miles a year for business. Under her employer's accountable plan, she accounts for the time (dates), place, and business purpose of each trip. Her employer pays her a mileage allowance of 20 cents a mile.

Since Nicole's $3,450 expenses computed under the standard mileage rate (10,000 miles × 34 1/2 cents) are more than her $2,000 reimbursement (10,000 miles × 20 cents), she itemizes her deductions to claim the excess expenses. Nicole completes Form 2106 (showing ***all*** of her expenses and reimbursements) and enters $1,450 ($3,450 − $2,000) as an itemized deduction.

Allowance MORE than the federal rate. If your allowance is more than the federal rate, your employer must include the allowance amount up to the federal rate in box 12 of your Form W-2. This amount is not taxable. However, the excess allowance will be included in box 1 of your Form W-2. You must report this part of your allowance as if it were wage income.

If your actual expenses are less than or equal to the federal rate, you do not complete Form 2106 or claim any of your expenses on your return.

However, if your actual expenses are more than the federal rate, you can complete Form 2106 and, generally, deduct those excess expenses. You must report on Form 2106 your reimbursements up to the federal rate (as shown in box 12 of your Form W-2) and all your expenses. You should be able to prove these amounts to the IRS.

Example. Joe lives and works in Austin. His employer sent him to San Diego for 4 days and paid the hotel directly for Joe's hotel bill. The employer reimbursed Joe $50 a day for his meals and incidental expenses. The federal rate for San Diego is $46 a day.

Joe can prove that his actual meal expenses totaled $290. His employer's accountable plan will not pay more than $50 a day for travel to San Diego, so Joe does not give his employer the records that prove that he actually spent $290. However, he does account for the time, place, and business purpose of the trip. This is Joe's only business trip this year.

Joe was reimbursed $200 ($50 × 4 days), which is $16 more than the federal rate of $184 ($46 × 4 days). The employer includes the $16 as income on Joe's Form W-2 in box 1. The employer also enters $184 in box 12 of Joe's Form W-2, along with a code **L**.

Joe completes Form 2106 to figure his deductible expenses. He enters the total of his actual expenses for the year ($290) on Form 2106. He also enters the reimbursements that were not included in his income ($184). His total deductible expense, before the 50% limit, is $106. After he figures the 50% limit on his unreimbursed meals and entertainment, he will include the balance, $53, as an itemized deduction.

Returning Excess Reimbursements

Under an accountable plan, you are required to return any excess reimbursement for your business expenses to the person paying the reimbursement or allowance. ***Excess reimbursement*** means any amount for which you did not adequately account within a reasonable period of time. For example, if you received a travel advance and you did not spend all the money on business-related expenses, or if you do not have proof of all your expenses, you have an excess reimbursement.

"Adequate accounting" and "reasonable period of time" were discussed earlier.

Travel advance. You receive a travel advance if your employer provides you with an expense allowance before you actually have the expense, and the allowance is reasonably expected to be no more than your expense. Under an accountable plan, you are required to adequately account to your employer for this advance and to return any excess within a reasonable period of time.

If you do not adequately account for or do not return any excess advance within a reasonable period of time, the amount you do not account for or return will be treated as having been paid under a nonaccountable plan (discussed later).

Unproved amounts. If you do not prove that you actually traveled on each day for which you received a per diem or car allowance (proving the elements described in *Table 28-2*), you must return this unproved amount of the travel advance within a reasonable period of time. If you do not do this, the unproved amount is considered paid under a nonaccountable plan (discussed later).

Per diem allowance MORE than federal rate. If your employer's accountable plan pays you an allowance that is higher than the federal rate, you do not have to return the difference between the two rates for the period you can prove business-related travel expenses. However, the difference will be reported as wages on your Form W-2. This excess amount is considered paid under a nonaccountable plan (discussed later).

Example. Your employer sends you on a 5-day business trip to Phoenix and gives you a $225 ($45 × 5 days) advance to cover your meals and incidental expenses. The federal per diem for meals and incidental expenses for Phoenix is $42. Your trip lasts only 3 days. Under your employer's accountable plan, you must return the $90 ($45 × 2 days) advance for the 2 days you did not travel. You do not have to return the $9 difference between the allowance you received and the federal rate for Phoenix [($45 − $42) × 3 days]. However, the $9 will be reported on your Form W-2 as wages.

Nonaccountable Plans

A nonaccountable plan is a reimbursement or expense allowance arrangement that does not meet one or more of the three rules listed earlier under *Accountable Plans.*

In addition, even if your employer has an accountable plan, the following payments will be treated as being paid under a nonaccountable plan.

1) Excess reimbursements you fail to return to your employer.
2) Reimbursement of nondeductible expenses related to your employer's business. See *Reimbursement of nondeductible expenses* earlier under *Accountable Plans.*

If you are not sure if the reimbursement or expense allowance arrangement is an accountable or nonaccountable plan, ask your employer.

Reporting your expenses under a nonaccountable plan. Your employer will combine the amount of any reimbursement or other expense allowance paid to you under a nonaccountable plan with your wages, salary, or other pay. Your employer will report the total in box 1 of your Form W-2.

You must complete Form 2106 or 2106-EZ and itemize your deductions to deduct your expenses for travel, transportation, meals, or entertainment. Your meal and entertainment expenses will be subject to the 50% limit discussed earlier under *Entertainment Expenses.* Also, your total expenses will be subject to the 2%-of-adjusted-gross-income limit that applies to most miscellaneous itemized deductions.

Example. Kim's employer gives her $500 a month ($6,000 for the year) for her business expenses. Kim does not have to provide any proof of her expenses to her employer, and Kim can keep any funds that she does not spend.

Kim is being reimbursed under a nonaccountable plan. Her employer will include the $6,000 on Kim's Form W-2 as if it were wages. If Kim wants to deduct her business expenses, she must complete Form 2106 or 2106-EZ and itemize her deductions.

Completing Forms 2106 and 2106-EZ

This section briefly describes how employees complete Forms 2106 and 2106-EZ. *Table 28-3* explains what the employer reports on Form W-2 and what the employee reports on Form 2106. The instructions for the forms have more information on completing them.

Form 2106-EZ. You may be able to use the shorter Form 2106-EZ to claim your employee business expenses. You can use this form if you meet all 3 of the following conditions.

1) You are an employee deducting expenses attributable to your job.
2) You were not reimbursed by your employer for your expenses (amounts included in box 1 of your Form W-2 are not considered reimbursements).
3) If you claim car expenses, you use the standard mileage rate.

Car expenses. If you used a car to perform your job as an employee, you may be able to deduct certain car expenses. These are generally figured in Part II of Form 2106, and then claimed on line 1, Column A, of Part I of Form 2106. Car expenses using the standard mileage rate can also be figured on Form 2106-EZ by completing Part II and line 1 of Part I.

Transportation expenses. Show your transportation expenses that did not involve overnight travel on line 2, Column A, of Form 2106 or on line 2, Part I, of Form 2106-EZ. Also include on this line business expenses you have for parking fees and tolls. Do not include expenses of operating your car or expenses of commuting between your home and work.

Employee business expenses other than meals and entertainment. Show your other employee business expenses on lines 3 and 4, Column A, of Form 2106 or lines 3 and 4 of Form 2106-EZ. Do not include expenses for meals and entertainment on those lines. Line 4 is for expenses such as gifts, educational expenses (tuition and books), office-in-the-home expenses, and trade and professional publications.

Tip. *If line 4 expenses are the only ones you are claiming, you received no reimbursements (or the reimbursements were all included in box 1 of your Form W-2), and the* Special Rules *discussed later do not apply to you, do not complete Form 2106 or 2106-EZ. Claim these amounts directly on line 20 of Schedule A (Form 1040). List the type and amount of each expense on the dotted lines and include the total on line 20.*

Meal and entertainment expenses. Show the full amount of your expenses for business-related meals and entertainment on line 5, Column B, of Form 2106. Include meals while away from your tax home overnight and other business meals and entertainment. Enter 50% of the line 8 meal and entertainment expenses on line 9, Column B, of Form 2106.

If you file Form 2106-EZ, enter the full amount of your meals and entertainment on the line to the left of line 5 and multiply the total by 50%. Enter the result on line 5.

Hours of service limits. If you are subject to the Department of Transportation's "hours of service" limits, use 60% instead of 50%.

Reimbursements. Enter on line 7 of Form 2106 the amounts your employer (or third party) reimbursed you that were ***not*** included in box 1 of your Form W-2. (You cannot use Form 2106-EZ.) This includes any reimbursement reported under code **L** in box 13 of Form W-2.

Allocating your reimbursement. If you were reimbursed under an accountable plan and want to deduct excess expenses that were not reimbursed, you may have to allocate your reimbursement. This is necessary if your employer pays your reimbursement in the following manner:

1) Pays you a single amount that covers meals and/or entertainment, as well as other business expenses, and
2) Does not clearly identify how much is for deductible meals and/or entertainment.

You must allocate the reimbursement so that you know how much to enter in Column A and Column B of line 7 of Form 2106.

Example. Rob's employer paid him an expense allowance of $5,000 this year under an accountable plan. The $5,000 payment consisted of $2,000 for airfare and $3,000 for entertainment and car expenses. The employer did not clearly show how much of the $3,000 was for the cost of deductible entertainment. Rob actually spent $6,500 during the year ($2,000 for airfare, $2,000 for entertainment, and $2,500 for car expenses).

Since the airfare allowance was clearly identified, Rob knows that $2,000 of the payment goes in Column A, line 7 of Form 2106. To allocate the remaining $3,000, Rob uses the worksheet from the instructions for Form 2106. His completed worksheet follows.

1. Enter the total amount of reimbursements your employer gave you that **were not** reported to you in box 1 of Form W–2	$3,000
2. Enter the total amount of your expenses for the periods covered by this reimbursement	4,500
3. Of the amount on line 2, enter your total expense for meals and entertainment	2,000
4. Divide line 3 by line 2. Enter the result as a decimal (rounded to at least three places)	.444
5. Multiply line 1 by line 4. Enter the result here and in Column B, line 7	1,332
6. Subtract line 5 from line 1. Enter the result here and in Column A, line 7	1,668

On line 7 of Form 2106, Rob enters $3,668 ($2,000 airfare and $1,668 of the $3,000) in Column A and $1,332 (of the $3,000) in Column B.

After you complete the form. After you have completed your Form 2106 or 2106-EZ, follow the directions on that form to deduct your expenses on the appropriate line of your tax return. For most taxpayers, this is line 20 of Schedule A (Form 1040). However, if you are

Table 28-3. **Reporting Travel, Entertainment, Gift, and Car Expenses and Reimbursements**

IF the type of reimbursement (or other expense allowance) arrangement is under:	THEN the employer reports on Form W-2:	AND the employee reports on Form 2106: *
An accountable plan with:		
Actual expense reimbursement: Adequate accounting made <u>and</u> excess returned	No amount.	No amount.
Actual expense reimbursement: Adequate accounting and return of excess both required <u>but</u> excess not returned	The excess amount as wages in box 1.	No amount.
Per diem or mileage allowance up to the federal rate: Adequate accounting made <u>and</u> excess returned.	No amount.	All expenses and reimbursements only if excess expenses are claimed. Otherwise, form is not filed.
Per diem or mileage allowance up to the federal rate: Adequate accounting and return of excess both required <u>but</u> excess not returned.	The excess amount as wages in box 1. The amount up to the federal rate is reported only in box 13—it is not reported in box 1.	No amount.
Per diem or mileage allowance exceeds the federal rate: Adequate accounting up to the federal rate only <u>and</u> excess not returned.	The excess amount as wages in box 1. The amount up to the federal rate is reported only in box 13—it is not reported in box 1.	All expenses (and reimbursement reported on Form W-2, box 13) only if expenses in excess of the federal rate are claimed. Otherwise, form is not required.
A nonaccountable plan with:		
Either adequate accounting or return of excess, or both, not required by plan	The entire amount as wages in box 1.	All expenses.
No reimbursement plan:	The entire amount as wages in box 1.	All expenses.
* You may be able to use Form 2106-EZ. See *Completing Forms 2106 and 2106-EZ.*		

a government official paid on a fee basis, a performing artist, or a disabled employee with impairment-related work expenses, see *Special Rules,* later.

Limits on employee business expenses. Your employee business expenses may be subject to any of the three limits described next. These limits are figured in the following order on the specified form.

1. Limit on meals and entertainment. Certain meal and entertainment expenses are subject to a 50% limit. Employees figure this limit on line 9 of Form 2106 or line 5 of Form 2106-EZ. See *50% Limit* under *Entertainment Expenses,* earlier.

2. Limit on miscellaneous itemized deductions. Employees deduct employee business expenses (as figured on Form 2106 or 2106-EZ) on line 20 of Schedule A (Form 1040). Most miscellaneous itemized deductions, including employee business expenses, are subject to a 2%-of-adjusted-gross-income limit. This limit is figured on line 25 of Schedule A (Form 1040).

3. Limit on total itemized deductions. If your adjusted gross income (line 34 of Form 1040) is more than $134,950 ($66,475 if you are

married filing separately), the total of certain itemized deductions, including employee business expenses, may be limited. See chapter 22 for more information on this limit.

Special Rules

This section discusses special rules that apply only to government officials who are paid on a fee basis, performing artists, and disabled employees with impairment-related work expenses.

Officials paid on a fee basis. Certain fee-basis officials can claim their employee business expenses whether or not they itemize their other deductions on Schedule A (Form 1040).

Fee-basis officials are persons who are employed by a state or local government and who are paid in whole or in part on a fee basis. They can deduct their business expenses in performing services in that job as an adjustment to gross income rather than as a miscellaneous itemized deduction.

If you are a fee-basis official, include your employee business expenses from line 10 of Form 2106 or line 6 of Form 2106-EZ in the total on line 32 of Form 1040. Write "FBO" and the amount of your employee business expenses in the space to the left of line 32 of Form 1040.

Expenses of certain performing artists. If you are a performing artist, you may qualify to deduct your employee business expenses as an adjustment to gross income rather than as a miscellaneous itemized deduction. To qualify, you must meet *all* of the following requirements.

1) During the tax year, you perform services in the performing arts for at least two employers.
2) You receive at least $200 each from any two of these employers.
3) Your related performing-arts business expenses are more than 10% of your gross income from the performance of those services.
4) Your adjusted gross income is not more than $16,000 before deducting these business expenses.

Special rules for married persons. If you are married, you must file a joint return unless you lived apart from your spouse at all times during the tax year.

If you file a joint return, you must figure requirements (1), (2), and (3) separately for both you and your spouse. However, requirement (4) applies to your and your spouse's combined adjusted gross income.

Where to report. If you meet all of the above requirements, you should first complete Form 2106 or 2106-EZ. Then you include your performing-arts-related expenses from line 10 of Form 2106 or line 6 of Form 2106-EZ in the total on line 32 of Form 1040. Write "QPA" and the amount of your performing-arts-related expenses in the space to the left of line 32 of Form 1040.

If you do not meet all of the above requirements, you do not qualify to deduct your expenses as an adjustment to gross income. Instead, you must complete Form 2106 or 2106-EZ and deduct your employee business expenses as an itemized deduction on line 20 of Schedule A (Form 1040).

Impairment-related work expenses of disabled employees. If you are an employee with a physical or mental disability, your impairment-related work expenses are not subject to the 2%-of-adjusted-gross-income limit that applies to most other employee business expenses. After you complete Form 2106 or 2106-EZ, enter your impairment-related work expenses from line 10 of Form 2106 or line 6 of Form 2106-EZ on line 27 of Schedule A (Form 1040), and identify the type and amount of this expense on the dotted line next to line 27. Enter your employee business expenses that are *unrelated* to your disability from line 10 of Form 2106 or line 6 of Form 2106-EZ on line 20 of Schedule A.

Impairment-related work expenses are your allowable expenses for attendant care at your workplace and other expenses you have in connection with your workplace that are necessary for you to be able to work. For more information, see chapter 23.

Illustrated Example

Bill Wilson is an employee of Fashion Clothing Co. in Manhattan, NY. In a typical week, Bill leaves his home on Long Island on Monday morning and drives to Albany to exhibit the Fashion line for 3 days to prospective customers. Then he drives to Troy to show Fashion's new line of merchandise to Town Department Store, an old customer. While in Troy, he talks with Tom Brown, purchasing agent for Town Department Store, to discuss the new line. He later takes John Smith of Attire Co. out to dinner to discuss Attire Co.'s buying Fashion's new line of clothing.

Bill purchased his car on January 3, 1998. He uses the standard mileage rate for car expense purposes. He records his total mileage, business mileage, parking fees, and tolls for the year. Bill timely records his expenses and other pertinent information in a travel expense log (not shown). He obtains receipts for his expenses for lodging and for any other expenses of $75 or more.

During the year, Bill drove a total of 25,000 miles of which 20,000 miles were for business. He answers all the questions in Part II of Form 2106. He figures his car expense to be $6,900 (20,000 business miles × 34 1/2 cents standard mileage rate).

His total employee business expenses are shown in the following table.

Type of Expense	Amount
Parking fees and tolls	$ 325
Car expenses	6,900
Meals	2,632
Lodging, laundry, dry cleaning	8,975
Entertainment	1,870
Gifts, education, etc.	430
Total	**$21,132**

Bill received an allowance of $3,600 ($300 per month) to help offset his expenses. Bill did not have to account to his employer for the reimbursement, and the $3,600 was included as income in box 1 of his Form W-2.

Because Bill's reimbursement was included in his income and he is using the standard mileage rate for his car expenses, he files **Form 2106-EZ** with his tax return. His filled-in form is shown on the next page.

TaxOrganizer

Records you should keep. Generally, you need documentary evidence of the business expenses you incur.

Adequate Evidence. Evidence is ordinarily considered adequate if it shows the amount, date, place, and essential character of the expense.

For example, a hotel receipt is sufficient to prove an expense for business travel if it has all of the following information:

1. The name and location of the hotel
2. The dates of your stay
3. Itemization of separate charges such as lodging, meals, and telephone calls

A restaurant receipt is enough to prove an expense for a business meal if it has all of the following:

1. The name and location of the restaurant
2. The number of people served
3. The date and amount of expense

Exceptions. Evidence not needed if:

1. You have meals or lodging expenses while traveling away from home for which you account to your employer under an accountable plan and you use a per diem allowance method that includes meals and/or lodging.
2. Your expense, other than lodging, is less than $75.
3. You have transportation expense for which a receipt is not readily available.

If a charge is made for item other than food and beverage, the receipt must show that this is the case.

Incomplete Records. If you do not have complete records to prove an element of expense, then you must prove the element by:

1. Your own statement, whether written or oral, that contains specific information about the element, and
2. Other supporting evidence that is sufficient to establish the element.

Form **2106-EZ**

Department of the Treasury
Internal Revenue Service

Unreimbursed Employee Business Expenses

▶ Attach to Form 1040.

OMB No. 1545-1441

20**01**

Attachment
Sequence No. **54A**

Your name	Occupation in which you incurred expenses	Social security number
Bill Wilson	Sales	555 00 5555

You May Use This Form Only if All of the Following Apply.

● You are an employee deducting expenses attributable to your job.

● You **do not** get reimbursed by your employer for any expenses (amounts your employer included in box 1 of your Form W-2 are not considered reimbursements).

● If you are claiming vehicle expense, you are using the standard mileage rate for 2001.

Caution: *You can use the standard mileage rate for 2001* **only if: (a)** *you owned the vehicle and used the standard mileage rate for the first year you placed the vehicle in service* **or (b)** *you leased the vehicle and used the standard mileage rate for the portion of the lease period after 1997.*

Part I   Figure Your Expenses

1	Vehicle expense using the standard mileage rate. Complete Part II and multipy line 8a by 34½¢ (.345)	**1**	6,900
2	Parking fees, tolls, and transportation, including train, bus, etc., that **did not** involve overnight travel or commuting to and from work	**2**	325
3	Travel expense while away from home overnight, including lodging, airplane, car rental, etc. **Do not** include meals and entertainment	**3**	8,975
4	Business expenses not included on lines 1 through 3. **Do not** include meals and entertainment	**4**	430
5	Meals and entertainment expenses: $ ___4,502___ x 50% (.50) (Employees subject to Department of Transportation (DOT) hours of service limits: Multiply meal expenses by 60% (.60) instead of 50%. For details, see instructions.)	**5**	2,251
6	**Total expenses.** Add lines 1 through 5. Enter here and **on line 20 of Schedule A (Form 1040).** (Fee-basis state or local government officials, qualified performing artists, and individuals with disabilities: See the instructions for special rules on where to enter this amount.)	**6**	18,881

Part II   Information on Your Vehicle. Complete this part **only** if you are claiming vehicle expense on line 1.

7   When did you place your vehicle in service for business use? (month, day, year) ▶ ___1___ / ___3___ / ___98___

8   Of the total number of miles you drove your vehicle during 2001, enter the number of miles you used your vehicle for:

a   Business ___20,000___   b Commuting ___2,600___   c Other ___2,400___

9   Do you (or your spouse) have another vehicle available for personal use? ☑ Yes ☐ No

10   Was your vehicle available for personal use during off-duty hours? ☑ Yes ☐ No

11a   Do you have evidence to support your deduction? ☑ Yes ☐ No

b   If "Yes," is the evidence written? ☑ Yes ☐ No

General Instructions

Section references are to the Internal Revenue Code.

A Change To Note

The standard mileage rate has been increased to 34½ cents for each mile of business use in 2001.

Purpose of Form

You may use Form 2106-EZ instead of Form 2106 to claim your unreimbursed employee business expenses if you meet all the requirements listed above Part I.

Recordkeeping

You cannot deduct expenses for travel (including meals, unless you used the standard meal allowance), entertainment, gifts, or use of a car or other listed property, unless you keep records to prove the time, place, business purpose, business relationship (for entertainment and gifts), and amounts of these expenses. Generally, you must also have receipts for all lodging expenses (regardless of the amount) and any other expense of $75 or more.

Additional Information

For more details about employee business expenses, see:

Pub. 463, Travel, Entertainment, Gift, and Car Expenses

Pub. 529, Miscellaneous Deductions

Pub. 587, Business Use of Your Home (Including Use by Day-Care Providers)

Pub. 946, How To Depreciate Property

For Paperwork Reduction Act Notice, see back of form.   Cat. No. 20604Q   Form **2106-EZ** (2001)

Tax Benefits for Work-Related Education

Introduction

Educational expenses are generally considered to be personal in nature and nondeductible. The law, however, does recognize that certain educational expenses are necessary for you as an employee. Deductions may be allowed for these expenses, as well as for reasonable expenses incurred in acquiring the education.

It's often difficult to determine if educational expenses are deductible. You do not necessarily have to earn a new degree for such expenses to be claimed. On the other hand, earning a degree doesn't necessarily make the expenses deductible. The expenses do have to meet certain tests. For example, they are deductible if the education either maintains or improves skills required in your trade or business or if the courses are required for you to retain your current job. The expenses are not deductible if they are spent on education that is required for you to meet the minimum educational requirements of your position. Also, you may not deduct expenses for

law school, medical school, or any other course of study that qualifies you for a new trade or business, even if you do not plan on entering the new trade or business. In addition, travel as a form of education is not deductible.

This chapter teaches you about deductible educational expenses. You'll learn that you may deduct not only your fees for educational instruction but also a number of other expenses that you incur because you are simultaneously working and in school.

Educational expenses and other miscellaneous itemized deductions are deductible only to the extent that they exceed 2% of your adjusted gross income.

It is also important to note that your 2001 itemized deductions may be subject to certain other limitations if your adjusted gross income exceeds $132,950 ($66,475 if married filing separately). See Chapter 22, Limit on Itemized Deductions, for more information on this subject.

Important Change for 2001

Standard mileage rate. Generally, if you drive your car to and from school, you can deduct 34 1/2 cents per mile. See *Using your car* under *What Educational Expenses Are Deductible.*

Important Change for 2002

Employer-provided educational assistance program extended. The tax-free status of up to $5,250 of employer-provided educational assistance benefits each year was scheduled to end for courses beginning after December 31, 2001. This benefit has been extended and, beginning January 1, 2002, the benefit also applies to graduate-level courses.

If you are working and have work-related educational expenses, you may be able to deduct all or part of the cost of your education as a business expense deduction. This chapter discusses:

- Qualifying education,
- What educational expenses are deductible, and
- Where to deduct expenses.

You cannot deduct educational expenses that are not work related, such as the costs of sending your children to college. However, you may be eligible for other tax benefits. Information on the education tax credits is in chapter 36, on making withdrawals from IRAs for educational expenses in chapter 18, and on cancellation of student loans in chapter 13. Information on student loan interest is in Publication 970, Tax Benefits for Higher Education.

Useful Items

You may want to see:

Publication

- ☐ **463**   Travel, Entertainment, Gift, and Car Expenses
- ☐ **508**   Tax Benefits for Work-Related Education
- ☐ **970**   Tax Benefits for Higher Education

Form (and Instructions)

- ☐ **2106**   Employee Business Expenses
- ☐ **2106-EZ**   Unreimbursed Employee Business Expenses
- ☐ **Schedule A (Form 1040)**   Itemized Deductions

Qualifying Education

You can deduct the costs of qualifying education. This is education that meets *at least one* of the following two tests.

1) The education is *required by your employer or the law* to keep your present salary, status, or job. The required education must serve a bona fide business purpose of your employer.
2) The education *maintains or improves skills* needed in your present work.

However, even if the education meets one or both of the above tests, it is not qualifying education if it:

1) Is needed to meet the *minimum educational requirements* of your present trade or business, or
2) Is part of a program of study that will *qualify you for a new trade or business.*

You can deduct the expenses for qualifying education even if the education could lead to a degree.

You can use *Figure 29-A* as a quick check to see if your education qualifies.

Explanation
In order to be deductible, educational expenses must relate to your current occupation.

Example
A college student obtaining employment through his or her college cooperative program or work/study program is not engaged in a trade or a business. His or her college fees are not deductible, because they are incurred in preparation for an occupation.

A full-time student does not have a trade or a business and may not deduct the cost of courses toward a college degree, even though the student may be employed full-time during the summer months.

TAXPLANNER

The IRS does not explicitly allow or disallow educational expenses for a semi-retired person. Therefore, it appears that educational expenses to maintain skills are deductible, even though the individual has reduced the scope of his or her trade or business.

An individual who abandons a former profession for a period of years and acquires a *new* profession may not deduct courses related to resuming his or her original profession.

A fully retired individual is not considered to have a trade or a business and is not entitled to a deduction for educational expenses.

Example
Gaby, an engineer, decides to teach math at a local high school. After teaching for a few years, she decides to resume her former career in engineering. Gaby takes refresher courses at a local college. The cost of these courses are *not* deductible.

Education Required by Employer or by Law

Once you have met the minimum educational requirements for your job, your employer or the law may require you to get more education. This additional education is qualifying education if all three of the following requirements are met.

1) It is required for you to keep your present salary, status, or job,
2) The requirement serves a business purpose of your employer, and
3) The education is not part of a program that will qualify you for a new trade or business.

Example 1
As a result of a corporate downsizing policy, you are taking courses to be retrained in another trade or business. If this education qualifies you to enter a new trade or business, even with the same employer, the costs are nondeductible.

Example 2
Your employer is restructuring its workforce. The company has said that additional education is required for you to retain your current job. Because the education serves a business purpose of your employer and is necessary for you to maintain your current position, the additional educational expenses are deductible.

When you get more education than your employer or the law requires, the additional education can be qualifying education only if it maintains or improves skills required in your present work. See *Education To Maintain or Improve Skills.*

Example. You are a teacher who has satisfied the minimum requirements for teaching. Your employer requires you to take an additional college course each year to keep your teaching job. If the courses

Figure 29-A. **Does Your Education Qualify?**

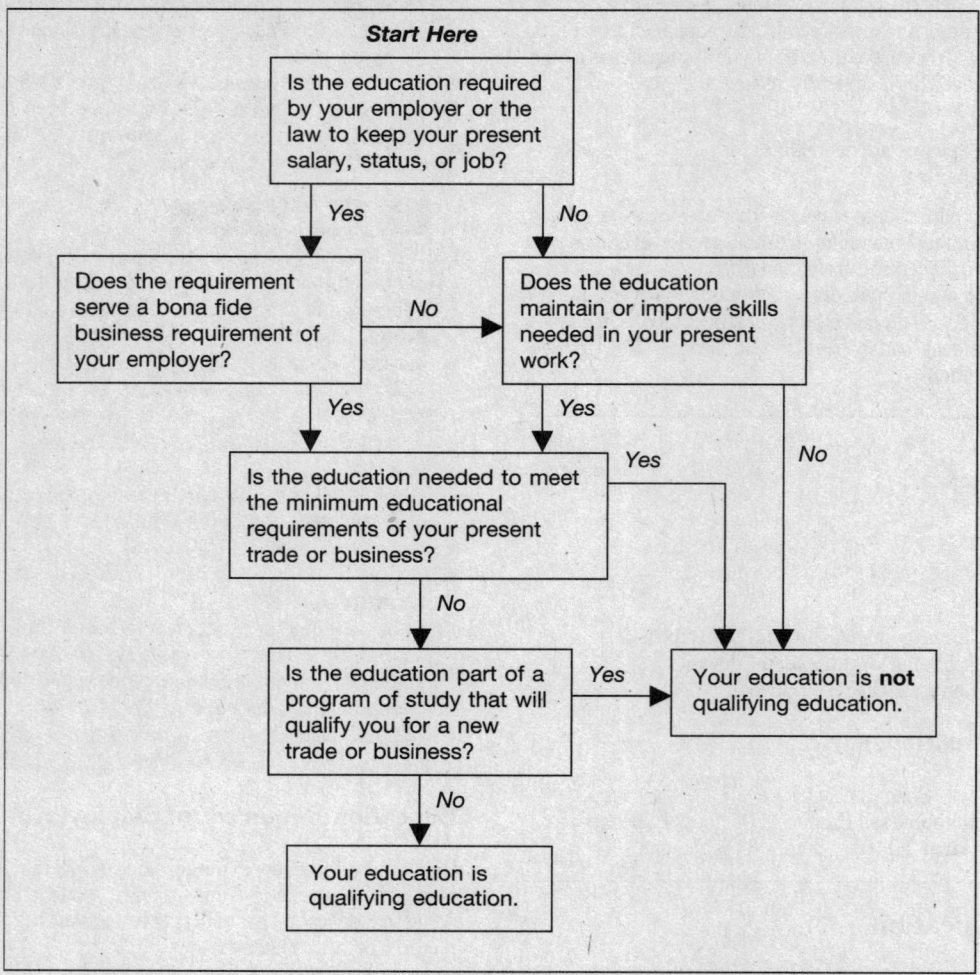

will not qualify you for a new trade or business, they are qualifying education even if you eventually receive a master's degree and an increase in salary because of this extra education.

Education To Maintain or Improve Skills

If your education is not required by your employer or the law, it can be qualifying education only if it maintains or improves skills needed in your present work. This could include refresher courses, courses on current developments, and academic or vocational courses.

Example. You repair televisions, radios, and stereo systems for XYZ Store. To keep up with the latest changes, you take special courses in radio and stereo service. These courses maintain and improve skills required in your work.

Explanation
For expenses to be deductible, they do not have to be spent on courses closely related to your duties, as long as the courses improve required skills.

Examples
The following are examples of educational expenses that were *deductible* because the courses maintained or improved skills:

- A tax attorney attended an out-of-town tax forum. The course was valuable for him in maintaining current knowledge of the tax laws.
- An engineering aide took night courses that improved his skills but were not required by his employer.
- A concert harpist took music lessons. The costs were deductible as maintaining or improving her skills.
- A doctor, engaged in the private practice of psychiatry, undertook a program of study and training at an accredited psychoanalytic institute that enabled him to qualify to practice psychoanalysis. The expenditures were deductible because the study and training maintained or improved skills required in the doctor's trade or business and didn't qualify the doctor for a new trade or a business.
- A farmer could deduct the cost of a welding course that improved his welding skills. Welding skills were necessary in the farming operation to keep the machinery repaired.
- An ordained minister could deduct the cost of undergraduate courses in psychology, education, and business. The court determined that the courses maintained and improved the skills that he needed to lead a congregation competently: counseling, teaching, and managing the financial affairs of the church.
- **Master of Laws in Taxation (LLM).** The Tax Court allows a deduction for the cost of obtaining a Master of Laws in

Taxation (LLM) provided the attorney has already passed the bar and is working in the field.

Maintaining skills vs. qualifying for new job. Education to maintain or improve skills needed in your present work is not qualifying education if it will also qualify you for a new trade or business.

Explanation
The following are examples of educational expenses that were *not deductible* because the courses qualified the taxpayer for a new trade or a business:

Examples

- A bookkeeper and tax return preparer returned to school and earned a bachelor's degree in accounting. The degree qualified her to sit for the certified public accounting examination. The costs incurred in earning the degree are not deductible because the courses were intended to obtain a new degree rather than to improve or maintain her skills; the new degree qualified her for a new trade or business.
- A quality control foreman took courses in business law, corporate strategy and business policies, and business finance. The costs were held to be nondeductible because they were only remotely related to his duties.

Temporary absence. If you stop working for a year or less in order to get education to maintain or improve skills needed in your present work and then return to the same work, your absence is considered temporary. Education that you get during a temporary absence is qualifying education if it maintains or improves skills needed in your present work.

Example. You quit your biology research job to become a full-time biology graduate student for one year. If you return to work in biology research after completing the courses, the education is related to your present work even if you do not go back to work with the same employer.

Indefinite absence. If you stop work for more than a year, your absence from your job is considered indefinite. Education during an indefinite absence, even if it maintains or improves skills needed in the work from which you are absent, is considered to qualify you for a new trade or business. Therefore, it is not qualifying education.

Explanation
While the IRS defines a temporary leave of absence as a period of 1 year or less, the courts have been more lenient, approving deductions for educational expenses for a leave of more than 1 year. The cases turn on whether or not the taxpayer expects to reenter the same trade or business, regardless of whether or not it is with a new employer.

Examples
A manager who quit his job to pursue a 2-year master of business administration course but who expected to reenter the same trade or business was allowed to deduct the cost of his courses.

A parochial schoolteacher ended her employment to raise a family. Over the next 23 years, she attended several different colleges until she was awarded a bachelor's degree in education. The following fall, she began employment again as a full-time teacher. The court determined that when she left the parochial school, there was no indication that she was on a leave of absence or that she planned to resume teaching in the future. Consequently, the court denied the deduction for the educational expenses.

Education To Meet Minimum Requirements

Education you need to meet the minimum educational requirements for your present trade or business is not qualifying education. The minimum educational requirements are determined by:

1) Laws and regulations,
2) Standards of your profession, trade, or business, and
3) Your employer.

Example
You have completed 2 years of a 3-year law school curriculum and are hired by a law firm to do legal research and to perform other functions on a full-time basis. As a condition of employment, you are required to obtain a law degree and to pass the state bar examination. You complete the law school education by attending night classes and take a bar review course in order to prepare for the bar examination. The law courses and the bar review course are considered the minimum educational requirements needed to qualify for your trade or business, and thus the costs of such courses are not deductible. However, courts have held that you may amortize over your life expectancy fees paid to state bar admission authorities.

Once you have met the minimum educational requirements that were in effect when you were hired, you do not have to meet any new minimum educational requirements. This means that if the minimum requirements change after you were hired, any education you need to meet the new requirements can be qualifying education.
Caution. *You have not necessarily met the minimum educational requirements of your trade or business simply because you are already doing the work.*

Example 1. You are a full-time engineering student. Although you have not received your degree or certification, you work part time as an engineer for a firm that will employ you as a full-time engineer after you finish college. Although your college engineering courses improve your skills in your present job, they are also needed to meet the minimum job requirements for a full-time engineer. The education is not qualifying education.

Example 2. You are an accountant and you have met the minimum educational requirements of your employer. Your employer later changes the minimum educational requirements and requires you to take college courses to keep your job. These additional courses can be qualifying education because you have already satisfied the minimum requirements that were in effect when you were hired.

Requirements for Teachers
States or school districts usually set the minimum educational requirements for teachers. The requirement is the college degree or the minimum number of college hours usually required of a person hired for that position.

If there are no requirements, you will have met the minimum educational requirements when you become a faculty member. You generally will be considered a faculty member when **one or more** of the following occurs.

1) You have tenure.
2) Your years of service count toward obtaining tenure.
3) You have a vote in faculty decisions.

4) Your school makes contributions for you to a retirement plan other than social security or a similar program.

Example 1. The law in your state requires beginning secondary school teachers to have a bachelor's degree, including ten professional education courses. In addition, to keep the job, a teacher must complete a fifth year of training within 10 years from the date of hire. If the employing school certifies to the state Department of Education that qualified teachers cannot be found, the school can hire persons with only 3 years of college. However, to keep their jobs, these teachers must get a bachelor's degree and the required professional education courses within 3 years.

Under these facts, the bachelor's degree, whether or not it includes the ten professional education courses, is considered the minimum educational requirement for qualification as a teacher in your state.

If you have all the required education except the fifth year, you have met the minimum educational requirements. The fifth year of training is qualifying education unless it is part of a program of study that will qualify you for a new trade or business.

Example 2. Assume the same facts as in *Example 1* except that you have a bachelor's degree and only six professional education courses. The additional four education courses can be qualifying education. Although you do not have all the required courses, you have already met the minimum educational requirements.

Example 3. Assume the same facts as in *Example 1* except that you are hired with only 3 years of college. The courses you take that lead to a bachelor's degree (including those in education) are not qualifying education. They are needed to meet the minimum educational requirements for employment as a teacher.

Example 4. You have a bachelor's degree and you work as a temporary instructor at a university. At the same time, you take graduate courses toward an advanced degree. The rules of the university state that you can become a faculty member only if you get a graduate degree. Also, you can keep your job as an instructor only as long as you show satisfactory progress toward getting this degree. You have not met the minimum educational requirements to qualify you as a faculty member. The graduate courses are not qualifying education.

TaxSaver

It's possible to maximize an education deduction by carefully limiting pre-employment education to minimum job requirements. Courses taken after employment is secured may then be deductible as maintaining or improving skills.

Example 1

Denise Thomas is starting her final semester of courses that will enable her to be a registered nurse. She needs 6 credit hours of nursing courses to reach the required level of education. In addition to the 6 credit hours, Denise also wants to take an advanced nursing course. To reduce her taxes, Denise should complete the minimum job requirements for nursing. If she takes the advanced nursing course after she qualifies to be a nurse and secures a nursing position, the cost is deductible.

Example 2

Robert Taylor is a recent law school graduate and is considering the pursuit of a full-time graduate law (LLM) program in international law. To qualify for a deduction, Robert should secure employment as a lawyer and complete the minimum requirements for practicing law (i.e., bar admission) before starting any graduate program.

After meeting these minimum requirements for practicing law, Robert may begin a graduate law program in international law and deduct the related educational expenses.

Certification in a new state. Once you have met the minimum educational requirements for teachers for your state, you are considered to have met the minimum educational requirements in all states. This is true even if you must get additional education to be certified in another state. Any additional education you need is qualifying education. You have already met the minimum requirements for teaching. Teaching in another state is not a new trade or business.

Example. You hold a permanent teaching certificate in State A and are employed as a teacher in that state for several years. You move to State B and are promptly hired as a teacher. You are required, however, to complete certain prescribed courses to get a permanent teaching certificate in State B. These additional courses are qualifying education because the teaching position in State B involves the same general kind of work for which you were qualified in State A.

Education That Qualifies You for a New Trade or Business

Education that is part of a program of study that will qualify you for a new trade or business is not qualifying education. This is true even if you do not plan to enter that trade or business.

If you are an employee, a change of duties that involves the same general kind of work is not a new trade or business.

Example 1. You are an accountant. Your employer requires you to get a law degree at your own expense. You register at a law school for the regular curriculum that leads to a law degree. Even if you do not intend to become a lawyer, the education is not qualifying because the law degree will qualify you for a new trade or business.

Example 2. You are a general practitioner of medicine. You take a 2-week course to review developments in several specialized fields of medicine. The course does not qualify you for a new profession. It is qualifying education because it maintains or improves skills required in your present profession.

Explanation

A change of duties is limited to employees. It does not pertain to self-employed individuals.

The IRS defines the phrase "the same general type of work" very narrowly. The burden is on the taxpayer to prove that he or she has not qualified for a new trade or business. However, teachers are generally given more latitude (see the following section, *Teaching and Related Duties*).

No deduction has been allowed for law school educational expenses, even if they are required by an employer. The courts have specifically disallowed a deduction for law school for employees in the following trades or businesses: accountant, insurance claims adjuster, industrial arts teacher, engineer, probation officer, patent examiner, mathematics teacher, IRS agent, hospital administrator, doctor, philosophy professor, and computer systems analyst.

Exceptions

Nevertheless, the courts have *allowed deductions* in some special cases:

- A night manager of a supermarket took food management courses at a local university. The courses elevated his rank within the management structure and also qualified him for a day manager position. The court held that the general management progression did not represent a change in business, and the court allowed the deductions.

- An engineer whose duties were changing to include more management and administrative skills took courses and received a degree in business management and administration. The courses were deductible because the education did not qualify him for a new trade or a business but was directly related to his current position. The courses also allowed him to maintain and improve skills required by his employer.
- Costs incurred in becoming a specialist within your trade or business are deductible.

TaxSaver

You may be able to deduct expenses incurred in gaining a specialty within a trade or a business if the expenses are delayed until after you have established yourself in the trade or business.

Example

A dentist engaged in general practice returned to dental school for full-time postgraduate study in orthodontics while continuing her practice on a part-time basis. After completing her postgraduate training, she limited her practice to orthodontic patients. The expenses incurred by the dentist in her studies were deductible because they improved her skills as a dentist and did not qualify her for a new trade or business.

Bar or CPA Review Course

Review courses to prepare for the bar examination or the certified public accountant (CPA) examination are not qualifying education. They are part of a program of study that can qualify you for a new profession.

Explanation

Bar review courses are not deductible, even if you are currently practicing in one state and are seeking admission to the bar in another state. However, you may be able to deduct the cost of graduate courses (LLM). See earlier examples under *Education to Maintain or Improve Skills*, and *Education to Meet Minimum Requirements*.

Teaching and Related Duties

All teaching and related duties are considered the same general kind of work. A change in duties in any of the following ways is not considered a change to a new business.

1) Elementary school teacher to secondary school teacher.
2) Teacher of one subject, such as biology, to teacher of another subject, such as art.
3) Classroom teacher to guidance counselor.
4) Classroom teacher to school administrator.

Explanation

If you are an employed teacher who meets the minimum education requirements of one state, you may deduct the cost of required courses to qualify as a teacher in another state. Changing employers and locations is not a significant change of duties and does not create a new trade or business. Like-

wise, deductions have been allowed for a Canadian teacher taking courses to qualify to teach in the United States. However, the IRS has ruled that the position of elementary school teacher does not involve the same general type of work and is not the same trade or business as a university professor.

Example

Lynn Arnold left her position as an elementary music teacher to obtain a Ph.D. degree in music. After obtaining her degree, she took a job as an assistant professor in the music department of a university. Lynn cannot deduct the expenses of getting her Ph.D.

What Educational Expenses Are Deductible?

If your education meets the requirements described earlier under *Qualifying Education,* you can generally deduct your educational expenses. If you are not self-employed, you can deduct educational expenses only if you itemize your deductions.

You cannot deduct expenses related to tax-exempt and excluded income.

Deductible expenses. The following educational expenses can be deducted.

- Tuition, books, supplies, lab fees, and similar items.
- Certain transportation and travel costs.
- Other educational expenses, such as costs of research and typing when writing a paper as part of an educational program.

TaxOrganizer

Records you should keep. In case the IRS challenges your deduction of educational expenses, you should keep the following information in order to support your claim for educational expenses incurred:

- Tuition statements and canceled checks
- Receipts for books, supplies, lab fees, and the like
- Records of travel and transportation expenses, including miles driven and parking receipts
- Receipts for meal expenses

Nondeductible expenses. Educational expenses do not include personal or capital expenses. For example, you cannot deduct the dollar value of vacation time or annual leave you take to attend classes. This amount is a personal expense.

Unclaimed reimbursement. If you do not claim reimbursement that you are entitled to receive from your employer, you cannot deduct the expenses that apply to the reimbursement.

Example. Your employer agrees to pay your educational expenses if you file a voucher showing your expenses. You do not file a voucher, and you do not get reimbursed. Because you did not file a voucher, you cannot deduct the expenses on your tax return.

Transportation Expenses

If your education qualifies, you can deduct local transportation costs of going directly from work to school. If you are regularly employed and go to school on a *temporary basis,* you can also deduct the costs of returning from school to home.

Temporary basis. If your attendance at school is realistically expected to last (and does in fact last) for 1 year or less, you go to school on a temporary basis (unless there are facts and circumstances that would indicate otherwise).

If your attendance at school is realistically expected to last for more than 1 year or if there is no realistic expectation that the attendance will last for 1 year or less, the attendance is not temporary, regardless of whether it actually lasts for more than 1 year.

If attendance at school initially is realistically expected to last for 1 year or less, but at some later date the attendance is realistically expected to last more than 1 year, that attendance will be treated as temporary (unless there are facts and circumstances that would indicate otherwise) until your expectation changes. It will not be treated as temporary after the date you determine it will last more than 1 year.

Caution. *Attendance at school on a temporary basis was formerly defined as attendance on an irregular or short-term basis (generally a matter of days or weeks).*

Tip. *You can file an amended return on Form 1040X,* Amended U.S. Individual Income Tax Return, *for any year in which you used the former definition of attendance on a temporary basis. However, you generally must file the amended return within 3 years from the time you filed the original return or within 2 years from the time you paid the tax, whichever is later.*

Deductible expenses. If you are regularly employed and go directly from home to school on a temporary basis, you can deduct the round-trip costs of transportation between your home and school. This is true regardless of the location of the school, the distance traveled, or whether you attend school on nonwork days.

Transportation expenses include the actual costs of bus, subway, cab, or other fares, as well as the costs of using your car. Transportation expenses do not include amounts spent for travel, meals, or lodging while you are away from home overnight.

Example 1. You regularly work in Camden, New Jersey, and go directly from work to home. You also attend school every night for 3 months to take a course that improves your job skills. Since you are attending school on a temporary basis, you can deduct your daily round-trip transportation expenses in going between home and school. This is true regardless of the distance traveled.

Example 2. Assume the same facts as in *Example 1* except that on certain nights you go directly from work to school and then home. You can deduct your transportation expenses from your regular work site to school and then home.

Example 3. Assume the same facts as in *Example 1* except that you attend the school for 9 months on Saturdays, nonwork days. Since you are attending school on a temporary basis, you can deduct your round-trip transportation expenses in going between home and school.

Example 4. Assume the same facts as in *Example 1* except that you attend classes twice a week for 15 months. Since your attendance in school is not considered temporary, you cannot deduct your transportation expenses in going between home and school. If you go directly from work to school, you can deduct the one-way transportation expenses of going from work to school. If you go from work to home to school and return home, your transportation expenses cannot be more than if you had gone directly from work to school.

Using your car. If you use your car (whether you own or lease it) for transportation to school, you can deduct your actual expenses or use the standard mileage rate to figure the amount you can deduct. The standard mileage rate for 2001 is 34 1/2 cents per mile. Whichever method you use, you can also deduct parking fees and tolls. See *Car Expenses* in chapter 28 for information on deducting your actual expenses of using a car.

Travel Expenses

You can deduct expenses for travel, meals (see *50% Limit,* later), and lodging if:

1) You travel overnight to obtain qualified education, and
2) The main purpose of the trip is to attend a work-related course or seminar.

Travel expenses for qualifying education are treated the same as travel expenses for other employee business purposes. For more information, see chapter 28.

Caution. *You cannot deduct expenses for personal activities, such as sightseeing, visiting, or entertaining.*

Mainly personal travel. If your travel away from home is mainly personal, you cannot deduct all of your expenses for travel, meals, and lodging. You can deduct only your expenses for lodging and 50% of your expenses for meals during the time you attend the qualified educational activities.

Whether a trip's purpose is mainly personal or educational depends upon the facts and circumstances. An important factor is the comparison of time spent on personal activities with time spent on educational activities. If you spend more time on personal activities, the trip is considered mainly educational only if you can show a substantial nonpersonal reason for traveling to a particular location.

Example 1. John works in Newark, New Jersey. He traveled to Chicago to take a deductible 1-week course at the request of his employer. His main reason for going to Chicago was to take the course.

While there, he took a sightseeing trip, entertained some friends, and took a side trip to Pleasantville for a day.

Since the trip was mainly for business, he can deduct his round-trip airfare to Chicago. He cannot deduct his transportation expenses of going to Pleasantville. He can deduct only the meals (subject to the 50% limit) and lodging connected with his educational activities.

Example 2. Dave works in Nashville and recently traveled to California to take a 2-week seminar. The seminar is qualifying education.

While there, he spent an extra 8 weeks on personal activities. The facts, including the extra 8-week stay, show that his main purpose was to take a vacation.

He cannot deduct his round-trip airfare or his meals and lodging for the 8 weeks. He can deduct only his expenses for meals (subject to the 50% limit) and lodging for the 2 weeks he attended the seminar.

TAXSAVER

Through careful planning and documentation, as well as recognition of the stringent tests applied by the courts, it's possible to mix business with pleasure and deduct some or all of your travel expenses. If you travel away from home primarily to obtain education, your expenditures for the education, as well as for travel, meals, and lodging while away from home, are deductible. It is helpful to be able to prove that the location you are visiting is unique and that, if education is involved, the education cannot be obtained elsewhere.

However, if you engage in some personal activity while on the trip, such as sight seeing, social visiting, entertaining, or other recreation, your expenses attributable to those personal activities are nondeductible personal expenses.

If your travel away from home is primarily personal, your expenditures for travel, meals, and lodging (other than meals and lodging during the time spent participating in deductible educational pursuits) are not deductible.

Whether a particular trip is primarily personal or primarily educational depends on all the facts and circumstances of each case, including the time devoted to personal activity as compared with the time devoted to educational pursuits.

Example

Shannon, a hair stylist, decides to attend a 4-day workshop on the latest trends of hair coloring and styling that is offered in Tampa, Florida, 400 miles from her home. Her primary purpose in going to Tampa is to take the course, but she also takes a side trip to Orlando (a couple of hours away from Tampa) for 2 days. Shannon's transportation expenses to Tampa are deductible, but her transportation to Orlando is not. Additionally, her expenses for meals and lodging while away from home must be allocated between her educational pursuits and her personal activities. Those expenses that are entirely personal, such as sight seeing in Orlando, are not deductible.

The cost of deductible meals must be reduced by 50%.

Cruises and conventions. Certain cruises and conventions offer seminars or courses as part of their itinerary. Even if the seminars or courses are work related, your deduction for travel may be limited. This applies to:

1) Travel by ocean liner, cruise ship, or other form of luxury water transportation, and
2) Conventions outside the North American area.

For a discussion of the limits on travel expense deductions that apply to cruises and conventions, see *Luxury Water Travel* and *Conventions* in Publication 463.

50% Limit

You can deduct only 50% of the cost of your qualifying meals while traveling away from home to obtain education. You cannot have been reimbursed for the meals.

Employees must use Form 2106 or Form 2106-EZ to apply the 50% limit.

Travel as Education

You cannot deduct the cost of travel as a form of education.

Example. You are a French language teacher. While on sabbatical leave granted for travel, you traveled through France to improve your knowledge of the French language. You chose your itinerary and most of your activities to improve your French language skills. You cannot deduct your travel expenses as educational expenses. This is true even if you spent most of your time learning French by visiting French schools and families, attending movies or plays, and engaging in similar activities.

Explanation
The cost of travel is not a deductible educational expense when the educational aspect of a trip is the trip itself. However, if you establish an ordinary and necessary business need for the travel, such as research that can only be done in a specific location, then a deduction may be allowed for travel expenses.

Student Loan Interest Expense

You may be able to deduct interest you pay on a qualified student loan. If you qualify, you can take this deduction whether or not the education is work related and even if you do not itemize deductions on Schedule A (Form 1040). For more information on the deduction of student loan interest, see Publication 970.

TAXALERT
Interest expense of up to $2,500 paid during 2001 on qualified student loans may be deducted from your income in determining your adjusted gross income. For more information, see Chapter 25, *Interest Expense.*

Expenses Relating to Tax-Exempt and Excluded Income

Some educational assistance you receive may be tax-exempt or excluded from your income. Since you do not pay tax on this income, you may not be able to deduct the related expenses. Examples of tax-exempt or excluded income include scholarships, veterans' educational assistance, and the Education Savings Bond Program. If you received assistance from any of these sources, see *Expenses Relating to Tax-Exempt and Excluded Income* in Publication 508.

TAXSAVER
You may be eligible to exclude from income the interest you receive from qualified U.S. savings bonds if you pay qualified higher education expenses. These are expenses for tuition and required fees at an eligible educational institution for you, your spouse, or your dependent. A qualified U.S. savings bond is a Series EE savings bond that is issued after December 31, 1989, to an individual who is 24 years of age or older. If your educational expenses qualify for deduction, you must reduce the expenses by the amount of interest excluded from income. For more information on the interest exclusion, see Chapter 8, *Interest Income.*

Employer-Provided Educational Assistance

If you receive educational assistance benefits from your employer under an educational assistance program, you can exclude up to $5,250 of those benefits each year. This means your employer should not include the benefits with your wages, tips, and other compensation shown in box 1 of your Form W-2. This also means that you do not have to include the benefits on your income tax return.

Caution. *You must reduce your deductible educational expenses by the amount of any tax-free educational assistance benefits you received for those expenses.*

Educational assistance program. To qualify as an educational assistance program, the plan must be written and must meet certain other requirements. Your employer can tell you whether there is a qualified program where you work.

Educational assistance. Tax-free educational assistance benefits include payments for tuition, fees and similar expenses, books, supplies, and equipment. The payments must be for undergraduate-level courses that begin before January 1, 2002. The payments do not have to be for work-related courses.

Tip. *Beginning January 1, 2002, this benefit has been expanded to include both undergraduate and graduate-level courses.*

Educational assistance benefits do **not** include payments for the following items.

1) Meals, lodging, transportation, or tools or supplies (other than textbooks) that you can keep after completing the course of instruction.
2) Education involving sports, games, or hobbies unless the education has a reasonable relationship to the business of your employer or is required as part of a degree program.
3) Graduate-level courses that are normally taken under a program leading to a law, business, medical, or other advanced academic or professional degree.

Benefit over $5,250. If your employer pays more than $5,250 for educational benefits for you during the year, you must generally pay tax on the amount over $5,250. Your employer should include in your wages (box 1 of your Form W-2) the amount you must include in income.

Working condition fringe benefit. However, if the payments also qualify as a working condition fringe benefit, your employer does not have to include them in your wages. A working condition fringe benefit is a benefit which, had you paid for it, you could deduct as an employee business expense.

Where To Deduct Expenses

Self-employed persons and employees report their educational expenses differently.

The following information explains what forms you must use to deduct the cost of your qualifying education.

Self-Employed Persons

If you are self-employed, you must report the cost of your qualifying education on the appropriate form used to report your business income and expenses (Schedule C, C-EZ, or F). If your educational expenses include expenses for a car or truck, travel, or meals, report them the same way you report other business expenses for those items. See the instructions for the form you file for information on how to complete it.

TaxSaver

From a tax perspective, it is more beneficial to report educational expenses on Schedules C, C-EZ, or F as appropriate. Reporting expenses on these forms will lower your adjusted gross income. As a result, a greater percentage of your itemized deductions may be allowed. In addition, reporting the expenses on Schedules C, C-EZ, or F will reduce your self-employment tax.

Employees

If you are an employee, you can deduct the cost of qualifying education only if you were not reimbursed by your employer or if the costs exceeded your reimbursement. (Amounts your employer paid under a nonaccountable plan and included in box 1 of your Form W-2 are not considered reimbursements.) How you treat any reimbursement you receive depends on the type of reimbursement arrangement and the amount of the reimbursement. For information on how to report your reimbursement, see chapter 28.

Include the cost of your qualifying education with your deduction for any other employee business expenses on line 20 of Schedule A (Form 1040). (Special rules for expenses of certain performing artists and fee-basis officials and for impairment-related work expenses are explained later.) This deduction is subject to the 2%-of-adjusted-gross-income limit that applies to most miscellaneous itemized deductions.

Form 2106 or 2106-EZ. To figure your deduction for employee business expenses, including qualifying education, you generally must complete Form 2106 or Form 2106-EZ.

Form not required. Do not complete either Form 2106 or Form 2106-EZ if:

• You were not reimbursed for any of your expenses, and
• You are not claiming travel, transportation, or meal expenses.

If you meet both of these requirements, enter the expenses directly on line 20 of Schedule A (Form 1040). (Special rules for expenses of certain performing artists and fee-basis officials and for impairment-related work expenses are explained later.)

Using Form 2106-EZ. This form is shorter and easier to use than Form 2106. Generally you can use this form if:

• You were not reimbursed for any of your expenses, and
• You are using the standard mileage rate if you are claiming vehicle expenses.

If you do not meet both of these requirements, use Form 2106.

Performing artists and fee-basis officials. If you are a qualified performing artist, or a state (or local) government official who is paid in whole or in part on a fee basis, you can deduct the cost of your qualifying education as an adjustment to gross income rather than as an itemized deduction.

For more information on qualified performing artists and fee-basis officials, see chapter 28.

Impairment-related work expenses. If you are disabled and have impairment-related work expenses that are necessary for you to be able to get qualifying education, you can deduct these expenses on line 27 of Schedule A (Form 1040). They are not subject to the 2%-of-adjusted-gross-income limit.

For more information on impairment-related work expenses, see chapter 28.

Recordkeeping

You must keep records as proof of any deduction claimed on your tax return. Generally, you should keep your records for 3 years from the date of filing the return and claiming the deduction.

For specific information about keeping records of business expenses, see *Recordkeeping* in chapter 28.

30

Miscellaneous Deductions

Introduction

This chapter covers a variety of expenses, both deductible and nondeductible. Deductible expenses can be broadly broken down into three categories: deductible employee expenses, deductible expenses of producing or collecting income, and other deductible expenses. The general rule is that you may deduct any "ordinary and
necessary" expense that is related to your trade or business, that is connected with producing or collecting other income, or that is paid to determine your tax. Note, however, that your deductions may be limited depending on the type of the expense and your income level. (See discussion below regarding Deductions Subject to the 2%

Limit *and Chapter 22,* Limit on Itemized Deductions, *for more information.)*

Nondeductible expenses, by definition, are all expenses that are not deductible. These expenses are typically personal in nature. The nondeductible expenses discussed in this chapter are not all-inclusive, but rather reflect the more common expenses that people may think are (or should be) deductible.

With proper planning, you may be able to deduct more than you think. Be sure to take note of the special comments throughout this chapter with respect to documenting the appropriateness of your deductions, and check out the list at the front of the book for 50 of the Most Easily Overlooked Deductions *to be sure you haven't missed anything.*

Important Reminder

Limit on itemized deductions. For 2001, if your adjusted gross income is more than $132,950 ($66,475 if you are married filing separately), you may have to reduce the amount of certain itemized deductions, including most miscellaneous deductions.

This chapter explains which expenses you can claim as miscellaneous itemized deductions on **Schedule A** (Form 1040). You must reduce the total of most miscellaneous itemized deductions by 2% of your adjusted gross income. This chapter covers the following topics.

- Deductions subject to the 2% limit.
- Deductions not subject to the 2% limit.
- Expenses you cannot deduct.

Recordkeeping. You must keep records to verify your deductions. You should keep receipts, canceled checks, financial account statements, and other documentary evidence. For more information on recordkeeping, get Publication 552, *Recordkeeping for Individuals.*

Useful Items

You may want to see:

Publication

- ☐ **463** Travel, Entertainment, Gift, and Car Expenses
- ☐ **525** Taxable and Nontaxable Income
- ☐ **529** Miscellaneous Deductions
- ☐ **535** Business Expenses
- ☐ **587** Business Use of Your Home (Including Use by Day-Care Providers)
- ☐ **946** How To Depreciate Property

Form (and Instructions)

- ☐ **2106** Employee Business Expenses
- ☐ **2106-EZ** Unreimbursed Employee Business Expenses

Deductions Subject to the 2% Limit

You can deduct certain expenses as miscellaneous itemized deductions on Schedule A (Form 1040). You can claim the amount of expenses that is more than 2% of your adjusted gross income. You figure your deduction on Schedule A by subtracting 2% of your adjusted gross income from the total amount of these expenses. Your adjusted gross income is the amount on line 34, Form 1040.

Generally, you apply the 2% limit after you apply any other deduction limit. For example, you apply the 50% (or 60%) limit on business-related meals and entertainment (discussed in chapter 28) before you apply the 2% limit.

Explanation
2% limitation. First, you must determine which expenses are deductible. Next, you must calculate the amount that is deductible, taking into account any limitation for certain types of expenses (e.g., 50% for meals and entertainment). The sum of all of your allowable miscellaneous deductions is then reduced by 2% of your adjusted gross income (AGI) on Schedule A.

Example
Assume an individual's adjusted gross income is $45,000 in 2001. This person paid $1,500 in 2001 for the preparation of his 2000 income tax returns and also had $200 of unreimbursed business-related meal expenses in 2001. Both of these expenses are deductible. The $1,500 tax preparation fee is fully deductible, whereas only 50% of the $200 meal expense is deductible. Therefore, total miscellaneous deductions are $1,600 ($1,500 + 50% x $200). However, 2% of the individual's AGI is $900 ($45,000 x 2%), so he is permitted a deduction of only $700 ($1,600 allowable deductions reduced by 2% of AGI, or $900).

Deductions subject to the 2% limit are discussed in the three categories in which you report them on Schedule A.

1) *Unreimbursed employee expenses* (line 20).
2) *Tax preparation fees* (line 21).
3) *Other expenses* (line 22).

Impairment-related work expenses. If you have a physical or mental disability, certain expenses you incur that allow you to work may not be subject to the 2% limit. See *Impairment-Related Work Expenses* under *Deductions Not Subject to the 2% Limit,* later.

Performing artists. If you are a qualified performing artist, you may be able to deduct your employee business expenses as an adjustment to gross income rather than as a miscellaneous itemized deduction. See *Special Rules* in chapter 28 if you need more information about this exception.

State and local government officials paid on a fee basis. If you performed services as an employee of a state or local government and you were paid in whole or in part on a fee basis, you can claim your trade or business expenses in performing those services as an adjustment to gross income, rather than as a miscellaneous deduction. See *Officials Paid on a Fee Basis* under *Deductions Not Subject to the 2% Limit,* later.

Unreimbursed Employee Expenses (Line 20)

You can deduct only unreimbursed employee expenses that are:

1) Paid or incurred during your tax year,
2) For carrying on your trade or business of being an employee, and
3) Ordinary and necessary.

An expense is *ordinary* if it is common and accepted in your type of trade or business. An expense is *necessary* if it is appropriate and helpful to your trade or business.

Explanation
Unreimbursed employee business expenses. If you are an employee and have business expenses either that are not reimbursed or that are more than the amount reimbursed by your employer, you can generally deduct them only as a miscellaneous deduction (subject to the 2% adjusted gross income limit) on Schedule A (Form 1040).

TAXPLANNER
If you can get your employer to reimburse you for what would otherwise be unreimbursed business expenses, in lieu of an equal amount of salary, you should do so. You benefit at no additional cost to your employer because reimbursed employee business expenses for which you have adequately accounted to your employer are deductible by your employer the same as wages. However, the reimbursement for those expenses is not included on your Form W-2 as income, which would increase your tax liability.

Examples of unreimbursed employee expenses are listed next. The list is followed by discussions of additional unreimbursed employee expenses that are more common.

- Business bad debt of an employee.
- Education that is work related. (See chapter 29.)
- Legal fees related to your job.
- Licenses and regulatory fees.
- Malpractice insurance premiums.
- Medical examinations required by an employer.
- Occupational taxes.
- Passport for a business trip.
- Subscriptions to professional journals and trade magazines related to your work.
- Travel, transportation, entertainment, gift, and car expenses related to your work. (See chapter 28.)

Explanation
Business bad debt of an employee. A business bad debt is a loss from a debt created or acquired in your trade or business, or a loss when there is a very close relationship between the debt and your trade or business when the debt becomes worthless (e.g., as an employee, your main motive for incurring the debt is a business reason). For example, if an employee makes a bona fide loan to his employer in order to keep his job, and the company fails to pay the debt, the employee has a business bad debt. See Publication 535 for more information on business bad debts.

Explanation
Business travel and entertainment. Generally, only 50% of the amount spent for business meals (including meals away from home on overnight business) and entertainment will be deductible. This limit must be applied before arriving at the amount subject to the 2% of AGI limitation.

TAXALERT
Prior to 1994, if your spouse or child accompanied you on a business trip, travel expenses attributable to the family member were deductible only if you could adequately show that the presence of a family member served a bona fide business purpose. Now, however, you are not allowed to deduct the travel expenses of family members, even if there is a business purpose for their presence on the trip unless the family member is also an employee. If your employer reimburses you for travel expenses, the portion of the expense attributable to family members who are not employees of the company may be included in your W-2 income. See Chapter 28, *Car Expenses and Other Employee Business Expenses,* for more information about travel expenses.

TAXALERT
The deduction percentage for meals consumed while away from home by individuals subject to hours of service limitations of the Department of Transportation, such as interstate truck and bus drivers, certain railroad employees, and certain merchant marines, is 60% in 2001. The deduction will gradually increase to 80% by 2008. Note that you must apply this percentage before applying the 2% of AGI limitation.

TAXORGANIZER
Records you should keep. Adequate records should be kept for the amount of your travel and entertainment expenses—the time and place they occurred, the business purpose of the expenses, and the business relationship to the persons entertained—in order for you to substantiate your deduction.

Explanation
Business gifts. You can deduct no more than $25 for business gifts to any one person per year. See Chapter 28, *Car Expenses and Other Employee Business Expenses,* for more information.

Business Liability Insurance
You can deduct insurance premiums you paid for protection against personal liability for wrongful acts on the job.

Damages for Breach of Employment Contract
If you break an employment contract, you can deduct damages you pay your former employer if the damages are attributable to the pay you received from that employer.

Depreciation on Computers or Cellular Telephones
You can claim a depreciation deduction for a computer or cellular telephone that you use in your work as an employee if its use is:

1) For the convenience of your employer, and
2) Required as a condition of your employment.

Explanation
"For the convenience of your employer" means that your use of the computer or cellular telephone is for a substantial business reason of your employer. All facts must be considered in making this determination. The use of your computer or cellular phone during your regular working hours to carry on your employer's business is generally for the convenience of your employer.

"Required as a condition of your employment" means that you cannot properly perform your duties without it. Whether or not you can properly perform your duties without the computer or cellular telephone depends on all the facts and circumstances. It is not necessary that your employer explicitly requires you to use your computer or cellular telephone. But neither is it sufficient that your employer merely states that your use of these items is a condition of your employment.

Example

You are an engineer with an engineering firm. You occasionally take work home at night rather than work late at the office. You own and use a computer that is similar to the one you use at the office to complete your work at home. Because your use of the computer is not for the convenience of your employer and is not required as a condition of your employment, you cannot claim a deduction.

TaxAlert

Which depreciation method you may use depends on whether or not your computer or cellular telephone is used predominantly (more than 50%) for business or personal purposes. See Publication 529 for more information.

TaxAlert

The rules for depreciation on a computer that you use in your work as an employee differ from the rules for depreciation on a computer owned or leased and used only in your home office. See the section below relating to home office and Publication 529 for more information.

TaxPlanner

Personal computers. Home computers are frequently used for both business and personal purposes. Video games, children's homework, holiday card lists, and personal finances are considered personal uses. If you don't have a separate personal computer and a separate business computer, some type of allocation should be made between business use and personal use of the same computer.

The point to remember is that it is difficult to claim a deduction for your home computer. The IRS position is that no deduction will be allowed for a personal computer unless it meets the "for the convenience of your employer" and "required as a condition of your employment" tests described above.

TaxOrganizer

Records you should keep. Adequate records must be maintained to support your business use of the property in order to claim a depreciation expense deduction.

In case the IRS challenges your deductions for depreciation on home computers or cellular telephones, you should keep the following information to support your claim for home computer and cellular telephone depreciation deductions:

- Documentation from your employer that use of the home computer or cellular telephone is required by the employer
- A log of time spent using the computer or cellular phone and whether such time was for personal or business use

For details on allowable methods of depreciation, see Chapter 10, *Rental Income and Expenses.* The Section 179 deduction is explained in Chapter 38, *If You Are Self-Employed: How to File Schedule C.*

For more information about the rules and exceptions to the rules affecting the allowable deductions for a home computer or cellular telephone, see Publication 529.

Dues to Chambers of Commerce and Professional Societies

You may be able to deduct dues paid to professional organizations (such as bar associations and medical associations) and to chambers of commerce and similar organizations, if membership helps you carry out the duties of your job. Similar organizations include:

- Boards of trade,
- Business leagues,
- Civic or public service organizations,
- Real estate boards, and
- Trade associations.

You **cannot** deduct dues paid to an organization if one of its main purposes is to:

1) Conduct entertainment activities for members or their guests, or
2) Provide members or their guests with access to entertainment facilities.

Dues paid to airline, hotel, and luncheon clubs are not deductible. See *Club Dues* under *Nondeductible Expenses,* later.

Lobbying and political activities. You may not be able to deduct that part of your dues that is for certain lobbying and political activities. See *Dues used for lobbying* under *Lobbying Expenses,* later.

Home Office

If you use a part of your home regularly and exclusively for business purposes, you may be able to deduct a part of the operating expenses and depreciation of your home.

TaxAlert

Home office deduction. It is easier for taxpayers to claim a home office deduction. *Even if you were not able to claim a home office deduction in prior years and your business use of your home has not changed, you may now be able to take a deduction.*

Explanation

Individuals claiming home office deductions on Schedule C are required to figure those deductions on Form 8829, *Expenses for Business Use of Your Home.* However, if you are an employee claiming unreimbursed job-related expenses, use Form 2106, *Employee Business Expenses,* if applicable, or include the amount directly on Schedule A.

You can claim this deduction for the business use of a part of your home only if you use that part of your home **regularly** and **exclusively:**

1) As your principal place of business for any trade or business,
2) As a place to meet or deal with your patients, clients, or customers in the normal course of your trade or business, or
3) In the case of a separate structure not attached to your home, in connection with your trade or business.

Explanation

A home may be a house, an apartment, a condominium, a mobile home, or even a boat. It may also be other structures on the same property as the house you live in, such as a studio, a barn, a greenhouse, or an unattached garage.

The regular and exclusive business use must be *for the convenience of your employer* and not just appropriate and helpful in your job. Get Publication 587 for more detailed information and a worksheet.

Explanation

A home office deduction will only be allowed if you use your home in connection with a **trade or business.** All profit-seeking activities are not trades or businesses (e.g., if you invest from home and are not a broker or dealer investing on behalf of clients, you are not in the business of investing). However, you may take a home office deduction for a trade or business that is not your full-time occupation, as long as all of the appropriate tests are met (an example would be an attorney who uses his home office for the management of rental properties he owns).

Once the trade or business test is met, the remaining tests for qualifying for a home office deduction are:

1. The "principal place of business" test
2. The "regular and exclusive use" test
3. If an employee, the "for the convenience of your employer" test

The deduction is then limited to your gross income from your trade or business.

TaxPlanner

Principal place of business. Administrative and management activities for your trade or business that are performed exclusively and regularly in your home will qualify your home as your **principal place of business** if you have no other fixed location where you perform substantial administrative or management activities. Activities that are considered administrative or managerial include billing clients, customers, or patients; keeping books and records; ordering supplies; setting up appointments; and writing reports.

In addition, certain administrative and management activities may be performed in other locations and *not* disqualify your home office as your principal place of business for purposes of meeting the above test. For example, you may hire another person or company to perform your administrative activities, such as computing employee payrolls, at locations other than your home. You may also conduct administrative and management activities at places that are not fixed locations, such as hotel rooms or airports, and you may occasionally conduct minimal administrative and managerial activities at a fixed location outside of your home. Also, performing substantial nonadministrative activities outside of your home, such as servicing clients or making sales calls, will not disqualify your home as your principal place of business. And, significantly, you may even have suitable space available to you outside your home for performing administrative and managerial tasks but choose to use your home instead. (Note, however, that if you are an employee, any use of your home must be for the convenience of your employer in order to qualify for the home office deduction.)

Example

Jeff is a self-employed anesthesiologist, working for three different local hospitals. One of the hospitals provides him with a small shared office where he could perform administrative or management activities. However, Jeff prefers to use a room in his home as an office. He regularly and exclusively uses this room to schedule patients, maintain patient logs, bill patients, and read medical journals.

Prior to 1999, Jeff's home office did not qualify as his principal place of business because his most important activity, administering anesthetics, was performed in the hospitals. Under the new rules, Jeff's office qualifies for the home office deduction in 2001 (i.e., his home office will qualify as his principal place of business) because he conducts administrative and managerial activities for his business there and has no other fixed location where these activities take place. Neither the fact that Jeff has available space at the hospital for performing administrative tasks nor the fact that his most important task is performed outside of his home disqualifies his home office as his principal place of business.

Explanation

To qualify for the **regular and exclusive use** test, you must use a specific area of your home *only* for your trade or business and on a continuing basis. The specific area can be a separate room or any identifiable space (the space does not need to be marked off by a permanent enclosure). Any personal use of the space will cause you to fail the requirements of the exclusive use test. Occasional or incidental use will cause you to fail the regular use test, even if that area of your house is not used for any other purposes.

Exceptions

Note that there is an exception to the regular and exclusive use test if you use part of your home as a day-care facility for children, persons age 65 or older, or individuals who are physically or mentally incapable of caring for themselves. The day-care provider must be licensed or certified under applicable state law, or exempt from licensing, for the exception to apply. There is also an exception to the regular and exclusive use test if you use part of your home to store inventory or product samples. If your home is the principal place of your business, the space used for inventory and sample storage qualifies for the home office deduction as long as it is used regularly, but not necessarily exclusively, for business.

TaxPlanner

Many home sales operations require a great deal of personal time and attention but produce a minimum of deductible expenses. The storage use concept may produce valuable deductions for otherwise underutilized spaces, such as attics and basements. Remember, the storage space must be a specific area that is used as a part of your principal place of business.

TaxSaver

Day-care providers. Day-care providers who operate businesses in their homes may benefit from a recent IRS ruling. The square footage of a room that is regularly used for day care and is available throughout the business day will be considered used for day care for the entire business day. Previously, taxpayers had to take partial days based on the hours of actual business use. The deduction for day-care providers is equal to the total costs of maintaining the home (e.g., electricity, gas, water, trash collection, general maintenance) to provide day care, multiplied by the following two fractions:

$$\frac{\text{Total square feet available and used regularly each day}}{\text{Total square feet of home}}$$

$$\frac{\text{Total hours each year home used for day-care business}}{\text{Total hours each year (8,760 hours)}}$$

The resulting deduction is subject to the income limitation, discussed below. IRS Form 8829 will help you work through this calculation.

Example

A day-care provider uses a bedroom (available for child care throughout the business day) for the children's morning and afternoon naps every day. Although the bedroom is not used during every hour of the business day, the total square footage of that room is considered as day-care usage for the entire business day when the total area for business is calculated.

Explanation

If you are an employee and you meet the above tests for the use of your home in your trade or business, you will only qualify for a home office deduction if your use of your home is for the **convenience of your employer** and you do not rent your home office to your employer. It is not sufficient that a home office is helpful to your job; it must be a requirement of your employer. Your home office must also be justified by the nature of your job, which depends on all the facts and circumstances.

How to figure the deduction. To figure the percentage of your home used for business, you may compare the square feet of space used for business to the total square feet in your home. Or, if the rooms in your home are approximately the same size, you may compare the number of rooms used for business to the total number of rooms in your home. You may also use any other reasonable method. Generally, you figure the business part of your expenses by applying the percentage to the total of each expense.

Example

The room in your home that you use for business measures 120 square feet. Your home measures 1,200 square feet. Therefore, you are using one-tenth, or 10%, of the total area for business.

If you use one room for business in a five-room house and the rooms in your home are about the same size, you are using one-fifth, or 20%, of the total area for business.

Basing the deduction on an approximation of the rental costs of comparable office space is not a proper method, according to one court ruling.

Explanation

The general rule is that the expenses you have for maintaining and running your entire home may be taken, in part, as deductions, because they benefit both the business and the personal parts of your home.

If you have purchased your home, you may deduct part of the interest you pay on your home mortgage as a business expense. To figure the business part of your mortgage interest, multiply the mortgage interest by the part of your home used for business. If you rent a home, you may deduct part of the rent you pay using a similar calculation.

If you have a casualty loss (see Chapter 27, *Casualty and Theft Losses*) on your home or other property that you use in business, you may deduct the business part of the loss as a business expense. The amount of the loss that qualifies for a deduction depends on what property is affected. If the loss is sustained on property that you use only in your business, the entire loss is treated as a business deduction. If the loss affects property used for both business and personal purposes, only the business part is a business deduction.

If you use part of your home for business, you may also deduct part of the expenses for utilities and services, such as electricity, gas, trash removal, and cleaning services. Expenses that are related only to your business, such as business long-distance telephone calls and depreciation of office furniture and equipment, are fully deductible.

Likewise, if you use part of your home for business, you may deduct part of your insurance on your home. However, if your insurance premium gives you coverage for a period that extends past the end of your tax year, you may deduct for business only the part of the premium that covers you for the tax year.

Example

If you paid a 2-year premium of $240 on September 1, 2001, only 4 months of the policy are included in your 2001 tax year. Therefore, only four twenty-fourths (1/6) of the premium may be used to figure your deduction in 2001. In 2002, you may use twelve twenty-fourths (1/2), and in 2003 eight twenty-fourths (1/3) would be used to figure your deduction. The premium must then be allocated between business and nonbusiness uses of your home.

Explanation

When it comes to repairs, you may deduct the cost of labor and supplies for the business part of your home. Your own labor, however, is not a deductible expense.

You can deduct part of the cost of painting the outside of your home or repairing the roof based on the percentage of your home used for business. However, you cannot deduct expenses for lawn care and landscaping.

Example

A repair to your furnace benefits the entire home. If 10% of the area of your home is used for business, 10% of the cost of the furnace repair is deductible.

Depreciation. You can deduct depreciation on the part of your home used for business subject to the *limit on the deduction* discussed above.

Home leased to employer. If you lease any part of your home to your employer, you cannot claim a home office deduction for that part for any period you use that part of your home to perform services for your employer. However, you may want to see Chapter 10, *Rental Income and Expenses,* as well as Publication 527, *Residential Rental Property*, for information on deducting rental expenses.

Income limitation. Deductions for the business use of your home may not create or add to a business loss. Therefore, if the total gross income for your business exceeds all of your business expenses (both direct business expenses and the expenses you have allocated for the use of a home office), you may deduct all of your expenses. However, if your business expenses exceed your gross business income, your deduction of certain expenses may be limited. You can carry any excess business expenses that are not currently deductible over to the next tax year, assuming that you have income from the business in the next tax year. If you do not have income from the business in the next tax year, the deductions may be carried to any later year in which you have gross income from the business.

Explanation
Your business deductions for the business use of your home are deducted in the following order:

1. The business percentage of the expenses that would otherwise be allowable as deductions, that is, mortgage interest, real estate taxes, and deductible casualty losses.
2. The direct expenses for your business in your home, such as expenses for supplies and compensation, but not the other expenses of the office in your home (such as those listed in item 3, below).
3. The other expenses for the business use of your home, such as maintenance, utilities, insurance, and depreciation. Deductions that adjust the basis in your home are taken last.

Example
Peggy Green is an employee who works in her home for the convenience of her employer. She uses 20% of her home regularly and exclusively for this business purpose. In 2001, her gross income, expenses for the business, and computation of the deduction for the business use of her home are as follows:

Gross income from business use of home		$7,500
Minus:		
Business percentage (20% of home use) of mortgage interest and real estate taxes	$2,000	
Other business expenses (supplies, transportation, etc.)	5,000	7,000
Modified net income		$ 500
Business use of home expenses		
Maintenance, insurance, utilities (20%)		$ 800
Depreciation (20%)		700
Total		$1,500
Deduction limited to modified net income		500
Carryover expenses to 2002 (subject to income limitation in 2002)		$1,000

The deduction of $500 is considered to be maintenance, insurance, and utilities. Peggy will not reduce the basis in her home for the $700 of depreciation until that amount is deducted in a future year.

TaxOrganizer

Records you should keep. If you intend to deduct home office expenses, it is extremely important that you keep adequate records. You should keep records of clients who come to your house, hours worked at home, type of work done at home, and office equipment purchases. Additionally, you should keep track of repairs that can be allocated to your home office. See the *Records You Should Keep* section at the front of this book for other items that you should keep.

For more information on using your home in your work and how to compute your allowable deduction, get Publication 587.

Job Search Expenses
You can deduct certain expenses you have in looking for a new job in your present occupation, even if you do not get a new job. You cannot deduct these expenses if:

1) You are looking for a job in a new occupation,
2) There was a substantial break between the ending of your last job and your looking for a new one, or
3) You are looking for a job for the first time.

Examples
- A certified public accountant employed by a national accounting firm was permitted to deduct expenses incurred in investigating whether or not he could practice his profession as a **self-employed** person.
- A corporate executive could deduct expenses involved in seeking a position as a corporate executive with another corporation.
- An attorney for a state agency could deduct the costs of taking an examination for a position as an attorney in another city because the new position would be in the same trade or business.
- An unemployed electrician was allowed to deduct transportation costs for going to the union hall to check on potential job opportunities. He was considered to be in the electrical trade, even though he was unemployed at the time.

Employment and outplacement agency fees. You can deduct employment and outplacement agency fees you pay in looking for a new job in your present occupation.

Employer pays you back. If, in a later year, your employer pays you back for employment agency fees, you must include the amount you receive in your gross income up to the amount of your tax benefit in the earlier year. (See *Recoveries* in chapter 13.)

Employer pays the employment agency. If your employer pays the fees directly to the employment agency and you are not responsible for them, you do not include them in your gross income.

Explanation
Job search expenses and fees are deductible, even if the agency does not find you a suitable job.

Expenses for career counseling are deductible if they are incurred in your effort to find other employment in the same trade or business.

Résumé. You can deduct amounts you spend for typing, printing, and mailing copies of a résumé to prospective employers if you are looking for a new job in your present occupation.

Travel and transportation expenses. If you travel to an area and, while there, you look for a new job in your present occupation, you may be able to deduct travel expenses to and from the area. You can deduct the travel expenses if the trip is primarily to look for a new job. The amount of time you spend on personal activity compared to the amount of time you spend in looking for work is important in determining whether the trip is primarily personal or is primarily to look for a new job.

Even if you cannot deduct the travel expenses to and from an area, you can deduct the expenses of looking for a new job in your present occupation while in the area.

You may choose to use the standard mileage rate to figure your car expenses. The standard mileage rate for 2001 is 34 1/2 cents per mile. See chapter 28 for more information.

TaxOrganizer

Records you should keep. In case the IRS challenges your deduction for job search expenses, you should keep the following information to support your claim for job search expense deductions:

- Evidence of your current occupation at the time the job search expenses were incurred
- Written records, such as a letter from a prospective employer or an employment agency contract, evidencing a search for employment and the nature of the job
- Receipts, canceled checks, credit card slips, plane tickets, and the like, evidencing the amount and payment of job search expenses
- Detailed records and evidence of costs, such as automobile mileage, for which a direct payment is not made
- A log allocating the time spent while traveling on personal activities compared to the time spent looking for a job

Licenses and Regulatory Fees

You can deduct the amount you pay each year to state or local governments for licenses and regulatory fees for your trade, business, or profession.

Occupational Taxes

You can deduct an occupational tax charged at a flat rate by a locality for the privilege of working or conducting a business in the locality. If you are an employee, you can claim occupational taxes only as a miscellaneous deduction subject to the 2% limit; you cannot claim them as a deduction for taxes elsewhere on your return.

Repayment of Income Aid Payment

An "income aid payment" is one that is received under an employer's plan to aid employees who lose their jobs because of lack of work. If you repay a lump-sum income aid payment that you received and included in income in an earlier year, you can deduct the repayment.

Research Expenses of a College Professor

If you are a college professor, you can deduct research expenses, including travel expenses, for teaching, lecturing, or writing and publishing on subjects that relate directly to the field of your teaching duties. You must have undertaken the research as a means of carrying out the duties expected of a professor and without expectation of profit apart from salary. However, you cannot deduct the cost of travel as a form of education.

Explanation

Travel as a form of education is never deductible. An example would be a French teacher who, in order to learn more about local customs in France, travels throughout the country. The travel in this case is not for research in writing or publishing and the person did not teach while traveling. Travel as a form of education tends to resemble travel for personal purposes, and the IRS will disallow a deduction for travel expenses as a form of educational expenses. See Chapter 29, *Tax Benefits for Work-Related Education,* for more information on educational expenses that are deductible.

Tools Used in Your Work

Generally, you can deduct amounts you spend for tools used in your work if the tools wear out and are thrown away within 1 year from the date of purchase. You can depreciate the cost of tools that have a useful life substantially beyond the tax year. For more information about depreciation, get Publication 946.

Union Dues and Expenses

You can deduct dues and initiation fees you pay for union membership.

You can also deduct assessments for benefit payments to unemployed union members. However, you cannot deduct the part of the assessments or contributions that provides funds for the payment of sick, accident, or death benefits. Also, you cannot deduct contributions to a pension fund, even if the union requires you to make the contributions.

You may not be able to deduct amounts you pay to the union that are related to certain lobbying and political activities. See *Lobbying Expenses* under *Nondeductible Expenses,* later.

Explanation

A fine paid by a union member is deductible if by not paying the fine the member would be dropped from the union.

If a union contract provides that all employees, regardless of whether or not they are union members, must pay union dues, the nonmembers may also deduct the union dues.

Work Clothes and Uniforms

You can deduct the cost and upkeep of work clothes if the following two requirements are met.

1) You must wear them as a condition of your employment.
2) The clothes are not suitable for everyday wear.

Caution. *It is not enough that you wear distinctive clothing. The clothing must be specifically required by your employer. Nor is it enough that you do not, in fact, wear your work clothes away from work. The clothing must not be suitable for taking the place of your regular clothing.*

Examples of workers who may be able to deduct the cost and upkeep of work clothes are: delivery workers, firefighters, health care workers, law enforcement officers, letter carriers, professional athletes, and transportation workers (air, rail, bus, etc.).

Musicians and entertainers can deduct the cost of theatrical clothing and accessories if they are not suitable for everyday wear.

However, work clothing consisting of white cap, white shirt or white jacket, white bib overalls, and standard work shoes, which a painter is required by his union to wear on the job, is not distinctive in character or in the nature of a uniform. Similarly, the costs of buying and maintaining blue work clothes worn by a welder at the request of a foreman are not deductible.

Protective clothing. You can deduct the cost of protective clothing required in your work, such as safety shoes or boots, safety glasses, hard hats, and work gloves.

Examples of workers who may be required to wear safety items are: carpenters, cement workers, chemical workers, electricians, fishing boat crew members, machinists, oil field workers, pipe fitters, steamfitters, and truck drivers.

Military uniforms. You generally cannot deduct the cost of your uniforms if you are on full-time active duty in the armed forces. However, if you are an armed forces reservist, you can deduct the unreimbursed cost of your uniform if military regulations restrict you from wearing it except while on duty as a reservist. In figuring the deduction, you must reduce the cost by any nontaxable allowance you receive for these expenses.

If local military rules do not allow you to wear fatigue uniforms when you are off duty, you can deduct the amount by which the cost of buying and keeping up these uniforms is more than the uniform allowance you receive.

You can deduct the cost of your uniforms if you are a civilian faculty or staff member of a military school.

Explanation

The initial expense and the costs of maintaining work clothes and business uniforms are deductible, not only if they must be worn as a condition of employment and they are not suitable for general or personal use but also if they are in fact not used for personal purposes. Taxpayers have been allowed to deduct costs relating to uniforms in the following cases:

- An art teacher deducted the costs of protective smocks.
- An airline clerk deducted the cost of "unfeminine, businesslike" shoes that she was required to wear and, in fact, wore only at work.
- A hospital worker deducted work clothes he kept in a locker at the hospital. He was in frequent contact with contagious persons and never brought the clothing home.
- A private-duty nurse deducted a uniform that served as a mark of her profession and was necessary for patient care.
- A member of the National Ski Patrol was allowed to deduct the cost of the parkas and ski trousers patrol members are required to wear.
- Scoutmasters, Red Cross volunteers, and others who wear uniforms while performing charitable activities may deduct the cost of the uniforms as charitable donations.

Tax Preparation Fees (Line 21)

You can usually deduct tax preparation fees in the year you pay them. Thus, on your 2001 return, you can deduct fees paid in 2001 for preparing your 2000 return. These fees include the cost of tax preparation software programs and tax publications. They also include any fee you paid for electronic filing of your return.

Deduct expenses of preparing tax schedules relating to profit or loss from business (Schedule C or C-EZ), rentals or royalties (Schedule E), or farm income and expenses (Schedule F) on the appropriate schedule. Deduct the expenses of preparing the remainder of the return on line 21, Schedule A (Form 1040).

Explanation

You may deduct expenses paid for the determination, collection, or refund of any tax—income tax, estate tax, gift tax, sales tax, or property tax. Fees paid to a consultant to advise you on the tax consequences of a transaction are deductible. If you contest a tax assessment, any fees you pay are deductible, even if the defense is unsuccessful. Professional fees incurred in obtaining federal tax rulings are deductible. However, the cost of filing a complaint in court relating to an IRS levy against property is considered a capital expenditure and therefore not currently deductible.

TAXPLANNER

Business related. Generally, most tax preparation fees are only deductible on Schedule A and are subject to the 2% adjusted gross income floor and the overall limitation on itemized deductions. However, according to the IRS, business owners can deduct the portion of tax preparation fees relating to a business directly on Schedule C, E, or F (and related business schedules).

TAXORGANIZER

In order to minimize controversy with the IRS over what portion of tax preparation fees applies to each activity, it's best to have your tax advisor give you a detailed breakdown of your bill, indicating the amounts attributable to each activity.

Example

Mark, an individual taxpayer, owns a consulting business and rental property. In 2001, he paid $900 in tax preparation fees, of which $400 was related to the consulting business, $300 to the rental property, and $200 to his individual return. Mark can deduct $400 as a business expense on Schedule C, $300 as a business expense on Schedule E, and $200 as a miscellaneous itemized deduction (subject to the 2%-adjusted-gross-income floor) on Schedule A.

Other Expenses (Line 22)

You can deduct certain other expenses as miscellaneous itemized deductions subject to the 2%-of-adjusted-gross-income limit. These are expenses you pay:

1) To produce or collect income that must be included in your gross income,
2) To manage, conserve, or maintain property held for producing such income, or
3) To determine, contest, pay, or claim a refund of any tax.

You can deduct expenses you pay for the purposes in (1) and (2) above only if they are reasonably and closely related to these purposes. Some of these other expenses are explained in the following discussions.

If the expenses you pay produce income that is only partially taxable, see *Tax-Exempt Income Expenses,* later, under *Nondeductible Expenses.*

Explanation

Deductions have also been allowed for the following:

- Monthly service charges paid to a bank to participate in an automatic investment service plan
- Service charges subtracted from cash dividends before the dividends are reinvested
- Premiums on indemnity bonds posted to secure replacement of lost taxable securities
- Trustee's commission for administering a revocable trust
- Expenses incurred by an official of the National Association of Investment Clubs in attending conventions
- Transportation and parking costs on trips to the taxpayer's stockbroker
- Packing, moving, and storage expenses of condominium furniture when the only tenant the taxpayer could find wanted the unit unfurnished
- Depreciation on a safe used to store securities and other financial certificates
- Expenses incurred in moving the office in which a taxpayer carries on his or her investment activities to a new location
- Postage related to investment activities
- A fee paid to a broker engaged to find another company that could be merged with the taxpayer's closely held company, even though no company was found
- Safe-deposit box rental when the box was used to store Series EE treasury bonds, even though no income is reportable in the tax year because the taxpayer elected to report the appreciation when the bonds matured (see Chapter 8, *Interest Income,* for details)
- Entertainment expenses in connection with taxable investments

- Investor's payment to a stockholders' committee that sought changes in corporate management
- Travel expenses to a director's meeting of a director who was also a substantial minority shareholder (The taxpayer feared that the policies of the majority would endanger his investment. Because the expense was incurred to protect his investment, it was deductible.)
- Costs incurred in a proxy fight opposing management

You may deduct a reward paid for the return of business property you have lost.

Example

A man left his briefcase on the train. A deduction was allowed for the reward given and for the cost of the ad offering the reward.

Appraisal Fees

You can deduct appraisal fees if you pay them to figure a casualty loss or the fair market value of donated property.

Certain Casualty and Theft Losses

You can deduct a casualty or theft loss as a miscellaneous itemized deduction subject to the 2% limit if you used the damaged or stolen property in performing services as an employee. First report the loss in Section B of Form 4684, *Casualties and Thefts.* You may also have to include the loss on Form 4797, *Sales of Business Property,* if you are otherwise required to file that form. Your deduction is the amount of the loss included on lines 32 and 38b of Form 4684 and line 18b of Form 4797. For other casualty and theft losses, see chapter 27.

Clerical Help and Office Rent

You can deduct office expenses, such as rent and clerical help, that you have in connection with your investments and collecting the taxable income on them.

Depreciation on Home Computer

You can deduct depreciation on your home computer if you use it to produce income (for example, to manage your investments that produce taxable income). You generally must depreciate the computer using the straight line method over the Alternative Depreciation System (ADS) recovery period. But if you work as an employee and also use the computer in that work, see Publication 946.

Excess Deductions of an Estate

If an estate's total deductions in its last tax year are more than its gross income for that year, the beneficiaries succeeding to the estate's property can deduct the excess. Do not include deductions for personal exemptions and charitable contributions when figuring the estate's total deductions. The beneficiaries can claim the deduction only for the tax year in which, or with which, the estate terminates, whether the year of termination is a normal year or a short tax year. For more information, see *Termination of Estate* in Publication 559, *Survivors, Executors, and Administrators.*

Fees to Collect Interest and Dividends

You can deduct fees you pay to a broker, bank, trustee, or similar agent to collect your taxable bond interest or dividends on shares of stock. But you cannot deduct a fee you pay to a broker to buy investment property, such as stocks or bonds. You must add the fee to the cost of the property.

You cannot deduct the fee you pay to a broker to sell securities. You can use the fee only to figure gain or loss from the sale. See the instructions for columns (d) and (e) of Schedule D (Form 1040) for information on how to report the fee.

Hobby Expenses

You can generally deduct hobby expenses, but only up to the amount of hobby income. A hobby is not a business because it is not carried on to make a profit. See *Activity not for profit* in chapter 13 under *Other Income.*

Indirect Deductions of Pass-Through Entities

Pass-through entities include partnerships, S corporations, and mutual funds that are not publicly offered. Deductions of pass-through entities are passed through to the partners or shareholders. The partners or shareholders can deduct their share of passed-through deductions for investment expenses as miscellaneous itemized deductions subject to the 2% limit.

Example. You are a member of an investment club that is formed solely to invest in securities. The club is treated as a partnership. The partnership's income is solely from taxable dividends, interest, and gains from sales of securities. In this case, you can deduct your share of the partnership's operating expenses as miscellaneous itemized deductions subject to the 2% limit. However, if the investment club partnership has investments that also produce nontaxable income, you cannot deduct your share of the partnership's expenses that produce the nontaxable income.

Publicly offered mutual funds. Publicly offered mutual funds do not pass deductions for investment expenses through to shareholders. A mutual fund is "publicly offered" if it is:

1) Continuously offered pursuant to a public offering,
2) Regularly traded on an established securities market, or
3) Held by or for at least 500 persons at all times during the tax year.

A publicly offered mutual fund will send you a Form 1099-DIV, or a substitute form, showing the net amount of dividend income (gross dividends minus investment expenses). This net figure is the amount you report on your return as income. You cannot deduct investment expenses.

Information returns. You should receive information returns from pass-through entities.

Partnerships and S corporations. These entities issue Schedule K-1, which lists the items and amounts you must report and identifies the tax return schedules and lines to use.

Nonpublicly offered mutual funds. These funds will send you a Form 1099-DIV, *Dividends and Distributions,* or a substitute form, showing your share of gross income and investment expenses. You can claim the expenses only as a miscellaneous itemized deduction subject to the 2% limit.

Investment Fees and Expenses

You can deduct investment fees, custodial fees, trust administration fees, and other expenses you paid for managing your investments that produce taxable income.

Legal Expenses

You can usually deduct legal expenses that you incur in attempting to produce or collect taxable income or that you pay in connection with the determination, collection, or refund of any tax.

TAXPLANNER

Professional fees. Legal, accounting, and professional fees often have deductible and nondeductible elements. Whether professional fees should be deducted, capitalized, or considered personal expenses depends on the reasons the fees were incurred. To be deductible as a miscellaneous expense on Schedule A, the expense must either be connected to producing income (advising you on your employment, collecting alimony, and the like) or be incurred for a tax-related matter.

TAXORGANIZER

Records you should keep. To minimize controversy with the IRS over what portion of a professional fee is deductible, it's best to have the professional give you a detailed breakdown of your bill, indicating which portions are tax-deductible.

You can also deduct legal expenses that are:

1) Related to either doing or keeping your job, such as those you paid to defend yourself against criminal charges arising out of your trade or business,
2) For tax advice related to a divorce if the bill specifies how much is for tax advice and it is determined in a reasonable way, or
3) To collect taxable alimony.

You can deduct expenses of resolving tax issues relating to profit or loss from business (Schedule C or C-EZ), rentals or royalties (Schedule E), or farm income and expenses (Schedule F) on the appropriate schedule. You deduct expenses of resolving nonbusiness tax issues on Schedule A (Form 1040).

Loss on Deposits
For information on whether, and if so, how, you may deduct a loss on your deposit in a qualified financial institution, see *Deposit in Insolvent or Bankrupt Financial Institution* in chapter 15.

Repayments of Income
If you had to repay an amount that you included in income in an earlier year, you may be able to deduct the amount you repaid. If the amount you had to repay was ordinary income of $3,000 or less, the deduction is subject to the 2% limit. If it was more than $3,000, see *Repayments Under Claim of Right* under *Deductions Not Subject to the 2% Limit,* later.

Repayments of Social Security Benefits
For information on how to deduct your repayments of certain social security benefits, see *Repayments More Than Gross Benefits* in chapter 12.

Safe Deposit Box Rent
You can deduct safe deposit box rent if you use the box to store taxable income-producing stocks, bonds, or investment-related papers and documents. You cannot deduct the rent if you use the box only for jewelry, other personal items, or tax-exempt securities.

Service Charges on Dividend Reinvestment Plans
You can deduct service charges you pay as a subscriber in a dividend reinvestment plan. These service charges include payments for:

1) Holding shares acquired through a plan,
2) Collecting and reinvesting cash dividends, and
3) Keeping individual records and providing detailed statements of accounts.

Trustee's Administrative Fees for IRA
Trustee's administrative fees that are billed separately and paid by you in connection with your individual retirement arrangement (IRA) are deductible (if they are ordinary and necessary) as a miscellaneous itemized deduction subject to the 2% limit. For more information about IRAs, see chapter 18.

TAXSAVER

Administrative fees paid to IRA trustees are deductible if the fees are billed to, and paid by, the account owner separate

from any IRA contribution. If the trustee takes the fee out of your $2,000 contribution, your total deduction is less than what it could be (only $2,000 instead of $2,000 plus the trustee's fee); also, you then have less money remaining in the IRA account for investment. Because the income in the IRA account accumulates tax free, the difference in these two amounts—the full $2,000 and the remainder of that sum after fees—compounded annually, becomes significant over the years.

Deductions Not Subject to the 2% Limit

You can deduct the items listed below as miscellaneous itemized deductions. They are not subject to the 2% limit. Report these items on line 27, Schedule A (Form 1040).

List of Deductions

Each of the following items are discussed in detail after the list.

- Amortizable premium on taxable bonds.
- Casualty and theft losses from income-producing property.
- Federal estate tax on income in respect of a decedent.
- Gambling losses up to the amount of gambling winnings.
- Impairment-related work expenses of persons with disabilities.
- Repayments of more than $3,000 under a claim of right.
- Unrecovered investment in an annuity.
- Expenses of officials paid on a fee basis.

Amortizable Premium on Taxable Bonds
In general, if the amount you pay for a bond is greater than its stated principal amount, the excess is bond premium. You can elect to amortize the premium on taxable bonds. The amortization of the premium is generally an offset to interest income on the bond rather than a separate deduction item.

Part of the premium on some bonds may be a miscellaneous deduction not subject to the 2% limit. For more information, see *Amortizable Premium on Taxable Bonds* in Publication 529 and *Bond Premium Amortization* in chapter 3 of Publication 550, *Investment Income and Expenses.*

TAXORGANIZER

You should keep documentation that shows the date of purchase, face value, and the purchase price of the bond. The types of documents you may want to keep include your broker's confirmation or monthly account statement.

Certain Casualty and Theft Losses
You can deduct a casualty or theft loss as a miscellaneous itemized deduction not subject to the 2% limit if the damaged or stolen property was income-producing property (property held for investment, such as stocks, notes, bonds, gold, silver, vacant lots, and works of art). First report the loss in Section B of Form 4684. You may also have to include the loss on Form 4797 if you are otherwise required to file that form. Your deduction is the amount of the loss included on lines 32 and 38b of Form 4684 and line 18b of Form 4797. For more information on casualty and theft losses, see chapter 27.

Federal Estate Tax on Income in Respect of a Decedent
You can deduct the federal estate tax attributable to income in respect of a decedent that you as a beneficiary include in your gross income. Income in respect of the decedent is gross income that the decedent would

have received had death not occurred and that was not properly includible in the decedent's final income tax return. See Publication 559 for more information.

Gambling Losses Up to the Amount of Gambling Winnings

You must report the full amount of your gambling winnings for the year on line 21, Form 1040. You deduct your gambling losses for the year on line 27, Schedule A (Form 1040). You cannot deduct gambling losses that are more than your winnings.

Caution. *You cannot reduce your gambling winnings by your gambling losses and report the difference. You must report the full amount of your winnings as income and claim your losses up to the amount of winnings as an itemized deduction. Therefore, your records should show your winnings separately from your losses.*

Diary of winnings and losses. You must keep an accurate diary or similar record of your losses and winnings.

Your diary should contain at least the following information.

1) The date and type of your specific wager or wagering activity.
2) The name and address or location of the gambling establishment.
3) The names of other persons present with you at the gambling establishment.
4) The amount(s) you won or lost.

See Publication 529 for more information.

Explanation
For specific wagering transactions, you can use the following items to support your winnings and losses:

Keno: Copies of the keno tickets you purchased that were validated by the gambling establishment, copies of your casino credit records, and copies of your casino check-cashing records.

Slot machines: A record of the machine number and all winnings by date and time the machine was played.

Table games [twenty-one (blackjack), craps, poker, baccarat, roulette, wheel of fortune, etc.]: The number of the table at which you were playing and casino credit card data indicating whether the credit was issued in the pit or at the cashier's cage.

Bingo: A record of the number of games played, cost of tickets purchased, and amounts collected on winning tickets. Supplemental records include any receipts from the casino, parlor, and the like.

Racing (horse, harness, dog, etc.): A record of the races, amounts of wagers, amounts collected on winning tickets, and amounts lost on losing tickets. Supplemental records include unredeemed tickets and payment records from the racetrack.

Lotteries: A record of ticket purchases, dates, winnings, and losses. Supplemental records include unredeemed tickest, payment slips, and winnings statements.

TaxAlert

The cost of transportation, meals, and lodging related to gambling is not deductible for tax purposes.

Impairment-Related Work Expenses

If you have a physical or mental disability that limits your being employed, or substantially limits one or more of your major life activities, such as performing manual tasks, walking, speaking, breathing, learning, and working, you can deduct your impairment-related work expenses.

Impairment-related work expenses are ordinary and necessary business expenses for attendant care services at your place of work and other expenses in connection with your place of work that are necessary for you to be able to work.

Where to report. If you are an employee, you enter impairment-related work expenses on Form 2106 or Form 2106-EZ. Enter on line 27, Schedule A (Form 1040) that part of the amount on line 10 of Form 2106, or line 6 of Form 2106-EZ, that is related to your impairment. Enter the amount that is unrelated to your impairment on line 20, Schedule A (Form 1040).

Repayments Under Claim of Right

If you had to repay more than $3,000 that you included in your income in an earlier year because at the time you thought you had an unrestricted right to it, you may be able to deduct the amount you repaid or take a credit against your tax. See *Repayments* in chapter 13 for more information.

Unrecovered Investment in Annuity

A retiree who contributed to the cost of an annuity can exclude from income a part of each payment received as a tax-free return of the retiree's investment. If the retiree dies before the entire investment is recovered tax free, any unrecovered investment can be deducted on the retiree's final income tax return. See chapter 11 for more information about the tax treatment of pensions and annuities.

TaxSaver

Performing Artist
If you are a performing artist, you may qualify to deduct your employee business expenses as an adjustment to income rather than as a miscellaneous itemized deduction. To qualify to deduct your expenses as an adjustment income, you must meet all three of the following requirements:

1. You perform services in the performing arts for at least two employers during your tax year.
2. Your related performing-arts business expenses are more than 10% of your gross income from the performance of such services.
3. Your adjusted gross income is not more than $16,000 before deducting these business expenses.

Explanation
You are not considered to have performed services in the performing arts for an employer unless that employer paid you $200 or more.

If you do not meet all of the above requirements, you do not qualify to deduct your expenses as an adjustment to gross income and the expenses are subject to the 2% limit.

Special rules for married persons. If you are married, you must file a joint return unless you lived apart from your spouse at all times during the tax year.

If you file a joint return, you must figure requirements (1) and (2) separately for both you and your spouse. However, requirement (3) applies to your and your spouse's combined adjusted gross income.

Where to report. If you meet all of the above requirements, you should first complete Form 2106 or Form 2106-EZ. Then you include your performing arts–related expenses from line 10 of Form 2106 or from line 6 of 2106-EZ on line 32 of Form 1040. Then print "QPA" and the amount of your performing arts–related expenses on the dotted line next to line 32 (Form 1040).

Officials Paid on a Fee Basis

If you are a fee-basis official, you can claim your expenses in performing services in that job as an adjustment to income rather than as a miscellaneous itemized deduction. To qualify as a fee-basis official, you must be employed by a state or local government and be paid in whole or in part on a fee basis.

Where to report. If you qualify as a fee-basis official, you should first complete Form 2106 or Form 2106-EZ. Then include your expenses in performing services in that job (line 10 of Form 2106 or line 6 of Form 2106-EZ) on line 32 of Form 1040. Then write "FBO" and the amount of those expenses on the dotted line next to line 32 of Form 1040.

Nondeductible Expenses

Examples of nondeductible expenses are listed next. The list is followed by discussions of additional nondeductible expenses that are more common.

List of Nondeductible Expenses

- Adoption expenses.
- Broker's commissions that you paid in connection with your IRA or other investment property.
- Burial or funeral expenses, including the cost of a cemetery lot.
- Capital expenses.
- Fees and licenses, such as car licenses, marriage licenses, and dog tags.
- Hobby losses—But see *Hobby Expenses,* earlier.
- Home repairs, insurance, and rent.
- Illegal bribes and kickbacks—See *Bribes and kickbacks* in chapter 13 of Publication 535.
- Losses from the sale of your home, furniture, personal car, etc.
- Personal disability insurance premiums.
- Personal, living, or family expenses.
- The value of wages never received or lost vacation time.

Exception
While funeral and burial expenses may not be deducted on your personal income tax return, they may be deducted on your federal estate tax return.

Campaign Expenses

You cannot deduct campaign expenses of a candidate for any office, even if the candidate is running for reelection to the office. These include qualification and registration fees for primary elections.

Legal fees. You cannot deduct legal fees paid to defend charges that arise from participation in a political campaign.

Check-Writing Fees on Personal Account

If you have a personal checking account, you cannot deduct fees charged by the bank for the privilege of writing checks, even if the account pays interest.

Club Dues

Generally, you cannot deduct the cost of membership in any club organized for business, pleasure, recreation, or other social purpose. This includes business, social, athletic, luncheon, sporting, airline, and hotel clubs. For exceptions, see *Dues to Chambers of Commerce and Professional Societies* under *Unreimbursed Employee Expenses,* earlier.

Explanation
No deduction is allowed for club dues if the club is organized for business, pleasure, recreation, or social purposes. These clubs include any organization whose principal purpose is the entertainment of its members or guests. The character of an organization is determined by its purposes and activities, not by its name. For example, no deduction is allowed for dues paid to country clubs, airline clubs, and hotel clubs.

The IRS has specified, however, that some club dues will continue to be deductible under the regular business-use rules. For example, dues paid to trade associations, bar and medical associations, and civic organizations—such as Rotary clubs or Kiwanis clubs—will continue to be deductible as long as the principal purpose of these organizations is not to conduct entertainment activities for their members.

TaxSaver
Meals and entertainment. Specific business expenses, such as meals and entertainment that occur at a club, are deductible to the extent that they otherwise satisfy the standard for deductibility. For details, see Chapter 28, *Car Expenses and Other Employee Business Expenses.*

Commuting Expenses

You cannot deduct commuting expenses (the cost of transportation between your home and your main or regular place of work). If you haul tools, instruments, or other items, in your car to and from work, you can deduct only the additional cost of hauling the items such as the rent on a trailer to carry the items.

Explanation
Commuting to a temporary work site can be a deductible expense. A work assignment is temporary if the individual has the expectation that it will last less than 1 year, and it actually does last for 1 year or less. If you have a regular place of business away from home, then travel expenses from home to a temporary work site are deductible, regardless of the distance.

An individual who has no regular place of business outside the home (or a home office), but who works at several locations within a metropolitan area, can deduct travel expenses to a temporary work site that is outside the metropolitan area. However, many people now commute as many as 2 hours or more one way. Therefore, the IRS interpretation of a "metropolitan area" is also expanding.

Another increasingly common scenario is an individual who loses his full-time job due to downsizing or outsourcing and subsequently works for several different employers on a part-time basis. This individual has no regular place of business. It is not clear whether his travel to a temporary work site outside the metropolitan area is deductible. A strict interpretation of the rules would indicate that such travel is deductible, because a regular business location is not a consideration. However, the IRS may argue that he has merely extended his personal commute, because he is working for a different employer in each location.

TaxSaver
If you drive to a location close to home to perform a bona fide job function and then drive to your regular work location, the second leg of the trip is deductible. See Chapter 28, *Car Expenses and Other Employee Business Expenses,* for details.

Example

An accountant drives to the local IRS office to represent clients and then goes to his office downtown later that day. The second leg of his travel is deductible.

TaxOrganizer

Records you should keep:

- Purchase price of car
- Monthly lease payments on car
- Gas receipts
- Toll receipts
- Receipts for repairs and maintenance

You should keep a written record of these expenses and the dates they were incurred to verify deductibility.

Fines or Penalties

You cannot deduct fines or penalties you pay to a governmental unit for violating a law. This includes an amount paid in settlement of your actual or potential liability for a fine or penalty (civil or criminal). Fines or penalties include parking tickets, tax penalties, and penalties deducted from teachers' paychecks after an illegal strike.

Explanation

Although state taxes are deductible when itemizing your deductions, the penalties and interest related to the underpayment of taxes or the late payment of taxes is not deductible.

Health Spa Expenses

You cannot deduct health spa expenses, even if there is a job requirement to stay in excellent physical condition, such as might be required of a law enforcement officer.

Home Security System

You cannot deduct the cost of a home security system as a miscellaneous deduction. However, you may be able to claim a deduction for a home security system as a business expense if you have a home office. See *Home Office* under *Unreimbursed Employee Expenses,* earlier, and *Security System* under *Deducting Expenses* in Publication 587.

Homeowners' Insurance Premiums

You cannot deduct premiums that you pay or that are placed in escrow for insurance on your home, such as fire and liability or mortgage insurance.

Investment-Related Seminars

You cannot deduct any expenses for attending a convention, seminar, or similar meeting for investment purposes.

Life Insurance Premiums

You cannot deduct premiums you pay on your life insurance. You may be able to deduct, as alimony, premiums you pay on life insurance policies assigned to your former spouse. See chapter 20 for information on alimony.

Lobbying Expenses

You generally cannot deduct amounts paid or incurred for lobbying expenses. These include expenses to:

1) Influence legislation,
2) Participate or intervene in any political campaign for, or against, any candidate for public office,
3) Attempt to influence the general public, or segments of the public, about elections, legislative matters, or referendums, or
4) Communicate directly with covered executive branch officials in any attempt to influence the official actions or positions of those officials.

Lobbying expenses also include any amounts paid or incurred for research, preparation, planning, or coordination of any of these activities.

Dues used for lobbying. If a tax-exempt organization notifies you that part of the dues or other amounts you pay to the organization are used to pay nondeductible lobbying expenses, you cannot deduct that part. See *Lobbying Expenses* in Publication 529 for information on exceptions.

Lost or Mislaid Cash or Property

You cannot deduct a loss based on the mere disappearance of money or property. However, an accidental loss or disappearance of property can qualify as a casualty if it results from an identifiable event that is sudden, unexpected, or unusual. See chapter 27.

Example. A car door is accidentally slammed on your hand, breaking the setting of your diamond ring. The diamond falls from the ring and is never found. The loss of the diamond is a casualty.

Lunches With Co-Workers

You cannot deduct the expenses of lunches with co-workers, except while traveling away from home on business. See chapter 28 for information on deductible expenses while traveling away from home.

Meals While Working Late

You cannot deduct the cost of meals while working late. However, you may be able to claim a deduction if the cost of meals is a deductible entertainment expense, or if you are traveling away from home. See chapter 28 for information on deductible entertainment expenses and expenses while traveling away from home.

Personal Legal Expenses

You cannot deduct personal legal expenses such as those for the following.

1) Custody of children.
2) Breach of promise (to marry) suit.
3) Civil or criminal charges resulting from a personal relationship.
4) Damages for personal injury.
5) Preparation of a title (or defense or perfection of a title).
6) Preparation of a will.
7) Property claims or property settlement in a divorce.

You cannot deduct these expenses even if a result of the legal proceeding is the loss of income-producing property.

Political Contributions

You cannot deduct contributions made to a political candidate, a campaign committee, or a newsletter fund. Advertisements in convention bulletins and admissions to dinners or programs that benefit a political party or political candidate are not deductible.

Professional Accreditation Fees

You cannot deduct professional accreditation fees such as the following.

1) Accounting certificate fees paid for the initial right to practice accounting.
2) Bar exam fees and incidental expenses in securing admission to the bar.
3) Medical and dental license fees paid to get initial licensing.

Professional Reputation

You cannot deduct expenses of radio and TV appearances to increase your personal prestige or establish your professional reputation.

Relief Fund Contributions

You cannot deduct contributions paid to a private plan that pays benefits to any covered employee who cannot work because of any injury or illness not related to the job.

Residential Telephone Service

You cannot deduct any charge (including taxes) for basic local telephone service for the first telephone line to your residence, even if it is used in a trade or business.

Stockholders' Meetings

You cannot deduct transportation and other expenses you pay to attend stockholders' meetings of companies in which you own stock but have no other interest. You cannot deduct these expenses even if you are attending the meeting to get information that would be useful in making further investments.

Explanation

The courts have allowed deductions for stockholders' meetings when the shareholders' interests are more extensive. Consider the following:

- A shareholder who went to a meeting to present a resolution that management stop diluting shareholder equity was entitled to deduct his travel expenses. (See Chapter 28, *Car Expenses and Other Employee Business Expenses*.)
- A court held that an investor's travel expenses to an investment convention were deductible because (1) the trip was part of a rationally planned, systematic investigation of business operations; (2) the costs were reasonable in relation to the size of the investment and the value of the information expected; (3) there was no disguised personal motive for the trip; and (4) there was evidence of practical application of the information obtained on the trip.

Nevertheless, if a person owns only a very small interest in a large corporation and cannot reasonably expect that his or her attendance at a stockholders' meeting would affect his or her income or investment, the deduction of travel expenses probably would not be allowed.

Tax-Exempt Income Expenses

You cannot deduct expenses to produce tax-exempt income. You cannot deduct interest on a debt incurred or continued to buy or carry tax-exempt securities.

If you have expenses to produce both taxable and tax-exempt income, but you cannot identify the expenses that produce each type of income, you must divide the expenses based on the amount of each type of income to determine the amount that you can deduct.

Example. During the year, you received taxable interest of $4,800 and tax-exempt interest of $1,200. In earning this income, you had total expenses of $500 during the year. You cannot identify the amount of each expense item that is for each income item. Therefore, 80% ($4,800/$6,000) of the expense is for the taxable interest and 20% ($1,200/$6,000) is for the tax-exempt interest. You can deduct, subject to the 2% limit, expenses of $400 (80% of $500).

Travel Expenses for Another Individual

You generally cannot deduct travel expenses you pay or incur for a spouse, dependent, or other individual who accompanies you (or your employee) on business travel. See chapter 28 for more information on deductible travel expenses.

Voluntary Unemployment Benefit Fund Contributions

You cannot deduct voluntary unemployment benefit fund contributions you make to a union fund or a private fund. However, you can deduct contributions as taxes if state law requires you to make them to a state unemployment fund that covers you for the loss of wages from unemployment caused by business conditions.

Wristwatches

You cannot deduct the cost of a wristwatch, even if there is a job requirement that you know the correct time to properly perform your duties.

Explanation

The courts have found the following to be nondeductible expenses:

- Amounts paid to guard a personal residence against burglary attempts
- The cost of a home security system installed to protect a collector's stamps and coins (The IRS reasoned that the activity was an investment activity and not a regular trade or business; consequently, the expense did not meet the home office rules, discussed earlier in this chapter.)
- Payments for general advice pertaining to a family trust
- Legal fees for defending a libel suit arising out of the purchase of the taxpayer's personal residence

TaxAlert

The cost of specific legal advice on the disposition of a stock is not deductible as a miscellaneous expense on Schedule A but must be treated as a selling expense and used to increase your basis in the stock.

TaxOrganizer

Records you should keep.

- Legal fees itemizing services performed
- Tax preparation fees that allocate amount between Schedules A, C, and E
- Financial account statements that indicate investment fees
- Logs substantiating the use of property (i.e., a cellular telephone, a home computer, an automobile) for both business and personal purposes
- Home office expenses and the calculation to allocate total expenses between business and personal use
- Evidence of job search expenses

PART IV

Figuring Your Taxes and Credits

The seven chapters in this part explain how to figure your tax and how to figure the tax of certain children who have more than $1,500 of investment income. They also discuss tax credits. Credits, unlike deductions, are subtracted directly from your tax and therefore reduce your tax dollar for dollar. There are tax credits for the elderly or for the permanently and totally disabled, for the expense of having your child or disabled dependent cared for so that you can work, for the purchase of a qualified electric vehicle, and for other kinds of expenses. Chapters 35 and 36, *Child Tax Credit* and *Education Credits*, discuss the child tax credit and education credits, respectively. Chapter 37, *Other Credits Including the Earned Income Credit*, discusses the earned income credit and how you might be able to get the credit paid to you in advance (from your employer) throughout the year rather than wait until you file your tax return. See *Changes in the Tax Law You Should Know About* at the beginning of this book for new rules about tax credits starting in 2001.

31

How to Figure Your Tax

Introduction

This chapter explains how to calculate your tax liability under all three available tax forms—Form 1040EZ, Form 1040A, and Form 1040. It also will help you decide which of the forms to file.

In particular, you should review the section of this chapter on the alternative minimum tax to determine if that tax may apply to you.

After you have figured your income and deductions as explained in *Parts One through Five,* your next step is to figure your tax. This chapter discusses:

- The general steps you take to figure your tax,
- An additional tax you may have to pay called the alternative minimum tax, and
- The conditions you must meet if you want the IRS to figure your tax.

Figuring Your Tax

TaxAlert: The 2001 Tax Act

A gradual reduction in the individual income tax rates starts in 2001, thanks to the 2001 Tax Act passed by Congress. In addition, a new tax rate bracket of 10% was created.

A rate reduction credit will apply in lieu of the 10% tax rate for 2001. Advanced refund checks equal to 5% of the amount of income eligible for the 10% rate were mailed to eligible taxpayers in the second half of 2001. If you did not receive a check this year, the credit for the first 5% along with the remaining 5% will be available on your 2001 return.

Your income tax is based on your taxable income. After you figure your income tax, subtract your tax credits and add any other taxes you may owe. The result is your total tax. Compare your total tax with your total payments to determine whether you are entitled to a refund or owe additional tax.

This section provides a general outline of how to figure your tax. You can find step-by-step directions in the instructions for Forms 1040EZ, 1040A, and 1040. If you are unsure of which tax form you should file, see *Which Form Should I Use?* in chapter 1.

Tax. Most taxpayers use either the Tax Table or the Tax Rate Schedules to figure their income tax. However, there are special methods if your income includes any of the following items.

- Capital gains (see chapter 17).
- Lump-sum distributions (see chapter 11).
- Farm income (see Schedule J (Form 1040), *Farm Income Averaging*).
- Investment income over $1,500 for children under age 14 (see chapter 32).

Credits. After you figure your income tax, determine your tax credits. This chapter does not explain whether you are eligible for these credits. You can find that information in chapters 33 through 37 and your form instructions. See the following table for credits you may be able to subtract from your income tax.

CREDITS

For information on:	See chapter:
Adoption	37
Child and dependent care	33
Child tax credit	35
Education	36
Elderly or disabled	34
Foreign tax	37
Mortgage interest	37
Prior year minimum tax	37
Qualified electric vehicle	37
Rate reduction	37

Some credits (such as the earned income credit) are not listed above because they are treated as payments. See *Payments,* later.

There are other credits that are not discussed in this publication. These include the following items.

- General business credit, which is made up of several separate business-related credits. These generally are reported on Form 3800, *General Business Credit,* and are discussed in chapter 4 of Publication 334, *Tax Guide for Small Business.*
- Empowerment zone employment credit, which is for certain employers whose employees work and live in an empowerment zone. See Publication 954, *Tax Incentives for Empowerment Zones and Other Distressed Communities,* and the instructions for Form 8844, *Empowerment Zone Employment Credit.*
- District of Columbia first-time homebuyer credit, which is for certain persons who buy a main home in the District. See the instructions for Form 8859, *District of Columbia First-Time Homebuyer Credit.*
- Credit for fuel from a nonconventional source, which is for the person who sold the fuel. See the instructions for line 51 of Form 1040 and section 29 of the Internal Revenue Code.

Other taxes. After you subtract your tax credits, determine whether there are any other taxes you must pay. This chapter does not explain these other taxes. You can find that information in other chapters of this publication and your form instructions. See the following table for other taxes you may need to add to your income tax.

OTHER TAXES

For information on:	See chapter:
Tax on qualified retirement plans and IRAs	11, 18
Advance earned income credit payments	37
Household employment taxes	33
Social security and Medicare tax on unreported tips	7
Uncollected social security and Medicare tax on tips	7

Another tax you may have to pay, the alternative minimum tax, is discussed later in this chapter.

There are other taxes that are not discussed in this publication. These include the following items.

1) *Self-employment tax.* You must figure this tax if either of the following applies to you (or your spouse if you file a joint return).
   a) You were self-employed and your net earnings from self-employment were $400 or more. The term "net earnings from self-employment" may include certain nonemployee compensation and other amounts reported to you on Form 1099-MISC, *Miscellaneous Income.* If you received a Form 1099-MISC, see the *Instructions to Recipients* on the back. Also see the instructions for Schedule SE (Form 1040), *Self-Employment Tax,* and Publication 533, *Self-Employment Tax.*
   b) You had church employee income of $108.28 or more.
2) *Recapture taxes.* You may have to pay these taxes if you previously claimed an education credit, an investment credit, a low-income housing credit, a mortgage interest credit, a qualified electric vehicle credit, or an Indian employment credit. For more information about recapture of an education credit, see chapter 36. For more information about other recapture taxes, see the instructions for line 58 of Form 1040.
3) *Section 72(m)(5) excess benefits tax.* If you are (or were) a 5% owner of a business and you received a distribution that exceeds the benefits provided for you under the qualified pension or annuity plan formula, you may have to pay this additional tax. See *Tax on Excess Benefits* in Publication 560, *Retirement Plans for Small Business (SEP, SIMPLE, and Qualified Plans).*
4) *Uncollected social security and Medicare tax on group-term life insurance.* If your former employer provides you with more than $50,000 of group-term life insurance coverage, you must pay the employee part of social security and Medicare taxes on those premiums.

The amount should be shown in box 12 of your Form W-2 with codes M and N.

5) *Tax on golden parachute payments.* This tax applies if you, as a key employee, received an "excess parachute payment" (EPP) due to a change in a corporation's ownership or control. See the instructions for line 58 of Form 1040.
6) *Tax on accumulation distribution of trusts.* This applies if you are the beneficiary of a trust that accumulated its income instead of distributing it currently. See the instructions for Form 4970, *Tax on Accumulation Distribution of Trusts.*
7) *Additional tax on MSAs.* If amounts contributed to, or distributed from, your medical savings account do not meet the rules for these accounts, you may have to pay additional taxes. See Publication 969, *Medical Savings Accounts (MSAs),* and Forms 8853, *Archer MSAs and Long-Term Care Insurance Contracts,* and 5329, *Additional Taxes on Qualified Plans (Including IRAs) and Other Tax-Favored Accounts.*

Payments. After you determine your total tax, figure the total payments you have already made for the year. Include credits that are treated as payments. This chapter does not explain these payments and credits. You can find that information in other chapters of this publication and your form instructions. See the following table for amounts you can include in your total payments.

PAYMENTS

For information on:	See chapter:
Child tax credit (additional)	35
Earned income credit	37
Estimated tax paid	5
Excess social security and RRTA tax withheld	37
Federal income tax withheld	5
Regulated investment company credit	37
Tax paid with extension	1

Another credit that is treated as a payment is the credit for federal excise tax paid on fuels. This credit is for persons who have a nontaxable use of certain fuels, such as diesel fuel and kerosene. It is claimed on line 65 of Form 1040. See Publication 378, *Fuel Tax Credits and Refunds,* and Form 4136, *Credit for Federal Tax Paid on Fuels.*

Refund or balance due. To determine whether you are entitled to a refund or owe additional tax, compare your total payments with your total tax. If you are entitled to a refund, see your form instructions for information on having it directly deposited into your financial account instead of receiving a paper check.

Explanation
For information on how to elect to pay your 2001 tax in installments, see Chapter 1, *Filing Information,* under the section entitled *Amount You Owe.*

Alternative Minimum Tax

This section briefly discusses an additional tax you may have to pay.

The tax law gives special treatment to some kinds of income and allows special deductions and credits for some kinds of expenses. Taxpayers who benefit from the law in these ways may have to pay at least a minimum amount of tax through an additional tax. This additional tax is called the alternative minimum tax (AMT).

You may have to pay the alternative minimum tax if your taxable income for regular tax purposes, combined with certain adjustments and tax preference items, is more than:

- $49,000 if your filing status is married filing a joint return (or a qualifying widow(er) with dependent child),
- $35,750 if your filing status is single or head of household, or
- $24,500 if your filing status is married filing a separate return.

Explanation

Individuals, trusts, and estates must pay the alternative minimum tax (AMT) if it exceeds their regular tax liability for the year. The amount subject to the AMT will be determined by adding a number of preference items to your taxable income and making various adjustments to your regular taxable income. This amount is reduced by the exemption amounts, and the balance is subject to the following AMT rates:

Rate	Married filing separately	All other filers
26%	Up to $87,500 over exemption amount	Up to $175,000 over exemption amount
28%	Greater than $87,500 over exemption amount	Greater than $175,000 over exemption amount

Exemption amount

Filing status	Base amount	Less 25% of the amount by which AMTI* exceeds
Single	$35,750	$112,500
Married filing jointly, surviving spouses	49,000	150,000
Married filing separately, estates and trusts	24,500	75,000

*Alternative minimum taxable income

TaxAlert

This table shows the amount of adjustments and preference items that single or joint filers at three different levels of taxable income can have before they would be subject to the AMT in 2001. For example, married taxpayers filing a joint return with $150,000 of regular taxable income in 2001 could have up to $32,497 of preferences and adjustments before they owe any AMT.

ALTERNATIVE MINIMUM TAX EXPOSURE
Adjustments and Preferences That Will Cause AMT to Apply in 2001

Regular taxable income	Joint filers	Single filers
$ 50,000	$30,151	$25,627
150,000	32,497	27,450
200,000	32,761	29,139

Adjustments and tax preference items. The more common adjustments and tax preference items include:

- Addition of *personal exemptions,*
- Addition of the *standard deduction* (if claimed),
- Addition of *itemized deductions* claimed for state and local taxes, certain interest, most miscellaneous deductions, and part of medical expenses,
- Subtraction of any *refund of state and local taxes* included in gross income,

- Changes to accelerated *depreciation* of certain property,
- Difference between *gain or loss* on the sale of property reported for regular tax purposes and AMT purposes,
- Addition of certain income from *incentive stock options,*
- Change in certain *passive activity loss* deductions,

TaxAlert

If your deduction for state taxes is unusually high—for example, perhaps you made a large payment with your 2000 state tax return when you filed in April of 2001; or perhaps you have substantial state tax withholding during 2001 on your regular income—you should take a closer look at the possibility of being subject to the AMT.

Explanation

Besides accounting for tax preference items, certain adjustments (increases or decreases) must be made to taxable income to arrive at alternative minimum taxable income. The adjustments are as follows:

1. An alternative depreciation deduction (using less accelerated methods and longer depreciable lives) is substituted for the regular tax depreciation deduction for real and personal property and certified pollution control facilities placed in service after 1986 and before 1999. Recomputations are done in the aggregate; that is, the amount of the adjustment is not determined on a property-by-property basis. *Note:* This adjustment does not apply if you have elected to apply the alternative depreciation system (ADS) for regular tax purposes. For tax years beginning in 1999, the recovery periods over which property is depreciated will be the same for regular and AMT purposes.
2. Mining exploration and development costs must be amortized over 10 years using the straight-line method.
3. The percentage-of-completion method of accounting must be used for long-term contracts entered into on or after March 1, 1986. Certain small construction contracts entered into on or after June 21, 1988, must use separate, simplified procedures for cost allocations in the percentage-of-completion calculation.
4. An alternative tax net operating loss deduction replaces the regular net operating loss deduction.
5. The installment method of accounting is disallowed for certain installment sales occurring after March 1, 1986.
6. The treatment of itemized deductions is modified as follows:
   - Medical expenses are deductible only to the extent that they exceed 10% of the taxpayer's adjusted gross income.
   - State, local, and foreign real property and income taxes, and state and local personal property taxes, are deductible for AMT purposes only if they are deductible for regular tax purposes in computing adjusted gross income. *Note:* These are taxes related to business, rental property, and farming that are deducted on Schedule C, E, or F.
   - Investment interest is deductible to the extent of net investment income that is adjusted for amounts relating to tax-exempt interest earned on certain private-activity bonds.
   - Home mortgage interest is allowed as a deduction for AMT purposes. However, the definition of such interest is narrower than that of "qualified residence

interest" for regular tax purposes. Refinanced home mortgage interest that is applicable to any mortgage in excess of the outstanding mortgage before refinancing is not deductible.

- No deduction is allowed for miscellaneous itemized deductions subject to the 2%-of-adjusted-gross-income limit.

7. No deduction is allowed for the standard deduction.
8. Circulation expenditures and research/experimental costs must be amortized over 3- and 10-year periods, respectively.
9. Deductions for passive farm losses are denied, except to the extent that the taxpayer is insolvent or the activity is disposed of during the year.
10. Rules limiting passive loss deductions also apply to the AMT, except that (a) otherwise disallowed losses are reduced by the amount by which the taxpayer is insolvent, and (b) all AMT adjustments and preferences are taken into consideration in computing income and/or losses from passive activities.
11. For beneficiaries of estates and trusts, the difference between a distribution included in income for regular tax and the AMT income shown on Schedule K-1 must be taken into account.
12. For property disposed of during the year, the gain or loss is refigured to take into consideration the impact that AMT adjustments, such as depreciation, have on the taxpayer's basis in the property.
13. For partners in partnerships and shareholders in S corporations, the income or loss is refigured to take into account AMT adjustments.
14. In exercising an incentive stock option (ISO), the taxpayer needs to adjust for the difference between the option price and the fair market value at the time the option is exercised. In calculating the AMT gain or loss on the subsequent sale of the ISO stock, the AMT basis in the stock is the sum of the option price paid and the AMT adjustment included in alternative minimum taxable income when the stock becomes substantially vested.

TaxAlert

If you plan to exercise incentive stock options that have been granted to you by your employer, you should always evaluate the potential AMT impact prior to doing so. Although you will not report any income for regular tax purposes when you exercise the incentive options, you will be required to report income (which is measured as the difference between what you paid to exercise the option and the fair market value of the stock on the day of exercise) for AMT purposes. See Chapter 46, *Planning Ahead for 2002 and Beyond*, for an additional discussion about AMT planning.

- Addition of certain *depletion* that is more than the adjusted basis of the property,
- Addition of part of the deduction for certain *intangible drilling costs,* and

TaxSaver

To avoid treating excess intangible drilling costs as a tax preference item, you may elect to capitalize and amortize these expenses over a 10-year period in your regular tax calculation.

- Addition of *tax-exempt interest* on certain private activity bonds.

TaxAlert

If you plan to make a substantial gift of appreciated property (e.g., stock) to a charity, you no longer need to consider the alternative minimum tax (AMT) impact. Under the 1993 Tax Act, you are able to recognize a charitable contribution deduction for the full fair market value of appreciated long-term capital gain property for both regular and AMT purposes. Under prior law, the amount of appreciation on donated property was considered a tax preference item for AMT purposes.

Explanation

You will only pay the AMT if it is higher than your regular tax. You may, however, offset your AMT liability by using any foreign tax credit, as computed under the AMT rules, that you are allowed to claim. Other nonrefundable credits cannot, under any circumstances, reduce your AMT liability. To the extent that no tax benefit is obtained for these nonrefundable credits for the year in which the AMT applies, such credits are generally carried back or forward.

The law provides a credit against the regular tax for all or a portion of the AMT you paid in previous years. The credit is the AMT attributable to deferral, rather than exclusion, items. Deferral items such as accelerated depreciation are those that have the effect of reducing your regular taxable income relative to alternative minimum taxable income in early years, but the situation reverses over time. Thus, the same total of deductions is eventually allowed under both tax systems. When you pay AMT as a result of deferral preferences, the law gives you a credit that can be used to reduce your regular tax liability in the future. This avoids double taxation on the same income. Exclusion preferences, such as certain tax-exempt interest income, reduce your regular taxable income permanently. Because these preferences never reverse in the future, you are not given a credit for AMT paid. The credit is carried forward indefinitely from the year of payment and cannot be carried back.

Example

The following example demonstrates how you would calculate your regular tax and your AMT for calendar year 2001 assuming your filing status is married filing jointly.

	Regular tax	Alternative minimum tax
Salary	$150,000	$150,000
Dividends	11,000	11,000
Long-term capital gains	80,000	80,000
Net passive losses	(25,000)	(25,000)
Passive losses disallowed by Tax Reform Act of 1986	25,000	25,000
Adjusted gross income	$241,000	$241,000
State taxes	(30,000)	n/a*
Charitable contributions	(40,000)	(40,000)

Interest expense—principal residence	(27,000)	(27,000)
Reduction in itemized deductions for adjusted gross income over $132,950	3,242	n/a
Exemptions (4)	(7,656)	n/a
Tax preference items: Incentive stock options	n/a	25,000
Alternative taxable income before exemption	n/a	$199,000
Exemption ($49,000 less 25% of alternative taxable income in excess of $150,000)	n/a	(36,750)
Taxable income	$139,586	$162,250
Tax due	$26,808	$42,185

*n/a means "not applicable."

Because your regular tax is less than your AMT, you must pay the AMT of $42,185.

The $30,000 you paid in state income tax was not allowed as a deduction from alternative minimum taxable income. Because deductions are based on actual payments made during the calendar year, good planning would require minimizing your state income taxes and your miscellaneous deductions to the extent that you are able in a year when it is possible you will be subject to the AMT.

TAXPLANNER

Even if you have benefited from the tax preference items that generally subject you to the AMT, you may avoid the AMT by controlling the timing of certain transactions. The trick is not to exceed the amount exempt from the AMT for a given year. If you know that you will be subject to the AMT this year, and provided your current AMT situation is due to exclusion items, you should consider realizing income this year that otherwise would be realized next year so that it is taxed at 26% or 28% rather than at a higher rate next year. Likewise, consider deferring deductions, especially those that are not deductible for AMT purposes.

The $49,000 exemption for joint returns is phased out beginning at $150,000 of alternative minimum taxable income. For unmarried taxpayers, the exemption amount is $35,750, and it is phased out beginning at $112,500. You lose $1 of exemption for every $4 over the base amount. Consequently, the exemption amount is completely phased out at $346,000 for joint returns and $255,500 for unmarried taxpayers.

More information. For more information about the alternative minimum tax, see the instructions for Form 1040, line 41, and Form 6251, *Alternative Minimum Tax—Individuals.*

Tax Figured by IRS

If you file by April 15, 2002, you can have the IRS figure your tax for you on Form 1040EZ, Form 1040A, or Form 1040.

If the IRS figures your tax and you paid too much, you will receive a refund. If you did not pay enough, you will receive a bill for the balance. To avoid interest or the penalty for late payment, you must pay the bill within 30 days of the date of the bill or by the due date for your return, whichever is later.

TAXPLANNER

If you make a preliminary calculation and see that you owe money to the IRS, you might consider waiting until April 15 to file your return and letting the IRS figure your tax. It will take the IRS some time to process your return and compute your tax. You will not have to come up with the money you owe until 30 days after the IRS sends you a bill. You will not have to pay any interest if you pay within 30 days of receiving your bill.

When the IRS cannot figure your tax. The IRS cannot figure your tax for you if any of the following apply.

1) You want your refund directly deposited.
2) You want any of your refund applied to your 2002 estimated tax.
3) Any of your income for the year was from *other than* wages, salaries, tips, interest, dividends, taxable social security benefits, unemployment compensation, IRA distributions, pensions, and annuities.
4) Your taxable income is $100,000 or more.
5) You itemize deductions.
6) You file any of the following forms.
   a) Form 2555, *Foreign Earned Income.*
   b) Form 2555-EZ, *Foreign Earned Income Exclusion.*
   c) Form 4137, *Social Security and Medicare Tax on Unreported Tip Income.*
   d) Form 4970, *Tax on Accumulation Distribution of Trusts.*
   e) Form 4972, *Tax on Lump-Sum Distributions.*
   f) Form 6198, *At-Risk Limitations.*
   g) Form 6251, *Alternative Minimum Tax—Individuals.*
   h) Form 8606, *Nondeductible IRAs and Coverdell ESAs.*
   i) Form 8615, *Tax for Children Under Age 14 Who Have Investment Income of More Than $1,500.*
   j) Form 8814, *Parents' Election To Report Child's Interest and Dividends.*
   k) Form 8839, *Qualified Adoption Expenses.*
   l) Form 8853, *Archer MSAs and Long-Term Care Insurance Contracts.*

Filing the Return

After you complete the line entries for the tax form you are filing (discussed next), attach the peel-off label, enter your social security number(s), sign the return, and mail it. If you do not have a peel-off label, fill in your name and address. See chapter 1 for more information.

Form 1040EZ Line Entries

Read lines 1 through 9 and fill in the lines that apply to you. If you are filing a joint return, write your taxable income and your spouse's taxable income to the left of line 6.

Earned income credit. If you can take this credit, as discussed in chapter 37, the IRS can figure it for you. Print "EIC" in the space to the right of line 9a. Enter the amount of any nontaxable earned income on line 9b.

If your credit for any year after 1996 was reduced or disallowed by the IRS, you may also have to file Form 8862, *Information To Claim Earned Income Credit After Disallowance,* with your return. For details, see that form and its instructions.

Form 1040A Line Entries

Read lines 1 through 25 and fill in the lines that apply to you. If you are filing a joint return, write your taxable income and your spouse's taxable income to the left of line 25. Complete lines 27 through 30, 35, and 37 through 40 if they apply to you. Do not fill in lines 28 and 39a if you want the IRS to figure the credits shown on those lines. Also, enter any write-in information that applies to you in the space to the left of line 41.

Credit for child and dependent care expenses. If you can take this credit, as discussed in chapter 33, complete Schedule 2 and attach it to your return. Enter the amount of the credit on line 27 (Form 1040A). The IRS will not figure this credit.

Credit for the elderly or the disabled. If you can take this credit, as discussed in chapter 34, attach Schedule 3 (1040A), *Credit for the Elderly or the Disabled for Form 1040A Filers.* Print "CFE" in the space to the left of line 28 (Form 1040A). The IRS will figure this credit for you. On Schedule 3, check the box in Part I for your filing status and age. Complete Part II and lines 11 and 13 of Part III if they apply.

Earned income credit. If you can take this credit, as discussed in chapter 37, the IRS will figure it for you. Print "EIC" directly to the right of line 39a. Enter the amount of any nontaxable earned income on line 39b. If you have a qualifying child, you must fill in Schedule EIC, *Earned Income Credit,* and attach it to your return.

If your credit for any year after 1996 was reduced or disallowed by the IRS, you may also have to file Form 8862 with your return. For details, see that form and its instructions.

Form 1040 Line Entries

Read lines 1 through 39 and fill in the lines that apply to you.

If you are filing a joint return, write your taxable income and your spouse's taxable income in the space under the words "Adjusted Gross Income" on the front of your return.

Read lines 41 through 65. Fill in the lines that apply to you, but do not fill in the "Total" lines. Do not fill in lines 45 and 61a if you want the IRS to figure the credits shown on those lines.

Fill in any forms or schedules asked for on the lines you completed, and attach them to your return.

Credit for child and dependent care expenses. If you can take this credit, as discussed in chapter 33, complete Form 2441 and attach it to your return. Enter the amount of the credit on line 44. The IRS will not figure this credit.

Credit for the elderly or the disabled. If you can take this credit, as discussed in chapter 34, attach Schedule R, *Credit for the Elderly or the Disabled.* Print "CFE" on the dotted line next to line 45 of Form 1040. The IRS will figure the credit for you. On Schedule R check the box in Part I for your filing status and age. Complete Part II and lines 11 and 13 of Part III if they apply.

Earned income credit. If you can take this credit, as discussed in chapter 37, the IRS will figure it for you. Print "EIC" directly to the right of line 61a of Form 1040. Enter the amount of any nontaxable earned in-

come in the space provided on line 61b. If you have a qualifying child, you must fill in Schedule EIC and attach it to your return.

If your credit for any year after 1996 was reduced or disallowed by the IRS, you may also have to file Form 8862 with your return. For details, see that form and its instructions.

TAX ORGANIZER

Records you should keep. The taxpayer should retain documentation for the following items:

1. *W-2:* Wages, salaries, tips; allocated tips; advance EIC payments; dependent care benefits; adoption benefits; employer contributions to a medical savings account
2. *W-2G:* Gambling winnings
3. *1098:* Mortgage interest; points; refund of overpaid interest
4. *1098-E:* Student loan interest
5. *1099-A:* Acquisition or abandonment of secured property
6. *1099-B:* Stocks and bonds; bartering; futures contracts
7. *1099-C:* Canceled debt
8. *1099-DIV:* Ordinary dividends; total capital gains distributions; nontaxable distributions; investment expenses; foreign tax paid
9. *1099-G:* Unemployment compensation; state or local income tax refund; taxable grants; agriculture payments
10. *1099-INT:* Interest income; early withdrawal penalty; interest on U.S. savings bonds and Treasury obligations
11. *1099-LTC:* Long-term care and accelerated death benefits
12. *1099-MISC:* Rents; royalties; other income (prizes, awards); nonemployee compensation
13. *1099-MSA:* Distributions from medical savings accounts
14. *1099-OID:* Original issue discount; other periodic interest; early withdrawal penalty
15. *1099-PATR:* Patronage dividends and other distributions from a cooperative; credits; patron's AMT adjustment
16. *1099-R:* Distributions from IRAs; distributions from pensions, annuities; capital gain
17. *1099-S:* Gross proceeds from real estate transactions; buyer's part of real estate tax

Tax on Investment Income of Certain Minor Children

Introduction

*There's nothing easy about bringing up children these days, and that applies to their tax returns as well. It is enormously complicated to determine the correct tax and fill out a proper tax return for children **under age 14** who have **unearned** income.*

Unearned income of children under age 14 is taxed at the marginal rate of their parents, as if the parents had received the income, rather than at the child's lower rate. Generally, this isn't going to give your child a break. Because most parents have a higher marginal tax rate than their children, these rules generally eliminate the benefits of transferring income-producing assets, such as stocks or bonds, to your minor children in order for the income to be taxed at the children's lower marginal rate.

The following are additional complications:

1. *A child may not claim a personal exemption for himself or herself if he or she is eligible to be claimed on a parent's return.*
2. *A child's unearned income falls under special rules.*

The child can use $750 of his or her standard deduction to offset unearned income. The next $750 of unearned income is taxed at the child's tax rate. The balance of a child's unearned income will be taxed at the parent's marginal tax rate. This is accomplished by including the child's income on the parents return (use Form 8814) OR by filing a tax return for the child (attach Form 8615). Note that copies of these forms are included in Chapter 48, 2001 Federal Tax Forms and Schedules You Can Use. You can also obtain these forms from the Ernst & Young Tax and Financial Planning Corner on the Internet at the following address: www.ey.com/pfc.

3. *If a child also has earned income, his or her tax return gets more complicated still. The earned income can increase his or her allowable standard deduction.*

This chapter will help you sort through all the complications. Here's hoping that, while you're muddling through it, your children will be out having fun.

Important Change

Tax computation for certain dependents. Generally, the tax computed for a dependent using the 2001 Tax Table or Tax Rate Schedules can be reduced to take into account the new 10% tax rate. To figure the reduced tax, use the *Tax Computation Worksheet for Certain Dependents* in the instructions for Form 1040 (line 40), Form 1040A (line 26), and Form 1040EZ (line 11).

This computation *does not apply to* the following.

- Dependents who received (before any offsets) an advance payment of their 2001 taxes.
- Dependents who file Form 1040NR, *Nonresident Alien Income Tax Return.*

Important Reminder

Parent's election to report child's interest and dividends. You may be able to elect to include your child's interest and dividends on your tax return. If you make this election, the child does not have to file a return. See *Parent's Election To Report Child's Interest and Dividends,* later.

This chapter discusses two special tax rules that apply to certain investment income of a child under age 14.

1) If the child's interest, dividends, and other investment income total more than $1,500, part of that income may be taxed at the parent's tax rate instead of the child's tax rate. (See *Tax for Children Under Age 14 Who Have Investment Income of More Than $1,500,* later.)
2) The child's parent may be able to choose to include the child's interest and dividend income (including capital gain distributions) on the parent's return rather than file a return for the child. (See *Parent's Election To Report Child's Interest and Dividends,* later.)

For these rules, the term "child" includes a legally adopted child and a stepchild. These rules apply whether or not the child is a dependent.

These rules do *not* apply if:

1) The child is not required to file a tax return, or
2) Neither of the child's parents were living at the end of the tax year.

Explanation
For the 2001 tax year, "under age 14" means that the child has not reached age 14 by January 1, 2002. If your child reached age 14 at any time during 2001, this chapter will not apply.

TaxSaver
The tax benefit of transferring investment property to your children is limited; however, some advantages still exist. First, keep in mind that the first $1,500 in investment income is taxed at a very low rate. Second, the child will eventually be 14 years old and have his or her own tax bracket (which will probably be lower than yours). Third, if the property appreciates in value while your child is a minor, the appreciation will not complicate your tax situation.

Useful Items

You may want to see:

Publication

☐ 929 Tax Rules for Children and Dependents

Form (and Instructions)

☐ 8615 Tax for Children Under Age 14 With Investment Income of More Than $1,500
☐ 8814 Parents' Election To Report Child's Interest and Dividends

Which Parent's Return To Use

If a child's parents are married to each other and file a joint return, use the joint return to figure the tax on the investment income of a child under age 14. For parents who do not file a joint return, the following discussions explain which parent's tax return must be used to figure the tax. Only the parent whose tax return is used can make the election described under *Parent's Election To Report Child's Interest and Dividends.* The tax rate and other return information from that parent's return are used to compute the child's tax as explained later under *Tax for Children Under Age 14 Who Have Investment Income of More Than $1,500.*

Parents are married. If the child's parents file separate returns, use the return of the parent with the greater taxable income.

Parents not living together. If the child's parents are married to each other but not living together, and the parent with whom the child lives (the custodial parent) is considered unmarried, use the return of the custodial parent. If the custodial parent is not considered unmarried, use the return of the parent with the greater taxable income.

For an explanation of when a married person living apart from his or her spouse is considered unmarried, see *Head of Household* in chapter 2.

Parents are divorced. If the child's parents are divorced or legally separated, and the parent who had custody of the child for the greater part of the year (the custodial parent) has not remarried, use the return of the custodial parent.

Custodial parent remarried. If the custodial parent has remarried, the stepparent (rather than the noncustodial parent) is treated as the child's other parent. Therefore, if the custodial parent and the stepparent file a joint return, use that joint return. Do not use the return of the noncustodial parent.

If the custodial parent and the stepparent are married, but file separate returns, use the return of the one with the greater taxable income. If the custodial parent and the stepparent are married but not living together, the earlier discussion under *Parents not living together* applies.

Explanation
When both parents have custody of a child with unearned income, the custodial parent is the parent with custody for the greater portion of the calendar year.

Parents never married. If a child's parents did not marry each other, but lived together all year, use the return of the parent with the greater taxable income. If the parents did not live together all year, the rules explained earlier under *Parents are divorced* apply.

Widowed parent remarried. If a widow or widower remarries, the new spouse is treated as the child's other parent. The rules explained earlier under *Custodial parent remarried* apply.

Parent's Election To Report Child's Interest and Dividends

You may be able to elect to include your child's interest and dividend income (including capital gain distributions) on your tax return. If you do, your child will not have to file a return.

You can make this election for 2001 only if *all* the following conditions are met.

1) Your child was under age 14 on January 1, 2002.
2) Your child is required to file a return for 2001 unless you make this election.
3) Your child had income only from interest and dividends (including capital gain distributions and Alaska Permanent Fund dividends).
4) The dividend and interest income was less than $7,500.
5) No estimated tax payment was made for 2001 and no 2000 overpayment was applied to 2001 under your child's name and social security number.
6) No federal income tax was taken out of your child's income under the backup withholding rules.
7) You are the parent whose return must be used when applying the special tax rules for children under age 14. (See *Which Parent's Return To Use,* earlier.)

These conditions are also shown in *Figure 32-A.*

How to make the election. Make the election by attaching **Form 8814** to your Form 1040 or Form 1040NR. (If you make this election, you cannot file Form 1040A or Form 1040EZ.) Attach a separate Form 8814 for each child for whom you make the election. You can make the election for one or more children and not for others.

Figure 32–A. **Can You Include Your Child's Income On Your Tax Return?**

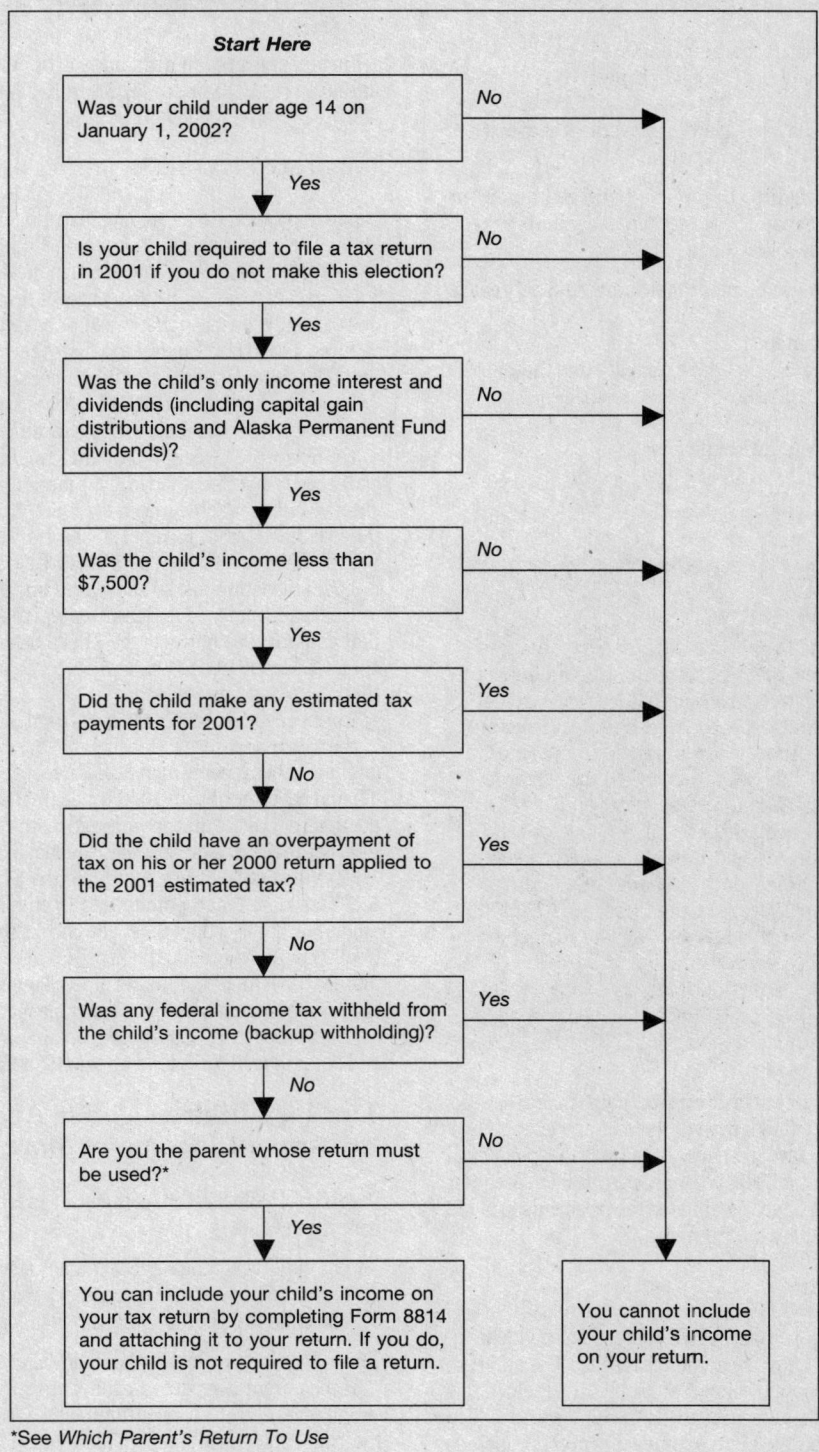

*See *Which Parent's Return To Use*

Effect of Making the Election

The federal income tax on your child's income may be more if you make the Form 8814 election rather than file a return for the child.

Rates may be higher. If you use Form 8814, the child's income may be taxed at a higher rate on your return than it would be on the child's own return.

TAXALERT

Most individuals will not want to elect to file Form 8814, because, as the IRS notes, in some cases it could result in more total tax.

Deductions you cannot take. By making the Form 8814 election, you cannot take any of the following deductions the child would be entitled to on his or her return.

1) The higher standard deduction for a blind child.
2) The deduction for a penalty on an early withdrawal of your child's savings.
3) Itemized deductions (such as your child's investment expenses or charitable contributions).

Reduced deductions or credits. If you use Form 8814, your increased adjusted gross income may reduce certain deductions or credits on your return including the following.

1) Deduction for contributions to a traditional individual retirement arrangement (IRA).
2) Deduction for student loan interest.
3) Itemized deductions for medical expenses, casualty and theft losses, and certain miscellaneous expenses.
4) Total itemized deductions.
5) Credit for child and dependent care expenses.
6) Child tax credit.
7) Education tax credits.
8) Earned income credit.

TaxAlert

If you use Form 8814 to add your child's income to yours, not only may your increased adjusted gross income reduce such items on your return as any itemized deductions for medical expenses, casualty and theft losses, and certain miscellaneous expenses, but it may also subject you to the personal exemption phaseout and the 3% reduction to itemized deductions (see Chapter 21, *Standard Deduction* and Chapter 22, *Limit on Itemized Deductions*), as well as limit your deduction for IRA contributions [*see* Chapter 18, *Individual Retirement Arrangements* (IRAs) *and Education Savings Accounts* (ESAs)], and your ability to claim the favorable $25,000 rental loss allowance under the passive activity rules (see Chapter 13, *Other Income*). Finally, adding your child's income to yours also may increase your state and local tax liability. Consider this election carefully before filing Form 8814.

Penalty for underpayment of estimated tax. If you make this election for 2001 and did not have enough tax withheld or pay enough estimated tax to cover the tax you owe, you may be subject to a penalty. If you plan to make this election for 2002, you may need to increase your federal income tax withholding or your estimated tax payments to avoid the penalty. See chapter 5 for more information.

Figuring Child's Income

Use *Part I* of Form 8814 to figure your child's interest and dividend income to report on your return. Only the amount over $1,500 is added to your income. This amount is shown on line 6 of Form 8814. Include this amount on line 21 of Form 1040 or Form 1040NR. Write "Form 8814" in the space next to line 21. If you file more than one Form 8814, include the total amounts from line 6 of all your Forms 8814 on line 21.

Capital gain distributions. If your child's dividend income included any capital gain distributions, see *Capital gain distributions* under *Figuring Child's Income* in Publication 929.

Figuring Additional Tax

Use *Part II* of Form 8814 to figure the tax on the $1,500 of your child's interest and dividends that you do not include in your income. This tax is added to the tax figured on your income.

This additional tax is the *smaller* of:

1) 10% × (your child's gross income − $750), or
2) $75.

Include the amount from line 9 of all your Forms 8814 in the total on line 40, Form 1040, or line 39, Form 1040NR. Check box **a** on Form 1040, line 40, or Form 1040NR, line 39.

Illustrated Example

David and Linda Parks are married and will file separate tax returns for 2001. Their only child, Philip, is 8. Philip received a Form 1099-INT showing $3,200 taxable interest income and a Form 1099-DIV showing $300 ordinary dividends. His parents decide to include that income on one of their returns so they will not have to file a return for Philip.

First, David and Linda each figure their taxable income (Form 1040, line 39) without regard to Philip's income. David's taxable income is $41,700 and Linda's is $59,300. Because her taxable income is greater, Linda can elect to include Philip's income on her return.

On Form 8814 (see illustrated form), Linda enters her name and social security number, then Philip's name and social security number. She enters Philip's taxable interest income, $3,200, on line 1a. Philip had no tax-exempt interest income, so she leaves line 1b blank. Linda enters Philip's ordinary dividends, $300, on line 2. Philip did not have any capital gain distributions, so she leaves line 3 blank.

Linda adds lines 1a and 2 and enters the result, $3,500, on line 4. From that amount she subtracts the $1,500 base amount shown on line 5 and enters the result, $2,000, on line 6. This is the part of Philip's income that Linda must add to her income.

Linda includes the $2,000 in the total on line 21 of her Form 1040 and in the space next to that line prints "Form 8814—$2,000." Adding that amount to her income increases each of the amounts on lines 22, 33, 34, 37, and 39 of her Form 1040 by $2,000. Linda is not claiming any deductions or credits that are affected by the increase to her income. Therefore, her revised taxable income on line 39 is $61,300 ($59,300 + $2,000).

On Form 8814, Linda subtracts the $750 shown on line 7 from the $3,500 on line 4 and enters the result, $2,750, on line 8. Because that amount is not less than $750, she checks the "No" box and enters $75 on line 9. This is the tax on the first $1,500 of Philip's income, which Linda did not have to add to her income. She must add this additional tax to the tax figured on her revised taxable income.

The tax on her $61,300 revised taxable income is $14,240. She adds $75, and enters the $14,315 total on line 40 of Form 1040, and checks box **a**.

Tax for Children Under Age 14 Who Have Investment Income of More Than $1,500

Part of a child's 2001 investment income may be subject to tax at the parent's tax rate if:

1) The child was under age 14 on January 1, 2002,
2) The child's investment income was more than $1,500, and
3) The child is required to file a return for 2001.

These conditions are also shown in *Figure 32-B.*

If the parent does not or cannot choose to include the child's income on the parent's return, use **Form 8615** to figure the child's tax. Attach the completed form to the child's Form 1040, Form 1040A, or Form 1040NR.

The following discussions explain the parental information needed for Form 8615 and the steps to follow in figuring the child's tax. Form 8615 is illustrated later.

Providing Parental Information (Form 8615, lines A-C)

On lines A and B of Form 8615, enter the parent's name and social security number. (If the parents filed a joint return, enter the name and so-

Figure 32–B. **Do You Have To Use Form 8615 To Figure Your Child's Tax?**

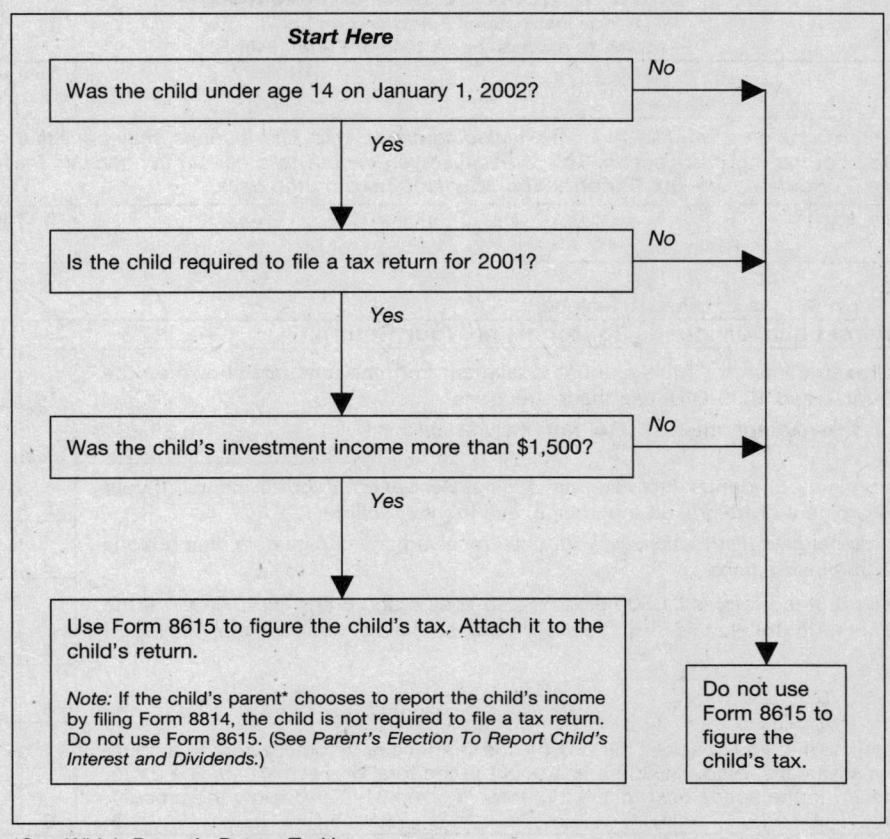

*See *Which Parent's Return To Use*

cial security number listed first on the joint return.) On line C, check the box for the parent's filing status.

See *Which Parent's Return To Use* at the beginning of this chapter for information on which parent's return information must be used on Form 8615.

Parent with different tax year. If the parent and the child do not have the same tax year, complete Form 8615 using the information on the parent's return for the tax year that ends in the child's tax year.

Parent's return information not known timely. If the information needed from the parent's return is not known by the time the child's return is due (usually April 15), you can file the return using estimates.

You can use any reasonable estimate. This includes using information from last year's return. If you use an estimated amount on Form 8615, write "Estimated" on the line next to the amount.

When you get the correct information, file an amended return on Form 1040X, *Amended U.S. Individual Income Tax Return.*

Instead of using estimated information, you may want to request an extension of time to file. Extensions are discussed in chapter 1.

Step 1. Figuring the Child's Net Investment Income (Form 8615, Part I)

The first step in figuring a child's tax using Form 8615 is to figure the child's net investment income. To do that, use Part I of Form 8615.
Line 1 (investment income). If the child had **no earned income,** enter on this line the adjusted gross income shown on the child's return. Adjusted gross income is shown on line 33 of Form 1040, line 19 of Form 1040A, or line 33 of Form 1040NR. Form 1040EZ cannot be used if Form 8615 must be filed.

If the child had **earned income,** figure the amount to enter on line 1 of Form 8615 by using the worksheet in the instructions for the form.

However, if the child has excluded any foreign earned income or deducted either a loss from self-employment or a net operating loss from another year, use the *Alternate Worksheet for Line 1 of Form 8615* in Publication 929 to figure the amount to enter on line 1 of Form 8615.

Investment income defined. Investment income is generally all income other than salaries, wages, and other amounts received as pay for work actually done. It includes taxable interest, dividends, capital gains, the taxable part of social security and pension payments, and certain distributions from trusts. Investment income includes amounts produced by assets the child obtained with earned income (such as interest on a savings account into which the child deposited wages).

Nontaxable income. For this purpose, investment income includes only amounts that the child must include in total income. Nontaxable investment income, such as tax-exempt interest and the nontaxable part of social security and pension payments, is not included.

Income from property received as a gift. A child's investment income includes all income produced by property belonging to the child. This is true even if the property was transferred to the child regardless of when the property was transferred or purchased or who transferred it.

A child's investment income includes income produced by property given as a gift to the child. This includes gifts to the child from grandparents or any other person and gifts made under the Uniform Gift to Minors Act.

Example. Amanda Black, age 13, received the following income.

- Dividends—$600
- Wages—$2,100

Form **8814**		**Parents' Election To Report** **Child's Interest and Dividends** ▶ See instructions below and on back. ▶ Attach to parents' Form 1040 or Form 1040NR.	OMB No. 1545-1128 **2001** Attachment Sequence No. **40**
Department of the Treasury Internal Revenue Service			

Name(s) shown on your return	**Your social security number**
Linda Parks	111 : 00 : 1111

Caution: *The Federal income tax on your child's income, including capital gain distributions, may be less if you file a separate tax return for the child instead of making this election. This is because you cannot take certain tax benefits that your child could take on his or her own return. For details, see **Tax Benefits You May Not Take** on the back.*

A	Child's name (first, initial, and last)	**B Child's social security number**
	Philip Parks	000 : 00 : 0000

c If more than one Form 8814 is attached, check here . . . . ▶ ☐

Part I   Child's Interest and Dividends To Report on Your Return

1a	Enter your child's **taxable** interest. If this amount is different from the amounts shown on the child's Forms 1099-INT and 1099-OID, see the instructions	**1a**	3,200
b	Enter your child's **tax-exempt** interest. **Do not** include this amount on line 1a **1b**		
2	Enter your child's ordinary dividends, including any Alaska Permanent Fund dividends. If your child received any ordinary dividends as a nominee, see the instructions	**2**	300
3	Enter your child's capital gain distributions. If your child received any capital gain distributions as a nominee, see the instructions	**3**	
4	Add lines 1a, 2, and 3. If the total is $1,500 or less, skip lines 5 and 6 and go to line 7. If the total is $7,500 or more, **do not** file this form. Your child **must** file his or her own return to report the income	**4**	3,500
5	Base amount	**5**	1,500 00
6	Subtract line 5 from line 4. If you checked the box on line C above or if you entered an amount on line 3, see the instructions. Also, include this amount in the total on Form 1040, line 21, or Form 1040NR, line 21. In the space next to line 21, enter "Form 8814" and show the amount. Go to line 7 below . . . . ▶	**6**	2,000

Part II   Tax on the First $1,500 of Child's Interest and Dividends

7	Amount not taxed	**7**	750 00
8	Subtract line 7 from line 4. If the result is zero or less, enter -0-	**8**	2,750
9	**Tax.** Is the amount on line 8 less than $750? ☑ **No.** Enter $75 here and see the **Note** below. ☐ **Yes.** Multiply line 8 by 10% (.10). Enter the result here and see the **Note** below.	**9**	75

Note: *If you checked the box on line C above, see the instructions. Otherwise, include the amount from line 9 in the tax you enter on Form 1040, line 40, or Form 1040NR, line 39. Be sure to check box **a** on Form 1040, line 40, or Form 1040NR, line 39.*

General Instructions

Purpose of Form. Use this form if you elect to report your child's income on your return. If you do, your child will not have to file a return. You can make this election if your child meets **all** of the following conditions.

● Was under age 14 on January 1, 2002.

● Is required to file a 2001 return.

● Had income only from interest and dividends, including Alaska Permanent Fund dividends.

● Had gross income for 2001 that was less than $7,500.

● Had no estimated tax payments for 2001 (including any overpayment of tax from his or her 2000 return applied to 2001 estimated tax).

● Had no Federal income tax withheld from his or her income.

You must also qualify. See **Parents Who Qualify To Make the Election** below.

How To Make the Election. To make the election, complete and attach Form(s) 8814 to your tax return and file your return by the due date (including extensions). A separate Form 8814 must be filed for **each** child whose income you choose to report.

Parents Who Qualify To Make the Election. You qualify to make this election if you file Form 1040 or Form 1040NR and **any** of the following apply.

● You are filing a joint return for 2001 with the child's other parent.

● You and the child's other parent were married to each other but file separate returns for 2001 **and** you had the **higher** taxable income.

● You were unmarried, treated as unmarried for Federal income tax purposes, or separated from the child's other parent by a divorce or separate maintenance decree. You must have had custody of your child for most of the year (you were the custodial parent). If you were the custodial parent and you remarried, you may make the election on a joint return with your new spouse. But if you and your new spouse do not file a joint return, you qualify to make the election only if you had **higher** taxable income than your new spouse.

(continued)

- Taxable interest—$1,200
- Tax-exempt interest—$100
- Net capital gains—$100.

The dividends were on stock given to her by her grandparents.

Amanda's investment income is $1,900. This is the total of the dividends ($600), taxable interest ($1,200), and net capital gains ($100). Her wages are earned (not investment) income because they are pay received for work actually done. Her tax-exempt interest is not included because it is nontaxable.

Trust income. If a child is the beneficiary of a trust, distributions of taxable interest, dividends, capital gains, and other investment income from the trust are investment income to the child.

Line 2 (deductions). If the child does not itemize deductions on Schedule A (Form 1040 or Form 1040NR), enter $1,500 on line 2.

If the child does itemize deductions, enter on line 2 the larger of:

1) $750 plus the child's itemized deductions that are directly connected with the production of investment income, or
2) $1,500.

Directly connected. Itemized deductions are directly connected with the production of investment income if they are for expenses paid to produce or collect taxable income or to manage, conserve, or maintain property held for producing income. These expenses include custodian fees and service charges, service fees to collect taxable interest and dividends, and certain investment counsel fees.

These expenses are added to certain other miscellaneous deductions on Schedule A (Form 1040). Only the amount greater than 2% of the child's adjusted gross income can be deducted. See chapter 30 for more information.

Explanation
Directly connected itemized deductions also include any investment interest expense deducted on the child's return that relates to debt incurred to finance the investments that produced the unearned income.

Example 1. Roger, age 12, has investment income of $8,000, no other income, no adjustments to income, and itemized deductions of $300 (net of the 2%-of-adjusted-gross-income limit) that are directly connected with his investment income. His adjusted gross income is $8,000, which is entered on line 1. Line 2 is $1,500 because that is more than the sum of $750 and his directly-connected itemized deductions of $300.

Example 2. Eleanor, 8, has investment income of $16,000 and an early withdrawal penalty of $100. She has no other income. She has itemized deductions of $1,050 (net of the 2% of adjusted gross income limit) that are directly connected with the production of her investment income. Her adjusted gross income, entered on line 1, is $15,900 ($16,000 − $100). Line 2 is $1,800. This is the larger of:

1) $750 plus the $1,050 of directly connected itemized deductions, or
2) $1,500.

TAXSAVER

Kids with investment income. If your child is under 14 years of age and has investment income and you are in the top income bracket, you may want to consider altering his or her investment strategy if it is financially appropriate. Because a child with over $1,500 in unearned income will be taxed at his or her parent's rate, it might be advisable to seek out deferred or tax-exempt income.

An example of deferred income might be generated by an investment in a growth-oriented stock or mutual fund. Such an investment may not pay high current dividends, and the realization of any appreciation in value may be deferred by holding the investment until the child reaches age 14. Tax-exempt income may be generated by municipal bonds or U.S. government EE bonds.

Step 2. Figuring Tentative Tax at the Parent's Tax Rate (Form 8615, Part II)

The tentative tax is the difference between the tax on the parent's taxable income figured with the child's net investment income (plus the net investment income of any other child whose Form 8615 includes the tax return information of that parent) and the tax figured without it.

When figuring the tentative tax, do not refigure any of the exclusions, deductions, or credits on the parent's return because of the child's net investment income. For example, do not refigure the medical expense deduction.

Figure the tentative tax on lines 6 through 13 of Form 8615.

Note. If the child has any capital gains or losses, get Publication 929 for help in completing Part II of Form 8615.

Tip. *You may be able to skip lines 7 through 16 of Form 8615. See the Form 8615 instructions for line 6 for details.*

Line 7 (net investment income of other children). If the tax return information of the parent is also used on any other child's Form 8615, enter on line 7 the total of the amounts from line 5 of all the other children's Forms 8615. Do not include the amount from line 5 of the Form 8615 being completed.

Example. Paul and Jane Persimmon have three children, Sharon, Jerry, and Mike, who must attach Form 8615 to their tax returns. The children's net investment income amounts on line 5 of their Forms 8615 are:

- Sharon—$800
- Jerry—$600
- Mike—$1,000

Line 7 of Sharon's Form 8615 will show $1,600 ($600 + $1,000), the total of the amounts on line 5 of Jerry's and Mike's Forms 8615.

Line 7 of Jerry's Form 8615 will show $1,800 ($800 + $1,000).

Line 7 of Mike's Form 8615 will show $1,400 ($800 + $600).

Other children's information not available. If the net investment income of the other children is not available when the return is due, either file the return using estimates or get an extension of time to file. See *Parent's return information not known timely,* earlier.

Line 11 (tentative tax). Subtract line 10 from line 9 and enter the result on this line. This is the tentative tax.

If line 7 is blank, skip lines 12a and 12b and enter the amount from line 11 on line 13.

Lines 12a and 12b (dividing the tentative tax). If an amount is entered on line 7, divide the tentative tax shown on line 11 among the children according to each child's share of the total net investment income. This is done on lines 12a, 12b, and 13. Add the amount on line 7 to the amount on line 5 and enter the total on line 12a. Divide the amount on line 5 by the amount on line 12a and enter the result as a decimal on line 12b.

Example. In the earlier example under *Line 7 (net investment income of other children),* Sharon's Form 8615 shows $1,600 on line 7. Line 12a is $2,400, the total of lines 5 and 7 ($800 + $1,600). The decimal on line 12b is .333, figured as follows and rounded to three places.

$$\frac{\$800}{\$2,400} = .333$$

Step 3. Figuring the Child's Tax (Form 8615, Part III)

The final step in figuring a child's tax using Form 8615 is to determine the *larger* of:

1) The total of:
   a) The child's share of the tentative tax based on the parent's tax rate, plus
   b) The tax on the child's taxable income in excess of net investment income, figured at the child's tax rate, or
2) The tax on the child's taxable income, figured at the child's tax rate.

This is the child's tax. It is figured on lines 14 through 18 of Form 8615.

Caution. Tax computation for certain dependents. *Generally, if the child can be claimed as a dependent on someone else's tax return, you can reduce any tax amount figured using the 2001 Tax Table or Tax Rate Schedules (including any line 15 tax figured on any worksheet or schedule described in the following paragraphs) by one-third of the tax amount or $300, whichever is smaller.*

*This reduction **does not apply to** the following dependents.*

- *A child who received (before any offsets) an advance payment of their 2001 taxes.*
- *A child who files Form 1040NR.*

Alternative minimum tax. A child may be subject to alternative minimum tax (AMT) if he or she has certain items given preferential treatment under the tax laws or certain adjustments to taxable income that total more than an exemption amount. See *Alternative Minimum Tax* in chapter 31.

AMT is figured on Form 6251. For information on special limits that apply to a child who files Form 6251, *Alternative Minimum Tax—Individuals,* see *Alternative Minimum Tax* in Publication 929.

Illustrated Example

The following example includes a completed Form 8615.

John and Laura Brown have one child, Sara. She is 13 and has $2,750 taxable interest and dividend income and $1,500 earned income. She does not itemize deductions and did not receive an advance payment of her 2001 taxes during 2001. John and Laura file a joint return with John's name and social security number listed first. They claim three exemptions, including an exemption for Sara, on their return.

Because Sara is under age 14 and has more than $1,500 investment income, part of her income may be subject to tax at her parents' rate. A completed Form 8615 must be attached to her return.

Sara's father, John, fills out Sara's return for her.

John enters his name and social security number on Sara's Form 8615 because his name and number are listed first on the joint return he and Laura are filing. He checks the box for married filing jointly.

He enters Sara's investment income, $2,750, on line 1. Sara does not itemize deductions, so John enters $1,500 on line 2. He enters $1,250 ($2,750 − $1,500) on line 3.

Sara's taxable income, as shown on line 25 of her Form 1040A, is $2,500. This is her total income ($4,250) minus her standard deduction ($1,750). Her standard deduction is limited to the amount of her earned income plus $250. John enters $2,500 on line 4.

John compares lines 3 and 4 and enters the smaller amount, $1,250, on line 5.

John enters $48,000 on line 6. This is the taxable income from line 39 of their joint Form 1040 return. Sara is an only child, so line 7 is blank. He adds line 5 ($1,250), line 6 ($48,000), and line 7 (blank), and enters $49,250 on line 8.

Using the column for married filing jointly in the Tax Table, John finds the tax on $49,250. He enters the tax, $7,901 on line 9. He enters $7,557 on line 10. This is the tax from line 40 of John and Laura's Form 1040. He enters $344 on line 11 ($7,901 − $7,557).

Because line 7 is blank, John skips lines 12a and 12b and enters $344 on line 13.

John subtracts line 5 ($1,250) from line 4 ($2,500) and enters the result, $1,250, on line 14. Using the column for single filing status in the Tax Table, John finds the tax on $1,250 and reduces it as explained earlier. He enters this tax, $126, on line 15. He adds lines 13 ($344) and 15 ($126) and enters $470 on line 16.

Using the column for single filing status in the Tax Table, John finds the tax on $2,500 (line 4) and reduces it as explained earlier. He enters this tax, $251, on line 17.

John compares lines 16 and 17 and enters the larger amount, $470, on line 18 of Sara's Form 8615. He also enters that amount on line 26 of Sara's Form 1040A.

John also completes Schedule 1 (Form 1040A) for Sara.

TAX**ORGANIZER**

Records you should keep. The taxpayer should retain documentation for the following items:

1. *1099-INT or 1099-OID:* Child's interest income.
2. *1099-DIV:* Child's dividend investment income; child's capital gain investment income.
3. *W-2:* Child's earned income; child's estimated tax payments for the year (if any).

Form **8615**	**Tax for Children Under Age 14 With Investment Income of More Than $1,500** ► Attach only to the child's Form 1040, Form 1040A, or Form 1040NR. ► See separate instructions.	OMB No. 1545-0998 **2001**
Department of the Treasury Internal Revenue Service		Attachment Sequence No. **33**

Child's name shown on return	Child's social security number
Sara L. Brown	117 00 1111

Before you begin: If the child, the parent, or any of the parent's other children under age 14 received capital gains (including capital gain distributions) or farm income, see **Pub. 929**, Tax Rules for Children and Dependents. It explains how to figure the tax for lines 9 and 15 using the **Capital Gain Tax Worksheet** in the Form 1040 or Form 1040A instructions, or **Schedule D or J** (Form 1040).

A	Parent's name (first, initial, and last). **Caution:** See instructions before completing.	**B** Parent's social security number
	John J. Brown	007 00 0001

C Parent's filing status (check one):

☐ Single   ☑ Married filing jointly   ☐ Married filing separately   ☐ Head of household   ☐ Qualifying widow(er)

Part I	**Child's Net Investment Income**		
1	Enter the child's investment income (see instructions)	**1**	2,750
2	If the child **did not** itemize deductions on Schedule A (Form 1040 or Form 1040NR), enter $1,500. If the child **did** itemize deductions, see instructions	**2**	1,500
3	Subtract line 2 from line 1. If zero or less, **do not** complete the rest of this form but **do** attach it to the child's return	**3**	1,250
4	Enter the child's taxable income from Form 1040, line 39; Form 1040A, line 25; or Form 1040NR, line 38	**4**	2,500
5	Enter the **smaller** of line 3 or line 4. If zero or less, **do not** complete the rest of this form but **do** attach it to the child's return	**5**	1,250

Part II	**Tentative Tax Based on the Tax Rate of the Parent**		
6	Enter the parent's taxable income from Form 1040, line 39; Form 1040A, line 25; Form 1040EZ, line 6; TeleFile Tax Record, line K; Form 1040NR, line 38; or Form 1040NR-EZ, line 14. If zero or less, enter -0-	**6**	48,000
7	Enter the total, if any, from Forms 8615, line 5, of **all other** children of the parent named above. **Do not** include the amount from line 5 above	**7**	
8	Add lines 5, 6, and 7. If the total is not more than $45,200, lines 9 through 16 **may not** have to be completed (see instructions)	**8**	49,250
9	Enter the tax on the amount on line 8 based on the **parent's** filing status above (see instructions). If the Capital Gain Tax Worksheet or Schedule D or J (Form 1040) is used, check here ► ☐	**9**	7,901
10	Enter the parent's tax from Form 1040, line 40; Form 1040A, line 26, minus any alternative minimum tax; Form 1040EZ, line 11; TeleFile Tax Record, line K; Form 1040NR, line 39; or Form 1040NR-EZ, line 15. **Do not** include any tax from Form 4972 or 8814. If the Capital Gain Tax Worksheet or Schedule D or J (Form 1040) was used to figure the tax, check here ► ☐	**10**	7,557
11	Subtract line 10 from line 9 and enter the result. If line 7 is blank, also enter this amount on line 13 and go to Part III	**11**	344
12a	Add lines 5 and 7 . . . . **12a**		
b	Divide line 5 by line 12a. Enter the result as a decimal rounded to at least three places	**12b**	× .
13	Multiply line 11 by line 12b	**13**	344

Part III	**Child's Tax—If lines 4 and 5 above are the same, enter -0- on lines 14 and 15 and go to line 16.**		
14	Subtract line 5 from line 4 . . . . **14**	1,250	
15	Enter the tax on the amount on line 14 based on the child's filing status (see instructions). If the Capital Gain Tax Worksheet or Schedule D or J (Form 1040) is used, check here ► ☐	**15**	126
16	Add lines 13 and 15	**16**	470
17	Enter the tax on the amount on line 4 based on the child's filing status (see instructions). If the Capital Gain Tax Worksheet or Schedule D or J (Form 1040) is used to figure the tax, check here ► ☐	**17**	251
18	Enter the **larger** of line 16 or line 17 here and on the child's Form 1040, line 40; Form 1040A, line 26; or Form 1040NR, line 39	**18**	470

For Paperwork Reduction Act Notice, see page 2 of the instructions.   Cat. No. 64113U   Form **8615** (2001)

Note: At the time this book went to press, Form 8615 had not yet been updated. The form is subject to change.

Child and Dependent Care Credit

Introduction

A credit that directly reduces your taxes is available for certain child and **dependent** *care expenses that enable you to work. The credit may be as much as $720 if you have one qualifying individual or $1,440 if you have more than one qualifying individual. The credit is designed to help ease the tax burden of persons who must work and who also have the responsibility for the care of children or disabled dependents and spouses.*

In general, to claim this credit, you must pay someone to care for a qualifying individual so that you can work or look for work. You must also have **earned income** *from your work during the year and must have maintained a home for yourself and the qualifying individual. This chapter spells out all the details.*

Important Reminders

Limit on credit. For 2001, your credit can offset both your regular tax (after reduction by any foreign tax credit) and your alternative minimum tax, if any. Previously, the credit could offset only your regular tax.

Taxpayer identification number needed for each qualifying person. You must include on line 2 of Form 2441 or Schedule 2 (Form 1040A) the name and taxpayer identification number (generally the social security number) of each qualifying person. See *Taxpayer identification number* under *Qualifying Person Test,* later.

You may have to pay employment taxes. If you pay someone to come to your home and care for your dependent or spouse, you may be a household employer who has to pay employment taxes. Usually, you are *not* a household employer if the person who cares for your dependent or spouse does so at his or her home or place of business.

> **Explanation**
> See Chapter 41, *What to Do if You Employ Domestic Help.*

This chapter discusses the *credit for child and dependent care expenses* and covers the following topics.

- Tests you must meet to claim the credit.
- How to figure the credit.
- How to claim the credit.
- Employment taxes you may have to pay as a household employer.

You may be able to claim the credit if you pay someone to care for your dependent who is under age 13 or for your spouse or dependent who is not able to care for himself or herself. The credit can be up to 30% of your expenses. To qualify, you must pay these expenses so you can work or look for work.

Caution. *This credit should not be confused with the* Child Tax Credit *discussed in chapter 35.*

Dependent care benefits. If you received any dependent care benefits from your employer during the year, you may be able to exclude from your income all or part of them. You must complete Part III of Form 2441 or Schedule 2 (Form 1040A) before you can figure the amount of your credit. See *Employer-Provided Dependent Care Benefits* under *How To Figure the Credit,* later.

Useful Items

You may want to see:

Publication

- ☐ **501** Exemptions, Standard Deduction, and Filing Information
- ☐ **503** Child and Dependent Care Expenses
- ☐ **926** Household Employer's Tax Guide

Form (and Instructions)

- ☐ **2441** Child and Dependent Care Expenses
- ☐ **Schedule 2 (Form 1040A)** Child and Dependent Care Expenses for Form 1040A Filers
- ☐ **Schedule H (Form 1040)** Household Employment Taxes
- ☐ **W-7** Application for IRS Individual Taxpayer Identification Number
- ☐ **W-10** Dependent Care Provider's Identification and Certification

Tests To Claim the Credit

To be able to claim the credit for child and dependent care expenses, you must file Form 1040 or Form 1040A, not Form 1040EZ, and meet *all* the following tests.

1) The care must be for one or more qualifying persons who are identified on the form you use to claim the credit. (See *Qualifying Person Test.*)
2) You (and your spouse if you are married) must keep up a home that you live in with the qualifying person or persons. (See *Keeping Up a Home Test,* later.)
3) You (and your spouse if you are married) must have earned income during the year. (However, see *Rule for student-spouse or spouse not able to care for self* under *Earned Income Test,* later.)
4) You must pay child and dependent care expenses so you (and your spouse if you are married) can work or look for work. (See *Work-Related Expense Test,* later.)
5) You must make payments for child and dependent care to someone you (or your spouse) cannot claim as a dependent. If you make payments to your child, he or she cannot be your dependent and must be age 19 or older by the end of the year. (See *Payments to Relatives* under *Work-Related Expense Test,* later.)
6) Your filing status must be single, head of household, qualifying widow(er) with dependent child, or married filing jointly. You must file a joint return if you are married, unless an exception applies to you. (See *Joint Return Test,* later.)
7) You must identify the care provider on your tax return. (See *Provider Identification Test,* later.)
8) If you exclude dependent care benefits provided by your employer, the amount you exclude must be less than the dollar limit for qualifying expenses (generally, $2,400 if one qualifying person was cared for or $4,800 if two or more qualifying persons were cared for). (See *Reduced Dollar Limit* under *How To Figure the Credit,* later.)

These tests are presented in *Figure 33–A* and are also explained in detail in this chapter.

Qualifying Person Test

Your child and dependent care expenses must be for the care of one or more qualifying persons.

A qualifying person is:

1) Your dependent who was under age 13 when the care was provided and for whom you can claim an exemption,

2) Your spouse who was physically or mentally not able to care for himself or herself, or
3) Your dependent who was physically or mentally not able to care for himself or herself and for whom you can claim an exemption (or could claim an exemption except the person had $2,900 or more of gross income).

If you are divorced or separated, see *Child of Divorced or Separated Parents,* later, to determine which parent may treat the child as a qualifying person.

Physically or mentally not able to care for oneself. Persons who cannot dress, clean, or feed themselves because of physical or mental problems are considered not able to care for themselves. Also, persons who must have constant attention to prevent them from injuring themselves or others are considered not able to care for themselves.

> **Explanation**
> Just because an individual is unable to engage in any substantial gainful activity, perform the normal household functions of a homemaker, or care for minor children does not necessarily establish that the person cannot care for himself or herself. For a person to be considered disabled, physical or mental incapacity must prevent the person from caring for himself or herself.

Person qualifying for part of year. You determine a person's qualifying status each day. For example, if the person for whom you pay child and dependent care expenses no longer qualifies on September 16, count only those expenses through September 15. Also see *Dollar Limit* under *How To Figure the Credit,* later.

Taxpayer identification number. You must include on your return the name and taxpayer identification number (generally the social security number) of the qualifying person(s). If the correct information is not shown, the credit may be reduced or disallowed.

Individual taxpayer identification number (ITIN) for aliens. If your qualifying person is a nonresident or resident alien who does not have and cannot get a social security number (SSN), use that person's ITIN. To apply for an ITIN, file Form W-7 with the IRS. The ITIN is entered wherever an SSN is requested on a tax return.

An ITIN is for tax use only. It does not entitle the holder to social security benefits or change the holder's employment or immigration status under U.S. law.

Adoption taxpayer identification number (ATIN). If your qualifying person is a child who was placed in your home for adoption and for whom you do not have an SSN, you must get an ATIN for the child. File Form W-7A, *Application for Taxpayer Identification Number for Pending U.S. Adoptions.*

Child of Divorced or Separated Parents

To be a qualifying person, your child usually must be your dependent for whom you can claim an exemption. But an exception may apply if you are divorced or separated. Under the exception, if you are the custodial parent, you can treat your child as a qualifying person even if you cannot claim the child's exemption. If you are the noncustodial parent, you cannot treat your child as a qualifying person even if you can claim the child's exemption.

This exception applies if *all* of the following are true.

1) One or both parents had custody of the child for more than half of the year.
2) One or both parents provided more than half of the child's support for the year.
3) Either—
   a) The custodial parent signed **Form 8332**, *Release of Claim to Exemption for Child of Divorced or Separated Parents,* or a sim-

Figure 33–A. **Can You Claim the Credit?**

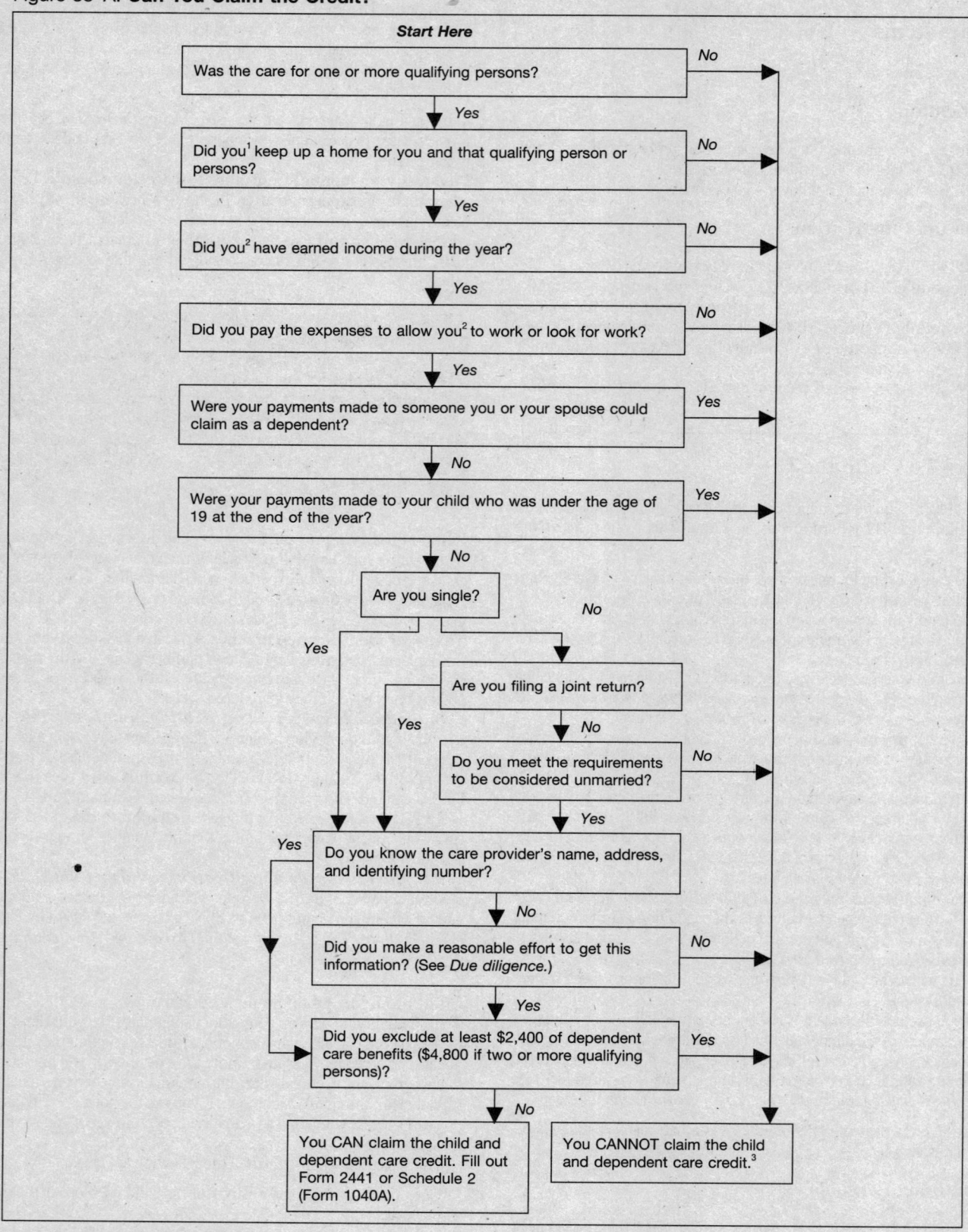

¹This includes your spouse if you were married.
²This also applies to your spouse, unless your spouse was disabled or a full-time student.
³If you had expenses that met the requirements for 2000, except that you did not pay them until 2001, you may be able to claim those expenses in 2001.
See *Expenses not paid until the following year* under *How To Figure the Credit.*

ilar statement, agreeing not to claim the child's exemption for the year, or

b) The noncustodial parent provided at least $600 for the child's support and can claim the child's exemption under a pre-1985 decree of divorce or separate maintenance or written agreement.

For purposes of 3(a), a similar statement includes a divorce decree or separation agreement that went into effect after 1984 that allows the noncustodial parent to claim the child's exemption without any conditions, such as payment of support.

You can use *Figure 33–B* to see whether this exception applies to you. If it applies, only the custodial parent can treat the child as a qualifying person. If the exception does not apply, follow the regular rules for a qualifying person under *Qualifying Person Test,* earlier.

Example. You are divorced and have custody of your 8-year-old child. You sign Form 8332 to allow your ex-spouse to take the exemption. You pay child care expenses so you can work. Your child is a qualifying person and you, the custodial parent, can claim the credit for those expenses, even though your ex-spouse claims an exemption for the child.

Custodial parent. You are the custodial parent if, during the year, you have custody of your child longer than your child's other parent has custody.

Explanation

To take the credit, you do not necessarily have to claim the child as a dependent. If you have custody of the child even though you have signed a statement that entitles your ex-spouse to the child's dependency exemption, you may still claim the credit. To receive the credit, however, you must write your child's name on line 2 of Form 2441, or Schedule 2 of Form 1040A. To avoid questions from the IRS, you may want to attach to your tax return a copy of the signed statement authorizing the release of your dependency claim.

Example

Charles and Margaret Collins are divorced and share custody of their 3-year-old son, Alan. Alan lives 10 months a year with Margaret and attends a day-care center while his mother works. Charles and Margaret provide all of Alan's support. Alan is a qualifying person, since he is under age 13, is in the custody of his parents for more than half the year, and receives more than half his support from his parents. He is a qualifying person for Margaret and not Charles because Margaret has custody of him for a longer period than does Charles. Alan is a qualifying person for Margaret, even if she has released her right to claim him as a dependent to Charles.

In no case may two taxpayers filing separate returns claim separate tax credits for the same qualifying individual.

Divorced or separated. For purposes of determining whether your child is a qualifying person, you are considered divorced or separated if *either* of the following applies.

1) You are divorced or separated under a decree of divorce or separate maintenance or a written separation agreement.
2) You lived apart from your spouse for all of the last 6 months of the year.

Keeping Up a Home Test

To claim the credit, you must keep up a home. You and one or more qualifying persons must live in the home.

You are keeping up a home if you (and your spouse if you are married) pay more than half the cost of running it for the year.

Home. The home you keep up must be the main home for both you and the qualifying person. Your home can be the qualifying person's main home even if he or she does not live there all year because of his or her:

1) Birth,
2) Death, or
3) Temporary absence due to:
   a) Sickness,
   b) School,
   c) Business,
   d) Vacation,
   e) Military service, or
   f) Custody agreement.

Costs of keeping up home. The costs of keeping up a home normally include property taxes, *mortgage interest,* rent, utility charges, home repairs, insurance on the home, and food eaten at home.

Costs not included. The costs of keeping up a home do not include payments for clothing, education, medical treatment, vacations, life insurance, transportation, or *mortgage principal.*

They also do not include the purchase, permanent improvement, or replacement of property. For example, you cannot include the cost of replacing a water heater. However, you can include the cost of repairing a water heater.

Explanation

It is not sufficient that you maintain a household without also living there. If more than one family occupies living quarters in common, each family constitutes a separate household.

Example 1

Ann Bailey and her children and Monica Stewart and her children share a house. Both Ann and Monica provide more than half the costs of maintaining their respective families. Each is treated as maintaining a household.

Example 2

Ruth Martin is the 10-year-old daughter of Lynne Martin. She lives with her mother, who provides more than half the costs of running their home. During the summer, Ruth spends 3 months with her father. Her absence does not prevent Lynne's home from being Ruth's residence.

Earned Income Test

To claim the credit, you (and your spouse if you are married) must have earned income during the year.

Earned income. Earned income includes wages, salaries, tips, other employee compensation, and net earnings from self-employment. A net loss from self-employment reduces earned income. Earned income also includes strike benefits and any disability pay you report as wages.

Certain nontaxable earned income included. It also includes nontaxable earned income such as parsonage allowances, meals and lodging furnished for the convenience of the employer, voluntary salary deferrals, military basic quarters and subsistence allowances and in-kind quarters and subsistence, and military pay earned in a combat zone.

Members of certain religious faiths opposed to social security. Certain income earned by persons who are members of certain religious faiths that are opposed to participation in Social Security Act Programs and have an IRS-approved form that exempts certain income from social security and Medicare taxes may not be considered earned income for this purpose. See *Earned Income Test* in Publication 503.

Not earned income. Earned income does not include pensions or annuities, social security payments, workers' compensation, interest, dividends, or unemployment compensation. It also does not include schol-

Figure 33–B. **Is a Child of Divorced or Separated Parents a Qualifying Person?**

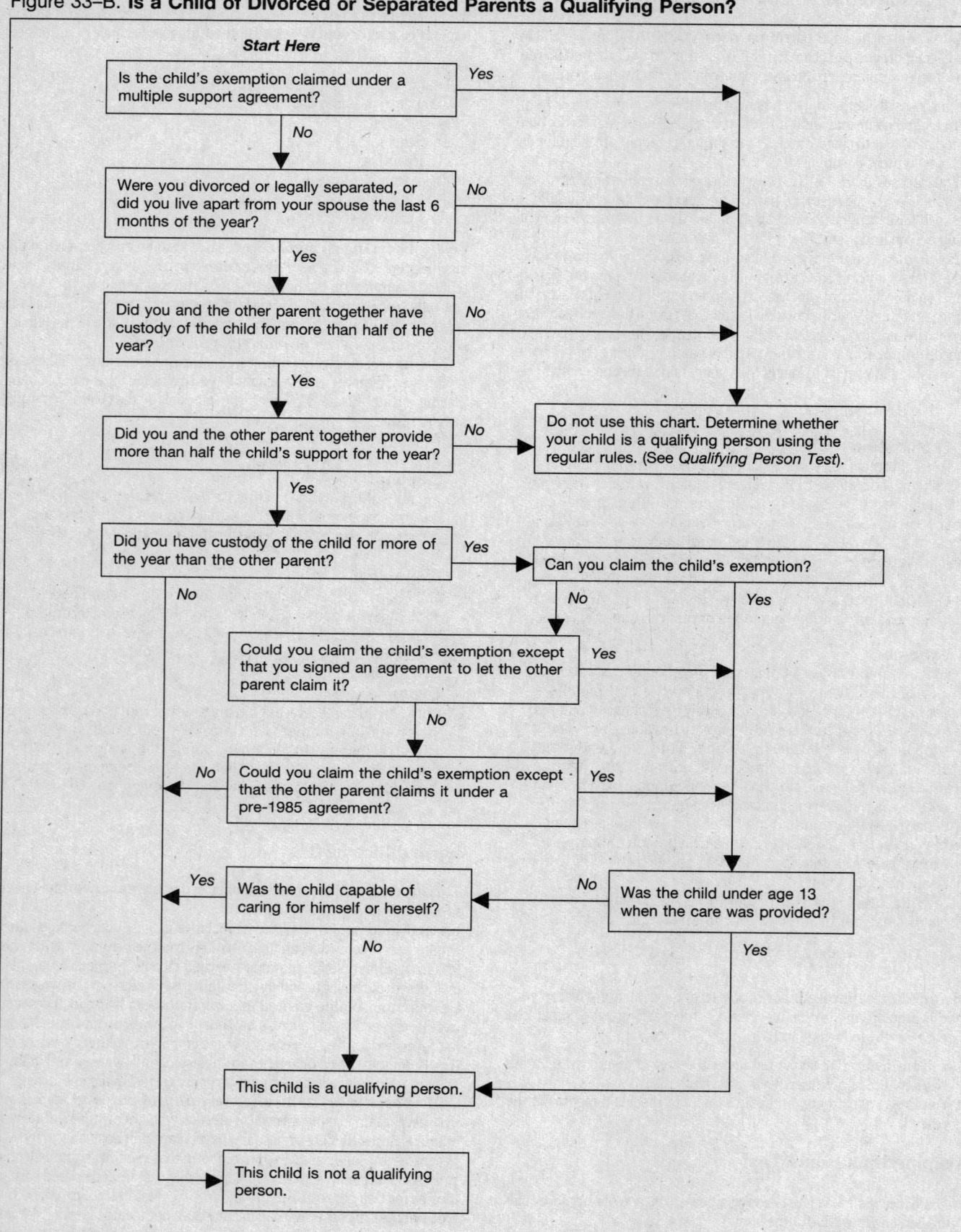

arship or fellowship grants, except amounts paid to you (and reported on Form W-2) for teaching, research, or other services.

Rule for student-spouse or spouse not able to care for self. Your spouse is treated as having earned income for any month that he or she is:

1) A full-time student, or
2) Physically or mentally not able to care for himself or herself.

Figure the earned income of the nonworking spouse described under (1) or (2) above as explained under *Earned Income Limit,* later.

This rule applies to only one spouse for any one month. If, in the same month, both you and your spouse do not work and are either full-time students or physically or mentally not able to care for yourselves, only one of you can be treated as having earned income in that month.

Full-time student. You are a full-time student if you are enrolled at and attend a school for the number of hours or classes that the school considers full time. You must have been a student for some part of each of 5 calendar months during the year. (The months need not be consecutive.) If you attend school only at night, you are not a full-time student. However, as part of your full-time course of study, you may attend some night classes.

School. The term "school" includes elementary schools, junior and senior high schools, colleges, universities, and technical, trade, and mechanical schools. It does not include on-the-job training courses, correspondence schools, and night schools.

Example

James and Janet are married and file a joint return. Janet works full-time. James was a full-time student from January through May and from September through December. Their 4-year-old son attends a day-care center while James is in school. Since James was a full-time student during at least 5 months of the year, the minimum required by the IRS, he is considered to have worked each of the 9 months he was a full-time student.

Assume the same facts, except that both James and Janet were full-time students for 9 months during the year. Only one of them may be considered as having worked during the months they were students. They would not be able to claim a credit for child care expenses.

Assume instead that while James and Janet were full-time students, James also held a part-time job. Both may now be considered as having worked during the 9 months they were students—James because he was working and Janet because she was a full-time student. They may claim a credit for child care expenses.

Work-Related Expense Test

Child and dependent care expenses must be work related to qualify for the credit. Expenses are considered work related only if both of the following are true.

- They allow you (and your spouse if you are married) to work or look for work.
- They are for a qualifying person's care.

Working or Looking for Work

To be work related, your expenses must allow you to work or look for work. If you are married, generally both you and your spouse must work or look for work. Your spouse is treated as working during any month he or she is a full-time student or is physically or mentally not able to care for himself or herself.

Your work can be for others or in your own business or partnership. It can be either full time or part time.

Work also includes actively looking for work. However, if you do not find a job and have no earned income for the year, you cannot take this credit. See *Earned Income Test,* earlier.

Whether your expenses allow you to work or look for work depends on the facts. For example, the cost of a sitter while you and your spouse go out to eat is not normally a work-related expense.

An expense is not considered work related merely because you had it while you were working. The purpose of the expense must be to enable you to work.

Volunteer work. You are not gainfully employed if you do unpaid volunteer work or volunteer work for a nominal salary.

Example 1

Susan Green is single. She began looking for a job in November 2001. Prior to this time, she had not worked. While looking for a job, she paid a sitter to watch her 4-year-old daughter. She finally found a job in February 2002. Her child care expenses during November and December 2001 were $125. Since Susan did not have income from work in 2001, she may not claim a credit for her child care expenses for that year.

Assume the same facts, except that Susan had worked until October 2001 when she was laid off and began looking for a new job. In this instance, she did have income from work during the year, so she may claim a credit for her child care expenses incurred while looking for work.

Example 2

Mary Smith works 12 hours per week as an unpaid volunteer in the library of the local elementary school. She pays a sitter to watch her 3-year-old twins while she is working. Since she is not compensated for her work, she may not claim a credit for her child care expenses.

If Mary were paid $15 per week for her services in the library, she still could not claim a credit for her child care expenses because her work is for a nominal salary. What is considered a nominal salary is determined by the facts and circumstances of each situation. As a general rule, however, if you are working for less than the minimum wage, you are probably working for a nominal salary.

Work for part of year. If you work or actively look for work during only part of the period covered by the expenses, then you must figure your expenses for each day. For example, if you work all year and pay care expenses of $200 a month ($2,400 for the year), all the expenses are work related. However, if you work or look for work for only 2 months and 15 days during the year and pay expenses of $200 a month, your work-related expenses are limited to $500 a month (2 1/2 months × $200).

Payments while you are out sick. Do not count as work-related expenses amounts you pay for child and dependent care while you are off work because of illness. These amounts are not paid to allow you to work. This applies even if you get sick pay and are still considered an employee.

Example

Samantha Street, a single parent, has a housekeeper on weekdays to watch her 9-year-old daughter while Samantha works. She pays the housekeeper $1,000 a month. As a result of illness, Samantha was home 10 business days during September. Samantha's work-related expenses for the month are $500 [(10 workdays ÷ 20 business days in September) × $1,000].

If you know that your total work-related expenses for the year will exceed the limits, it is not necessary to perform this calculation.

Care of a Qualifying Person

To be work related, your expenses must be to provide care for a qualifying person. You do not have to choose the least expensive way of providing the care.

Expenses are for the care of a qualifying person only if their main purpose is the person's well-being and protection.

Expenses for *household services* qualify if part of the services is for the care of qualifying persons. See *Household services,* later.

Expenses not for care. Expenses for care do not include amounts you pay for food, clothing, education, and entertainment. However, you can include small amounts paid for these items if they are incident to and cannot be separated from the cost of caring for the qualifying person.

Education. Expenses to attend first grade or a higher grade are not expenses for care. Do not use these expenses to figure your credit.

Explanation
You can use the total cost of schooling below first grade only if the cost of schooling cannot be separated from the cost of the child's care.

Example 1. You take your 3-year-old child to a nursery school that provides lunch and educational activities as a part of its preschool child-care service. You can count the total cost when you figure the credit.

Example 2. You place your 10-year-old child in a boarding school so you can work full time. Only the part of the boarding school expense that is for the care of your child is a work-related expense. You can count that part of the expense in figuring your credit if it can be separated from the cost of education. You cannot count any part of the amount you pay the school for your child's education.

Care outside your home. You can count the cost of care provided outside your home if the care is for your dependent under age 13 or any other qualifying person who regularly spends at least 8 hours each day in your home.

Dependent care center. You can count care provided outside your home by a dependent care center only if the center complies with all state and local regulations that apply to these centers.

A dependent care center is a place that provides care for more than six persons (other than persons who live there) and receives a fee, payment, or grant for providing services for any of those persons, even if the center is not run for profit.

Explanation
If a care center has six or fewer individuals enrolled on the day on which you enroll a qualified person, you may presume that it is not a dependent care center for the tax year. You may also presume that if a center was not a dependent care center in the prior year and has six or fewer individuals enrolled on January 1, it will not be considered a dependent care center during the current year.

As the IRS text notes, if care is provided by a dependent care center, the center must meet local and state regulations for your expenses to qualify for the credit. For example, most states stipulate the maximum permissible ratio of children to adult workers in a day-care center. You may wish to inquire at a center if it meets all state and local regulations. Ask to see a copy of the center's most recent cer-

tification from the proper authorities. However, if care is provided by a center that is not a dependent care center, the center need not meet local and state regulations for your expenses to qualify for the credit.

Example
Sam Anderson attends a child care center during the week while his mother works. The center regularly cares for 15 children and does not meet local and state regulations. The center is a dependent care center, but since the center does not meet the appropriate government regulations, expenses for Sam's care do not qualify for the tax credit.

Assume the same facts, except that the center regularly cares for five children. Now the center is not a dependent care center. Expenses for Sam's care qualify for the tax credit, although the center does not meet government regulations.

Camp. The cost of sending your child to an overnight camp is *not* considered a work-related expense.

Transportation. The cost of getting a qualifying person from your home to the care location and back, or from the care location to school and back, is *not* considered a work-related expense. This includes the costs of bus, subway, taxi, or private car. Also, if you pay the transportation cost for the care provider to come to your home, you cannot count this cost as a work-related expense.

Household services. Expenses you pay for household services meet the work-related expense test if they are at least partly for the well-being and protection of a qualifying person.

Household services are ordinary and usual services done in and around your home that are necessary to run your home. They include the services of a housekeeper, maid, or cook. However, they do not include the services of a chauffeur, bartender, or gardener. See *Household Services* in Publication 503 for more information.

▮ TAX PLANNER

Allocating expenses. There are no hard-and-fast rules that govern when an allocation is reasonable or when the expense for other services is small in relation to the total expense. The facts and circumstances of each case are the determining factors. Use your best judgment. If you must make an allocation, you should document how the allocation is made. If you decide that an allocation is not necessary, you should also document the basis for your decision. A note in your personal records should be sufficient.

In this chapter, the term housekeeper refers to any household employee whose services include the care of a qualifying person.

Taxes paid on wages. The taxes you pay on wages for qualifying child and dependent care services are work-related expenses.

Explanation
See Chapter 41, *What to Do if You Employ Domestic Help.*

Payments to Relatives

You can count work-related payments you make to relatives who are not your dependents, even if they live in your home. However, do not count any amounts you pay to:

1) A dependent for whom you (or your spouse if you are married) can claim an exemption, or
2) Your child who was under age 19 at the end of the year, even if he or she is not your dependent.

> **Example**
> Georgia Stephens lives with her daughter Sara and cares for her granddaughter Marie after school while Sara is at work. Sara pays her mother $300 per month and cannot claim her as a dependent. These payments qualify as work-related expenses for Sara.
>
> Assume, instead, that Sara pays her other daughter, Frances, $150 per month to look after Marie, Frances's sister. Frances turns 19 during the year and can be claimed as a dependent by Sara. Sara's payments to Frances are not qualified work-related expenses.

Joint Return Test

Generally, married couples must file a joint return to take the credit. However, if you are legally separated or living apart from your spouse, you may be able to file a separate return and still take the credit.

Legally separated. You are not considered married if you are legally separated from your spouse under a decree of divorce or separate maintenance. You are eligible to take the credit on a separate return.

Married and living apart. You are not considered married and are eligible to take the credit if *all* the following apply.

1) You file a separate return.
2) Your home is the home of a qualifying person for more than half the year.
3) You pay more than half the cost of keeping up your home for the year.
4) Your spouse does not live in your home for the last 6 months of the year.

> **Example**
> Mark and Katherine Bristol separated in April. They are not **legally separated** at the end of the year and plan to file separate returns. Their two children lived with Katherine for the entire year, and she provided more than half the costs of maintaining her household for the year. Katherine may claim a credit on her separate return.
>
> Assume, instead, that Mark and Katherine were separated in August. Since Mark lived in Katherine's home during part of the last 6 months of the year, a joint return must be filed to claim the credit.

Death of spouse. If your spouse died during the year and you do not remarry before the end of the year, you generally must file a joint return to take the credit. If you do remarry before the end of the year, the credit can be claimed on your deceased spouse's separate return.

Provider Identification Test

You must identify all persons or organizations that provide care for your child or dependent. Use Part I of Form 2441 or Schedule 2 (Form 1040A) to show the information.

Information needed. To identify the care provider, you must give the provider's:

1) Name,
2) Address, and
3) Taxpayer identification number.

If the care provider is an individual, the taxpayer identification number is his or her social security number or individual taxpayer identification number. If the care provider is an organization, then it is the employer identification number (EIN).

You do not have to show the taxpayer identification number if the care provider is one of certain tax-exempt organizations (such as a church or school). In this case, write "Tax-Exempt" in the space where the tax form calls for the number.

If you cannot provide all of the information or if the information you provide is incorrect you must be able to show that you used due diligence (discussed later) in trying to furnish the necessary information.

Getting the information. You can use **Form W-10** to request the required information from the care provider. If you do not use Form W-10, you can get the information from:

1) A copy of the provider's social security card,
2) A copy of the provider's driver's license (in a state where the license includes the social security number),
3) A copy of the provider's completed Form W-4 if he or she is your household employee,
4) A copy of the statement furnished by your employer if the provider is your employer's dependent care plan, or
5) A letter or invoice from the provider if it shows the information.

> **Explanation**
> Also see *Records You Need* in Chapter 41, *What to Do if You Employ Domestic Help,* if the care provider does not have a Social Security number.

Recordkeeping. You should keep this information with your tax records. Do not send Form W-10 (or other document containing this information) to the Internal Revenue Service.

> **Explanation**
> Keep Form W-10 with your tax records to substantiate the name, address, and taxpayer identification number(s) of your day-care provider(s). If Form W-10 is not used, keep any other documents that substantiate the required information.

Due diligence. If the care provider information you give is incorrect or incomplete, your credit may not be allowed. However, if you can show that you used due diligence in trying to supply the information, you can still claim the credit.

You can show due diligence by getting and keeping the provider's completed Form W-10 or one of the other sources of information listed earlier. Care providers can be penalized if they do not provide this information to you or if they provide incorrect information.

Provider refusal. If the provider refuses to give you their identifying information, you should report whatever information you have (such as the name and address) on the form you use to claim the credit. Write "See page 2" in the columns calling for the information you do not have. On the bottom of page 2, explain that you requested the information from the care provider, but the provider did not give you the information. This statement will show that you used due diligence in trying to furnish the necessary information.

How To Figure the Credit

Your credit is a percentage of your work-related expenses. Your expenses are subject to the earned income limit and the dollar limit. The percentage is based on your adjusted gross income.

Figuring Total Work-Related Expenses

To figure the credit for 2001 work-related expenses, count only those you paid by December 31, 2001.

Expenses prepaid in an earlier year. If you pay for services before they are provided, you can count the prepaid expenses only in the year the care is received. Claim the expenses for the later year as if they were actually paid in that later year.

Example

Martha Winters paid $1,800 in November 2001 to the daycare center her son attends. The payment was for the 6-month period from November 2001 through April 2002. She may use $600 (2/6 × $1,800) of this payment in calculating her credit for 2001. This amount represents payment for services rendered in November and December 2001. She may use $1,200 (4/6 × $1,800) of this payment in 2002. This amount represents payment for services rendered in January through April 2002.

Expenses not paid until the following year. Do *not* count 2000 expenses that you paid in 2001 as work-related expenses for 2001. You may be able to claim an additional credit for them on your 2001 return, but you must figure it separately. See *Payments for previous year's expenses* under *Amount of Credit* in Publication 503.

Tip. *If you had expenses in 2001 that you did not pay until 2002, you cannot count them when figuring your 2001 credit. You may be able to claim a credit for them on your 2002 return.*

TAXPLANNER

The general rule is that expenses used in computing your child care credit are included in figuring your tax for the year in which the expenses are paid or for the year in which the services are provided, whichever is later. However, regardless of when they are paid, expenses are subject to the dollar limitation for the year in which the services are provided. You may not reap an additional tax advantage by paying your expenses in a year that is different from the one in which the services are provided.

Example

Jennifer Reid, who is divorced and files a separate return, paid $300 in January 2001 for care provided for her daughter in November and December 2000. Her adjusted gross income and earned income in 2000 were $25,000, and she paid $1,200 for work-related expenses in 2000. Jennifer may increase her 2001 child care credit by $66 (as calculated in Column A below).

	Column A	Column B
1) 2000 expenses paid in 2000	$ 1,200	$ 2,500
2) 2000 expenses paid in 2001	300	300
3) Total 2000 expenses	$ 1,500	$ 2,800
4) Limitation for one qualifying person	$ 2,400	$ 2,400
5) Earned income limitation	25,000	25,000
6) Smallest of lines 3, 4, and 5	1,500	2,400
7) Child care expenses used in calculating 2000 credit	(1,200)	(2,400)
8) 2000 expenses carried over to 2001	$ 300	$ -0-

---

9) Credit percentage applicable for 2000 adjusted gross income	22%	22%
10) Increase in 2001 credit (line 8 × line 9)	$ 66	$ -0-

Jennifer should attach a statement to her 2001 return, showing the above calculation in Column A as support for her inclusion of $66 on line 9, Form 2441.

Assume, instead, that Jennifer paid $2,500 in work-related expenses during 2000. No increase in her 2001 credit is available (see Column B above), since the maximum amount of expenses for 2000 is already used in calculating the credit. She receives no benefit for the $300 paid in 2001, as she would have received no benefit if it had been paid in 2000.

Expenses reimbursed. If a state social services agency pays you a nontaxable amount to reimburse you for some of your child and dependent care expenses, you cannot count the expenses that are reimbursed as work-related expenses.

Example. You paid work-related expenses of $3,000. You are reimbursed $2,000 by a state social services agency. You can use only $1,000 to figure your credit.

Medical expenses. Some expenses for the care of qualifying persons who are not able to care for themselves may qualify as work-related expenses and also as medical expenses. You can use them either way, but you cannot use the same expenses to claim both a credit and a medical expense deduction.

If you use these expenses to figure the credit and they are more than the earned income limit or the dollar limit, discussed later, you can add the excess to your medical expenses. However, if you use your total expenses to figure your medical expense deduction, you cannot use any part of them to figure your credit.

Example

During the year, you pay $2,750 to a private-duty nurse for the care of your physically handicapped dependent daughter, who is not able to care for herself. These expenses are for work done in your home and qualify as medical expenses. Your earned income for the year is $25,000. Because your work-related expenses are for one qualifying person, you may take a maximum of $2,400 of these expenses into account in figuring your tax credit. You may treat the remaining $350 as a medical expense.

Caution. *Amounts excluded from your income under your employer's dependent care benefits plan **cannot** be used to claim a medical expense deduction.*

Explanation

Keep copies of receipts and cancelled checks to document the amount of dependent care expenses that you paid for the year. The fact that you have provided these to your employer's plan may not be sufficient without such records.

Employer-Provided Dependent Care Benefits

Dependent care benefits include:

1) Amounts your employer pays directly to either you or your care provider for the care of your qualifying person while you work, and

2) The fair market value of care in a day-care facility provided or sponsored by your employer.

Your salary may have been reduced to pay for these benefits. If you received benefits, they should be shown on your W-2 form. See *Statement for employee,* later.

Exclusion. If your employer provides dependent care benefits under a qualified plan, you may be able to exclude these benefits from your income. Your employer can tell you whether your benefit plan qualifies. If it does, you must complete Part III of either Form 2441 or Schedule 2 (Form 1040A) to claim the exclusion even if you cannot take the credit. You cannot use Form 1040EZ.

The amount you can exclude is limited to the smallest of:

1) The total amount of dependent care benefits you received during the year,
2) The total amount of qualified expenses you incurred during the year,
3) Your earned income,
4) Your spouse's earned income, or
5) $5,000 ($2,500 if married filing separately).

> **Explanation**
> You cannot claim any credit if your employer has reduced your income by the full $5,000 and you have been reimbursed the full $5,000. See *Reduced Dollar Limit* later.

> **TAXSAVER**
> Before you sign up for your employer's plan, you should determine which will give you the greater tax savings: the child care credit or excluding the expenses from earnings under your employer's plan.

Statement for employee. Your employer must give you a **Form W-2** (or similar statement), showing in box 10 the total amount of dependent care benefits provided to you during the year under a qualified plan. Your employer will also include any dependent care benefits over $5,000 in your wages shown in box 1 of your Form W-2.

Forfeitures. Forfeitures are amounts credited to your dependent care benefit account (flexible spending account) and included in the amount shown in box 10 of your Form W-2, but not received because you did not incur the expense. When figuring your exclusion, subtract any forfeitures from the total dependent care benefits reported by your employer. To do this, enter the forfeited amount on line 11 of Form 2441 or Schedule 2 (Form 1040A).

Caution. *Forfeitures do not include amounts that you expect to receive in the future.*

Effect of exclusion. If you exclude dependent care benefits from your income, the amount of the excluded benefits:

1) Is not included in your work-related expenses, and
2) Reduces the dollar limit, discussed later.

Earned Income Limit

The amount of work-related expenses you use to figure your credit cannot be more than:

1) Your earned income for the year if you are *single* at the end of the year, or
2) The smaller of your or your spouse's earned income for the year if you are *married* at the end of the year.

Earned income is defined under *Earned Income Test,* earlier.

Tip. *For purposes of item (2), use your spouse's earned income for the entire year, even if you were married for only part of the year.*

> **TAXPLANNER**
> At year-end, if you are self-employed, you should review your income and expenses for the year. To the extent it is possible, income and expenses for the remaining part of the year should be timed to take maximum advantage of the dependent care credit.

Separated spouse. If you are legally separated or married and living apart from your spouse (as described under *Joint Return Test,* earlier), you are not considered married for purposes of the earned income limit. Use only your income in figuring the earned income limit.

Surviving spouse. If your spouse died during the year and you file a joint return as a surviving spouse, you are not considered married for purposes of the earned income limit. Use only your income in figuring the earned income limit.

Community property laws. You should disregard community property laws when you figure earned income for this credit.

> **Example**
> Harry and Elizabeth Jones are married and live in a community property state. Harry earns $52,000 as an engineer, while Elizabeth earns $15,000 as a nurse. Under community property laws, each is considered to have earned half the other's compensation. Hence, each is considered to bring in $33,500 [(50% × $52,000) + (50% × $15,000)]. For the purpose of calculating this tax credit, however, Harry has $52,000 of earned income and Elizabeth has $15,000.

Student-spouse or spouse not able to care for self. Your spouse who is either a full-time student or not able to care for himself or herself is treated as having earned income. His or her earned income for each month is considered to be at least $200 if there is one qualifying person in your home, or at least $400 if there are two or more.

Spouse works. If your spouse works during that month, use the higher of $200 (or $400) or his or her actual earned income for that month.

Spouse qualifies for part of month. If your spouse is a full-time student or not able to care for himself or herself for only part of a month, the full $200 (or $400) still applies for that month.

Both spouses qualify. If, in the same month, both you and your spouse are either full-time students or not able to care for yourselves, only one spouse can be considered to have this earned income of $200 (or $400) for that month.

> **Example**
> Mary Smith works full-time as a real estate broker and earns $25,000. John Smith is a full-time medical student for 11 months during the year and has no earned income. They have a 5-year-old son whose day-care expenses for the year are $5,000. John is treated as earning $2,200 for the year ($200 per month for the 11 months he is a student). Their work-related expenses for the year may therefore not exceed $2,200.

Dollar Limit

There is a dollar limit on the amount of your work-related expenses you can use to figure the credit. This limit is $2,400 for one qualifying person, or $4,800 for two or more qualifying persons.

Yearly limit. The dollar limit is a yearly limit. The amount of the dollar limit remains the same no matter how long, during the year, you have a qualifying person in your household. Use the $2,400 limit if you paid work-related expenses for the care of one qualifying person at any time during the year. Use $4,800 if you paid work-related expenses for the care of more than one qualifying person at any time during the year.

> ### Example
> Patricia Ellis employs a full-time housekeeper to care for her two children while she works. Her older child turned 13 years old during the year. The dollar limit on her work-related expenses is $4,800, since at some time during the year she had two qualifying persons.
>
> Assume the same facts, except that Patricia has only one child, who turned 13 years old on August 31. The dollar limit on her work-related expenses is $2,400. Only her expenses through August 31 may be used. The limit is the maximum amount that may be used in calculating the credit. If her actual expenses through August are less than $2,400, she must use that amount in calculating her tax credit.

Reduced Dollar Limit

If you received dependent care benefits from your employer that you exclude from your income, you must subtract that amount from the dollar limit that applies to you. Your reduced dollar limit is figured on lines 20 through 24 of Form 2441 or Schedule 2 (Form 1040A). See *Employer-Provided Dependent Care Benefits,* earlier, for information on excluding these benefits.

Example. George is a widower with one child and earns $24,000 a year. He pays work-related expenses of $1,900 for the care of his 4-year-old child and qualifies to claim the credit for child and dependent care expenses. His employer pays an additional $1,000 under a dependent care benefit plan. This $1,000 is excluded from George's income.

Although the dollar limit for his work-related expenses is $2,400 (one qualifying person), George figures his credit on only $1,400 of the $1,900 work-related expenses he paid. This is because his dollar limit is reduced as shown next.

George's Reduced Dollar Limit

1) Maximum allowable expenses for one qualifying person	$2,400
2) *Minus:* Dependent care benefits George excludes from income	−1,000
3) Reduced dollar limit on expenses George can use for the credit	$1,400

Amount of Credit

To determine the amount of your credit, multiply your work-related expenses (after applying the earned income and dollar limits) by a percentage. This percentage depends on your adjusted gross income shown on line 34 of Form 1040 or line 19 of Form 1040A. The following table shows the percentage to use based on adjusted gross income.

IF your adjusted gross income is		THEN the percentage is
Over	**But not over**	
$0	$10,000	30%
10,000	12,000	29%
12,000	14,000	28%
14,000	16,000	27%
16,000	18,000	26%
18,000	20,000	25%
20,000	22,000	24%
22,000	24,000	23%
24,000	26,000	22%
26,000	28,000	21%
28,000	No limit	20%

> ### Example
> Nathan Smith is single, has adjusted gross income of $23,500, and has $1,800 in qualified expenses for 2001. The credit available to him is $414 (23% × $1,800).
>
> Assume, instead, that Nathan has adjusted gross income of $28,500. Now his available tax credit is $360 (20% × $1,800).

> ### Example
> Sharon White has a tax liability of $400 before credits and a potential child care credit of $720. She may use $400 of the child care credit to bring her tax liability to zero. The excess credit of $320 is effectively lost. It may not be refunded, carried forward to a future year, or carried back to a prior year.

How to Claim the Credit

To claim the credit, you can file Form 1040 or Form 1040A. You cannot claim the credit on Form 1040EZ.

Form 1040. You must complete **Form 2441** and attach it to your Form 1040. Enter the credit on line 44 of your Form 1040. An example of a filled-in Form 2441 is at the end of this chapter.

Form 1040A. You must complete **Schedule 2** (Form 1040A) and attach it to your Form 1040A. Enter the credit on line 27 of your Form 1040A.

Limit on credit. The amount of credit you can claim is limited to the amount of your regular tax (after reduction by any allowable foreign tax credit) plus your alternative minimum tax, if any. For more information, see the instructions for Form 2441 or Schedule 2 (Form 1040A).

Tax credit not refundable. You cannot get a refund for any part of the credit that is more than this limit.

Recordkeeping. You should keep records of your work-related expenses. Also, if your dependent or spouse is not able to care for himself or herself, your records should show both the nature and the length of the disability. Other records you should keep to support your claim for the credit are described earlier under *Provider Identification Test.*

> ### Explanation
> Your records of work-related expenses may be either cancelled checks or cash receipt tickets. A note in your files recording the nature and length of a person's disability should be sufficient documentation in most cases.

Example

The following example shows how to figure the credit for child and dependent care expenses for two children when employer dependent care benefits are involved. The filled-in Form 2441 is shown at the end of this chapter.

Illustrated example. Joan Thomas is divorced and has two children, ages 3 and 9. She works at ACME Computers. Her adjusted gross income (AGI) is $29,000, and the entire amount is earned income.

Joan's younger child (Susan) stays at her employer's on-site child-care center while she works. The benefits from this child-care center qualify to be excluded from her income. Her employer reports the value of this service as $3,000 for the year. This $3,000 is shown in box 10 of her Form W-2, but is not included in taxable wages in box 1.

A neighbor cares for Joan's older child (Seth) after school, on holidays, and during the summer. She pays her neighbor $2,400 for this care.

Joan figures her credit on Form 2441 as follows.

Work-related expenses Joan paid	$2,400
Dollar limit	$4,800
Minus: Dependent care benefits excluded from Joan's income	-3,000
Reduced dollar limit	$1,800
Lesser of expenses paid ($2,400) or dollar limit ($1,800)	$1,800
Percentage for AGI of $29,000	x .20
Amount of credit (20% of $1,800)	$ 360

Explanation

Note: The dollar limit for two or more qualifying persons ($4,800) is reduced by the amount of excluded benefits, as discussed earlier under *Reduced Dollar Limit.*

Example

Janice Johnson is single and works to keep up a home for herself and her dependent father. Her adjusted gross income of $25,000 is entirely earned income.

Her father was disabled and incapable of self-care for 6 months. To keep working, she paid a housekeeper $500 per month to care for her father, prepare lunch and dinner, and do housework.

Her credit is as follows:

Total work-related expenses (6 × $500)	$3,000
Maximum allowable expenses	$2,400
Amount of credit (22% of $2,400)	$ 528

TaxAlert

As stated earlier under *Qualifying Person Test*, if the dependent for whom you have work-related expenses is dis-

abled for only part of a month, the total work-related expenses are limited to that part of the month.

Example 1

Diane and Richard are married and file a joint return. Because of an accident, Richard is incapable of self-care for the entire tax year. To keep working, Diane pays a neighbor $2,000 to take care of him. Diane's adjusted gross income is $29,000. The entire amount is earned income.

They figure their credit on the smallest of the following amounts:

1) Total work-related expenses	$ 2,000
2) Diane's earned income	$29,000
3) Income considered earned by Richard (12 × $200)	$ 2,400
Allowable credit (20% of $2,000)	$ 400

Example 2

John Harris works and keeps up a home for himself, his wife Peggy, and their two children (both under age 13). John has adjusted gross income of $35,000. The entire amount is earned income.

Peggy is a full-time student at State University from January 4 through June 10. She does not return to school after June 10.

They paid a neighbor $500 per month from January 4 to June 10 (total $3,000) to care for their two children in her home while the children are not in school.

They figure the credit on the smallest of the following amounts:

1) Total work-related expenses	$ 3,000
2) John's earned income	$35,000
3) Income considered earned by Peggy (6 × $400)	$ 2,400
Allowable credit (20% of $2,400)	$ 480

Form **2441**

Department of the Treasury
Internal Revenue Service

Child and Dependent Care Expenses

▶ Attach to Form 1040.

▶ See separate instructions.

OMB No. 1545-0068

2001

Attachment
Sequence No. **21**

Name(s) shown on Form 1040

Joan Thomas

Your social security number

559 : 00 : 3436

Before you begin: You need to understand the following terms. See **Definitions** on page 1 of the instructions.

● **Dependent Care Benefits**   ● **Qualifying Person(s)**   ● **Qualified Expenses**   ● **Earned Income**

Part I	Persons or Organizations Who Provided the Care—You **must** complete this part. (If you need more space, use the bottom of page 2.)

1	**(a)** Care provider's name	**(b)** Address (number, street, apt. no., city, state, and ZIP code)	**(c)** Identifying number (SSN or EIN)	**(d)** Amount paid (see instructions)
	Pat Green	12 Ash Avenue Hometown, TX 75240	240-00-3811	2,400
	ACME Computers	(See W-2)		

Did you receive **dependent care benefits?**

No ──────▶ Complete only Part II below.

Yes ──────▶ Complete Part III on the back next.

Caution. If the care was provided in your home, you may owe employment taxes. See the instructions for Form 1040, line 57.

Part II	Credit for Child and Dependent Care Expenses

2 Information about your **qualifying person(s)**. If you have more than two qualifying persons, see the instructions.

(a) Qualifying person's name — First	Last	**(b)** Qualifying person's social security number	**(c)** Qualified expenses you incurred and paid in 2001 for the person listed in column (a)
Seth	Thomas	559 : 00 : 1234	2,400
Susan	Thomas	559 : 00 : 5678	

3 Add the amounts in column (c) of line 2. **Do not** enter more than $2,400 for one qualifying person or $4,800 for two or more persons. If you completed Part III, enter the amount from line 24 . . . . **3**   1,800

4 Enter your **earned income** **4**   29,000

5 If married filing a joint return, enter your spouse's earned income (if your spouse was a student or was disabled, see the instructions); **all others,** enter the amount from line 4 . . . . . . **5**   29,000

6 Enter the **smallest** of line 3, 4, or 5 . . . . . **6**   1,800

7 Enter the amount from Form 1040, line 34 . . . . **7**   29,000

8 Enter on line 8 the decimal amount shown below that applies to the amount on line 7

If line 7 is:			If line 7 is:		
Over	**But not over**	**Decimal amount is**	**Over**	**But not over**	**Decimal amount is**
$0	10,000	.30	$20,000	22,000	.24
10,000	12,000	.29	22,000	24,000	.23
12,000	14,000	.28	24,000	26,000	.22
14,000	16,000	.27	26,000	28,000	.21
16,000	18,000	.26	28,000	No limit	.20
18,000	20,000	.25			

8   × . 20

9 Multiply **line 6** by the decimal amount on line 8. Enter the result here and on Form 1040, line 44. But if this amount is more than the amount on Form 1040, line 42, minus any amount on line 43, **or** you paid 2000 expenses in 2001, see the instructions for the amount to enter on line 44 . . . . **9**   360

For Paperwork Reduction Act Notice, see page 3 of the instructions.   Cat. No. 11862M   Form **2441** (2001)

Part III Dependent Care Benefits

10 Enter the total amount of **dependent care benefits** you received for 2001. This amount should be shown in box 10 of your W-2 form(s). **Do not** include amounts that were reported to you as wages in box 1 of Form(s) W-2	10	3,000
11 Enter the amount forfeited, if any. See the instructions	11	
12 Subtract line 11 from line 10	12	3,000

13 Enter the total amount of **qualified expenses** incurred in 2001 for the care of the **qualifying person(s)**. . .	13	5,400		
14 Enter the **smaller** of line 12 or 13	14	3,000		
15 Enter your **earned income**	15	29,000		
16 If married filing a joint return, enter your spouse's earned income (if your spouse was a student or was disabled, see the instructions for line 5); if married filing a separate return, see the instructions for the amount to enter; **all others,** enter the amount from line 15	16	29,000		
17 Enter the **smallest** of line 14, 15, or 16.	17	3,000		

18 **Excluded benefits.** Enter here the **smaller** of the following:

- The amount from line 17 or
- $5,000 ($2,500 if married filing a separate return **and** you were required to enter your spouse's earned income on line 16).

. . . .	18	3,000
19 **Taxable benefits.** Subtract line 18 from line 12. Also, include this amount on Form 1040, line 7. On the dotted line next to line 7, enter "DCB"	19	-0-

To claim the child and dependent care
credit, complete lines 20–24 below.

20 Enter $2,400 ($4,800 if two or more qualifying persons)	20	4,800
21 Enter the amount from line 18.	21	3,000
22 Subtract line 21 from line 20. If zero or less, **stop.** You cannot take the credit. **Exception.** If you paid 2000 expenses in 2001, see the instructions for line 9	22	1,800
23 Complete line 2 on the front of this form. **Do not** include in column (c) any benefits shown on line 18 above. Then, add the amounts in column (c) and enter the total here . . .	23	2,400
24 Enter the **smaller** of line 22 or 23. Also, enter this amount on line 3 on the front of this form and complete lines 4–9	24	1,800

Form **2441** (2001)

34

Credit for the Elderly or the Disabled

Introduction

When Congress passed legislation giving the elderly a tax credit, the idea was to provide a measure of tax relief for older citizens who were not receiving adequate amounts of Social Security or other nontaxable **pensions.** *Consequently, if you or your spouse is 65 years old or older, you may be entitled to a credit of as much as $1,125 against your tax.*

Taxpayers under 65 years of age who are permanently and totally disabled may also be eligible for the credit.

In general, if you file as a **single** *individual, you do* **not** *qualify for the tax credit if (1) you receive nontaxable Social Security or other nontaxable pensions of $5,000 or more, (2) your* **adjusted gross income** *is $17,500 or more, or (3) your tax is zero.*

This chapter tells you specifically if you are eligible for the credit for the elderly and, if so, how you may claim it—whether you are single or married.

If you qualify, the law provides a number of credits that can reduce the tax you owe for a year. One of these credits is the credit for the elderly or the disabled.

This chapter explains:

- Who qualifies for the credit for the elderly or the disabled, and
- How to figure this credit.

The maximum credit available is $1,125. You may be able to take this credit if you are:

- Age 65 or older, or
- Retired on permanent and total disability.

Useful Items

You may want to see:

Publication

- ☐ **524** Credit for the Elderly or the Disabled
- ☐ **554** Older Americans' Tax Guide
- ☐ **967** The IRS Will Figure Your Tax

Forms (and Instructions)

- ☐ **Schedule 3 (Form 1040A)** Credit for the Elderly or the Disabled for Form 1040A Filers
- ☐ **Schedule R (Form 1040)** Credit for the Elderly or the Disabled

Explanation
See Chapter 12, *Social Security and Equivalent Railroad Retirement Benefits,* for a discussion of how Social Security and equivalent railroad retirement benefits are taxed.

Can You Take the Credit?

You can take the credit for the elderly or the disabled if you meet *both* of the following requirements.

1) You are a *qualified individual.*
2) Your income is not more than certain limits.

Figure 34–A. **Are You a Qualified Individual?**

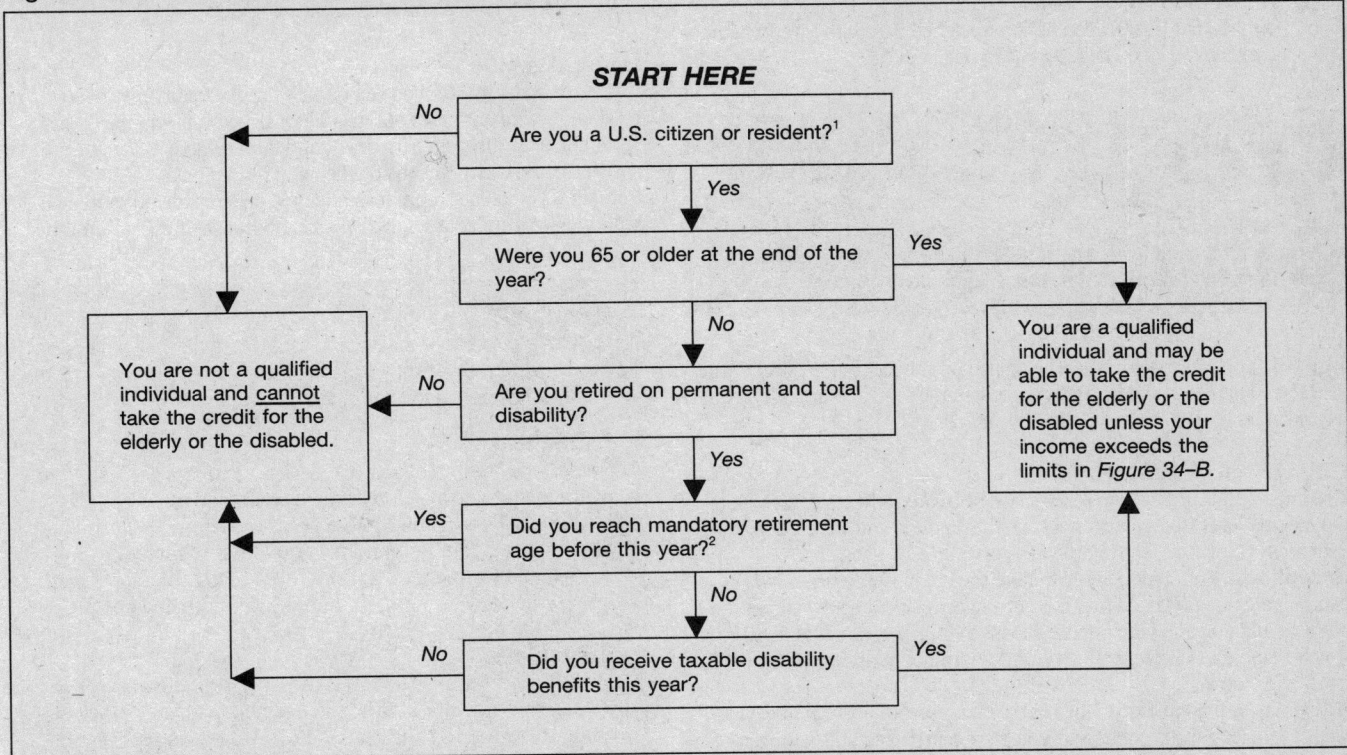

[1]If you were a nonresident alien at any time during the tax year and were married to a U.S. citizen or resident at the end of the tax year, see *U.S. Citizen or Resident* under *Qualified Individual.* If you and your spouse choose to treat you as a U.S. resident, answer "yes" to this question.
[2]Mandatory retirement age is the age set by your employer at which you would have been required to retire, had you not become disabled.

Figure 34–B. **Income Limits**

IF your filing status is ...	THEN even if you qualify (see *Figure 34–A*), you CANNOT take the credit if ...	
	Your adjusted gross income (AGI)* is equal to or more than ...	OR your nontaxable social security and other nontaxable pension(s) is equal to or more than ...
Single, Head of household, or Qualifying widow(er) with dependent child	$17,500	$5,000
Married filing a joint return *and* both spouses qualify in *Figure 34–A*	$25,000	$7,500
Married filing a joint return *and* only one spouse qualifies in *Figure 34–A*	$20,000	$5,000
Married filing a separate return *and* you did not live with your spouse at any time during the year	$12,500	$3,750

*AGI is the amount on Form 1040A, line 19, or Form 1040, line 34.

You can use *Figure 34-A* and *Figure 34-B* as guides to see if you qualify.

Use *Figure 34-A* first to see if you are a qualified individual. If you are, go to *Figure 34-B* to make sure your income is not too high to take the credit.

Tip. *You can take the credit only if you file Form 1040 or Form 1040A. You cannot take the credit if you file Form 1040EZ.*

Qualified Individual

You are a qualified individual for this credit if you are a U.S. citizen or resident and either of the following applies.

1) You were age 65 or older at the end of 2001.
2) You were under age 65 at the end of 2001 and all three of the following statements are true.

a) You retired on permanent and total disability (explained later).
b) You received taxable disability income for 2001.
c) On January 1, 2001, you had not reached mandatory retirement age (defined later under *Disability Income*).

Explanation
To qualify for the credit, you cannot have reached your employer's mandatory retirement age before the beginning of the year. The reason for the requirement is that any amount received from your employer *after* you have reached mandatory retirement age is *not* disability income.

Age 65. You are considered to be age 65 on the day before your 65th birthday. Therefore, you are 65 at the end of the year if your 65th birthday is on January 1 of the following year.

U.S. Citizen or Resident
You must be a U.S. citizen or resident (or be treated as a resident) to take the credit. Generally, you cannot take the credit if you were a nonresident alien at any time during the tax year.

Exceptions. You may be able to take the credit if you are a nonresident alien who is married to a U.S. citizen or resident at the end of the tax year and you and your spouse choose to treat you as a U.S. resident. If you make that choice, both you and your spouse are taxed on your worldwide income.

If you were a nonresident alien at the beginning of the year and a resident at the end of the year, and you were married to a U.S. citizen or resident at the end of the year, you may be able to choose to be treated as a U.S. resident for the entire year. In that case, you may be allowed to take the credit. For information on these choices, see chapter 1 of Publication 519, *U.S. Tax Guide for Aliens.*

Explanation
For more information about nonresident aliens, see Chapter 43, *Foreign Citizens Living in the United States.*

Married Persons
Generally, if you are married at the end of the tax year, you and your spouse must file a joint return to take the credit. However, if you and your spouse did not live in the same household at any time during the tax year, you can file either joint or separate returns and still take the credit.

Example 1
Tom and Betsy Fitch are both past the age of 65 and are married at year's end, but they have been living apart since May. They must file a joint return to claim the credit. Next year, if they remain married and live apart for the entire year, they may file separate returns and claim the credit.

Example 2
George and Sylvia Thompson are married at year's end and have lived apart for the entire year. Sylvia is 63 years old and receives a disability pension from her former employer. George is 69 years old. They may file separate returns, and each may claim a credit, since both meet the basic tests for eligibility.

Head of household. You can file as head of household and qualify to take the credit, even if your spouse lived with you during the first 6 months of the year, if you meet all the tests. See *Head of Household* in chapter 2 for the tests you must meet.

Under Age 65
If you are under age 65, you can qualify for the credit only if you are retired on permanent and total disability. If you retired after January 1, 1977, you are retired on permanent and total disability if you were permanently and totally disabled when you retired.

Even if you do not retire formally, you are considered retired on disability when you have stopped working because of your disability.

Example 1
Bill Russell is 62 years old and receives a disability pension from his former employer. He is eligible for the disability credit if he meets the other tests.

Example 2
Harry Carter retired at age 60 and is receiving a pension from his former employer. Harry was not disabled when he retired. In 2001, when Harry was 62 years old, he was in an accident that left him permanently and totally disabled. Harry is not eligible for the disability credit in 2001, because when he retired, he was not permanently and totally disabled.

Example 3
Marian Sloan retired in 1976 at age 30 on disability, even though she was not at the time permanently and totally disabled. However, by January 1, 1977, she was permanently and totally disabled. In 2001, she is still receiving disability payments from her former employer and has not yet reached her employer's mandatory retirement age. Marian is eligible for the credit in 2001.

Permanent and total disability. You are permanently and totally disabled if you cannot engage in any substantial gainful activity because of your physical or mental condition. A physician must certify that the condition has lasted or can be expected to last continuously for 12 months or more, or that the condition can be expected to result in death. See *Physician's statement,* later.

Substantial gainful activity. Substantial gainful activity is the performance of significant duties over a reasonable period of time while working for pay or profit, or in work generally done for pay or profit.

Full-time work (or part-time work done at your employer's convenience) in a competitive work situation for at least the minimum wage conclusively shows that you are able to engage in substantial gainful activity.

Substantial gainful activity is not work you do to take care of yourself or your home. It is not unpaid work on hobbies, institutional therapy or training, school attendance, clubs, social programs, and similar activities. However, doing this kind of work may show that you are able to engage in substantial gainful activity.

The fact that you have not worked for some time is not, of itself, conclusive evidence that you cannot engage in substantial gainful activity.

Explanation
The test of whether you are able to engage in substantial gainful activity is dependent on the facts and circumstances of your particular situation. No strict rule governs every case. The most important guideline to keep in mind is whether you hold a job that pays at least the minimum wage. This means any job, not just the job you held before your disability.

Sheltered employment. Certain work offered at qualified locations to physically or mentally impaired persons is considered sheltered employment. These qualified locations are in sheltered workshops, hospitals and similar institutions, homebound programs, and Department of Veterans Affairs (VA) sponsored homes.

Compared to commercial employment, pay is lower for sheltered employment. Therefore, one usually does not look for sheltered employment if he or she can get other employment. The fact that one has accepted sheltered employment is not proof of that person's ability to engage in substantial gainful activity.

Physician's statement. If you are under age 65, you must have your physician complete a statement certifying that you were permanently and totally disabled on the date you retired. You can use the statement in the instructions for Schedule R (Form 1040) or Schedule 3 (Form 1040A).

You do not have to file this statement with your Form 1040 or Form 1040A, but you **must** keep it for your records.

Veterans. If the Department of Veterans Affairs (VA) certifies that you are permanently and totally disabled, you can substitute VA Form 21-0172, *Certification of Permanent and Total Disability,* for the physician's statement you are required to keep. VA Form 21-0172 must be signed by a person authorized by the VA to do so. You can get this form from your local VA regional office.

Physician's statement obtained in earlier year. If you got a physician's statement in an earlier year **and,** due to your continued disabled condition, you were unable to engage in any substantial gainful activity during 2001, you may not need to get another physician's statement for 2001. For a detailed explanation of the conditions you must meet, see the instructions for Part II of Schedule R (Form 1040) or Schedule 3 (Form 1040A). If you meet the required conditions, check the box on line 2 of Part II of Schedule R (Form 1040) or Schedule 3 (Form 1040A).

If you checked box 4, 5, or 6 in Part I of either Schedule R or Schedule 3, print in the space above the box on line 2 in Part II, the first name(s) of the spouse(s) for whom the box is checked.

Disability income. If you are under age 65, you can qualify for the credit only if you have taxable disability income. Disability income must meet both of the following requirements.

1) It must be paid under your employer's accident or health plan or pension plan.
2) It must be included in your income as wages (or payments instead of wages) for the time you are absent from work because of permanent and total disability.

Payments that are not disability income. Any payment you receive from a plan that does not provide for disability retirement is not disability income. Any lump-sum payment for accrued annual leave that you receive when you retire on disability is a salary payment and is not disability income.

For purposes of the credit for the elderly or the disabled, disability income does not include amounts you receive after you reach mandatory retirement age. *Mandatory retirement age* is the age set by your employer at which you would have had to retire, had you not become disabled.

Example 1
Marie Carter retired in June at age 55 with a total and permanent disability. At retirement, she received a $5,000 payment for accrued vacation and sick leave days. The amount is not disability income, since it is not paid to her as wages or in lieu of wages because of her permanent and total disability.

Example 2
George Martin turned 62 years old on September 9, 2001. He had retired several years earlier as a result of a total and permanent disability. He has received disability payments from his employer since retirement. His former employer's mandatory retirement age is 62. As a result, any amount George receives after he reaches the age of 62 will *not* be disability income.

Income Limits

To determine if you can claim the credit, you must consider two income limits. The first limit is the amount of your adjusted gross income (AGI). The second limit is the amount of nontaxable social security and other nontaxable pensions you received. The limits are shown in *Figure 34-B,* earlier.

If both your AGI and nontaxable pensions are less than the income limits, you may be able to claim the credit. See *Figuring the Credit,* next. **Caution.** *If either your AGI or your nontaxable pensions are equal to or more than the income limits, you cannot take the credit.*

Figuring the Credit

You can figure the credit yourself (see the explanation that follows) or the IRS will figure it for you. See *Credit Figured for You,* later.

TAXALERT

With the aid of this book, you should not have to rely on the IRS to calculate your credit. Although the IRS routinely checks the mathematics on a return, it, too, can make computational errors. Also, as noted in Chapter 31, *How to Figure Your Tax,* you must still provide certain information to enable the IRS to calculate the credit. Therefore, our advice is to give the calculation of your credit a try.

Figuring the credit yourself. If you figure the credit yourself, fill out the front of either Schedule R (if you are filing Form 1040) or Schedule 3 (if you are filing Form 1040A). Next, fill out Part III of either Schedule R or Schedule 3.

There are four steps in Part III to determine the amount of your credit:

1) Determine your *initial amount* (lines 10–12).
2) Total any *nontaxable social security* and certain other nontaxable pensions and disability benefits you received (lines 13a, 13b, and 13c).
3) Determine your *excess adjusted gross income* (lines 14–17).
4) Determine your credit (lines 18–20).

These steps are discussed in more detail next.

Step 1. Determine Initial Amount

To figure the credit, you must first determine your initial amount. See *Table 34-1.*
Initial amounts for persons under age 65. If you are a qualified individual under age 65, your initial amount cannot be more than your taxable disability income.

Example 1
Thomas Washington, who is 59 years old and single, retired during the year because of a total and permanent physical disability. He received $4,300 in income during the year from his prior employer because of his disability. He received no other income. The initial amount Thomas uses in calculating his credit is $4,300.

Table 34–1. **Initial Amounts**

IF your filing status is ...	THEN enter on line 10 of Schedule R (Form 1040) or Schedule 3 (Form 1040A)...
Single, head of household, or qualifying widow or widower with dependent child and by the end of 2001, you were	
• 65 or older	$5,000
• under 65 and retired on permanent and total disability1	$5,000
Married filing a joint return and by the end of 2001	
• both of you were 65 or older	$7,500
• both of you were under 65 and one of you retired on permanent and total disability^1	$5,000
• both of you were under 65 and both of you retired on permanent and total disability^2	$7,500
• one of you was 65 or older, and the other was under 65 and retired on permanent and total disability^3	$7,500
• one of you was 65 or older, and the other was under 65 and **not** retired on permanent and total disability	$5,000
Married filing a separate return return and did not live with your spouse at any time during the year and, by the end of 2001, you were	
• 65 or older	$3,750
• under 65 and retired on permanent and total disability^1	$3,750

^{1}Amount cannot be more than the taxable disability income.
^{2}Amount cannot be more than your combined taxable disability income.
^{3}Amount is $5,000 plus the taxable disability income of the spouse under age 65, but not more than $7,500.

If Thomas had received $6,900 in disability income, his initial amount would be $5,000.

Example 2

Henry Jefferson is 72 years old and files a joint return with his wife, Abigail. Abigail is 63 years old and is permanently and totally disabled. She received $3,000 from her previous employer because of her disability. The initial amount they use in calculating their credit is $7,500, which is the lesser of (1) the $7,500 initial amount for married couples filing joint returns or (2) $5,000 plus the $3,000 disability income received by the person under the age of 65.

Step 2. Total Certain Nontaxable Pensions and Benefits

Step 2 is to figure the total amount of nontaxable social security and certain other nontaxable payments (listed below) you received during the year.

Enter these nontaxable payments on lines 13a or 13b, and total them on line 13c. If you are married filing a joint return, you must enter the combined amount of nontaxable payments both you and your spouse receive.

Tip. *Worksheets are provided in the Form 1040 or Form 1040A instructions to help you determine if any part of your social security benefits (or equivalent railroad retirement benefits) is taxable.*

Include the following nontaxable payments in the amounts you enter on lines 13a and 13b.

• Nontaxable social security payments. This is the nontaxable part of the amount of benefits shown in box 5 of Form SSA-1099, which includes disability benefits, before deducting any amounts withheld to pay premiums on supplementary Medicare insurance, and before any reduction because of receipt of a benefit under workers' compensation.

Do not include a lump-sum death benefit payment you may receive as a surviving spouse, or a surviving child's insurance benefit payment you may receive as a guardian.

Example 1

Jim and Jeanette are married and file a joint return. He is 69 years old and she is 64, and each receives $1,000 in Social Security. The initial amount used to figure their credit is $5,000, since only Jim is 65 years of age or older. This initial amount must be reduced by the $2,000 in Social Security that they received during the year. Next year, when Jeanette becomes 65 years old, their initial amount will rise to $7,500.

Example 2

Jean Blair retired in January 2001 at age 62 because of a permanent disability and collected $4,600 from her former employer as a disability pension. She also received $3,600 in Social Security benefits in 2001. Jean is single, and her adjusted gross income is less than $7,500. Jean must subtract the Social Security income from her disability income in computing the adjusted initial amount. Her credit is $150 [15% × ($4,600 − $3,600)].

- Social security equivalent part of tier 1 railroad retirement pension payments that is not taxed. This is the nontaxable part of the amount of benefits shown in box 5 of Form RRB-1099.
- Nontaxable pension or annuity payments or disability benefits that are paid under a law administered by the Department of Veterans Affairs (VA).

  Do not include amounts received as a pension, annuity, or similar allowance for personal injuries or sickness resulting from active service in the armed forces of any country or in the National Oceanic and Atmospheric Administration or the Public Health Service, or as a disability annuity under section 808 of the Foreign Service Act of 1980.
- Pension or annuity payments or disability benefits that are excluded from income under any provision of federal law other than the Internal Revenue Code.

  Do not include amounts that are a return of your cost of a pension or annuity. These amounts do not reduce your initial amount.

Caution. *You should be sure to take into account all of the nontaxable amounts you receive. These amounts are verified by the IRS through information supplied by other government agencies.*

EXPLANATION

Do not reduce the initial amount used to figure your credit by any of the following:

  Amounts that are treated as a return of your cost of an annuity or a pension
  Veterans Administration service-connected disability compensation
  Payments from accident or health insurance policies
  Basic or supplementary Medicare benefits
  Death compensation paid by the Veterans Administration to the surviving spouse of a veteran who died from sickness or injury incurred in active service
  Life insurance payments received when the insured person dies

---

Step 3. Determine Excess Adjusted Gross Income

You also must reduce your initial amount by your excess adjusted gross income. Figure your excess adjusted gross income on lines 14 through 17.

You figure your excess adjusted gross income as follows:

1) Subtract from your adjusted gross income (line 34 of Form 1040 or line 19 of Form 1040A) the amount shown for your filing status in the following list:
   a) **$7,500** if you are single, a head of household, or a qualifying widow(er) with a dependent child,
   b) **$10,000** if you are married filing a joint return, or
   c) **$5,000** if you are married filing a separate return and you and your spouse did not live in the same household at any time during the tax year.
2) Divide the result of (1) by 2.

Example 1

Henry is over age 65 and single, with $8,900 in adjusted gross income, which is in excess of the $7,500 allowed

for his single filing status. He must reduce his initial amount by $700 (one-half of the $1,400 difference between $8,900 and $7,500). Henry also receives $1,000 in nontaxable Social Security payments. The adjusted initial amount he uses to compute his credit is $3,300, calculated as follows:

Initial amount	$5,000
Less:	
Nontaxable Social Security	1,000
Excess adjusted gross income	700
Adjusted initial amount	$3,300
Tentative credit (15% of $3,300)	$ 495

Note: 15% times the adjusted initial amount is the method you use in calculating your tentative credit.

Example 2

Dennis and Constance are married, both are over age 65, and they file a joint return. Their adjusted gross income for the year is $12,000. They receive $1,750 in nontaxable Social Security. Their adjusted initial amount used to figure their credit is $4,750, calculated as follows:

Initial amount	$7,500
Less:	
Nontaxable Social Security	1,750
Excess adjusted gross income [½ ($12,000 − $10,000)]	1,000
Adjusted initial amount	$4,750
Tentative credit (15% of $4,750)	$ 713

Step 4. Determine Your Credit

To determine if you can take the credit, you must add the amounts you figured in Step 2 and Step 3.

IF the total of Steps 2 and 3 is ...	THEN ...
Equal to or more than the amount in Step 1	You **cannot** take the credit.
Less than the amount in Step 1	You **can** take the credit.

Figuring the credit. If you can take the credit, subtract the total of Step 2 and Step 3 from the amount in Step 1 and multiply the result by 15%. This is your credit.

In certain cases, the amount of your credit may be limited. See *Limit on Credit,* later.

Explanation

To summarize the situations outlined above, based on your filing status, you may not claim the credit for the elderly and disabled if (1) your nontaxable Social Security and other nontaxable pensions or (2) 50% of your excess adjusted gross income or (3) the sum of (1) and (2) equals or exceeds your initial amount.

A simple way to compute your credit is as follows:

1. Subtract from your initial amount the sum of your nontaxable Social Security income, other nontaxable pensions, and your excess adjusted gross income.
2. Multiply the amount from step 1 by 15%. This is your credit for the year.

Example. You are 66 years old and your spouse is 64. Your spouse is not disabled. You file a joint return on Form 1040. Your adjusted gross income is $14,630. Together you received $3,200 from social security, which was nontaxable. You figure the credit as follows:

1) Initial amount		$5,000
2) Subtract the total of:		
a) Nontaxable social security and other nontaxable pensions	$3,200	
b) Excess adjusted gross income [($14,630 – $10,000) ÷ 2]	2,315	5,515
3) Balance (Not less than –0–)		–0–
4) **Credit**		–0–

You cannot take the credit since your nontaxable social security (line 2a) plus your excess adjusted gross income (line 2b) is more than your amount on line 1.

Limit on Credit

The amount of credit you can claim may be limited. Use one of the following worksheets (or the worksheet in the instructions for Schedule 3, Form 1040A, or Schedule R, Form 1040, whichever applies) to determine the amount of credit you can claim if any of the following apply.

1) You file Form 1040A and the credit you figured on line 20 of Schedule 3 is more than the tax on Form 1040A, line 26.
2) You file Form 1040 and the credit you figured on line 20 of Schedule R is more than the amount on Form 1040, line 42 (regular tax plus any alternative minimum tax), minus any foreign tax credit on Form 1040, line 43.
3) You are claiming the credit for child and dependent care expenses on:
   a) Form 1040A, line 27, or
   b) Form 1040, line 44.

If (1), (2), and (3) above do not apply, you do not need to use a worksheet to figure a limit on your credit. Claim the full amount of the credit you figured on Schedule 3 (Form 1040A) or Schedule R (Form 1040).

Credit Limit Worksheet (Form 1040)

1) Enter the amount from 1040, line 42, minus any amount on Form 1040, line 43 ....

2) Enter the amount, if any, from Form 1040, line 44 ....

3) Subtract line 2 from line 1 ....

4) Enter the credit you first figured on Schedule R, line 20 ....

5) **Credit.** Enter the smaller of line 3 or line 4 here and on Form 1040, line 45. If line 3 is the smaller amount, also replace the amount on Schedule R, line 20, with that amount ....

Credit Limit Worksheet (Form 1040A)

1) Enter the amount from 1040A, line 26 ....

2) Enter the amount, if any from Form 1040A, line 27 ....

3) Subtract line 2 from line 1 ....

4) Enter the credit you first figured on Schedule 3, line 20 ....

5) **Credit.** Enter the smaller of line 3 or line 4 here and on Form 1040A, line 28. If line 3 is the smaller amount, also replace the amount on Schedule 3, line 20, with that amount ....

Credit Figured for You

If you choose to have the Internal Revenue Service (IRS) figure the credit for you, read the following discussion for the form you will file (Form 1040 or 1040A). If you want the IRS to figure your tax, see chapter 31. **Form 1040.** If you want the IRS to figure your credit, see *Form 1040 Line Entries* under *Tax Figured by IRS* in chapter 31. **Form 1040A.** If you want the IRS to figure your credit, see *Form 1040A Line Entries* under *Tax Figured by IRS* in chapter 31.

Examples

The following examples illustrate the credit for the elderly or the disabled. The initial amounts are taken from *Table 34-1,* shown earlier.

Example 1. James Davis is 58 years old, single, and files Form 1040A. In 1998 he retired on permanent and total disability, and he is still permanently and totally disabled. He got the required physician's statement in 1998, and kept it with his records. His physician signed on line B of the statement. This year James checks the box in Part II of Schedule 3. He does not need to get another statement for 2001.

He received the following income for the year:

Nontaxable social security	$2,500
Interest (taxable)	100
Taxable disability pension	9,400

James' adjusted gross income is $9,500 ($9,400 + $100). He figures the credit on Schedule 3 as follows:

1) Initial amount		$5,000
2) Taxable disability pension		$9,400
3) Smaller of (1) or (2)		$5,000
4) Subtract the total of:		
a) Nontaxable disability benefits (social security)	$2,500	
b) Excess adjusted gross income [($9,500 – $7,500) ÷ 2]	1,000	3,500
5) Balance (Not less than 0)		$1,500
6) **Credit** (15% of $1,500)		$ 225

Example 2. William White is 53. His wife Helen is 49. William had a stroke 3 years ago and retired on permanent and total disability. He is still permanently and totally disabled because of the stroke. In November of last year, Helen was injured in an accident at work and retired on permanent and total disability.

William received nontaxable social security disability benefits of $3,000 during the year and a taxable disability pension of $6,000. Helen earned $9,200 from her job and received a taxable disability pension of $1,000. Their joint return on Form 1040 shows adjusted gross income of $16,200 ($6,000 + $9,200 + $1,000).

Helen got her doctor to complete the physician's statement in the instructions for Schedule R. Helen is not required to include the statement with her return, but she must keep it for her records.

William got a physician's statement for the year he had the stroke. His doctor had signed on line B of that physician's statement to certify that William was permanently and totally disabled. William has kept the physicians's statement with his records. He checks the box in Part II of Schedule R and writes his first name in the space above line 2.

William and Helen use Schedule R to figure their $135 credit for the elderly or the disabled. They attach Schedule R to their joint return and enter $135 on line 45 of Form 1040. See their filled-in Schedule R and Helen's filled-in physician's statement on the next three pages.

Instructions for Physician's Statement

Taxpayer

If you retired after 1976, enter the date you retired in the space provided on the statement below.

Physician

A person is permanently and totally disabled if **both** of the following apply:

1. He or she cannot engage in any substantial gainful activity because of a physical or mental condition, and

2. A physician determines that the disability has lasted or can be expected to last continuously for at least a year or can lead to death.

Physician's Statement (keep for your records)

I certify that _____ Helen A. White _____

Name of disabled person

was permanently and totally disabled on January 1, 1976, or January 1, 1977, **OR** was permanently and totally disabled on the date he or she retired. If retired after 1976, enter the date retired. ▶ _November 30, 2001_

Physician: Sign your name on **either** line A or B below.

A The disability has lasted or can be expected to last continuously for at least a year . . _____

Physician's signature   Date

B There is no reasonable probability that the disabled condition will ever improve . . _Juanita D. Doctor_ ____ 2/7/2002

Physician's signature   Date

Physician's name

Juanita D. Doctor

Physician's address

1900 Green St., Hometown, MD 20000

Schedule R
(Form 1040)

Department of the Treasury
Internal Revenue Service

Credit for the Elderly or the Disabled

▶ **Attach to Form 1040.**   ▶ **See Instructions for Schedule R (Form 1040).**

OMB No. 1545-0074

2001

Attachment
Sequence No. **16**

Name(s) shown on Form 1040
William M. White and Helen A. White

Your social security number
220 : 00 : 3333

You may be able to take this credit and reduce your tax if by the end of 2001:

- You were age 65 or older **or** • You were under age 65, you retired on **permanent and total** disability, and you received taxable disability income.

But you must also meet other tests. See page R-1.

TIP In most cases, the IRS can figure the credit for you. See page R-1.

Part I   **Check the Box for Your Filing Status and Age**

If your filing status is:	And by the end of 2001:		Check only one box:
Single, Head of household, or Qualifying widow(er) with dependent child	**1** You were 65 or older	**1**	☐
	2 You were under 65 and you retired on permanent and total disability	**2**	☐
Married filing a joint return	**3** Both spouses were 65 or older	**3**	☐
	4 Both spouses were under 65, but only one spouse retired on permanent and total disability	**4**	☐
	5 Both spouses were under 65, and both retired on permanent and total disability	**5**	☑
	6 One spouse was 65 or older, and the other spouse was under 65 and retired on permanent and total disability	**6**	☐
	7 One spouse was 65 or older, and the other spouse was under 65 and **not** retired on permanent and total disability	**7**	☐
Married filing a separate return	**8** You were 65 or older and you lived apart from your spouse for all of 2001	**8**	☐
	9 You were under 65, you retired on permanent and total disability, and you lived apart from your spouse for all of 2001	**9**	☐

Did you check box 1, 3, 7, or 8? —— **Yes** ——▶ Skip Part II and complete Part III on back.

—— **No** ——▶ Complete Parts II and III.

Part II   **Statement of Permanent and Total Disability** (Complete **only** if you checked box 2, 4, 5, 6, or 9 above.)

If: 1 You filed a physician's statement for this disability for 1983 or an earlier year, or you filed or got a statement for tax years after 1983 and your physician signed line B on the statement, **and**

William

2 Due to your continued disabled condition, you were unable to engage in any substantial gainful activity in 2001, check this box . . . . ▶ ☑

- If you checked this box, you do not have to get another statement for 2001.

- If you **did not** check this box, have your physician complete the statement on page R-4. You **must** keep the statement for your records.

For Paperwork Reduction Act Notice, see Form 1040 instructions.   Cat. No. 11359K   **Schedule R (Form 1040) 2001**

Schedule R (Form 1040) 2001   Page **2**

Part III   **Figure Your Credit**

10 If you checked (in Part I):   Enter:
   Box 1, 2, 4, or 7 . . . .$5,000 ⎫
   Box 3, 5, or 6 . . . .$7,500 ⎬ **10**   7,500
   Box 8 or 9 . . . .$3,750 ⎭

   ┌──────────────┐
   │ Did you check│────── **Yes** ──────▶ You **must** complete line 11.
   │ box 2, 4, 5, 6,│
   │ or 9 in Part I?│────── **No** ──────▶ Enter the amount from line 10
   └──────────────┘   on line 12 and go to line 13.

11 If you checked:
   ● Box 6 in Part I, add $5,000 to the taxable disability income   ⎫
     of the spouse who was under age 65. Enter the total.   │
   ● Box 2, 4, or 9 in Part I, enter your taxable disability income.   ⎬ **11**   7,000
   ● Box 5 in Part I, add your taxable disability income to your   │
     spouse's taxable disability income. Enter the total.   ⎭

   TIP For more details on what to include on line 11, see page R-3.

12 If you completed line 11, enter the **smaller** of line 10 or line 11; **all others,** enter the
   amount from line 10 . . . .   **12**   7,000

13 Enter the following pensions, annuities, or disability income
   that you (and your spouse if filing a joint return) received in
   2001:
 a Nontaxable part of social security benefits and   ⎫
   Nontaxable part of railroad retirement benefits   ⎬ . .   **13a**   3,000
   treated as social security. See page R-3.   ⎭

 b Nontaxable veterans' pensions and   ⎫
   Any other pension, annuity, or disability benefit that   ⎬ . .   **13b**
   is excluded from income under any other provision   │
   of law. See page R-3.   ⎭

 c Add lines 13a and 13b. (Even though these income items are
   not taxable, they **must** be included here to figure your credit.)
   If you did not receive any of the types of nontaxable income
   listed on line 13a or 13b, enter -0- on line 13c **13c**   3,000

14 Enter the amount from Form 1040,   **14**   16,200
   line 34 . . . .

15 If you checked (in Part I):   Enter:
   Box 1 or 2 . . . . . . $7,500   ⎫
   Box 3, 4, 5, 6, or 7. . . .$10,000   ⎬   **15**   10,000
   Box 8 or 9 . . . . . . $5,000   ⎭
16 Subtract line 15 from line 14. If zero or
   less, enter -0- **16**   6,200

17 Enter one-half of line 16 . . . .   **17**   3,100

18 Add lines 13c and 17 . . . .   **18**   6,100

19 Subtract line 18 from line 12. If zero or less, **stop;** you **cannot** take the credit. Otherwise,
   go to line 20 . . . .   **19**   900

20 Multiply line 19 by 15% (.15). Enter the result here and on Form 1040, line 45. But if
   this amount is more than the amount on Form 1040, line 42, minus any amount on line
   43, **or** you are filing Form 2441, see page R-3 for the amount of credit you may take   **20**   135

Schedule R (Form 1040) 2001

Child Tax Credit

Introduction

A tax credit of $600 is available for each qualifying child under age 17. A qualifying child is an individual for whom the taxpayer can claim a dependency exemption and who is the child, grandchild, step-child, or eligible foster-child of the taxpayer. The credit is phased out de- *pending on your adjusted gross income and the number of qualifying children. The child tax credit is not the same as the credit for child and dependent care expenses, which is explained in Chapter 33,* Child and Dependent Care Credit.

Important Changes

TaxAlert: The 2001 Tax Act

The child tax credit has been increased from $500 per child in 2000 to $600 per child in 2001 and will gradually increase to $1,000 per child in 2010. At least a portion of the new child tax credit will now be a *refundable* tax credit. This means that you may be able to receive a refund of the credit even if it exceeds your tax liability. The refundable portion of the child tax credit is equal to 10% of a taxpayer's earned income in excess of $10,000, not to exceed the amount of the child tax credit. The credit continues to be reduced or eliminated for higher income individuals as described below.

Child tax credit increased. The maximum child tax credit for each qualifying child is increased to $600 for 2001.

Additional child tax credit expanded. For tax years after 2000, the qualifications for claiming the additional child tax credit have been expanded to include qualifying individuals with fewer than three children. See *Additional Child Tax Credit,* later, for more information.

The child tax credit is a credit that can reduce your tax. You may be able to take a credit on your tax return of up to $600 for each of your qualifying children.

The child tax credit is not the same as the credit for child and dependent care expenses. For information on the credit for child and dependent care expenses, see chapter 33.

This chapter gives you information about the child tax credit. It explains:

• Who is a qualifying child.
• How much is the credit.
• How do I claim the credit.
• Why should I check my tax withholding.

If you have no tax. Credits, such as the child tax credit, the adoption credit, or the credit for child and dependent care expenses, are used to reduce tax. If your tax on line 42 (Form 1040) or line 26 (Form 1040A) is zero, do not figure the child tax credit because there is no tax to reduce. However, you may qualify for the additional child tax credit on line 63 (Form 1040) or line 40 (Form 1040A).

Useful Items

You may want to see:

Form (and Instructions)

☐ **8812**   Additional Child Tax Credit
☐ **W-4**   Employee's Withholding Allowance Certificate

Qualifying Child

A qualifying child for purposes of the child tax credit must be all of the following.

1) Under age 17 at the end of 2001.
2) A citizen or resident of the United States.
3) Claimed as your dependent.
4) Your:
   a) Son or daughter,
   b) Stepson or stepdaughter,
   c) Adopted child,
   d) Grandchild, or
   e) Eligible foster child.

Example. Your son turned 17 on December 30, 2001. He is a citizen of the United States and you claimed him as a dependent on your return. He is ***not*** a qualifying child for the child tax credit because he was ***not*** under age 17 at the end of 2001.

Adopted child. A child placed with you by an authorized placement agency for legal adoption is an adopted child even if the adoption is not final.

Grandchild. A grandchild is any descendant of your son, daughter, or adopted child and includes your great-grandchild, great-great-grandchild, etc.

Explanation

Grandparents can claim a child credit for grandchildren if the grandchildren can be claimed as dependents on the grandparents' tax return.

Eligible foster child. An eligible foster child is any child you cared for as your own and who is:

1) Your brother, sister, stepbrother, stepsister, or
2) A descendent (such as a child) of your brother, sister, stepbrother, stepsister, or
3) A child placed with you by an authorized placement agency.

In addition, the child must have lived with you for all of 2001. A child who was born or died in 2001 is considered to have lived with you for all of 2001 if your home was the child's home for the entire time he or she was alive.

Kidnapped child. A kidnapped child is treated as a qualifying child for the child tax credit if the child is presumed by law enforcement authorities to have been kidnapped by someone who is not a member of your family or the child's family. This treatment applies for all years that the child remains kidnapped. However, the last year this treatment can apply is the earlier of:

1) The year the child is determined to be dead, or
2) The year the child would have reached age 17.

Amount of Credit

The maximum credit you can claim is $600 for each qualifying child.

Limits on the Credit

You must reduce your child tax credit if either (1) or (2) applies.

1) The amount on line 42 (Form 1040) or line 26 (Form 1040A) is less than the credit. If this amount is zero, you cannot take this credit because there is no tax to reduce. But you may be able to take the ***additional child tax credit.*** See *Additional Child Tax Credit,* later.
2) Your modified adjusted gross income (AGI) is above the amount shown below for your filing status.

- Married filing jointly—$110,000.
- Single, head of household, or qualifying widow(er)—$75,000.
- Married filing separately—$55,000.

Explanation

There is a phaseout of the credit based on the taxpayer's adjusted gross income and on the number of qualifying children. The maximum child credit available to the taxpayer ($600 times the number of qualifying children) would phase down by $50 for each $1,000 by which the tax-

---

payer's AGI exceeds the threshold amounts (i.e., $75,000 for single filers and head of household, $110,000 for couples filing jointly, and $55,000 for married persons filing separately).

Modified AGI. For purposes of the child tax credit, your modified AGI is your AGI plus the following amounts that may apply to you.

- Any amount excluded from income because of the exclusion of income from Puerto Rico.
- Any amount on lines 43 and 48 of Form 2555, *Foreign Earned Income.*
- Any amount on line 18 of Form 2555-EZ, *Foreign Earned Income Exclusion.*
- Any amount on line 15 of Form 4563, *Exclusion of Income for Bona Fide Residents of American Samoa.*

If you do not have any of the above, modified AGI is the AGI amount on line 34 (Form 1040) or line 20 (Form 1040A).

Claiming the Credit

To claim the child tax credit, you must file Form 1040 or Form 1040A. You must provide the name and identification number (usually a social security number) on your tax return for each qualifying child.

Answer the *Questions* in your form instructions for line 48 (Form 1040) or line 31 (Form 1040A) to find out which child tax credit worksheet you can use to figure the credit.

If you answer "Yes" to question 1, 2, or 3 in your Form 1040 instructions or question 1 or 2 in your Form 1040A instructions, you must complete the child tax credit worksheet in Publication 972, *Child Tax Credit.* Otherwise, you can use the *Child Tax Credit Worksheet* in your Form 1040 or Form 1040A instructions. (See the filled-in example, later.)

Example

Amy Brown files as head of household and has two dependent children under age 17. The children are qualifying children for purposes of the child tax credit. Amy's only income is her salary of $23,500. She had $1,439 of social security and Medicare taxes withheld. Amy chooses to itemize her deductions and files Form 1040. Her AGI, shown on line 34 of her Form 1040, is $23,500. This is her taxable earned income.

Amy does not file Form 2555, 2555-EZ, or 4563. She does not exclude income from Puerto Rico. Her modified AGI is $23,500.

Amy's tax, shown on line 42 of her Form 1040, is $1,226. She claims a $960 credit for child and dependent care expenses on line 44. She claims a $1,810 earned income credit on line 61a. She has no other credits.

After answering the *Questions* in the Form 1040 instructions for line 48, she completes the child tax credit worksheet to figure her child tax credit of $266. Amy's completed questions and child tax credit worksheet are shown later.

Amy reads the *TIP* in the worksheet and finds that she may be able to take the additional child tax credit. See *Additional Child Tax Credit* and Amy's completed Form 8812, later.

Additional Child Tax Credit

This credit is for certain individuals who get less than the full amount of the child tax credit. The additional child tax credit may give you a refund even if you do not owe any tax.

How to claim the additional child tax credit. To claim the additional child tax credit, follow the steps below.

1) Make sure you figured the amount, if any, of your child tax credit. See *Claiming the Credit,* earlier.
2) Use Form 8812 to see if you can take the additional child tax credit

only if you answered "Yes" on line 4 or line 5 of the *Child Tax Credit Worksheet*.

3) If you have an additional child tax credit on line 13 of Form 8812, carry it to line 63 (Form 1040) or line 40 (Form 1040A).

Taxable earned income. Generally, for purposes of the additional child tax credit, your taxable earned income is the amount on line 7 of Form 1040 or Form 1040A. See the instructions for Form 8812 to figure your taxable earned income.

Checking Your Withholding

The child tax credit decreases your tax. You can check your tax withholding by using Worksheet 7 in Publication 919, *How Do I Adjust My Tax Withholding*.

If you are having too much tax withheld, and you prefer to have the money during the year, you may be able to decrease your withholding. You do this by completing a new Form W-4 and giving it to your employer.

Filled-in Questions for Amy Brown
(Page references are to the Form 1040 instructions.)

Questions **Who Must Use Pub. 972** Pub. 972

1. Are you excluding income from Puerto Rico **or** are you filing any of the following forms?

   - Form 2555 or 2555-EZ (relating to foreign earned income)

   - Form 4563 (exclusion of income for residents of American Samoa)

   ☑ **No.** *Continue* ↘   ☐ **Yes.** (STOP) You must use Pub. 972 to figure your credit.

2. Is the amount on Form 1040, line 34, more than the amount shown below for your filing status?

   - Married filing jointly – $110,000

   - Single, head of household, or qualifying widow(er) – $75,000

   - Married filing separately – $55,000

   ☑ **No.** *Continue* ↘   ☐ **Yes.** (STOP) You must use Pub. 972 to figure your credit.

3. Are you claiming any of the following credits?

   - Adoption credit, Form 8839 (see the instructions for Form 1040, line 49, on page 39)

   - Mortgage interest credit, Form 8396 (see the instructions for Form 1040, line 50, on page 39)

   - District of Columbia first-time homebuyer credit, Form 8859

   ☑ **No.** Use the worksheet on page 38 to figure your child tax credit.   ☐ **Yes.** You must use Pub. 972 to figure your child tax credit. You will also need the form(s) listed above for any credit(s) you are claiming.

Filled-in Child Tax Credit Worksheet—Amy Brown
(Page references are to the Form 1040 instructions.)

Form 1040—Line 48

Child Tax Credit Worksheet—Line 48

Keep for Your Records

Do not use this worksheet if you answered "Yes" to question 1, 2, or 3 on page 37. Instead, use Pub. 972.

1. Number of qualifying children: ___2___ × $600. Enter the result.   **1** | 1,200

2. Enter the amount from Form 1040, line 42.   **2** | 1,226

3. Add the amounts from Form 1040:

   Line 43 _____
   Line 44 + ___960___
   Line 45 + _____
   Line 46 + _____
   Line 47 + _____   Enter the total.   **3** | 960

4. Are the amounts on lines 2 and 3 the same?

   ☐ **Yes.** (STOP)
   You cannot take this credit because there is no tax to reduce. However, see the **TIP** below before completing the rest of your Form 1040.

   ☑ **No.** Subtract line 3 from line 2.   **4** | 266

5. Is the amount on line 1 more than the amount on line 4?

   ☑ **Yes.** Enter the amount from line 4.
   Also, see the **TIP** below.

   ☐ **No.** Enter the amount from line 1.

   } **This is your child tax credit.**

   5 | 266

   Enter this amount on Form 1040, line 48.

   1040

TIP
You may be able to take the **additional child tax credit** on Form 1040, line 63, if you answered "Yes" on line 4 **or** line 5 above.

• First, complete your Form 1040 through line 62.

• Then, use Form 8812 to figure any additional child tax credit.

Form **8812**

Department of the Treasury
Internal Revenue Service

Additional Child Tax Credit

Complete and attach to Form 1040 or Form 1040A.

OMB No. 1545-1620

2001

Attachment
Sequence No. **47**

Name(s) shown on return	Your social security number
Amy Brown	012 : 00 : 5678

Part I   All Filers

1	Enter the amount from line 1 of your Child Tax Credit Worksheet on page 38 of the Form 1040 instructions or page 37 of the Form 1040A instructions. If you used Pub. 972, enter the amount from line 8 of the worksheet on page 3 of the publication	**1**	1,200
2	Enter the amount from Form 1040, line 48, or Form 1040A, line 31	**2**	266
3	Subtract line 2 from line 1. If zero, **stop**; you cannot take this credit	**3**	934

4	Enter your total taxable earned income. See the instructions on back .	**4**	23,500	
5	Is the amount on line 4 more than $10,000?			
	☐ **No.** Leave line 5 blank and enter -0- on line 6.			
	☑ **Yes.** Subtract $10,000 from the amount on line 4. Enter the result.	**5**	13,500	

6	Multiply the amount on line 5 by 10% (.10) and enter the result	**6**	1,350

Next. Do you have three or more qualifying children?

☑ **No.** If line 6 is zero, **stop**; you cannot take this credit. Otherwise, skip Part II and enter the **smaller** of line 3 or line 6 on line 13.

☐ **Yes.** If line 6 is equal to or more than line 3, skip Part II and enter the amount from line 3 on line 13. Otherwise, go to line 7.

Part II   Certain Filers Who Have Three or More Qualifying Children

7	Enter the total of the withheld social security and Medicare taxes from Form(s) W-2, boxes 4 and 6. If married filing jointly, include your spouse's amounts with yours. If you worked for a railroad, see the instructions on back .	**7**	
8	**1040 filers:** Enter the total of the amounts from Form 1040, lines 27 and 54, plus any uncollected social security and Medicare or RRTA taxes included on line 58. **1040A filers:** Enter -0-.	**8**	
9	Add lines 7 and 8	**9**	
10	**1040 filers:** Enter the total of the amounts from Form 1040, lines 61a and 62. **1040A filers:** Enter the total of the amount from Form 1040A, line 39a, plus any excess social security and RRTA taxes withheld that you entered to the left of line 41 (see the instructions on back).	**10**	
11	Subtract line 10 from line 9. If zero or less, enter -0-	**11**	
12	Enter the **larger** of line 6 or line 11 here	**12**	
	Next, enter the **smaller** of line 3 or line 12 on line 13.		

Part III   Your Additional Child Tax Credit

13	**This is your additional child tax credit**	**13**	934

Enter this amount on Form 1040, line 63, or Form 1040A, line 40.

For Paperwork Reduction Act Notice, see back of form.   Cat. No. 10644E   Form **8812** (2001)

36

Education Credits

Introduction

Generally, you may not deduct education and training expenses unless they are required by your employer or improve your job skills. However, two tax credits broaden the tax benefits available for education costs. You can elect either a nonrefundable Hope scholarship tax credit or a Lifetime Learning credit for eligible education expenses.

These two credits, as well as the tax-free withdrawals from Coverdell ESAs (formerly education IRAs) [see Chapter 18, Individual Retirement Arrangements (IRAs) and Education Savings Accounts (ESAs)] are mutually exclusive in 2001. For each eligible student in 2001,

you must elect either of the tax credits or the exclusion from gross income for withdrawals from Coverdell ESAs.

The credits are phased out for single taxpayers with modified adjusted gross income (AGI) of $40,000–$50,000 and for couples filing jointly with modified AGI between $80,000–$100,000. After the year 2001, the income phaseout ranges will be indexed for inflation.

For both the Hope scholarship credit and the Lifetime Learning credit, qualified tuition does not include any amounts otherwise excludable from gross income or amounts deductible as a business expense.

This chapter discusses the Hope credit and the lifetime learning credit. It will:

- Give you general information that applies to both of the credits,
- Give you specific information about each of the credits,
- Help you choose which of the credits to claim, and
- Show you how to figure the credit you choose.

Useful Items

You may want to see:

Publication

☐ **970** Tax Benefits for Higher Education

Form (and Instructions)

☐ **8863** Education Credits (Hope and Lifetime Learning Credits)

Education Tax Credits

The following two tax credits are available to persons who pay higher education costs.

- The Hope credit.
- The lifetime learning credit.

Table 36-1 compares the Hope and lifetime learning credits. If you are eligible to claim both credits based on the higher education expenses of one student, it will generally be to your benefit to claim the Hope credit. **Caution.** *If a student receives a tax-free withdrawal from an education IRA in a particular tax year, none of that student's expenses can be used as the basis of a higher education credit for that tax year. However, the student can waive the tax-free treatment. See* Waiver of tax-free treatment *under* No double benefit allowed.

Rules That Apply to Both Credits

The amount of each credit is determined by the amount you pay for qualified tuition and related expenses for students and the amount of your modified adjusted gross income. Education credits are subtracted from your tax but they are nonrefundable. This means if the credits are more than your tax, the excess is not refunded to you.
Caution. *If you are married filing separately you cannot claim the higher education credits.*

TAXALERT

One credit per customer. The Hope credit and Lifetime Learning credit, as well as the tax-free withdrawals from education savings accounts [see Chapter 18, *Individual Retirement Arrangements (IRAs) and Education Savings Accounts (ESAs)*], are mutually exclusive. For each eligible student in each tax year, the taxpayer must elect either one

---

Table 36–1. **Comparison of Education Credits**

Hope Scholarship Credit	Lifetime Learning Credit
Up to $1,500 credit per **eligible student**	Up to $1,000 credit per **return**
Available **ONLY** for the first two years of postsecondary education	Available for all years of postsecondary education
Available **ONLY** for 2 years per eligible student	Available for an unlimited number of years
Student must be pursuing a degree or other recognized educational credential	Student does not need to be pursuing a degree or other recognized educational credential
Student must be enrolled at least half time for at least one academic period during the year	Available for one or more courses
No felony drug conviction on student's record	Felony drug conviction rule does not apply

of the tax credits or the exclusion from gross income for withdrawals from education savings accounts. Beginning in 2002, the Hope and Lifetime Learning credits can be claimed in the same year that a distribution from an education savings account is made, as long as the distribution is not used to cover the same expenses for which the education credits are claimed.

The credits are phased out for single taxpayers with modified adjusted gross income (AGI) of $40,000 to $50,000 and for couples filing jointly with modified AGI between $80,000 and $100,000. Unlike the child tax credit (see Chapter 35, *Child Tax Credit*), the income phaseout ranges for the education credits will be indexed for inflation rounded down to the closest multiple of $1,000. The first tax year for which the inflation adjustment could be made to increase the income phaseout ranges will be 2002. The credits are not available to married taxpayers filing separately.

What expenses qualify. The credits are based on qualified tuition and related expenses you pay for yourself, your spouse, or a dependent for whom you claim an exemption on your tax return. Generally the credits are allowed for qualified tuition and related expenses paid for an academic period beginning in the same year as the year the payment is made (but see *Prepaid expenses,* later).

In general, qualified tuition and related expenses are tuition and fees required for enrollment or attendance at an eligible educational institution. Student-activity fees and fees for course-related books, supplies, and equipment are included in qualified tuition and related expenses *only if* the fees must be paid *to the institution* as a condition of enrollment or attendance.

Prepaid expenses. If you paid qualified tuition and related expenses in 2001 for an academic period that begins in the first three months of 2002, you can use the prepaid amount in figuring your credit.

For example, if you paid $2,000 in December 2001 for qualified tuition for the winter 2002 semester beginning in January 2002, you can use that $2,000 in figuring your 2001 credit.

Payments with borrowed funds. You can claim an education credit for qualified tuition and related expenses paid with the proceeds of a loan. You claim the credit in the year in which the expenses are paid, not in the year in which the loan is repaid.

Expenses that do not qualify. Qualified tuition and related expenses do not include the cost of:

- Insurance,
- Medical expenses (including student health fees),
- Room and board,
- Transportation, or
- Similar personal, living or family expenses.

This is true even if the fee must be paid to the institution as a condition of enrollment or attendance.

Qualified tuition and related expenses generally do not include expenses that relate to any course of instruction or other education that involves sports, games, or hobbies, or any noncredit course. However, if the course of instruction or other education is part of the student's degree program or, in the case of the lifetime learning credit, is taken by the student to acquire or improve job skills, these expenses can qualify.

Dependent for whom you claim an exemption. You claim an exemption for a dependent if you list his or her name on line 6c, Form 1040 (or Form 1040A). (See chapter 3 for details on exemptions for dependents.)

Eligible educational institution. An eligible educational institution is any college, university, vocational school, or other postsecondary educational institution eligible to participate in a student aid program administered by the Department of Education. It includes virtually all accredited, public, nonprofit, and proprietary (privately owned profit-making) postsecondary institutions. The educational institution should be able to tell you if it is an eligible educational institution.

Academic period. An academic period includes a semester, trimester, quarter, or other period of study (such as a summer school session) as reasonably determined by an educational institution.

No double benefit allowed. You cannot:

- Deduct higher education expenses on your income tax return and also claim a Hope credit based on those same expenses,
- Claim a Hope credit and a lifetime learning credit based on the same qualified education expenses, or
- Claim a credit based on expenses paid with tax-free scholarship, grant, or employer-provided educational assistance. See *Adjustments to qualified expenses,* next.

Adjustments to qualified expenses. If you pay higher education expenses with certain *tax-free* funds, you cannot claim a credit for those amounts. You must reduce the qualified expenses by the amount of any tax-free educational assistance you received. Tax-free educational assistance could include:

- Scholarships,
- Pell grants,

- Employer-provided educational assistance,
- Veterans' educational assistance, and
- Any other nontaxable payments (other than gifts, bequests, or inheritances) received for education expenses.

Do not reduce the qualified expenses by amounts paid with the student's:

- Earnings,
- Loans,
- Gifts,
- Inheritances, and
- Personal savings.

Also, do not reduce the qualified expenses by any scholarship reported as income on the student's return or any scholarship which, by its terms, cannot be applied to qualified tuition and related expenses.

Waiver of tax-free treatment. The designated beneficiary of a Coverdell ESA (formerly known as an education IRA) can waive the tax-free treatment of the withdrawal and elect to pay any tax that would otherwise be owed on the withdrawal. The beneficiary or the beneficiary's parents may then be eligible to claim a Hope credit or lifetime learning credit for qualified higher education expenses paid in that tax year. See *Coverdell ESAs* in Publication 970.

Refunds. Qualified tuition and related expenses do not include expenses for which you receive a refund. If you paid expenses in 2001, and you received a refund of those expenses before you file your tax return for 2001, simply reduce the amount of the expenses by the amount of the refund received. If you receive the refund after you file your tax return, see *When must the credit be repaid,* next.

When must the credit be repaid? If, after you file your 2001 tax return, you receive tax-free educational assistance for, or a refund of, an expense you used to figure a higher education credit on that return, you may have to repay all or part of the credit. You must refigure your education credits as if the assistance or refund was received in 2001. Subtract the amount of the refigured credit from the amount of the credit you claimed. See the instructions for your 2001 tax return for information about how and where to report the repayment (recapture).

Who can claim the credit. If there are higher education costs for your dependent for a year, either you or your dependent, but not both of you, can claim a credit for that dependent's expenses for that year. If you claim an exemption for your dependent on your tax return, only you can claim a credit. If you do not claim an exemption for your dependent on your tax return, only your dependent can claim a credit.

Expenses paid by dependent. If you claim an exemption on your tax return for an eligible student who is your dependent, treat any expenses paid by the student as if you had paid them. Include these expenses when figuring the amount of your Hope or lifetime learning credit.

Tip. *Qualified tuition and related expenses paid directly to an eligible educational institution for your dependent under a court-approved divorce decree are treated as paid by your dependent.*

Expenses paid by others. If someone other than you, your spouse, or your dependent (such as a relative or former spouse) makes a payment directly to an eligible educational institution to pay for an eligible student's qualified tuition and related expenses, the student is treated as receiving the payment from the other person. The student is treated as paying the qualified tuition and related expenses to the institution. If you claim an exemption on your tax return for the student, you are considered to have paid the expenses.

Example. Ms. Allen makes a payment directly to an eligible educational institution in 2001 for her grandson Todd's qualified tuition and related expenses. For purposes of claiming an education credit, Todd is treated as receiving the money from Ms. Allen and, in turn, paying his qualified tuition and related expenses himself.

If Todd's exemption is not claimed on anyone's return, he can use the payment to claim an education credit.

If anyone, such as his parents, claims an exemption for him on their tax return, whoever lists him as a dependent may be able to use the expenses to claim an education credit.

Nonresident alien. You cannot claim an education credit if you (or your spouse) were a nonresident alien for any part of 2001, and the nonresident alien did not elect to be treated as a resident alien. More information on nonresident aliens can be found in Publication 519, *Tax Guide for U.S. Aliens.*

Does the Amount of Your Income Affect the Amount of Your Credit?

Your education credits are phased out (gradually reduced) if your modified adjusted gross income is between $40,000 and $50,000 ($80,000 and $100,000 if you file a joint return). You cannot claim **any** higher education credits if your modified adjusted gross income is $50,000 or more ($100,000 or more if you file a joint return).

How the phaseout works. The phaseout (reduction) works on a sliding scale. The higher your modified adjusted gross income, the more your credits are reduced. You figure the reduction, if any, in Part III of Form 8863.

Modified adjusted gross income. For most taxpayers, modified adjusted gross income (MAGI) will be their adjusted gross income (AGI) as figured on their federal income tax return.

On Form 1040, AGI is line 34. On Form 1040A, AGI is line 19.

However, you must file using Form 1040 and make adjustments to your AGI if you excluded income earned abroad or from certain U.S. territories or possessions.

If this applies to you, increase your AGI by the following amounts you excluded from your income.

1) Foreign earned income of U.S. citizens or residents living abroad.
2) Housing costs of U.S. citizens or residents living abroad.
3) Income from sources within Puerto Rico, Guam, American Samoa, or the Northern Mariana Islands.

At present, no implementation agreement has been signed with Guam or the Northern Marianna Islands to allow exclusion of income from those sources. Until an implementation agreement is signed, there is no exclusion from these sources which must be added to your AGI to determine MAGI.

Hope Credit

You may be able to claim a Hope credit of up to $1,500 for qualified tuition and related expenses paid for *each* eligible student.

Eligible student for the Hope credit. For purposes of the Hope credit an eligible student is a student who meets *all* of the following requirements.

1) Did not have expenses that were used to figure a Hope credit in any 2 earlier years.
2) Had not *completed the first 2 years* of postsecondary education (generally, the freshman and sophomore years of college).
3) Was *enrolled at least half-time* in a program that leads to a degree, certificate, or other recognized educational credential, for at least one *academic period* beginning in 2001.
4) Was free of any federal or state felony conviction for possessing or distributing a controlled substance as of the end of 2001.

Completion of first 2 years. A student who was awarded 2 years of academic credit for postsecondary work completed before 2001 has completed the first 2 years of postsecondary education. This student would not be an eligible student for purposes of the Hope credit.

Any academic credit awarded solely on the basis of the student's performance on proficiency examinations is disregarded in determining whether the student has completed 2 years of postsecondary education.

Enrolled at least half-time. A student was enrolled at least half-time if the student was taking at least half the normal full-time work load for his or her course of study.

The standard for what is half of the normal full-time work load is determined by each eligible educational institution. However, the standards may not be lower than those established by the Department of Education under the Higher Education Act of 1965.

Amount of credit. The amount of the Hope credit is the sum of:

1) 100% of the first $1,000 qualified tuition and related expenses you paid for each eligible student, ***and***
2) 50% of the next $1,000 qualified tuition and related expenses you paid for each eligible student.

The maximum amount of Hope credit you can claim in 2001 is $1,500 times the number of eligible students. You can claim the full $1,500 for each eligible student for whom you paid at least $2,000 of qualified expenses. However, the credit may be reduced based on your modified adjusted gross income. See *Does the Amount of Your Income Affect the Amount of Your Credit?,* earlier.

TAX PLANNER

For tax years beginning after 2001, the $1,500 maximum Hope credit amount will be indexed for inflation.

Example. Jon and Karen are married and file a joint tax return. For 2001, they claim an exemption for their dependent daughter on their tax return and their modified adjusted gross income is $70,000. Their daughter is in her sophomore (second) year of studies at the local university and Jon and Karen pay qualified tuition and related expenses of $4,300 in 2001.

Jon and Karen, their daughter, and the local university meet all of the requirements for the Hope credit. Jon and Karen can claim a $1,500 Hope credit in 2001. This is 100% of the first $1,000 qualified tuition and related expenses, plus 50% of the next $1,000.

How to figure the Hope credit. The Hope credit is figured in Parts I and III of Form 8863. An illustrated example using Form 8863 appears later.

Lifetime Learning Credit

You may be able to claim a lifetime learning credit of up to $1,000 for qualified tuition and related expenses paid for ***all*** students enrolled in eligible educational institutions.

The lifetime learning credit is different than the Hope credit in the following ways.

1) The lifetime learning credit is not based on the student's work load. It is allowed for one or more courses.
2) Expenses for graduate-level degree work are eligible.
3) Expenses related to a course of instruction or other education that involves sports, games, hobbies, or other noncredit courses are eligible ***if*** they are part of a course of instruction to acquire or improve job skills.
4) There is no limit on the number of years for which the lifetime learning credit can be claimed for each student. It is not limited to students in the first 2 years of postsecondary education.
5) The amount you can claim as a lifetime learning credit does not vary (increase) based on the number of students for whom you pay qualified expenses.

Amount of credit. The amount of the lifetime learning credit is 20% of the first $5,000 qualified tuition and related expenses you pay for all eligible students. The maximum amount of lifetime learning credit you can claim for 2001 is $1,000 (20% × $5,000). However, that amount may be reduced based on your modified adjusted gross income. See

Does the Amount of Your Income Affect the Amount of Your Credit, earlier.

Explanation

The Lifetime Learning credit is equal to 20% of qualified tuition and fees incurred during the tax year on behalf of the taxpayer, the taxpayer's spouse, or any dependents. For expenses paid after June 30, 1998, and before January 1, 2003, up to $5,000 of qualified tuition and fees per taxpayer return will be eligible for the 20% Lifetime Learning credit (i.e., the maximum credit per taxpayer return will be $1,000). For expenses paid after December 31, 2002, up to $10,000 of qualified tuition and fees per taxpayer return will be eligible for the 20% Lifetime Learning credit (i.e., the maximum credit per taxpayer return will be $2,000). Qualified tuition and fees for the Lifetime Learning credit include amounts incurred for undergraduate or graduate-level (and professional degree) courses. The credit is available for the tuition and fees of a student who attends classes on at least a half-time basis as part of a degree or certificate program. It also is available for any course of instruction at an eligible educational institution (whether the student is enrolled on a full-time, half-time, or less than half-time basis) to acquire or improve the student's job skills.

Example. Bruce and Toni are married and file a joint tax return. For 2001, their modified adjusted gross income is $50,000. Toni is attending the community college (an eligible educational institution) to earn credits towards an associate's degree in nursing. She already has a bachelor's degree in history and wants to become a nurse. In August 2001, Toni paid $4,000 for her fall 2001 semester. Bruce and Toni can claim an $800 (20% × $4,000) lifetime learning credit on their 2001 joint tax return.

How to figure the lifetime learning credit. The lifetime learning credit is figured in Parts II and III of Form 8863. An illustrated example using Form 8863 appears later.

Choosing Which Credit To Claim

For each student, you can elect for any tax year only ***one*** of the credits ***or*** a tax-free withdrawal from a Coverdell ESA. (See *Coverdell ESAs* in chapter 4, Publication 970, for more information.)

For example, if you elect to take the Hope credit for a child on your 2001 tax return, you cannot, for that same child, also claim the lifetime learning credit for 2001 or take a tax-free withdrawal from a Coverdell ESA for 2001.

Lifetime learning credit after Hope credit. You can claim the Hope credit for the first 2 years of a student's postsecondary education and claim the lifetime learning credit for that same student in later tax years.

Tax credits for more than one student. If you pay qualified expenses for more than one student in the same year, you can choose to take credits on a per-student, per-year basis. This means that, for example, you can claim the Hope credit for one student and the lifetime learning credit for another student in the same tax year.

TAX ALERT

Who should claim the education credit. If you claim your child as a dependent, only you may claim the education credit for the child's qualified tuition and related expenses. If, however, you are eligible to claim your child as a dependent but choose not to do so, your child may claim the education credit for his or her qualified tuition and related expenses *even if* the tuition and expenses were paid by you, the parent. It is important to note, however, that if a parent who is eligible to claim a dependency exemption for a student does not do so, the student is not allowed to take a personal exemption for himself or herself on his or her own return. As a result, the exemption for the student may be lost. If you are subject to the income phaseout limitation of the education credits, you should consider not claiming an exemption for your child and allowing your child to claim the education credits.

How Is the Credit Claimed?

You elect to claim education credits and you figure their amount by completing **Form 8863.** A filled-in Form 8863 is shown in the *Illustrated Example* at the end of this chapter.

An eligible educational institution (such as a college or university) that received payment of qualified tuition and related expenses in 2001, generally must issue **Form 1098-T,** *Tuition Payments Statement,* to each student by February 1, 2002. The eligible educational institution may ask for a completed **Form W-9S,** *Request for Student's or Borrower's Social Security Number and Certification,* or similar statement, to obtain the student's name, address, and taxpayer identification number.

Illustrated Example

Dave and Valerie are married and file a joint tax return. For 2001, they claim exemptions for their two dependent children on their tax return. Their modified adjusted gross income is $72,000. Their tax is $9,475. Their son, Sean, will receive his bachelor's degree in psychology from the state college in May 2002. Their daughter, Corey, enrolled full-time at that same college in August 2000 to begin working on her bachelor's degree in physical education. In December 2000, Dave and Valerie paid $2,000 for each child's tuition for the winter 2001 semester. In July 2001, they paid $2,200 in tuition costs for each of them for the fall 2001 semester.

Dave and Valerie, their children, and the college meet all of the requirements for the higher education credits. Because Sean is beyond the second (sophomore) year of his postsecondary education, his expenses do not qualify for the Hope credit. But, amounts paid for Sean's expenses in 2001 for academic periods after 2000 and before April 1, 2002, qualify for the lifetime learning credit. Corey is in her first (freshman) year of postsecondary education and expenses paid for her in 2001 for academic periods beginning after 2000 and before April 1, 2002, qualify for the Hope credit.

Dave and Valerie figure their total higher education credits for 2001, $1,940, as shown in the completed Form 8863. They can claim the full amount because their modified adjusted gross income is not more than $80,000. They carry the amount from Form 8863 to line 46 of Form 1040, and they attach the **Form 8863** to their return.

Form 8863

Department of the Treasury
Internal Revenue Service

Education Credits
(Hope and Lifetime Learning Credits)

► See instructions on pages 2 and 3.   ► Attach to Form 1040 or Form 1040A.

OMB No. 1545-1618

2001

Attachment
Sequence No. **50**

Name(s) shown on return: Dave and Valerie Jones

Your social security number: 987 00 6543

Part I   Hope Credit. Caution: *The Hope credit may be claimed for no more than **2** tax years for the **same** student.*

1

(a) Student's name (as shown on page 1 of your tax return) First, Last	(b) Student's social security number (as shown on page 1 of your tax return)	(c) Qualified expenses (but **do not** enter more than $2,000 for each student). See instructions	(d) Enter the **smaller** of the amount in column (c) or $1,000	(e) Subtract column (d) from column (c)	(f) Enter one-half of the amount in column (e)
Corey Jones	137 00 9642	2,000	1,000		500

2 Add the amounts in columns (d) and (f) . . . . . **2** | 1,000 | ▨▨▨ | 500

3 Tentative Hope credit. Add the amounts on line 2, columns (d) and (f) . . . . . . ► **3** | 1,500

Part II   Lifetime Learning Credit

4

Caution: *You cannot take the Hope credit and the lifetime learning credit for the same student.*

(a) Student's name (as shown on page 1 of your tax return) First Last	(b) Student's social security number (as shown on page 1 of your tax return)	(c) Qualified expenses. See instructions
Sean Jones	246 00 9731	2,200

5 Add the amounts on line 4, column (c), and enter the total . . . . **5** | 2,200

6 Enter the **smaller** of line 5 or $5,000 . . . . **6** | 2,200

7 Tentative lifetime learning credit. Multiply line 6 by 20% (.20) . . . . ► **7** | 440

Part III   Allowable Education Credits

8 Tentative education credits. Add lines 3 and 7. . . . . **8** | 1,940

9 Enter: $100,000 if married filing jointly; $50,000 if single, head of household, or qualifying widow(er) . . . . . . **9** | 100,000

10 Enter the amount from Form 1040, line 34 (or Form 1040A, line 20)* **10** | 72,000

11 Subtract line 10 from line 9. If line 10 is equal to or more than line 9, **stop;** you cannot take any education credits. . . . . . **11** | 28,000

12 Enter: $20,000 if married filing jointly; $10,000 if single, head of household, or qualifying widow(er) . . . . **12** | 20,000

13 If line 11 is equal to or more than line 12, enter the amount from line 8 on line 14 and go to line 15. If line 11 is less than line 12, divide line 11 by line 12. Enter the result as a decimal (rounded to at least three places) . . . . **13** | × .

14 Multiply line 8 by line 13. . . . . ► **14** | 1,940

15 Enter the amount from Form 1040, line 42 (or Form 1040A, line 26) **15** | 9,475

16 Enter the total, if any, of your credits from Form 1040, lines 43 through 45 (or from Form 1040A, lines 27 and 28). . . . . **16** | -0-

17 Subtract line 16 from line 15. If line 16 is equal to or more than line 15, **stop;** you cannot take any education credits . . . . **17** | 9,475

18 **Education credits.** Enter the **smaller** of line 14 or line 17 here and on Form 1040, line 46 (or Form 1040A, line 29) . . . . ► **18** | 1,940

*See Pub. 970 for the amount to enter if you are filing Form 2555, 2555-EZ, or 4563 or you are excluding income from Puerto Rico.

For Paperwork Reduction Act Notice, see page 4.   Cat. No. 25379M   Form **8863** (2001)

37

Other Credits Including the Earned Income Credit

Introduction

This chapter discusses eight credits you may use to reduce your tax liability. Five of these credits are nonrefundable; that is, although they may be used to bring your tax liability to zero, any credit in excess of your liability is not refunded to you. Three of these credits are refundable. That means that any unused credit is refunded to you.

The five nonrefundable credits are:

1. The Adoption Credit
2. The Foreign Tax Credit
3. The Mortgage Interest Credit

4. The Minimum Tax Credit
5. The Electric Vehicle Credit

Depending on the credit, part or all of a nonrefundable credit that is not utilized in the current year generally may be carried back or carried forward and utilized in another year.

The three refundable credits are:

1. The excess Social Security or Railroad Retirement Tax Credit
2. The Regulated Investment Company Credit
3. The Earned Income Credit

Important Change

Rate reduction credit. You may qualify for the rate reduction credit if you did not receive the maximum advance payment in 2001. See Rate Reduction Credit, later.

Excess withholding of social security tax and tier 1 railroad retirement tax. Social Security and tier 1 railroad retirement tax (RRTA) are both withheld at a rate of 6.2% of wages. The maximum wages subject to this tax increased to $80,400 in 2001. If you had two or more employers and they withheld too much Social Security or RRTA tax during 2001, you may be entitled to a credit of the excess withholding. For more information about the credit, see *Credit for Excess Social Security Tax or Railroad Retirement Tax Withheld* under *Refundable Credits,* later.

This chapter discusses the following credits.

- Rate reduction credit.
- Adoption credit.
- Foreign tax credit.
- Mortgage interest credit.

- Credit for prior year minimum tax.
- Credit for electric vehicles.
- Credit for excess Social Security tax or railroad retirement tax withheld.
- Credit for tax on undistributed capital gain.
- Earned income credit

Several other credits are discussed in other chapters in this publication.

- Child and dependent care credit (chapter 33).
- Credit for the elderly or the disabled (chapter 34).
- Child tax credit (chapter 35).
- Education credits (chapter 36).

Nonrefundable credits. The first part of this chapter, Nonrefundable Credits, covers six credits that you subtract directly from your tax. These credits may reduce your tax to zero. If these credits are more than your tax, the excess is not refunded to you.

Refundable credits. The second part of this chapter, *Refundable Credits,* covers three credits that are treated as payments and are refundable to you. These credits are added to the federal income tax withheld and any estimated tax payments you made. If this total is more than your total tax, the excess will be refunded to you.

Useful Items

You may want to see:

Publication

☐ **514**   Foreign Tax Credit for Individuals
☐ **564**   Mutual Fund Distributions
☐ **936**   Home Mortgage Interest Deduction
☐ **968**   Tax Benefits of Adoption

Form (and Instructions)

☐ **1116**   Foreign Tax Credit (Individual, Estate, Trust, or Nonresident Alien Individual)
☐ **8396**   Mortgage Interest Credit
☐ **8801**   Credit For Prior Year Minimum Tax—Individuals, Estates, and Trusts
☐ **8828**   Recapture of Federal Mortgage Subsidy
☐ **8834**   Qualified Electric Vehicle Credit
☐ **8839**   Qualified Adoption Expenses

Nonrefundable Credits

The following credits are discussed in this part.

- Rate reduction credit.
- Adoption credit.
- Foreign tax credit.
- Mortgage interest credit.
- Credit for prior year minimum tax.
- Credit for electric vehicles.

Rate Reduction Credit

For 2001, the lowest tax rate is 10%. Most individuals received the benefits of the new 10% rate in an advance payment of income tax based on their 2000 tax returns. You can use the worksheet in your form instructions to determine whether you can claim the rate reduction credit based on your 2001 return.

Advance payment. Any advance payment of income tax that you received (before offset) during 2001 was based on your 2000 tax return. This payment is not subject to federal income tax. If you filed a joint return for 2000, you and your spouse are each considered to have received one-half of the advance payment.

This advance payment reduces your rate reduction credit. You cannot claim the credit if the advance payment is equal to the amount shown for your 2001 filing status.

- Single or married filing separately—$300.
- Head of household—$500.
- Married filing jointly or qualifying widow(er)—$600.

If your advance payment does not equal the amount shown, you may be able to claim the rate reduction credit.

Offsets. You are considered to have received the full amount of the advance payment even though all or part of that amount was used to offset (pay) certain past-due amounts. For information on offsets, see *Offsets against debts,* in chapter 1.

How to figure the credit. Use the *Rate Reduction Credit Worksheet* in your form instructions to figure your credit based on your 2001 tax return. If the credit is more than your advance payment, you can claim the

difference as the rate reduction credit. If the credit is not more than your advance payment, you cannot claim the rate reduction credit. You do not have to pay back the advance payment that is more than your credit.

Caution. *If you are filing a joint return for 2001, you must add your and your spouse's advance payments (before offsets) to determine the total advance payment received.*

Example 1. For 2001, you are single and, based on your 2001 tax return, you qualify for a rate reduction credit of $250. During 2001, you received $300 as an advance payment of income tax. Since the advance payment is more than your rate reduction credit, you cannot claim the credit. You do not have to pay back any of your advance payment.

Example 2. You get married during 2001 and file a joint return for that year. Based on your 2001 tax return, you qualify for the maximum rate reduction credit of $600. During 2001, you received $225 and your spouse received $300 as advance payments of income tax based on your individual tax returns for 2000. You must reduce your maximum rate reduction credit by the advance payments you and your spouse received. Your credit for 2001 is $75.

Dependents. If you, or your spouse if filing a joint return, can be claimed as a dependent on someone else's return, you cannot claim the credit. Figure your tax using the *Tax Computation Worksheet for Certain Dependents* in your form instructions unless you, or your spouse if filing a joint return, received an advance payment of income tax during 2001.

Nonresident alien. If you were a nonresident alien at the end of the year you cannot claim the credit. See your Form 1040NR instructions for how to figure your tax.

Adoption Credit

You may be able to take a tax credit of up to $5,000 for qualifying expenses paid to adopt an eligible child. The credit can be as much as $6,000 if the expenses are for the adoption of a child with special needs.

If your modified adjusted gross income (AGI) is more than $75,000, your credit is reduced. If your modified AGI is $115,000 or more, you cannot claim the credit.

TaxAlert: The 2001 Tax Act

Beginning in 2002, the maximum adoption credit has been doubled. You may now claim a credit for up to $10,000 qualified adoption expenses. Beginning in 2003, in the case of the adoption of a child with special needs, you may claim a credit of $10,000 when the adoption becomes finalized regardless of whether you have actually paid qualified adoption expenses.

Qualifying expenses. Qualifying adoption expenses are reasonable and necessary adoption fees, court costs, attorney fees, traveling expenses (including amounts spent for meals and lodging) while away from home, and other expenses directly related to, and whose principal purpose is for, the legal adoption of an eligible child.

Nonqualifying expenses. Qualifying adoption expenses do not include expenses:

- That violate state or federal law,
- For carrying out any surrogate parenting arrangement,
- For the adoption of your spouse's child,
- Paid using funds received from any federal, state, or local program,
- Allowed as a credit or deduction under any other federal income tax rule, or
- Paid or reimbursed by your employer or any other person or organization.

Eligible child. The term "eligible child" means any individual:

1) Under 18 years old, or
2) Physically or mentally incapable of caring for himself or herself.

TAXALERT

Qualified adoption expenses eligible for the credit include expenses paid or incurred in an unsuccessful effort to adopt an otherwise eligible child who is a citizen or resident of the United States. In the case of a child who is not a citizen or resident of the United States, the credit is available only for adoptions that become final.

Child with special needs. An eligible child is a child with special needs if:

1) He or she is a citizen or resident of the United States (including the District of Columbia and U.S. possessions) and
2) A state determines that the child cannot or should not be returned to his or her parents' home and probably will not be adopted unless adoption assistance is provided to the adoptive parents.

Factors used by states to determine if a child has special needs could include:

- The child's ethnic background,
- The child's age,
- Whether the child is a member of a minority or sibling group, or
- Whether the child has a medical condition or physical, mental, or emotional handicap.

Caution. A foreign child cannot be treated as a child with special needs.
When to claim the credit. Generally, you cannot take any credit before the year the adoption becomes final. See Publication 968 for information on when to claim expenses paid before the year the adoption becomes final.

TAXALERT

You may claim a credit for qualified adoption expenses of up to $5,000 ($6,000 in the case of a child with special needs). The credit is phased out for taxpayers with an adjusted gross income between $75,000 and $115,000. Taxpayers with adjusted gross income of more than $115,000 are not entitled to the credit. Qualified adoption expenses include reasonable and necessary adoption fees, court costs, attorney fees, and other expenses that are directly related to the adoption of a child by the taxpayer. The principal purpose of the expenses must be the adoption of an eligible child. An eligible child is an individual who has not attained the age of 18 or who is physically or mentally incapable of caring for himself or herself. The expenses cannot be in violation of federal or state law or for carrying out any surrogate parenting arrangement. You may not claim a credit for expenses incurred in adopting the child of your spouse. You may also not claim a credit for expenses reimbursed by a program of your employer; a federal, state, or local program; or other types. You are eligible for a separate credit for each child whom you adopt. Thus, you may claim a credit of up to $10,000 if you adopt two children and meet all of the other requirements.

For 2001, you may claim a credit only for qualified adoption expenses paid in 2000 or 2001 if the adoption becomes final in 2001. If you incur qualified adoption expenses in 2001 and the adoption becomes final in a later year, you must wait until 2002 to claim the credit.

How to claim the credit. To claim the credit, you must complete Form 8839 and attach it to your Form 1040 or Form 1040A. Enter the credit on line 49, Form 1040, or line 31, Form 1040A.

Foreign Tax Credit

You generally can choose to claim income taxes you paid or accrued during the year to a foreign country or U.S. possession as a credit against your U.S. income tax. Or, you can deduct them as an itemized deduction (see chapter 24).

You cannot take a credit (or deduction) for foreign income taxes paid on income that is exempt from U.S. tax under the foreign earned income exclusion or the foreign housing exclusion.
Limit on the credit. Your foreign tax credit cannot be more than your U.S. tax liability (line 40, Form 1040) multiplied by a fraction. The numerator of the fraction is your taxable income from sources outside the United States. The denominator is your total taxable income from U.S. and foreign sources. See Publication 514 for more information.

Explanation

To take the foreign tax credit, the foreign taxes must have been imposed on you, and you must have paid or accrued the taxes during your tax year. Furthermore, if you work overseas and elect to claim the foreign earned income exclusion or the foreign housing exclusion, the amount of foreign taxes eligible for credit is reduced. The foreign earned income exclusion allows U.S. citizens or residents who meet one of the tests for living abroad to exclude up to $76,000 of foreign earned income from their **gross income.** The foreign housing exclusion allows U.S. citizens or residents to exclude excess foreign housing costs from their gross income. See Chapter 42, *U.S. Citizens Working Abroad: Tax Treatment of Foreign Earned Income,* for a more complete discussion of these subjects.

The amount you may claim as a foreign tax credit is limited. You can figure your maximum credit by performing the following calculation:

$$\frac{\text{Taxable income from sources outside the U.S.}}{\text{Taxable income from all sources}} \times \text{U.S. income tax} = \text{Maximum credit}$$

Separate foreign tax credit limitations must be calculated for passive income and several other categories.

However, while you are limited in the amount of credit for foreign taxes you may claim in any one year, you are able to carry back the unused credits for 2 years and carry forward the unused credits for 5 years. See Chapter 42, *U.S. Citizens Working Abroad: Tax Treatment of Foreign Earned Income,* for a further discussion of how to calculate your foreign tax credit.

TAXPLANNER

It is usually better to claim a credit for foreign taxes than to deduct them as itemized deductions. Credits reduce your U.S. tax on a dollar-for-dollar basis, whereas a deduction just reduces the amount of income subject to tax. (For an example of this point, see Chapter 24, *Taxes You May Deduct.*)

How to claim the credit. Complete Form 1116 and attach it to your Form 1040. Enter the credit on line 43, Form 1040.
Election not to file Form 1116. You will not be subject to the limit and may be able to claim the credit without using Form 1116 if all the following requirements are met.

1) You are an individual.
2) Your only foreign source income for the tax year is passive income (dividends, interest, royalties, etc.) that is reported to you on a payee statement (such as a Form 1099-DIV, *Dividends and Distributions,* or 1099-INT, *Interest Income*).
3) Your qualified foreign taxes for the tax year are not more than $300 ($600 if filing a joint return) and are reported on a payee statement.
4) You elect this procedure for the tax year.

If you qualify and elect not to file Form 1116, enter the amount of your foreign taxes paid on line 43, Form 1040.

Caution. *If you make this election, you cannot carry back or carry over any unused foreign tax to or from this tax year.*

Mortgage Interest Credit

Mortgage credit certificates issued by state and local governments may entitle a certificate holder to a mortgage interest credit. The certificate must be used in connection with the purchase, qualified rehabilitation, or qualified home improvement of the certificate holder's main home.

Who qualifies. You may be able to claim a mortgage interest credit if you were issued a *mortgage credit certificate (MCC)* under a qualified MCC program. The MCC must relate to your main home.

Amount of credit. If your mortgage is equal to (or smaller than) the certified indebtedness amount (loan) shown on your MCC, you multiply the certified credit rate, shown on your MCC, by all the interest you paid on your mortgage during the year.

If your mortgage is larger than the certified indebtedness amount shown on your MCC, you multiply the certified credit rate, shown on your MCC, by only the interest allocated to the certified indebtedness amount shown on your MCC.

Caution. *If the certificate credit rate is more than 20%, the credit cannot be more than $2,000.*

Carryforward. If your allowable credit is more than your tax liability reduced by certain credits, you can carry forward the unused portion of the credit to your next 3 tax years or until used, whichever comes first.

If you are subject to the $2,000 limit because your certificate credit rate is more than 20%, no amount over the $2,000 (or your prorated share of the $2,000 if you must allocate the credit) may be carried forward.

Reduced home mortgage interest deduction. If you claim the credit and itemize your deductions on Schedule A (Form 1040), you must reduce your home mortgage interest deduction. Reduce your deduction by the amount on line 3 of Form 8396, even if part of that amount is to be carried forward to 2002. For more information about the home mortgage interest deduction, see chapter 25.

Recapture of federal mortgage subsidy. If your home was financed with a mortgage from a qualified mortgage bond program or you received an MCC, you may be subject to a recapture rule. The recapture would generally occur if you sold or disposed of your home during the first 9 years after the date you closed your mortgage loan. See Publication 523, *Selling Your Home,* for more information.

How to claim the credit. Figure your 2001 credit and any carryforward to 2002 on Form 8396, and attach it to your Form 1040. Be sure to include any credit carry forward from 1998, 1999, and 2000.

Include the credit in your total for line 50, Form 1040, and check box b.

Credit for Prior Year Minimum Tax

The tax laws give special treatment to some kinds of income and allow special deductions and credits for some kinds of expenses. If you benefit from these laws, you may have to pay at least a minimum amount of tax in addition to any other tax on these items. This is called the alternative minimum tax.

The special treatment of some items of income and expenses only allows you to postpone paying tax until a later year. If in prior years you paid alternative minimum tax because of these tax postponement items, you may be able to claim a credit for prior year minimum tax against your current year's regular tax. The amount of the credit cannot reduce your current year's tax below your current year's tentative alternative minimum tax.

You may be able to take a credit against your regular tax if you:

1) Paid alternative minimum tax in 2000,
2) Had on an unused minimum tax credit that you are carrying forward from 2000 to 2001, or
3) Had unallowed qualified electric vehicle credits in 2000.

How to claim the credit. Figure your 2001 credit and any carryforward to 2002 on Form 8801, and attach it to your Form 1040. Include the credit in your total for line 50, Form 1040, and check box c. You can carry forward any unused credit for prior year minimum tax to later years until it is completely used.

For additional information about the credit, see the instructions for Form 8801.

TAXPLANNER

Taxpayers reporting varying income from year to year may find themselves in a regular tax position in one year and in an AMT position the next. By accelerating income into an AMT year and deferring expenses until a regular tax year, you may take advantage of the different tax rates between the regular tax and the AMT. The effect of such a strategy is reduced due to the AMT credit, which is designed to even out the effect of AMT over time. However, the AMT credit will be of no benefit for AMT arising from certain itemized deductions, certain tax-exempt interest, depletion, and the exclusion for gains on the sale of certain small business stock. This should be considered if you undertake any plans to defer or accelerate income or expenses.

TAXPLANNER

Where possible, you should arrange income and deductions so that any AMT incurred will result in an AMT credit that is quickly usable.

Credit for Electric Vehicles

You may be allowed a tax credit if you placed a qualified electric vehicle in service during the year.

Qualified electric vehicle. This is a motor vehicle that:

1) Has at least four wheels and is manufactured primarily for use on public streets, roads, and highways,
2) Is powered *primarily* by an electric motor that draws its power from rechargeable batteries, fuel cells, or other portable sources of electrical current,
3) Is originally used by you, and
4) Is acquired for your own use, not for resale.

Amount of credit. The credit is equal to 10% of the cost of the vehicle. However, if the vehicle is a depreciable business asset, you must reduce the cost by any section 179 deduction before figuring the credit. Get Publication 463, Travel, Entertainment, Gift, and Car Expenses, for information on the section 179 deduction.

The credit is limited to $4,000 for each vehicle placed in service in 2001.

Special rules. You cannot take the credit if you use the vehicle predominately outside the United States.

The credit will be subject to recapture if, within 3 years after the date you place the vehicle in service, the vehicle is used predominantly outside the United States or is modified so that it is no longer eligible for the credit.

How to claim the credit. To claim the credit, complete Form 8834, and attach it to your Form 1040. Include the credit in your total for line 50, Form 1040. Check box d, and print "8834" on the line next to box d.

Refundable Credits

The following credits are refundable and are treated as payments of tax.

- Credit for excess social security tax or railroad retirement tax withheld.
- Credit for tax on undistributed capital gain.
- Earned income credit.

Credit for Excess Social Security Tax or Railroad Retirement Tax Withheld

TaxAlert

Since 1994, there has not been a cap on wages subject to the 1.45% Medicare tax. However, there is still a cap for Social Security taxes. In 2001, employees are subject to the 6.2% Social Security tax on the first $80,400 of wages. If you worked for two or more employers in 2001, you may still claim a credit for any excess Social Security or railroad retirement taxes withheld on your wages.

Most employers must withhold Social Security tax from your wages. If you work for a railroad employer, that employer must withhold tier 1 railroad retirement (RRTA) tax and tier 2 RRTA tax.

If you worked for two or more employers in 2001, you may have had too much Social Security tax or RRTA withheld from your pay. You can claim the excess as a credit against your income tax. The following table shows the maximum amount of wages subject to tax and the maximum amount of tax that should have been withheld in 2001.

Type of Tax	Maximum wages subject to tax	Maximum tax that should have been withheld
Social Security or RRTA tier 1	$80,400	$4,984.80
RRTA tier 2	$59,700	$2,925.30

Caution. All wages are subject to Medicare tax withholding.

One employer. If any one employer withheld Social Security or RRTA tax that exceeded the amounts in the preceding table, you cannot claim the extra amount withheld by that employer as a credit against your income tax. Your employer must adjust this for you.

Joint return. If you are filing a joint return, you cannot add the Social Security or RRTA tax withheld from your spouse's wages to the amount withheld from your wages. Figure the credit separately for both you and your spouse to determine if either of you has excess withholding.

How to claim the credit. If you file Form 1040, enter the credit on line 62. If you file Form 1040A, include the credit in the total on line 41 and put "Excess SST" and the amount of the credit in the space to the left of the line.

Example 1

Marie Gibson earned $84,000 during 2001. Her sole employer for the year inadvertently withheld $6,426 in Social Security and Medicare taxes from her salary. The amount that should have been withheld was $6,202.80 (6.2% × $80,400 plus 1.45% × $84,000). She may not claim the $223.20 overwithholding as a credit on her return. Instead, her employer should adjust her next check for this amount.

Example 2

Assume instead that Marie worked for two firms during the year and that her total withholding for Social Security and Medicare taxes was $6,426. Each firm withheld no more than $6,202.80. She should now claim the $223.20 overwithholding as a credit.

How to figure the credit if you did not work for a railroad. If you did not work for a railroad during 2001, figure the credit as follows:

1. Add all Social Security tax withheld (but not more than $4,984.80 for each employer). Enter the total here .... _____

2. Enter any uncollected Social Security tax on tips or group-term life insurance included in the total on Form 1040, line 58 .... _____

3. Add lines 1 and 2. If $4,984.80 or less, stop here. You cannot claim the credit .... _____

4. Social Security tax limit 4,984.80

5. Credit. Subtract line 4 from line 3. Enter the result here and on Form 1040, line 62 (or Form 1040A, line 41) .... _____

Example. You are married and file a joint return with your spouse who had no gross income in 2001. During 2001 you worked for the Brown Shoe Company and earned $45,000 in wages. Social Security tax of $2,790 was withheld. You also worked for another employer in 2001 and earned $40,000 in wages. $2,480 of Social Security tax was withheld from these wages. Because you worked for more than one employer and your total wages were more than $80,400 you can claim a credit of $285.20 for the excess Social Security tax withheld.

1. Add all Social Security tax withheld (but not more than $4,984.80 for each employer). Enter the total here $5,270.00

2. Enter any uncollected Social Security tax on tips or group-term life insurance included in the total on Form 1040, line 58 .... –0–

3. Add lines 1 and 2. If $4,984.80 or less, stop here. You cannot claim the credit 5,270.00

4. Social Security tax limit 4,984.80

5. Credit. Subtract line 4 from line 3. Enter the result here and on Form 1040, line 62 (or Form 1040A, line 41) $285.20

How to figure the credit if you worked for a railroad. If you were a railroad employee during 2001, figure the credit as follows:

1. Add all Social Security and tier 1 RRTA tax withheld (but not more than $4,984.80 for each employer). Enter the total here .... _____

2. Enter any uncollected Social Security and tier 1 RRTA tax on tips or group-term life insurance included in the total on Form 1040, line 58 .... _____

3. Add lines 1 and 2. If $4,984.80 or less, enter –0– on line 5 and go to line 6. .... _____

4. Social Security and tier 1 RRTA tax limit 4,984.80

5. Subtract line 4 from line 3 .... _____

6. Add all tier 2 RRTA tax withheld (but not more than $2,925.30 for each employer). Enter the total here .... _____

7. Enter any uncollected tier 2 railroad retirement tax on tips or group-term life insurance included in the total on Form 1040, line 58 .... _____

8. Add lines 6 and 7. If $2,925.30 or less, enter –0– on line 10 and go to line 11 .... _____

9. RRTA tier 2 limit 2,925.30

10. Subtract line 9 from line 8 .... _____

11. Credit. Add lines 5 and 10. Enter the result here and on Form 1040, line 62 (or Form 1040A, line 41) .... _____

Example

In 2001, Maurice Evans worked for a railroad for 7 months and had $2,573.00 in tier 1 railroad retirement tax, $601.75 in Medicare tax, and $2,033.50 in tier 2 railroad retirement tax withheld. He worked the remaining 5 months for a nonrailroad employer and had $2,705 in Social Security tax and $632.62 in Medicare tax withheld. He had no income from tips or group-term life insurance on either job. His credit is calculated as follows:

1.	Total Social Security and tier 1 RRTA tax withheld (do not include more than $4,984.80 for each employer	$5,278.00
2.	Total Social Security and tier 1 RRTA tax on tips or group-term life insurance included on line 53, Form 1040	0
3.	Total: Add lines 1 and 2	5,278.00
4.	Limit	$4,984.80
5.	Credit: Subtract line 4 from line 3	$293.20

Credit for Tax on Undistributed Capital Gain

You must include in your income any amounts that regulated investment companies (commonly called mutual funds) or real estate investment trusts (REITs) allocated to you as capital gain distributions, even if you did not actually receive them. If the mutual fund or REIT paid a tax on the capital gain, you are allowed a credit for the tax since it is considered paid by you. The mutual fund or REIT will send you Form 2439, Notice to Shareholder of Undistributed Long-Term Capital Gains, showing the undistributed capital gains and the tax paid, if any. Claim the credit for the tax paid by entering the amount on line 65, Form 1040, and checking box a. Attach Copy B of Form 2439 to your return. See Capital Gain Distributions in chapter 9 for more information on undistributed capital gains.

Earned Income Credit

The earned income credit (EIC) is a tax credit for certain people who work and have earned income under $32,121. A tax credit usually means more money in your pocket. It reduces the amount of tax you owe. The EIC may also give you a refund.

Important Changes for 2001

Earned income amount is more. The amount you can earn and still get the credit has increased for 2001. The amount you earn must be less than:

- $28,281 with one qualifying child,
- $32,121 with more than one qualifying child, or
- $10,710 if you do not have a qualifying child.

Investment income amount is more. The maximum amount of investment income you can have and still get the credit has increased for 2001. You can have investment income up to $2,450. For most people, investment income is taxable interest and dividends, tax-exempt interest, and capital gain net income. To get more detailed information, see *Rule 5*.

Kidnapped child. You may be able to claim the EIC for persons with a qualifying child even though your child has been kidnapped. To get more detailed information, see *Kidnapped child* under *Rule 7*.

Important Changes for 2002

New definition of earned income. For tax years after 2001, earned income will no longer include employee compensation that is nontaxable. This will change *Rule 6* and *Rule 14*.

Elimination of modified adjusted gross income (AGI). For tax years after 2001, you will no longer need to figure modified AGI. Your EIC will be figured using your AGI, *not* modified AGI. This will change *Rule 15*.

New rules for persons with same qualifying child. For tax years after 2001, new rules will be used to determine which person can claim the EIC on the basis of a qualifying child when two or more persons have the same qualifying child. This will change *Rule 8*. For details, see Publication 553, *Highlights of 2001 Tax Changes.*

New definition of eligible foster child. For tax years after 2001, the definition of an eligible foster child in *Rule 7* will change. The child will have to live with you only for more than half of the year, instead of the whole year.

Reduction of EIC by alternative minimum tax eliminated. For tax years after 2001, your EIC will no longer be reduced by the amount of alternative minimum tax shown on your return.

Important Reminders

Certain people must use Publication 596. Certain people must use Publication 596 to see if they meet the rules to take the EIC and to figure the amount of the credit. You must use Publication 596 if any of the following situations applies to you.

- The amount on Form 1040, line 21, includes an amount from Form 8814, *Parent's Election To Report Child's Interest and Dividends.*
- Your investment income *(Rule 5)* is $2,450 or more **and** you are filing Form 4797, *Sales of Business Property.*
- You are filing Schedule E, *Supplemental Income and Loss,* (Form 1040).
- You are reporting income or a loss from the rental of personal property not used in a trade or business.
- You are claiming a loss on Form 1040, line 12, 13, or 18.
- You (or your spouse if filing a joint return) received distributions from a pension, annuity, or IRA that are not fully taxable.
- You owe alternative minimum tax (AMT), found on Form 1040, line 41, or included in the total found on Form 1040A, line 35.

For information on how you can get Publication 596, *Earned Income Credit,* or other free IRS publications, see *How To Get Tax Help* in the back of this publication.

Modified AGI (adjusted gross income). Your modified AGI used to limit your credit includes:

1) Tax-exempt interest, and
2) The nontaxable part of a pension, annuity, or individual retirement arrangement (IRA) distribution, except any amount that is nontaxable because it was a trustee-to-trustee transfer or a rollover distribution.

Also, the amount of business losses that must be added back to AGI to figure modified AGI is 75%.

See *Rule 15* in this chapter or for more detailed information get Publication 596.

Advance payment of the earned income credit in your paycheck. If you qualify for the earned income credit in 2002, you can receive part of it in each paycheck throughout the year. See *Advance Earned Income Credit,* later, for more information.

Earned income credit has no effect on certain welfare benefits. Any refund you receive because of the EIC and any advance EIC payments you receive generally will not be used to determine whether you are eligible for the following benefit programs, or how much you can receive from these programs.

- Temporary assistance for needy families (TANF).
- Medicaid and supplemental security income (SSI).
- Food stamps.
- Low-income housing.

Social Security numbers. To claim the EIC, you must have a valid Social Security number (SSN) for you and your spouse (if filing a joint return) and any qualifying children. If an SSN is missing or incorrect, you may not get the credit. See *Rule 1,* later.

Form 8862 to claim EIC after disallowance. If your EIC for any year after 1996 was denied or reduced for any reason other than a mathematical or clerical error, you must attach a completed Form 8862, *Information To Claim Earned Income Credit After Disallowance,* to your next return if you wish to claim the EIC. The date on which your EIC was denied and the date on which you file your 2001 return affect whether you need to attach Form 8862 to your 2001 return or to a later return. See chapter 5 in Publication 596 for more information.

How do you get the earned income credit? To claim the EIC, you must:

1) Qualify by meeting certain rules, and
2) File a tax return, even if you:
   a) Do not owe any tax,
   b) Did not earn enough money to file a return, or
   c) Did not have income taxes withheld from your pay.

TaxAlert

You may be eligible for the earned income credit. This credit is available to certain low-income taxpayers. For 2001, a taxpayer without any qualifying children (see later) may be eligible for a maximum credit of $364.

A taxpayer with one child may be eligible for a maximum credit of $2,428, while a taxpayer with two or more qualifying children may be eligible for a maximum credit of $4,008.

TaxAlert

You are not eligible to claim the earned income credit if your investment income exceeds $2,400. Investment income includes dividends, interest, tax-exempt interest, net capital gain, net passive income, and net rental and royalty income not derived in the ordinary course of a trade or business.

TaxAlert

Taxpayers claiming the earned income credit must include a taxpayer identification number for themselves, their spouses (if married), and any qualifying children on the return. For this purpose only, a taxpayer identification number is a Social Security number issued by the Social Security Administration, other than one issued to an individual for the purpose of applying for federally funded benefits.

When you complete your return, you can figure your EIC by using a worksheet in the instructions for Form 1040, Form 1040A, or Form 1040EZ. Or, if you prefer, you can let the IRS figure the credit for you.

Table 37–1. Earned Income Credit in a Nutshell

Part A Rules for Everyone	Part B Rules If You Have a Qualifying Child	Part C Rules If You Do Not Have a Qualifying Child
Rule 1. You must have a valid social security number.	**Rule 7.** Your child must meet the relationship, age, and residency tests.	**Rule 10.** You must be at least age 25 but under age 65.
Rule 2. Your filing status cannot be "Married filing separately."	**Rule 8.** Your qualifying child cannot be the qualifying child of another person with a higher modified AGI.	**Rule 11.** You cannot be the dependent of another person.
Rule 3. You must be a U.S. citizen or resident alien all year.	**Rule 9.** You cannot be a qualifying child of another person.	**Rule 12.** You cannot be a qualifying child of another person.
Rule 4. You cannot file Form 2555 or Form 2555–EZ (relating to foreign earned income).		**Rule 13.** You must have lived in the United States more than half the year.
Rule 5. Your investment income must be $2,450 or less.		
Rule 6. You must have earned income.		

**Part D
Figuring and Claiming the EIC**

Rule 14. Your earned income must be less than:
- $32,121 if you have more than one qualifying child,
- $28,281 if you have one qualifying child, or
- $10,710 if you do not have a qualifying child.

Rule 15. Your modified AGI must be less than:
- $32,121 if you have more than one qualifying child,
- $28,281 if you have one qualifying child, or
- $10,710 if you do not have a qualifying child.

Useful Items

You may want to see:

Publication

- ☐ **504** Divorced or Separated Individuals
- ☐ **533** Self-Employment Tax
- ☐ **596** Earned Income Credit

Form (and Instructions)

- ☐ **Schedule EIC** Earned Income Credit (Qualifying Child Information)
- ☐ **Schedule SE (Form 1040)** Self-Employment Tax
- ☐ **W-5** Earned Income Credit Advance Payment Certificate
- ☐ **8862** Information To Claim Earned Income Credit After Disallowance

---

TAXSAVER

You *must* file a tax return to receive the earned income credit. If the tax you owe is less than the amount of the earned income credit, you will receive a refund from the government. Therefore, even if you are not required to file a tax return because your income is less than the income required to file, you still must do so in order to receive the credit.

Do You Qualify for the Credit?

To see if you can claim the EIC, you must first meet all of the rules explained in Part A, *Rules for Everyone.* Then you must meet the rules in Part B, *Rules If you Have a Qualifying Child,* or Part C, *Rules If You Do Not Have a Qualifying Child.* There are two final rules you must meet in Part D, *Figuring and Claiming the EIC.* You qualify for the credit if you meet all the rules in each part that applies to you. For example:

- If you have a qualifying child, the rules in *Parts A, B,* and *D* apply to you, or
- If you do not have a qualifying child, the rules in *Parts A, C,* and *D* apply to you.

Table 37–1, Earned Income Credit in a Nutshell. Use *Table 37–1* as a guide to *Parts A, B, C,* and *D.* The table is a summary list of all the rules in each part. Each rule listed has a rule number. Use the rule number to find a discussion of that rule in this chapter.

Do you have a qualifying child? Basically, a qualifying child is a child who:

1) Is your son, daughter, adopted child, grandchild, stepchild, or eligible foster child, **and**
2) Was (at the end of 2001) under age 19, under age 24 and a full-time student, or any age and permanently and totally disabled during the year, **and**
3) Lived with you in the United States for more than half of 2001 (for all of 2001 if the child is your eligible foster child).

See *Rule 7* for more detailed information.

If Improper Claim Made in Prior Year

You must file Form 8862 if for any year after 1996 your EIC was denied or reduced for any reason other than a math or clerical error. But do not file Form 8862 if, after your EIC was denied or reduced in an earlier year, you filed Form 8862 (or other documents) and your EIC was then allowed.

If it was determined that your error was due to reckless or intentional disregard of the EIC rules or fraud, you cannot claim the EIC for the next 2 years (10 years in the case of fraud).

More information. See chapter 5 in Publication 596 for more detailed information about the disallowance period and Form 8862.

EIC Eligibility Checklist

*You may claim the EIC if you answer YES to all the following questions.**	YES	NO
1. Do you, your spouse, and your qualifying child each have a valid SSN? (See Rule 1.)	❏	❏
2. Is your filing status married filing jointly, head of household, qualifying widow(er), or single? (See Rule 2.) **Caution:** If you are a nonresident alien, answer **YES** only if your filing status is married filing jointly and you are married to a U.S. citizen or resident alien. (See Rule 3.)	❏	❏
3. Answer **YES** if you are not filing Form 2555 or Form 2555–EZ. Otherwise, answer **NO**. (See Rule 4.)	❏	❏
4. Is your investment income $2,450 or less? (See Rule 5.)	❏	❏
5. Is your total earned income at least $1 but less than: • $10,710 if you do not have a qualifying child. • $28,281 if you have one qualifying child, or • $32,121 if you have more than one qualifying child? (See Rules 6 and 14.)	❏	❏
6. Is your modified AGI less than: • $10,710 if you do not have a qualifying child. • $28,281 if you have one qualifying child, or • $32,121 if you have more than one qualifying child? (See Rule 15.)	❏	❏
7. Answer **YES** if you (and your spouse if filing a joint return) are not a qualifying child of another person. (See Rules 9 and 12.)	❏	❏
STOP If you have a qualifying child, answer questions 8 and 9 and skip 10–12. If you do not have a qualifying child, skip answers 8 and 9 and answer 10–12.*		
8. Does your child meet the age, residency, and relationship tests for a qualifying child? (See Rule 7.)	❏	❏
9. Is your child a qualifying child only for you? Answer **YES** if your qualified child is also a qualifying child for another person but your modified AGI is higher than the other person's. (See Rule 8.)	❏	❏
10. Was your main home (and your spouse's if filing a joint return) in the United States for more than half the year? (See Rule 13.)	❏	❏
11. Were you (or your spouse if filing a joint return) at least age 25 but under 65 at the end of 2001? (See Rule 10.)	❏	❏
12. Answer **YES** if you (and your spouse if filing a joint return) cannot be claimed as a dependent on anyone else's return. Answer **NO** if you (and your spouse if filing a joint return) can be claimed as a dependent on someone else's return. (See Rule 11.)	❏	❏

* **PERSONS WITH A QUALIFYING CHILD:** If you answered **YES** to questions 1 through 9, you can claim the EIC. Remember to fill out Schedule EIC and attach it to your Form 1040 or Form 1040A. You cannot use Form 1040EZ.

PERSONS WITHOUT A QUALIFYING CHILD: If you answered **YES** to questions 1 through 7, and 10 through 12, you can claim the EIC.

If you answered NO to any question that applies to you: You cannot claim the EIC.

PART V

Special Situations and Tax Planning

The first four chapters in this part discuss some special situations. Chapter 38 is essential reading for anybody who is self-employed—freelancers, artists, and small business owners. Mutual fund investors will want to pay special attention to Chapter 39. It discusses what you need to know about the tax treatment of gains, losses, dividends, and distributions from a mutual fund. Chapter 41 will be of interest to taxpayers who employ domestic help, whether it be to care for their children or a disabled or elderly dependent. Chapter 42 discusses how U.S. citizens working abroad should handle their taxes. Among other matters, it explains how you can get a credit against your U.S. taxes for taxes you have paid to a foreign government. Chapter 43 discusses the tax rules applicable to foreign citizens living in the United States. Chapter 44 tells you how to prepare your tax records for your accountant. Ernst & Young prepares tax returns for thousands of individuals, so you won't be surprised to learn this is a matter that we've considered quite carefully. The next chapters offer a further helping hand. With luck, you won't need to refer to Chapter 45, but, in case your tax return is examined, you will find it useful. Chapter 46 can help you save money on your taxes next year. It discusses likely tax developments in 2002 and beyond.

If You Are Self-Employed: How to File Schedule C

Introduction

Many people work for themselves. Whether a business—already existing or new—is your sole source of income or whether it supplements other income, you will face a number of perplexing tax questions that ordinary wage earners do not. What income do you report? What expenses can you deduct? What forms do you need to file?

Unlike a partnership or a regular corporation, a sole proprietorship is not a separate entity. In a sole proprietorship, you and your business are one and the same. You report net profit or loss for the year from a sole

proprietorship on Form 1040, Schedule C (or C-EZ), and it becomes part of your adjusted gross income. In addition to owing income tax on such income, you, as the sole proprietor, usually will be liable for self-employment tax and will also be required to make payments of estimated taxes. A net loss from the business generally can be deducted when you compute your adjusted gross income.

This chapter concentrates on how a sole proprietorship recognizes business profit and losses on federal Form 1040, Schedule C and Schedule SE.

Who Must File Schedule C

If you are a sole proprietor, an independent contractor, a statutory employee, or a statutory nonemployee, you may be required to report business income and expenses on Schedule C.

Sole proprietor. If you operate a business as a sole proprietor, you must file Schedule C to report your income and expenses from your business. If you operate more than one business, or if you and your spouse had separate businesses, you must prepare a separate Schedule C for each business.

Independent contractor. A person whose work hours and procedures are not controlled by another and who is therefore deemed to be self-employed for tax purposes must also file a Schedule C. (Refer to page 509 for a further discussion on independent contractors.)

Statutory employee. If you are a statutory employee, you should file Schedule C. If you file Schedule C, you can

deduct certain business expenses when computing your adjusted gross income. A statutory employee's business expenses will not be subject to the 2% reduction of his or her adjusted gross income that applies to business expenses reported as a part of Schedule A, Itemized Deductions. A statutory employee includes the following occupations:

1. Certain agent and commission drivers
2. Full-time life insurance sales representatives
3. Certain home workers performing work, according to specifications furnished by the person for whom the services are performed
4. Certain traveling or city salespeople who work full-time (except for sideline sales activities) for one firm or person, soliciting orders from customers

If you meet the definition of a statutory employee, your employer must indicate this classification by checking box 15 on your Form W-2. This indicates to the IRS that you have the right to report your income and expenses on Schedule C.

As a statutory employee, you are considered an employee for Social Security and Medicare purposes. However, if you and your employer agree, federal income tax withholding is optional rather than mandatory.

A statutory employee reports his or her wages from box 1 of Form W-2 on line 1 of Schedule C. He or she then deducts allowable expenses on Part II of Schedule C to arrive at reportable income.

Statutory nonemployee. If you are a statutory nonemployee, you must file Schedule C to report your income and expenses.

Explanation

There are two categories of statutory nonemployees. The two categories are a direct seller of consumer products and a licensed real estate agent. They are treated as self-employed for federal income tax and employment tax purposes if:

1. Substantially all payments for their services as direct sellers or real estate agents are directly related to sales or other output, rather than to the number of hours worked; and
2. Their services are performed under a written contract providing that they will not be treated as employees for federal tax purposes.

Direct sellers. Direct sellers are persons:

1. Engaged in selling (or soliciting the sale of) consumer products in the home or at a place of business other than in a permanent retail establishment; or
2. Engaged in selling (or soliciting the sale of) consumer products to any buyer on a buy-sell basis, a deposit-commission basis, or any similar basis prescribed by regulations for resale in the home or at a place of business other than in a permanent retail establishment.

Direct selling also includes activities of individuals who attempt to increase direct sales activities of their direct sellers and who earn income based on the productivity of their direct sellers. Such activities include providing motivation and encouragement; imparting skills, knowledge, or experience; and recruiting.

Licensed real estate agents. This category includes individuals engaged in appraisal activities for real estate sales if they earn income based on sales or other output.

TAXALERT

Unlike a statutory employee, a statutory nonemployee is not subject to Social Security and Medicare withholding. Therefore, he or she is required to pay self-employment tax on net earnings. Additionally, federal income tax withholding is not required; therefore, estimated taxes must be paid.

What's Included on Schedule C

Schedule C is used to report income and related expenses applicable to the above activities. Income includes cash, property, and services received from all sources, unless specifically excluded under the tax code. Expenses include all ordinary and necessary expenses incurred in connection with the activity.

For sole proprietorships in the business of selling goods or inventory, the primary expense will be the cost of goods sold. The cost of goods sold represents the cost of materials, labor, and overhead included in the inventory sold during the year. Other expenses that you deduct on Schedule C include salaries and wages, interest on loans used in the activity, rent, depreciation, bad debts, travel, 50% of entertainment expenses, insurance, real estate taxes, state and local taxes, and an allocable portion of your tax return preparation fee.

TAXPLANNER

Schedule C-EZ. You may use Schedule C-EZ instead of Schedule C if you operated a business or practiced a profession as a sole proprietorship and you have met all of the requirements listed below:

- Had business expenses of $2,500 or less
- Used the cash method of accounting
- Did not have an inventory at any time during the year
- Did not have a net loss from your business
- Had only one business as a sole proprietor

and you:

- Had no employees during the year
- Are not required to file Form 4562, *Depreciation and Amortization,* for this business
- Do not deduct expenses for business use of your home
- Do not have prior-year, unallowed passive activity losses from this business

Where to Report on Your Return

Adjusted gross income (AGI). The net income or net loss arrived at on Schedule C should be reported on page 1 of Form 1040. The net income or net loss (subject to certain limitations) generated on your Schedule C will cause either an increase or a decrease in your AGI.

TAXALERT

It is important to note that if you are filing Schedule C, you must use Form 1040, not Form 1040A or Form 1040EZ.

Losses. If Schedule C expenses exceed Schedule C income, a loss will result. There is a possibility that the amount of Schedule C loss that can be deducted on your current year's income tax return may be limited. The amount of the loss that can be deducted on your return depends on whether or not you materially participate in the operation of the business or whether or not you have enough investment at risk to cover the loss.

Defining material participation. You are treated as a material participant only if you are involved in the operations of the activity on a regular, continuous, and substantial basis. If you are not a material participant in an activity but your spouse is, you are treated as being a material participant and the activity is not considered passive. A passive activity involves the conduct of any trade or business in which you do not materially participate.

For more information about passive activities and the at-risk limitation, see Chapter 13, *Other Income,* and IRS Publication 925, *Passive Activity and At-Risk Rules.*

Carrybacks and Carryforwards. If you have incurred a Schedule C loss, it is possible that the loss may be large enough to offset all taxable income reported on your Form 1040. If this is the case, you may have generated a net operating loss (NOL).

TaxAlert

Net operating loss. If you have incurred a net operating loss (NOL), you can carry back or carry forward the loss and utilize it to offset income in other years. An NOL can be carried back 2 years and forward 20 years. NOLs from pre-1998 tax years still expire after 15 carryforward years.

You may elect not to carry back your NOL. If you make this election, you may use your NOL only during the 20-year carryforward period with respect to losses arising for tax years beginning after August 5, 1997. To make this election, attach a statement to your tax return for the NOL year. This statement must show that you are electing to forgo the carryback period under Section 172(b)(3) of the Internal Revenue Code.

· Proprietorships with less than $5 million in gross receipts that incurred losses attributable to presidentially declared disaster areas are subject to a 3-year carryback period.

Example

In 2001, Robert Jones, the sole proprietor of a small business, has a net operating loss of $66,000. In past years, Jones reported the following amounts of taxable income: 1998—$82,000, 1999—$10,000, and 2000—$4,000. The NOL can be carried back 2 years to 1999 and 2000 and can offset $14,000 ($10,000 + $4,000) of taxable income from those years. The remaining NOL of $52,000 ($66,000 – $14,000) can be carried forward for 20 years.

TaxSaver

If your income was subject to tax at a lower tax bracket during the carryback period and you expect your future income to be subject to tax at a higher tax bracket, you may wish to elect to forgo the carryback of the NOL.

Example

In 2001, you incur an NOL of $20,000. You have been profitable in the 2 previous years, and the profits have been taxed at a 15% tax rate. You expect to generate large income in future years, and you expect to be taxed at a 38.6% tax rate. By electing to forgo the carryback of the NOL, you can save $4,720 in taxes [$20,000 × (38.6% – 15%)].

For more information on net operating losses, see Form 1045 and Publication 536, *Net Operating Losses.*

Self-Employment Income and Social Security Tax

Income reported on Schedule C is classified as self-employment income for the sole proprietor, the independent contractor, and the statutory nonemployee. It is not classified as self-employment income for a statutory employee and is therefore not subject to self-employment tax.

Self-employment tax is calculated on Form 1040 Schedule SE. Self-employment tax is composed of a Social Security tax of 12.4% and a Medicare tax of 2.9%. For 2001, the maximum amount of wages and/or self-employment income subject to the Social Security part of the self-employment tax is $80,400. Therefore, if your salary income as an employee is $80,400 or above you would have already paid all the Social Security tax you owe. Your self-employment income would, however, be subject to the Medicare tax of 2.9%. There is no limit on the amount of earnings subject to the Medicare portion of the self-employment tax. A comprehensive example at the end of this chapter shows you how to calculate your self-employment tax when you also have salary income.

You may be able to use the short Schedule SE if:

1. Your self-employment earnings and wages subject to Social Security were less than $80,400;
2. You did not receive tips reported to your employer;
3. You are not a minister or member of a religious order.

Exception

If your net self-employment income multiplied by .9235 is below $400, you are not subject to self-employment tax on your self-employment income.

TaxAlert

Estimated income taxes. You may be required to pay estimated tax on your self-employment income. This depends on how much income and self-employment tax you expect for the year and how much of your income will be subject to withholding tax. For more information, see Chapter 5, *Tax Withholding and Estimated Tax.*

TaxPlanner

If you are a salaried employee as well, you may cover your estimated self-employment tax payments by having your employer increase the amount of income tax withheld from your pay.

TaxSaver

If you have more than one trade or business, you must combine the net earnings from each business to determine your net self-employment income. A loss that you incur in one business will offset your income in another business.

When an individual's self-employment earnings are less than $400, he or she is not required to file Form 1040 Schedule SE or to pay self-employment tax.

Joint returns show the name of the spouse with self-employment income on Schedule SE. If both spouses have self-employment income, each must file a separate Schedule SE. If one spouse qualifies to use Short Schedule SE and the other has to use Long Schedule SE, both can use one Schedule SE. One spouse should complete the front and the other the back.

Include the total profits or losses from all businesses on Form 1040, as appropriate. Enter the combined Schedule SE tax on Form 1040.

TaxSaver

Self-employment tax deduction. You can deduct one-half of your self-employment tax in figuring your adjusted gross income. This is an income tax adjustment only. It does not affect either your net earnings from self-employment or your self-employment tax. To deduct the tax, enter on Form 1040, line 25, the amount shown on the "Deduction for one-half of self-employment tax" line of Schedule SE.

What Is Included in Net Self-Employment Earnings?

In most cases, net earnings include your net profit from a farm or nonfarm business, plus the following items:

- Rental income from a farm if, as landlord, you materially participated in the production or management of the production of farm products on this land.

- Cash or a payment in kind from the Department of Agriculture for participating in a land diversion program.

- Payments for the use of rooms or other space when you also provided substantial services. Examples are hotel rooms, boarding houses, tourist camps or homes, parking lots, warehouses, and storage garages.

- Income from the retail sale of newspapers and magazines if you were age 18 or older and kept the profits.

- Amounts received by current or former self-employed insurance agents that are:

1. Paid after retirement but calculated as a percentage of commissions received from the paying company before retirement;
2. Renewal commissions; or
3. Deferred commissions paid after retirement for sales made before retirement.

- Fees as a state or local government employee if you were paid only on a fee basis and the job was not covered under a federal-state Social Security coverage agreement.

- Interest received in the course of any trade or business, such as interest on notes or accounts receivable.

- Fees and other payments received by you for services as a director of a corporation.

- Fees you received as a professional fiduciary.

- Gain or loss from Section 1256 contracts or related property by an options or commodities dealer in the normal course of dealing in or trading Section 1256 contracts.

Income and Losses Not Included in Net Earnings from Self-Employment

- Salaries, fees, and so on, subject to Social Security or Medicare tax that you received for performing services as an employee.

- Income you received as a retired partner under a written partnership plan that provides for lifelong periodic retirement payments if you had no other interest in the partnership and did not perform services for it during the year.

- Income from real estate rentals (including rentals paid in crop shares), if you did not receive the income in the course of a trade or business as a real estate dealer. This includes cash and crop shares received from a tenant or sharefarmer.

- Dividends on shares of stock and interest on bonds, notes, and so on, if you did not receive the income in the course of your trade or business as a dealer in stocks or securities.

- Gain or loss from:

1. The sale or exchange of a capital asset;
2. The sale, exchange, involuntary conversion, or other disposition of property unless the property is stock in trade or other property that would be considered inventory, or held primarily for sale to customers in the ordinary course of the business; or
3. Certain transactions in timber, coal, or domestic iron ore.

- Net operating losses from other years.

Statutory employee income. If you were a statutory employee, **do not** include the net profit or (loss) from that Schedule C (or the net profit from Schedule C-EZ) on Schedule SE. A statutory employee is defined above.

Self-Employment Tax Calculation
Self-employment tax can be calculated under one of the following methods: the regular method, the farm optional method, and the nonfarm optional method.

Regular Method. Under the regular method, your self-employment tax should be calculated as follows:

1. Figure your net self-employment income. The net profit from your business or profession is generally your net self-employment income.
2. After you figure your net self-employment income, determine how much is subject to self-employment tax. The amount subject to self-employment tax is called net earnings from self-employment. It is figured on Short Schedule SE, line 4, or Long Schedule SE, line 4a. It is generally 92.35% of net self-employment income.
3. Figure your self-employment tax as follows:

- If, for 2001, your net earnings from self-employment plus any wages and tips are not more than $80,400 and you do not have to use Long Schedule SE, use Short Schedule SE. On line 5, multiply your net earnings by 15.3% (.153). The result is the amount of your self-employment tax.
- If you had no wages or tips in 2001, your net earnings from self-employment are more than $80,400, and you do not have to use Long Schedule SE, use Short Schedule SE. On line 5, multiply the line 4 net earnings by 2.9% (.029) Medicare tax and add the result to $9,970 (12.4% of $80,400). The total is the amount of your self-employment tax.
- If you received wages or tips in 2001 and your net earnings from self-employment *plus* any wages and tips are more than $80,400, you must use Long Schedule SE. Subtract your total wages and tips from $80,400 to find the maximum amount of earnings subject to the 12.4% Social Security part of the tax. If more than zero, multiply the amount by 12.4% (.124). The result is the Social Security tax amount. Then multiply your net earnings from self-employment by 2.9% (.029). The result is the Medicare tax amount. The total of the Social Security tax amount and the Medicare tax amount is your self-employment tax.

Optional Methods. Generally, you can use the optional methods when you have a loss or small amount of net income from self-employment and:

1. You want to receive credit for Social Security benefit coverage,
2. You incurred child or dependent care expenses for which you could claim a credit (this method will increase your earned income, which could increase your credit), or
3. You are entitled to the earned income credit (this method will increase your earned income, which could increase your credit).

How to Determine Items of Income and Expenses

Start-up and Pre-operating Expenses
Start-up expenditures are the costs of getting started in business before you actually begin business operations. Start-up costs may include expenses for such things as ad-

vertising, travel, utilities, repairs, or employees' wages. These are often the same kinds of costs that can be deducted when they occur after you open for business.

Start-up costs include what you pay for both investigating a prospective business and getting the business started. For example, they may include costs for the following items:

- A survey of potential markets
- An analysis of available facilities, labor, supplies, and so forth
- Advertisements for the opening of the business
- Salaries and wages for employees who are being trained and their instructors
- Travel and other necessary costs for securing prospective distributors, suppliers, or customers
- Salaries and fees for executives and consultants or for other professional services

Start-up costs do not include deductible interest, taxes, and research and experimental costs. Therefore, subject to other limitations, these items are currently deductible.

Whether or not you can deduct your start-up expenditures depends on whether you actually begin the active trade or business.

If you go into business. When your business actually begins, all of the costs you incurred to start it up are not currently deductible and must be capitalized. However, an election can be made to amortize these start-up costs ratably over a minimum of 60 months. To amortize your start-up costs, the costs must meet the following tests:

1. They must be costs that would be deductible if they were paid or incurred to operate an existing trade or business (i.e., wages, advertising) but not to purchase machinery.
2. They must be paid or incurred by you before you actually begin business operations.

Electing to amortize expenses. An election to amortize expenses must be made by the due date of the return (including extensions) for the year in which active business begins.

The election must include a description of the expenditures, the amounts, the dates they were incurred, the month in which the business began, and the number of months in the amortization period. The amount of amortization is reported on Form 4562, Part VI.

Example

John's repair shop started business on June 1, 2001. Prior to starting business, John incurred various expenses totaling $6,000 to set up shop. John makes an election on his 2001 income tax return to amortize these expenses over a 60-month period. John is permitted a tax deduction for amortization of start-up expenses of $700 in 2001 [$6,000 ÷ 60 months) × 7 months in 2001].

TaxAlert

Though the IRS has been instructed to do so, it has not issued any guidance as to when a trade or a business begins. When it does, the IRS is likely to take a conservative stance. In the meantime, there has been substantial litigation about this issue. The generally accepted rule seems to be that even though a taxpayer has made a firm decision to enter into a business and over a considerable period of time has spent money in preparation for entering that business, he or she still has not engaged in carrying on any trade or business until such time as the business has begun to function as a going concern and has performed those activities for which it was organized.

If you fail to go into business. If your attempt to go into business is not successful, whether or not you can deduct the expenses you incurred in trying to establish yourself in business depends on the type of expenses you incurred.

Investigatory expenses. The costs you incurred before making a decision to acquire or to begin a specific business are classified as personal and therefore are not deductible. Investigatory expenses include costs incurred in the course of a general search for, or preliminary investigation of, a business prior to reaching a decision to acquire or enter any business. Examples include expenses incurred for the analysis or survey of potential markets, products, labor supply, transportation facilities, and so on.

Start-up expenses. The costs that you incur after you've made a decision to acquire or to establish a particular business and prior to its actual operation are classified as capital expenditures and may be deductible in the year in which your attempt to go into business fails.

Business sold. If you completely dispose of a trade or a business before the end of the amortization period you have selected, any deferred start-up costs for the trade or business that have not yet been deducted may be deducted to the extent that they qualify as a loss from a trade or a business.

Tax Year

Every taxpayer must determine taxable income and file a tax return on the basis of an annual accounting period. The term "tax year" is the annual accounting period you use for keeping your records and for reporting your income and expenses. The accounting periods you can use are as follows:

1. A calendar year
2. A fiscal year

You adopt a tax year when you file your first income tax return. It cannot be longer than 12 months.

Calendar tax year. If you adopt the calendar year for your annual accounting period, you must maintain your books and records, and report your income and expenses for the period from January 1 through December 31 of each year.

TaxAlert

If you filed your first return using the calendar tax year and you later begin business as a sole proprietor, you must continue to use the calendar tax year, unless you get permission from the IRS to change. You must report your income from all sources, including your sole proprietorship, using the same tax year.

Fiscal tax year. A regular fiscal tax year is 12 consecutive months, ending on the last day of any month except December.

If you adopt a fiscal tax year, you must maintain your books and records, and report your income and expenses using the same tax year.

Accounting Methods

Accounting methods are described in Chapter 1, *Filing Information.* The discussion that follows relates mainly to self-employed entrepreneurs, sole proprietors, and others who file Schedule C. No single accounting method is required for all taxpayers. Generally, you may figure your taxable income under any of the following accounting methods:

1. Cash method
2. Accrual method
3. Special methods of accounting for certain items of income and expenses
4. Combination (hybrid) method using elements of (1), (2), or (3)

Cash method. The cash method of accounting is used by most individuals and many small businesses with no inventories. However, if inventories are necessary in accounting for your income, you must use the accrual method for your sales and purchases. If you are not required to maintain inventories, it is often advisable to use the cash method, because it allows you more flexibility and control over your income.

Income. Under the cash method, your gross income includes all items of income you actually receive during the year. You must include in your income property and services you recieve at their fair market value.

Expenses. Usually, you must deduct expenses in the tax year in which you actually pay them. However, you may be required to postpone the deduction for expenses you pay in advance. In addition, you may have to capitalize certain costs.

Accrual method. Under an accrual method of accounting, income generally is reported in the year in which it is earned, regardless of when the income is actually collected, and expenses generally are deducted in the year in which they are incurred, regardless of when the expenses are paid. The purpose of an accrual method of accounting is to match your income and your expenses. If inventories are necessary in your business, only the accrual method of accounting can be used for purchases and sales.

Income. All items of income are generally included in your gross income when you earn them, even though you may receive payment in another tax year. All events that fix your right to receive the income must have happened, and you must be able to determine the amount with reasonable accuracy.

Example

You are a calendar year taxpayer. You sold a radio on November 28, 2001. You billed the customer 3 days later but did not receive payment until February 2002. You must include the amount of the sale in your income for 2001 because you earned the income in 2001.

Income received in advance. Prepaid income is generally included in gross income in the year you receive it. Your method of accounting does not matter as long as the income is available to you. Prepaid income includes rents or interest received in advance and compensation for services to be performed later.

If, under an agreement, you receive advance payment for services to be performed by the end of the next tax year, you can defer the inclusion in income of the payments received until you earn them by performing the service. You **must** be an accrual method taxpayer to defer recognition of income on advance payments for services. You cannot defer the income beyond the year after the year you receive the payment.

Example 1

You are in the television repair business. In 2001, you received payment for 1-year contracts under which you agree to repair or replace certain parts that fail to function properly in television sets that were sold by an unrelated party. You include the payments in gross income as you earn them by performing the services as specified under the accrual method of including advance payments.

If for any reason you do not perform part of the services by the end of the following tax year, 2002, you must include in gross income for 2002 the amount of the advance payments that are for the unperformed services.

Example 2

You own a dance studio. On November 4, 2001, you received payment for a 1-year contract, beginning on that date and providing for 48 1-hour lessons. You gave 8 lessons in 2001. If you recognize income under the accrual method of including advance payments, you must include one-sixth (8/48) of the payment in income for 2001 and five-sixths (40/48) of the payment in 2002.

Expenses. You deduct expenses when you become liable for them, whether or not you pay them in the same year. Before you can deduct expenses, all events that set the amount of the liability must have happened, you must be able to determine the amount of the liability with reasonable accuracy, and economic performance (see below) must occur.

Economic performance rule. Even if all of the events that determine the amount of your expenses have occurred, you still cannot deduct business expenses until economic performance occurs. If your expense is for property or services provided to you, or for use of property by you, economic performance occurs as the property or services are provided or as the property is used. If your expense is for property or services that you provide to others, economic performance occurs as the property or services are provided or as the property is used.

Special rules for related persons. An accrual basis taxpayer cannot deduct business expenses and interest owed to a related cash basis taxpayer until the amount is paid.

For purposes of applying this rule, related persons include, but are not limited to:

1. Members of the immediate family, including only brothers and sisters, husband and wife, ancestors, and lineal descendants
2. An individual and a corporation, if more than 50% in value of the outstanding stock is owned, directly or indirectly, by or for such individual
3. An S corporation and any individual who owns any of the stock of such S corporation
4. A partnership and any person who owns any capital interest or profits interest of such partnership

Special methods. In addition to the cash or accrual methods, certain items of income or expenses are accounted for under special methods. They include:

- Depreciation
- Amortization and depletion
- Bad debts
- Installment sales

The method of accounting for depreciation and bad debts is discussed later in this chapter. Methods for deducting amortization and depletion are discussed in IRS Publication 535, *Business Expenses*. Methods for reporting installment sales are discussed in IRS Publication 537, *Installment Sales.*

Combination (hybrid) method. Any combination of cash, accrual, and special methods of accounting can be used if the combination clearly reflects income and is consistently used. As an example, if you maintain inventory, the accrual method of accounting for purchases and sales must be used; however, you may use the cash method for all other items of income and expenses.

Two or more businesses. If you operate more than one business, you generally may use a different accounting method for each separate and distinct business if the method you use for each clearly reflects your income. For example, if you operate a personal-service business and a manufacturing business, you may use the cash method for the personal-service business, but you must use the accrual method for the manufacturing business.

How to Complete Schedule C

Schedule C is divided into five parts:

> Part I: Income
> Part II: Expenses
> Part III: Cost of Goods Sold
> Part IV: Information on Your Vehicle
> Part V: Other Expenses

In addition, Schedule C requires that you answer a number of general questions about the activity.

General Information

Line A asks for the principal business or profession, including the product or service that provided your principal source of income.

Line B asks for the four-digit code that identifies your principal business or professional activity. The instructions to Schedule C contain a list of the principal business or professional activity codes that you should use.

Line C asks for your business name. If none, leave this line blank.

Line D asks for your employer identification number (EIN). An EIN is needed only if you had a Keogh plan [discussed later in this chapter and in Chapter 18, *Individual Retirement Arrangements (IRAs)*] or if you were required to file an employment or excise tax return. If you do not have an EIN, do not enter your Social Security number. To apply for an EIN, you must file Form SS-4 with the IRS where you file your individual tax return. For your convenience, Form SS-4 is found in the back of this book.

Line E requests your business address. If you conducted business out of your home, you do not have to complete this line.

Line F asks for your accounting method, as discussed earlier in this chapter and in Chapter 1, *Filing Information*.

Line G asks whether or not you "materially participated" in the business. If you did not, your losses from the business that you can deduct currently may be limited. See Chapter 13, *Other Income*.

Line H must be checked if this is the initial Schedule C filed for this particular business.

In addition, Part III of the form asks two additional questions. Line 33 asks for the method used to value closing inventory, if your business maintains inventory. The inventory can be valued under any one of the following three methods: (1) cost, (2) lower of cost or market, or (3) any other method approved by the IRS. Methods of valuing inventory will be discussed later in this chapter.

Line 34 does not need to be answered if your business does not have inventory. If the business does maintain inventory and there was a change in determining quantities, costs, or valuations between opening and closing inventories, answer the question "yes" and attach an explanation for the change.

Income

Part I of Schedule C is used to report the gross income from the business. You should include on line 1 gross receipts or sales from your business. Do not combine receipts from two separate businesses on this line. Remember that you must file a separate Schedule C for each business. Statutory employees enter the amount from box 1 of Form W-2 and check the box on line 1.

On line 2, report such items as sales returns, rebates, and allowances. For example, if an item you previously sold is returned for a cash refund, the cash refund should be reported here and not included as a reduction of the gross receipts or sales reported on line 1.

Subtract line 2 from line 1, and enter the difference on line 3. From this amount, deduct the cost of goods sold. After deducting the cost of goods sold, you arrive at the gross profit from the business.

Costs of Goods Sold

Part III of Schedule C is used to determine your cost of goods sold. If you make or buy goods to sell, you are entitled to deduct the cost of the goods sold on your tax return. One of the most important costs that must be determined is the cost of your inventory.

Inventories are required to be determined at the beginning and end of each tax year for manufacturers, wholesalers, retailers, and every other business that makes, buys, or sells goods to produce income. Inventories include goods held for sale in the normal course of business, work in process, and raw materials and supplies that will physically become a part of merchandise intended for sale.

Add to your beginning inventory the cost of inventory items purchased during the year, including all other items entering into the cost of obtaining or producing the inventory. From this total, subtract your inventory at the end of the year. The remainder represents the cost of goods sold during the tax period. It should not include selling expenses or any other expenses that are not directly related to obtaining or producing the goods sold.

Inventory methods. To determine the value of your inventory, you need a method for identifying the items in your inventory and a method for valuing these items. In general, there are three methods of identifying items in inventory: (1) specific identification, (2) first in, first out (FIFO), and (3) last in, first out (LIFO).

The specific identification method is used to identify the cost of each inventoried item by matching the item with its cost of acquisition in addition to other allocable costs, such as labor and transportation. This method is most often used by retailers of unique items.

If there is no specific identification of items with their costs, you must make an assumption to decide which items were sold and which remain in inventory. You make this identification by either the FIFO or the LIFO method.

The FIFO method assumes that the items you purchased or produced first are the first items you sold, consumed, or otherwise disposed of.

The LIFO method assumes that the items of inventory that

you purchased or produced last are sold or removed from inventory first.

The FIFO method and the LIFO method produce different results in income, depending on the trend of price levels of the goods included in those inventories. In times of inflation, when prices are rising, LIFO will produce a larger cost of goods sold and a lower closing inventory. Under FIFO, the cost of goods sold will be lower and the closing inventory will be higher. However, in times of falling prices, LIFO will produce a smaller cost of goods sold and a higher closing inventory. Under FIFO, the reverse will be true.

Valuing inventory. Valuing the items in your inventory is a major factor in figuring your taxable income. The two common ways to value your inventory if you use the FIFO method are the specific-cost identification method and the lower-of-cost-or-market method.

Adopting LIFO method. To adopt the LIFO method, you are required to file Form 970, *Application to Use LIFO Inventory Method,* or a statement that has all the information required in Form 970. You must file the form (or the statement) with your timely filed tax return for the year in which you first use LIFO.

Once a method is selected you may not change to another method without the permission of the IRS. For a further discussion of inventory, see Publication 334, *Tax Guide for Small Business.*

Expenses

Part II of Schedule C is used to report expenses associated with your business. To be deductible, a business expense must be both ordinary and necessary. An ordinary expense is one that is common and accepted in your field of business, trade, or profession. A necessary expense is one that is helpful and appropriate for your trade, business, or profession. An expense does not have to be indispensable to be considered necessary. Examples of deductible business expenses include (1) reasonable allowance for salaries and other compensation, (2) traveling expenses while away from home, and (3) rentals or other payments for property used in a trade or a business.

You must keep business expenses separate from personal expenses. If you have any expense that is partly business and partly personal, a reasonable allocation should be made to separate the personal part from the business part.

Capital expenditures. A capital expenditure is defined as an expense that must be capitalized rather than deducted. These costs are considered a part of your investment in your business. There are, in general, three types of costs that must be capitalized: (1) costs of going into business, (2) costs to purchase business assets, and (3) cost of improvements.

Although you generally cannot directly deduct a capital expenditure, you may be able to take deductions for the amount you spend through a method of depreciation, amortization, or depletion.

A discussion of some of the more common expenses you will encounter in your business follows.

Bad Debts. If someone owes you money that you cannot collect, you have a bad debt. You may be able to deduct the amount owed to you when you figure your business income in the year in which the debt becomes worthless. There are two kinds of bad debts: business bad debts and nonbusiness bad debts. A business bad debt generally is one that comes from your trade or business. All other bad debts are nonbusiness bad debts. For a discussion of nonbusiness

bad debts and when a debt becomes worthless, see Chapter 15, *Sale of Property.*

Business bad debts usually occur because of credit sales to customers. They can also be loans to suppliers, employees, and others associated with your trade or business. These debts are usually shown on your books as either accounts receivable or notes receivable. If you are unable to collect any part of these accounts or notes receivable, the uncollectible part is a business bad debt.

You may take a bad debt deduction on your accounts and notes receivable only if you have basis in the debt; that is, you already included the amount you are owed in your current or earlier gross income (i.e., accounts receivable), or you actually loaned the money (i.e., notes receivable). Only individuals filing a Schedule C using either the accrual or hybrid (cash accrual) accounting method will be able to deduct bad debts relating to accounts receivable. Cash method taxpayers do not report income that is due them until they actually receive payment. Therefore, they cannot take a bad debt deduction on payments they cannot collect.

Example 1
Paul, who uses the accrual method on his Schedule C, reported income in 2000 of $1,000 related to an account receivable from a customer. In 2001, that account receivable became worthless. Because Paul is on the accrual method and has already included the $1,000 in income, he is permitted to recognize a bad debt deduction in 2001.

Example 2
Assume the same facts as in Example 1, except that Paul is on the cash method. Because Paul has not recognized the $1,000 income in 2000, he cannot take a bad debt deduction when the debt becomes worthless in 2001.

The net effect on Paul's income in either situation is the same.

	Accrual	Cash
Income recognized in 2000	$1,000	-0-
Less bad debt deduction in 2001	1,000	-0-
Net effect	-0-	-0-

Methods of treating bad debts. The method of accounting for bad debts is referred to as the "specific charge-off method," because it requires the specific identification of the debt that has become worthless. Using the specific charge-off method, you can deduct specific business bad debts that become either partly or totally worthless during the tax year.

Partially worthless debts. You may deduct specific bad debts that are partially uncollectible. To take the deduction, however, the amount must be written off on your books; that is, you must eliminate the worthless portion of the debt from your books as an asset. You do not have to write off and deduct your partially worthless debts annually. Instead, you may delay the write-off until a later year. Also, you may wait until more of the debt has become worthless or until you have collected all you can on the debt and it is totally worthless. You may not, however, deduct any part of the bad debt in a year after the year in which the debt becomes totally worthless. This rule permits you the opportunity to select the year in which to claim the partial bad debt deduction.

Totally worthless debts. A totally worthless debt is deducted only in the tax year in which it becomes totally worthless. The deduction for the debt must not include any amount deducted in an earlier tax year when the debt was only partially worthless. You are not required to make an actual write-off on your books to claim a bad debt deduction for a totally worthless debt. However, you may want to do so. If a debt you claim to be totally worthless is not written off on your books and the IRS later rules that the debt is only partially worthless, you will not be allowed a deduction until the amount is actually written off your books.

Recovery of bad debt. If you deducted a bad debt and in a later tax year recover (collect) all or part of it, you may have to include the amount you recover in your gross income. However, you may exclude from gross income the amount recovered, up to the amount of the deduction that did not reduce your tax in the year in which it was deducted.

Example

In 1999, John had a $25,000 bad debt loss relating to his Schedule C. He also had $25,000 of income from the activity. John had no taxable income for 1999.

In 2001, John recovered the entire $25,000 debt. To figure how much he should include in his 2001 income, see the calculation below.

	1999 with bad debt	1999 without bad debt
Income:		
Schedule C	$25,000	$25,000
Bad debt loss	(25,000)	-0-
Adjusted gross income	-0-	25,000
Less:		
Standard deductions	-0-	4,250
Personal exemption	-0-	2,700
Taxable income	-0-	18,050

The calculations show that John's 1999 taxable income was reduced by $18,050 by including the bad debt. Therefore, $18,050 is included in John's taxable income for 2001, the year in which he collected the $25,000 debt.

Automobile and Truck Expenses

If you use your automobile for business purposes, you may be able to deduct expenses associated with the business use of the automobile. You generally can use one of two methods to figure your expense: actual expenses or the standard mileage rate. Refer to Chapter 28, *Car Expenses and Other Employee Business Expenses,* for more information on expenses for business use of your automobile.

TAXALERT

You can report business vehicle information on Part IV of Schedule C instead of Form 4562 if you are claiming the standard mileage rate, you lease your vehicle, or your vehicle is fully depreciated. However, if you wish to deduct actual automobile expenses or if you must file Form 4562 for any other reason, you must continue to use Part V of Form 4562 to report the vehicle information.

Depreciation and Expensing Certain Assets

When you use property in your business, you are permitted to recover your investment in the property through tax deductions. You do this by "depreciating" the property—that is, deducting some of your cost on your income tax return each year. You can depreciate "tangible" property, such as a car, a building, or machinery, and amortize "intangible" property, such as a copyright or a patent. Depreciation is reported on Part II or Part III of Form 4562, whereas amortization is reported on Part VI of Form 4562. You cannot depreciate land, property you rent, or inventory.

Property is depreciable if it meets the following requirements:

1. It must be used in business or held for the production of income.
2. It must have a determinable life, and that life must be longer than 1 year.
3. It must be something that wears out, decays, gets used up, becomes obsolete, or loses value from natural causes.

In general, if property does not meet all three of these conditions, it is not depreciable.

The amount of depreciation you can deduct depends on (1) how much the property costs, (2) when you began using it, (3) how long it will take to recover your cost, and (4) which one of the several depreciation methods you use.

You begin to claim depreciation on property when you place it in service in your trade or business or for the production of income. You continue to depreciate the property until you recover your basis (generally the cost) in it, dispose of it, or stop using it for business or investment purposes.

Form 4562, *Depreciation and Amortization,* is used to report your depreciation. For a further discussion of depreciation, see Chapter 10, *Rental Income and Expenses.* Additional information can be found in Publication 534, *Depreciation.*

Expensing certain assets (Section 179 deduction). You can elect to treat all or part of the cost, not to exceed $20,000, of certain qualifying property as an expense in the year in which the property is purchased, rather than capitalize the cost and depreciate it over its life. This means that you can deduct all or part of the cost in 1 year rather than take depreciation deductions spread out over several years. You must decide for each item of qualifying property whether to deduct, subject to the yearly limit, or capitalize and depreciate its cost.

Qualifying property is property purchased for use in your trade or business and property that would have qualified for the investment tax credit.

Basis of qualifying property. The amount you elect to deduct is subtracted from the basis of the qualifying property. If you elect the Section 179 deduction, the amount of your allowable ACRS or MACRS deduction for this property will be reduced. If you and your spouse file separate returns, you can each deduct only $10,000, unless you and your spouse agree on a different split of the $20,000.

Other restrictions. The amount of the Section 179 deduction cannot be greater than the income derived from the active conduct by the taxpayer of any business during such taxable year (computed without regard to the property to be expensed). Any Section 179 deductions disallowed under this income limitation are carried forward to the succeeding taxable year and added to the allowable amount for such year. Therefore, in the following year, you are eligible to receive the $20,000 deduction plus the carryover from the preceding year, limited to the amount of income. Also, the $20,000 amount is reduced dollar for dollar for property investments in excess of $200,000.

Cost. The cost of property for the Section 179 deduction does not include any part of the basis of the property that is determined by reference to the basis of other property held at any time by the person acquiring this property. For example, if you buy a new truck to use in your business, your cost for purposes of the Section 179 deduction does not include the adjusted basis of the truck you trade in on the new vehicle.

Example

You buy a new piece of equipment, paying $2,500 cash and trading in your old equipment, which had an undepreciated cost to you of $4,000. Even though the new equipment has a tax basis to you of $6,500, you may claim only the Section 179 deduction on the $2,500 you paid out.

When to elect. You must make an election to take the Section 179 deduction. You can only make this election in the first tax year in which the property is placed in service.

If you elect to deduct the cost of qualifying property, you must specify the items to which the election applies and the part of the cost of each you elect to deduct. If in 2001, you purchase and place in service two items of qualifying property costing $8,700 and $15,300, and you want to elect the $20,000 deduction, you must specify what part of the $8,700 property or the $15,300 property you want to deduct. You may arbitrarily allocate the maximum $20,000 between the two properties.

Use Form 4562 to make your election and report your Section 179 deduction. You make the election by taking the deduction on Form 4562, filed with your original tax return. The election cannot be made on an amended tax return filed after the due date (including extensions), and once made can be revoked only with the consent of the Internal Revenue Service.

You should consult your tax advisor regarding the Section 179 rules, particularly when you acquire or dispose of assets.

Computers. If you use a computer for both business and personal use, there are special rules that may limit the amount of depreciation that can be deducted.

The amount of depreciation you are allowed to deduct depends on what percentage of use was business and what percentage was personal. The allocation is made on the basis of the most appropriate unit of time. For example, determine the percentage of use in a trade or a business for a tax year by dividing the number of hours the computer is used for business purposes by the total number of hours the computer is used for any purpose for that tax year.

Luxury automobiles. See Chapter 28, *Car Expenses and Other Employee Business Expenses,* for a discussion of luxury cars and depreciation.

Amortization. Capitalized costs of certain intangible property that is acquired and is held in connection with the conduct of a trade or business or an activity engaged in for the production of income may be amortized. The amount of the deduction is determined by amortizing the adjusted basis (generally the cost) of the intangible property ratably over a 15-year period. The amortization period begins with the month that the intangible property is acquired.

The new amortization rules apply to "Section 197 intangible" property. "Section 197 intangible" property is defined as any property that is included in any one or more of the following categories:

1. Goodwill and going concern value;
2. Certain specified types of intangible property that generally relate to workforce, information base, know-how, customers, suppliers, or other similar items;
3. Any license, permit, or other right granted by a governmental unit or an agency or instrumentality thereof;
4. Any covenant not to compete (or other arrangement to the extent that the arrangement has substantially the same effect as a covenant not to compete) entered into in connection with the direct or indirect acquisition of an interest in a trade or business (or substantial portion thereof); and
5. Any franchise, trademark, or trade name.

Special rules apply if a taxpayer disposes of some, but not all, of Section 197 intangible property that was acquired in a transaction. No loss is to be recognized by reason of such a disposition. Instead, the adjusted bases of the retained Section 197 intangible properties that were acquired in connection with such transaction are increased by the amount of any loss that is not recognized.

Leasing Business Assets

Many sole proprietors decide to lease a business asset, rather than purchase it. This is ideal if the asset is only needed for a limited period of time. For example, a tax practitioner may only need a computer for the months of February through April. Instead of incurring the large capital outlay required to purchase the asset, he or she can free up cash by leasing a computer.

Generally, the entire expense for leasing a business asset is deductible. This assumes that the asset is used 100% of the time for business purposes. If, however, the asset is used for both business and personal use, only the portion attributable to business use is allowed as a deduction. The most common business asset that is leased by a sole proprietor and a statutory employee is an automobile.

If you lease an automobile, you can deduct the part of each lease payment that is for the use of the automobile in your business or work. You cannot deduct any part of a lease payment that is for commuting to your regular job or other personal use of the automobile. You must amortize any advance payments made on the lease over the entire lease period.

If you leased an automobile after December 31, 1986, that you use in your business, for a lease term of 30 days or more, you may have to include in your income for each tax year in which you lease the car an "inclusion amount." If the fair market value of the automobile when the lease began was more than $12,800 ($13,400 for leases beginning in 1991, $13,700 for leases beginning in 1992, $14,300 for leases beginning in 1993, $14,600 for leases beginning in 1994, $15,500 for leases beginning in 1995 and 1996, $15,800 for leases beginning in 1997 and 1998, $15,500 for leases beginning in 1999, 2000, and 2001), you must include in your gross income an inclusion amount each tax year during which you lease the automobile. For more about leasing see Chapter 28, *Car Expenses and Other Employee Business Expenses.*

Health Insurance

Self-employed individuals, including those filing Schedule C, may deduct part of the amount paid for health insurance premiums on behalf of themselves, their spouses, and dependents. This deduction is only available if you had net profits from self-employment for the year and were not eligible to participate in a subsidized health plan maintained by you or your spouse's employer. The determination of whether a self-employed individual or his or her spouse may be eligible for employer-provided health benefits is made on a monthly basis.

The allowable deduction is limited to the lesser of (1) 60% of the amount paid for health insurance premiums during 2001 for the self-employed individual, spouse, and dependent, or (2) the net profit from the trade or business less the amount claimed for a Keogh plan or a SEP deduction on Form 1040, line 27.

The deduction is not claimed on Schedule C and is not allowed as a deduction for self-employment tax purposes. However, the deduction is claimed on Form 1040, line 26 as an adjustment to income. Any medical insurance expenses in excess of the allowable deduction may be claimed as an itemized deduction on Schedule A (Form 1040), subject to the 7.5% of adjusted gross income floor for medical expenses.

Employees

Who are employees? Before you can know how to treat payments that you make for services rendered to you, you must first know the business relationship that exists between you and the person performing those services. The person performing the services may be: (1) an independent contractor, (2) a common-law employee, (3) a statutory employee, or (4) a statutory independent contractor.

The determination of a worker's classification can have significant tax consequences to an employer. When workers are not treated as employees, the employer can avoid employment tax and wage withholding responsibilities, as well as costs related to pension plans, health insurance, and other fringe benefits.

Independent contractors. People, such as lawyers, contractors, subcontractors, public stenographers, auctioneers, and so on, who follow an independent trade, business, or profession in which they offer their services to the general public are generally not employees. However, whether such people are employees or independent contractors depends on the facts in each case. The general rule is that an individual is an independent contractor if you, the employer, have the right to control or direct only the result of the work and not the means and methods of accomplishing the result.

You do not have to withhold or pay taxes on payments that you make to independent contractors.

Common-law employees. Under common-law rules, every individual who performs services subject to the will and control of an employer, as to both what must be done and how it must be done, is an employee. It does not matter that the employer allows the employee discretion and freedom of action, so long as the employer has the legal right to control both the method and the result of the services.

Two usual characteristics of an employer–employee relationship are that the employer has the right to discharge the employee and that the employer supplies the employee with tools and a place to work.

No distinction is made between classes of employees. Superintendents, managers, and other supervisory personnel are all employees. An officer of a corporation is generally an employee, but a director is not. An officer who performs no services or only minor services, and neither receives nor is entitled to receive any pay, is not considered an employee.

You generally must withhold and pay federal, Social Security, and Medicare taxes on wages you pay to common-law employees.

Statutory employees and statutory independent contractors are discussed at the beginning of this chapter.

Salaries, wages, and other forms of pay that you make to employees are generally deductible business expenses. However, a deduction for salaries and wages must be reduced by any work opportunity credit determined for the tax year. This will be discussed later in this chapter.

Tests for Deductibility

To be deductible, employees' pay must meet all of the following four tests:

- **Test 1—Ordinary and necessary.** You must be able to show that salaries, wages, and other payments for employees' services are ordinary and necessary expenses directly connected with your trade or business.
- **Test 2—Reasonable.** What is reasonable pay is determined by the facts. Generally, it is the amount that would ordinarily be paid for these services by like enterprises under similar circumstances.
- **Test 3—For services performed.** You must be able to prove that the payments were made for services actually performed.
- **Test 4—Paid or incurred.** You must have actually made the payments or incurred the expense during the tax year.

If you use the cash method of accounting, the expense for salaries and wages can be deducted only in the year in which the salaries and wages were paid. If you use the accrual method of accounting, the expense for salaries and wages is deducted when your obligation to make the payments is established and economic performance occurs (generally, when an employee performs his or her services for you). In addition, the expense must be paid within 2½ months after the end of the tax year. However, the deduction of an accrual of salary to an owner may be limited. (See the previous discussion on the deduction of an accrual to a related party.)

Payroll Taxes

General Rules for Withholding

As an employer, you must generally withhold income taxes, Social Security, and Medicare taxes from wages that you pay employees. In addition, the amounts withheld with respect to Social Security and Medicare taxes will have to be matched by you, the employer. Also, unemployment tax payments may be required.

For information about the payroll tax deposit rules, see Publication 15, as well as IRS Circular E, *Employer's Tax Guide.*

TaxSaver

You may find it helpful to remember the following general rules for withholding:

1. *Independent contractors.* You do not withhold income tax or Social Security and Medicare taxes from amounts you pay an independent contractor.

2. *Common-law employees.* You generally have to withhold income tax, Social Security tax, and Medicare tax from the wages you pay common-law employees. You also have to pay federal unemployment tax and your share of Social Security and Medicare taxes on these wages.
3. *Statutory employees.* You are not required to withhold income tax from the wages of statutory employees. You must withhold and pay Social Security and Medicare taxes. Unless they are full-time life insurance sales agents or work at home, you must also pay federal unemployment tax on their wages.
4. *Statutory nonemployees.* You do not withhold or pay taxes on payments to statutory nonemployees.

Reporting payments to independent contractors and statutory nonemployees. If you pay an independent contractor or a statutory nonemployee $600 or more during the year in the course of your trade or business, you must file with the IRS and provide the independent contractor a Form 1099-MISC, *Miscellaneous Income.*

Reporting payments to common-law employees. To report wages paid to a common-law employee, you must complete a Form W-2. The Form W-2 must show the total wages and other compensation paid, total wages subject to Social Security taxes, total wages subject to Medicare taxes, the amounts deducted for income, Social Security, and Medicare taxes, and any other information required on the statement. For information on preparing Form W-2, see the Instructions that come with Form W-2.

Reporting payments to statutory employees. To report wages paid to a statutory employee, you must complete a Form W-2. You must report the same information that you reported for common-law employees. If the statutory employee and employer have elected not to withhold income tax, this information does not have to be furnished. Also, the employer must check box 15, "statutory employee," on Form W-2.

When hiring new employees, you are required to have the employee complete a Form W-4, *Employee's Withholding Allowance Certificate,* and a Form I-9, *Employment Eligibility Verification Form.* In addition, the employee is required to file various payroll forms with the government. For more information on which payroll forms the employee must file, see IRS Circular E, *Employer's Tax Guide.*

Office in the Home and Form 8829

It is not unusual for a person filing a Schedule C to use part of his or her home for business. If you use part of your home regularly and exclusively for business, you may be able to deduct certain operating and depreciation expenses on your home.

Requirements for claiming the deduction. You may deduct certain expenses for operating out of a part of your home only if that part of your home is used regularly and exclusively as

1. Your principal place of business for any trade or business in which you engage
2. A place to meet or deal with your patients, clients, or customers in the normal course of your trade or business

For tax years beginning before January 1, 1999, the U.S. Supreme Court had established a very restrictive approach to determine if a home office constituted a principal place of business. Under the Supreme Court's approach, the primary considerations in determining if a home office constituted a principal place of business were: (1) the relative importance of activities performed at each business location, and (2) the time spent at each business location.

For example, under this approach a plumber's principal place of business was generally considered to be the customers' kitchens and bathrooms, so no home office deductions were allowed.

TaxAlert

The Taxpayer Relief Act of 1997 overruled the U.S. Supreme Court by providing that for tax years beginning after December 31, 1998, a home office qualifies as the principal place of business if:

1. You use the office to conduct administrative or management activities of a trade or business, and
2. There is no other fixed location of the trade or business where you conduct substantial administrative or management activities

Example

John Smith is a salesperson. His only office is a room in his house used regularly and exclusively to set up appointments and write up orders and other reports for the companies whose products he sells. John's tax year is the calendar year.

John's business is selling products to customers at various locations within the metropolitan area where he lives. To make these sales, he regularly visits the customers to explain the available products and to take orders. John makes only a few sales from his home office. John spends an average of 30 hours a week visiting customers and 12 hours a week working at his home office.

The essence of John's business as a salesperson requires him to meet with customers primarily at the customer's place of business. The home office activities are less important to John's business than the sales activities he performs when visiting customers. Prior to 1999, John would not have been allowed to deduct expenses of a home office. John will be entitled to deduct home office expenses after 1999.

You may also deduct certain expenses for operating out of a separate structure that is not attached to your home, if you use it regularly and exclusively for your trade or business. (See Chapter 30, *Miscellaneous Deductions,* for more about deducting these expenses.)

TaxSaver

Even if you do *not* qualify for a business use of the home deduction, you may be allowed to take a depreciation deduction or elect a Section 179 deduction for furniture and equipment you use in your home for business or work as an employee.

If you use part of your home for business and meet the requirements discussed earlier, you must divide the expenses of operating out of your home between personal and business use. Some expenses are divided on an area basis. Some of these are further divided on a time–usage basis. If neither of these methods is appropriate, you can choose any other reasonable method to figure the business part of the expense.

What to deduct. Some expenses you pay to maintain your home are directly related to its business use; others are indirectly related; some are unrelated. You can deduct direct expenses and part of your indirect expenses, both subject to certain limitations. If you are a cash basis taxpayer, you can deduct only the expenses you pay during the tax year.

TaxAlert

The deduction for expenses related to a storage unit in the taxpayer's home that is regularly used for inventory of the taxpayer's business of selling products in which the home is the sole fixed location of the business has been expanded to cover product samples as well as inventory.

Taxpayers are not required to use the space *exclusively* for the storage of inventory or product samples in order to be eligible for the deduction. The new rule adds "product samples" to clarify the current rule, so taxpayers need not attempt to distinguish between inventory and product samples.

Example

Joe Smith is in the business of selling cosmetics. Joe's residence is the only location of his business. He uses space in the study of his home to store cosmetic samples. Joe may deduct the expenses related to the portion of his residence used to store the product samples. It does not matter if Joe uses the study for additional purposes.

Direct Expenses

Direct expenses benefit only the business part of your home. They include painting or repairs made to the specific area or room used for business. You can deduct direct expenses in full.

Indirect Expenses

Indirect expenses are for keeping up and running your entire home. They benefit both the business and personal parts of your home. Examples of indirect expenses include:

> Real estate taxes
> Deductible mortgage interest
> Casualty losses
> Rent
> Utilities and services
> Insurance
> Repairs
> Security systems
> Depreciation

You can deduct the business percentage of your indirect expenses.

Figuring the business percentage. To figure deductions for the business use of your home, find the business percentage. You can do this by dividing the area used for business by the total area of your home. You may measure the area in square feet. To figure the percentage of your home used for business, divide the number of square feet of space used for business by the total number of square feet of space in your home. If the rooms in your home are about the same size, figure the business percentage by dividing the number of rooms used for business by the number of rooms in the home. You can also use any other reasonable method to determine the business percentage.

> **Example 1.** Your home measures 1,200 square feet. You use one room that measures 240 square feet for business. Therefore, you use one-fifth (240 ÷ 1,200), or 20%, of the total area for business.

> **Example 2.** If the rooms in your home are about the same size, and you use one room in a five-room house for business, you use one-fifth, or 20%, of the total area for business.

Real Estate Taxes

If you own your home, you can deduct part of the real estate taxes on your home as a business expense. To figure the business part of your real estate taxes, multiply the real estate taxes paid by the percentage of your home used for business.

Deductible Mortgage Interest

If you pay deductible mortgage interest, you can generally deduct part of it as a business expense. To figure the business part of your deductible mortgage interest, multiply this interest by the percentage of your home used in business. You can include interest on a second mortgage in this computation.

Casualty Losses

If you have a casualty loss on your home or other property you use in business, you can deduct the business part of the loss as a business expense. Treat a casualty loss as an unrelated expense, a direct expense, or an indirect expense depending on the property affected.

In a partial destruction, the deductible loss is the decrease in fair market value of the property or the adjusted basis of the property, whichever is less. You must reduce this amount by any insurance or other reimbursement you receive or expect to receive.

If your business property is completely destroyed (becomes totally worthless), your deductible loss is the adjusted basis of the property, minus any salvage value and any insurance or other reimbursement you receive or expect to receive. Figure the loss without taking into account any decrease in fair market value.

Rent

If you rent, rather than own, a home and meet the requirements for business use of the home, you can deduct part of the rent you pay. To figure your deduction, multiply your rent payments by the percentage of your home used for business.

Utilities and Services

Expenses for utilities and services, such as electricity, gas, trash removal, and cleaning services, are primarily personal expenses. However, if you use part of your home for business, you can deduct the business part of these expenses.

Telephone

The basic local telephone service charge, including taxes, for the first telephone line into your home is a nondeductible personal expense. However, charges for business long-distance phone calls on that line, as well as the cost of a second line into your home used exclusively for business, are deductible business expenses for the business use of your home. Deduct these charges separately on the appropriate schedule. Do not include them in your home office deduction.

Insurance

You can deduct the cost of insurance that covers the business part of your home.

Repairs

The cost of repairs and supplies that relate to your business, including labor (other than your own labor), is a deductible expense. For example, a furnace repair benefits the entire home. If you use 10% of your home for business, you can deduct 10% of the cost of the furnace repair.

Repairs keep your home in good working order over its useful life. Examples of common repairs are patching walls and floors, painting, wallpapering, repairing roofs and gutters, and mending leaks.

Security System

If you install a security system that protects all the doors and windows in your home, you can deduct the business part of the expenses you incur to maintain and monitor the system. You can also take a depreciation deduction for the part of the cost of the security system relating to the business use of your home.

Depreciation

The cost of property that can be used for more than 1 year, such as a building, a permanent improvement, or furniture, is a capital expenditure.

Land is not depreciable property. You generally cannot recover the cost of land until you dispose of it.

Permanent improvements. A permanent improvement increases the value of property, adds to its life, or gives it a new or different use. Examples of improvements are replacement of electric wiring or plumbing, a new roof, an addition, paneling, remodeling, or major modifications.

Depreciating your home. If you use part of your home for business, depreciate that part as nonresidential real property under the Modified Accelerated Cost Recovery System (MACRS). Under MACRS, nonresidential real property is depreciated using the straight-line method over 39 years.

To figure depreciation on the business part of your home, you need to know:

1. The business-use percentage of your home;
2. The first month in your tax year for which you can deduct business use of your home expenses; and
3. The adjusted basis and fair market value of your home at the time you qualify for a deduction.

Adjusted basis of home. The adjusted basis of your home is generally its cost plus the cost of any permanent improvements that you made to it minus any casualty losses deducted in earlier tax years.

When you change part of your home from personal to business use, your basis for depreciation is the business-use percentage times the lesser of:

1. The adjusted basis of your home (excluding land) on the date of change; or
2. The fair market value of your home (excluding land) on the date of change.

Unrelated expenses benefit only the parts of your home that you do not use for business. These include repairs to personal areas of your home, lawn care, and landscaping. You cannot deduct unrelated expenses. For more information, also see Chapter 30, *Miscellaneous Deductions.*

Recordkeeping. You do not have to use a particular method of recordkeeping, but you must keep records that provide the information needed to figure your deductions for the business use of your home. Your records must show the following:

1. The part of your home you use for business
2. That you use this part of your home exclusively and regularly for business as either your principal place of business or as the place where you meet or deal with clients or customers in the normal course of your business
3. The depreciation and expenses for the business part of your home

Generally, you must keep your records for at least 3 years from the date the return was filed or 2 years from the date the tax was paid, whichever is later. Keep records that support your basis in your home for as long as they are needed to figure the correct basis of your home.

Deduction Limit

If your gross income from the business use of your home equals or exceeds your total business expenses (including depreciation), you can deduct all of your expenses for the business use of your home. But if your gross income from that use is less than your total business expenses, your deduction for certain expenses for the business use of your home is limited. The total of your deductions for otherwise nondeductible expenses, such as utilities, insurance, and depreciation (with depreciation taken last) cannot be more than your gross income from the business use of your home minus the sum of:

1. The business percentage of the otherwise deductible mortgage interest, real estate taxes, and casualty and theft losses, and
2. The business expenses that are not attributable to the business use of your home (e.g., salaries or supplies).

If you are self-employed, do not include in (2) above your deduction for half of your self-employment tax.

You can carry forward to your next tax year deductions over the current year's limit. These deductions are subject to the gross income limit from the business use of your home for the next tax year. The amount carried forward will be allowable only up to your gross income in the next tax year from the business in which the deduction arose, whether or not you live in the home during the year.

Figuring deduction limit and carryover. If you file Schedule C (Form 1040), figure your deduction limit on Form 8829, *Expenses for Business Use of Your Home.* Enter the amount from line 34 of Form 8829 on Schedule C, line 30.

Deductible mortgage interest. After you have figured the business part of the mortgage interest on Form 8829, subtract that amount from the total mortgage interest. The *remainder* is deductible on Schedule A; do not deduct any of the business part on Schedule A. If the amount of interest you deduct on Schedule A for your home mortgage is limited, enter the excess on Form 8829.

Real estate taxes. If you file Schedule C, enter all your deductible real estate taxes on Form 8829. After you have figured the business part of your taxes on Form 8829, subtract that amount from your total real estate taxes. The *remainder* is deductible on Schedule A; do not deduct any of the business part of real estate taxes on Schedule A.

Day-Care Facility

You can deduct expenses for using part of your home on a regular basis to provide day-care services if you meet the following requirements:

1. You must be in the trade or business of providing day care for children, for persons age 65 or older, or for persons who are physically or mentally unable to care for themselves.
2. You must have applied for, been granted, or be exempt from having a license, certification, registration, or approval as a day-care center or as a family or group day-care home under applicable state law. You do not meet this requirement if your application was rejected or your license or other authorization was revoked.

Meals. If you provide food for your day-care business, do not include the expense as a cost of using your home for business. Claim it as a separate deduction on your Schedule C. You can deduct 100% of the cost of food consumed by your day-care recipients and 50% of the cost of food consumed by your employees as a business expense. You cannot deduct the cost of food consumed by you and your family.

Do not deduct the cost of meals for which you were reimbursed under the Child and Adult Care Food Program administered by the Department of Agriculture. The reimbursements are not included in your income to the extent you used them to provide food for the eligible children.

Retirement Plans

If you are self-employed, you can take an income tax deduction for certain contributions that you make for yourself to a retirement plan. You can also deduct a trustee's fees if contributions to the plan do not cover them.

TAXALERT

Commencing in 2002, small businesses with 100 or fewer employees will be eligible for a tax credit for expenses of establishing a new retirement plan. Deductible contributions plus the plan's earnings on them are tax free until you receive distributions from the plan in later years. If you are a sole proprietor, you can deduct contributions you make for your common-law employees, as well as contributions you make for yourself. A common-law employee cannot take a deduction for your contributions.

There are two types of plans that a self-employed person may set up: a Keogh plan or a Simplified Employee Pension (SEP) plan.

Keogh Plans

A Keogh (HR 10) plan is a retirement plan that can be established by a sole proprietor. The plan must be for the exclusive benefit of employees or their beneficiaries. As an employer, you can usually deduct, subject to limits, contributions you make to a Keogh plan, including those made for your own retirement.

For further information about Keogh plans, see Chapter 18, *Individual Retirement Arrangements (IRAs)* and *Education Savings Accounts (ESAs)*.

Where to deduct on Form 1040. Take the deduction for contributions for yourself on line 27 of Form 1040. Deduct the contributions for your common-law employees on Schedule C.

Because the deduction for your contribution to a Keogh plan for your benefit is reported on Form 1040, line 27, not on Schedule C, the contribution does not reduce your self-employment income that is subject to tax.

Reporting requirements. As the Keogh plan administrator or the employer, you may have to file an annual return/report form by the last day of the seventh month following the end of the plan year.

Simplified Employee Pension (SEP)

A simplified employee pension (SEP) is a written plan that allows an employer to make contributions toward an employee's retirement, and his or her own, if the employer is self-employed, without becoming involved in a more complex Keogh retirement plan.

For further information about SEPs, see Chapter 18, *Individual Retirement Arrangements (IRAs) and Education Savings Accounts (ESAs)*.

Individual Retirement Arrangements (IRAs)

In addition to the retirement plans already discussed, a self-employed person may also make a contribution, which may or may not be deductible, to an Individual Retirement Arrangement (IRA).

TAXALERT

The earnings on your contributions generated by the plan are generally not subject to tax. The distributions of your deductible contributions and the earnings from the plan, which are subject to certain limitations, may be taxable to you upon withdrawal.

For further information about IRAs, see Chapter 18, *Individual Retirement Arrangements (IRAs) and Education Savings Accounts (ESAs)*.

New SIMPLE Retirement Plan. Small businesses that normally employ 100 or fewer employees, paid them at least $5,000 in compensation in the preceding year, and do not maintain another qualified plan may establish a Savings Incentive Match Plan for Employees (SIMPLE plan). A SIMPLE plan can be in the form of either an individual retirement account (IRA) for each employee or part of a qualified cash or deferred arrangement [401(k) plan]. Employees may make elective contributions of up to $6,000 per year to a SIMPLE plan, and employers must make matching contributions. Employees are not taxed on account assets until distributions are made, and employers generally may deduct their contributions to the plan.

Travel and Entertainment

Business travel and meals and entertainment expenses are deductible, subject to certain limits, assuming that these amounts are both ordinary and necessary, as defined earlier in the chapter.

For a self-employed person, the meals and entertainment expenses to be deducted are subject to the 50% limit and certain documentation requirements as discussed in Chapter 28, *Car Expenses and Other Employee Business Expenses*. (Also see Chapter 28 for a more complete discussion of the deductibility of both travel and meals and entertainment expenses.)

Other Schedule C Deductions

Various other expenses not previously mentioned are allowed as a deduction on Schedule C. Examples of these expenses are advertising, commissions and fees, insurance (other than health), interest, legal and professional services, office expenses, including supplies and other items used in the office, general rent, repairs and maintenance, taxes, utilities, and any other business expense that can be classified as ordinary and necessary.

Sales of Business Property Used in Your Business

How Different Assets Are Treated

A sole proprietorship usually has many assets. When sold, these assets must be classified as either depreciable personal property used in the business, real property used in the business, or property held for sale to customers, such as inventory or stock in trade or capital assets.

The gain or loss on each asset is figured separately. The sale of inventory results in ordinary income or loss and is reported on Schedule C. The sale of a capital asset results in a capital gain or loss and is reported on Schedule D. The sale of depreciable personal property and real property used in the business results in Section 1231 gains or losses and is reported on Form 4797. (For further information about Section 1231 transactions, see Chapter 17, *Reporting Gains and Losses*).

Any gain realized on sales and certain other dispositions of depreciable personal property and, under certain circumstances depreciable real property, is treated as ordinary income to the extent of depreciation deductions taken prior to the sale. The amount of depreciation recapture is the lesser of (1) the gain recognized or (2) depreciation taken on the property. For more information, see Chapters 14, *Basis of Property*, 15, *Sale of Property*, and 17, *Reporting Gains and Losses*.

Section 1231 business gain or loss. Once you have determined your gain or loss on your personal and real property that is not subject to depreciation recapture, you must combine all gains and losses from the sale and disposition of Section 1231 property for the tax year including Section 1231 gains and losses reported to you through partnerships and S corporations in which you have an interest. In general, if all of your Section 1231 transactions resulted in a net gain, the gain is treated as a long-term capital gain. If all of your Section 1231 transactions resulted in a net loss, the loss is treated as an ordinary loss. See Chapter 17, *Reporting Gains and Losses*, for a further discussion of how to treat Section 1231 gains and losses.

Recapture of net ordinary losses. A net Section 1231 gain is treated as ordinary income to the extent that it does not exceed your nonrecaptured net Section 1231 losses taken in prior years. Nonrecaptured losses are net Section 1231 losses deducted for your 5 most recent tax years that have not yet been applied (recaptured) against any net Section 1231 gains in a tax year beginning after 1984. Your losses are recaptured, beginning with the earliest year that is subject to recapture.

Sale of the Entire Business

Because a sole proprietorship is not a separate entity, a sale of the business will be treated as if each asset in the business had been sold separately. The gain or loss on such a sale is the total of the gains or losses as separately computed for each individual asset.

Both the buyer and the seller of a group of assets constituting a trade or a business must report to the IRS on Form 8594 various information about the acquisition of assets, including the following:

1. The name of the buyer and seller of the assets
2. The fair market value of the assets transferred
3. The allocation of the sales price to the assets transferred
4. Whether the buyer purchased a license, covenant not to compete or entered into a lease agreement, employment contract, management contract, or similar arrangement with the seller.

Business Tax Credit

Tax credits are distinguished from deductions in that a deduction reduces taxable income and a credit reduces tax liability. Consequently, $1 in tax credit is more valuable than $1 in tax deduction.

Form 3800. The general business tax credit includes the following:

1. The investment credit (Form 3468)
2. The work opportunity credit (Form 5884)
3. The credit for increasing research activities (Form 6765)
4. The low-income housing credit (Form 8586)
5. The welfare-to-work credit

If you have more than one of these credits, if you have a carryback or carryforward of any of these credits, or if any of these credits is from a passive activity, you must attach the appropriate credit forms and summarize them on Form 3800. If you have only one of these credits and that credit is not from a passive activity, you do not have to file Form 3800. Instead, use the applicable form to claim the credit. For example, if you have only a 2001 work opportunity credit, you may use Form 5884, *Work Opportunity Credit*. You do not have to file Form 3800.

TaxAlert

Work opportunity credit. The work opportunity tax credit provides an incentive to hire persons from targeted groups that have a particularly high unemployment rate or other special employment needs. The employer is entitled to a credit equal to 25% of qualified first-year wages for hiring an eligible employee who works 120 to 399 hours and a 40% credit for employees who work 400 hours or more.

TaxAlert

The credit for increasing research activities, which was set to expire on June 30, 1999, was extended through June 30, 2004 by the Tax Relief Extension Act of 1999.

TaxAlert

Credit for hiring long-term family assistance recipients. A credit, called the welfare-to-work credit, is available for employers who paid wages to long-term family assistance recipients who began work after 1997. The amount of the credit for a tax year is 35% of the qualified first-year wages for such year plus 50% of the qualified second-year wages for such year. The credit applies only to the first $10,000 of wages in each year with respect to any individual. Thus, the maximum total credit per qualified employee is $8,500 for the 2 years.

Any unused credit can be carried back 1 year or forward 20 tax years as part of the general business credit for years beginning after December 31, 1997.

Special Situations

Hobby Losses
Frequently, individuals carry on an activity that has no profit motive. The IRS will not classify this as a business. Instead, it will be classified as a hobby, and it will be subject to the hobby loss rules.

If your activity or the activity you invest in is not carried on to make a profit, the deductions you can take are limited to the income of the hobby, if any, and no loss is allowed to offset other income.

To determine whether an activity is carried on for profit, all of the facts with regard to the activity are taken into account. No one factor alone is decisive. For a discussion of Hobby Losses see the discussion of them in Chapter 13, *Other Income*.

Artists and Authors
The proper way for artists and authors to account for their expenses has been the topic of much debate in recent years. A special exception excludes authors and artists from the uniform capitalization rules for certain qualified creative expenses that they incur in their trade or business. As a result, these expenses can be currently deducted and not capitalized. A "qualified creative expense" is defined as any expense that is paid or incurred by an individual in the trade or business of being a writer or an artist and that would be allowable as a deduction for the taxable year.

Although you are allowed currently to deduct those expenses that are classified as qualified creative expenses, there are some expenses that need to be capitalized. Examples of such expenses include any expense related to printing, photographic plates, motion pictures, videotapes, and similar items.

There is an alternative way for an artist or an author to treat his or her qualified creative expenses. If the artist or author so chooses, he or she can capitalize all qualified creative costs. In the current year he or she is able to deduct 50% of the eligible costs and then deduct the remaining 50% ratably over the next 2 years. The reason one may choose this method over deducting all qualified creative expenses currently is that the meaning of a qualified creative cost is broader in this instance. It includes the costs of films, sound recordings, videotapes, and books. These expenses would normally need to be capitalized and amortized over their estimated useful lives.

How to Complete Schedule SE

Line by Line, Briefly
Self-employed individuals filing Schedule C may be required to pay self-employment tax. Self-employment income and the related tax are discussed earlier in this chapter.

When completing Form 1040, Schedule SE, you must first determine whether you need to file the short Schedule SE form or the long Schedule SE form. You must use the long Schedule SE form if any of the following apply:

- You received wages or tips and the total of all of your wages (and tips) subject to Social Security, Medicare, or railroad retirement taxes plus your net earnings from self-employment is more than $80,400.
- You use either "optional method" to figure your net earnings from self-employment.
- You are a minister, a member of a religious order, or a Christian Science practitioner and you received IRS approval (by filing Form 4361) not to be taxed on your earnings from these sources, but you owe self-employment tax on other earnings.
- You had church employee income of $108.28 or more that was reported to you on Form W-2.
- You received tips subject to Social Security, Medicare, or railroad retirement taxes, but you did not report those tips to your employer.

If none of these conditions exist, you are able to use the Short Schedule SE form.

As a Schedule C filer, you would report your Schedule C income on line 2 of Section A for the Short form Schedule SE or Section B for the Long form Schedule SE (remember do not include the income reported on Schedule C as a statutory employee).

Example
Pete Thirsty owns a refreshment stand on the beach. His net income from self-employment on Schedule C in 2001 is $54,000. He had no other earned income for that year. Pete is eligible to use the Short Schedule SE form. Pete's self-employment tax liability for 2001 is calculated as follows:

Net earnings from self-employment ($54,000 × .9235)	$49,869
SE tax rate	15.3%
SE tax	$ 7,630

One-half of self-employment tax can be deducted. The deduction is taken on line 25 of Form 1040. In this example, Pete would be able to take a deduction of $3,815.

Comprehensive Schedule C/Self-Employment Example

John Paul Jones is a self-employed comic book salesman. He does business as JPJ Comics. The majority of his business consists of retail sales of comic books. John Paul works out of his home, located at 64-09 79th Street, Queens, New York 11379, where he has been running the business since 1992. One-fourth of his home is used solely for the purpose of running his business. John accounts for his purchases and sales on the accrual method. All other income and expense items are accounted for by use of the cash method. He is also a professor and has $54,000 of W-2 wages in 2001.

John Paul had the following income and expenses during 2001:

Gross receipts from sales of comic books—accrual basis	$35,000
Beginning inventory	2,200
Purchases	13,000
Ending inventory	2,700
Business subscriptions	350

Advertising	1,700
Bad debts	200
Supplies	1,200
Meals and entertainment	600
Travel	900
Telephone	600
Annual home insurance	2,000
Annual mortgage interest	6,000

Annual real estate taxes	4,000
Annual utilities	1,200
Basis of home purchased on 6/1/88	220,000
Amount attributable to land	40,000
Amount attributable to house	180,000

John Paul has established a money purchase pension plan, providing for a maximum contribution of 25% of compensation. For 2001, John Paul has made the maximum contribution before filing his tax return.

SCHEDULE C (Form 1040)	Profit or Loss From Business	OMB No. 1545-0074

Profit or Loss From Business
(Sole Proprietorship)

► **Partnerships, joint ventures, etc., must file Form 1065 or Form 1065-B.**

Department of the Treasury
Internal Revenue Service   (99)

► **Attach to Form 1040 or Form 1041.**   ► **See Instructions for Schedule C (Form 1040).**

2001

Attachment
Sequence No. **09**

Name of proprietor: **John Paul Jones**

Social security number (SSN): **111 : 22 : 3344**

A Principal business or profession, including product or service (see page C-1 of the instructions)
Retail sales of comic books

B Enter code from pages C-7 & 8: **5 0 1 1 7**

C Business name. If no separate business name, leave blank.
J P J Comics

D Employer ID number (EIN), if any: **1 3 2 9 9 9 9 0 9**

E Business address (including suite or room no.) ► **64-09 79th Street**
City, town or post office, state, and ZIP code **Queens, New York 11379**

F Accounting method: **(1)** ☐ Cash **(2)** ☐ Accrual **(3)** ☒ Other (specify) ► **Hybrid**

G Did you "materially participate" in the operation of this business during 2001? If "No," see page C-2 for limit on losses   ☒ Yes ☐ No

H If you started or acquired this business during 2001, check here . . . . ► ☐

Part I   Income

1	Gross receipts or sales. **Caution:** If this income was reported to you on Form W-2 and the "Statutory employee" box on that form was checked, see page C-2 and check here . . . . . ► ☐	**1**	35,000
2	Returns and allowances	**2**	
3	Subtract line 2 from line 1	**3**	35,000
4	Cost of goods sold (from line 42 on page 2)	**4**	12,500
5	**Gross profit.** Subtract line 4 from line 3	**5**	22,500
6	Other income, including Federal and state gasoline or fuel tax credit or refund (see page C-2) . . .	**6**	
7	**Gross income.** Add lines 5 and 6 . . . . ►	**7**	22,500

Part II   Expenses. Enter expenses for business use of your home **only** on line 30.

8	Advertising	**8**	1,700	**19**	Pension and profit-sharing plans	**19**	
9	Bad debts from sales or services (see page C-3) . .	**9**	200	**20**	Rent or lease (see page C-4):		
				a	Vehicles, machinery, and equipment .	**20a**	
10	Car and truck expenses (see page C-3)	**10**		**b**	Other business property . .	**20b**	
11	Commissions and fees . .	**11**		**21**	Repairs and maintenance . .	**21**	
12	Depletion	**12**		**22**	Supplies (not included in Part III) .	**22**	1,200
13	Depreciation and section 179 expense deduction (not included in Part III) (see page C-3) . .	**13**		**23**	Taxes and licenses	**23**	
				24	Travel, meals, and entertainment:		
14	Employee benefit programs (other than on line 19) . . .	**14**		**a**	Travel	**24a**	900
15	Insurance (other than health) .	**15**		**b**	Meals and entertainment .	600	
16	Interest:			**c**	Enter nondeductible amount included on line 24b (see page C-5) .	300	
a	Mortgage (paid to banks, etc.) .	**16a**					
b	Other	**16b**		**d**	Subtract line 24c from line 24b .	**24d**	300
17	Legal and professional services	**17**		**25**	Utilities	**25**	600
18	Office expense	**18**		**26**	Wages (less employment credits) .	**26**	
				27	Other expenses (from line 48 on page 2)	**27**	350

28	**Total expenses** before expenses for business use of home. Add lines 8 through 27 in columns . ►	**28**	5,250
29	Tentative profit (loss). Subtract line 28 from line 7	**29**	17,250
30	Expenses for business use of your home. Attach **Form 8829**	**30**	4,729
31	**Net profit or (loss).** Subtract line 30 from line 29.		
	• If a profit, enter on **Form 1040, line 12,** and **also** on **Schedule SE, line 2** (statutory employees, see page C-5). Estates and trusts, enter on Form 1041, line 3.	**31**	12,521
	• If a loss, you **must** go on to line 32.		

32 If you have a loss, check the box that describes your investment in this activity (see page C-5).

• If you checked 32a, enter the loss on **Form 1040, line 12,** and **also** on **Schedule SE, line 2** (statutory employees, see page C-5). Estates and trusts, enter on Form 1041, line 3.

• If you checked 32b, you **must** attach **Form 6198.**

32a ☐ All investment is at risk.
32b ☐ Some investment is not at risk.

For Paperwork Reduction Act Notice, see Form 1040 instructions.   Cat. No. 11334P   Schedule C (Form 1040) 2001

Schedule C (Form 1040) 2001

Page **2**

Part III   Cost of Goods Sold   (see page C-6)

33 Method(s) used to value closing inventory: a ☒ Cost   b ☐ Lower of cost or market   c ☐ Other (attach explanation)

34 Was there any change in determining quantities, costs, or valuations between opening and closing inventory? If "Yes," attach explanation . . . . ☐ **Yes**   ☒ **No**

35	Inventory at beginning of year. If different from last year's closing inventory, attach explanation . .	**35**	2,200
36	Purchases less cost of items withdrawn for personal use	**36**	13,000
37	Cost of labor. Do not include any amounts paid to yourself	**37**	
38	Materials and supplies	**38**	
39	Other costs	**39**	
40	Add lines 35 through 39	**40**	15,200
41	Inventory at end of year	**41**	2,700
42	**Cost of goods sold.** Subtract line 41 from line 40. Enter the result here and on page 1, line 4 . .	**42**	12,500

Part IV   Information on Your Vehicle.   Complete this part **only** if you are claiming car or truck expenses on line 10 and are not required to file Form 4562 for this business. See the instructions for line 13 on page C-3 to find out if you must file.

43 When did you place your vehicle in service for business purposes? (month, day, year) ▶ .... / .... / ....

44 Of the total number of miles you drove your vehicle during 2001, enter the number of miles you used your vehicle for:

 a Business ....   **b** Commuting ....   **c** Other ....

45 Do you (or your spouse) have another vehicle available for personal use? . . . . ☐ **Yes**   ☐ **No**

46 Was your vehicle available for use during off-duty hours? . . . . ☐ **Yes**   ☐ **No**

47a Do you have evidence to support your deduction? . . . . ☐ **Yes**   ☐ **No**

 b If "Yes," is the evidence written? . . . . ☐ **Yes**   ☐ **No**

Part V   Other Expenses.   List below business expenses not included on lines 8 –26 or line 30.

.... Subscriptions	350

48	**Total other expenses.** Enter here and on page 1, line 27	**48**	350

Schedule C (Form 1040) 2001

SCHEDULE SE **(Form 1040)** Department of the Treasury Internal Revenue Service (99)	**Self-Employment Tax** ▶ See Instructions for Schedule SE (Form 1040). ▶ Attach to Form 1040.	OMB No. 1545-0074 **2001** Attachment Sequence No. **17**

Name of person with **self-employment** income (as shown on Form 1040) John Paul Jones	Social security number of person with **self-employment** income ▶ 111 : 22 : 3344

Who Must File Schedule SE

You must file Schedule SE if:

- You had net earnings from self-employment from **other than** church employee income (line 4 of Short Schedule SE or line 4c of Long Schedule SE) of $400 or more, **or**
- You had church employee income of $108.28 or more. Income from services you performed as a minister or a member of a religious order **is not** church employee income. See page SE-1.

Note: Even if you had a loss or a small amount of income from self-employment, it may be to your benefit to file Schedule SE and use either "optional method" in Part II of Long Schedule SE. See page SE-3.

Exception. If your only self-employment income was from earnings as a minister, member of a religious order, or Christian Science practitioner **and** you filed Form 4361 and received IRS approval not to be taxed on those earnings, **do not** file Schedule SE. Instead, write "Exempt–Form 4361" on Form 1040, line 52.

May I Use Short Schedule SE or Must I Use Long Schedule SE?

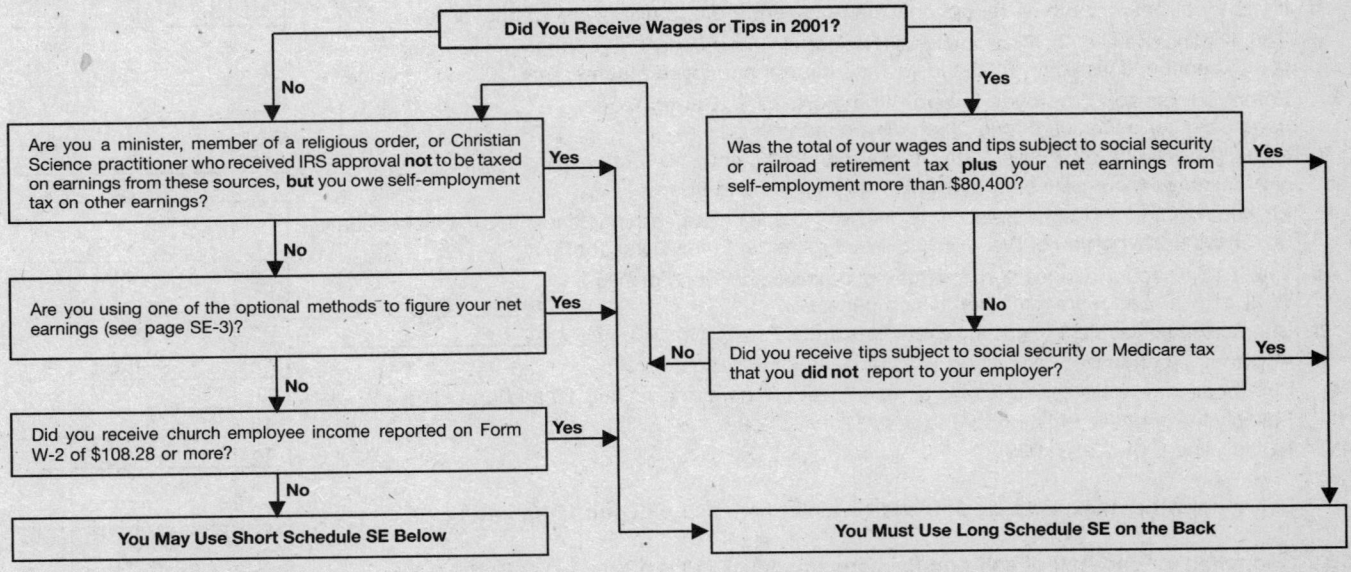

Section A—Short Schedule SE. Caution: Read above to see if you can use Short Schedule SE.

1	Net farm profit or (loss) from Schedule F, line 36, and farm partnerships, Schedule K-1 (Form 1065), line 15a	**1**
2	Net profit or (loss) from Schedule C, line 31; Schedule C-EZ, line 3; Schedule K-1 (Form 1065), line 15a (other than farming); and Schedule K-1 (Form 1065-B), box 9. Ministers and members of religious orders, see page SE-1 for amounts to report on this line. See page SE-2 for other income to report	**2**
3	Combine lines 1 and 2	**3**
4	**Net earnings from self-employment.** Multiply line 3 by 92.35% (.9235). If less than $400, **do not** file this schedule; you do not owe self-employment tax . . . . ▶	**4**
5	**Self-employment tax.** If the amount on line 4 is: • $80,400 or less, multiply line 4 by 15.3% (.153). Enter the result here and on **Form 1040, line 52.** • More than $80,400, multiply line 4 by 2.9% (.029). Then, add $9,969.60 to the result. Enter the total here and on **Form 1040, line 52.**	**5**
6	**Deduction for one-half of self-employment tax.** Multiply line 5 by 50% (.5). Enter the result here and on **Form 1040, line 27**	**6**	

Schedule SE (Form 1040) 2001   Attachment Sequence No. **17**   Page **2**

Name of person with **self-employment** income (as shown on Form 1040) *John Paul Jones*	Social security number of person with **self-employment** income ► 111 : 22 : 3344

Section B—Long Schedule SE

Part I   Self-Employment Tax

Note: If your only income subject to self-employment tax is **church employee income,** skip lines 1 through 4b. Enter -0- on line 4c and go to line 5a. Income from services you performed as a minister or a member of a religious order **is not** church employee income. See page SE-1.

A   If you are a minister, member of a religious order, or Christian Science practitioner **and** you filed Form 4361, but you had $400 or more of **other** net earnings from self-employment, check here and continue with Part I . . . . . . ▶ ☐

1	Net farm profit or (loss) from Schedule F, line 36, and farm partnerships, Schedule K-1 (Form 1065), line 15a. **Note.** Skip this line if you use the farm optional method. See page SE-3 . .	**1**	
2	Net profit or (loss) from Schedule C, line 31; Schedule C-EZ, line 3; Schedule K-1 (Form 1065), line 15a (other than farming); and Schedule K-1 (Form 1065-B), box 9. Ministers and members of religious orders, see page SE-1 for amounts to report on this line. See page SE-2 for other income to report. **Note.** Skip this line if you use the nonfarm optional method. See page SE-3 .	**2**	12,521
3	Combine lines 1 and 2	**3**	12,521
4a	If line 3 is more than zero, multiply line 3 by 92.35% (.9235). Otherwise, enter amount from line 3	**4a**	11,563
b	If you elect one or both of the optional methods, enter the total of lines 15 and 17 here . .	**4b**	
c	Combine lines 4a and 4b. If less than $400, **do not** file this schedule; you do not owe self-employment tax. **Exception.** If less than $400 and you had **church employee income,** enter -0- and continue ▶	**4c**	11,563
5a	Enter your **church employee income** from Form W-2. **Caution.** *See page SE-1 for definition of church employee income* **5a**		
b	Multiply line 5a by 92.35% (.9235). If less than $100, enter -0-	**5b**	
6	**Net earnings from self-employment.** Add lines 4c and 5b	**6**	11,563
7	Maximum amount of combined wages and self-employment earnings subject to social security tax or the 6.2% portion of the 7.65% railroad retirement (tier 1) tax for 2001	**7**	80,400
8a	Total social security wages and tips (total of boxes 3 and 7 on Form(s) W-2) and railroad retirement (tier 1) compensation **8a** 54,000		
b	Unreported tips subject to social security tax (from Form 4137, line 9) **8b**		
c	Add lines 8a and 8b	**8c**	54,000
9	Subtract line 8c from line 7. If zero or less, enter -0- here and on line 10 and go to line 11 ▶	**9**	26,400
10	Multiply the **smaller** of line 6 or line 9 by 12.4% (.124)	**10**	1,434
11	Multiply line 6 by 2.9% (.029)	**11**	335
12	**Self-employment tax.** Add lines 10 and 11. Enter here and on **Form 1040, line 52**	**12**	1,769
13	**Deduction for one-half of self-employment tax.** Multiply line 12 by 50% (.5). Enter the result here and on **Form 1040, line 27** **13** 885		

Part II   Optional Methods To Figure Net Earnings   (See page SE-3.)

Farm Optional Method. You may use this method **only** if:

• Your gross farm income[1] was not more than $2,400, **or**

• Your net farm profits[2] were less than $1,733.

14	Maximum income for optional methods	**14**	1,600	00
15	Enter the **smaller** of: two-thirds (⅔) of gross farm income[1] (not less than zero) **or** $1,600. Also include this amount on line 4b above	**15**	

Nonfarm Optional Method. You may use this method **only** if:

• Your net nonfarm profits[3] were less than $1,733 and also less than 72.189% of your gross nonfarm income[4] **and**

• You had net earnings from self-employment of at least $400 in 2 of the prior 3 years.

Caution: *You may use this method no more than five times.*

16	Subtract line 15 from line 14	**16**	
17	Enter the **smaller** of: two-thirds (⅔) of gross nonfarm income[4] (not less than zero) **or** the amount on line 16. Also include this amount on line 4b above	**17**	

[1] From Sch. F, line 11, and Sch. K-1 (Form 1065), line 15b.
[2] From Sch. F, line 36, and Sch. K-1 (Form 1065), line 15a.
[3] From Sch. C, line 31; Sch. C-EZ, line 3; Sch. K-1 (Form 1065), line 15a; and Sch. K-1 (Form 1065-B), box 9.
[4] From Sch. C, line 7; Sch. C-EZ, line 1; Sch. K-1 (Form 1065), line 15c; and Sch. K-1 (Form 1065-B), box 9.

Form **8829**	**Expenses for Business Use of Your Home**	OMB No. 1545-1266
Department of the Treasury Internal Revenue Service (99)	▶ File only with Schedule C (Form 1040). Use a separate Form 8829 for each home you used for business during the year. ▶ See separate instructions.	**2001** Attachment Sequence No. **66**

Name(s) of proprietor(s)   Your social security number

John Paul Jones   111 : 22 : 3344

Part I   Part of Your Home Used for Business

1	Area used regularly and exclusively for business, regularly for day care, or for storage of inventory or product samples. See instructions	1	200 SQ. FT.
2	Total area of home	2	800 SQ. FT.
3	Divide line 1 by line 2. Enter the result as a percentage	3	25%

• **For day-care facilities not used exclusively for business, also complete lines 4–6.**
• **All others, skip lines 4–6 and enter the amount from line 3 on line 7.**

4	Multiply days used for day care during year by hours used per day	4	hr.
5	Total hours available for use during the year (365 days x 24 hours). See instructions	5	8,760 hr.
6	Divide line 4 by line 5. Enter the result as a decimal amount	6	.
7	Business percentage. For day-care facilities not used exclusively for business, multiply line 6 by line 3 (enter the result as a percentage). All others, enter the amount from line 3 ▶	7	25%

Part II   Figure Your Allowable Deduction

8	Enter the amount from Schedule C, line 29, **plus** any net gain or (loss) derived from the business use of your home and shown on Schedule D or Form 4797. If more than one place of business, see instructions		8	17,250	

See instructions for columns (a) and (b) before completing lines 9–20.

		(a) Direct expenses	(b) Indirect expenses		
9	Casualty losses. See instructions	9			
10	Deductible mortgage interest. See instructions	10	6,000		
11	Real estate taxes. See instructions	11	4,000		
12	Add lines 9, 10, and 11	12	10,000		
13	Multiply line 12, column (b) by line 7	13	2,500		
14	Add line 12, column (a) and line 13			14	2,500
15	Subtract line 14 from line 8. If zero or less, enter -0-			15	14,750
16	Excess mortgage interest. See instructions	16			
17	Insurance	17	2,000		
18	Repairs and maintenance	18			
19	Utilities	19	1,200		
20	Other expenses. See instructions	20			
21	Add lines 16 through 20	21	3,200		
22	Multiply line 21, column (b) by line 7	22	800		
23	Carryover of operating expenses from 2000 Form 8829, line 41	23			
24	Add line 21 in column (a), line 22, and line 23			24	800
25	Allowable operating expenses. Enter the **smaller** of line 15 or line 24			25	800
26	Limit on excess casualty losses and depreciation. Subtract line 25 from line 15			26	13,950
27	Excess casualty losses. See instructions	27			
28	Depreciation of your home from Part III below	28	1,429		
29	Carryover of excess casualty losses and depreciation from 2000 Form 8829, line 42	29			
30	Add lines 27 through 29			30	1,429
31	Allowable excess casualty losses and depreciation. Enter the **smaller** of line 26 or line 30			31	1,429
32	Add lines 14, 25, and 31			32	4,729
33	Casualty loss portion, if any, from lines 14 and 31. Carry amount to **Form 4684**, Section B			33	
34	Allowable expenses for business use of your home. Subtract line 33 from line 32. Enter here and on Schedule C, line 30. If your home was used for more than one business, see instructions ▶			34	4,729

Part III   Depreciation of Your Home

35	Enter the **smaller** of your home's adjusted basis or its fair market value. See instructions	35	220,000
36	Value of land included on line 35	36	40,000
37	Basis of building. Subtract line 36 from line 35	37	180,000
38	Business basis of building. Multiply line 37 by line 7	38	45,000
39	Depreciation percentage. See instructions	39	3,175 %
40	Depreciation allowable. Multiply line 38 by line 39. Enter here and on line 28 above. See instructions	40	1,429

Part IV   Carryover of Unallowed Expenses to 2002

41	Operating expenses. Subtract line 25 from line 24. If less than zero, enter -0-	41	0
42	Excess casualty losses and depreciation. Subtract line 31 from line 30. If less than zero, enter -0-	42	0

For Paperwork Reduction Act Notice, see page 4 of separate instructions.   Cat. No. 13232M   Form **8829** (2001)

Mutual Funds

Introduction

Mutual funds come in all shapes and sizes. Generally, mutual funds are classified according to their investment objectives. Aggressive growth funds, for example, are characterized by high risk and high return. These funds typically seek capital appreciation and do not produce significant interest income or dividends. The objectives of balanced funds, on the other hand, are to conserve an investor's initial principal, pay high current income through dividends, and promote the long-term growth of both principal and income. While aggressive growth funds generally invest only in stocks, balanced funds typically invest in both bonds and stocks. There are many other kinds of mutual funds—growth and income funds, bond funds, sector funds, index funds, and

the like—all with differing investing objectives and different strategies to achieve them. A general rule to keep in mind: The higher the potential reward from your investment, the greater the risk that you may not achieve the expected return.

A **money market fund** *is a mutual fund that tries to increase current income available to shareholders by purchasing short-term market investments.*

This chapter explains how differing distributions that you may receive from a mutual fund are taxed as well as the different methods by which you may calculate your gain or loss when you sell your mutual fund shares. It also discusses some of the expenses you may incur when investing in mutual funds.

The following chapter incorporates excerpts from IRS Publication 564 (Mutual Fund Distributions), *Chapter 8* (Mutual Funds) *from* The Ernst & Young Tax Saver's Guide 2002, *and Chapter 6 of the* Personal Financial Planning Guide, Special Tax Edition. *The Ernst & Young comments are reproduced with permission from the copyright holder. For more tax-saving tips and strategies see* The Ernst & Young Tax Saver's Guide 2002.

Kinds of Mutual Funds

A mutual fund is a regulated investment company generally created by "pooling" funds of investors to allow them to take advantage of a diversity of investments and professional management.

The advantages that investment companies can offer you are numerous, including:

- Professional investment management of assets at a relatively low cost
- Ownership in a diversified portfolio
- Potentially lower commissions, because the investment company buys and sells in large blocks
- Prospectuses and reports of various periodicals to assist people in readily accessing information needed to perform fund comparisons
- Other special services, such as dividend reinvestment

plans, periodic withdrawal and investment plans, the ability to switch between funds by telephone or over the Internet, and in some cases, check writing privileges

Investment Objectives

Mutual funds are classified according to their investment objectives. Following is a summary of the various types of funds categorized by their investment objective.

Aggressive Growth Funds. These funds are characterized by high risk and high return: They typically seek capital appreciation and do not produce significant interest income or dividends.

Growth Funds. Growth funds aim to achieve an increase in the value of their investments over the long term (capital gains) rather than paying dividends.

Growth and Income Funds. Also called "equity-income" and "total return" funds, these funds aim to balance the objectives of long-term growth and current income.

Balanced Funds. These funds have three objectives: to conserve investors' initial principal, to pay high current income through dividends and interest, and to promote long-term growth of both principal and income. Balanced funds invest in both bonds and stocks.

Bond Funds. Bond mutual funds invest primarily in bonds. Some funds may concentrate on short-term bonds, others on intermediate-term bonds, and still others on long-term bonds.

Sector Funds. Sector funds invest in one industry, such as biotechnology or retail, and therefore do not offer the diversity you generally receive from a growth mutual fund, for example.

Index Funds. Index mutual funds re-create a particular market index (e.g., the S&P 500). The holdings and the return should mirror that of the index.

Types of Regulated Investment Companies

In addition to categorizing investment companies by their investment objectives, investment companies are classified according to their capital structure. The three types are:

- Closed-end funds
- Unit investment trusts
- Open-end funds

Closed-End Funds. Closed-end investment companies have a set capital structure with a specified number of shares. For this reason, investors must generally purchase existing shares of closed-end funds from current stockholders. Investors who wish to liquidate their position in closed-end investment companies must sell their shares to other investors. Shares in closed-end funds are therefore traded on the open market just like the stock of publicly held corporations. As a result, closed-end funds have an additional risk that isn't present in open-end funds—their price does not necessarily equal their net asset value. Closed-end funds that are sold at a discount from the value of the underlying investments can produce an opportunity for greater return.

Unit Investment Trusts. Unit investment trusts are a variation of closed-end funds. Unit trusts typically invest in a fixed portfolio of bonds that are held until maturity rather than managed and traded, as is the case with bond mutual funds. As an investor you purchase units that represent an ownership in the trust assets. Because the bonds are not traded, the annual fees charged for unit trusts may be lower than those charged by bond mutual funds. The unit trust collects the interest income and repayment of principal of the bonds held in the portfolio and distributes these funds to the unit holders. Unit investment trusts can provide you with a portfolio of bonds that have different maturity dates and an average holding period that meets your objectives. Cash flow is relatively predictable, because the intention is to hold the bonds until maturity.

Open-End Funds. Commonly referred to as mutual funds, open-end funds differ from closed-end funds in that they do not have a fixed number of shares to issue. Instead, the number of shares outstanding varies as investors purchase and redeem them directly from the open-end investment company. An investor who wants a position in a particular mutual fund purchases the shares from the fund either through a stockbroker or by contacting the fund directly. Conversely, mutual fund shareholders who want to liquidate their position sell their shares back to the company. The value of a share in a mutual fund is determined by the net asset value (NAV). Funds compute NAV by dividing the value of the fund's total net assets by the number of shares outstanding.

Mutual Funds Fees

The costs associated with open-end fund shares resemble those for closed-end funds. Like closed-end funds, open-end funds bear the trading costs and investment management fees of the investment company. However, mutual fund investors may or may not be subject to a sales charge referred to as a "load."

Depending on the type of load charged (if any), open-end mutual funds are classified as:

- No-load funds
- 12b-1 funds
- Load funds

No-Load Funds. No-load funds don't impose a sales charge on their investors. Purchases and sales of shares in a no-load fund are made at the fund's NAV per share. Consequently, every dollar invested gets allocated to the fund for investment rather than having a portion permanently kept back to cover sales charges.

12b-1 Funds. 12b-1 funds are a variation on no-load funds. While every dollar paid into the fund is committed to investment, the 12b-1 fund shareholders indirectly pay an annual fee to cover the fund's sales and marketing costs. This 12-b-1 fee typically ranges from 0.1% to the maximum 1% of total fund assets. [*Note*: The 12b-1 fee is assessed every year (instead of only once); thus, the longer you hold your 12b-1 fund shares, the greater the sales charge you will bear.]

Load Funds. By contrast, load funds charge the shareholder a direct commission at the time of purchase and/or when the shares are redeemed. "Front-end loads" are charged to the investor at the time of purchase and can be as high as 8.5% of the gross amount invested. On the other hand, some load funds charge their shareholders the load at the time their shares are redeemed. This cost will be either a "back-end load" or a "redemption fee." A back-end load is based on the lesser of the initial cost or final value of the shares redeemed and may disappear after a few years. A redemption fee is similar to a back-end load, but is based on the value of the shares you choose to redeem rather than your initial investment. It typically applies if the investor sells within a very short period of time (usually 30 to 60 days). The purpose of such fees is to discourage shareholders from short-term trading of fund shares.

All fees, loads, and charges reduce your investment return. Therefore, you should consider not only a fund's return, but all of the expenses that affect this return.

Foreign Stock Mutual Funds

Many stock mutual funds invest in foreign stocks. They are divided into the following categories:

- *Global or world funds.* These funds invest anywhere in the world, including the United States.
- *International or foreign funds.* Such funds invest anywhere in the world except the United States.
- *Regional funds.* These invest in specific geographic areas, such as Europe, Latin America, or the Pacific Rim.

- *Country funds.* Funds of this sort invest entirely in a specific country. For the most part, single country funds are closed-end mutual funds that typically trade on either the New York Stock Exchange or the American Stock Exchange.
- *International index funds.* These are mutual funds that parallel the concept of a domestic equity index fund. They are designed and operated so that their portfolios mirror the composition of the market index after which the funds are named.

Foreign Bond Mutual Funds

In addition to foreign stock funds, numerous foreign bond funds are available for investment. Because economic conditions differ from country to country, interest rates vary as well. At any given time, you can usually find several countries with interest rates higher than those in the United States. There is a downside to consider, though. Overseas interest rates may be more attractive, but language barriers, differing regulations, and illiquid markets all increase the challenge of foreign investments. Fluctuating currency values, although a potential advantage, can work against you if the currency of your foreign investment loses value relative to the U.S. dollar.

For more about mutual fund investing see *Ernst & Young's Personal Financial Planning Guide, Special Tax Edition.*

Tax Treatment of Distributions

A mutual fund will send you a Form 1099-DIV, *Dividends and Distributions,* or a substitute form containing substantially the same language, to tell you what you must report or take into account on your income tax return. See *How To Report,* later.

TaxPlanner

How mutual funds are taxed. Which mutual fund or funds you choose will depend largely on your own investment objectives. But one factor you should definitely consider is how your mutual fund investment will be taxed. Generally, a mutual fund is a conduit for tax purposes—that is, the fund does not ordinarily pay income taxes, but its shareholders do. Interest, dividends, gains, and losses are generally passed through to shareholders in a fund in the form of dividends and capital gains distributions. As a shareholder, you are liable for any taxes due on these distributions. Consequently, it can matter enormously how those gains and losses are taxed.

Dividends declared one year but not paid until the next. Often, a mutual fund will declare a dividend at the end of the calendar year but not pay it until January of the following year. Nevertheless, you are treated as having received the dividend in the year in which it was declared.

Example

A fund declares a dividend in December 2001 payable to shareholders owning stock on that date. This is known as the record date. The dividend is not paid until January 2002. You are treated as having received the dividend on December 31, 2001.

TaxSaver

Timing your purchase of a mutual fund. You should pay close attention to the timing of your purchase of a mutual fund. For example, if you invest in a fund near the end of the year and the fund shortly thereafter makes a year-end distribution, you will have to pay tax on the distribution even though from your point of view you are simply getting back the capital you just invested in the fund. In effect, all you've done is "bought" taxable income that the fund earned earlier in the year but had not yet paid out to shareholders. Typically, the fund's share price drops by the amount of the distribution. Your cost basis in the mutual fund, however, will be the predistribution price you paid for the shares.

There is one consolation. Your higher basis will reduce any capital gain on a later sale. Moreover, if you sell the fund at a loss, it will increase your capital loss. If you want to limit your tax liability and lower your basis in the shares, you should delay your purchase of fund shares until after the

□ CORRECTED (if checked)

PAYER'S name, street address, city, state, ZIP code, and telephone no.		**1** Ordinary dividends $	OMB No. 1545-0110	**Dividends and Distributions**
		2a Total capital gain distr. $	**2001**	
		2b 28% rate gain $	Form **1099-DIV**	
PAYER'S Federal identification number	RECIPIENT'S identification number	**2c** Qualified 5-year gain $	**2d** Unrecap. sec. 1250 gain $	**Copy B For Recipient**
RECIPIENT'S name		**2e** Section 1202 gain $	**3** Nontaxable distributions $	This is important tax information and is being furnished to the Internal Revenue Service. If you are required to file a return, a negligence penalty or other sanction may be imposed on you if this income is taxable and the IRS determines that it has not been reported.
Street address (including apt. no.)		**4** Federal income tax withheld $	**5** Investment expenses $	
City, state, and ZIP code		**6** Foreign tax paid $	**7** Foreign country or U.S. possession	
Account number (optional)		**8** Cash liquidation distr. $	**9** Noncash liquidation distr. $	

Form **1099-DIV**   (Keep for your records.)   Department of the Treasury - Internal Revenue Service record date for the distribution. Usually, a fund can tell you when distributions, if any, for the year are expected. Alternatively, you can consult investment publications, such as *Morningstar Mutual Funds,* which indicate distribution dates for the previous year.

Example
ABC Fund declares and distributes a $1 dividend on December 1. If you had purchased 1,000 shares at $10 per share on November 30, you will have to report $1,000 of income for 2001. If instead you bought the shares on December 2, after the record date, you will pay $9 per share and have no taxable income to report. Of course, for the shares bought on November 30, your basis would be $10 per share instead of $9.

TAXSAVER
Year-end selling. If you are thinking of *selling* shares in a mutual fund, particularly near the end of the year when many funds pay dividends, you should consider redeeming your shares before any upcoming dividend payments are made by the fund. If your shares are worth more than you paid, you can take a capital gain on the redemption and avoid paying the higher tax rate on ordinary income that you would pay on an ordinary dividend. If your shares are worth less than you paid for them, you can minimize your capital losses by selling before the dividend. Remember, the net asset value per share of the fund (that is, the amount you would receive on the redemption of your shares) decreases by the amount of the dividend.

Community property states. If you are married and receive a distribution that is community income, one-half of the distribution is generally considered to be received by each spouse. If you file separate returns, you must each report one-half of any taxable distribution. Get Publication 555, *Community Property,* for more information on community income.

If the distribution is not considered community income under state law and you and your spouse file separate returns, each of you must report your separate taxable distributions.

Kinds of Distributions

There are several kinds of distributions that you, as a shareholder, may receive from a mutual fund. They include:

- Ordinary dividends,
- Capital gain distributions,
- Exempt-interest dividends, and
- Return of capital (nontaxable) distributions.

Tax-exempt mutual fund. Distributions from a tax-exempt mutual fund (one that invests primarily in tax-exempt securities) may consist of ordinary dividends, capital gain distributions, undistributed capital gains, or return of capital like any other mutual fund. These distributions generally are treated the same as distributions from a regular mutual fund. Distributions designated as exempt-interest dividends are not taxable.

All other distributions generally follow the same rules as a regular mutual fund. Regardless of what type of mutual fund you have (whether regular or tax-exempt), when you dispose of your shares (sell, exchange, or redeem), you usually will have a taxable gain or a deductible loss to report.

For more information on figuring taxable gains and losses see *Sales Exchanges and Redemptions,* later. Also see Chapter 17, *Reporting Capital Gains and Losses,* for further information.

Ordinary Dividends

An ordinary dividend is a distribution by a mutual fund out of its earnings and profits. Include ordinary dividends that you receive from a mutual fund as dividend income on your individual income tax return.

Explanation
Dividend distributions from a mutual fund, such as interest or dividends earned from the fund's investment securities, are generally considered ordinary income for tax purposes. Ordinary dividend distributions also can include any net short-term capital gains—short-term capital gains minus short-term losses—realized by the fund when it sells securities.

Ordinary dividends are the most common type of dividends. They will be reported in box 1 of the Form 1099-DIV or on a similar statement you receive from the mutual fund.

Capital Gain Distributions

These distributions are paid by mutual funds from their net realized long-term capital gains. The Form 1099-DIV (box 2a) or the fund's statement will tell you the amount you are to report as a capital gain distribution. Capital gain distributions are taxed as long-term capital gains regardless of how long you have owned the shares in the mutual fund.

Explanation
A capital gains distribution from a fund represents net long-term capital gains realized by the fund. While a fund may also realize net long-term losses from the sale of securities, it is not permitted to pass through these losses to shareholders. Instead, the fund must carry net capital losses forward to offset any future capital gains. Generally, all dividend and capital gains distributions from a fund are subject to federal and state income taxes. Dividends from municipal bond or municipal money market funds are the exception. These dividends are usually exempt from federal income tax and may also be exempt from state and local income taxes, depending on where you live and your state's tax law. See the above discussion on tax-exempt mutual funds. For more information on reporting capital gains and losses from the sale of mutual fund shares, see the discussion on gains and losses later in this chapter.

TAXSAVER
High-turnover funds. Before you invest in a mutual fund, you should consider the rate at which the fund turns over its assets. A fund with a high turnover rate will generate frequent gains and losses, increasing the chances that capital distributions will be short-term, rather than long-term. Short-term capital gain distributions are reported and taxed as ordinary income dividends; long-term capital gains are eligible for the lower long-term capital gain rate.

Undistributed capital gains. Mutual funds may keep some of their long-term capital gains and pay taxes on those undistributed amounts. You must report your share of these amounts as long-term capital gains, even though you did not actually receive a distribution. You can take a credit for any tax paid because you are considered to have paid it.

Form 2439. The fund will send you Form 2439, *Notice to Shareholder of Undistributed Long-Term Capital Gains,* showing your share of the undistributed capital gains and any tax paid by the mutual fund. You can take a credit for any tax paid because you are considered to have paid it.

The undistributed capital gain reported on Form 2439 should be reported as a capital gain distribution in addition to any other capital gain distributions reported on Form 1099-DIV.

TaxOrganizer

Undistributed capital gains. A mutual fund will report the amount of undistributed capital gains to you on Form 2439, not on Form 1099-DIV.

A special rule exists for capital gain distributions you receive when you sell your shares in the fund at a loss within 6 months of the date of original purchase. In this case, the portion of your capital loss attributable to the capital gain dividend is treated as a long-term—not a short-term—capital loss.

Increase to basis. When a mutual fund allocates undistributed capital gains to you, you can increase your basis in the shares. For more information see Chapter 14, *Basis of Property.*

Exempt-Interest Dividends

A mutual fund may pay exempt-interest dividends to its shareholders if it meets certain requirements. These dividends are paid from tax-exempt interest earned by the fund. Since the exempt-interest dividends keep their tax-exempt character, do not include them in income. However, you may need to report them on your return. See *Information reporting requirement,* next. The mutual fund will send you a statement within 60 days after the close of its tax year showing your exempt-interest dividends. Exempt-interest dividends are not shown on Form 1099-DIV.

Information reporting requirement. Although exempt-interest dividends are not taxable, you must report them on your tax return if you are required to file. This is an information reporting requirement and does *not* convert tax-exempt interest to taxable interest.

TaxPlanner

"Tax-preference" dividends. Some or all of your tax-exempt dividends may be treated as a "tax preference item" and may be subject to the alternative minimum tax (AMT). The mutual fund company will let you know what percentage of your dividends is a tax preference. If you receive exempt-interest dividends, you should obtain Form 6251, *Alternative Minimum Tax—Individuals,* for more information.

Return of Capital (Nontaxable) Distributions

A distribution that is not out of earnings and profits is a return of your investment, or capital, in the mutual fund and is shown in box 3 of Form 1099-DIV. These returns of capital distributions are not taxed as ordinary dividends and are sometimes called tax-free dividends or nontaxable distributions. However, they may be fully or partly taxable as capital gains.

A return of capital distribution reduces your basis in the shares. Basis is explained in Chapter 14, *Basis of Property.* Your basis cannot be reduced below zero. If your basis is reduced to zero, you must report the return of capital distribution on your tax return as a capital gain. The distribution is taxable if it, when added to all return of capital distributions received in past years, is more than your basis in the shares. Report this capital gain on Schedule D (Form 1040). Whether it is a long-term or short-term capital gain depends on how long you held the shares.

Example

In 1992, Jane Smith bought shares in ABC Mutual Fund for $10 a share. In 1993, she received a return of capital distribution of $2 a share, which reduces her basis in each share by $2 to an adjusted basis of $8. In 1994, Jane received a return of capital of $4 per share, reducing her basis in each share from $8 to $4. In 2001, the return of capital distribution from the mutual fund is $5 a share. Jane will report the $1 excess per share as a long-term capital gain on Schedule D.

Reinvestment of dividends. Many mutual funds offer dividend reinvestment plans in which you may use your dividends to buy more shares of stock in the mutual fund instead of receiving the dividends in cash. If you reinvest your dividends, you still must report the dividends on your return. Whether you include the reinvested dividends in income depends on the nature of the dividend. For example, if you reinvest your tax-exempt dividends, you do not have to include them in income.

How To Report

You must report mutual fund distributions on Form 1040 or Form 1040A. You cannot report mutual fund distributions on Form 1040EZ.

You *cannot* use Form 1040A and *must* use Form 1040 in either of the following situations.

- You received a return of capital distribution that must be reported as a capital gain because it is more than your basis in your mutual fund shares.
- You must report an undistributed capital gain.

Table 1, *Reporting Mutual Fund Distributions on Form 1040,* shown below, explains where on Form 1040 or its related schedules to report distributions from mutual funds.

If your only capital gains are from mutual funds distributions, you should report them on line 13 of Form 1040 and not on Schedule D. Make sure you calculate the tax using the table in the instructions.

TaxSaver

If you did not have any capital gain or nontaxable distributions, you may be able to file Form 1040A rather than Form 1040. See Chapter 1, *Filing Information,* for further details.

Foreign tax deduction or credit. Some mutual funds invest in foreign securities or other instruments. Your mutual fund may choose to allow you to claim a deduction or credit for the taxes it paid to a foreign country or U.S. possession. The fund will notify you if this applies to you. The notice will include your share of the foreign taxes paid to each country or possession and the part of the dividend derived from sources in each country or possession.

Explanation

You must complete Form 1116 if you choose to claim the credit for income tax paid to a foreign country. You do not have to complete Form 1116 if your total foreign taxes paid is $300 or less for the year ($600 if married filing jointly). You can claim the credit for the full amount of the taxes paid as long as your foreign income is all passive (i.e., interest

Table 1. Reporting Mutual Fund Distributions on Form 1040

Type of Distribution	Where To Report if Total Dividends From All Payers Are:	
	$400 or Less	**More than $400**
Ordinary Dividends Form 1099-DIV, Box 1	Form 1040, line 9	Schedule B, line 5
Capital Gain Distributions Form 1099-DIV, Boxes 2a-2d	Schedule D, line 13, column (f) (Form 1040, line 13 if no other capital gains)	Schedule D, line 13, column (f) (Form 1040, line 13 if no other capital gains)
Nontaxable Distributions Form 1099-DIV, Box 3	Basis of shares reduced to zero? No—Nontaxable until zero Yes—Report on Schedule D	Basis of shares reduced to zero? No—Nontaxable until zero Yes—Report on Schedule D
Exempt-Interest Dividends (Not included on Form 1099-DIV)	Form 1040, line 8b	Form 1040, line 8b
Undistributed Capital Gains Form 2439, Box 1a	**Gain**—Schedule D, line 11, column (f)	**Gain**—Schedule D, line 11, column (f)

dividends, etc.). Under certain circumstances, however, it may be to your benefit to treat the tax as an itemized deduction on Schedule A (Form 1040).

For a discussion of the foreign tax credit and whether you should claim the credit or a tax deduction, see Chapter 24, *Taxes You May Deduct.*

Sales, Exchanges, and Redemptions

When you sell or exchange your mutual fund shares, or if they are redeemed (a redemption), you will generally have a taxable gain or a deductible loss. This also applies to shares of a tax-exempt mutual fund. Sales, exchanges, and redemptions are all treated as sales of capital assets. The amount of the gain or loss is the difference between your adjusted basis (defined earlier) in the shares and the amount you realize from the sale, exchange, or redemption.

In general, a sale is a transfer of shares for money only. An exchange is a transfer of shares in return for other shares. A redemption occurs when a fund reacquires its shares from you in exchange for money or other property.

TAX ORGANIZER

When there is a sale, exchange, or redemption of your shares in a fund, keep the confirmation statement you receive. The statement shows the price you received for the shares and other information you need to report gain or loss on your return.

TAXSAVER

Exchanging funds in the same family. You will have a capital gain or loss when you exchange shares of one mutual fund for another mutual fund in the same mutual fund family. So, for example, if you exchange shares in ABC Growth Fund for shares in ABC Technology Fund, you may have to recognize a capital gain or loss. Generally, any service fee charged for the exchange may be added to your basis of the shares you acquired.

You will not have to recognize a capital gain or loss, however, if the shares in one mutual fund are converted to the shares of another pursuant to a merger of the two funds or if the redemption of your shares is treated as a dividend.

Information returns. Brokers must report to the Internal Revenue Service the proceeds from sales, exchanges, or redemptions. Brokers must give each customer a written statement with that information by January 31 of the year following the calendar year the transaction occurred. Form 1099-B, *Proceeds From Broker and Barter Exchange Transactions,* or a substitute, may be used for this purpose. Report your sales shown on Form(s) 1099-B (or substitute) on Schedule D (Form 1040) along with your other gains and losses. If the total sales reported on Form(s) 1099-B is more than the total you report on Schedule D, attach a statement to your return explaining the difference.

Taxpayer identification number. You must give the broker your correct taxpayer identification number (TIN). Generally, an individual will use his or her social security number as the TIN. If you do not provide your TIN, your broker is required to withhold tax at a rate of 31% (30% beginning January 1, 2002) on the gross proceeds of a transaction, and you may be penalized.

Keeping Track of Your Basis

You should keep track of your basis in mutual fund shares because you need the basis to figure any gain or loss on the shares when you sell, exchange, or redeem them. The basis depends on how the shares were acquired.

Shares Acquired by Purchase

The original basis of mutual fund shares you bought is usually their cost or purchase price. The purchase price usually includes any commissions or load charges paid for the purchase.

Example

Martin Brown bought 200 shares of XYZ Mutual Fund for $10 a share. He paid a $100 commission to the broker for the purchase. His cost basis for each share is $10.50 ($2,100 ÷ 200).

TAX ORGANIZER

When you buy or sell shares in a fund, keep the confirmation statements you receive. The statements show the price you paid for the shares when you bought them and the price you received for the shares when you disposed of them. The information from the confirmation statement when you purchased the shares will help you figure your basis in the fund.

Commissions and load charges. The fees and charges you pay to acquire or redeem shares of a mutual fund are not deductible. You can usually add acquisition fees and charges to your cost of the shares and thereby increase your basis. A fee paid to redeem the shares is usually a reduction in the redemption price (sales price).

You cannot add your entire acquisition fee or load charge to the cost of mutual fund shares if *all* of the following conditions apply.

1) You get a reinvestment right because of the purchase of the shares or the payment of the fee or charge.
2) You dispose of the shares within 90 days of the purchase date.
3) You acquire new shares in the same mutual fund or another mutual fund, for which the fee or charge is reduced or waived because of the reinvestment right.

The amount of the original load charge in excess of the reduction in (3) is added to the cost of the original shares. The rest of the original load charge is added to the cost basis of the new shares (unless all three conditions above apply to the purchase of the new shares).

Reinvestment right. This is the right to acquire mutual fund shares in the same or another mutual fund without paying a fee or load charge, or by paying a reduced fee or load charge.

Shares Acquired by Reinvestment

The original cost basis of mutual fund shares you acquire by reinvesting your distributions is the amount of the distributions used to purchase each full or fractional share. This rule applies even if the distribution is an exempt-interest dividend that you do not report as income.

TAX ORGANIZER

Dividend reinvestment plan. If you participate in a dividend reinvestment plan, you should keep a record of the dividends and of the shares purchased with the reinvestment. The reinvested dividends are part of your cost basis for the shares. You will need these records to figure your cost basis when you sell all or some of your shares. See *Identifying the Shares Sold,* later in this chapter.

Shares Acquired by Gift or Inheritance

See Chapter 14, *Basis of Property.*

Adjusted Basis

After you acquire mutual fund shares, you may need to make adjustments to your basis. The adjusted basis of your shares is your original basis (defined earlier), increased or reduced as described here.

Addition to basis. Increase the basis in your shares by the difference between the amount of undistributed capital gain you include in income and the tax considered paid by you on that income.

The mutual fund reports the amount of your undistributed capital gain in box 1a of Form 2439. You should keep Copy C of all Forms 2439 to show increases in the basis of your shares.

TAX ORGANIZER

Confirmation statements. You should keep all confirmation statements for purchases of mutual fund shares as well as records of dividends that are automatically reinvested in your account. Your basis is increased by amounts reported to you by the fund on Form 2439 as undistributed capital gains you are required to report as income less the tax paid by the fund on the undistributed gains. Your basis is reduced by non-taxable dividends that are a return of your investment.

Reduction of basis. You must reduce your basis in your shares by any return of capital distributions that you receive from the fund.

No reduction of basis. You do not reduce your basis for distributions from the fund that are exempt-interest dividends.

Identifying the Shares Sold

To figure your gain or loss when you dispose of mutual fund shares, you need to determine which shares were sold and the basis of those shares. If your shares in a mutual fund were acquired all on the same day and for the same price, figuring their basis is not difficult. However, shares are generally acquired at various times, in various quantities, and at various prices. Therefore, figuring your basis can be more difficult. You can choose to use either a cost basis or an average basis to figure your gain or loss. See Table 2, *Choosing a Basis Method.*

Table 2. Choosing a Basis Method

Basis Method	Advantages/Disadvantages
Specific identification	The most flexible way to determine your gains and losses. But there are important restrictions governing its use.
FIFO	The simplest approach. But it may mean a large gain if your shares have appreciated significantly and you are redeeming only part of your account.
Average cost (single category)	The middle ground. A more modest tax burden than the FIFO method but more tedious calculations if you sell shares frequently.
Average cost (double category)	Only makes sense if (1) you have elected it in the past and are required to continue using it and (2) there is a tax benefit from maintaining separate short-and long-term average costs.

Cost Basis

Under the *cost basis,* you can choose one of the following methods:

- Specific share identification, or
- First-in first-out (FIFO)

Specific share identification. If you can definitely identify the shares you sold, you can use the adjusted basis of those particular shares to figure your gain or loss.

You will adequately identify your mutual fund shares, even if you bought the shares in different lots at various prices and times, if you:

1) Specify to your broker or other agent the particular shares to be sold or transferred at the time of the sale or transfer, and
2) Receive confirmation of your specification from your broker in writing within a reasonable time.

Table 3. **How To Figure Basis of Shares Sold**

This is an example showing two different ways to figure basis. It compares the cost basis using the FIFO method and the average basis using the single-category method.

Date	Action	Share Price	No. of Shares	Total Shares Owned
02/4/00	Invest $4,000	$25	160	160
08/5/00	Invest $4,800	$20	240	400
12/16/00	Reinvest $300 dividend	$30	10	410
09/29/01	Sell $6,720	$32	210	200

COST BASIS (FIFO)

To figure the basis of the 210 shares sold on 9/29/01, use the share price of the first 210 shares you bought, namely the 160 shares you purchased on 2/4/00 and 50 of those purchased on 8/5/00.

$4,000 (cost of 160 shares on 2/4/00)
+ $1,000 (cost of 50 shares on 8/5/00)
Basis = $5,000

AVERAGE BASIS (single-category)

To figure the basis of the 210 shares sold on 9/29/01 use the average basis of all 410 shares owned on 9/29/01.

$9,100 (cost of 410 shares)
÷ 410 (number of shares)
$22.20 (average basis per share)

$22.20
× 210
Basis = $4,662

The confirmation by the mutual fund must confirm that you instructed your broker to sell particular shares. You continue to have the burden of proving that you owned the specified shares at the time of sale or transfer.

First-in first-out (FIFO). If the shares were acquired at different times or at different prices and you cannot identify which shares you sold, use the basis of the shares you acquired first as the basis of the shares sold. Therefore, the oldest shares still available are considered sold first. You should keep a separate record of each purchase and any dispositions of the shares until all shares purchased at the same time have been disposed of completely. Table 3, *How To Figure Basis of Shares Sold,* shows how to figure a gain or loss on a sale of shares in a mutual fund using the FIFO method.

Average Basis

You may choose to use an average basis to figure your gain or loss when you sell all or part of your shares in a regulated investment company, if you acquired the shares at various times and prices, and you left the shares on deposit in an account handled by a custodian or agent who acquires or redeems those shares.

Once you elect to use an average basis, you must continue to use it for all accounts in the same fund. However, you may specify cost basis for shares in other funds, even those within the same family of funds.

Example
You own two accounts in the income fund issued by Company A. You also own 100 shares of the growth fund issued by Company A. If you elect to use average basis for the first account of the income fund, you must use average basis for the second account. However, you may use cost basis for the growth fund.

To figure average basis, you can use one of the following methods:

- Single-category method
- Double-category method

Single-category method. All shares are included in a single category. The adjusted basis of each share is the total adjusted basis of all shares in the category at the time of a disposition, divided by the number of shares in the category. In determining the holding period, the shares disposed of are considered to be those shares acquired first.

Example
John Smith bought the following shares in the GLM Mutual Fund: 100 shares in 1999 at $10 per share, 100 shares in 2000 at $12 a share, and 100 shares in 2001 at $26 a share. The 300 shares cost a total of $4,800. The average basis per share is $16 ($4,800 ÷ 300).

Remaining shares. The basis of your shares determined under average basis is the basis of *all* your shares in the account. That is, the basis of the remaining shares is the same as the basis of the shares sold.

Double-category method. All shares in an account at the time of each disposition are divided into two categories: short-term and long-term. Shares held one year or less are short-term. Shares held longer than one year are long-term.

The adjusted basis of each share in a category is the total adjusted basis of all shares in that category at the time of disposition divided by the total shares in the category. You may specify, to the custodian or agent handling your account, from which category the shares are to be sold or transferred. The custodian or agent must confirm *in writing* your specification. If you do not specify or receive confirmation, you must first charge the shares sold against the long-term category and then, any remaining shares sold against the short-term category.

Changing categories. After you have held a mutual fund share for more than one year, you must transfer that share from the short-term category to the long-term category. When you make the change, the basis of a transferred share is its actual cost or adjusted basis to you, or if some of the shares in the short-term category have been disposed of, its basis under the average basis method. The basis of the undisposed shares left in the short-term category that are changed to the long-term category is the average basis of the shares in the short-term category at the time of the most recent disposition from this category.

Making the choice. You choose to use the average basis of mutual fund shares by clearly showing on your income tax return, for each year the choice applies, that you used an average basis in reporting gain or loss from the sale or transfer of the shares. You must specify whether you used the single-category method or the double-category method in determining average basis. This choice is effective until you get permission from the IRS to revoke it.

Making the choice for gift shares. If your account includes shares that you received by gift, and the fair market value of the shares at the time of the gift was less than the donor's basis, special rules apply. To use the average basis, you must submit a statement with your initial choice to use one of the average basis methods. It must state that the basis used in figuring the average basis of the gift shares under either method will be the FMV at the time of the gift. This statement applies to gift shares you receive before and after making the choice, as long as the choice to use the average basis is in effect. If you do not make this statement, you cannot choose to use the average basis for any account that contains gift shares.

Gains and Losses

You figure gain or loss on the disposition of your shares by comparing the *amount you realize* with the *adjusted basis* of your shares. If the amount you realize is more than the adjusted basis of the shares, you have a gain. If the amount you realize is less than the adjusted basis of the shares, you have a loss.

Amount you realize. The amount you realize from a disposition of your shares is the money and value of any property you receive for the shares disposed of, minus your expenses of sale (such as redemption fees, sales commissions, sales charges, or exit fees).

Adjusted basis. Adjusted basis is explained under *Keeping Track of Your Basis,* earlier.

Reporting on Schedule D. Mutual funds and brokers report dispositions of mutual fund shares on Form 1099-B, or a substitute form containing substantially the same language. The form shows the amount of the sales price and indicates whether the amount reported is the gross amount or the net amount (gross amount minus commissions).

If your Form 1099-B or similar statement from the payer shows the gross sales price, do not subtract the expenses of sale from it when reporting your sales price in column (d) on Schedule D. Instead, report the gross amount in column (d) and increase your cost or other basis, column (e), by any expense of the sale. If your Form 1099-B shows that the gross sales price less commissions was reported to IRS, enter the net amount in column (d) of Schedule D and *do not* increase your basis in column (e) by the sales commission.

Example 1
Linda Jones sold 200 shares of Fund B for $5,000. She paid a $150 commission to the broker for handling the sale. Her Form 1099-B shows that the net sales proceeds, $4,850 ($5,000 – $150), were reported to IRS. Report this amount in column (d) of Schedule D.

Example 2
Joe Green sold 100 shares of Fund KLM for $5,000. He paid a $50 commission to the broker for handling the sale. He bought the shares for $2,500. Joe's broker reported the gross proceeds to IRS on Form 1099-B, so he must increase his basis in column (e) of Schedule D to $2,550.

Holding Period

When you dispose of your mutual fund shares, you must determine your holding period. Your holding period determines whether the gain or loss is a short-term capital gain or loss or a long-term capital gain or loss.

Short-term gain or loss. If you hold the shares for one year or less, your gain or loss will be a short-term gain or loss.

Long-term gain or loss. If you hold the shares for more than one year, your gain or loss will be a long-term gain or loss.

Determining period held. Determine your holding period by using the trade dates of your purchases and your sales. The **trade date** is the date on which you contract to buy or sell shares. Most mutual funds will show the trade dates on confirmation statements showing your purchases and sales.

To find out how long you have held your shares, begin counting on the day after the trade date on which you bought the shares. (Do not count the trade date itself.) The trade date on which you dispose of the shares is counted as part of your holding period.

Example
Assume Lori Hill bought shares in XYZ Mutual Fund on January 13, 2000 (trade date). She starts counting on January 14, and the 14th of each following month is the beginning of a new month. Therefore, if she sells the shares on January 13, 2001 (trade date), her holding period would not be more than 1 year. However, if she sells them on January 14, 2001, her holding period would be more than 1 year (12 months plus 1 day).

Mutual fund shares received as a gift. If you receive a gift of mutual fund shares and your basis is determined by the donor's basis, your holding period is considered to have started on the same day that the donor's holding period started.

Inherited mutual fund shares. If you inherit mutual fund shares, you are considered to have held the shares for more than 1 year (even if you disposed of the shares within 1 year after the decedent's death) if your basis is:

1. The fair market value at the date of the decedent's death (or the alternate valuation date), or
2. The decedent's adjusted basis (in the case of shares decedent received as a gift from you in the year prior to decedent's death).

Report the sale of inherited mutual fund shares on line 8 of Schedule D and write "Inherited" in column (b) instead of the date you acquired the shares.

Reinvested distributions. If your dividends and capital gain distributions are reinvested in new shares, the holding period of each new share begins the day after that share was purchased. Therefore, if you sell both the new shares and the original shares, you might have both short-term and long-term gains and losses.

Certain short-term losses. Special rules may apply if you have a short-term loss on the sale of shares on which you received an exempt-interest dividend or a capital gain distribution.

Exempt-interest dividends before short-term loss. If you received exempt-interest dividends on mutual fund shares that you held for 6 months or less and sold at a loss, you may claim only the part of the loss that is more than the exempt-interest dividends. On Schedule D, column (d), increase the sales price by the amount of exempt-interest dividends. Report the loss as a short-term capital loss.

Example

On January 6, 2001, you bought a mutual fund share for $50. On February 1, 2001, the mutual fund paid a $3 dividend from tax-exempt interest, which is not taxable to you. On February 8, 2001, you sold the share for $45. If it were not for the tax-exempt dividend, your loss would be $5 ($50 − $45). However, you can deduct only $2, the part of the loss that is more than the exempt-interest dividend ($5 − $3). On Schedule D, column (d), increase the sales price from $45 to $48 (the $3 portion of the loss that is not deductible). You may deduct only $2 as a short-term capital loss.

Capital gain distribution before short-term loss. Generally, if you received capital gain distributions (or had to report undistributed capital gains) on mutual fund shares that you held for 6 months or less and sold at a loss, report only the part of the loss that is more than the capital gain distribution (or undistributed capital gain) as a short-term capital loss. The rest of the loss is reported as a long-term capital loss.

Example

On April 12, 2001, Ben Simms bought one share of ABC Mutual Fund for $25. On June 29, 2001, the mutual fund paid a capital gain distribution of $1 a share, which is taxed as a long-term capital gain. On July 11, 2001, he sold the share for $22.50. If it were not for the capital gain distribution, Ben would have had a $2.50 ($25 − $22.50) short-term loss. However, the part of the loss that is not more than the capital gain distribution ($1) must be reported as a long-term capital loss. The remaining $1.50 of the loss can be reported as a short-term capital loss.

Wash sales. If you sell mutual fund shares at a loss and within 30 days before or after the sale you buy, acquire in a taxable exchange, or acquire a contract or option to buy substantially identical property, you have a wash sale. You cannot deduct losses from wash sales. In determining whether the shares are substantially identical, you must consider all the facts and circumstances. Ordinarily, shares issued by one company are not considered to be substantially identical to shares issued by another company.

How to Figure Gains and Losses on Schedule D

Separate your short-term gains and losses from your long-term gains and losses on all the mutual fund shares and other capital assets you disposed of during the year. Then determine your net short-term gain or loss and your net long-term gain or loss.

Explanation
Net capital loss. If you have a net capital loss, your allowable capital loss deduction is the smaller of:

1. $3,000 ($1,500 if you are married and filing a separate return)
2. Your net capital loss

Enter your allowable loss on line 13 of Form 1040.

Example 1
Bob and Gloria sold all of their shares in a mutual fund. The sale resulted in a capital loss of $7,000. They had no other sales of capital assets during the year. On their joint return, they can deduct $3,000, which is the smaller of their loss or the net capital loss limit.

If Bob and Gloria's capital loss had been $2,000, their capital loss deduction would have been $2,000 because it is less than the $3,000 limit.

Example 2
Margaret has capital gains and losses for the year as follows:

	Short-term	Long-term
Gains	$700	$400
Losses	(800)	(2,000)

Margaret's deductible capital loss is $1,700, which she figures as follows:

Short-term capital losses	($800)
Subtract short-term capital gains	700
Net short-term capital loss	($100)
Long-term capital losses	($2,000)
Subtract long-term capital gains	400
Net long-term capital loss	($1,600)
Deductible capital loss	($1,700)

Example 3
Art and Karen file a joint return. They have a net long-term capital loss of $5,600 and a net short-term capital gain of $450. Their net capital loss is $5,150 ($5,600−$450). Because their net capital loss exceeds $3,000, the amount they can deduct for the year is limited to $3,000.

Capital loss carryovers. If your net capital losses are more than your allowable net capital loss deduction, you may carry over the excess to later years until it is completely used up. To determine your capital loss carryover, subtract from your capital loss the lesser of:

1) Your allowable capital loss deduction for the year, or
2) Your taxable income increased by your allowable capital loss deduction for the year and by your deduction for personal exemptions.

If your deductions exceed your gross income, you start the computation with a negative number.

When carried over, the loss will keep its original character as long-term or short-term. Therefore, a long-term capital loss carried over from a previous year will offset long-term gains of the current year before it offsets short-term gains of the current year.

In determining your capital loss carryover, apply your capital loss deduction to reduce your net short-term losses first. If after applying the short-term losses, the capital loss limit has not been reached, then apply the long-term losses until you reach the limit.

Use the *Capital Loss Carryover Worksheet* at the end of Chapter 17, *Reporting Gains and Losses,* to figure your capital loss carryover.

Capital loss carryovers from separate returns are combined if you file a joint return for the current year. However, if you once filed jointly and are now filing separately, a capital loss carryover from the joint return can be deducted only on the separate return of the spouse who actually had the loss.

Investment Expenses

You can generally deduct the expenses of producing investment income. These include expenses for investment counseling and advice, legal and accounting fees, and investment newsletters. These expenses are deductible as miscellaneous itemized deductions to the extent that they exceed 2% of your adjusted gross income. See Chapter 30, *Miscellaneous Deductions,* for further information.

Publicly offered mutual funds. Generally, mutual funds are publicly offered funds. These mutual funds report only the net amount of investment income after your share of the investment expenses has been deducted.

TAX*SAVER*

If you own shares in a publicly offered mutual fund, you do not have to pay tax on your share of the fund's expenses. There should be no entry in box 5 of Form 1099-DIV. However, expenses of a nonpublicly offered fund may be subject to tax. You should consult your tax advisor for details.

TAX*SAVER*

Front-end fees. "Front-end," or purchase, fees (also known as "load charges") reduce your investment in a mutual fund, but they are still considered part of your cost basis for tax purposes.

Example

You invest $10,000 in a fund that charges a 1% load on portfolio transaction (purchase) fee. Your account statement reports a net balance of $9,900 ($10,000 minus the 1% fee). For tax purposes, however, your cost remains at $10,000.

Exception

Your basis in mutual fund shares does not include load charges (sales fees) paid after October 3, 1989, on the purchase of shares if you held the shares for 90 days or less and then reinvested the proceeds in a fund within the same fund family with a reduced load charge. Instead, the load charges become part of your basis in the shares of the new fund into which you put your investment.

TAX*SAVER*

Sales charges and redemption fees. Before you buy a mutual fund, you should examine the sales charges and redemption fees it charges, if any. No-load funds do not have a sales charge. Mutual fund listings in newspapers generally indicate whether there is a sales charge. No-load funds have the same purchase and redemption price for fund shares. Your broker should be able to tell you which funds charge commissions.

Explanation

Back-end fees. Fees may also be deducted from your fund when you redeem or sell shares. These are generally called redemption or "back-end" fees. (Certain back-end fees called "contingent deferred sales charges" or "contingent deferred sales loads" typically decline and eventually disappear over a set period of time.) If your mutual fund reports all proceeds net of redemption fees on your Form 1099-B, you do not need to adjust your tax cost. However, if your mutual fund reports gross proceeds before any redemption fees on Form 1099-B, you should increase your cost basis by the amount of the fee you paid when calculating your capital gain or loss.

Other fees. Custodial and account maintenance fees are deductible as investment expenses on Schedule A of your income tax return, subject to certain caveats. See Investment Expenses, above, and Chapter 2, *Filing Status.*

Nonpublicly Offered Mutual Funds

If you own shares in a nonpublicly offered mutual fund during the year, you can deduct your share of the investment expenses on your Schedule A (Form 1040) as a miscellaneous itemized deduction to the extent your miscellaneous deductions exceed 2% of your adjusted gross income. Your share of the expenses will be shown in box 1e of Form 1099-DIV. A nonpublicly offered mutual fund is one that:

1. Is not continuously offered pursuant to a public offering
2. Is not regularly traded on an established securities market
3. Is not held by at least 500 persons at all times during the tax year

Contact your mutual fund if you are not sure whether it is nonpublicly offered.

Expenses allocable to exempt-interest dividends. You cannot deduct expenses that are for the collection or production of exempt-interest dividends. Expenses must be allocated if they were partly for both taxable and tax-exempt income. One accepted method for allocating expenses is to divide them in the same proportion that your tax-exempt income from the mutual fund is to your total income from the fund.

Limit on Investment Interest Expense

The amount you can deduct as an investment interest expense may be limited. See Chapter 25, *Interest Expense.*

40

The Gift Tax

Introduction

Birthdays. Anniversaries. Holidays. Graduations. Special occasions. For most of us, we are continually giving something to someone. Surely, we cannot be taxed on our generosity. Or can we? The answer generally depends on how generous you are.

If you make a gift to an individual during the year, you *might be required to pay a gift tax. Not surprisingly, what constitutes a gift is not a simple answer. This chapter shows you what constitutes a gift for gift tax purposes, explains how to calculate your gift tax liability, and informs you when to use either of the two available gift tax forms—Form 709 and Form 709-A.*

What Is a Gift?

Unlike the income tax, which imposes a tax on the receipt of property, the gift tax imposes a tax on the *transfer of property*. Thus, when a father *gives* his daughter a gold watch on her graduation, he has made a gift that is potentially subject to tax.

Determining If a Gift Has Occurred

Step 1—To determine whether a gift has occurred, you first need to identify the donor. While at first glance this might seem relatively easy, the donor is not always the person who actually delivers the property. For instance, if you give property to someone who acts on your behalf with instructions to distribute the property to another, your agent is not the donor; you are, even though you did not physically hand the property to the ultimate recipient.

Step 2—Once the donor is identified, your next step is to determine whether the transfer is subject to the gift tax. Almost anything can be considered a gift. Obvious examples include the transfer by gift of cash, stock, land, and personal property. Less-well-known items include forgiving a debt owed to you, making interest-free or below market loans, allowing rent-free use of property, and assigning the benefits of an insurance policy. Performing free personal services, however, generally is not subject to gift tax.

In addition to the transfer of any kind of property mentioned above, the gift tax can also apply to sales or exchanges *not* made in the ordinary course of business where the money or value exchanged is worth less than the value of what is sold or exchanged.

Three types of transfers, however, are *not* subject to the gift tax. The first is a transfer to political organizations for the use of the organization. The second is a transfer of property made on behalf of an individual to an educational organization as tuition for education or training. The payment must be made directly to the qualifying educational organization and it must be for tuition only. The third is a transfer made on behalf of an individual to a person or institution that provides medical care for the individual. If the payment for a medical expense is reimbursed by the recipient's insurance company, however, your payment for that expense, to the extent of the reimbursed amount, is not eligible for the medical exclusion.

Step 3—Next, you must determine whether a completed transfer occurred. To constitute a completed transfer, the rights to ownership must be passed to the recipient voluntarily and the donor generally may not retain any rights of ownership. If a person makes a qualified disclaimer with respect to any interest in property, the property will be treated as if it had never been transferred to that person.

Step 4—Finally, you must determine the fair market value of the property transferred. For some items of property, this is an easy determination, such as cash and marketable securities (the average of the high and low value as quoted in an established securities exchange). Other items may require an appraisal to establish fair market value (i.e., artwork, real estate, interest in the family business). The Treasury regulations define fair market value to be the price at which a willing buyer and seller would establish with each other, with each being knowledgeable of all the relevant facts and neither being under any compulsion to sell.

TaxALERT

The law requires adequate disclosure of your taxable gifts. This essentially means that you must provide adequate information about the gift made and your method for valuing the transfer. Failure to adequately disclose a gift permits the IRS to challenge the gift tax return at any time.

Example

A father loans his son $400 interest free payable on demand. The father also agrees to pay off his son's credit card debts. The forgone interest, and the satisfaction of his son's debts, all are gifts subject to tax, although, as seen below, a gift tax may not necessarily be imposed.

It's important to note that the gift tax will not apply to the satisfaction of a support obligation. A parent will not be subject to gift tax on anything he or she gives to a child which is considered support. So providing a college education, giving a car to a dependent child, and the like, will not subject you to a gift tax.

Exclusions from Gift Tax

Given the broad definition of what constitutes a gift, many of us are guilty of making gifts almost every day. So why aren't we all required to pay a gift tax? Part of the reason is that each of us is entitled to transfer gift tax free up to $10,000 per donee each year (the annual exclusion) to as many donees as we wish, provided, however, that the gift is of a *present* interest.

Present vs. future interest. A gift is considered a *present* interest if the donee has all immediate rights to the use, possession, and enjoyment of the property and income from the property. Gifts made to a trust for the benefit of a minor (Minor's trust) have special rules. A gift to a minor trust is considered a *present* interest if all of the following conditions are met by the terms of the trust:

1. Both the property and its income may be expended by, or for the benefit of, the minor before the minor reaches age 21;
2. All remaining trust property and its income must pass to the minor on the minor's twenty-first birthday; and
3. If the minor dies before the age of 21, the property and its income will be payable either to the minor's estate or to whomever the minor may appoint under a general power of appointment.

A gift of a *future* interest, however, cannot be excluded under the $10,000 annual exclusion. A gift is considered a *future* interest if the donee's rights to the use, possession, and enjoyment of the property and income from the property will not begin until some future date. *Future* interests include reversions, remainders, and other similar interests or estates. Putting property in trust for future use by the beneficiary, other than the minor's trust discussed above, is a gift of a future interest.

TaxSAVER

The $10,000 "annual exclusion" eliminates many of our token gifts from the gift tax. The annual exclusion also can be used over time to transfer a significant amount of wealth. For instance, if a mother transferred $10,000 a year for 10 years to her adult son, a total of $100,000 would be transferred gift tax free. Moreover, if the mother transferred $10,000 a year for 10 years to both her adult son and her adult daughter, $200,000 would be transferred gift tax free.

TaxALERT

As a result of a change in the law, the $10,000 annual exclusion will now be indexed for inflation. As a consequence, inflation should no longer erode the effectiveness of the annual exclusion.

Gift-splitting. There is a further benefit to the $10,000 annual exclusion if the donor is married and the donor's spouse consents to the giving of the gift. In that case, all gifts either spouse made to third parties during the calendar year will be considered as made one-half by each, so long as:

1. The spouses were married to one another at the time of the gift;
2. If the spouses were divorced or widowed after the gift, neither former spouse (nor surviving spouse) remarried during the rest of the calendar year;
3. Neither spouse was a nonresident alien at the time of the gift; and
4. The donor did not give the other spouse a general power of appointment over the property interest transferred.

In order for a spouse's consent to be valid, the spouse must sign the gift tax return of the donor spouse. If the consenting spouse is deceased, the executor of the deceased spouse may sign the consent. Likewise, if the consenting spouse is legally incompetent, the guardian of the spouse may sign the consent. The consent is effective for the entire calendar year; therefore, all gifts made by the donor and the donor's spouse (while married) to third parties during the calendar year must be split. If the consent is effective, each spouse is jointly and severally liable for any gift tax.

TaxSAVER

By "splitting" gifts, a married couple can give up to $20,000 a year gift tax free to as many recipients as they wish. In essence, each spouse is giving $10,000 worth of the gift.

The Marital and Charitable Deductions

There are only two deductions permitted under the gift tax rules: a charitable deduction and a marital deduction. As with the income tax, the charitable deduction under the gift tax is available only if the contributions are made to a qualified organization. Refer to Chapter 26, *Contributions,* for more details on charitable giving. It is important to note, however, that, unlike for income tax purposes, to qualify for the gift tax charitable deduction, the donee organization does not have to be domestic—that is, a foreign charity will qualify for this deduction. With respect to the marital deduction, unless the spouse of the donor is not a citizen of the United States, the donor spouse may deduct the entire amount of property transferred to his or her spouse. If the recipient spouse is not a U.S. citizen, special rules apply. For the gift tax, the marital deduction is eliminated and replaced by an expanded $106,000 annual gift tax exclusion. For the estate tax, the marital deduction is allowed if the property transferred to the noncitizen spouse is placed in a special trust known as a qualified domestic trust.

TaxAlert

Effective for gifts made after August 5, 1997, a donor is not required to report a charitable contribution on a gift tax return so long as (1) the donor has transferred his entire interest in the property and (2) either no other interest in such property is or has been transferred (for less than adequate consideration) for a noncharitable purpose or such transfer is of a qualified real property interest.

Computing the Gift Tax

In order to compute the gift tax, two computations are necessary. First, you must determine the tax under current tax tables for the combination of all prior gifts, whether reported or not, and the current year's gifts. Second, you must determine the tax under current tax tables only for the prior gifts, again whether reported or not. The difference between the first figure and the second figure is the amount of tax due on the current year's gift.

Table for Computing Tax

The gift tax is computed on a cumulative basis as follows:

Column A Taxable Amount Over —	Column B Taxable Amount Not Over —	Column C Tax on Amount in Column A	Column D Rate of Tax on Excess Over Amount in Column A
—	$10,000	—	18%
10,000	20,000	$1,800	20%
20,000	40,000	3,800	22%
40,000	60,000	8,200	24%
60,000	80,000	13,000	26%
80,000	100,000	18,200	28%
100,000	150,000	23,800	30%
150,000	250,000	38,800	32%
250,000	500,000	70,800	34%
500,000	750,000	155,800	37%
750,000	1,000,000	248,300	39%
1,000,000	1,250,000	345,800	41%
1,250,000	1,500,000	448,300	43%
1,500,000	2,000,000	555,800	45%
2,000,000	2,500,000	780,800	49%
2,500,000	3,000,000	1,025,800	53%
3,000,000	10,000,000	1,290,800	55%
10,000,000	17,184,000	5,140,800	60%
17,184,000	—	9,451,200	55%

TaxAlert: The 2001 Tax Act

The top gift tax rate will be gradually reduced from 2002 until 2010, when the top gift tax rate will be 35%. Note that the Unified Credit Exemption (explained below) amount for gift tax purposes will remain frozen at one million dollars after 2002. The increase in the unified credit amount in 2003-2009 is only for estate tax purposes, upon death. So, a wealthy individual who has already used his/her gift tax exemption of $1 million by 2004 by gifting that amount will not be able to give away, tax-free, another $500,000 when the estate tax exemption rises to $1.5 million in 2004. However, if that person dies in 2004, the additional $500,000 will be passed on to his or her heirs tax-free.

Unified Credit

If the donor is a citizen or resident of the United States, he or she is entitled to a tax credit. This credit, called the unified credit, must be used to offset any gift tax liability until it is exhausted. In 2001, a donor is entitled to a unified credit of $220,550, which permits a donor to transfer up to $675,000 in taxable gifts without paying a gift tax. In 2002, the unified credit exemption amount will increase to $1,000,000. This gift tax exemption amount will not increase beyond $1,000,000. After 2002, this amount is *not* indexed for inflation. The following table illustrates the increase in the estate and generation-skipping transfer tax-exemption amounts.

Table 3

Estate and GST Tax Rates and Unified Credit Exemption Amount

Calendar Year	Estate and GST tax deathtime transfer exemption	Highest estate and gift tax rates (GST tax rate)
2001	$675,000 for estate tax; $1,060,000 for GST tax	55%, plus 6% surtax on certain estates over $10 million
2002	$1 million for estate tax; $1,060,000 indexed from 2001 for GST tax	50% (and surtax repealed)
2003	$1 million for estate tax; $1,060,000 indexed from 2001 for GST tax	49%
2004	$1.5 million	48%
2005	$1.5 million	47%
2006	$2 million	46%
2007	$2 million	45%
2008	$2 million	45%
2009	$3.5 million	45%
2010	N/A (estate and GST taxes repealed)	Gift tax remains, equal to top individual income tax rate of 35%
2011	$1 million for estate tax; $1,060,000 indexed from 2001 for GST tax	55% (plus 5% surtax)

TaxPlanner

Any unused unified credit may be used to offset any subsequent estate tax liability. If you have a sizable estate—one considerably in excess of what you need to live on—you might consider how paying gift taxes (or utilizing your unified credit) now can save on estate taxes later. By gifting property now, any appreciation will not be subject to tax.

Do You Need to File a Gift Tax Return?

Only individuals are required to file a gift tax return. If a trust, estate, partnership, or corporation makes a gift, the individual beneficiaries, partners, or stockholders are considered donors and may be liable for the gift tax. If a donor dies before filing a return, the donor's executor must file the gift tax return.

Although you may have made gifts during the year, you

do not need to file a gift tax return so long as you meet all of the following requirements:

1. You made no gifts during the year to your spouse;
2. You gave no more than $10,000 during the year to any one recipient; and
3. All of the gifts you made were of present interests.

Additionally, except in limited circumstances, you do not have to file a gift tax return solely to report gifts to your spouse (regardless of the amount of these gifts and regardless of whether the gifts are present or future interests). You must file a gift tax return, however, if:

- Your spouse is not a U.S. citizen and the total gifts you made to your spouse during the year exceeds $106,000, or if you made any gift of a terminable interest that does not meet certain exceptions;
- You make a Qualified Terminable Interest Property election;
- You gave gifts to any donee other than your spouse that are not fully excluded under the $10,000 annual exclusion. Thus, you must file a gift tax return to report any gift of a future interest (regardless of amount) or to report gifts to any donee that total more than $10,000 for the year; or
- You elect to split gifts with your spouse (regardless of the amount of the gifts).

If you are required to file a gift tax return, use Form 709, *United States Gift Tax Return*, unless, as explained later, you are entitled to use Form 709-A, *United States Short Form Gift Tax Return* in lieu of Form 709.

When to File the Gift Tax Return

The gift tax return is an annual return. In general, you must file a gift tax return on or after January 1 but not later than April 15 (without extensions) of the year following the calendar year when the gifts were made. If the donor of the gifts died during the year in which the gifts were made, the executor must file the donor's gift tax return not later than the earlier of: (1) the due date (with extensions) for filing the donor's estate tax return; or (2) April 15 of the year following the calendar year when the gifts were made. If no estate tax return is required to be filed, the due date for the gift tax return (without extensions) is April 15.

Extension of Time to File

You can extend the time to file the gift tax return in either of two ways. First, you can request an extension by writing to the IRS district director or service center for your area. In the letter, you must explain the reasons for the delay. Second, you can request an extension by using one of the extension forms used to extend the filing of your income tax return. Income tax return extensions are made by using Forms 4868, 2688, or 2350, which have checkboxes for the gift tax return. You may only use one of these forms to extend the time for filing your gift tax return if you are also requesting an extension of time to file your income tax return. If you are not requesting an extension to file your income tax return, only the first method of extension is available to you.

TAXPLANNER

Like the income tax return, an extension to file a gift tax return does not extend the time to pay the gift tax due. If you want an extension of time to pay the gift tax, you must make a separate request.

Gift Tax Return—Form 709

Form 709 is used to report transfers subject to the federal gift tax (as well as the generation-skipping transfer tax, not discussed here) and also to compute the tax, if any, due on those transfers. A married couple may not file a joint Form 709, even if the spouses elect gift splitting. Instead, both the donor spouse and the consenting spouse must each file a separate gift tax return unless either of two situations are met:

Situation 1. During the calendar year:

- Only one spouse made any gifts;
- The total value of these gifts to each third-party donee does not exceed $20,000; and
- All of the gifts were of present interests.

Situation 2. During the calendar year:

- Only one spouse (the donor spouse) made gifts of more than $10,000 but not more than $20,000 to any third-party donee;
- The only gifts made by the other spouse (the consenting spouse) were gifts of not more than $10,000 to third-party donees other than those to whom the donor spouse made gifts; and
- All of the gifts by both spouses were of present interests. If either of these two situations is met, only the donor spouse must file a return and the consenting spouse signifies consent on that return.

Gift Tax Return—Form 709-A

When You May File a Form 709-A Instead of a Form 709. Form 709-A is the short form gift tax return and may be used only by certain married couples to report nontaxable gifts that they consent to split. If you were married during the entire calendar year, you may use Form 709-A instead of Form 709, so long as all of the following requirements are met:

1. You are a citizen or resident of the United States, and were married during the entire calendar year to one individual who is also a citizen or resident of the United States. Both you and your spouse must have been alive at the end of the calendar year.
2. Your only gifts (other than gifts for tuition or medical care) to a third party consisted entirely of present interests in tangible personal property, cash, U.S. Savings Bonds, or stocks and bonds listed on a stock exchange. You cannot use Form 709-A to report gifts of closely held stock, partnership interests, fractional interests in real estate, or gifts for which the value has been reduced to reflect a valuation discount.
3. Your gifts to any one third-party donee (other than gifts for tuition or medical care) during the calendar year did not total more than $20,000. If the donee is a charity, no part of that gift may be given to a noncharitable donee.
4. During the calendar year, you did not make any gifts of terminable interests to your spouse.
5. During the calendar year, your spouse did not make any gifts to any of the donees listed on the form, did not make gifts of terminable interests to you, did not make gifts (other than gifts for tuition or medical care) of over $10,000 to any other donee, and did not make any gifts of future interests to any other donee.
6. You and your spouse agree to split all of the gifts either of you made during the calendar year.
7. You did not file a Form 709 for the calendar year in which you are filing the Form 709-A.

41

What to Do If You Employ Domestic Help

Introduction

If you have a domestic helper who qualifies as your **employee,** *you may have to pay Social Security and Medicare taxes, as well as federal and state unemployment taxes. You may also have to withhold federal income tax and make* **earned income credit** *advance payments. In general, a person who works in or around your house qualifies as your employee if you control his or her working conditions—pay, work schedule, conduct, and appearance. This chapter spells out what federal tax rules govern domestic help and advises you on how to comply with them.*

Both you and your employee are subject to Social Security and Medicare taxes if you pay your employee $1,200 or more during any calendar year. If you have paid any employee $1,000 or more in any calendar quarter during the current or preceding year, you are subject to federal unemployment taxes on every employee during the current year.

Your employee may ask you to withhold federal income tax from compensation. If you decide to do so, you must withhold the proper amount from each

paycheck. This withholding must be remitted to the IRS.

Use Schedule H (Form 1040) to compute federal taxes for your household employees and attach it to your personal income tax return.

If you pay your income taxes late, penalties and interest will be due by you on the taxes described in this chapter as well as on your personal income taxes.

This chapter only discusses the federal taxes applying to household employees. There may be additional taxes due depending on the state and city where the services are rendered.

You may also be subject to federal and/or state rules regarding employees' pay and benefits. For example, state laws may dictate the maximum number of hours an employee may work, the amount to be paid for overtime, and/or the number of days of paid vacation and holidays the employee is entitled to.

Even if your domestic employee does not have legal authorization to work in the United States, you are still liable for the payroll taxes discussed in this chapter.

TaxAlert

The rules in this chapter relate to someone who works for you in the United States or who is a U.S. citizen or green card holder. If you are employing someone to work outside of the United States, you will need to investigate your responsibilities under the laws of that country.

Employment Taxes for Household Employers

If you pay someone to come to your home and care for your dependent or spouse, you may be a household employer. If you are a household employer, you will need an employer identification number

(EIN) and you may have to pay employment taxes. If the individuals who work in your home are self-employed, you are not liable for any of the taxes discussed in this section. Self-employed persons who are in business for themselves are not household employees. Usually, you are *not* a household employer if the person who cares for your dependent or spouse does so at his or her home or place of business.

Exception

Baby-sitters and yard workers under the age of 18 are exempt, regardless of how much they earn, provided they are full-time students. In addition, the wages that they earn in the year in which they turn 18 are also exempted.

TAXPLANNER

Paying the "nanny" tax. Employers are required to report the Social Security and federal unemployment taxes due on domestic workers' wages on the employers' Form 1040. The taxes must be paid through the employers' estimated tax payments. Alternatively, the employer could increase federal withholding on his or her own wages and pay the Social Security tax on the domestic worker in that manner. Federal unemployment taxes on domestics are payable the same way.

If you use a placement agency that exercises control over what work is done and how it will be done by a babysitter or companion who works in your home, that person is not your employee. This control could include providing rules of conduct and appearance and requiring regular reports. In this case, you do not have to pay employment taxes. But, if an agency merely gives you a list of sitters and you hire one from that list, the sitter may be your employee.

If you have a household employee you may be subject to:

1) Social Security and Medicare taxes,
2) Federal unemployment tax, and
3) Federal income tax withholding.

Social Security and Medicare taxes are generally withheld from the employee's pay and matched by the employer. Federal unemployment (FUTA) tax is paid by the employer only and provides for payments of unemployment compensation to workers who have lost their jobs. Federal income tax is withheld from the employee's total pay if the employee asks you to do so and you agree.

For more information on a household employer's tax responsibilities, see Publication 926 and Schedule H (Form 1040) and its instructions.

State employment taxes. You may also have to pay state unemployment tax. Contact your state unemployment tax office for information. You should also find out whether you need to pay or collect other state employment taxes or carry workers' compensation insurance. A list of state employment tax agencies, including addresses and phone numbers, is in Publication 926.

Explanation

Employee or independent contractor? Whether or not a person who provides services in and around your house is your employee depends on the facts and circumstances of the situation. In general, a person is your employee if you control his or her working conditions and compensation. A person does not have to work for you full-time to qualify as your employee.

Generally, workers are classified based on how they perform their work and their accountability for it. By definition, independent contractors are responsible for *results*, not how their tasks are accomplished. On the other hand, individuals who are instructed as to when, where, and how to complete their jobs would probably be considered employees. If you determine that your domestic helpers are employees, you must withhold and match Social Security payments and may be subject to paying federal and state unemployment taxes as well.

To gain a better understanding of the distinction between an independent contractor and an employee, consider the person who mows your lawn. If the person works for an independent lawn service and is supervised by the lawn company that also provides its own equipment—all you provide is the grass—there's little question that the provider is an independent contractor. However, if a college student cuts your lawn using your mower, and you give specific instructions as to how and when to do the job, he or she will be considered your employee.

To enable you to determine whether a person is indeed an independent contractor, there are certain common indicators that can help. An independent contractor:

- Works for several homeowners;
- Provides his or her own tools and supplies to perform the job;
- Can bring in additional help if he or she deems necessary;
- Determines how the results will be accomplished;
- Is paid by the job, not by the hour;
- Advertises his or her services;
- May be fired at will; and
- Can set his or her own hours and leave when the job is completed.

If you have reason to believe that a person is an independent contractor and not your employee, you should not withhold Social Security tax from his or her compensation. You may want to get a signed letter from this person indicating that he or she is an independent contractor and is responsible for his or her own employment taxes.

TAXPLANNER

Records you need. When you hire a household employee, make a record of that person's name and Social Security number exactly as it appears on his or her Social Security card. You will need this information when you remit Social Security, Medicare, federal unemployment, and withholding of federal income taxes.

An employee who does not have a Social Security number should apply for one on Form SS-5, *Application for a Social Security Card.* This form is available at all Social Security Administration offices as well as at most IRS offices and post offices.

If your employee is not eligible to obtain a Social Security number, he or she may obtain an individual taxpayer identification number (ITIN) by filing Form W-7 with the IRS. The ITIN can be used on a tax return wherever a Social Security number should be used. You should note that the ITIN is for IRS records only. It does not change the employee's status with the Immigration and Naturalization Service or his or her entitlement to Social Security or other employment benefits.

Employer Identification Number (EIN). In order to pay federal taxes for your household employee, you will need an employer identification number (EIN). This is a nine-digit number issued by the IRS. It is not the same as your Social Security number. If you already have an EIN, use that number. If you do not have an EIN, use Form SS-4, *Application for Employer Identification Number,* from Chapter 48, *2001 Federal Tax Forms and Schedules You Can Use.* You will need to send it to the IRS office listed in Table 41–1 for your location. If you need further information regarding the IRS process for issuing an EIN number, call or fax the IRS office in your area.

Social Security and Medicare Taxes

If you pay a household employee cash wages of $1,200 or more during a calendar year, those wages are subject to So-

Table 41–1. **IRS Offices for EIN Application**

Your residence location	IRS' address and phone/fax number
Florida, Georgia, South Carolina	Attn: Entity Control Atlanta, GA 39901 (770) 455-2360
New Jersey, New York City, and counties of Nassau, Rockland, Suffolk, and Westchester	Attn: Entity Control Holtsville, NY 00501 (631) 447-4955
New York (all other counties), Connecticut, Maine, Massachusetts, New Hampshire, Rhode Island, Vermont	Attn: Entity Control Andover, MA 05501 (978) 474-9717
Illinois, Iowa, Minnesota, Missouri, Wisconsin	Attn: Entity Control Stop 6800 2306 E. Bannister Rd. Kansas City, MO 64999 (816) 926-5999
Delaware, District of Columbia, Maryland, Pennsylvania, Virginia and persons having no state residency	Attn: Entity Control Philadelphia, PA 19255 (215) 516-6999
Indiana, Kentucky, Michigan, Ohio, West Virginia	Attn: Entity Control Cincinnati, OH 45999 (859) 292-5467
Kansas, New Mexico, Oklahoma, Texas	Attn: Entity Control Austin, TX 73301 (512) 460-7843
Alaska, Arizona, California (counties of Alpine, Amador, Butte, Calaveras, Colusa, Contra Costa, Del Norte, El Dorado, Glenn, Humboldt, Lake, Lassen, Marin, Mendocino, Modoc, Napa, Nevada, Placer, Plumas, Sacramento, San Joaquin, Shasta, Sierra, Siskiyou, Solano, Sonoma, Sutter, Tehama, Trinity, Yolo, and Yuba), Colorado, Idaho, Montana, Nebraska, Nevada, North Dakota, Oregon, South Dakota, Utah, Washington, Wyoming	Attn: Entity Control Mail Stop 6271 P.O. Box 9941 Ogden, UT 84201 (801) 620-7645
California (all other counties), Hawaii	Attn: Entity Control Fresno, CA 93888 (559) 452-4010
Alabama, Arkansas, Louisiana, Mississippi, North Carolina, Tennessee	Attn: Entity Control Memphis, TN 37501 fax (901) 546-3920

cial Security and Medicare taxes. Payments in kind (meals, transportation, etc.) are not used to figure the $1,200 amount or to figure the taxes. The taxes are figured on all cash wage payments in the year, regardless of when they were earned.

What is taxable compensation? Table 41–2 may help to clarify what is reportable income to your employee. Remember that state and local income tax and unemployment or disability and other employment tax rules may be different.

Family members. Social Security and Medicare taxes do not apply to household services performed by your spouse or by your child under 21. Social Security and Medicare taxes **apply** to wages you pay your parents for household services if:

1. Your child lives with you and is under age 18 or requires adult supervision for at least 4 continuous weeks in a calendar quarter due to a mental or physical condition, and

2. You are divorced and have not remarried, are widowed, or are married to a person who cannot care for your child because of a mental or physical condition.

TAXALERT

If a person is an employee whom you pay a total of $1,200 or more per year, you have tax filing and payment responsibilities.

TAXPLANNER

Baby-sitters. If the baby-sitter watches your children in your house at the time you specify, IRS rulings conclude that the person is an employee. It's not enough to stop giving the sitter a ride home in an attempt to make him or her appear more independent. You would need to use sitters who watch children in *their* homes or other facilities during set business hours. Or you can rotate sitters to avoid paying any one more than $1,200 per year. As previously noted, sitters under age 18 who are full-time students are exempt from Social Security taxes.

Paying the tax. Both you and the employee pay a share of the Social Security and Medicare taxes on the employee's wages. For 2001, the tax rate for Social Security is 6.2% for both you and the employee (a total of 12.4%). The tax rate for Medicare is 1.45% for both you and the employee (a total of 2.9%). The 6.2% Social Security tax applies only to the first $80,400 you paid each employee during calendar year 2001. The 1.45% Medicare tax applies to all wages.

TAXALERT

For 2002, the Social Security and Medicare tax rates will not change. The wage base on which the Social Security tax is calculated will remain at $84,900.

You must pay the total of these taxes (your employee's and your share) yourself if you do not deduct the employee's share from his or her wages. Any of the employee's share you pay is added income to the employee. This income must be included in box 1, *Wages, tips, other compensation*, on Form W-2, *Wage and Tax Statement*, but do not count it as cash wages for Social Security and Medicare purposes. You must also include the employee Social Security and Medicare taxes you pay in boxes 4 and 6 of the employee's Form W-2, even though the taxes were not actually withheld.

TAXPLANNER

If you would rather pay your employee's share of Social Security and Medicare taxes without deducting it from wages, you may do so. Any portion you do pay, however, is added to the compensation to your employee, even though it does not constitute cash wages for Social Security and Medicare purposes. Although it may be easier if you pay your employee's share of Social Security and Medicare taxes, it does raise *your* cost. You should come to an agreement with your employee on this issue before he or she begins work.

TAXPLANNER

If you and your employee agree that the employee will be responsible for his or her own share of the Social Security and Medicare taxes, you should also reach agreement on

Table 41–2. **What Is Taxable Compensation?**

	Federal Income Tax	Social Security and Medicare (FICA)	Federal Unemployment Tax (FUTA)
Salary paid by cash, check, or other means	Yes	Yes	Yes
Cash bonus (overtime, holiday, etc.)[1]	Yes	Yes	Yes
Cash gifts (holiday, birthday, wedding, etc.)[1]	Yes	Yes	Yes
Gifts of property (holiday, birthday, etc.)[2]	Yes	Yes	Yes
Vacation Pay	Yes	Yes	Yes
Sign-on bonus	Yes	Yes	Yes
Value of meals & lodging on your premises as part of job and for your convenience	No	No	No
Car provided to employee for commutation	Yes	Yes	Yes
Value of public transit tokens provided (less than $65 per month)	No	No	No
Car provided to employee to do work for you only	No	No	No
Insurance for employee's own car	Yes	Yes	Yes
Employee's medical insurance bills you pay	No	No	No
Uniforms you give to employee to wear on your premises	No	No	No
Cash uniform allowance	Yes	Yes	Yes
Value of vacation when nanny accompanies family to care for children	No	No	No
Employee's legal fees you pay	Yes	Yes	Yes
Employee's social security taxes you pay	Yes	No	Yes
Employee's income taxes you pay	Yes	Yes	Yes

[1]Unless less than $30, then nontaxable.

[2]Taxable value is lesser of cost or fair market value. Gifts valued at less than $30 are not taxable.

how it is to be paid. To minimize difficulties, you may want to start withholding immediately rather than wait until $1,200 has been earned each year. This avoids the problem of the employee having to pay you $91.80 (7.65% × $1,200) once the threshold has been met.

Example

Meredith Cabot pays her full-time housekeeper a $15,000 salary. She also pays both the employer's share of the Social Security and Medicare taxes (7.65% of $15,000, or $1,147.50) and the employee's share (7.65% of $15,000, or $1,147.50). For federal income tax purposes, the housekeeper's total compensation for the year is $16,147.50 ($15,000 plus $1,147.50), even though only $15,000 is subject to Social Security and Medicare taxes.

Federal Income Tax Withholding

If your household employee requests income tax withholding, and you agree, you must withhold an amount from each payment based on the information shown on the **Form W-4**, *Employee's Withholding Allowance Certificate*, given to you by the employee. See Chapter 6, *Wages, Salaries, and Other Earnings*, for more information about Form W-4. Publication 15 (Circular E), *Employer's Tax Guide*, explains how to figure the amount to withhold.

TAXPLANNER

It is your decision whether or not to withhold income tax from your employee's compensation, even if withholding is requested by your employee. However, if you do withhold for an employee, everything that you pay your employee—whether cash or noncash—is income subject to withholding. Some of the more common forms of compensation for household employees are (1) salaries; (2) overtime and bonuses; (3) meals, unless provided in your home and for your convenience; and (4) lodging, unless provided in your home, for your convenience, and as a condition of employ-

ment. As a general rule, if you have live-in domestic help, any meals and lodging you provide are *not* considered compensation. A car that you provide solely for use in transporting family members and doing household errands would not be considered compensation. However, a car provided to a domestic employee for his or her personal use (including getting to and from your house) would be considered income to him or her. Other forms of compensation include cash reimbursement for the employee's personal expenses, such as car insurance and vacation expenses. However, up to $65 per month in public transit passes can be provided to an employee without any federal tax effect. State tax laws may be different.

Any income tax withholding you pay for an employee without deducting it from the employee's wages is added income to the employee and subject to income, Social Security, and Medicare taxes.

Copies of Form W-4 and Publication 15 are available from the IRS Center where you file your income tax return.

Earned income credit advance payment. You must make advance payments of the earned income credit to any employee who is eligible to claim the earned income credit and requests advance payment of it. Who is eligible to claim the credit is explained in Chapter 37, *Other Credits Including the Earned Income Credit*.

The employee makes the request by giving you a completed **Form W-5**, *Earned Income Credit Advance Payment Certificate*. Each payday, you make the payments to your employee from the Social Security, Medicare, and withheld income taxes that you would otherwise pay to the Internal Revenue Service. For more information, see Publication 15.

You must notify any employees not having federal income tax withheld that they may be eligible for an income tax refund because of the earned income credit.

For more information about employment, see Publication 926, *Employment Taxes for Household Employers*.

Federal Unemployment Tax (FUTA)

Federal unemployment tax (FUTA) is for your employee's unemployment insurance. If you paid cash wages of $1,000 or more to household employees in any calendar quarter this year or last year, you are liable for FUTA for any employees you have this year. However, the tax does not apply to wages paid to your spouse, your parents, or your children under 21 years old.

Rate. The rate for 2001 and 2002 is 6.2% on the first $7,000 of cash wages paid to each employee during the calendar year.

The tax is imposed on you as the employer. Unlike Social Security, Medicare, and federal income tax, federal unemployment tax is *solely* an employer's responsibility. It is an additional cost to you of having domestic help. You must not collect or deduct it from the wages of your employees.

You may claim a credit against your federal unemployment tax for the state unemployment tax you paid by the due date for filing your Form 1040. The credit can be up to 5.4% of the federal tax. So your net federal tax may be as low as 0.8% if you pay the state tax on time.

When you hire a household employee, you should contact your state employment tax office to get information on how to file the state return and to get a state reporting number. The state will help you to figure the amount of tax you will pay the state. See the instructions to Schedule H for how to claim the credit.

Example 1

George Darby paid his housekeeper $3,000 in cash during the first quarter of 2001. He must pay federal unemployment tax (FUTA) for any employees he has during any part of 2001. Since he was liable for FUTA in 2001, any cash wages he pays to his employees in 2002 will also be subject to FUTA.

Example 2

George Darby paid his housekeeper and sole employee $12,000 for all of 2001. Since FUTA is assessed only on the first $7,000 of cash compensation paid to each employee during the calendar year, George's FUTA liability (before any credit for state unemployment taxes) was $434 ($7,000 × 6.2%).

Reporting and paying taxes on wages paid to household employees. Unless you own a business as a sole proprietor, you should report these taxes on Schedule H attached to your 2001 Form 1040. These taxes are added to your income taxes. The total must be paid during the course of the year. See Chapter 5, *Tax Withholding and Estimated Tax.*

If you are a sole proprietor who has nonhousehold employees, you should be filing Form 940 (or 940-EZ) annually to report FUTA (unemployment taxes) and Form 941 quarterly to report and remit federal income tax and FICA (Social Security and Medicare) tax withholdings. The IRS gives sole proprietors the option of including withholdings and taxes paid for domestic employees with withholdings and taxes paid for nondomestic employees on Forms 940 and 941. Alternatively, sole proprietors can exclude domestic employees from Forms 940 and 941 and file Schedule H with their own income tax returns.

Whether or not you are a sole proprietor, once you withhold tax from an employee, you must remit the tax to the IRS. If you do not, you could be responsible for substantial fines and penalties.

Example

Paul and Irene Jurgens employ Emily Whitney as a housekeeper and baby-sitter. Emily's weekly salary is $200, which is paid by Paul in cash each Friday. In addition, Irene pays Emily $50 for helping once a month on weekends when the Jurgens entertain. Emily uses her own car to drive to and from the Jurgens' home but is reimbursed weekly by Irene for gas to drive the children to school. Emily gives Irene a list of the actual miles driven and Irene pays her 34.5 cents per mile. Four times a year Paul pays $400 for Emily's medical insurance. Irene pays Emily's $300 vacation airfare in June and gives her a $500 bonus in December. Since Emily's annual compensation is expected to be over $1,200, the Jurgens decide to deduct FICA from Emily's salary from the beginning of the year. Emily completes and provides to the Jurgens a Form W-4. The Jurgens agree to deduct income tax from Emily's compensation. Emily does not qualify for the earned income credit. The state in which they reside has a flat income tax of 4% and unemployment taxes of 2% to be paid by Emily, and 7% to be paid by the Jurgens on income up to $7,000.

Since Emily has provided documentation indicating how many miles were driven, for what purpose and when, and since the reimbursement is within the IRS guideline of 34.5 cents per mile, Emily's reimbursement for gas is not taxable income to her. Also, since Emily does not have the option of receiving cash for the medical insurance premiums, the reimbursement for medical insurance is not taxable to her. The following worksheet (Figure 41–1) summarizes the taxable compensation paid to Emily and the taxes required to be deducted from her pay. The Jurgens would provide a Form W-2 to Emily showing taxable earnings of $11,800 and withholdings as indicated on Figure 41–1. A copy would be sent to the Social Security Administration. They would report the federal income tax withholding and FICA and pay the required FUTA and their portion of Social Security ($903) with their Form 1040, reflected on Schedule H. The state income tax and unemployment tax withholdings would be remitted as required by the state authorities. In addition, the Jurgens would be liable for $490 of state unemployment tax, which would also be remitted as required but not later than the due date for filing the Jurgens' Form 1040. The employer is responsible for FUTA, which in this case would be $56 ($7,000 × 6.2% less 5.4% maximum credit).

The Jurgens will have to either increase the withholding from their wages or increase their estimated tax payments by $2,875 in order to pay their household employee's taxes during the course of the year.

TAXORGANIZER

Forms you will need. You will need the following federal tax forms if you employ household help:

> Schedule H
> Form W-2, Wage and Tax Statement
> Form W-3, Transmittal of Wage and Tax Statements
> Form W-4, Employees' Withholding Allowance Certificate

You will need to contact your state tax authorities for applicable state tax forms.

As an employer, you must keep records of any cash or noncash wages paid to your employee as well as any taxes withheld from those wages. Figure 41–1 is designed to help you accumulate this information. You will need this infor-

Figure 41–1. **Worksheet for Domestic Employee's Wages**

Employee's Name Emily Whitney   **Employee's Social Security Number** 123-45-6789

	Cash Paid Directly to Employee	Cash Paid to Third Parties	Non-Cash Amounts	Taxes Paid on Behalf of Employee	Total Earnings for W-2 Purposes	Social Security and Medicare Tax Deducted	Federal Income Tax Deducted	State Income Tax Deducted	Other State Taxes Deducted	Earned Income Credit Advanced
January	$850				$850	$65	$65	$34	$17	
February	850				850	65	65	34	17	
March	1,050				1,050	80	95	42	21	
April	850				850	65	65	34	17	
May	850				850	65	65	34	17	
June	1,050		$300		1,350	103	137	54	27	
July	850				850	65	65	34	17	
August	850				850	65	65	34	7	
September	1,050				1,050	80	95	42		
October	850				850	65	65	34		
November	850				850	65	65	34		
December	1,550				1,550	119	167	62		
Total	$11,500		$300		$11,800	$902	$1,014	$472	$140	

mation at year-end to prepare the employee's Form W-2, which must be given to the employee by January 31 of the following year. If you are preparing more than one Form W-2, you also will need Form W-3, *Transmittal of Wage and Tax Statements*, to send copies to the Social Security Administration. The government copies must be sent by the last day of February of the following year.

A sample of a completed Schedule H is included in this chapter for the preceding example. You may want to see the IRS instructions to Schedule H for further information.

SCHEDULE H (Form 1040) Department of the Treasury Internal Revenue Service (99)	**Household Employment Taxes** (For Social Security, Medicare, Withheld Income, and Federal Unemployment (FUTA) Taxes) ▶ **Attach to Form 1040, 1040NR, 1040NR-EZ, 1040-SS, or 1041.** ▶ **See separate instructions.**	OMB No. 1545-0074 **2001** Attachment Sequence No. **44**

Name of employer	Social security number
Paul and Irene Jurgens	923 : 45 : 6789
	Employer identification number l l l : l l l l : l l l l

A Did you pay **any one** household employee cash wages of $1,200 or more in 2001? (If any household employee was your spouse, your child under age 21, your parent, or anyone under age 18, see the line A instructions on page 3 before you answer this question.)

☒ **Yes.** Skip lines B and C and go to line 1.
☐ **No.** Go to line B.

B Did you withhold Federal income tax during 2001 for any household employee?

☐ **Yes.** Skip line C and go to line 5.
☐ **No.** Go to line C.

C Did you pay **total** cash wages of $1,000 or more in **any** calendar **quarter** of 2000 or 2001 to household employees? (**Do not** count cash wages paid in 2000 or 2001 to your spouse, your child under age 21, or your parent.)

☐ **No.** **Stop.** Do not file this schedule.
☐ **Yes.** Skip lines 1-9 and go to line 10 on the back.

Part I   **Social Security, Medicare, and Income Taxes**

1	Total cash wages subject to social security taxes (see page 3) . .	**1** 11,800	
2	Social Security taxes. Multiply line 1 by 12.4% (.124)		**2** 1,463
3	Total cash wages subject to Medicare taxes (see page 3)	**3** 11,800	
4	Medicare taxes. Multiply line 3 by 2.9% (.029)		**4** 342
5	Federal income tax withheld, if any		**5** 1,014
6	**Total social Security, Medicare, and income taxes** (add lines 2, 4, and 5)		**6** 2,819
7	Advance earned income credit (EIC) payments, if any		**7** —
8	**Net taxes** (subtract line 7 from line 6)		**8** 2,819

9 Did you pay **total** cash wages of $1,000 or more in **any** calendar **quarter** of 2000 or 2001 to household employees? (**Do not** count cash wages paid in 2000 or 2001 to your spouse, your child under age 21, or your parent.)

☐ **No.** **Stop.** Enter the amount from line 8 above on Form 1040, line 56. If you are not required to file Form 1040, see the line 9 instructions on page 4.

☒ **Yes.** Go to line 10 on the back.

For Paperwork Reduction Act Notice, see Form 1040 instructions.	Cat. No. 12187K	**Schedule H (Form 1040) 2001**

Part II   Federal Unemployment (FUTA) Tax

			Yes	No
10	Did you pay unemployment contributions to only one state?	10	X	
11	Did you pay all state unemployment contributions for 2001 by April 15, 2002? Fiscal year filers, see page 4	11	X	
12	Were all wages that are taxable for FUTA tax also taxable for your state's unemployment tax? . . .	12	X	

Next: If you checked the **"Yes"** box on **all** the lines above, complete Section A.

If you checked the **"No"** box on **any** of the lines above, skip Section A and complete Section B.

Section A

13	Name of the state where you paid unemployment contributions ▶ Any State			
14	State reporting number as shown on state unemployment tax return ▶ 22-222			
15	Contributions paid to your state unemployment fund (see page 4) .	15	490	
16	Total cash wages subject to FUTA tax (see page 4)	16	7,000	
17	**FUTA tax.** Multiply line 16 by .008. Enter the result here, skip Section B, and go to line 26 . .	17	56	

Section B

18   Complete all columns below that apply (if you need more space, see page 4):

(a) Name of state	(b) State reporting number as shown on state unemployment tax return	(c) Taxable wages (as defined in state act)	(d) State experience rate period		(e) State experience rate	(f) Multiply col. (c) by .054	(g) Multiply col. (c) by col. (e)	(h) Subtract col. (g) from col. (f). If zero or less, enter -0-.	(i) Contributions paid to state unemployment fund
			From	To					

19	Totals	19	
20	Add columns (h) and (i) of line 19	20	
21	Total cash wages subject to FUTA tax (see the line 16 instructions on page 4)	21	
22	Multiply line 21 by 6.2% (.062)	22	
23	Multiply line 21 by 5.4% (.054)	23	
24	Enter the **smaller** of line 20 or line 23	24	
25	**FUTA tax.** Subtract line 24 from line 22. Enter the result here and go to line 26	25	

Part III   Total Household Employment Taxes

26	Enter the amount from line 8	26	2,819
27	Add line 17 (or line 25) and line 26	27	2,875

28   Are you required to file Form 1040?

    ☒ **Yes.**   **Stop.** Enter the amount from line 27 above on Form 1040, line 56. **Do not** complete Part IV below.

    ☐ **No.**   You may have to complete Part IV. See page 4 for details.

Part IV   Address and Signature—Complete this part **only** if required. See the line 28 instructions on page 4.

Address (number and street) or P.O. box if mail is not delivered to street address	Apt., room, or suite no.

City, town or post office, state, and ZIP code

Under penalties of perjury, I declare that I have examined this schedule, including accompanying statements, and to the best of my knowledge and belief, it is true, correct, and complete. No part of any payment made to a state unemployment fund claimed as a credit was, or is to be, deducted from the payments to employees.

▶ _____   ▶ _____
   Employer's signature   Date

Schedule H (Form 1040) 2001

U.S. Citizens Working Abroad: Tax Treatment of Foreign Earned Income

Introduction

U.S. citizens and **resident aliens** *are taxed on their worldwide income regardless of where it is earned, paid, or received. But U.S. citizens living abroad get certain tax benefits that are not available back home.* **Employees** *and* **self-employed** *individuals living abroad may elect to exclude up to $78,000 of their foreign-earned income*

from taxation in 2001. This exclusion will increase to $80,000 in 2002. Employees and self-employed individuals may also exclude or deduct part of their housing costs from **taxable** *income. This chapter tells you about all the tax benefits you get from living abroad and what you have to do to qualify for them.*

How to Qualify for the Foreign Earned Income Exclusion

You qualify for the foreign earned income exclusion if you are a U.S. citizen, you have a **tax home** in a foreign country, and you meet either the foreign residence test or the physical presence test, described below.

Generally, if you are a resident alien of the United States, you may qualify for the foreign earned income exclusion if you satisfy the physical presence test. This assumes that you have not permanently left the United States and that you plan to continue your resident alien status.

Tax home. Your tax home generally is the location of your principal place of employment, which may or may not coincide with the location of your family's residence. Among the factors that are important in determining whether or not your tax home is outside the United States are the anticipated duration of your overseas assignment and whether or not you will return to the same employment location in the United States. Under IRS guidelines, an anticipated short-term (less than 1-year) assignment overseas, followed by a return to the same place of employment in the United

States, would indicate that you do not have a tax home outside the United States.

If you meet either the foreign residence test or the physical presence test, you are eligible for two exclusions—the foreign earned income exclusion and the foreign housing exclusion. Self-employed individuals are eligible for a housing **deduction** rather than the housing exclusion (see the discussion later in this chapter).

Foreign residence test. The foreign residence test requires that you be a "bona fide resident" of a foreign country (or several foreign countries) for an uninterrupted period that includes an entire tax year. Whether or not you are a bona fide resident is a subjective question of your intent, the answer to which is determined by the facts and circumstances of each situation, including the purpose of your trip and the nature and length of your term abroad.

The following types of factors are considered by the IRS in determining your intent to reside in a specific place:

1. The type of quarters you occupy (hotel or rooming house, rented quarters, purchased quarters, or quarters furnished by your employer)

2. How long your family resided with you during the tax year
3. The length of the uninterrupted period during which you have been living outside the United States
4. The nature of any conditions or limitations concerning your employment agreement and the type and term of your visa
5. Whether you maintain a home in the United States and, if so, its rental status and the relationship of any tenants to you

If you make a statement to the authorities of a foreign country that you are not a resident of that country, and if you are not taxed as a resident of that country, you do not qualify as a bona fide resident of that country.

Once you have met the foreign residence test for an entire tax year, your qualification is retroactive to the first day you established your bona fide residence. Occasional trips to the United States for business or vacation do not affect your qualification.

Example 1

You moved from the United States to a foreign country, arriving on September 15, 2001. You entered the country under a resident visa with your family for a 3-year assignment. You did not declare to the foreign authorities that you were not a resident. You qualify as a bona fide resident of the foreign country if these facts remain the same through December 31, 2002. You may file your 2001 U.S. income tax return (or amend your original 2001 tax return) to claim the benefits of a bona fide resident of a foreign country for the period September 15, 2001, through December 31, 2001.

Example 2

George has been a resident of the United Kingdom for 5 consecutive years. If he moves to France this year, he continues to be a bona fide resident of a foreign country. An uninterrupted period of bona fide residence may include residence in more than one foreign country.

Example 3

Amy moved to France with her family on June 15, 2000, for a job assignment of indefinite length. On December 3, 2001, she was transferred back to the United States. She did not satisfy the bona fide residence test in either year, since she did not maintain a bona fide residence in a foreign country for a period that includes a complete tax year. However, she may qualify under the physical presence test.

Physical presence test. This test simply requires that you be physically present in a foreign country (or countries) for 330 full days during any consecutive 12-month period. This is a purely objective test. There is no reference to your intentions or to any other factors that determine bona fide residence abroad.

Two important rules regarding this test are the following:

1. A full day is a 24-hour period commencing at midnight. Thus, a day in which you travel to or from the United States is not a full day in a foreign country.
2. When you travel *between foreign countries,* the travel days will qualify as full days in a foreign country, provided that the time spent outside of either foreign country during the journey (i.e., time spent over international waters and/or time spent in the United States) is less than 24 hours.

TaxOrganizer

Keep a calendar. Keep a copy of your calendar of days in and out of the United States. The calendar can be supported by airline tickets or stamped passports documenting arrival and departure dates.

The Foreign Earned Income Exclusion

If you qualify, you may elect to exclude a maximum of $78,000 in foreign earned income from your U.S. taxable income in 2001. The exclusion will increase to $80,000 in 2002, then it will be indexed for inflation beginning in 2008.

The amount of income you may exclude depends on (1) the number of days during the year in which you were a bona fide resident or (2) the number of days you were physically present in the country during a 12-month period. If you are out of the country for the entire year, you may exclude all of your earned income up to the $78,000 limit. However, if you are out of the country for only part of the year, you generally must prorate the exclusion based on your number of qualifying days during the taxable year.

Example

You were a bona fide resident of a foreign country for 300 days during 2001. The maximum amount of income you may exclude from U.S. taxes is 300/365 × $78,000, or $64,116. Your exclusion is, of course, limited by the amount of foreign income you earn. If you earn less than the maximum allowed, you may exclude only that amount.

Only foreign earned income is eligible for the exclusion. Earned income is income received for the performance of personal services. It does *not* include **dividends, interest, capital gains,** and **rental property income.** For example, interest earned on a bank account in the United Kingdom by a U.S. expatriate on assignment in London is not eligible for the exclusion, since it is not foreign *earned* income.

Earned income may be received in cash or benefits in kind, including the following:

- Salaries, wages, bonuses, commissions, overseas incentive premiums, and so on
- A housing allowance. This may take the form of a cash payment or housing provided by your employer. When a cash payment is received, you must report the full amount as income. When housing is provided, your employer should furnish you with an estimate of its **fair market value.**
- An automobile allowance. A cash allowance for an automobile should be included in your income. When an automobile is provided by your employer, an amount representing the value of its personal use to you should be included in your income.
- A cost-of-living allowance
- An education allowance
- Home leave. The value of home leave benefits provided to you and your family is included in your income. However, if you spend a significant portion of your home leave on business, you may be justified in characterizing your portion of the trip as a business trip and thereby exclude your travel expenses from income.
- Rest and relaxation airfare
- A moving expense reimbursement or allowance
- A tax reimbursement or allowance

Source of earned income. The source of earned income depends on the place where the services are rendered. If the services are performed in the United States, the income is considered U.S. source income. If the services are performed in a foreign country, the income is foreign source. For the income to be excluded from your U.S. income, the earned income must be from sources within a foreign country (or countries).

How to compute your foreign source income. To compute your foreign source income for purposes of the foreign earned income exclusion, you must determine your earned income from sources outside the United States.

Foreign source earned income includes *all* income received for personal services performed outside the United States. The place of payment is irrelevant. A payment made in the United States by a U.S.-based employer for services performed outside the United States is foreign source income. If you have performed services both within and without the United States during the tax year, you must determine what portion of your income was from U.S. sources and what portion was from foreign sources.

Example 1

You received $50,000 for services performed in 2001. You worked a total of 240 days during the year, 235 days in the United Kingdom on foreign assignment and 5 days in the United States for a technical meeting. The source of your earned income is as follows:

$$\frac{\text{5 days worked in the United States}}{\text{240 days worked worldwide}} \times \$50,000 = \$1,042$$

$$\frac{\text{235 days worked outside the United States}}{\text{240 days worked worldwide}} \times \$50,000 = \$48,958$$

Your U.S. source income is $1,042. Your foreign source income is $48,958.

There are several other considerations to keep in mind when you are figuring out the source of your income:

1. If there has been a significant change in your rate of compensation during the year, it may be appropriate to allocate your compensation separately for the days worked and income earned in the respective periods.
2. If payment is received during the year for services performed in a prior year, it may be appropriate to report that payment based on the days worked in the prior year. Such income cannot be excluded under the current year's foreign earned income exclusion, but it can be excluded on your current year's tax return to the extent that your prior year's exclusion was not fully utilized.
3. Do not figure travel to the United States for a vacation as part of your calculation.

Example 2

In 2000, you were eligible for the full $76,000 foreign earned income exclusion but only had $68,000 of foreign source earned income that was excluded on your 2000 tax return. Therefore, you have $8,000 of unused exclusion from 2000. In 2001, your compensation includes $10,000 of foreign source income earned in 2000. You can exclude $8,000 of the $10,000 on your 2001 tax return. The $8,000 exclusion is in addition to any exclusion you might have for compensation earned and paid in 2001.

The Foreign Housing Exclusion

If you qualify as a U.S. citizen living abroad, you may elect to exclude from your U.S. taxable income the excess of reasonable housing expenses over a "base housing amount." The base housing amount ($10,557 for 2001) is 16% of the salary for a U.S. government employee at the GS–14, step 1 level. The base amount is prorated by the ratio of the number of qualifying days to the total days in the year.

Example

You had $16,000 of qualified housing expenses in 2001. Based on an allocation of your earned income, you determine that you had $98,000 of foreign source income. Furthermore, you had a qualifying period of 330 days in the tax year. Assume that the base housing amount is $10,557. Your housing exclusion is computed as follows:

1) Housing expenses	$16,000
2) Number of qualifying days	330
3) Total days in the tax year	365
4) Assumed base housing amount	$10,557
5) 330/365 × $10,557	$9,544
6) Housing exclusion (line 1 – line 5)	$6,456

Assuming the same facts, you calculate your foreign earned income exclusion as follows:

1) Maximum foreign earned income exclusion	$78,000
2) Number of qualifying days	330
3) Total days in tax year	365
4) 330/365 × $78,000	$70,512
5) Total foreign source income	$98,000
6) Less: Housing exclusion	($6,456)
7) Total foreign source income available for exclusion	$91,544
8) Smaller of line 4 or 7	$70,512

Your foreign earned income exclusion is $70,512. In addition, your foreign housing exclusion is $6,456. Your total exclusion is $76,968.

Foreign housing deduction for self-employed individuals. If you are a self-employed individual and you do not have an employer to provide housing, you may *deduct* the cost of foreign housing in computing your **adjusted gross income.** Your housing deduction is limited to the amount of foreign earned income that exceeds your foreign earned income exclusion for that year.

If you are both an employee and a self-employed individual during the same tax year, see Publication 54, *Tax Guide for U.S. Citizens and Resident Aliens Abroad.*

TAXPLANNER

When to elect the foreign earned income exclusion and the foreign housing exclusion. You elect and calculate the foreign earned income exclusion and the foreign housing exclusion separately using Form 2555 or, in some cases, Form 2555-EZ. The elections can be made on a tax return that you file on time, on an amended tax return, or on a late-filed tax return that is filed within 1 year of the original due date. The IRS also allows the elections to be made later under certain circumstances. When you are deciding whether or not to use the exclusions, you should take into account a number of factors, including the level of taxation in the foreign country in which you are living, the type of foreign assignment you are on, and your employer's international assignee policy.

When you elect the foreign income exclusion, you are required to reduce your deductible expenses associated with the excluded income. Similarly, foreign taxes available for the foreign tax credit must also be reduced (see *Foreign Tax Credit,* later).

If you are living in a foreign country with a high tax rate, you may be better off forgoing the exclusions and claiming a larger foreign tax credit. In this case, forgoing the exclusions may result in a higher current tax liability but may also create large foreign tax credits that may be carried forward and used to offset the tax in years after you return to the United States and receive foreign source income.

In countries with moderate or low tax rates, it is usually to your advantage to claim the exclusions. You should calculate your taxes with and without the exclusions to see which is more beneficial.

You may revoke your election of the foreign earned income exclusion or the foreign housing exclusion for any tax year by attaching a statement to your return or your amended return saying that you do not wish to claim the exclusion. Once revoked, you may not claim the exclusions again for the next 5 years without obtaining IRS approval.

Employer-Provided Meals and Lodging

Meals and lodging provided in kind by, or on behalf of, an employer to an employee or to his or her spouse or **dependents** are excluded from taxable income if certain requirements are met:

1. The meals are provided by the employer on his or her business premises and for his or her convenience.
2. Lodging is provided by the employer on his or her premises and for his or her convenience, and the employee is required to accept such lodging as a condition of employment.

The IRS has taken a narrow view of the lodging exclusion. As a result, most employer-provided lodging is not excludable from your income. However, the exclusion applies if the employee resides in a camp that is provided by the employer because the employee's work site is in a remote area where satisfactory housing is not available on the open market. The camp has to be located as near as is practicable to the work site and should be furnished with a common area or enclave that is not available to the general public and normally accommodates 10 or more employees.

TaxAlert

You do not have to be living abroad to take advantage of this exclusion for employer-provided meals and lodging. All taxpayers are entitled to exclude the value of meals and lodging from taxable income when they are provided on the employer's premises for the employer's convenience and when the lodging must be accepted as a condition of employment.

Foreign Tax Credit

You may elect to claim a credit for foreign income taxes paid or accrued during the tax year, or you may claim the taxes paid as an itemized deduction. Generally, claiming a credit is more beneficial. The foreign tax credit on your U.S. return is limited to the lesser of (1) the actual foreign income taxes paid or accrued during the year (including carrybacks or carryforwards) or (2) the amount of U.S. tax attributable to foreign source taxable income for the year. The foreign tax credit is elected and calculated on Form 1116 (see Chapter 37, *Other Credits Including the Earned Income Credit*).

If you elect to take either the foreign earned income exclusion or the foreign housing exclusion, the amount of foreign taxes that you may receive credit for is reduced.

TaxOrganizer

Keep your foreign tax return. Keep a copy of your foreign tax return and receipts for taxes paid supporting the tax credit calculations. This may be needed if your return is audited.

Example 1

You had $98,000 of foreign source income and $16,000 of qualified housing expenses in 2001. The total amount you may exclude from your income is $76,968. (See the foreign housing exclusion example above to learn how this number is calculated.) You paid $4,000 in foreign taxes for the year. You figure the amount that you may claim as a foreign tax credit as follows:

$$\frac{\$76,968}{\$98,000} \times \$4,000 = \$3,142$$

A maximum of $858 ($4,000 − $3,142) may be claimed as a foreign tax credit.

Example 2

You are an unmarried U.S. citizen currently residing in the United Kingdom. Your total **gross income** for the year is $120,000, all of which is compensation. You qualify for a foreign earned income exclusion of $78,000 and a housing exclusion of $5,000, for a total of $83,000. You spent 10% of your working days in the United States. You have $6,200 of **itemized deductions,** none of which directly relate to a class (or classes) of income. The amount you may claim as a foreign tax credit is computed as follows:

Compensation from foreign sources (90% of $120,000)	$108,000
Deductions allocated to foreign source compensation: $\frac{\$108,000}{\$120,000} \times \$6,200$	($5,580)
	$102,420
Less: Foreign earned income and housing exclusions	($83,000)
Foreign source taxable income	$19,420
U.S. source compensation (10% of $120,000)	$12,000
Balance of itemized deductions ($6,200 minus $5,580)	($620)
U.S. taxable income before personal exemptions	$ 30,800

The foreign tax credit limitation is calculated by determining the ratio of foreign source taxable income to U.S. taxable income (as shown above). The ratio in the above example would be

$$\frac{\$19,420}{\$30,800} = .6305$$

This ratio is then multiplied by the U.S. tax liability for the year to determine the maximum amount of credit usable for the year. If the U.S. tax were, say, $4,500, the maximum credit would be $2,837 (.6305 × $4,500).

Carryback and carryforward of foreign tax credit. Example 1 (above) shows how to determine the amount of foreign taxes that may be used as a credit. Example 2 shows how to determine the maximum amount of foreign tax credit that may be currently used as a credit against your U.S. taxes. If the amount of the foreign tax credit that is generated exceeds the amount that can be used currently, you may carry back the excess 2 years. The remainder, if any, may be carried forward 5 years.

TAXPLANNER

Planning tips for individuals on international assignment. Here is a list of items you should consider in planning and preparing your tax return:

1. **Rental of your personal residence.** The vacation home rules disallowing certain deductions in excess of rental income (see Chapter 10, *Rental Income and Expenses*) do not apply when you rent your principal residence during a qualified rental period, which consists of 12 or more months during which your residence is rented or available to be rented. A period of less than 12 months qualifies if the period ends because your residence was sold or exchanged.

2. **Sale of your principal residence.** A taxpayer may claim an exclusion of up to $250,000 for single taxpayers ($500,000 for joint filers) once every 2 years if the taxpayer owned the residence and occupied it as a principal residence for at least 2 of the 5 years before the sale or exchange.

   There are no special rules for home sales by expatriates. If you have significant gain in your home and you expect your assignment to last more than 3 years, you should give consideration to selling your home. Otherwise, if you decide to sell at a later date, you may fail the 2-year out of 5-year test and some or all of the exclusion may be lost (see Chapter 16, *Selling Your Home*).

3. **Individual Retirement Arrangements (IRAs).** An expatriate who contributes to an **IRA** [see Chapter 18, *Individual Retirement Arrangements (IRAs)*] must have earned income in excess of the total of his or her foreign earned income and foreign housing exclusions if he or she elects to use the exclusions.

   If you are covered by a company pension plan, your modified **adjusted gross income** must be below a certain level for your IRA contribution to be tax deductible. Similarly, your modified **adjusted gross income** must be below a certain level in order to make a contribution to a **Roth IRA** or an **education IRA**. Note that for purposes of computing modified **adjusted gross income**, the foreign earned income exclusion and the foreign housing exclusion amounts must be disregarded. For a more detailed discussion of IRAs, please refer to Chapter 18, *Individual Retirement Arrangements (IRAs)*.

4. **Alternative minimum tax (AMT).** For taxable years beginning after December 31, 1986, the maximum amount of AMT (see Chapter 31, *How to Figure Your Tax*) that can be offset with foreign tax credits is 90%. Prior to this effective date, the entire amount of AMT may be offset by foreign tax credits to the extent that such credits are available.

Foreign Citizens Living in the United States

Introduction

Almost everybody living in the United States—whether a U.S. citizen or not—is subject to U.S. income tax laws.

*Foreign nationals working in the United States are either **resident aliens** or **nonresident aliens**. Resident aliens, like U.S. citizens, are subject to U.S. tax on their worldwide income. Nonresident aliens are subject to U.S. tax only on their U.S. source income. Some foreign citizens living in the United States are not taxed at all—at least not by the U.S. government. A foreign citizen resi-*
dent in the United States who works for a foreign government doing normal diplomatic work is exempt from the U.S. tax laws, provided that U.S. government employees working in that foreign country are exempt from its tax laws. Tax treaties between the United States and some foreign governments contain numerous other exceptions.

This chapter tells you how to determine if you are a resident or nonresident alien and how you should calculate your tax.

Determining Your Status

Whether you are a resident alien or nonresident alien is of critical importance when you determine how much U.S. income tax you will pay. Your residency status will determine your filing status, the tax rate schedule applicable to your income, and the amount of your income that will be subject to U.S. income tax. Under rules that became effective in 1985, an alien must meet *either* of two tests in order to be considered a resident of the United States for tax purposes. The tests are as follows:

1. **The green card test.** Have you been lawfully admitted to the United States for permanent residency? In other words, do you have a green card?
2. **The substantial presence test.** Have you been present in the United States for a substantial period of time? If you have been present in the United States for at least 31 days in the current year and if the total days you are present in the United States during the calendar year, plus one-third of the days present in the preceding calendar year, plus one-sixth of the days present in the second preceding calendar year are equal to at least 183 days, you will meet the substantial presence test and will be considered a resident alien in the current year.

If you are considered a U.S. resident under the substantial presence test (and you were not a U.S. resident in the prior year), your residency period generally begins on the first day on which you were present in the United States in the current year. However, if you visit the United States, and the total days you spend in the United States during the visit amount to 10 days or less, you may, under certain circumstances, ignore those days for purposes of determining when your residency period begins.

Example

You move to the United States on June 1, 2001, and spend a sufficient number of days in this country in 2001 to meet the substantial presence test. Prior to your actual arrival on June 1, you spent 10 days in the United States from February 2 through February 11 to house hunt and to meet with your U.S. employer while you maintained your tax home in a foreign country. Your U.S. residency period begins on June 1. If you had stayed in the United States until February 12 (11 days), your U.S. residency period would have begun on February 2.

A similar rule applies in the year in which your U.S. residency terminates. Your residency period generally ends on the last day of the year. However, if you can show that you have closer connections to a foreign country for the remainder of the year, your U.S. residency generally ends on the last day on which you are present in the United States. Visits to the United States totaling 10 days or less following your departure may be disregarded in determining the last day of your U.S. residency.

TaxAlert

To take advantage of this closer connection rule and terminate your residency on the last day on which you are present in the United States, you may be required to attach a statement to your U.S. tax return for that year detailing those facts that support your connections to a foreign country.

Example

In 2001 you lived in the United States continuously from January 1 through October 31, when you moved to a foreign country. Generally, you are considered to be a resident of the United States through October 31. If you return to the United States on business trips or on vacation during November and December and spend 10 days or less in total in the United States, your residency period terminates on October 31. If you spend more than 10 days in total in the United States in November and December, your U.S. residency period will be extended beyond October 31. The actual termination date will depend on the specific dates of your visits.

TaxOrganizer

Arrival and departure dates. To substantiate your arrival and departure dates to and from the United States, copies of travel tickets (airline, boat, etc.) or stamped passports should be retained in your tax files.

TaxAlert

Resident alien status. Even if you meet the substantial presence test, you can avoid being considered a resident alien if you are present in the United States for less than 183 days in the current year *and* you can show closer ties to a tax home in a foreign country (or in the case of a move, no more than two foreign countries) than to the United States for the entire year. Whether you have closer ties to the United States or to a foreign country depends on the facts and circumstances. Consult a tax advisor for details. You may be required to furnish a statement to the IRS to this effect.

Election to Be Treated as a Resident

The Tax Reform Act of 1986 contains a provision that allows an alien to elect to be treated as a resident of the United States for tax purposes, even though he or she does not meet the green card or substantial presence test. The provision allows an alien with significant U.S. presence toward the end of one year and who meets the substantial presence test in the following year to elect to be treated as a U.S. resident alien in the earlier year. The alien can only make this election after he or she has met the substantial presence test in the next year. This may necessitate the filing of an extension. This election will be advantageous to some aliens, such as those who incur significant expenses when they first arrive in the United States (interest, deductible mortgage points, and real estate taxes incurred in connection with a new U.S. residence, for example), which would be deductible for a resident but not for a nonresident.

The election could also benefit married aliens who would be required to file using married filing separate rates as nonresidents. As U.S. residents under this election, they would be permitted to make a further election to be treated as residents for the entire year (see the following Example), thus permitting the filing of a joint return and the use of the more favorable joint return rates. An alien who meets the following criteria may make the election:

1. Doesn't meet the green card or substantial presence tests for the current year,
2. Was not a resident alien in the prior year,
3. Meets the substantial presence test in the following year,
4. Is present in the United States for at least 31 consecutive days in the current year, and
5. Spends at least 75% of the days between the first of the 31 consecutive days and year-end in the United States. (*Note:* Up to 5 non-U.S. days will be counted as U.S. days for the purposes of this test.)

Under 1992 final IRS regulations, an alien who makes the election to be treated as a resident may also make a similar election on his or her tax return on behalf of dependent children if the children are not required to file tax returns on their own, assuming, of course, that the children also meet the requirements of the election. The filing of the election will enable an alien to take dependency exemptions for the children.

Example

Assume that an alien is present in the United States for the following periods:

7/4–8/15	43 days
9/16–11/25	71 days
12/16–12/31	16 days

During the testing period of July 4 through December 31, the individual is in the United States 130 days out of 181 days total. Including the 5 additional non-U.S. days, which can be counted as U.S. days, the individual is present in the United States on less than 75% of the days and cannot make the election for this period.

$$\frac{130 \text{ plus } 5}{181} = 74.6\%$$

However, since, during the testing period of September 16 through December 31, the individual was in the United States 87 days out of 107, which exceeds 75%, the individual could elect to be treated as a resident for the period of September 16 through December 31 (assuming that the other tests regarding the prior and subsequent years are also met).

TaxPlanner

If you have a green card, you should be aware that you are considered a resident alien and are subject to tax on all of your income. If you have substantial U.S. or foreign investment income, you may want to transfer the income-producing assets to somebody else, for example, a spouse or other close relative who is still living abroad.

TaxPlanner

Substantial presence test. If you meet the substantial presence test described above, but you are present in the

United States less than 183 days each year, you should examine your ties to another country. You might qualify for the exception to the substantial presence test if you can demonstrate that your ties to another country are stronger than your ties to the United States. You must file a statement with your tax return supporting your claim, or, if no return is required, a statement alone must be filed with the IRS.

If your ties are weak and you want to try to strengthen them, consider

1. Maintaining a home in that country
2. Obtaining a driver's license issued by that country
3. Joining a religious, political, or cultural organization in that country
4. Maintaining or establishing a membership in a social organization in that country
5. Having a bank account in that country
6. Having personal property in that country such as cars, clothing, or jewelry
7. Continuing to vote in that country

If you spend a significant amount of time in the United States each year, you should carefully monitor the days to keep them below the 183-day threshold during the 3-year period considered under the substantial presence test.

TaxPlanner

Do not assume that nonresident alien filing status necessarily results in greater savings than resident alien status. Resident alien status may result in a lower U.S. tax if you can use the lower joint return rates (for married resident aliens), are eligible for greater itemized deductions, and/or can benefit from the foreign tax credit.

Income tax treaties. Some existing or proposed income tax treaties may have the effect of overriding the provisions of the law. Consult a tax advisor for details.

Generally, tax treaties are consulted when an individual is a dual resident, that is, a resident of both the United States and a foreign country. When a treaty is used to claim that an individual is a nonresident of the United States, the individual must file Form 1040-NR and attach Form 8833, *Treaty-Based Return Position Disclosure*, to the return presenting facts to support the claim of U.S. nonresidence.

An election to be treated as a nonresident of the United States under a treaty will apply for *all* purposes in computing the alien's income tax liability for the dual residency period.

TaxAlert

Filing Form 1040-NR may affect the determination by the Immigration and Naturalization Service as to whether you qualify as a U.S. resident for immigration purposes (i.e., green card). Consult with immigration counsel to evaluate the impact of this rule on your personal situation.

Dual-status aliens. A dual-status alien is a person who is considered a resident alien and a nonresident alien during the same tax year.

You are most likely to have dual status in the year of your arrival in or departure from the United States. You could, for example, be a resident alien until your departure from the United States. At that time, you would become a nonresident alien.

For purposes of computing your tax liability, different rules apply to the time when you are a resident alien and the time when you are a nonresident alien. However, it is necessary to fill out only one tax return. You may make a special election that may decrease your taxes for some years in which you have dual status. This election is discussed in the following section.

TaxPlanner

An alien's residency status may not be the same for all purposes. The definition discussed above applies for federal income tax laws. Different rules apply in determining residency for state income tax and federal estate tax purposes.

How Resident Aliens Are Taxed
Like U.S. citizens, resident aliens are subject to tax on the worldwide income they receive, regardless of its source. Resident aliens compute their **taxable income** and file their income tax in the same way in which U.S. citizens do. They include the same items in income and are entitled to take the same **deductions** as U.S. citizens.

TaxAlert

Rules for Individuals Giving up U.S. Citizenship or U.S. Residency
The 1996 Tax Act contains a provision which treats long-term resident aliens who terminate their U.S. residency similar to individuals who relinquish their U.S. citizenship. Under these rules, these individuals will continue to be subject to U.S. tax for 10 years on certain categories of U.S. source income and gains, provided they terminated residency principally for the purpose of avoiding U.S. income tax.

An individual (other than a U.S. citizen) is a long-term U.S. resident if the individual is a lawfully permanent U.S. resident in at least 8 out of 15 tax years ending with the tax year of expatriation. An individual is presumed to have a tax avoidance motive if the individual's average annual net income tax liability for 5 tax years ending before the loss of citizenship is greater than $100,000 or if his/her net worth on such date is $500,000 or more. However, individuals may challenge the presumption of tax avoidance by submitting a complete and good faith request for a ruling to the IRS. The tax rules are effective for individuals losing U.S. citizenship and long-term residents terminating residency after February 5, 1995.

Note: If you are contemplating terminating residency or relinquishing U.S. citizenship consult your tax advisor and immigration attorney. The rules are complex and special filings may be warranted.

Dual-Status Aliens
Dual-status aliens who are resident aliens for part of the tax year are taxed somewhat differently from U.S. citizens.

If you file an individual return, you are taxed on your worldwide income for the part of the year in which you are a resident alien. For the part of the year in which you are a nonresident alien, only your U.S. source income is taxed.

Dual-status aliens who are married may not file a **joint return** or claim the standard deduction. Married taxpayers are taxed on their worldwide income for the part of the year in which they are resident aliens and only on their U.S.

source income for the part of the year in which they are non-residents. They are not, however, able to file a joint return and take advantage of the joint return rate schedule.

Exceptions. Dual-status aliens who are married have two other alternatives in the year in which they arrive in the United States:

1. **The Section 6013(h) election.** This election is available only in cases in which a U.S. citizen or resident alien is married to an individual who is a resident alien at the close of the tax year. An alien choosing this alternative is treated as a resident of the United States for the *entire tax year*. The most significant consequences of making this choice are:

   a) All income, both U.S. and foreign source, is subject to tax, including any income you had during the period in which you were not a resident of the United States. This income would have been exempt from U.S. taxes or taxed at a reduced rate if you had not made the Section 6013(h) election.

   b) You may claim **itemized deductions** for the period in which you were not a resident of the United States, if such items would otherwise qualify for deduction. Some examples are foreign real property taxes, mortgage interest, and medical expenses.

   c) You may deduct, or elect to claim as a credit, foreign income taxes attributable to the period during which you were not a U.S. resident, which may substantially eliminate U.S. income tax. Other benefits, however, like being able to file a joint return and thus be taxed at accordingly lower rates, are left intact. The result is that your net U.S. tax liability may be reduced.

2. **The Section 6013(g) election.** Under the Section 6013(g) election, a married couple may file a joint return as full-year residents of the United States if, at the end of the tax year, one spouse is a nonresident alien and the other is a citizen or resident of the United States.

   The effects of making this election are the same as choosing the Section 6013(h) election, with one very significant and beneficial distinction. The Section 6013(g) election is valid for all subsequent years in which you and your spouse qualify, including the year in which the resident alien leaves the United States. The fact that you may qualify for this status in the year of your departure may eventually give you a big tax break. Once made, the Section 6013(g) election can be revoked. However, if you revoke the election, you cannot make another such election in the future. Similarly the Section 6013(h) election cannot be made by the same two individuals in any future tax year.

Example

You and your spouse became U.S. residents on April 1, 2001. Prior to your arrival in the United States, you earned $5,000 in wages and your spouse earned $1,000 in wages. Both of you also had $500 in joint interest income for the first 3 months of the year. Once in the United States, you earned $75,000 from April through December. Your spouse did not work in the United States. You had an additional $700 in joint interest income. Your itemized deductions equal the standard deduction. Your tax liabilities are computed as follows:

Alternative 1: Dual-status return, married filing separately (for period while a U.S. resident)

Salary	$75,000
Interest	350
Itemized deductions	(3,800)
Exemptions	(2,900)
Taxable income	$68,650
Tax	$16,475

You would not be taxed on your non-U.S. source income.

Alternative 2: Full-year election, joint return

Salary	$81,000
Interest	1,200
Itemized deductions	(7,600)
Exemptions	(5,800)
Taxable income	$68,800
Tax	$13,270

By electing to be treated as a resident alien for the entire tax year, you save $3,205 in income taxes. Note that your spouse could not be claimed as a dependent under Alternative 1, since your spouse had income during the U.S. residency period. Your spouse does not need to file a return under Alternative 1, since your spouse's income did not exceed the amount that requires you to file. (See Chapter 1, *Filing Information.*)

The $6,500 in income that you and your spouse earned in your home country would probably be subject to tax there. If so, you would be eligible for the foreign tax credit if you filed under Alternative 2. The tax credit would further lower your taxes. See Chapter 37, *Other Credits Including the Earned Income Credit,* for a discussion of the foreign tax credit.

TAXPLANNER

In order to claim exemptions for a resident alien's spouse and/or children, a tax ID number is required for each person. Obtaining such a tax ID number no longer necessitates going to the Social Security office with the family. Rather, these numbers are now obtained directly from the IRS. Alternatively, certain tax advisors are now registered with the IRS to review your original documentation and obtain the tax ID for you.

How Nonresident Aliens Are Taxed

A nonresident alien is taxed as follows:

Compensation for services rendered in the United States or other income that is effectively connected with a U.S. trade or business is generally taxed on a net basis at graduated rates. A nonresident alien may deduct certain expenses incurred in producing that income, such as business expenses and state and local taxes. In addition, he or she may deduct casualty losses and qualifying charitable contributions. However, a nonresident alien may not benefit from the standard deduction.

TAXALERT

For taxable years beginning after 1986, income that is effectively connected with a U.S. trade or business at the time it is earned will be considered "effectively connected" at the time it is received, even if receipt occurs in a different tax year.

A nonresident alien is generally able to claim a personal exemption for only himself or herself. However, a nonresident alien who is a resident of Mexico or Canada or a national of the United States is also entitled to claim personal exemptions for

1. A spouse, if the spouse had no gross income for U.S. tax purposes and was not the dependent of another taxpayer
2. Other dependents, if they meet the same requirements as a U.S. citizen

A married nonresident alien is taxed under the "married filing separately" Tax Rate Schedule, which is the highest Tax Rate Schedule applicable to individuals. You may not claim **head of household** status if you are a nonresident alien. A nonresident alien who is **single** would use the "unmarried" Tax Rate Schedule.

Dividends, interest, royalties, pensions, annuities, and other types of U.S. source income that are not effectively connected with a U.S. trade or business are usually subject to a 30% tax rate unless a lesser rate has been established by a tax treaty. No deductions or exemptions are allowed against this income. Interest earned on bank accounts, as well as certain other investments (known as "portfolio" debt instruments), is exempt from U.S. taxes.

Gains and losses from the sale of **capital assets,** other than real property from U.S. sources, may be taxed in either of two ways. If the gains and losses are not connected with a trade or business in the United States, any gain (after deducting losses) is taxed at a 30% rate if the nonresident alien is in the United States for 183 days or more during the tax year. If a gain is derived from the sale of capital assets effectively connected with a trade or a business in the United States, it is taxed as though a U.S. citizen had incurred the gain. Capital gains from the sale of real property located in the United States are considered to be connected with a U.S. trade or business and are subject to special U.S. tax laws. (For a more detailed discussion of the tax treatment of gains and losses, see IRS Publication 519, *U.S. Tax Guide for Aliens.*)

Foreign students. Foreign students who enter the U.S. under an "F" visa (academic or language student) or a "J" visa (educational and cultural exchange visitor) are nonresidents for U.S. tax purposes, as long as they substantially comply with the terms of their visa.

▌TAXPLANNER

Foreign nationals who become U.S. residents. Foreign nationals who become U.S. residents are taxed on their worldwide income from the day on which they become residents. You may, however, take several steps before you become a U.S. resident that limit your U.S. tax liability. Consider the following:

1. If you anticipate receiving a payment of compensation for past services, such as a bonus, arrange to receive this payment before becoming a resident of the United States. If this payment is received after you become a U.S. resident alien, it will be taxable in full by the United States, even though the related services were rendered prior to coming to the United States.
2. If you anticipate incurring expenses that will be deductible for U.S. income tax purposes, such as mortgage points, interest, or certain charitable contributions, con-

sider deferring these payments until after you are a resident of the United States.
3. If you sell a stock for a gain prior to your arrival in the United States, the entire gain is not subject to U.S. tax. However, if you sell a stock at a profit after you become a U.S. resident, the entire gain is subject to U.S. tax, even if the entire appreciation of the stock occurred before you became a U.S. resident. You should consider selling stocks in which you have a profit before you become a U.S. resident.

If you have a loss and the entire loss was generated before you became a U.S. resident, but you did not realize the loss until after you took up residency, you may deduct the loss.
4. If you receive a **lump-sum distribution** from a government or private retirement plan after you have become a U.S. resident, the entire amount may be subject to U.S. tax. If at all possible, arrange to receive the payment before you become a U.S. resident, when it is not subject to U.S. tax.
5. If you sell your principal residence before becoming a U.S. resident, the proceeds are not normally subject to any U.S. tax. However, if you become a U.S. resident and elect to be taxed as a resident alien for the entire year to take advantage of lower joint filing rates (see *Exceptions,* earlier), you may end up paying tax on the sale of your principal residence, as well as tax on any exchange gain associated with the mortgage. Be sure to consider this fact before you elect to be taxed as a resident alien for the entire year.

A $250,000 exclusion for single taxpayers ($500,000 married filers) on home sale gain exists if you have lived in the home as your principal residence for 2 of the last 5 years. The use of the exclusion by foreign nationals who have ceased to be residents of the United States is permitted if the expatriation provisions do not apply (see *Rules for Individuals Giving Up U.S. Citizenship or U.S. Residency,* earlier in this chapter). This area is complex. Tax advice should be sought prior to disposing of your primary residence.
6. You may be able to take advantage of a "window," a situation in which certain income is never taxed. This requires analyzing the tax laws of your home country and the United States. A window may be created if you come from a country that does not tax income of its nonresident citizens.

Example

Humphrey Benson is a citizen of the United Kingdom who decides to move to the United States. He owns securities that have appreciated by $100,000. On his move to the United States, Humphrey goes to Bermuda for 2 weeks. While there, he sells all his securities. The result is that he does not have to pay any tax in the United Kingdom, in the United States, or in Bermuda.

▌TAXPLANNER

Minimizing your tax burden. The main point to remember is that the best time for you to minimize your U.S. tax burden is *before* you make an investment in the United States and *before* you become a U.S. resident.

Departing from the United States

Before you depart from the United States, you must obtain a certificate of compliance, indicating that you have satisfied your federal tax liability. This certificate, frequently referred to as a "sailing permit" or an "exit permit," is obtained by filing Form 1040C or Form 2063. To get the permit, you must either pay all of the U.S. income tax due prior to departure or demonstrate that your departure from the United States will not impair the collection of the tax. The forms may be obtained from your nearest IRS office. An exit permit is valid only for 30 days. If you postpone your departure, you probably have to apply for a new exit permit. See IRS Publication 519, *U.S. Tax Guide for Aliens,* for more details.

TaxOrganizer

Sailing permits. The IRS representative must see actual departure tickets in order to issue your "sailing permit." Make sure you bring these along to the IRS.

A certificate of compliance is not a substitute for an annual income tax return. A federal tax return still must be filed in accordance with regular filing procedures. Any payment in conjunction with the filing of Form 1040C is treated as a payment on your annual tax return.

TaxPlanner

For tax years beginning after 1986, effectively connected salary income that is paid in a tax year after the alien's year of departure will be considered effectively connected and taxed at the regular graduated rates. If the alien was in the highest tax bracket in the year in which the income was earned, the receipt of the income in a subsequent year will cause it to be taxed at the lowest marginal tax rate first, for example, 10% in 2001.

How to Prepare for Your Accountant

Introduction

Millions of Americans prepare their own tax returns every year, while others rely on accountants to do the work for them. In fact, over half of those filing individual tax returns seek some kind of professional assistance. Which path you should take depends primarily on how compli-cated your financial affairs are and, of course, your willingness to puzzle through IRS forms. This chapter will help you organize your financial affairs, whether or not you have an accountant.

Who Needs an Accountant?

You will probably benefit from the advice and expertise of an accountant if you find yourself in one or more of the following conditions:

1. You have more than one source of income.
2. You think you are eligible for a lot of deductions.
3. You want to take advantage of a tax credit.

You probably do *not* need an accountant if your return appears to be relatively simple. *If you are planning to file using Form 1040EZ, there is probably no reason for you to seek professional help.*

Choosing an Accountant

Finding an accountant. Choosing an accountant is not something that should be done casually. There are over 300,000 certified public accountants in the United States. Most of them are single practitioners or in business with a few other people. The bread and butter of their work is preparing tax returns for individuals. The rest of the nation's accountants work mostly for larger accounting firms or for individual companies.

Questions to ask your tax return preparer. Before choosing your tax preparer, you may want to get satisfactory answers to the following questions:

1. Are you a certified public accountant? What are your professional qualifications? Are you affiliated with any financial institution or investment company?
2. Do you have experience in preparing returns for others in my occupation and in handling tax issues similar to mine?
3. How much will it cost to prepare my tax return?
4. Is there anything I can do to reduce the cost of return preparation?
5. What type of information do you need to prepare my return? In what format would you like it submitted and by what date?
6. If I am owed a refund, when can I expect to receive it?
7. Will you inform me if any items on my return are likely to be challenged by the IRS or state authorities?
8. Will you inform me if I am passing up any opportunities to reduce my tax liability?
9. What should I do if I receive a notice from the IRS or state authorities concerning my return?
10. Will you represent me before the IRS or state authorities if my return is audited?
11. Who in your office would work on my return? Do you use outside computer service firms to help prepare tax returns?
12. Can you give me the names of clients who would be references for your work?

What an accountant should do for you. You should be able to rely on your accountant for more than preparing your annual tax return. As your accountant becomes increasingly familiar with your personal and financial affairs, he or she should become a valuable and trusted financial advisor.

Any time you are entering into a major financial transaction, it is a good idea to give your accountant a call and review the alternatives available. Your accountant should advise you of any possibilities that will minimize your taxes. If you're buying or selling a house, for example, your accountant should be consulted regarding certain procedures that may have significant tax consequences. While an accountant certainly cannot take the place of your broker, he or she can remind you of the tax consequences of buying or selling stocks and bonds.

The cost of an accountant. The cost of having your tax return prepared by an accountant can vary widely. Although some charge a fixed fee for the preparation of a return, the cost usually depends on the time your accountant spends on your return. You can help reduce this time by gathering, organizing, and summarizing your information yourself.

While you do not need to furnish your accountant with supporting cancelled checks or other documents, you should provide those documents about which you have questions. Considerable time may have to be spent on your return if the law governing some of your transactions is particularly difficult or unclear.

The hourly rates charged by national accounting firms are ordinarily higher than those charged by local firms. However, the fees charged by some of the larger local firms approximate those of the national firms. *The fee structure should be discussed and agreed on before your accountant begins work.*

Getting good service. You should expect good service from your accountant. Your telephone calls should be returned promptly. Your questions should be answered willingly and in understandable language. Your return should be completed and available to you with adequate time for you to review it before it must be filed.

A key factor in choosing your accountant is whether he or she is "independent." For example, you should know the relationship, if any, that your accountant has to any investment he or she recommends to you. Does your accountant have a significant financial interest in the investment that he or she recommends? Is your accountant an officer, director, or otherwise related to the investment? In addition, you should know the nature and amount of compensation, if any, that your accountant receives from any other person for his or her recommendations.

Switching accountants. If you are dissatisfied with your present accountant, you may wish to consider switching to another. As a matter of professional courtesy, most accountants will cooperate with a new accountant to make the transition as smooth as possible.

You may want your new accountant to have copies of your prior accountant's work papers. Although these work papers are the property of the prior accountant, most will make them available to you or your new accountant. If your files with your prior accountant are extensive, you should discuss an acceptable billing arrangement to cover the cost of providing them to your new accountant.

Preparing for Your Accountant
When to see your accountant. You probably do not need to see your accountant more than once a year, especially if he or she has prepared your return in prior years. If you have a new accountant, however, you might also want to get together for an initial meeting to go over your personal situation before your return is prepared. If your accountant is already familiar with your tax situation, you can alternatively send whatever documentation is necessary to prepare your return and talk on the telephone if need be.

A good time to see your accountant is after he or she has prepared your return so that you can go over it together. It is usually wise to do this as soon as possible so that, if any mistakes have been made, they can be easily corrected before the filing deadline.

TaxOrganizer

Documents you will need. The remainder of this chapter discusses the documentation you should keep to support the information contained in your tax return.

What to bring to your accountant. Whether you prepare your own tax return or let an accountant do the work, the task of gathering your tax information together is unavoidable. The better prepared you are to discuss your affairs with your accountant, the more efficient the entire process of preparing your return will be. In general, you should have documentation that supports all income, deductions, and credits that will appear on your return. In addition, if you are using a new accountant, you should also bring a copy of your prior year's returns.

Supporting documentation comes in many forms. The most common types of documentation and the items they substantiate are outlined in the following table.

Item	Documentation
1) Wages and salaries	W–2 forms; usually provided by your employer
2) Dividends and interest	Form 1099-DIV and Form 1099-INT; usually provided by the bank or company paying the dividend or interest
3) Capital gains and losses	Broker's statements for purchase and sale of assets disposed of during the year and Form 1099-B; usually provided by the broker who sold the assets
4) Business income from sole proprietorships, rents, and royalties	Books and records (Form 1099-MISC *may* also be provided by the payor of the income)
5) Income from partnerships, estates, trusts, and S corporations	Form K-1; usually provided by the partnership, etc.
6) Unemployment compensation	Form 1099-G; usually provided by the governmental agency paying the unemployment compensation
7) Social Security benefits	Form SSA-1099; usually provided by the federal government
8) State and local income tax refunds	Form 1099-G; usually provided by the state or city that refunded the taxes
9) Original issue discount	Form 1099-OID; usually provided by the issuer of the long-term debt obligation
10) All distributions, both total and partial, from pensions, annuities, insurance contracts, retirement or profit-sharing plans, and Individual Retirement Arrangements (IRAs)	Form 1099-R; usually provided by the trustee for the plan making the distribution
11) Barter income	Form 1099-B; usually provided by the barter exchange through which property or services were exchanged
12) Sale of your home	Form 1099-S; provided by the person responsible for closing a real estate transaction
13) IRA contributions	Form 5498; provided by the trustee or custodian of the IRA

Check Analysis

Date	Check #	Payee	Amount	Medical	Taxes	Interest	Contributions	Other	Description
2/17	1459	Dr. Broline	$ 55.00	$ 55.00					
3/04	1502	Cancer Society	25.00				$25.00		
3/26	1542	State Comptroller	494.00		$494.00				
4/20	1590	First National Bank	350.00			$350.00			
5/16	1630	Church	75.00				75.00		
6/12	1665	Acme Trucking	783.00					$783.00	Moving
7/18	1721	Dr. Broline	40.00	40.00					
7/18	1722	Ace Pharmacy	27.00	27.00					
10/22	1853	Church	75.00				75.00		
11/15	1902	First National Bank	300.00			300.00			
Totals			$2,224.00	$122.00	$494.00	$650.00	$175.00	$783.00	

14) Moving and employee business expenses	Receipts and canceled checks and Form 4782, if moving expenses are paid or reimbursed by your employer (see Chapter 19, *Moving Expenses,* for details)
15) Medical expenses	Receipts and canceled checks
16) Mortgage interest and points paid on the purchase of a principal residence	Form 1098 or mortgage company statement; usually provided by mortgage company
17) Business and investment interest	Canceled checks and brokers' statements
18) Real estate taxes	Receipts, canceled checks, and mortgage company statements (if applicable)
19) Other taxes	Receipts and canceled checks
20) Contributions	Receipts, canceled checks; written acknowledgment from the charitable organization is generally required for contributions of $250 or more (see Chapter 26, *Contributions,* for details).

What *not* to bring to your accountant. You need not bring all of your documentation to your accountant. For example, if you prepare a summary of your dividends or charitable contributions, just provide your accountant with the summary. If you are providing a summary of your capital gains and losses to your accountant, make sure that the total of all your sales proceeds agrees to the total reported to you on Form 1099-B(s). If you do give your accountant all of your documentation, he or she will probably feel obligated to verify the accuracy of your summaries, which, as you well know, can be a time-consuming process. Your fee increases accordingly. However, you should be able to provide full documentation on request.

Collecting Your Tax Information

1. **Study last year's tax return.** A good place to start when you are gathering information is your prior year's tax return. This return is a record of your taxable transactions during the previous year. If your economic activities have not significantly changed during the current year, then your prior year's return will give you a good indication of the kinds of documentation you should gather for your accountant. The old return may also serve as a powerful reminder of a little-used bank account that paid you interest or some other source of income, great or small, that you otherwise might forget. You should retain copies of prior years' returns for future reference.

2. **Review all checks.** At some point, you should be sure to review all the checks you have written during the year to search for possible tax deductions. To simplify your task, it's wise, if possible, to pay all of your checks from a single account. If, for example, you have a money market account and a checking account at your bank, it might be easier for recordkeeping purposes to transfer money into your checking account as necessary rather than to write checks on both accounts. If you want to be absolutely certain not to miss anything, prepare a worksheet like the one above. Do so each month throughout the year as you reconcile your bank statement. Various computer software programs are also available to help simplify the task of recordkeeping.

3. **Fill out a tax questionnaire.** To make sure that you don't miss anything, many accountants use questionnaires or checklists to obtain information about all of your taxable transactions during the year. Even if you're not planning to use an accountant, it might be a good idea to fill out an accountant's questionnaire. Some accountants may ask for this information in electronic format to facilitate preparation of your return. For a sample questionnaire, refer to the Individual Tax Organizer in the front of this book.

A final reminder: The common goal that you share with your accountant is the preparation of a complete and accurate return. The closer you work together, the more likely it is that your return will be satisfactory. Just as important, the closer you work together, the better your chances will be of saving money on your taxes.

45

If Your Return Is Examined

Introduction

This chapter is probably not for you. Overall, the IRS examines only a small fraction of all tax returns that are filed. However, if you are contacted by the IRS about your tax return, this material may be very important to you. Just how important will depend on how carefully your return was prepared and the sources and amount of your income.

An IRS examination is nothing to be feared, if you have kept accurate records to support your deductions and all of your income has been reported. In most cases, IRS audits are rather routine. In fact, in about 25% of the cases, the IRS makes no changes or issues a refund. Whatever the result, you won't do yourself much good by making things difficult for the IRS. An IRS examiner has the legal power to force a taxpayer to produce books and records to complete the examination. The best strategy is almost invariably one of concluding the examina-

tion as quickly as possible by providing the facts needed and by meeting deadlines.

On the other hand, an IRS examination is nothing to take lightly. You should be prepared, and that preparation starts with keeping receipts and records, followed by careful preparation of your return. The IRS examiner must follow certain rules in conducting the examination. Since you'd be well advised to know what they are, this chapter tells you about them.

You will find a summary of your rights as a taxpayer at the beginning of this chapter. It may be especially helpful in cases that involve the delinquent payment of assessed taxes. This chapter tells you about your rights when your return is examined. You should know these rights, since they affect you and your pocketbook. You should also read the IRS Publication 1, Your Rights as a Taxpayer.

The first part of this chapter explains some of your most important rights as a taxpayer. The second part explains the examination, appeal, collection, and refund processes.

Declaration of Taxpayer Rights

Protection of your rights. IRS employees will explain and protect your rights as a taxpayer throughout your contact with us.

Privacy and confidentiality. The IRS will not disclose to anyone the information you give us, except as authorized by law. You have the right to know why we are asking you for information, how we will use it, and what happens if you do not provide requested information.

Professional and courteous service. If you believe that an IRS employee has not treated you in a professional, fair, and courteous manner, you should tell that employee's supervisor. If the supervisor's response is not satisfactory, you should write to the IRS director for your area or the center where you filed your return.

Representation. You may either represent yourself or, with proper written authorization, have someone else represent you in your place. Your representative must be a person allowed to practice before the IRS,

such as an attorney, certified public accountant, or enrolled agent. If you are in an interview and ask to consult such a person, then we must stop and reschedule the interview in most cases.

You can have someone accompany you at an interview. You may make sound recordings of any meetings with our examination, appeal, or collection personnel, provided you tell us in writing 10 days before the meeting.

Payment of only the correct amount of tax. You are responsible for paying only the correct amount of tax due under the law—no more, no less. If you cannot pay all of your tax when it is due, you may be able to make monthly installment payments.

Help with unresolved tax problems. See *How To Get Tax Help.*

Appeals and judicial review. If you disagree with us about the amount of your tax liability or certain collection actions, you have the right to ask the Appeals Office to review your case. You may also ask a court to review your case.

Relief from certain penalties and interest. The IRS will waive penalties when allowed by law if you can show you acted reasonably and in good faith or relied on the incorrect advice of an IRS employee. We will waive interest that is the result of certain errors or delays caused by an IRS employee.

The Examination and Appeals Process

The IRS examines returns for correctness of income, exemptions, credits, and deductions.

Who gets audited? The odds that your return will be examined by the IRS are, in fact, quite low. According to the most recent Treasury tables, the IRS examined approximately 1% of all individual returns, down from about 5% in the mid-1960s. The odds shift substantially, depending on your income level and types of income. However, recent pressure by the U.S. Congress to block the Taxpayer Compliance Measurement Program (TCMP) has prevented the IRS from updating its individual return selection systems, so for the time being the IRS is using old data and relying more heavily on supplemental systems. This may alter the traditional odds of getting audited.

Here is a list of some items or circumstances that can frequently draw the IRS's attention:

- Reported income does not agree with information on information returns, Forms 1099 and W2.
- Married taxpayers filing separately. Many such taxpayers do not report items consistently between returns (e.g., itemized deductions, zero bracket or standard deduction amount elections).
- Returns with significant items that may trigger alternative minimum tax (e.g., significant miscellaneous itemized deductions and state, local, and property taxes).
- Taxpayers who may receive substantial cash payments in the normal course of business (e.g., doctors, lawyers, retail establishments, waiters).
- Deductions that seem unusually large compared to your income level.
- Total Schedule C (business income) gross receipts of $100,000 or more. According to one recent study, the IRS has concluded that individuals filing Schedule C are most likely not to report income.
- Large business expenses in relation to your income.
- A return submitted by an accountant or a tax preparer who is on an IRS list of problem preparers because they have repeatedly violated the law.
- Complex investment or business transactions without clear explanations.
- Schedule F (farm) losses, particularly where the taxpayer has significant salary income.
- Earned income credit. Because there is the perception of potential abuse in this area, returns claiming the earned income credit are more closely scrutinized.
- Taxpayers' returns that fall in an area included in the IRS Market Segment Specialization Program (MSSP) such as automobile dealers, taxi services, air charters, attorneys, gas retailers, and others in a series of businesses or occupations that the IRS believes to need examination attention.

Other areas of noncompliance have been identified by IRS district offices as part of a project commonly referred to as "Compliance 2001." In addition, a local IRS district may undertake an Information Gathering Project (IGP) to more specifically focus on what they perceive as local compliance problems.

Fairness if Your Return Is Examined

Most taxpayers' returns are accepted as filed. But if your return is selected for examination, it does not suggest that you are dishonest. The inquiry or examination may or may not result in more tax. Your case may be closed without change. Or, you may receive a refund.

Courtesy and consideration. You are entitled to courteous and considerate treatment from IRS employees at all times. If you ever feel that you are not being treated with fairness, courtesy, and consideration by an IRS employee, you should tell the employee's supervisor. Publication 1, *Your Rights as a Taxpayer,* explains the many rights you have as a taxpayer. You can get free publications by calling 1-800-829-3676.

Your rights as a taxpayer. While the taxpayer bill of rights did not break new legal ground, it did create a single document that informs you of your rights. It is useful to review it to be aware of the rights you have. A summary of the most important points follow.

Pay only the required tax. You have the right to plan your business and personal finances in such a way that you will pay the least tax that is due under the law. You are liable only for the correct amount of tax. The IRS's purpose is to apply the law consistently and fairly to all taxpayers.

Privacy and confidentiality. You have the right to have your tax case kept confidential. Under the law, the IRS must protect the privacy of your tax information. However, if a lien or a lawsuit is filed, certain aspects of your tax case will become public record. People who prepare your return or represent you must also keep your information confidential.

You also have the right to know why the IRS is asking you for the information, exactly how the agency will use it, and what might happen if you do not give it.

Examination of Returns

An examination usually begins when the IRS notifies you that your return has been selected. The IRS will tell you which records you will need. If you gather your records before the examination, it can be completed with the least amount of effort.

How returns are selected. The IRS selects returns for examination by several methods. A computer program called the Discriminant Function System (DIF) is used to select most returns. In this method, the computer uses historical data to give parts of the return a score. IRS personnel then screen the return.

Some returns are selected at random. The IRS uses the results of examining these returns to update and improve its selection process.

The IRS also selects returns by examining claims for credit or refund and by matching information documents, such as Forms W-2 and the 1099 series, with returns.

Verification methods for proper payment. The IRS uses several methods and techniques to attempt to verify that the proper amount of tax is being paid by taxpayers:

1. **Document perfection.** Every return is checked for mathematical, tax calculation, and clerical errors in initial processing. If a mistake is discovered, a recalculation of the tax due and a notice of explanation are sent to the taxpayer. This procedure is not an **audit**—an important distinction.

   The IRS determines whether the return is in "processible form." The law lets the IRS avoid payment of interest on any refund until the return contains the taxpayer's name, address, identifying number, and required signature. Furthermore, the return must be on the permitted form and contain sufficient information to permit the mathematical verification of the tax liability shown on the return. The IRS has carried this to extremes by sending tax returns back to taxpayers for failing to check a box, not attaching all required forms, and not making alternative minimum tax computations when it is obvious no such action is due. While the IRS concentrates on refund returns with small errors that permit them to avoid large refunds, it has also sent balance-due returns back after depositing any checks attached. If the return is not perfected and returned before the due date, the IRS says the return is delinquent. The IRS has lost this issue in the Tax Court but persists in its position.

2. **Discriminant Function System (DIF).** Basically, DIF assigns a numerical value to certain items on your return. If the total of all the values equals or exceeds a minimum set by the IRS, the computer will single out the return for a possible audit. IRS agents will then check the return to see if it is worth the IRS's time to conduct an audit. This will depend on, among other things, staffing in your IRS district office. Even if your return is selected for an audit, it is likely that only specific items, such as charitable contributions or employee business expenses, would be examined, not your entire return.

It's a closely guarded secret what weight DIF assigns to which items. Some things this computer program is on the lookout for include:

- Large amounts of income not subject to withholding
- More deductions than seem to be reasonable for your income level
- Claims for an unusual number of dependency deductions as compared to withholding and other items on the return
- Discrepancies such as a change of address combined with deductions claimed for owning a residence when you have not reported that you sold your old residence

The DIF system is being used less as a selection source in recent years, especially in the case of Schedule C filers. The Audit Specialization Program is taking its place (see later in this chapter).

3. **Taxpayer Compliance Measurement Program (TCMP).** The type of examination triggered by TCMP is more intensive than that generated by DIF. You will be advised by the IRS that your return is being examined under the TCMP.

The bad news about a TCMP examination is that almost every item on your return can be examined, and you must substantiate everything. If you are married, you may be required to produce your marriage certificate. If you claim exemptions for your children, the IRS may ask to see their birth certificates. The IRS uses TCMP examinations to construct a computer model and to keep its taxpayer profile up-to-date.

TCMP audits focus on "economic reality" and a search for off-the-book items. "Economic reality," simply put, is a comparison of the taxpayer's economic activity to items reported on the return. For example, a taxpayer's mortgage expense deduction would be considered in determining if income reported appeared to be realistic.

Example

Your house payment is $1,500 a month. Your annual housing expenses are:

$13,000	interest
3,000	property tax
2,000	insurance and principal
$18,000	

A reasonable rule of thumb is that about 20% of an individual's income is allocated to house payment ($18,000 × 5 = $90,000 projected income). Consequently, the IRS would figure that you should be reporting roughly $90,000 in income.

TaxAlert

Future audits. TCMP examinations were suspended in 1997 because of expected cuts in the IRS budget but will doubtless resume in some form. Now that TCMP has been cancelled, IRS revenue agents are expected to apply economic reality principles to other taxpayer examinations. Legislation is pending in Congress that would restrict use of "economic reality" examination techniques.

4. **Document-matching program.** The IRS matches the information supplied by your bank, your employer, and others on Forms W-2 and 1099 and other information documents with the information supplied on your return. If an item is omitted from your return or conflicts with what is reported to the IRS, the IRS computer will generate a notice that recalculates your tax with corrections for the omitted income or overstated deduction. The Revenue Reconciliation Act of 1989 repealed the section of the tax law that gave the IRS the presumption of being correct in asserting a negligence penalty if you fail to report correctly relevant amounts reflected on information returns. The change applies to returns filed after December 31, 1989. It is probable that the IRS will continue to assert not only the negligence penalty but also the substantial understatement penalty. This procedure does not technically constitute a formal examination.

5. **The Market Segment Specialization Program (MSSP) and other special projects.** In 1991, the Internal Revenue Service began a project in the Los Angeles District Office focusing on developing highly trained revenue agents for a particular business market segment. Prior to this initiative, the IRS had not been training their revenue agents to be specialists within any certain business market segment. From that initiative in Los Angeles, the IRS has expanded the program to cover more business market segments and has formally named the program the Market Segment Specialization Program (MSSP). The following is a list of these market segments:

IRC Section 936 corporations	Beauty shops/barber shops
Air charter	Bed & breakfast
Alaska commercial fishing	Building maintenance
Alaska placer gold mining	services
Architectural services	Cable TV
Art dealers	Carwashing and detailing
Attorneys	Casino gambling
Auto body shops	Cattle
Auto repair shops	Check cashing
Bail bondsmen	establishments
Bankruptcy	Child care

Citrus industry
Commercial banking
Community banks
Construction/general building
  contractors
Construction industry
Cooperative housing
  corporations
Electronic components
Emergency care clinics
Employment tax—pizza drivers
Entertainment industry:
• Contracts—audit
   applications
• Foreign athletes and
   entertainers
• Motion pictures/television
• Music (Nashville)
• Theater—live performances
Escort service
Federal excise tax, coal mining
Financial institutions
Foreign tourism
Form 1042S withholding
  agents
Furniture manufacturing
Garment industry
Gas retailers
Golf courses
Grain and milo growers
Grocery stores
Health care
Insurance agencies
Jewelry dealers
Laundromat
Life insurance
Liquor stores
Low-income housing credit
Ministers
Mobile cart vendors

Mortuaries
Motor fuel tax
Nursing/rest homes
Offshore captive insurance
  co.
Oil and gas operators
Parking lots
Passive activity losses
Pawn shops
Petroleum contamination
  cleanup
Pizza parlors
Plastic surgeons
Port of Houston
Poultry
Printing
Real estate agents/brokers
Real estate developers
Recycling
Reforestation
Rehabilitation credit
Rent to own
Restaurants/bars/eating
  places
RTC project (forgiveness of
  debt)
Scrap metal
Seafood purchases
Selling door-to-door/
  telephone
Taxicabs
Timber sales
Time-sharing
Tobacco
Tour bus industry
Travel agency
Trucking industry
Used auto dealers
Wine industry

The scope of the MSSP will affect virtually every taxpayer who has a Schedule C attached to his or her return whose business operations come under one of the many business market segments. Once a business market segment is identified, the IRS issues detailed audit guidelines to their specialists as a guide to conduct an audit of the tax return. These guidelines will detail various issues and practices within a market segment that should be scrutinized by all revenue agents for potential adjustment. The IRS has issued formal audit guidelines to their examiners with respect to 27 market segments, including, but not limited to, gas retailers, attorneys, trucking, mortuaries, air charters, bed and breakfasts, taxicabs, the music industry, foreign athletes and entertainers, architectural services, bars and restaurants, mobile food vendors, resolution trust corporations, the wine industry, passive activity losses, and the rehabilitation credit.

In addition, the IRS initiates "Compliance 2001" projects on a district-by-district basis to identify areas of noncompliance. For example, one district examined all the drywall contractors in a major metro area and claims to have found widespread underreporting of gross receipts as well as nonfilers. Another district selected returns of individuals who had renegotiated loans and examined them to determine if they were subject to tax because an indebtedness had been forgiven.

IRS service centers conduct other projects. Several service centers screened returns to determine if taxpayers who requested extensions of time to file were understating the tax that would be due. The IRS then treated extensions as invalid when the difference between the tax shown on the return and the extension exceeded certain tolerances. Other IRS service centers screened tax returns to detect failure to report gain on residences that were not replaced.

6. **Economic reality audits**. The IRS has begun a program of gathering information about a taxpayer that is a reflection of the individual's financial status. This technique involves an examination of the taxpayer's lifestyle as an additional check on whether the taxpayer had unreported income. Areas of inquiry may include standard of living, accumulated wealth, economic history, business environment, and potential nontaxable income. The intent is to audit the taxpayer and not just the tax return.

Problems can arise when the examiner decides that the taxpayer cannot afford the style in which the taxpayer lives, if such a decision is made without knowledge of what mortgage indebtedness (if any) the taxpayer may owe. If the taxpayer has nontaxable trust, or other income, determinations based on inadequate information can be the start of a troublesome IRS investigation that is unwarrantedly seeking criminal evasion evidence. Because of the delicate balance between what is and what is not a proper subject of inquiry of the IRS examiner, some care should be exercised. Particular attention should be given if there is any indication that the matter could be tied to a Market Segment inquiry (see above). The issues are serious to the IRS and the inquiry is a serious matter.

With the passage of the Internal Revenue Service Restructuring and Reform Act of 1998, economic reality audits have been severely restricted. These audit techniques were extremely intrusive and their use has been limited to situations where the IRS already has indications of unreported income. In these cases, the examiners have been instructed to tell the taxpayer that there appears to be a problem regarding income and give him or her an opportunity to explain and/or resolve any discrepancies. However, due to the potential serious nature of this type of issue, the well-informed taxpayer should consider contacting a tax advisor.

Arranging the examination. Many examinations are handled by mail. However, if the IRS notifies you that your examination is to be conducted through a personal interview, or if you request an interview, you have the right to ask that the examination take place at a reasonable time and place that are convenient for both you and the IRS. If the time or place the IRS suggests is not convenient, the examiner will try to work out something more suitable. However, the IRS will make the final determination on how, when, and where an examination takes place. The difference between the correspondence and office audit is as follows:

Correspondence audit. After a tax return is initially selected for examination, the IRS may first conduct a correspondence audit, requesting that documentation of a specific item on your tax return be submitted by mail. If it is more convenient, you may request that the audit be held at the IRS's local district office. However, by law, the IRS has the right to make the final decision on where and how an examination will be conducted, as long as it is not unreasonable in exercising its discretion. The Taxpayer Bill of Rights directed the IRS to publish regulations defining reasonable time and place. These regulations were published in temporary form, effective June 4, 1990.

Office audit. If the examination is conducted at an IRS office, its scope may be expanded to cover all questionable items. Although correspondence audits may be resolved more quickly than examinations conducted at an IRS office, there is no rule of thumb for which type of audit would be more beneficial to you. However, it is generally to your disadvantage to request that a correspondence audit be changed to an office audit or a field audit. Correspondence audits are limited in scope. You open the opportunity for the examiner to question other items if you request an interview audit at an IRS office or an audit at your place of business.

The easier you make the IRS's job, the less the amount of time required to conclude the audit and the greater the likelihood that you will avoid any arbitrary adjustments.

An examination verifies the accuracy of your tax liability on a specific item as reported on a tax return, claim, or other filing. An examination is generally limited to the study of those matters bearing directly on the tax question at hand. The IRS has the authority to examine information that may not appear to be directly related to your tax liability. For example, the IRS may study your living expenses to determine if your reported income can support your lifestyle or whether you may have unreported income.

Transfers to another district. Generally, your individual return is examined in the IRS district office nearest your home. However, not all offices have examination facilities. Your business return is examined where your books and records are maintained. If the place of examination is not convenient, you may ask to have the examination done in another office or transferred to a different district.

Representation. Throughout the examination, you may represent yourself, have someone else accompany you, or, with proper written authorization, have someone represent you in your absence. If you want to consult an attorney, an enrolled agent, a CPA, or any other person permitted to represent a taxpayer during an examination, the IRS will stop and reschedule the interview. The IRS cannot suspend the interview if you are there because of an administrative summons.

If you use Form 8821, *Tax Information Authorization*, to name a representative for you, the representative is only authorized to receive information and cannot fully represent you by taking action on the information. If you use Form 2848, *Power of Attorney*, to name your representative, the representative is fully authorized to represent you and take any action necessary, including signing an agreement for a deficiency or overassessment of tax to conclude the case.

In recent years, some districts and some examiners have been very aggressive in demanding that the taxpayer, even though represented by a qualified practitioner with a power of attorney, appear personally to answer questions. This practice was admittedly to probe for unreported income and to establish if the taxpayer's lifestyle might suggest other

problems in compliance with tax laws. The Taxpayer Bill of Rights now specifies that the IRS "may not require a taxpayer to accompany the representative in the absence of an administrative summons," and a properly qualified practitioner with a power of attorney is authorized to represent a client in any interview without the taxpayer's presence, except for criminal cases or matters involving the integrity of an IRS employee. Furthermore, the law specifies that "if a taxpayer clearly states at any time during an interview," except where an administrative summons has been enforced or accepted, "that the taxpayer wishes to consult with an attorney, certified public accountant, enrolled agent, enrolled actuary, or any other person permitted to represent the taxpayer," the IRS "shall suspend such interview, regardless of whether the taxpayer may have answered one or more questions."

TAXPLANNER

Do you need professional help? The answer is: It depends on the issues involved and your ability to represent yourself. If the amounts involved are small, it may not be worth it to pay for an advisor's time. If your return was prepared by a certified public accountant or a lawyer, you will want to inquire whether his or her fee included representing you at an audit. If it didn't and you want him or her to represent you, you should agree on a fee at the beginning of the process. You will certainly want an accountant or a lawyer to represent you if (1) the law involved in the audit is unclear or complicated, (2) highly technical supporting information may be required, (3) you think other issues may come up, or (4) you are too nervous or emotionally involved to handle the matter yourself.

Tape recording meetings with the IRS. You can generally make an audio recording of an interview with an IRS examination officer. Your request to record the interview should be made in writing. You must notify the IRS at least 10 days before the meeting and bring your own recording equipment. The IRS also can record an interview. If the IRS initiates the recording, it will notify you 10 days before the meeting, and you can get a copy of the recording at your expense.

Repeat examinations. The IRS tries to avoid repeat examinations of the same items, but sometimes this happens. If the IRS examines your tax return for the same items in either of the 2 previous years and proposed no change to your tax liability, please contact it as soon as possible so that the agency can see if it should discontinue the examination.

Generally, in connection with auditing your return for a particular year, the IRS may inspect your books only once. But there may be a second examination if you request it or if the IRS notifies you in writing that an additional audit is necessary. A further investigation could be considered necessary simply if the IRS suspects that additional tax is owed.

You may refuse the IRS's request to make a second examination. In fact, if you do not object, you have, in effect, given your consent for the examination to take place. If you refuse to produce records, the IRS must issue a summons. If you still resist, the IRS will be forced to obtain court assistance to enforce the summons.

The ban on second examinations does not apply when

1. The original audit, although prolonged and characterized by IRS staffing changes, is still going on.
2. The examination is not considered an examination as such (e.g., when the IRS contacts you to verify the

amount of dividends or interest on your return because that figure does not match what was otherwise reported).

3. The second examination is for a different kind of tax (e.g., employment or excise tax, instead of income tax) than was dealt with in the first examination.
4. A mere visual inspection of the return has taken place, not an examination of your books and records.
5. Cases involving the year of deduction of a net operating loss carryback (or similar type of carryback).
6. Cases in which there have been involuntary conversions and the taxpayer has not recomputed the tax liability after the replacement period has expired.

In sum, it is difficult for the IRS to justify a second examination of your books and records for the same year, but if there is a legitimate reason to do so, the IRS is usually within its rights.

Explanation of changes. If the IRS proposes any changes to your return, it will explain the reasons for the changes. It is important that you understand the reasons for any proposed change. You should not hesitate to ask about anything that is unclear to you.

Agreement with changes. If you agree with the proposed changes, you may sign an agreement form and pay any additional tax you may owe. You must pay interest on any additional tax. If you pay when you sign the agreement, the interest is generally figured from the due date of your return to the date you paid.

The IRS uses misleading language when it describes this consent form as an "agreement form." When you sign a Form 870 or Form 4549, you are simply permitting the IRS to make its assessment of tax without waiting 90 days, as required by law, and you are forfeiting your right to go to the Tax Court. You are not bound to follow the IRS position in subsequent years and may even file a claim for a refund for the years covered by the Form 870 after the tax has been paid.

If you do not pay the additional tax when you sign the agreement, you will receive a bill. The interest on the additional tax is generally figured from the due date of your return to the billing date. However, you will not be billed for more than 30 days' additional interest, even if the bill is delayed. Also, you will not have to pay any additional interest or penalties if you pay the amount due within 10 days of the billing date.

If you are due a refund, the IRS can refund your money more quickly if you sign the agreement form. You will be paid interest on the refund.

An IRS examiner's authority. An IRS examiner has virtually unlimited authority to determine the facts. Since most examination issues concern factual matters, the examiner has considerable discretion in accepting secondary evidence and in deciding what constitutes acceptable proof. On technical legal issues, though, he or she must adhere to established IRS policy. Therefore, even if certain court cases support your argument, the examiner must disallow it if the IRS has decided not to follow the precedents established by these cases.

In theory, IRS examiners are also not permitted to trade off items, letting you take one deduction in return for disallowing another. In practice, negotiations with the IRS are commonplace.

An important reminder. IRS examiners are under considerable pressure to close cases by reaching an agreement at the initial examination. An agent is given high marks for explaining the IRS position in a convincing manner. Contrary to popular belief, examiners are not rated by the amount of money they bring in or by the number of cases they close.

While all examination reports have a chance of being reviewed, except for cases that fall into a mandatory review category, the review is on a sample basis, so only a small percentage of cases are actually reviewed. The mandatory categories include cases involving refunds in excess of $1 million, tax shelters, TCMP, and fraud. All unagreed cases are subject to a limited review on receipt of a protest asking for an Appeals hearing. This review is primarily focused on perfecting the IRS case based on your arguments in the protest.

Appealing the Examination Findings

If you and the IRS auditor reach an agreement on the issue under examination, the auditor will be on your side if his or her report is reviewed by his or her boss.

If you do not agree with the examiner's report, you can meet with the examiner's supervisor to discuss your case further. If you still do not agree after receiving the examiner's findings, you have the right to appeal them. The examiner will explain your appeal rights and give you a copy of Publication 5, *Appeal Rights and Preparation of Protests for Unagreed Cases*. This free publication explains your appeal rights in detail and tells you exactly what to do if you want to appeal.

If you disagree with the IRS. If you and the IRS examiner disagree over the proper interpretation of a point of law, either you or the examiner may request technical advice from the IRS national office. Technical advice will be given only if the issue is unusual or complex, or if there is a lack of uniformity within the IRS about its treatment. If you ask for technical advice and the examiner denies the request, you may appeal to the Chief of the Examination Division. If he or she also denies the request and you disagree with the denial, all data will be forwarded to the Assistant Commissioner (Examination) in the national office for review. Action on the disputed issue generally will be suspended until it is decided whether or not technical advice will be issued.

Technical disagreements may be resolved by taking them to the agent's supervisor. However, this course of action is not recommended unless you are absolutely certain you are correct. The supervisor could point out an alternative position that might be more favorable to the examining agent.

Appeals. There is a single level of administrative appeal within the IRS. You make your appeal about the findings of the examiner to the Appeals Office in your region. Appeals conferences are conducted as informally as possible.

If you want an appeals conference, address your request to your District Director, according to the instructions in the IRS letter to you. Your District Director will forward your request to the Appeals Office, which will arrange for a conference at a convenient time and place. You or your representative should be prepared to discuss all disputed issues and to present your views at this meeting in order to save the time and expense of additional conferences. Most differences are resolved at this level.

If agreement is not reached at your appeals conference, you may, at any stage of the proceedings, take your case to court. See *Appeals to the Courts*, later.

Written protests. Along with your request for a conference, you may be required to file a written protest with your District Director.

You do not have to file a written protest if

1. The proposed increase or decrease in tax, or claimed refund, is not more than $2,500 for any of the tax periods involved.
2. Your examination was conducted by correspondence or in an IRS office by a tax auditor.

If a written protest is required, you should send it within the period granted in the letter that you received with the examination report. Your protest should contain all the following:

1. A statement that you want to appeal the findings of the examiner to the Appeals Office.
2. Your name and address and a daytime phone number.
3. The date and symbols from the letter, showing the adjustments and findings you are protesting.
4. The tax periods or years involved.
5. An itemized schedule of the adjustments with which you do not agree and why you do not agree.
6. A statement of facts supporting your position in any issue with which you do not agree.
7. A statement outlining the law or other authority on which you rely.

If the additional tax exceeds $2,500 but does not exceed $10,000, items 6 and 7 above are not required.

The statement of facts under item 6 must be declared true under penalties of perjury. This may be done by adding to the protest the following signed declaration: "Under the penalties of perjury, I declare that I have examined the facts stated in this protest and in any accompanying schedules and, to the best of my knowledge and belief, they are true, correct, and complete."

If your representative submits the protest for you, he or she may substitute a declaration stating the following:

1. That he or she prepared the protest and accompanying documents.
2. Whether he or she knows personally that the statement of facts contained in the protest and accompanying documents is true and correct.

Representation. You may represent yourself at your appeals conference, or you may be represented by an attorney, a certified public accountant, or a person enrolled to practice before the IRS.

If your representative attends a conference without you, he or she may receive or inspect confidential information only if a power of attorney or a tax information authorization has been filed. Form 2848, *Power of Attorney and Declaration of Representative*, or Form 8821, *Tax Information Authorization*, or any other properly written power of attorney or authorization may be used for this purpose.

You may also bring witnesses to support your position. You should consider consulting an attorney specializing in tax law before you do this.

Bargaining with the IRS. Whereas an IRS examiner must follow established IRS policy on statutory and procedural points, the appeals officer may bargain with you. He or she may consider whether litigation is worthwhile, given the strength of the views at odds with the IRS's position. If you make an unsuitable good faith settlement offer, the appeals officer may reject it but indicate a settlement he or she would recommend be accepted. In arriving at a figure, the appeals officer may calculate the chances of the IRS prevailing in

court. Generally, however, the IRS will not settle a case just because it is a nuisance to continue to pursue it.

Appeals officers do not have final settlement authority in all cases and for all issues. Accordingly, it is good practice in negotiating a settlement to ask the appeals officer if any part of a settlement proposed is subject to a supervisory review.

If no agreement can be reached at the appeals conference, you have two options:

1. Pay the additional tax generated by the disputed issue and sue for the refund of this payment in your District Court or the U.S. Court of Federal Claims (formerly the U.S. Claims Court) (see *Appeals to the courts*, below).
2. Wait for the arrival of your closing letter, and select a course of action at that point. If you do not pay the disputed amount, you will receive from the IRS a notice of deficiency, which is also known as a 90-day letter. This notice authorizes you to file a petition in the U.S. Tax Court with first having to pay the tax. A Tax Court suit may not be filed before receipt of the 90-day letter.

TaxAlert

Partnerships and S Corporations. Special procedures apply to certain partnerships and S corporations. The amount of any adjustment is determined at the partnership or S corporation level. The procedures are complex, regular statutory notices are not issued, and you should consult a professional if you want to contest a partnership or S corporation issue raised in the examination of your return.

Appeals to the courts. Depending on whether you first pay the disputed tax, you can take your case to the U.S. Tax Court, the U.S. Court of Federal Claims, or your U.S. District Court. These courts are entirely independent of the IRS. However, a U.S. Tax Court case is generally reviewed by an Appeals Office before it is heard by the Tax Court. As always, you can represent yourself or have someone admitted to practice before the court represent you.

Tax Court. If your case involves a disagreement over whether you owe additional income tax, estate tax, gift tax, windfall profit tax on domestic crude oil, or certain excise taxes of private foundations, public charities, qualified pension and other retirement plans, or real estate investment trusts, you may take it to the U.S. Tax Court. For you to appeal your case to the Tax Court, the IRS must first issue a formal letter, called a *notice of deficiency*. You have 90 days from the date this notice is mailed to you to file a petition with the Tax Court (150 days if it is addressed to you outside the United States). If you do not file your petition within the 90 or 150 days, you lose your opportunity to appeal to the Tax Court.

Generally, the Tax Court hears cases only if the tax has not been assessed and paid; however, you may pay the tax after the notice of deficiency has been issued and still petition the Tax Court for review. You must be sure that your petition to the Tax Court is filed on time. If it is not, the proposed liability will be automatically assessed against you. Once the tax is assessed, a notice of tax due (a bill) will be sent to you, and you may no longer take your case to the Tax Court. Once the assessment has been made, collection of the full amount due may proceed, even if you believe that the assessment was excessive. Publication 586A, *The Collection Process (Income Tax Accounts)*, explains IRS collection procedures.

If you filed your petition on time, the Tax Court will schedule your case for trial at a location that is convenient to you. You may represent yourself before the Tax Court, or you may be represented by anyone admitted to practice before the Tax Court.

If your case involves a dispute of not more than $10,000 ($50,000 after July 22, 1998) for any 1 tax year, the Tax Court provides a simple alternative for resolving disputes. At your request, and with the approval of the Tax Court, your case may be handled under the *small case* procedures, whereby you can present your own case to the Tax Court for a binding decision. If your case is handled under this procedure, the decision of the Tax Court is final and cannot be appealed. You can get more information about the small case procedures and other Tax Court matters from the U.S. Tax Court, 400 Second Street, N.W., Washington, D.C. 20217.

TaxAlert

Representing yourself. Since many taxpayers represent themselves in small cases, the IRS has a very high win record. Filing your own petition may not be a good idea, especially if the amount is substantial to you. In any event, be careful in following the instructions *to the letter,* especially regarding the date for filing, the required fee, and the address of the Tax Court. The date of mailing a petition to the Tax Court is the filing date, but you should use certified mail and carefully retain the receipt with a legible postmark.

District Court and U.S. Court of Federal Claims. Generally, the District Court and the U.S. Court of Federal Claims hear tax cases only after you have paid the tax and have filed a claim for a credit or a refund. As explained later under *Claims for Refund,* you may file a claim for a credit or a refund with the IRS if, after you pay your tax, you believe that the tax is incorrect or too high. If your claim is rejected, you will receive a notice of disallowance of the claim, unless you signed a Form 2297, *Waiver of Statutory Notification of Claim Disallowance.* If the IRS has not acted on your claim within 6 months from the date on which you filed it, you may then file suit for refund. You must file suit for a credit or a refund no later than 2 years after the IRS disallows your claim or a Form 2297 is issued.

You may file your credit or refund suit in your U.S. District Court or in the U.S. Court of Federal Claims. However, the U.S. Court of Federal Claims does not have jurisdiction if your claim was filed after July 18, 1984, and is for credit or refund of a penalty that relates to promoting an abusive tax shelter or to aiding and abetting the understatement of tax liability on someone else's return.

For information about procedures for filing suit in either court, contact the Clerk of your U.S. District Court or the Clerk of the U.S. Court of Federal Claims. The addresses of the District Courts and the U.S. Court of Federal Claims are in Publication 556, *Examination of Returns, Appeal Rights, and Claims for Refund.*

Before you file suit. Here are some of the factors that you might want to consider before you decide to file your suit in Tax Court, District Court, or U.S. Court of Federal Claims:

1. Which court has most recently arrived at favorable rulings on similar disputed issues.
2. The amount of tax involved. You may file a suit in Tax Court without paying the IRS the amount it claims you owe. If the tax has already been paid and you wish to file suit to obtain a refund, the U.S. District Court and the U.S. Court of Federal Claims are your only choices. However, to stop the accumulation of interest, you can at any time make a deposit in the nature of a cash bond of the tax that an examiner says you owe. *Note:* Such a remittance must be clearly labeled as a deposit. If you are successful in an appeal, you will draw no interest on the deposits returned. A deposit does not prevent you from going to the Tax Court. Once you file a suit in Tax Court, you may then pay the alleged tax deficiency and your suit will not be thrown out of court. If you do make the payment at this point in the process, you will not be liable for interest charges past the payment date. If you win, the government will then owe you interest from the date on which you made the payment. A deposit will be converted to a payment of the tax when you file a petition with the Tax Court. It is important to distinguish between payments of tax and deposits to stop the accumulation of interest.
3. Jury trials are available only in the District Courts. If your case rests on a question of equity, rather than on a finer point of tax law, a jury might be more responsive to your arguments. Remember, however, that both parties may appeal a District Court or a Tax Court decision.
4. A representative who is not an attorney may appear before the Tax Court if admitted to practice before that court.
5. Filing a suit before the Tax Court suspends the statute of limitation for assessment on the tax return that you are contesting. Consequently, if the IRS chooses, it could raise new issues and assert additional tax while your case is pending in court.
6. You're more likely to avoid embarrassing publicity before the Court of Federal Claims. The U.S. Court of Federal Claims is located in Washington, D.C. There is a U.S. District Court near your hometown. The Tax Court tries cases on a circuit-riding basis in most major cities.
7. You may file suit in Tax Court within 90 days (150 days if outside the United States) after the IRS issues a statutory notice of deficiency. You have more time to file before the U.S. District Court and the U.S. Court of Federal Claims.
8. In Tax Court, attorneys from the Office of Chief Counsel represent the IRS. In District Court and U.S. Court of Federal Claims, attorneys from the Tax Division of the Department of Justice will oppose your case.
9. Tax Court and District Court cases are appealed to the Circuit Court of Appeals and then to the Supreme Court. U.S. Court of Federal Claims decisions may be appealed to the Court of Appeals for the Federal Circuit and then to the Supreme Court.
10. Any court of the United States may now award attorney's fees and other costs for cases initiated after December 31, 1985, including certain costs incurred in an administrative appeal if the IRS's position was not substantially justified.

Recovering litigation expenses. If the court agrees with you on most of the issues in your case and finds the IRS's position to be largely unjustified, you may be able to recover some of your litigation expenses from the IRS. But to do this, you must have used up all the administrative remedies available to you within the IRS, including going through the appeals system. You may also be able to recover administrative expenses from the IRS. Free Publication 556, *Examination of Returns, Appeal Rights, and Claims for Refund*, explains your appeal rights.

The Taxpayer Bill of Rights corrects an inequity in prior law by permitting the courts to award costs, not only for litigating but also for administrative proceedings once a taxpayer's administrative appeal rights have been exhausted and a "notice of decision" by the IRS or a statutory notice of deficiency has been issued, whichever occurs earlier. The prior law had been interpreted to permit recovery only after the IRS's attorneys had taken a position before the courts. To recover, a taxpayer must substantially prevail through a determination in an administrative proceeding, after the point specified above, or in a court of law and must establish that the position of the United States in the proceeding was not substantially justified. In collection matters, when neither notice is issued, only litigation costs are recoverable.

Reasonable administrative costs include the following:

- Fees or charges imposed by the IRS
- Reasonable expert witness fees
- Reasonable costs of studies and analyses
- Costs associated with engineering or test reports
- Reasonable fees (generally not in excess of $125 per hour) for a qualified representative of the taxpayer in connection with the administrative action

Other remedies. If you believe that tax, penalty, or interest was unjustly charged, you have rights that can remedy the situation.

Claims for refund. Once you have paid your tax, you have the right to file a claim for a credit or refund if you believe the tax is too much. Be aware that informal claims that mention vague and general future possibilities to justify a refund will not be considered valid. The procedure for filing a claim is explained in Chapter 1, *Filing Information.*

Some courts have held that an informal claim for a refund will, under certain circumstances, prevent the statutory period from expiring before you can accumulate and submit all your data. An informal claim should be in writing, should notify the IRS that a right to a refund is being asserted, and should tell as fully as possible the reasons why you feel the refund would be valid. A formal claim for the refund filed on official IRS forms should be made as soon as practical thereafter.

If you file with the wrong IRS center. If you file an amended return with the wrong IRS Service Center, it is under no obligation to forward that return to the correct Service Center. If you do not hear from the IRS within 6 months of filing Form 1040X, you should make a point of contacting it to determine the source of the delay.

Claims (Form 1040X) should always ask for a specific dollar amount or "for such greater amount as is legally refundable" to ensure that you receive a refund of interest and interest on such interest where appropriate.

Cancellation of penalties. You have the right to ask that certain penalties (but not interest, as discussed later) be cancelled (abated) if you can show reasonable cause for the failure that led to the penalty (or can show that you exercised due diligence, if that is the standard for the penalty).

If you relied on wrong advice from IRS employees given to you by phone, the agency will cancel certain penalties that may result. But you have to show that your reliance on the advice was reasonable.

Reduction of interest. If the IRS's error caused a delay in your case, and this is grossly unfair, you may be entitled to a reduction of the interest that would otherwise be due. Only delays caused by procedural or mechanical acts that do not involve exercising judgment or discretion qualify. If you think the IRS caused such a delay, please discuss it with the examiner and file a claim.

TaxSaver

If the IRS makes an error. If the IRS made an error, sent you a refund check, and then made you pay interest when you repaid it, you now can strike back. According to the Tax Reform Act of 1986, the IRS may not charge you interest from the date of the erroneous refund to the date they demanded you repay it. The law has also given the IRS the discretion to refund or abate excessive interest that you may have paid on an underpayment of your tax if an IRS employee was dilatory or made an error in processing it. To qualify, you must not have caused the error in any way. The erroneous refund must have been less than $50,000. Use Form 843 to file your claim.

Past-due taxes. The Taxpayer Bill of Rights recognized that taxpayers occasionally may have problems paying taxes due on their returns because of unanticipated changes on examination or other unexpected difficulties. To ensure fair treatment, the Taxpayer Bill of Rights made some changes in how notices are issued, how much time is allowed for payment, how taxpayers can get help, and so on. The key provisions relating to past-due taxes are as follows:

1. The period from when the IRS provides written notice to a taxpayer to the first permissible date on which the IRS can levy on bank accounts, wages, and so on is increased from 10 days to 30 days. The IRS also cannot levy on property on any day on which the person appears before the IRS in response to a summons, unless the IRS determines the collection of the tax is in jeopardy. In addition, financial institutions are required to hold accounts garnished by the IRS for 21 days after receipt of the notice of levy.
2. The IRS was required to establish a formal system for the appeal of liens similar to that existing in the income tax deficiency area. The appeals procedures are printed on the notice of lien.
3. The IRS now has the legal right to enter into installment agreements with taxpayers so that they can more easily pay delinquent taxes. The agreement will remain in effect unless the taxpayer has provided inaccurate information, does not pay an installment when it is due, fails to respond to a reasonable request for updated financial information, or the collection of the balance is in jeopardy. In addition, the IRS may only modify or terminate an agreement if the taxpayer's financial condition has significantly changed. Notification of the reason for the action has to be given at least 30 days prior to any action.
4. The Taxpayer Advocate is authorized to issue a taxpayer assistance order (TAO) in any situation in which the taxpayer is suffering or about to suffer a significant hardship as a result of the manner in which the IRS laws are being administered. During the period in which the order is in effect, the statute of limitations is suspended and any further IRS action is halted. Only the Commissioner, Deputy Commissioner, or Taxpayer Advocate can modify or rescind the order. The Taxpayer Advocate administers the

IRS Problem Resolution Program, which was created to resolve problems not remedied through normal operating channels.

The IRS has designed a form (Form 911) to assist taxpayers in applying for a TAO.

The Taxpayer Bill of Rights and the Taxpayer Bill of Rights 2, which passed August 1996, have many other provisions that may be helpful to you. If you have further problems with the IRS and believe that you are being treated unfairly, you should contact the district Problem Resolution Officer or a knowledgeable professional.

Examinations, Appeals, Collections, and Refunds

Examinations (Audits)

We accept most taxpayers' returns as filed. If we inquire about your return or select it for examination, it does not suggest that you are dishonest. The inquiry or examination may or may not result in more tax. We may close your case without change; or, you may receive a refund.

The process of selecting a return for examination usually begins in one of two ways. First, we use computer programs to identify returns that may have incorrect amounts. These programs may be based on information returns, such as Forms 1099 and W-2, on studies of past examinations, or on certain issues identified by compliance projects. Second, we use information from outside sources that indicates that a return may have incorrect amounts. These sources may include newspapers, public records, and individuals. If we determine that the information is accurate and reliable, we may use it to select a return for examination.

Publication 556, *Examination of Returns, Appeal Rights, and Claims for Refund,* explains the rules and procedures that we follow in examinations. The following sections give an overview of how we conduct examinations.

By mail. We handle many examinations and inquiries by mail. We will send you a letter with either a request for more information or a reason why we believe a change to your return may be needed. You can respond by mail or you can request a personal interview with an examiner. If you mail us the requested information or provide an explanation, we may or may not agree with you, and we will explain the reasons for any changes. Please do not hesitate to write to us about anything you do not understand.

By interview. If we notify you that we will conduct your examination through a personal interview, or you request such an interview, you have the right to ask that the examination take place at a reasonable time and place that is convenient for both you and the IRS. If our examiner proposes any changes to your return, he or she will explain the reasons for the changes, if you do not agree with these changes, you can meet with the examiner's supervisor.

Repeat examinations. If we examined your return for the same items in either of the 2 previous years and proposed no change to your tax liability, please contact us as soon as possible so we can see if we should discontinue the examination.

Appeals

If you do not agree with the examiner's proposed changes, you can appeal them to the Appeals Office of IRS. Most differences can be settled without expensive and time-consuming court trials. Your appeal rights are explained in detail in both Publication 5, *Your Appeal Rights and How To Prepare a Protest If You Don't Agree,* and Publication 556, *Examination of Returns, Appeal Rights, and Claims for Refund.*

If you do not wish to use the Appeals Office or disagree with its findings, you may be able to take your case to the U.S. Tax Court, U.S. Court of Federal Claims, or the U.S. District Court where you live. If you take your case to court, the IRS will have the burden of proving certain facts if you kept adequate records to show your tax liability, cooperated with the IRS, and meet certain other conditions. If the court agrees with you on most issues in your case and finds that our position was largely unjustified, you may be able to recover some of your administrative and litigation costs. You will not be eligible to recover these costs unless you tried to resolve your case administratively, including going through the appeals system, and you gave us the information necessary to resolve the case.

Collections

Publication 594, *The IRS Collection Process,* explains your rights and responsibilities regarding payment of federal taxes. It describes:

- What to do when you owe taxes. It describes what to do if you get a tax bill and what to do if you think your bill is wrong. It also covers making installment payments, delaying collection action, and submitting an offer in compromise.
- IRS collection actions. It covers liens, releasing a lien, levies, releasing a levy, seizures and sales, and release of property.

Your collection appeal rights are explained in detail in Publication 1660, *Collection Appeal Rights.*

Innocent spouse relief. Generally, both you and your spouse are responsible, jointly and individually, for paying the full amount of any tax, interest, or penalties due on your joint return. However, if you qualify for innocent spouse relief, you may not have to pay the tax, interest, and penalties related to your spouse (or former spouse). For information on innocent spouse relief and two other ways to get relief, see Publication 971, *Innocent Spouse Relief,* and Form 8857, *Request for Innocent Spouse Relief (And Separation of Liability and Equitable Relief).*

Refunds

You may file a claim for refund if you think you paid too much tax. You must generally file the claim within 3 years from the date you filed your original return or 2 years from the date you paid the tax, whichever is later. The law generally provides for interest on your refund if it is not paid within 45 days of the date you filed your return or claim for refund. Publication 556, *Examination of Returns, Appeals Rights, and Claims for Refund,* has more information on refunds.

If you were due a refund but you did not file a return, you must file within 3 years from the date the return was originally due to get that refund.

Planning Ahead for 2002 and Beyond

Introduction

The 2001 Tax Act, which President George W. Bush signed into law on June 7, 2001, represents a historic change in the tax law for individuals. When all the provisions in the bill—formally called The Economic Growth and Tax Relief Reconciliation Act of 2001—are added up, it amounts to a $1.35 trillion tax cut, but the cuts are spread out over a 10-year period and fraught with complexities—not the least of which is that the new law will expire in 2010 unless a future Congress takes some action to the contrary.

The good new for taxpayers is that the focus of the new law is broad based individual tax cuts. Among the major new provisions are:

- *An across-the-board individual income tax rate reduction (with the top rate eventually reduced to 35%—down from 39.6%).*
- *Marriage penalty relief*
- *A phased-in repeal of the estate tax and generation-skipping transfer tax*
- *A phased-in refundable and increased child tax credit.*

In addition, the tax package includes select education tax incentives and some relief for taxpayers subject to the alternative minimum tax.

The new law also contains numerous new retirement savings incentives designed to help Americans focus on building a secure retirement. Among other things, the new law increases certain retirement contribution limits, expands pension coverage and increases the portability of retirement assets. For employers, the new law reduces some of the regulatory burdens on employer-provided retirement plans.

Many of the new provisions will be phased-in gradually forcing taxpayers and their advisors to remain vigilant and flexible in order to benefit fully from the rules. The most significant changes contained in the new law begin to take effect in 2002—not 2001. Prudent taxpayers will begin planning, however, even before their 2001 taxes are due on April 15, 2002. This chapter serves as a roadmap to what lies ahead.

Tax Changes for 2002 You Should Know About

Tax Rate Reduction

Beginning July 1, 2001, individual income tax rates will be reduced gradually. A new 10% tax rate bracket has been created, the 15% tax rate bracket will be expanded for joint filers, and cuts in the tax rates above 15% are phased in over a five-year period. Table 1 shows the phase-in of the reductions for individual tax brackets greater than 15%.

TABLE 1
PHASE-IN OF INDIVIDUAL RATE REDUCTIONS

TAX YEAR	TAX RATES			
2000	28%	31%	36%	39.6%
2001	27.5%	30.5%	35.5%	39.1%
2002–2003	27%	30%	35%	38.6%
2004–2005	26%	29%	34%	37.6%
2006 and later	25%	28%	33%	35%

TAXPLANNER

To take advantage of the scheduled tax rate reductions, you may want to defer the recognition of income (to have it taxed at lower rates) and accelerate the payment of tax-deductible expenses (to get a larger tax benefit). Some methods of deferring income include participating in an employer's deferred compensation program and buying tax-deferred treasury securities like E- or I-bonds. You can accelerate expenses by making earlier payment of some investment expenses, mortgage interest, real estate taxes, and state and local taxes. You should consult with your tax advisor on these and other potential strategies.

Adoption Credit

For 2001, you can claim an adoption credit for up to $5,000 of qualified adoption expenses per eligible child ($6,000 for a special needs child). Beginning in 2002, the credit will increase to as much as $10,000 for any child, including special needs children. Also, the credit will be available to many more people since the beginning of the phase-out range will double from $75,000 to $150,000 of modified adjusted gross income.

Education Savings Accounts

An education savings account (ESA) is an account created exclusively to pay the qualified education expenses of a single named beneficiary. Contributions to ESAs (formally known as Coverdell education savings accounts after the Georgia politician who championed them) are made with after-tax dollars and grow tax-free as long as distributions are used to pay qualifying expenses. The new law significantly increased the amount that can be contributed annually, the types of expenses that qualify, and the number of taxpayers that can use these accounts.

Beginning in 2002, the annual contribution that can be made for each designated beneficiary will increase from $500 to $2,000. In another significant change, qualifying expenses will no longer be limited to those related to higher education. Elementary (including kindergarten) and secondary public, private, or religious school tuition and expenses will now qualify. The new law also specifically permits as elementary and secondary school expenses: academic tutoring; certain computer technology; and expenses for uniforms, transportation, and extended day programs.

The new law substantially increased the phase-out range for married taxpayers filing a joint return. Starting in 2002, joint filers with adjusted gross income below $190,000 (increased from $150,000) may make a full contribution to an ESA, and those with income below $220,000 (increased from $160,000) may make a partial contribution. Corporations and other entities can make contributions to ESAs regardless of the entity's income.

Qualified Tuition (Section 529) Programs

Section 529 plans allow a taxpayer to either buy tuition credits or to contribute to a special higher education savings account for a designated beneficiary. These programs have become even more valuable as a result of changes made by the new law.

The most significant change made by the new law is that qualifying distributions from these programs will no longer be subject to tax. Under prior law, account earnings used for qualifying expenses were taxable to the student at the time withdrawn. Under the new law, post-2001 distributions from qualified state tuition plans will be fully excluded from gross income.

Private educational institutions will also be able to establish prepaid educational services accounts and sell credits or certificates for the payment at a future date of qualified higher education expenses. Beginning in 2004, qualifying distributions from those programs will be excluded from gross income.

The new law also expands the definition of "room and board" for students who live off campus and not at home. Under prior law, only $2,500 per year of room and board expenses for such students was considered a qualifying expense. Beginning in 2002, the new law removes the dollar limit for both qualified tuition programs and education IRAs allowing "reasonable" expenses for room and board.

TAXPLANNER

Parents and grandparents should take a close look at the revised qualified tuition (Section 529) program. The combination of benefits and flexibility offered by these programs and their availability to all taxpayers will likely make them the most widely used education incentive program. Be sure to discuss with your financial advisor the investment options and limitations of the various programs.

Employer-Provided Educational Assistance (Section 127) Plans

Under current law, up to $5,250 in employer-paid educational expenses may be excluded annually from income, and will not be considered wages for purposes of federal income tax and employment tax withholding, if provided under a plan meeting the requirements of Section 127. This exclusion did not extend to graduate-level courses beginning after June 30, 1996, or to undergraduate level courses beginning after December 31, 2001. Effective with courses beginning after December 31, 2001, the Act extends the annual exclusion of up to $5,250 under Section 127 to cover both undergraduate and graduate-level courses.

Student-Loan Interest Deduction

Under current law, qualifying taxpayers can claim a deduction for up to $2,500 of interest paid on student loans during the first 60 months that payments are required.

The deduction is an adjustment to gross income and thus is available even if you do not claim itemized deductions. Under the new law, the 60-month limit is repealed. In addition, for interest paid after December 31, 2001, the phase-out ranges have been raised for single taxpayers to $50,000-$65,000 (from $40,000-$55,000) and to $100,000-$130,000 (from $60,000-$75,000) for taxpayers filing joint returns.

Deduction for Higher-Education Expenses

Eligible taxpayers will be able to claim an annual deduction for up to $3,000 ($4,000 in 2004) of qualified higher education expenses. This deduction is also an adjustment to gross income and available even if you do not claim itemized deductions. The deductions will be available beginning in 2002 to a single taxpayer with adjusted gross income up to $65,000, or $130,000 if married and filing jointly.

Health Insurance Deductibility

The gradual increase in the deduction for health insurance that is available to self-employed taxpayers (and more-than-2% employee shareholders of S corporations) will increase to the following levels: 60% for 2001; 70% for 2002; and 100% for 2003 and beyond.

Higher IRA Contribution Limits

The maximum annual contribution limits for both traditional and Roth IRAs will gradually rise from the current $2,000 to $5,000 by 2008 with annual inflation adjustments after 2008. Starting in 2002, taxpayers who have attained age 50 by the end of the year will be able to make additional "catch-up" contributions of $500 for 2002 through 2005, and $1,000 for 2006 and thereafter.

TABLE 2
TRADITIONAL AND ROTH IRA ANNUAL CONTRIBUTION LIMITS

CALENDAR YEAR	INDIVIDUALS UNDER AGE 50	INDIVIDUALS AGE 50 AND ABOVE
2001	$2,000	$2,000
2002-2004	$3,000	$3,500
2005	$4,000	$4,500
2006-2007	$4,000	$5,000
2008	$5,000	$6,000

These larger contribution amounts may increase the attractiveness of IRAs relative to variable annuities.

Although the 2001 Tax Act substantially increases the amount that can be contributed to an IRA, the limitations in the current law on deductibility and the ability to use a Roth IRA remain the same. Also retained is the current law limit on converting to a Roth IRA—you're only eligible to do so if your adjusted gross income is not more than $100,000.

Defined Contribution Plans

The dollar limit of the amount you can contribute on an elective deferral basis to your 401(k) or other defined contribution plan will increase to $11,000 in 2002 and will reach $15,000 by 2006. The limit will then be indexed for inflation. The applicable dollar limit is larger for taxpayers who are age 50 by the end of the year. Table 3 shows the limits.

TABLE 3
QUALIFIED EMPLOYER-SPONSORED RETIREMENT PLAN: ANNUAL ELECTIVE DEFERRAL LIMITS

CALENDAR YEAR	INDIVIDUALS UNDER AGE 50	INDIVIDUALS AGE 50 AND ABOVE
2001	$10,500	$10,500
2002	$11,000	$12,000
2003	$12,000	$14,000
2004	$13,000	$16,000
2005	$14,000	$18,000
2006	$15,000	$20,000

SIMPLE Plans

The new law increases the maximum annual elective deferrals that may be made to a SIMPLE plan to $7,000 in 2002 and in $1,000 annual increments thereafter until the limit reaches $10,000 in 2005. For taxpayers who reach age 50 before the end of the plan year, these limits are increased to $7,500 for 2002; $9,000 for 2003; $10,500 for 2004; $12,000 for 2005; and $12,500 for 2006.

Tax-Exempt Organization and State or Local Governmental (Section 457) Plans

Under current law, the maximum annual deferral under all of an individual's Section 457 plans is the lesser of $8,500 (the "inflation adjusted dollar limit") or 33% of your compensation.

For years beginning after 2001, the new law repeals the rules that coordinate the Section 457 plan inflation-adjusted dollar limit with contributions to other types of plans. The new law also increases the inflation-adjusted dollar limit on 457 plans to $11,000 in 2002. The limit increases in $1,000 annual increments until it reaches $15,000 in 2006. The limit in the three years prior to retirement is twice the otherwise applicable dollar limit.

Maximum Compensation for Qualified Plan Purposes

For purposes of determining plan contributions, benefits, nondiscrimination testing, and applying the deduction rules, the maximum annual compensation of each plan participant that may be taken into account under current law is limited to $170,000. For years beginning in 2002, the 2001 Tax Act raises the amount of annual compensation that may be taken into account for qualified plan purposes to $200,000.

Increase in Deduction Limit for Contributions to Profit-Sharing Plans

Under current law, the deduction for contributions to a profit-sharing plan is limited to 15% of compensation. Beginning in 2002, the limit will increase to 25% of compensation. This is especially important for self-employed individuals considering the adoption of a Keogh plan. Under current law, in order to maximize deductibility and flexibility, a combination of a profit-sharing plan and a money purchase plan was necessary. Under the new law, adopting a profit-sharing plan alone would provide maximum flexibility and allow the largest deduction provided by law.

Tax Credit to Encourage Certain Taxpayers to Save for Retirement

Beginning in 2002, a taxpayer meeting applicable income requirements can qualify for a tax credit of up to $1,000 for contributions or deferrals to retirement savings plans. The maximum credit is 50% of the contribution or deferral (up to $2,000). The amount of the credit is determined on a sliding scale. The credit is fully phased out for joint filers with adjusted gross income over $50,000 and over $25,000 for single taxpayers and those that are married and filing separately.

Tax-Free Employee Transportation Benefits

Under current law, employees are permitted to exclude up to $65 of employer-provided transit and vanpool benefits and up to $180, per month of employer-provided parking without regard to whether such benefits are offered in lieu of other compensation. Under prior law, transit and vanpool benefits were excludable only if offered in addition to (not in lieu of) other compensation, whereas employer-paid parking was excludable if offered in lieu of or in addition to other compensation. These amounts will be indexed for inflation. In addition, beginning in 2002, the exclusion for transit passes and vanpooling will be increased to $100 per month and indexed thereafter.

Planning Ideas to Consider

AMT Calculation

Current law permits taxpayers to take full advantage of the nonrefundable personal tax credits (i.e., the dependent care credit, credit for the elderly and disabled, adoption tax credit, credit for interest on certain home mortgages, the HOPE Scholarship and Lifetime Learning tax credits, and the D.C. homebuyer's tax credit). Therefore, for the 2001 tax year, the nonrefundable personal tax credits can be used to offset your regular tax in full, not just to the extent by which your tentative alternative minimum tax (AMT) is exceeded. This provision will expire as of December 31, 2001, unless extended by Congress. As this book went to press, such legislation was pending in Congress.

The Alternative Minimum Tax was devised by Congress as a tax system imposed on top of the regular tax system to prevent taxpayers from taking too great of an advantage of special tax breaks such as accelerated depreciation, interest on certain tax-exempt bonds, and so on. Taxpayers who do not use these tax preferences to lower their regular income tax are not subject to the AMT.

However, Congress did not index the income thresholds for the AMT, and each year more and more Americans discover they must perform AMT calculations. Taxpayers who do not consider themselves "high income" are often surprised to find that items such as the child tax credit and various educational credits can lower their regular tax liability so much that they are subject to the AMT. Table 4 shows how a typical taxpayer with ordinary income as low as $50,000 can trigger the AMT:

TABLE 4
ADJUSTMENTS AND PREFERENCES THAT WILL CAUSE AMT
TO APPLY IN 2001

REGULAR TAXABLE INCOME	JOINT	SINGLE
50,000	30,183	25,660
100,000	33,041	28,493
150,000	32,503	27,456
200,000	32,767	29,145
300,000	34,467	49,681
400,000	71,227	89,324
500,000	110,870	128,967

Dependent Care Credit

Beginning in 2003, eligible taxpayers will be able to claim a larger dependent care credit for expenses incurred to enable a spouse to be employed. The eligible employment-related expenses increase frm $2,400 to $3,000 for one qualifying individual (from $4,800 to $6,000 for two or more) and the maximum credit rate increases from 30% to 35%. The beginning point of income phase-out increases from $10,000 to $15,000 of adjusted gross income. The credit percentage will be reduced to 20% for taxpayers with adjusted gross income over $43,000. Once this provision becomes effective, a qualifying taxpayer with two children and more than $43,000 of income will be able to claim a $1,200 credit, up from $960 under current law.

Contributions to Charity

Most taxpayers make many of their charitable contributions at the end of the tax year. The reason is simple: you can have use of the money for the entire year and, at the same time, you can take the tax deduction for that year. If you made your contribution in January, you would be entitled to the same deduction but would not have use of the money for the rest of the year. Charitable contributions are available only if you itemize your deductions.

A few points to consider, especially at year-end:

1. If cash is not readily available, you can use a credit card to charge donations to charity. They will be deductible in 2001, even though you don't pay the charge until 2002.
2. If you are going to give publicly traded stock to a charity, check with your stockbroker to ensure that you have a readily transferable title to the property that you want to donate to charity.
3. A contribution of appreciated long-term capital gain publicly traded stock to a private foundation will qualify for a full fair market value deduction.

Remember that your 2001 itemized deductions may be subject to certain limitations if your adjusted gross income exceeds $132,950 ($66,475 if married filing separately).

PART VI

Filling Out Your Tax Return and Tax Forms You Can Use

The chapters in this part provide you with forms, schedules, and tables you can use. Chapter 47, *Filling Out Form 1040* has line-by-line instructions for filling out Form 1040. Chapter 48, *2001 Federal Tax Forms and Schedules You Can Use* includes most of the 2001 Federal Tax Forms and Schedules you will need to complete your return. The final chapter includes the tax tables and tax rate schedules that you need to complete your tax return.

47

Filling Out Form 1040

Introduction

Form 1040 is designed to handle every taxpayer's situation regardless of the size and complexity of his or her economic activity.

The line-by-line instructions that follow should guide you through the sometimes cumbersome and always mind-numbing process of filling out your tax return. If you *have to cope with a situation that is not covered in the following pages, you should turn to the appropriate chapter in the book. To make your task easier, many of the sample tax forms in this chapter contain circles directing you to the pages in this chapter where more information can be found.*

Line Instructions for Form 1040

Name and Address

Use the Peel-Off Label

Using your peel-off name and address label in this booklet will speed the processing of your return. It also prevents common errors that can delay refunds or result in unnecessary notices. Put the label on your return **after** you have finished it. Cross out any errors and print the correct information. Add any missing items, such as your apartment number.

Address Change

If the address on your peel-off label is not your current address, cross out your old address and print your new address.

Name Change

If you changed your name, be sure to report the change to your local Social Security Administration office **before** filing your return. This prevents delays in processing your return and issuing refunds. It also safeguards your future social security benefits. If you received a peel-off label, cross out your former name and print your new name.

What If You Do Not Have a Label?

Print or type the information in the spaces provided. If you are married filing a separate return, enter your husband's or wife's name on line 3 instead of below your name.

Tip. If you filed a joint return for 2000 and you are filing a joint return for 2001 with the same spouse, be sure to enter your names and SSNs in the same order as on your 2000 return.

P.O. Box

Enter your box number **only** if your post office does not deliver mail to your home.

Foreign Address

Enter the information in the following order: City, province or state, and country. Follow the country's practice for entering the postal code. **Do not** abbreviate the country name.

Death of a Taxpayer

See Chapter 4.

Social Security Number (SSN)

An incorrect or missing SSN may increase your tax or reduce your refund. **To apply for an SSN,** get **Form SS-5** from your local Social Security Administration (SSA) office or call the SSA at 1-800-772-1213. Fill in Form SS-5 and return it to the SSA. It usually takes about 2 weeks to get an SSN.

Check that your SSN is correct on your Forms W-2 and 1099.

IRS Individual Taxpayer Identification Numbers (ITINs) for Aliens

The IRS will issue you an ITIN if you are a nonresident or resident alien and you do not have and are not eligible to get an SSN. **To apply for**

Questions about what to put on a line? Help is on the page number in the circle.

Form 1040
Department of the Treasury—Internal Revenue Service
U.S. Individual Income Tax Return
2001 (99) IRS Use Only—Do not write or staple in this space.

For the year Jan. 1–Dec. 31, 2001, or other tax year beginning ____, 2001, ending ____, 20__

OMB No. 1545-0074

Label
(575)

(See instructions on page 575.)

Use the IRS label. Otherwise, please print or type.

L A B E L   H E R E

| Your first name and initial | Last name | Your social security number (575) |

| If a joint return, spouse's first name and initial | Last name | Spouse's social security number (575) |

Home address (number and street). If you have a P.O. box, see page 575. | Apt. no.

City, town or post office, state, and ZIP code. If you have a foreign address, see page 575.

▲ **Important!** ▲
You **must** enter your SSN(s) above.

Presidential Election Campaign
(See page 580.) (580)

Note. Checking "Yes" will not change your tax or reduce your refund.

Do you, or your spouse if filing a joint return, want $3 to go to this fund? . . . . ▶

You: ☐ Yes ☐ No Spouse: ☐ Yes ☐ No

Filing Status

Check only one box. (580)

1 ☐ Single
2 ☐ Married filing joint return (even if only one had income)
3 ☐ Married filing separate return. Enter spouse's social security no. above and full name here. ▶ _____
4 ☐ Head of household (with qualifying person). (See page 580.) If the qualifying person is a child but not your dependent, enter this child's name here. ▶ _____
5 ☐ Qualifying widow(er) with dependent child (year spouse died ▶ ____). (See page 580.)

Exemptions (580)

6a ☐ **Yourself.** If your parent (or someone else) can claim you as a dependent on his or her tax return, **do not** check box 6a1 . . . .

b ☐ **Spouse** . . . .

c **Dependents:**

If more than six dependents, see page 580. (580)

(1) First name Last name	(2) Dependent's social security number (580)	(3) Dependent's relationship to you	(4)✓ if qualifying child for child tax credit (see page 580) (580)
____	____	____	☐
____	____	____	☐
____	____	____	☐
____	____	____	☐
____	____	____	☐
____	____	____	☐

No. of boxes checked on 6a and 6b ____

No. of your children on 6c who:
• lived with you ____
• did not live with you due to divorce or separation (see page 581) (581) ____

Dependents on 6c not entered above ____

Add numbers entered on lines above ▶ ☐

d Total number of exemptions claimed . . . .

Income (611)

Attach Forms W-2 and W-2G here. Also attach Form(s) 1099-R if tax was withheld.

If you did not get a W-2, see page 581. (581)

Enclose, but do not attach, any payment. Also, please use Form 1040-V. (610)

7 Wages, salaries, tips, etc. Attach Form(s) W-2 . . . | 7 (581)
8a **Taxable** interest. Attach Schedule B if required . (582) . | 8a (582)
b **Tax-exempt** interest. **Do not** include on line 8a . . | 8b (582)
9 Ordinary dividends. Attach Schedule B if required (582) | 9 (582)
10 Taxable refunds, credits, or offsets of state and local income taxes (see page 582). . | 10 (582)
11 Alimony received . . . . | 11 (583)
12 Business income or (loss). Attach Schedule C or C-EZ . . . | 12 (583)
13 Capital gain or (loss). Attach Schedule D if required. If not required, check here ▶ ☐ | 13 (583)
14 Other gains or (losses). Attach Form 4797 . . . | 14 (583)
15a Total IRA distributions . | 15a (583) | b Taxable amount (see page 583) | 15b (583)
16a Total pensions and annuities | 16a (583) | b Taxable amount (see page 583) | 16b (583)
17 Rental real estate, royalties, partnerships, S corporations, trusts, etc. Attach Schedule E | 17
18 Farm income or (loss). Attach Schedule F . . . | 18
19 Unemployment compensation . . . . . . | 19 (585)
20a Social security benefits | 20a (585) | b Taxable amount (see page 585) | 20b (585)
21 Other income. List type and amount (see page 585) ____ (585) | 21
22 Add the amounts in the far right column for lines 7 through 21. This is your **total income** ▶ | 22

Adjusted Gross Income

23 IRA deduction (see page 587). . . . . . . | 23 (587)
24 Student loan interest deduction (see page 588) . . . | 24 (588)
25 Archer MSA deduction. Attach Form 8853 . . . . | 25 (588)
26 Moving expenses. Attach Form 3903 . . . . . | 26 (588)
27 One-half of self-employment tax. Attach Schedule SE . | 27 (588)
28 Self-employed health insurance deduction (see page 588) | 28 (588)
29 Self-employed SEP, SIMPLE, and qualified plans . . | 29 (590)
30 Penalty on early withdrawal of savings . . . . . | 30 (590)
31a Alimony paid b Recipient's SSN ▶ ____ | 31a (590)
32 Add lines 23 through 31a . . . . | 32 (590)
33 Subtract line 32 from line 22. This is your **adjusted gross income** . . . . ▶ | 33 (590)

Cat. No. 11320B

Form **1040** (2001)

Questions about what to put on a line? Help is on the page number in the circle.

Form 1040 (2001) ⟨590⟩ Page **2**

Tax and Credits	34	Amount from line 33 (adjusted gross income)	**34**	
	35a	Check if: ☐ **You** were 65 or older, ☐ Blind; ☐ **Spouse** was 65 or older, ☐ Blind. Add the number of boxes checked above and enter the total here **35a**		⟨590⟩
Standard Deduction for—	b	If you are married filing separately and your spouse itemizes deductions, or you were a dual-status alien, see page 590 and check here ⟨590⟩ . . . . **35b** ☐		
People who checked any box on line 35a or 35b **or** who can be claimed as a dependent, see page 590.	36	**Itemized deductions** (from Schedule A) **or** your **standard deduction** (see left margin) . .	**36**	⟨590⟩
	37	Subtract line 36 from line 34	**37**	
	38	If line 34 is $99,725 or less, multiply $2,900 by the total number of exemptions claimed on line 6d. If line 34 is over $99,725, see the worksheet on page 590	**38**	⟨590⟩
	39	**Taxable income.** Subtract line 38 from line 37. If line 38 is more than line 37, enter -0-	**39**	⟨590⟩
All others:	40	**Tax** (see page 590). Check if any tax is from **a** ☐ Form(s) 8814 **b** ☐ Form 4972	**40**	⟨590⟩
Single, $4,550	41	**Alternative minimum tax** (see page 592). Attach Form 6251 . .	**41**	⟨592⟩
Head of household, $6,650	42	Add lines 40 and 41	**42**	

Married filing jointly or Qualifying widow(er), $7,600	43	Foreign tax credit. Attach Form 1116 if required	**43**		⟨592⟩	
	44	Credit for child and dependent care expenses. Attach Form 2441	**44**	⟨593⟩		
	45	Credit for the elderly or the disabled. Attach Schedule R . .	**45**		⟨593⟩	
Married filing separately, $3,800	46	Education credits. Attach Form 8863	**46**	⟨593⟩		
	47	Rate reduction credit. See the worksheet on page 596	**47**			
⟨590⟩	48	Child tax credit (see page 593)	**48**		⟨593⟩	
	49	Adoption credit. Attach Form 8839	**49**	⟨594⟩		
	50	Other credits from: **a** ☐ Form 3800 **b** ☐ Form 8396 **c** ☐ Form 8801 **d** ☐ Form (specify) _____	**50**	⟨594⟩		

	51	Add lines 43 through 50. These are your **total credits**	**51**	
	52	Subtract line 51 from line 42. If line 51 is more than line 42, enter -0-	**52**	
Other Taxes	53	Self-employment tax. Attach Schedule SE	**53**	
	54	Social security and Medicare tax on tip income not reported to employer. Attach Form 4137 . .	**54**	⟨594⟩
	55	Tax on qualified plans, including IRAs, and other tax-favored accounts. Attach Form 5329 if required . .	**55**	⟨595⟩
	56	Advance earned income credit payments from Form(s) W-2	**56**	⟨595⟩
	57	Household employment taxes. Attach Schedule H	**57**	⟨596⟩
	58	Add lines 52 through 57. This is your **total tax**	**58**	⟨596⟩

Payments	59	Federal income tax withheld from Forms W-2 and 1099 . .	**59**	⟨597⟩	
	60	2001 estimated tax payments and amount applied from 2000 return .	**60**		⟨597⟩
If you have a qualifying child, attach Schedule EIC.	61a	**Earned income credit (EIC)**	**61a**	⟨597⟩	
	b	Nontaxable earned income . . . **61b** ⟨598⟩			
	62	Excess social security and RRTA tax withheld (see page 597)	**62**		⟨597⟩
	63	Additional child tax credit. Attach Form 8812	**63**	⟨609⟩	
	64	Amount paid with request for extension to file (see page 609)	**64**		⟨609⟩
	65	Other payments. Check if from **a** ☐ Form 2439 **b** ☐ Form 4136	**65**	⟨609⟩	
	66	Add lines 59, 60, 61a, and 62 through 65. These are your **total payments**	**66**		

Refund	67	If line 66 is more than line 58, subtract line 58 from line 66. This is the amount you **overpaid**	**67**	⟨609⟩
Direct deposit? See page 609 and fill in 68b, 68c, and 68d.	68a	Amount of line 67 you want **refunded to you** . . . ⟨609⟩	**68a**	
	b	Routing number ☐☐☐☐☐☐☐☐☐ **c** Type ☐ Checking ☐ Savings		
	d	Account number ☐☐☐☐☐☐☐☐☐☐☐☐☐☐☐☐☐		
	69	Amount of line 67 you want **applied to your 2002 estimated tax** **69** ⟨609⟩		
Amount You Owe	70	**Amount you owe.** Subtract line 66 from line 58. For details on how to pay, see page 610	**70**	⟨610⟩
	71	Estimated tax penalty. Also include on line 70 . . . . . **71** ⟨610⟩		

Third Party Designee

Do you want to allow another person to discuss this return with the IRS (see page 610)? ☐ **Yes.** Complete the following. ☐ **No**

Designee's name	Phone no. ( )	Personal identification number (PIN) ☐☐☐☐☐

Sign Here

Joint return? See page 575.

Keep a copy for your records.

Under penalties of perjury, I declare that I have examined this return and accompanying schedules and statements, and to the best of my knowledge and belief, they are true, correct, and complete. Declaration of preparer (other than taxpayer) is based on all information of which preparer has any knowledge.

Your signature ⟨611⟩	Date	Your occupation	Daytime phone number ( ) ⟨611⟩
Spouse's signature. If a joint return, **both** must sign.	Date	Spouse's occupation	

Paid Preparer's Use Only

Preparer's signature ⟨611⟩	Date	Check if self-employed ☐	Preparer's SSN or PTIN
Firm's name (or yours if self-employed), address, and ZIP code		EIN	
		Phone no. ( )	

Form **1040** (2001)

Where To Report Certain Items From 2001 Forms W-2, 1098, and 1099

Report on Form 1040, line 59, any amounts shown on these forms as **Federal income tax withheld.** If you itemize your deductions, report on Schedule A, line 5, any amounts shown on these forms as **state or local income tax withheld.**

Form	Item and Box in Which it Should Appear	Where To Report if Filing Form 1040
W-2	Wages, salaries, tips, etc. (box 1)	Form 1040, line 7
	Allocated tips (box 8)	See **Tip income** on page 581
	Advance EIC payment (box 9)	Form 1040, line 56
	Dependent care benefits (box 10)	Form 2441, line 10
	Adoption benefits (box 12, code **T**)	Form 8839, line 18
	Employer contributions to an MSA (box 12, code **R**)*	Form 8853, line 3b
W-2G	Gambling winnings (box 1)	Form 1040, line 21 (Schedule C or C-EZ for professional gamblers)
1098	Mortgage interest (box 1)	Schedule A, line 10**
	Points (box 2)	
	Refund of overpaid interest (box 3)	Form 1040, line 21, but first see the instructions on Form 1098**
1098-E	Student loan interest (box 1)	See the instructions for Form 1040, line 24**
1099-A	Acquisition or abandonment of secured property	See Pub. 544
1099-B	Stocks, bonds, etc. (box 2)	Schedule D
	Bartering (box 3)	See Pub. 525
	Aggregate profit or (loss) on futures contracts (box 9)	Form 6781
1099-C	Canceled debt (box 2)	Form 1040, line 21, but first see the instructions on Form 1099-C**
1099-DIV	Ordinary dividends (box 1)	Form 1040, line 9
	Total capital gain distributions (box 2a)	Form 1040, line 13, or, if required, Schedule D, line 13, column (f)
	28% rate gain (box 2b)	Schedule D, line 13, column (g)
	Qualified 5-year gain (box 2c)	See the worksheet for Schedule D, line 29
	Unrecaptured section 1250 gain (box 2d)	See the worksheet for Schedule D, line 19
	Section 1202 gain (box 2e)	See the instructions for Schedule D
	Nontaxable distributions (box 3)	See the instructions for Form 1040, line 9
	Investment expenses (box 5)	Schedule A, line 22
	Foreign tax paid (box 6)	Form 1040, line 43, or Schedule A, line 8
1099-G	Unemployment compensation (box 1)	Form 1040, line 19. But if you repaid any unemployment compensation in 2001, see the instructions for line 19
	State or local income tax refunds (box 2)	See the instructions for Form 1040, line 10**
	Qualified state tuition program earnings (box 5)	Form 1040, line 21
	Taxable grants (box 6)	Form 1040, line 21**
	Agriculture payments (box 7)	See the Schedule F instructions or Pub. 225

* *MSAs were renamed Archer MSAs after Form W-2 was released for print.*
** *If the item relates to an activity for which you are required to file Schedule C, C-EZ, E, or F or Form 4835, report the taxable or deductible amount allocable to the activity on that schedule or form instead.*

Form	Item and Box in Which it Should Appear	Where To Report if Filing Form 1040
1099-INT	Interest income (box 1)	Form 1040, line 8a
	Early withdrawal penalty (box 2)	Form 1040, line 30
	Interest on U.S. savings bonds and Treasury obligations (box 3)	See the instructions for Form 1040, line 8a
	Investment expenses (box 5)	Schedule A, line 22
	Foreign tax paid (box 6)	Form 1040, line 43, or Schedule A, line 8
1099-LTC	Long-term care and accelerated death benefits	See Pub. 502 and the instructions for Form 8853
1099-MISC	Rents (box 1)	See the instructions for Schedule E
	Royalties (box 2)	Schedule E, line 4 (timber, coal, iron ore royalties, see Pub. 544)
	Other income (box 3)	Form 1040, line 21*
	Nonemployee compensation (box 7)	Schedule C, C-EZ, or F. But if you were not self-employed, see the instructions on Form 1099-MISC.
	Other (boxes 5, 6, 8, 9, 10, 13, and 14)	See the instructions on Form 1099-MISC
1099-MSA	Distributions from MSAs**	Form 8853
1099-OID	Original issue discount (box 1)	See the instructions on Form 1099-OID
	Other periodic interest (box 2)	
	Early withdrawal penalty (box 3)	Form 1040, line 30
1099-PATR	Patronage dividends and other distributions from a cooperative (boxes 1, 2, 3, and 5)	Schedule C, C-EZ, or F or Form 4835, but first see the instructions on Form 1099-PATR
	Credits (boxes 7 and 8)	Form 3468 or Form 5884
	Patron's AMT adjustment (box 9)	Form 6251, line 14j
1099-R	Distributions from IRAs***	See the instructions for Form 1040, lines 15a and 15b
	Distributions from pensions, annuities, etc.	See the instructions for Form 1040, lines 16a and 16b
	Capital gain (box 3)	See the instructions on Form 1099-R
1099-S	Gross proceeds from real estate transactions (box 2)	Form 4797, Form 6252, or Schedule D. But if the property was your home, see the instructions for Schedule D to find out if you must report the sale or exchange.
	Buyer's part of real estate tax (box 5)	See the instructions for Schedule A, line 6*

* If the item relates to an activity for which you are required to file Schedule C, C-EZ, E, or F or Form 4835, report the taxable or deductible amount allocable to the activity on that schedule or form instead.

** This includes distributions from Archer and Medicare+Choice MSAs.

*** This includes distributions from Roth, SEP, and SIMPLE IRAs; and Coverdell education savings accounts (ESAs).

an ITIN, file **Form W-7** with the IRS. It usually takes about 4–6 weeks to get an ITIN. **Enter your ITIN wherever your SSN is requested on your tax return.**

Note. An ITIN is for tax use only. It does not entitle you to social security benefits or change your employment or immigration status under U.S. law.

Nonresident Alien Spouse

If your spouse is a nonresident alien and you file a joint or separate return, your spouse must have either an SSN or an ITIN.

Presidential Election Campaign Fund

This fund helps pay for Presidential election campaigns. The fund reduces candidates' dependence on large contributions from individuals and groups and places candidates on an equal financial footing in the general election. If you want $3 to go to this fund, check the "Yes" box. If you are filing a joint return, your spouse may also have $3 go to the fund. If you check "Yes," your tax or refund will not change.

Filing Status

Check **only** the filing status that applies to you. The ones that will usually give you the lowest tax are listed last.

- Married filing separately.
- Single.
- **Head of household.** This status is for unmarried people who paid over half the cost of keeping up a home for a qualifying person, such as a child who lived with you or your dependent parent. Certain married people who lived apart from their spouse for the last 6 months of 2001 may also be able to use this status.
- Married filing jointly or Qualifying widow(er) with dependent child. The **Qualifying widow(er)** status is for certain people whose spouse died in 1999 or 2000 and who had a child living with them whom they can claim as a dependent.

Joint and Several Tax Liability. If you file a joint return, both you and your spouse are generally responsible for the tax and any interest or penalties due on the return. This means that if one spouse does not pay the tax due, the other may have to.

Tip. More than one filing status may apply to you. Choose the one that will give you the lowest tax. If you are not sure about your filing status, use TeleTax topic 353 or see **Pub. 501.**

Exemptions

You usually can deduct $2,900 on line 38 for each exemption you can take.

Line 6b Spouse

Check the box on line 6b if you file either **(a)** a joint return or **(b)** a separate return and your spouse had no income and is not filing a return. However, **do not** check the box if your spouse can be claimed as a dependent on another person's return.

Line 6c Dependents

You can take an exemption for each of your dependents. The following is a brief description of the five tests that must be met for a person to qualify as your dependent. If you have **more than six** dependents, attach a statement to your return with the required information.

Relationship Test. The person must be either your relative or have lived in your home as a family member all year. If the person is not your relative, the relationship must not violate local law.

Joint Return Test. If the person is married, he or she cannot file a joint return. But the person can file a joint return if the return is filed only as a claim for refund **and** no tax liability would exist for either spouse if they had filed separate returns.

Citizen or Resident Test. The person must be a U.S. citizen or resident alien, or a resident of Canada or Mexico. There is an exception for certain adopted children. To find out who is a **resident alien,** use TeleTax topic 851 or see **Pub. 519.**

Income Test. The person's gross income must be less than $2,900. But your child's gross income can be $2,900 or more if he or she was either **(a) under age 19** at the end of 2001 or **(b) under age 24** at the end of 2001 and was a **student.**

Support Test. You must have provided over half of the person's total support in 2001. But there are two exceptions to this test: One for children of divorced or separated parents and one for persons supported by two or more taxpayers.

Tip. For more details about the tests, including any exceptions that apply, see **Pub. 501.**

Line 6c, Column (2)

You must enter each dependent's social security number (SSN). Be sure the name and SSN entered agree with the dependent's social security card. Otherwise, at the time we process your return, we may disallow the exemption claimed for the dependent and reduce or disallow any other tax benefits (such as the child tax credit and the earned income credit) based on that dependent. If the name or SSN on the dependent's social security card is not correct, call the Social Security Administration at 1-800-772-1213.

Tip. For details on how your dependent can get an SSN, see page 575. If your dependent will not have a number by April 15, 2002, see **What if You Cannot File on Time?**

If your dependent child was born and died in 2001 and you do not have an SSN for the child, you may attach a copy of the child's birth certificate instead and enter "Died" in column (2).

Adoption Taxpayer Identification Numbers (ATINs). If you have a dependent who was placed with you by an authorized placement agency and you do not know his or her SSN, you must get an ATIN for the dependent from the IRS. An authorized placement agency includes any person authorized by state law to place children for legal adoption. See **Form W-7A** for details.

Line 6c, Column (4)

Check the box in this column if your dependent is a qualifying child for the child tax credit (defined below). If you have at least one qualifying child, you may be able to take the child tax credit on line 48 and the additional child tax credit on line 63.

Qualifying Child for Child Tax Credit. A qualifying child for purposes of the child tax credit is a child who:

- Is claimed as your dependent on line 6c, **and**
- Was **under age 17** at the end of 2001, **and**
- Is your son, daughter, adopted child, grandchild, stepchild, or foster child, **and**
- Is a U.S. citizen or resident alien.

Note. The above requirements are not the same as the requirements to be a qualifying child for the earned income credit.

A child placed with you by an authorized placement agency for legal adoption is an **adopted child** even if the adoption is not final. An authorized placement agency includes any person authorized by state law to place children for legal adoption.

A **grandchild** is any descendant of your son, daughter, or adopted child and includes your great-grandchild, great-great-grandchild, etc.

A **foster child** is any child you cared for as your own child and who:

- Is **(a)** your brother, sister, stepbrother, or stepsister; **(b)** a descendant (such as a child, including an adopted child) of your brother, sister, stepbrother, or stepsister; **or (c)** a child placed with you by an authorized placement agency **and**
- Lived with you for all of 2001. A child who was born or died in 2001 is considered to have lived with you for all of 2001 if your home was the child's home for the entire time he or she was alive during 2001.

Children Who Did Not Live With You Due to Divorce or Separation

If you are claiming a child who did not live with you under the rules explained in **Pub. 501** for children of divorced or separated parents, attach **Form 8332** or similar statement to your return. But see **Exception** below. If your divorce decree or separation agreement went into effect after 1984 and it states you can claim the child as your dependent without regard to any condition, such as payment of support, you may attach a copy of the following pages from the decree or agreement instead.

- Cover page (put the other parent's SSN on that page),
- The page that states you can claim the child as your dependent, and
- Signature page with the other parent's signature and date of agreement.

Note. You must attach the required information even if you filed it in an earlier year.

Exception. You do not have to attach Form 8332 or similar statement if your divorce decree or written separation agreement went into effect before 1985 and it states that you can claim the child as your dependent.

Other Dependent Children

Include the total number of children who did not live with you for reasons other than divorce or separation on the line labeled "Dependents on 6c not entered above." Include dependent children who lived in Canada or Mexico during 2001.

Income

Foreign-Source Income

You must report unearned income, such as interest, dividends, and pensions, from sources outside the United States unless exempt by law or a tax treaty. You must also report earned income, such as wages and tips, from sources outside the United States.

If you worked abroad, you may be able to exclude part or all of your earned income. For details, see **Pub. 54** and **Form 2555** or **2555-EZ**.

Community Property States

Community property states are Arizona, California, Idaho, Louisiana, Nevada, New Mexico, Texas, Washington, and Wisconsin. If you and your spouse lived in a community property state, you must usually follow state law to determine what is community income and what is separate income. For details, see **Pub. 555**.

Rounding Off to Whole Dollars

To round off cents to the nearest whole dollar on your forms and schedules, drop amounts under 50 cents and increase amounts from 50 to 99 cents to the next dollar. If you do round off, do so for all amounts. But if you have to add two or more amounts to figure the amount to enter on a line, include cents when adding and only round off the total.

Line 7 Wages, Salaries, Tips, etc.

Enter the total of your wages, salaries, tips, etc. If a joint return, also include your spouse's income. For most people, the amount to enter on this line should be shown in box 1 of their **Form(s) W-2.** But the following types of income must also be included in the total on line 7.

- Wages received as a **household employee** for which you did not receive a W-2 form because your employer paid you less than $1,300 in 2001. Also, enter "HSH" and the amount not reported on a W-2 form on the dotted line next to line 7.
- **Tip income** you did not report to your employer. Also include **allocated tips** shown on your W-2 form(s) unless you can prove that you received less. Allocated tips should be shown in box 8 of your W-2 form(s). They are not included as income in box 1. See **Pub. 531** for more details.

Caution. You may owe social security and Medicare tax on unreported or allocated tips. See the instructions for line 54 on page 594.

- **Dependent care benefits,** which should be shown in box 10 of your W-2 form(s). But first complete **Form 2441** to see if you may exclude part or all of the benefits.
- **Employer-provided adoption benefits,** which should be shown in box 12 of your W-2 form(s) with code **T.** But first complete **Form 8839** to see if you may exclude part or all of the benefits.
- **Scholarship and fellowship grants** not reported on a W-2 form. Also, enter "SCH" and the amount on the dotted line next to line 7. **Exception.** If you were a degree candidate, include on line 7 **only** the amounts you used for expenses other than tuition and course-related expenses. For example, amounts used for room, board, and travel must be reported on line 7.
- **Excess salary deferrals.** The amount deferred should be shown in box 12 of your W-2 form and the "Retirement plan" box in box 13 should be checked. If the total amount you (or your spouse if filing jointly) deferred for 2001 under **all** plans was more than $10,500, include the excess on line 7. But a different limit may apply if amounts were deferred under a tax-sheltered annuity plan or an eligible plan of a state or local government or tax-exempt organization. See **Pub. 525** for details.

Caution. You may **not** deduct the amount deferred. It is not included as income in box 1 of your W-2 form.

- **Disability pensions** shown on **Form 1099-R** if you have not reached the minimum retirement age set by your employer. Disability pensions received after you reach that age and other pensions shown on Form 1099-R (other than payments from an IRA* or a Coverdell education savings account (ESA)) are reported on lines 16a and 16b. Payments from an IRA or a Coverdell ESA are reported on lines 15a and 15b.
- **Corrective distributions** shown on **Form 1099-R** of **(a)** excess salary deferrals plus earnings and **(b)** excess contributions plus earnings to a retirement plan. But do not include distributions from an IRA* or a Coverdell ESA on line 7. Instead, report them on lines 15a and 15b.

Were You a Statutory Employee?

If you were, the "Statutory employee" box in box 13 of your W-2 form should be checked. Statutory employees include full-time life insurance salespeople, certain agent or commission drivers and traveling salespeople, and certain homeworkers. If you have related business expenses to deduct, report the amount shown in box 1 of your W-2 form on **Schedule C** or **C-EZ** along with your expenses.

Missing or Incorrect Form W-2?

If you do not get a W-2 form from your employer by January 31, 2002, use TeleTax topic 154 to find out what to do. Even if you do not get a

*This includes a Roth, SEP, or SIMPLE IRA.

Form W-2, you must still report your earnings on line 7. If you lose your Form W-2 or it is incorrect, ask your employer for a new one.

Line 8a Taxable Interest

Each payer should send you a **Form 1099-INT** or **Form 1099-OID.** Enter your total taxable interest income on line 8a. But you must fill in and attach **Schedule B** if the total is over $400 or any of the other conditions listed at the beginning of the Schedule B instructions apply to you.

Interest credited in 2001 on deposits that you could not withdraw because of the bankruptcy or insolvency of the financial institution may not have to be included in your 2001 income. For details, see **Pub. 550.**
Tip. If you get a 2001 Form 1099-INT for U.S. savings bond interest that includes amounts you reported before 2001, see Pub. 550.

Line 8b Tax-Exempt Interest

If you received any tax-exempt interest, such as from municipal bonds, report it on line 8b. Include any exempt-interest dividends from a mutual fund or other regulated investment company. **Do not** include interest earned on your IRA or Coverdell education savings account.

Line 9 Ordinary Dividends

Each payer should send you a **Form 1099-DIV.** Enter your total ordinary dividends on line 9. But you must fill in and attach **Schedule B** if the total is over $400 or you received, as a nominee, ordinary dividends that actually belong to someone else.
Capital Gain Distributions If you received any capital gain distributions, see the instructions for line 13.

Nontaxable Distributions

Some distributions are nontaxable because they are a return of your cost (or other basis). They will not be taxed until you recover your cost (or other basis). You must reduce your cost (or other basis) by these distributions. After you get back all of your cost (or other basis), you must report these distributions as capital gains on **Schedule D.** For details, see **Pub. 550.**
Tip. Dividends on insurance policies are a partial return of the premiums you paid. **Do not** report them as dividends. Include them in income only if they exceed the total of all net premiums you paid for the contract.

Line 10 Taxable Refunds, Credits, or Offsets of State and Local Income Taxes

Tip. None of your refund is taxable if, in the year you paid the tax, you **did not** itemize deductions.

If you received a refund, credit, or offset of state or local income taxes in 2001, you may receive a **Form 1099-G.** If you chose to apply part or all of the refund to your 2001 estimated state or local income tax, the amount applied is treated as received in 2001. If the refund was for a tax you paid in 2000 and you itemized deductions for 2000, use the worksheet below to see if any of your refund is taxable.
Exception. See **Recoveries** in **Pub. 525** instead of using the worksheet below if **any** of the following apply.

- You received a refund in 2001 that is for a tax year other than 2000.
- You received a refund other than an income tax refund, such as a real property tax refund, in 2001 of an amount deducted or credit claimed in an earlier year.

State and Local Income Tax Refund Worksheet—Line 10   *Keep for Your Records*

1. Enter the income tax refund from **Form(s) 1099-G** (or similar statement). But **do not** enter more than the amount on your 2000 Schedule A (Form 1040), line 5 . . . . **1.** _____

2. Enter your total allowable itemized deductions from your 2000 Schedule A (Form 1040), line 28 . . . . **2.** _____

   Note. If the filing status on your 2000 Form 1040 was married filing separately and your spouse itemized deductions in 2000, skip lines 3, 4, and 5, and enter the amount from line 2 on line 6.

3. Enter the amount shown below for the filing status claimed on your **2000** Form 1040.
   - Single—$4,400
   - Married filing jointly or qualifying widow(er)—$7,350 } . . . **3.** _____
   - Married filing separately—$3,675
   - Head of household—$6,450

4. Did you fill in line 35a on your 2000 Form 1040?
   ☐ **No.** Enter -0-.
   ☐ **Yes.** Multiply the number on line 35a of your 2000 Form 1040 by: $850 if your 2000 filing status was married filing jointly or separately or qualifying widow(er); $1,100 if your 2000 filing status was single or head of household } **4.** _____

5. Add lines 3 and 4 . . . . **5.** _____

6. Is the amount on line 5 less than the amount on line 2?
   ☐ **No.** (STOP) None of your refund is taxable.
   ☐ **Yes.** Subtract line 5 from line 2 . . . . **6.** _____

7. **Taxable part of your refund.** Enter the **smaller** of line 1 or line 6 here and on Form 1040, line 10 . . . . **7.** _____

- Your 2000 taxable income was less than zero.
- You made your last payment of 2000 estimated state or local income tax in 2001.
- You owed alternative minimum tax in 2000.
- You could not deduct the full amount of credits you were entitled to in 2000 because the total credits exceeded the amount shown on your 2000 Form 1040, line 42, minus any foreign tax credit shown on line 43 of that form.
- You could be claimed as a dependent by someone else in 2000.

Also, see **Tax Benefit Rule** in Pub. 525 instead of using the worksheet below if **all three** of the following apply.

1. You had to use the Itemized Deductions Worksheet in the 2000 Schedule A instructions because your 2000 adjusted gross income was over: $128,950 if single, married filing jointly, head of household, or qualifying widow(er); $64,475 if married filing separately.
2. You could not deduct all of the amount on line 1 of the 2000 Itemized Deductions Worksheet.
3. The amount on line 8 of that 2000 worksheet would be more than the amount on line 4 of that worksheet if the amount on line 4 were reduced by 80% of the refund you received in 2001.

Line 11 Alimony Received

Enter amounts received as alimony or separate maintenance. You must let the person who made the payments know your social security number. If you do not, you may have to pay a $50 penalty. For more details, use TeleTax topic 406 (see page 11) or see **Pub. 504.**

Line 12 Business Income or (Loss)

If you operated a business or practiced your profession as a sole proprietor, report your income and expenses on **Schedule C or C-EZ.**

Line 13 Capital Gain or (Loss)

If you had a capital gain or loss, including any **capital gain distributions** from a mutual fund, you **must** complete and attach **Schedule D.**
Exception. You do not have to file Schedule D if **all three** of the following apply.

1. The only amounts you have to report on Schedule D are capital gain distributions from box 2a of **Forms 1099-DIV** or substitute statements.
2. None of the Forms 1099-DIV or substitute statements have an amount in box 2b (28% rate gain), box 2c (qualified 5-year gain), box 2d (unrecaptured section 1250 gain), or box 2e (section 1202 gain).
3. You are not filing **Form 4952** (relating to investment interest expense deduction) **or** the amount on line 4e of that form is zero or blank.

If all three of the above apply, enter your capital gain distributions on line 13 and check the box on that line. Also, be sure you use the **Capital Gain Tax Worksheet** on page 594 to figure your tax.

Line 14 Other Gains or (Losses)

If you sold or exchanged assets used in a trade or business, see the Instructions for **Form 4797.**

Lines 15a and 15b IRA Distributions

Note. If you converted part or all of an individual retirement arrangement (IRA) to a Roth IRA in 1998 and you chose to report the taxable amount over 4 years, see **1998 Roth IRA Conversions** on this page.
You should receive a **Form 1099-R** showing the amount of any distribution from your IRA or Coverdell education savings account (ESA).

Unless otherwise noted in the line 15a and 15b instructions, an IRA includes a traditional IRA, Roth IRA, simplified employee pension (SEP) IRA, and a savings incentive match plan for employees (SIMPLE) IRA. Except as provided below, leave line 15a blank and enter the total distribution on line 15b.
Exception 1. Enter the total distribution on line 15a if you rolled over part or all of the distribution from one:

- IRA to another IRA of the same type (for example, from one traditional IRA to another traditional IRA),
- Coverdell ESA to another, or
- SEP or SIMPLE IRA to a traditional IRA.

Also, put "Rollover" next to line 15b. If the total distribution was rolled over, enter zero on line 15b. If the total was not rolled over, enter the part not rolled over on line 15b unless **Exception 2** applies to the part not rolled over.
If you rolled over the distribution **(a)** in 2002 or **(b)** from a conduit IRA into a qualified plan, attach a statement explaining what you did.
Exception 2. If **any** of the following apply, enter the total distribution on line 15a and use **Form 8606** and its instructions to figure the amount to enter on line 15b.

- You received a distribution from an IRA (other than a Roth IRA) and you made nondeductible contributions to any of your traditional or SEP IRAs for 2001 or an earlier year. If you made nondeductible contributions to these IRAs for 2001, also see **Pub. 590.**
- You received a distribution from a Roth IRA or Coverdell ESA.
- You converted part or all of a traditional, SEP, or SIMPLE IRA to a Roth IRA in 2001.
- You had a 2000 or 2001 IRA or Coverdell ESA contribution returned to you, with the related earnings or less any loss, by the due date (including extensions) of your tax return for that year.
- You made excess contributions to your IRA for an earlier year and had them returned to you in 2001.
- You recharacterized part or all of a contribution to a Roth IRA as a traditional IRA contribution, or vice versa.

Note. If you received more than one distribution, figure the taxable amount of each distribution and enter the total of the taxable amounts on line 15b. Enter the total amount of those distributions on line 15a.
Caution. You may have to pay an additional tax if **(a)** you received an early distribution from your IRA and the total was not rolled over or **(b)** you were born before July 1, 1930, and received less than the minimum required distribution from your traditional, SEP, and SIMPLE IRAs. See the instructions for line 55 on page 39 for details.
1998 Roth IRA Conversions. If you converted an IRA to a Roth IRA to 1998 and you chose to report the taxable amount over 4 years, leave line 15a blank and enter on line 15b the amount from your **1998 Form 8606,** line 17. But see the 2001 Instructions for Form 8606 for the amount to enter on line 15b if **(a)** you rounded the amount on line 17 of your 1998 Form 8606 to the next higher whole dollar or **(b)** you received a distribution from a Roth IRA in 1998, 1999, or 2000.

Lines 16a and 16b Pensions and Annuities

You should receive a **Form 1099-R** showing the amount of your pension and annuity payments. See page 25 for details on rollovers and lump-sum distributions. **Do not** include the following payments on lines 16a and 16b. Instead, report them on line 7.

- Disability pensions received before you reach the minimum retirement age set by your employer.
- Corrective distributions of excess salary deferrals or excess contributions to retirement plans.

Tip. Attach Form(s) 1099-R to Form 1040 if any Federal income tax was withheld.

Simplified Method Worksheet—Lines 16a and 16b

Keep for Your Records

Before you begin: ✓ If you are the beneficiary of a deceased employee or former employee who died **before** August 21, 1996, see Pub. 939 to find out if you are entitled to a death benefit exclusion of up to $5,000. If you are, include the exclusion in the amount entered on line 2 below.

Note. If you had more than one partially taxable pension or annuity, figure the taxable part of each separately. Enter the total of the taxable parts on Form 1040, line 16b. Enter the total pension or annuity payments received in 2001 on Form 1040, line 16a.

1. Enter the total pension or annuity payments received in 2001. Also, enter this amount on Form 1040, line 16a . . . . **1.** _____

2. Enter your cost in the plan at the annuity starting date . . . . **2.** _____

3. Enter the appropriate number from **Table 1** below. **But** if your annuity starting date was **after** 1997 **and** the payments are for your life and that of your beneficiary, enter the appropriate number from **Table 2** below . . . . **3.** _____

4. Divide line 2 by the number on line 3 . . . . **4.** _____

5. Multiply line 4 by the number of months for which this year's payments were made. If your annuity starting date was **before** 1987, skip lines 6 and 7 and enter this amount on line 8. Otherwise, go to line 6 . . . . **5.** _____

6. Enter the amount, if any, recovered tax free in years after 1986 . . . . . . **6.** _____

7. Subtract line 6 from line 2 . . . . **7.** _____

8. Enter the **smaller** of line 5 or line 7 . . . . **8.** _____

9. **Taxable amount.** Subtract line 8 from line 1. Enter the result, but not less than zero. Also, enter this amount on Form 1040, line 16b. If your Form 1099-R shows a larger amount, use the amount on this line instead of the amount from Form 1099-R . . . . **9.** _____

Table 1 for Line 3 Above

IF the age at annuity starting date (see page 25) was . . .	AND your annuity starting date was—	
	before November 19, 1996, enter on line 3 . . .	**after** November 18, 1996, enter on line 3 . . .
55 or under	300	360
56–60	260	310
61–65	240	260
66–70	170	210
71 or older	120	160

Table 2 for Line 3 Above

IF the combined ages at annuity starting date (see page 25) were . . .	THEN enter on line 3 . . .
110 or under	410
111–120	360
121–130	310
131–140	260
141 or older	210

Fully Taxable Pensions and Annuities

If your pension or annuity is fully taxable, enter it on line 16b; **do not** make an entry on line 16a. Your payments are fully taxable if **either** of the following applies.

- You did not contribute to the cost of your pension or annuity **or**
- You got your entire cost back tax free before 2001.

Fully taxable pensions and annuities also include military retirement pay shown on Form 1099-R. For details on military disability pensions, see **Pub. 525.** If you received a **Form RRB-1099-R,** see **Pub. 575** to find out how to report your benefits.

Partially Taxable Pensions and Annuities

Enter the total pension or annuity payments you received in 2001 on line 16a. If your Form 1099-R does not show the taxable amount, you must use the General Rule explained in **Pub. 939** to figure the taxable part to enter on line 16b. But if your annuity starting date (defined on page 25) was **after** July 1, 1986, see page 585 to find out if you must use the Simplified Method to figure the taxable part.

You can ask the IRS to figure the taxable part for you for an $85 fee. For details, see Pub. 939.

If your Form 1099-R shows a taxable amount, you may report that amount on line 16b. But you may be able to report a lower taxable amount by using the General Rule or the Simplified Method.

Annuity Starting Date

Your annuity starting date is the later of the first day of the first period for which you received a payment, or the date the plan's obligations became fixed.

Simplified Method

You **must** use the Simplified Method if **(a)** your annuity starting date (defined above) was **after** July 1, 1986, and you used this method last year to figure the taxable part or **(b)** your annuity starting date was **after** November 18, 1996, and **all three** of the following apply.

1. The payments are for **(a)** your life or **(b)** your life and that of your beneficiary.
2. The payments are from a qualified employee plan, a qualified employee annuity, or a tax-sheltered annuity.
3. On your annuity starting date, either you were under age 75 or the number of years of guaranteed payments was fewer than 5. See Pub. 575 for the definition of guaranteed payments.

If you must use the Simplified Method, complete the worksheet on page 584 to figure the taxable part of your pension or annuity. For more details on the Simplified Method, see Pub. 575 or **Pub. 721** for U.S. Civil Service retirement.
Caution. If you received U.S. Civil Service retirement benefits and you chose the alternative annuity option, use the worksheet in Pub. 721. **Do not** use the worksheet on page 584.

Age (or Combined Ages) at Annuity Starting Date

If you are the retiree, use your age on the annuity starting date. If you are the survivor of a retiree, use the retiree's age on his or her annuity starting date. **But** if your annuity starting date was after 1997 and the payments are for your life and that of your beneficiary, use your combined ages on the annuity starting date.

If you are the beneficiary of an employee who died, see Pub. 575. If there is more than one beneficiary, see Pub. 575 or Pub. 721 to figure each beneficiary's taxable amount.

Cost

Your cost is generally your net investment in the plan as of the annuity starting date. It does not include pre-tax contributions. Your net investment should be shown in box 9b of Form 1099-R for the first year you received payments from the plan.

Rollovers

A rollover is a tax-free distribution of cash or other assets from one retirement plan that is contributed to another plan. Use lines 16a and 16b to report a rollover, including a direct rollover, from one qualified employer's plan to another or to an IRA or SEP.

Enter on line 16a the total distribution before income tax or other deductions were withheld. This amount should be shown in box 1 of **Form 1099-R.** From the total on line 16a, subtract any contributions (usually shown in box 5) that were taxable to you when made. From that result, subtract the amount that was rolled over either directly or within 60 days of receiving the distribution. Enter the remaining amount, even if zero, on line 16b. Also, put "Rollover" next to line 16b.

Special rules apply to partial rollovers of property. For more details on rollovers, including distributions under qualified domestic relations orders, see Pub. 575.

Lump-Sum Distributions

If you received a lump-sum distribution from a profit-sharing or retirement plan, your Form 1099-R should have the "Total distribution" box in box 2b checked. You may owe an additional tax if you received an early distribution from a qualified retirement plan and the total amount was not rolled over. For details, see the instructions for line 55.

Enter the total distribution on line 16a and the taxable part on line 16b.
Tip. You may be able to pay less tax on the distribution if you were born before 1936, you meet certain other conditions, and you choose to use **Form 4972** to figure the tax on any part of the distribution. You may also be able to use Form 4972 if you are the beneficiary of a deceased employee who was born before 1936. For details, see Form 4972.

Line 19 Unemployment Compensation

You should receive a **Form 1099-G** showing the total unemployment compensation paid to you in 2001.

If you received an overpayment of unemployment compensation in 2001 and you repaid any of it in 2001, subtract the amount you repaid from the total amount you received. Enter the result on line 19. Also, enter "Repaid" and the amount you repaid on the dotted line next to line 19. If, in 2001, you repaid unemployment compensation that you included in gross income in an earlier year, you may deduct the amount repaid on **Schedule A,** line 22. But if you repaid more than $3,000, see **Repayments** in Pub. 525 for details on how to report the repayment.

Lines 20a and 20b Social Security Benefits

You should receive a **Form SSA-1099** showing in box 3 the total social security benefits paid to you. Box 4 will show the amount of any benefits you repaid in 2001. If you received railroad retirement benefits treated as social security, you should receive a **Form RRB-1099.**

Use the worksheet on page 586 to see if any of your benefits are taxable.
Exception. Do not use the worksheet on page 586 if **any** of the following apply.

- You made contributions to a traditional IRA for 2001 and you were covered by a retirement plan at work or through self-employment. Instead, use the worksheets in **Pub. 590** to see if any of your social security benefits are taxable and to figure your IRA deduction.
- You repaid any benefits in 2001 and your total repayments (box 4) were more than your total benefits for 2001 (box 3). **None** of your benefits are taxable for 2001. In addition, you may be able to take an itemized deduction for part of the excess repayments if they were for benefits you included in gross income in an earlier year. For more details, see **Pub. 915.**
- You file **Form 2555, 2555-EZ, 4563,** or **8815,** or you exclude employer-provided adoption benefits or income from sources within Puerto Rico. Instead, use the worksheet in Pub. 915.

Line 21 Other Income

Caution. Do not report on this line any income from **self-employment** or fees received as a notary public. Instead, you **must** use **Schedule C, C-EZ,** or **F,** even if you do not have any business expenses. Also, **do not** report on line 21 any nonemployee compensation shown on **Form 1099-MISC.** Instead, see the chart on page 18 to find out where to report that income.

Use line 21 to report any other income not reported on your return or other schedules. See examples below. List the type and amount of income. If necessary, show the required information on an attached statement. For more details, see **Miscellaneous Taxable Income** in **Pub. 525.**

Social Security Benefits Worksheet—Lines 20a and 20b

Keep for Your Records

Before you begin:
- √ Complete Form 1040, lines 21, 23, and 25 through 31a, if they apply to you.
- √ Figure any amount to be entered on the dotted line next to line 32.
- √ If you are married filing separately and you **lived apart** from your spouse for all of 2001, enter "D" to the right of the word "benefits" on line 20a.
- √ Be sure you have read the **Exception** on page 585 to see if you can use this worksheet instead of a publication to find out if any of your benefits are taxable.

1. Enter the total amount from **box 5** of **all** your **Forms SSA-1099** and **RRB-1099** . . . . **1.** _____

2. Is the amount on line 1 more than zero?

   ☐ **No.** (STOP) None of your social security benefits are taxable.

   ☐ **Yes.** Enter one-half of line 1 . . . . **2.** _____

3. Add the amounts on Form 1040, lines 7, 8a, 9 through 14, 15b, 16b, 17 through 19, and 21. Do not include amounts from box 5 of Forms SSA-1099 or RRB-1099 . . . . . . **3.** _____

4. Enter the amount, if any, from Form 1040, line 8b . . . . **4.** _____

5. Add lines 2, 3, and 4 . . . . **5.** _____

6. Add the amounts on Form 1040, lines 23, and 25 through 31a, and any amount you entered on the dotted line next to line 32 . . . . **6.** _____

7. Subtract line 6 from line 5. If zero or less, **stop here.** None of your social security benefits are taxable . . . . **7.** _____

8. Enter: $25,000 if single, head of household, qualifying widow(er), or married filing separately and you **lived apart** from your spouse for all of 2001; $32,000 if married filing jointly; -0- if married filing separately and you lived with your spouse at any time in 2001. . . . . **8.** _____

9. Is the amount on line 8 less than the amount on line 7?

   ☐ **No.** (STOP) None of your social security benefits are taxable. You do not have to enter any amounts on lines 20a or 20b of Form 1040. **But** if you are married filing separately and you **lived apart** from your spouse for all of 2001, enter -0- on line 20b. Be sure you entered "D" to the right of the word "benefits" on line 20a.

   ☐ **Yes.** Subtract line 8 from line 7 . . . . **9.** _____

10. Enter: $9,000 if single, head of household, qualifying widow(er), or married filing separately and you **lived apart** from your spouse for all of 2001; $12,000 if married filing jointly; -0- if married filing separately and you lived with your spouse at any time in 2001. . . . . **10.** _____

11. Subtract line 10 from line 9. If zero or less, enter -0- . . . . **11.** _____

12. Enter the **smaller** of line 9 or line 10. . . . . **12.** _____

13. Enter one-half of line 12 . . . . **13.** _____

14. Enter the **smaller** of line 2 or line 13. . . . . **14.** _____

15. Multiply line 11 by 85% (.85). If line 11 is zero, enter -0- . . . . **15.** _____

16. Add lines 14 and 15 . . . . **16.** _____

17. Multiply line 1 by 85% (.85). . . . . **17.** _____

18. **Taxable social security benefits.** Enter the **smaller** of line 16 or line 17 . . . . **18.** _____

   - Enter the amount from line 1 above on Form 1040, line 20a.
   - Enter the amount from line 18 above on Form 1040, line 20b.

(TIP) If part of your benefits are taxable for 2001 **and** they include benefits paid in 2001 that were for an earlier year, you may be able to reduce the taxable amount. See Pub. 915 for details.

Tip. Do not report any nontaxable income on line 21, such as an advance payment of your 2001 taxes; child support; money or property that was inherited, willed to you, or received as a gift; or life insurance proceeds received because of a person's death.

Examples of **income to report** on line 21 are:

- Prizes and awards.
- Gambling winnings, including lotteries, raffles, a lump-sum payment

from the sale of a right to receive future lottery payments, etc. For details on gambling losses, see the instructions for **Schedule A**, line 27, on page A-6.

- Jury duty fees. Also, see the instructions for line 32.
- Alaska Permanent Fund dividends.
- Qualified state tuition program earnings.
- Reimbursements or other amounts received for items deducted in an earlier year, such as medical expenses, real estate taxes, or home mort-

gage interest. See **Recoveries** in Pub. 525 for details on how to figure the amount to report.
- Income from the rental of personal property if you engaged in the rental for profit but were not in the business of renting such property. Also, see the instructions for line 32.
- Income from an activity not engaged in for profit. See **Pub. 535.**
- Loss on certain corrective distributions of excess deferrals. See Pub. 525.

Adjusted Gross Income

Line 23 IRA Deduction

Tip. If you made any nondeductible contributions to a traditional individual retirement arrangement (IRA) for 2001, you **must** report them on **Form 8606.**

If you made contributions to a traditional IRA for 2001, you may be able to take an IRA deduction. But you, or your spouse if filing a joint return, must have had earned income to do so. For IRA purposes, earned income includes certain alimony received. See **Pub. 590** for details. You should receive a statement by May 31, 2002, that shows all contributions to your traditional IRA for 2001.

Use the worksheet on page 587 to figure the amount, if any, of your IRA deduction. **But read the following list before you fill in the worksheet.**

- If you were age 70 1/2 or older at the end of 2001, you **cannot** deduct any contributions made to your traditional IRA for 2001 or treat them as nondeductible contributions.
- You **cannot** deduct contributions to a Roth IRA or a Coverdell education savings account.

IRA Deduction Worksheet—Line 23   *Keep for Your Records*

Before you begin:
- ✓ Complete Form 1040, lines 25 through 31a, if they apply to you.
- ✓ Figure any amount to be entered on the dotted line next to line 32 (see page 590).
- ✓ Be sure you have read the list above.

		Your IRA	Spouse's IRA
1a.	Were you covered by a retirement plan (see page 588)?	1a. ☐ Yes ☐ No	
1b.	If married filing jointly, was your spouse covered by a retirement plan?		1b. ☐ Yes ☐ No

Next. If you checked "No" on line 1a, and, if married filing jointly, "No" on line 1b, skip lines 2–6, enter $2,000 on line 7a (and 7b if applicable), and go to line 8. Otherwise, go to line 2.

2. Enter the amount shown below that applies to you.
   - Single, head of household, or married filing separately and you **lived apart** from your spouse for all of 2001, enter $43,000
   - Qualifying widow(er), enter $63,000
   - Married filing jointly, enter $63,000 in both columns. But if you checked "No" on either line 1a or 1b, enter $160,000 for the person who was not covered by a plan
   - Married filing separately and you lived with your spouse at any time in 2001, enter $10,000   **2a.** _____   **2b.** _____

3. Enter the amount from Form 1040, line 22 . . . . . . **3.** _____
4. Add amounts on Form 1040, lines 25 through 31a, and any amount you entered on the dotted line next to line 32 . . . **4.** _____
5. Subtract line 4 from line 3. Enter the result in both columns . . . **5a.** _____   **5b.** _____
6. Is the amount on line 5 less than the amount on line 2?

   ☐ **No.** (STOP) None of your IRA contributions are deductible. For details on nondeductible IRA contributions, see Form 8606.

   ☐ **Yes.** Subtract line 5 from line 2 in each column. **If the result is $10,000 or more, enter $2,000 on line 7 for that column** . . . . **6a.** _____   **6b.** _____

7. Multiply lines 6a and 6b by 20% (.20). If the result is not a multiple of $10, increase it to the next multiple of $10 (for example, increase $490.30 to $500). If the result is $200 or more, enter the result. But if it is less than $200, enter $200 . . . **7a.** _____   **7b.** _____

8. Enter your wages, and your spouse's if filing jointly, and other earned income from Form 1040, minus any deductions on Form 1040, lines 27 and 29. Do not reduce wages by any loss from self-employment . . . . **8.** _____

⚠ CAUTION If married filing jointly and line 8 is less than $4,000, **stop here** and see Pub. 590 to figure your IRA deduction.

9. Enter traditional IRA contributions made, or that will be made by April 15, 2002, for 2001 to your IRA on line 9a and to your spouse's IRA on line 9b . . . . **9a.** _____   **9b.** _____
10. On line 10a, enter the **smallest** of line 7a, 8, or 9a. On line 10b, enter the **smallest** of line 7b, 8, or 9b. This is the most you can deduct. Add the amounts on lines 10a and 10b and enter the total on Form 1040, line 23. Or, if you want, you may deduct a smaller amount and treat the rest as a nondeductible contribution (see Form 8606) **10a.** _____   **10b.** _____

Caution. If you made contributions to both a traditional IRA and a Roth IRA for 2001, **do not** use the worksheet on page 28. Instead, use the worksheet in **Pub. 590** to figure the amount, if any, of your IRA deduction.

- You **cannot** deduct contributions to a 401(k) plan, section 457 plan, SIMPLE plan, or the Federal Thrift Savings Plan. These amounts are not included as income in box 1 of your W-2 form.
- If you made contributions to your IRA in 2001 that you deducted for 2000, **do not** include them in the worksheet.
- If you received a distribution from a nonqualified deferred compensation plan or section 457 plan that is included in box 1 of your W-2 form, **do not** include that distribution on line 8 of the worksheet. The distribution should be shown in box 11 of your W-2 form. If it is not, contact your employer for the amount of the distribution.
- You must file a joint return to deduct contributions to your spouse's IRA. Enter the total IRA deduction for you and your spouse on line 23.
- Do not include rollover contributions in figuring your deduction. Instead, see the instructions for lines 15a and 15b on page 23.
- Do not include trustees' fees that were billed separately and paid by you for your IRA. These fees can be deducted only as an itemized deduction on **Schedule A.**
- If the total of your IRA deduction on line 23 plus any nondeductible contribution to your traditional IRAs shown on Form 8606 is less than your total traditional IRA contributions for 2001, see Pub. 590 for special rules.

Tip. By April 1 of the year after the year in which you turn age 70 1/2, you must start taking minimum required distributions from your traditional IRA. If you do not, you may have to pay a 50% additional tax on the amount that should have been distributed. For details, including how to figure the minimum required distribution, see Pub. 590.

Were You Covered by a Retirement Plan?

If you were covered by a retirement plan (qualified pension, profit-sharing (including 401(k)), annuity, SEP, SIMPLE, etc.) at work or through self-employment, your IRA deduction may be reduced or eliminated. But you can still make contributions to an IRA even if you cannot deduct them. In any case, the income earned on your IRA contributions is not taxed until it is paid to you.

The "Retirement plan" box in box 13 of your W-2 form should be checked if you were covered by a plan at work even if you were not vested in the plan. You are also covered by a plan if you were self-employed and had a SEP, SIMPLE, or qualified retirement plan.

If you were covered by a retirement plan and you file **Form 2555, 2555-EZ,** or **8815,** or you exclude employer-provided adoption benefits, see Pub. 590 to figure the amount, if any, of your IRA deduction. **Married Persons Filing Separately.** If you were not covered by a retirement plan but your spouse was, **you** are considered covered by a plan unless you **lived apart** from your spouse for all of 2001.

Line 24 Student Loan Interest Deduction

Use the worksheet on page 589 to figure your student loan interest deduction if **all five** of the following apply.

1. You paid interest in 2001 on a qualified student loan.
2. At least part of the interest paid in 2001 was paid during the first 60 months that interest payments were required to be made. See **Example** on page 29.
3. Your filing status is any status **except** married filing separately.
4. Your modified adjusted gross income (AGI) is less than: $55,000 if single, head of household, or qualifying widow(er); $75,000 if married filing jointly. Use lines 3 through 5 of the worksheet on page 29 to figure your modified AGI.
5. You are not claimed as a dependent on someone's (such as your parent's) 2001 tax return.

Exception. Use **Pub. 970** instead of the worksheet on page 29 to figure your student loan interest deduction if you file **Form 2555, 2555-EZ,** or **4563,** or you exclude income from sources within Puerto Rico. **Example.** You took out a qualified student loan in 1994 while in college. You had 6 years to repay the loan and your first monthly payment was due July 1996, after you graduated. You made a payment every month as required. If you meet items **3** through **5** listed on page 28, you may use only the interest you paid for January through June 2001 to figure your deduction. June is the end of the 60-month period (July 1996–June 2001).

Qualified Student Loan. This is any loan you took out to pay the qualified higher education expenses for yourself, your spouse, or anyone who was your dependent when the loan was taken out. The person for whom the expenses were paid must have been an eligible student (defined on this page). However, a loan is not a qualified student loan if **(a)** any of the proceeds were used for other purposes or **(b)** the loan was from either a related person or a person who borrowed the proceeds under a qualified employer plan or a contract purchased under such a plan. To find out who is a related person, see Pub. 970.

Qualified higher education expenses generally include tuition, fees, room and board, and related expenses such as books and supplies. The expenses must be for education in a degree, certificate, or similar program at an eligible educational institution. An eligible educational institution includes most colleges, universities, and certain vocational schools. You must reduce the expenses by the following nontaxable benefits.

- Employer-provided educational assistance benefits that are not included in box 1 of your W-2 form(s).
- Excludable U.S. series EE and I savings bond interest from **Form 8815.**
- Qualified distributions from a Coverdell education savings account.
- Any scholarship, educational assistance allowance, or other payment (but **not** gifts, inheritances, etc.) excluded from income.

For more details on these expenses, see Pub. 970.
An **eligible student** is a person who:

- Was enrolled in a degree, certificate, or other program (including a program of study abroad that was approved for credit by the institution at which the student was enrolled) leading to a recognized educational credential at an eligible educational institution **and**
- Carried at least half the normal full-time workload for the course of study he or she was pursuing.

Line 25 Archer MSA Deduction

If you made a contribution to an Archer MSA for 2001, you may be able to take this deduction. See **Form 8853.**

Line 26 Moving Expenses

If you moved in connection with your job or business or started a new job, you may be able to take this deduction. But your new workplace must be at least 50 miles farther from your old home than your old home was from your old workplace. If you had no former workplace, your new workplace must be at least 50 miles from your old home. Use TeleTax topic 455 or see **Form 3903.**

Line 27 One-Half of Self-Employment Tax

If you were self-employed and owe self-employment tax, fill in **Schedule SE** to figure the amount of your deduction.

Line 28 Self-Employed Health Insurance Deduction

You may be able to deduct part of the amount paid for health insurance for yourself, your spouse, and dependents if **either** of the following applies.

Student Loan Interest Deduction Worksheet—Line 24

Keep for Your Records

Before you begin:
✓ Complete Form 1040, lines 25 through 31a, if they apply to you.
✓ Figure any amount to be entered on the dotted line next to line 32 (see page 30).
✓ See the instructions for line 24.
✓ Be sure you have read the **Exception** on page 28 to see if you can use this worksheet instead of Pub. 970 to figure your deduction.

1. Enter the total interest you paid in 2001 on qualified student loans (defined above). Do not include interest that was required to be paid after the first 60 months . . . . **1.** _____

2. Enter the **smaller** of line 1 or $2,500 . . . . **2.** _____

3. Enter the amount from Form 1040, line 22 . . . . **3.** _____

4. Enter the total of the amounts from Form 1040, line 23, lines 25 through 31a, plus any amount you entered on the dotted line next to line 32 . . . . **4.** _____

5. Subtract line 4 from line 3 . . . . **5.** _____

6. Enter the amount shown below for your filing status.
   - Single, head of household, or qualifying widow(er)—$40,000 ⎱ . . . **6.** _____
   - Married filing jointly—$60,000 ⎰

7. Is the amount on line 5 more than the amount on line 6?
   ☐ **No.** Skip lines 7 and 8, enter -0- on line 9, and go to line 10.
   ☐ **Yes.** Subtract line 6 from line 5 . . . . **7.** _____

8. Divide line 7 by $15,000. Enter the result as a decimal (rounded to at least three places). Do not enter more than "1.000" . . . . **8.** ___ . _____

9. Multiply line 2 by line 8 . . . . **9.** _____

10. **Student loan interest deduction.** Subtract line 9 from line 2. Enter the result here and on Form 1040, line 24. **Do not** include this amount in figuring any other deduction on your return (such as on Schedule A, C, E, etc.) . . . . **10.** _____

Self-Employed Health Insurance Deduction Worksheet—Line 28

Keep for Your Records

Before you begin:
✓ Complete Form 1040, line 29, if it applies to you.
✓ Be sure you have read the **Exception** above to see if you can use this worksheet instead of Pub. 535 to figure your deduction.

1. Enter the total amount paid in 2001 for health insurance coverage established under your business for 2001 for you, your spouse, and dependents. But do not include amounts for any month you were eligible to participate in an employer-sponsored health plan . . . . **1.** _____

2. Multiply line 1 by 60% (.60) . . . . **2.** _____

3. Enter your net profit and any other earned income* from the business under which the insurance plan is established, minus any deductions you claim on Form 1040, lines 27 and 29 . . . . **3.** _____

4. **Self-employed health insurance deduction.** Enter the **smaller** of line 2 or line 3 here and on Form 1040, line 28. **Do not** include this amount in figuring any medical expense deduction on Schedule A (Form 1040) . . . . **4.** _____

* ***Earned income*** *includes net earnings and gains from the sale, transfer, or licensing of property you created. It does not include capital gain income. If you were a more-than-2% shareholder in the S corporation under which the insurance plan is established, earned income is your wages from that corporation.*

- You were self-employed and had a net profit for the year.
- You received wages in 2001 from an S corporation in which you were a more-than-2% shareholder. Health insurance benefits paid for you may be shown in box 14 of your W-2 form.

The insurance plan must be established under your business. But if you were also eligible to participate in any subsidized health plan maintained by your or your spouse's employer for any month or part of a month in 2001, amounts paid for health insurance coverage for that month cannot be used to figure the deduction. For example, if you were eligible to participate in a subsidized health plan maintained by your spouse's employer from September 30 through December 31, you cannot use amounts paid for health insurance coverage for September through December to figure your deduction. For more details, see **Pub. 535.**

If you qualify to take the deduction, use the worksheet below to figure the amount you can deduct.

Exception. Use Pub. 535 instead of the worksheet below to find out how to figure your deduction if **any** of the following apply.

- You had more than one source of income subject to self-employment tax.

- You file **Form 2555** or **2555-EZ**.
- You are using amounts paid for qualified long-term care insurance to figure the deduction.

Line 29 Self-Employed SEP, SIMPLE, and Qualified Plans

If you were self-employed or a partner, you may be able to take this deduction. See **Pub. 560** or, if you were a minister, **Pub. 517.**

Line 30 Penalty on Early Withdrawal of Savings

The **Form 1099-INT** or **Form 1099-OID** you received will show the amount of any penalty you were charged.

Lines 31a and 31b Alimony Paid

If you made payments to or for your spouse or former spouse under a divorce or separation instrument, you may be able to take this deduction. Use TeleTax topic 452 or see **Pub. 504.**

Line 32

Include in the total on line 32 any of the following adjustments. To find out if you can take the deduction, see the form or publication indicated. On the dotted line next to line 32, enter the amount of your deduction and identify it as indicated.

- Performing-arts-related expenses (see **Form 2106** or **2106-EZ**). Identify as "QPA."
- Jury duty pay given to your employer (see **Pub. 525**). Identify as "Jury Pay."
- Deductible expenses related to income reported on line 21 from the rental of personal property engaged in for profit. Identify as "PPR."
- Reforestation amortization (see **Pub. 535**). Identify as "RFST."
- Repayment of supplemental unemployment benefits under the Trade Act of 1974 (see **Pub. 525**). Identify as "Sub-Pay TRA."
- Contributions to section 501(c)(18) pension plans (see **Pub. 525**). Identify as "501(c)(18)."
- Contributions by certain chaplains to section 403(b) plans (see **Pub. 517**). Identify as "403(b)."
- Deduction for clean-fuel vehicles (see **Pub. 535**). Identify as "Clean-Fuel."
- Employee business expenses of fee-basis state or local government officials (see **Form 2106** or **2106-EZ**). Identify as "FBO."

Line 33

If line 33 is less than zero, you may have a net operating loss that you can carry to another tax year. See **Pub. 536.**

Tax and Credits

Line 35a

If you were age 65 or older or blind, check the appropriate box(es) on line 35a. If you were married and checked the box on line 6b of Form 1040 and your spouse was age 65 or older or blind, also check the appropriate box(es) for your spouse. Be sure to enter the total number of boxes checked.

Age

If you were age 65 or older on January 1, 2002, check the "65 or older" box on your 2001 return.

Blindness

If you were partially blind as of December 31, 2001, you must get a statement certified by your eye doctor or registered optometrist that:

- You cannot see better than 20/200 in your better eye with glasses or contact lenses or
- Your field of vision is 20 degrees or less.

If your eye condition is not likely to improve beyond the conditions listed above, you can get a statement certified by your eye doctor or registered optometrist to this effect instead.

You must keep the statement for your records.

Line 35b

If your spouse itemizes deductions on a separate return or if you were a dual-status alien, check the box on line 35b. But if you were a dual-status alien and you file a joint return with your spouse who was a U.S. citizen or resident at the end of 2001 and you and your spouse agree to be taxed on your combined worldwide income, **do not** check the box.

Line 36 Itemized Deductions or Standard Deduction

In most cases, your Federal income tax will be less if you take the **larger** of:

- Your itemized deductions or
- Your standard deduction.

Caution. If you checked the box on **line 35b,** your standard deduction is zero.

Itemized Deductions

To figure your itemized deductions, fill in **Schedule A.**

Standard Deduction

Most people can find their standard deduction by looking at the amounts listed under "All others" to the left of line 36 of Form 1040. But if you checked **any** box on **line 35a, or** you (or your spouse if filing jointly) can be claimed as a dependent on someone's 2001 return, use the worksheet below or the chart on page 32, whichever applies, to figure your standard deduction. Also, if you checked the box on **line 35b,** your standard deduction is zero, even if you were age 65 or older or blind.

Electing To Itemize for State Tax or Other Purposes

If you itemize even though your itemized deductions are less than your standard deduction, enter "IE" on the dotted line next to line 36.

Line 40 Tax

Do you want the IRS to figure your tax for you?
- ☐**Yes.** See **Pub. 967** for details, including who is eligible and what to do. If you have paid too much, we will send you a refund. If you did not pay enough, we will send you a bill.
- ☐**No.** Use one of the following methods to figure your tax. Also include in the total on line 40 any of the following taxes.

  - Tax from **Forms 8814** and **4972.** Be sure to check the appropriate box(es).
  - Tax from recapture of an education credit. You may owe this tax if **(a)** you claimed an education credit in an earlier year **and (b)** you, your spouse if filing jointly, or your dependent received in 2001 either tax-free educational assistance or a refund or qualified expenses. See **Form 8863** for more details. If you owe this tax, enter the amount and "ECR" on the dotted line next to line 40.

Tax Table or Tax Rate Schedules. If your taxable income is less than $100,000, you **must** use the Tax Table, which starts on page 685,

Standard Deduction Worksheet for Dependents—Line 36   *Keep for Your Records*

Use this worksheet **only** if someone can claim you, or your spouse if filing jointly, as a dependent.

1. Add $250 to your **earned income***. Enter the total . . . . **1.** _____
2. Minimum standard deduction . . . . **2.** __750.00__
3. Enter the **larger** of line 1 or line 2 . . . . **3.** _____
4. Enter the amount shown below for your filing status.
   - Single—$4,550
   - Married filing separately—$3,800
   - Married filing jointly or qualifying widow(er)—$7,600   } . . . . **4.** _____
   - Head of household—$6,650
5. **Standard deduction.**
   a. Enter the **smaller** of line 3 or line 4. If under 65 and not blind, **stop here** and enter this amount on Form 1040, line 36. **Otherwise,** go to line 5b . . . . **5a.** _____
   b. If 65 or older or blind, multiply the number on Form 1040, line 35a, by: $1,100 if single or head of household; $900 if married filing jointly or separately, or qualifying widow(er) . . . . **5b.** _____
   c. Add lines 5a and 5b. Enter the total here and on Form 1040, line 36 . . . . **5c.** _____

*Earned income *includes wages, salaries, tips, professional fees, and other compensation received for personal services you performed. It also includes any amount received as a scholarship that you must include in your income. Generally, your earned income is the total of the amount(s) you reported on Form 1040, lines 7, 12, and 18, minus the amount, if any, on line 27.*

Standard Deduction Chart for People Age 65 or Older or Blind—Line 36

Do not use this chart if someone can claim you, or your spouse if filing jointly, as a dependent. Instead use the worksheet on page 31.

Enter the number from the box on line 35a of Form 1040 . . . . ▶ [ ]   ⚠ CAUTION   Do not use the number of exemptions from line 6d.

IF your filing status is . . .	AND the number in the box above is . . .	THEN your standard deduction is . . .
Single	1	$5,650
	2	6,750
Married filing jointly or Qualifying widow(er)	1	$8,500
	2	9,400
	3	10,300
	4	11,200
Married filing separately	1	$4,700
	2	5,600
	3	6,500
	4	7,400
Head of household	1	$7,750
	2	8,850

to figure your tax. Be sure you use the correct column. If your taxable income is $100,000 or more, use the Tax Rate Schedules on page 685. **Exception. Do not** use the Tax Table or Tax Rate Schedules to figure your tax if **either 1** or **2** below applies.

1. You are required to figure your tax using the **Tax Computation Worksheet for Certain Dependents** below, **Form 8615, Schedule D,** or the **Capital Gain Tax Worksheet** on page 594.
2. You use **Schedule J** (for farm income) to figure your tax.

Tax Computation Worksheet for Certain Dependents. If you, or your spouse if filing jointly, can be claimed as a dependent on some-

one's 2001 return, you must use the worksheet below to figure your tax unless you received (before offset) an advance payment of your 2001 taxes. If any of the other methods listed in item **1** or **2** above apply to you, follow the **Special Rules** on the worksheet to figure your tax. Your tax may be less if this worksheet applies.

Form 8615. Form 8615 must generally be used to figure the tax for any child who was under age 14 on January 1, 2002, and who had more than $1,500 of investment income, such as taxable interest, ordinary dividends, or capital gains (includng capital gain distributions). But if neither of the child's parents was alive on December 31, 2001, do not use Form 8615 to figure the child's tax.

Deduction for Exemptions Worksheet—Line 38

Keep for Your Records

1. Is the amount on Form 1040, line 34, more than the amount shown on line 4 below for your filing status?

   ☐ **No.** (STOP) Multiply $2,900 by the total number of exemptions claimed on Form 1040, line 6d, and enter the result on line 38.

   ☐ **Yes.** *Continue* ↘

2. Multiply $2,900 by the total number of exemptions claimed on Form 1040, line 6d . . . .   2. _____

3. Enter the amount from Form 1040, line 34 . . . .   3. _____

4. Enter the amount shown below for your filing status.

   • Single—$132,950
   • Married filing jointly or qualifying widow(er)—$199,450
   • Married filing separately—$99,725
   • Head of household—$166,200

   } . . .   4. _____

5. Subtract line 4 from line 3 . . . .   5. _____

   Note. If line 5 is more than: $122,500 if single, married filing jointly, head of household, or qualifying widow(er); $61,250 if married filing separately, **stop here.** You **cannot** take a deduction for exemptions.

6. Divide line 5 by: $2,500 if single, married filing jointly, head of household, or qualifying widow(er); $1,250 if married filing separately. If the result is not a whole number, increase it to the next higher whole number (for example, increase 0.0004 to 1) . . . .   6. _____

7. Multiply line 6 by 2% (.02) and enter the result as a decimal . . . .   7. _____

8. Multiply line 2 by line 7 . . . .   8. _____

9. **Deduction for exemptions.** Subtract line 8 from line 2. Enter the result here and on Form 1040, line 38   9. _____

Schedule D. If you had a net capital gain on Schedule D (both lines 16 and 17 of Schedule D are gains) and the amount on Form 1040, line 39, is more than zero, use Part IV of Schedule D to figure your tax.

Capital Gain Tax Worksheet. If you received capital gain distributions but you are not required to file Schedule D, use the worksheet on page 34 to figure your tax.

Schedule J. If you had income from farming, your tax may be less if you choose to figure it using income averaging on Schedule J.

Line 41 Alternative Minimum Tax

Use the worksheet on page 35 to see if you should fill in **Form 6251.**
Exception. Fill in Form 6251 instead of using the worksheet on page 35 if you claimed or received **any** of the following items.

1. Accelerated depreciation.
2. Stock by exercising an incentive stock option and you did not dispose of the stock in the same year.
3. Tax-exempt interest from private activity bonds.
4. Intangible drilling, circulation, research, experimental, or mining costs.
5. Amortization of pollution-control facilities or depletion.
6. Income or (loss) from tax-shelter farm activities or passive activities.
7. Percentage-of-completion income from long-term contracts.
8. Interest paid on a home mortgage **not** used to buy, build, or substantially improve your home.
9. Investment interest expense reported on **Form 4952.**
10. Net operating loss deduction.
11. Alternative minimum tax adjustments from an estate, trust, electing large partnership, or cooperative.
12. Section 1202 exclusion.

Caution. Form 6251 should be filled in for a child under age 14 if the child's adjusted gross income from Form 1040, line 34, exceeds the child's earned income by more than $5,350.

Line 43 Foreign Tax Credit

If you paid income tax to a foreign country, you may be able to take this credit. Generally, you must complete and attach **Form 1116** to do so.
Exception. You do not have to file Form 1116 to take this credit if **all five** of the following apply.

1. All of your gross foreign-source income is from interest and dividends and all of that income and the foreign tax paid on it is reported to you on **Form 1099-INT** or **Form 1099-DIV** (or substitute statement).
2. If you have dividend income from shares of stock, you held those shares for at least 16 days.
3. You are not filing **Form 4563** or excluding income from sources within Puerto Rico.
4. The total of your foreign taxes is not more than $300 (not more than $600 if married filing jointly).
5. All of your foreign taxes were:

• Legally owed and not eligible for a refund and
• Paid to countries that are recognized by the United States and do not support terrorism.

For more details on these requirements, see the Instructions for Form 1116.

Do you meet all five requirements above?

☐**Yes.** Enter on line 43 the **smaller** of your total foreign taxes or the amount on Form 1040, line 40.

Tax Computation Worksheet for Certain Dependents—Line 40   *Keep for Your Records*

Before you begin: ✓ Be sure you can use this worksheet (see **Tax Computation Worksheet for Certain Dependents** above).

✓ **Do not** use this worksheet if you, or your spouse if filing jointly, received (before offset) an advance payment of your 2001 taxes.

✓ Be sure you read the **Special Rules** below.

---

1. Figure the tax on the amount on Form 1040, line 39 (or the applicable line of the worksheet, schedule, or form listed below). Use the Tax Table or Tax Rate Schedules, whichever applies . . . . . .   **1.** _____

2. Is the amount on line 1 more than the amount shown below for your filing status?

   • Single or married filing separately—$900

   • Married filing jointly or qualifying widow(er)—$1,800

   • Head of household—$1,500

   ☐ **Yes.** Enter: $300 if single or married filing separately; $500 if head of household; $600 if married filing jointly or qualifying widow(er).   } . . . . . .   **2.** _____

   ☐ **No.** Divide the amount on line 1 by 3.0.

3. Subtract line 2 from line 1. Enter the result here and on Form 1040, line 40 (or the applicable line of the worksheet, schedule, or form listed below) . . . .   **3.** _____

Special Rules. If you use:

   • The **Capital Gain Tax Worksheet** on page 34, use the worksheet above to figure the tax on lines 4 and 14 of the Capital Gain Tax Worksheet.

   • **Schedule D, Part IV,** use the worksheet above to figure the tax on lines 25 and 39 of Part IV. If you use the **Schedule D Tax Worksheet** on page D-9, use the worksheet above to figure the tax on lines 15 and 36 of the Schedule D Tax Worksheet.

   • **Schedule J,** use the worksheet above to figure the tax on line 4 of Schedule J.

   • **Form 8615,** use the worksheet above to figure the tax on lines 15 and 17 of Form 8615 (and line 9 if the parent used this worksheet).

   • **Other forms or worksheets** that require you to figure the tax using the 2001 Tax Table or Tax Rate Schedules, use the worksheet above to figure the tax on any line that would otherwise be figured using the 2001 Tax Table or Tax Rate Schedules.

☐**No.** See Form 1116 to find out if you can take the credit and, if you can, if you have to file Form 1116.

Line 44 Credit for Child and Dependent Care Expenses

You may be able to take this credit if you paid someone to care for your child **under age 13** or your dependent or spouse who could not care for himself or herself. For details, use TeleTax topic 602 or see **Form 2441.**

Line 45 Credit for the Elderly or the Disabled

You may be able to take this credit if by the end of 2001 **(a)** you were age 65 or older or **(b)** you retired on **permanent and total disability** and you had taxable disability income. But you usually **cannot** take the credit if the amount on Form 1040, line 34, is $17,500 or more ($20,000 if married filing jointly and only one spouse is eligible for the credit; $25,000 if married filing jointly and both spouses are eligible; $12,500 if married filing separately). See **Schedule R** and its instructions for details.

Credit Figured by the IRS. If you can take this credit and you want us to figure it for you, see the Instructions for Schedule R.

Line 46 Education Credits

If you (or your dependent) paid qualified expenses in 2001 for yourself, your spouse, or your dependent to enroll in or attend an eligible educa-

tional institution, you may be able to take an education credit. See **Form 8863** for details. However, you **cannot** take an education credit if **any** of the following apply.

   • You are claimed as a dependent on someone's (such as your parent's) 2001 tax return.

   • Your filing status is married filing separately.

   • The amount on Form 1040, line 34, is $50,000 or more ($100,000 or more if married filing jointly).

   • You (or your spouse) were a nonresident alien for any part of 2001 unless your filing status is married filing jointly.

Line 48—Child Tax Credit

What Is the Child Tax Credit?

This credit is for people who have a qualifying child as defined in the instructions for line 6c, column (4), on page 20. It is in addition to the credit for child and dependent care expenses on Form 1040, line 44, and the earned income credit on Form 1040, line 61a.

Three Steps To Take the Child Tax Credit!

Step 1. Make sure you have a qualifying child for the child tax credit. See the instructions for line 6c, column (4), on page 20.

Step 2. Make sure you checked the box in column (4) of line 6c on Form 1040 for each qualifying child.

Capital Gain Tax Worksheet—Line 40   *Keep for Your Records*

Before you begin: √ Be sure you do not have to file Schedule D (see the instructions for Form 1040, line 13).

                     √ Be sure you checked the box on line 13 of Form 1040.

1. Enter the amount from Form 1040, line 39 . . . .   **1.** _____

2. Enter the amount from Form 1040, line 13 . . . .   **2.** _____

3. Subtract line 2 from line 1. If zero or less, enter -0- . . . .   **3.** _____

4. Figure the tax on the amount on line 3. Use the Tax Table or Tax Rate Schedules, whichever applies   **4.** _____

5. Enter the **smaller** of:

   • The amount on line 1 or

   • $27,050 if single; $45,200 if married filing jointly or qualifying widow(er); $22,600 if married filing separately; or $36,250 if head of household.   }. . .   **5.** _____

6. Is the amount on line 3 equal to or more than the amount on line 5?

   ☐ **Yes.** Leave lines 6 through 8 blank; go to line 9 and check the "No" box.

   ☐ **No.** Enter the amount from line 3 . . . .   **6.** _____

7. Subtract line 6 from line 5 . . . .   **7.** _____

8. Multiply line 7 by 10% (.10) . . . .   **8.** _____

9. Are the amounts on lines 2 and 7 the same?

   ☐ **Yes.** Leave lines 9 through 12 blank; go to line 13.

   ☐ **No.** Enter the **smaller** of line 1 or line 2 . . . . . .   **9.** _____

10. Enter the amount, if any, from line 7 . . . .   **10.** _____

11. Subtract line 10 from line 9. If zero or less, enter -0- . . . . . .   **11.** _____

12. Multiply line 11 by 20% (.20) . . . .   **12.** _____

13. Add lines 4, 8, and 12 . . . .   **13.** _____

14. Figure the tax on the amount on line 1. Use the Tax Table or Tax Rate Schedules, whichever applies   **14.** _____

15. **Tax on all taxable income (including capital gain distributions).** Enter the **smaller** of line 13 or line 14 here and on Form 1040, line 40 . . . .   **15.** _____

Step 3. Answer the questions on this page to see if you may use the worksheet on page 38 to figure your credit or if you must use Pub. 972, Child Tax Credit.

Line 49 Adoption Credit

You may be able to take this credit if you paid expenses in 2001 to adopt a child. See **Form 8839** for details.

Line 50 Other Credits

Include in the total on line 50 any of the following credits and check the appropriate box(es). If box **d** is checked, also enter the form number. To find out if you can take the credit, see the form or publication indicated.

- Mortgage interest credit. If a state or local government gave you a mortgage credit certificate, see **Form 8396.**
- Credit for prior year minimum tax. If you paid alternative minimum tax in a prior year, see **Form 8801.**
- Qualified electric vehicle credit. If you placed a new electric vehicle in service in 2001, see **Form 8834.**
- General business credit. This credit consists of a number of credits that usually apply only to individuals who are partners, shareholders in an S corporation, self-employed, or who have rental property. See **Form 3800** or **Pub. 334.**

- Empowerment zone employment credit. See **Form 8844.**
- District of Columbia first-time home-buyer credit. See **Form 8859.**

Line 51

If you sold fuel produced from a nonconventional source, see Internal Revenue Code section 29 to find out if you can take the **nonconventional source fuel credit.** If you can, attach a schedule showing how you figured the credit. Include the credit in the total on line 51. Enter the amount and "FNS" on the dotted line next to line 51.

Other Taxes

Line 54 Social Security and Medicare Tax on Tip Income Not Reported to Employer

If you received tips of $20 or more in any month and you did not report the full amount to your employer, you must pay the social security and Medicare or railroad retirement (RRTA) tax on the unreported tips. You must also pay this tax if your W-2 form(s) shows allocated tips that you are including in your income on Form 1040, line 7.

    To figure the tax, use **Form 4137.** To pay the RRTA tax, contact your employer. Your employer will figure and collect the tax.

Caution. You may be charged a penalty equal to 50% of the social security and Medicare tax due on tips you received but did not report to your employer.

Worksheet To See if You Should Fill in Form 6251—Line 41

Keep for Your Records

Before you begin: √ Be sure you have read the **Exception** on page 591 to see if you must fill in Form 6251 instead of using this worksheet.

√ If you are claiming the foreign tax credit (see the instructions for Form 1040, line 43), enter that credit on line 43.

1. Enter the amount from Form 1040, line 37 . . . .   **1.** _____

2. Are you filing **Schedule A?**

☐ **Yes.** Leave line 2 blank and go to line 3.

☐ **No.** Enter your standard deduction from Form 1040, line 36, and go to line 5. . . . . . .   **2.** _____

3. Enter the **smaller** of the amount on Schedule A, line 4, or 2.5% (.025) of the amount on Form 1040, line 34 . . . .   **3.** _____

4. Add lines 9 and 26 of Schedule A and enter the total . . . .   **4.** _____

5. Add lines 1 through 4 above . . . .   **5.** _____

6. Enter the amount shown below for your filing status.
    • Single or head of household—$35,750
    • Married filing jointly or qualifying widow(er)—$49,000   . . . .   **6.** _____
    • Married filing separately—$24,500

7. Is the amount on line 5 more than the amount on line 6?

☐ **No.** (STOP) You do not need to fill in Form 6251.

☐ **Yes.** Subtract line 6 from line 5 . . . .   **7.** _____

8. Enter the amount shown below for your filing status.
    • Single or head of household—$112,500
    • Married filing jointly or qualifying widow(er)—$150,000   . . . .   **8.** _____
    • Married filing separately—$75,000

9. Is the amount on line 5 more than the amount on line 8?
    ☐ **No.** Enter -0- here and on line 10 and go to line 11.
    ☐ **Yes.** Subtract line 8 from line 5.   . . . .   **9.** _____

10. Multiply line 9 by 25% (.25) and enter the result but do not enter more than line 6 above . . .   **10.** _____

11. Add lines 7 and 10 . . . .   **11.** _____

12. Is the amount on line 11 more than the amount shown below for your filing status?
    • Single, married filing jointly, head of household, or qualifying widow(er)—$175,000
    • Married filing separately—$87,500

☐ **Yes.** (STOP) Fill in Form 6251 to see if you owe the alternative minimum tax.

☐ **No.** Multiply line 11 by 26% (.26) . . . .   **12.** _____

13. Enter the amount from Form 1040, line 40, minus the total of any tax from Form 4972 and any amount on Form 1040, line 43 . . . .   **13.** _____

Next. Is the amount on line 12 more than the amount on line 13?

☐ **Yes.** Fill in Form 6251 to see if you owe the alternative minimum tax.

☐ **No.** You do not need to fill in Form 6251.

Line 55 Tax on Qualified Plans Including IRAs, and Other Tax-Favored Accounts

If **any** of the following apply, see **Form 5329** and its instructions to find out if you owe this tax and if you must file Form 5329.

1. You received any early distributions from **(a)** an IRA or other qualified retirement plan, **(b)** an annuity, or **(c)** a modified endowment contract entered into after June 20, 1988.

2. Excess contributions were made to your IRAs, Coverdell ESAs, or Archer MSAs.

3. You received distributions from Coverdell ESAs in excess of your qualified higher education expenses.

4. You were born before July 1, 1930, and did not take the minimum required distribution from your IRA or other qualified retirement plan.

Exception. If **only** item 1 applies to you **and** distribution code 1 is correctly shown in box 7 of your **Form 1099-R,** you do not have to file Form 5329. Instead, multiply the taxable amount of the distribution by 10% (.10) and enter the result on line 55. The taxable amount of the distribution is the part of the distribution you reported on line 15b or line 16b of Form 1040 or on Form 4972. Also, put "No" under the heading "Other Taxes" to the left of line 55 to indicate that you do not have to file Form 5329. **But** if distribution code 1 is incorrectly shown in box 7 of Form 1099-R, you must file Form 5329.

Line 56 Advance Earned Income Credit Payments

Enter the total amount of advance earned income credit (EIC) payments you received. These payments are shown in box 9 of your W-2 form(s).

Rate Reduction Credit Worksheet—Line 47   *Keep for Your Records*

Before you begin:

✓ If you received (before offset) an advance payment of your 2001 taxes equal to the amount shown below for your 2001 filing status, **stop.** You cannot take the credit because you have received the maximum amount of the credit.

- Single or married filing separately — $300
- Head of household — $500
- Married filing jointly or qualifying widow(er) — $600

✓ If you, or your spouse if filing a joint return, can be claimed as a dependent on another person's return, **stop.** You cannot take the credit.

✓ If you received (before offset) an advance payment and you filed a joint return for 2000, you and your spouse are each considered to have received one-half of the payment.

 If you received Notice 1275, 1277, or 1278 have it available. The notice shows the amount of your advance payment (before offset).

1. Enter the amount from Form 1040, line 39. If line 39 is zero or blank, **stop;** you cannot take the credit   1. _____

2. Enter the amount shown below for your filing status.
   - Single or married filing separately — $6,000
   - Head of household — $10,000
   - Married filing jointly or qualifying widow(er) — $12,000   } . . . .   2. _____

3. Is the amount on line 1 less than the amount on line 2?

   No.   Enter: $300 if single or married filing separately; $500 if head of household; $600 if married filing jointly or qualifying widow(er).   } . . . .   3. _____

   Yes.   Multiply the amount on line 1 by 5% (.05). Enter the result.

4. Enter the amount from Form 1040, line 42 . . . .   4. _____

5. Add the amounts from Form 1040, lines 43 through 46. Enter the total . . .   5. _____

6. Subtract line 5 from line 4. If the result is zero or less, **stop;** you cannot take the credit . . . . .   6. _____

7. Enter the **smaller** of line 3 or line 6 . . . .   7. _____

8. Enter the amount, if any, of your advance payment (before offset). If filing a joint return, include your spouse's advance payment with yours . . . .   8. _____

9. **Rate reduction credit.** Subtract line 8 from line 7. Enter the result here and, if more than zero, on Form 1040, line 47. If line 8 is more than line 7, you do not have to pay back the difference . . . .   9. _____

Line 57 Household Employment Taxes

If **any** of the following apply, see **Schedule H** and its instructions to find out if you owe these taxes.

1. You paid **any one** household employee (defined below) cash wages of $1,300 or more in 2001. Cash wages include wages paid by checks, money orders, etc.
2. You withheld Federal income tax during 2001 at the request of any household employee.
3. You paid **total** cash wages of $1,000 or more in **any** calendar **quarter** of 2000 or 2001 to household employees.

Tip. For item **1**, do not count amounts paid to an employee who was under age 18 at any time in 2001 and was a student.

Household Employee. Any person who does household work is a household employee if you can control what will be done and how it will be done. Household work includes work done in or around your home by babysitters, nannies, health aides, maids, yard workers, and similar domestic workers.

Line 58 Total Tax

Include in the total on line 58 any of the following taxes. To find out if you owe the tax, see the form or publication indicated. On the dotted line next to line 58, enter the amount of the tax and identify it as indicated.

Recapture of the Following Credits.

- Investment credit (see **Form 4255**). Identify as "ICR."
- Low-income housing credit (see **Form 8611**). Identify as "LIHCR."
- Qualified electric vehicle credit (see **Pub. 535**). Identify as "QEVCR."
- Indian employment credit. Identify as "IECR."

Recapture of Federal Mortgage Subsidy. If you sold your home in 2001 and it was financed (in whole or in part) from the proceeds of any tax-exempt qualified mortgage bond or you claimed the mortgage interest credit, see **Form 8828**. Identify as "FMSR."

Section 72(m)(5) Excess Benefits Tax (see **Pub. 560**). Identify as "Sec. 72(m)(5)."

Line 48—Child Tax Credit

Questions   **Who Must Use Pub. 972**

1. Are you excluding income from Puerto Rico **or** are you filing any of the following forms?

    - Form 2555 or 2555-EZ (relating to foreign earned income)

    - Form 4563 (exclusion of income for residents of American Samoa)

    ☐ **No.** *Continue* ➘   ☐ **Yes.** (STOP)
    You must use Pub. 972 to figure your credit.

2. Is the amount on Form 1040, line 34, more than the amount shown below for your filing status?

    - Married filing jointly – $110,000

    - Single, head of household, or qualifying widow(er) – $75,000

    - Married filing separately – $55,000

    ☐ **No.** *Continue* ➘   ☐ **Yes.** (STOP)
    You must use Pub. 972 to figure your credit.

3. Are you claiming any of the following credits?

    - Adoption credit, Form 8839 (see the instructions for Form 1040, line 49)

    - Mortgage interest credit, Form 8396 (see the instructions for Form 1040, line 50)

    - District of Columbia first-time homebuyer credit, Form 8859

    ☐ **No.** Use the worksheet on page 38 to figure your child tax credit.   ☐ **Yes.** You must use Pub. 972 to figure your child tax credit. You will also need the form(s) listed above for any credit(s) you are claiming.

Uncollected Social Security and Medicare or RRTA Tax on Tips or Group-Term Life Insurance. This tax should be shown in box 12 of your Form W-2 with codes **A** and **B** or **M** and **N.** Identify as "UT."

Golden Parachute Payments. If you received an excess parachute payment (EPP), you must pay a 20% tax on it. This tax should be shown in box 12 of your W-2 form with code **K.** If you received a **Form 1099-MISC,** the tax is 20% of the EPP shown in box 13. Identify as "EPP."

Tax on Accumulation Distribution of Trusts. Enter the amount from **Form 4970** and identify as "ADT."

Payments

Line 59 Federal Income Tax Withheld

Add the amounts shown as Federal income tax withheld on your **Forms W-2, W-2G,** and **1099-R.** Enter the total on line 59. The amount withheld should be shown in box 2 of Form W-2 or W-2G, and in box 4 of Form 1099-R. If line 59 includes amounts withheld as shown on Form 1099-R, attach the Form 1099-R to the front of your return.

If you received a 2001 Form 1099 showing Federal income tax withheld on dividends, interest income, unemployment compensation, social security benefits, or other income you received, include the amount withheld in the total on line 59. This should be shown in box 4 of the 1099 form or box 6 of **Form SSA-1099.**

Line 60 2001 Estimated Tax Payments

Enter any payments you made on your estimated Federal income tax (**Form 1040-ES**) for 2001. Include any overpayment from your 2000 return that you applied to your 2001 estimated tax.

If you and your spouse paid joint estimated tax but are now filing separate income tax returns, you can divide the amount paid in any way you choose as long as you both agree. If you cannot agree, you must divide the payments in proportion to each spouse's individual tax as shown on your separate returns for 2001. For an example of how to do this, see **Pub. 505.** Be sure to show both social security numbers (SSNs) in the space provided on the separate returns. If you or your spouse paid separate estimated tax but you are now filing a joint return, add the amounts you each paid. Follow these instructions even if your spouse died in 2001 or in 2002 before filing a 2001 return.

Divorced Taxpayers

If you got divorced in 2001 and you made joint estimated tax payments with your former spouse, put your former spouse's SSN in the space provided on the front of Form 1040. If you were divorced and remarried in 2001, put your present spouse's SSN in the space provided on the front of Form 1040. Also, under the heading "Payments" to the left of line 60, put your former spouse's SSN, followed by "DIV."

Name Change

If you changed your name because of marriage, divorce, etc., and you made estimated tax payments using your former name, attach a statement to the front of Form 1040. On the statement, explain all the payments you and your spouse made in 2001 and the name(s) and SSN(s) under which you made them.

Line 62 Excess Social Security and RRTA Tax Withheld

If you, or your spouse if filing a joint return, had more than one employer for 2001 and total wages of more than $80,400, too much social security

Child Tax Credit Worksheet—Line 48

Keep for Your Records

Do not use this worksheet if you answered "Yes" to question 1, 2, or 3 on page 37. Instead, use Pub. 972.

1. Number of qualifying children: _____ × $600. Enter the result.   **1** [ ]

2. Enter the amount from Form 1040, line 42.   **2** [ ]

3. Add the amounts from Form 1040:

    Line 43   _____

    Line 44   + _____

    Line 45   + _____

    Line 46   + _____

    Line 47   + _____   Enter the total.   **3** [ ]

4. Are the amounts on lines 2 and 3 the same?

    ☐ **Yes.** (STOP)
       You cannot take this credit because there is no tax to reduce. However, see the **TIP** below before completing the rest of your Form 1040.

    ☐ **No.** Subtract line 3 from line 2.   **4** [ ]

5. Is the amount on line 1 more than the amount on line 4?

    ☐ **Yes.** Enter the amount from line 4.
       Also, see the **TIP** below.   } **This is your child tax**   **5** [ ]
    ☐ **No.** Enter the amount from line 1. } **credit.**

       Enter this amount on Form 1040, line 48.

TIP

You may be able to take the **additional child tax credit** on Form 1040, line 63, if you answered "Yes" on line 4 **or** line 5 above.

● First, complete your Form 1040 through line 62.

● Then, use Form 8812 to figure any additional child tax credit.

Lines 61a and 61b—
Earned Income Credit (EIC)

What Is the EIC?

The EIC is a credit for certain people who work. The credit may give you a refund even if you do not owe any tax.

To Take the EIC:

● Follow the steps below.

● Complete the worksheet that applies to you **or** let the IRS figure the credit for you.

● If you have a qualifying child, complete and attach Schedule EIC.

**You
Will
Need:**

 If you take the EIC even though you are not eligible and it is determined that your error is due to reckless or intentional disregard of the EIC rules, you will not be allowed to take the credit for 2 years even if you are otherwise eligible to do so. If you fraudulently take the EIC, you will not be allowed to take the credit for 10 years. You may also have to pay penalties.

Step 1   All Filers

1. Is the amount on Form 1040, line 34, less than $32,121 (or $10,710 if a child did not live with you in 2001)?

   ☐ **Yes.** *Continue* ↘   ☐ **No.** (STOP)
   You cannot take the credit.

2. Do you, and your spouse if filing a joint return, have a social security number that allows you to work or is valid for E 594)?·poses (see page 602)?

   ☐ **Yes.** *Continue* ↘   ☐ **No.** (STOP)
   You cannot take the credit.
   Put "No" directly to the right of line 61a.

3. Is your filing status married filing separately?

   ☐ **Yes.** (STOP)   ☐ **No.** *Continue* ↘
   You cannot take
   the credit.

4. Are you filing Form 2555 or 2555-EZ (relating to foreign earned income)?

   ☐ **Yes.** (STOP)   ☐ **No.** *Continue* ↘
   You cannot take
   the credit.

5. Were you a nonresident alien for any part of 2001?

   ☐ **Yes.** *See Nonresident*   ☐ **No.** *Go to Step 2.*
   Aliens on page 602.

Step 2   Investment Income

1. Add the amounts from   Line 8a   _____
   Form 1040:   Line 8b + _____
                           Line 9   + _____
                           Line 13 + _____

   Investment Income = [   ]

2. Is your investment income more than $2,450?

   ☐ **Yes.** *Continue* ↘   ☐ **No.** *Skip the next
                                         question; go to Step 3.*

3. Are you filing Form 4797 (relating to sales of business property)?

   ☐ **Yes.** *See Form 4797*   ☐ **No.** (STOP)
   Filers on page 602.   You cannot take the credit.

Step 3   Who Must Use Pub. 596

Some people must use Pub. 596, Earned Income Credit, to see if they can take the credit and how to figure it. To see if you must use Pub. 596, answer the following questions.

1. Are you filing Schedule E?

   ☐ **No.** *Continue* ↘   ☐ **Yes.** →

2. Are you claiming a loss on Form 1040, line 12, 13, or 18?

   ☐ **No.** *Continue* ↘   ☐ **Yes.** →

3. Are you reporting income or a loss from the rental of personal property not used in a trade or business?

   ☐ **No.** *Continue* ↘   ☐ **Yes.** →

4. Did you, or your spouse if filing a joint return, receive a distribution from a pension, annuity, IRA, or Coverdell ESA that is not fully taxable?

   ☐ **No.** *Continue* ↘   ☐ **Yes.** →

5. Are you reporting income on Form 1040, line 21, from Form 8814 (relating to election to report child's interest and dividends)?

   ☐ **No.** *Continue* ↘   ☐ **Yes.** →

6. Did you enter an amount other than zero on Form 1040, line 41?

   ☐ **No.** *Continue* ↘   ☐ **Yes.** →

(STOP) You must use Pub. 596 to see if you can take the credit and how to figure it.

7. Did a child live with you in 2001?

   ☐ **Yes.** *Go to Step 4*   ☐ **No.** *Go to Step 5 on*
   on page 600.   *page 600.*

Continued from page 599

Step 4 **Qualifying Child**

A qualifying child is a child who is your...

Son	Grandchild
Daughter	Stepchild
Adopted child	Foster child (see page 602)

If the child was married, see page 602.

AND

was at the end of 2001...

Under age 19

or

Under age 24 and a student (see page 602)

or

Any age and permanently and totally disabled (see page 602)

AND

who...

Lived with you in the United States for more than half of 2001 or, if a foster child, for all of 2001.
If the child did not live with you for the required time, see Exception to "Time Lived With You" Condition on page 602.

1. Look at the qualifying child conditions above. Could you, or your spouse if filing a joint return, be a qualifying child of another person in 2001?

   ☐ **Yes.** (STOP) You cannot take the credit. *Put "No" directly to the right of line 61a.*

   ☐ **No.** *Continue* ↘

2. Do you have at least one child who meets the above conditions to be your qualifying child?

   ☐ **Yes.** *Continue* ↘

   ☐ **No.** *Skip the next question; go to Step 5, question 2.*

3. Does the child meet the conditions to be a qualifying child of any other person (other than your spouse if filing a joint return) for 2001?

   ☐ **Yes.** *See Qualifying Child of More Than One Person on page 602.*

   ☐ **No.** This child is your qualifying child. The child must have a social security number as defined on page 602 unless the child was born and died in 2001. *Skip Step 5; go to Step 6.*

Step 5 **Filers Without a Qualifying Child**

1. Look at the qualifying child conditions in Step 4. Could you, or your spouse if filing a joint return, be a qualifying child of another person in 2001?

   ☐ **Yes.** (STOP) You cannot take the credit. *Put "No" directly to the right of line 61a.*

   ☐ **No.** *Continue* ↘

2. Can you, or your spouse if filing a joint return, be claimed as a dependent on someone else's 2001 tax return?

   ☐ **Yes.** (STOP) You cannot take the credit.

   ☐ **No.** *Continue* ↘

3. Were you, or your spouse if filing a joint return, at least age 25 but under age 65 at the end of 2001?

   ☐ **Yes.** *Continue* ↘

   ☐ **No.** (STOP) You cannot take the credit. *Put "No" directly to the right of line 61a.*

4. Was your home, and your spouse's if filing a joint return, in the United States for more than half of 2001? Members of the military stationed outside the United States, see page 602 before you answer.

   ☐ **Yes.** *Go to Step 6.*

   ☐ **No.** (STOP) You cannot take the credit. *Put "No" directly to the right of line 61a.*

Step 6 **Modified Adjusted Gross Income**

1. Add the amounts from Form 1040:

   Line 8b _____

   Line 34 + _____

   Modified Adjusted Gross Income = | Box A | _____ |

2. If you have:

   • 2 or more qualifying children, is Box A less than $32,121?

   • 1 qualifying child, is Box A less than $28,281?

   • No qualifying children, is Box A less than $10,710?

   ☐ **Yes.** *Go to Step 7 on page 601.*

   ☐ **No.** (STOP) You cannot take the credit.

Continued from page 600

Step 7 Nontaxable and Taxable Earned Income

1. Add all your nontaxable earned income, including your spouse's if filing a joint return. This includes anything of value (money, goods, or services) that is not taxable that you received from your employer for your work. Types of nontaxable earned income are listed below.

- Salary deferrals, such as a 401(k) plan or the Federal Thrift Savings Plan, shown in box 12 of your W-2 form. See page 602.
- Salary reductions, such as under a cafeteria plan, unless they are included in box 1 of your W-2 form. See page 602.
- Mandatory contributions to a state or local retirement plan.
- Military employee basic housing, subsistence, and combat zone compensation. These amounts are shown in box 12 of your W-2 form with code Q.
- Meals and lodging provided for the convenience of your employer.
- Housing allowances or rental value of a parsonage for clergy members. If filing Schedule SE, see Clergy on this page.
- Excludable dependent care benefits from Form 2441, line 18, employer-provided adoption benefits from Form 8839, line 26, and educational assistance benefits (these benefits may be shown in box 14 of your W-2 form).
- Certain amounts received by Native Americans. See Pub. 596.

Note. Nontaxable earned income does not include welfare benefits or workfare payments (see page 602), or qualified foster care payments.

Nontaxable Earned Income = [Box B] _____

Enter this amount on Form 1040, line 61b.  ◄ ∙ ∙ ∙ ∙ ∙

2. Are you filing Schedule SE because you had church employee income of $108.28 or more?

☐ **Yes.** *See Church Employees on this page.* ☐ **No.** *Continue* ↘

3. Figure taxable earned income:

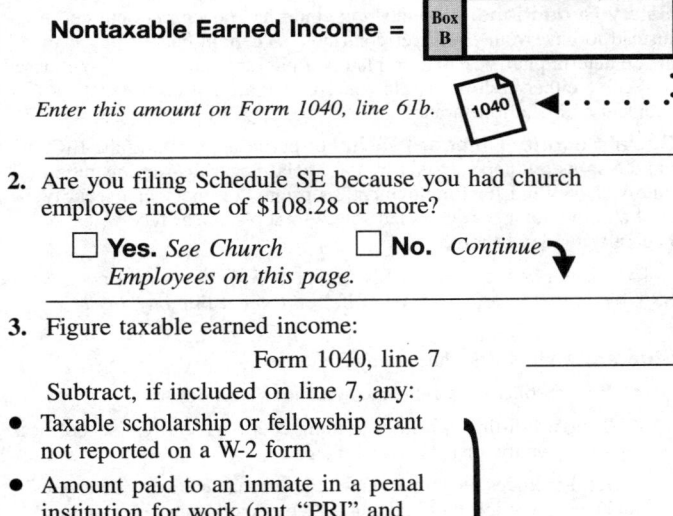

Form 1040, line 7 _____

Subtract, if included on line 7, any:

- Taxable scholarship or fellowship grant not reported on a W-2 form
- Amount paid to an inmate in a penal institution for work (put "PRI" and the amount subtracted on the dotted line next to line 7 of Form 1040)
- Amount received as a pension or annuity from a nonqualified deferred compensation plan or a section 457 plan (put "DFC" and the amount subtracted on the dotted line next to line 7 of Form 1040). This amount may be shown in box 11 of your W-2 form. If you received such an amount but box 11 is blank, contact your employer for the amount received as a pension or annuity.

— _____

Taxable Earned Income = [Box C] _____

Go to question 4.

4. Were you self-employed, or are you filing Schedule SE because you had church employee income, or are you filing Schedule C or C-EZ as a statutory employee?

☐ **Yes.** *Skip Steps 8 and 9; go to Worksheet B on page 604.* ☐ **No.** *Go to Step 8.*

Step 8 Total Earned Income

1. Nontaxable Earned Income (Step 7, Box B) _____

Taxable Earned Income (Step 7, Box C) + _____

Total Earned Income = [Box D] _____

2. If you have:

- 2 or more qualifying children, is Box D less than $32,121?
- 1 qualifying child, is Box D less than $28,281?
- No qualifying children, is Box D less than $10,710?

☐ **Yes.** *Go to Step 9.* ☐ **No.** (STOP) You cannot take the credit. *Put "No" directly to the right of line 61a.*

Step 9 How To Figure the Credit

1. Do you want the IRS to figure the credit for you?

☐ **Yes.** *See Credit Figured by the IRS below.* ☐ **No.** *Go to Worksheet A on page 603.*

Definitions and Special Rules *(listed in alphabetical order)*

Adopted Child. Any child placed with you by an authorized placement agency for legal adoption. An authorized placement agency includes any person authorized by state law to place children for legal adoption. The adoption does not have to be final.

Church Employees. Determine how much of the amount on Form 1040, line 7, was also reported on Schedule SE, line 5a. Subtract that amount from the amount on Form 1040, line 7, and enter the result in the first space of Step 7, line 3. Be sure to answer "Yes" on line 4 of Step 7.

Clergy. If you are filing Schedule SE and the amount on line 2 of that schedule includes an amount that was also reported on Form 1040, line 7:

1. Put "Clergy" directly to the right of line 61a of Form 1040.
2. Do not include any housing allowance or rental value of the parsonage as nontaxable earned income in Box B if it is required to be included on Schedule SE, line 2.
3. Determine how much of the amount on Form 1040, line 7, was also reported on Schedule SE, line 2.
4. Subtract that amount from the amount on Form 1040, line 7. Enter the result in the first space of Step 7, line 3.
5. Be sure to answer "Yes" on line 4 of Step 7.

Credit Figured by the IRS. To have the IRS figure the credit for you:

1. Put "EIC" directly to the right of line 61a of Form 1040.
2. Be sure you entered the amount of any nontaxable earned income (Step 7, Box B, on this page) on Form 1040, line 61b.

Continued from page 601

3. If you have a qualifying child, complete and attach Schedule EIC. If your EIC for a year after 1996 was reduced or disallowed, see Form 8862, Who Must File, below.

Exception to "Time Lived With You" Condition. A child is considered to have lived with you for all of 2001 if the child was born or died in 2001 and your home was this child's home for the entire time he or she was alive in 2001. Temporary absences, such as for school, vacation, medical care, or detention in a juvenile facility, count as time lived at home. If your child is presumed to have been kidnapped by someone who is not a family member, see Pub. 596 to find out if that child is a qualifying child for the EIC. If you were in the military stationed outside the United States, see Members of the Military below.

Form 4797 Filers. If the amount on Form 1040, line 13, includes an amount from Form 4797, you must use Pub. 596 to see if you can take the EIC and how to figure it. Otherwise, stop; you cannot take the EIC.

Form 8862, Who Must File. You must file Form 8862 if your EIC for a year after 1996 was reduced or disallowed for any reason other than a math or clerical error. But do not file Form 8862 if, after your EIC was reduced or disallowed in an earlier year:

- You filed Form 8862 (or other documents) and your EIC was then allowed and
- Your EIC has not been reduced or disallowed again for any reason other than a math or clerical error.

Also, do not file Form 8862 or take the credit if it was determined that your error was due to reckless or intentional disregard of the EIC rules or fraud.

Foster Child. Any child you cared for as your own child **and** who is **(a)** your brother, sister, stepbrother, or stepsister; **(b)** a descendant (such as a child, including an adopted child) of your brother, sister, stepbrother, or stepsister; or **(c)** a child placed with you by an authorized placement agency. For example, if you acted as the parent of your niece or nephew, this child is considered your foster child.

Grandchild. Any descendant of your son, daughter, or adopted child. For example, a grandchild includes your great-grandchild, great-great-grandchild, etc.

Married Child. A child who was married at the end of 2001 is a qualifying child only if **(a)** you can claim him or her as your dependent on Form 1040, line 6c, or **(b)** this child's other parent claims him or her as a dependent under the rules in Pub. 501 for children of divorced or separated parents.

Members of the Military. If you were on extended active duty outside the United States, your home is considered to be in the United States during that duty period. Extended active duty is military duty ordered for an indefinite period or for a period of more than 90 days. Once you begin serving extended active duty, you are considered to be on extended active duty even if you serve fewer than 90 days.

Nonresident Aliens. If your filing status is married filing jointly, go to Step 2 on page 599. Otherwise, stop; you cannot take the EIC.

Permanently and Totally Disabled Child. A child who cannot engage in any substantial gainful activity because of a physical or mental condition and a doctor has determined that this condition:

- Has lasted or can be expected to last continuously for at least a year or
- Can lead to death.

Qualifying Child of More Than One Person. If the child meets the conditions to be a qualifying child of more than one person, only the person who had the **highest** modified adjusted gross income (AGI) for 2001 may treat that child as a qualifying child. The other person(s) cannot take the EIC for people who do not have a qualifying child. If the other person is your spouse and you are filing a joint return, this rule does not apply. If you have the highest modified AGI, this child is your qualifying child. The child must have a social security number as defined below unless the child was born and died in 2001. Skip Step 5; go to Step 6 on page 600. If you do not have the highest modified AGI, stop; you cannot take the EIC. Put "No" directly to the right of line 61a.

Modified AGI is the total of the amounts on Form 1040, lines 8b and 34, increased by:

- Any loss claimed on Form 1040, line 13,
- Any loss from the rental of personal property not used in a trade or business,
- 75% of any losses on Form 1040, lines 12 and 18,
- Certain nontaxable distributions from a pension, annuity, or IRA (see Pub. 596), and
- Certain amounts reported on Schedule E (see Pub. 596).

Example. You and your 5-year-old daughter moved in with your mother in April 2001. You are not a qualifying child of your mother. Your daughter meets the conditions to be a qualifying child for both you and your mother. Your modified AGI for 2001 was $8,000 and your mother's was $14,000. Because your mother's modified AGI was higher, your daughter is your mother's qualifying child. You **cannot** take any EIC even if your mother does not claim the credit. You would put "No" directly to the right of line 61a.

Salary Deferrals. Contributions from your pay to certain retirement plans, such as a 401(k) plan or the Federal Thrift Savings Plan, shown in box 12 of your W-2 form. The "Retirement plan" box in box 13 of your W-2 form should be checked.

Salary Reductions. Amounts you could have been paid but chose instead to have your employer contribute to certain benefit plans, such as a cafeteria plan. A cafeteria plan is a plan that allows you to choose to receive either cash or certain benefits that are not taxed (such as accident and health insurance).

Social Security Number (SSN). For purposes of taking the EIC, a valid SSN is a number issued by the Social Security Administration unless "Not Valid for Employment" is printed on the social security card and the number was issued solely to apply for or receive a Federally funded benefit.

To find out how to get an SSN, see page 575. If you will not have an SSN by April 15, 2002, see What if You Cannot File on Time?

Student. A child who during any 5 months of 2001:

- Was enrolled as a full-time student at a school or
- Took a full-time, on-farm training course given by a school or a state, county, or local government agency.

A **school** includes technical, trade, and mechanical schools. It does not include on-the-job training courses, correspondence schools, or night schools.

Welfare Benefits, Effect of Credit on. Any refund you receive as a result of taking the EIC will not be used to determine if you are eligible for the following programs, or how much you can receive from them.

- Temporary Assistance for Needy Families (TANF).
- Medicaid and supplemental security income (SSI).
- Food stamps and low-income housing.

Workfare Payments. Cash payments certain people receive from a state or local agency that administers public assistance programs funded under the Federal Temporary Assistance for Needy Families (TANF) program in return for certain work activities such as:

- Work experience activities (including work associated with remodeling or repairing publicly assisted housing) if sufficient private sector employment is not available or
- Community service program activities.

Worksheet A—Earned Income Credit (EIC)—Lines 61a and 61b   *Keep for Your Records*

Before you begin: √ Be sure you are using the correct worksheet. **Do not** use this worksheet if you were self-employed, or you are filing Schedule SE because you had church employee income, or you are filing Schedule C or C-EZ as a statutory employee. Instead, use Worksheet B on page 604.

Part 1

All Filers Using Worksheet A

1. Enter your total earned income from Step 8, Box D, on page 601.

| 1 | |

2. Look up the amount on line 1 above in the EIC Table on pages 606–608 to find the credit. Enter the credit here.

If line 2 is zero, **STOP** You cannot take the credit.
Put "No" directly to the right of line 61a.

| 2 | |

3. Enter your modified adjusted gross income from Step 6, Box A, on page 600.

| 3 | |

4. Are the amounts on lines 3 and 1 the same?

☐ **Yes.** *Skip line 5; enter the amount from line 2 on line 6.*

☐ **No.** *Go to line 5.*

Part 2

Filers Who Answered "No" on Line 4

5. Is the amount on line 3 less than:

- $5,950 if you do not have a qualifying child **or**
- $13,100 if you have one or more qualifying children?

☐ **Yes.** *Leave line 5 blank; enter the amount from line 2 on line 6.*

☐ **No.** Look up the amount on line 3 in the EIC Table on pages 606–608 to find the credit. Enter the credit here.

Look at the amounts on lines 5 and 2.
*Then, enter the **smaller** amount on line 6.*

| 5 | |

Part 3

Your Earned Income Credit

6. **This is your earned income credit.**

| 6 | |

Enter this amount on Form 1040, line 61a.

Reminder—

√ Be sure you entered the amount of any nontaxable earned income (Step 7, Box B, on page 601) on Form 1040, line 61b.

√ If you have a qualifying child, complete and attach Schedule EIC.

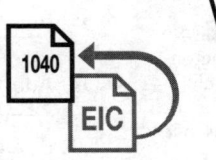

 If your EIC for a year after 1996 was reduced or disallowed, see page 602 to find out if you must file Form 8862 to take the credit for 2001.

Worksheet **B**—Earned Income Credit (EIC)—Lines 61a and 61b   *Keep for Your Records*

Use this worksheet if you were self-employed, or you are filing Schedule SE because you had church employee income, or you are filing Schedule C or C-EZ as a statutory employee.

✓ Complete the parts below (Parts 1 through 3) that apply to you. Then, continue to Part 4.

✓ If you are married filing a joint return, include your spouse's amounts, if any, with yours to figure the amounts to enter in Parts 1 through 3.

Part 1	**1a.** Enter the amount from Schedule SE, Section A, line 3, or Section B, line 3, whichever applies.	**1a**	
Self-Employed and People With Church Employee Income Filing Schedule SE	**b.** Enter any amount from Schedule SE, Section B, line 4b, and line 5a.	+ **1b**	
	c. Add lines 1a and 1b.	= **1c**	
	d. Enter the amount from Schedule SE, Section A, line 6, or Section B, line 13, whichever applies.	− **1d**	
	e. Subtract line 1d from 1c.	= **1e**	

Part 2	**2.** Do not include on these lines any statutory employee income or any amount exempt from self-employment tax as the result of the filing and approval of Form 4029 or Form 4361.		
Self-Employed NOT Required To File Schedule SE	**a.** Enter any net farm profit or (loss) from Schedule F, line 36, and from farm partnerships, Schedule K-1 (Form 1065), line 15a*.	**2a**	
For example, your net earnings from self-employment were less than $400.	**b.** Enter any net profit or (loss) from Schedule C, line 31; Schedule C-EZ, line 3; Schedule K-1 (Form 1065), line 15a (other than farming); and Schedule K-1 (Form 1065-B), box 9*.	+ **2b**	
	c. Add lines 2a and 2b.	= **2c**	

*If you have any Schedule K-1 amounts, complete the appropriate line(s) of Schedule SE, Section A. Put your name and social security number on Schedule SE and attach it to your return.

Part 3			
Statutory Employees Filing Schedule C or C-EZ	**3.** Enter the amount from Schedule C, line 1, or Schedule C-EZ, line 1, that you are filing as a statutory employee.	**3**	

Part 4	**4a.** Add lines 1e, 2c, and 3.	**4a**	
All Filers Using Worksheet B	**b.** Enter your nontaxable earned income from Step 7, Box B, on page 601.	+ **4b**	
Note. If line 4d includes income on which you should have paid self-employment tax but did not, we may reduce your credit by the amount of self-employment tax not paid.	**c.** Enter your taxable earned income from Step 7, Box C, on page 601.	+ **4c**	
	d. Add lines 4a, 4b, and 4c. **This is your total earned income.**	= **4d**	

5. If you have:

- 2 or more qualifying children, is line 4d less than $32,121?
- 1 qualifying child, is line 4d less than $28,281?
- No qualifying children, is line 4d less than $10,710?

☐ **Yes.** If you want the IRS to figure your credit, see page 601. *If you want to figure the credit yourself, enter the amount from line 4d on line 6 (page 605).*

☐ **No.** 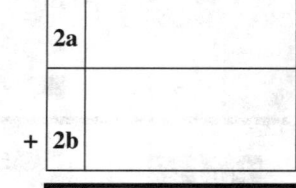 You cannot take the credit. *Put "No" directly to the right of line 61a.*

Worksheet B—*Continued from page 604*

Part 5 **All Filers Using Worksheet B**	**6.** Enter your total earned income from Part 4, line 4d, on page 604.	**6**	

7. Look up the amount on line 6 above in the EIC Table on pages 48–50 to find the credit. Enter the credit here.

	7	

If line 7 is zero, You cannot take the credit.
Put "No" directly to the right of line 61a.

8. Enter your modified adjusted gross income from Step 6, Box A, on page 600.

8	

9. Are the amounts on lines 8 and 6 the same?

☐ **Yes.** *Skip line 10; enter the amount from line 7 on line 11.*

☐ **No.** *Go to line 10.*

10. Is the amount on line 8 less than:
- $5,950 if you do not have a qualifying child **or**
- $13,100 if you have one or more qualifying children?

☐ **Yes.** *Leave line 10 blank; enter the amount from line 7 on line 11.*

☐ **No.** Look up the amount on line 8 in the EIC Table on pages 606–608 to find the credit. Enter the credit here.

10	

Look at the amounts on lines 10 and 7.
*Then, enter the **smaller** amount on line 11.*

Part 6 **Your Earned Income Credit**	**11.** **This is your earned income credit.**	**11**	

Enter this amount on Form 1040, line 61a.

Reminder—

√ Be sure you entered the amount of any nontaxable earned income (Step 7, Box B, on page 601) on Form 1040, line 61b.

√ If you have a qualifying child, complete and attach Schedule EIC.

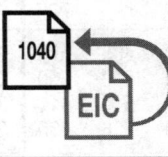

 If your EIC for a year after 1996 was reduced or disallowed, see page 602 to find out if you must file Form 8862 to take the credit for 2001.

2001 Earned Income Credit (EIC) Table

 CAUTION

This is **not** a tax table.

1. To find your credit, read down the "At least – But less than" columns and find the line that includes the amount you were told to look up from your EIC Worksheet.

2. Then, read across to the column that includes the number of qualifying children you have. Enter the credit from that column on your EIC Worksheet.

Example. If you have one qualifying child and the amount you are looking up from your EIC Worksheet is $4,875, you would enter $1,658.

If the amount you are looking up from the worksheet is—		And you have—		
		No children	One child	Two children
At least	But less than	Your credit is—		
4,800	4,850	364	1,641	1,930
4,850	4,900	364	1,658	1,950
4,900	4,950	364	1,675	1,970
4,950	5,000	364	1,692	1,990

If the amount you are looking up from the worksheet is—		And you have—		
		No children	One child	Two children
At least	But less than	Your credit is—		
$1	$50	$2	$9	$10
50	100	6	26	30
100	150	10	43	50
150	200	13	60	70
200	250	17	77	90
250	300	21	94	110
300	350	25	111	130
350	400	29	128	150
400	450	33	145	170
450	500	36	162	190
500	550	40	179	210
550	600	44	196	230
600	650	48	213	250
650	700	52	230	270
700	750	55	247	290
750	800	59	264	310
800	850	63	281	330
850	900	67	298	350
900	950	71	315	370
950	1,000	75	332	390
1,000	1,050	78	349	410
1,050	1,100	82	366	430
1,100	1,150	86	383	450
1,150	1,200	90	400	470
1,200	1,250	94	417	490
1,250	1,300	98	434	510
1,300	1,350	101	451	530
1,350	1,400	105	468	550
1,400	1,450	109	485	570
1,450	1,500	113	502	590
1,500	1,550	117	519	610
1,550	1,600	120	536	630
1,600	1,650	124	553	650
1,650	1,700	128	570	670
1,700	1,750	132	587	690
1,750	1,800	136	604	710
1,800	1,850	140	621	730
1,850	1,900	143	638	750
1,900	1,950	147	655	770
1,950	2,000	151	672	790
2,000	2,050	155	689	810
2,050	2,100	159	706	830
2,100	2,150	163	723	850
2,150	2,200	166	740	870

If the amount you are looking up from the worksheet is—		And you have—		
		No children	One child	Two children
At least	But less than	Your credit is—		
2,200	2,250	170	757	890
2,250	2,300	174	774	910
2,300	2,350	178	791	930
2,350	2,400	182	808	950
2,400	2,450	186	825	970
2,450	2,500	189	842	990
2,500	2,550	193	859	1,010
2,550	2,600	197	876	1,030
2,600	2,650	201	893	1,050
2,650	2,700	205	910	1,070
2,700	2,750	208	927	1,090
2,750	2,800	212	944	1,110
2,800	2,850	216	961	1,130
2,850	2,900	220	978	1,150
2,900	2,950	224	995	1,170
2,950	3,000	228	1,012	1,190
3,000	3,050	231	1,029	1,210
3,050	3,100	235	1,046	1,230
3,100	3,150	239	1,063	1,250
3,150	3,200	243	1,080	1,270
3,200	3,250	247	1,097	1,290
3,250	3,300	251	1,114	1,310
3,300	3,350	254	1,131	1,330
3,350	3,400	258	1,148	1,350
3,400	3,450	262	1,165	1,370
3,450	3,500	266	1,182	1,390
3,500	3,550	270	1,199	1,410
3,550	3,600	273	1,216	1,430
3,600	3,650	277	1,233	1,450
3,650	3,700	281	1,250	1,470
3,700	3,750	285	1,267	1,490
3,750	3,800	289	1,284	1,510
3,800	3,850	293	1,301	1,530
3,850	3,900	296	1,318	1,550
3,900	3,950	300	1,335	1,570
3,950	4,000	304	1,352	1,590
4,000	4,050	308	1,369	1,610
4,050	4,100	312	1,386	1,630
4,100	4,150	316	1,403	1,650
4,150	4,200	319	1,420	1,670
4,200	4,250	323	1,437	1,690
4,250	4,300	327	1,454	1,710
4,300	4,350	331	1,471	1,730
4,350	4,400	335	1,488	1,750

If the amount you are looking up from the worksheet is—		And you have—		
		No children	One child	Two children
At least	But less than	Your credit is—		
4,400	4,450	339	1,505	1,770
4,450	4,500	342	1,522	1,790
4,500	4,550	346	1,539	1,810
4,550	4,600	350	1,556	1,830
4,600	4,650	354	1,573	1,850
4,650	4,700	358	1,590	1,870
4,700	4,750	361	1,607	1,890
4,750	4,800	364	1,624	1,910
4,800	4,850	364	1,641	1,930
4,850	4,900	364	1,658	1,950
4,900	4,950	364	1,675	1,970
4,950	5,000	364	1,692	1,990
5,000	5,050	364	1,709	2,010
5,050	5,100	364	1,726	2,030
5,100	5,150	364	1,743	2,050
5,150	5,200	364	1,760	2,070
5,200	5,250	364	1,777	2,090
5,250	5,300	364	1,794	2,110
5,300	5,350	364	1,811	2,130
5,350	5,400	364	1,828	2,150
5,400	5,450	364	1,845	2,170
5,450	5,500	364	1,862	2,190
5,500	5,550	364	1,879	2,210
5,550	5,600	364	1,896	2,230
5,600	5,650	364	1,913	2,250
5,650	5,700	364	1,930	2,270
5,700	5,750	364	1,947	2,290
5,750	5,800	364	1,964	2,310
5,800	5,850	364	1,981	2,330
5,850	5,900	364	1,998	2,350
5,900	5,950	364	2,015	2,370
5,950	6,000	362	2,032	2,390
6,000	6,050	358	2,049	2,410
6,050	6,100	355	2,066	2,430
6,100	6,150	351	2,083	2,450
6,150	6,200	347	2,100	2,470
6,200	6,250	343	2,117	2,490
6,250	6,300	339	2,134	2,510
6,300	6,350	335	2,151	2,530
6,350	6,400	332	2,168	2,550
6,400	6,450	328	2,185	2,570
6,450	6,500	324	2,202	2,590
6,500	6,550	320	2,219	2,610
6,550	6,600	316	2,236	2,630

If the amount you are looking up from the worksheet is—		And you have—		
		No children	One child	Two children
At least	But less than	Your credit is—		
6,600	6,650	313	2,253	2,650
6,650	6,700	309	2,270	2,670
6,700	6,750	305	2,287	2,690
6,750	6,800	301	2,304	2,710
6,800	6,850	297	2,321	2,730
6,850	6,900	293	2,338	2,750
6,900	6,950	290	2,355	2,770
6,950	7,000	286	2,372	2,790
7,000	7,050	282	2,389	2,810
7,050	7,100	278	2,406	2,830
7,100	7,150	274	2,428	2,850
7,150	7,200	270	2,428	2,870
7,200	7,250	267	2,428	2,890
7,250	7,300	263	2,428	2,910
7,300	7,350	259	2,428	2,930
7,350	7,400	255	2,428	2,950
7,400	7,450	251	2,428	2,970
7,450	7,500	247	2,428	2,990
7,500	7,550	244	2,428	3,010
7,550	7,600	240	2,428	3,030
7,600	7,650	236	2,428	3,050
7,650	7,700	232	2,428	3,070
7,700	7,750	228	2,428	3,090
7,750	7,800	225	2,428	3,110
7,800	7,850	221	2,428	3,130
7,850	7,900	217	2,428	3,150
7,900	7,950	213	2,428	3,170
7,950	8,000	209	2,428	3,190
8,000	8,050	205	2,428	3,210
8,050	8,100	202	2,428	3,230
8,100	8,150	198	2,428	3,250
8,150	8,200	194	2,428	3,270
8,200	8,250	190	2,428	3,290
8,250	8,300	186	2,428	3,310
8,300	8,350	182	2,428	3,330
8,350	8,400	179	2,428	3,350
8,400	8,450	175	2,428	3,370
8,450	8,500	171	2,428	3,390
8,500	8,550	167	2,428	3,410
8,550	8,600	163	2,428	3,430
8,600	8,650	160	2,428	3,450
8,650	8,700	156	2,428	3,470
8,700	8,750	152	2,428	3,490
8,750	8,800	148	2,428	3,510

2001 Earned Income Credit (EIC) Table Continued   (Caution. This is **not** a tax table.)

If the amount you are looking up from the worksheet is—		And you have—		
At least	But less than	No children	One child	Two children
		Your credit is—		
8,800	8,850	144	2,428	3,530
8,850	8,900	140	2,428	3,550
8,900	8,950	137	2,428	3,570
8,950	9,000	133	2,428	3,590
9,000	9,050	129	2,428	3,610
9,050	9,100	125	2,428	3,630
9,100	9,150	121	2,428	3,650
9,150	9,200	117	2,428	3,670
9,200	9,250	114	2,428	3,690
9,250	9,300	110	2,428	3,710
9,300	9,350	106	2,428	3,730
9,350	9,400	102	2,428	3,750
9,400	9,450	98	2,428	3,770
9,450	9,500	94	2,428	3,790
9,500	9,550	91	2,428	3,810
9,550	9,600	87	2,428	3,830
9,600	9,650	83	2,428	3,850
9,650	9,700	79	2,428	3,870
9,700	9,750	75	2,428	3,890
9,750	9,800	72	2,428	3,910
9,800	9,850	68	2,428	3,930
9,850	9,900	64	2,428	3,950
9,900	9,950	60	2,428	3,970
9,950	10,000	56	2,428	3,990
10,000	10,050	52	2,428	4,008
10,050	10,100	49	2,428	4,008
10,100	10,150	45	2,428	4,008
10,150	10,200	41	2,428	4,008
10,200	10,250	37	2,428	4,008
10,250	10,300	33	2,428	4,008
10,300	10,350	29	2,428	4,008
10,350	10,400	26	2,428	4,008
10,400	10,450	22	2,428	4,008
10,450	10,500	18	2,428	4,008
10,500	10,550	14	2,428	4,008
10,550	10,600	10	2,428	4,008
10,600	10,650	7	2,428	4,008
10,650	10,700	3	2,428	4,008
10,700	10,750	*	2,428	4,008
10,750	13,100	0	2,428	4,008
13,100	13,150	0	2,422	4,001
13,150	13,200	0	2,414	3,990
13,200	13,250	0	2,406	3,980
13,250	13,300	0	2,398	3,969
13,300	13,350	0	2,390	3,959
13,350	13,400	0	2,382	3,948
13,400	13,450	0	2,374	3,937
13,450	13,500	0	2,366	3,927
13,500	13,550	0	2,358	3,916
13,550	13,600	0	2,350	3,906
13,600	13,650	0	2,342	3,895
13,650	13,700	0	2,334	3,885
13,700	13,750	0	2,326	3,874
13,750	13,800	0	2,318	3,864
13,800	13,850	0	2,310	3,853
13,850	13,900	0	2,302	3,843

If the amount you are looking up from the worksheet is—		And you have—		
At least	But less than	No children	One child	Two children
		Your credit is—		
13,900	13,950	0	2,294	3,832
13,950	14,000	0	2,286	3,822
14,000	14,050	0	2,278	3,811
14,050	14,100	0	2,270	3,801
14,100	14,150	0	2,262	3,790
14,150	14,200	0	2,254	3,779
14,200	14,250	0	2,246	3,769
14,250	14,300	0	2,238	3,758
14,300	14,350	0	2,230	3,748
14,350	14,400	0	2,222	3,737
14,400	14,450	0	2,214	3,727
14,450	14,500	0	2,206	3,716
14,500	14,550	0	2,198	3,706
14,550	14,600	0	2,190	3,695
14,600	14,650	0	2,182	3,685
14,650	14,700	0	2,174	3,674
14,700	14,750	0	2,166	3,664
14,750	14,800	0	2,158	3,653
14,800	14,850	0	2,150	3,643
14,850	14,900	0	2,142	3,632
14,900	14,950	0	2,134	3,622
14,950	15,000	0	2,126	3,611
15,000	15,050	0	2,118	3,600
15,050	15,100	0	2,110	3,590
15,100	15,150	0	2,102	3,579
15,150	15,200	0	2,094	3,569
15,200	15,250	0	2,086	3,558
15,250	15,300	0	2,078	3,548
15,300	15,350	0	2,070	3,537
15,350	15,400	0	2,062	3,527
15,400	15,450	0	2,054	3,516
15,450	15,500	0	2,046	3,506
15,500	15,550	0	2,038	3,495
15,550	15,600	0	2,030	3,485
15,600	15,650	0	2,023	3,474
15,650	15,700	0	2,015	3,464
15,700	15,750	0	2,007	3,453
15,750	15,800	0	1,999	3,443
15,800	15,850	0	1,991	3,432
15,850	15,900	0	1,983	3,421
15,900	15,950	0	1,975	3,411
15,950	16,000	0	1,967	3,400
16,000	16,050	0	1,959	3,390
16,050	16,100	0	1,951	3,379
16,100	16,150	0	1,943	3,369
16,150	16,200	0	1,935	3,358
16,200	16,250	0	1,927	3,348
16,250	16,300	0	1,919	3,337
16,300	16,350	0	1,911	3,327
16,350	16,400	0	1,903	3,316
16,400	16,450	0	1,895	3,306
16,450	16,500	0	1,887	3,295
16,500	16,550	0	1,879	3,285
16,550	16,600	0	1,871	3,274
16,600	16,650	0	1,863	3,264
16,650	16,700	0	1,855	3,253

If the amount you are looking up from the worksheet is—		And you have—		
At least	But less than	No children	One child	Two children
		Your credit is—		
16,700	16,750	0	1,847	3,242
16,750	16,800	0	1,839	3,232
16,800	16,850	0	1,831	3,221
16,850	16,900	0	1,823	3,211
16,900	16,950	0	1,815	3,200
16,950	17,000	0	1,807	3,190
17,000	17,050	0	1,799	3,179
17,050	17,100	0	1,791	3,169
17,100	17,150	0	1,783	3,158
17,150	17,200	0	1,775	3,148
17,200	17,250	0	1,767	3,137
17,250	17,300	0	1,759	3,127
17,300	17,350	0	1,751	3,116
17,350	17,400	0	1,743	3,106
17,400	17,450	0	1,735	3,095
17,450	17,500	0	1,727	3,085
17,500	17,550	0	1,719	3,074
17,550	17,600	0	1,711	3,063
17,600	17,650	0	1,703	3,053
17,650	17,700	0	1,695	3,042
17,700	17,750	0	1,687	3,032
17,750	17,800	0	1,679	3,021
17,800	17,850	0	1,671	3,011
17,850	17,900	0	1,663	3,000
17,900	17,950	0	1,655	2,990
17,950	18,000	0	1,647	2,979
18,000	18,050	0	1,639	2,969
18,050	18,100	0	1,631	2,958
18,100	18,150	0	1,623	2,948
18,150	18,200	0	1,615	2,937
18,200	18,250	0	1,607	2,927
18,250	18,300	0	1,599	2,916
18,300	18,350	0	1,591	2,906
18,350	18,400	0	1,583	2,895
18,400	18,450	0	1,575	2,884
18,450	18,500	0	1,567	2,874
18,500	18,550	0	1,559	2,863
18,550	18,600	0	1,551	2,853
18,600	18,650	0	1,543	2,842
18,650	18,700	0	1,535	2,832
18,700	18,750	0	1,527	2,821
18,750	18,800	0	1,519	2,811
18,800	18,850	0	1,511	2,800
18,850	18,900	0	1,503	2,790
18,900	18,950	0	1,495	2,779
18,950	19,000	0	1,487	2,769
19,000	19,050	0	1,479	2,758
19,050	19,100	0	1,471	2,748
19,100	19,150	0	1,463	2,737
19,150	19,200	0	1,455	2,726
19,200	19,250	0	1,447	2,716
19,250	19,300	0	1,439	2,705
19,300	19,350	0	1,431	2,695
19,350	19,400	0	1,423	2,684
19,400	19,450	0	1,415	2,674
19,450	19,500	0	1,407	2,663

If the amount you are looking up from the worksheet is—		And you have—		
At least	But less than	No children	One child	Two children
		Your credit is—		
19,500	19,550	0	1,399	2,653
19,550	19,600	0	1,391	2,642
19,600	19,650	0	1,383	2,632
19,650	19,700	0	1,375	2,621
19,700	19,750	0	1,367	2,611
19,750	19,800	0	1,359	2,600
19,800	19,850	0	1,351	2,590
19,850	19,900	0	1,343	2,579
19,900	19,950	0	1,335	2,569
19,950	20,000	0	1,327	2,558
20,000	20,050	0	1,319	2,547
20,050	20,100	0	1,311	2,537
20,100	20,150	0	1,303	2,526
20,150	20,200	0	1,295	2,516
20,200	20,250	0	1,287	2,505
20,250	20,300	0	1,279	2,495
20,300	20,350	0	1,271	2,484
20,350	20,400	0	1,263	2,474
20,400	20,450	0	1,255	2,463
20,450	20,500	0	1,247	2,453
20,500	20,550	0	1,239	2,442
20,550	20,600	0	1,231	2,432
20,600	20,650	0	1,224	2,421
20,650	20,700	0	1,216	2,411
20,700	20,750	0	1,208	2,400
20,750	20,800	0	1,200	2,390
20,800	20,850	0	1,192	2,379
20,850	20,900	0	1,184	2,368
20,900	20,950	0	1,176	2,358
20,950	21,000	0	1,168	2,347
21,000	21,050	0	1,160	2,337
21,050	21,100	0	1,152	2,326
21,100	21,150	0	1,144	2,316
21,150	21,200	0	1,136	2,305
21,200	21,250	0	1,128	2,295
21,250	21,300	0	1,120	2,284
21,300	21,350	0	1,112	2,274
21,350	21,400	0	1,104	2,263
21,400	21,450	0	1,096	2,253
21,450	21,500	0	1,088	2,242
21,500	21,550	0	1,080	2,232
21,550	21,600	0	1,072	2,221
21,600	21,650	0	1,064	2,211
21,650	21,700	0	1,056	2,200
21,700	21,750	0	1,048	2,189
21,750	21,800	0	1,040	2,179
21,800	21,850	0	1,032	2,168
21,850	21,900	0	1,024	2,158
21,900	21,950	0	1,016	2,147
21,950	22,000	0	1,008	2,137
22,000	22,050	0	1,000	2,126
22,050	22,100	0	992	2,116
22,100	22,150	0	984	2,105
22,150	22,200	0	976	2,095
22,200	22,250	0	968	2,084
22,250	22,300	0	960	2,074

*If the amount you are looking up from the worksheet is at least $10,700 but less than $10,710, your credit is $1. Otherwise, you cannot take the credit.

2001 Earned Income Credit (EIC) Table Continued (Caution. This is **not** a tax table.)

If the amount you are looking up from the worksheet is—		And you have— No children	One child	Two children
At least	But less than	Your credit is—		
22,300	22,350	0	952	2,063
22,350	22,400	0	944	2,053
22,400	22,450	0	936	2,042
22,450	22,500	0	928	2,032
22,500	22,550	0	920	2,021
22,550	22,600	0	912	2,010
22,600	22,650	0	904	2,000
22,650	22,700	0	896	1,989
22,700	22,750	0	888	1,979
22,750	22,800	0	880	1,968
22,800	22,850	0	872	1,958
22,850	22,900	0	864	1,947
22,900	22,950	0	856	1,937
22,950	23,000	0	848	1,926
23,000	23,050	0	840	1,916
23,050	23,100	0	832	1,905
23,100	23,150	0	824	1,895
23,150	23,200	0	816	1,884
23,200	23,250	0	808	1,874
23,250	23,300	0	800	1,863
23,300	23,350	0	792	1,853
23,350	23,400	0	784	1,842
23,400	23,450	0	776	1,831
23,450	23,500	0	768	1,821
23,500	23,550	0	760	1,810
23,550	23,600	0	752	1,800
23,600	23,650	0	744	1,789
23,650	23,700	0	736	1,779
23,700	23,750	0	728	1,768
23,750	23,800	0	720	1,758
23,800	23,850	0	712	1,747
23,850	23,900	0	704	1,737
23,900	23,950	0	696	1,726
23,950	24,000	0	688	1,716
24,000	24,050	0	680	1,705
24,050	24,100	0	672	1,695
24,100	24,150	0	664	1,684
24,150	24,200	0	656	1,673
24,200	24,250	0	648	1,663
24,250	24,300	0	640	1,652
24,300	24,350	0	632	1,642
24,350	24,400	0	624	1,631
24,400	24,450	0	616	1,621
24,450	24,500	0	608	1,610
24,500	24,550	0	600	1,600
24,550	24,600	0	592	1,589
24,600	24,650	0	584	1,579
24,650	24,700	0	576	1,568
24,700	24,750	0	568	1,558
24,750	24,800	0	560	1,547
24,800	24,850	0	552	1,537
24,850	24,900	0	544	1,526

If the amount you are looking up from the worksheet is—		And you have— No children	One child	Two children
At least	But less than	Your credit is—		
24,900	24,950	0	536	1,516
24,950	25,000	0	528	1,505
25,000	25,050	0	520	1,494
25,050	25,100	0	512	1,484
25,100	25,150	0	504	1,473
25,150	25,200	0	496	1,463
25,200	25,250	0	488	1,452
25,250	25,300	0	480	1,442
25,300	25,350	0	472	1,431
25,350	25,400	0	464	1,421
25,400	25,450	0	456	1,410
25,450	25,500	0	448	1,400
25,500	25,550	0	440	1,389
25,550	25,600	0	432	1,379
25,600	25,650	0	425	1,368
25,650	25,700	0	417	1,358
25,700	25,750	0	409	1,347
25,750	25,800	0	401	1,337
25,800	25,850	0	393	1,326
25,850	25,900	0	385	1,315
25,900	25,950	0	377	1,305
25,950	26,000	0	369	1,294
26,000	26,050	0	361	1,284
26,050	26,100	0	353	1,273
26,100	26,150	0	345	1,263
26,150	26,200	0	337	1,252
26,200	26,250	0	329	1,242
26,250	26,300	0	321	1,231
26,300	26,350	0	313	1,221
26,350	26,400	0	305	1,210
26,400	26,450	0	297	1,200
26,450	26,500	0	289	1,189
26,500	26,550	0	281	1,179
26,550	26,600	0	273	1,168
26,600	26,650	0	265	1,158
26,650	26,700	0	257	1,147
26,700	26,750	0	249	1,136
26,750	26,800	0	241	1,126
26,800	26,850	0	233	1,115
26,850	26,900	0	225	1,105
26,900	26,950	0	217	1,094
26,950	27,000	0	209	1,084
27,000	27,050	0	201	1,073
27,050	27,100	0	193	1,063
27,100	27,150	0	185	1,052
27,150	27,200	0	177	1,042
27,200	27,250	0	169	1,031
27,250	27,300	0	161	1,021
27,300	27,350	0	153	1,010
27,350	27,400	0	145	1,000
27,400	27,450	0	137	989
27,450	27,500	0	129	979

If the amount you are looking up from the worksheet is—		And you have— No children	One child	Two children
At least	But less than	Your credit is—		
27,500	27,550	0	121	968
27,550	27,600	0	113	957
27,600	27,650	0	105	947
27,650	27,700	0	97	936
27,700	27,750	0	89	926
27,750	27,800	0	81	915
27,800	27,850	0	73	905
27,850	27,900	0	65	894
27,900	27,950	0	57	884
27,950	28,000	0	49	873
28,000	28,050	0	41	863
28,050	28,100	0	33	852
28,100	28,150	0	25	842
28,150	28,200	0	17	831
28,200	28,250	0	9	821
28,250	28,300	0	**	810
28,300	28,350	0	0	800
28,350	28,400	0	0	789
28,400	28,450	0	0	778
28,450	28,500	0	0	768
28,500	28,550	0	0	757
28,550	28,600	0	0	747
28,600	28,650	0	0	736
28,650	28,700	0	0	726
28,700	28,750	0	0	715
28,750	28,800	0	0	705
28,800	28,850	0	0	694
28,850	28,900	0	0	684
28,900	28,950	0	0	673
28,950	29,000	0	0	663
29,000	29,050	0	0	652
29,050	29,100	0	0	642
29,100	29,150	0	0	631
29,150	29,200	0	0	620
29,200	29,250	0	0	610
29,250	29,300	0	0	599
29,300	29,350	0	0	589
29,350	29,400	0	0	578
29,400	29,450	0	0	568
29,450	29,500	0	0	557
29,500	29,550	0	0	547
29,550	29,600	0	0	536
29,600	29,650	0	0	526
29,650	29,700	0	0	515
29,700	29,750	0	0	505
29,750	29,800	0	0	494
29,800	29,850	0	0	484
29,850	29,900	0	0	473
29,900	29,950	0	0	463
29,950	30,000	0	0	452
30,000	30,050	0	0	441
30,050	30,100	0	0	431

If the amount you are looking up from the worksheet is—		And you have— No children	One child	Two children
At least	But less than	Your credit is—		
30,100	30,150	0	0	420
30,150	30,200	0	0	410
30,200	30,250	0	0	399
30,250	30,300	0	0	389
30,300	30,350	0	0	378
30,350	30,400	0	0	368
30,400	30,450	0	0	357
30,450	30,500	0	0	347
30,500	30,550	0	0	336
30,550	30,600	0	0	326
30,600	30,650	0	0	315
30,650	30,700	0	0	305
30,700	30,750	0	0	294
30,750	30,800	0	0	284
30,800	30,850	0	0	273
30,850	30,900	0	0	262
30,900	30,950	0	0	252
30,950	31,000	0	0	241
31,000	31,050	0	0	231
31,050	31,100	0	0	220
31,100	31,150	0	0	210
31,150	31,200	0	0	199
31,200	31,250	0	0	189
31,250	31,300	0	0	178
31,300	31,350	0	0	168
31,350	31,400	0	0	157
31,400	31,450	0	0	147
31,450	31,500	0	0	136
31,500	31,550	0	0	126
31,550	31,600	0	0	115
31,600	31,650	0	0	105
31,650	31,700	0	0	94
31,700	31,750	0	0	83
31,750	31,800	0	0	73
31,800	31,850	0	0	62
31,850	31,900	0	0	52
31,900	31,950	0	0	41
31,950	32,000	0	0	31
32,000	32,050	0	0	20
32,050	32,100	0	0	10
32,100	32,121	0	0	2
32,121 or more		0	0	0

**If the amount you are looking up from the worksheet is at least $28,250 but less than $28,281, your credit is $3. Otherwise, you cannot take the credit.

tax may have been withheld. You can take a credit on this line for the amount withheld in excess of $4,984.80. But if any one employer withheld more than $4,984.80, you must ask that employer to refund the excess to you. You cannot claim it on your return. Figure this amount separately for you and your spouse.

If you had more than one railroad employer for 2001 and your total compensation was over $59,700, too much railroad retirement (RRTA) tax may have been withheld.

For more details, see **Pub. 505.**

Line 63 Additional Child Tax Credit

What Is the Additional Child Tax Credit?

This credit is for certain people who have at least one qualifying child as defined in the instructions for line 6c, column (4). The additional child tax credit may give you a refund even if you do not owe any tax.

Two Steps To Take the Additional Child Tax Credit!

Step 1. Be sure you figured the amount, if any, of your child tax credit. See the instructions for line 48.
Step 2. Read the **TIP** at the end of your Child Tax Credit Worksheet. Use Form 8812 to see if you can take the additional child tax credit only if you meet the condition given in that TIP.

Line 64 Amount Paid With Request for Extension To File

If you filed **Form 4868** to get an automatic extension of time to file Form 1040, enter any amount you paid with that form or by electronic funds withdrawal or credit card. If you paid by credit card, do not include on line 64 the convenience fee you were charged. Also, include any amounts paid with **Form 2688** or **2350.**

Line 65 Other Payments

Check the box(es) on line 65 to report any credit from **Form 2439** or **4136.**

Refund

Line 67 Amount Overpaid

If line 67 is under $1, we will send a refund only on written request.

If you want to check the status of your refund, please wait at least 4 weeks from the date you filed your return to do so.
Tip. If the amount you overpaid is large, you may want to decrease the amount of income tax withheld from your pay by filing a new **Form W-4.**

Refund Offset

If you owe past-due Federal tax, state income tax, child support, spousal support, or certain Federal nontax debts, such as student loans, all or part of the overpayment on line 67 may be used (offset) to pay the past-due amount. Offsets for Federal taxes are made by the IRS. All other offsets are made by the Treasury Department's Financial Management Service (FMS). You will receive a notice from FMS showing the amount of the offset and the agency receiving it. To find out if you may have an offset or if you have any questions about it, contact the agency(ies) you owe the debt to.

Injured Spouse Claim

If you file a joint return and your spouse has not paid past-due Federal tax, state income tax, child support, spousal support, or a Federal nontax debt, such as a student loan, part or all of the overpayment on line 67 may be used (offset) to pay the past-due amount. But **your** part of the overpayment may be refunded to you after the offset occurs if certain conditions apply and you complete **Form 8379.** For details, use TeleTax topic 203 or see Form 8379.

Lines 68b Through 68d

Direct Deposit of Refund

Complete lines 68b through 68d if you want us to directly deposit the amount shown on line 68a into your account at a bank or other financial institution (such as a mutual fund, brokerage firm, or credit union) instead of sending you a check.

Why Use Direct Deposit?

- You get your refund fast—even faster if you *e-file!*
- Payment is more secure—there is no check to get lost.
- More convenient. No trip to the bank to deposit your check.
- Saves tax dollars. A refund by direct deposit costs less than a check.

Tip. You can check with your financial institution to make sure your deposit will be accepted and to get the correct routing and account numbers. The IRS is not responsible for a lost refund if you enter the wrong account information.

If you file a joint return and fill in lines 68b through 68d, you are appointing your spouse as an agent to receive the refund. This appointment cannot be changed later.

Line 68b

The routing number **must** be **nine** digits. The first two digits must be 01 through 12 or 21 through 32. Otherwise, the direct deposit will be rejected and a check sent instead. On the sample check on page 610, the routing number is 250250025.

Your check may state that it is payable through a financial institution different from the one at which you have your checking account. If so, **do not** use the routing number on that check. Instead, contact your financial institution for the correct routing number to enter on line 68b.

Line 68d

The account number can be up to 17 characters (both numbers and letters). Include hyphens but omit spaces and special symbols. Enter the number from left to right and leave any unused boxes blank. On the sample check on page 610, the account number is 20202086. Be sure **not** to include the check number.
Caution. Some financial institutions will not allow a joint refund to be deposited into an individual account. If the direct deposit is rejected, a check will be sent instead. The IRS is not responsible if a financial institution rejects a direct deposit.

Line 69 Applied to Your 2002 Estimated Tax

Enter on line 69 the amount, if any, of the overpayment on line 67 you want applied to your 2002 estimated tax. We will apply this amount to your account unless you attach a statement requesting us to apply it to your spouse's account. Include your spouse's social security number in the attached statement.
Caution. This election to apply part or all of the amount overpaid to your 2002 estimated tax cannot be changed later.

Sample Check—Lines 68b Through 68d

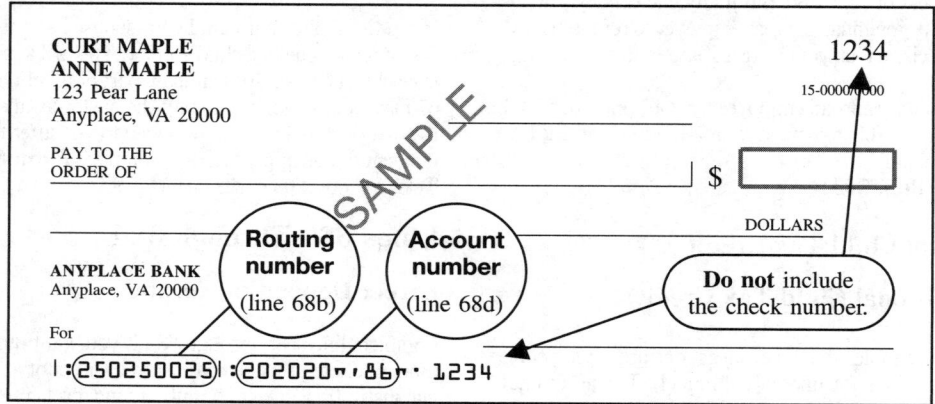

Amount You Owe

Line 70 Amount You Owe

Tip. You do not have to pay if line 70 is under $1.

Include any estimated tax penalty from line 71 in the amount you enter on line 70.

You can pay by check, money order, or credit card. **Do not** include any estimated tax payment in your check, money order, or amount you charge. Instead, make the estimated tax payment separately.

To Pay by Check or Money Order. Make your check or money order payable to the **"United States Treasury"** for the full amount due. **Do not** send cash. **Do not** attach the payment to your return. Write "2001 Form 1040" and your name, address, daytime phone number, and social security number (SSN) on your payment. If you are filing a joint return, enter the SSN shown first on your tax return.

To help us process your payment, enter the amount on the right side of the check like this: $ XXX.XX. Do not use dashes or lines (for example, do not enter "$ XXX.-" or "$ XXX XX/100").

Then, please complete **Form 1040-V** following the instructions on that form and enclose it in the envelope with your tax return and payment. Although you do not have to use Form 1040-V, doing so allows us to process your payment more accurately and efficiently.

To Pay by Credit Card. You may use your American Express® Card, Discover® Card, or MasterCard® card. To pay by credit card, call toll free or access by Internet one of the service providers listed on this page and follow the instructions. A convenience fee will be charged by the service provider based on the amount you are paying. Fees may vary between the providers. You will be told what the fee is during the transaction and you will have the option to either continue or cancel the transaction. You can also find out what the fee will be by calling the provider's toll-free automated customer service number or visiting the provider's Web Site shown below. **If you paid by credit card,** enter on page 1 of Form 1040 in the upper left corner the confirmation number you were given at the end of the transaction and the amount you charged (not including the convenience fee).

PhoneCharge, Inc.
1-888-ALLTAXX (1-888-255-8299)
1-877-851-9964 (Customer Service)
www.1888ALLTAXX.com
Official Payments Corporation
1-800-2PAY-TAX (1-800-272-9829)
1-877-754-4413 (Customer Service)
www.officialpayments.com

Tip. You may need to **(a)** increase the amount of income tax withheld from your pay by filing a new **Form W-4** or **(b)** make estimated tax payments for 2002.

What if You Cannot Pay?

If you cannot pay the full amount shown on line 70 when you file, you may ask to make monthly **installment payments.** You may have up to 60 months to pay. However, you will be charged interest and may be charged a late payment penalty on the tax not paid by April 15, 2002, even if your request to pay in installments is granted. You must also pay a fee. To limit the interest and penalty charges, pay as much of the tax as possible when you file. But before requesting an installment agreement, you should consider other less costly alternatives, such as a bank loan.

To ask for an installment agreement, use **Form 9465.** You should receive a response to your request for installments within 30 days. But if you file your return after March 31, it may take us longer to reply.

Line 71 Estimated Tax Penalty

Caution. You must include household employment taxes reported on line 57 to see if you owe the penalty if line 59 is more than zero **or** you would owe the penalty even if you did not include those taxes. But if you entered an amount on Schedule H, line 7, include the total of that amount plus the amount on Form 1040, line 57.

You may owe this penalty if:

• Line 70 is at least $1,000 and it is more than 10% of the tax shown on your return or
• You did not pay enough estimated tax by any of the due dates. This is true even if you are due a refund.

For most people, the "tax shown on your return" is the amount on line 58 minus the total of any amounts shown on lines 61a and 63 and Forms 8828, 4137, 4136, and 5329 (Parts III, IV, V, VI, and VII only).

Exception. You will not owe the penalty if your 2000 tax return was for a tax year of 12 full months **and either** of the following applies.

1. You had no tax liability for 2000 and you were a U.S. citizen or resident for all of 2000 **or**
2. The total of lines 59, 60, and 62 on your 2001 return is at least as much as the tax liability shown on your 2000 return. Your estimated tax payments for 2001 must have been made on time and for the required amount.

Caution. If your 2000 adjusted gross income was over $150,000 (over $75,000 if your 2001 filing status is married filing separately), item **2** above applies only if the total of lines 59, 60, and 62 on your 2001 return is at least 110% of the tax liability shown on your 2000 return. This rule does not apply to farmers and fishermen.

Figuring the Penalty

If the **Exception** above does not apply and you choose to figure the penalty yourself, see **Form 2210** (or **2210-F** for farmers and fishermen) to find out if you owe the penalty. If you do, you can use the form to figure the amount. In certain situations, you may be able to lower your penalty. For details, see the Instructions for Form 2210 (or 2210-F).

Enter the penalty on line 71. Add the penalty to any tax due and enter the total on line 70. If you are due a refund, subtract the penalty from the overpayment you show on line 67. **Do not** file Form 2210 with your return unless Form 2210 indicates that you must do so. Instead, keep it for your records.

Tip. Because Form 2210 is complicated, if you want to, you can leave line 71 blank and the IRS will figure the penalty and send you a bill. We will not charge you interest on the penalty if you pay by the date specified on the bill.

Third Party Designee

If you want to allow a friend, family member, or any other person you choose to discuss your 2001 tax return with the IRS, check the "Yes" box in the "Third Party Designee" area of your return. Also, enter the designee's name, phone number, and any five numbers the designee chooses as his or her personal identification number (PIN). **But** if you want to allow the paid preparer who signed your return to discuss it with the IRS, just enter "Preparer" in the space for the designee's name. You do not have to provide the other information requested.

If you check the "Yes" box, you, and your spouse if filing a joint return, are authorizing the IRS to call the designee to answer any questions that may arise during the processing of your return. You are also authorizing the designee to:

- Give the IRS any information that is missing from your return,
- Call the IRS for information about the processing of your return or the status of your refund or payment(s), and
- Respond to certain IRS notices that you have shared with the designee about math errors, offsets, and return preparation. The notices will not be sent to the designee.

You are not authorizing the designee to receive any refund check, bind you to anything (including any additional tax liability), or otherwise represent you before the IRS. If you want to expand the designee's authorization, see **Pub. 947.**

The authorization cannot be revoked. However, the authorization will automatically end no later than the due date (without regard to extensions) for filing your 2002 tax return. This is April 15, 2003, for most people.

Sign Your Return

Form 1040 is not considered a valid return unless you sign it. If you are filing a joint return, your spouse must also sign. If your spouse cannot sign the return, see **Pub. 501.** If you have someone prepare your return, you are still responsible for the correctness of the return.
Child's Return If your child cannot sign the return, either parent may sign the child's name in the space provided. Then, add "By (your signature), parent for minor child."

Daytime Phone Number

Providing your daytime phone number may help speed the processing of your return. We may have questions about items on your return, such as the earned income credit, credit for child and dependent care expenses, etc. By answering our questions over the phone, we may be able to continue processing your return without mailing you a letter. If you are filing a joint return, you may enter either your or your spouse's daytime phone number.

Paid Preparer Must Sign Your Return

Generally, anyone you pay to prepare your return must sign it by hand in the space provided. Signature stamps or labels cannot be used. The preparer must give you a copy of the return for your records. Someone who prepares your return but does not charge you should not sign your return.

Assemble Your Return

Assemble any schedules and forms behind Form 1040 in order of the "Attachment Sequence No." shown in the upper right corner of the schedule or form. If you have supporting statements, arrange them in the same order as the schedules or forms they support and attach them last. **Do not** attach correspondence or other items unless required to do so. Attach a copy of Forms W-2, W-2G, and 2439 to the front of Form 1040. Also attach Form(s) 1099-R to the front of Form 1040 if tax was withheld.

2001 Federal Tax Forms and Schedules You Can Use

Introduction

This chapter contains many of the official IRS tax forms that you need to complete your income tax return. The forms can be easily torn out and used. It is perfectly acceptable to use these forms in filling out your return.

A listing of all the tax forms included in this book—some of which are samples and others of which are provided for your use—can be found in the Table of Contents.

Here are the forms that are included in this chapter:

Form SS-4: Application for Employer Identification Number

Form 1040X: Amended U.S. Individual Income Tax Return

Form 1040EZ: Income Tax Return for Single and Joint Filers with No Dependents

Form 1040A: U.S. Individual Income Tax Return

Schedule 1: Interest and Ordinary Dividends for Form 1040A Filers

Schedule 2: Child and Dependent Care Expenses for Form 1040A Filers

Schedule 3: Credit for the Elderly or the Disabled for Form 1040A Filers

Form 1040: U.S. Individual Income Tax Return

Schedule A: Itemized Deductions

Schedule B: Interest and Ordinary Dividends

Schedule C: Profit or Loss from Business (Sole Proprietorship)

Schedule D: Capital Gains and Losses

Schedule E: Supplemental Income and Loss

Schedule F: Profit or Loss from Farming

Schedule R: Credit for the Elderly or the Disabled

Schedule SE: Self-Employment Tax

Form 1040-ES: Estimated Tax for Individuals—Payment Voucher

Form 1040-V: Payment Voucher

Form 709: United States Gift (and Generation-Skipping Transfer) Tax Return

Form 1116: Foreign Tax Credit

Form 2441: Child and Dependent Care Expenses

Form 3903: Moving Expenses

Form 4684: Casualties and Thefts

Form 4797: Sales of Business Property

Form 4868: Application for Automatic Extension of Time to File U.S. Individual Income Tax Return

Form 4952: Investment Interest Expense Deduction

Form 6251: Alternative Minimum Tax—Individuals

Form 8283: Noncash Charitable Contributions

Form 8812: Additional Child Tax Credit

Form 8814: Parents' Election to Report Child's Interests and Dividends

Form 8822: Change of Address

Form 8829: Expenses for Business Use of Your Home

Form 8839: Qualified Adoption Expenses

Form 8863: Education Credits (Hope and Lifetime Learning Credits)

Form **SS-4**

(Rev. April 2000)

Department of the Treasury
Internal Revenue Service

Application for Employer Identification Number

(For use by employers, corporations, partnerships, trusts, estates, churches, government agencies, certain individuals, and others. See instructions.)

▶ **Keep a copy for your records.**

EIN

OMB No. 1545-0003

Please type or print clearly.

1 Name of applicant (legal name) (see instructions)

2 Trade name of business (if different from name on line 1)

3 Executor, trustee, "care of" name

4a Mailing address (street address) (room, apt., or suite no.)

5a Business address (if different from address on lines 4a and 4b)

4b City, state, and ZIP code

5b City, state, and ZIP code

6 County and state where principal business is located

7 Name of principal officer, general partner, grantor, owner, or trustor—SSN or ITIN may be required (see instructions) ▶

8a Type of entity (Check only one box.) (see instructions)

Caution: *If applicant is a limited liability company, see the instructions for line 8a.*

- ☐ Sole proprietor (SSN) _____
- ☐ Partnership   ☐ Personal service corp.
- ☐ REMIC   ☐ National Guard
- ☐ State/local government ☐ Farmers' cooperative
- ☐ Church or church-controlled organization
- ☐ Other nonprofit organization (specify) ▶ _____
- ☐ Other (specify) ▶

- ☐ Estate (SSN of decedent) _____
- ☐ Plan administrator (SSN) _____
- ☐ Other corporation (specify) ▶ _____
- ☐ Trust
- ☐ Federal government/military
- (enter GEN if applicable) _____

8b If a corporation, name the state or foreign country (if applicable) where incorporated

State

Foreign country

9 Reason for applying (Check only one box.) (see instructions)
- ☐ Started new business (specify type) ▶ _____
- ☐ Hired employees (Check the box and see line 12.)
- ☐ Created a pension plan (specify type) ▶

- ☐ Banking purpose (specify purpose) ▶ _____
- ☐ Changed type of organization (specify new type) ▶ _____
- ☐ Purchased going business
- ☐ Created a trust (specify type) ▶ _____
- ☐ Other (specify) ▶

10 Date business started or acquired (month, day, year) (see instructions)

11 Closing month of accounting year (see instructions)

12 First date wages or annuities were paid or will be paid (month, day, year). **Note:** *If applicant is a withholding agent, enter date income will first be paid to nonresident alien. (month, day, year)* . . . . ▶

13 Highest number of employees expected in the next 12 months. **Note:** *If the applicant does not expect to have any employees during the period, enter -0-. (see instructions)* . . . . ▶

Nonagricultural	Agricultural	Household

14 Principal activity (see instructions) ▶

15 Is the principal business activity manufacturing? . . . . ☐ **Yes** ☐ **No**
If "Yes," principal product and raw material used ▶

16 To whom are most of the products or services sold? Please check one box. ☐ Business (wholesale)
☐ Public (retail)   ☐ Other (specify) ▶   ☐ N/A

17a Has the applicant ever applied for an employer identification number for this or any other business? . . . . ☐ **Yes** ☐ **No**
Note: *If "Yes," please complete lines 17b and 17c.*

17b If you checked "Yes" on line 17a, give applicant's legal name and trade name shown on prior application, if different from line 1 or 2 above.
Legal name ▶   Trade name ▶

17c Approximate date when and city and state where the application was filed. Enter previous employer identification number if known.
Approximate date when filed (mo., day, year) | City and state where filed | Previous EIN

Under penalties of perjury, I declare that I have examined this application, and to the best of my knowledge and belief, it is true, correct, and complete.

Business telephone number (include area code)
( )

Fax telephone number (include area code)
( )

Name and title (Please type or print clearly.) ▶

Signature ▶   Date ▶

Note: *Do not write below this line. For official use only.*

Please leave blank ▶	Geo.	Ind.	Class	Size	Reason for applying

For Privacy Act and Paperwork Reduction Act Notice, see page 4.

Cat. No. 16055N

Form **SS-4** (Rev. 4-2000)

Form 1040X
(Rev. November 2000)

Department of the Treasury—Internal Revenue Service

Amended U.S. Individual Income Tax Return
► See separate instructions.

OMB No. 1545-0091

This return is for calendar year ► , or fiscal year ended ► , .

Please print or type

Your first name and initial	Last name

Your social security number

If a joint return, spouse's first name and initial	Last name

Spouse's social security number

Home address (no. and street) or P.O. box if mail is not delivered to your home — Apt. no.

Phone number ( )

City, town or post office, state, and ZIP code. If you have a foreign address, see page 2 of the instructions.

For Paperwork Reduction Act Notice, see page 6.

A If the name or address shown above is different from that shown on the original return, check here . . . . . . ► ☐

B Has the original return been changed or audited by the IRS or have you been notified that it will be? . . ☐ **Yes** ☐ **No**

C Filing status. Be sure to complete this line. **Note.** You cannot change from joint to separate returns after the due date.

On original return ► ☐ Single ☐ Married filing joint return ☐ Married filing separate return ☐ Head of household ☐ Qualifying widow(er)

On this return ► ☐ Single ☐ Married filing joint return ☐ Married filing separate return ☐ Head of household* ☐ Qualifying widow(er)

* If the qualifying person is a child but not your dependent, see page 2.

Use Part II on the Back to Explain any Changes

		A. Original amount or as previously adjusted (see page 2)	B. Net change—amount of increase or (decrease)—explain in Part II	C. Correct amount
Income and Deductions (see pages 2–6)				
1 Adjusted gross income (see page 3)	1			
2 Itemized deductions or standard deduction (see page 3) . .	2			
3 Subtract line 2 from line 1	3			
4 Exemptions. If changing, fill in Parts I and II on the back .	4			
5 Taxable income. Subtract line 4 from line 3	5			
Tax Liability				
6 Tax (see page 4). Method used in col. C_____	6			
7 Credits (see page 4)	7			
8 Subtract line 7 from line 6. Enter the result but not less than zero .	8			
9 Other taxes (see page 4)	9			
10 Total tax. Add lines 8 and 9	10			
Payments				
11 Federal income tax withheld and excess social security and RRTA tax withheld. If changing, see page 5	11			
12 Estimated tax payments, including amount applied from prior year's return	12			
13 Earned income credit (EIC)	13			
14 Additional child tax credit from Form 8812	14			
15 Credits from Form 2439 or Form 4136	15			
16 Amount paid with request for extension of time to file (see page 5)	16			
17 Amount of tax paid with original return plus additional tax paid after it was filed	17			
18 Total payments. Add lines 11 through 17 in column C	18			
Refund or Amount You Owe				
19 Overpayment, if any, as shown on original return or as previously adjusted by the IRS . . .	19			
20 Subtract line 19 from line 18 (see page 5)	20			
21 **Amount you owe.** If line 10, column C, is more than line 20, enter the difference and see page 5 .	21			
22 If line 10, column C, is less than line 20, enter the difference	22			
23 Amount of line 22 you want **refunded to you**	23			
24 Amount of line 22 you want **applied to your** estimated tax	24			

Sign Here

Joint return? See page 2. Keep a copy for your records.

Under penalties of perjury, I declare that I have filed an original return and that I have examined this amended return, including accompanying schedules and statements, and to the best of my knowledge and belief, this amended return is true, correct, and complete. Declaration of preparer (other than taxpayer) is based on all information of which the preparer has any knowledge.

► Your signature — Date

► Spouse's signature. If a joint return, **both** must sign. — Date

Paid Preparer's Use Only

Preparer's signature ►	Date	Check if self-employed ☐

Preparer's SSN or PTIN

Firm's name (or yours if self-employed), address, and ZIP code ►

EIN

Phone no. ( )

Cat. No. 11360L

Form **1040X** (Rev. 11-2000)

Part I	**Exemptions.** See Form 1040 or 1040A instructions.	**A. Original number** of exemptions reported or as previously adjusted	**B. Net change**	**C. Correct number** of exemptions

If you are **not changing your exemptions,** do not complete this part.
If claiming **more exemptions,** complete lines 25–31.
If claiming **fewer exemptions,** complete lines 25–30.

25	Yourself and spouse **25**			
	Caution. If your parents (or someone else) can claim you as a dependent (even if they chose not to), you cannot claim an exemption for yourself.			
26	Your dependent children who lived with you **26**			
27	Your dependent children who did not live with you due to divorce or separation **27**			
28	Other dependents **28**			
29	Total number of exemptions. Add lines 25 through 28 . . . . . **29**			
30	Multiply the number of exemptions claimed on line 29 by the amount listed below for the tax year you are amending. Enter the result here and on line 4. **30**			

Tax year	Exemption amount	But see the instructions for line 4 on page 3 if the amount on line 1 is over:
2000	$2,800	$96,700
1999	2,750	94,975
1998	2,700	93,400
1997	2,650	90,900

31 Dependents (children and other) not claimed on original (or adjusted) return:

Note. For tax years after 1997, do not complete column (e) below. For tax year 1997, do not complete column (d) below.

(a) First name Last name	**(b)** Dependent's social security number	**(c)** Dependent's relationship to you	**(d)** ✔ if qualifying child for child tax credit (see page 5)	**(e)** No. of months lived in your home
			☐	
			☐	
			☐	
			☐	
			☐	
			☐	

No. of your children on line 31 who:
- **lived with you** . . ▶ ☐
- **did not live** with you due to divorce or separation (see page 5). . ▶ ☐
- Dependents on line 31 not entered above ▶ ☐

Part II	**Explanation of Changes to Income, Deductions, and Credits**

Enter the line number from the front of the form for each item you are changing and give the reason for each change. Attach only the supporting forms and schedules for the items changed. If you do not attach the required information, your Form 1040X may be returned. Be sure to include your name and social security number on any attachments.

If the change relates to a net operating loss carryback or a general business credit carryback, attach the schedule or form that shows the year in which the loss or credit occurred. See page 2 of the instructions. Also, check here . . . . . ▶ ☐

Part III	**Presidential Election Campaign Fund.** Checking below will not increase your tax or reduce your refund.

If you did not previously want $3 to go to the fund but now want to, check here . . . . ▶ ☐
If a joint return and your spouse did not previously want $3 to go to the fund but now wants to, check here . . . . ▶ ☐

Department of the Treasury—Internal Revenue Service

Form 1040EZ

Income Tax Return for Single and Joint Filers With No Dependents (99) **2001**

OMB No. 1545-0675

Label
(See page 12.)
Use the IRS label. Otherwise, please print or type.

L A B E L

H E R E

| Your first name and initial | Last name | Your social security number |

| If a joint return, spouse's first name and initial | Last name | Spouse's social security number |

| Home address (number and street). If you have a P.O. box, see page 12. | Apt. no. |

| City, town or post office, state, and ZIP code. If you have a foreign address, see page 12. |

▲ **Important!** ▲
You **must** enter your SSN(s) above.

Presidential Election Campaign
(page 12)

Note. Checking "Yes" will not change your tax or reduce your refund.
Do you, or spouse if a joint return, want $3 to go to this fund? . . . . ▶

	You	Spouse
	☐ Yes ☐ No	☐ Yes ☐ No

Income

Attach Form(s) W-2 here.
Enclose, but do not attach, any payment.

1 Total wages, salaries, and tips. This should be shown in box 1 of your W-2 form(s). Attach your W-2 form(s). **1**

2 Taxable interest. If the total is over $400, you cannot use Form 1040EZ. **2**

3 Unemployment compensation, qualified state tuition program earnings, and Alaska Permanent Fund dividends (see page 14). **3**

4 Add lines 1, 2, and 3. This is your **adjusted gross income.** **4**

Note. You **must** check Yes or No.

5 Can your parents (or someone else) claim you on their return?
Yes. Enter amount from worksheet on back. ☐
No. If **single,** enter 7,450.00.
If **married,** enter 13,400.00.
See back for explanation. **5**

6 Subtract line 5 from line 4. If line 5 is larger than line 4, enter 0. This is your **taxable income.** ▶ **6**

Credits, payments, and tax

7 Rate reduction credit. See the worksheet on page 14. **7**

8 Enter your Federal income tax withheld from box 2 of your W-2 form(s). **8**

9a **Earned income credit (EIC).** See page 15. **9a**

b Nontaxable earned income. **9b**

10 Add lines 7, 8, and 9a. These are your **total credits and payments.** ▶ **10**

11 **Tax.** If you checked "Yes" on line 5, see page 20. Otherwise, use the amount on **line 6 above** to find your tax in the tax table on pages 24–28 of the booklet. Then, enter the tax from the table on this line. **11**

Refund

Have it directly deposited! See page 20 and fill in 12b, 12c, and 12d.

12a If line 10 is larger than line 11, subtract line 11 from line 10. This is your **refund.** ▶ **12a**

b Routing number

▶ c Type: ☐ Checking ☐ Savings

d Account number

Amount you owe

13 If line 11 is larger than line 10, subtract line 10 from line 11. This is the **amount you owe.** See page 21 for details on how to pay. ▶ **13**

Third party designee

Do you want to allow another person to discuss this return with the IRS (see page 22)? ☐ **Yes.** Complete the following. ☐ **No**

Designee's name ▶
Phone no. ▶ ( )
Personal identification number (PIN) ▶

Sign here

Joint return? See page 11.
Keep a copy for your records.

Under penalties of perjury, I declare that I have examined this return, and to the best of my knowledge and belief, it is true, correct, and accurately lists all amounts and sources of income I received during the tax year. Declaration of preparer (other than the taxpayer) is based on all information of which the preparer has any knowledge.

| Your signature | Date | Your occupation | Daytime phone number ( ) |

| Spouse's signature. If a joint return, **both** must sign. | Date | Spouse's occupation | |

Paid preparer's use only

| Preparer's signature ▶ | Date | Check if self-employed ☐ | Preparer's SSN or PTIN |

| Firm's name (or yours if self-employed), address, and ZIP code ▶ | | EIN |
| | | Phone no. ( ) |

For Disclosure, Privacy Act, and Paperwork Reduction Act Notice, see page 23. Cat. No. 11329W Form **1040EZ** (2001)

617

Use this form if	• Your filing status is single or married filing jointly. • You (and your spouse if married) were under 65 on January 1, 2002, and not blind at the end of 2001.

Use this form if

- Your filing status is single or married filing jointly.
- You do not claim any dependents.
- You (and your spouse if married) were under 65 on January 1, 2002, and not blind at the end of 2001.
- Your taxable income (line 6) is less than $50,000.
- You do not claim a student loan interest deduction (see page 8) or an education credit.
- You had **only** wages, salaries, tips, taxable scholarship or fellowship grants, unemployment compensation, qualified state tuition program earnings, or Alaska Permanent Fund dividends, and your taxable interest was not over $400. **But** if you earned tips, including allocated tips, that are not included in box 5 and box 7 of your W-2, you may not be able to use Form 1040EZ. See page 13. If you are planning to use Form 1040EZ for a child who received Alaska Permanent Fund dividends, see page 14.
- You did not receive any advance earned income credit payments.

If you are not sure about your filing status, see page 11. If you have questions about dependents, use TeleTax topic 354 (see page 6). If you **cannot use this form,** use TeleTax topic 352 (see page 6).

Filling in your return

For tips on how to avoid common mistakes, see page 30.

If you received a scholarship or fellowship grant or tax-exempt interest income, such as on municipal bonds, see the booklet before filling in the form. Also, see the booklet if you received a Form 1099-INT showing Federal income tax withheld or if Federal income tax was withheld from your unemployment compensation or Alaska Permanent Fund dividends. **Remember,** you must report all wages, salaries, and tips even if you do not get a W-2 form from your employer. You must also report all your taxable interest, including interest from banks, savings and loans, credit unions, etc., even if you do not get a Form 1099-INT.

Worksheet for dependents who checked "Yes" on line 5

(keep a copy for your records)

Use this worksheet to figure the amount to enter on line 5 if someone can claim you (or your spouse if married) as a dependent, even if that person chooses not to do so. To find out if someone can claim you as a dependent, use TeleTax topic 354 (see page 6).

A. Amount, if any, from line 1 on front . . . . +   250.00 Enter total ▶   **A.** _____

B. Minimum standard deduction . . . . **B.** _____ 750.00

C. Enter the **larger** of line A or line B here . . . . **C.** _____

D. Maximum standard deduction. If **single,** enter 4,550.00; if **married,** enter 7,600.00 . . . . **D.** _____

E. Enter the **smaller** of line C or line D here. This is your standard deduction . . . . **E.** _____

F. Exemption amount.
- If single, enter 0.
- If married and—
  —both you and your spouse can be claimed as dependents, enter 0.
  —only one of you can be claimed as a dependent, enter 2,900.00.

                                          F. _____

G. Add lines E and F. Enter the total here and on line 5 on the front . . . . **G.** _____

If you checked "No" on line 5 because no one can claim you (or your spouse if married) as a dependent, enter on line 5 the amount shown below that applies to you.
- Single, enter 7,450.00. This is the total of your standard deduction (4,550.00) and your exemption (2,900.00).
- Married, enter 13,400.00. This is the total of your standard deduction (7,600.00), your exemption (2,900.00), and your spouse's exemption (2,900.00).

Mailing return

Mail your return by **April 15, 2002.** Use the envelope that came with your booklet. If you do not have that envelope, see the back cover for the address to use.

Form **1040A**

Department of the Treasury—Internal Revenue Service

U.S. Individual Income Tax Return (99) **2001**

IRS Use Only—Do not write or staple in this space.

OMB No. 1545-0085

Label
(See page 19.)

Use the IRS label.

Otherwise, please print or type.

L A B E L H E R E	Your first name and initial	Last name

Your social security number

If a joint return, spouse's first name and initial | Last name

Spouse's social security number

Home address (number and street). If you have a P.O. box, see page 20. | Apt. no.

City, town or post office, state, and ZIP code. If you have a foreign address, see page 20.

▲ **Important!** ▲
You **must** enter your SSN(s) above.

Presidential Election Campaign
(See page 20.)

▶ **Note.** Checking "Yes" will not change your tax or reduce your refund.
Do you, or your spouse if filing a joint return, want $3 to go to this fund? . . . ▶

	You		Spouse	
	☐ Yes ☐ No		☐ Yes ☐ No	

Filing status

Check only one box.

1 ☐ Single
2 ☐ Married filing joint return (even if only one had income)
3 ☐ Married filing separate return. Enter spouse's social security number above and full name here. ▶ _____
4 ☐ Head of household (with qualifying person). (See page 21.) If the qualifying person is a child but not your dependent, enter this child's name here. ▶ _____
5 ☐ Qualifying widow(er) with dependent child (year spouse died ▶ ____). (See page 22.)

Exemptions

If more than seven dependents, see page 22.

6a ☐ **Yourself.** If your parent (or someone else) can claim you as a dependent on his or her tax return, **do not** check box 6a.

b ☐ **Spouse**

c **Dependents:**

(1) First name Last name	(2) Dependent's social security number	(3) Dependent's relationship to you	(4) ✓ if qualifying child for child tax credit (see page 23)
			☐
			☐
			☐
			☐
			☐
			☐
			☐

No. of boxes checked on 6a and 6b ____

No. of your children on 6c who:
• lived with you ____
• did not live with you due to divorce or separation (see page 24) ____

Dependents on 6c not entered above ____

Add numbers entered on lines above ☐

d Total number of exemptions claimed.

Income

Attach Form(s) W-2 here. Also attach Form(s) 1099-R if tax was withheld.

If you did not get a W-2, see page 25.

Enclose, but do not attach, any payment.

7 Wages, salaries, tips, etc. Attach Form(s) W-2. | 7

8a **Taxable** interest. Attach Schedule 1 if required. | 8a
b **Tax-exempt** interest. **Do not** include on line 8a. | 8b

9 Ordinary dividends. Attach Schedule 1 if required. | 9

10 Capital gain distributions (see page 25). | 10

11a Total IRA distributions. | 11a | **11b** Taxable amount (see page 25). | 11b

12a Total pensions and annuities. | 12a | **12b** Taxable amount (see page 26). | 12b

13 Unemployment compensation, qualified state tuition program earnings, and Alaska Permanent Fund dividends. | 13

14a Social security benefits. | 14a | **14b** Taxable amount (see page 28). | 14b

15 Add lines 7 through 14b (far right column). This is your **total income.** ▶ | 15

Adjusted gross income

16 IRA deduction (see page 28). | 16
17 Student loan interest deduction (see page 31). | 17
18 Add lines 16 and 17. These are your **total adjustments.** | 18

19 Subtract line 18 from line 15. This is your **adjusted gross income.** ▶ | 19

For Disclosure, Privacy Act, and Paperwork Reduction Act Notice, see page 53. Cat. No. 11327A Form **1040A** (2001)

Tax, credits, and payments	**20**	Enter the amount from line 19 (adjusted gross income).	20	

Standard Deduction for—

- **People who checked any box on line 21a or 21b or who can be claimed as a dependent, see page 33.**
- **All others:** Single, $4,550
  Head of household, $6,650
  Married filing jointly or Qualifying widow(er), $7,600
  Married filing separately, $3,800

21a	Check if: ☐ **You** were 65 or older ☐ Blind ☐ **Spouse** was 65 or older ☐ Blind **Enter number of boxes checked ▶** 21a		
b	If you are married filing separately and your spouse itemizes deductions, see page 32 and check here . . . . ▶ 21b ☐		
22	Enter your **standard deduction** (see left margin).	22	
23	Subtract line 22 from line 20. If line 22 is more than line 20, enter -0-.	23	
24	Multiply $2,900 by the total number of exemptions claimed on line 6d.	24	
25	Subtract line 24 from line 23. If line 24 is more than line 23, enter -0-. This is your **taxable income.** ▶	25	
26	**Tax,** including any alternative minimum tax (see page 33).	26	
27	Credit for child and dependent care expenses. Attach Schedule 2.	27	
28	Credit for the elderly or the disabled. Attach Schedule 3.	28	
29	Education credits. Attach Form 8863.	29	
30	Rate reduction credit. See the worksheet on page 36.	30	
31	Child tax credit (see page 36).	31	
32	Adoption credit. Attach Form 8839.	32	
33	Add lines 27 through 32. These are your **total credits.**	33	
34	Subtract line 33 from line 26. If line 33 is more than line 26, enter -0-.	34	
35	Advance earned income credit payments from Form(s) W-2.	35	
36	Add lines 34 and 35. This is your **total tax.** ▶	36	
37	Federal income tax withheld from Forms W-2 and 1099.	37	
38	2001 estimated tax payments and amount applied from 2000 return.	38	

If you have a qualifying child, attach Schedule EIC.

39a	**Earned income credit (EIC).**	39a
b	Nontaxable earned income. 39b	
40	Additional child tax credit. Attach Form 8812.	40
41	Add lines 37, 38, 39a, and 40. These are your **total payments.** ▶	41

Refund Direct deposit? See page 47 and fill in 43b, 43c, and 43d.	**42**	If line 41 is more than line 36, subtract line 36 from line 41. This is the amount you **overpaid.**	42
	43a	Amount of line 42 you want **refunded to you.** ▶	43a
	▶ **b**	Routing number ☐☐☐☐☐☐☐☐☐ ▶ **c** Type: ☐ Checking ☐ Savings	
	▶ **d**	Account number ☐☐☐☐☐☐☐☐☐☐☐☐☐☐☐☐☐	
	44	Amount of line 42 you want **applied to your 2002 estimated tax.** 44	
Amount you owe	**45**	**Amount you owe.** Subtract line 41 from line 36. For details on how to pay, see page 48. ▶	45
	46	Estimated tax penalty (see page 48). 46	

Third party designee	Do you want to allow another person to discuss this return with the IRS (see page 49)? ☐ **Yes.** Complete the following. ☐ **No**

Designee's name ▶   Phone no. ▶ (   )   Personal identification number (PIN) ▶ ☐☐☐☐☐

Sign here

Joint return? See page 20.

Keep a copy for your records.

Under penalties of perjury, I declare that I have examined this return and accompanying schedules and statements, and to the best of my knowledge and belief, they are true, correct, and accurately list all amounts and sources of income I received during the tax year. Declaration of preparer (other than the taxpayer) is based on all information of which the preparer has any knowledge.

Your signature	Date	Your occupation	Daytime phone number ( )
Spouse's signature. If a joint return, **both** must sign.	Date	Spouse's occupation	

Paid preparer's use only

Preparer's signature ▶	Date	Check if self-employed ☐	Preparer's SSN or PTIN
Firm's name (or yours if self-employed), address, and ZIP code ▶		EIN	
		Phone no. ( )	

Form **1040A** (2001)

Schedule 1
(Form 1040A)

Department of the Treasury—Internal Revenue Service

**Interest and Ordinary Dividends
for Form 1040A Filers** (99)   **2001**

OMB No. 1545-0085

Name(s) shown on Form 1040A

Your social security number

Part I

Interest

(See page 61 and the instructions for Form 1040A, line 8a.)

Note. If you received a Form 1099-INT, Form 1099-OID, or substitute statement from a brokerage firm, enter the firm's name and the total interest shown on that form.

1 List name of payer. If any interest is from a seller-financed mortgage and the buyer used the property as a personal residence, see page 61 and list this interest first. Also, show that buyer's social security number and address.

Amount

	1	

2 Add the amounts on line 1.   **2**

3 Excludable interest on series EE and I U.S. savings bonds issued after 1989 from Form 8815, line 14. You **must** attach Form 8815.   **3**

4 Subtract line 3 from line 2. Enter the result here and on Form 1040A, line 8a.   **4**

Part II

Ordinary dividends

(See page 61 and the instructions for Form 1040A, line 9.)

Note. If you received a Form 1099-DIV or substitute statement from a brokerage firm, enter the firm's name and the ordinary dividends shown on that form.

5 List name of payer. Include only ordinary dividends. If you received any capital gain distributions, see the instructions for Form 1040A, line 10.

Amount

	5	

6 Add the amounts on line 5. Enter the total here and on Form 1040A, line 9.   **6**

For Paperwork Reduction Act Notice, see Form 1040A instructions.   Cat. No. 12075R   **Schedule 1 (Form 1040A) 2001**

621

Schedule 2
(Form 1040A)

Department of the Treasury—Internal Revenue Service

Child and Dependent Care Expenses for Form 1040A Filers   (99)   **2001**

OMB No. 1545-0085

Name(s) shown on Form 1040A | Your social security number

Before you begin: You need to understand the following terms. See **Definitions** on page 1 of the separate instructions.

- **Dependent Care Benefits**   - **Qualifying Person(s)**   - **Qualified Expenses**   - **Earned Income**

Part I

Persons or organizations who provided the care

You **must** complete this part.

1

	(a) Care provider's name	(b) Address (number, street, apt. no., city, state, and ZIP code)	(c) Identifying number (SSN or EIN)	(d) Amount paid (see instructions)

(If you need more space, use the bottom of page 2.)

Did you receive **dependent care benefits?**

No ⟶ Complete only Part II below.

Yes ⟶ Complete Part III on the back next.

Caution. If the care was provided in your home, you may owe employment taxes. If you do, you must use Form 1040. See **Schedule H** and its instructions for details.

Part II

Credit for child and dependent care expenses

2 Information about your **qualifying person(s).** If you have more than two qualifying persons, see the instructions.

(a) Qualifying person's name		(b) Qualifying person's social security number	(c) Qualified expenses you incurred and paid in 2001 for the person listed in column (a)
First	Last		

3 Add the amounts in column (c) of line 2. **Do not** enter more than $2,400 for one qualifying person or $4,800 for two or more persons. If you completed Part III, enter the amount from line 24. | **3** |

4 Enter your **earned income.** | **4** |

5 If married filing a joint return, enter your spouse's earned income (if your spouse was a student or was disabled, see the instructions); **all others,** enter the amount from line 4. | **5** |

6 Enter the **smallest** of line 3, 4, or 5. | **6** |

7 Enter the amount from Form 1040A, line 20.   **7** | |

8 Enter on line 8 the decimal amount shown below that applies to the amount on line 7.

If line 7 is:			If line 7 is:		
Over	But not over	Decimal amount is	Over	But not over	Decimal amount is
$0—10,000		.30	$20,000—22,000		.24
10,000—12,000		.29	22,000—24,000		.23
12,000—14,000		.28	24,000—26,000		.22
14,000—16,000		.27	26,000—28,000		.21
16,000—18,000		.26	28,000—No limit		.20
18,000—20,000		.25			

8   ✕ .

9 Multiply **line 6** by the decimal amount on line 8. Enter the result here and on Form 1040A, line 27. But if this amount is more than the amount on Form 1040A, line 26, **or** you paid 2000 expenses in 2001, see the instructions for the amount to enter on line 27. | **9** |

For Paperwork Reduction Act Notice, see Form 1040A instructions.   Cat. No. 10749I   Schedule 2 (Form 1040A) 2001

Part III

Dependent care benefits

10   Enter the total amount of **dependent care benefits** you received for 2001. This amount should be shown in box 10 of your W-2 form(s). **Do not** include amounts that were reported to you as wages in box 1 of Form(s) W-2.   10

11   Enter the amount forfeited, if any. See the instructions.   11

12   Subtract line 11 from line 10.   12

13   Enter the total amount of **qualified expenses** incurred in 2001 for the care of the qualifying person(s).   13

14   Enter the **smaller** of line 12 or 13.   14

15   Enter your **earned income.**   15

16   If married filing a joint return, enter your spouse's earned income (if your spouse was a student or was disabled, see the instructions for line 5); if married filing a separate return, see the instructions for the amount to enter; **all others,** enter the amount from line 15.   16

17   Enter the **smallest** of line 14, 15, or 16.   17

18   **Excluded benefits.** Enter here the **smaller** of the following:
   ● The amount from line 17 or
   ● $5,000 ($2,500 if married filing a separate return **and** you were required to enter your spouse's earned income on line 16).   18

19   **Taxable benefits.** Subtract line 18 from line 12. Also, include this amount on Form 1040A, line 7. In the space to the left of line 7, enter "DCB."   19

To claim the child and dependent care credit, complete lines 20–24 below.

20   Enter $2,400 ($4,800 if two or more qualifying persons).   20

21   Enter the amount from line 18.   21

22   Subtract line 21 from line 20. If zero or less, **stop.** You cannot take the credit. **Exception.** If you paid 2000 expenses in 2001, see the instructions for line 9.   22

23   Complete line 2 on the front of this schedule. **Do not** include in column (c) any benefits shown on line 18 above. Then, add the amounts in column (c) and enter the total here.   23

24   Enter the **smaller** of line 22 or 23. Also, enter this amount on line 3 on the front of this schedule and complete lines 4–9.   24

Schedule 2 (Form 1040A) 2001

624

Schedule 3
(Form 1040A)

Department of the Treasury—Internal Revenue Service

**Credit for the Elderly or the Disabled
for Form 1040A Filers**

(99) **2001**

OMB No. 1545-0085

Name(s) shown on Form 1040A

Your social security number

You may be able to take this credit and reduce your tax if by the end of 2001:
- You were age 65 or older   **or**   • You were under age 65, you retired on **permanent and total** disability, and you received taxable disability income.

But you must also meet other tests. See the separate instructions for Schedule 3.

TIP In most cases, the IRS can figure the credit for you. See the instructions.

Part I **Check the box for your filing status and age**	**If your filing status is:**	**And by the end of 2001:**	**Check only one box:**
	Single, Head of household, or Qualifying widow(er) with dependent child	**1** You were 65 or older	1 ☐
		2 You were under 65 and you retired on permanent and total disability	2 ☐
	Married filing a joint return	**3** Both spouses were 65 or older	3 ☐
		4 Both spouses were under 65, but only one spouse retired on permanent and total disability . . .	4 ☐
		5 Both spouses were under 65, and both retired on permanent and total disability	5 ☐
		6 One spouse was 65 or older, and the other spouse was under 65 and retired on permanent and total disability	6 ☐
		7 One spouse was 65 or older, and the other spouse was under 65 and **not** retired on permanent and total disability	7 ☐
	Married filing a separate return	**8** You were 65 or older and you lived apart from your spouse for all of 2001.	8 ☐
		9 You were under 65, you retired on permanent and total disability, and you lived apart from your spouse for all of 2001	9 ☐

Did you check box 1, 3, 7, or 8?

Yes ➞ Skip Part II and complete Part III on the back.

No ➞ Complete Parts II and III.

Part II **Statement of permanent and total disability** Complete this part **only** if you checked box 2, 4, 5, 6, or 9 above.	**If:**	**1** You filed a physician's statement for this disability for 1983 or an earlier year, or you filed or got a statement for tax years after 1983 and your physician signed line B on the statement, **and**
		2 Due to your continued disabled condition, you were unable to engage in any substantial gainful activity in 2001, check this box . . . . ▶ ☐
		• If you checked this box, you do not have to get another statement for 2001.
		• If you **did not** check this box, have your physician complete the statement on page 4 of the instructions. You **must** keep the statement for your records.

For Paperwork Reduction Act Notice, see Form 1040A instructions.   Cat. No. 12064K   Schedule 3 (Form 1040A) 2001

625

Part III

Figure your credit

10 If you checked (in Part I):   **Enter:**

      Box 1, 2, 4, or 7 . . . . $5,000

      Box 3, 5, or 6 . . . . $7,500

      Box 8 or 9 . . . . $3,750   10

| **Did you check box 2, 4, 5, 6, or 9 in Part I?** | — Yes ——▶ | You **must** complete line 11. |
| | — No ——▶ | Enter the amount from line 10 on line 12 and go to line 13. |

11   • If you checked box 6 in Part I, add $5,000 to the taxable disability income of the spouse who was under age 65. Enter the total.

     • If you checked box 2, 4, or 9 in Part I, enter your taxable disability income.

     • If you checked box 5 in Part I, add your taxable disability income to your spouse's taxable disability income. Enter the total.

     TIP   For more details on what to include on line 11, see the instructions.   11

12 If you completed line 11, enter the **smaller** of line 10 or line 11; **all others,** enter the amount from line 10.   12

13 Enter the following pensions, annuities, or disability income that you (and your spouse if filing a joint return) received in 2001.

  a Nontaxable part of social security benefits and

      Nontaxable part of railroad retirement benefits treated as social security. See instructions.   13a

  b Nontaxable veterans' pensions and

      Any other pension, annuity, or disability benefit that is excluded from income under any other provision of law. See instructions.   13b

  c Add lines 13a and 13b. (Even though these income items are not taxable, they **must** be included here to figure your credit.) If you did not receive any of the types of nontaxable income listed on line 13a or 13b, enter -0- on line 13c.   13c

14 Enter the amount from Form 1040A, line 20.   14

15 **If you checked (in Part I):**   **Enter:**

      Box 1 or 2 . . . . $7,500

      Box 3, 4, 5, 6, or 7 . . . . . . $10,000

      Box 8 or 9 . . . . $5,000   15

16 Subtract line 15 from line 14. If zero or less, enter -0-.   16

17 Enter one-half of line 16.   17

18 Add lines 13c and 17.   18

19 Subtract line 18 from line 12. If zero or less, **stop;** you **cannot** take the credit. Otherwise, go to line 20.   19

20 Multiply line 19 by 15% (.15). Enter the result here and on Form 1040A, line 28. But if this amount is more than the amount on Form 1040A, line 26, **or** you are filing Schedule 2 (Form 1040A), see the instructions for the amount of credit you may take.   20

Department of the Treasury—Internal Revenue Service

U.S. Individual Income Tax Return **2001** (99) IRS Use Only—Do not write or staple in this space.

			OMB No. 1545-0074

For the year Jan. 1–Dec. 31, 2001, or other tax year beginning , 2001, ending , 20

Label

(See instructions on page 19.)

Use the IRS label. Otherwise, please print or type.

L A B E L   H E R E

Your first name and initial	Last name	Your social security number
If a joint return, spouse's first name and initial	Last name	Spouse's social security number
Home address (number and street). If you have a P.O. box, see page 19.		Apt. no.
City, town or post office, state, and ZIP code. If you have a foreign address, see page 19.		

▲ **Important!** ▲

You **must** enter your SSN(s) above.

Presidential Election Campaign
(See page 19.)

Note. Checking "Yes" will not change your tax or reduce your refund.

Do you, or your spouse if filing a joint return, want $3 to go to this fund? . . . ▶

You ☐ Yes ☐ No   Spouse ☐ Yes ☐ No

Filing Status

Check only one box.

1 ☐ Single
2 ☐ Married filing joint return (even if only one had income)
3 ☐ Married filing separate return. Enter spouse's social security no. above and full name here. ▶
4 ☐ Head of household (with qualifying person). (See page 19.) If the qualifying person is a child but not your dependent, enter this child's name here. ▶
5 ☐ Qualifying widow(er) with dependent child (year spouse died ▶). (See page 19.)

Exemptions

If more than six dependents, see page 20.

6a ☐ **Yourself.** If your parent (or someone else) can claim you as a dependent on his or her tax return, **do not** check box 6a . . . .

b ☐ **Spouse** . . . .

c **Dependents:**	(2) Dependent's social security number	(3) Dependent's relationship to you	(4) ✓ if qualifying child for child tax credit (see page 20)
(1) First name Last name			
			☐
			☐
			☐
			☐
			☐
			☐

No. of boxes checked on 6a and 6b ____

No. of your children on 6c who:
● lived with you ____
● did not live with you due to divorce or separation (see page 20) ____

Dependents on 6c not entered above ____

Add numbers entered on lines above ▶ ☐

d Total number of exemptions claimed . . . .

Income

Attach Forms W-2 and W-2G here. Also attach Form(s) 1099-R if tax was withheld.

If you did not get a W-2, see page 21.

Enclose, but do not attach, any payment. Also, please use **Form 1040-V.**

7	Wages, salaries, tips, etc. Attach Form(s) W-2	7	
8a	**Taxable** interest. Attach Schedule B if required	8a	
b	**Tax-exempt** interest. **Do not** include on line 8a . . 8b		
9	Ordinary dividends. Attach Schedule B if required	9	
10	Taxable refunds, credits, or offsets of state and local income taxes (see page 22) . .	10	
11	Alimony received	11	
12	Business income or (loss). Attach Schedule C or C-EZ	12	
13	Capital gain or (loss). Attach Schedule D if required. If not required, check here ▶ ☐	13	
14	Other gains or (losses). Attach Form 4797	14	
15a	Total IRA distributions . 15a	b Taxable amount (see page 23)	15b	
16a	Total pensions and annuities 16a	b Taxable amount (see page 23)	16b	
17	Rental real estate, royalties, partnerships, S corporations, trusts, etc. Attach Schedule E	17	
18	Farm income or (loss). Attach Schedule F	18	
19	Unemployment compensation	19	
20a	Social security benefits . 20a	b Taxable amount (see page 25)	20b	
21	Other income. List type and amount (see page 27)	21	
22	Add the amounts in the far right column for lines 7 through 21. This is your **total income** ▶	22	

Adjusted Gross Income

23	IRA deduction (see page 27)	23	
24	Student loan interest deduction (see page 28) . . .	24	
25	Archer MSA deduction. Attach Form 8853	25	
26	Moving expenses. Attach Form 3903	26	
27	One-half of self-employment tax. Attach Schedule SE .	27	
28	Self-employed health insurance deduction (see page 30)	28	
29	Self-employed SEP, SIMPLE, and qualified plans	29	
30	Penalty on early withdrawal of savings	30	
31a	Alimony paid b Recipient's SSN ▶	31a	
32	Add lines 23 through 31a		32	
33	Subtract line 32 from line 22. This is your **adjusted gross income** ▶		33	

For Disclosure, Privacy Act, and Paperwork Reduction Act Notice, see page 72.   Cat. No. 11320B   Form **1040** (2001)

Tax and Credits	**34**	Amount from line 33 (adjusted gross income)	**34**	

Standard Deduction for—

- People who checked any box on line 35a or 35b **or** who can be claimed as a dependent, see page 31.
- All others:

Single, $4,550

Head of household, $6,650

Married filing jointly or Qualifying widow(er), $7,600

Married filing separately, $3,800

35a	Check if: ☐ **You** were 65 or older, ☐ Blind; ☐ **Spouse** was 65 or older, ☐ Blind.	
	Add the number of boxes checked above and enter the total here . . . . ▶ **35a**	
b	If you are married filing separately and your spouse itemizes deductions, or you were a dual-status alien, see page 31 and check here . . . . . . ▶ **35b** ☐	
36	**Itemized deductions** (from Schedule A) **or** your **standard deduction** (see left margin) . .	**36**
37	Subtract line 36 from line 34	**37**
38	If line 34 is $99,725 or less, multiply $2,900 by the total number of exemptions claimed on line 6d. If line 34 is over $99,725, see the worksheet on page 32	**38**
39	**Taxable income.** Subtract line 38 from line 37. If line 38 is more than line 37, enter -0-	**39**
40	**Tax** (see page 33). Check if any tax is from **a** ☐ Form(s) 8814 **b** ☐ Form 4972 .	**40**
41	**Alternative minimum tax** (see page 34). Attach Form 6251	**41**
42	Add lines 40 and 41 . . . . ▶	**42**

43	Foreign tax credit. Attach Form 1116 if required . . .	**43**	
44	Credit for child and dependent care expenses. Attach Form 2441	**44**	
45	Credit for the elderly or the disabled. Attach Schedule R .	**45**	
46	Education credits. Attach Form 8863	**46**	
47	Rate reduction credit. See the worksheet on page 36 .	**47**	
48	Child tax credit (see page 37)	**48**	
49	Adoption credit. Attach Form 8839	**49**	
50	Other credits from: **a** ☐ Form 3800 **b** ☐ Form 8396		
	c ☐ Form 8801 **d** ☐ Form (specify) _____	**50**	

51	Add lines 43 through 50. These are your **total credits**	**51**
52	Subtract line 51 from line 42. If line 51 is more than line 42, enter -0- . . . ▶	**52**

Other Taxes			
	53	Self-employment tax. Attach Schedule SE	**53**
	54	Social security and Medicare tax on tip income not reported to employer. Attach Form 4137 . .	**54**
	55	Tax on qualified plans, including IRAs, and other tax-favored accounts. Attach Form 5329 if required .	**55**
	56	Advance earned income credit payments from Form(s) W-2	**56**
	57	Household employment taxes. Attach Schedule H	**57**
	58	Add lines 52 through 57. This is your **total tax** . . . . ▶	**58**

Payments			
	59	Federal income tax withheld from Forms W-2 and 1099 . .	**59**
	60	2001 estimated tax payments and amount applied from 2000 return	**60**

If you have a qualifying child, attach Schedule EIC.

61a	**Earned income credit (EIC)**	**61a**	
b	Nontaxable earned income . . **61b**		
62	Excess social security and RRTA tax withheld (see page 51)	**62**	
63	Additional child tax credit. Attach Form 8812	**63**	
64	Amount paid with request for extension to file (see page 51)	**64**	
65	Other payments. Check if from **a** ☐ Form 2439 **b** ☐ Form 4136	**65**	

66	Add lines 59, 60, 61a, and 62 through 65. These are your **total payments** . . . . ▶	**66**

Refund			
	67	If line 66 is more than line 58, subtract line 58 from line 66. This is the amount you **overpaid**	**67**
Direct deposit? See page 51 and fill in 68b, 68c, and 68d.	**68a**	Amount of line 67 you want **refunded to you** . . . . ▶	**68a**
▶ **b**		Routing number [ ] ▶ **c** Type: ☐ Checking ☐ Savings	
▶ **d**		Account number [ ]	
	69	Amount of line 67 you want **applied to your 2002 estimated tax** ▶ **69**	

Amount You Owe			
	70	**Amount you owe.** Subtract line 66 from line 58. For details on how to pay, see page 52 ▶	**70**
	71	Estimated tax penalty. Also include on line 70 . . . . **71**	

Third Party Designee		
	Do you want to allow another person to discuss this return with the IRS (see page 53)? ☐ **Yes.** Complete the following. ☐ **No**	
	Designee's name ▶	Phone no. ▶ ( )	Personal identification number (PIN) ▶ [ ]

Sign Here

Joint return? See page 19.

Keep a copy for your records.

Under penalties of perjury, I declare that I have examined this return and accompanying schedules and statements, and to the best of my knowledge and belief, they are true, correct, and complete. Declaration of preparer (other than taxpayer) is based on all information of which preparer has any knowledge.

Your signature	Date	Your occupation	Daytime phone number ( )
Spouse's signature. If a joint return, **both** must sign.	Date	Spouse's occupation	

Paid Preparer's Use Only

Preparer's signature ▶	Date	Check if self-employed ☐	Preparer's SSN or PTIN
Firm's name (or yours if self-employed), address, and ZIP code ▶		EIN	
		Phone no. ( )	

Form **1040** (2001)

628

SCHEDULES A&B
(Form 1040)

Department of the Treasury
Internal Revenue Service (99)

OMB No. 1545-0074

Schedule A—Itemized Deductions

(Schedule B is on back)

► Attach to Form 1040. ► See Instructions for Schedules A and B (Form 1040).

2001

Attachment
Sequence No. 07

Name(s) shown on Form 1040

Your social security number

Medical and Dental Expenses

Caution. Do not include expenses reimbursed or paid by others.

1 Medical and dental expenses (see page A-2)

2 Enter amount from Form 1040, line 34. | 2 |

3 Multiply line 2 above by 7.5% (.075)

4 Subtract line 3 from line 1. If line 3 is more than line 1, enter -0-

Taxes You Paid

(See page A-2.)

5 State and local income taxes

6 Real estate taxes (see page A-2)

7 Personal property taxes

8 Other taxes. List type and amount ► _____

9 Add lines 5 through 8

Interest You Paid

(See page A-3.)

Note.
Personal interest is not deductible.

10 Home mortgage interest and points reported to you on Form 1098

11 Home mortgage interest not reported to you on Form 1098. If paid to the person from whom you bought the home, see page A-3 and show that person's name, identifying no., and address ►

_____

_____

12 Points not reported to you on Form 1098. See page A-3 for special rules

13 Investment interest. Attach Form 4952 if required. (See page A-3.)

14 Add lines 10 through 13

Gifts to Charity

If you made a gift and got a benefit for it, see page A-4.

15 Gifts by cash or check. If you made any gift of $250 or more, see page A-4

16 Other than by cash or check. If any gift of $250 or more, see page A-4. You **must** attach Form 8283 if over $500

17 Carryover from prior year

18 Add lines 15 through 17

Casualty and Theft Losses

19 Casualty or theft loss(es). Attach Form 4684. (See page A-5.)

Job Expenses and Most Other Miscellaneous Deductions

(See page A-5 for expenses to deduct here.)

20 Unreimbursed employee expenses—job travel, union dues, job education, etc. You **must** attach Form 2106 or 2106-EZ if required. (See page A-5.) ► _____

_____

21 Tax preparation fees

22 Other expenses—investment, safe deposit box, etc. List type and amount ► _____

23 Add lines 20 through 22

24 Enter amount from Form 1040, line 34. | 24 |

25 Multiply line 24 above by 2% (.02)

26 Subtract line 25 from line 23. If line 25 is more than line 23, enter -0-

Other Miscellaneous Deductions

27 Other—from list on page A-6. List type and amount ► _____

_____

Total Itemized Deductions

28 Is Form 1040, line 34, over $132,950 (over $66,475 if married filing separately)?

☐ **No.** Your deduction is not limited. Add the amounts in the far right column for lines 4 through 27. Also, enter this amount on Form 1040, line 36. ►

☐ **Yes.** Your deduction may be limited. See page A-6 for the amount to enter.

For Paperwork Reduction Act Notice, see Form 1040 instructions.   Cat. No. 11330X   Schedule A (Form 1040) 2001

629

Name(s) shown on Form 1040. Do not enter name and social security number if shown on other side.

Your social security number

Schedule B—Interest and Ordinary Dividends

Attachment
Sequence No. **08**

			Amount
Part I **Interest** (See page B-1 and the instructions for Form 1040, line 8a.)	**1**	List name of payer. If any interest is from a seller-financed mortgage and the buyer used the property as a personal residence, see page B-1 and list this interest first. Also, show that buyer's social security number and address ▶	
			1
Note. If you received a Form 1099-INT, Form 1099-OID, or substitute statement from a brokerage firm, list the firm's name as the payer and enter the total interest shown on that form.			
	2	Add the amounts on line 1	**2**
	3	Excludable interest on series EE and I U.S. savings bonds issued after 1989 from Form 8815, line 14. You **must** attach Form 8815	**3**
	4	Subtract line 3 from line 2. Enter the result here and on Form 1040, line 8a ▶	**4**

Note. If line 4 is over $400, you must complete Part III.

			Amount
Part II **Ordinary** **Dividends** (See page B-1 and the instructions for Form 1040, line 9.)	**5**	List name of payer. Include only ordinary dividends. If you received any capital gain distributions, see the instructions for Form 1040, line 13 ▶	
			5
Note. If you received a Form 1099-DIV or substitute statement from a brokerage firm, list the firm's name as the payer and enter the ordinary dividends shown on that form.			
	6	Add the amounts on line 5. Enter the total here and on Form 1040, line 9 . ▶	**6**

Note. If line 6 is over $400, you must complete Part III.

	You must complete this part if you **(a)** had over $400 of taxable interest or ordinary dividends; **(b)** had a foreign account; or **(c)** received a distribution from, or were a grantor of, or a transferor to, a foreign trust.	Yes	No
Part III **Foreign** **Accounts** **and Trusts** (See page B-2.)	**7a** At any time during 2001, did you have an interest in or a signature or other authority over a financial account in a foreign country, such as a bank account, securities account, or other financial account? See page B-2 for exceptions and filing requirements for Form TD F 90-22.1		
	b If "Yes," enter the name of the foreign country ▶		
	8 During 2001, did you receive a distribution from, or were you the grantor of, or transferor to, a foreign trust? If "Yes," you may have to file Form 3520. See page B-2		

For Paperwork Reduction Act Notice, see Form 1040 instructions.   Schedule B (Form 1040) 2001

SCHEDULE C
(Form 1040)

Department of the Treasury
Internal Revenue Service   (99)

Profit or Loss From Business
(Sole Proprietorship)

▶ **Partnerships, joint ventures, etc., must file Form 1065 or Form 1065-B.**

▶ **Attach to Form 1040 or Form 1041.**   ▶ **See Instructions for Schedule C (Form 1040).**

OMB No. 1545-0074

2001

Attachment
Sequence No. **09**

Name of proprietor | Social security number (SSN)

A Principal business or profession, including product or service (see page C-1 of the instructions)	**B** Enter code from pages C-7 & 8 ▶
C Business name. If no separate business name, leave blank.	**D** Employer ID number (EIN), if any

E Business address (including suite or room no.) ▶
City, town or post office, state, and ZIP code

F Accounting method: **(1)** ☐ Cash   **(2)** ☐ Accrual   **(3)** ☐ Other (specify) ▶

G Did you "materially participate" in the operation of this business during 2001? If "No," see page C-2 for limit on losses . ☐ Yes ☐ No

H If you started or acquired this business during 2001, check here . . . . ▶ ☐

Part I   Income

1	Gross receipts or sales. **Caution.** If this income was reported to you on Form W-2 and the "Statutory employee" box on that form was checked, see page C-2 and check here . . . . . . ▶ ☐	**1**
2	Returns and allowances	**2**
3	Subtract line 2 from line 1	**3**
4	Cost of goods sold (from line 42 on page 2)	**4**
5	**Gross profit.** Subtract line 4 from line 3	**5**
6	Other income, including Federal and state gasoline or fuel tax credit or refund (see page C-3) . . .	**6**
7	**Gross income.** Add lines 5 and 6 . . . . ▶	**7**

Part II   Expenses. Enter expenses for business use of your home **only** on line 30.

8	Advertising	**8**	**19** Pension and profit-sharing plans	**19**	
9	Bad debts from sales or services (see page C-3) . .	**9**	**20** Rent or lease (see page C-4):		
10	Car and truck expenses (see page C-3)	**10**	**a** Vehicles, machinery, and equipment .	**20a**	
11	Commissions and fees . .	**11**	**b** Other business property . . .	**20b**	
12	Depletion	**12**	**21** Repairs and maintenance	**21**	
13	Depreciation and section 179 expense deduction (not included in Part III) (see page C-3) . .	**13**	**22** Supplies (not included in Part III) . .	**22**	
			23 Taxes and licenses	**23**	
			24 Travel, meals, and entertainment:		
14	Employee benefit programs (other than on line 19) . . .	**14**	**a** Travel	**24a**	
15	Insurance (other than health) .	**15**	**b** Meals and entertainment		
16	Interest:		**c** Enter nondeduct-ible amount in-cluded on line 24b (see page C-5) .		
a	Mortgage (paid to banks, etc.) .	**16a**			
b	Other	**16b**	**d** Subtract line 24c from line 24b .	**24d**	
17	Legal and professional services	**17**	**25** Utilities	**25**	
			26 Wages (less employment credits) .	**26**	
18	Office expense	**18**	**27** Other expenses (from line 48 on page 2)	**27**	

28	**Total expenses** before expenses for business use of home. Add lines 8 through 27 in columns . ▶	**28**
29	Tentative profit (loss). Subtract line 28 from line 7	**29**
30	Expenses for business use of your home. Attach **Form 8829**	**30**
31	**Net profit or (loss).** Subtract line 30 from line 29.	
	• If a profit, enter on **Form 1040, line 12,** and **also** on **Schedule SE, line 2** (statutory employees, see page C-5). Estates and trusts, enter on Form 1041, line 3.	**31**
	• If a loss, you **must** go to line 32.	
32	If you have a loss, check the box that describes your investment in this activity (see page C-6).	
	• If you checked 32a, enter the loss on **Form 1040, line 12,** and **also** on **Schedule SE, line 2** (statutory employees, see page C-5). Estates and trusts, enter on Form 1041, line 3.	**32a** ☐ All investment is at risk.
	• If you checked 32b, you **must** attach **Form 6198.**	**32b** ☐ Some investment is not at risk.

For Paperwork Reduction Act Notice, see Form 1040 instructions.   Cat. No. 11334P   Schedule C (Form 1040) 2001

Part III **Cost of Goods Sold** (see page C-6)

33 Method(s) used to value closing inventory: **a** ☐ Cost **b** ☐ Lower of cost or market **c** ☐ Other (attach explanation)

34 Was there any change in determining quantities, costs, or valuations between opening and closing inventory? If "Yes," attach explanation . . . . ☐ **Yes** ☐ **No**

35	Inventory at beginning of year. If different from last year's closing inventory, attach explanation . .	**35**	
36	Purchases less cost of items withdrawn for personal use	**36**	
37	Cost of labor. Do not include any amounts paid to yourself	**37**	
38	Materials and supplies	**38**	
39	Other costs	**39**	
40	Add lines 35 through 39	**40**	
41	Inventory at end of year	**41**	
42	**Cost of goods sold.** Subtract line 41 from line 40. Enter the result here and on page 1, line 4 . .	**42**	

Part IV **Information on Your Vehicle.** Complete this part **only** if you are claiming car or truck expenses on line 10 and are not required to file Form 4562 for this business. See the instructions for line 13 on page C-3 to find out if you must file.

43 When did you place your vehicle in service for business purposes? (month, day, year) ▶ _____ / _____ / _____ .

44 Of the total number of miles you drove your vehicle during 2001, enter the number of miles you used your vehicle for:

a Business _____ **b** Commuting _____ **c** Other _____

45 Do you (or your spouse) have another vehicle available for personal use? . . . . ☐ **Yes** ☐ **No**

46 Was your vehicle available for personal use during off-duty hours? . . . . ☐ **Yes** ☐ **No**

47a Do you have evidence to support your deduction? . . . . ☐ **Yes** ☐ **No**

  b If "Yes," is the evidence written? . . . . ☐ **Yes** ☐ **No**

Part V **Other Expenses.** List below business expenses not included on lines 8–26 or line 30.

-----------------------------------	
48 **Total other expenses.** Enter here and on page 1, line 27	**48**

SCHEDULE D
(Form 1040)

Department of the Treasury
Internal Revenue Service   (99)

Capital Gains and Losses

▶ Attach to Form 1040.   ▶ See Instructions for Schedule D (Form 1040).

▶ Use Schedule D-1 to list additional transactions for lines 1 and 8.

OMB No. 1545-0074

2001

Attachment
Sequence No. **12**

Name(s) shown on Form 1040

Your social security number

Part I — Short-Term Capital Gains and Losses—Assets Held One Year or Less

(a) Description of property (Example: 100 sh. XYZ Co.)	(b) Date acquired (Mo., day, yr.)	(c) Date sold (Mo., day, yr.)	(d) Sales price (see page D-5 of the instructions)	(e) Cost or other basis (see page D-5 of the instructions)	(f) Gain or (loss) Subtract (e) from (d)	
1						

2 Enter your short-term totals, if any, from Schedule D-1, line 2 . . . . | **2** | | |

3 **Total short-term sales price amounts.** Add lines 1 and 2 in column (d) . . . . . | **3** | | |

4 Short-term gain from Form 6252 and short-term gain or (loss) from Forms 4684, 6781, and 8824 . . . . | **4** | |

5 Net short-term gain or (loss) from partnerships, S corporations, estates, and trusts from Schedule(s) K-1 . . . . | **5** | |

6 Short-term capital loss carryover. Enter the amount, if any, from line 8 of your 2000 Capital Loss Carryover Worksheet . . . . | **6** ( ) |

7 **Net short-term capital gain or (loss).** Combine lines 1 through 6 in column (f). | **7** | |

Part II — Long-Term Capital Gains and Losses—Assets Held More Than One Year

(a) Description of property (Example: 100 sh. XYZ Co.)	(b) Date acquired (Mo., day, yr.)	(c) Date sold (Mo., day, yr.)	(d) Sales price (see page D-5 of the instructions)	(e) Cost or other basis (see page D-5 of the instructions)	(f) Gain or (loss) Subtract (e) from (d)	(g) 28% rate gain or (loss) * (see instr. below)
8						

9 Enter your long-term totals, if any, from Schedule D-1, line 9 . . . . | **9** | | |

10 **Total long-term sales price amounts.** Add lines 8 and 9 in column (d) . . . . | **10** | | |

11 Gain from Form 4797, Part I; long-term gain from Forms 2439 and 6252; and long-term gain or (loss) from Forms 4684, 6781, and 8824 . . . . | **11** | |

12 Net long-term gain or (loss) from partnerships, S corporations, estates, and trusts from Schedule(s) K-1 . . . . | **12** | |

13 Capital gain distributions. See page D-1 of the instructions . . . . . . | **13** | |

14 Long-term capital loss carryover. Enter in both columns (f) and (g) the amount, if any, from line 13 of your 2000 Capital Loss Carryover Worksheet . . . . . | **14** ( ) ( ) |

15 Combine lines 8 through 14 in column (g) . . . . | **15** | |

16 **Net long-term capital gain or (loss).** Combine lines 8 through 14 in column (f) | **16** | |
Next: Go to Part III on the back.

*___**28% rate gain or loss** includes **all** "collectibles gains and losses" (as defined on page D-6 of the instructions) and up to 50% of the eligible gain on qualified small business stock (see page D-4 of the instructions).

For Paperwork Reduction Act Notice, see Form 1040 instructions.   Cat. No. 11338H   **Schedule D (Form 1040) 2001**

Part III	Taxable Gain or Deductible Loss

17 Combine lines 7 and 16 and enter the result. **If a loss, go to line 18. If a gain,** enter the gain on Form 1040, line 13, and complete Form 1040 through line 39 . . . . | **17** |

> **Next:** • If both lines 16 and 17 are gains **and** Form 1040, line 39, is more than zero, complete Part IV below.
> • Otherwise, skip the rest of Schedule D and complete Form 1040.

18 If line 17 is a loss, enter here and on Form 1040, line 13, the **smaller** of **(a)** that loss or **(b)** ($3,000) (or, if married filing separately, ($1,500)). Then complete Form 1040 through line 37 | **18** ( ) |

> **Next:** • If the loss on line 17 is more than the loss on line 18 **or** if Form 1040, line 37, is less than zero, skip **Part IV** below and complete the **Capital Loss Carryover Worksheet** on page D-6 of the instructions before completing the rest of Form 1040.
> • Otherwise, skip **Part IV** below and complete the rest of Form 1040.

Part IV	Tax Computation Using Maximum Capital Gains Rates

19 Enter your unrecaptured section 1250 gain, if any, from line 17 of the worksheet on page D-7 of the instructions . . . . | **19** |

If line 15 or line 19 is more than zero, complete the worksheet on page D-9 of the instructions to figure the amount to enter on lines 22, 29, and 40 below, and skip all other lines below. Otherwise, go to line 20.

20 Enter your taxable income from Form 1040, line 39 . . . . . . | **20** |

21 Enter the **smaller** of line 16 or line 17 of Schedule D . . . . | **21** |

22 If you are deducting investment interest expense on Form 4952, enter the amount from Form 4952, line 4e. Otherwise, enter -0- | **22** |

23 Subtract line 22 from line 21. If zero or less, enter -0- . . . . | **23** |

24 Subtract line 23 from line 20. If zero or less, enter -0- . . . . | **24** |

25 Figure the tax on the amount on line 24. Use the Tax Table or Tax Rate Schedules, whichever applies | **25** |

26 Enter the **smaller** of:
  • The amount on line 20 **or**
  • $45,200 if married filing jointly or qualifying widow(er);
    $27,050 if single;
    $36,250 if head of household; or
    $22,600 if married filing separately | **26** |

If line 26 is greater than line 24, go to line 27. Otherwise, skip lines 27 through 33 and go to line 34.

27 Enter the amount from line 24 . . . . | **27** |

28 Subtract line 27 from line 26. If zero or less, enter -0- and go to line 34 | **28** |

29 Enter your qualified 5-year gain, if any, from line 7 of the worksheet on page D-8 . . | **29** |

30 Enter the **smaller** of line 28 or line 29 . . . . | **30** |

31 Multiply line 30 by 8% (.08) . . . . | **31** |

32 Subtract line 30 from line 28 . . . . | **32** |

33 Multiply line 32 by 10% (.10) . . . . | **33** |

If the amounts on lines 23 and 28 are the same, skip lines 34 through 37 and go to line 38.

34 Enter the **smaller** of line 20 or line 23 . . . . | **34** |

35 Enter the amount from line 28 (if line 28 is blank, enter -0-) . . . | **35** |

36 Subtract line 35 from line 34 . . . . | **36** |

37 Multiply line 36 by 20% (.20) . . . . | **37** |

38 Add lines 25, 31, 33, and 37 . . . . | **38** |

39 Figure the tax on the amount on line 20. Use the Tax Table or Tax Rate Schedules, whichever applies | **39** |

40 **Tax on all taxable income (including capital gains).** Enter the **smaller** of line 38 or line 39 here and on Form 1040, line 40 . . . . | **40** |

SCHEDULE E **(Form 1040)** Department of the Treasury Internal Revenue Service (99)	**Supplemental Income and Loss** (From rental real estate, royalties, partnerships, S corporations, estates, trusts, REMICs, etc.) ▶ **Attach to Form 1040 or Form 1041.** ▶ **See Instructions for Schedule E (Form 1040).**	OMB No. 1545-0074 **2001** Attachment Sequence No. **13**

Name(s) shown on return   Your social security number

Part I   **Income or Loss From Rental Real Estate and Royalties**   **Note.** If you are in the business of renting personal property, use **Schedule C** or **C-EZ** (see page E-1). Report farm rental income or loss from **Form 4835** on page 2, line 39.

1 Show the kind and location of each **rental real estate property:**	2 For each rental real estate property listed on line 1, did you or your family use it during the tax year for personal purposes for more than the greater of: ● 14 days **or** ● 10% of the total days rented at fair rental value? (See page E-1.)		Yes	No
A		**A**		
B		**B**		
C		**C**		

Income:

			Properties A	Properties B	Properties C		Totals (Add columns A, B, and C.)
3	Rents received	3				3	
4	Royalties received	4				4	

Expenses:

			A	B	C		Totals
5	Advertising	5					
6	Auto and travel (see page E-2) .	6					
7	Cleaning and maintenance. . .	7					
8	Commissions	8					
9	Insurance	9					
10	Legal and other professional fees	10					
11	Management fees.	11					
12	Mortgage interest paid to banks, etc. (see page E-2)	12				12	
13	Other interest	13					
14	Repairs	14					
15	Supplies	15					
16	Taxes	16					
17	Utilities	17					
18	Other (list) ▶	18					
19	Add lines 5 through 18	19				19	
20	Depreciation expense or depletion (see page E-3)	20				20	
21	Total expenses. Add lines 19 and 20	21					
22	Income or (loss) from rental real estate or royalty properties. Subtract line 21 from line 3 (rents) or line 4 (royalties). If the result is a (loss), see page E-3 to find out if you must file **Form 6198**. . .	22					
23	Deductible rental real estate loss. **Caution.** Your rental real estate loss on line 22 may be limited. See page E-3 to find out if you must file **Form 8582.** Real estate professionals must complete line 42 on page 2	23	( )	( )	( )		
24	**Income.** Add positive amounts shown on line 22. **Do not** include any losses					24	
25	**Losses.** Add royalty losses from line 22 and rental real estate losses from line 23. Enter total losses here					25	( )
26	**Total rental real estate and royalty income or (loss).** Combine lines 24 and 25. Enter the result here. If Parts II, III, IV, and line 39 on page 2 do not apply to you, also enter this amount on Form 1040, line 17. Otherwise, include this amount in the total on line 40 on page 2					26	

For Paperwork Reduction Act Notice, see Form 1040 instructions.   Cat. No. 11344L   **Schedule E (Form 1040) 2001**

635

Name(s) shown on return. Do not enter name and social security number if shown on other side.	Your social security number

Note. If you report amounts from farming or fishing on Schedule E, you must enter your gross income from those activities on line 41 below. Real estate professionals must complete line 42 below.

Part II   Income or Loss From Partnerships and S Corporations

Note. If you report a loss from an at-risk activity, you **must** check either column **(e)** or **(f)** on line 27 to describe your investment in the activity. See page E-5. If you check column **(f)**, you must attach **Form 6198**.

27	(a) Name	(b) Enter P for partnership; S for S corporation	(c) Check if foreign partnership	(d) Employer identification number	Investment At Risk? (e) All is at risk	(f) Some is not at risk
A						
B						
C						
D						
E						

	Passive Income and Loss		Nonpassive Income and Loss		
	(g) Passive loss allowed (attach **Form 8582** if required)	(h) Passive income from **Schedule K–1**	(i) Nonpassive loss from **Schedule K–1**	(j) Section 179 expense deduction from **Form 4562**	(k) Nonpassive income from **Schedule K–1**
A					
B					
C					
D					
E					
28a Totals					
b Totals					

29	Add columns (h) and (k) of line 28a	29
30	Add columns (g), (i), and (j) of line 28b	30 ( )
31	Total partnership and S corporation income or (loss). Combine lines 29 and 30. Enter the result here and include in the total on line 40 below	31

Part III   Income or Loss From Estates and Trusts

32	(a) Name	(b) Employer identification number
A		
B		

	Passive Income and Loss		Nonpassive Income and Loss	
	(c) Passive deduction or loss allowed (attach **Form 8582** if required)	(d) Passive income from **Schedule K–1**	(e) Deduction or loss from **Schedule K–1**	(f) Other income from **Schedule K–1**
A				
B				
33a Totals				
b Totals				

34	Add columns (d) and (f) of line 33a	34
35	Add columns (c) and (e) of line 33b	35 ( )
36	Total estate and trust income or (loss). Combine lines 34 and 35. Enter the result here and include in the total on line 40 below	36

Part IV   Income or Loss From Real Estate Mortgage Investment Conduits (REMICs)—Residual Holder

37	(a) Name	(b) Employer identification number	(c) Excess inclusion from Schedules Q, line 2c (see page E-6)	(d) Taxable income (net loss) from Schedules Q, line 1b	(e) Income from Schedules Q, line 3b

38	Combine columns (d) and (e) only. Enter the result here and include in the total on line 40 below	38

Part V   Summary

39	Net farm rental income or (loss) from **Form 4835**. Also, complete line 41 below	39
40	**Total** income or (loss). Combine lines 26, 31, 36, 38, and 39. Enter the result here and on Form 1040, line 17 ▶	40
41	**Reconciliation of Farming and Fishing Income.** Enter your **gross** farming and fishing income reported on Form 4835, line 7; Schedule K-1 (Form 1065), line 15b; Schedule K-1 (Form 1120S), line 23; and Schedule K-1 (Form 1041), line 14 (see page E-6)	41
42	**Reconciliation for Real Estate Professionals.** If you were a real estate professional (see page E-4), enter the net income or (loss) you reported anywhere on Form 1040 from all rental real estate activities in which you materially participated under the passive activity loss rules . . .	42

SCHEDULE F
(Form 1040)

Department of the Treasury
Internal Revenue Service (99)

Profit or Loss From Farming

▶ Attach to Form 1040, Form 1041, Form 1065, or Form 1065-B.

▶ See Instructions for Schedule F (Form 1040).

OMB No. 1545-0074

2001

Attachment
Sequence No. **14**

Name of proprietor

Social security number (SSN)

A Principal product. Describe in one or two words your principal crop or activity for the current tax year.

B Enter code from Part IV
▶

D Employer ID number (EIN), if any

C Accounting method: **(1)** ☐ Cash **(2)** ☐ Accrual

E Did you "materially participate" in the operation of this business during 2001? If "No," see page F-2 for limit on passive losses. ☐ Yes ☐ No

Part I Farm Income—Cash Method. Complete Parts I and II (Accrual method taxpayers complete Parts II and III, and line 11 of Part I.)
Do not include sales of livestock held for draft, breeding, sport, or dairy purposes; report these sales on Form 4797.

1	Sales of livestock and other items you bought for resale	**1**	
2	Cost or other basis of livestock and other items reported on line 1	**2**	
3	Subtract line 2 from line 1	**3**	
4	Sales of livestock, produce, grains, and other products you raised	**4**	
5a	Total cooperative distributions (Form(s) 1099-PATR)	**5a**	**5b** Taxable amount	**5b**
6a	Agricultural program payments (see page F-2)	**6a**	**6b** Taxable amount	**6b**
7	Commodity Credit Corporation (CCC) loans (see page F-3):		
a	CCC loans reported under election	**7a**	
b	CCC loans forfeited	**7b**	**7c** Taxable amount	**7c**
8	Crop insurance proceeds and certain disaster payments (see page F-3):		
a	Amount received in 2001	**8a**	**8b** Taxable amount	**8b**
c	If election to defer to 2002 is attached, check here ▶ ☐	**8d** Amount deferred from 2000	**8d**
9	Custom hire (machine work) income	**9**	
10	Other income, including Federal and state gasoline or fuel tax credit or refund (see page F-3)	**10**	
11	**Gross income.** Add amounts in the right column for lines 3 through 10. If accrual method taxpayer, enter the amount from page 2, line 51 ▶	**11**	

Part II Farm Expenses—Cash and Accrual Method. Do not include personal or living expenses such as taxes, insurance, repairs, etc., on your home.

12	Car and truck expenses (see page F-4—also attach **Form 4562**)	**12**		25	Pension and profit-sharing plans	**25**
13	Chemicals	**13**		26	Rent or lease (see page F-5):	
14	Conservation expenses (see page F-4)	**14**		a	Vehicles, machinery, and equipment	**26a**
15	Custom hire (machine work)	**15**		b	Other (land, animals, etc.)	**26b**
16	Depreciation and section 179 expense deduction not claimed elsewhere (see page F-4)	**16**		27	Repairs and maintenance	**27**
				28	Seeds and plants purchased	**28**
				29	Storage and warehousing	**29**
17	Employee benefit programs other than on line 25	**17**		30	Supplies purchased	**30**
18	Feed purchased	**18**		31	Taxes	**31**
19	Fertilizers and lime	**19**		32	Utilities	**32**
20	Freight and trucking	**20**		33	Veterinary, breeding, and medicine	**33**
21	Gasoline, fuel, and oil	**21**		34	Other expenses (specify):	
22	Insurance (other than health)	**22**		a	....	**34a**
23	Interest:			b	....	**34b**
a	Mortgage (paid to banks, etc.)	**23a**		c	....	**34c**
b	Other	**23b**		d	....	**34d**
24	Labor hired (less employment credits)	**24**		e	....	**34e**
				f		**34f**

35	**Total expenses.** Add lines 12 through 34f ▶	**35**	
36	**Net farm profit or (loss).** Subtract line 35 from line 11. If a profit, enter on **Form 1040, line 18,** and also on Schedule SE, line 1. If a loss, you **must** go on to line 37 (estates, trusts, and partnerships, see page F-6)	**36**	

37	If you have a loss, you **must** check the box that describes your investment in this activity (see page F-6). • If you checked 37a, enter the loss on **Form 1040, line 18,** and **also** on **Schedule SE, line 1.** • If you checked 37b, you **must** attach **Form 6198.**	**37a** ☐ All investment is at risk. **37b** ☐ Some investment is not at risk.

For Paperwork Reduction Act Notice, see Form 1040 instructions.

Cat. No. 11346H

Schedule F (Form 1040) 2001

637

Part III **Farm Income—Accrual Method** (see page F-6)

Do not include sales of livestock held for draft, breeding, sport, or dairy purposes; report these sales on Form 4797 and do not include this livestock on line 46 below.

38 Sales of livestock, produce, grains, and other products during the year.	**38**	
39a Total cooperative distributions (Form(s) 1099-PATR)	**39a**	
	39b Taxable amount	**39b**
40a Agricultural program payments	**40a**	
	40b Taxable amount	**40b**
41 Commodity Credit Corporation (CCC) loans:		
a CCC loans reported under election	**41a**	
b CCC loans forfeited	**41b**	
	41c Taxable amount	**41c**
42 Crop insurance proceeds	**42**	
43 Custom hire (machine work) income	**43**	
44 Other income, including Federal and state gasoline or fuel tax credit or refund	**44**	
45 Add amounts in the right column for lines 38 through 44	**45**	
46 Inventory of livestock, produce, grains, and other products at beginning of the year.	**46**	
47 Cost of livestock, produce, grains, and other products purchased during the year.	**47**	
48 Add lines 46 and 47	**48**	
49 Inventory of livestock, produce, grains, and other products at end of year	**49**	
50 Cost of livestock, produce, grains, and other products sold. Subtract line 49 from line 48*	**50**	
51 **Gross income.** Subtract line 50 from line 45. Enter the result here and on page 1, line 11 . . . . ▶	**51**	

*If you use the unit-livestock-price method or the farm-price method of valuing inventory and the amount on line 49 is larger than the amount on line 48, subtract line 48 from line 49. Enter the result on line 50. Add lines 45 and 50. Enter the total on line 51.

Part IV **Principal Agricultural Activity Codes**

Caution. File **Schedule C** (Form 1040), Profit or Loss From Business, or **Schedule C-EZ** (Form 1040), Net Profit From Business, instead of Schedule F if:

● Your principal source of income is from providing agricultural services such as soil preparation, veterinary, farm labor, horticultural, or management for a fee or on a contract basis or

● You are engaged in the business of breeding, raising, and caring for dogs, cats, or other pet animals.

These codes for the Principal Agricultural Activity classify farms by the type of activity they are engaged in to facilitate the administration of the Internal Revenue Code. These six-digit codes are based on the North American Industry Classification System (NAICS).

Select one of the following codes and enter the six-digit number on page 1, line B.

Crop Production

111100	Oilseed and grain farming
111210	Vegetable and melon farming
111300	Fruit and tree nut farming
111400	Greenhouse, nursery, and floriculture production
111900	Other crop farming

Animal Production

112111	Beef cattle ranching and farming
112112	Cattle feedlots
112120	Dairy cattle and milk production
112210	Hog and pig farming
112300	Poultry and egg production
112400	Sheep and goat farming
112510	Animal aquaculture
112900	Other animal production

Forestry and Logging

113000	Forestry and logging (including forest nurseries and timber tracts)

Schedule R (Form 1040)	Credit for the Elderly or the Disabled	OMB No. 1545-0074 **2001**
Department of the Treasury Internal Revenue Service (99)	▶ **Attach to Form 1040.** ▶ **See Instructions for Schedule R (Form 1040).**	Attachment Sequence No. **16**

Name(s) shown on Form 1040	Your social security number

You may be able to take this credit and reduce your tax if by the end of 2001:

- You were age 65 or older **or**
- You were under age 65, you retired on **permanent and total** disability, and you received taxable disability income.

But you must also meet other tests. See page R-1.

(TIP) In most cases, the IRS can figure the credit for you. See page R-1.

Part I Check the Box for Your Filing Status and Age

If your filing status is:	And by the end of 2001:	Check only one box:
Single, Head of household, or Qualifying widow(er) with dependent child	**1** You were 65 or older **1**	☐
	2 You were under 65 and you retired on permanent and total disability **2**	☐
Married filing a joint return	**3** Both spouses were 65 or older. **3**	☐
	4 Both spouses were under 65, but only one spouse retired on permanent and total disability **4**	☐
	5 Both spouses were under 65, and both retired on permanent and total disability **5**	☐
	6 One spouse was 65 or older, and the other spouse was under 65 and retired on permanent and total disability **6**	☐
	7 One spouse was 65 or older, and the other spouse was under 65 and **not** retired on permanent and total disability. **7**	☐
Married filing a separate return	**8** You were 65 or older and you lived apart from your spouse for all of 2001 . . . . **8**	☐
	9 You were under 65, you retired on permanent and total disability, and you lived apart from your spouse for all of 2001 . . . . **9**	☐

Did you check box 1, 3, 7, or 8?	Yes ——▶ Skip Part II and complete Part III on back.
	No ——▶ Complete Parts II and III.

Part II Statement of Permanent and Total Disability (Complete **only** if you checked box 2, 4, 5, 6, or 9 above.)

If: 1 You filed a physician's statement for this disability for 1983 or an earlier year, or you filed or got a statement for tax years after 1983 and your physician signed line B on the statement, **and**

2 Due to your continued disabled condition, you were unable to engage in any substantial gainful activity in 2001, check this box . . . . ▶ ☐

- If you checked this box, you do not have to get another statement for 2001.

- If you **did not** check this box, have your physician complete the statement on page R-4. You **must** keep the statement for your records.

For Paperwork Reduction Act Notice, see Form 1040 instructions. Cat. No. 11359K Schedule R (Form 1040) 2001

639

Part III **Figure Your Credit**

10 If you checked (in Part I):   **Enter:**

Box 1, 2, 4, or 7 . . . . $5,000
Box 3, 5, or 6 . . . . $7,500 } **10**
Box 8 or 9 . . . . $3,750

> **Did you check box 2, 4, 5, 6, or 9 in Part I?** ─── **Yes** ──▶ You **must** complete line 11.
>
> ─── **No** ──▶ Enter the amount from line 10 on line 12 and go to line 13.

11 If you checked:

- Box 6 in Part I, add $5,000 to the taxable disability income of the spouse who was under age 65. Enter the total.
- Box 2, 4, or 9 in Part I, enter your taxable disability income. } **11**
- Box 5 in Part I, add your taxable disability income to your spouse's taxable disability income. Enter the total.

(TIP) For more details on what to include on line 11, see page R-3.

12 If you completed line 11, enter the **smaller** of line 10 or line 11; **all others,** enter the amount from line 10 . . . . **12**

13 Enter the following pensions, annuities, or disability income that you (and your spouse if filing a joint return) received in 2001:

a Nontaxable part of social security benefits and

Nontaxable part of railroad retirement benefits treated as social security. See page R-3. } . . . **13a**

b Nontaxable veterans' pensions and

Any other pension, annuity, or disability benefit that is excluded from income under any other provision of law. See page R-3. } . . . **13b**

c Add lines 13a and 13b. (Even though these income items are not taxable, they **must** be included here to figure your credit.) If you did not receive any of the types of nontaxable income listed on line 13a or 13b, enter -0- on line 13c **13c**

14 Enter the amount from Form 1040, line 34 . . . . **14**

15 If you checked (in Part I):   **Enter:**

Box 1 or 2 . . . . . . $7,500
Box 3, 4, 5, 6, or 7 . . . $10,000 } **15**
Box 8 or 9 . . . . . . $5,000

16 Subtract line 15 from line 14. If zero or less, enter -0- **16**

17 Enter one-half of line 16 . . . . **17**

18 Add lines 13c and 17 . . . . **18**

19 Subtract line 18 from line 12. If zero or less, **stop; you cannot** take the credit. Otherwise, go to line 20 . . . . **19**

20 Multiply line 19 by 15% (.15). Enter the result here and on Form 1040, line 45. But if this amount is more than the amount on Form 1040, line 42, minus any amount on line 43, **or** you are filing Form 2441, see page R-3 for the amount of credit you may take **20**

SCHEDULE SE	Self-Employment Tax	OMB No. 1545-0074

SCHEDULE SE
(Form 1040)

Department of the Treasury
Internal Revenue Service (99)

Self-Employment Tax

▶ **See Instructions for Schedule SE (Form 1040).**

▶ **Attach to Form 1040.**

OMB No. 1545-0074

20**01**

Attachment
Sequence No. **17**

Name of person with **self-employment** income (as shown on Form 1040)

Social security number of person
with **self-employment** income ▶

Who Must File Schedule SE

You must file Schedule SE if:

- You had net earnings from self-employment from **other than** church employee income (line 4 of Short Schedule SE or line 4c of Long Schedule SE) of $400 or more **or**
- You had church employee income of $108.28 or more. Income from services you performed as a minister or a member of a religious order **is not** church employee income. See page SE-1.

Note. Even if you had a loss or a small amount of income from self-employment, it may be to your benefit to file Schedule SE and use either "optional method" in Part II of Long Schedule SE. See page SE-3.

Exception. If your only self-employment income was from earnings as a minister, member of a religious order, or Christian Science practitioner **and** you filed Form 4361 and received IRS approval not to be taxed on those earnings, **do not** file Schedule SE. Instead, write "Exempt–Form 4361" on Form 1040, line 53.

May I Use Short Schedule SE or Must I Use Long Schedule SE?

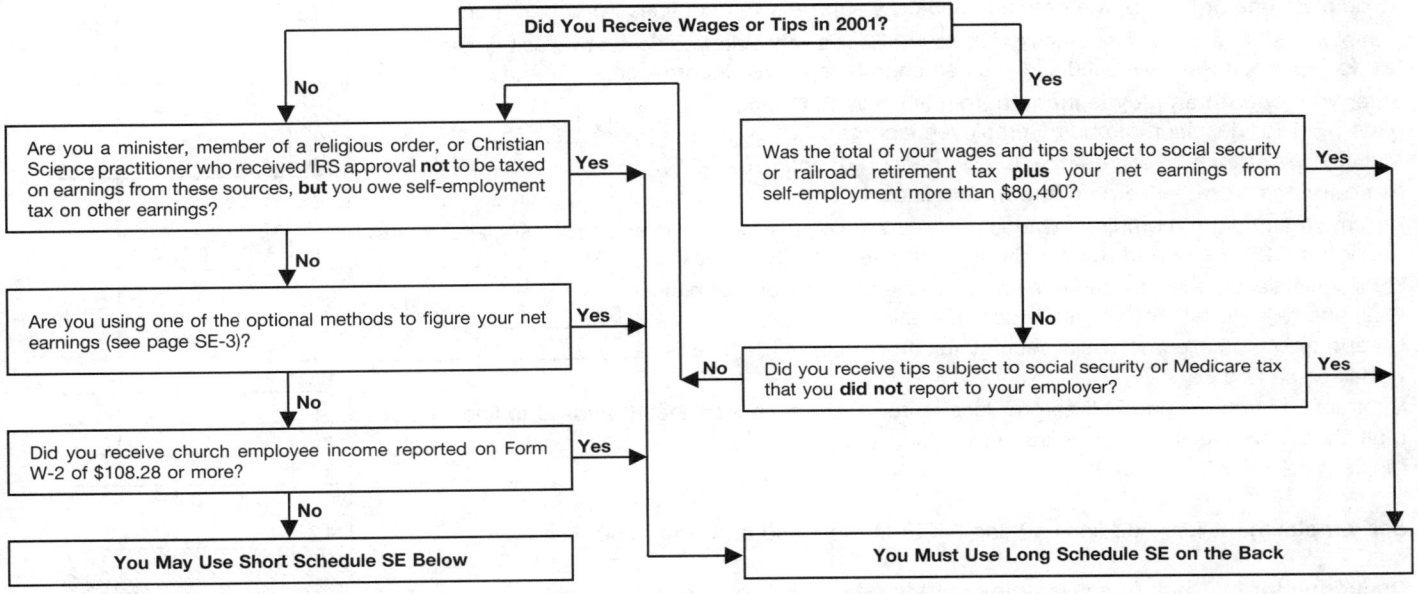

Section A—Short Schedule SE. Caution. Read above to see if you can use Short Schedule SE.

1	Net farm profit or (loss) from Schedule F, line 36, and farm partnerships, Schedule K-1 (Form 1065), line 15a	**1**	
2	Net profit or (loss) from Schedule C, line 31; Schedule C-EZ, line 3; Schedule K-1 (Form 1065), line 15a (other than farming); and Schedule K-1 (Form 1065-B), box 9. Ministers and members of religious orders, see page SE-1 for amounts to report on this line. See page SE-2 for other income to report	**2**	
3	Combine lines 1 and 2	**3**	
4	**Net earnings from self-employment.** Multiply line 3 by 92.35% (.9235). If less than $400, **do not** file this schedule; you do not owe self-employment tax . . . . ▶	**4**	
5	**Self-employment tax.** If the amount on line 4 is: ● $80,400 or less, multiply line 4 by 15.3% (.153). Enter the result here and on **Form 1040, line 53.** ● More than $80,400, multiply line 4 by 2.9% (.029). Then, add $9,969.60 to the result. Enter the total here and on **Form 1040, line 53.**	**5**	
6	**Deduction for one-half of self-employment tax.** Multiply line 5 by 50% (.5). Enter the result here and on **Form 1040, line 27**	**6**	

For Paperwork Reduction Act Notice, see Form 1040 instructions.   Cat. No. 11358Z   **Schedule SE (Form 1040) 2001**

Name of person with **self-employment** income (as shown on Form 1040)	Social security number of person with **self-employment** income ▶		

Section B—Long Schedule SE

Part I   Self-Employment Tax

Note. If your only income subject to self-employment tax is **church employee income,** skip lines 1 through 4b. Enter -0- on line 4c and go to line 5a. Income from services you performed as a minister or a member of a religious order **is not** church employee income. See page SE-1.

A   If you are a minister, member of a religious order, or Christian Science practitioner **and** you filed Form 4361, but you had $400 or more of **other** net earnings from self-employment, check here and continue with Part I . . . . ▶ ☐

1	Net farm profit or (loss) from Schedule F, line 36, and farm partnerships, Schedule K-1 (Form 1065), line 15a. **Note.** Skip this line if you use the farm optional method. See page SE-3 . .	**1**		
2	Net profit or (loss) from Schedule C, line 31; Schedule C-EZ, line 3; Schedule K-1 (Form 1065), line 15a (other than farming); and Schedule K-1 (Form 1065-B), box 9. Ministers and members of religious orders, see page SE-1 for amounts to report on this line. See page SE-2 for other income to report. **Note.** Skip this line if you use the nonfarm optional method. See page SE-3.	**2**		
3	Combine lines 1 and 2	**3**		
4a	If line 3 is more than zero, multiply line 3 by 92.35% (.9235). Otherwise, enter amount from line 3	**4a**		
b	If you elect one or both of the optional methods, enter the total of lines 15 and 17 here . . .	**4b**		
c	Combine lines 4a and 4b. If less than $400, **do not** file this schedule; you do not owe self-employment tax. **Exception.** If less than $400 and you had **church employee income,** enter -0- and continue ▶	**4c**		
5a	Enter your **church employee income** from Form W-2. **Caution.** See page SE-1 for definition of church employee income **5a**			
b	Multiply line 5a by 92.35% (.9235). If less than $100, enter -0-	**5b**		
6	**Net earnings from self-employment.** Add lines 4c and 5b	**6**		
7	Maximum amount of combined wages and self-employment earnings subject to social security tax or the 6.2% portion of the 7.65% railroad retirement (tier 1) tax for 2001	**7**	80,400	00
8a	Total social security wages and tips (total of boxes 3 and 7 on Form(s) W-2) and railroad retirement (tier 1) compensation **8a**			
b	Unreported tips subject to social security tax (from Form 4137, line 9) **8b**			
c	Add lines 8a and 8b	**8c**		
9	Subtract line 8c from line 7. If zero or less, enter -0- here and on line 10 and go to line 11 . ▶	**9**		
10	Multiply the **smaller** of line 6 or line 9 by 12.4% (.124)	**10**		
11	Multiply line 6 by 2.9% (.029)	**11**		
12	**Self-employment tax.** Add lines 10 and 11. Enter here and on **Form 1040, line 53**	**12**		
13	**Deduction for one-half of self-employment tax.** Multiply line 12 by 50% (.5). Enter the result here and on **Form 1040, line 27** . . . **13**			

Part II   Optional Methods To Figure Net Earnings (See page SE-3.)

Farm Optional Method. You may use this method **only** if:

- Your gross farm income[1] was not more than $2,400 **or**
- Your net farm profits[2] were less than $1,733.

14	Maximum income for optional methods	**14**	1,600	00
15	Enter the **smaller** of: two-thirds (⅔) of gross farm income[1] (not less than zero) **or** $1,600. Also include this amount on line 4b above	**15**		

Nonfarm Optional Method. You may use this method **only** if:

- Your net nonfarm profits[3] were less than $1,733 and also less than 72.189% of your gross nonfarm income[4] **and**
- You had net earnings from self-employment of at least $400 in 2 of the prior 3 years.

Caution. You may use this method no more than five times.

16	Subtract line 15 from line 14	**16**		
17	Enter the **smaller** of: two-thirds (⅔) of gross nonfarm income[4] (not less than zero) **or** the amount on line 16. Also include this amount on line 4b above	**17**		

[1]From Sch. F, line 11, and Sch. K-1 (Form 1065), line 15b.   [3]From Sch. C, line 31; Sch. C-EZ, line 3; Sch. K-1 (Form 1065), line 15a; and Sch. K-1 (Form 1065-B), box 9.
[2]From Sch. F, line 36, and Sch. K-1 (Form 1065), line 15a.   [4]From Sch. C, line 7; Sch. C-EZ, line 1; Sch. K-1 (Form 1065), line 15c; and Sch. K-1 (Form 1065-B), box 9.

| Form **1040-ES** | Estimated Tax for Individuals | OMB No. 1545-0087 |

Department of the Treasury
Internal Revenue Service

This package is primarily for first-time filers of estimated tax.

2001

Record of Estimated Tax Payments (Farmers, fishermen, and fiscal year taxpayers, see page 3 for payment due dates.)

Payment number	Payment due date	(a) Date paid	(b) Check or money order number or credit card confirmation number	(c) Amount paid (**do not** include any credit card convenience fee)	(d) 2000 overpayment credit applied	(e) Total amount paid and credited (add (c) and (d))
1	4/16/2001					
2	6/15/2001					
3	9/17/2001					
4	1/15/2002*					
Total . . . . ▶						

*You do not have to make this payment if you file your 2001 tax return by January 31, 2002, **and** pay the entire balance due with your return.

Where To File Your Payment Voucher if Paying by Check or Money Order

Mail your payment voucher and check or money order to the Internal Revenue Service at the address shown below for the place where you live. **Do not** mail your tax return to this address **or** send an estimated tax payment without a payment voucher. Also, do not mail your estimated tax payments to the address shown in the Form 1040 or 1040A instructions. If you need more payment vouchers, use another Form 1040-ES package.

Note: *For proper delivery of your estimated tax payment to a P.O. box, you must include the box number in the address. Also, note that only the U.S. Postal Service can deliver to P.O. boxes.*

IF you live in . . . ▼	THEN use . . . ▼
Delaware, New Jersey, New York (New York City and counties of Nassau, Rockland, Suffolk, and Westchester)	P.O. Box 162 Newark, NJ 07101-0162
New York (all other counties), Connecticut, Maine, Massachusetts, New Hampshire, Rhode Island, Vermont	P.O. Box 371999 Pittsburgh, PA 15250-7999
District of Columbia, Indiana, Maryland, Pennsylvania, Virginia	P.O. Box 8318 Philadelphia, PA 19162-8318

Florida, Georgia, South Carolina, West Virginia	P.O. Box 105900 Atlanta, GA 30348-5900
Michigan, Ohio	P.O. Box 7422 Chicago, IL 60680-7422
Alabama, Arkansas, Kentucky, Louisiana, Mississippi, Nebraska, North Carolina, Tennessee	P.O. Box 1219 Charlotte, NC 28201-1219
Illinois, Iowa, Kansas, Minnesota, Missouri, Oregon, Wisconsin	P.O. Box 970006 St. Louis, MO 63197-0006
Colorado, Idaho, Montana, New Mexico, Oklahoma, Texas, Wyoming	P.O. Box 970001 St. Louis, MO 63197-0001
Arizona, California (counties of Alpine, Amador, Butte, Calaveras, Colusa, Contra Costa, Del Norte, El Dorado, Glenn, Humboldt, Lake, Lassen, Marin, Mendocino, Modoc, Napa, Nevada, Placer, Plumas, Sacramento, San Joaquin, Shasta, Sierra, Siskiyou, Solano, Sonoma, Sutter, Tehama, Trinity, Yolo, and Yuba), Nevada, North Dakota, South Dakota, Utah, Washington	P.O. Box 510000 San Francisco, CA 94151-5100

California (all other counties), Alaska, Hawaii	P.O. Box 54030 Los Angeles, CA 90054-0030
All APO and FPO addresses, American Samoa, the Commonwealth of the Northern Mariana Islands, nonpermanent residents of Guam or the Virgin Islands, Puerto Rico (or if excluding income under section 933), or a foreign country (U.S. citizens and those filing Form 2555, Form 2555-EZ, or Form 4563)	P.O. Box 8318 Philadelphia, PA 19162-8318
Permanent residents of Guam*	Department of Revenue and Taxation Government of Guam P.O. Box 23607 GMF, GU 96921
Permanent residents of the Virgin Islands*	V.I. Bureau of Internal Revenue 9601 Estate Thomas Charlotte Amalie St. Thomas, VI 00802

* Permanent residents must prepare separate vouchers for estimated income tax and self-employment tax payments. Send the income tax vouchers to the address for permanent residents and the self-employment tax vouchers to the address for nonpermanent residents.

Form **1040-ES**
Department of the Treasury
Internal Revenue Service

2001 Payment Voucher **1**

OMB No. 1545-0087

File only if you are making a payment of estimated tax by check or money order. Mail this voucher with your check or money order payable to the **"United States Treasury."** Write your social security number and "2001 Form 1040-ES" on your check or money order. Do not send cash. Enclose, but do not staple or attach, your payment with this voucher.

Calendar year—Due April 16, 2001

Amount of estimated tax you are paying by check or money order. **$**

Your first name and initial	Your last name	Your social security number
If joint payment, complete for spouse		
Spouse's first name and initial	Spouse's last name	Spouse's social security number
Address (number, street, and apt. no.)		
City, state, and ZIP code (If a foreign address, enter city, province or state, postal code, and country.)		

Type or print

2001 Form 1040-V

What Is Form 1040-V and Do You Have To Use It?

It is a statement you send with your check or money order for any balance due on line 70 of your **2001 Form 1040.** Using Form 1040-V allows us to process your payment more accurately and efficiently. We strongly encourage you to use Form 1040-V, but there is no penalty if you do not do so.

How To Fill In Form 1040-V

Line 1. Enter your social security number (SSN). If you are filing a joint return, enter the SSN shown **first** on your return.

Line 2. If you are filing a joint return, enter the SSN shown **second** on your return.

Line 3. Enter the amount you are paying by check or money order.

Line 4. Enter your name(s) and address **exactly** as shown on your return. Please print your name(s) clearly.

How To Prepare Your Payment

● Make your check or money order payable to the **"United States Treasury." Do not** send cash.

● Make sure your name and address appear on your check or money order.

● Enter "2001 Form 1040," your daytime phone number, and your SSN on your check or money order. If you are filing a joint return, enter the SSN shown **first** on your return.

● To help us process your payment, enter the amount on the right side of your check like this: $ XXX.XX. **Do not** use dashes or lines (for example, do not enter "$ XXX—" or "$ XXX $\frac{XX}{100}$").

How To Send In Your Return, Payment, and Form 1040-V

● Detach Form 1040-V along the dotted line.

● **Do not** staple or otherwise attach your payment or Form 1040-V to your return or to each other. Instead, just put them loose in the envelope.

● If an envelope came with your tax package, please use it to mail your 2001 tax return, payment, and Form 1040-V.

● If you do not have that envelope or you moved or used a paid preparer, mail your tax return, payment, and Form 1040-V to the Internal Revenue Service at the address shown on the back that applies to you.

Paperwork Reduction Act Notice. We ask for the information on Form 1040-V to help us carry out the Internal Revenue laws of the United States. If you use Form 1040-V, you must provide the requested information. Your cooperation will help us ensure that we are collecting the right amount of tax.

You are not required to provide the information requested on a form that is subject to the Paperwork Reduction Act unless the form displays a valid OMB control number. Books or records relating to a form or its instructions must be retained as long as their contents may become material in the administration of any Internal Revenue law. Generally, tax returns and return information are confidential, as required by Internal Revenue Code section 6103.

The time needed to complete and mail Form 1040-V will vary depending on individual circumstances. The estimated average time is 19 minutes. If you have comments about the accuracy of this time estimate or suggestions for making Form 1040-V simpler, we would be happy to hear from you. See the Instructions for Form 1040.

Cat. No. 20975C   ▼ **Detach Here and Mail With Your Payment and Return** ▼   Form **1040-V** (2001)

Form 1040-V
Department of the Treasury
Internal Revenue Service (99)

Payment Voucher

► **Do not staple or attach this voucher to your payment or return.**

OMB No. 1545-0074

2001

1 Your social security number (SSN)	2 If a joint return, SSN shown second on that return	3 Amount you are paying by check or money order	Dollars	Cents

4 Your first name and initial		Last name	
If a joint return, spouse's first name and initial		Last name	
Home address (number and street)			Apt. no.
City, town or post office, state, and ZIP code			

Cat. No. 20975C

IF you live in . . .	THEN use this address if you:	
	Prepared your own return . . .	**Used a paid preparer . . .**
Florida, Georgia, North Carolina, South Carolina, West Virginia	Atlanta, GA 39901-0102	P.O. Box 105093 Atlanta, GA 30348-5093
New Jersey, New York *(New York City and counties of Nassau, Rockland, Suffolk, and Westchester)*	Holtsville, NY 00501-0102	P.O. Box 1187 Newark, NJ 07101-1187
New York *(all other counties)*, Massachusetts, Michigan, Rhode Island	Andover, MA 05501-0102	P.O. Box 13757 Philadelphia, PA 19101-3757
Illinois, Iowa, Kansas, Minnesota, Missouri, Wisconsin	Kansas City, MO 64999-0102	P.O. Box 970011 St. Louis, MO 63197-0011
Oklahoma	Kansas City, MO 64999-0102	P.O. Box 105017 Atlanta, GA 30348-5017
Utah	Kansas City, MO 64999-0102	P.O. Box 660308 Dallas, TX 75266-0308
Maine, New Hampshire, Vermont	Philadelphia, PA 19255-0102	P.O. Box 13757 Philadelphia, PA 19101-3757
Connecticut, Delaware	Philadelphia, PA 19255-0102	P.O. Box 1187 Newark, NJ 07101-1187
District of Columbia, Indiana, Maryland, Pennsylvania	Philadelphia, PA 19255-0102	P.O. Box 80101 Cincinnati, OH 45280-0001
Ohio	Cincinnati, OH 45999-0102	P.O. Box 80101 Cincinnati, OH 45280-0001
Arizona, Colorado, Idaho, Montana, New Mexico, Texas, Wyoming	Austin, TX 73301-0102	P.O. Box 660308 Dallas, TX 75266-0308
Nebraska, North Dakota, South Dakota, Washington	Ogden, UT 84201-0102	P.O. Box 60840 Los Angeles, CA 90060-0840
Alaska, California, Hawaii, Nevada	Fresno, CA 93888-0102	P.O. Box 7704 San Francisco, CA 94120-7704
Oregon	Fresno, CA 93888-0102	P.O. Box 970011 St. Louis, MO 63197-0011
Alabama, Arkansas, Kentucky, Louisiana, Mississippi, Tennessee, Virginia	Memphis, TN 37501-0102	P.O. Box 105017 Atlanta, GA 30348-5017
All APO and FPO addresses, American Samoa, nonpermanent residents of Guam or the Virgin Islands*, Puerto Rico *(or if excluding income under Internal Revenue Code section 933)*, a foreign country *(or if a dual-status alien):* U.S. citizens or those filing Form 2555, Form 2555-EZ, or Form 4563	Philadelphia, PA 19255-0215	P.O. Box 80101 Cincinnati, OH 45280-0001

* Permanent residents of Guam or the Virgin Islands should not use Form 1040-V.

Form **709**

Department of the Treasury
Internal Revenue Service

United States Gift (and Generation-Skipping Transfer) Tax Return

(Section 6019 of the Internal Revenue Code) (For gifts made during calendar year 2001)

▶ **See separate instructions.**

OMB No. 1545-0020

2001

Part 1—General Information

1 Donor's first name and middle initial	2 Donor's last name	3 **Donor's social security number**

4 Address (number, street, and apartment number)	5 Legal residence (domicile) (county and state)

6 City, state, and ZIP code	7 Citizenship

		Yes	No
8	If the donor died during the year, check here ▶ ☐ and enter date of death................ , ...		
9	If you received an extension of time to file this Form 709, check here ▶ ☐ and attach the Form 4868, 2688, 2350, or extension letter .		
10	Enter the total number of separate donees listed on Schedule A—count each person only once. ▶		
11a	Have you (the donor) previously filed a Form 709 (or 709-A) for any other year? If the answer is "No," do not complete line 11b .		
11b	If the answer to line 11a is "Yes," has your address changed since you last filed Form 709 (or 709-A)?		
12	Gifts by husband or wife to third parties.—Do you consent to have the gifts (including generation-skipping transfers) made by you and by your spouse to third parties during the calendar year considered as made one-half by each of you? (See instructions.) (If the answer is "Yes," the following information must be furnished and your spouse must sign the consent shown below. **If the answer is "No," skip lines 13–18 and go to Schedule A.)**		
13	Name of consenting spouse **14** SSN		
15	Were you married to one another during the entire calendar year? (see instructions)		
16	If the answer to 15 is "No," check whether ☐ married ☐ divorced or ☐ widowed, and give date (see instructions) ▶		
17	Will a gift tax return for this calendar year be filed by your spouse?		
18	**Consent of Spouse**—I consent to have the gifts (and generation-skipping transfers) made by me and by my spouse to third parties during the calendar year considered as made one-half by each of us. We are both aware of the joint and several liability for tax created by the execution of this consent.		

Consenting spouse's signature ▶   Date ▶

Part 2—Tax Computation

1	Enter the amount from Schedule A, Part 3, line 15	**1**		
2	Enter the amount from Schedule B, line 3	**2**		
3	Total taxable gifts (add lines 1 and 2)	**3**		
4	Tax computed on amount on line 3 (see Table for Computing Tax in separate instructions). . .	**4**		
5	Tax computed on amount on line 2 (see Table for Computing Tax in separate instructions). . .	**5**		
6	Balance (subtract line 5 from line 4)	**6**		
7	Maximum unified credit (nonresident aliens, see instructions)	**7**	220,550	00
8	Enter the unified credit against tax allowable for all prior periods (from Sch. B, line 1, col. C) . .	**8**		
9	Balance (subtract line 8 from line 7)	**9**		
10	Enter 20% (.20) of the amount allowed as a specific exemption for gifts made after September 8, 1976, and before January 1, 1977 (see instructions)	**10**		
11	Balance (subtract line 10 from line 9)	**11**		
12	Unified credit (enter the smaller of line 6 or line 11)	**12**		
13	Credit for foreign gift taxes (see instructions)	**13**		
14	Total credits (add lines 12 and 13)	**14**		
15	Balance (subtract line 14 from line 6) (do not enter less than zero)	**15**		
16	Generation-skipping transfer taxes (from Schedule C, Part 3, col. H, Total)	**16**		
17	Total tax (add lines 15 and 16)	**17**		
18	Gift and generation-skipping transfer taxes prepaid with extension of time to file	**18**		
19	If line 18 is less than line 17, enter **balance due** (see instructions)	**19**		
20	If line 18 is greater than line 17, enter **amount to be refunded**	**20**		

Attach check or money order here.

Sign Here

Under penalties of perjury, I declare that I have examined this return, including any accompanying schedules and statements, and to the best of my knowledge and belief, it is true, correct, and complete. Declaration of preparer (other than donor) is based on all information of which preparer has any knowledge.

▶ Signature of donor   Date

Paid Preparer's Use Only

Preparer's signature ▶	Date	Check if self-employed ▶ ☐
Firm's name (or yours if self-employed), address, and ZIP code ▶		Phone no. ▶ ( )

For Disclosure, Privacy Act, and Paperwork Reduction Act Notice, see page 12 of the separate instructions for this form.   Cat. No. 16783M   Form **709** (2001)

SCHEDULE A	Computation of Taxable Gifts (Including Transfers in Trust)

A Does the value of any item listed on Schedule A reflect any valuation discount? If the answer is "Yes," see instructions   . . Yes ☐ No ☐

B ☐ ◄ Check here if you elect under section 529(c)(2)(B) to treat any transfers made this year to a qualified state tuition program as made ratably over a 5-year period beginning this year. See instructions. Attach explanation.

Part 1—Gifts Subject Only to Gift Tax. *Gifts less political organization, medical, and educational exclusions—see instructions*

A Item number	**B** • Donee's name and address • Relationship to donor (if any) • Description of gift • If the gift was made by means of a trust, enter trust's EIN and attach a description or copy of the trust instrument (see instructions) • If the gift was of securities, give CUSIP number	**C** Donor's adjusted basis of gift	**D** Date of gift	**E** Value at date of gift
1				

Total of Part 1 (add amounts from Part 1, column E) . . . . ►

Part 2—Gifts That are Direct Skips and are Subject to Both Gift Tax and Generation-Skipping Transfer Tax. You must list the gifts in chronological order. *Gifts less political organization, medical, and educational exclusions—see instructions. (Also list here direct skips that are subject only to the GST tax at this time as the result of the termination of an "estate tax inclusion period." See instructions.)*

A Item number	**B** • Donee's name and address • Relationship to donor (if any) • Description of gift • If the gift was made by means of a trust, enter trust's EIN and attach a description or copy of the trust instrument (see instructions) • If the gift was of securities, give CUSIP number	**C** Donor's adjusted basis of gift	**D** Date of gift	**E** Value at date of gift
1				

Total of Part 2 (add amounts from Part 2, column E) . . . . ►

Part 3—Taxable Gift Reconciliation

1	Total value of gifts of donor (add totals from column E of Parts 1 and 2)	**1**	
2	One-half of items _____ attributable to spouse (see instructions)	**2**	
3	Balance (subtract line 2 from line 1)	**3**	
4	Gifts of spouse to be included (from Schedule A, Part 3, line 2 of spouse's return—see instructions) .	**4**	
	If any of the gifts included on this line are also subject to the generation-skipping transfer tax, check here ► ☐ and enter those gifts also on Schedule C, Part 1.		
5	Total gifts (add lines 3 and 4)	**5**	
6	Total annual exclusions for gifts listed on Schedule A (including line 4, above) (see instructions) . . .	**6**	
7	Total included amount of gifts (subtract line 6 from line 5)	**7**	

Deductions (see instructions)

8	Gifts of interests to spouse for which a marital deduction will be claimed, based on items _____ of Schedule A	**8**		
9	Exclusions attributable to gifts on line 8	**9**		
10	Marital deduction—subtract line 9 from line 8	**10**		
11	Charitable deduction, based on items _____ less exclusions . .	**11**		
12	Total deductions—add lines 10 and 11		**12**	
13	Subtract line 12 from line 7		**13**	
14	Generation-skipping transfer taxes payable with this Form 709 (from Schedule C, Part 3, col. H, Total) .		**14**	
15	Taxable gifts (add lines 13 and 14). Enter here and on line 1 of the Tax Computation on page 1 . . .		**15**	

(If more space is needed, attach additional sheets of same size.)   Form **709** (2001)

SCHEDULE A	Computation of Taxable Gifts *(continued)*

16 Terminable Interest (QTIP) Marital Deduction. (See instructions for line 8 of Schedule A.)

If a trust (or other property) meets the requirements of qualified terminable interest property under section 2523(f), and

    a. The trust (or other property) is listed on Schedule A, and

    b. The value of the trust (or other property) is entered in whole or in part as a deduction on line 8, Part 3 of Schedule A,

then the donor shall be deemed to have made an election to have such trust (or other property) treated as qualified terminable interest property under section 2523(f).

If less than the entire value of the trust (or other property) that the donor has included in Part 1 of Schedule A is entered as a deduction on line 8, the donor shall be considered to have made an election only as to a fraction of the trust (or other property). The numerator of this fraction is equal to the amount of the trust (or other property) deducted on line 10 of Part 3, Schedule A. The denominator is equal to the total value of the trust (or other property) listed in Part 1 of Schedule A.

If you make the QTIP election (see instructions for line 8 of Schedule A), the terminable interest property involved will be included in your spouse's gross estate upon his or her death (section 2044). If your spouse disposes (by gift or otherwise) of all or part of the qualifying life income interest, he or she will be considered to have made a transfer of the entire property that is subject to the gift tax (see Transfer of Certain Life Estates on page 4 of the instructions).

17 Election Out of QTIP Treatment of Annuities

☐ ◄ Check here if you elect under section 2523(f)(6) **NOT** to treat as qualified terminable interest property any joint and survivor annuities that are reported on Schedule A and would otherwise be treated as qualified terminable interest property under section 2523(f). (See instructions.) Enter the item numbers (from Schedule A) for the annuities for which you are making this election ►

SCHEDULE B	Gifts From Prior Periods

If you answered "Yes" on line 11a of page 1, Part 1, see the instructions for completing Schedule B. If you answered "No," skip to the Tax Computation on page 1 (or Schedule C, if applicable).

A Calendar year or calendar quarter (see instructions)	B Internal Revenue office where prior return was filed	C Amount of unified credit against gift tax for periods after December 31, 1976	D Amount of specific exemption for prior periods ending before January 1, 1977	E Amount of taxable gifts

1 Totals for prior periods (without adjustment for reduced specific exemption)	**1**	
2 Amount, if any, by which total specific exemption, line 1, column D, is more than $30,000	**2**	
3 Total amount of taxable gifts for prior periods (add amount, column E, line 1, and amount, if any, on line 2). (Enter here and on line 2 of the Tax Computation on page 1.)	**3**	

(If more space is needed, attach additional sheets of same size.)

Form **709** (2001)

SCHEDULE C	Computation of Generation-Skipping Transfer Tax

Note: *Inter vivos direct skips that are completely excluded by the GST exemption must still be fully reported (including value and exemptions claimed) on Schedule C.*

Part 1—Generation-Skipping Transfers

A Item No. (from Schedule A, Part 2, col. A)	B Value (from Schedule A, Part 2, col. E)	C Split Gifts (enter ½ of col. B) (see instructions)	D Subtract col. C from col. B	E Nontaxable portion of transfer	F Net Transfer (subtract col. E from col. D)
1					
2					
3					
4					
5					
6					

	Split gifts from spouse's Form 709 (enter item number)	Value included from spouse's Form 709	Nontaxable portion of transfer	Net transfer (subtract col. E from col. D)
If you elected gift splitting and your spouse was required to file a separate Form 709 (see the instructions for "Split Gifts"), you must enter all of the gifts shown on Schedule A, Part 2, of your spouse's Form 709 here.	S-			
	S-			
In column C, enter the item number of each gift in the order it appears in column A of your spouse's Schedule A, Part 2. We have preprinted the prefix "S-" to distinguish your spouse's item numbers from your own when you complete column A of Schedule C, Part 3.	S-			
	S-			
	S-			
	S-			
In column D, for each gift, enter the amount reported in column C, Schedule C, Part 1, of your spouse's Form 709.	S-			
	S-			

Part 2—GST Exemption Reconciliation (Section 2631) and Section 2652(a)(3) Election

Check box ▶ ☐   if you are making a section 2652(a)(3) (special QTIP) election (see instructions)

Enter the item numbers (from Schedule A) of the gifts for which you are making this election ▶ ....

1	Maximum allowable exemption (see instructions)	1	
2	Total exemption used for periods before filing this return	2	
3	Exemption available for this return (subtract line 2 from line 1)	3	
4	Exemption claimed on this return (from Part 3, col. C total, below)	4	
5	Exemption allocated to transfers not shown on Part 3, below. **You must attach a Notice of Allocation.** (See instructions.)	5	
6	Add lines 4 and 5	6	
7	Exemption available for future transfers (subtract line 6 from line 3)	7	

Part 3—Tax Computation

A Item No. (from Schedule C, Part 1)	B Net transfer (from Schedule C, Part 1, col. F)	C GST Exemption Allocated	D Divide col. C by col. B	E Inclusion Ratio (subtract col. D from 1.000)	F Maximum Estate Tax Rate	G Applicable Rate (multiply col. E by col. F)	H Generation-Skipping Transfer Tax (multiply col. B by col. G)
1					55% (.55)		
2					55% (.55)		
3					55% (.55)		
4					55% (.55)		
5					55% (.55)		
6					55% (.55)		
					55% (.55)		
					55% (.55)		
					55% (.55)		
					55% (.55)		

Total exemption claimed. Enter here and on line 4, Part 2, above. May not exceed line 3, Part 2, above		**Total generation-skipping transfer tax.** Enter here, on line 14 of Schedule A, Part 3, and on line 16 of the Tax Computation on page 1	

(If more space is needed, attach additional sheets of same size.)   Form **709** (2001)

Form **1116**	**Foreign Tax Credit**	OMB No. 1545-0121

Form 1116

Department of the Treasury
Internal Revenue Service (99)

Foreign Tax Credit
(Individual, Estate, Trust, or Nonresident Alien Individual)
► Attach to Form 1040, 1040NR, 1041, or 990-T.
► See separate instructions.

OMB No. 1545-0121

2001

Attachment
Sequence No. **19**

Name

Identifying number as shown on page 1 of your tax return

Use a separate Form 1116 for each category of income listed below. See **Categories of Income** on page 3 of the instructions. Check only one box on each Form 1116. Report all amounts in U.S. dollars except where specified in Part II below.

a ☐ Passive income
b ☐ High withholding tax interest
c ☐ Financial services income
d ☐ Shipping income
e ☐ Dividends from a DISC or former DISC
f ☐ Certain distributions from a foreign sales corporation (FSC) or former FSC
g ☐ Lump-sum distributions
h ☐ Section 901(j) income
i ☐ Certain income re-sourced by treaty
j ☐ General limitation income

k Resident of (name of country) ►

Note: If you paid taxes to only one foreign country or U.S. possession, use column A in Part I and line A in Part II. If you paid taxes to **more than one** foreign country or U.S. possession, use a separate column and line for each country or possession.

Part I   Taxable Income or Loss From Sources Outside the United States (for Category Checked Above)

		Foreign Country or U.S. Possession			Total
		A	**B**	**C**	(Add cols. A, B, and C.)
l	Enter the name of the foreign country or U.S. possession . . . . ►				
1	Gross income from sources within country shown above and of the type checked above. See page 8 of the instructions:				
					1
	Deductions and losses (*Caution: See pages 8 and 9 of the instructions*):				
2	Expenses **definitely related** to the income on line 1 (attach statement)				
3	Pro rata share of other deductions **not definitely related:**				
a	Certain itemized deductions or standard deduction. See instructions				
b	Other deductions (attach statement)				
c	Add lines 3a and 3b				
d	Gross foreign source income. See instructions .				
e	Gross income from all sources. See instructions				
f	Divide line 3d by line 3e. See instructions . .				
g	Multiply line 3c by line 3f				
4	Pro rata share of interest expense. See instructions:				
a	Home mortgage interest (use worksheet on page 9 of the instructions)				
b	Other interest expense				
5	Losses from foreign sources				
6	Add lines 2, 3g, 4a, 4b, and 5				**6**
7	Subtract line 6 from line 1. Enter the result here and on line 14, page 2 . . . . ►				**7**

Part II   Foreign Taxes Paid or Accrued (See page 9 of the instructions.)

Country	Credit is claimed for taxes (you must check one)	Foreign taxes paid or accrued								
		In foreign currency				In U.S. dollars				
	(m) ☐ Paid (n) ☐ Accrued	Taxes withheld at source on:			(s) Other foreign taxes paid or accrued	Taxes withheld at source on:			(w) Other foreign taxes paid or accrued	(x) Total foreign taxes paid or accrued (add cols. (t) through (w))
	(o) Date paid or accrued	(p) Dividends	(q) Rents and royalties	(r) Interest		(t) Dividends	(u) Rents and royalties	(v) Interest		
A										
B										
C										
8	Add lines A through C, column (x). Enter the total here and on line 9, page 2 . . . . ►								**8**	

For Paperwork Reduction Act Notice, see page 12 of the instructions.   Cat. No. 11440U   Form **1116** (2001)

Part III **Figuring the Credit**

9 Enter the amount from line 8. These are your total foreign taxes paid
or accrued for the category of income checked above Part I . . . | **9**

10 Carryback or carryover (attach detailed computation) . . . . . | **10**

11 Add lines 9 and 10 . . . . | **11**

12 Reduction in foreign taxes. See page 10 of the instructions . . . | **12**

13 Subtract line 12 from line 11. This is the total amount of foreign taxes available for credit . . . . | **13**

14 Enter the amount from line 7. This is your taxable income or (loss) from
sources outside the United States (before adjustments) for the category
of income checked above Part I. See page 10 of the instructions . . | **14**

15 Adjustments to line 14. See page 10 of the instructions . . . . | **15**

16 Combine the amounts on lines 14 and 15. This is your net foreign
source taxable income. (If the result is zero or less, you have no foreign
tax credit for the category of income you checked above Part I. Skip
lines 17 through 21. However, if you are filing more than one Form
1116, you must complete line 19.) . . . . | **16**

17 **Individuals:** Enter the amount from Form 1040, line 37. If you are a
nonresident alien, enter the amount from Form 1040NR, line 36.
Estates and trusts: Enter your taxable income without the deduction
for your exemption . . . . | **17**

   Caution: *If you figured your tax using the special rates on capital gains, see page 12 of the instructions.*

18 Divide line 16 by line 17. If line 16 is more than line 17, enter "1" . . . . | **18**

19 **Individuals:** Enter the amount from Form 1040, line 40. If you are a nonresident alien, enter the
amount from Form 1040NR, line 39.

   Estates and trusts: Enter the total of Form 1041, Schedule G, lines 1a and 1b, or the total of Form 990-T,
lines 36 and 37 . . . . | **19**

20 Multiply line 19 by line 18 (maximum amount of credit) . . . . | **20**

21 Enter the **smaller** of line 13 or line 20. If this is the only Form 1116 you are filing, skip lines 22 through
30 and enter this amount on line 31. Otherwise, complete the appropriate line in Part IV. See page
12 of the instructions . . . . ▶ | **21**

Part IV **Summary of Credits From Separate Parts III** (See page 12 of the instructions.)

22 Credit for taxes on passive income . . . . | **22**

23 Credit for taxes on high withholding tax interest . . . . . . | **23**

24 Credit for taxes on financial services income . . . . | **24**

25 Credit for taxes on shipping income . . . . | **25**

26 Credit for taxes on dividends from a DISC or former DISC and certain
distributions from a FSC or former FSC . . . . . . | **26**

27 Credit for taxes on lump-sum distributions . . . . | **27**

28 Credit for taxes on certain income re-sourced by treaty . . . . . | **28**

29 Credit for taxes on general limitation income . . . . | **29**

30 Add lines 22 through 29 . . . . | **30**

31 Enter the **smaller** of line 19 or line 30 . . . . | **31**

32 Reduction of credit for international boycott operations. See instructions for line 12 on page 10 . | **32**

33 Subtract line 32 from line 31. This is your **foreign tax credit.** Enter here and on Form 1040, line 43;
Form 1040NR, line 42; Form 1041, Schedule G, line 2a; or Form 990-T, line 40a . . . . . ▶ | **33**

Form **2441**	**Child and Dependent Care Expenses**	OMB No. 1545-0068
Department of the Treasury Internal Revenue Service (99)	▶ **Attach to Form 1040.** ▶ **See separate instructions.**	**2001** Attachment Sequence No. **21**

Name(s) shown on Form 1040	**Your social security number**

Before you begin: You need to understand the following terms. See **Definitions** on page 1 of the instructions.

- **Dependent Care Benefits**
- **Qualifying Person(s)**
- **Qualified Expenses**
- **Earned Income**

Part I **Persons or Organizations Who Provided the Care—You must complete this part.**
(If you need more space, use the bottom of page 2.)

1	(a) Care provider's name	(b) Address (number, street, apt. no., city, state, and ZIP code)	(c) Identifying number (SSN or EIN)	(d) Amount paid (see instructions)

Did you receive dependent care benefits?

No ──────▶ Complete only Part II below.

Yes ──────▶ Complete Part III on the back next.

Caution. If the care was provided in your home, you may owe employment taxes. See the instructions for Form 1040, line 57.

Part II **Credit for Child and Dependent Care Expenses**

2 Information about your **qualifying person(s).** If you have more than two qualifying persons, see the instructions.

(a) Qualifying person's name		(b) Qualifying person's social security number	(c) Qualified expenses you incurred and paid in 2001 for the person listed in column (a)
First	Last		

3 Add the amounts in column (c) of line 2. **Do not** enter more than $2,400 for one qualifying person or $4,800 for two or more persons. If you completed Part III, enter the amount from line 24 . . . . **3**

4 Enter your **earned income** **4**

5 If married filing a joint return, enter your spouse's earned income (if your spouse was a student or was disabled, see the instructions); **all others,** enter the amount from line 4 . . . . **5**

6 Enter the **smallest** of line 3, 4, or 5 . . . . **6**

7 Enter the amount from Form 1040, line 34 . . . . . **7**

8 Enter on line 8 the decimal amount shown below that applies to the amount on line 7

If line 7 is:				If line 7 is:		
Over	But not over	Decimal amount is		Over	But not over	Decimal amount is
$0—10,000		.30		$20,000—22,000		.24
10,000—12,000		.29		22,000—24,000		.23
12,000—14,000		.28		24,000—26,000		.22
14,000—16,000		.27		26,000—28,000		.21
16,000—18,000		.26		28,000—No limit		.20
18,000—20,000		.25				

8 × .

9 Multiply **line 6** by the decimal amount on line 8. Enter the result here and on Form 1040, line 44. But if this amount is more than the amount on Form 1040, line 42, minus any amount on line 43, **or** you paid 2000 expenses in 2001, see the instructions for the amount to enter on line 44 . . . . **9**

For Paperwork Reduction Act Notice, see page 3 of the instructions.   Cat. No. 11862M   Form **2441** (2001)

Part III Dependent Care Benefits

10 Enter the total amount of **dependent care benefits** you received for 2001. This amount should be shown in box 10 of your W-2 form(s). **Do not** include amounts that were reported to you as wages in box 1 of Form(s) W-2 . . . . | **10** |

11 Enter the amount forfeited, if any. See the instructions . . . . | **11** |

12 Subtract line 11 from line 10 . . . . | **12** |

13 Enter the total amount of **qualified expenses** incurred in 2001 for the care of the **qualifying person(s)** . . . | **13** |

14 Enter the **smaller** of line 12 or 13 . . . . | **14** |

15 Enter your **earned income** . . . . | **15** |

16 If married filing a joint return, enter your spouse's earned income (if your spouse was a student or was disabled, see the instructions for line 5); if married filing a separate return, see the instructions for the amount to enter; **all others,** enter the amount from line 15 . . . . . | **16** |

17 Enter the **smallest** of line 14, 15, or 16 . . . . . . | **17** |

18 **Excluded benefits.** Enter here the **smaller** of the following:

- The amount from line 17 or
- $5,000 ($2,500 if married filing a separate return **and** you were required to enter your spouse's earned income on line 16).   } . . . . | **18** |

19 **Taxable benefits.** Subtract line 18 from line 12. Also, include this amount on Form 1040, line 7. On the dotted line next to line 7, enter "DCB" . . . . | **19** |

To claim the child and dependent care credit, complete lines 20–24 below.

20 Enter $2,400 ($4,800 if two or more qualifying persons) . . . . | **20** |

21 Enter the amount from line 18 . . . . | **21** |

22 Subtract line 21 from line 20. If zero or less, **stop.** You cannot take the credit. **Exception.** If you paid 2000 expenses in 2001, see the instructions for line 9 . . . . | **22** |

23 Complete line 2 on the front of this form. **Do not** include in column (c) any benefits shown on line 18 above. Then, add the amounts in column (c) and enter the total here . . . | **23** |

24 Enter the **smaller** of line 22 or 23. Also, enter this amount on line 3 on the front of this form and complete lines 4–9 . . . . | **24** |

Moving Expenses

▶ **Attach to Form 1040.**

OMB No. 1545-0062

Attachment
Sequence No. **62**

Name(s) shown on Form 1040 | **Your social security number**

Before you begin: See the **Distance Test** and **Time Test** in the instructions to find out if you can deduct your moving expenses. If you are a member of the armed forces, see the instructions to find out how to complete this form.

1	Enter the amount you paid for transportation and storage of household goods and personal effects (see instructions)	**1**
2	Enter the amount you paid for travel and lodging expenses in moving from your old home to your new home. **Do not** include the cost of meals (see instructions)	**2**
3	Add lines 1 and 2	**3**
4	Enter the total amount your employer paid you for the expenses listed on lines 1 and 2 that is **not** included in the wages box (box 1) of your W-2 form. This amount should be identified with code **P** in box 12 of your W-2 form	**4**

5 Is line 3 **more than** line 4?

☐ **No.** You **cannot** deduct your moving expenses. If line 3 is less than line 4, subtract line 3 from line 4 and include the result on the "Wages, salaries, tips, etc." line of Form 1040.

☐ **Yes.** Subtract line 4 from line 3. Enter the result here and on the "Moving expenses" line of Form 1040. This is your **moving expense deduction** . . . . | **5**

General Instructions

A Change To Note

Beginning in 2001, the standard mileage rate for using your vehicle to move to a new home is 12 cents a mile.

Purpose of Form

Use Form 3903 to figure your moving expense deduction for a move related to the start of work at a new principal place of work (workplace) that is either:

● Within the United States or its possessions or

● Outside the United States or its possessions and you are a U.S. citizen or resident alien.

If you qualify to deduct expenses for more than one move, use a separate Form 3903 for each move.

For more details, see **Pub. 521,** Moving Expenses.

Who May Deduct Moving Expenses

If you move to a new home because of a new principal workplace, you may be able to deduct your moving expenses whether you are self-employed or an employee. But you must meet both of the tests explained next.

Distance Test

Your new principal workplace must be at least 50 miles farther from your old home than your old workplace was. For example, if your old workplace was 3 miles from your old home, your new workplace must be at least 53 miles from that home. If you did not have an old workplace, your new workplace must be at least 50 miles from your old home. The distance between the two points is the shortest of the more commonly traveled routes between them.

TIP: *To see if you meet the distance test, use the worksheet on this page.*

Time Test

If you are an employee, you must work full time in the general area of your new workplace for at least 39 weeks during the 12 months right after you move. If you are self-employed, you must work full time in the general area of your new workplace for at least 39 weeks during the first 12 months and a total of at least 78 weeks during the 24 months right after you move.

What If You Do Not Meet the Time Test Before Your Return Is Due? If you expect to meet the time test, you may deduct your moving expenses in the year you move. Later, if you do not meet the time test, you must either:

● Amend your tax return for the year you claimed the deduction by filing **Form 1040X,** Amended U.S. Individual Income Tax Return **or**

● For the year you cannot meet the time test, report as income the amount of your moving expense deduction that reduced your income tax for the year you moved.

Distance Test Worksheet *(Keep for Your Records)*

1. Enter the number of miles from your **old home** to your **new workplace**	**1.** _____ miles
2. Enter the number of miles from your **old home** to your **old workplace**	**2.** _____ miles
3. Subtract line 2 from line 1. If zero or less, enter -0- . . .	**3.** _____ miles

Is line 3 at least 50 miles?

☐ **Yes.** You meet this test.

☐ **No.** You do not meet this test. You **cannot** deduct your moving expenses. **Do not** complete Form 3903.

If you do not deduct your moving expenses in the year you move and you later meet the time test, you may take the deduction by filing an amended return for the year you moved. To do this, use Form 1040X.

Exceptions to the Time Test. You do not have to meet the time test if any of the following apply.

- Your job ends because of disability.
- You are transferred for your employer's benefit.
- You are laid off or discharged for a reason other than willful misconduct.
- You meet the requirements (explained later) for retirees or survivors living outside the United States.
- You are filing this form for a decedent.

More Information. For more information on the time test, see Pub. 521.

Members of the Armed Forces

If you are in the armed forces, you do not have to meet the **distance** and **time tests** if the move is due to a permanent change of station. A permanent change of station includes a move in connection with and within 1 year of retirement or other termination of active duty.

How To Complete the Form

Do not include on lines 1 and 2 any expenses for moving services that were provided by the government. If you and your spouse and dependents are moved to or from different locations, treat the moves as a single move.

On line 4, enter the total reimbursements and allowances you received from the government in connection with the expenses you claimed on lines 1 and 2. **Do not** include the value of moving services provided by the government. Complete line 5 if applicable.

Retirees or Survivors Living Outside the United States

If you are a retiree or survivor who moved to a home in the United States or its possessions and you meet the following requirements, you are treated as if you moved to a new workplace located in the United States. You are subject to the distance test.

Retirees

You may deduct moving expenses for a move to a new home in the United States when you actually retire if both your old principal workplace and your old home were outside the United States.

Survivors

You may deduct moving expenses for a move to a home in the United States if you are the spouse or dependent of a person whose principal workplace at the time of death was outside the United States. In addition, the expenses must be for a move **(a)** that begins within 6 months after the decedent's death and **(b)** from a former home outside the United States that you lived in with the decedent at the time of death.

Reimbursements

You may choose to deduct moving expenses in the year you are reimbursed by your employer, even though you paid the expenses in a different year. However, special rules apply. See **How To Report** in Pub. 521.

Filers of Form 2555

If you file **Form 2555,** Foreign Earned Income, to exclude any of your income or housing costs, report the full amount of your deductible moving expenses on Form 3903 and on Form 1040. Report the part of your moving expenses that is not allowed because it is allocable to the excluded income on the appropriate line of Form 2555. For details on how to figure the part allocable to the excluded income, see **Pub. 54,** Tax Guide for U.S. Citizens and Resident Aliens Abroad.

Specific Instructions

You may deduct the following expenses you paid to move your family and dependent household members. Do not deduct expenses for employees such as a maid, nanny, or nurse.

Line 1

Moves Within or to the United States or its Possessions. Enter the amount you paid to pack, crate, and move your household goods and personal effects. You may also include the amount you paid to store and insure household goods and personal effects within any period of 30 days in a row after the items were moved from your old home and before they were delivered to your new home.

Moves Outside the United States or its Possessions. Enter the amount you paid to pack, crate, move, store, and insure your household goods and personal effects. Also, include the amount you paid to move your personal effects to and from storage and to store them for all or part of the time the new workplace continues to be your principal workplace.

TIP: *You do not have to complete this form if **(a)** you moved in an earlier year, **(b)** you are claiming only storage fees during your absence from the United States, and **(c)** any amount your employer paid for the storage fees is included in the wages box of your W-2 form. Instead, enter the storage fees on the "Moving expenses" line of Form 1040, and write "Storage" next to the amount.*

Line 2

Enter the amount you paid to travel from your old home to your new home. This includes transportation and lodging on the way. Include costs for the day you arrive. Although not all the members of your household have to travel together or at the same time, you may only include expenses for one trip per person.

If you use your own vehicle(s), you may figure the expenses by using either:

- Actual out-of-pocket expenses for gas and oil or
- Mileage at the rate of 12 cents a mile.

You may add parking fees and tolls to the amount claimed under either method. Keep records to verify your expenses.

Paperwork Reduction Act Notice. We ask for the information on this form to carry out the Internal Revenue laws of the United States. You are required to give us the information. We need it to ensure that you are complying with these laws and to allow us to figure and collect the right amount of tax.

You are not required to provide the information requested on a form that is subject to the Paperwork Reduction Act unless the form displays a valid OMB control number. Books or records relating to a form or its instructions must be retained as long as their contents may become material in the administration of any Internal Revenue law. Generally, tax returns and return information are confidential, as required by Internal Revenue Code section 6103.

The time needed to complete and file this form will vary depending on individual circumstances. The estimated average time is: **Recordkeeping,** 33 min.; **Learning about the law or the form,** 9 min.; **Preparing the form,** 15 min.; and **Copying, assembling, and sending the form to the IRS,** 13 min.

If you have comments concerning the accuracy of these time estimates or suggestions for making this form simpler, we would be happy to hear from you. See the Instructions for Form 1040.

Form **4684**

Department of the Treasury
Internal Revenue Service

Casualties and Thefts

▶ See separate instructions.
▶ Attach to your tax return.
▶ Use a separate Form 4684 for each casualty or theft.

OMB No. 1545-0177

2001

Attachment
Sequence No. **26**

Name(s) shown on tax return

Identifying number

SECTION A—Personal Use Property (Use this section to report casualties and thefts of property **not** used in a trade or business or for income-producing purposes.)

1 Description of properties (show type, location, and date acquired for each):

Property **A** ....

Property **B** ....

Property **C** ....

Property **D** ....

		Properties (Use a separate column for each property lost or damaged from the same casualty or theft.)			
		A	**B**	**C**	**D**
2 Cost or other basis of each property	**2**				
3 Insurance or other reimbursement (whether or not you filed a claim). See instructions . . . . . **Note:** *If line 2 is **more** than line 3, skip line 4.*	**3**				
4 Gain from casualty or theft. If line 3 is **more** than line 2, enter the difference here and skip lines 5 through 9 for that column. See instructions if line 3 includes insurance or other reimbursement you did not claim, or you received payment for your loss in a later tax year	**4**				
5 Fair market value **before** casualty or theft . . .	**5**				
6 Fair market value **after** casualty or theft	**6**				
7 Subtract line 6 from line 5	**7**				
8 Enter the **smaller** of line 2 or line 7	**8**				
9 Subtract line 3 from line 8. If zero or less, enter -0-	**9**				

10 Casualty or theft loss. Add the amounts on line 9 in columns A through D	**10**	
11 Enter the **smaller** of line 10 or $100	**11**	
12 Subtract line 11 from line 10 . . . . **Caution:** *Use only one Form 4684 for lines 13 through 18.*	**12**	
13 Add the amounts on line 12 of all Forms 4684	**13**	
14 Add the amounts from line 4 of all Forms 4684	**14**	
15 ● If line 14 is **more** than line 13, enter the difference here and on Schedule D. **Do not** complete the rest of this section. See instructions. ● If line 14 is **less** than line 13, enter -0- here and go to line 16. ● If line 14 is **equal** to line 13, enter -0- here. **Do not** complete the rest of this section.	**15**	
16 If line 14 is **less** than line 13, enter the difference	**16**	
17 Enter 10% of your adjusted gross income from Form 1040, line 34. Estates and trusts, see instructions. . .	**17**	
18 Subtract line 17 from line 16. If zero or less, enter -0-. Also enter result on Schedule A (Form 1040), line 19. Estates and trusts, enter on the "Other deductions" line of your tax return	**18**	

For Paperwork Reduction Act Notice, see page 4 of the instructions.

Cat. No. 12997O

Form **4684** (2001)

Name(s) shown on tax return. Do not enter name and identifying number if shown on other side. | Identifying number

SECTION B—Business and Income-Producing Property

Part I   **Casualty or Theft Gain or Loss** (Use a separate Part I for each casualty or theft.)

19 Description of properties (show type, location, and date acquired for each):

Property **A** ....

Property **B** ....

Property **C** ....

Property **D** ....

Properties (Use a separate column for each property lost or damaged from the same casualty or theft.)

		A	B	C	D
20	Cost or adjusted basis of each property				
21	Insurance or other reimbursement (whether or not you filed a claim). See the instructions for line 3. **Note:** *If line 20 is more than line 21, skip line 22.*				
22	Gain from casualty or theft. If line 21 is **more** than line 20, enter the difference here and on line 29 or line 34, column (c), except as provided in the instructions for line 33. Also, skip lines 23 through 27 for that column. See the instructions for line 4 if line 21 includes insurance or other reimbursement you did not claim, or you received payment for your loss in a later tax year.				
23	Fair market value **before** casualty or theft				
24	Fair market value **after** casualty or theft				
25	Subtract line 24 from line 23				
26	Enter the **smaller** of line 20 or line 25. **Note:** *If the property was totally destroyed by casualty or lost from theft, enter on line 26 the amount from line 20.*				
27	Subtract line 21 from line 26. If zero or less, enter -0-				
28	Casualty or theft loss. Add the amounts on line 27. Enter the total here and on line 29 **or** line 34 (see instructions).	**28**			

Part II   **Summary of Gains and Losses** (from separate Parts I)

(a) Identify casualty or theft	(b) Losses from casualties or thefts		(c) Gains from casualties or thefts includible in income
	(i) Trade, business, rental or royalty property	(ii) Income-producing and employee property	

Casualty or Theft of Property Held One Year or Less

29		( )	( )	
		( )	( )	
30	Totals. Add the amounts on line 29 **30**	( )	( )	

31 Combine line 30, columns (b)(i) and (c). Enter the net gain or (loss) here and on Form 4797, line 14. If Form 4797 is not otherwise required, see instructions   **31**

32 Enter the amount from line 30, column (b)(ii) here. Individuals, enter the amount from income-producing property on Schedule A (Form 1040), line 27, and enter the amount from property used as an employee on Schedule A (Form 1040), line 22. Estates and trusts, partnerships, and S corporations, see instructions   **32**

Casualty or Theft of Property Held More Than One Year

33	Casualty or theft gains from Form 4797, line 32 **33**			
34		( )	( )	
		( )	( )	
35	Total losses. Add amounts on line 34, columns (b)(i) and (b)(ii) **35**	( )	( )	
36	Total gains. Add lines 33 and 34, column (c) **36**			
37	Add amounts on line 35, columns (b)(i) and (b)(ii) **37**			

38 If the loss on line 37 is **more** than the gain on line 36:

a Combine line 35, column (b)(i) and line 36, and enter the net gain or (loss) here. Partnerships (except electing large partnerships) and S corporations, see the note below. All others, enter this amount on Form 4797, line 14. If Form 4797 is not otherwise required, see instructions.   **38a**

b Enter the amount from line 35, column (b)(ii) here. Individuals, enter the amount from income-producing property on Schedule A (Form 1040), line 27, and enter the amount from property used as an employee on Schedule A (Form 1040), line 22. Estates and trusts, enter on the "Other deductions" line of your tax return. Partnerships (except electing large partnerships) and S corporations, see the note below. Electing large partnerships, enter on Form 1065-B, Part II, line 11.   **38b**

39 If the loss on line 37 is **less** than or **equal** to the gain on line 36, combine lines 36 and 37 and enter here. Partnerships (except electing large partnerships), see the note below. All others, enter this amount on Form 4797, line 3   **39**

Note: *Partnerships, enter the amount from line 38a, 38b, or line 39 on Form 1065, Schedule K, line 7. S corporations, enter the amount from line 38a or 38b on Form 1120S, Schedule K, line 6.*

Form **4797**	**Sales of Business Property**	OMB No. 1545-0184

Form 4797

Department of the Treasury
Internal Revenue Service   (99)

Sales of Business Property
(Also Involuntary Conversions and Recapture Amounts
Under Sections 179 and 280F(b)(2))
► **Attach to your tax return.**   ► **See separate instructions.**

OMB No. 1545-0184

2001

Attachment
Sequence No. **27**

Name(s) shown on return | Identifying number

1 Enter the gross proceeds from sales or exchanges reported to you for 2001 on Form(s) 1099-B or 1099-S (or substitute statement) that you are including on line 2, 10, or 20 (see instructions) . . . . | **1**

Part I — Sales or Exchanges of Property Used in a Trade or Business and Involuntary Conversions From Other Than Casualty or Theft—Most Property Held More Than 1 Year (See instructions.)

(a) Description of property	(b) Date acquired (mo., day, yr.)	(c) Date sold (mo., day, yr.)	(d) Gross sales price	(e) Depreciation allowed or allowable since acquisition	(f) Cost or other basis, plus improvements and expense of sale	(g) Gain or (loss) Subtract (f) from the sum of (d) and (e)
2						

3 Gain, if any, from Form 4684, line 39 . . . . | **3** |

4 Section 1231 gain from installment sales from Form 6252, line 26 or 37 . . . . . | **4** |

5 Section 1231 gain or (loss) from like-kind exchanges from Form 8824 . . . . . | **5** |

6 Gain, if any, from line 32, from other than casualty or theft . . . . | **6** |

7 Combine lines 2 through 6. Enter the gain or (loss) here and on the appropriate line as follows: . . . . . . | **7** |

Partnerships (except electing large partnerships). Report the gain or (loss) following the instructions for Form 1065, Schedule K, line 6. Skip lines 8, 9, 11, and 12 below.

S corporations. Report the gain or (loss) following the instructions for Form 1120S, Schedule K, lines 5 and 6. Skip lines 8, 9, 11, and 12 below, unless line 7 is a gain and the S corporation is subject to the capital gains tax.

All others. If line 7 is zero or a loss, enter the amount from line 7 on line 11 below and skip lines 8 and 9. If line 7 is a gain and you did not have any prior year section 1231 losses, or they were recaptured in an earlier year, enter the gain from line 7 as a long-term capital gain on Schedule D and skip lines 8, 9, 11, and 12 below.

8 Nonrecaptured net section 1231 losses from prior years (see instructions) . . . . | **8** |

9 Subtract line 8 from line 7. If zero or less, enter -0-. Also enter on the appropriate line as follows (see instructions): | **9** |
S corporations. Enter any gain from line 9 on Schedule D (Form 1120S), line 15, and skip lines 11 and 12 below.
All others. If line 9 is zero, enter the gain from line 7 on line 12 below. If line 9 is more than zero, enter the amount from line 8 on line 12 below, and enter the gain from line 9 as a long-term capital gain on Schedule D.

Part II — Ordinary Gains and Losses

10 Ordinary gains and losses not included on lines 11 through 17 (include property held 1 year or less):

11 Loss, if any, from line 7 . . . . | **11** ( ) |

12 Gain, if any, from line 7 or amount from line 8, if applicable . . . . | **12** |

13 Gain, if any, from line 31 . . . . | **13** |

14 Net gain or (loss) from Form 4684, lines 31 and 38a . . . . | **14** |

15 Ordinary gain from installment sales from Form 6252, line 25 or 36 . . . . . . | **15** |

16 Ordinary gain or (loss) from like-kind exchanges from Form 8824 . . . . . . | **16** |

17 Recapture of section 179 expense deduction for partners and S corporation shareholders from property dispositions by partnerships and S corporations (see instructions) . . . . | **17** |

18 Combine lines 10 through 17. Enter the gain or (loss) here and on the appropriate line as follows: . . . . . | **18** |

a **For all except individual returns.** Enter the gain or (loss) from line 18 on the return being filed.

b **For individual returns:**

(1) If the loss on line 11 includes a loss from Form 4684, line 35, column (b)(ii), enter that part of the loss here. Enter the part of the loss from income-producing property on Schedule A (Form 1040), line 27, and the part of the loss from property used as an employee on Schedule A (Form 1040), line 22. Identify as from "Form 4797, line 18b(1)." See instructions . . . . | **18b(1)** |

(2) Redetermine the gain or (loss) on line 18 excluding the loss, if any, on line 18b(1). Enter here and on Form 1040, line 14 . . . . | **18b(2)** |

For Paperwork Reduction Act Notice, see page 7 of the instructions.   Cat. No. 130861   Form **4797** (2001)

659

Part III Gain From Disposition of Property Under Sections 1245, 1250, 1252, 1254, and 1255

19	(a) Description of section 1245, 1250, 1252, 1254, or 1255 property:	(b) Date acquired (mo., day, yr.)	(c) Date sold (mo., day, yr.)
A			
B			
C			
D			

	These columns relate to the properties on lines 19A through 19D. ▶		Property A	Property B	Property C	Property D
20	Gross sales price (**Note:** See line 1 before completing.)	**20**				
21	Cost or other basis plus expense of sale	**21**				
22	Depreciation (or depletion) allowed or allowable	**22**				
23	Adjusted basis. Subtract line 22 from line 21	**23**				
24	Total gain. Subtract line 23 from line 20	**24**				
25	**If section 1245 property:**					
a	Depreciation allowed or allowable from line 22	**25a**				
b	Enter the **smaller** of line 24 or 25a	**25b**				
26	**If section 1250 property:** If straight line depreciation was used, enter -0- on line 26g, except for a corporation subject to section 291.					
a	Additional depreciation after 1975 (see instructions)	**26a**				
b	Applicable percentage multiplied by the **smaller** of line 24 or line 26a (see instructions)	**26b**				
c	Subtract line 26a from line 24. If residential rental property **or** line 24 is not more than line 26a, skip lines 26d and 26e	**26c**				
d	Additional depreciation after 1969 and before 1976	**26d**				
e	Enter the **smaller** of line 26c or 26d	**26e**				
f	Section 291 amount (corporations only)	**26f**				
g	Add lines 26b, 26e, and 26f	**26g**				
27	**If section 1252 property:** Skip this section if you did not dispose of farmland or if this form is being completed for a partnership (other than an electing large partnership).					
a	Soil, water, and land clearing expenses	**27a**				
b	Line 27a multiplied by applicable percentage (see instructions)	**27b**				
c	Enter the **smaller** of line 24 or 27b	**27c**				
28	**If section 1254 property:**					
a	Intangible drilling and development costs, expenditures for development of mines and other natural deposits, and mining exploration costs (see instructions)	**28a**				
b	Enter the **smaller** of line 24 or 28a	**28b**				
29	**If section 1255 property:**					
a	Applicable percentage of payments excluded from income under section 126 (see instructions)	**29a**				
b	Enter the **smaller** of line 24 or 29a (see instructions)	**29b**				

Summary of Part III Gains. Complete property columns A through D through line 29b before going to line 30.

30	Total gains for all properties. Add property columns A through D, line 24	**30**	
31	Add property columns A through D, lines 25b, 26g, 27c, 28b, and 29b. Enter here and on line 13	**31**	
32	Subtract line 31 from line 30. Enter the portion from casualty or theft on Form 4684, line 33. Enter the portion from other than casualty or theft on Form 4797, line 6	**32**	

Part IV Recapture Amounts Under Sections 179 and 280F(b)(2) When Business Use Drops to 50% or Less (See instructions.)

			(a) Section 179	(b) Section 280F(b)(2)
33	Section 179 expense deduction or depreciation allowable in prior years	**33**		
34	Recomputed depreciation. See instructions	**34**		
35	Recapture amount. Subtract line 34 from line 33. See the instructions for where to report	**35**		

Form **4868**	**Application for Automatic Extension of Time**	OMB No. 1545-0188
Department of the Treasury Internal Revenue Service (99)	**To File U.S. Individual Income Tax Return**	20**01**

It's Convenient, Safe, and Secure

IRS *e-file* is the IRS's electronic filing program. Now you can get an automatic extension of time to file your tax return by filing Form 4868 electronically by April 15, 2002. You will receive an electronic acknowledgment or confirmation number once you complete the transaction. Keep it with your records. **Do not send in Form 4868 if you file electronically.**

Complete Form 4868 to use as a worksheet. If you think you may owe tax when you file your return, you will need to estimate your total tax liability and subtract how much you have already paid (lines 4, 5, and 6 below).

If you think you may owe tax and wish to make a payment, you may pay by electronic funds withdrawal (direct debit) using option 1 or 2 below or you may pay by credit card using option 3.

1  *E-file* by Phone—March 1–April 15
Call toll free **1-888-796-1074**

Anyone who filed a tax return last year can file Form 4868 by phone. The telephone system will accept extensions any time from March 1 through April 15, 2002, and your extension will be good through August 15, 2002. Filing by telephone is advantageous because you get a confirmation number.

If you wish to make a payment by electronic funds withdrawal (direct debit), you will be asked for last year's adjusted gross income (AGI). AGI is located on line 33 of your 2000 Form 1040, line 19 of your 1040A, line 4 of your 1040EZ, or line I of your 2000 TeleFile Tax Record. If you choose, you may also file your extension by phone and mail a paper check to the address shown in the middle column on page 4.

2 *E-file* Using Your Personal Computer or Through a Tax Professional

Refer to your tax software package or tax preparer for ways to file electronically. Be sure to have a copy of last year's tax return — you will be asked to provide information from the return for

taxpayer verification. If you wish to make a payment, you can pay by electronic funds withdrawal (see page 4) or send your check to the address shown on page 4.

3 *E-file* and Pay by Credit Card

You can get an extension if you pay part or all of your estimate of income tax due by using a credit card (American Express® Card, Discover® Card or MasterCard® card). Your payment must be at least $1. You may pay by phone or over the Internet through one of the service providers listed below.

Each service provider will charge a convenience fee based on the amount of the tax payment you are making. Fees may vary between service providers. You will be told what the fee is during the transaction and will have the option to continue or cancel the transaction. You may also obtain the convenience fee by calling the service providers' automated customer service numbers or visiting their Web Sites. All calls are toll free. Do not add the convenience fee to your tax payment.

PhoneCharge, Inc.
1-888-ALLTAXX
(1-888-255-8299)
1-877-851-9964 (Customer Service)
www.1888ALLTAXX.com

Official Payments Corporation
1-800-2PAY-TAX
(1-800-272-9829)
1-877-754-4413 (Customer Service)
www.officialpayments.com

Form 709 or 709-A. Although an extension of time to file your income tax return also extends the time to file Form 709 or 709-A, you cannot make payments of the gift or GST tax with a credit card. To make a payment of the gift or GST tax, send a check or money order to the service center where the donor's income tax return will be filed. Enter "2001 Form 709" and the donor's name and social security number on the payment.

File a Paper Form 4868

If you wish to file on paper instead of electronically, fill in the Form 4868 below and mail it to the address shown on page 4.

▼ DETACH HERE ▼

Form **4868**	**Application for Automatic Extension of Time**	OMB No. 1545-0188
Department of the Treasury Internal Revenue Service (99)	**To File U.S. Individual Income Tax Return** **For calendar year 2001, or other tax year beginning , 2001, ending , .**	20**01**

Part I Identification

1 Your name(s) (see instructions)

Address (see instructions)

City, town or post office, state, and ZIP code

2 Your social security number	**3 Spouse's social security number**

Part II Complete ONLY If Filing Gift/GST Tax Return

Caution: *Only for gift/GST tax extension! Checking box(es) may result in correspondence if Form 709 or 709-A is not filed.*

This form also extends the time for filing a gift or generation-skipping transfer (GST) tax return if you file a calendar (not fiscal) year income tax return. Enter your gift or GST tax payment(s) in Part IV and:

Check this box ▶ ☐ if **you** are requesting a **Gift or GST tax** return extension.

Check this box ▶ ☐ if **your spouse** is requesting a **Gift or GST tax** return extension.

Part III Individual Income Tax

4 Estimate of total tax liability for 2001 $ _____

5 Total 2001 payments . . . . . . _____

6 **Balance due.** Subtract 5 from 4 . . _____

Part IV Gift/GST Tax—If you are **not filing** a gift or GST tax return, go to Part V now. See the instructions.

7 Your gift or GST tax payment . $ _____

8 **Your spouse's** gift/GST tax payment

Part V Total

9 **Total liability.** Add lines 6, 7, and 8 $ _____

10 Amount you are paying. . . . . ▶ _____

Confirmation Number

If you file electronically, you will receive a confirmation number telling you that your Form 4868 has been accepted. Enter the confirmation number here and keep it for your records . . . . . . ▶ _____

For Privacy Act and Paperwork Reduction Act Notice, see page 4.   Cat. No. 13141W   Form **4868** (2001)

General Instructions

Purpose of Form

Use Form 4868 to apply for 4 more months to file **Form 1040, 1040A, 1040EZ, 1040NR,** or **1040NR-EZ.**

To get the extra time you **must:**

• Properly estimate your 2001 tax liability using the information available to you,

• Enter your tax liability on line 9 of Form 4868, **and**

• File Form 4868 by the regular due date of your return.

Caution: *Although you are not required to make a payment of the tax you estimate as due, Form 4868 does not extend the time to pay taxes. If you do not pay the amount due by the regular due date, you will owe interest. You may also be charged penalties. For more details, see* **Interest** *on this page and* **Late Payment Penalty** *on page 3. Any remittance you make with your application for extension will be treated as a payment of tax.*

You do not have to explain why you are asking for the extension. We will contact you only if your request is denied.

Do not file Form 4868 if you want the IRS to figure your tax or you are under a court order to file your return by the regular due date.

If you need an additional extension, see **If You Need Additional Time** on this page.

Form 709 or 709-A. Generally, an extension of time to file your 2001 **calendar year** income tax return also extends the time to file a gift or generation-skipping transfer (GST) tax return for 2001. Special rules apply if the donor dies during the year in which the gifts were made. See the Instructions for Form 709.

When To File Form 4868

File Form 4868 by April 15, 2002. Fiscal year taxpayers, file Form 4868 by the regular due date of the return.

If you had 2 extra months to file your return because you were out of the country, file Form 4868 by June 17, 2002, for a 2001 calendar year return.

Out of the Country

If you already had 2 extra months to file because you were a U.S. citizen or resident and were out of the country, use this form to obtain an additional 2 months to file. You can only file a paper Form 4868. Write "Taxpayer Abroad" across the top of Form 4868. "Out of the country" means either:

1. You live outside the United States and Puerto Rico **and** your main place of work is outside the United States and Puerto Rico **or**

2. You are in military or naval service outside the United States and Puerto Rico.

If You Need Additional Time

If the automatic 4-month extension (until August 15, 2002, for most calendar year taxpayers) does not give you enough time, you can ask for additional time later. But you will have to give a good reason, and it must be approved by the IRS. To ask for the additional time, you must **either:**

1. File **Form 2688,** Application for Additional Extension of Time To File U.S. Individual Income Tax Return or

2. Explain your reason in a letter. Mail it to the address in the right column under **Where To File a Paper Form 4868** on page 4.

File Form 4868 **before** you file Form 2688 or write a letter asking for more time. Only in cases of undue hardship will the IRS approve your request for an additional extension without receiving Form 4868 first. Ask early for this extra time. Then, you can still file your return on time if your request is not approved.

Filing Your Tax Return

You may file your tax return any time before the extension expires.

Do not attach a copy of Form 4868 to your return.

Interest

You will owe interest on any tax not paid by the regular due date of your return. The interest runs until you pay the tax. Even if you had a good reason for not paying on time, you will still owe interest.

Late Payment Penalty

The penalty is usually ½ of 1% of any tax (other than estimated tax) not paid by the regular due date. It is charged for each month or part of a month the tax is unpaid. The maximum penalty is 25%.

The late payment penalty will not be charged if you can show reasonable cause for not paying on time. Attach a statement to your return fully explaining the reason. **Do not** attach the statement to Form 4868.

You are considered to have "reasonable cause" for the period covered by this automatic extension if at least 90% of your actual 2001 tax liability is paid before the regular due date of your return through withholding, estimated tax payments, or with Form 4868.

Late Filing Penalty

A penalty is usually charged if your return is filed after the due date (including extensions). It is usually 5% of the tax not paid by the regular due date for each month or part of a month your return is late. Generally, the maximum penalty is 25%. If your return is more than 60 days late, the minimum penalty is $100 or the balance of the tax due on your return, whichever is smaller. You might not owe the penalty if you have a good reason for filing late. Attach a statement to your return fully explaining the reason. **Do not** attach the statement to Form 4868.

How To Claim Credit for Payment Made With This Form

When you file your return, include the amount of any payment you made with Form 4868 on the appropriate line of your tax return.

The instructions for the following line of your tax return will tell you how to report the payment:

- Form 1040, line 64.
- Form 1040A, line 41.
- Form 1040EZ, line 10.
- Form 1040NR, line 59.
- Form 1040NR-EZ, line 21.

If you and your spouse each filed a separate Form 4868 but later file a joint return for 2001, enter the total paid with both Forms 4868 on the appropriate line of your joint return.

If you and your spouse jointly file Form 4868 but later file separate returns for 2001, you may enter the total amount paid with Form 4868 on either of your separate returns. Or you and your spouse may divide the payment in any agreed amounts. Be sure each separate return has the social security numbers of both spouses.

Specific Instructions

How To Complete Form 4868

Caution: *Skip Parts II and IV unless you are requesting an extension of time to file a gift or GST tax return.*

Part I—Identification

Enter your name(s) and address. If you plan to file a joint return, include both spouses' names in the order in which they will appear on the return.

If you want correspondence regarding this extension to be sent to you at an address other than your own or to an agent acting for you, include the agent's name, if any, and enter that address instead.

If you changed your name after you filed your last return because of marriage, divorce, etc., be sure to report this to your local Social Security Administration office before filing Form 4868. This prevents delays in processing your extension request.

If you changed your mailing address after you filed your last return, you should use **Form 8822,** Change of Address, to notify the IRS of the change. Showing a new address on Form 4868 will not update your record. You can get IRS forms by calling 1-800-TAX-FORM (1-800-829-3676). You can also download forms from the IRS Web Site at **www.irs.gov.**

If you plan to file jointly, enter on line 2 the social security number (SSN) that you will show first on your return. Enter your spouse's SSN on line 3.

If you are filing Form 1040NR or 1040NR-EZ, and do not have (and are not eligible to obtain) an SSN, enter your IRS-issued individual taxpayer identification number (ITIN). For information on obtaining an ITIN, get **Form W-7,** Application for IRS Individual Taxpayer Identification Number.

Part III—Individual Income Tax

Line 4—Estimate of Total Tax Liability for 2001

Enter on line 4 the total tax liability you expect to report on your 2001:

- Form 1040, line 58.
- Form 1040A, line 36.
- Form 1040EZ, line 11.
- Form 1040NR, line 54.

- Form 1040NR-EZ, line 17.

If you expect this amount to be zero, enter zero.

Caution: *Make your estimate as accurate as you can with the information you have. If we later find that the estimate was not reasonable, the extension will be null and void.*

Line 5—Total Payments for 2001

Enter on line 5 the total payments from:

- Form 1040, line 66 (excluding line 64).
- Form 1040A, line 41.
- Form 1040EZ, line 10.
- Form 1040NR, line 64 (excluding line 59).
- Form 1040NR-EZ, line 21.

Note: *For Forms 1040A, 1040EZ, and 1040NR-EZ, do not include on line 5 the amount you are paying with this Form 4868.*

Line 6—Balance

Subtract line 5 from line 4. If line 5 is more than line 4, enter zero.

If you find you cannot pay the amount shown on line 6, you can still get the extension. But you should pay as much as you can to limit the amount of interest you will owe. Also, you may be charged the late payment penalty on the unpaid tax from the regular due date of your return. See **Late Payment Penalty** on this page.

Part IV—Gift/GST Tax

Fill in this part **only** if you or your spouse plan to file Form 709 or 709-A **and** you are also using Form 4868 to apply for an extension of time to file your 2001 **calendar year** income tax return. **Do not** include income tax on lines 7 and 8.

Enter the amount of gift and GST tax you (or your spouse) are paying on these lines. If your spouse files a **separate** Form 4868, **do not** check the box in Part II for your spouse; enter on your form only the total gift and GST tax **you** are paying. Pay in full with this form to avoid interest and penalties.

Part V—Total

Enter the total of line 6 (and 7 and 8, if applicable) on line 9. If you are paying your entire estimate of tax liability, lines 9 and 10 should both be the same.

How To Make a Payment With Your Extension

Paying by Electronic Funds Withdrawal (Direct Debit)

You can e-file Form 4868 using IRS e-file option 1 or 2 on page 1 and make a payment by authorizing an electronic funds withdrawal (direct debit) from your checking or savings account. You can authorize an electronic funds withdrawal for your extension tax payment and/or for payment of your gift or GST tax. Check with your financial institution to make sure that an electronic funds withdrawal is allowed and to get the correct routing and account numbers.

If you owe tax and wish to have the money electronically withdrawn from your account, you will be asked to make the following declaration:

I authorize the U.S. Treasury and its designated Financial Agent to initiate an ACH electronic funds withdrawal (direct debit) entry to the financial institution account indicated for payment of my Federal taxes owed, and the financial institution to debit the entry to this account. This authorization is to remain in full force and effect until I notify the U.S. Treasury Financial Agent to terminate the authorization. To revoke a payment, I must contact the U.S. Treasury Financial Agent at **1-888-353-4537** no later than 2 business days prior to the payment (settlement) date. I also authorize the financial institutions involved in the processing of the electronic payment of taxes to receive confidential information necessary to answer inquiries and resolve issues related to the payment.

Note: *This is your written copy of the electronic funds withdrawal authorization you made to have the amount you owe withdrawn.* **Keep it for your records.**

Paying by Credit Card

You can e-file Form 4868 using IRS e-file option 3 on page 1 and pay by credit card.

Paying by Check or Money Order

- When paying by check or money order with Form 4868, use the addresses in the middle column under **Where To File a Paper Form 4868** below.
- Make your check or money order payable to the **"United States Treasury."** Do not send cash.
- Write your social security number, daytime phone number, and "2001 Form 4868" on your check or money order.
- Do not staple or attach your payment to the form.

Where To File a Paper Form 4868

If you live in:	And you are making a payment, send Form 4868 with your payment to IRS:	And you are not making a payment, send Form 4868 to Internal Revenue Service Center:
Florida, Georgia, North Carolina, South Carolina, West Virginia	P.O. Box 105073 Alanta, GA 30348-5073	Atlanta, GA 39901
Connecticut, Delaware	P.O. Box 22423 Newark, NJ 07101-2423	Philadelphia, PA 19255
New Jersey, New York (*New York City and counties of Nassau, Rockland, Suffolk, and Westchester*)	P.O. Box 22423 Newark, NJ 07101-2423	Holtsville, NY 00501
New York (*all other counties*), Massachusetts, Michigan, Rhode Island	P.O. Box 13843 Philadelphia, PA 19101-3843	Andover, MA 05501
Maine, New Hampshire, Vermont	P.O. Box 13843, Philadelphia, PA 19101-3843	Philadelphia, PA 19255
Illinois, Iowa, Kansas, Minnesota, Missouri, Wisconsin	P.O. Box 970028 St. Louis, MO 63197-0028	Kansas City, MO 64999
Oregon	P.O. Box 970028 St. Louis, MO 63197-0028	Fresno, CA 93888
District of Columbia, Indiana, Maryland, Pennsylvania	P.O. Box 80109 Cincinnati, OH 45280-0009	Philadelphia, PA 19255
Ohio	P.O. Box 80109 Cincinnati, OH 45280-0009	Cincinnati, OH 45999
Arizona, Colorado, Idaho, Montana, New Mexico, Texas, Wyoming	P.O. Box 660575 Dallas, TX 75266-0575	Austin, TX 73301
Utah	P.O. Box 660575 Dallas, TX 75266-0575	Kansas City, MO 64999
Alaska, California, Hawaii, Nevada	P.O. Box 7122 San Francisco, CA 94120-7122	Fresno, CA 93888
Alabama, Arkansas, Kentucky, Louisiana, Mississippi, Tennessee, Virginia	P.O. Box 105050 Atlanta, GA 30348-5050	Memphis, TN 37501
Nebraska, North Dakota, South Dakota, Washington	P.O. Box 30659 Los Angeles, CA 90030-0659	Ogden, UT 84201
Oklahoma	P.O. Box 105050 Atlanta, GA 30348-5050	Kansas City, MO 64999
American Samoa or Puerto Rico (*or exclude income under section 933*); are a nonpermanent resident of Guam or the Virgin Islands; have an APO, FPO, or foreign address; are a dual-status alien; or file Form 2555, 2555-EZ, or 4563	P.O. Box 80109 Cincinnati, OH 45280-0009	Philadelphia, PA 19255
Guam: Permanent residents	Send Form 4868 and payments to:	Department of Revenue and Taxation Government of Guam P.O. Box 23607 GMF, GU 96921
Virgin Islands: Permanent residents	Send Form 4868 and payments to:	V.I. Bureau of Internal Revenue 9601 Estate Thomas Charlotte Amalie, St. Thomas, VI 00802

Privacy Act and Paperwork Reduction Act Notice. We ask for the information on this form to carry out the Internal Revenue laws of the United States. We need this information so that our records will reflect your intention to file your individual income tax return within 4 months after the regular due date. If you choose to apply for an automatic extension of time to file, you are required by Internal Revenue Code section 6081 to provide the information requested on this form. Under section 6109, you must disclose your social security number (SSN) or individual taxpayer identification number (ITIN). Routine uses of this information include giving it to the Department of Justice for civil and criminal litigation, and to cities, states, and the District of Columbia for use in administering their tax laws. If you fail to provide this information in a timely manner or provide incomplete or false information, you may be liable for penalties and interest.

You are not required to provide the information requested on a form that is subject to the Paperwork Reduction Act unless the form displays a valid OMB control number. Books or records relating to a form or its instructions must be retained as long as their contents may become material in the administration of any Internal Revenue law. Generally, tax returns and return information are confidential, as required by Internal Revenue Code section 6103.

The time needed to complete and file this form will vary depending on individual circumstances. The estimated average time is: **Recordkeeping,** 26 min.; **Learning about the law or the form,** 13 min.; **Preparing the form,** 18 min.; and **Copying, assembling, and sending the form to the IRS,** 10 min.

If you have comments concerning the accuracy of these time estimates or suggestions for making this form simpler, we would be happy to hear from you. You can write to the Tax Forms Committee, Western Area Distribution Center, Rancho Cordova, CA 95743-0001. **Do not** send the form to this address. Instead, see **Where To File a Paper Form 4868** above.

Form **4952**	**Investment Interest Expense Deduction**	**2001**
Department of the Treasury Internal Revenue Service (99)	▶ **Attach to your tax return.**	Attachment Sequence No. **72**

Name(s) shown on return

Identifying number

Part I — Total Investment Interest Expense

1	Investment interest expense paid or accrued in 2001. See instructions	**1**
2	Disallowed investment interest expense from 2000 Form 4952, line 7	**2**
3	**Total investment interest expense.** Add lines 1 and 2	**3**

Part II — Net Investment Income

4a	Gross income from property held for investment (excluding any net gain from the disposition of property held for investment)	**4a**
b	Net gain from the disposition of property held for investment . . . **4b**	
c	Net capital gain from the disposition of property held for investment **4c**	
d	Subtract line 4c from line 4b. If zero or less, enter -0-	**4d**
e	Enter the amount from line 4c that you elect to include in investment income. Do not enter more than the amount on line 4b. See instructions . . . . ▶	**4e**
f	Investment income. Add lines 4a, 4d, and 4e. See instructions	**4f**
5	Investment expenses. See instructions	**5**
6	**Net investment income.** Subtract line 5 from line 4f. If zero or less, enter -0-	**6**

Part III — Investment Interest Expense Deduction

7	Disallowed investment interest expense to be carried forward to 2002. Subtract line 6 from line 3. If zero or less, enter -0-	**7**
8	**Investment interest expense deduction.** Enter the **smaller** of line 3 or 6. See instructions . .	**8**

Section references are to the Internal Revenue Code unless otherwise noted.

General Instructions

Purpose of Form

Use Form 4952 to figure the amount of investment interest expense you can deduct for 2001 and the amount you can carry forward to future years. Your investment interest expense deduction is limited to your net investment income.

For additional information, see **Pub. 550,** Investment Income and Expenses.

Who Must File

If you are an individual, estate, or a trust and you claim a deduction for investment interest expense, you must complete Form 4952 and attach it to your tax return unless **all** of the following apply.

● Your investment interest expense is not more than your investment income from interest and ordinary dividends.

● You have no other deductible investment expenses.

● You have no disallowed investment interest expense from 2000.

Allocation of Interest Expense Under Temporary Regulations Section 1.163-8T

If you paid or accrued interest on a loan and used the loan proceeds for more than one purpose, you may have to allocate the interest. This is necessary because different rules apply to investment interest, personal interest, trade or business interest, home mortgage interest, and passive activity interest. See **Pub. 535,** Business Expenses.

Specific Instructions

Part I—Total Investment Interest Expense

Line 1

Enter the investment interest expense paid or accrued during the tax year, regardless of when you incurred the indebtedness.

Investment interest expense is interest paid or accrued on a loan or part of a loan that is allocable to property held for investment (as defined on page 2).

Include investment interest expense reported to you on Schedule K-1 from a partnership or an S corporation. Include

amortization of bond premium on taxable bonds purchased after October 22, 1986, but before January 1, 1988, unless you elected to offset amortizable bond premium against the interest payments on the bond. A taxable bond is a bond on which the interest is includible in gross income.

Investment interest expense **does not** include any of the following:

● Home mortgage interest.

● Interest expense that is properly allocable to a passive activity. Generally, a passive activity is any business activity in which you **do not** materially participate and any rental activity. See the separate instructions for **Form 8582,** Passive Activity Loss Limitations, for details.

● Any interest expense that is capitalized, such as construction interest subject to section 263A.

● Interest expense related to tax-exempt interest income under section 265.

● Interest expense, disallowed under section 264, on indebtedness with respect to life insurance, endowment, or annuity contracts issued after June 8, 1997, even if the proceeds were used to purchase any property held for investment.

For Paperwork Reduction Act Notice, see back.   Cat. No. 13177Y   Form **4952** (2001)

Property held for investment. Property held for investment includes property that produces income, **not** derived in the ordinary course of a trade or business, from interest, dividends, annuities, or royalties. It also includes property that produces gain or loss, **not** derived in the ordinary course of a trade or business, from the disposition of property that produces these types of income or is held for investment. However, it does not include an interest in a passive activity.

Exception. A working interest in an oil or gas property that you held directly or through an entity that did **not** limit your liability is property held for investment, but only if you did not materially participate in the activity.

Part II—Net Investment Income

Line 4a

Enter your gross income from property held for investment. This includes income, unless derived in the ordinary course of a trade or business, from:

- Interest,
- Ordinary dividends (except Alaska Permanent Fund dividends),
- Annuities, and
- Royalties.

Include investment income reported to you on Schedule K-1 from a partnership or an S corporation. Also include net investment income from an estate or a trust.

Also include on line 4a (or 4b, if applicable) net passive income from a passive activity of a publicly traded partnership (as defined in section 469(k)(2)). See Notice 88-75, 1988-2 C.B. 386, for details.

Net income from certain passive activities, such as rental of substantially nondepreciable property, may have to be recharacterized and included on line 4a. For details, see **Pub. 925,** Passive Activity and At-Risk Rules, or Regulations section 1.469-2(f)(10).

If you are filing **Form 8814,** Parents' Election To Report Child's Interest and Dividends, part or all of your child's income may be included on line 4a. See Form 8814 for details.

Caution: *Do not include on line 4a any net gain from the disposition of property held for investment. Instead, enter it on line 4b.*

Line 4b

Enter your net gain from the disposition of property held for investment. This is the excess of your total gains over your total losses from the disposition of property held for investment. When figuring this amount, include capital gain distributions from mutual funds.

Line 4c

Enter your net capital gain from the disposition of property held for investment. This is the excess of your net long-term capital gain over your net short-term capital loss from the disposition of property held for investment.

Capital gain distributions from mutual funds are treated as long-term capital gains.

Line 4e

Net capital gain from the disposition of property held for investment, line 4c, is excluded from investment income. However, you may elect to include in investment income part or all of the net capital gain from the disposition of property held for investment. If you make this election, you must reduce the amount of net capital gain eligible for capital gains tax rates by the amount of net capital gain you include in investment income. Therefore, you should consider the tax effect of using the capital gains tax rates before making this election. Once made, the election may only be revoked with IRS consent.

To make the election, enter on line 4e the amount you elect to include in investment income. Also enter this amount on line 22 of Schedule D (Form 1040), or on line 20 of Schedule D (Form 1041), if applicable.

You must generally make this election on a timely filed return, including extensions. However, if you timely filed your return without making the election, you can make the election on an amended return filed within 6 months of the due date of your return (excluding extensions). Write "Filed pursuant to section 301.9100-2" on the amended return and file it at the same place you filed the original return.

Line 5

Investment expenses are your allowed deductions, other than interest expense, directly connected with the production of investment income. For example, depreciation or depletion allowed on assets that produce investment income is an investment expense.

Include investment expenses reported to you on Schedule K-1 from a partnership or an S corporation.

Investment expenses **do not** include any deductions used in determining your income or loss from a passive activity.

If you have investment expenses that are included as a miscellaneous itemized deduction on Schedule A (Form 1040), line 22, the 2% adjusted gross income limitation on Schedule A (Form 1040), line 25, may reduce the amount you must include on Form 4952, line 5. Include on line 5 the **smaller** of:

- The investment expenses included on Schedule A (Form 1040), line 22, or
- The total on Schedule A (Form 1040), line 26.

Example. Schedule A, line 22, includes investment expenses of $3,000, and line 26 is $1,300 after the 2% adjusted gross income limitation. Investment expenses from Schedule A of $1,300 are used to figure line 5. If line 22 included investment expenses of $800 and line 26 was $1,300, investment expenses from Schedule A of $800 would be used.

Part III—Investment Interest Expense Deduction

Line 8

You may deduct the amount on line 8 as investment interest expense.

Individuals. Generally, enter the amount from line 8 on Schedule A (Form 1040), line 13, even if all or part of it is attributable to a partnership or an S corporation. However, if any part of the interest expense is attributable to royalties, enter that part on Schedule E (Form 1040). Also, if any part of the interest is attributable to a trade or business that is not a passive activity, enter that part on the schedule where you report other expenses for that trade or business.

Estates and trusts. Enter the amount from line 8 on Form 1041, line 10.

Form 6198. If any of your deductible investment interest expense is attributable to an activity for which you are not at risk, you must also use **Form 6198,** At-Risk Limitations, to figure your deductible investment interest expense. Enter the part attributable to the at-risk activity on Form 6198, line 4. Reduce Form 4952, line 8, by the amount entered on Form 6198.

Alternative minimum tax (AMT). Deductible interest expense may be an adjustment for the AMT. For details, see **Form 6251,** Alternative Minimum Tax—Individuals, or Form 1041, Schedule I, for estates and trusts.

Paperwork Reduction Act Notice. We ask for the information on this form to carry out the Internal Revenue laws of the United States. You are required to give us the information. We need it to ensure that you are complying with these laws and to allow us to figure and collect the right amount of tax.

You are not required to provide the information requested on a form that is subject to the Paperwork Reduction Act unless the form displays a valid OMB control number. Books or records relating to a form or its instructions must be retained as long as their contents may become material in the administration of any Internal Revenue law. Generally, tax returns and return information are confidential, as required by section 6103.

The time needed to complete and file this form will vary depending on individual circumstances. The estimated average time is:

Recordkeeping . . . . 13 min.

Learning about the law or the form . . . . . . 16 min.

Preparing the form . . . . . 21 min.

Copying, assembling, and sending the form to the IRS . . 10 min.

If you have comments concerning the accuracy of these time estimates or suggestions for making this form simpler, we would be happy to hear from you. See the instructions for the tax return with which this form is filed.

Alternative Minimum Tax—Individuals

► See separate instructions.

► Attach to Form 1040 or Form 1040NR.

OMB No. 1545-0227

2001

Department of the Treasury
Internal Revenue Service (99)

Attachment
Sequence No. **32**

Name(s) shown on Form 1040

Your social security number

Part I — Alternative Minimum Taxable Income

1	If you itemized deductions on Schedule A (Form 1040), go to line 2. Otherwise, enter your standard deduction from Form 1040, line 36, here and go to line 6	1
2	Medical and dental. Enter the **smaller** of Schedule A (Form 1040), line 4 **or** 2½% of Form 1040, line 34 .	2
3	Taxes. Enter the amount from Schedule A (Form 1040), line 9	3
4	Certain interest on a home mortgage **not** used to buy, build, or improve your home	4
5	Miscellaneous itemized deductions. Enter the amount from Schedule A (Form 1040), line 26 . . .	5
6	Refund of taxes. Enter any tax refund from Form 1040, line 10 or line 21	6 ( )
7	Investment interest. Enter difference between regular tax and AMT deduction	7
8	Post-1986 depreciation. Enter difference between regular tax and AMT depreciation	8
9	Adjusted gain or loss. Enter difference between AMT and regular tax gain or loss	9
10	Incentive stock options. Enter excess of AMT income over regular tax income	10
11	Passive activities. Enter difference between AMT and regular tax income or loss	11
12	Beneficiaries of estates and trusts. Enter the amount from Schedule K-1 (Form 1041), line 9	12
13	Tax-exempt interest income from private activity bonds issued after August 7, 1986	13
14	Other. Enter the amount, if any, for each item below and enter the total on line 14.	

a Circulation expenditures .	**i** Mining costs .	
b Depletion	**j** Patron's adjustment . .	
c Depreciation (pre-1987) . .	**k** Pollution control facilities .	
d Installment sales	**l** Research and experimental .	
e Intangible drilling costs . .	**m** Section 1202 exclusion . .	
f Large partnerships . . .	**n** Tax shelter farm activities .	
g Long-term contracts . . .	**o** Related adjustments . .	
h Loss limitations		14

15	Total adjustments and preferences. Combine lines 1 through 14	15
16	Enter the amount from Form 1040, line 37. If less than zero, enter as a (loss)	16
17	Enter as a positive amount any net operating loss deduction from Form 1040, line 21	17
18	If Form 1040, line 34, is over $132,950 (over $66,475 if married filing separately) and you itemized deductions, enter the amount, if any, from line 9 of the worksheet for Schedule A (Form 1040), line 28	18 ( )
19	Combine lines 15 through 18	19
20	Alternative tax net operating loss deduction (see page 6 of the instructions) . .	20
21	**Alternative minimum taxable income.** Subtract line 20 from line 19. (If married filing separately and line 21 is more than $173,000, see page 7 of the instructions.)	21

Part II — Alternative Minimum Tax

22	Exemption amount. (If this form is for a child under age 14, see page 7 of the instructions.)

IF your filing status is . . .	AND line 21 is not over . . .	THEN enter on line 22 . . .
Single or head of household	$112,500	$35,750
Married filing jointly or qualifying widow(er) . .	150,000	49,000
Married filing separately	75,000	24,500

If line 21 is **over** the amount shown above for your filing status, see page 7 of the instructions.

22	

	If line 21 is **over** the amount shown above for your filing status, see page 7 of the instructions.	
23	Subtract line 22 from line 21. If zero or less, enter -0- here and on lines 26 and 28 and stop here . .	23
24	Go to Part III of Form 6251 to figure line 24 if you reported capital gain distributions directly on Form 1040, line 13, **or** you had a gain on both lines 16 and 17 of Schedule D (Form 1040) (as refigured for the AMT, if necessary). **All others:** If line 23 is $175,000 or less ($87,500 or less if married filing separately), multiply line 23 by 26% (.26). Otherwise, multiply line 23 by 28% (.28) and subtract $3,500 ($1,750 if married filing separately) from the result	24
25	Alternative minimum tax foreign tax credit (see page 7 of the instructions)	25
26	Tentative minimum tax. Subtract line 25 from line 24	26
27	Enter your tax from Form 1040, line 40 (minus any tax from Form 4972 and any foreign tax credit from Form 1040, line 43)	27
28	**Alternative minimum tax.** Subtract line 27 from line 26. If zero or less, enter -0-. Enter here and on Form 1040, line 41	28

For Paperwork Reduction Act Notice, see page 8 of the instructions.   Cat. No. 13600G   Form **6251** (2001)

Part III   **Line 24 Computation Using Maximum Capital Gains Rates**

Caution: *If you **did not** complete Part IV of Schedule D (Form 1040), see page 8 of the instructions before you complete this part.*

29	Enter the amount from Form 6251, line 23	**29**
30	Enter the amount from Schedule D (Form 1040), line 23, or line 9 of the Schedule D Tax Worksheet on page D-9 of the instructions for Schedule D (Form 1040), whichever applies (as refigured for the AMT, if necessary) (see page 8 of the instructions) **30**	
31	Enter the amount from Schedule D (Form 1040), line 19 (as refigured for the AMT, if necessary) (see page 8 of the instructions) **31**	
32	Add lines 30 and 31 . . . . **32**	
33	Enter the amount from Schedule D (Form 1040), line 23, or line 4 of the Schedule D Tax Worksheet on page D-9 of the instructions for Schedule D (Form 1040), whichever applies (as refigured for the AMT, if necessary) (see page 8 of the instructions) **33**	
34	Enter the **smaller** of line 32 or line 33	**34**
35	Subtract line 34 from line 29. If zero or less, enter -0-	**35**
36	If line 35 is $175,000 or less ($87,500 or less if married filing separately), multiply line 35 by 26% (.26). Otherwise, multiply line 35 by 28% (.28) and subtract $3,500 ($1,750 if married filing separately) from the result	**36**
37	Enter the amount from Schedule D (Form 1040), line 28, or line 16 of the Schedule D Tax Worksheet on page D-9 of the instructions for Schedule D (Form 1040), whichever applies (as figured for the regular tax) (see page 8 of the instructions) **37**	
38	Enter the **smallest** of line 29, line 30, or line 37. If zero, go to line 44 . . **38**	
39	Enter your qualified 5-year gain, if any, from Schedule D (Form 1040), line 29 (as refigured for the AMT, if necessary) (see page 8 of the instructions) **39**	
40	Enter the **smaller** of line 38 or line 39 . . . . **40**	
41	Multiply line 40 by 8% (.08)	**41**
42	Subtract line 40 from line 38 . . . . **42**	
43	Multiply line 42 by 10% (.10)	**43**
44	Enter the **smaller** of line 29 or line 30 . . . . **44**	
45	Enter the amount from line 38 . . . . **45**	
46	Subtract line 45 from line 44 . . . . **46**	
47	Multiply line 46 by 20% (.20)	**47**

If line 31 is zero or blank, skip lines 48 through 51 and go to line 52. Otherwise, go to line 48.

48	Enter the amount from line 29 . . . . **48**	
49	Add lines 35, 38, and 46 . . . . **49**	
50	Subtract line 49 from line 48 . . . . **50**	
51	Multiply line 50 by 25% (.25)	**51**
52	Add lines 36, 41, 43, 47, and 51	**52**
53	If line 29 is $175,000 or less ($87,500 or less if married filing separately), multiply line 29 by 26% (.26). Otherwise, multiply line 29 by 28% (.28) and subtract $3,500 ($1,750 if married filing separately) from the result	**53**
54	Enter the **smaller** of line 52 or line 53 here and on line 24	**54**

Form **6251** (2001)

Form 8283
(Rev. October 1998)

Department of the Treasury
Internal Revenue Service

Noncash Charitable Contributions

▶ Attach to your tax return if you claimed a total deduction of over $500 for all contributed property.

▶ See separate instructions.

OMB No. 1545-0908

Attachment
Sequence No. **55**

Name(s) shown on your income tax return

Identifying number

Note: *Figure the amount of your contribution deduction before completing this form. See your tax return instructions.*

Section A—List in this section **only** items (or groups of similar items) for which you claimed a deduction of $5,000 or less. Also, list certain publicly traded securities even if the deduction is over $5,000 (see instructions).

Part I	Information on Donated Property—If you need more space, attach a statement.

1	(a) Name and address of the donee organization	(b) Description of donated property
A		
B		
C		
D		
E		

Note: *If the amount you claimed as a deduction for an item is $500 or less, you do not have to complete columns (d), (e), and (f).*

	(c) Date of the contribution	(d) Date acquired by donor (mo., yr.)	(e) How acquired by donor	(f) Donor's cost or adjusted basis	(g) Fair market value	(h) Method used to determine the fair market value
A						
B						
C						
D						
E						

Part II	Other Information—Complete line 2 if you gave less than an entire interest in property listed in Part I. Complete line 3 if conditions were attached to a contribution listed in Part I.

2 If, during the year, you contributed less than the entire interest in the property, complete lines a–e.

a Enter the letter from Part I that identifies the property ▶ _____. If Part II applies to more than one property, attach a separate statement.

b Total amount claimed as a deduction for the property listed in Part I: **(1)** For this tax year ▶ _____ .
(2) For any prior tax years ▶ _____ .

c Name and address of each organization to which any such contribution was made in a prior year (complete only if different from the donee organization above):

Name of charitable organization (donee)

Address (number, street, and room or suite no.)

City or town, state, and ZIP code

d For tangible property, enter the place where the property is located or kept ▶ _____

e Name of any person, other than the donee organization, having actual possession of the property ▶ _____

3 If conditions were attached to any contribution listed in Part I, answer questions a – c and attach the required statement (see instructions).

		Yes	No
a	Is there a restriction, either temporary or permanent, on the donee's right to use or dispose of the donated property?		
b	Did you give to anyone (other than the donee organization or another organization participating with the donee organization in cooperative fundraising) the right to the income from the donated property or to the possession of the property, including the right to vote donated securities, to acquire the property by purchase or otherwise, or to designate the person having such income, possession, or right to acquire?		
c	Is there a restriction limiting the donated property for a particular use?		

For Paperwork Reduction Act Notice, see page 4 of separate instructions.   Cat. No. 62299J   Form **8283** (Rev. 10-98)

Name(s) shown on your income tax return

Identifying number

Section B—Appraisal Summary—List in this section only items (or groups of similar items) for which you claimed a deduction of more than $5,000 per item or group. **Exception.** Report contributions of certain publicly traded securities only in Section A.

If you donated art, you may have to attach the complete appraisal. See the **Note** in Part I below.

Part I	Information on Donated Property—To be completed by the taxpayer and/or appraiser.

4 Check type of property:

☐ Art* (contribution of $20,000 or more) ☐ Real Estate ☐ Gems/Jewelry ☐ Stamp Collections

☐ Art* (contribution of less than $20,000) ☐ Coin Collections ☐ Books ☐ Other

*Art includes paintings, sculptures, watercolors, prints, drawings, ceramics, antique furniture, decorative arts, textiles, carpets, silver, rare manuscripts, historical memorabilia, and other similar objects.

Note: If your total art contribution deduction was $20,000 or more, you must attach a complete copy of the signed appraisal. See instructions.

5	(a) Description of donated property (if you need more space, attach a separate statement)	(b) If tangible property was donated, give a brief summary of the overall physical condition at the time of the gift	(c) Appraised fair market value
A			
B			
C			
D			

	(d) Date acquired by donor (mo., yr.)	(e) How acquired by donor	(f) Donor's cost or adjusted basis	(g) For bargain sales, enter amount received	See instructions	
					(h) Amount claimed as a deduction	(i) Average trading price of securities
A						
B						
C						
D						

Part II	Taxpayer (Donor) Statement—List each item included in Part I above that the appraisal identifies as having a value of $500 or less. See instructions.

I declare that the following item(s) included in Part I above has to the best of my knowledge and belief an appraised value of not more than $500 (per item). Enter identifying letter from Part I and describe the specific item. See instructions. ▶ _____

Signature of taxpayer (donor) ▶   Date ▶

Part III	Declaration of Appraiser

I declare that I am not the donor, the donee, a party to the transaction in which the donor acquired the property, employed by, or related to any of the foregoing persons, or married to any person who is related to any of the foregoing persons. And, if regularly used by the donor, donee, or party to the transaction, I performed the majority of my appraisals during my tax year for other persons.

Also, I declare that I hold myself out to the public as an appraiser or perform appraisals on a regular basis; and that because of my qualifications as described in the appraisal, I am qualified to make appraisals of the type of property being valued. I certify that the appraisal fees were not based on a percentage of the appraised property value. Furthermore, I understand that a false or fraudulent overstatement of the property value as described in the qualified appraisal or this appraisal summary may subject me to the penalty under section 6701(a) (aiding and abetting the understatement of tax liability). I affirm that I have not been barred from presenting evidence or testimony by the Director of Practice.

Sign Here Signature ▶   Title ▶   Date of appraisal ▶

Business address (including room or suite no.)

Identifying number

City or town, state, and ZIP code

Part IV	Donee Acknowledgment—To be completed by the charitable organization.

This charitable organization acknowledges that it is a qualified organization under section 170(c) and that it received the donated property as described in Section B, Part I, above on ▶ _____

(Date)

Furthermore, this organization affirms that in the event it sells, exchanges, or otherwise disposes of the property described in Section B, Part I (or any portion thereof) within 2 years after the date of receipt, it will file **Form 8282,** Donee Information Return, with the IRS and give the donor a copy of that form. This acknowledgment does not represent agreement with the claimed fair market value.

Does the organization intend to use the property for an unrelated use? . . . . ▶ ☐ Yes ☐ No

Name of charitable organization (donee)

Employer identification number

Address (number, street, and room or suite no.)

City or town, state, and ZIP code

Authorized signature

Title

Date

Additional Child Tax Credit

1040
1040A
8812

Complete and attach to Form 1040 or Form 1040A.

OMB No. 1545-1620

20 01

Attachment
Sequence No. **47**

Name(s) shown on return

Your social security number

Part I — All Filers

1	Enter the amount from line 1 of your Child Tax Credit Worksheet on page 38 of the Form 1040 instructions or page 37 of the Form 1040A instructions. If you used Pub. 972, enter the amount from line 8 of the worksheet on page 3 of the publication	**1**
2	Enter the amount from Form 1040, line 48, or Form 1040A, line 31	**2**
3	Subtract line 2 from line 1. If zero, **stop**; you cannot take this credit	**3**
4	Enter your total taxable earned income. See the instructions on back . .	**4**
5	Is the amount on line 4 more than $10,000? ☐ **No.** Leave line 5 blank and enter -0- on line 6. ☐ **Yes.** Subtract $10,000 from the amount on line 4. Enter the result .	**5**
6	Multiply the amount on line 5 by 10% (.10) and enter the result . . . . **Next.** Do you have three or more qualifying children? ☐ **No.** If line 6 is zero, **stop**; you cannot take this credit. Otherwise, skip Part II and enter the **smaller** of line 3 or line 6 on line 13. ☐ **Yes.** If line 6 is equal to or more than line 3, skip Part II and enter the amount from line 3 on line 13. Otherwise, go to line 7.	**6**

Part II — Certain Filers Who Have Three or More Qualifying Children

7	Enter the total of the withheld social security and Medicare taxes from Form(s) W-2, boxes 4 and 6. If married filing jointly, include your spouse's amounts with yours. If you worked for a railroad, see the instructions on back . .	**7**
8	**1040 filers:** Enter the total of the amounts from Form 1040, lines 27 and 54, plus any uncollected social security and Medicare or RRTA taxes included on line 58. **1040A filers:** Enter -0-.	**8**
9	Add lines 7 and 8	**9**
10	**1040 filers:** Enter the total of the amounts from Form 1040, lines 61a and 62. **1040A filers:** Enter the total of the amount from Form 1040A, line 39a, plus any excess social security and RRTA taxes withheld that you entered to the left of line 41 (see the instructions on back).	**10**
11	Subtract line 10 from line 9. If zero or less, enter -0-	**11**
12	Enter the **larger** of line 6 or line 11 here . . . . **Next,** enter the **smaller** of line 3 or line 12 on line 13.	**12**

Part III — Your Additional Child Tax Credit

13	**This is your additional child tax credit**	**13**

Enter this amount on Form 1040, line 63, or Form 1040A, line 40.

Instructions

Purpose of Form

Use Form 8812 to figure your additional child tax credit.

 The additional child tax credit may give you a refund even if you do not owe any tax.

Who Should Use Form 8812

First, complete the Child Tax Credit Worksheet that applies to you. See the instructions for Form 1040, line 48, or Form 1040A, line 31. If you meet the condition given in the **TIP** at the end of your Child Tax Credit Worksheet, use Form 8812 to see if you can take the additional child tax credit.

Effect of Credit on Welfare Benefits

Any refund you receive as a result of taking the additional child tax credit will not be used to determine if you are eligible for the following programs, or how much you can receive from them.

- Temporary Assistance for Needy Families (TANF).
- Medicaid and supplemental security income (SSI).
- Food stamps and low-income housing.

Taxable Earned Income

1. Did you, or your spouse if filing a joint return, have net earnings from self-employment and use either optional method to figure those net earnings?

☐ **No.** Go to question 2.

☐ **Yes.** Use Pub. 972 to figure the amount to enter on Form 8812, line 4.

2. Are you claiming the earned income credit (EIC) on Form 1040, line 61a, or Form 1040A, line 39a?

☐ **Yes.** Use the following chart to find the amount to enter on Form 8812, line 4.

IF you are filing Form...	AND you completed...	THEN enter on Form 8812, line 4, the amount from...
1040	Worksheet B on page 46 of your 1040 instructions or on page 30 of Pub. 596	Worksheet B, lines 4a and 4c (combine lines 4a and 4c and enter the result on Form 8812, line 4)*
	Step 7 on page 43 of your 1040 instructions (but not Worksheet B)	Step 7, Box C
	Worksheet 2 on page 22 of Pub. 596	Worksheet 2, line 8
1040A	Step 7 on page 41 of your 1040A instructions	Step 7, Box C
	Worksheet 2 on page 22 of Pub. 596	Worksheet 2, line 8

* If you were a minister, member of a religious order who has not taken a vow of poverty, or a Christian Science practitioner, subtract the following from the total of lines 4a and 4c: **(a)** the rental value of a home or the nontaxable portion of an allowance for a home furnished to you (including payments for utilities) and **(b)** the value of meals and lodging provided to you, your spouse, and your dependents for your employer's convenience.

☐ **No.** **1040 filers:** Go to question 3.
        1040A filers: Skip question 3 and go to question 4.

3. Were you, or your spouse if filing a joint return, self-employed, or are you filing Schedule SE because you had church employee income, or are you filing Schedule C or C-EZ as a statutory employee?

☐ **No.** Go to question 4.

☐ **Yes.** Use Pub. 972 to figure the amount to enter on Form 8812, line 4.

4. Does the amount on line 7 of Form 1040 or Form 1040A include any of the following amounts?

- Scholarship or fellowship grants not reported on a W-2 form.
- Amounts paid to an inmate in a penal institution for work (put "PRI" and the amount paid in the space next to line 7 of Form 1040 or 1040A).
- Amounts received as a pension or annuity from a nonqualified deferred compensation plan or a section 457 plan (put "DFC" and the amount received in the space next to line 7 of Form 1040 or 1040A). This amount may be reported in box 11 of your W-2 form. If you received such an amount but box 11 is blank, contact your employer for the amount received as a pension or annuity.
- Amounts from Form 2555, line 41, or Form 2555-EZ, line 18.

☐ **No.** Enter the amount from line 7 of Form 1040 or Form 1040A on Form 8812, line 4.

☐ **Yes.** Subtract the total of those amounts from the amount on line 7 of Form 1040 or Form 1040A. (If an amount is included in more than one of the above categories, include it only once in figuring the total amount to subtract.) Enter the result on Form 8812, line 4.

Railroad Employees

If you worked for a railroad, include the following taxes in the total on Form 8812, line 7.

- Tier 1 tax withheld from your pay. This tax should be shown in box 14 of your W-2 form(s) and identified as "Tier 1 tax."
- If you were an employee representative, 50% of the total Tier 1 tax and Tier 1 Medicare tax you paid for 2001.

1040A Filers

If you, or your spouse if filing a joint return, had more than one employer for 2001 and total wages of over $59,700, figure any excess social security and railroad retirement (RRTA) taxes withheld. See the instructions for Form 1040A, line 41. Include any excess on Form 8812, line 10.

Paperwork Reduction Act Notice. We ask for the information on this form to carry out the Internal Revenue laws of the United States. You are required to give us the information. We need it to ensure that you are complying with these laws and to allow us to figure and collect the right amount of tax.

You are not required to provide the information requested on a form that is subject to the Paperwork Reduction Act unless the form displays a valid OMB control number. Books or records relating to a form or its instructions must be retained as long as their contents may become material in the administration of any Internal Revenue law. Generally, tax returns and return information are confidential, as required by Internal Revenue Code section 6103.

The time needed to complete and file this form will vary depending on individual circumstances. The estimated average time is: **Recordkeeping,** 6 min.; **Learning about the law or the form,** 5 min.; **Preparing the form,** 28 min.; **Copying, assembling, and sending the form to the IRS,** 20 min.

If you have comments concerning the accuracy of these time estimates or suggestions for making this form simpler, we would be happy to hear from you. See the Instructions for Form 1040 or Form 1040A.

Form **8814**

Department of the Treasury
Internal Revenue Service (99)

Parents' Election To Report
Child's Interest and Dividends

▶ See instructions below and on back.
▶ Attach to parents' Form 1040 or Form 1040NR.

OMB No. 1545-1128

2001

Attachment
Sequence No. **40**

Name(s) shown on your return

Your social security number

Caution: *The Federal income tax on your child's income, including capital gain distributions, may be less if you file a separate tax return for the child instead of making this election. This is because you cannot take certain tax benefits that your child could take on his or her own return. For details, see* **Tax Benefits You May Not Take** *on the back.*

A Child's name (first, initial, and last)

B Child's social security number

C If more than one Form 8814 is attached, check here . . . . ▶

Part I Child's Interest and Dividends To Report on Your Return

1a Enter your child's **taxable** interest. If this amount is different from the amounts shown on the child's Forms 1099-INT and 1099-OID, see the instructions . . . . | **1a** |

b Enter your child's **tax-exempt** interest. **Do not** include this amount on line 1a | **1b** |

2 Enter your child's ordinary dividends, including any Alaska Permanent Fund dividends. If your child received any ordinary dividends as a nominee, see the instructions . . . . . . | **2** |

3 Enter your child's capital gain distributions. If your child received any capital gain distributions as a nominee, see the instructions . . . . | **3** |

4 Add lines 1a, 2, and 3. If the total is $1,500 or less, skip lines 5 and 6 and go to line 7. If the total is $7,500 or more, **do not** file this form. Your child **must** file his or her own return to report the income | **4** |

5 Base amount | **5** | 1,500 | 00 |

6 Subtract line 5 from line 4. If you checked the box on line C above or if you entered an amount on line 3, see the instructions. Also, include this amount in the total on Form 1040, line 21, or Form 1040NR, line 21. In the space next to line 21, enter "Form 8814" and show the amount. Go to line 7 below . . . . ▶ | **6** |

Part II Tax on the First $1,500 of Child's Interest and Dividends

7 Amount not taxed . . . . | **7** | 750 | 00 |

8 Subtract line 7 from line 4. If the result is zero or less, enter -0- . . . . | **8** |

9 **Tax.** Is the amount on line 8 less than $750?
☐ **No.** Enter $75 here and see the **Note** below.
☐ **Yes.** Multiply line 8 by 10% (.10). Enter the result here and see the **Note** below. | **9** |

Note: *If you checked the box on line C above, see the instructions. Otherwise, include the amount from line 9 in the tax you enter on Form 1040, line 40, or Form 1040NR, line 39. Be sure to check box* **a** *on Form 1040, line 40, or Form 1040NR, line 39.*

General Instructions

Purpose of Form. Use this form if you elect to report your child's income on your return. If you do, your child will not have to file a return. You can make this election if your child meets **all** of the following conditions.

● Was under age 14 on January 1, 2002.

● Is required to file a 2001 return.

● Had income only from interest and dividends, including Alaska Permanent Fund dividends.

● Had gross income for 2001 that was less than $7,500.

● Had no estimated tax payments for 2001 (including any overpayment of tax from his or her 2000 return applied to 2001 estimated tax).

● Had no Federal income tax withheld from his or her income.

You must also qualify. See **Parents Who Qualify To Make the Election** below.

How To Make the Election. To make the election, complete and attach Form(s) 8814 to your tax return and file your return by the due date (including extensions). A separate Form 8814 must be filed for **each** child whose income you choose to report.

Parents Who Qualify To Make the Election. You qualify to make this election if you file Form 1040 or Form 1040NR and **any** of the following apply.

● You are filing a joint return for 2001 with the child's other parent.

● You and the child's other parent were married to each other but file separate returns for 2001 **and** you had the **higher** taxable income.

● You were unmarried, treated as unmarried for Federal income tax purposes, or separated from the child's other parent by a divorce or separate maintenance decree. You must have had custody of your child for most of the year (you were the custodial parent). If you were the custodial parent and you remarried, you may make the election on a joint return with your new spouse. But if you and your new spouse do not file a joint return, you qualify to make the election only if you had **higher** taxable income than your new spouse.

(continued)

For Paperwork Reduction Act Notice, see back of form.

Cat. No. 10750J

Form **8814** (2001)

673

Note: *If you and the child's other parent were not married but lived together during the year with the child, you qualify to make the election only if you are the parent with the **higher** taxable income.*

Tax Benefits You May Not Take. If you elect to report your child's income on your return, you may not take any of the following deductions that your child could take on his or her own return.

● Standard deduction of $1,850 for a blind child.

● Penalty on early withdrawal of child's savings.

● Itemized deductions such as child's investment expenses or charitable contributions.

If your child received capital gain distributions that included qualified 5-year gain and had a net capital gain, you may pay up to $15 more tax if you make this election instead of filing a separate tax return for the child. This is because the tax rate on the child's income between $750 and $1,500 is 10% if you make this election. However, if you file a separate return for the child, the tax rate on the qualified 5-year gain may be 8% because of the preferential capital gains tax rates.

If any of the above apply to your child, first figure the tax on your child's income as if he or she is filing a return. Next, figure the tax as if you are electing to report your child's income on **your** return. Then, compare the methods to determine which results in the lower tax.

Alternative Minimum Tax. If your child received tax-exempt interest (or exempt-interest dividends paid by a regulated investment company) from certain private activity bonds, you must take this into account in determining if you owe the alternative minimum tax. See **Form 6251,** Alternative Minimum Tax—Individuals, and its instructions for details.

Investment Interest Expense. Your child's income (other than Alaska Permanent Fund dividends and capital gain distributions) that you report on your return is considered to be **your** investment income for purposes of figuring your investment interest expense deduction. If your child received Alaska Permanent Fund dividends or capital gain distributions, see **Pub. 550,** Investment Income and Expenses, to figure the amount you may treat as your investment income.

Foreign Accounts and Trusts. Complete Part III of **Schedule B** (Form 1040) for your child if he or she **(a)** had a foreign financial account or **(b)** received a distribution from, or was the grantor of, or transferor to, a foreign trust. If you answer "Yes" to either question, you must file this Schedule B with **your** return. Enter "Form 8814" next to line 7a or line 8, whichever applies. Also, complete line 7b if applicable.

Change of Address. If your child filed a return for a previous year and the address shown on the last return filed is not your child's current address, be sure to notify the IRS, in writing, of the new address. To do this, you may use **Form 8822,** Change of Address.

Additional Information. See Pub. 929 for more details.

Line Instructions

Name and Social Security Number. If filing a joint return, include your spouse's name but enter the social security number of the person whose name is shown first on the return.

Line 1a. Enter **all** taxable interest income received by your child in 2001. If your child received a **Form 1099-INT** for tax-exempt interest, such as from municipal bonds, enter the amount and "Tax-exempt interest" on the dotted line next to line 1a. **Do not** include this interest in the total for line 1a but be sure to include it on line 1b.

If your child received, as a **nominee,** interest that actually belongs to another person, enter the amount and "ND" (for nominee distribution) on the dotted line next to line 1a. **Do not** include amounts received as a nominee in the total for line 1a.

If your child had accrued interest that was paid to the seller of a bond, amortizable bond premium (ABP) allowed as a reduction to interest income, or if any original issue discount (OID) is less than the amount shown on your child's **Form 1099-OID,** enter the nontaxable amount on the dotted line next to line 1a and "Accrued interest," "ABP adjustment," or "OID adjustment," whichever applies. **Do not** include any nontaxable amounts in the total for line 1a.

Line 1b. If your child received any tax-exempt interest income, such as from certain state and municipal bonds, report it on line 1b. Also, include any exempt-interest dividends your child received as a shareholder in a mutual fund or other regulated investment company.

Note: *If line 1b includes tax-exempt interest or exempt-interest dividends paid by a regulated investment company from private activity bonds, see **Alternative Minimum Tax** on this page.*

Line 2. Enter the ordinary dividends received by your child in 2001. Ordinary dividends should be shown in box 1 of **Form 1099-DIV.** Also, include ordinary dividends your child received through a partnership, an S corporation, or an estate or trust.

If your child received, as a **nominee,** ordinary dividends that actually belong to another person, enter the amount and "ND" on the dotted line next to line 2. **Do not** include amounts received as a nominee in the total for line 2.

Line 3. Enter the capital gain distributions received by your child in 2001. Capital gain distributions should be shown in box 2a of Form 1099-DIV. Also, see the instructions for line 6.

If your child received, as a **nominee,** capital gain distributions that actually belong to another person, enter the amount and "ND" on the dotted line next to line 3. **Do not** include amounts received as a nominee in the total for line 3.

Line 6. If you checked the box on line C, add the amounts from line 6 of **all** your Forms 8814. Include the total on line 21 of Form 1040 or Form 1040NR, whichever applies. Be sure to enter "Form 8814" and the total of the line 6 amounts in the space next to line 21.

If your child received capital gain distributions, part or all of those distributions must be reported on your **Schedule D** (Form 1040) **or** on Form 1040 or on Form 1040NR instead of on Form 8814, line 6. See Pub. 929 for details.

Line 9. If you checked the box on line C, add the amounts from line 9 of **all** your Forms 8814. Include the total on Form 1040, line 40, or Form 1040NR, line 39. Be sure to check box **a** on that line.

Paperwork Reduction Act Notice. We ask for the information on this form to carry out the Internal Revenue laws of the United States. You are required to give us the information. We need it to ensure that you are complying with these laws and to allow us to figure and collect the right amount of tax.

You are not required to provide the information requested on a form that is subject to the Paperwork Reduction Act unless the form displays a valid OMB control number. Books or records relating to a form or its instructions must be retained as long as their contents may become material in the administration of any Internal Revenue law. Generally, tax returns and return information are confidential, as required by Internal Revenue Code section 6103.

The time needed to complete and file this form will vary depending on individual circumstances. The estimated average time is: **Recordkeeping,** 26 min.; **Learning about the law or the form,** 10 min.; **Preparing the form,** 24 min.; and **Copying, assembling, and sending the form to the IRS,** 17 min.

If you have comments concerning the accuracy of these time estimates or suggestions for making this form simpler, we would be happy to hear from you. See the instructions for the tax return with which this form is filed.

Form **8822**
(Rev. Oct. 2000)
Department of the Treasury
Internal Revenue Service

Change of Address

▶ **Please type or print.**

▶ **See instructions on back.** ▶ **Do not attach this form to your return.**

OMB No. 1545-1163

Part I Complete This Part To Change Your Home Mailing Address

Check **all** boxes this change affects:

1 ☐ Individual income tax returns (Forms 1040, 1040A, 1040EZ, TeleFile, 1040NR, etc.)

   ▶ If your last return was a joint return and you are now establishing a residence separate from the spouse with whom you filed that return, check here . . . . ▶ ☐

2 ☐ Gift, estate, or generation-skipping transfer tax returns (Forms 706, 709, etc.)

   ▶ For Forms 706 and 706-NA, enter the decedent's name and social security number below.

   ▶ Decedent's name   ▶ Social security number

3a Your name (first name, initial, and last name)	**3b** Your social security number
4a Spouse's name (first name, initial, and last name)	**4b** Spouse's social security number

5 Prior name(s). See instructions.

6a Old address (no., street, city or town, state, and ZIP code). If a P.O. box or foreign address, see instructions.	Apt. no.
6b Spouse's old address, if different from line 6a (no., street, city or town, state, and ZIP code). If a P.O. box or foreign address, see instructions.	Apt. no.
7 New address (no., street, city or town, state, and ZIP code). If a P.O. box or foreign address, see instructions.	Apt. no.

Part II Complete This Part To Change Your Business Mailing Address or Business Location

Check **all** boxes this change affects:

8 ☐ Employment, excise, and other business returns (Forms 720, 940, 940-EZ, 941, 990, 1041, 1065, 1120, etc.)
9 ☐ Employee plan returns (Forms 5500 and 5500-EZ).
10 ☐ Business location

11a Business name	**11b** Employer identification number
12 Old mailing address (no., street, city or town, state, and ZIP code). If a P.O. box or foreign address, see instructions.	Room or suite no.
13 New mailing address (no., street, city or town, state, and ZIP code). If a P.O. box or foreign address, see instructions.	Room or suite no.
14 New business location (no., street, city or town, state, and ZIP code). If a foreign address, see instructions.	Room or suite no.

Part III Signature

Daytime telephone number of person to contact (optional) ▶ (   )

Sign Here ▶

Your signature	Date	If Part II completed, signature of owner, officer, or representative	Date
If joint return, spouse's signature	Date	Title	

For Privacy Act and Paperwork Reduction Act Notice, see back of form.   Cat. No. 12081V   Form **8822** (Rev. 10-2000)

675

Purpose of Form

You may use Form 8822 to notify the Internal Revenue Service if you changed your home or business mailing address or your business location. If this change also affects the mailing address for your children who filed income tax returns, complete and file a separate Form 8822 for each child. If you are a representative signing for the taxpayer, attach to Form 8822 a copy of your power of attorney.

Changing Both Home and Business Addresses? If you are, use a separate Form 8822 to show each change unless the service center under **Where To File** is the same for both home and business.

Prior Name(s)

If you or your spouse changed your name because of marriage, divorce, etc., complete line 5. Also, be sure to notify the **Social Security Administration** of your new name so that it has the same name in its records that you have on your tax return. This prevents delays in processing your return and issuing refunds. It also safeguards your future social security benefits.

Addresses

Be sure to include any apartment, room, or suite number in the space provided.

P.O. Box

Enter your box number instead of your street address **only** if your post office does not deliver mail to your street address.

Foreign Address

Enter the information in the following order: city, province or state, and country. Follow the country's practice for entering the postal code. Please **do not** abbreviate the country name.

Signature

If you are completing Part II, the owner, an officer, or a representative must sign. An officer is the president, vice president, treasurer, chief accounting officer, etc. A representative is a person who has a valid power of attorney to handle tax matters.

Where To File

Send this form to the **Internal Revenue Service Center** shown below that applies to you.

Filers Who Completed Part I

IF your old home mailing address was in. . .	THEN use this address. . .
Florida, Georgia, South Carolina, West Virginia	Atlanta, GA 39901
Colorado, Idaho, Montana, New Mexico, Oklahoma, Texas, Wyoming	Austin, TX 73301
Delaware, New Jersey, New York (New York City and counties of Nassau, Rockland, Suffolk, and Westchester)	Holtsville, NY 00501
New York (all other counties), Connecticut, Maine, Massachusetts, New Hampshire, Rhode Island, Vermont	Andover, MA 05501
Arizona, California (counties of Alpine, Amador, Butte, Calaveras, Colusa, Contra Costa, Del Norte, El Dorado, Glenn, Humboldt, Lake, Lassen, Marin, Mendocino, Modoc, Napa, Nevada, Placer, Plumas, Sacramento, San Joaquin, Shasta, Sierra, Siskiyou, Solano, Sonoma, Sutter, Tehama, Trinity, Yolo, and Yuba), Nevada, North Dakota, South Dakota, Utah, Washington	Ogden, UT 84201
Alaska, California (all other counties), Hawaii	Fresno, CA 93888
Michigan, Ohio	Cincinnati, OH 45999
District of Columbia, Indiana, Maryland, Pennsylvania, Virginia	Philadelphia, PA 19255
Alabama, Arkansas, Kentucky, Louisiana, Mississippi, Nebraska, North Carolina, Tennessee	Memphis, TN 37501
Illinois, Iowa, Kansas, Minnesota, Missouri, Oregon, Wisconsin	Kansas City, MO 64999
American Samoa	Philadelphia, PA 19255
Guam: Permanent residents	Department of Revenue and Taxation Government of Guam P.O. Box 23607 GMF, GU 96921
Guam: Nonpermanent residents Puerto Rico (or if excluding income under Internal Revenue Code section 933) Virgin Islands: Nonpermanent residents	Philadelphia, PA 19255
Virgin Islands: Permanent residents	V. I. Bureau of Internal Revenue 9601 Estate Thomas Charlotte Amalie St. Thomas, VI 00802
Foreign country: U.S. citizens and those filing Form 2555, Form 2555-EZ, or Form 4563 All APO and FPO addresses	Philadelphia, PA 19255

Filers Who Completed Part II

IF your old business address was in. . .	THEN use this address. . .
Virginia or Outside the United States	Philadelphia, PA 19255
Delaware, District of Columbia, Indiana, Kentucky, Maryland, Michigan, New Jersey, North Carolina, Ohio, Pennsylvania, South Carolina, West Virginia, Wisconsin	Cincinnati, OH 45999
Kansas, New Mexico, Oklahoma	Austin, TX 73301
Alabama, Tennessee	Memphis, TN 37501
Illinois	Kansas City, MO 64999

Alaska, Arizona, Arkansas, California (counties of Alpine, Amador, Butte, Calaveras, Colusa, Contra Costa, Del Norte, El Dorado, Glenn, Humboldt, Lake, Lassen, Marin, Mendocino, Modoc, Napa, Nevada, Placer, Plumas, Sacramento, San Joaquin, Shasta, Sierra, Siskiyou, Solano, Sonoma, Sutter, Tehama, Trinity, Yolo, and Yuba), Colorado, Hawaii, Idaho, Iowa, Louisiana, Minnesota, Mississippi, Missouri, Montana, Nebraska, Nevada, North Dakota, Oregon, South Dakota, Texas, Utah, Washington, Wyoming	Ogden, UT 84201
California (all other counties)	Fresno, CA 93888
Florida, Georgia	Atlanta, GA 39901
New York (New York City and counties of Nassau, Rockland, Suffolk, and Westchester)	Holtsville, NY 00501
New York (all other counties), Connecticut, Maine, Massachusetts, New Hampshire, Rhode Island, Vermont	Andover, MA 05501

Privacy Act and Paperwork Reduction Act Notice. We ask for the information on this form to carry out the Internal Revenue laws of the United States. We may give the information to the Department of Justice and to other Federal agencies, as provided by law. We may also give it to cities, states, the District of Columbia, and U.S. commonwealths or possessions to carry out their tax laws. And we may give it to foreign governments because of tax treaties they have with the United States.

You are not required to provide the information requested on a form that is subject to the Paperwork Reduction Act unless the form displays a valid OMB control number. Books or records relating to a form or its instructions must be retained as long as their contents may become material in the administration of any Internal Revenue law. Generally, tax returns and return information are confidential, as required by Internal Revenue Code section 6103.

The use of this form is voluntary. However, if you fail to provide the Internal Revenue Service with your current mailing address, you may not receive a notice of deficiency or a notice and demand for tax. Despite the failure to receive such notices, penalties and interest will continue to accrue on the tax deficiencies.

The time needed to complete and file this form will vary depending on individual circumstances. The estimated average time is 16 minutes.

If you have comments concerning the accuracy of this time estimate or suggestions for making this form simpler, we would be happy to hear from you. You can write to the Tax Forms Committee, Western Area Distribution Center, Rancho Cordova, CA 95743-0001. **Do not** send the form to this address. Instead, see **Where To File** on this page.

676

Form **8829**	**Expenses for Business Use of Your Home**	OMB No. 1545-1266

Form 8829

Department of the Treasury
Internal Revenue Service (99)

► File only with Schedule C (Form 1040). Use a separate Form 8829 for each home you used for business during the year.

► See separate instructions.

2001

Attachment
Sequence No. **66**

Name(s) of proprietor(s)

Your social security number

Part I — Part of Your Home Used for Business

1	Area used regularly and exclusively for business, regularly for day care, or for storage of inventory or product samples. See instructions	1	
2	Total area of home	2	
3	Divide line 1 by line 2. Enter the result as a percentage	3	%

- **For day-care facilities not used exclusively for business, also complete lines 4–6.**
- **All others, skip lines 4–6 and enter the amount from line 3 on line 7.**

4	Multiply days used for day care during year by hours used per day	4		hr.
5	Total hours available for use during the year (365 days × 24 hours). See instructions	5	8,760	hr.
6	Divide line 4 by line 5. Enter the result as a decimal amount	6	.	

7	Business percentage. For day-care facilities not used exclusively for business, multiply line 6 by line 3 (enter the result as a percentage). All others, enter the amount from line 3 ►	7	%

Part II — Figure Your Allowable Deduction

8	Enter the amount from Schedule C, line 29, **plus** any net gain or (loss) derived from the business use of your home and shown on Schedule D or Form 4797. If more than one place of business, see instructions		8	

See instructions for columns (a) and (b) before completing lines 9–20.

		(a) Direct expenses	(b) Indirect expenses	
9	Casualty losses. See instructions			
10	Deductible mortgage interest. See instructions			
11	Real estate taxes. See instructions			
12	Add lines 9, 10, and 11			
13	Multiply line 12, column (b) by line 7	13		
14	Add line 12, column (a) and line 13			14
15	Subtract line 14 from line 8. If zero or less, enter -0-			15
16	Excess mortgage interest. See instructions			
17	Insurance			
18	Repairs and maintenance			
19	Utilities			
20	Other expenses. See instructions			
21	Add lines 16 through 20			
22	Multiply line 21, column (b) by line 7	22		
23	Carryover of operating expenses from 2000 Form 8829, line 41	23		
24	Add line 21 in column (a), line 22, and line 23			24
25	Allowable operating expenses. Enter the **smaller** of line 15 or line 24			25
26	Limit on excess casualty losses and depreciation. Subtract line 25 from line 15			26
27	Excess casualty losses. See instructions	27		
28	Depreciation of your home from Part III below	28		
29	Carryover of excess casualty losses and depreciation from 2000 Form 8829, line 42	29		
30	Add lines 27 through 29			30
31	Allowable excess casualty losses and depreciation. Enter the **smaller** of line 26 or line 30			31
32	Add lines 14, 25, and 31			32
33	Casualty loss portion, if any, from lines 14 and 31. Carry amount to **Form 4684**, Section B			33
34	Allowable expenses for business use of your home. Subtract line 33 from line 32. Enter here and on Schedule C, line 30. If your home was used for more than one business, see instructions ►			34

Part III — Depreciation of Your Home

35	Enter the **smaller** of your home's adjusted basis or its fair market value. See instructions	35	
36	Value of land included on line 35	36	
37	Basis of building. Subtract line 36 from line 35	37	
38	Business basis of building. Multiply line 37 by line 7	38	
39	Depreciation percentage. See instructions	39	%
40	Depreciation allowable. Multiply line 38 by line 39. Enter here and on line 28 above. See instructions	40	

Part IV — Carryover of Unallowed Expenses to 2002

41	Operating expenses. Subtract line 25 from line 24. If less than zero, enter -0-	41	
42	Excess casualty losses and depreciation. Subtract line 31 from line 30. If less than zero, enter -0-	42	

For Paperwork Reduction Act Notice, see page 4 of separate instructions.　　Cat. No. 13232M　　Form **8829** (2001)

677

Form **8839**

Department of the Treasury
Internal Revenue Service

Qualified Adoption Expenses

▶ Attach to Form 1040 or 1040A.

▶ See separate instructions.

OMB No. 1545-1552

2001

Attachment
Sequence No. **38**

Name(s) shown on return | Your social security number

Before you begin: You need to understand the following terms. See **Definitions** on page 1 of the instructions.

- **Eligible Child**
- **Employer-Provided Adoption Benefits**
- **Qualified Adoption Expenses**

Part I | Information About Your Eligible Child or Children—You **must** complete this part. See the instructions for details, including what to do if you need more space.

1

| | (a) Child's name | | (b) Child's year of birth | Check if child was— | | | (f) Child's identifying number |
	First — Last			(c) born **before 1983** and was disabled	(d) a child with special needs	(e) a foreign child	
Child 1				☐	☐	☐	
Child 2				☐	☐	☐	

Caution: *If the child was a foreign child, see **Special Rules** in the instructions for line 1, column (e), before you complete Part II or Part III. If you received **employer-provided adoption benefits,** complete Part III on the back next.*

Part II | Adoption Credit

			Child 1		Child 2		
2	Enter $5,000 ($6,000 for a child with special needs)	**2**					
3	Did you file Form 8839 for a prior year? ☐ **No.** Enter -0-. ☐ **Yes.** See the instructions for the amount to enter.	**3**					
4	Subtract line 3 from line 2	**4**					
5	Enter the total **qualified adoption expenses** you paid in: • 2000 if the adoption was not final by the end of 2001. • 2000 and 2001 if the adoption was final in 2001. • 2001 if the adoption was final before 2001.	**5**					
6	Enter the **smaller** of line 4 or line 5 . . .	**6**					
7	Add the amounts on line 6. If zero, skip lines 8-11 and enter -0- on line 12				**7**		
8	Enter your modified adjusted gross income (see instructions) . .	**8**					
9	Is line 8 more than $75,000? ☐ **No.** Skip lines 9 and 10, and enter -0- on line 11. ☐ **Yes.** Subtract $75,000 from line 8.	**9**					
10	Divide line 9 by $40,000. Enter the result as a decimal (rounded to at least three places). Do not enter more than "1.000"			**10**	✕ .		
11	Multiply line 7 by line 10			**11**			
12	Subtract line 11 from line 7			**12**			
13	Carryforward of adoption credit from prior years (see instructions)			**13**			
14	Add lines 12 and 13. Then, see the instructions for the amount of credit to enter on Form 1040, line 49, or Form 1040A, line 32			**14**			

For Paperwork Reduction Act Notice, see page 4 of instructions. | Cat. No. 22843L | Form **8839** (2001)

Part III Employer-Provided Adoption Benefits

		Child 1	Child 2		
15	Enter $5,000 ($6,000 for a child with special needs)	**15**			
16	Did you receive **employer-provided adoption benefits** for a prior year? ☐ **No.** Enter -0-. ☐ **Yes.** See the instructions for the amount to enter.	**16**			
17	Subtract line 16 from line 15. If zero or less, enter -0-	**17**			
18	Enter the total amount of employer-provided adoption benefits you received in 2001. This amount should be shown in box 12 of your 2001 W-2 form(s) with code **T**	**18**			
19	Add the amounts on line 18				**19**
20	Enter the **smaller** of line 17 or line 18	**20**			
21	Add the amounts on line 20. If zero, skip lines 22-25, enter -0- on line 26, and go to line 27		**21**		
22	Enter your modified adjusted gross income (from the worksheet in the instructions)	**22**			
23	Is line 22 more than $75,000? ☐ **No.** Skip lines 23 and 24, and enter -0- on line 25. ☐ **Yes.** Subtract $75,000 from line 22.	**23**			
24	Divide line 23 by $40,000. Enter the result as a decimal (rounded to at least three places). Do not enter more than "1.000" . . .	**24**	✕ .		
25	Multiply line 21 by line 24	**25**			
26	**Excluded benefits.** Subtract line 25 from line 21				**26**
27	**Taxable benefits.** Subtract line 26 from line 19. Also, include this amount on Form 1040, line 7, or Form 1040A, line 7. On the line next to line 7, enter "AB".				**27**

Note: If the total adoption expenses you paid in 2001 were not fully reimbursed by your employer **and** the adoption was final in or before 2001, you may be able to claim the adoption credit in Part II on the front of this form.

Form **8863**		
Department of the Treasury Internal Revenue Service		

Education Credits
(Hope and Lifetime Learning Credits)

▶ See instructions on pages 2 and 3.   ▶ Attach to Form 1040 or Form 1040A.

OMB No. 1545-1618

2001

Attachment Sequence No. **50**

Name(s) shown on return

Your social security number

Part I   **Hope Credit. Caution:** *The Hope credit may be claimed for no more than* **2** *tax years for the* **same** *student.*

1

(a) Student's name (as shown on page 1 of your tax return) First, Last	(b) Student's social security number (as shown on page 1 of your tax return)	(c) Qualified expenses (but **do not** enter more than $2,000 for each student). See instructions	(d) Enter the **smaller** of the amount in column (c) or $1,000	(e) Subtract column (d) from column (c)	(f) Enter one-half of the amount in column (e)

------------------					

2 Add the amounts in columns (d) and (f) . . . . . | **2** | | ///////// | |

3 Tentative Hope credit. Add the amounts on line 2, columns (d) and (f) . . . . ▶ | **3** |

Part II   **Lifetime Learning Credit**

4

Caution: *You cannot take the Hope credit and the lifetime learning credit for the same student.*

(a) Student's name (as shown on page 1 of your tax return) First Last	(b) Student's social security number (as shown on page 1 of your tax return)	(c) Qualified expenses. See instructions

5 Add the amounts on line 4, column (c), and enter the total . . . . | **5** |

6 Enter the **smaller** of line 5 or $5,000 . . . . | **6** |

7 Tentative lifetime learning credit. Multiply line 6 by 20% (.20) . . . . ▶ | **7** |

Part III   **Allowable Education Credits**

8 Tentative education credits. Add lines 3 and 7 . . . . | **8** |

9 Enter: $100,000 if married filing jointly; $50,000 if single, head of household, or qualifying widow(er) . . . . | **9** |

10 Enter the amount from Form 1040, line 34 (or Form 1040A, line 20)* | **10** |

11 Subtract line 10 from line 9. If line 10 is equal to or more than line 9, **stop;** you cannot take any education credits . . . . . | **11** |

12 Enter: $20,000 if married filing jointly; $10,000 if single, head of household, or qualifying widow(er) . . . . | **12** |

13 If line 11 is equal to or more than line 12, enter the amount from line 8 on line 14 and go to line 15. If line 11 is less than line 12, divide line 11 by line 12. Enter the result as a decimal (rounded to at least three places) . . . . . | **13** | × . |

14 Multiply line 8 by line 13 . . . . ▶ | **14** |

15 Enter the amount from Form 1040, line 42 (or Form 1040A, line 26) . . . . | **15** |

16 Enter the total, if any, of your credits from Form 1040, lines 43 through 45 (or from Form 1040A, lines 27 and 28) . . . . | **16** |

17 Subtract line 16 from line 15. If line 16 is equal to or more than line 15, **stop;** you cannot take any education credits . . . . | **17** |

18 **Education credits.** Enter the **smaller** of line 14 or line 17 here and on Form 1040, line 46 (or Form 1040A, line 29) . . . . ▶ | **18** |

*See Pub. 970 for the amount to enter if you are filing Form 2555, 2555-EZ, or 4563 or you are excluding income from Puerto Rico.

For Paperwork Reduction Act Notice, see page 4.   Cat. No. 25379M   Form **8863** (2001)

General Instructions

Purpose of Form

Use Form 8863 to figure and claim your education credits. The education credits are:

- The Hope credit and
- The lifetime learning credit.

Who May Claim the Credits

You may be able to claim the credits if you, your spouse, or a dependent you claim on your tax return was a student enrolled at or attending an eligible educational institution. The credits are based on the amount of **qualified expenses** paid for the student in 2001 for academic periods beginning in 2001 and the first 3 months of 2002. However, qualified expenses **do not** include expenses paid directly or indirectly using tax-free educational assistance (see below).

Note: *If a student is claimed as a dependent on another person's tax return, only the person who claims the student as a dependent may claim the credits for the student's qualified expenses. If a student is not claimed as a dependent on another person's tax return, only the student may claim the credits.*

Generally, qualified expenses paid on behalf of the student by someone other than the student (such as a relative) are treated as paid by the student. In addition, qualified expenses paid (or treated as paid) by a student who is claimed as a dependent on your tax return are treated as paid by you. Therefore, you are treated as having paid expenses that were paid from your dependent student's earnings, gifts, inheritances, savings, etc.

You **cannot** claim the education credits if **any** of the following apply.

1. You are claimed as a dependent on another person's tax return, such as your parent's return (but see the note above).

2. Your filing status is married filing separately.

3. Your adjusted gross income (from Form 1040, line 34, or Form 1040A, line 20) is:

- $100,000 or more if married filing jointly or
- $50,000 or more if single, head of household, or qualifying widow(er).

4. You (or your spouse) were a nonresident alien for any part of 2001 and the nonresident alien did not elect to be treated as a resident alien.

Additional Information

See **Pub. 970,** Tax Benefits for Higher Education, for more information about these credits.

Rules That Apply to Both Credits

What Expenses Qualify?

Generally, **qualified expenses** are amounts paid in 2001 for tuition and fees **required** for the student's enrollment or attendance at an eligible educational institution. It does not matter whether the expenses were paid in cash, by check, by credit card, or with borrowed funds.

Qualified expenses **do not** include the following.

- Amounts paid for room and board, insurance, medical expenses (including student health fees), transportation, or other similar personal, living, or family expenses.
- Amounts paid for course-related books, supplies, equipment, and nonacademic activities, except for fees **required** to be paid to the institution as a condition of enrollment or attendance.
- Amounts paid for any course or other education involving sports, games, or hobbies, unless such course or other education is part of the student's degree program or (for the lifetime learning credit only) helps the student to acquire or improve job skills.

If you or the student take a deduction for higher education expenses, such as on Schedule A or Schedule C (Form 1040), you **cannot** use those expenses when figuring your education credits.

Tax-Free Educational Assistance and Refunds of Qualified Expenses

You must reduce the total of your qualified expenses by any tax-free educational assistance and by any refunds of qualified expenses. If the refund or tax-free assistance is received in the same year in which the expenses were paid or in the following year before you file your

tax return, reduce your qualified expenses by the amount received and figure your education credits using the reduced amount of qualified expenses. If the refund or tax-free assistance is received after you file your return for the year in which the expenses were paid, you must figure the amount by which your education credits would have been reduced if the refund or tax-free assistance had been received in the year for which you claimed the education credits. Include that amount as an additional tax for the year the refund or tax-free assistance was received on the tax line of your tax return (line 40 of the 2001 Form 1040 or line 26 of the 2001 Form 1040A). Enter the amount and "ECR" next to that line.

Example. You paid $2,250 tuition on December 26, 2000, and your child began college on January 29, 2001. You filed your 2000 tax return on February 1, 2001, and claimed a Hope credit of $1,500. After you filed your return, your child dropped two courses (but maintained one-half of a full-time workload), and you received a refund of $750. You must refigure your 2000 Hope credit using $1,500 of qualified expenses instead of $2,250. The refigured credit is $1,250. You must include the difference of $250 on line 40 of your 2001 Form 1040 or line 26 of your 2001 Form 1040A.

Tax-free educational assistance includes a tax-free scholarship or Pell grant or tax-free employer-provided educational assistance.

 *If a student received a tax-free distribution from a Coverdell education savings account (ESA) in 2001, none of that student's expenses may be used to figure any 2001 education credits. However, the student may elect to be taxed on the distribution and the expenses may then be used to figure 2001 education credits. See* **Form 8606,** *Nondeductible IRAs and Coverdell ESAs, for details.*

Prepaid Expenses

Qualified expenses paid in 2001 for an academic period that **begins** in the first 3 months of 2002 can be used in figuring your 2001 education credits. For example, if you pay $2,000 in December 2001 for qualified tuition for the 2002 winter quarter that begins in January 2002, you can use that $2,000 in figuring your 2001 education credits (if you meet all the other requirements).

 *You **cannot** use any amount paid in 2000 or 2002 to figure your 2001 education credits.*

What Is an Eligible Educational Institution?

An **eligible educational institution** is generally any accredited public, nonprofit, or proprietary (private) college, university, vocational school, or other postsecondary institution. Also, the institution must be eligible to participate in a student aid program administered by the Department of Education. Virtually all accredited postsecondary institutions meet this definition.

Specific Instructions

Part I
Hope Credit

You may be able to claim a credit of up to $1,500 for qualified expenses (defined earlier) paid for **each** student who qualifies for the Hope credit. You can claim the Hope credit for a student if **all five** of the following apply.

1. As of the beginning of 2001, the student had not completed the first 2 years of postsecondary education (generally, the freshman and sophomore years of college), as determined by the eligible educational institution. For this purpose, **do not** include academic credit awarded solely because of the student's performance on proficiency examinations.

2. The student was enrolled in 2001 in a program that leads to a degree, certificate, or other recognized educational credential.

3. The student was taking at least one-half the normal full-time workload for his or her course of study for at least one academic period beginning in 2001.

4. The Hope credit was **not** claimed for that student's expenses in more than one prior tax year.

5. The student has not been convicted of a felony for possessing or distributing a controlled substance.

If a student does not meet **all five** of the qualifications, you may be able to take the lifetime learning credit for part or all of that student's qualified expenses instead.

Line 1

Complete columns (a) through (f) on line 1 for each student who qualifies for and for whom you elect to take the Hope credit.

Column (a)

Enter the first name of the student above the dotted line, and enter the student's last name below the dotted line.

Column (c)

Enter **only** qualified expenses paid for the student in 2001 for academic periods beginning after 2000 but before April 1, 2002, as explained on page 2. If the student's expenses are more than $2,000, enter $2,000.

Note: *If you have more than three students who qualify for the Hope credit, write "See attached" next to line 1 and attach a statement with the required information for each additional student. Include the totals from line 1, columns (d) and (f), for all students in the amount you enter in columns (d) and (f) on line 2.*

Part II
Lifetime Learning Credit

The maximum lifetime learning credit for 2001 is $1,000, regardless of the number of students. For the lifetime learning credit, you **cannot** use any qualified expenses of a student for whom you elect to take the Hope credit.

Line 4

Complete columns (a) through (c) for each student for whom you are claiming the lifetime learning credit.

 *You **cannot** claim the lifetime learning credit for any student for whom you are claiming the Hope credit.*

Column (c)

Enter **only** qualified expenses paid for the student in 2001 for academic periods beginning after 2000 but before April 1, 2002, as explained on page 2.

Note: *If you are claiming the lifetime learning credit for more than five students, write "See attached" next to line 4 and attach a statement with the required information for each additional student. Include the totals from line 4, column (c), in the amount you enter on line 5.*

Part III
Allowable Education Credits

The amount of your education credits may be limited by the amount of your modified adjusted gross income or the amount of tax you owe. Part III figures these limits.

Paperwork Reduction Act Notice. We ask for the information on this form to carry out the Internal Revenue laws of the United States. You are required to give us the information. We need it to ensure that you are complying with these laws and to allow us to figure and collect the right amount of tax.

You are not required to provide the information requested on a form that is subject to the Paperwork Reduction Act unless the form displays a valid OMB control number. Books or records relating to a form or its instructions must be retained as long as their contents may become material in the administration of any Internal Revenue law. Generally, tax returns and return information are confidential, as required by Internal Revenue Code section 6103.

The time needed to complete and file this form will vary depending on individual circumstances. The estimated average time is: **Recordkeeping,** 13 min.; **Learning about the law or the form,** 10 min.; **Preparing the form,** 34 min.; **Copying, assembling, and sending the form to the IRS,** 34 min.

If you have comments concerning the accuracy of these time estimates or suggestions for making this form simpler, we would be happy to hear from you. See the instructions for the tax return with which this form is filed.

49

Tax Table and Tax Rate Schedules

Introduction

This chapter includes the official 2001 Tax Table and the 2001 Tax Rate Schedules.

The Tax Table is used to determine the tax on **taxable income** of less than $50,000 for Form 1040EZ (line 6), and Form 1040A (line 25), and less than $100,000 for Form 1040 (line 39). The Tax Rate Schedules are generally used by individuals with $100,000 or more in taxable income to determine their tax.

2001 Tax Table

Use if your taxable income is less than $100,000.
If $100,000 or more, use the Tax Rate Schedules.

Caution. Dependents, see *Tax Computation Worksheet for Certain Dependents* in your tax form package.

Example. Mr. and Mrs. Brown are filing a joint return. Their taxable income on line 39 of Form 1040 is $25,300. First, they find the $25,300–25,350 income line. Next, they find the column for married filing jointly and read down the column. The amount shown where the income line and filing status column meet is $3,799. This is the tax amount they should enter on line 40 of their Form 1040.

Sample Table

At least	But less than	Single	Married filing jointly *	Married filing separately	Head of a household
			Your tax is—		
25,200	25,250	3,784	3,784	4,112	3,784
25,250	25,300	3,791	3,791	4,126	3,791
25,300	25,350	3,799	3,799	4,139	3,799
25,350	25,400	3,806	3,806	4,153	3,806

If (taxable income) is—		And you are—			
At least	But less than	Single	Married filing jointly *	Married filing separately	Head of a household
			Your tax is—		
0	5	0	0	0	0
5	15	2	2	2	2
15	25	3	3	3	3
25	50	6	6	6	6
50	75	9	9	9	9
75	100	13	13	13	13
100	125	17	17	17	17
125	150	21	21	21	21
150	175	24	24	24	24
175	200	28	28	28	28
200	225	32	32	32	32
225	250	36	36	36	36
250	275	39	39	39	39
275	300	43	43	43	43
300	325	47	47	47	47
325	350	51	51	51	51
350	375	54	54	54	54
375	400	58	58	58	58
400	425	62	62	62	62
425	450	66	66	66	66
450	475	69	69	69	69
475	500	73	73	73	73
500	525	77	77	77	77
525	550	81	81	81	81
550	575	84	84	84	84
575	600	88	88	88	88
600	625	92	92	92	92
625	650	96	96	96	96
650	675	99	99	99	99
675	700	103	103	103	103
700	725	107	107	107	107
725	750	111	111	111	111
750	775	114	114	114	114
775	800	118	118	118	118
800	825	122	122	122	122
825	850	126	126	126	126
850	875	129	129	129	129
875	900	133	133	133	133
900	925	137	137	137	137
925	950	141	141	141	141
950	975	144	144	144	144
975	1,000	148	148	148	148

1,000

At least	But less than	Single	Married filing jointly *	Married filing separately	Head of a household
1,000	1,025	152	152	152	152
1,025	1,050	156	156	156	156
1,050	1,075	159	159	159	159
1,075	1,100	163	163	163	163
1,100	1,125	167	167	167	167
1,125	1,150	171	171	171	171
1,150	1,175	174	174	174	174
1,175	1,200	178	178	178	178
1,200	1,225	182	182	182	182
1,225	1,250	186	186	186	186
1,250	1,275	189	189	189	189
1,275	1,300	193	193	193	193

If (taxable income) is—		And you are—			
At least	But less than	Single	Married filing jointly *	Married filing separately	Head of a household
			Your tax is—		
1,300	1,325	197	197	197	197
1,325	1,350	201	201	201	201
1,350	1,375	204	204	204	204
1,375	1,400	208	208	208	208
1,400	1,425	212	212	212	212
1,425	1,450	216	216	216	216
1,450	1,475	219	219	219	219
1,475	1,500	223	223	223	223
1,500	1,525	227	227	227	227
1,525	1,550	231	231	231	231
1,550	1,575	234	234	234	234
1,575	1,600	238	238	238	238
1,600	1,625	242	242	242	242
1,625	1,650	246	246	246	246
1,650	1,675	249	249	249	249
1,675	1,700	253	253	253	253
1,700	1,725	257	257	257	257
1,725	1,750	261	261	261	261
1,750	1,775	264	264	264	264
1,775	1,800	268	268	268	268
1,800	1,825	272	272	272	272
1,825	1,850	276	276	276	276
1,850	1,875	279	279	279	279
1,875	1,900	283	283	283	283
1,900	1,925	287	287	287	287
1,925	1,950	291	291	291	291
1,950	1,975	294	294	294	294
1,975	2,000	298	298	298	298

2,000

At least	But less than	Single	Married filing jointly *	Married filing separately	Head of a household
2,000	2,025	302	302	302	302
2,025	2,050	306	306	306	306
2,050	2,075	309	309	309	309
2,075	2,100	313	313	313	313
2,100	2,125	317	317	317	317
2,125	2,150	321	321	321	321
2,150	2,175	324	324	324	324
2,175	2,200	328	328	328	328
2,200	2,225	332	332	332	332
2,225	2,250	336	336	336	336
2,250	2,275	339	339	339	339
2,275	2,300	343	343	343	343
2,300	2,325	347	347	347	347
2,325	2,350	351	351	351	351
2,350	2,375	354	354	354	354
2,375	2,400	358	358	358	358
2,400	2,425	362	362	362	362
2,425	2,450	366	366	366	366
2,450	2,475	369	369	369	369
2,475	2,500	373	373	373	373
2,500	2,525	377	377	377	377
2,525	2,550	381	381	381	381
2,550	2,575	384	384	384	384
2,575	2,600	388	388	388	388
2,600	2,625	392	392	392	392
2,625	2,650	396	396	396	396
2,650	2,675	399	399	399	399
2,675	2,700	403	403	403	403

If (taxable income) is—		And you are—			
At least	But less than	Single	Married filing jointly *	Married filing separately	Head of a household
			Your tax is—		
2,700	2,725	407	407	407	407
2,725	2,750	411	411	411	411
2,750	2,775	414	414	414	414
2,775	2,800	418	418	418	418
2,800	2,825	422	422	422	422
2,825	2,850	426	426	426	426
2,850	2,875	429	429	429	429
2,875	2,900	433	433	433	433
2,900	2,925	437	437	437	437
2,925	2,950	441	441	441	441
2,950	2,975	444	444	444	444
2,975	3,000	448	448	448	448

3,000

At least	But less than	Single	Married filing jointly *	Married filing separately	Head of a household
3,000	3,050	454	454	454	454
3,050	3,100	461	461	461	461
3,100	3,150	469	469	469	469
3,150	3,200	476	476	476	476
3,200	3,250	484	484	484	484
3,250	3,300	491	491	491	491
3,300	3,350	499	499	499	499
3,350	3,400	506	506	506	506
3,400	3,450	514	514	514	514
3,450	3,500	521	521	521	521
3,500	3,550	529	529	529	529
3,550	3,600	536	536	536	536
3,600	3,650	544	544	544	544
3,650	3,700	551	551	551	551
3,700	3,750	559	559	559	559
3,750	3,800	566	566	566	566
3,800	3,850	574	574	574	574
3,850	3,900	581	581	581	581
3,900	3,950	589	589	589	589
3,950	4,000	596	596	596	596

4,000

At least	But less than	Single	Married filing jointly *	Married filing separately	Head of a household
4,000	4,050	604	604	604	604
4,050	4,100	611	611	611	611
4,100	4,150	619	619	619	619
4,150	4,200	626	626	626	626
4,200	4,250	634	634	634	634
4,250	4,300	641	641	641	641
4,300	4,350	649	649	649	649
4,350	4,400	656	656	656	656
4,400	4,450	664	664	664	664
4,450	4,500	671	671	671	671
4,500	4,550	679	679	679	679
4,550	4,600	686	686	686	686
4,600	4,650	694	694	694	694
4,650	4,700	701	701	701	701
4,700	4,750	709	709	709	709
4,750	4,800	716	716	716	716
4,800	4,850	724	724	724	724
4,850	4,900	731	731	731	731
4,900	4,950	739	739	739	739
4,950	5,000	746	746	746	746

(Continued on next page)

* This column must also be used by a qualifying widow(er).

If (taxable income) is—		And you are—			
At least	But less than	Single	Married filing jointly *	Married filing separately	Head of a household
		Your tax is—			

5,000

At least	But less than	Single	Married filing jointly *	Married filing separately	Head of a household
5,000	5,050	754	754	754	754
5,050	5,100	761	761	761	761
5,100	5,150	769	769	769	769
5,150	5,200	776	776	776	776
5,200	5,250	784	784	784	784
5,250	5,300	791	791	791	791
5,300	5,350	799	799	799	799
5,350	5,400	806	806	806	806
5,400	5,450	814	814	814	814
5,450	5,500	821	821	821	821
5,500	5,550	829	829	829	829
5,550	5,600	836	836	836	836
5,600	5,650	844	844	844	844
5,650	5,700	851	851	851	851
5,700	5,750	859	859	859	859
5,750	5,800	866	866	866	866
5,800	5,850	874	874	874	874
5,850	5,900	881	881	881	881
5,900	5,950	889	889	889	889
5,950	6,000	896	896	896	896

6,000

At least	But less than	Single	Married filing jointly *	Married filing separately	Head of a household
6,000	6,050	904	904	904	904
6,050	6,100	911	911	911	911
6,100	6,150	919	919	919	919
6,150	6,200	926	926	926	926
6,200	6,250	934	934	934	934
6,250	6,300	941	941	941	941
6,300	6,350	949	949	949	949
6,350	6,400	956	956	956	956
6,400	6,450	964	964	964	964
6,450	6,500	971	971	971	971
6,500	6,550	979	979	979	979
6,550	6,600	986	986	986	986
6,600	6,650	994	994	994	994
6,650	6,700	1,001	1,001	1,001	1,001
6,700	6,750	1,009	1,009	1,009	1,009
6,750	6,800	1,016	1,016	1,016	1,016
6,800	6,850	1,024	1,024	1,024	1,024
6,850	6,900	1,031	1,031	1,031	1,031
6,900	6,950	1,039	1,039	1,039	1,039
6,950	7,000	1,046	1,046	1,046	1,046

7,000

At least	But less than	Single	Married filing jointly *	Married filing separately	Head of a household
7,000	7,050	1,054	1,054	1,054	1,054
7,050	7,100	1,061	1,061	1,061	1,061
7,100	7,150	1,069	1,069	1,069	1,069
7,150	7,200	1,076	1,076	1,076	1,076
7,200	7,250	1,084	1,084	1,084	1,084
7,250	7,300	1,091	1,091	1,091	1,091
7,300	7,350	1,099	1,099	1,099	1,099
7,350	7,400	1,106	1,106	1,106	1,106
7,400	7,450	1,114	1,114	1,114	1,114
7,450	7,500	1,121	1,121	1,121	1,121
7,500	7,550	1,129	1,129	1,129	1,129
7,550	7,600	1,136	1,136	1,136	1,136
7,600	7,650	1,144	1,144	1,144	1,144
7,650	7,700	1,151	1,151	1,151	1,151
7,700	7,750	1,159	1,159	1,159	1,159
7,750	7,800	1,166	1,166	1,166	1,166
7,800	7,850	1,174	1,174	1,174	1,174
7,850	7,900	1,181	1,181	1,181	1,181
7,900	7,950	1,189	1,189	1,189	1,189
7,950	8,000	1,196	1,196	1,196	1,196

8,000

At least	But less than	Single	Married filing jointly *	Married filing separately	Head of a household
8,000	8,050	1,204	1,204	1,204	1,204
8,050	8,100	1,211	1,211	1,211	1,211
8,100	8,150	1,219	1,219	1,219	1,219
8,150	8,200	1,226	1,226	1,226	1,226
8,200	8,250	1,234	1,234	1,234	1,234
8,250	8,300	1,241	1,241	1,241	1,241
8,300	8,350	1,249	1,249	1,249	1,249
8,350	8,400	1,256	1,256	1,256	1,256
8,400	8,450	1,264	1,264	1,264	1,264
8,450	8,500	1,271	1,271	1,271	1,271
8,500	8,550	1,279	1,279	1,279	1,279
8,550	8,600	1,286	1,286	1,286	1,286
8,600	8,650	1,294	1,294	1,294	1,294
8,650	8,700	1,301	1,301	1,301	1,301
8,700	8,750	1,309	1,309	1,309	1,309
8,750	8,800	1,316	1,316	1,316	1,316
8,800	8,850	1,324	1,324	1,324	1,324
8,850	8,900	1,331	1,331	1,331	1,331
8,900	8,950	1,339	1,339	1,339	1,339
8,950	9,000	1,346	1,346	1,346	1,346

9,000

At least	But less than	Single	Married filing jointly *	Married filing separately	Head of a household
9,000	9,050	1,354	1,354	1,354	1,354
9,050	9,100	1,361	1,361	1,361	1,361
9,100	9,150	1,369	1,369	1,369	1,369
9,150	9,200	1,376	1,376	1,376	1,376
9,200	9,250	1,384	1,384	1,384	1,384
9,250	9,300	1,391	1,391	1,391	1,391
9,300	9,350	1,399	1,399	1,399	1,399
9,350	9,400	1,406	1,406	1,406	1,406
9,400	9,450	1,414	1,414	1,414	1,414
9,450	9,500	1,421	1,421	1,421	1,421
9,500	9,550	1,429	1,429	1,429	1,429
9,550	9,600	1,436	1,436	1,436	1,436
9,600	9,650	1,444	1,444	1,444	1,444
9,650	9,700	1,451	1,451	1,451	1,451
9,700	9,750	1,459	1,459	1,459	1,459
9,750	9,800	1,466	1,466	1,466	1,466
9,800	9,850	1,474	1,474	1,474	1,474
9,850	9,900	1,481	1,481	1,481	1,481
9,900	9,950	1,489	1,489	1,489	1,489
9,950	10,000	1,496	1,496	1,496	1,496

10,000

At least	But less than	Single	Married filing jointly *	Married filing separately	Head of a household
10,000	10,050	1,504	1,504	1,504	1,504
10,050	10,100	1,511	1,511	1,511	1,511
10,100	10,150	1,519	1,519	1,519	1,519
10,150	10,200	1,526	1,526	1,526	1,526
10,200	10,250	1,534	1,534	1,534	1,534
10,250	10,300	1,541	1,541	1,541	1,541
10,300	10,350	1,549	1,549	1,549	1,549
10,350	10,400	1,556	1,556	1,556	1,556
10,400	10,450	1,564	1,564	1,564	1,564
10,450	10,500	1,571	1,571	1,571	1,571
10,500	10,550	1,579	1,579	1,579	1,579
10,550	10,600	1,586	1,586	1,586	1,586
10,600	10,650	1,594	1,594	1,594	1,594
10,650	10,700	1,601	1,601	1,601	1,601
10,700	10,750	1,609	1,609	1,609	1,609
10,750	10,800	1,616	1,616	1,616	1,616
10,800	10,850	1,624	1,624	1,624	1,624
10,850	10,900	1,631	1,631	1,631	1,631
10,900	10,950	1,639	1,639	1,639	1,639
10,950	11,000	1,646	1,646	1,646	1,646

11,000

At least	But less than	Single	Married filing jointly *	Married filing separately	Head of a household
11,000	11,050	1,654	1,654	1,654	1,654
11,050	11,100	1,661	1,661	1,661	1,661
11,100	11,150	1,669	1,669	1,669	1,669
11,150	11,200	1,676	1,676	1,676	1,676
11,200	11,250	1,684	1,684	1,684	1,684
11,250	11,300	1,691	1,691	1,691	1,691
11,300	11,350	1,699	1,699	1,699	1,699
11,350	11,400	1,706	1,706	1,706	1,706
11,400	11,450	1,714	1,714	1,714	1,714
11,450	11,500	1,721	1,721	1,721	1,721
11,500	11,550	1,729	1,729	1,729	1,729
11,550	11,600	1,736	1,736	1,736	1,736
11,600	11,650	1,744	1,744	1,744	1,744
11,650	11,700	1,751	1,751	1,751	1,751
11,700	11,750	1,759	1,759	1,759	1,759
11,750	11,800	1,766	1,766	1,766	1,766
11,800	11,850	1,774	1,774	1,774	1,774
11,850	11,900	1,781	1,781	1,781	1,781
11,900	11,950	1,789	1,789	1,789	1,789
11,950	12,000	1,796	1,796	1,796	1,796

12,000

At least	But less than	Single	Married filing jointly *	Married filing separately	Head of a household
12,000	12,050	1,804	1,804	1,804	1,804
12,050	12,100	1,811	1,811	1,811	1,811
12,100	12,150	1,819	1,819	1,819	1,819
12,150	12,200	1,826	1,826	1,826	1,826
12,200	12,250	1,834	1,834	1,834	1,834
12,250	12,300	1,841	1,841	1,841	1,841
12,300	12,350	1,849	1,849	1,849	1,849
12,350	12,400	1,856	1,856	1,856	1,856
12,400	12,450	1,864	1,864	1,864	1,864
12,450	12,500	1,871	1,871	1,871	1,871
12,500	12,550	1,879	1,879	1,879	1,879
12,550	12,600	1,886	1,886	1,886	1,886
12,600	12,650	1,894	1,894	1,894	1,894
12,650	12,700	1,901	1,901	1,901	1,901
12,700	12,750	1,909	1,909	1,909	1,909
12,750	12,800	1,916	1,916	1,916	1,916
12,800	12,850	1,924	1,924	1,924	1,924
12,850	12,900	1,931	1,931	1,931	1,931
12,900	12,950	1,939	1,939	1,939	1,939
12,950	13,000	1,946	1,946	1,946	1,946

13,000

At least	But less than	Single	Married filing jointly *	Married filing separately	Head of a household
13,000	13,050	1,954	1,954	1,954	1,954
13,050	13,100	1,961	1,961	1,961	1,961
13,100	13,150	1,969	1,969	1,969	1,969
13,150	13,200	1,976	1,976	1,976	1,976
13,200	13,250	1,984	1,984	1,984	1,984
13,250	13,300	1,991	1,991	1,991	1,991
13,300	13,350	1,999	1,999	1,999	1,999
13,350	13,400	2,006	2,006	2,006	2,006
13,400	13,450	2,014	2,014	2,014	2,014
13,450	13,500	2,021	2,021	2,021	2,021
13,500	13,550	2,029	2,029	2,029	2,029
13,550	13,600	2,036	2,036	2,036	2,036
13,600	13,650	2,044	2,044	2,044	2,044
13,650	13,700	2,051	2,051	2,051	2,051
13,700	13,750	2,059	2,059	2,059	2,059
13,750	13,800	2,066	2,066	2,066	2,066
13,800	13,850	2,074	2,074	2,074	2,074
13,850	13,900	2,081	2,081	2,081	2,081
13,900	13,950	2,089	2,089	2,089	2,089
13,950	14,000	2,096	2,096	2,096	2,096

* This column must also be used by a qualifying widow(er).

(Continued on next page)

If (taxable income) is—		And you are—				If (taxable income) is—		And you are—				If (taxable income) is—		And you are—			
At least	But less than	Single	Married filing jointly *	Married filing separately	Head of a house-hold	At least	But less than	Single	Married filing jointly *	Married filing separately	Head of a house-hold	At least	But less than	Single	Married filing jointly *	Married filing separately	Head of a house-hold
		Your tax is—						Your tax is—						Your tax is—			
14,000						**17,000**						**20,000**					
14,000	14,050	2,104	2,104	2,104	2,104	17,000	17,050	2,554	2,554	2,554	2,554	20,000	20,050	3,004	3,004	3,004	3,004
14,050	14,100	2,111	2,111	2,111	2,111	17,050	17,100	2,561	2,561	2,561	2,561	20,050	20,100	3,011	3,011	3,011	3,011
14,100	14,150	2,119	2,119	2,119	2,119	17,100	17,150	2,569	2,569	2,569	2,569	20,100	20,150	3,019	3,019	3,019	3,019
14,150	14,200	2,126	2,126	2,126	2,126	17,150	17,200	2,576	2,576	2,576	2,576	20,150	20,200	3,026	3,026	3,026	3,026
14,200	14,250	2,134	2,134	2,134	2,134	17,200	17,250	2,584	2,584	2,584	2,584	20,200	20,250	3,034	3,034	3,034	3,034
14,250	14,300	2,141	2,141	2,141	2,141	17,250	17,300	2,591	2,591	2,591	2,591	20,250	20,300	3,041	3,041	3,041	3,041
14,300	14,350	2,149	2,149	2,149	2,149	17,300	17,350	2,599	2,599	2,599	2,599	20,300	20,350	3,049	3,049	3,049	3,049
14,350	14,400	2,156	2,156	2,156	2,156	17,350	17,400	2,606	2,606	2,606	2,606	20,350	20,400	3,056	3,056	3,056	3,056
14,400	14,450	2,164	2,164	2,164	2,164	17,400	17,450	2,614	2,614	2,614	2,614	20,400	20,450	3,064	3,064	3,064	3,064
14,450	14,500	2,171	2,171	2,171	2,171	17,450	17,500	2,621	2,621	2,621	2,621	20,450	20,500	3,071	3,071	3,071	3,071
14,500	14,550	2,179	2,179	2,179	2,179	17,500	17,550	2,629	2,629	2,629	2,629	20,500	20,550	3,079	3,079	3,079	3,079
14,550	14,600	2,186	2,186	2,186	2,186	17,550	17,600	2,636	2,636	2,636	2,636	20,550	20,600	3,086	3,086	3,086	3,086
14,600	14,650	2,194	2,194	2,194	2,194	17,600	17,650	2,644	2,644	2,644	2,644	20,600	20,650	3,094	3,094	3,094	3,094
14,650	14,700	2,201	2,201	2,201	2,201	17,650	17,700	2,651	2,651	2,651	2,651	20,650	20,700	3,101	3,101	3,101	3,101
14,700	14,750	2,209	2,209	2,209	2,209	17,700	17,750	2,659	2,659	2,659	2,659	20,700	20,750	3,109	3,109	3,109	3,109
14,750	14,800	2,216	2,216	2,216	2,216	17,750	17,800	2,666	2,666	2,666	2,666	20,750	20,800	3,116	3,116	3,116	3,116
14,800	14,850	2,224	2,224	2,224	2,224	17,800	17,850	2,674	2,674	2,674	2,674	20,800	20,850	3,124	3,124	3,124	3,124
14,850	14,900	2,231	2,231	2,231	2,231	17,850	17,900	2,681	2,681	2,681	2,681	20,850	20,900	3,131	3,131	3,131	3,131
14,900	14,950	2,239	2,239	2,239	2,239	17,900	17,950	2,689	2,689	2,689	2,689	20,900	20,950	3,139	3,139	3,139	3,139
14,950	15,000	2,246	2,246	2,246	2,246	17,950	18,000	2,696	2,696	2,696	2,696	20,950	21,000	3,146	3,146	3,146	3,146
15,000						**18,000**						**21,000**					
15,000	15,050	2,254	2,254	2,254	2,254	18,000	18,050	2,704	2,704	2,704	2,704	21,000	21,050	3,154	3,154	3,154	3,154
15,050	15,100	2,261	2,261	2,261	2,261	18,050	18,100	2,711	2,711	2,711	2,711	21,050	21,100	3,161	3,161	3,161	3,161
15,100	15,150	2,269	2,269	2,269	2,269	18,100	18,150	2,719	2,719	2,719	2,719	21,100	21,150	3,169	3,169	3,169	3,169
15,150	15,200	2,276	2,276	2,276	2,276	18,150	18,200	2,726	2,726	2,726	2,726	21,150	21,200	3,176	3,176	3,176	3,176
15,200	15,250	2,284	2,284	2,284	2,284	18,200	18,250	2,734	2,734	2,734	2,734	21,200	21,250	3,184	3,184	3,184	3,184
15,250	15,300	2,291	2,291	2,291	2,291	18,250	18,300	2,741	2,741	2,741	2,741	21,250	21,300	3,191	3,191	3,191	3,191
15,300	15,350	2,299	2,299	2,299	2,299	18,300	18,350	2,749	2,749	2,749	2,749	21,300	21,350	3,199	3,199	3,199	3,199
15,350	15,400	2,306	2,306	2,306	2,306	18,350	18,400	2,756	2,756	2,756	2,756	21,350	21,400	3,206	3,206	3,206	3,206
15,400	15,450	2,314	2,314	2,314	2,314	18,400	18,450	2,764	2,764	2,764	2,764	21,400	21,450	3,214	3,214	3,214	3,214
15,450	15,500	2,321	2,321	2,321	2,321	18,450	18,500	2,771	2,771	2,771	2,771	21,450	21,500	3,221	3,221	3,221	3,221
15,500	15,550	2,329	2,329	2,329	2,329	18,500	18,550	2,779	2,779	2,779	2,779	21,500	21,550	3,229	3,229	3,229	3,229
15,550	15,600	2,336	2,336	2,336	2,336	18,550	18,600	2,786	2,786	2,786	2,786	21,550	21,600	3,236	3,236	3,236	3,236
15,600	15,650	2,344	2,344	2,344	2,344	18,600	18,650	2,794	2,794	2,794	2,794	21,600	21,650	3,244	3,244	3,244	3,244
15,650	15,700	2,351	2,351	2,351	2,351	18,650	18,700	2,801	2,801	2,801	2,801	21,650	21,700	3,251	3,251	3,251	3,251
15,700	15,750	2,359	2,359	2,359	2,359	18,700	18,750	2,809	2,809	2,809	2,809	21,700	21,750	3,259	3,259	3,259	3,259
15,750	15,800	2,366	2,366	2,366	2,366	18,750	18,800	2,816	2,816	2,816	2,816	21,750	21,800	3,266	3,266	3,266	3,266
15,800	15,850	2,374	2,374	2,374	2,374	18,800	18,850	2,824	2,824	2,824	2,824	21,800	21,850	3,274	3,274	3,274	3,274
15,850	15,900	2,381	2,381	2,381	2,381	18,850	18,900	2,831	2,831	2,831	2,831	21,850	21,900	3,281	3,281	3,281	3,281
15,900	15,950	2,389	2,389	2,389	2,389	18,900	18,950	2,839	2,839	2,839	2,839	21,900	21,950	3,289	3,289	3,289	3,289
15,950	16,000	2,396	2,396	2,396	2,396	18,950	19,000	2,846	2,846	2,846	2,846	21,950	22,000	3,296	3,296	3,296	3,296
16,000						**19,000**						**22,000**					
16,000	16,050	2,404	2,404	2,404	2,404	19,000	19,050	2,854	2,854	2,854	2,854	22,000	22,050	3,304	3,304	3,304	3,304
16,050	16,100	2,411	2,411	2,411	2,411	19,050	19,100	2,861	2,861	2,861	2,861	22,050	22,100	3,311	3,311	3,311	3,311
16,100	16,150	2,419	2,419	2,419	2,419	19,100	19,150	2,869	2,869	2,869	2,869	22,100	22,150	3,319	3,319	3,319	3,319
16,150	16,200	2,426	2,426	2,426	2,426	19,150	19,200	2,876	2,876	2,876	2,876	22,150	22,200	3,326	3,326	3,326	3,326
16,200	16,250	2,434	2,434	2,434	2,434	19,200	19,250	2,884	2,884	2,884	2,884	22,200	22,250	3,334	3,334	3,334	3,334
16,250	16,300	2,441	2,441	2,441	2,441	19,250	19,300	2,891	2,891	2,891	2,891	22,250	22,300	3,341	3,341	3,341	3,341
16,300	16,350	2,449	2,449	2,449	2,449	19,300	19,350	2,899	2,899	2,899	2,899	22,300	22,350	3,349	3,349	3,349	3,349
16,350	16,400	2,456	2,456	2,456	2,456	19,350	19,400	2,906	2,906	2,906	2,906	22,350	22,400	3,356	3,356	3,356	3,356
16,400	16,450	2,464	2,464	2,464	2,464	19,400	19,450	2,914	2,914	2,914	2,914	22,400	22,450	3,364	3,364	3,364	3,364
16,450	16,500	2,471	2,471	2,471	2,471	19,450	19,500	2,921	2,921	2,921	2,921	22,450	22,500	3,371	3,371	3,371	3,371
16,500	16,550	2,479	2,479	2,479	2,479	19,500	19,550	2,929	2,929	2,929	2,929	22,500	22,550	3,379	3,379	3,379	3,379
16,550	16,600	2,486	2,486	2,486	2,486	19,550	19,600	2,936	2,936	2,936	2,936	22,550	22,600	3,386	3,386	3,386	3,386
16,600	16,650	2,494	2,494	2,494	2,494	19,600	19,650	2,944	2,944	2,944	2,944	22,600	22,650	3,394	3,394	3,397	3,394
16,650	16,700	2,501	2,501	2,501	2,501	19,650	19,700	2,951	2,951	2,951	2,951	22,650	22,700	3,401	3,401	3,411	3,401
16,700	16,750	2,509	2,509	2,509	2,509	19,700	19,750	2,959	2,959	2,959	2,959	22,700	22,750	3,409	3,409	3,424	3,409
16,750	16,800	2,516	2,516	2,516	2,516	19,750	19,800	2,966	2,966	2,966	2,966	22,750	22,800	3,416	3,416	3,438	3,416
16,800	16,850	2,524	2,524	2,524	2,524	19,800	19,850	2,974	2,974	2,974	2,974	22,800	22,850	3,424	3,424	3,452	3,424
16,850	16,900	2,531	2,531	2,531	2,531	19,850	19,900	2,981	2,981	2,981	2,981	22,850	22,900	3,431	3,431	3,466	3,431
16,900	16,950	2,539	2,539	2,539	2,539	19,900	19,950	2,989	2,989	2,989	2,989	22,900	22,950	3,439	3,439	3,479	3,439
16,950	17,000	2,546	2,546	2,546	2,546	19,950	20,000	2,996	2,996	2,996	2,996	22,950	23,000	3,446	3,446	3,493	3,446

* This column must also be used by a qualifying widow(er).

(Continued on next page)

23,000

At least	But less than	Single	Married filing jointly *	Married filing separately	Head of a household
23,000	23,050	3,454	3,454	3,507	3,454
23,050	23,100	3,461	3,461	3,521	3,461
23,100	23,150	3,469	3,469	3,534	3,469
23,150	23,200	3,476	3,476	3,548	3,476
23,200	23,250	3,484	3,484	3,562	3,484
23,250	23,300	3,491	3,491	3,576	3,491
23,300	23,350	3,499	3,499	3,589	3,499
23,350	23,400	3,506	3,506	3,603	3,506
23,400	23,450	3,514	3,514	3,617	3,514
23,450	23,500	3,521	3,521	3,631	3,521
23,500	23,550	3,529	3,529	3,644	3,529
23,550	23,600	3,536	3,536	3,658	3,536
23,600	23,650	3,544	3,544	3,672	3,544
23,650	23,700	3,551	3,551	3,686	3,551
23,700	23,750	3,559	3,559	3,699	3,559
23,750	23,800	3,566	3,566	3,713	3,566
23,800	23,850	3,574	3,574	3,727	3,574
23,850	23,900	3,581	3,581	3,741	3,581
23,900	23,950	3,589	3,589	3,754	3,589
23,950	24,000	3,596	3,596	3,768	3,596

24,000

At least	But less than	Single	Married filing jointly *	Married filing separately	Head of a household
24,000	24,050	3,604	3,604	3,782	3,604
24,050	24,100	3,611	3,611	3,796	3,611
24,100	24,150	3,619	3,619	3,809	3,619
24,150	24,200	3,626	3,626	3,823	3,626
24,200	24,250	3,634	3,634	3,837	3,634
24,250	24,300	3,641	3,641	3,851	3,641
24,300	24,350	3,649	3,649	3,864	3,649
24,350	24,400	3,656	3,656	3,878	3,656
24,400	24,450	3,664	3,664	3,892	3,664
24,450	24,500	3,671	3,671	3,906	3,671
24,500	24,550	3,679	3,679	3,919	3,679
24,550	24,600	3,686	3,686	3,933	3,686
24,600	24,650	3,694	3,694	3,947	3,694
24,650	24,700	3,701	3,701	3,961	3,701
24,700	24,750	3,709	3,709	3,974	3,709
24,750	24,800	3,716	3,716	3,988	3,716
24,800	24,850	3,724	3,724	4,002	3,724
24,850	24,900	3,731	3,731	4,016	3,731
24,900	24,950	3,739	3,739	4,029	3,739
24,950	25,000	3,746	3,746	4,043	3,746

25,000

At least	But less than	Single	Married filing jointly *	Married filing separately	Head of a household
25,000	25,050	3,754	3,754	4,057	3,754
25,050	25,100	3,761	3,761	4,071	3,761
25,100	25,150	3,769	3,769	4,084	3,769
25,150	25,200	3,776	3,776	4,098	3,776
25,200	25,250	3,784	3,784	4,112	3,784
25,250	25,300	3,791	3,791	4,126	3,791
25,300	25,350	3,799	3,799	4,139	3,799
25,350	25,400	3,806	3,806	4,153	3,806
25,400	25,450	3,814	3,814	4,167	3,814
25,450	25,500	3,821	3,821	4,181	3,821
25,500	25,550	3,829	3,829	4,194	3,829
25,550	25,600	3,836	3,836	4,208	3,836
25,600	25,650	3,844	3,844	4,222	3,844
25,650	25,700	3,851	3,851	4,236	3,851
25,700	25,750	3,859	3,859	4,249	3,859
25,750	25,800	3,866	3,866	4,263	3,866
25,800	25,850	3,874	3,874	4,277	3,874
25,850	25,900	3,881	3,881	4,291	3,881
25,900	25,950	3,889	3,889	4,304	3,889
25,950	26,000	3,896	3,896	4,318	3,896

26,000

At least	But less than	Single	Married filing jointly *	Married filing separately	Head of a household
26,000	26,050	3,904	3,904	4,332	3,904
26,050	26,100	3,911	3,911	4,346	3,911
26,100	26,150	3,919	3,919	4,359	3,919
26,150	26,200	3,926	3,926	4,373	3,926
26,200	26,250	3,934	3,934	4,387	3,934
26,250	26,300	3,941	3,941	4,401	3,941
26,300	26,350	3,949	3,949	4,414	3,949
26,350	26,400	3,956	3,956	4,428	3,956
26,400	26,450	3,964	3,964	4,442	3,964
26,450	26,500	3,971	3,971	4,456	3,971
26,500	26,550	3,979	3,979	4,469	3,979
26,550	26,600	3,986	3,986	4,483	3,986
26,600	26,650	3,994	3,994	4,497	3,994
26,650	26,700	4,001	4,001	4,511	4,001
26,700	26,750	4,009	4,009	4,524	4,009
26,750	26,800	4,016	4,016	4,538	4,016
26,800	26,850	4,024	4,024	4,552	4,024
26,850	26,900	4,031	4,031	4,566	4,031
26,900	26,950	4,039	4,039	4,579	4,039
26,950	27,000	4,046	4,046	4,593	4,046

27,000

At least	But less than	Single	Married filing jointly *	Married filing separately	Head of a household
27,000	27,050	4,054	4,054	4,607	4,054
27,050	27,100	4,064	4,061	4,621	4,061
27,100	27,150	4,078	4,069	4,634	4,069
27,150	27,200	4,092	4,076	4,648	4,076
27,200	27,250	4,106	4,084	4,662	4,084
27,250	27,300	4,119	4,091	4,676	4,091
27,300	27,350	4,133	4,099	4,689	4,099
27,350	27,400	4,147	4,106	4,703	4,106
27,400	27,450	4,161	4,114	4,717	4,114
27,450	27,500	4,174	4,121	4,731	4,121
27,500	27,550	4,188	4,129	4,744	4,129
27,550	27,600	4,202	4,136	4,758	4,136
27,600	27,650	4,216	4,144	4,772	4,144
27,650	27,700	4,229	4,151	4,786	4,151
27,700	27,750	4,243	4,159	4,799	4,159
27,750	27,800	4,257	4,166	4,813	4,166
27,800	27,850	4,271	4,174	4,827	4,174
27,850	27,900	4,284	4,181	4,841	4,181
27,900	27,950	4,298	4,189	4,854	4,189
27,950	28,000	4,312	4,196	4,868	4,196

28,000

At least	But less than	Single	Married filing jointly *	Married filing separately	Head of a household
28,000	28,050	4,326	4,204	4,882	4,204
28,050	28,100	4,339	4,211	4,896	4,211
28,100	28,150	4,353	4,219	4,909	4,219
28,150	28,200	4,367	4,226	4,923	4,226
28,200	28,250	4,381	4,234	4,937	4,234
28,250	28,300	4,394	4,241	4,951	4,241
28,300	28,350	4,408	4,249	4,964	4,249
28,350	28,400	4,422	4,256	4,978	4,256
28,400	28,450	4,436	4,264	4,992	4,264
28,450	28,500	4,449	4,271	5,006	4,271
28,500	28,550	4,463	4,279	5,019	4,279
28,550	28,600	4,477	4,286	5,033	4,286
28,600	28,650	4,491	4,294	5,047	4,294
28,650	28,700	4,504	4,301	5,061	4,301
28,700	28,750	4,518	4,309	5,074	4,309
28,750	28,800	4,532	4,316	5,088	4,316
28,800	28,850	4,546	4,324	5,102	4,324
28,850	28,900	4,559	4,331	5,116	4,331
28,900	28,950	4,573	4,339	5,129	4,339
28,950	29,000	4,587	4,346	5,143	4,346

29,000

At least	But less than	Single	Married filing jointly *	Married filing separately	Head of a household
29,000	29,050	4,601	4,354	5,157	4,354
29,050	29,100	4,614	4,361	5,171	4,361
29,100	29,150	4,628	4,369	5,184	4,369
29,150	29,200	4,642	4,376	5,198	4,376
29,200	29,250	4,656	4,384	5,212	4,384
29,250	29,300	4,669	4,391	5,226	4,391
29,300	29,350	4,683	4,399	5,239	4,399
29,350	29,400	4,697	4,406	5,253	4,406
29,400	29,450	4,711	4,414	5,267	4,414
29,450	29,500	4,724	4,421	5,281	4,421
29,500	29,550	4,738	4,429	5,294	4,429
29,550	29,600	4,752	4,436	5,308	4,436
29,600	29,650	4,766	4,444	5,322	4,444
29,650	29,700	4,779	4,451	5,336	4,451
29,700	29,750	4,793	4,459	5,349	4,459
29,750	29,800	4,807	4,466	5,363	4,466
29,800	29,850	4,821	4,474	5,377	4,474
29,850	29,900	4,834	4,481	5,391	4,481
29,900	29,950	4,848	4,489	5,404	4,489
29,950	30,000	4,862	4,496	5,418	4,496

30,000

At least	But less than	Single	Married filing jointly *	Married filing separately	Head of a household
30,000	30,050	4,876	4,504	5,432	4,504
30,050	30,100	4,889	4,511	5,446	4,511
30,100	30,150	4,903	4,519	5,459	4,519
30,150	30,200	4,917	4,526	5,473	4,526
30,200	30,250	4,931	4,534	5,487	4,534
30,250	30,300	4,944	4,541	5,501	4,541
30,300	30,350	4,958	4,549	5,514	4,549
30,350	30,400	4,972	4,556	5,528	4,556
30,400	30,450	4,986	4,564	5,542	4,564
30,450	30,500	4,999	4,571	5,556	4,571
30,500	30,550	5,013	4,579	5,569	4,579
30,550	30,600	5,027	4,586	5,583	4,586
30,600	30,650	5,041	4,594	5,597	4,594
30,650	30,700	5,054	4,601	5,611	4,601
30,700	30,750	5,068	4,609	5,624	4,609
30,750	30,800	5,082	4,616	5,638	4,616
30,800	30,850	5,096	4,624	5,652	4,624
30,850	30,900	5,109	4,631	5,666	4,631
30,900	30,950	5,123	4,639	5,679	4,639
30,950	31,000	5,137	4,646	5,693	4,646

31,000

At least	But less than	Single	Married filing jointly *	Married filing separately	Head of a household
31,000	31,050	5,151	4,654	5,707	4,654
31,050	31,100	5,164	4,661	5,721	4,661
31,100	31,150	5,178	4,669	5,734	4,669
31,150	31,200	5,192	4,676	5,748	4,676
31,200	31,250	5,206	4,684	5,762	4,684
31,250	31,300	5,219	4,691	5,776	4,691
31,300	31,350	5,233	4,699	5,789	4,699
31,350	31,400	5,247	4,706	5,803	4,706
31,400	31,450	5,261	4,714	5,817	4,714
31,450	31,500	5,274	4,721	5,831	4,721
31,500	31,550	5,288	4,729	5,844	4,729
31,550	31,600	5,302	4,736	5,858	4,736
31,600	31,650	5,316	4,744	5,872	4,744
31,650	31,700	5,329	4,751	5,886	4,751
31,700	31,750	5,343	4,759	5,899	4,759
31,750	31,800	5,357	4,766	5,913	4,766
31,800	31,850	5,371	4,774	5,927	4,774
31,850	31,900	5,384	4,781	5,941	4,781
31,900	31,950	5,398	4,789	5,954	4,789
31,950	32,000	5,412	4,796	5,968	4,796

* This column must also be used by a qualifying widow(er).

(Continued on next page)

32,000 / 33,000 / 34,000

At least	But less than	Single	Married filing jointly *	Married filing separately	Head of a household
32,000					
32,000	32,050	5,426	4,804	5,982	4,804
32,050	32,100	5,439	4,811	5,996	4,811
32,100	32,150	5,453	4,819	6,009	4,819
32,150	32,200	5,467	4,826	6,023	4,826
32,200	32,250	5,481	4,834	6,037	4,834
32,250	32,300	5,494	4,841	6,051	4,841
32,300	32,350	5,508	4,849	6,064	4,849
32,350	32,400	5,522	4,856	6,078	4,856
32,400	32,450	5,536	4,864	6,092	4,864
32,450	32,500	5,549	4,871	6,106	4,871
32,500	32,550	5,563	4,879	6,119	4,879
32,550	32,600	5,577	4,886	6,133	4,886
32,600	32,650	5,591	4,894	6,147	4,894
32,650	32,700	5,604	4,901	6,161	4,901
32,700	32,750	5,618	4,909	6,174	4,909
32,750	32,800	5,632	4,916	6,188	4,916
32,800	32,850	5,646	4,924	6,202	4,924
32,850	32,900	5,659	4,931	6,216	4,931
32,900	32,950	5,673	4,939	6,229	4,939
32,950	33,000	5,687	4,946	6,243	4,946
33,000					
33,000	33,050	5,701	4,954	6,257	4,954
33,050	33,100	5,714	4,961	6,271	4,961
33,100	33,150	5,728	4,969	6,284	4,969
33,150	33,200	5,742	4,976	6,298	4,976
33,200	33,250	5,756	4,984	6,312	4,984
33,250	33,300	5,769	4,991	6,326	4,991
33,300	33,350	5,783	4,999	6,339	4,999
33,350	33,400	5,797	5,006	6,353	5,006
33,400	33,450	5,811	5,014	6,367	5,014
33,450	33,500	5,824	5,021	6,381	5,021
33,500	33,550	5,838	5,029	6,394	5,029
33,550	33,600	5,852	5,036	6,408	5,036
33,600	33,650	5,866	5,044	6,422	5,044
33,650	33,700	5,879	5,051	6,436	5,051
33,700	33,750	5,893	5,059	6,449	5,059
33,750	33,800	5,907	5,066	6,463	5,066
33,800	33,850	5,921	5,074	6,477	5,074
33,850	33,900	5,934	5,081	6,491	5,081
33,900	33,950	5,948	5,089	6,504	5,089
33,950	34,000	5,962	5,096	6,518	5,096
34,000					
34,000	34,050	5,976	5,104	6,532	5,104
34,050	34,100	5,989	5,111	6,546	5,111
34,100	34,150	6,003	5,119	6,559	5,119
34,150	34,200	6,017	5,126	6,573	5,126
34,200	34,250	6,031	5,134	6,587	5,134
34,250	34,300	6,044	5,141	6,601	5,141
34,300	34,350	6,058	5,149	6,614	5,149
34,350	34,400	6,072	5,156	6,628	5,156
34,400	34,450	6,086	5,164	6,642	5,164
34,450	34,500	6,099	5,171	6,656	5,171
34,500	34,550	6,113	5,179	6,669	5,179
34,550	34,600	6,127	5,186	6,683	5,186
34,600	34,650	6,141	5,194	6,697	5,194
34,650	34,700	6,154	5,201	6,711	5,201
34,700	34,750	6,168	5,209	6,724	5,209
34,750	34,800	6,182	5,216	6,738	5,216
34,800	34,850	6,196	5,224	6,752	5,224
34,850	34,900	6,209	5,231	6,766	5,231
34,900	34,950	6,223	5,239	6,779	5,239
34,950	35,000	6,237	5,246	6,793	5,246

35,000 / 36,000 / 37,000

At least	But less than	Single	Married filing jointly *	Married filing separately	Head of a household
35,000					
35,000	35,050	6,251	5,254	6,807	5,254
35,050	35,100	6,264	5,261	6,821	5,261
35,100	35,150	6,278	5,269	6,834	5,269
35,150	35,200	6,292	5,276	6,848	5,276
35,200	35,250	6,306	5,284	6,862	5,284
35,250	35,300	6,319	5,291	6,876	5,291
35,300	35,350	6,333	5,299	6,889	5,299
35,350	35,400	6,347	5,306	6,903	5,306
35,400	35,450	6,361	5,314	6,917	5,314
35,450	35,500	6,374	5,321	6,931	5,321
35,500	35,550	6,388	5,329	6,944	5,329
35,550	35,600	6,402	5,336	6,958	5,336
35,600	35,650	6,416	5,344	6,972	5,344
35,650	35,700	6,429	5,351	6,986	5,351
35,700	35,750	6,443	5,359	6,999	5,359
35,750	35,800	6,457	5,366	7,013	5,366
35,800	35,850	6,471	5,374	7,027	5,374
35,850	35,900	6,484	5,381	7,041	5,381
35,900	35,950	6,498	5,389	7,054	5,389
35,950	36,000	6,512	5,396	7,068	5,396
36,000					
36,000	36,050	6,526	5,404	7,082	5,404
36,050	36,100	6,539	5,411	7,096	5,411
36,100	36,150	6,553	5,419	7,109	5,419
36,150	36,200	6,567	5,426	7,123	5,426
36,200	36,250	6,581	5,434	7,137	5,434
36,250	36,300	6,594	5,441	7,151	5,444
36,300	36,350	6,608	5,449	7,164	5,458
36,350	36,400	6,622	5,456	7,178	5,472
36,400	36,450	6,636	5,464	7,192	5,486
36,450	36,500	6,649	5,471	7,206	5,499
36,500	36,550	6,663	5,479	7,219	5,513
36,550	36,600	6,677	5,486	7,233	5,527
36,600	36,650	6,691	5,494	7,247	5,541
36,650	36,700	6,704	5,501	7,261	5,554
36,700	36,750	6,718	5,509	7,274	5,568
36,750	36,800	6,732	5,516	7,288	5,582
36,800	36,850	6,746	5,524	7,302	5,596
36,850	36,900	6,759	5,531	7,316	5,609
36,900	36,950	6,773	5,539	7,329	5,623
36,950	37,000	6,787	5,546	7,343	5,637
37,000					
37,000	37,050	6,801	5,554	7,357	5,651
37,050	37,100	6,814	5,561	7,371	5,664
37,100	37,150	6,828	5,569	7,384	5,678
37,150	37,200	6,842	5,576	7,398	5,692
37,200	37,250	6,856	5,584	7,412	5,706
37,250	37,300	6,869	5,591	7,426	5,719
37,300	37,350	6,883	5,599	7,439	5,733
37,350	37,400	6,897	5,606	7,453	5,747
37,400	37,450	6,911	5,614	7,467	5,761
37,450	37,500	6,924	5,621	7,481	5,774
37,500	37,550	6,938	5,629	7,494	5,788
37,550	37,600	6,952	5,636	7,508	5,802
37,600	37,650	6,966	5,644	7,522	5,816
37,650	37,700	6,979	5,651	7,536	5,829
37,700	37,750	6,993	5,659	7,549	5,843
37,750	37,800	7,007	5,666	7,563	5,857
37,800	37,850	7,021	5,674	7,577	5,871
37,850	37,900	7,034	5,681	7,591	5,884
37,900	37,950	7,048	5,689	7,604	5,898
37,950	38,000	7,062	5,696	7,618	5,912

38,000 / 39,000 / 40,000

At least	But less than	Single	Married filing jointly *	Married filing separately	Head of a household
38,000					
38,000	38,050	7,076	5,704	7,632	5,926
38,050	38,100	7,089	5,711	7,646	5,939
38,100	38,150	7,103	5,719	7,659	5,953
38,150	38,200	7,117	5,726	7,673	5,967
38,200	38,250	7,131	5,734	7,687	5,981
38,250	38,300	7,144	5,741	7,701	5,994
38,300	38,350	7,158	5,749	7,714	6,008
38,350	38,400	7,172	5,756	7,728	6,022
38,400	38,450	7,186	5,764	7,742	6,036
38,450	38,500	7,199	5,771	7,756	6,049
38,500	38,550	7,213	5,779	7,769	6,063
38,550	38,600	7,227	5,786	7,783	6,077
38,600	38,650	7,241	5,794	7,797	6,091
38,650	38,700	7,254	5,801	7,811	6,104
38,700	38,750	7,268	5,809	7,824	6,118
38,750	38,800	7,282	5,816	7,838	6,132
38,800	38,850	7,296	5,824	7,852	6,146
38,850	38,900	7,309	5,831	7,866	6,159
38,900	38,950	7,323	5,839	7,879	6,173
38,950	39,000	7,337	5,846	7,893	6,187
39,000					
39,000	39,050	7,351	5,854	7,907	6,201
39,050	39,100	7,364	5,861	7,921	6,214
39,100	39,150	7,378	5,869	7,934	6,228
39,150	39,200	7,392	5,876	7,948	6,242
39,200	39,250	7,406	5,884	7,962	6,256
39,250	39,300	7,419	5,891	7,976	6,269
39,300	39,350	7,433	5,899	7,989	6,283
39,350	39,400	7,447	5,906	8,003	6,297
39,400	39,450	7,461	5,914	8,017	6,311
39,450	39,500	7,474	5,921	8,031	6,324
39,500	39,550	7,488	5,929	8,044	6,338
39,550	39,600	7,502	5,936	8,058	6,352
39,600	39,650	7,516	5,944	8,072	6,366
39,650	39,700	7,529	5,951	8,086	6,379
39,700	39,750	7,543	5,959	8,099	6,393
39,750	39,800	7,557	5,966	8,113	6,407
39,800	39,850	7,571	5,974	8,127	6,421
39,850	39,900	7,584	5,981	8,141	6,434
39,900	39,950	7,598	5,989	8,154	6,448
39,950	40,000	7,612	5,996	8,168	6,462
40,000					
40,000	40,050	7,626	6,004	8,182	6,476
40,050	40,100	7,639	6,011	8,196	6,489
40,100	40,150	7,653	6,019	8,209	6,503
40,150	40,200	7,667	6,026	8,223	6,517
40,200	40,250	7,681	6,034	8,237	6,531
40,250	40,300	7,694	6,041	8,251	6,544
40,300	40,350	7,708	6,049	8,264	6,558
40,350	40,400	7,722	6,056	8,278	6,572
40,400	40,450	7,736	6,064	8,292	6,586
40,450	40,500	7,749	6,071	8,306	6,599
40,500	40,550	7,763	6,079	8,319	6,613
40,550	40,600	7,777	6,086	8,333	6,627
40,600	40,650	7,791	6,094	8,347	6,641
40,650	40,700	7,804	6,101	8,361	6,654
40,700	40,750	7,818	6,109	8,374	6,668
40,750	40,800	7,832	6,116	8,388	6,682
40,800	40,850	7,846	6,124	8,402	6,696
40,850	40,900	7,859	6,131	8,416	6,709
40,900	40,950	7,873	6,139	8,429	6,723
40,950	41,000	7,887	6,146	8,443	6,737

* This column must also be used by a qualifying widow(er).

(Continued on next page)

41,000

At least	But less than	Single	Married filing jointly *	Married filing separately	Head of a household
41,000	41,050	7,901	6,154	8,457	6,751
41,050	41,100	7,914	6,161	8,471	6,764
41,100	41,150	7,928	6,169	8,484	6,778
41,150	41,200	7,942	6,176	8,498	6,792
41,200	41,250	7,956	6,184	8,512	6,806
41,250	41,300	7,969	6,191	8,526	6,819
41,300	41,350	7,983	6,199	8,539	6,833
41,350	41,400	7,997	6,206	8,553	6,847
41,400	41,450	8,011	6,214	8,567	6,861
41,450	41,500	8,024	6,221	8,581	6,874
41,500	41,550	8,038	6,229	8,594	6,888
41,550	41,600	8,052	6,236	8,608	6,902
41,600	41,650	8,066	6,244	8,622	6,916
41,650	41,700	8,079	6,251	8,636	6,929
41,700	41,750	8,093	6,259	8,649	6,943
41,750	41,800	8,107	6,266	8,663	6,957
41,800	41,850	8,121	6,274	8,677	6,971
41,850	41,900	8,134	6,281	8,691	6,984
41,900	41,950	8,148	6,289	8,704	6,998
41,950	42,000	8,162	6,296	8,718	7,012

42,000

At least	But less than	Single	Married filing jointly *	Married filing separately	Head of a household
42,000	42,050	8,176	6,304	8,732	7,026
42,050	42,100	8,189	6,311	8,746	7,039
42,100	42,150	8,203	6,319	8,759	7,053
42,150	42,200	8,217	6,326	8,773	7,067
42,200	42,250	8,231	6,334	8,787	7,081
42,250	42,300	8,244	6,341	8,801	7,094
42,300	42,350	8,258	6,349	8,814	7,108
42,350	42,400	8,272	6,356	8,828	7,122
42,400	42,450	8,286	6,364	8,842	7,136
42,450	42,500	8,299	6,371	8,856	7,149
42,500	42,550	8,313	6,379	8,869	7,163
42,550	42,600	8,327	6,386	8,883	7,177
42,600	42,650	8,341	6,394	8,897	7,191
42,650	42,700	8,354	6,401	8,911	7,204
42,700	42,750	8,368	6,409	8,924	7,218
42,750	42,800	8,382	6,416	8,938	7,232
42,800	42,850	8,396	6,424	8,952	7,246
42,850	42,900	8,409	6,431	8,966	7,259
42,900	42,950	8,423	6,439	8,979	7,273
42,950	43,000	8,437	6,446	8,993	7,287

43,000

At least	But less than	Single	Married filing jointly *	Married filing separately	Head of a household
43,000	43,050	8,451	6,454	9,007	7,301
43,050	43,100	8,464	6,461	9,021	7,314
43,100	43,150	8,478	6,469	9,034	7,328
43,150	43,200	8,492	6,476	9,048	7,342
43,200	43,250	8,506	6,484	9,062	7,356
43,250	43,300	8,519	6,491	9,076	7,369
43,300	43,350	8,533	6,499	9,089	7,383
43,350	43,400	8,547	6,506	9,103	7,397
43,400	43,450	8,561	6,514	9,117	7,411
43,450	43,500	8,574	6,521	9,131	7,424
43,500	43,550	8,588	6,529	9,144	7,438
43,550	43,600	8,602	6,536	9,158	7,452
43,600	43,650	8,616	6,544	9,172	7,466
43,650	43,700	8,629	6,551	9,186	7,479
43,700	43,750	8,643	6,559	9,199	7,493
43,750	43,800	8,657	6,566	9,213	7,507
43,800	43,850	8,671	6,574	9,227	7,521
43,850	43,900	8,684	6,581	9,241	7,534
43,900	43,950	8,698	6,589	9,254	7,548
43,950	44,000	8,712	6,596	9,268	7,562

44,000

At least	But less than	Single	Married filing jointly *	Married filing separately	Head of a household
44,000	44,050	8,726	6,604	9,282	7,576
44,050	44,100	8,739	6,611	9,296	7,589
44,100	44,150	8,753	6,619	9,309	7,603
44,150	44,200	8,767	6,626	9,323	7,617
44,200	44,250	8,781	6,634	9,337	7,631
44,250	44,300	8,794	6,641	9,351	7,644
44,300	44,350	8,808	6,649	9,364	7,658
44,350	44,400	8,822	6,656	9,378	7,672
44,400	44,450	8,836	6,664	9,392	7,686
44,450	44,500	8,849	6,671	9,406	7,699
44,500	44,550	8,863	6,679	9,419	7,713
44,550	44,600	8,877	6,686	9,433	7,727
44,600	44,650	8,891	6,694	9,447	7,741
44,650	44,700	8,904	6,701	9,461	7,754
44,700	44,750	8,918	6,709	9,474	7,768
44,750	44,800	8,932	6,716	9,488	7,782
44,800	44,850	8,946	6,724	9,502	7,796
44,850	44,900	8,959	6,731	9,516	7,809
44,900	44,950	8,973	6,739	9,529	7,823
44,950	45,000	8,987	6,746	9,543	7,837

45,000

At least	But less than	Single	Married filing jointly *	Married filing separately	Head of a household
45,000	45,050	9,001	6,754	9,557	7,851
45,050	45,100	9,014	6,761	9,571	7,864
45,100	45,150	9,028	6,769	9,584	7,878
45,150	45,200	9,042	6,776	9,598	7,892
45,200	45,250	9,056	6,787	9,612	7,906
45,250	45,300	9,069	6,801	9,626	7,919
45,300	45,350	9,083	6,814	9,639	7,933
45,350	45,400	9,097	6,828	9,653	7,947
45,400	45,450	9,111	6,842	9,667	7,961
45,450	45,500	9,124	6,856	9,681	7,974
45,500	45,550	9,138	6,869	9,694	7,988
45,550	45,600	9,152	6,883	9,708	8,002
45,600	45,650	9,166	6,897	9,722	8,016
45,650	45,700	9,179	6,911	9,736	8,029
45,700	45,750	9,193	6,924	9,749	8,043
45,750	45,800	9,207	6,938	9,763	8,057
45,800	45,850	9,221	6,952	9,777	8,071
45,850	45,900	9,234	6,966	9,791	8,084
45,900	45,950	9,248	6,979	9,804	8,098
45,950	46,000	9,262	6,993	9,818	8,112

46,000

At least	But less than	Single	Married filing jointly *	Married filing separately	Head of a household
46,000	46,050	9,276	7,007	9,832	8,126
46,050	46,100	9,289	7,021	9,846	8,139
46,100	46,150	9,303	7,034	9,859	8,153
46,150	46,200	9,317	7,048	9,873	8,167
46,200	46,250	9,331	7,062	9,887	8,181
46,250	46,300	9,344	7,076	9,901	8,194
46,300	46,350	9,358	7,089	9,914	8,208
46,350	46,400	9,372	7,103	9,928	8,222
46,400	46,450	9,386	7,117	9,942	8,236
46,450	46,500	9,399	7,131	9,956	8,249
46,500	46,550	9,413	7,144	9,969	8,263
46,550	46,600	9,427	7,158	9,983	8,277
46,600	46,650	9,441	7,172	9,997	8,291
46,650	46,700	9,454	7,186	10,011	8,304
46,700	46,750	9,468	7,199	10,024	8,318
46,750	46,800	9,482	7,213	10,038	8,332
46,800	46,850	9,496	7,227	10,052	8,346
46,850	46,900	9,509	7,241	10,066	8,359
46,900	46,950	9,523	7,254	10,079	8,373
46,950	47,000	9,537	7,268	10,093	8,387

47,000

At least	But less than	Single	Married filing jointly *	Married filing separately	Head of a household
47,000	47,050	9,551	7,282	10,107	8,401
47,050	47,100	9,564	7,296	10,121	8,414
47,100	47,150	9,578	7,309	10,134	8,428
47,150	47,200	9,592	7,323	10,148	8,442
47,200	47,250	9,606	7,337	10,162	8,456
47,250	47,300	9,619	7,351	10,176	8,469
47,300	47,350	9,633	7,364	10,189	8,483
47,350	47,400	9,647	7,378	10,203	8,497
47,400	47,450	9,661	7,392	10,217	8,511
47,450	47,500	9,674	7,406	10,231	8,524
47,500	47,550	9,688	7,419	10,244	8,538
47,550	47,600	9,702	7,433	10,258	8,552
47,600	47,650	9,716	7,447	10,272	8,566
47,650	47,700	9,729	7,461	10,286	8,579
47,700	47,750	9,743	7,474	10,299	8,593
47,750	47,800	9,757	7,488	10,313	8,607
47,800	47,850	9,771	7,502	10,327	8,621
47,850	47,900	9,784	7,516	10,341	8,634
47,900	47,950	9,798	7,529	10,354	8,648
47,950	48,000	9,812	7,543	10,368	8,662

48,000

At least	But less than	Single	Married filing jointly *	Married filing separately	Head of a household
48,000	48,050	9,826	7,557	10,382	8,676
48,050	48,100	9,839	7,571	10,396	8,689
48,100	48,150	9,853	7,584	10,409	8,703
48,150	48,200	9,867	7,598	10,423	8,717
48,200	48,250	9,881	7,612	10,437	8,731
48,250	48,300	9,894	7,626	10,451	8,744
48,300	48,350	9,908	7,639	10,464	8,758
48,350	48,400	9,922	7,653	10,478	8,772
48,400	48,450	9,936	7,667	10,492	8,786
48,450	48,500	9,949	7,681	10,506	8,799
48,500	48,550	9,963	7,694	10,519	8,813
48,550	48,600	9,977	7,708	10,533	8,827
48,600	48,650	9,991	7,722	10,547	8,841
48,650	48,700	10,004	7,736	10,561	8,854
48,700	48,750	10,018	7,749	10,574	8,868
48,750	48,800	10,032	7,763	10,588	8,882
48,800	48,850	10,046	7,777	10,602	8,896
48,850	48,900	10,059	7,791	10,616	8,909
48,900	48,950	10,073	7,804	10,629	8,923
48,950	49,000	10,087	7,818	10,643	8,937

49,000

At least	But less than	Single	Married filing jointly *	Married filing separately	Head of a household
49,000	49,050	10,101	7,832	10,657	8,951
49,050	49,100	10,114	7,846	10,671	8,964
49,100	49,150	10,128	7,859	10,684	8,978
49,150	49,200	10,142	7,873	10,698	8,992
49,200	49,250	10,156	7,887	10,712	9,006
49,250	49,300	10,169	7,901	10,726	9,019
49,300	49,350	10,183	7,914	10,739	9,033
49,350	49,400	10,197	7,928	10,753	9,047
49,400	49,450	10,211	7,942	10,767	9,061
49,450	49,500	10,224	7,956	10,781	9,074
49,500	49,550	10,238	7,969	10,794	9,088
49,550	49,600	10,252	7,983	10,808	9,102
49,600	49,650	10,266	7,997	10,822	9,116
49,650	49,700	10,279	8,011	10,836	9,129
49,700	49,750	10,293	8,024	10,849	9,143
49,750	49,800	10,307	8,038	10,863	9,157
49,800	49,850	10,321	8,052	10,877	9,171
49,850	49,900	10,334	8,066	10,891	9,184
49,900	49,950	10,348	8,079	10,904	9,198
49,950	50,000	10,362	8,093	10,918	9,212

* This column must also be used by a qualifying widow(er).

(Continued on next page)

If (taxable income) is—		And you are—			
At least	But less than	Single	Married filing jointly *	Married filing separately	Head of a house-hold
		Your tax is—			

50,000

At least	But less than	Single	Married filing jointly	Married filing separately	Head of a household
50,000	50,050	10,376	8,107	10,932	9,226
50,050	50,100	10,389	8,121	10,946	9,239
50,100	50,150	10,403	8,134	10,959	9,253
50,150	50,200	10,417	8,148	10,973	9,267
50,200	50,250	10,431	8,162	10,987	9,281
50,250	50,300	10,444	8,176	11,001	9,294
50,300	50,350	10,458	8,189	11,014	9,308
50,350	50,400	10,472	8,203	11,028	9,322
50,400	50,450	10,486	8,217	11,042	9,336
50,450	50,500	10,499	8,231	11,056	9,349
50,500	50,550	10,513	8,244	11,069	9,363
50,550	50,600	10,527	8,258	11,083	9,377
50,600	50,650	10,541	8,272	11,097	9,391
50,650	50,700	10,554	8,286	11,111	9,404
50,700	50,750	10,568	8,299	11,124	9,418
50,750	50,800	10,582	8,313	11,138	9,432
50,800	50,850	10,596	8,327	11,152	9,446
50,850	50,900	10,609	8,341	11,166	9,459
50,900	50,950	10,623	8,354	11,179	9,473
50,950	51,000	10,637	8,368	11,193	9,487

51,000

At least	But less than	Single	Married filing jointly	Married filing separately	Head of a household
51,000	51,050	10,651	8,382	11,207	9,501
51,050	51,100	10,664	8,396	11,221	9,514
51,100	51,150	10,678	8,409	11,234	9,528
51,150	51,200	10,692	8,423	11,248	9,542
51,200	51,250	10,706	8,437	11,262	9,556
51,250	51,300	10,719	8,451	11,276	9,569
51,300	51,350	10,733	8,464	11,289	9,583
51,350	51,400	10,747	8,478	11,303	9,597
51,400	51,450	10,761	8,492	11,317	9,611
51,450	51,500	10,774	8,506	11,331	9,624
51,500	51,550	10,788	8,519	11,344	9,638
51,550	51,600	10,802	8,533	11,358	9,652
51,600	51,650	10,816	8,547	11,372	9,666
51,650	51,700	10,829	8,561	11,386	9,679
51,700	51,750	10,843	8,574	11,399	9,693
51,750	51,800	10,857	8,588	11,413	9,707
51,800	51,850	10,871	8,602	11,427	9,721
51,850	51,900	10,884	8,616	11,441	9,734
51,900	51,950	10,898	8,629	11,454	9,748
51,950	52,000	10,912	8,643	11,468	9,762

52,000

At least	But less than	Single	Married filing jointly	Married filing separately	Head of a household
52,000	52,050	10,926	8,657	11,482	9,776
52,050	52,100	10,939	8,671	11,496	9,789
52,100	52,150	10,953	8,684	11,509	9,803
52,150	52,200	10,967	8,698	11,523	9,817
52,200	52,250	10,981	8,712	11,537	9,831
52,250	52,300	10,994	8,726	11,551	9,844
52,300	52,350	11,008	8,739	11,564	9,858
52,350	52,400	11,022	8,753	11,578	9,872
52,400	52,450	11,036	8,767	11,592	9,886
52,450	52,500	11,049	8,781	11,606	9,899
52,500	52,550	11,063	8,794	11,619	9,913
52,550	52,600	11,077	8,808	11,633	9,927
52,600	52,650	11,091	8,822	11,647	9,941
52,650	52,700	11,104	8,836	11,661	9,954
52,700	52,750	11,118	8,849	11,674	9,968
52,750	52,800	11,132	8,863	11,688	9,982
52,800	52,850	11,146	8,877	11,702	9,996
52,850	52,900	11,159	8,891	11,716	10,009
52,900	52,950	11,173	8,904	11,729	10,023
52,950	53,000	11,187	8,918	11,743	10,037

53,000

At least	But less than	Single	Married filing jointly	Married filing separately	Head of a household
53,000	53,050	11,201	8,932	11,757	10,051
53,050	53,100	11,214	8,946	11,771	10,064
53,100	53,150	11,228	8,959	11,784	10,078
53,150	53,200	11,242	8,973	11,798	10,092
53,200	53,250	11,256	8,987	11,812	10,106
53,250	53,300	11,269	9,001	11,826	10,119
53,300	53,350	11,283	9,014	11,839	10,133
53,350	53,400	11,297	9,028	11,853	10,147
53,400	53,450	11,311	9,042	11,867	10,161
53,450	53,500	11,324	9,056	11,881	10,174
53,500	53,550	11,338	9,069	11,894	10,188
53,550	53,600	11,352	9,083	11,908	10,202
53,600	53,650	11,366	9,097	11,922	10,216
53,650	53,700	11,379	9,111	11,936	10,229
53,700	53,750	11,393	9,124	11,949	10,243
53,750	53,800	11,407	9,138	11,963	10,257
53,800	53,850	11,421	9,152	11,977	10,271
53,850	53,900	11,434	9,166	11,991	10,284
53,900	53,950	11,448	9,179	12,004	10,298
53,950	54,000	11,462	9,193	12,018	10,312

54,000

At least	But less than	Single	Married filing jointly	Married filing separately	Head of a household
54,000	54,050	11,476	9,207	12,032	10,326
54,050	54,100	11,489	9,221	12,046	10,339
54,100	54,150	11,503	9,234	12,059	10,353
54,150	54,200	11,517	9,248	12,073	10,367
54,200	54,250	11,531	9,262	12,087	10,381
54,250	54,300	11,544	9,276	12,101	10,394
54,300	54,350	11,558	9,289	12,114	10,408
54,350	54,400	11,572	9,303	12,128	10,422
54,400	54,450	11,586	9,317	12,142	10,436
54,450	54,500	11,599	9,331	12,156	10,449
54,500	54,550	11,613	9,344	12,169	10,463
54,550	54,600	11,627	9,358	12,183	10,477
54,600	54,650	11,641	9,372	12,197	10,491
54,650	54,700	11,654	9,386	12,212	10,504
54,700	54,750	11,668	9,399	12,227	10,518
54,750	54,800	11,682	9,413	12,243	10,532
54,800	54,850	11,696	9,427	12,258	10,546
54,850	54,900	11,709	9,441	12,273	10,559
54,900	54,950	11,723	9,454	12,288	10,573
54,950	55,000	11,737	9,468	12,304	10,587

55,000

At least	But less than	Single	Married filing jointly	Married filing separately	Head of a household
55,000	55,050	11,751	9,482	12,319	10,601
55,050	55,100	11,764	9,496	12,334	10,614
55,100	55,150	11,778	9,509	12,349	10,628
55,150	55,200	11,792	9,523	12,365	10,642
55,200	55,250	11,806	9,537	12,380	10,656
55,250	55,300	11,819	9,551	12,395	10,669
55,300	55,350	11,833	9,564	12,410	10,683
55,350	55,400	11,847	9,578	12,426	10,697
55,400	55,450	11,861	9,592	12,441	10,711
55,450	55,500	11,874	9,606	12,456	10,724
55,500	55,550	11,888	9,619	12,471	10,738
55,550	55,600	11,902	9,633	12,487	10,752
55,600	55,650	11,916	9,647	12,502	10,766
55,650	55,700	11,929	9,661	12,517	10,779
55,700	55,750	11,943	9,674	12,532	10,793
55,750	55,800	11,957	9,688	12,548	10,807
55,800	55,850	11,971	9,702	12,563	10,821
55,850	55,900	11,984	9,716	12,578	10,834
55,900	55,950	11,998	9,729	12,593	10,848
55,950	56,000	12,012	9,743	12,609	10,862

56,000

At least	But less than	Single	Married filing jointly	Married filing separately	Head of a household
56,000	56,050	12,026	9,757	12,624	10,876
56,050	56,100	12,039	9,771	12,639	10,889
56,100	56,150	12,053	9,784	12,654	10,903
56,150	56,200	12,067	9,798	12,670	10,917
56,200	56,250	12,081	9,812	12,685	10,931
56,250	56,300	12,094	9,826	12,700	10,944
56,300	56,350	12,108	9,839	12,715	10,958
56,350	56,400	12,122	9,853	12,731	10,972
56,400	56,450	12,136	9,867	12,746	10,986
56,450	56,500	12,149	9,881	12,761	10,999
56,500	56,550	12,163	9,894	12,776	11,013
56,550	56,600	12,177	9,908	12,792	11,027
56,600	56,650	12,191	9,922	12,807	11,041
56,650	56,700	12,204	9,936	12,822	11,054
56,700	56,750	12,218	9,949	12,837	11,068
56,750	56,800	12,232	9,963	12,853	11,082
56,800	56,850	12,246	9,977	12,868	11,096
56,850	56,900	12,259	9,991	12,883	11,109
56,900	56,950	12,273	10,004	12,898	11,123
56,950	57,000	12,287	10,018	12,914	11,137

57,000

At least	But less than	Single	Married filing jointly	Married filing separately	Head of a household
57,000	57,050	12,301	10,032	12,929	11,151
57,050	57,100	12,314	10,046	12,944	11,164
57,100	57,150	12,328	10,059	12,959	11,178
57,150	57,200	12,342	10,073	12,975	11,192
57,200	57,250	12,356	10,087	12,990	11,206
57,250	57,300	12,369	10,101	13,005	11,219
57,300	57,350	12,383	10,114	13,020	11,233
57,350	57,400	12,397	10,128	13,036	11,247
57,400	57,450	12,411	10,142	13,051	11,261
57,450	57,500	12,424	10,156	13,066	11,274
57,500	57,550	12,438	10,169	13,081	11,288
57,550	57,600	12,452	10,183	13,097	11,302
57,600	57,650	12,466	10,197	13,112	11,316
57,650	57,700	12,479	10,211	13,127	11,329
57,700	57,750	12,493	10,224	13,142	11,343
57,750	57,800	12,507	10,238	13,158	11,357
57,800	57,850	12,521	10,252	13,173	11,371
57,850	57,900	12,534	10,266	13,188	11,384
57,900	57,950	12,548	10,279	13,203	11,398
57,950	58,000	12,562	10,293	13,219	11,412

58,000

At least	But less than	Single	Married filing jointly	Married filing separately	Head of a household
58,000	58,050	12,576	10,307	13,234	11,426
58,050	58,100	12,589	10,321	13,249	11,439
58,100	58,150	12,603	10,334	13,264	11,453
58,150	58,200	12,617	10,348	13,280	11,467
58,200	58,250	12,631	10,362	13,295	11,481
58,250	58,300	12,644	10,376	13,310	11,494
58,300	58,350	12,658	10,389	13,325	11,508
58,350	58,400	12,672	10,403	13,341	11,522
58,400	58,450	12,686	10,417	13,356	11,536
58,450	58,500	12,699	10,431	13,371	11,549
58,500	58,550	12,713	10,444	13,386	11,563
58,550	58,600	12,727	10,458	13,402	11,577
58,600	58,650	12,741	10,472	13,417	11,591
58,650	58,700	12,754	10,486	13,432	11,604
58,700	58,750	12,768	10,499	13,447	11,618
58,750	58,800	12,782	10,513	13,463	11,632
58,800	58,850	12,796	10,527	13,478	11,646
58,850	58,900	12,809	10,541	13,493	11,659
58,900	58,950	12,823	10,554	13,508	11,673
58,950	59,000	12,837	10,568	13,524	11,687

* This column must also be used by a qualifying widow(er).

(Continued on next page)

Caution. Dependents, see *Tax Computation Worksheet for Certain Dependents* in your tax form package.

If (taxable income) is— At least	But less than	Single	Married filing jointly *	Married filing separately	Head of a household
59,000					
59,000	59,050	12,851	10,582	13,539	11,701
59,050	59,100	12,864	10,596	13,554	11,714
59,100	59,150	12,878	10,609	13,569	11,728
59,150	59,200	12,892	10,623	13,585	11,742
59,200	59,250	12,906	10,637	13,600	11,756
59,250	59,300	12,919	10,651	13,615	11,769
59,300	59,350	12,933	10,664	13,630	11,783
59,350	59,400	12,947	10,678	13,646	11,797
59,400	59,450	12,961	10,692	13,661	11,811
59,450	59,500	12,974	10,706	13,676	11,824
59,500	59,550	12,988	10,719	13,691	11,838
59,550	59,600	13,002	10,733	13,707	11,852
59,600	59,650	13,016	10,747	13,722	11,866
59,650	59,700	13,029	10,761	13,737	11,879
59,700	59,750	13,043	10,774	13,752	11,893
59,750	59,800	13,057	10,788	13,768	11,907
59,800	59,850	13,071	10,802	13,783	11,921
59,850	59,900	13,084	10,816	13,798	11,934
59,900	59,950	13,098	10,829	13,813	11,948
59,950	60,000	13,112	10,843	13,829	11,962
60,000					
60,000	60,050	13,126	10,857	13,844	11,976
60,050	60,100	13,139	10,871	13,859	11,989
60,100	60,150	13,153	10,884	13,874	12,003
60,150	60,200	13,167	10,898	13,890	12,017
60,200	60,250	13,181	10,912	13,905	12,031
60,250	60,300	13,194	10,926	13,920	12,044
60,300	60,350	13,208	10,939	13,935	12,058
60,350	60,400	13,222	10,953	13,951	12,072
60,400	60,450	13,236	10,967	13,966	12,086
60,450	60,500	13,249	10,981	13,981	12,099
60,500	60,550	13,263	10,994	13,996	12,113
60,550	60,600	13,277	11,008	14,012	12,127
60,600	60,650	13,291	11,022	14,027	12,141
60,650	60,700	13,304	11,036	14,042	12,154
60,700	60,750	13,318	11,049	14,057	12,168
60,750	60,800	13,332	11,063	14,073	12,182
60,800	60,850	13,346	11,077	14,088	12,196
60,850	60,900	13,359	11,091	14,103	12,209
60,900	60,950	13,373	11,104	14,118	12,223
60,950	61,000	13,387	11,118	14,134	12,237
61,000					
61,000	61,050	13,401	11,132	14,149	12,251
61,050	61,100	13,414	11,146	14,164	12,264
61,100	61,150	13,428	11,159	14,179	12,278
61,150	61,200	13,442	11,173	14,195	12,292
61,200	61,250	13,456	11,187	14,210	12,306
61,250	61,300	13,469	11,201	14,225	12,319
61,300	61,350	13,483	11,214	14,240	12,333
61,350	61,400	13,497	11,228	14,256	12,347
61,400	61,450	13,511	11,242	14,271	12,361
61,450	61,500	13,524	11,256	14,286	12,374
61,500	61,550	13,538	11,269	14,301	12,388
61,550	61,600	13,552	11,283	14,317	12,402
61,600	61,650	13,566	11,297	14,332	12,416
61,650	61,700	13,579	11,311	14,347	12,429
61,700	61,750	13,593	11,324	14,362	12,443
61,750	61,800	13,607	11,338	14,378	12,457
61,800	61,850	13,621	11,352	14,393	12,471
61,850	61,900	13,634	11,366	14,408	12,484
61,900	61,950	13,648	11,379	14,423	12,498
61,950	62,000	13,662	11,393	14,439	12,512
62,000					
62,000	62,050	13,676	11,407	14,454	12,526
62,050	62,100	13,689	11,421	14,469	12,539
62,100	62,150	13,703	11,434	14,484	12,553
62,150	62,200	13,717	11,448	14,500	12,567
62,200	62,250	13,731	11,462	14,515	12,581
62,250	62,300	13,744	11,476	14,530	12,594
62,300	62,350	13,758	11,489	14,545	12,608
62,350	62,400	13,772	11,503	14,561	12,622
62,400	62,450	13,786	11,517	14,576	12,636
62,450	62,500	13,799	11,531	14,591	12,649
62,500	62,550	13,813	11,544	14,606	12,663
62,550	62,600	13,827	11,558	14,622	12,677
62,600	62,650	13,841	11,572	14,637	12,691
62,650	62,700	13,854	11,586	14,652	12,704
62,700	62,750	13,868	11,599	14,667	12,718
62,750	62,800	13,882	11,613	14,683	12,732
62,800	62,850	13,896	11,627	14,698	12,746
62,850	62,900	13,909	11,641	14,713	12,759
62,900	62,950	13,923	11,654	14,728	12,773
62,950	63,000	13,937	11,668	14,744	12,787
63,000					
63,000	63,050	13,951	11,682	14,759	12,801
63,050	63,100	13,964	11,696	14,774	12,814
63,100	63,150	13,978	11,709	14,789	12,828
63,150	63,200	13,992	11,723	14,805	12,842
63,200	63,250	14,006	11,737	14,820	12,856
63,250	63,300	14,019	11,751	14,835	12,869
63,300	63,350	14,033	11,764	14,850	12,883
63,350	63,400	14,047	11,778	14,866	12,897
63,400	63,450	14,061	11,792	14,881	12,911
63,450	63,500	14,074	11,806	14,896	12,924
63,500	63,550	14,088	11,819	14,911	12,938
63,550	63,600	14,102	11,833	14,927	12,952
63,600	63,650	14,116	11,847	14,942	12,966
63,650	63,700	14,129	11,861	14,957	12,979
63,700	63,750	14,143	11,874	14,972	12,993
63,750	63,800	14,157	11,888	14,988	13,007
63,800	63,850	14,171	11,902	15,003	13,021
63,850	63,900	14,184	11,916	15,018	13,034
63,900	63,950	14,198	11,929	15,033	13,048
63,950	64,000	14,212	11,943	15,049	13,062
64,000					
64,000	64,050	14,226	11,957	15,064	13,076
64,050	64,100	14,239	11,971	15,079	13,089
64,100	64,150	14,253	11,984	15,094	13,103
64,150	64,200	14,267	11,998	15,110	13,117
64,200	64,250	14,281	12,012	15,125	13,131
64,250	64,300	14,294	12,026	15,140	13,144
64,300	64,350	14,308	12,039	15,155	13,158
64,350	64,400	14,322	12,053	15,171	13,172
64,400	64,450	14,336	12,067	15,186	13,186
64,450	64,500	14,349	12,081	15,201	13,199
64,500	64,550	14,363	12,094	15,216	13,213
64,550	64,600	14,377	12,108	15,232	13,227
64,600	64,650	14,391	12,122	15,247	13,241
64,650	64,700	14,404	12,136	15,262	13,254
64,700	64,750	14,418	12,149	15,277	13,268
64,750	64,800	14,432	12,163	15,293	13,282
64,800	64,850	14,446	12,177	15,308	13,296
64,850	64,900	14,459	12,191	15,323	13,309
64,900	64,950	14,473	12,204	15,338	13,323
64,950	65,000	14,487	12,218	15,354	13,337
65,000					
65,000	65,050	14,501	12,232	15,369	13,351
65,050	65,100	14,514	12,246	15,384	13,364
65,100	65,150	14,528	12,259	15,399	13,378
65,150	65,200	14,542	12,273	15,415	13,392
65,200	65,250	14,556	12,287	15,430	13,406
65,250	65,300	14,569	12,301	15,445	13,419
65,300	65,350	14,583	12,314	15,460	13,433
65,350	65,400	14,597	12,328	15,476	13,447
65,400	65,450	14,611	12,342	15,491	13,461
65,450	65,500	14,624	12,356	15,506	13,474
65,500	65,550	14,638	12,369	15,521	13,488
65,550	65,600	14,653	12,383	15,537	13,502
65,600	65,650	14,668	12,397	15,552	13,516
65,650	65,700	14,683	12,411	15,567	13,529
65,700	65,750	14,698	12,424	15,582	13,543
65,750	65,800	14,714	12,438	15,598	13,557
65,800	65,850	14,729	12,452	15,613	13,571
65,850	65,900	14,744	12,466	15,628	13,584
65,900	65,950	14,759	12,479	15,643	13,598
65,950	66,000	14,775	12,493	15,659	13,612
66,000					
66,000	66,050	14,790	12,507	15,674	13,626
66,050	66,100	14,805	12,521	15,689	13,639
66,100	66,150	14,820	12,534	15,704	13,653
66,150	66,200	14,836	12,548	15,720	13,667
66,200	66,250	14,851	12,562	15,735	13,681
66,250	66,300	14,866	12,576	15,750	13,694
66,300	66,350	14,881	12,589	15,765	13,708
66,350	66,400	14,897	12,603	15,781	13,722
66,400	66,450	14,912	12,617	15,796	13,736
66,450	66,500	14,927	12,631	15,811	13,749
66,500	66,550	14,942	12,644	15,826	13,763
66,550	66,600	14,958	12,658	15,842	13,777
66,600	66,650	14,973	12,672	15,857	13,791
66,650	66,700	14,988	12,686	15,872	13,804
66,700	66,750	15,003	12,699	15,887	13,818
66,750	66,800	15,019	12,713	15,903	13,832
66,800	66,850	15,034	12,727	15,918	13,846
66,850	66,900	15,049	12,741	15,933	13,859
66,900	66,950	15,064	12,754	15,948	13,873
66,950	67,000	15,080	12,768	15,964	13,887
67,000					
67,000	67,050	15,095	12,782	15,979	13,901
67,050	67,100	15,110	12,796	15,994	13,914
67,100	67,150	15,125	12,809	16,009	13,928
67,150	67,200	15,141	12,823	16,025	13,942
67,200	67,250	15,156	12,837	16,040	13,956
67,250	67,300	15,171	12,851	16,055	13,969
67,300	67,350	15,186	12,864	16,070	13,983
67,350	67,400	15,202	12,878	16,086	13,997
67,400	67,450	15,217	12,892	16,101	14,011
67,450	67,500	15,232	12,906	16,116	14,024
67,500	67,550	15,247	12,919	16,131	14,038
67,550	67,600	15,263	12,933	16,147	14,052
67,600	67,650	15,278	12,947	16,162	14,066
67,650	67,700	15,293	12,961	16,177	14,079
67,700	67,750	15,308	12,974	16,192	14,093
67,750	67,800	15,324	12,988	16,208	14,107
67,800	67,850	15,339	13,002	16,223	14,121
67,850	67,900	15,354	13,016	16,238	14,134
67,900	67,950	15,369	13,029	16,253	14,148
67,950	68,000	15,385	13,043	16,269	14,162

* This column must also be used by a qualifying widow(er).

(Continued on next page)

Header (applies to all columns):

If (taxable income) is—		And you are—			
At least	But less than	Single	Married filing jointly *	Married filing separately	Head of a household
		Your tax is—			

68,000

At least	But less than	Single	MFJ	MFS	HoH
68,000	68,050	15,400	13,057	16,284	14,176
68,050	68,100	15,415	13,071	16,299	14,189
68,100	68,150	15,430	13,084	16,314	14,203
68,150	68,200	15,446	13,098	16,330	14,217
68,200	68,250	15,461	13,112	16,345	14,231
68,250	68,300	15,476	13,126	16,360	14,244
68,300	68,350	15,491	13,139	16,375	14,258
68,350	68,400	15,507	13,153	16,391	14,272
68,400	68,450	15,522	13,167	16,406	14,286
68,450	68,500	15,537	13,181	16,421	14,299
68,500	68,550	15,552	13,194	16,436	14,313
68,550	68,600	15,568	13,208	16,452	14,327
68,600	68,650	15,583	13,222	16,467	14,341
68,650	68,700	15,598	13,236	16,482	14,354
68,700	68,750	15,613	13,249	16,497	14,368
68,750	68,800	15,629	13,263	16,513	14,382
68,800	68,850	15,644	13,277	16,528	14,396
68,850	68,900	15,659	13,291	16,543	14,409
68,900	68,950	15,674	13,304	16,558	14,423
68,950	69,000	15,690	13,318	16,574	14,437

69,000

At least	But less than	Single	MFJ	MFS	HoH
69,000	69,050	15,705	13,332	16,589	14,451
69,050	69,100	15,720	13,346	16,604	14,464
69,100	69,150	15,735	13,359	16,619	14,478
69,150	69,200	15,751	13,373	16,635	14,492
69,200	69,250	15,766	13,387	16,650	14,506
69,250	69,300	15,781	13,401	16,665	14,519
69,300	69,350	15,796	13,414	16,680	14,533
69,350	69,400	15,812	13,428	16,696	14,547
69,400	69,450	15,827	13,442	16,711	14,561
69,450	69,500	15,842	13,456	16,726	14,574
69,500	69,550	15,857	13,469	16,741	14,588
69,550	69,600	15,873	13,483	16,757	14,602
69,600	69,650	15,888	13,497	16,772	14,616
69,650	69,700	15,903	13,511	16,787	14,629
69,700	69,750	15,918	13,524	16,802	14,643
69,750	69,800	15,934	13,538	16,818	14,657
69,800	69,850	15,949	13,552	16,833	14,671
69,850	69,900	15,964	13,566	16,848	14,684
69,900	69,950	15,979	13,579	16,863	14,698
69,950	70,000	15,995	13,593	16,879	14,712

70,000

At least	But less than	Single	MFJ	MFS	HoH
70,000	70,050	16,010	13,607	16,894	14,726
70,050	70,100	16,025	13,621	16,909	14,739
70,100	70,150	16,040	13,634	16,924	14,753
70,150	70,200	16,056	13,648	16,940	14,767
70,200	70,250	16,071	13,662	16,955	14,781
70,250	70,300	16,086	13,676	16,970	14,794
70,300	70,350	16,101	13,689	16,985	14,808
70,350	70,400	16,117	13,703	17,001	14,822
70,400	70,450	16,132	13,717	17,016	14,836
70,450	70,500	16,147	13,731	17,031	14,849
70,500	70,550	16,162	13,744	17,046	14,863
70,550	70,600	16,178	13,758	17,062	14,877
70,600	70,650	16,193	13,772	17,077	14,891
70,650	70,700	16,208	13,786	17,092	14,904
70,700	70,750	16,223	13,799	17,107	14,918
70,750	70,800	16,239	13,813	17,123	14,932
70,800	70,850	16,254	13,827	17,138	14,946
70,850	70,900	16,269	13,841	17,153	14,959
70,900	70,950	16,284	13,854	17,168	14,973
70,950	71,000	16,300	13,868	17,184	14,987

71,000

At least	But less than	Single	MFJ	MFS	HoH
71,000	71,050	16,315	13,882	17,199	15,001
71,050	71,100	16,330	13,896	17,214	15,014
71,100	71,150	16,345	13,909	17,229	15,028
71,150	71,200	16,361	13,923	17,245	15,042
71,200	71,250	16,376	13,937	17,260	15,056
71,250	71,300	16,391	13,951	17,275	15,069
71,300	71,350	16,406	13,964	17,290	15,083
71,350	71,400	16,422	13,978	17,306	15,097
71,400	71,450	16,437	13,992	17,321	15,111
71,450	71,500	16,452	14,006	17,336	15,124
71,500	71,550	16,467	14,019	17,351	15,138
71,550	71,600	16,483	14,033	17,367	15,152
71,600	71,650	16,498	14,047	17,382	15,166
71,650	71,700	16,513	14,061	17,397	15,179
71,700	71,750	16,528	14,074	17,412	15,193
71,750	71,800	16,544	14,088	17,428	15,207
71,800	71,850	16,559	14,102	17,443	15,221
71,850	71,900	16,574	14,116	17,458	15,234
71,900	71,950	16,589	14,129	17,473	15,248
71,950	72,000	16,605	14,143	17,489	15,262

72,000

At least	But less than	Single	MFJ	MFS	HoH
72,000	72,050	16,620	14,157	17,504	15,276
72,050	72,100	16,635	14,171	17,519	15,289
72,100	72,150	16,650	14,184	17,534	15,303
72,150	72,200	16,666	14,198	17,550	15,317
72,200	72,250	16,681	14,212	17,565	15,331
72,250	72,300	16,696	14,226	17,580	15,344
72,300	72,350	16,711	14,239	17,595	15,358
72,350	72,400	16,727	14,253	17,611	15,372
72,400	72,450	16,742	14,267	17,626	15,386
72,450	72,500	16,757	14,281	17,641	15,399
72,500	72,550	16,772	14,294	17,656	15,413
72,550	72,600	16,788	14,308	17,672	15,427
72,600	72,650	16,803	14,322	17,687	15,441
72,650	72,700	16,818	14,336	17,702	15,454
72,700	72,750	16,833	14,349	17,717	15,468
72,750	72,800	16,849	14,363	17,733	15,482
72,800	72,850	16,864	14,377	17,748	15,496
72,850	72,900	16,879	14,391	17,763	15,509
72,900	72,950	16,894	14,404	17,778	15,523
72,950	73,000	16,910	14,418	17,794	15,537

73,000

At least	But less than	Single	MFJ	MFS	HoH
73,000	73,050	16,925	14,432	17,809	15,551
73,050	73,100	16,940	14,446	17,824	15,564
73,100	73,150	16,955	14,459	17,839	15,578
73,150	73,200	16,971	14,473	17,855	15,592
73,200	73,250	16,986	14,487	17,870	15,606
73,250	73,300	17,001	14,501	17,885	15,619
73,300	73,350	17,016	14,514	17,900	15,633
73,350	73,400	17,032	14,528	17,916	15,647
73,400	73,450	17,047	14,542	17,931	15,661
73,450	73,500	17,062	14,556	17,946	15,674
73,500	73,550	17,077	14,569	17,961	15,688
73,550	73,600	17,093	14,583	17,977	15,702
73,600	73,650	17,108	14,597	17,992	15,716
73,650	73,700	17,123	14,611	18,007	15,729
73,700	73,750	17,138	14,624	18,022	15,743
73,750	73,800	17,154	14,638	18,038	15,757
73,800	73,850	17,169	14,652	18,053	15,771
73,850	73,900	17,184	14,666	18,068	15,784
73,900	73,950	17,199	14,679	18,083	15,798
73,950	74,000	17,215	14,693	18,099	15,812

74,000

At least	But less than	Single	MFJ	MFS	HoH
74,000	74,050	17,230	14,707	18,114	15,826
74,050	74,100	17,245	14,721	18,129	15,839
74,100	74,150	17,260	14,734	18,144	15,853
74,150	74,200	17,276	14,748	18,160	15,867
74,200	74,250	17,291	14,762	18,175	15,881
74,250	74,300	17,306	14,776	18,190	15,894
74,300	74,350	17,321	14,789	18,205	15,908
74,350	74,400	17,337	14,803	18,221	15,922
74,400	74,450	17,352	14,817	18,236	15,936
74,450	74,500	17,367	14,831	18,251	15,949
74,500	74,550	17,382	14,844	18,266	15,963
74,550	74,600	17,398	14,858	18,282	15,977
74,600	74,650	17,413	14,872	18,297	15,991
74,650	74,700	17,428	14,886	18,312	16,004
74,700	74,750	17,443	14,899	18,327	16,018
74,750	74,800	17,459	14,913	18,343	16,032
74,800	74,850	17,474	14,927	18,358	16,046
74,850	74,900	17,489	14,941	18,373	16,059
74,900	74,950	17,504	14,954	18,388	16,073
74,950	75,000	17,520	14,968	18,404	16,087

75,000

At least	But less than	Single	MFJ	MFS	HoH
75,000	75,050	17,535	14,982	18,419	16,101
75,050	75,100	17,550	14,996	18,434	16,114
75,100	75,150	17,565	15,009	18,449	16,128
75,150	75,200	17,581	15,023	18,465	16,142
75,200	75,250	17,596	15,037	18,480	16,156
75,250	75,300	17,611	15,051	18,495	16,169
75,300	75,350	17,626	15,064	18,510	16,183
75,350	75,400	17,642	15,078	18,526	16,197
75,400	75,450	17,657	15,092	18,541	16,211
75,450	75,500	17,672	15,106	18,556	16,224
75,500	75,550	17,687	15,119	18,571	16,238
75,550	75,600	17,703	15,133	18,587	16,252
75,600	75,650	17,718	15,147	18,602	16,266
75,650	75,700	17,733	15,161	18,617	16,279
75,700	75,750	17,748	15,174	18,632	16,293
75,750	75,800	17,764	15,188	18,648	16,307
75,800	75,850	17,779	15,202	18,663	16,321
75,850	75,900	17,794	15,216	18,678	16,334
75,900	75,950	17,809	15,229	18,693	16,348
75,950	76,000	17,825	15,243	18,709	16,362

76,000

At least	But less than	Single	MFJ	MFS	HoH
76,000	76,050	17,840	15,257	18,724	16,376
76,050	76,100	17,855	15,271	18,739	16,389
76,100	76,150	17,870	15,284	18,754	16,403
76,150	76,200	17,886	15,298	18,770	16,417
76,200	76,250	17,901	15,312	18,785	16,431
76,250	76,300	17,916	15,326	18,800	16,444
76,300	76,350	17,931	15,339	18,815	16,458
76,350	76,400	17,947	15,353	18,831	16,472
76,400	76,450	17,962	15,367	18,846	16,486
76,450	76,500	17,977	15,381	18,861	16,499
76,500	76,550	17,992	15,394	18,876	16,513
76,550	76,600	18,008	15,408	18,892	16,527
76,600	76,650	18,023	15,422	18,907	16,541
76,650	76,700	18,038	15,436	18,922	16,554
76,700	76,750	18,053	15,449	18,937	16,568
76,750	76,800	18,069	15,463	18,953	16,582
76,800	76,850	18,084	15,477	18,968	16,596
76,850	76,900	18,099	15,491	18,983	16,609
76,900	76,950	18,114	15,504	18,998	16,623
76,950	77,000	18,130	15,518	19,014	16,637

* This column must also be used by a qualifying widow(er).

(Continued on next page)

77,000

At least	But less than	Single	Married filing jointly *	Married filing separately	Head of a household
77,000	77,050	18,145	15,532	19,029	16,651
77,050	77,100	18,160	15,546	19,044	16,664
77,100	77,150	18,175	15,559	19,059	16,678
77,150	77,200	18,191	15,573	19,075	16,692
77,200	77,250	18,206	15,587	19,090	16,706
77,250	77,300	18,221	15,601	19,105	16,719
77,300	77,350	18,236	15,614	19,120	16,733
77,350	77,400	18,252	15,628	19,136	16,747
77,400	77,450	18,267	15,642	19,151	16,761
77,450	77,500	18,282	15,656	19,166	16,774
77,500	77,550	18,297	15,669	19,181	16,788
77,550	77,600	18,313	15,683	19,197	16,802
77,600	77,650	18,328	15,697	19,212	16,816
77,650	77,700	18,343	15,711	19,227	16,829
77,700	77,750	18,358	15,724	19,242	16,843
77,750	77,800	18,374	15,738	19,258	16,857
77,800	77,850	18,389	15,752	19,273	16,871
77,850	77,900	18,404	15,766	19,288	16,884
77,900	77,950	18,419	15,779	19,303	16,898
77,950	78,000	18,435	15,793	19,319	16,912

78,000

At least	But less than	Single	Married filing jointly *	Married filing separately	Head of a household
78,000	78,050	18,450	15,807	19,334	16,926
78,050	78,100	18,465	15,821	19,349	16,939
78,100	78,150	18,480	15,834	19,364	16,953
78,150	78,200	18,496	15,848	19,380	16,967
78,200	78,250	18,511	15,862	19,395	16,981
78,250	78,300	18,526	15,876	19,410	16,994
78,300	78,350	18,541	15,889	19,425	17,008
78,350	78,400	18,557	15,903	19,441	17,022
78,400	78,450	18,572	15,917	19,456	17,036
78,450	78,500	18,587	15,931	19,471	17,049
78,500	78,550	18,602	15,944	19,486	17,063
78,550	78,600	18,618	15,958	19,502	17,077
78,600	78,650	18,633	15,972	19,517	17,091
78,650	78,700	18,648	15,986	19,532	17,104
78,700	78,750	18,663	15,999	19,547	17,118
78,750	78,800	18,679	16,013	19,563	17,132
78,800	78,850	18,694	16,027	19,578	17,146
78,850	78,900	18,709	16,041	19,593	17,159
78,900	78,950	18,724	16,054	19,608	17,173
78,950	79,000	18,740	16,068	19,624	17,187

79,000

At least	But less than	Single	Married filing jointly *	Married filing separately	Head of a household
79,000	79,050	18,755	16,082	19,639	17,201
79,050	79,100	18,770	16,096	19,654	17,214
79,100	79,150	18,785	16,109	19,669	17,228
79,150	79,200	18,801	16,123	19,685	17,242
79,200	79,250	18,816	16,137	19,700	17,256
79,250	79,300	18,831	16,151	19,715	17,269
79,300	79,350	18,846	16,164	19,730	17,283
79,350	79,400	18,862	16,178	19,746	17,297
79,400	79,450	18,877	16,192	19,761	17,311
79,450	79,500	18,892	16,206	19,776	17,324
79,500	79,550	18,907	16,219	19,791	17,338
79,550	79,600	18,923	16,233	19,807	17,352
79,600	79,650	18,938	16,247	19,822	17,366
79,650	79,700	18,953	16,261	19,837	17,379
79,700	79,750	18,968	16,274	19,852	17,393
79,750	79,800	18,984	16,288	19,868	17,407
79,800	79,850	18,999	16,302	19,883	17,421
79,850	79,900	19,014	16,316	19,898	17,434
79,900	79,950	19,029	16,329	19,913	17,448
79,950	80,000	19,045	16,343	19,929	17,462

80,000

At least	But less than	Single	Married filing jointly *	Married filing separately	Head of a household
80,000	80,050	19,060	16,357	19,944	17,476
80,050	80,100	19,075	16,371	19,959	17,489
80,100	80,150	19,090	16,384	19,974	17,503
80,150	80,200	19,106	16,398	19,990	17,517
80,200	80,250	19,121	16,412	20,005	17,531
80,250	80,300	19,136	16,426	20,020	17,544
80,300	80,350	19,151	16,439	20,035	17,558
80,350	80,400	19,167	16,453	20,051	17,572
80,400	80,450	19,182	16,467	20,066	17,586
80,450	80,500	19,197	16,481	20,081	17,599
80,500	80,550	19,212	16,494	20,096	17,613
80,550	80,600	19,228	16,508	20,112	17,627
80,600	80,650	19,243	16,522	20,127	17,641
80,650	80,700	19,258	16,536	20,142	17,654
80,700	80,750	19,273	16,549	20,157	17,668
80,750	80,800	19,289	16,563	20,173	17,682
80,800	80,850	19,304	16,577	20,188	17,696
80,850	80,900	19,319	16,591	20,203	17,709
80,900	80,950	19,334	16,604	20,218	17,723
80,950	81,000	19,350	16,618	20,234	17,737

81,000

At least	But less than	Single	Married filing jointly *	Married filing separately	Head of a household
81,000	81,050	19,365	16,632	20,249	17,751
81,050	81,100	19,380	16,646	20,264	17,764
81,100	81,150	19,395	16,659	20,279	17,778
81,150	81,200	19,411	16,673	20,295	17,792
81,200	81,250	19,426	16,687	20,310	17,806
81,250	81,300	19,441	16,701	20,325	17,819
81,300	81,350	19,456	16,714	20,340	17,833
81,350	81,400	19,472	16,728	20,356	17,847
81,400	81,450	19,487	16,742	20,371	17,861
81,450	81,500	19,502	16,756	20,386	17,874
81,500	81,550	19,517	16,769	20,401	17,888
81,550	81,600	19,533	16,783	20,417	17,902
81,600	81,650	19,548	16,797	20,432	17,916
81,650	81,700	19,563	16,811	20,447	17,929
81,700	81,750	19,578	16,824	20,462	17,943
81,750	81,800	19,594	16,838	20,478	17,957
81,800	81,850	19,609	16,852	20,493	17,971
81,850	81,900	19,624	16,866	20,508	17,984
81,900	81,950	19,639	16,879	20,523	17,998
81,950	82,000	19,655	16,893	20,539	18,012

82,000

At least	But less than	Single	Married filing jointly *	Married filing separately	Head of a household
82,000	82,050	19,670	16,907	20,554	18,026
82,050	82,100	19,685	16,921	20,569	18,039
82,100	82,150	19,700	16,934	20,584	18,053
82,150	82,200	19,716	16,948	20,600	18,067
82,200	82,250	19,731	16,962	20,615	18,081
82,250	82,300	19,746	16,976	20,630	18,094
82,300	82,350	19,761	16,989	20,645	18,108
82,350	82,400	19,777	17,003	20,661	18,122
82,400	82,450	19,792	17,017	20,676	18,136
82,450	82,500	19,807	17,031	20,691	18,149
82,500	82,550	19,822	17,044	20,706	18,163
82,550	82,600	19,838	17,058	20,722	18,177
82,600	82,650	19,853	17,072	20,737	18,191
82,650	82,700	19,868	17,086	20,752	18,204
82,700	82,750	19,883	17,099	20,767	18,218
82,750	82,800	19,899	17,113	20,783	18,232
82,800	82,850	19,914	17,127	20,798	18,246
82,850	82,900	19,929	17,141	20,813	18,259
82,900	82,950	19,944	17,154	20,828	18,273
82,950	83,000	19,960	17,168	20,844	18,287

83,000

At least	But less than	Single	Married filing jointly *	Married filing separately	Head of a household
83,000	83,050	19,975	17,182	20,859	18,301
83,050	83,100	19,990	17,196	20,874	18,314
83,100	83,150	20,005	17,209	20,889	18,328
83,150	83,200	20,021	17,223	20,905	18,342
83,200	83,250	20,036	17,237	20,920	18,356
83,250	83,300	20,051	17,251	20,936	18,369
83,300	83,350	20,066	17,264	20,954	18,383
83,350	83,400	20,082	17,278	20,972	18,397
83,400	83,450	20,097	17,292	20,990	18,411
83,450	83,500	20,112	17,306	21,007	18,424
83,500	83,550	20,127	17,319	21,025	18,438
83,550	83,600	20,143	17,333	21,043	18,452
83,600	83,650	20,158	17,347	21,061	18,466
83,650	83,700	20,173	17,361	21,078	18,479
83,700	83,750	20,188	17,374	21,096	18,493
83,750	83,800	20,204	17,388	21,114	18,507
83,800	83,850	20,219	17,402	21,132	18,521
83,850	83,900	20,234	17,416	21,149	18,534
83,900	83,950	20,249	17,429	21,167	18,548
83,950	84,000	20,265	17,443	21,185	18,562

84,000

At least	But less than	Single	Married filing jointly *	Married filing separately	Head of a household
84,000	84,050	20,280	17,457	21,203	18,576
84,050	84,100	20,295	17,471	21,220	18,589
84,100	84,150	20,310	17,484	21,238	18,603
84,150	84,200	20,326	17,498	21,256	18,617
84,200	84,250	20,341	17,512	21,274	18,631
84,250	84,300	20,356	17,526	21,291	18,644
84,300	84,350	20,371	17,539	21,309	18,658
84,350	84,400	20,387	17,553	21,327	18,672
84,400	84,450	20,402	17,567	21,345	18,686
84,450	84,500	20,417	17,581	21,362	18,699
84,500	84,550	20,432	17,594	21,380	18,713
84,550	84,600	20,448	17,608	21,398	18,727
84,600	84,650	20,463	17,622	21,416	18,741
84,650	84,700	20,478	17,636	21,433	18,754
84,700	84,750	20,493	17,649	21,451	18,768
84,750	84,800	20,509	17,663	21,469	18,782
84,800	84,850	20,524	17,677	21,487	18,796
84,850	84,900	20,539	17,691	21,504	18,809
84,900	84,950	20,554	17,704	21,522	18,823
84,950	85,000	20,570	17,718	21,540	18,837

85,000

At least	But less than	Single	Married filing jointly *	Married filing separately	Head of a household
85,000	85,050	20,585	17,732	21,558	18,851
85,050	85,100	20,600	17,746	21,575	18,864
85,100	85,150	20,615	17,759	21,593	18,878
85,150	85,200	20,631	17,773	21,611	18,892
85,200	85,250	20,646	17,787	21,629	18,906
85,250	85,300	20,661	17,801	21,646	18,919
85,300	85,350	20,676	17,814	21,664	18,933
85,350	85,400	20,692	17,828	21,682	18,947
85,400	85,450	20,707	17,842	21,700	18,961
85,450	85,500	20,722	17,856	21,717	18,974
85,500	85,550	20,737	17,869	21,735	18,988
85,550	85,600	20,753	17,883	21,753	19,002
85,600	85,650	20,768	17,897	21,771	19,016
85,650	85,700	20,783	17,911	21,788	19,029
85,700	85,750	20,798	17,924	21,806	19,043
85,750	85,800	20,814	17,938	21,824	19,057
85,800	85,850	20,829	17,952	21,842	19,071
85,850	85,900	20,844	17,966	21,859	19,084
85,900	85,950	20,859	17,979	21,877	19,098
85,950	86,000	20,875	17,993	21,895	19,112

* This column must also be used by a qualifying widow(er).

(Continued on next page)

86,000

At least	But less than	Single	Married filing jointly *	Married filing separately	Head of a household
86,000	86,050	20,890	18,007	21,913	19,126
86,050	86,100	20,905	18,021	21,930	19,139
86,100	86,150	20,920	18,034	21,948	19,153
86,150	86,200	20,936	18,048	21,966	19,167
86,200	86,250	20,951	18,062	21,984	19,181
86,250	86,300	20,966	18,076	22,001	19,194
86,300	86,350	20,981	18,089	22,019	19,208
86,350	86,400	20,997	18,103	22,037	19,222
86,400	86,450	21,012	18,117	22,055	19,236
86,450	86,500	21,027	18,131	22,072	19,249
86,500	86,550	21,042	18,144	22,090	19,263
86,550	86,600	21,058	18,158	22,108	19,277
86,600	86,650	21,073	18,172	22,126	19,291
86,650	86,700	21,088	18,186	22,143	19,304
86,700	86,750	21,103	18,199	22,161	19,318
86,750	86,800	21,119	18,213	22,179	19,332
86,800	86,850	21,134	18,227	22,197	19,346
86,850	86,900	21,149	18,241	22,214	19,359
86,900	86,950	21,164	18,254	22,232	19,373
86,950	87,000	21,180	18,268	22,250	19,387

87,000

At least	But less than	Single	Married filing jointly *	Married filing separately	Head of a household
87,000	87,050	21,195	18,282	22,268	19,401
87,050	87,100	21,210	18,296	22,285	19,414
87,100	87,150	21,225	18,309	22,303	19,428
87,150	87,200	21,241	18,323	22,321	19,442
87,200	87,250	21,256	18,337	22,339	19,456
87,250	87,300	21,271	18,351	22,356	19,469
87,300	87,350	21,286	18,364	22,374	19,483
87,350	87,400	21,302	18,378	22,392	19,497
87,400	87,450	21,317	18,392	22,410	19,511
87,450	87,500	21,332	18,406	22,427	19,524
87,500	87,550	21,347	18,419	22,445	19,538
87,550	87,600	21,363	18,433	22,463	19,552
87,600	87,650	21,378	18,447	22,481	19,566
87,650	87,700	21,393	18,461	22,498	19,579
87,700	87,750	21,408	18,474	22,516	19,593
87,750	87,800	21,424	18,488	22,534	19,607
87,800	87,850	21,439	18,502	22,552	19,621
87,850	87,900	21,454	18,516	22,569	19,634
87,900	87,950	21,469	18,529	22,587	19,648
87,950	88,000	21,485	18,543	22,605	19,662

88,000

At least	But less than	Single	Married filing jointly *	Married filing separately	Head of a household
88,000	88,050	21,500	18,557	22,623	19,676
88,050	88,100	21,515	18,571	22,640	19,689
88,100	88,150	21,530	18,584	22,658	19,703
88,150	88,200	21,546	18,598	22,676	19,717
88,200	88,250	21,561	18,612	22,694	19,731
88,250	88,300	21,576	18,626	22,711	19,744
88,300	88,350	21,591	18,639	22,729	19,758
88,350	88,400	21,607	18,653	22,747	19,772
88,400	88,450	21,622	18,667	22,765	19,786
88,450	88,500	21,637	18,681	22,782	19,799
88,500	88,550	21,652	18,694	22,800	19,813
88,550	88,600	21,668	18,708	22,818	19,827
88,600	88,650	21,683	18,722	22,836	19,841
88,650	88,700	21,698	18,736	22,853	19,854
88,700	88,750	21,713	18,749	22,871	19,868
88,750	88,800	21,729	18,763	22,889	19,882
88,800	88,850	21,744	18,777	22,907	19,896
88,850	88,900	21,759	18,791	22,924	19,909
88,900	88,950	21,774	18,804	22,942	19,923
88,950	89,000	21,790	18,818	22,960	19,937

89,000

At least	But less than	Single	Married filing jointly *	Married filing separately	Head of a household
89,000	89,050	21,805	18,832	22,978	19,951
89,050	89,100	21,820	18,846	22,995	19,964
89,100	89,150	21,835	18,859	23,013	19,978
89,150	89,200	21,851	18,873	23,031	19,992
89,200	89,250	21,866	18,887	23,049	20,006
89,250	89,300	21,881	18,901	23,066	20,019
89,300	89,350	21,896	18,914	23,084	20,033
89,350	89,400	21,912	18,928	23,102	20,047
89,400	89,450	21,927	18,942	23,120	20,061
89,450	89,500	21,942	18,956	23,137	20,074
89,500	89,550	21,957	18,969	23,155	20,088
89,550	89,600	21,973	18,983	23,173	20,102
89,600	89,650	21,988	18,997	23,191	20,116
89,650	89,700	22,003	19,011	23,208	20,129
89,700	89,750	22,018	19,024	23,226	20,143
89,750	89,800	22,034	19,038	23,244	20,157
89,800	89,850	22,049	19,052	23,262	20,171
89,850	89,900	22,064	19,066	23,279	20,184
89,900	89,950	22,079	19,079	23,297	20,198
89,950	90,000	22,095	19,093	23,315	20,212

90,000

At least	But less than	Single	Married filing jointly *	Married filing separately	Head of a household
90,000	90,050	22,110	19,107	23,333	20,226
90,050	90,100	22,125	19,121	23,350	20,239
90,100	90,150	22,140	19,134	23,368	20,253
90,150	90,200	22,156	19,148	23,386	20,267
90,200	90,250	22,171	19,162	23,404	20,281
90,250	90,300	22,186	19,176	23,421	20,294
90,300	90,350	22,201	19,189	23,439	20,308
90,350	90,400	22,217	19,203	23,457	20,322
90,400	90,450	22,232	19,217	23,475	20,336
90,450	90,500	22,247	19,231	23,492	20,349
90,500	90,550	22,262	19,244	23,510	20,363
90,550	90,600	22,278	19,258	23,528	20,377
90,600	90,650	22,293	19,272	23,546	20,391
90,650	90,700	22,308	19,286	23,563	20,404
90,700	90,750	22,323	19,299	23,581	20,418
90,750	90,800	22,339	19,313	23,599	20,432
90,800	90,850	22,354	19,327	23,617	20,446
90,850	90,900	22,369	19,341	23,634	20,459
90,900	90,950	22,384	19,354	23,652	20,473
90,950	91,000	22,400	19,368	23,670	20,487

91,000

At least	But less than	Single	Married filing jointly *	Married filing separately	Head of a household
91,000	91,050	22,415	19,382	23,688	20,501
91,050	91,100	22,430	19,396	23,705	20,514
91,100	91,150	22,445	19,409	23,723	20,528
91,150	91,200	22,461	19,423	23,741	20,542
91,200	91,250	22,476	19,437	23,759	20,556
91,250	91,300	22,491	19,451	23,776	20,569
91,300	91,350	22,506	19,464	23,794	20,583
91,350	91,400	22,522	19,478	23,812	20,597
91,400	91,450	22,537	19,492	23,830	20,611
91,450	91,500	22,552	19,506	23,847	20,624
91,500	91,550	22,567	19,519	23,865	20,638
91,550	91,600	22,583	19,533	23,883	20,652
91,600	91,650	22,598	19,547	23,901	20,666
91,650	91,700	22,613	19,561	23,918	20,679
91,700	91,750	22,628	19,574	23,936	20,693
91,750	91,800	22,644	19,588	23,954	20,707
91,800	91,850	22,659	19,602	23,972	20,721
91,850	91,900	22,674	19,616	23,989	20,734
91,900	91,950	22,689	19,629	24,007	20,748
91,950	92,000	22,705	19,643	24,025	20,762

92,000

At least	But less than	Single	Married filing jointly *	Married filing separately	Head of a household
92,000	92,050	22,720	19,657	24,043	20,776
92,050	92,100	22,735	19,671	24,060	20,789
92,100	92,150	22,750	19,684	24,078	20,803
92,150	92,200	22,766	19,698	24,096	20,817
92,200	92,250	22,781	19,712	24,114	20,831
92,250	92,300	22,796	19,726	24,131	20,844
92,300	92,350	22,811	19,739	24,149	20,858
92,350	92,400	22,827	19,753	24,167	20,872
92,400	92,450	22,842	19,767	24,185	20,886
92,450	92,500	22,857	19,781	24,202	20,899
92,500	92,550	22,872	19,794	24,220	20,913
92,550	92,600	22,888	19,808	24,238	20,927
92,600	92,650	22,903	19,822	24,256	20,941
92,650	92,700	22,918	19,836	24,273	20,954
92,700	92,750	22,933	19,849	24,291	20,968
92,750	92,800	22,949	19,863	24,309	20,982
92,800	92,850	22,964	19,877	24,327	20,996
92,850	92,900	22,979	19,891	24,344	21,009
92,900	92,950	22,994	19,904	24,362	21,023
92,950	93,000	23,010	19,918	24,380	21,037

93,000

At least	But less than	Single	Married filing jointly *	Married filing separately	Head of a household
93,000	93,050	23,025	19,932	24,398	21,051
93,050	93,100	23,040	19,946	24,415	21,064
93,100	93,150	23,055	19,959	24,433	21,078
93,150	93,200	23,071	19,973	24,451	21,092
93,200	93,250	23,086	19,987	24,469	21,106
93,250	93,300	23,101	20,001	24,486	21,119
93,300	93,350	23,116	20,014	24,504	21,133
93,350	93,400	23,132	20,028	24,522	21,147
93,400	93,450	23,147	20,042	24,540	21,161
93,450	93,500	23,162	20,056	24,557	21,174
93,500	93,550	23,177	20,069	24,575	21,188
93,550	93,600	23,193	20,083	24,593	21,202
93,600	93,650	23,208	20,097	24,611	21,216
93,650	93,700	23,223	20,111	24,628	21,230
93,700	93,750	23,238	20,124	24,646	21,245
93,750	93,800	23,254	20,138	24,664	21,261
93,800	93,850	23,269	20,152	24,682	21,276
93,850	93,900	23,284	20,166	24,699	21,291
93,900	93,950	23,299	20,179	24,717	21,306
93,950	94,000	23,315	20,193	24,735	21,322

94,000

At least	But less than	Single	Married filing jointly *	Married filing separately	Head of a household
94,000	94,050	23,330	20,207	24,753	21,337
94,050	94,100	23,345	20,221	24,770	21,352
94,100	94,150	23,360	20,234	24,788	21,367
94,150	94,200	23,376	20,248	24,806	21,383
94,200	94,250	23,391	20,262	24,824	21,398
94,250	94,300	23,406	20,276	24,841	21,413
94,300	94,350	23,421	20,289	24,859	21,428
94,350	94,400	23,437	20,303	24,877	21,444
94,400	94,450	23,452	20,317	24,895	21,459
94,450	94,500	23,467	20,331	24,912	21,474
94,500	94,550	23,482	20,344	24,930	21,489
94,550	94,600	23,498	20,358	24,948	21,505
94,600	94,650	23,513	20,372	24,966	21,520
94,650	94,700	23,528	20,386	24,983	21,535
94,700	94,750	23,543	20,399	25,001	21,550
94,750	94,800	23,559	20,413	25,019	21,566
94,800	94,850	23,574	20,427	25,037	21,581
94,850	94,900	23,589	20,441	25,054	21,596
94,900	94,950	23,604	20,454	25,072	21,611
94,950	95,000	23,620	20,468	25,090	21,627

* This column must also be used by a qualifying widow(er).

(Continued on next page)

If (taxable income) is—		And you are—				If (taxable income) is—		And you are—			
At least	But less than	Single	Married filing jointly *	Married filing separately	Head of a household	At least	But less than	Single	Married filing jointly *	Married filing separately	Head of a household
		Your tax is—						Your tax is—			

95,000 / 98,000

At least	But less than	Single	Married filing jointly *	Married filing separately	Head of a household	At least	But less than	Single	Married filing jointly *	Married filing separately	Head of a household
95,000	95,050	23,635	20,482	25,108	21,642	98,000	98,050	24,550	21,307	26,173	22,557
95,050	95,100	23,650	20,496	25,125	21,657	98,050	98,100	24,565	21,321	26,190	22,572
95,100	95,150	23,665	20,509	25,143	21,672	98,100	98,150	24,580	21,334	26,208	22,587
95,150	95,200	23,681	20,523	25,161	21,688	98,150	98,200	24,596	21,348	26,226	22,603
95,200	95,250	23,696	20,537	25,179	21,703	98,200	98,250	24,611	21,362	26,244	22,618
95,250	95,300	23,711	20,551	25,196	21,718	98,250	98,300	24,626	21,376	26,261	22,633
95,300	95,350	23,726	20,564	25,214	21,733	98,300	98,350	24,641	21,389	26,279	22,648
95,350	95,400	23,742	20,578	25,232	21,749	98,350	98,400	24,657	21,403	26,297	22,664
95,400	95,450	23,757	20,592	25,250	21,764	98,400	98,450	24,672	21,417	26,315	22,679
95,450	95,500	23,772	20,606	25,267	21,779	98,450	98,500	24,687	21,431	26,332	22,694
95,500	95,550	23,787	20,619	25,285	21,794	98,500	98,550	24,702	21,444	26,350	22,709
95,550	95,600	23,803	20,633	25,303	21,810	98,550	98,600	24,718	21,458	26,368	22,725
95,600	95,650	23,818	20,647	25,321	21,825	98,600	98,650	24,733	21,472	26,386	22,740
95,650	95,700	23,833	20,661	25,338	21,840	98,650	98,700	24,748	21,486	26,403	22,755
95,700	95,750	23,848	20,674	25,356	21,855	98,700	98,750	24,763	21,499	26,421	22,770
95,750	95,800	23,864	20,688	25,374	21,871	98,750	98,800	24,779	21,513	26,439	22,786
95,800	95,850	23,879	20,702	25,392	21,886	98,800	98,850	24,794	21,527	26,457	22,801
95,850	95,900	23,894	20,716	25,409	21,901	98,850	98,900	24,809	21,541	26,474	22,816
95,900	95,950	23,909	20,729	25,427	21,916	98,900	98,950	24,824	21,554	26,492	22,831
95,950	96,000	23,925	20,743	25,445	21,932	98,950	99,000	24,840	21,568	26,510	22,847

96,000 / 99,000

At least	But less than	Single	Married filing jointly *	Married filing separately	Head of a household	At least	But less than	Single	Married filing jointly *	Married filing separately	Head of a household
96,000	96,050	23,940	20,757	25,463	21,947	99,000	99,050	24,855	21,582	26,528	22,862
96,050	96,100	23,955	20,771	25,480	21,962	99,050	99,100	24,870	21,596	26,545	22,877
96,100	96,150	23,970	20,784	25,498	21,977	99,100	99,150	24,885	21,609	26,563	22,892
96,150	96,200	23,986	20,798	25,516	21,993	99,150	99,200	24,901	21,623	26,581	22,908
96,200	96,250	24,001	20,812	25,534	22,008	99,200	99,250	24,916	21,637	26,599	22,923
96,250	96,300	24,016	20,826	25,551	22,023	99,250	99,300	24,931	21,651	26,616	22,938
96,300	96,350	24,031	20,839	25,569	22,038	99,300	99,350	24,946	21,664	26,634	22,953
96,350	96,400	24,047	20,853	25,587	22,054	99,350	99,400	24,962	21,678	26,652	22,969
96,400	96,450	24,062	20,867	25,605	22,069	99,400	99,450	24,977	21,692	26,670	22,984
96,450	96,500	24,077	20,881	25,622	22,084	99,450	99,500	24,992	21,706	26,687	22,999
96,500	96,550	24,092	20,894	25,640	22,099	99,500	99,550	25,007	21,719	26,705	23,014
96,550	96,600	24,108	20,908	25,658	22,115	99,550	99,600	25,023	21,733	26,723	23,030
96,600	96,650	24,123	20,922	25,676	22,130	99,600	99,650	25,038	21,747	26,741	23,045
96,650	96,700	24,138	20,936	25,693	22,145	99,650	99,700	25,053	21,761	26,758	23,060
96,700	96,750	24,153	20,949	25,711	22,160	99,700	99,750	25,068	21,774	26,776	23,075
96,750	96,800	24,169	20,963	25,729	22,176	99,750	99,800	25,084	21,788	26,794	23,091
96,800	96,850	24,184	20,977	25,747	22,191	99,800	99,850	25,099	21,802	26,812	23,106
96,850	96,900	24,199	20,991	25,764	22,206	99,850	99,900	25,114	21,816	26,829	23,121
96,900	96,950	24,214	21,004	25,782	22,221	99,900	99,950	25,129	21,829	26,847	23,136
96,950	97,000	24,230	21,018	25,800	22,237	99,950	100,000	25,145	21,843	26,865	23,152

97,000

At least	But less than	Single	Married filing jointly *	Married filing separately	Head of a household
97,000	97,050	24,245	21,032	25,818	22,252
97,050	97,100	24,260	21,046	25,835	22,267
97,100	97,150	24,275	21,059	25,853	22,282
97,150	97,200	24,291	21,073	25,871	22,298
97,200	97,250	24,306	21,087	25,889	22,313
97,250	97,300	24,321	21,101	25,906	22,328
97,300	97,350	24,336	21,114	25,924	22,343
97,350	97,400	24,352	21,128	25,942	22,359
97,400	97,450	24,367	21,142	25,960	22,374
97,450	97,500	24,382	21,156	25,977	22,389
97,500	97,550	24,397	21,169	25,995	22,404
97,550	97,600	24,413	21,183	26,013	22,420
97,600	97,650	24,428	21,197	26,031	22,435
97,650	97,700	24,443	21,211	26,048	22,450
97,700	97,750	24,458	21,224	26,066	22,465
97,750	97,800	24,474	21,238	26,084	22,481
97,800	97,850	24,489	21,252	26,102	22,496
97,850	97,900	24,504	21,266	26,119	22,511
97,900	97,950	24,519	21,279	26,137	22,526
97,950	98,000	24,535	21,293	26,155	22,542

Caution.

- Dependents, see *Tax Computation Worksheet for Certain Dependents* in your tax form package

- **$100,000 or over** — use the Tax Rate Schedules

* This column must also be used by a qualifying widow(er).

2001
Tax Rate
Schedules

Use **only** if your taxable income (Form 1040, line 39) is $100,000 or more. If less, use the **Tax Table.** Even though you cannot use the Tax Rate Schedules below if your taxable income is less than $100,000, all levels of taxable income are shown so taxpayers can see the tax rate that applies to each level.

Schedule X—Use if your filing status is **Single**

If the amount on Form 1040, line 39, is: Over—	But not over—	Enter on Form 1040, line 40	of the amount over—
$0	$27,050	.... 15%	$0
27,050	65,550	$4,057.50 + 27.5%	27,050
65,550	136,750	14,645.00 + 30.5%	65,550
136,750	297,350	36,361.00 + 35.5%	136,750
297,350	....	93,374.00 + 39.1%	297,350

Schedule Y-1—Use if your filing status is **Married filing jointly** or **Qualifying widow(er)**

If the amount on Form 1040, line 39, is: Over—	But not over—	Enter on Form 1040, line 40	of the amount over—
$0	$45,200	.... 15%	$0
45,200	109,250	$6,780.00 + 27.5%	45,200
109,250	166,500	24,393.75 + 30.5%	109,250
166,500	297,350	41,855.00 + 35.5%	166,500
297,350	....	88,306.75 + 39.1%	297,350

Schedule Y-2—Use if your filing status is **Married filing separately**

If the amount on Form 1040, line 39, is: Over—	But not over—	Enter on Form 1040, line 40	of the amount over—
$0	$22,600	.... 15%	$0
22,600	54,625	$3,390.00 + 27.5%	22,600
54,625	83,250	12,196.88 + 30.5%	54,625
83,250	148,675	20,927.50 + 35.5%	83,250
148,675	....	44,153.38 + 39.1%	148,675

Schedule Z—Use if your filing status is **Head of household**

If the amount on Form 1040, line 39, is: Over—	But not over—	Enter on Form 1040, line 40	of the amount over—
$0	$36,250	.... 15%	$0
36,250	93,650	$5,437.50 + 27.5%	36,250
93,650	151,650	21,222.50 + 30.5%	93,650
151,650	297,350	38,912.50 + 35.5%	151,650
297,350	....	90,636.00 + 39.1%	297,350

Dependents, see *Tax Computation Worksheet for Certain Dependents* in your tax form package.

Order Blank for Forms and Publications

The most frequently ordered forms and publications are listed on the order blank below. We will mail you two copies of each form and one copy of each publication you order. To help reduce waste, please order only the items you need to prepare your return.

TIP For faster ways of getting the items you need, such as by computer or fax, see the front cover of 1040 Instructions.

How To Use the Order Blank

Circle the items you need on the order blank below. Use the blank spaces to order items not listed. If you need more space, attach a separate sheet of paper.

Print or type your name and address accurately in the space provided below. An accurate address is necessary to ensure delivery of your order. Cut the order blank on the dotted line. Enclose the order blank in your own envelope and send it to the IRS address shown on this page that applies to you. You should receive your order within 10 days after we receive your request.

Where To Mail Your Order Blank for Free Forms and Publications

IF you live in the . . .	THEN mail to . . .	AT this address . . .
Western United States	Western Area Distribution Center	Rancho Cordova, CA 95743-0001
Central United States	Central Area Distribution Center	P.O. Box 8903 Bloomington, IL 61702-8903
Eastern United States or a foreign country	Eastern Area Distribution Center	P.O. Box 85074 Richmond, VA 23261-5074

Detach at this line

Order Blank

Fill in your name and address.

Name

Number and street   Apt./Suite/Room

City   State   ZIP code

Foreign country   International postal code

Daytime telephone number (optional)
(   )

Some items may be picked up at many IRS offices, post offices, and libraries. You may also download all these items from the Internet at www.irs.gov or place an electronic order for them.

Circle the forms and publications you need. The instructions for any form you order will be included.

1040	Schedule F (1040)	Schedule 3 (1040A)	2441	8812	Pub. 463	Pub. 527	Pub. 910
Schedules A&B (1040)	Schedule H (1040)	**1040EZ**	3903	8822	Pub. 501	Pub. 529	Pub. 926
Schedule C (1040)	Schedule J (1040)	1040-ES (2000)	4562	8829	Pub. 502	Pub. 535	Pub. 929
Schedule C-EZ (1040)	Schedule R (1040)	1040-V	4868	8863	Pub. 505	Pub. 550	Pub. 936
Schedule D (1040)	Schedule SE (1040)	1040X	5329	9465	Pub. 508	Pub. 554	Pub. 970
Schedule D-1 (1040)	**1040A**	2106	8283	Pub. 1	Pub. 521	Pub. 575	Pub. 972
Schedule E (1040)	**Schedule 1 (1040A)**	2106-EZ	8582	Pub. 17	Pub. 523	Pub. 590	
Schedule EIC (1040A or 1040)	**Schedule 2 (1040A)**	2210	8606	Pub. 334	Pub. 525	Pub. 596	

What Is TeleTax?

Call TeleTax at **1-800-829-4477** for:

- **Refund information.** Check the status of your **2001** refund.
- **Recorded tax information.** There are about 150 topics that answer many Federal tax questions.
- **2001 advance payment (rebate) information.** Find out the amount of your advance payment (before offset). You may need this information to complete the Rate Reduction Credit Worksheet on page 596.

How Do You Use Tele-Tax?

Refund Information

Refund information is not available until at least 4 weeks after you file your return (3 weeks if you file electronically), and sometimes is not available for up to 6 weeks. Please wait at least 4 weeks from the date you filed before calling to check the status of your refund. Do not send in a copy of your return unless asked to do so.

Be sure to have a copy of your 2001 tax return available because you will need to know the first social security number shown on your return, the filing status, and the **exact** whole-dollar amount of your refund. Then, call **1-800-829-4477** and follow the recorded instructions.

 TIP Refunds are sent out weekly on Fridays. If you call to check the status of your refund and are not given the date it will be issued, please wait until the next week before calling back.

Recorded Tax Information

Recorded tax information is available 24 hours a day, 7 days a week. Select the number of the topic you want to hear. Then, call **1-800-829-4477**. Have paper and pencil handy to take notes.

Topics by Personal Computer

TeleTax topics are also available using a personal computer and modem (go to **www.irs.gov**).

TeleTax Topics

All topics are available in Spanish.

TeleTax Topics

(Continued)

Topic numbers are effective January 1, 2002.

Calling the IRS

If you cannot answer your question by using one of the methods listed on page 7, please call us for assistance at **1-800-829-1040.** You will not be charged for the call unless your phone company charges you for local calls. Our normal hours of operation are Monday through Friday from 7:00 a.m. to 10:00 p.m. local time. Beginning December 31, 2001, through April 16, 2002, assistance will also be available on Saturday from 9:00 a.m. to 5:00 p.m. local time. Assistance provided to callers from Alaska and Hawaii will be based on the hours of operation in the Pacific Time zone.

 If you want to check the status of your **2001 refund,** call **TeleTax** at **1-800-829-4477** (see page 11 for instructions).

Employee Plans. If you own a business and have questions about starting a pension or other employee plan, an existing plan, or filing **Form 5500,** call our **Tax Exempt/Government Entities Customer Account Services** at **1-877-829-5500.** Assistance is available Monday through Friday from 8:00 a.m. to 9:30 p.m. EST. If you have questions about an individual retirement arrangement (IRA), call **1-800-829-1040.**

Exempt Organizations. If you have questions about exempt organizations, including the types of tax-exempt organizations, or you want to verify an organization's charitable status, call our **Tax Exempt/Government Entities Customer Account Services** at **1-877-829-5500.** Assistance is available Monday through Friday from 8:00 a.m. to 9:30 p.m. EST.

Before You Call

IRS representatives care about the quality of the service we provide to you, our customer. You can help us provide accurate, complete answers to your questions by having the following information available.

- The tax form, schedule, or notice to which your question relates.
- The facts about your particular situation. The answer to the same question often varies from one taxpayer to another because of differences in their age, income, whether they can be claimed as a dependent, etc.
- The name of any IRS publication or other source of information that you used to look for the answer.

To maintain your account security, you may be asked for the following information, which you should also have available.

- Your social security number.
- The amount of refund and filing status shown on your tax return.
- The "Caller ID Number" shown at the top of any notice you received.
- Your personal identification number (PIN) if you have one.
- Your date of birth.
- The numbers in your street address.
- Your ZIP code.

If you are asking for an installment agreement to pay your tax, you will be asked for the highest amount you can pay each month and the date on which you can pay it.

Evaluation of Services Provided. The IRS uses several methods to evaluate the quality of this telephone service. One method is for a second IRS representative to sometimes listen in on or record telephone calls. Another is to ask some callers to complete a short survey at the end of the call.

Making the Call

Call **1-800-829-1040** (for TTY/TDD help, call 1-800-829-4059). We have redesigned our menus to allow callers with pulse or rotary dial telephones to speak their responses when requested to do so. First, you will be provided a series of options that will request touch-tone responses. If a touch-tone response is not received, you will then hear a series of options and be asked to speak your selections. After your touch-tone or spoken response is received, the system will direct your call to the appropriate assistance. You can do the following within the system.

- Order tax forms and publications.
- Find out the status of your refund or what you owe.
- Determine if we have adjusted your account or received payments you made.
- Request a transcript of your account.
- Find out where to send your tax return or payment.
- Request more time to pay or set up a monthly installment agreement.

Before You Hang Up

If you do not fully understand the answer you receive, or you feel our representative may not fully understand your question, our representative needs to know this. He or she will be happy to take additional time to be sure your question is answered fully.

By law, you are responsible for paying your share of Federal income tax. If we should make an error in answering your question, you are still responsible for the payment of the correct tax. Should this occur, however, you will not be charged any penalty.

A Glossary of Tax and Financial Terms

A

Accelerated Cost Recovery System (ACRS). A method of **depreciation** that, in general, allowed you to deduct the cost of a **capital asset** at a faster rate than was previously possible. ACRS is used for almost all **assets** you began depreciating in the years 1981–1986. See Chapter 10, *Rental Income and Expenses.*

Accelerated Death Benefit. Certain payments received under a life insurance contract on the life of a terminally or chronically ill individual before the individual's death.

Accelerated depreciation. A method of **depreciation** that allows you to deduct the cost of property more rapidly than **straight-line depreciation.** Accelerated depreciation rates are included in **ACRS** rates and most Modified Accelerated Cost Recovery System **(MACRS)** rates if you want to use them. See Chapter 10, *Rental Income and Expenses.*

Accountable plan. An employer's plan for reimbursing employees for business-related expenses, under which the employees are required to substantiate each business expense to the employer and return any reimbursement in excess of the substantiated expenses. Reimbursements received under an accountable plan are generally excluded from wages and are not subject to employment taxes. See Chapter 28, *Car Expenses and Other Employee Business Expenses.*

Accounting to an employer. Providing an employer with documents (a diary, a statement of expenses, etc.) that support expenses you have incurred.

Accrual method of accounting. A method of accounting in which income is reported in the year in which it is earned and expenses are reported in the year in which they are incurred. See and compare **cash method of accounting.** See Chapter 1, *Filing Information.*

Acquisition debt. Indebtedness (subject to a $1 million ceiling) used to acquire a principal residence or a second home, the interest on which is fully deductible. See Chapter 25, *Interest Expense.*

ACRS. See **Accelerated Cost Recovery System.**

Adjusted basis. The measure used as a starting point for determining a gain or a loss on the sale or exchange of property. Your **basis** in property is adjusted by certain increases (**capital expenditures,** for example) or decreases (**depreciation**). See Chapter 14, *Basis of Property.*

Adjusted gross income. Your **gross income** reduced by certain adjustments allowed by law. For example, you may reduce your gross income by your deductible **IRA** contribution. See Chapter 31, *How to Figure Your Tax.*

Administrator. Person who is usually appointed by the court if no will exists, if no executor was named in the will, or if the named executor cannot or will not serve. The administrator will have to administer the estate (property or debts left by the decedent) and distribute properties as the decedent has directed.

ADS. See **Alternative Depreciation System.**

Alimony. Periodic payments made under (1) a decree of divorce or **separate maintenance,** (2) a written separation agreement, or (3) a decree of **support.** Alimony that you pay may be taken as a deduction in calculating your adjusted gross income. Alimony that you receive must be included as income in calculating your adjusted gross income. See Chapter 20, *Alimony.*

Alternative Depreciation System (ADS). A way of depreciating assets using the straight-line depreciation method and longer recovery periods than are available under **MACRS.** Mandatory for such items as foreign assets, luxury automobiles, and tax-exempt use property. See Chapter 10, *Rental Income and Expenses.*

Alternative Minimum Tax (AMT). A tax that may apply in lieu of income tax when a taxpayer has **tax preference items** or certain deductions allowed in determining regular taxable income. How to calculate the alternative minimum tax is explained in Chapter 31, *How to Figure Your Tax.*

Amended return. A return (Form 1040X) filed within a 3-year period to correct a mistake on an original income tax return or to claim a refund.

Amortization. A deductible expense allowed as a means of recovering your investment in an intangible asset. Compare with **depreciation.**

Amount realized. The **fair market value** of property, including money (at face value), received in a sale or an exchange.

AMT. See **Alternative Minimum Tax.**

Annuity. A sum of money paid periodically that includes the return of your invested capital plus income generated by it. An annuity is frequently purchased by an individual for investment purposes and is used by retirement plans to pay **pensions.** See Chapter 11, *Retirement Plans, Pensions, and Annuities.*

Annuity trust. A type of **trust** in which one of the beneficiaries is paid a specified amount of income at least annually. See Chapter 11, *Retirement Plans, Pensions, and Annuities.*

Applicable federal rate. Interest rates published by the IRS for use in determining imputed interest on transactions providing for below-market interest.

Asset. Property that has value.

At-risk limitations. Generally, partnership losses are deductible up to the amount you have at risk in the activity. The amount at risk is your basis in the activity and any amounts borrowed for use in the activity for which you are personally liable. See Chapter 13, *Other Income.*

Audit. An examination of your financial records. When the **IRS** examines your tax records, it is called an audit. See Chapter 45, *If Your Return Is Examined.*

Away from home overnight. A period substantially longer than an ordinary workday during which you are away from your **tax home.** The period you are away from home must include time for sleep or rest.

B

Bad debt. An amount owed you representing a cash outlay or an item already included in income that you are unable to collect. See Chapter 15, *Sale of Property.*

Basis. Generally, the cost of an **asset.** See Chapter 14, *Basis of Property.*

Boot. The taxable receipt of cash or its equivalent as part of an exchange of properties.

C

Calendar year. A 12-month period ending on December 31. Most individual taxpayers are required to file their returns on the basis of such a year. Compare **fiscal year.**

Capital asset. In general, property held for personal purposes or investment, rather than for business purposes.

Capital expenditures. The costs for additions or improvements that increase the value or **useful life** of your property.

Capital gain dividend (capital gain distribution). A distribution to shareholders in a **mutual fund** of a **capital gain** realized by the fund on the sale of a part of its investment portfolio. See Chapter 9, *Dividends and Other Corporate Distributions.*

Capital gain or loss. A gain or loss arising from the sale or exchange of **capital assets.** You compute your capital gain or loss by comparing the amount you realize on the sale or exchange of an **asset** with the **adjusted basis** of the asset. See Chapter 17, *Reporting Gains and Losses.*

Capital loss carryover. The excess of **capital losses** over **capital gains** that cannot be deducted in a particular year and must be carried over to the succeeding year.

Capitalize. To treat an expenditure as a cost or an additional cost of property that increases the property's **basis**—as opposed to treating the expenditure as a current deduction.

Cash method of accounting. A method of accounting in which income is reported when it is actually or **constructively received** and expenses are reported when they are paid.

Casualty loss. A loss arising from fire, storm, shipwreck, or other similar and unexpected occurrences. See Chapter 27, *Casualty and Theft Losses.*

Child support. Payments made to support a minor child following a divorce or a separation. The payments cannot be deducted from your **gross income** and are not taxable to the recipient parent. Starting in 1985, the parent with custody of the child is generally entitled to the dependency **exemption** unless such a right is expressly waived. See Chapter 20, *Alimony.*

Child tax credit. For tax years beginning after 1997, a tax credit is allowed against income with respect to each qualifying child for taxpayers with modified adjusted gross income below certain thresholds.

Clifford trust. A short-term **trust** in which the beneficiary receives the income from the property placed in the trust. When the trust expires, after 10 years or on the death of the beneficiary, if earlier, the property that remains in the trust is returned to the original donor. Current tax rules have terminated the tax benefits of such trusts.

Community income. Income that is treated as belonging equally to each spouse, no matter which spouse actually earns or receives it. See **community property.**

Community property. Property that belongs equally to husband and wife. This concept of property ownership is used in Arizona, California, Idaho, Louisiana, Nevada, New Mexico, Texas, Washington, and Wisconsin.

Condemnation. The seizure of property for compensation by a government agency for a public purpose.

Constructive receipt. Income you are taxed on because it was made available to you to draw on, even if it has not yet been physically transferred to you.

Consumer interest. Interest incurred on personal and consumer purchases. Consumer interest has not been deductible since 1991. Also called personal interest.

Corporation. A business entity owned by shareholders that is generally treated as a separate taxpayer.

D

Decedent. The deceased taxpayer.

Declining balance depreciation. A method of **accelerated depreciation** by which each year's **depreciation** is a percentage of the reduced **basis** of the **asset.** See Chapter 10, *Rental Income and Expenses.*

Deductions. Expenses allowed by law to reduce your **gross income** to **adjusted gross income** or **taxable income.**

Deferred gain. A gain realized but not recognized as **taxable income** until a later time.

Deficiency. The difference between your correct tax liability and the amount reported on your return.

Dependency exemption. An exemption of $2,900 (for 2001) allowed to a taxpayer for a qualifying **dependent.** See Chapter 3, *Personal Exemptions and Dependents.*

Dependent. An individual who is supported by a taxpayer in a manner that entitles the taxpayer to claim an **exemption** allowance on his or her income tax return. See Chapter 3, *Personal Exemptions and Dependents.*

Dependent care credit. A credit to reduce your taxes dollar-for-dollar based on expenses incurred in caring for a **dependent** so that you can be gainfully employed. See Chapter 33, *Child and Dependent Care Credit.*

Depletion. A deductible expense that reflects the decrease of a depletable natural resource, such as oil and gas, as it is extracted. See Chapter 10, *Rental Income and Expenses.*

Depreciable asset. Property used in a trade or a business or held for the production of income with a **useful life** of more than 1 year.

Depreciation. A deductible expense that reflects a reasonable allowance for wear and tear of tangible property. Only property that has a **useful life** of more than 1 year and is used for business or income-producing purposes can be depreciated. Depreciation can be calculated under various prescribed methods. See Chapter 10, *Rental Income and Expenses.*

Direct rollover. An eligible rollover distribution that is paid directly to an eligible retirement plan for the benefit of the distributee. See Chapter 11, *Retirement Plans, Pensions, and Annuities.*

Discount income. Income on an obligation purchased at a discount and maturing at face value.

Dividend. Generally, a share of a corporation's profits that is distributed to shareholders and is taxable to them.

Domicile. The place that an individual intends to be his or her permanent residence.

DRIP (Dividend Reinvestment Plan). A plan that allows you to choose to use your dividends to buy (through an agent or possibly directly from the company) more shares of stock in the corporation instead of receiving the dividends in cash.

Dual-status alien. An individual who is a **nonresident alien** for part of the year and a **resident alien** or U.S. citizen for the rest of the year. See Chapter 43, *Foreign Citizens Living in the United States.*

E

Earned income. Compensation for personal services rendered. Earned income does not include amounts received from an **annuity** or a **pension.**

Earned income credit. A refundable credit, based on **earned income,** available to taxpayers with low income.

Education IRA. An IRA created exclusively for the purpose of paying the trust beneficiary's qualified higher education expenses.

Eligible retirement plan. A qualified retirement plan, an individual retirement account, or an individual retirement annuity.

Eligible rollover distribution. Any distribution of all or any portion of the balance to the credit of the employee in a qualified retirement plan.

Employee. An individual whose work is performed under the control or direction of an employer.

Estimated tax. A direct quarterly payment of taxes that is required, for example, when the taxes withheld from your wages are inadequate. See Chapter 5, *Tax Withholding and Estimated Tax.*

Exclusion. An amount that is excluded from **gross income.**

Executor. Person named in the decedent's will to administer the estate (property or debts left by the decedent) and distribute properties as the decedent has directed.

Exemption. An amount allowed to a taxpayer as a **deduction** for himself or herself and for each **dependent.** See Chapter 3, *Personal Exemptions and Dependents.*

F

Fair market value. The price a willing buyer would pay and a willing seller would accept, neither of whom is under any compulsion to buy or to sell.

Fiduciary. An individual who has discretionary authority to receive and manage another's income. Also, an individual who holds **assets** in a **trust** in which another person has an interest.

Finance charges. Interest paid on purchases made on a deferred-payment basis.

Fiscal year. A 12-month period ending on the last day of any month other than December.

Foreign corporation. A corporation organized outside the laws of the United States.

Foreign tax credit. A credit allowed for income taxes paid to a foreign tax jurisdiction (e.g., a foreign country) to mitigate double taxation.

401(k) plan. A tax-favored deferred compensation plan under which a portion of an employee's salary is withheld on a pretax basis and allowed to earn income on a tax-deferred basis until withdrawal is authorized at age 59½, separation from service or other qualifying events.

G

Gross income. All of the **income** of a taxpayer before subtracting any allowable **deductions.**

H

Head of household. A taxpayer who is unmarried and pays more than 50% of the cost of maintaining a residence for the entire year for a qualifying individual. If you are a head of household, you qualify for special tax rates. See Chapter 2, *Filing Status.*

Holding period. The length of time an **asset** is held. The holding period of a capital asset determines whether a sale or an exchange results in a **long-term** or a **short-term capital gain** or **loss.** See Chapter 17, *Reporting Gains and Losses.*

Home equity debt. Debt secured by a principal residence or a second residence in excess of acquisition debt. Interest on home equity indebtedness not in excess of $100,000 is generally fully deductible.

Hope Scholarship Credit. Election to take an income tax credit with respect to qualified tuition and related expenses of each eligible student. Credit is only allowed for first 2 years of undergraduate education.

I

Imputed interest. Interest deemed to have been earned or charged on a debt if the stated interest rate is below the rate set by law.

Incentive stock option (ISO). A type of stock option that can be received and exercised without recognition of income until the option stock is sold, if certain statutory requirements are met. See Chapter 6, *Wages, Salaries, and Other Earnings.*

Income averaging. A method that taxes some of the income in a high-income year as if it were spread over a 4-year period. Income averaging is not available for years after 1986.

Income with respect to a decedent. Income earned by an individual before death but taxed to the survivor who receives it after the earner dies.

Independent contractor. A person whose work hours and procedures (as opposed to end product) are not controlled by another and who is therefore deemed to be self-employed for tax purposes.

Individual Retirement Account. See **Individual Retirement Arrangement.**

Individual Retirement Annuity. See **Individual Retirement Arrangement.**

Individual Retirement Arrangement (IRA). An account under which certain individuals are permitted to establish a retirement plan and to deduct their contributions to the account. The maximum contribution that can be deducted each year is $2,000 per person. See Chapter 18, *Individual Retirement Arrangements (IRAs).*

Inflation adjustment. The adjustment by which, beginning in 1989, the tax rate brackets, standard deduction, and personal exemption amounts are adjusted for inflation.

Installment sale method of accounting. A method of reporting the gain from a sale during the years in which the installment payments of the purchase price are received instead of reporting the entire amount of the gain in the year of sale.

Intangible personal property. Property whose value consists of rights rather than material attributes. Some examples are patents, notes receivable, and accounts receivable.

Internal Revenue Service (IRS). The division of the U.S. Treasury Department that is responsible for the enforcement of the tax laws.

Investment credit. A tax credit (now repealed) based on the cost of **tangible personal property** used for business purposes.

Involuntary conversion. The forced disposition of property as a result of casualty, theft, or **condemnation.** Upon conversion, you usually receive cash through insurance proceeds or condemnation awards.

IRA. See **Individual Retirement Arrangement.**

IRS. See **Internal Revenue Service.**

Itemized deductions. Expenses claimed on your individual tax return that are subtracted from your **adjusted gross income** to arrive at **taxable income.** Some examples are medical expenses, interest, taxes, and charitable contributions. See Part III, *Standard Deduction and Itemized Deductions.*

J

Joint return. A tax return filed by a husband and wife that combines their incomes and **deductions.**

K

Keogh plan. A retirement plan for **self-employed** individuals. Contributions to Keogh plans, within specified limits, are deductible, and income accumulates tax free until it is withdrawn. The money in the plan is subject to various restrictions. Keogh plans are also sometimes known as HR 10 plans. See Chapter 18, *Individual Retirement Arrangements (IRAs).*

Kiddie tax. The popular name for the tax on the investment income in excess of $1,500 of a dependent child under age 14, based on the parent's marginal tax rate. See Chapter 32, *Tax on Investment Income of Certain Minor Children.*

L

Legally separated. A husband and wife who are separated and required to live apart under a decree of separate maintenance.

Lifetime Learning Credit. 20% credit for up to $5,000 of qualified tuition and related expenses for undergraduate or graduate level courses.

Like-kind exchange. A tax-free exchange of properties held for either productive use in a trade or a business or for investment that are of the same nature or character. The term is also used in connection with **involuntary conversions.**

Long-term capital gain or loss. Gain or loss on the sale or exchange of a **capital asset** that has been held for a legislatively mandated **holding period.** See Chapter 17, *Reporting Gains and Losses.*

Long-term Care Insurance Contract. Insurance contract that only provides coverage for qualified long-term care services.

Lump-sum distribution. The distribution or payment within 1 taxable year of the total balance due from an employer-funded qualified **pension** or profit-sharing plan triggered by a specified event (e.g., retirement, separation from service).

Luxury Auto Tax. An excise tax imposed on the excess of the cost of luxury automobiles over threshold amounts. See Chapter 24, *Taxes You May Deduct.*

M

MACRS. See Modified Accelerated Cost Recovery System.

Marginal tax rate. The tax rate at which each additional dollar of income over a specified ceiling is taxed.

Market discount. A bond purchased in the secondary market at a discount from the face value, attributable to an increase in interest rates or other factors affecting the quality of the debt.

Marital deduction. Provision that allows unlimited transfers to a spouse free of estate and gift tax.

Material participant. A taxpayer who participates in an activity on a regular, continuous, and substantial basis. The term is used in connection with passive activity losses.

Miscellaneous itemized deductions. A class of itemized deductions (e.g., investment expenses, fee for tax advice, union dues) that is deductible only to the extent that the total exceeds 2% of adjusted gross income.

Modified Accelerated Cost Recovery System (MACRS). A method of depreciation generally used for assets acquired after 1986. See Chapter 10, *Rental Income and Expenses.*

Mutual fund. A company that is in the business of investing its shareholders' funds, usually in stocks or bonds; sometimes known as a **regulated investment company.**

N

Net operating loss. Generally, a business loss that exceeds current income. A net operating loss may be carried back 2 years and carried forward for 20 years to reduce taxes in 1 or more of those years.

Nominee. Someone who receives income that belongs to another person.

Nonqualified stock option. A type of stock option that when exercised creates **ordinary income** for the taxpayer.

Nonrecourse financing. A type of debt for which, in the event of forfeiture, the lender may not seek recovery from the borrower personally but must look only to the financed property.

Nonrecovery property. A term that applies to most tangible depreciable property that was in use *prior* to 1981. See Chapter 10, *Rental Income and Expenses.*

Nonresident alien. An individual who is not a citizen or permanent resident of the United States. See Chapter 43, *Foreign Citizens Living in the United States.*

Nontaxable exchange. An exchange of property in which no gain or loss is recognized for tax purposes.

O

OID. See **original issue discount.**

Ordinary gain or loss. A gain or loss other than a **capital gain or loss.**

Ordinary income. Income that does not arise from the sale or exchange of a **capital asset** or a **Section 1231 asset** and is not subject to any preferential tax treatment.

Original issue discount (OID). Applies to debt instruments initially sold at prices below their face value. The difference between the face value and the amount paid is OID. Generally, the OID must be included in taxable income over the life of the debt instrument. See Chapter 8, *Interest Income.*

Outside salesperson. An **employee** who engages in selling, principally away from his or her employer's place of business.

Owner-employee. An **employee** who is the **proprietor** of a business. Also, a partner who owns more than 10% of either the capital or the profit interest in a partnership.

P

Passive activity loss. A loss from a trade or a business in which the taxpayer is not a **material participant.** Passive activity losses are subject to deduction limitations. Passive activities include rental activities and investments in limited partnerships. See *Tax Shelters and Passive Activity Losses* in Chapter 13, *Other Income.*

Patronage dividend. A taxable distribution made by a cooperative to its members or patrons.

Pension. An arrangement under which payments are made to retired employees from an employer-funded retirement plan for past services rendered.

Percentage depletion. A method of calculating **depletion** that applies a fixed percentage to the **gross income** generated by the mineral property. See Chapter 10, *Rental Income and Expenses.*

Personal-use property. Property that is not held for investment or use in a trade or a business.

Points. Certain charges paid by a borrower, calculated as a percentage of the loan proceeds; each point is 1%. They are also called loan origination fees, maximum loan charges, or premium charges. See Chapter 25, *Interest Expense.*

Proprietor. An individual who is the sole owner of his or her trade or business.

Q

QTIP Trust. See **Qualified Terminal Interest Property Trust.**

Qualified state tuition program (QSTP). A program established and maintained by a state under which a person may: (1) prepay tuition benefits on behalf of a beneficiary so that the beneficiary is entitled to a waiver or payment of qualified higher education expenses, or (2) contribute to an account that is established for paying qualified higher education expenses of the beneficiary.

Qualified charitable organization. A nonprofit philanthropic organization specifically approved by the U.S. Treasury as a recipient of charitable contributions that are deductible for tax purposes. See Chapter 26, *Contributions.*

Qualified plan. An **employee** benefit plan established by an employer that meets certain requirements and therefore qualifies for certain tax benefits. Two examples are **pension** and profit-sharing plans.

Qualified real estate professionals. Taxpayers who satisfy certain eligibility thresholds and materially participate in rental real estate activities may offset these rental real estate losses against all sources of taxable income.

Qualified residence interest. Interest paid or accrued during the taxable year on acquisition indebtedness (limited to $1 million) or home equity indebtedness (limited to $100,000). See Chapter 25, *Interest Expense.*

Qualified Retirement Plan. See **Qualified plan.**

Qualified small business stock (QSBS). Certain stock issued after August 10, 1993, and held for more than 5 years. The gain from the sale of this stock is eligible for a 50% exclusion from gross income.

Qualified Terminal Interest Property Trust (QTIP Trust). A trust that allows you to transfer property to your spouse for life only, while still qualifying for the marital deduction. See Chapter 46, *Planning Ahead for 2001 and Beyond.*

Qualifying widow(er). A filing status for a surviving spouse with dependents that allows the individual to use the same tax rates and tables as if he or she were married filing jointly.

R

Real estate investment trust (REIT). A **trust** that invests principally in **real estate** and mortgages. It is taxed only on the income that it does not distribute to its beneficiaries or shareholders.

Real property (real estate). Physical property that is permanent and nonmovable in nature. Two examples are land and buildings.

Realized gain or loss. The difference between the amount you are entitled to receive on a sale or exchange of property and the **adjusted basis** of the property.

Recognized gain or loss. The amount of gain or loss realized that must be included in your **taxable income.**

Recovery property. A term that applies to most tangible depreciable property placed in use *after* 1980 and *before* 1987.

Regulated investment company. An investment company subject to Security and Exchange Commission regulations. If the investment company distributes its income to its shareholders, it does not pay any taxes.

Reinvested dividends. Dividends that are used to purchase additional shares of stock in the company rather than being distributed in cash. A reinvested dividend is taxable income in the year in which it is **constructively received.**

REIT. See **Real estate investment trust.**

Remainder interest. An interest in property or a **trust** that is left after the income beneficiaries have received their income interest.

Resident alien. An individual who is not a citizen of the United States but is a permanent resident of the United States.

Rollover. A distribution from a qualified plan that is reinvested tax-free in another qualified plan or IRA within 60 days of the date of receipt.

Roth IRA. Contributions to a Roth IRA are nondeductible, and, if certain specified conditions are met, distributions are tax free. The contribution may be limited by certain threshold amounts.

Royalty income. Income received for the use of certain kinds of property (e.g., mineral and literary properties, patents).

S

S corporation. A corporation that meets the requirements of, and elects to be taxed under, Subchapter S of the Internal Revenue Code. Generally, this type of corporation acts as a conduit, passing through to the shareholders its **taxable income** or loss, much like a partnership.

Salvage value. The estimated value of an **asset** at the end of its **useful life.**

Section 179 deduction. A tax rule whereby you can elect to deduct, instead of depreciate, up to $24,000 (for 2001) of certain trade or business property in the year in which the property is placed in service. See Chapter 38, *If You Are Self-Employed: How to File Schedule C.*

Section 1231 assets. Generally, **depreciable assets** used in a trade or a business and held for the required long-term holding period. Net gains from the sale or exchange of Section 1231 assets (after recapture of **depreciation**) are treated as **capital gains;** net losses are treated as **ordinary losses.** See Chapter 17, *Reporting Gains and Losses.*

Self-employed. An individual who works in his or her own trade or business.

SEP. See Simplified Employee Pension.

Separate maintenance payments. Payments made from one spouse to another when they are living apart. The payments are made in accordance with a court order or an agreement between the parties. See Chapter 20, *Alimony.*

Service business. A business that derives income from providing personal services. Two examples are law and accounting firms.

Short sale. A sale of borrowed securities made either to fix a gain to be reported in a subsequent year or to profit from an expected decline in price.

Short-term capital gain or loss. A gain or loss on the sale or exchange of a **capital asset** that has been held for less than the legislatively mandated **holding period.** See Chapter 17, *Reporting Gains and Losses.*

Simplified Employee Pension (SEP). An individual retirement arrangement that permits your employer to contribute the lesser of $30,000 or 15% of your compensation, subject to limitations, to your IRA each year. See Chapter 18, *Individual Retirement Arrangements (IRAs).*

Single. The filing status of an individual who is unmarried on the last day of a calendar year.

Single premium annuity contract. An **annuity** contract with a life insurance company. In exchange for a single premium, the life insurance company agrees to make periodic annuity payments, beginning on a specified date.

Specialized small business investment company (SSBIC). A licensed partnership or corporation under the Small Business Administration's Small Business Investment Act of 1958, + 301(d). Corporations and individuals can elect to roll over, without the payment of any capital gain tax, the capital gain from the sale of publicly traded securities into the purchase of common stock or a partnership interest in a SSBIC.

Standard deduction. A **deduction** used to reduce income by taxpayers who do not itemize their deductions. The amount of the deduction depends on your filing status, whether you are 65 or older or blind, and whether you can be claimed as a **dependent** on another taxpayer's return. Adjusted annually for inflation since 1989. See Chapter 21, *Standard Deduction.*

Standard mileage rate. An IRS-approved optional amount used to claim a **deduction** for business transportation expenses in lieu of deducting actual expenses (not including parking, tolls, interest, and taxes). The standard mileage rate is 34.5 cents for 2001 for all business miles.

Statute of limitations. The time period within which the IRS can assess and collect taxes and taxpayers can file for refunds.

Stock appreciation right (SAR). A right granted to an **employee** for additional compensation based on the amount of the appreciation in the company's stock between the date on which the right is granted and the date on which the right is exercised.

Stock dividend. A distribution by a corporation of additional shares of its stock to existing shareholders.

Stock option. An option to buy stock at a specified price.

Straddle. Offsetting investment positions.

Straight-line depreciation. A method of **depreciation** in which the cost or other **basis** of the asset is deducted in equal amounts over the property's **useful life.** See Chapter 10, *Rental Income and Expenses.*

Sum of the years' digits depreciation. A method of **accelerated depreciation** that is based on a formula developed from the expected **useful life** of the property.

Support. Payments made for the care and maintenance of a **dependent.** Expenditures for support include payments for food, lodging, medical expenses, and so on.

Surviving Spouse. See **Qualifying widow(er).**

T

Tangible personal property. Physical property that can be moved. Two examples are machinery and automobiles.

Tax credit carryforward (or carryover). Tax credit that you were unable to use to reduce previous year's tax and that can be applied to offset future tax.

Tax-exempt income. Income that is not subject to federal income tax. An example is income from state and municipal bonds.

Tax home. Generally, a taxpayer's place of business, employment, or post of duty. A tax home's location is used to determine if certain travel expenses are deductible as incurred away from home.

Tax loss carryforward (or carryover). Generally, a **net operating loss** that you were not able to apply against your income during the 2-year carryback period and that may now be applied against future income. The tax benefit of the loss expires if it is not utilized within a 20-year carryover period.

Tax preference items. Items that could subject you to the alternative minimum tax (AMT). Two examples are **accelerated depreciation** of **real property** and **percentage depletion.**

Tax Rate Schedules. Schedules issued by the IRS that must be used in figuring individual income tax for persons who may not use **Tax Tables** (i.e., persons with taxable income of at least $100,000).

Tax-Sheltered Annuities [Section 403(b) plans]. A tax-favored, deferred compensation plan only for employees of tax-exempt organizations and public schools, under which a portion of an employee's salary is withheld on a pretax basis and allowed to earn income on a tax-deferred basis until withdrawal is authorized at age 59½, separation from service, or other qualifying events.

Tax Tables. Tables issued by the IRS that must be used in figuring individual income tax for persons with **taxable income** of less than $100,000.

Taxable income. Your **gross income** minus all allowable **deductions** and **exemptions.** (This is the amount on which income tax is computed, before tax credits.)

Tenants by the entirety. Generally, husband and wife who own property jointly. At the death of one, the survivor takes the entire estate.

Tenants in common. Two or more parties, each of whom holds an undivided share of an entire property. After the death of one party, the survivor does not take the entire estate. The decedent's will or state law determines what happens to the decedent's share.

Tip Reporting Alternative Commitment Program (TRAC). A voluntary IRS program for tip reporting by food and beverage establishments. The program was established to increase tip reporting and compliance levels by both employees and employers.

Trade date. The date on which a purchase or sale of securities occurs. The trade date is used in determining the **holding period** of a security.

Trust. An entity to which **assets** are transferred for protection, management, and distribution to others.

U

Unitrust. A charitable remainder **trust** of which there is an income beneficiary who is not a charitable organization. The income beneficiary receives annual payments based on a fixed percentage of the net **fair market value** of the trust's **assets.**

Useful life. The number of years a **depreciable asset** may reasonably be expected to be in use in a trade or a business.

W

Wash sale. A transaction in which you sell stock at a loss and 30 days before or after the sale you buy substantially identical stock. Losses from wash sales are not deductible.

Index

NOTE: Boldface numerals indicate Ernst & Young Explanations, TaxAlerts, TaxPlanners, and TaxSavers

NOTE: Boldface numerals indicate Ernst & Young Explanations, TaxAlerts, TaxPlanners, and TaxSavers

E